D0461227

ROBERTSON'S BOOK OF FIRSTS

ROBERTSON'S
BOOK OF FIRSTS
WHO DID WHAT FOR THE FIRST TIME

Patrick Robertson

BLOOMSBURY
NEW YORK BERLIN LONDON SYDNEY

Published by Bloomsbury USA, New York

All papers used by Bloomsbury USA are natural, recyclable products made from wood grown in well-managed forests. The manufacturing processes conform to the environmental regulations of the country of origin.

LIBRARY OF CONGRESS CATALOGING-IN-PUBLICATION DATA

Robertson, Patrick, 1940–
The book of firsts : who did what for the first time / Patrick Robertson.—1st U.S. ed.
p. cm.
ISBN: 978-1-59691-579-4 (hardback)
1. Curiosities and wonders—Encyclopedias. 2. Curiosities and wonders—United States—Encyclopedias.
3. Handbooks, vade-mecums, etc. I. Title.
AG243.R553 2011
031.02—dc22
2010032081

First U.S. edition 2011

1 3 5 7 9 10 8 6 4 2

Designed by Sara E. Stemen
Printed in the U.S.A. by Quad/Graphics, Fairfield, Pennsylvania

FOR KARLA, WITH LOVE

INTRODUCTION

THIS IS A BOOK about *innovation* rather than *invention*, because it ranges much wider than technological breakthroughs and looks at the historical changes chronicled from the perspective of the user or consumer. So while books about invention will describe the process by which, for example, television developed from its primitive mechanical form to the electronic, high-definition system we know today, I have devoted rather more space to the origins of various program formats—how TV emerged as a cultural medium. What was the first soap opera or game show? And when could you first walk into a store and buy a television receiver?

Do we need to know? Naturally I think we do, or I would not have spent over fifty years traveling the world in search of significant firsts! What has impelled me to do so is a fascination with historical and social change and how that has affected everyday lives. Most conventional history is concerned with change wrought by wise or not so wise men in the councils of state, by prelates of the church molding the spiritual and often social advancement of all men under God, and by military commanders employing their martial skills to determine the fate of nations. But the day-to-day life of the citizenry of those nations is as often, perhaps more often, the outcome of change fostered by fellow citizens who hold no place in the hierarchy of governance. A need for improvement is identified, sometimes one long sought, other times spontaneously. A man, or less often a woman (why?), of imagination and enterprise finds a means of doing things differently. The result is not always the advancement sought—did Clarence Saunders benefit our communities by introducing the supermarket concept and thereby ensuring the eventual demise of the family-run neighborhood grocery store? We could argue that one until the bar codes hum, but what cannot be gainsaid is that Saunders, and those who embraced his idea of achieving economies through self-service and took it further, changed the lives of every shopper in the Western world.

I believe that is significant, historically and socially. And on the same basis I think we can look at any element of our daily lives, whether it is catching the school bus in the morning, or choosing the newspapers and magazines we read, or watching our favorite sport, or staying in a motel, or working on the laptop, or picking up messages on voice mail, or relaxing with an ice-cold canned beer out of the refrigerator, or picking up a paperback at the airport when we fly off on vacation, maybe with a burger in one hand and trying to pay by credit card with the other... and ask how did all those things start, because that is not how the first settlers at St. Augustine, Jamestown, and Plymouth Rock conducted their lives. Firsts are like pieces of a jigsaw, which, when fitted together, give us a coherent picture of how we got from where we were *then* to where we are *now*.

This is what I have sought to address, and I have done so with a wary eye. Few topics are subject to such a degree of partisanship, obfuscation, chauvinism, and misinformation as firsts. In this book I have sought to unravel fact from legend and determine who really did do what for the first time and where and when, but ever skeptical of claims based on special interests. And given America's tendency to cherish celebrity, I have found that anything attributed to a famous name needs to be subjected to particularly rigorous scrutiny.

The where is as important as the who. Something I have attempted in this book that has scarcely been attempted before is to place America's record of innovative achievement into a global context. The United States is incomparably the most innovative nation on Earth, with over 44 percent (my own estimate) of all significant firsts of the modern era. Moreover, since the 1870s the number of innovations originating in the United States has exceeded, in each decade, the total from all other nations combined. The reasons for this are too many and too diverse for examination here, but I believe this book provides a starting point for anyone who seeks to address the question of why America became, and remains, preeminent in so many fields of endeavor. True, she is now being challenged in a number of these, particularly from the emerging economies of Asia, but if Americans seek a blueprint for sustained innovation in the future, then it may help to know how it was achieved in the past.

The subjects covered in this volume were selected on the basis of several criteria. Some are ones where I wanted to question conventional wisdom (first woman doctor, radio station, electric power plant, sex change, etc.). Others appealed to me because they have attracted scant or inadequate attention elsewhere (first use of photography in advertising, hotel, character merchandising, newspaper headlines, mobile home, etc.) or because I have new information to impart (first television performer, women in the armed forces, children's novel, beauty pageant, black head of a white government, etc.).

There is still, though, a huge range of subjects for which there is no space in this volume. Therefore a supplementary volume is in preparation. *Robertson's Timeline of World & American Firsts* will list some 12,000 firsts in chronological order, with brief details of each, and will also present the same firsts according to place—by country and, within the United States, by state and by city. As the book aims to cover firsts relating to every facet of modern life, it will be possible to make a statistically robust assessment of which American states and cities have been the most innovative.

I invite readers of this volume to contribute to the supplementary volume if they have knowledge of firsts they would like to see included. I only ask them to bear in mind that items for consideration need to have some historic or social significance and should be supported by evidence (i.e., sources). Also, for a first to be eligible, it needs to be the first in the world or the first within the present boundaries of the United States (regional firsts, such as the first of something west of the Alleghenies, are not eligible). That said, I look forward to a rich harvest of firsts, especially those to be recorded for the first time!

PATRICK ROBERTSON
Chapel Hill, North Carolina
London, England
www.robertsonsfirsts.com
patrick@robertsonsfirsts.com

NOTES

1. *First* as used in the text refers to the first in the modern world. It does not preclude the possibility of earlier examples in classical antiquity, usually in a different form.

2. *United States* or *U.S.* as used in the text signifies the territory encompassed by the present boundaries of the United States, regardless of the date.

~~~~~~~~~~~~~~~~~~~~~~~ **A** ~~~~~~~~~~~~~~~~~~~~~~~

ABORTION, COUNTRY TO LEGALIZE

was the Soviet Union under a decree of 1920. Although in effect the decree allowed abortion on demand, physicians were ordered to discourage patients from having the operation, particularly in the case of first pregnancies. They were not, however, allowed to refuse an abortion unless the pregnancy had lasted more than two and a half months. Despite the official policy of limiting abortion as much as possible, the practice grew to such an extent that in 1934 there were a reported 700,000 legal abortions in the Russian Autonomous Republic alone. In order to remedy this situation, the original decree was revoked in 1936 and a new law introduced restricting the carrying out of abortions to cases in which pregnancy endangered life or was calculated to be a serious threat to the health of the patient, or the child was likely to inherit a specified disease. These conditions remained in force until 1955, when abortion on demand was reintroduced subject to certain safeguards.

The first country to introduce legalized abortion on medico-social grounds was Iceland under Law No. 38 of 28 January 1935. This law decreed that abortion might be carried out within the first 28 weeks of a pregnancy clearly demonstrated to constitute a threat to the physical or mental well-being of the patient. Most Western European nations followed Iceland's lead and prescribed medico-social conditions.

U.S.: The first state to partially legalize abortion was Colorado on 25 April 1967. Hospital abortions only were allowed, subject to the consent of a panel of three doctors, in cases where there was a threat to the woman's physical or mental health, she was likely to give birth to a severely deformed child, or she had been the victim of rape or incest.

The first state to decriminalize abortion, in effect allowing abortion on demand subject to certain safeguards, was Hawaii on 11 March 1970. On 9 April of the same year New York State enacted legislation allowing abortion through the twenty-fourth week of pregnancy if performed by a licensed physician. On the first day that the law became effective, 1 July, the nation's first legal abortion clinic, the Planned Parenthood Center of Syracuse, N.Y., performed four abortions. Executive director Ellen Fairchild recalled: "We had the young and we had the desperate. We even had one whole family of sharecroppers who came up from Mississippi because their thirteen- or fourteen-year-old girl was pregnant. They had read in the paper that we did abortions and we were the only place they had to turn."

State anti-abortion laws were ruled unconstitutional following the U.S. Supreme Court's 22 January 1973 decision in *Roe v. Wade*, striking down the 1859 Texas law prohibiting abortions other than to save a woman's life. The court ruled 7–2 that the constitutional right to privacy extended to a woman's decision, in consultation with her physician, to have an abortion in the first three months of pregnancy. Ironically, "Roe" (Norma McCorvey) later became an ardent pro-life campaigner.

ADVERTISEMENT, PRINTED

known is a handbill printed in German by Heinrich Eggerstein of the free republic of Strasbourg and promoted the bible he published in 1468. The earliest surviving example in English is a 5" x 7" in notice of 1477 by London's first printer, William Caxton, advertising his "Salisbury pyes"—not fast food, but rules to be observed by the clergy at Easter. These ads were posted on church doors and concluded with the admonition in Latin *Supplico stet cedula*, meaning "Please do not tear down." The earliest known **illustrated advertisement** was a handbill puffing a romance called *The Lovely Melusina* and was printed in Antwerp in what is now Belgium in 1491. The woodcut illustration depicted the heroine in her bath, undoubtedly the start of sex in advertising.

Press advertisements: These first appeared in the *Journal Général d'Affiches*, better known as the *Petites Affiches*, which commenced publication in Paris on 14 October 1612. Although no early issues of the paper survive, it is reasonable to suppose from its title, and from the nature of its contents during the succeeding three centuries of continued publication, that it was intended as an advertising medium (and solely as that) from its inception.

The first newspaper proper to contain an advertisement was an untitled Dutch coranto published in Amsterdam on 21 November 1626, which had a notice inserted beneath the editorial matter announcing that an auction sale was to be held for the disposal of a cargo of sugar, ivory, pepper, tobacco, and wood taken from a prize-ship.

The earliest paid press advertisements in English made their debut when Samuel Pecke's *Perfect Diurnall* (1643) began carrying regular book advertisements on 23 November 1646. The rate was 6d per insertion. Although there are earlier examples of book announcements in the journals of the day, these generally appeared as items of news, and there is no evidence that they were paid for by the publishers. In 1660 *Mercurius Politicus* carried the first known advertisement for a branded product:

> Most excellent and improved Dentifrices to scour and cleanse the teeth, making them as white as Ivory, preserves from the Toothache; it fastens the Teeth, sweetens the Breath, and preserves the Gums and Mouth from Cankers and Imposthumes. Made by Robert Taylor, Gentleman, and the right only are to be had at Thomas Rookes, Stationer, at the Holy Lamb, at East End of St. Paul's Church, near the School, in sealed papers, at 12d the paper. The reader is desired to beware of Counterfeits.

U.S.: The first paid advertisements appeared in the third issue of John Campbell's *Boston News-Letter* (SEE **newspaper**) for 1 May 1704. Two of these concerned thefts, one of men's clothing from the home of James Cooper by a twenty-two-year-old Irishman who "speaks bad English" and the other of improbably heavy goods:

> Lost on the 10. of *April* last off of Mr. Shippen's Wharf in *Boston*, Two Iron Anvils, weighing between 120 and140 pounds each: Whoever has taken them up and will bring or give true Intelligence of them to John Campbell Postmaster, shall have a sufficient reward.

Inserted between these announcements was America's first real-estate ad:

> At Oysterbay on Long Island in the province of New York there is a very good Fulling Mill to be let or sold, as also a Plantation, having on it a large Brick House, and other good house by it for a Kitchen and Workhouse, with a Barn, Stable &c. a young Orchard and about 20 acres clear land.

Rates were from 1s to 5s per announcement, the circulation of the *News-Letter* being about 200–300, though the readership (in coffeehouses, taverns, etc.) probably many times that.

Nearly all early ads were single-column classifieds. The first double-column, illustrated newspaper advertisement in the United States, a precursor of the large-space display advertising that only became dominant at the end of the nineteenth century, was for an "Unparalleled Attraction at the American Museum" and appeared in the *New York Herald* in 1836 with a striking woodcut, across both columns, depicting "Harrington's New Grand Moving Deorance (*sic*), showing the Awful and Devastating Conflagration of a Large Part of the City of New York."

The first **full-page advertisement** in the United States was placed by Robert Bonner, Irish-born proprietor of the *New York Ledger*, in his rival James Gordon Bennett's *New York Herald* on 7 June 1856. Bonner had contracted with popular novelist Fanny Fern to provide him with a serial to be paid for at the fabulous rate of $100 a column. The advertisement for this story created such demand for the *Ledger* that its circulation nearly doubled to 50,000.

The first **full-color advertisement** in the United States was a chromolithograph inset advertising the *New York Sun* newspaper, which was bound into the January 1880 issue of *Frank Leslie's Popular Monthly* (New York). It depicted a montage of events (horse racing, wedding, train crossing trestle, procession, political oration, hanging telegraph wires, concert, sailor fighting with cutlass, etc.) and the strap-line A MILLION A WEEK. The first to appear in the regular pagination of a magazine was a full-page ad for Mellin's baby food illustrated with a lithograph of Perrault's *The Awakening of Cupid*, which appeared on the back cover of the World's Columbian Exhibition number of the *Youth's Companion* (Boston) on 4 May 1893. The circulation of the magazine, normally 400,000, shot up to 650,000 for the special number, and the rate charged for the ad was a record $14,000.

Color advertising in newspapers in the United States began with the adoption of four-color rotary presses by the *Chicago Inter-Ocean* in May 1892, used for weekend supplements only. The first newspaper able to accept color ads in its editorial pages was the *Minneapolis Star*, which acquired two four-color run-of-paper presses in 1930. By 1935 there were 8 morning, 21 evening, and 20 Sunday papers that could accommodate four-color run-of-paper advertising (i.e., excluding supplements and rotogravure sections).

SEE **advertising photography**.

THE FIRST **ADVERTISING AGENCY**

of which record survives was established in London in 1786 by William Tayler, who booked advertisements in the provincial press for a handling fee of 6d or 1s. The early agencies confined their attention to placing advertisements and space brokering, albeit there is some evidence of creative involvement as early as 1809, when the essayist Charles Lamb was working as a freelance copywriter on a lottery account for James White's agency. It was only in the 1880s, though, that English and American agencies began to hire full-time creative staff, starting with copywriters (SEE **advertising copywriter**).

U.S.: The first agency was established in 1841 by Volney B. Palmer, of whom it was said by pioneering ad man George P. Rowell that "his stout figure, florid countenance, gray hair, bold head, blue coat with brass buttons, gold bowed spectacles, gold headed cane and bandanna handkerchief were known and, to some extent, respected by advertisers and publishers for a considerable term of years." This qualified respect may have been on account of the characteristics attributed to him by Rowell: "rather pompous; rather irascible." On one occasion Palmer told the distinguished and highly respected Samuel Bowles of the *Springfield Republican* that he could tell him the principles on which business could be conducted, but could not furnish him with the intellect necessary to comprehend the same.

It has been claimed that Palmer set up his agency in Philadelphia, but Rowell states that when Palmer first came to Boston in 1856 he worked out of offices in the Scollays Building there, though noting that the agency had branches in Philadelphia and New York. Palmer's terms for doing business were what would now be regarded as an extortionate 25-percent commission on the cost of the advertising space, and moreover, he also charged newspapers for his stationery and postage expenses. Any newspaper that subsequently accepted a direct booking from any of Palmer's former clients would find itself billed for the agency's standard 25 percent.

Palmer died c. 1860, and the Philadelphia and New York branches of his agency passed through several owners before being merged with N. W. Ayer & Son of Philadelphia toward the end of the century. Ayer in turn merged with the Kaplan Thaler Group in 2002 and closed. Another legacy from Volney B. Palmer has survived even longer, for he it was who invested the English language with the term "advertising agency," in a promotional insert in *M'Elroy's Philadelphia Directory for 1849*.

The first full-service agency was founded by the choleric George Batten, who established the Batten Co. (now BBDO) on Park Row in New York City in 1891. From the outset Batten would only accept accounts from clients prepared to allow him total control, developing the strategy, writing the copy, designing the ads, selecting the media, etc. It was certainly in the interest of advertising agencies to be this prescriptive. Already one of the magazines with the highest circulation in America, the *Youth's Companion*, had established an advertising department which would undertake the entire creative process for its advertisers.

International agency: The first was Gordon & Gotch, originally established in Melbourne, Australia, in 1855, which opened its first overseas branch in London in 1867. Other branches followed in South Africa and New Zealand. The London office rapidly became the main advertising agency for British manufacturers seeking to advertise their goods in the colonies.

U.S.: The first American agency to set up an overseas shop was Chicago's J. Walter Thompson in London in 1899. By the early 1920s JWT had a global network with branch agencies in Europe, India, and Latin America. The London office became the largest British agency after World War II, while JWT worldwide became British-owned when it was acquired by the WPP Group in a hostile takeover in June 1987. In 2000 WPP was ranked by *Advertising Age* the largest global network, with gross income of $7.97 billion.

Advertising agency headed by a woman: The first was Gumaelius, established in Stockholm, Sweden, by Sofia Gumaelius in 1877. The first ad agency in Sweden, by the time Sofia died in 1915 it had branches in Malmö and Gothenburg and overseas offices in Oslo and London.

THE FIRST **ADVERTISING COPYWRITER**

known by name was the essayist Charles Lamb, who wrote lottery advertisements for the London ad agency James White as early as 1809. Another distinguished writer similarly engaged at about the same time was the romantic poet and sexually rapacious rake Lord Byron, who did not work for an agency but seems to have been employed to write copy by at least two clients, who perhaps not coincidentally were the two highest spenders on advertising in Britain at the time. One was Warren's Blacking, sometimes claimed to have been the first nationally advertised brand and in whose London factory Charles Dickens toiled as a child. Warren's copy was done in verse, and in

February 1843 the *Edinburgh Review*, not normally known for tittle-tattle, observed: "When 'Childe Harold' was accused of receiving six hundred a year for his services as Poet-Laureate to Mrs Warren,—of being, in short, the actual personage alluded to in her famous boast, 'We keeps a poet,'—he showed no anxiety to repudiate the charge." According to the rival *Quarterly Review* (June 1855) it was the proprietor of Packwood's Razor Strops who declared, "La, sir, we keeps a poet," in response to an inquiry about the provenance of his advertising and indicated that the copywriter in question was Byron. Given that the poet was perpetually short of money, despite the huge royalties from his published works, he may well have been moonlighting for both advertisers.

The first **full-time copywriter** was John E. Powers, hired by John Wanamaker in May 1880 to write the ads for his Philadelphia department store. Powers was notable for his use of direct, simple English, short, punchy headlines, and total honesty at a time when most advertising copy was circumlocutory and polysyllabic, indulged in lengthy headlines, and was hyperbolic to the point sometimes of absurdity. A later advertising director for Wanamaker's, Joseph H. Appel, recalled how Powers had been buttonholed by a rubber-goods buyer who asked if his department could be featured in the next ad. Powers asked if there was anything in particular to push, to which the buyer responded, "Well, between you and me, we have a lot of rotten gossamers that we wish to get rid of." Copy for the ad when it appeared included the line "We have a lot of rotten gossamers and things we want to get rid of." By noon on that day the whole surplus had been snapped up by eager shoppers impressed with the store's candor. John Wanamaker shared Powers's integrity and devotion to literal truth, whether in advertising or daily conduct, and it was probably their mutual unbending rectitude that caused these stubborn and inflexible personalities to come into conflict. Powers was fired in 1883, hired back a year later, and fired for good in 1886, but he went on to craft equally direct and persuasive copy for Beecham's Pills, *Nation Magazine*, Murphy Varnish, Scott's Emulsion, and Vacuum Oil.

The first **advertising agency to hire a full-time copywriter** was N. W. Ayer of Philadelphia, who engaged the services of Jarvis Wood in 1888. The following year London's Thomas Smith Agency could offer its clients the resources of an "Ad-writing and Designing Department."

THE FIRST **ADVERTISING ENDORSEMENT**

The practice of quoting testimonials in advertising is first noted in 1752, the issue of London's *General Advertiser* for 19 January of that year containing a puff in which Elizabeth Gardiner, headmistress of a girls' boarding school, recommended the use of Mr. Parson's stays, which she declared were compulsory items of apparel for her charges. Nearly a hundred years later the celebrity endorsement had already made its appearance, an article on advertising in the February 1843 issue of the *Edinburgh Review* heaping ridicule on the advertisers of Cockle's Antibilious Pills, recommended by ten dukes, five marquises, seventeen earls, eight viscounts, sixteen lords, one archbishop (Armagh), fifteen bishops, the adjutant general, the attorney general, Sir Francis Burdett, Sir Andrew Agnew, Alderman Ward, and legal luminary Mr. Sergeant Talfourd. This list, the writer asserted, made one wonder about "the comparative biliousness of the higher classes." Celebrity endorsement by the entertainment profession followed in 1878 when Lillie Langtry, the "Jersey Lily," cherished by both the Prince of Wales and frontier hanging judge Roy Bean, declared her fidelity to Pears' Soap in large display ads illustrated with the matchless beauty's portrait and inscribed with the words attributed to her: "Since using Pears' Soap, I have discarded all others." These are believed to have been the earliest advertisements for which the featured celebrity was paid.

U.S.: The first celebrity endorsements were for Bull Durham Tobacco, manufactured by the Blackwell Tobacco Co. of Durham, N.C., and extolled during the late 1870s and 1880s by such luminaries of pipe and pen as Thomas Carlyle, William Thackeray, and James Russell Lowell. The company's advertising budget of $150,000 per annum was rivaled only by British manufacturing giants Pears' Soap and Cadbury's Cocoa. Lillie Langtry repeated her career-enhancing alliance with commerce in Britain by becoming the first show business personality to endorse a product in America.

This was in 1886 when Harriet Hubbard Ayer, proprietor of the Madame Récamier face cream business, persuaded her to lend her name to testimonials in exchange for a luxuriously appointed apartment in New York.

THE FIRST **ADVERTISING FILMS**

were made in France, Britain, and the United States in 1897. The single surviving American example of that year was copyrighted by the Edison Co. of West Orange, N.J., on 5 August 1897. The Library of Congress Catalog records:

> The film shows a large, poster-type backdrop with the words "Admiral Cigarettes." Sitting in front of the backdrop are four people in costume: Uncle Sam, a clergyman, an Indian, and a businessman. To the left of the screen is an ash-can size box that breaks apart and a girl, attired in a striking costume, goes across the stage toward the seated men and hands them cigarettes. Then she unfolds a banner that reads, "We All Smoke."

Advertising films were also made by the New York firm of Kuhn & Webster in 1897 for Haig Whisky, Pabst's Milwaukee Beer, and Maillard's Chocolate. These were shown by back projection on an open-air screen facing Broadway at 34th Street, Herald Square. The projectionist was Edwin S. Porter, later to achieve fame as director of *The Great Train Robbery* (SEE **film: westerns**). On this occasion, however, the only celebrity he achieved was in the police court, where he was charged with being a public nuisance and causing obstruction to traffic by encouraging crowds to linger on the sidewalk.

The French advertising films were the work of Georges Méliès, and were first shown in the open air on the boulevard des Italiens, near the Paris Opéra, in 1898. However, it is probable that some of them were made the previous year, and may have predated the Admiral cigarettes commercial. They were made at Méliès's studio at Montreuil-sous-Bois for clients who included Delion hats, Mystère corsets, Chocolat Menier, and Moritz beer.

Britain's first advertising film was made in 1897 for Bird's Custard Powder by Arthur Melbourne-Cooper of St. Albans, Hertfordshire, and brought to life a contemporary poster that showed an elderly chef slipping on the stairs and demolishing the tray of eggs he is carrying. The message was that he had no cause to worry as he used Bird's Custard Powder. The company undertook to pay Melbourne-Cooper £1 ($5) for every copy of the film distributed.

SEE ALSO **television commercial**.

THE FIRST **ADVERTISING JINGLE**

was performed live on 24 December 1926 over the airwaves of WCCO Minneapolis, which was owned by the Washburn Crosby Co. (later General Mills). Among its products was a new cereal called Wheaties, which was enjoying only sluggish sales. Washburn Crosby asked the station manager, Earl Gammons, to devise a novel means of promoting the underperformer. It would also, executive Donald Davis put it somewhat bluntly, help the company "find out what that radio station of ours is good for." Gammons responded to the challenge with a four-line lyric:

Have you tried Wheaties?
They're whole wheat with all the bran.
Won't you try Wheaties?
For wheat is the best food of man.

Sung to the tune of "She's a Jazz Baby," the first jingle was delivered by a volunteer quartet composed of a local businessman, a printer, a bailiff, and an undertaker. Known as the Wheaties Quartet, the group performed a half-hour program of jingles and other vocals for the next six years at a fee of $6 a week, which the WCCO suits cautiously appraised as "not too much if it works." It did when the quartet went national on the CBS network under a new name, the Gold Medal Fast Freight, with Wheaties sales tripling during the first year of coast-to-coast radio advertising.

TV jingle: The first was sung to a musical score by Joe Rines for the Sherman & Marquette advertising

agency's Ajax Cleanser commercial aired by Colgate-Palmolive in 1948. Featuring the energetic Ajax Pixies, the ad's jingle assured housewives, "You'll stop paying the elbow tax, when you start cleaning with Ajax." This was also the first fully animated TV commercial (qv).

THE FIRST **ADVERTISING PHOTOGRAPHY**

The earliest known photographically illustrated advertisement was a real estate poster for housing lots in Saint-Germain outside Paris for which Bisson Frères made a landscape photograph in 1854. According to a description in *La Lumière* for 23 September of that year, these were displayed at railroad ticket offices. The illustration, placed in the middle of the poster, showed the view that purchasers would enjoy from their houses when they had built them.

U.S.: The earliest known example is a wanted poster issued in Augusta, Ga., in April 1863 by rice planter Louis Manigault, with a photograph of his household slave Dolly, who had run away on the seventh of that month. A reward of $50 was offered for the return of the thirty-year-old woman, who is described as "rather good looking, with a fine set of teeth." The only surviving copy is in the Southern Historical Collection at the University of North Carolina, Chapel Hill.

Sporadic examples of product photography for sales literature followed. The earliest on record was a catalog of mourning clothes issued by the Peter Robinson dry goods store in London in 1865 with tipped-in photographs. According to advertising historian Frank Presbrey, occasional use of halftone illustrations was made in booklets put out by Montreal advertisers from about 1872. The first advertising halftone in the United States, Presbrey claimed, was made by Frederick Ives (SEE **halftone; photograph in color**) in 1881 for a brochure put out by an unnamed railroad. The oldest surviving American example of a photographically illustrated catalog is believed to be one issued in 1890 by the Northwestern Knitting Co. of Minneapolis for Munsingwear underclothes, featuring albumen prints of mustachioed male models sporting woolen combinations. The earliest reference to color photography in advertising, a brief mention in *Anthony's*

Photographic Bulletin, relates to "advertisements of rugs" (probably a catalog) in 1894. The first example of known provenance was a seed, plant, and bulb catalog issued in the fall of 1895 by Henry A. Dreer, nurseryman of Chestnut Street, Pa.

Press advertisement illustrated with a photograph: The earliest known was placed by the Harrison Patent Knitting Machine Co. of Manchester, England, in the 11 November 1887 issue of the *Parrot*, a locally produced humorous periodical, and depicted the company's display stand and attendant staff at the Manchester Jubilee Exhibition. The whole-page halftone was reproduced by the Meisenbach process (SEE **halftone**) and the advertisement was handled by Pratt & Co., advertising agents of Manchester.

U.S.: Two photographically illustrated advertisements appeared in the first issue of *Vogue* (New York) of 17 December 1892. One was by *Cosmopolitan* magazine offering a thousand scholarships at leading colleges to boys who sold the most subscriptions and was illustrated with a photograph of young men competing in a cycle race (presumably intended to signify college athletics). The other was for Howard & Co. of Fifth Avenue silverware and showed the company's products. Two weeks later there appeared the first photo-ad for a branded product. This promoted Louis Sherry eating chocolate and depicted Le Petit Chocolatier, the Gallic provenance lending distinction to what was, pre-Hershey, a luxury product targeted at a niche market. The halftone photographs are believed to have been by the Ives process. The first national (and international) advertiser to use photography in magazines was Mellin's Food, the Boston manufacturers licensed to produce Liebig's infant formula for the U.S. market. These advertisements depicted bouncing babies reared on the product and began appearing in most of the mass-circulation American and British middle-class weeklies and monthlies during 1894.

The first photographic press advertisement in color was a halftone pack-shot for the N. K. Fairbank Co.'s vegetable oil shortening Cottolene and appeared on the back cover of the *Christian Herald* (New York City) of 11 December 1896. (This was exceptional. Generally color was little-used in advertising photography until the 1940s.)

The progress of advertising photography in the closing years of the century was rapid. Richard Ohmann noted in *Selling Culture* (1996) that there were twenty photo-illustrated advertisements in *McClure's Magazine* for December 1895 and sixty-one in October 1899; eleven in *Munsey's* for October 1895 and thirty-six in May 1900. It was during this period that the Tonnesen Sisters of Chicago became the first **commercial photographers** to specialize in advertising. They had founded the business in 1896 as a portrait studio. It was the following year, Beatrice Tonnesen later recalled, that "one day we thought up a fine scheme. We would make advertising pictures using live models. It had never been done before." In fact it had been done before, not only in the examples noted above, but also in their own city of Chicago, where there were models earning a living doing advertising work (SEE **photographic model**) as early as 1894. But Beatrice Tonnesen and her sister Clara, who managed the business side of the studio while Beatrice concentrated on the creative input, were undoubtedly the first professional photographers to cater directly to the needs of advertisers. In 1903 they founded the world's first model agency (qv), which they ran successfully until their retirement in 1930.

THE FIRST **AERIAL CROP-DUSTING**

....

was carried out on behalf of the Ohio Agricultural Experimental Station by Lt. John B. Macready, then holder of the world altitude record, who used a Curtiss JN6 light aircraft to dust a six-acre catalpa grove infested with leaf caterpillars in Troy, Ohio, on 3 August 1921. Powdered arsenate of lead was released from a specially designed hopper secured to the side of the fuselage of the aircraft, which flew at a height of 20 to 35 feet above the ground, with 175 pounds of powder distributed over the 4,815 trees in the orchard in six 9-second discharges. Thus the actual time spent on the work of dusting was less than one minute.

Two days after the experiment C. R. Neillie, the Cleveland entomologist who had first suggested the idea, was able to report that "evidences of the wholesale destruction of the insects were everywhere apparent" and that not more than 1 percent remained alive on the trees.

The first commercially operated crop-dusting service was offered by Huff-Daland Dusters, Inc., founded in 1925 in Macon, Ga., by C. E. Woolman, who used a Petrel aircraft to discharge calcium arsenate over Georgia cotton plantations infested with boll weevil. The company eventually became Delta Air Lines.

THE FIRST **AERIAL PROPAGANDA**

raid took place in May 1806. Adm. Thomas Cochrane, 10th Earl of Dundonald, had been asked, in common with a number of other naval commanders, to distribute a quantity of "printed proclamations addressed to the French people." The Admiralty suggested that the leaflets should be handed to French fishermen encountered near the coast, with instructions to pass them on to their countrymen. Cochrane did not share Their Lordships' cynical—or perhaps naïve—assessment of the French fishing fleet's willingness to aid and abet the enemy, and sought a surer means of landing his cargo in France. The previous year he had conducted a series of experiments about HMS *Pallas* with enormous kites designed to supplement sailpower and give the ship greater impetus. Adapting this idea, the admiral had a number of smaller kites constructed. The leaflets were attached in bundles at spaced intervals along a slow-burning fuse, so that they would be released every mile or so as the ship progressed along the coast. The system worked, and Cochrane reported that the proclamations "became widely distributed over the country."

Aerial propaganda raid by airplane: The first was made by the Italian Servizi Aeronautici over Libya during the Italo-Turkish War of 1911–12. The leaflet, signed "Cavena" and dated Tripoli, 15 January 1912, was addressed to the Arabs of Tripolitania and promised a gold napoleon and a sack of wheat or barley to every man who surrendered. Aerial propaganda reached the American continent soon afterward. Didier Masson (SEE **aerial warfare**), hired as a one-man air force by Gen. Álvaro Obregón during the Mexican Revolution, dropped propaganda leaflets over the city of Guaymas in May 1913.

THE FIRST **AERIAL WARFARE**

The first use of an airplane on active service was a reconnaissance undertaken on behalf of the Mexican government forces by French aviator René Simon, leader of the Moisant International Aviators flying troupe, who flew from El Paso across the Rio Grande in a Blériot monoplane on 1 February 1911 to locate the rebel positions near Cuidad Juárez. Other reconnaissance flights were made by Simon's fellow stunt flier Roland Garros, neither pilot coming under fire—possibly on account of their forethought in stocking up with oranges and cigarettes with which to "bombard" the enemy.

Simon and Garros were both contract fliers, or mercenaries. The first military fliers to go to war were the members of the Italian Servizi Aeronautici who flew operations over Libya during the Italo-Turkish War of 1911–12. The original strength of the unit that arrived at Tripoli on 19 October 1911 was ten officers, twenty-nine troopers, and nine aircraft (two Blériots, two Etrichs, two Henri Farmans, and three Nieuports), later supplemented by some Deperdussins and several airships. The command for the aerial campaign in Libya consisted of an airplane battalion, an airship battalion (operational 4 March 1912), a factory for construction and repairs, and a laboratory for experimental work. The functions performed by the corps were fivefold: aerial reconnaissance, photogrammetry, artillery ranging, leaflet raids (SEE **aerial propaganda**), and bombing from the air. Thus the only two major uses of the airplane in modern warfare that were not foreshadowed during the Libyan campaign were the transport of troops and supplies, obviously beyond the capacity of the ultralight aircraft of 1911, and aerial combat (SEE BELOW). It is more than likely that fighting in the air would have taken place had the enemy succeeded in its attempt to acquire aircraft.

The first aerial operation carried out by the Italians was a reconnaissance flight made by Capt. Piazza, commander of the air base at Tripoli, who flew over the Turkish encampment at El Azizia on 23 October 1911 in a Blériot XI *bis*, causing consternation and alarm in the enemy ranks.

Air raid: The first took place on 1 November 1911, when Lt. Giulio Gavotti took off from Tripoli in an

Etrich monoplane and dropped a 4½-pound Cipelli-type bomb on the Turkish position at Ain Zara. After circling the camp to estimate the effect of the detonation, he flew to the oasis at Tagiura and released his three remaining bombs. A second raid on Ain Zara three days later brought a strong protest from the Turks that the Italians were contravening the Geneva Convention, and a considerable discussion ensued on the ethics of air bombardment, not only in the Turkish and Italian press but also in the newspapers of many non-aligned countries.

Casualty in aerial warfare: The first occurred on 31 March 1912, when civilian flier Carlo Montù was wounded by gunfire from the Arab encampment at Tobruk while dropping bombs from the observer's seat. The aircraft was being piloted by Lt. Rossi at a height of 1,800 feet when four bullets struck the fuselage, one of them hitting his passenger.

Capt. Riccardo Moizo came through the campaign unscathed, but earned the unenviable distinction of becoming the first **pilot to be captured in warfare** when his Nieuport made a forced landing near Azizia on 11 September 1912. Moizo had been the first pilot to arrive in Tripoli and during his eleven months on active service had made 82 sorties, more than any other member of the Aviation Corps. It was reported about this time that the longest an airman could last under war conditions was six months, and that he would then require a "considerable period of recuperation before he can take up military flying again."

Pilot killed in warfare: The first fatality occurred in Libya during the Italo-Turkish War of 1911–12 when Lt. Piero Manzini, seconded from the Italian army's 2nd Cavalry to the Aviation Corps, crashed into the sea on 25 August 1912 immediately after take-off from Tripoli on a photo reconnaissance mission. The first to be killed as a result of enemy action was Lt. Hristo Toprakchiev, a member of the 1st Aircraft Squadron of the Bulgarian army during the 1st Balkan War of 1912–13. He flew reconnaissance missions over Adrianople during the siege of the Turkish-held city on 17 and 18 October 1912. On the second of these his Russian-built Bleriot monoplane was hit nine times by ground fire, causing serious damage to the rudder and tail-plane. Repairs were made at the base at Simeonovgrad and on the following day, 19 October,

Toprakchiev took off on a test flight, but on landing back at base the tail-plane collapsed and the wrecked plane caught fire, resulting in the death of the pilot.

Although Toprakchiev was killed on active service, he was not flying a combat mission at the time. The first pilot to be shot down and killed was a Russian volunteer with the Bulgarian forces named M. Popov (first name unrecorded). His aircraft was hit by Turkish shrapnel shells over Adrianople on 30 October 1912.

Apart from the three campaigns already noted, aircraft were employed in several other wars prior to 1914—by the French and Spanish in their respective Moroccan campaigns, and during the Second Balkan War (1913), which was also the first conflict to see aircraft being used by both sides. In April 1914, a few weeks before the outbreak of World War I, the Americans gained a baptism of fire in the air when a short campaign was mounted in Mexico (SEE BELOW). While received opinion has it that aircraft were first used in warfare in World War I, in fact seven aerial campaigns had preceded it.

Air battle: The earliest recorded, albeit one-sided, is shrouded in the anonymity of a scrupulously censored Reuters dispatch dated 15 August 1914: "In another place a French aeroplane yesterday encountered a German aeroplane. The French pilot chased the German, firing with a Browning. The German aviator did not reply, but fled."

The first decisive aerial engagement, resulting in the death of the enemy, took place on 5 October 1914, when Joseph Frantz, of the French Air Corps' V24 squadron, encountered a German Aviatik while returning from a reconnaissance over enemy lines in his Voisin biplane. Frantz's mechanic, Louis Quénault, had charge of a Hotchkiss machine gun mounted in the nacelle of the plane; the Aviatik's observer was armed only with a rifle, which he had difficulty in aiming as the aircraft's tail was in the line of fire. Quénault riddled the German airplane with bullets until the Hotchkiss jammed, at which moment the Aviatik burst into flames and crashed behind the French lines. The battle was watched by ground troops of both sides, who climbed onto the parapets of their trenches to obtain a better view. The German aviators, first to be killed in air-to-air combat, were Wilhelm Sclienting of Alterdorf and Fritz von Zangen of Darmstadt. A letter found in the dead pilot's pocket, addressed to his mother, was delivered to a nearby German airfield by a French aircraft, a mark of compassion that became customary during the early period of the air war, when duels in the sky were still fought with a certain élan and without malice to the enemy.

U.S.: The first American pilot to fly on active service was a New York–born Cherokee Indian named John Hector Worden, who had learned to fly at the Blériot flying school in Étampes in France. In 1912 he was engaged by the Moisant company to demonstrate its planes to the military authorities in Mexico City, the Mexican Revolution still taking its toll of the *federales*. The enthusiastic Mexican officers persuaded him that the best kind of demonstration was a practical one, and he soon found himself in uniform as an acting captain in the Federal Army. As such he flew scouting missions to seek out the rebel positions. In particular, as he argued in the December 1912 issue of *Aircraft* on his return to the United States, airplanes were effective in locating prospective ambushes of trains carrying troops and supplies on the vulnerable single-track rail network. He did not advocate bombing from the air, believing it to be impracticable. It was left to the next American to fly as a military pilot in the Mexican Revolution to test that theory, albeit on behalf of the enemy.

French born, but a U.S. citizen, Didier Masson was an instructor at the Glenn L. Martin Flying School at Dominguez Field outside Los Angeles, when he was engaged by Gen. Álvaro Obregón to fly the Martin pusher-biplane *Sonora*, as it was named in its military guise, which the revolutionary commander had purchased from the Aero Club of Southern California for $5,000. Masson's contract gave him a retainer of $300 per month plus flight money ($50 for reconnaissance, $250 for bomb attacks) and the temporary rank of captain in Obregón's army. A bomb sight and a bomb rack were added to the machine on arrival, and Masson's mechanic, Thomas Dean, fashioned bombs out of lengths of iron pipe stuffed with dynamite and steel rivets. Masson became the **first American to make an air raid** on 30 May 1913, taking off from Moreno accompanied by Capt. Joaquin

Alcalde to bomb the Federal gunboats lying in the Bay of Guaymas 40 miles distant. They dropped Dean's 30-pound bombs from a height of 2,500 feet aiming for the *Guerrero* and two other vessels, the *Guerrero* returning fire but failing to hit the aircraft. Nor did the bombs hit the gunboats. Masson and Alcalde returned the following day, again failing to strike the target, but at least having the satisfaction of seeing the sailors jump overboard in terror. On the third attempt the plane crashed on takeoff, and Masson was grounded while replacement parts were smuggled over the border. A month later two more attacks were made, but whether any of the bombs reached their targets remains a matter of dispute; most accounts say they missed, though according to Masson's own testimony he caused minor damage.

It is alleged that one of Masson's air raids was an attack on the city of Guaymas itself, which if true would have been the first on a civilian target. According to one report "bombs fell in the principal business street, causing some loss of life and doing great damage to property." Masson claimed, shortly before he died in 1950, that he had refused Obregón's demand to bomb towns, so this "reign of terror" by his "dragon of war" may have been no more than imaginative Federalist propaganda. On the other hand, Masson did have an ax to grind. He quit Obregón's service in August 1913 because his pay was a month in arrears. Before he did so he handed the biplane over to Gustavo Salinas, nephew of the Constitutionalist Army's leader, Venustiano Carranza, whom he taught to fly. Even if Masson did not inaugurate terror bombing from the skies, it is possible that the young daredevil Salinas did so. Federalists claimed that he bombed the Pacific port of Mazatlán, before crash-landing and writing off the plane. A certain veracity is accorded to this by the fact that the commander of the U.S. Pacific Fleet sent two aides to the Constitutionalist camp to protest the use of airplanes in warfare. The United States was, however, about to use them itself, and in the same country, Mexico.

The first **use of airplanes by U.S. forces on active service** took place during the brief Mexican campaign of 1914. The USS *Birmingham* was sent to Tampico carrying two Curtiss aircraft but saw no action, while the USS *Mississippi* arrived at Vera Cruz carrying a C3 flying boat and a Curtiss A3 seaplane. The latter made reconnaissance flights on 43 consecutive days. The first patrol was made by Lt. P. N. L. Bellinger (U.S. Naval Aviator No. 8), accompanied by his observer, Ensign M. L. Stolz, on 25 April, spotting for mines and photographing enemy positions from the flying boat. On 2 May Bellinger flew the first ground-support mission with Ensign W. D. Lamont as observer in the seaplane after U.S. Marines encamped at Tejar had come under attack, and the fliers were able to report on enemy dispositions. Bellinger scored a third "first" on 6 May when the seaplane he was piloting over enemy positions became the first U.S. airplane hit by hostile fire. He succeeded in alighting safely alongside the *Birmingham*.

American pilot to shoot down an enemy aircraft: The first was Sgt. Kiffin Rockwell of the French Army's Escadrille Américaine (later known as the Lafayette Escadrille), who scored a kill in his Nieuport Scout on 18 May 1916 while escorting bombers near Mulhouse on the Western Front. Rockwell fired just four bullets at a distance of 25 yards, which hit the pilot, the observer, and the engine. He was triply fortunate—he had not flown in combat before, nor seen a German aircraft in the air, nor fired his machine gun. The first **American pilot to be shot down** was H. Clyde Balsley in a dogfight over Verdun on 18 June 1916, and the **first killed** was Victor Emmanuel Chapman of the Lafayette Escadrille near Verdun on 23 June 1916.

The first American pilot of the U.S. armed forces to shoot down an enemy aircraft was Lt. Stephen W. Thompson of the 103rd Pursuit Squadron (formerly the Lafayette Escadrille) over the Western Front on 5 February 1918. His victim was a German Albatros.

Strategic bombing raid by a formation of aircraft: The first was led by Sqn. Cdr. E. F. Briggs of Britain's Royal Naval Air Service, who took off from Belfort, France, on 21 November 1914 accompanied by Flt. Cdr. J. T. Babington and Flt. Lt. S. V. Sippe to attack the zeppelin sheds at Friedrichshafen, Germany. The three Avro 504s each carried four 20-pound bombs. One of the zeppelins, LZ32, was damaged in its shed, and the gas plant was destroyed. Heavy defensive fire by machine guns resulted in Briggs's airplane being forced to the ground, he himself being wounded in the head and taken prisoner on landing.

U.S.: The first was by eight Breguet 14s of the 96th Aero Squadron, which attacked the railway marshaling yard at Dommary-Baroncourt, France, on 12 June 1918.

THE FIRST **AEROBICS**

technique was developed c. 1966 by Dr. Kenneth H. Cooper, director of the Aerospace Medical Laboratory in San Antonio, Tex., who was assigned to develop a physical fitness regime for recruits falling below the U.S. Air Force's exacting standards. Dr. Cooper characterized his initial intake as "overweight, overanxious, chain-smoking slobs." He aimed to stimulate the heart and lungs through a sustained exercise program designed to make the participant increase his oxygen intake. The technique found a wider audience with the publication of Dr. Cooper's *Aerobics* in 1968 and the founding of the Cooper Aerobics Center in Dallas, Tex., two years later.

The first aerobics dance class, harbinger of many millions of Jane Fonda–style "go for the burn!" workouts, was started with six students in a church basement in Malibu, Calif., in 1971 by dancer-turned-fitness-expert Jacki Sorensen.

THE FIRST **AEROSOL**

was patented on 23 November 1927 by Norwegian engineer Erik Rotheim as a means of dispensing liquid soap, paint, insecticide, and cosmetics. Reputedly he was inspired by the need for a more effective way of applying wax to his skis. The first commercially available aerosol containers were produced for paint and polish by manufacturer Alf Bjerke of Oslo a year or so later. This venture did not survive, nor did a further attempt by instrument maker Frode Mortensen to package insecticide in aerosol cans. Rotheim died in 1938, before the significance of his invention had been proved.

U.S.: The first aerosol product was insecticide for the U.S. Army, using a canister developed by research chemist L. D. Goodhue of the Department of Agriculture. He had been working on aerosol insecticides since 1935 but had encountered a series of technical problems. The program was due to be discussed at a high-level Washington meeting scheduled for 14 April 1941. Faced with the prospect of an admission of failure, Goodhue decided to go into the lab the day before, Easter Sunday. There it occurred to him to try a previously abandoned solution one more time. Having filled a fumigation chamber with cockroaches, he squirted the aerosol at them, and this time it worked: ten minutes later all the cockroaches were dead.

Manufacture of what U.S. troops named "bug bombs" began under a contract signed by the Bridgeport Brass Co. of Connecticut in July 1942, and nearly fifty million were produced before the end of World War II. The canisters were too heavy and the cost of manufacture was too high to make the bug bomb readily adaptable to consumer use. Following much experimentation, a solution was found by adopting lightweight casings based on beer cans and substituting plastic valves for metal ones. The initial delivery of American-made aerosols for commercial use was 105,000 canisters delivered by Airosol, Inc., of Neodesha, Kans., on 21 November 1946. The following year the first food product packed in an aerosol can was launched, Reddi-wip whipped cream, introduced by Aaron Lapin of St. Louis in Spra-tainer cans produced by Crown Cork & Seal. Sold initially by milkmen in the St. Louis area, the product rapidly achieved national distribution, and within five years "Bunny" Lapin had become the first aerosol millionaire. "He bought Cadillacs two at a time," reported an admiring *Aerosol Age*, "and lived in Gloria Swanson's furnished mansion in Hollywood."

THE FIRST **AFFIRMATIVE ACTION**

The term "affirmative action" was coined by a young black attorney, Hobart Taylor Jr., who had been hired by Vice President Lyndon B. Johnson to draft President John F. Kennedy's Executive Order 10925 of March 1961 establishing the President's Committee on Equal Employment Opportunity. The government was to

> consider and recommend additional affirmative steps which should be taken by executive departments and agencies to realize more fully the national policy of non-discrimination ... The contractor will take affirmative action to ensure that applicants are employed, and that employees are treated during employment, without regard to their race, creed, color or national origin.

Taylor later recalled that he had been "searching for something that would give a sense of positiveness to performance under that executive order and I was torn between 'positive action' and the words 'affirmative action'.... And I took 'affirmative' because it was alliterative."

The original meaning of the phrase, given the context of *equal* opportunity, was different from that which it was soon to acquire. The government intended that there be a more proactive approach to nondiscriminatory hiring practices. The Congress of Racial Equality (CORE) was not satisfied that this was sufficient. In 1962 CORE demanded not only that employers hire a prescribed percentage of black workers but also that they adopt *preferential* hiring. The first company to comply was the Sealtest Dairy Co. of New York, which had only 1 percent of blacks among its workforce of 1,400. After a two-month boycott organized by the local CORE chapter, Sealtest agreed that in 1963 it would give "initial exclusive priority to all job openings to Negroes and Spanish Americans." Other successes followed CORE boycotts elsewhere in New York and in California, as well as in Baltimore, Denver, Detroit, and Seattle.

Affirmative action in the preferential sense was first enshrined in law with the adoption of the Nixon administration's so-called Philadelphia Plan by a majority vote of both the House and the Senate on 23 December 1969. This required contractors to the federal government in the construction industry to adopt plans to correct any city-based underrepresentation of ethnic minorities (black, Asian, Native American, and Spanish American) in their workforces. In February 1970 Secretary of Labor George Shultz's Order No. 4 extended the provision beyond the construction industry to all companies accepting a $50,000 federal contract and having more than fifty employees.

THE FIRST **AIDS VICTIM**

to have been publicly identified by name was a forty-seven-year-old Danish physician, Margrethe P. Rask, who succumbed to the malady in Copenhagen on 12 December 1977. She had been working since 1972 at hospitals in Zaire, where she had been exposed to African patients' secretions and blood. Chronic symptoms only diagnosed as AIDS several years after her death began appearing early in 1976.

It seems likely, though, that the disease had been incubating unrecognized in Central Africa for at least two decades. In 1957 a number of patients from the Belgian Congo (now the Democratic Republic of the Congo) were admitted to the Johannesburg Fever Hospital in South Africa suffering from a wasting disease, to which most succumbed. A medical missionary from the area affected was asked to advise on lifestyle habits the victims might have in common and the hospital's conclusion was that the virus was contracted by men who had contact with green monkeys. It was dubbed "green monkey disease," the symptoms of which were later identified by the Fever Hospital's Prof. Jock Gear as those of full-blown AIDS.

The first known American victim was a young gay New York man known as "Nick" who died on 15 January 1981, having begun to suffer general debilitation the previous March. The cause of death was not then known and attracted no public attention. The earliest reference to AIDS in print (though not by that name) was a sadly unprescient article by gay physician and writer Lawrence Mass in the *New York Native* of 18 May 1981, "Disease Rumors Largely Unfounded." On 3 July the *New York Times* devoted a brief report to "Rare Cancer Seen in 41 Homosexuals." AIDS did not become front-page news until the *Los Angeles Times* headlined on 31 May 1982 "Mysterious Fever Now Epidemic," nearly a year after the U.S. Centers for Disease Control and Prevention in Atlanta had issued a warning (5 June 1981) about a rare form of pneumonia among a promiscuous group of Los Angeles gays, later identified as AIDS-related.

From the United States the disease spread to Europe. In December 1981 a forty-nine-year-old British homosexual, who vacationed each year in Miami, died at London's Brompton Hospital—nine months after his last visit to Florida. At this date there were thirty-six cases of the then unnamed syndrome in Europe: seventeen in France, six in Belgium, five in Switzerland, three in Denmark, two in Britain, two in West Germany, and one in Spain. Two gay Italian men traveling together in the United States were diagnosed the same year. By then the number of American cases was already into three figures, many of the victims infected by a highly promiscuous Air Canada flight attendant, Gaetan Dugas, who refused to give up his lifestyle of one-night stands even after he had been diagnosed as a carrier. By 1983 the disease had spread to most other countries of Western Europe and to Czechoslovakia, Japan, and Australia.

THE FIRST **AIR-CONDITIONING**

in the sense of mechanical refrigeration for human comfort was installed in 1891 at the Ice Palace, a restaurant and beer hall on Market Street in St. Louis, Mo. The system consisted of three banks of expansion coils fitted halfway up the wall and was supplied with refrigerant from a central station operated by the Automatic Refrigerating Co. The inside temperature of the restaurant was maintained at 72°–75°F when the outside temperature registered up to 90°F. To enhance the effect the Ice Palace's walls were decorated with scenes of snow and ice, including paintings of the Kane Polar Expedition.

The first air-conditioning systems proper, able to control humidity as well as temperature, were designed by two engineers working separately but at the same time. Willis Carrier of the Buffalo Forge Co. in Buffalo, N.Y., often hailed as the "inventor" of air-conditioning, installed an apparatus capable of maintaining a summer temperature of 80°F with humidity of 72 percent for the Sackett-Wilhelms Lithographing & Publishing Co. of Brooklyn, where atmospheric conditions caused paper to expand or contract, with the result that colors were out of register. In operation by the spring of 1903, this was strictly an industrial application of air-conditioning. The other pioneer, heating and ventilation consultant Alfred R. Wolff, had, however, preceded Carrier with a cooling and dehumidification system he had installed in the dissecting room of Cornell Medical College in New York City in 1899. This was not intended for human comfort, as the humans to be kept cool were already dead, but in 1903, the same year that Carrier made his industrial installation, Wolff became the first to use air-conditioning for the purpose most common today. On 22 April that year the plant he had installed at the new New York Stock Exchange building at 18 Broad Street became operative, using three ammonia absorption machines to cool the vast 183' x 100' x 79' trading floor. Supplied by the Carbondale Machinery Co., each had a cooling capacity of 150 tons, and the system was designed to maintain a temperature of 75°F and 55 percent relative humidity. It also controlled the cleanliness and distribution of air.

The first **domestic air conditioner** marketed as such was designed by a team led by Harry Blair Hull and manufactured by Frigidaire of Fort Wayne, Ind., in 1929. This was a split-system design, the 28" x 18"x 49" cabinet being supplied from a sulfur dioxide condensing unit located in the basement. The cooler cabinet weighed 200 pounds and the condenser another 400 pounds. At this bulk it had rather more appeal to small businesses than to suburban home-owners, and one of the earliest purchasers was the Hollywood Night Club in New York. The first self-contained, plug-in air-conditioning units for home and office were launched by De La Vergne Machine Co. of New York and the Baldwin-Southwark Corp. of Philadelphia in 1932. Although a large number of refrigeration and ventilation manufacturers went into production during the 1930s, uptake was understandably modest for installations that cost nearly $2,000 to air-condition an average house. In 1938, when the smallest portable unit cost some $400, fewer than 0.25 percent of wired homes had even a single air-conditioned room. After World War II, prices fell and the market opened, with sales rising from just over 1,000 in 1945 to 30,000 the following year, 193,000 in 1950, and a staggering 1.3 million units in 1952. As one cold war was starting, another had been won.

THE FIRST **AIRCRAFT CARRIER**

to be designed as such was preceded by naval vessels equipped with improvised flight decks. The first of these was the U.S. light cruiser *Birmingham*, from which exhibition pilot Eugene Ely took off in a 50 hp Curtiss pusher biplane at 3:16 P.M. on 14 November 1910 while the ship lay at anchor in Chesapeake Bay. He landed 2½ miles away at Willoughby Spit, near Norfolk, Va.

The first landing on the deck of a ship was performed by Ely at 11:01 A.M. on 18 January 1911, when he touched down on a 120-foot-long platform erected on the stern of the armored cruiser *Pennsylvania*, moored in San Francisco Bay. His Curtiss aircraft was fitted with three pairs of spring-loaded hooks on the undercarriage, designed to engage a series of 22 cables stretched between sandbags across the flight deck at 3-foot intervals. This arrester system brought the plane to a halt after a deck run of only 30 feet.

The first **takeoff from a ship under way** was made from the Royal Navy's HMS *Hibernia* by Lt. Charles Samson in a Short S.38, while the vessel was moving at a speed of 10½ knots during a Review of the Fleet by King George V at Weymouth on 8 May 1912.

Aircraft carriers on active service: In April 1914 the battleship USS *Mississippi* and the cruiser USS *Birmingham* were ordered to Vera Cruz with four U.S. Navy seaplanes. The aircraft were used to make reconnaissance flights over the Mexican lines, being lowered over the side of their carriers for takeoff from the water. (SEE ALSO **aerial warfare.**)

The first successful **catapult launch** took place on 12 November 1914 when an airplane piloted by the U.S. Navy's first pilot, Theodore G. Ellyson, was launched at Washington Navy Yard. The first from aboard ship was made by Lt. Cdr. H. C. Mustin in an AB-2 flying boat from USS *North Carolina* in Pensacola Bay, Fla., on 5 November 1915.

Purpose-built aircraft carrier: The first warship built as an aircraft carrier, though not originally designed as such, was Britain's HMS *Ark Royal*, a 366-foot-long vessel of 7,020 tons displacement, launched at Blyth, Northumberland, in September 1914 and commissioned on 9 December. Intended as a merchantman, she was acquired by the Admiralty while under construction and converted for use as a carrier with below-deck hangars accommodating ten seaplanes. The *Ark Royal* was dispatched to the Dardanelles immediately on completing her trials and conducted her first offensive operation on arrival at Tenedos on 17 February 1915, when one of her aircraft took off on a reconnaissance mission.

The first warship built for the use of wheeled aircraft was HMS *Furious*, a 19,100-ton-displacement combination battle cruiser/carrier, which joined the fleet on completion in June 1917. At this time she had only a takeoff deck, her six wheeled aircraft being expected to proceed to a land base on fulfillment of a mission, but in November 1917 she returned to dock for installation of a landing deck. A notable feature of the *Furious* was a hydraulic lift for raising aircraft from hangar to flight deck.

Even before the installation of a landing deck, an aircraft had succeeded in landing on *Furious*. On 2 August 1917 Sqn. Cdr. Edwin Dunning took off in a Sopwith Pup from a field at Smoogro, overlooking Scapa Flow in the Orkneys, and landed on the 75-foot flight deck after cutting his engine. This was the first **landing on a moving ship** anywhere in the world. The *Furious* was traveling at 20 knots into a 22-knot wind. Dunning made a second successful landing on 7 August but was killed at the third attempt five days later.

The first carrier for wheeled aircraft to be designed and completed as such was the Japanese navy's 7,470-ton-displacement *Hosho*, which was laid down on 19 December 1919 and made her first sea trials off Tateyama on 30 November 1922. She carried twenty-one aircraft and had a maximum speed of 25 knots.

U.S.: America's first carrier for wheeled aircraft, USS *Langley*, was a conversion from a collier, *Jupiter*, which was equipped with a 53-foot flight deck and commissioned on 20 March 1922. The first to be purpose-built, USS *Saratoga*, was originally intended as a heavy battle cruiser but was completed as a carrier and commissioned at Camden, N.J., on 16 November 1927 under the command of Capt. H. E. Yarnall. Carrying ninety aircraft and with a displacement of 36,000 tons, she was the second-largest carrier in the world, and her 880-foot flight deck was the longest of any carrier at sea, a record sustained (together with USS *Lexington*, commissioned a month later) for eighteen years. *Saratoga* and *Lexington*, each with sixteen boilers developing 18,000 shp, were also the world's most powerful warships prior to World War II. First to be built as a carrier from the keel up was the 14,500-ton-displacement USS *Ranger*, launched at Newport News, Va., and commissioned on 4 June 1934.

Jet aircraft to take off from and land aboard an aircraft carrier: The first was an XFD-1 Phantom, which was flown from the USS *Franklin D. Roosevelt* by Lt. Cdr. James J. Davidson as she lay off Cape Henry, Va., on 21 July 1946. The deck run for takeoff was 460 feet.

The first carrier-based squadron of jet aircraft was U.S. Navy Squadron 17-A, comprising sixteen Phantoms, which qualified for cruiser operation aboard the USS *Saipan* on 5–7 May 1948.

Nuclear-powered aircraft carrier: The first was the 72,500-ton-displacement USS *Enterprise*, launched at Newport News, Va., on 24 September 1960 and commissioned on 25 November 1961. Fitted with eight pressurized water-cooled nuclear reactors, she was the most powerful warship ever built until then (approximately 300,000 hp), as well as the largest (1,101½ feet long) and the costliest ($445 million). The total complement of the *Enterprise* was 440 officers and 4,160 enlisted men. She was designed to carry one hundred aircraft, and her flight deck was described as being the size of four American football fields.

THE FIRST **AIR FORCE**

unit was the Aeronautical Division of the Office of the Chief Signal Officer of the U.S. Army, established under the command of Capt. Charles deForest Chandler on 1 July 1907. The original strength of the force was one officer, one NCO, and one enlisted man. A contract was placed with the Wright brothers for an aircraft that had to be able to reach a speed of at least 36 mph and remain in the air continuously for at least one hour. The biplane was delivered to Fort Myer, Va., for flight tests in August 1908 but crashed the following month. A new Wright Flyer was constructed and, after successful flight trials, formally handed over to the Aeronautical Division on 2 August 1909. It was then taken to College Park, Md., where it made its maiden flight as the world's first regularly commissioned **military aircraft**. The first pilot officer to solo was 2nd Lt. Frederick E. Humphreys, who made two circuits of the field at College Park in 3 minutes on 26 October 1909. Although the first to show heavier-than-air aircraft a formal military recognition, the U.S. Army was slow to develop its aviation resources, and by the outbreak of war in Europe in 1914 it could boast no more than six airworthy planes.

The first nation to build up an effective force of military aircraft was France, which by the end of 1910 had 34 fully qualified army pilots, another 20 under instruction, and 32 service aircraft. By the summer of 1911, French air power had increased to 100 aircraft and a comparable number of pilots. At the beginning of 1912, the number had doubled, with 234 aircraft and nearly 300 pilots.

Independent air force: The first subordinate to neither naval nor military command was Britain's Royal Air Force, formed by amalgamation of the Royal Flying Corps and the Royal Naval Air Service on 1 April 1918.

America's air force underwent many changes of name and status before it acquired its present designation and parity of command with the older services. The Aeronautical Division of the Signal Corps became the Aviation Section on 18 July 1914. This in turn was renamed the Airplane Division (aka the Air Service) on 2 June 1917, becoming an autonomous unit of the U.S. Army on 20 May 1918 when it separated from the Signal Corps. The Army Reorganization Act of 4 June 1920 formally recognized the commonly used name U.S. Air Service, which metamorphosed into the U.S. Army Air Corps on 2 July 1926. This changed to USAAF (U.S. Army Air Forces) on 20 June 1941, succeeded by the current, independent U.S. Air Force that came into being on 18 September 1947. Thus the world's first air force was one of the last in the developed world to cast off the shackles that bound it to the army, despite the fact that it was by then incomparably the most powerful.

SEE ALSO **aerial warfare**.

THE FIRST AIRLINE

to establish scheduled passenger service by airplane was the St. Petersburg–Tampa Airboat Line of St. Petersburg, Fla., which commenced flight operations on 1 January 1914. Passengers were carried across the 20-mile-wide Tampa Bay one at a time in a Benoist flying boat piloted by Tony Jannus. The first paying passenger was Mayor A. C. Phiel of St. Petersburg, who bought the world's first airline ticket at auction for $400. The mayor had a practical reason for this considerable outlay: He needed to buy some machinery in Tampa, and he was in a hurry. The first female passenger, Mrs. L. A. Whitney, flew on 8 January at the regular fare of $5, which saved the affluent and intrepid a 36-mile journey around the bay by road. Freight was also carried, at $5 per 100 pounds, minimum charge 25¢. The service continued for four months, with two return flights a day.

The first land-based airline and the first in the world to achieve a sustained service and multiple routes was Germany's DLR (Deutsche Luft-Reederei), which began flying between Johannesthal airfield in Berlin and the new capital, Weimar, on a regular daily schedule on 5 February 1919. Only mail and newspapers were carried on the initial flights, the first passenger being Reich Minister Albertz, who made the 2-hour 18-minute flight on 10 February. Other distinguished passengers in the first month of service were Reich President Friedrich Ebert, the first head of state to fly on government business, and Germany's most popular male film star, Hans Albers. The aircraft used were open-cockpit LVG C.IV biplanes, which meant that passengers had to be issued with flying suits, helmets and goggles, and fur-lined flying boots. Shortly, however, DLR began using AEG J.II biplanes with a five-seater passenger compartment. Further internal routes opened up during the course of 1919 included Berlin–Hamburg (1 March), Berlin–Hannover–Rotthausen (15 April), and Berlin–Warnemünde (15 April). One standard airline feature that had been pioneered by DLR before the end of the year was the adoption of a corporate emblem for display on its aircraft, and this symbol—a crane rising in flight, designed by Prof. Otto Firle—is still used as the fleet emblem of Lufthansa. DLR merged with Aero Lloyd AG in 1923, which itself merged with Junkers Luftverkehr to become Lufthansa in 1926.

The first **international airline route** was Paris, France–Brussels, Belgium, inaugurated on a weekly schedule by Lignes Farman on 22 March 1919 using a Farman F60 Goliath piloted by Lucien Bossoutrot. Flight duration was 2 hours 50 minutes, and the fare was 365 francs. For the first two flights there was no customs inspection on arrival. By the next, on 6 April, for the first time anywhere in the world customs officers were on hand at Brussels to check for forbidden or dutiable goods carried by the passengers.

The first international route on a daily schedule began with Air Transport & Travel's 9:10 A.M. flight from London (Hounslow) to Paris (Le Bourget) on 25 August 1919. A converted DH4a biplane bomber piloted by Lt. E. H. Lawford carried newspapers, a consignment of leather, several brace of grouse, some jars of Devonshire cream, and George Stevenson-Reece, who paid a one-way fare of £21 ($105) for the 2½-hour journey. The cost of traveling by rail and boat to Paris at this date was £3 8s 5d ($17).

U.S.: The first international service was inaugurated by floatplane operator Florida West Indies Airways from Key West, Fla., to Havana, Cuba, on 1 November 1919. On 25 August 1920 the company secured the first airmail contract from the U.S. Post Office Department, but was unable to secure the funding needed to activate it and was taken over in October by Aeromarine Airways, which renamed itself Aeromarine West Indies Airways. Founded by Inglis M. Uppercue of Keyport, N.J., Aeromarine had been flying summer vacation services from New York City to Newport, Southampton, and Atlantic City using the first **airliners** in the United States, which were adaptations of the Curtiss F-SL naval flying boat built at Uppercue's Aeromarine Plane and Motor at Raritan Bay, N.J. The first of these fourteen-seater 400 hp twin-engine Curtiss-type 75 Aeromarine Cruisers, the Santa Maria, had been christened at the Columbia Yacht Club on 22 June 1920 by Gov. Edward Edwards of New Jersey with a Prohibition-era illegal bottle of champagne. On 1 November 1920 the interrupted service from Key West to Havana was resumed, and this may have been America's first regular international route, as it is unclear whether Florida West Indies Airways had ever achieved sustained service. The two Type 75 Cruisers in operation, Santa Maria and Perita, made twice-daily return mail and passenger flights (fare $75) of 2½ hours each way at an average speed of 90 mph. Four other Cruisers were subsequently added to the fleet.

On 22 September 1921 service out of New York began with 1,521-mile flights to Havana via Atlantic City, Beaufort, S.C., Miami, and Key West, the 19-hour, $250 service dubbed the "Highball Express" because of its popularity with those fleeing the rigors of Prohibition. Scheduled daily service to Nassau in the Bahamas from Miami started on 1 November 1922, with fares for the 185-mile, 3-hour flight at $85 one-way, $150 round-trip. Ads invited, "Breakfast in Miami, Lunch in Nassau and Dinner in Miami—All in the same day." At this time the airline also undertook unscheduled and strictly clandestine rum-running flights.

Aeromarine's operations came to an end with the abrupt withdrawal of the airmail contract, and the final flight, to Nassau, took place on 1 May 1924. Including domestic charter and demonstration flights, more than thirty thousand passengers had been carried more than a million miles with only a single fatal accident (SEE **airline disaster**).

Prior to 1925 all the pioneer U.S. airlines used floatplanes or flying boats, thereby avoiding the need for costly airport (qv) facilities. America's first **land-based airline** was the Los Angeles–San Diego Air Line, aka Ryan Airlines, founded by aircraft engineer Claude Ryan with six war-surplus Lincoln Standard J biplane trainers, each of which he converted into a six-seat airliner powered by a new Hispano-Suiza 150-hp engine. Scheduled service began on the 120-mile route between Los Angeles and San Diego on 1 March 1925, with one-way fares of $17.50 for the 90-minute flight or $26.50 round-trip. Another aircraft, The Cloudster, was acquired during the year from Los Angeles–based Donald Douglas. The large 11-seat biplane had made its maiden flight on 24 February 1921 and was not only the first Douglas but the first purpose-designed airliner in the United States to go into service. A further distinction was being the first aircraft able to lift its own weight. Los Angeles–San Diego Air Line continued in operation during 1926, flying 5,600 passengers without a mishap until Cloudster met its end flying a wealthy Chinese businessman on charter to Ensenada, Mexico, in December. By this time the U.S. Post Office had begun letting contracts for flying domestic airmail, thus providing the subvention that would enable civil aviation to get properly started in the United States. Ryan, however, with his aero-engineering background, decided he would be better off manufacturing mail planes than operating them, and he did this with conspicuous success—his most celebrated creation being Charles Lindbergh's *Spirit of St. Louis.*

The inception of the Los Angeles–San Diego Air Line in 1925 marks the point at which passenger airlines in the United States began their continuous history and (from 1926–27) rapidly began to multiply. Hitherto lack of government support and the efficiency of ground communications had hindered progress, so that air transportation was practically unknown in the United States when almost the whole of Europe was accessible to paying passengers as were many parts of North Africa (linked to Europe by air in September 1919), South America (where Société des Transports Aériens Guyanais of French Guiana had started operating in November 1919), Russia, Asia, and Australia. America, the birthplace of the airplane, was thus the last of the advanced nations of the world to enter the field of commercial aviation as a regular and permanent means of passenger transport.

Economy fares: The first airline to offer a choice at varying fares was Imperial Airways on the London–Paris route in October 1927. First-class passengers were carried in "Silver Wing" Argosies with steward service for £9 ($45) round-trip and made the trip in 2 hours 30 minutes; second-class passengers paid £7.10s ($37.50) round-trip for a 2-hour 50-minute flight in a Handley Page biplane without food or drinks en route. Business class was first introduced by KLM on its North Atlantic route in 1978.

Transatlantic airline service: The first across the North Atlantic began with the inaugural passenger flight of Pan American Airways' Boeing 314 flying boat *Yankee Clipper* from Port Washington on Long Island, New York, via Botwood, Newfoundland, to Southampton, England, on 28 June 1939. The Atlantic leg took 18 hours and 42 minutes flying time. The standard of accommodation has scarcely been surpassed since on scheduled air routes: separate passenger cabins, a dining saloon, ladies' dressing room, recreation lounge, sleeping berths, and a bridal suite. The fare was $625 round-trip.

The new service also put an aerial girdle around Earth. Among the twenty-two passengers were two who were the first to fly around the world by scheduled airlines. Mrs. Clara Adams and Julius Rapoport, traveling together, had onward tickets for the Imperial Airways flight from London to Hong Kong, then returned to the United States aboard Pan Am's *Pacific Clipper.* The way in which transatlantic flying had annihilated the travails of distance was exemplified by one of the six women passengers, whose small daughter shouted out as she boarded, "Write me a letter." Her mother chuckled and called back, "Honey, I'll be back before the letter!"

Jet airline service: The first was inaugurated by British Overseas Airways Corp. (BOAC) with the flight of a De Havilland Comet from London to Johannesburg (6,724 miles) in 23 hours 34 minutes on 2–3 May 1952. Jet service by Comet to Sri Lanka followed on 11 August and to Singapore on 20 October. BOAC's weekly service to Tokyo began on 3 April 1953, and Air France started flying Comets from Paris to Beirut via Rome on 26 August 1953. Comets were grounded and the certificate of airworthiness withdrawn on 12 April 1954 after two crashes in a period of three months, one of them of the first Comet in scheduled service, G-ALYP, known by its call letters "Yoke Peter." A court of inquiry established metal fatigue as the cause. The aircraft was redesigned and took to the air again as the first jet airliner in transatlantic service.

The first jet services across the North Atlantic were flown between London and New York by BOAC Comet 4, G-APDC (pilot Capt. R. E. Millichap), and from New York to London by BOAC Comet 4, G-APDB (pilot Capt. T. B. Stoney), both on 4 October 1958. The NY–London run established a new Atlantic record of 6 hours 11 minutes. The fare was £279 15s ($785).

U.S.: Pan American became the first U.S. carrier to offer transatlantic jet service three weeks after BOAC, 26 October 1958, when it started flying Boeing 707s on the New York–Paris route.

The number of transatlantic passengers crossing by air exceeded the number crossing by ship for the first time in 1958. Another twelve years were to pass before the last regular passenger sailing (as opposed to cruise liners) in 1970. By that time the price advantage, which still existed in the 1960s with one-way economy class fares on immigrant ships of $180, had been wiped out with the adoption of the jumbo jet by Pan Am in January of that year.

Around-the-world passenger service: The first was inaugurated by Australia's Qantas Empire Airways on 14 January 1958, flying the Super Constellation *Southern Aurora* eastbound from Sydney to London via the United States in five and a half days and another Super Constellation, the *Southern Zephyr*, westbound from Sydney to London via India and the Middle East in six and a half days.

Supersonic airliners: The first in scheduled passenger service were a British Airways Concorde flying London (Heathrow)–Bahrain and an Air France Concorde flying Paris–Rio de Janeiro, both of which took off simultaneously at 11:40 A.M. on 21 January 1976. The pilots were Capt. Norman Todd and Capt. Pierre Chanoine, respectively. The first transatlantic passenger flights were made on 24 May 1976 with separate arrivals at Dulles International Airport, Washington, D.C., from both London and Paris.

Following a sharp decrease in airline travel post 9/11, the Concorde was withdrawn from service when British Airways's last supersonic flight from New York, BA 002, landed at Heathrow at 4:05 P.M. on 24 October 2003. Among the passengers was one of the Concorde's most frequent fliers, Sir David Frost, who once described it as the only means of being in two places at once. (With a fastest transatlantic crossing of under 2 hours 53 minutes, it was indeed possible to be in New York earlier than the hour of departure.) Total number of passengers in just under fifty thousand Concorde flights was 2.5 million.

THE FIRST **AIRLINE DISASTER**

on a scheduled passenger flight occurred at Golders Green, a suburb of north London, shortly after noon on Tuesday, 14 December 1920. The airliner, belonging to Handley Page Continental Air Services, had just left Cricklewood Aerodrome for Paris, carrying a two-man crew and six passengers. It crashed into the back of a newly built house, 6 Basinghill, the Ridgeway, and fell in flames into the garden. Four of the passengers managed to jump clear just before the aircraft hit the ground, two of them surviving unhurt, and the other two being only slightly injured. The four other occupants of the plane were killed, including the pilot, R. Bager, and his engineer.

U.S.: Aeromarine Airways' Type 75 Cruiser *Columbus* was forced down in the sea by engine failure 20 miles from Havana on 13 January 1923 while on a scheduled flight from Key West, Fla. The seven passengers managed to climb onto the hull of the flying boat, but four of them, Cuba-based sugar planter Edwin Atkins, his sons aged five and three, and their governess, were swept overboard by high waves and lost.

The first **jet airliner to crash** during a scheduled flight was BOAC's Comet 1 G-ALYV, which disintegrated through structural failure near Calcutta, India, on 2 May 1953 with the loss of forty-three lives. Subsequent accidents resulted in the British-built Comet, the world's first operational jet airliner, being grounded and the eventual dominance of the American-built Boeing 707.

THE FIRST **AIRLINE FLIGHT ATTENDANT**

was fourteen-year-old Jack Sanderson, who started duty on a De Havilland 34 operated by Britain's Daimler Airways between London and Paris on 2 April 1922. He wore a peaked cap and a cutaway jacket, his principal duties being handling baggage, serving beverages and sandwiches, and calming nervous passengers who were on their maiden flight. Steward Sanderson was killed in an air crash the following year.

U.S.: The first was Miles Davis, who joined Western Air Express on the Los Angeles–San Francisco route in 1927. At a time when most labor was arduous, the duties of a Western Air Express steward, with a maximum of only ten passengers on the Fokker F.10 trimotors, were comparatively light, consisting mainly of handing out newspapers and the deep-filled sandwiches prepared in advance by the Pig 'n Whistle restaurant in Los Angeles. By contrast, stewards on Britain's Imperial Airways cross-Channel flights were required to serve a six-course meal with wines to up to twenty passengers at a time, irrespective of the turbulence experienced at low altitude.

The first **female flight attendant** was Miss Ellen Church, a registered nurse from Iowa, who on 15 May 1930 welcomed her first eleven passengers aboard United Airlines trimotor Boeing 80A at Oakland (Calif.) Airport, preparatory to the five-stage flight to Cheyenne, Wyo. Miss Church, a private pilot herself, had written to the airline a month or two previously suggesting that suitably qualified young ladies like herself might be employed as cabin attendants. She was not only engaged but given the task of selecting and training seven others for the same work. Aspiring applicants had to be registered nurses of twenty-five or under, weigh not more than 115 pounds, and not exceed 5' 4" in height. The chosen few received a chic woolen twill uniform with gray and silver buttons, a salary of $125 a month, and the sometimes doubtful pleasure of spending a basic 100 hours per month flying in an unheated and unpressurized aircraft. Their duties, which were not confined to the air, included carrying the passengers' baggage, cleaning the interior of the airplane, helping the pilot and mechanics to push the machine in and out of hangars, and wielding a refueling hose. At each embarkation point they collected tickets and once in the air dispensed unvarying meals of fruit cocktail, fried chicken, and rolls, along with tea or coffee. Scheduled time for the 950-mile flight was 18 hours, but according to one of the pioneer attendants it generally took something closer to 24. At the beginning Miss Church and the other seven ex-nurses suffered undisguised hostility from pilots and the even fiercer resentment of their wives, who deluged the airline with letters demanding that the girls should go. Expressions of appreciation from passengers weighed more heavily with United, and the young ladies stayed, harbingers of a new profession for women.

Outside the United States, the first air stewardesses were recruited by Air France in 1931, and these were also the first to fly on international routes. Swissair followed suit in 1934, KLM a year later, Britain's Air Dispatch in 1936, and Lufthansa in 1938.

The first **black flight attendant** in the United States was Ruth Carol Taylor, hired by Mohawk Airlines of Ithaca, N.Y., on 11 February 1958 for its New York City–Ithaca run.

THE FIRST **AIRLINE MEALS**

were introduced in a modest way by Handley Page Transport with prepacked lunchboxes on its London–Brussels flights from 11 October 1919. The price was 3s (75¢). Hot meals were first served on London–Paris flights by two competing airlines in 1927. The three-engined Armstrong Whitworth Argosies employed by Imperial Airways' luxury "Silver Wing" flights beginning on 1 May of that year were furnished with a galley at the rear from which lunch accompanied by wines was served to up to eighteen passengers. The Rayon d'Or lunchtime service of France's Air Union, launched three months later, offered hors d'oeuvres, crayfish à la Parisienne, chicken chasseur, York ham in gelatine, salade Niçoise, ice cream, cheese, and fruit washed down with champagne, red or white Bordeaux, spirits, soft drinks, and coffee. This haute cuisine was served in sumptuous cabins designed specially by the Compagnie des Wagons-Lits. The flight time in Air Union's red, white, and gold–liveried LeO 21s was only 20 minutes longer that it would be over the same route fifty years later.

U.S.: The earliest airline meals consisted of deep-filled sandwiches from the Pig 'n Whistle cafeteria in Los Angeles which were loaded on to Western Air's Fokkers for their flights to San Francisco, starting with the appointment of their first airline flight attendant (qv) in 1927. Hot meals followed with the introduction of Transcontinental Air Transport's service from New York to Los Angeles on 7 July 1929, long sections of which had to be made by train. While actually in the air, passengers were indulged with bouillon and finger sandwiches in the morning, lunch served on silverware with starched linen napkins—invariably boiled chicken kept hot in thermos jugs, but elegantly presented on the finest Dirigold plates—and tea and toast in the afternoon. Unlike its European predecessors, TAT did not grace the repast with fine wines. Prohibition applied in the air just as it did on the ground.

The standard economy-class airline meal in which three courses are served at the same time on one tray was devised by hotelier Don Magarrell, who had earlier designed the kitchens on the United States Line's SS *Leviathan*, to fit the dimensions of a passenger's lap on a United Airlines DC3. A special flight kitchen was established at Oakland, Calif., in August 1937 and a Swiss chef was hired from San Francisco's Clift Hotel to prepare the meals on the ground, the hot part being dispensed from thermos flasks in the air. The pressed-pulp disposable tray measured 24" x 30" and had a 12-inch-wide depression to hold the main course; the appetizer lay in the top right corner, dessert was top left, and salad occupied a paper cup top center, with salt and pepper dispensers slotted into holes. To complete this gastronomic wonder, coffee, cream, and sugar lay to the right of the entrée. The whole was covered by a cardboard lid with blue and buff stripes.

THE FIRST **AIRMAIL**

flight by airplane was made by French pilot Henri Piquet in a Humber-Sommer biplane at the United Provinces Exhibition, Allahabad, India, on 18 February 1911. A load of six thousand letters and cards was flown 5 miles from Allahabad to Naini Junction, and then sent on by rail.

U.S.: The first unofficial airmail flight (i.e., carrying letters that had not been transmitted via the post office) was made by Fred Wiseman from Petaluma to Santa Rosa, Calif., in a 12-minute flight on 17 February 1911. In addition to letters from the mayor of Petaluma to the mayor of Santa Rosa, the homemade airplane, which Wiseman had copied from photographs of the Wright Flyer, also carried a sack of groceries and the morning newspapers. Wiseman said later, "I know I flew the first airmail, but Earl Ovington's widow used to get a big kick out of her husband being first, so I never said anything about it." Of aviation, the pioneer remarked, "I got out in 1913. Didn't see much future in it."

The Earl Ovington whom Wiseman magnanimously allowed to grab the glory was the first to make official flights under the auspices of the U.S. Post Office. These took place 23–30 September 1911 during the International Aviation Tournament at Garden City, N.Y. On the inaugural flight he carried 640 letters and 1,280 postcards in a Blériot monoplane 6 miles from Nassau Boulevard Aerodrome on Long Island and then dropped the mailbags from above the Mineola Post Office.

Regular commercially operated airmail service: The first was inaugurated in the German Colony of South West Africa (now Namibia) with a Roland biplane, which made its initial mail-carrying flight between the coastal resort of Swakopmund and the capital, Windhoek, on 18 May 1914. The service came to a premature end when Union troops invaded the country from South Africa on the outbreak of World War I.

U.S.: Regular service was started by the U.S. Army Signal Corps and the U.S. Post Office between Washington, D.C., Philadelphia, and New York on 15 May 1918.

International airmail service was first operated experimentally by Italian military aircraft between Brindisi, Italy, and Valona, Albania, in May–June 1917. The first regular international airmail service was the Austrian civil airmail inaugurated under the direction of A. R. von Marwil, a former fighter pilot, on 11 March 1918. Mail was carried by Hansa-Brandenburg C.I two-seater from Vienna, Austria, to Lvov (then Lemberg) and Proskurov, via Kraków, Poland, with a branch service from Proskurov to Odessa in Ukraine. From 4 July 1918 the route was extended to Budapest. The service ended with the collapse of the Austro-Hungarian Empire in November 1918.

U.S.: The first international airmail flight was made in a Boeing C-3 seaplane piloted by Eddie Hubbard from Vancouver, B.C., to Seattle, Wash., on 3 March 1919. Regular international contract airmail service was inaugurated between Seattle and Victoria, B.C., by Aeromarine Airways on 15 October 1920. The plane used was a B-1 flying boat, and the reason Victoria was chosen as the terminus was that it was the port for the Japanese ship *Africa Maru*, which carried mail to the Far East. Two weeks later Aeromarine began flying mail between Key West, Fla., and Havana, Cuba.

Transatlantic airmail was first flown by Capt. John Alcock and Lt. Whitten-Brown in a Vickers Vimy from St. John's, Newfoundland, to Clifden, County Galway, in Ireland on 14 June 1919. Earlier the same year, an attempt by Harry Hawker and Cmdr. Mackenzie-Grieve had ended when they were forced to ditch in the sea, abandoning the mail when they were rescued. Several days later a passing ship succeeded in extracting it from the fuselage of the still-drifting aircraft, and the sea-stained letters marked "First Transatlantic Air Post" were ultimately delivered to their destinations.

The first regular transatlantic airmail was inaugurated by Deutsche Lufthansa between Berlin and Buenos Aires, via Stuttgart, Seville, Bathurst, and Natal, Brazil, on 3 February 1934. Initially the service was run every fourteen days; from May 1935, weekly. Delivery time was four days.

The first regular North Atlantic airmail service was inaugurated by Pan American Airways between New York and Lisbon/Marseilles on 20 May 1939. Flying time for the Boeing 314 flying boats was 29 hours. BOAC began flying the first U.S.–UK route from New York/Montreal to Southampton two weeks later.

Jet airmail: The first service was inaugurated by Avro Canada Jetliner between Toronto and New York on 18 April 1950.

Airmail label: Inscribed FLUGPOST, the first was used on mail flown between Bork and Brueck in Germany on 18 February 1912. The words PAR AVION were first used on an airmail label for a flight by Lt. Rouin from Villacoublay to Bordeaux, France, on 15 October 1913. The French initiated the general issue of PAR AVION labels on 17 August 1918. These were imperforate labels, or *etiquettes*, printed in black on magenta paper for use on letters carried by the French civil airmail service inaugurated between Paris and Saint-Nazaire on 17 August 1918. *Etiquettes* continue to be inscribed PAR AVION in many countries, as French is the principal language recognized by the Universal Postal Union.

SEE ALSO **envelope: airmail; postage stamps: airmail**.

THE FIRST **AIRPLANE EJECTION SEAT**

was a compressed-air-operated device fitted to the experimental German Heinkel He 280 jet fighter, which made its maiden flight at Rostock-Marienehe on 2 April 1941. The first emergency ejection was made over Rechlin, Germany, on 13 January 1942, when the prototype crashed due to heavy icing. The

pilot, Maj. Schenk, ejected at 7,875 feet and made a safe landing. The He 280 did not go into production, as government contracts were canceled in favor of the Messerschmitt Me 262 jet fighter.

The first aircraft fitted with an ejection seat fired by an explosive charge was the Swedish-built Saab 21, which flew for the first time on 30 July 1943. This ballistic system of ejection completely superseded the use of compressed-air cylinders, and Saab can claim credit for developing in practical form the principle upon which nearly all modern ejection seats are operated.

The first production aircraft to become operational with an ejection seat as standard equipment was the Heinkel He 162, which made its maiden flight on 6 December 1944 and went into service with the German Luftwaffe Squadron L/JG1 at Leck-Holstein on 14 April 1945. Powder-charged ballistic catapult-type seats were fitted to a total of 116 pre-production and production aircraft. The Saab 21, which had been developed earlier than the He 162, did not become operational with the Royal Swedish Air Force until December 1945.

U.S.: The first ejection was by Sgt. Lawrence Lambert, USAAF, on 17 August 1946 from a Northrop P-61 Black Widow flying at 7,800 feet and a speed of 302 mph over Dayton, Ohio. First to use an ejection seat in an emergency was Lt. J. L. Fruin, USN, when he bailed out of a McDonnell F2H-1 Banshee on 9 August 1949 while it was flying at 575 mph over Waterboro, S.C. On 26 February 1955 North American Aviation Corporation test pilot George Franklin Smith became the first flier in the world to survive ejection at supersonic speed after he had bailed out from a Super Sabre at 6,000 feet off Laguna Beach, Calif., at Mach 1.05 (>700 mph). He remained unconscious for five days but nine months later was fit enough to resume flying.

While the United States did not pioneer the ejection seat, experimental work did engender another significant innovation. The first crash test dummy, precursor of those used in automobile testing, was "Sierra Sam," developed by the Sierra Engineering Co. of Sierra Madre, Calif., on behalf of the U.S. Air Force in 1949 for evaluation of ejection seats in rocket sled tests.

THE FIRST **AIRPLANE EQUIPPED WITH RADIO**

was a Curtiss biplane trailing a 49-foot aerial that was flown over the racetrack at Sheepshead Bay, N.Y., on 27 August 1910 by the Canadian pilot J. A. D. McCurdy, who transmitted the following message to the ground station operated by H. M. Horton: "Another chapter in aerial achievement is hereby written in the receiving of this first message ever recorded from an aeroplane in flight."

The first complete and coherent message transmitted from an aircraft beyond visual range of the receiving station was sent by Capt. Brenôt of the French Army from a position between Saint-Cyr and Rambouillet, some 35 miles from the Eiffel Tower radio station, early in July 1911.

The first use of airborne radio by the U.S. military was by Lt. Paul W. Beck of the U.S. Army Signal Corps, who transmitted from a Wright biplane at an altitude of about 100 feet to Selfridge Field, Mich., about 1½ miles away, on 21 January 1911. Two-way air-ground communication was achieved by the American military for the first time on 16 December 1914 in the Philippines, messages being exchanged between Signal Corps officers Lt. H. A. Dargue, flying a Burgess-Wright biplane, and Lt. J. O. Mauborgne, designer of the radio sets used. Dargue pioneered again when he participated in the first plane-to-plane radio transmission on 2 September 1916, he and Capt. C. C. Culver communicating with Lt. W. A. Roberts and Capt. A. D. Smith at a distance of about 2 miles over North Island Flying School, San Diego.

Airborne radio in warfare: First used on 24 September 1914, when British officers Lt. D. S. Lewis and Lt. B. T. James of No. 4 Squadron Royal Flying Corps directed artillery fire from the air during the First Battle of the Aisne. The radio log for that date begins at 4:02 P.M. with the message "A very little short. Fire! Fire!" and concludes at 4:42 P.M. with the words "I am coming home now." Both officers were killed in action shortly after.

Airborne radiotelephone: The first was the Aerophone, developed by British radio engineer Harry Grindell Matthews and used for ground-to-air communication with pilot C. B. Hucks flying 700 feet over the racecourse at Ely, Cambridgeshire, on 23 September 1911. Air-to-ground communication was first achieved in February 1916 in a demonstration of the Wireless Telephone Mark I, developed by former Marconi engineer Maj. C. E. Prince, held in the presence of Lord Kitchener "somewhere in France."

The first squadron to be equipped with two-way radio telephones was London Defence Squadron (No. 141) Royal Flying Corps in 1917. Training and installation was under the direction of Wireless Officer F. S. Mockford, who was to win greater renown after the war as the originator of the Mayday distress signal.

Civil airliner to be equipped with radio: The first was the DH 42 G-EALU operated by Aircraft Transport & Travel Ltd. between London and Paris in 1919. The AD I/S set was installed by the Marconi Company.

THE FIRST **AIRPLANE FLIGHT**

sustained and controlled in a powered aircraft was made by Orville Wright of Dayton, Ohio, in the 16-hp Flyer I at Kill Devil Hills, Kittyhawk, N.C., at 10:35 A.M. on 17 December 1903. The flight lasted for 12 seconds at a height of 8–12 feet and an airspeed of 30–35 mph. It was witnessed by Orville Wright's brother and co-inventor Wilbur and by five coast guards. Three other flights were made the same day, the longest by Wilbur, who covered 852 feet in 59 seconds before crash-landing—the Flyer being damaged beyond repair. The first press reports of the Wright brothers' achievement were based on a story filed by James J. Gray, an employee of the Weather Bureau at Norfolk, Va., who had relayed Wilbur's telegram home announcing the success. Articles appeared in the *Virginian Pilot*, the *Cincinnati Enquirer*, and other papers on 18 December. None was based on eyewitness reports, and most treated the announcement of the conquest of the air with levity.

The first eyewitness report of an airplane flight appeared, improbably, in *Gleanings in Bee Culture* (Medina, Ohio) for January 1905. Describing the Wrights' first circular flight at Huffman's Pasture, near Dayton, on 20 September 1904, the editor, A. I. Root, began his account on this cautionary note: "In order to make the story a helpful one I may stop and turn aside a good many times to point a moral."

Airplane flight with passenger: The first was made by sculptor Léon Delagrange at Issy-les-Moulineaux, Paris, France, on 28 March 1908, accompanied in his Voisin biplane by the Anglo-French aviator Henri Farman.

U.S.: At Kill Devil Hills, Kittyhawk, N. C., on 14 May 1908, Wilbur Wright carried his mechanic, Charles W. Furnas of Dayton, Ohio, on a 1,968-foot flight of 29 seconds duration in the Wright Flyer III.

The first **woman to fly as an airplane passenger** was the French sculptress Mme. Thérèse Peltier, who was taken for a 656-foot flight by Léon Delagrange in a Voisin at Turin on 8 July 1908. The first in the United States was Mrs. Ralph Henry Van Deman, wife of a U.S. Army Signal Corps officer, who was taken on a 4-minute flight at College Park, Md., by Wilbur Wright on 27 October 1909. Wright was giving flight instruction to Signal Corps officers at the time. He had not offered to take her aloft; she simply and unceremoniously climbed into the passenger seat beside him. Mrs. Van Deman came well prepared, binding her long skirts with string lest they billow in the slipstream. Afterward she exclaimed, "Now I know why birds sing. It was wonderful. There is no earthly sensation I can compare with it."

THE FIRST **AIRPLANE, JET**

was the Heinkel He 178, which was powered by a centrifugal-flow engine designed by Dr. Hans von Ohain, and first flown by Flug Kapitän Erich Warsitz at Rostock-Marienehe, Germany, early on the morning of 24 August 1939. A longer flight three days later is often erroneously described as the first. Dr. von Ohain had joined Heinkel in 1936, and his first test-bed turbojet engine, designated He S1, was run the following year. The experiments were carried out in secret without the knowledge of the German Air Ministry, and it was not until October 1939 that the He 178 was officially demonstrated before high-ranking officers of the Luftwaffe.

The first turbojet to fly with a performance superior to any piston-engined aircraft was Britain's Gloster-Whittle E.28 39, designed by Flying Officer (later Sir) Frank Whittle and test-flown for the first time at the RAF College Cranwell by Flt. Lt. P. E. G. Sayer on 15 May 1941. It attained speeds of up to 466 mph, compared with under 400 mph by the He 178. Whittle had taken out the first patent for a gas-turbine system of jet propulsion as early as 1930 while still an RAF cadet at Cranwell. He subsequently formed a company called British Power Jets Ltd. to exploit his patents, and the first test-bed run of the experimental Whittle Unit took place on 12 August 1937, about the same time as von Ohain's earliest experiments. Had the Air Ministry been less dilatory in supporting Whittle's visionary ideas for the future of flight, it is probable that the RAF would have had jet fighters in the Battle of Britain in 1940, and the war might have taken a different course. As it was, the Gloster-Whittle was beaten into the air not only by the Heinkel He 178 but also by Italy's Caproni-Caprini.

The first **turbojet aircraft in series production** and the first **jet fighter used in warfare** was the Messerschmitt Me 262A, the prototype making its maiden jet-powered flight at Leipheim on 18 July 1942. It was powered by Junkers Jumo 004 engines giving a maximum speed of 540 mph, and armed with four MK-108 30-millimeter short-barreled guns. Thirteen pre-production A-1 fighters were delivered to test centers at Lechfeld and Rechlin for service evaluation in March and April 1944, followed by the first production models in May. On 30 June 1944 the world's first operational jet-fighter unit, Erprobungskommando EK 262, was formed at Lechfeld under Hauptmann Werner Thierfelder. A total of 1,433 Me 262s were delivered to the Luftwaffe during WWII.

U.S.: The first jet aircraft was the Bell Airacomet fighter, powered by two GE A1 turbojets rated at 1,250-pound thrust, which was test-flown by Bell's chief test pilot, Bob Stanley, on 2 October 1942 at Muroc Dry Lake, Calif., (now Edwards Air Force Base). The pioneer American jet had been brought to fruition in an astonishingly short space of time. The project was authorized after Gen. H. H. "Hap" Arnold, deputy chief of staff for air, had witnessed a proving flight of the experimental Gloster-Whittle E.28/39 in Britain in May 1941. Under the Anglo-American Lend-Lease agreement, Britain's Air Ministry licensed the U.S. Army to manufacture the Whittle engine without fee. Accordingly General Electric was assigned to replicate the British design at its Lynn, Mass., aero engine factory, and the job of building the airframe was given to Bell Aircraft of Buffalo, N.Y. A sample Whittle engine was flown out to America in great secrecy in late September 1941, and by 18 April 1942 the initial American-built jet engine had been successfully tested. With the test flight in October, the first American jet fighter had been conceived and built in just one year, taking to the air five months before Britain's first jet fighter, the Gloster Meteor F Mk 1, was test-flown in March 1943. Despite this achievement, no American jet became operational during World War II, and the Meteor was the only Allied jet fighter to see active service. The sixty-six Airacomets completed out of an order for a hundred were confined to training duties; their comparatively low speed of 404 mph and disappointing performance in the air would have put them at a serious disadvantage in combat.

Jet fighter to engage an enemy in combat: The first was an Me 262 from the EK 262 experimental unit at Lechfeld, which intercepted a Mosquito of 544 Squadron RAF over Munich on 25 July 1944. The pilot of the British plane, Flt. Lt. Wall, evaded five firing passes from the Me 262 before escaping into a cloudbank. Two days later the RAF's first jet fighters, Gloster Meteor F Mk 1s of 614 Squadron based at Manston, Kent, were flown in combat operations for the first time. On 4 August F. O. Dean of 616 Squadron became the first jet fighter pilot to score a "kill" when he deflected and grounded a V-1 flying bomb targeted at London.

The first jet fighter to down an enemy in air-to-air combat is not known for certain, but an Me 262 of the Luftwaffe's Kommando Nowotny, pilot unnamed, is believed to have shot down a Boeing B-17 Flying Fortress of the U.S. 8th Air Force during the first week of October 1944. The effectiveness of jet fighters in World War II was greater than is sometimes credited; at least 12 Luftwaffe pilots became jet "aces" (i.e., scored five kills or more), with Oberstleutnant Heinz Bar being credited with no fewer than 16.

U.S.: The first American jet to fly on active service was a Lockheed RF-80F in which Lt. Bryce D. Poe II undertook a reconnaissance of Korean troop movements on 28 June 1950. The first jets to engage in combat were U.S. Navy Grumman F9F-2 Panthers, powered by British-made Rolls-Royce turbojets, which began operating against North Korean forces from the carrier USS *Valley Forge* on 3 July 1950. They raided military facilities in Pyongyang and shot down two Yak fighters.

The first **jet-to-jet aerial combat** took place over the Yalu River in North Korea on 8 November 1950, when Lt. Russell John Brown of the U.S. Air Force, flying a Lockheed F-80 jet fighter, engaged and destroyed a Chinese MiG-15.

Jet bomber: The first was the Messerschmitt Me 262A-2 *Sturmvögel* (Stormbird), delivered to the Kommando Schenk at Rheine for evaluation in June 1944. The first operational jet-bomber unit was 3. Staffel of I./KG 51, which arrived at Juvincourt, near Rheims, with five *Sturmvögel* in August. It was at Hitler's personal insistence that this bomber version of the Me 262 was produced, though the basic design was plainly unsuitable for such a role.

The first jet bomber to be designed as such and to be employed on bombing raids was the Arado 234 Blitz, powered by twin Junkers Jumo 0004B engines with 1,985-pound thrust, which undertook a bombing mission with the Luftwaffe's Kampfgeschwader 76 over the Ardennes during the Battle of the Bulge on 24 December 1944. Led by Capt. Dieter Lukesch, the bombers hit a factory and marshaling yards at Liège.

U.S.: The first experimental jet bomber was the Douglas XB-43, powered by a General Electric TG-180 axial-flow engine rated at 4,000 pounds of thrust, which made its maiden flight on 17 May 1946. This never achieved its planned production status, and the first jet bomber to become operational was the North American B-45A Tornado with the 84th and 8th Bombardment Wing, USAF, in March 1949. The first production block was powered by Allison J35-A-9 and -11 turbojets, the second by General Electric J47-GE-7 and -9 engines.

FOR JET AIRLINERS, SEE **airline**.

THE FIRST

AIRPLANE MANUFACTURING COMPANY

for the production of powered aircraft was the firm of Voisin Frères, established in rue de la Ferme, Billancourt, France, in November 1906 by twenty-six-year-old Gabriel Voisin and his brother Charles, twenty-four. Their cash assets at the time they decided to found a new industry, Gabriel remembered in his autobiography, amounted to four or five francs in the bank and some loose change. There were originally two employees, a former boat-builder called Métayer and a cabinetmaker named Brost. The company's first order was received in December 1906 from a M. Florencie, inventor of a flapping-wing ornithopter, but the machine was based on unsound principles and failed to leave the ground. The brothers' first successful, commercially built aircraft was a box-kite biplane of their own design powered by a 50-hp eight-cylinder Antoinette engine, which was ordered the same month by Paris sculptor Léon Delagrange and test-flown by Charles Voisin at Bagatelle on 30 March 1907. The aircraft was handed over to the customer the same day, and this date can be regarded as marking the birth of the worldwide aviation industry.

The first **commercially built aircraft in series production** was the American designed Wright Model A, of which six were built by Short Brothers at Leysdown, Essex, England, in 1909 under an agreement between Wilbur Wright and Eustace Short signed in February of that year. Production began at a purpose-built factory on the Aero Club's flying ground at Shellbeach, completed the following month.

U.S.: The first sale of an airplane was by the Wright brothers of Dayton, Ohio (SEE **airplane flight**), who signed a contract with the U.S. Army on 10 February 1908 for a trainer at a price of $25,000. The Wright Model A biplane was delivered to the Signal Corps Aeronautic Section (SEE **air force**) at Fort Myer, Va., on 20 August 1908. The airplane crashed the following month due to a faulty propeller, causing the first air fatality, but the army displayed resolve by ordering a replacement. This was delivered on 28 June 1909 and earned a $5,000 bonus for bettering the 40-mph speed required under the specification by 2 mph. Its success attracted the interest of investors, and the Wright Co. was incorporated on 22 November under Wilbur's presidency with headquarters in New York and a purpose-built factory in Dayton. Here they began producing the model B, the first airplane in series production in America, of which ten had been completed by the end of 1909 with another dozen on the order books.

This briefly made the Wright Co. the most productive airplane manufacturer in the world. It was not, however, the first airplane manufacturing company to be founded in the United States. This distinction belonged to the Herring-Curtiss Co., formed on 19 March 1909 by financier Augustus Herring and engineer Glenn H. Curtiss. Six airplanes were manufactured during 1909 at its factory in Hammondsport, N.J., the first of which, the $7,500 *Golden Bug*, was built for the American Aeronautical Society and delivered on 26 June 1909. Herring proved to be a braggart and a speculator who had misled Curtiss about claimed patent holdings and highly placed connections in Wall Street. Production was suspended when the Wright brothers brought suit for patent infringement, and in 1910 the company went bankrupt. Curtiss then formed the Curtiss Aeroplane Co. without Herring on 1 December 1910. This was the first truly successful airplane manufacturing enterprise in the United States, building the first U.S. Navy plane in 1911 and coming into its own during World War I, when 5,221 military aircraft and more than five thousand engines were produced at nine factories for the British and American forces.

The Wright Co. never attained mass production. As the pusher-engine biplane became obsolete, the main focus switched to exploiting the brothers' original patents in order to derive royalties. In 1929 what had evolved into the Wright Aeronautical Corp. amalgamated with its old rival the Curtiss Co., though by this time the respective founders, Orville Wright (Wilbur had died in 1912) and Glenn Curtiss, were no longer involved in company management. After prodigious efforts in World War II, when Curtiss-Wright produced 30,000 aircraft and more than 220,000 engines, the company lost its way as the jet age emerged, and in 1951 the company's airplane division, with its order books completely empty, was sold to North American Aviation.

THE FIRST **AIRPORT**

purpose-built for passenger traffic was laid out at Königsberg, East Prussia (now Kaliningrad, Russia), in 1921–22 with a three-story terraced terminal building designed by Hanns Hopp, flanked at either side by hangars. Earlier airports (SEE **airline**) such as Berlin's Johannisthal, London's Hounslow, Le Bourget at Paris, and Amsterdam's Schiphol, all dating from 1919, were ex-military airfields with existing buildings adapted for civilian use, though a purpose-built terminal was completed at Le Bourget in 1922, the same year as Königsberg. The reason that such a seemingly out-of-the-way place as Königsberg should have had the first modern airport was the result of the Treaty of Versailles, which separated East Prussia from the rest of Germany by the Polish Corridor. This made Königsberg an aerial junction linking Berlin with the Baltics, Finland, and the Soviet Union. The 56-hour rail journey from Königsberg to Moscow was cut to 8 hours by air.

U.S.: The first airport with a purpose-designed passenger terminal was the Ford Airport at Dearborn, Mich., dedicated on 15 January 1926. The terminal was designed by Albert Kahn, who also built America's first airport hotel there in 1931. The first international airport in the United States was established by Pan American at Miami in 1928 for services to Cuba and the Caribbean, later extended to Central and South America. The two-story Mediterranean-style stucco terminal building was designed by the New York architectural practice Delano & Aldrich.

Airport with hard-surfaced runways: The first was the Halle-Leipzig Airport in Germany in 1926. These were concrete and were designed for takeoff only. Newark, N.J., had the first hard-surface takeoff-and-landing runway in 1928. This was macadamized, the first concrete runways in the United States being laid at the Ford Airport at Dearborn, Mich., the following year.

Airport control tower: The first was erected at Croydon, then the international airport for London, and became operational in 1928.

U.S.: The first was designed for Cleveland Municipal Airport by Claude King and opened in 1930. There were twenty radio control towers in the United States by 1935.

Airport hotel: SEE **hotel**.

Airport with telescoping passageways from the terminal to the aircraft: The first was Oakland, Calif., in 1929.

Airport car rental: SEE **automobile rental service**.

Airport club lounge: The first was the Admirals Club established by American Airlines at La Guardia, Long Island, N.Y., in 1939.

Airport duty-free: The first was opened by airport restaurant manager Brendan O'Regan on 21 April 1947 in a kiosk at Shannon Airport, Co. Clare, Ireland, to sell linens and souvenirs. Takings on a good day could amount to as much as £5 ($20). Shannon's duty-free became the first in the world to stock liquor and tobacco in 1952.

Airport luggage carts: The first were designed in 1956 by Sylvanus Goldman's Folding Carrier Co. of Oklahoma City (SEE **supermarket: shopping cart**), not for airports but for use on stations of the Santa Fe Railroad. When the Redcaps (baggage handlers) went on strike, the order was canceled, and Goldman offered a dozen free to Oklahoma City Airport. Here they proved so successful that orders came in from all over the United States.

Airport moving walkway: The first was the 1,425-foot-long travolator that began scrolling at Love Field Air Terminal, Dallas, Tex., on 30 January 1958.

Airport baggage carousel: The first was installed at the Pan American terminal of New York City's Idlewild Airport (later John F. Kennedy International Airport) in May 1960.

Airport purpose-built for jets: The first was John Foster Dulles International, in Washington, D.C., opened on 17 November 1962.

Airport rapid transit system: The first in the United States providing direct connection with downtown linked Cleveland, Ohio, with Hopkins International when the four-mile-long Rapid Transit from West Park Station was opened on 15 November 1968.

Airport baggage scanners: SEE **X-rays**.

THE FIRST **AIR TROOP TRANSPORT**

operation took place during the Kurdish uprising in Iraq in April 1923 when a fully equipped fighting force of 280 Sikh troops was flown by Britain's Royal Air Force from Kingarban to Kirkuk in 12-seater Vickers Vernon transports. Each man carried a rifle and 15 pounds of equipment, and the aircraft bore an additional load of 30,000 rounds of small-arms ammunition. The time taken to transport the whole force over the 75-mile distance was a day and a half, or about 10 flying hours—a journey normally taking five days on the march.

The first use of long-range air troop transport took place in June 1932, when 21 Vickers Victoria transports, belonging to 70 and 216 Squadron RAF, flew the 1st Northamptonshire Regiment from Egypt to Iraq, once again in ferment, in two airlifts during the course of six days.

U.S.: In December 1927 the U.S. Marines received a trimotor Fokker transport at Managua, the capital of Nicaragua, and used it for transporting up to eight fully equipped soldiers at a time to various jungle outposts. There the task of the airlifted troops was to contain the Sandino rebels, and they were supplied with ammunition, rations, medical equipment, and their pay by the same aircraft and the four other transports in use by August 1928. Elsewhere in Central America, larger-scale troop movements were to follow. In 1931 Battery B, 2nd Field Artillery Battalion, U.S. Army was transported by six airplanes 90 miles across the Isthmus of Panama from France Field on the Caribbean side to Rio Hato on the Pacific side. Two years later, also in Panama, the entire 2nd Field Battalion was airlifted the 35 miles from Rejuca to Cherrea.

Aerial invasion: The first took place starting on 28 July 1936 and continuing through to early September when 20 Junkers 52/3 Mg bomber-transports of the German Luftwaffe Transport Squadron under the command of Oberleutnant Rudolf Freiherr von Moreau were used to carry 8,899 Moorish troops, 44 field guns, 90 machine guns, and 137 tons of ammunition from Spanish Morocco to Seville in Spain in support of Gen. Francisco Franco's rebel forces.

THE FIRST **AMBULANCE**

was designed in 1792 by Baron Dominique-Jean Larrey, Napoleon's personal surgeon, as a means of removing wounded men from the field of battle without their sustaining further injury from jolting over rough ground in the unsprung carts previously employed. Together with the chief surgeon of the French Army, Pierre-François Percy, Larrey established an ambulance corps which first saw service in Napoleon's Italian campaign in 1796. For each 10,000 men there was a chief surgeon commanding three medical divisions. A division would be supported by a mobile unit comprising eight two-wheeled two-horse ambulances for flat country and four four-wheeled four-horse ambulances for hilly terrain, four storage wagons, and a hundred medical personnel, of whom fourteen were surgeons. Amputations were carried out on the battlefield, while the patient was in shock and the injured limb numb. Formerly the practice had been for the medical teams to stay in the rear, off the field of battle, and attend only those wounded able to reach them through their own efforts or the support of their comrades. Percy added trained **stretcher-bearers** to the arrangements for evacuation of the wounded during Gen. Jean-Victor Moreau's Spanish campaign of 1808.

U.S.: The first purpose-designed ambulances were four-wheeled Tripler and two-wheeled Finley & Coolidge models acquired by the U.S. Army for evaluation in the western service in 1859. The four-wheeler had been designed by Surgeon Charles S. Tripler; the two-wheelers, by Surgeon Clement A. Finley and Assistant Surgeon Richard H. Coolidge. These latter were abandoned within two or three years, one commentator asserting that "no man who has ever ridden in the two-wheeled ambulance would willingly get into one ever again, even if he were well." At the outset of the Civil War there was no organized ambulance system. The vehicles were under the control of the Quartermaster's Department, which allocated them at will without any trained personnel. A regiment of 600–700 men might have one ambulance per 100 men or so, though Gen. Irvin McDowell considered 50 to be more than adequate for his army of 35,000.

The only thing that could be said in favor of the Union Army's arrangements for evacuating the wounded and ensuring prompt attention to their needs was that the Confederate Army's were even more woeful. Improvement only came with the appointment of Jonathan Letterman as medical director of the Army of the Potomac. He it was who wrested control of ambulances from the Quartermaster's Department, ensured that the wounded were taken to clearing hospitals for onward evacuation to general hospitals (rather than leaving them in the care of the ill-equipped regiments), and introduced trained stretcher-bearers in place of the bandsmen formerly given the task of clearing the battlefield of casualties. These reforms were first put to the test at the Battle of Fredericksburg (13 December 1862), which saw the successful evacuation of more than 9,000 wounded in 12 hours despite a Union defeat, freezing temperatures, and continual harassment by the enemy. Letterman's system was given permanence and general adoption by the U.S. Army with the creation of the Ambulance Corps on 16 March 1864.

The most commonly used ambulance types throughout the war were the 10-foot-long by 4-foot-wide four-horse Tripler of 1859, which held four litters and also had seating for six walking wounded, and the lighter two-horse Wheeling (aka Rosecrans after the general of that name), which could accommodate two lying and two or three sitting. The Confederates did not use purpose-designed ambulances, relying on whatever wagons could be commandeered as and when needed.

Although the first civilian ambulance in the United States is usually credited to New York's Bellevue Hospital in 1869, the Commercial Hospital at Cincinnati (later Cincinnati General) was operating one at least as early as 1865. A list of employees for the year ending 28 February 1866 records that James R. Jackson was retained as ambulance driver at an annual salary of $360.

Motor ambulance: The first was a Daimler-engined vehicle exhibited by Panhard et Levassor at the Salon du Cycle held in the Palais d'Industrie in Paris in December 1895. There is no record that it went into service, and it would appear that the United States had the first motor ambulance to actually carry patients. The *New York Herald* under dateline Chicago, 24 February 1899, reported, "The first automobile ambulance ever constructed was presented today to Michael Reese Hospital of this city. It was built in Chicago and was the gift of five prominent businessmen. The ambulance weighs sixteen hundred pounds and its speed approximates sixteen miles per hour." That this vehicle was fully operative was confirmed by a reference to it in *McClure's Magazine* of July 1899, though no details are given about its maker.

The first air-conditioned ambulance, enhancing patients' prospects of survival in high temperatures, was the Springdale, built on a Buick chassis by Sayers & Scovill of Cincinnati and launched in 1937. The Springdale has special significance as the world's first air-conditioned motor vehicle on regular sale.

THE FIRST AMERICAN ACCENT

evolved from regional English, Irish, and Germanic speech patterns. The earliest allusion to a distinctive manner of speech common to Americans dates from 1717, when Harvard graduate Thomas Prince, later to distinguish himself as a journalist and historian and as pastor of Old South Church in Boston, returned from an extended trip to England "splendidly bewigged" and boasting that many cultivated Englishmen had mistaken him for one of their own. He asserted that unlike many of his fellow countrymen, he could not be distinguished by his accent. Prince had gone to London in 1709, so presumably there were already those of colonial birth who spoke differently from the English by that date. It would probably have taken at least a generation to emerge and therefore it would be reasonable to suppose that an American form of pronunciation and rhythm of speech was developing by the end of the seventeenth century.

THE FIRST
AMERICAN CITIZEN, NATURALIZED

was the Bohemian- (Czech-)born Augustine Herrmann (aka Heerman) who, together with his sons, was granted citizenship of Maryland by an act of the colony's Assembly in 1666. Herrmann was a highly educated man, the son of a prosperous merchant of Prague and his noblewoman wife. Although a surveyor by profession, he had served in the Thirty Years' War and subsequently came to New Netherland as an agent of the Dutch West India Company, settling in New Amsterdam in 1643. There he represented the great Amsterdam firm of Gabry & Co., trading with his brothers-in-law in Virginia and instituting tobacco imports from that colony. In 1659 the

Maryland connection was established when Herrmann was a member of the diplomatic mission sent by Gov. Peter Stuyvesant of New York to treat with the Marylanders on their claim to New Netherland. He was subsequently commissioned by the governor of Maryland to exercise his surveying skills in producing a detailed map of the colony and also of Virginia, in return for which he received a large grant of land at the head of Chesapeake Bay, where he established a manorial estate he named New Bohemia or Bohemia Manor. He moved there from Manhattan in 1661. According to family tradition, Herrmann paid one further visit to New Amsterdam while Stuyvesant was in power, quarreled with his former master, and was imprisoned in the fort. Feigning insanity, he asked for his favorite horse to keep him company in his cell, then made a daring escape by leaping from the ramparts mounted on this trusty steed and swam the North River to make an eventual escape to his adopted home country of Maryland.

The first general provision for naturalization was made by the New York Assembly in 1683. At this time there was no legislative provision for naturalization in the motherland, Britain, though Parliament was to pass an act in 1740 applying to all the American colonies and allowing naturalization as a British subject to any Protestant with seven years residence.

The first federal naturalization law, 26 March 1790, granted U.S. citizenship to free white applicants of two years' residence. African Americans only became eligible for citizenship in 1870.

THE FIRST **AMERICANISMS**

were coined by the Jamestown settlers probably shortly after their arrival in 1607 and not surprisingly consisted of loanwords from local Indian languages for which there was no equivalent in English. *Opossum* (spelled *apossoun*) appears in a manuscript of 1610, and John Smith used a number in his *Virginia* of 1612: *moccasins, persimmon, pone, tomahawk*. The following year *moose* (spelled *mus*) made its first known appearance in literature.

All the earliest Americanisms relate to flora, fauna, topography, or Indian life and lore. The first

wholly new word was *selectman*, which originated at Charlestown, Mass., in 1635 to denote one of a board of town officers chosen annually. It was soon adopted by most other New England municipalities.

The earliest known colloquial Americanism and the first to enter British English from America was *tote*, first noted in February 1677 in a manuscript of *Grievances of Gloucester County* (Va.): "[The governor's out-guard] were by Beverly commanded to go to work, fell trees and mawle and toat rails, which many... refusing to doe, he presently disarmed them." (It is possible that the obsolescent *mawle*, meaning to split rails for fencing, was also an Americanism, as the only definition given in the Oxford English Dictionary is "to mew like a cat.") Some philologists have suggested an African, Native American, or French derivation for *tote*. Webster says that it is improbable that it is African, as the word was already widely used in New England before any significant numbers of blacks resided there. The OED states flatly that African or Indian attribution is incorrect. As for French, there was little contact between the English colonists and their neighbors to the north in Canada, nor is there any French word of similar meaning that approximates it. *Tote*, it seems, was an Anglo-American neologism.

The earliest **expression known to have been minted in America** was "Under the rose a merkin," meaning that behind a thing of beauty or worth lies something shameful, an axiom long obsolescent but maybe ripe for revival. Its origin was explained by the anonymous "J. W." in the now extremely rare *Letter from New-England*, published in London in 1682:

> A vintner in Boston put up a new sign called The Rose and Crown, with two Naked Boys being Supporters, and their Nudities Pendent: the sight disturbed one Justice S——s, who commanded it down and away were the boys sent to the carvers to be dismembered: but the unlucky Dog of a Carver sent them back again two chopping Girles with Merkins exposed. This enraged the Justice more, and the Sign was summoned before the wise Court, where they gravely Determined (to keep the Girles from blushing) they should have Roses Clapt upon their Merkin, which is the original of our new proverb *Under the Rose a Merkin*.

Nominations are invited for the earliest American expression still current in the twenty-first century.

THE FIRST **AMERICAN, WHITE**

to be born and raised within the present boundaries of the United States was Martín de Argüelles Jr., son of Martín de Argüelles Sr. and his wife, the former Leonor Morales of St. Augustine, Fla. Martín Sr. and Leonor had been among the company of soldiers and their families who had come to Spanish Florida to garrison the *presidio* at St. Augustine under the command of Adm. Pedro Menéndez de Avilés in 1565 and established what may have been the first tavern in America. Martín Jr. was born there the following year, twenty-one years before the birth of the short-lived Virginia Dare to English settlers in the ill-fated colony on Roanoke Island.

All the early local records of St. Augustine, including the parish registers, were destroyed in Sir Francis Drake's attack on the settlement in 1586. What is known about Martín Jr. is owing to the fact that he followed his father into the king's service and petitioned in 1598, while serving in the Yucatán in Mexico, for four years' back pay. The previous occupant of the post had decamped, and there was nothing to prove that Sargento Major Argüelles was entitled to his salary. In order to establish his credentials, Martin needed to prove, inter alia, that he was of Spanish parentage. One witness was Don Tomé de Villaseca, who had known Martín Sr. while he served both as a soldier and as an *alcalde ordinario* (a functionary of the civil administration) at the infant settlement of St. Augustine. Furthermore he stated that the petitioner was known not only to himself but to many others as "*el primer español que nacio en el fuerte de San Agustín*" (the first Spaniard born in the garrison of St. Augustine). Another witness recounted how Martín Sr. had fallen sick after many years of service and removed his family to Havana. There Martín Jr. had joined the Spanish army, trained in Cuba, and served in several overseas campaigns before receiving the inadequately documented post in Yucatán. It is not known whether he ever received his back pay.

Martín de Argüelles certainly appears to have been the first Caucasian native of America to grow up in the country, but was he the first white child born in the United States? Shortly before the founding of St. Augustine, the French Huguenots had established the nearby Fort Caroline. In 1565 this was sacked by Adm. Menéndez, who put to the sword all the male settlers his forces succeeded in capturing. He spared the lives of thirty-two women and children, who were taken to Havana and later repatriated to France. According to Menéndez, some eight or twelve children had been born in the settlement. This seems improbable, because the reinforcements, which included families (the original garrison being all male), had only landed three weeks before the massacre. It is possible that there had been births in the brief interim, but it's more likely that the children had been brought to the colony. Whatever the reality of this scantily recorded episode of America's early European settlement, the fact remains that none of the children of French parentage, whether born in the United States or not, grew up as Martín de Argüelles or the other sixty-one white children known to be living in Spanish Florida in 1577 did—in the land of their birth.

THE FIRST **ANESTHESIA**

was probably administered in Rochester, N.Y., by William Clarke, a medical student who had been entertaining his friends with ether inhalations since 1839. At a date unknown, but possibly as early as January 1842, he applied ether on a towel to a Miss Hobbie, whose dentist, Elijah Pope, then proceeded to extract a tooth without any pain. Neither Clarke nor Pope seems to have realized the huge historical and medical significance of what they had just done, and it was not reported in print until H. M. Lyman published his *Artificial Anaesthesia and Anaesthetics* in 1881. Clarke became a prominent surgeon in Chicago, but never claimed to have discovered anesthesia, and no mention was made of the episode in the biography of him.

The first **anesthetic for a surgical operation** was administered on 30 March 1842 by Dr. Crawford Long of Jefferson, Ga., who removed a cyst from the neck of a student at the local academy, James Venable, while he was insensible under ether. The invoice for this pioneering endeavor was \$2. Ether had been introduced to the isolated community of Jefferson by an itinerant science lecturer who would demonstrate the effects of the gas at his exhibitions. The young people of the town, unbeknown to their parents, persuaded Dr. Long to let them try it out for themselves, and he readily gave them whiffs of ether and joined in the fun at their mild intoxication. Realizing that a stronger dose of the gas could have the effect of deadening a person's consciousness, Long persuaded Venable to undergo the experiment, with entirely successful results. Altogether he performed eight operations with ether, including the amputation of a slave boy's finger, before October 1846, when Morton administered ether at Massachusetts General Hospital (SEE BELOW), for which he was hailed as the pioneer of anesthesia. Long also became the first to use anesthesia for childbirth, delivering his wife of their second child on 27 December 1845. He was deprived of the credit for this as well, nearly every history of medicine attributing priority for anesthetized birth to Dr. James Young Simpson of Edinburgh, who used chloroform to deliver the infant Wilhelmina Carstairs on 9 November 1847. The reason that Crawford Long's precedence could not be established was, it has been claimed, owing to the vanity of his daughter, who became his biographer. Despite her pride in his achievements, she was not prepared to reveal the date of her birth or even that it had preceded that of Wilhelmina Carstairs.

Of larger moment is the matter of why Dr. Crawford Long's initial operations under anesthesia were overlooked. We can set aside the picturesque myth that he abandoned anesthesia when visited by a delegation of outraged citizens who accused him of sorcery and declared that he would be lynched should he not desist. The truth, according to his own testimony, is rather more prosaic. He did not want to announce his discovery until he had performed sufficient operations under ether to be able to report on them with a degree of scientific authority. The number of opportunities for surgery that came the way of a country doctor were few, averaging in Long's case about two a year. By the time he did finally publish a report, in the *Southern Medical and Surgical Journal* in December 1849, Morton's spectacular work in Boston had

firmly entrenched him in the popular imagination, as well as in medical circles, as the only begetter of painless surgery. Contrary to the many reports that Dr. Long abandoned anesthesia early in his career, there is ample evidence that he continued with its use until his death in 1878, performing such major operations as the amputation of a leg and a woman's breast as well as field surgery with ether during his service in the Civil War.

Anesthesia in major surgery: The first application was made at Massachusetts General Hospital, Boston, on 16 October 1846, when Dr. John Collins Warren excised a tumor from the jaw of a twenty-year-old printer called Gilbert Abbot. It was with the greatest reluctance that Warren had been persuaded by William Morton, the Boston dentist who administered the ether, to agree to the experiment. A plaque on the wall of the theater records: "The patient declared that he had felt no pain during the operation and was discharged well December 7. Knowledge of this discovery spread from this room throughout the civilized world and a new era for surgery began." The word *anesthesia* was coined by Oliver Wendell Holmes in a letter to Morton dated 21 November 1846.

Local anesthetic: The pain-killing properties of cocaine were first discovered by Karl Koller of the Allgemeines Krankenhaus, Vienna, while he was working with Sigmund Freud on the use of the drug as a treatment for morphine addiction. It was first demonstrated as an anesthetic on the eye of a patient from the Heidelberg Clinic by Josef Brettauer of Trieste, using a vial of cocaine forwarded by Koller, at the Heidelberg Congress of Ophthalmology on 15 September 1884.

Local anesthesia by injection, or neuro-regional anesthesia, was introduced by Prof. William Halsted of Johns Hopkins University, Baltimore, in 1885 a few weeks later when he used a hypodermic needle to inject cocaine into the lower jaw of a dentist and extracted a tooth painlessly. The patient reported in *Dental Cosmos*:

> This evening, Dr. Halsted gave me an injection of seventeen minims . . . In three minutes there was numbness and tingling of the skin . . . In six minutes there was complete anesthesia of the left

half of the lower lip... A pin thrust completely through the lip caused no sensation whatever... Hard blows upon the teeth with the back of a knife caused no sensation.

As with many medical advances, there was a price to pay. Halsted revealed in a letter to Sir William Osler in 1919 that three of his assistants had become addicted to cocaine during experiments with the drug, and all had died without recovering from the habit.

Intravenous general anesthetic: The first was Pentothal, which was synthesized in 1936 after trials with two hundred compounds by Ernest H. Volwiler and Donalee L. Tabern of Abbott Laboratories of Chicago. A sulfa-bearing analogue of Nembutal, it could be injected directly into the bloodstream without the side effects that had rendered previous attempts at intravenous anesthesia impracticable. It would be employed prior to the administration of ether or other gaseous anesthetics, to relieve the patient of the stress of breathing in gas while conscious. It is also known as the "truth serum" from its application in small doses to relax inhibitions during interrogation.

THE FIRST

ANTIQUE AUTOMOBILE MOVEMENT
....

began with a vintage car rally held in Munich on 12 July 1925, in celebration of the 25th anniversary of the Allgemeiner Schnaufer-Club ("Tin Lizzy Club"). The historical Automobil-Korso included the oldest gasoline-driven car in the world, a three-wheeled Benz of 1886 (SEE ALSO **automobile**), driven by the eighty-one-year-old Karl Benz himself. Also in attendance, driving or riding in vehicles a little more juvenile, were Karl Opel, Emil Stoever, August Horch, Heinrich Kleyer, and other pioneers of the German motor industry.

U.S.: The first meet was the Antique Automobile Derby inaugurated as a lighthearted sidebar to the annual show of the Philadelphia Automobile Trade Association in January 1931. Intended as an inexpensive way of attracting press coverage for the show, the event was for cars twenty-five years old or older (i.e., pre 1907). It was sufficiently successful to be repeated annually, but while it gave a huge amount of pleasure

to the spectators, who regarded the funny-looking old cars as objects of derision, the owners were sometimes less happy for their vehicles to be treated as part of an auto burlesque. Among those who believed that many of these rattletrap old-timers were in fact valuable examples of developing automotive technology deserving of preservation were Ted Fiala and Frank Abramson, who formed the first club for like-minded enthusiasts, the Antique Automobile Club of America, in Philadelphia in November 1935. It was the second such organization in the world, preceded only by Britain's Veteran Car Club, which had been founded five years earlier. There were fourteen founder members who each paid a subscription of $1 per year. By 1944, when many historic vehicles were being broken up for scrap, there were already four hundred members, whose strenuous efforts to save notable early marques from the wreckers were often deemed unpatriotic. At the end of the war, the first regional chapter was formed in Cleveland, and by 1960 more than eighty spanned the United States and Canada with over nine thousand members. It now has sixty thousand members in four hundred chapters and is the largest such organization in the world.

The first **antique car auction** in the United States was in May 1962, when nine items from the Wallace C. Bird collection of classic cars were sold for $37,850 by O'Reilly Brothers on Long Island, N.Y. While prices of $5,300 for a Duesenberg, $3,700 for a Hispano-Suiza, and $1,850 for a Bugatti Type-43 were reckoned sky-high at the time, an observer from a New York fine art and antiques auction house saw the future and saw that it was good (for vendors and auctioneers): "Friend, I would advise you to buy your heart's desire now. I warn you that in ten years most of you guys will be standing outside the hobby looking in."

THE FIRST **APARTMENT HOUSE**
....

in the United States was the Renaissance-style Pontalba Building, which lines two sides of Jackson Square in the Vieux Carré of New Orleans, the uptown side completed in 1849 and the other in 1851. It was commissioned at a cost of $302,000 by Baroness Micaela Pontalba whose father, Don Andrés Almonester, had initiated the construction of the historic square in the 1790s. The redheaded, strong-willed Micaela consulted several architects, among them the celebrated James Gallier Jr., but supervised most of the building work herself, wearing trousers the better to clamber up ladders and check that the workmen were not laying bricks inferior to those she had paid for. The ironwork that encloses the second-floor galleries she designed herself, having it fabricated in New York, and it incorporates her initials. The first floors consisted of rows of shops, while the two-story apartments above were rented by well-to-do Creole families of the city. Today the lower Pontalba Building, maintained by the Louisiana State Museum, contains an apartment decorated in the late Empire style fashionable when it was first inhabited. New York, the archetypal city of apartment dwellers, did not have its first apartment building until the construction of the Stuyvesant Apartments, designed in 1869 by Richard Morris Hunt. They became known as the "French flats" (at a time when the English term *flat* was still used—*apartment* was coined in the 1880s), reflecting the Gallic provenance of multi-occupancy in America.

THE FIRST **APPENDECTOMY**

was carried out on a kitchen table by Dr. Abraham Groves (1847–1935) of Fergus, Ontario, Canada, on 10 May 1883. The patient was a twelve-year-old boy suffering from pain and tenderness in the right iliac region. On making an incision, an inflamed appendix was found, and Dr. Groves removed the organ, sterilizing the appendiceal stump with a probe heated in the flame of a lamp. The only other instruments used in the operation were a knife and a needle.

Three days later the boy was well on his way to recovery, but his father was far from satisfied. A neighbor suffering from similar pain had been treated by another doctor simply by poulticing, and the boy's father accused Dr. Groves of having put his son's life at risk through ignorance. When the doctor reported the case at a medical meeting a short time later, he found that his peers took the same view, one of them

declaring that if such treatment became widespread the death rate would be appalling.

Dr. Groves, who performed more than twenty thousand operations during his sixty-three years of practice in the village of Fergus, was not only an archetype of the skillful and kindly backwoods doctor but also a remarkable innovator. In 1874 he had pioneered the practice of sterilizing surgical instruments by boiling them, and in November 1885 he became the first medical practitioner known to have used sterilized rubber gloves for surgery. This was some four years earlier than Prof. William Halsted (SEE ALSO **anesthesia**) of Johns Hopkins University in Baltimore, the celebrated American surgeon usually credited as the first to have adopted rubber gloves.

U.S.: Dr. William West Grant removed the vermiform appendix of Mary Gartside at St. Luke's Hospital in Davenport, Iowa, on 4 January 1885.

THE FIRST **ARCHAEOLOGICAL DIG**

in America to be carried out systematically and with scientific intention (as opposed to digging up artifacts to sell to antiquarians) was described by Thomas Jefferson in his *Notes on the State of Virginia*. Although eventually published, this originally comprised jottings compiled in 1781–82 in response to questions about the state of which he was governor addressed to Jefferson by François Marbois, secretary of the French legation in Philadelphia. The chapter devoted to Native Americans contains an account of Jefferson's excavation, at a date unrecorded, of a burial mound on the banks of the south branch of the Rivanna River, near an Indian town some 5 miles north of Charlottesville. The question he sought to address was whether these mounds were repositories for the bones of those who had fallen in battle, or a charnal house for periodic tribal burials, or a "general sepulchre for towns." His methodology was to dig a cross-section trench through the mound to determine the soil layers in relation to time ("stratification," which became standard archaeological practice only in the 1930s) and to observe the disposition and nature of the bones. This enabled him to produce a list of findings leading to the unexciting but scientifically sound conclusion that the Native Americans had buried general collections of bones periodically.

Jefferson pioneered the archaeology of sites associated with aboriginal peoples, a science practiced in America mainly in the Southwest, where pre-Columbian society was at its most advanced. The other principal branch of American archaeology, known as "historical archaeology," involves the excavation and analysis of sites that represent the transplanting of European cultures to this alien environment and the development of a lifestyle adapted to North American conditions. It began with a dig conducted in 1863–64 at Duxbury, Mass., by James Hall at the site of the sixteenth-century home of his ancestor Myles Standish, the Mayflower voyager of military renown. Hall made a scale map of the foundations and anticipated the mid-twentieth-century archaeological practice of "piece plotting" by listing the artifacts found according to the precise location of their excavation. Another of his innovations was the use of "datum points," permanent topographical features that allow the site to be identified by later researchers; in this case two springs, still there today. Hall carried out his pioneering work solely for his own satisfaction, and it was not until exactly a century later that it came to light when his descendants, living in Mexico, found the map and some of the artifacts and presented them to Pilgrim Hall, the historical foundation at Plymouth, Mass. By studying these relics the experts there were able to date the building of the house to the period 1637–50.

There were no further attempts at historical archaeology until 1894, when workmen were hired by the owners of Jamestown Island, the earliest English settlement (qv) in America, to excavate the ruins on the waterfront in the New Towne area. This was a strictly amateur effort, but more scientific excavations were made at the site of the old church tower three years later under the supervision of Mary Jeffery Galt, founder of the Association for the Preservation of Virginia Antiquities, and of the town house known as the Ludwell Statehouse Group by Col. Samuel H. Yonge of the Corps of Engineers in 1903. The continuous development of historical archaeology in the United States dates from excavations begun at Plymouth, Mass., in the 1920s and at Jamestown and Colonial Williamsburg in the 1930s.

THE FIRST **ARMY**

raised in America was recruited from the settlers of Jamestown, Va., by Capt. John Smith in March 1608 as a fighting force to defend the infant settlement (qv), established only the previous year, from the depredations of the mighty Indian warrior Powhatan (father of Pocahontas) and the thirty or so tribes under his command. Smith recorded in his *True Relation*:

> Six or seven days we spent only in trayning our men to march, fight, and scirmish in the woods. Their willing minds to this action so quickened their understanding in this exercise as, in all judgements, wee were better able to fight with Powhatans whole force, in our order of battle amongst the trees . . . then the Fort was to repulse 400 at the first assault, with some tenne or twenty shot not knowing what to doe, nor how to use a Piece.

"A piece" referred to artillery. Training continued, with some of the soldiers being posted as sentries at Jamestown and others manning the blockhouse guarding the narrow peninsula joining the island community to the mainland. Skirmishes with the Indians in the forest proved to Smith that a more effective tactic was to attack their villages. By the time he returned to England in the fall of 1609, there were about a hundred men under arms out of a total of 490, described as "well trained and expert soldiers." Armament comprised twenty-four pieces of artillery and three hundred muskets as well as pikes and swords. After Smith's departure, Indian depredations on the settlement increased during that winter's "Starving Time." Reinforcements arrived the following summer with the aptly named governor, Lord De la Warr, on 10 June 1610. The governor brought with him a hundred "Old Soldiers," veterans of the campaigns in the Low Countries, and these, together with conscripts from the civilian population, were formed into fifty-strong companies, each under the command of an experienced captain. This force went on active service for the first time on 9 July, less than a month after De la Warr's arrival, when a punitive attack was led by Lt. Gov. Sir Thomas Gates on the Indian village of Kecoughton in response to the murder of a settler. The inhabitants having been killed or dispersed, Fort Charles was built on the site.

De la Warr continued the campaign against the tribes owing fealty to the great warrior Powhatan in order to deter the harassment to which the settlers had been subjected and which had cost many lives. The raids, known as "feedfights," were also intended to prevent a repetition of the Starving Time. The Indians having been put to flight, their crops were harvested and brought back to the settlement to feed the populace. Powhatan, however, rallied his forces and laid siege to De la Warr's fort for three months, eventually forcing the Virginian garrison to abandon it after the loss of thirty-two soldiers. De la Warr, a broken and dejected man, departed for Nevis in the West Indies to recuperate.

On 12 May 1611 Marshal of Virginia Sir Thomas Dale arrived with further reinforcements, 300 veterans of the Low Countries with arms and armor, but was disgusted to find the settlers bowling in the streets rather than attending to their military and agrarian duties. There followed an administration known to modern historians as the "military regime." The Indian war was resumed and the effectiveness of the new armor against arrows proved during a devastating attack on the Nansemonds. When Sir Thomas Gates returned to Virginia in August 1611, the army was further enlarged with an additional 250 veterans accompanying him. This relatively large and now well equipped force was able to bring a conclusion to this first war fought by American forces with the expulsion of the Appomattoc tribe in December 1611.

America's first **standing army** (i.e. the regular U.S. Army) originally comprised the junior officers and eighty men of the one remaining regiment of the Revolutionary force authorized by Congress to be retained in peacetime by an act of 2 June 1784:

> Resolved, that the commanding officer . . . is hereby directed to discharge the troops now in the service of the United States, except twenty-five privates to guard the stores at Fort Pitt and fifty-five to guard the stores at West Point and other magazines, with a proportional number of officers, no officers to remain in service above the rank of captain.

This band of what amounted to little more than security guards was almost immediately augmented by an act passed the following day allowing for a force of seven hundred men enlisted for twelve months (later increased to three years) to garrison the frontier posts evacuated by the British. The highest-ranking officer, a lieutenant colonel, was to be paid $82 a month, and the privates, belonging to eight companies of infantry and two artillery batteries, were to receive $4. The force was to be supported by an officer corps of two majors, eight captains, ten lieutenants, ten ensigns, and a surgeon.

In fact, during the early years of the U.S. Army these figures were never attained. The force was supposed to be raised by the individual states, but initially only Pennsylvania complied. The actual number, therefore, raised to defend the new nation was twelve officers, two surgeons, and two hundred privates. Under the command of Lt. Col. Josiah Harmar, at thirty-one a veteran with eight years of war service, this small force set about its appointed task: to drive squatters off the land they had settled on the frontier of western Pennsylvania. Later there would be hostile Indians to confront, but for two years the army's inglorious task was to burn the settlers' houses and destroy their crops in order to preserve the land on behalf of the government.

Little is known about the rank and file of those pioneer Pennsylvanian troops. According to a congressional study, the main inducement to enlist was free clothing; one officer reported that his new recruits were naked. The $2 bounty on enlistment must also have attracted men suffering such dire poverty. As to their background, a list of sixty deserters—once clothed and fed, some found the harsh and lonely life of the frontier lacked appeal—reveals that thirty were foreign born, nineteen of them Irish, and that thirty-one were unskilled laborers. It is also known that one of the companies under a German captain was almost entirely composed of Germans. By no means all were veterans—Capt. Hamtramck had to ask the commandant for some ammunition because his men were "unacquainted with firing."

At least one recruit, though, Yorkshire-born John Robert Shaw, had fought on both sides during the Revolutionary War. And another Briton, the remarkable Andrew Wallace (1730–1835), had fought with the Young Pretender at Culloden as a sixteen-year-old stripling, fled to Pennsylvania after the defeat of the Scots, joined Braddock's Army in 1756 and become a sergeant in the French and Indian War, reenlisted for service in the Revolutionary War, served with the nascent U.S. Army for four years from 1784–88, rejoined in 1791, and was finally discharged at the age of 81 in 1811. At his death in New York in 1835 he was a month short of his 105th birthday, and his funeral at St. Patrick's Cathedral was attended by the mayor of the city.

The permanence of the U.S. Army, doubtful in its formative years, was recognized by the Constitution of the United States in 1788 with the appointment of the president as commander in chief. The forces at his command totaled just 595 men.

THE FIRST **ARMY NURSES**

in America were recruited by the Army Medical Department established by the Second Continental Congress on 27 July 1775, following a request by Gen. George Washington for female nurses and matrons so that male orderlies could be released for battle. The establishment allowed for one nurse per ten patients and one supervisory matron per one hundred. Nurses were paid $2 a month in addition to rations (rising to $8 per month by the end of the Revolutionary War) and matrons $15 per month, compared to $50 per month for surgeon's mates.

When the Army Nursing Corps was established under Dorothea Dix in 1861, the qualifications for nursing recruits were that they be religious, of high moral character, thirty years old or more... and plain.

SEE ALSO **women in the armed forces**.

THE FIRST **ART EXHIBITION**

was held by the Académie de Peinture et de Sculpture at the Palais-Royale in Paris, 9–23 April 1667. They were continued biennially, though after 1671 the exhibition was usually held in the Grande Galerie of the Louvre, then a royal palace.

U.S.: Boston portrait painter John Smibert, originally of Edinburgh, settled in America in 1729 and in the spring of the following year held an exhibition of his paintings at his studio on Green Lane (Salem Street), Boston. This would probably have included his best-known work, *Bishop Berkeley and Friends*, a massive canvas with eight life-size portraits that Smibert had painted at Newport, R.I., shortly after his arrival in the bishop's entourage the previous year. Certainly one of his earliest Boston portraits, of Judge Samuel Sewall, was exhibited. Also on show were a number of paintings by other artists that Smibert had brought with him to America. According to a contemporary poem by Cotton Mather's nephew Mather Byles about the show, the exhibits included a ribald, anti-Catholic canvas showing how "gloating monks their amorous rights debate" and another painting in which "Roman ruins nod their awful head." Other exhibits were copies of works by Raphael, Titian, Tintoretto, Van Dyck, and Rubens by Smibert himself, as well as casts of the Venus de Medici and Homer and a bust of Scottish painter Allan Ramsay. Smibert was to become America's foremost portrait painter. Whether he was the first, as often claimed, depends on definition, but he was undoubtedly the earliest to make a substantial living from portraiture alone.

Exhibition of paintings by American artists: The first was organized by Charles Willson Peale (SEE ALSO **art museum**) of the Columbianum or American Academy of Fine Arts and opened at Philosophy Hall, Philadelphia, in May 1795. Thirty-seven artists were represented, of whom about half exhibited portraits. Most of the other paintings were landscapes and still lifes. The most popular exhibit was by Peale himself. Titled *The Staircase Group*, this early example of trompe l'oeil showed with a photographic fidelity life-size figures of his son Raphaelle [*sic*] mounting a stairway and his son Titian peering around a corner from above. In order to enhance the illusion of reality, Peale had mounted the picture in an actual door frame and placed a real step at the base of the painted staircase. It was reported that dogs would run against it in an attempt to ascend.

THE FIRST ART MUSEUM

to be established primarily for the benefit of the public (as opposed to royal, ducal, and papal collections) was opened at the Abbey of Saint Vincent de Besançon at Besançon, France, in 1694. Abbot J. B. Bloizot had died, bequeathing his collection of paintings and medallions to the abbey "with the stipulation that the whole form a public collection." The gallery was open to all on Wednesdays and Saturdays from 8 A.M. to 10 A.M. and from 2 P.M. to 4 P.M.

U.S.: The first was opened in 1784 at his own house on the corner of Third and Lombard Streets, Philadelphia, by artist Charles Willson Peale, who had studied under Benjamin West. The collection comprised mainly paintings of Revolutionary heroes by Peale himself, together with other patriotic representations. The gallery was combined with a museum of curiosities collected by Peale and, after it had moved to the Philosophical Society's building on Fifth Street in September 1794, a small zoo. Sometimes there was synergy between the museum exhibits and the gallery exhibits, as in 1818 when the "Great Sea-Serpent," a thitherto unknown monster of the deep caught off the coast of Massachusetts the previous year, was put on display together with John Ritto Penniman's enormous 19' x 9' painting of its capture. Peale's Museum and Gallery of the Fine Arts was the first building in America lit by gas, the installation being made by Peale—himself a skilled mechanic—and his son Rubens in the spring of 1816. It became incorporated as the Philadelphia Museum Co. in 1821 and two years later moved into the Arcade, where it remained until the opening of the purpose-built Philadelphia Museum on Ninth Street in 1835. By that time the collection of paintings numbered between two and three hundred. When the museum failed financially, the art exhibits were moved to the Old Masonic Hall on Chestnut Street, renamed the Academy of Fine Arts (no connection with the Academy named below), but survived for less than a year, closing in July 1847. The paintings were then sold at auction for a total of $11,672.06, the City of Philadelphia purchasing some of the choicest for display at Independence Hall.

The first purpose-built gallery in the United States was the Pennsylvania Academy of the Fine Arts, founded by Charles Willson Peale and William Rush and opened in Philadelphia in a Greek-style building by John Dorsey on Chestnut Street between 11th and 12th in April 1807. The inaugural annual exhibition at the Academy—the first such regular event in the United States—was held in May 1811 in association with the Society of Artists. Some five hundred works of art were shown. The building was destroyed in 1845 by a fire that also engulfed most of the exhibits, including a Murillo of the "Roman Daughter" and the collection of fine casts from the antique presented to the Academy by the Emperor Napoleon.

National gallery: The first was the Musée des Arts opened in the Louvre Palace in Paris (known today simply as the Louvre) on 10 August 1793, the first anniversary of the fall of the French monarch—whose collection it was that now became public property.

U.S.: A rather modest National Gallery opened under that name in a wing of the Smithsonian Institution in Washington, D.C., in 1910, exhibiting European old masters and pre–Civil War American artists. This was renamed the National Collection when the National Gallery of Washington opened in 1941.

Museum of contemporary art: The first was the Musée des Artistes Vivants, opened in the Luxembourg Palace, Paris (and usually known as the Musée de Luxembourg) on 24 April 1818—the second anniversary of the restoration of the monarchy. In order to maintain its role as a *musée de passage*, the collections were changed as artists died or their reputations were eclipsed by those younger and more fashionable. In practice ten years' grace was allowed after the death of an artist, those whose reputations had survived intact having works deemed of enduring significance moved to the hallowed halls of the Louvre, which contained only paintings by artists dead for at least ten years. It moved from the Luxembourg Palace to the old Orangery of the Luxembourg Gardens in 1886, a building that was too small to adequately accommodate representative selections of the burgeoning Paris art world of the fin de siècle and was unsuitable given the heat and humidity of what was in fact a vast conservatory. The museum survived until 1938, though by that time the collection was fixed and no longer conformed to the original intention to exhibit only contemporary art.

U.S.: With no "old masters" to conserve and cherish, it followed that most early American art museums housed principally recent or contemporary work, since there was little else available before the tycoon collectors of the later nineteenth and early twentieth centuries began buying European art wholesale. The first American gallery with an avowed policy of modernism was the Albright Art Gallery of the Fine Arts Academy, Buffalo, N.Y., opened on 31 May 1905 and from its inception closely in touch with the Musée de Luxembourg, which lent it some notable examples of contemporary French art. Successful exhibitions were held of modern German art, French Impressionists, pictorial photography, designs for the Russian Ballet, etc. Picasso proved a step too far, however, and when the vice president of the Fine Arts Academy, A. Conger Goodyear, acquired *La Toilette* for the gallery in 1928 without reference to his fellow trustees he was forced off the board. Not as bad a career move as might have been expected; the following year Goodyear was appointed first president of the newly established Museum of Modern Art in New York.

THE FIRST **ARTIFICIAL INSEMINATION**

between humans was conducted by Dr. Thouret, doyen of the medical faculty at Paris University, who made an intra-vaginal injection of sperm on his sterile wife in 1785 with a tin syringe. This resulted in the birth of a healthy baby, the achievement being described by Thouret in an anonymous pamphlet.

U.S.: Gynecologist Dr. James Marion Sims, chief of the Women's Hospital in New York City, treated fifty-five women with cervical abnormalities by injection of sperm during 1866–67. One pregnancy resulted.

The first artificial insemination with semen other than that of the husband (AID, or artificial insemination with donor) was conducted by Prof. William Pancoast of Jefferson Medical College, Philadelphia, on a chloroformed woman without her knowledge in 1884. Her husband, a Quaker merchant fifteen years her senior, was sterile. Together they had come to Dr. Pancoast for advice, and he in turn discussed it with his students. One of them suggested that semen should be collected from the "best-looking" member of the class, and the professor acceded to this novel suggestion. He called the woman back to his office and conducted the procedure under the pretense that he was carrying out a further examination that required her to be anesthetized.

Artificial insemination was first legalized in the United States by the state of Oklahoma on 18 May 1967.

THE FIRST **ASPIRIN**

was introduced commercially in powder form by Bayer AG of Leverkusen, Germany, in May 1899. Acetylsalicylic acid ("Aspirin" was a registered trade name) had been synthesized as early as 1853 by an Alsatian chemist, Charles Gerhardt; it was not until 10 August 1897 that young research chemist Dr. Felix Hoffmann of Bayer succeeded in producing it in a form sufficiently pure to be employed therapeutically. He did so, he wrote in 1934, because his father had complained about the bitter taste of salicylic acid, the only drug then available for treating rheumatism and closely related to aspirin chemically.

What was to become the most successful pharmaceutical drug in history then languished for the better part of two years after Bayer's pharmacology consultant Dr. Heinrich Dreser rejected it out of hand on the specious grounds that acetylsalicylic acid would enfeeble the heart. Besides, they already had a product that would do all that was claimed for Aspirin; it was called Heroin. Hoffmann's colleague Arthur Eichengrun eventually took matters into his own hands and clandestinely distributed it to a number of Berlin doctors, who reported back that their patients not only found that it relieved fevers and aching joints, as Bayer's Berlin agent Dr. Felix Goldmann had told them, but also cured headaches. When Goldmann wrote an enthusiastic appraisal, Dreser dismissed it with an angry growl: "That's just the usual Berlin bragging; the product has no value." On this occasion he did not get his way. Bayer CEO Friedrich Carl Duisberg insisted on an independent pharmacologist's report. This proving wholly positive, Dreser changed tack and wrote up a scientific paper for publication in which he extolled the value of the new drug. No mention was made in it of Hoffmann or Eichengrün.

Originally Aspirin was only available in Germany by prescription, but this did not impede its instantaneous success. Dreser, who received royalties on all drugs tested in his laboratory, made so much money from Aspirin that he was able to retire early as a rich man. Hoffmann and Eichengrun received nothing.

U.S.: Aspirin was imported by Bayer's sales agents Schieffelin & Co. and by its New York sales subsidiary Farbenfabriken of Elberfeld Co. in 1900. Manufacture of the powder began at Bayer's new factory at Rensselaer, N.Y., in 1903. Aspirin tablets were first manufactured in the United States in early 1914, Germany following suit the next year.

Aspirin and its users got a new lease on life with the discovery in 1971 by Sir John Vane, professor of experimental pharmacology at London University, that it had the formerly unknown property of blocking the action of prostaglandins. Only a small dose of 75 mg a day is necessary to inhibit blood from clotting, with the potential to prevent leg thromboses, strokes, and heart attacks (ironic in view of Dr. Dreser's assertion that it could cause heart attacks). For this and later work on prostacyclin, Sir John Vane shared the Nobel Prize in Physiology or Medicine 1982.

THE FIRST ATOMIC BOMB

was detonated experimentally at Alamogordo Air Base, N.M. on 16 July 1945.

The first **atomic bomb used in warfare** was the 9,000-pound, 10-foot-long "Little Boy," dropped over Hiroshima, Japan, from the USAAF B-29 bomber *Enola Gay* at a height of 31,000 feet on the morning of 6 August 1945. The pilot was Col. Paul W. Tibbets of Miami, Fla., and the bomb was released by Maj. Thomas W. Ferebee of Mocksville, N.C. The number of deaths caused by the explosion has been put at 78,150, with some 70,000 injured. The second bomb, exploded over Nagasaki on 9 August, killed some 40,000 and injured a further 25,000, precipitating the surrender of Japan on 15 August. The Japanese were unaware that the Allies had no further atomic bombs at their disposal.

The development of the first atomic bomb, estimated to have cost a total of $1.6 billion, was a joint project sponsored by the British, American, and Canadian governments. It began with a meeting held at the Royal Society's Rooms at Burlington House in London on 10 April 1940, when a working party under Prof. Sir George Thomson, later known as the Maud Committee, was convened to consider the feasibility of proposals for an atomic bomb that had been put forward by Rudolph Peierls and Otto Frisch, two German-Jewish refugees then engaged in nuclear research at the University of Birmingham. Following intensive research by teams of scientists at Liverpool, Birmingham, and Cambridge universities, the Maud Committee issued its report in July 1941, and on October 17 of the same year the government made its decision that the atomic bomb was to be built. Practical development was put in hand immediately under the direction of the Department of Scientific and Industrial Research, and a company registered in the cover name of Tube Alloys was set up to produce nuclear explosives.

The American S-1 Uranium Committee—equivalent to Britain's Maud Committee—was formed in December 1941 after a fact-finding tour of British nuclear research establishments by a team of American nuclear physicists. On 20 June 1942 Churchill proposed to Roosevelt that resources and information be pooled and the results shared. It was also decided that the bomb should be built in the United States, owing to Britain's vulnerability to air attack. Accordingly the Americans set up an organization called the Manhattan Project to construct the bomb, the British team crossing the Atlantic to join their American and Canadian colleagues on the undertaking. The project team at Los Alamos, N.M., was under the overall direction of Berkeley physicist Robert Oppenheimer.

Under the terms of the Quebec Agreement, signed in August 1943, it was agreed that all postwar and peaceful benefits of the joint research should accrue to the United States, that the bomb should not be used without mutual consent, that no information should be exchanged with outside parties, and that a combined Policy Committee be set up. The most controversial clause, the first, is thought to have been imposed on Britain at a time when she was in no position, after nearly four years of total war, to refuse any conditions if the bomb was to be brought to successful fruition.

Consequently, at the end of the war the United States was the world's only nuclear power, remaining so until 29 August 1949, when the Soviet Union tested its first atomic bomb. Britain was obliged to inaugurate a new nuclear program, joining the "nuclear club" when she exploded her first atomic bomb on the Monte Bello Islands off the northwest coast of Western Australia on 3 October 1952. The other nuclear powers (with dates of first tests) are France (13 February 1960), China (16 October 1964), India (11 May 1998), Pakistan (28 May 1998), and North Korea (9 October 2006). Israel may have detonated a nuclear device in the Indian Ocean on 22 September 1979, according to satellite data. Iran is known to have a nuclear program, believed to be directed at the development of offensive weapons.

Hydrogen bomb: The first was a thermonuclear weapon with the code name "Mike" that was detonated in a series of tests conducted by the United States at the Eniwetok [Enewetak] Proving Ground in the Marshall Islands, 31 October–4 November 1952. The principal test island of Elugelab was completely obliterated in an explosion described as "250 times more powerful than the A-bomb that leveled Hiroshima." Thermonuclear bombs were subsequently tested by the Soviet Union (22 November 1955), the United Kingdom (15 May 1957), China (17 June 1967), and France (24 August 1968).

THE FIRST **AUTOMATIC TELLER MACHINE**

was the Bankmatic, invented by Turkish-born Luther George Simjian and installed at the City Bank of New York in Manhattan for a six-month trial in 1939. It was withdrawn owing to lack of demand. According to Simjian, the only regular customers were late-night gamblers and prostitutes.

Nearly thirty years were to pass before the first permanent installation. The machine in question was developed by John Shepherd-Barron, of Britain's De La Rue Instruments, who was frustrated by not having ready access to cash on weekends. Installed at Barclays Bank in Enfield, North London, it was formally inaugurated on 27 June 1967 by television comedy actor Reg Varney. During the same year Shepherd-Barron

was given just 12 minutes to speak about cash dispensers at an international banking conference in Miami, but it was sufficient to gain him an order for six machines from First Pennsylvania Bank for installation in its Philadelphia branches. These were the first ATMs in the United States.

The De La Rue cash dispenser was activated by chemically encoded vouchers resembling traveler's checks issued to customers in packs of ten. In Britain a voucher was good for £10 ($26), which was the amount Shepherd-Barron deemed sufficient to tide one over the weekend. The first ATM to be operated with a plastic card was devised by Don Wetzel, vice president of product planning at online baggage-handling equipment manufacturer Docutel of Dallas, who was inspired with the idea while standing impatiently in a long line at his local bank. The inaugural unit was installed in January 1969 at a branch of Chemical Bank of New York at Rockville Center, Long Island, and activated with a Master Charge credit card (today's MasterCard).

The first network to link the ATMs of competing banks, enabling customers of one bank to draw money at another bank's branches, was developed in 1981 by First Data Network of Denver, Colo.

THE FIRST **AUTOMOBILE**

with an internal-combustion engine was built by the Luxembourg-born engineer J. J. Étienne Lenoir at the factory of the Société des Moteurs Lenoir (SEE ALSO **internal-combustion engine**) in rue de la Roquette, Paris, in May 1862. Lenoir had originally trained as an enameler but later turned his attention to railroads, inventing electric brakes and a new kind of railway signaling system. While employed as consulting engineer to the Paris engineering firm of Gautier et Cie, he began experimenting with internal-combustion engines fueled with illuminating gas. His first essays in this direction were of immense size, but by 1862 he had produced an engine small enough to fit to a carriage. The 1½-hp engine ran on liquid hydrocarbon fuel at 100 rpm.

It was some time before Lenoir felt sufficient confidence in his new vehicle to take it out on the public highway, and only in September 1863 did he summon up the courage to drive from rue de Roquette through the Bois de Vincennes to Joinville-le-Point, a distance of about 6 miles. The journey there and back took a driving time of 3 hours, an average speed of 4 mph.

The following year Lenoir received the world's first order for a motorcar from no less a customer than Tsar Alexander II of Russia. How the tsar heard about Lenoir's car is not known, for it received comparatively little publicity at the time. He is remembered, though, for the interest he took in technical progress, and many of the innovations he made in Russia were based on French example. The car was built and set out for the railway station at Vincennes under its own power. There it was entrained for St. Petersburg. What happened to it on arrival is an unsolved mystery. There is no evidence that the tsar ever rode in his motor carriage, and it is quite possible that there was no one attached to the Imperial Court with sufficient engineering skill to make it start. Nor is it known whether any arrangements were made for a supply of fuel. Indeed, nothing seems to have been known about the sale until 1906, when a set of papers detailing the transaction was found in Paris. A hunt for the car was then set on foot in Russia, but with negative results. It had vanished without trace, and if it was still in existence at that time, hidden away in a barn or storeroom, it seems unlikely that it would have long survived the chaos of the Bolshevik Revolution. Lenoir himself abandoned work on automobiles to concentrate his energies on developing a practical motorboat (qv).

Gasoline-driven automobile: The first was built in 1883 by twenty-seven-year-old Édouard Delamare-Deboutteville, son of a cotton-mill proprietor, who was inspired with the idea of seeking an alternative to horse transport for carrying cotton goods from his father's factories at Montgrimont and Fontaine-le-Bourg to the railhead at Rouen. With the help of his mechanic, Charles Malandin, Delamare-Deboutteville modified an 8-hp stationary gas engine for use with petroleum as a fuel and fitted it to a four-wheeled hunting brake. Road tests were carried out between Deboutteville's home at Fontaine-le-Bourg and nearby Cailly. The effect of the brake's iron-tired wheels on the rough stone *pavé* was too much for it,

and the vehicle was eventually abandoned as too fragile for the power of the motor. Deboutteville subsequently built a rubber-tired tricycle, but the motor was too heavy and the frame collapsed. After this setback the inventor abandoned the idea of self-propelled carriages and concentrated his attention on stationary engines, winning a number of awards for his improvements and receiving the Légion d'honneur in 1896.

The first successful gasoline-engine car, representing the beginning of the continuous development of commercially practicable motor vehicles, was built by the Rheinische Gasmotoren-Fabrik Karl Benz of Mannheim, Germany, in the fall of 1885. The three-wheeled single-cylinder vehicle weighed about 560 pounds and was powered by a ¾-hp water-cooled engine with electric ignition and a mechanically operated inlet valve. The engine drove the two rear wheels. An advanced feature of the car was its remarkably sophisticated differential gear. Benz was granted a patent on the design of the car on 29 January 1886.

The first public demonstration of Benz's three-wheeler took place on 3 July 1886, when it was driven for about a kilometer in Mannheim at a speed of 15 kph (9.3 mph). This historic event was reported the next day in the *Neue Badische Landeszeitung* under the heading "Miscellaneous."

During the winter of 1886–87 Benz built a more powerful 1½-hp car, and this was followed by a 2-hp model, which won a Gold Medal at the Munich Industrial Exhibition in September 1888. Meanwhile Gottlieb Daimler of Cannstatt had produced the first successful four-wheeled gasoline-engine car at the Maschinenfabrik Esslinger in August 1886. The single-cylinder engine was mounted onto an ordinary horse-drawn carriage, but Daimler soon realized that if motor transport was to have a future, it was essential for the vehicle to be designed as an entity. His *Stahlradwagen* (steel-wheeled carriage) of 1889 marked this departure and is also notable as the first car with a two-cylinder high-revving V-engine. It had a respectable maximum speed of 17.5 kph (10.9 mph) and was remarkably reliable for its time.

The motor-manufacturing concerns founded by Karl Benz and Gottlieb Daimler (SEE ALSO **automobile manufacture**) were eventually united in 1926 as Daimler-Benz, but during their lifetimes the two fathers of the industry worked quite independently and never met each other.

U.S.: At least two gasoline-powered vehicles were built in 1891. One, built by John William Lambert, is claimed by the man who was commissioned to photograph it to have been operated in the streets of Ohio City, Ohio, in August of that year. Lambert, the proprietor of a grain elevator, intended to manufacture the surrey-topped three-wheeler for sale at $550, but when the prototype was destroyed in a fire later in 1891 these plans were abandoned. The other pioneer vehicle was a four-wheeler constructed at Allentown, Pa., by Henry Nadig. Powered by a one-cylinder gasoline engine developing 2 hp at 600 to 800 rpm, the vehicle, according to Nadig's later testimony, ran "under its own power . . . on Fourth Street probably a dozen times in 1891." He continued to drive it until 1900.

There is also a third possible contender for earliest gasoline-powered American car. In 1891 Marshall McCluer of Spring Lake, Mich., built a motor buggy said to have been driven at 20 mph. There is, unfortunately, no record of the motive power, though a surviving photograph suggests a gasoline or electric motor rather than steam.

The oldest surviving American car is the horseless carriage fitted with a one-cylinder two-cycle Sintz marine gas engine by Gottfried Schloemer and Frank Toepfer in Milwaukee in 1892. It is preserved at the Milwaukee Public Museum.

THE FIRST **AUTOMOBILE FATALITY**

occurred on 17 August 1896 at the Crystal Palace, an exhibition and recreational center in London. The victim was Mrs. Bridget Driscoll from the London suburb of Croydon, the forty-four-year-old wife of a laborer, who was on her way to a Catholic temperance fete in the grounds with her teenage daughter and two friends when she was run over and suffered a fractured skull. The driver was Arthur Edsell, who was employed by the Anglo-French Motor Co. to give joyrides in a Roger-Benz on the terrace of the Crystal Palace. Edsell's vision was obstructed by two other cars in front, and Mrs. Driscoll, in a state of panic, stood still in the path of the approaching vehicle. At the inquest it was stated that Edsell had been driving at high speed and zigzagging to show off to his girlfriend, but it was established that in fact the vehicle had been traveling at 4 mph at the moment of impact. The verdict was accidental death.

U.S.: The first fatality happened in New York on 13 September 1899, when sixty-eight-year-old real estate broker Henry H. Bliss was run over by an electric cab driven by Arthur Smith at 74th Street and Central Park West. He was taken to Roosevelt Hospital, where he died the next day. Smith was charged with manslaughter and held on $1,000 bail, but he was later acquitted on grounds that there had been no intention to take life. On the centenary of the accident a plaque was dedicated to Henry Bliss on the site and a service was held outside the American Embassy in London in his memory and to commemorate the estimated 17 million people who had since died on the highways of the world.

THE FIRST
AUTOMOBILE FITTED
WITH AN ELECTRIC STARTER

was the prototype of the Arnold Sociable, the first gasoline-driven car in series production in Britain, built by W. Arnold & Son Ltd. of East Peckham in November 1896 and sold to H. J. Dowsing of Ealing, London, the following month. Dowsing, an electrical engineer by profession, added an electric self-starter of his own design (Patent No. 10781 of 1896) to the car. This consisted of a dynamotor, coupled to a flywheel, which would act as a dynamo to charge the battery and as a motor when required to start the engine.

The first production car to be sold with an electric self-starter system as a standard fitting was the Belgian-made 1902 Dechamps, manufactured by Atelier HP Dechamps of 31 rue Frère Orban, Brussels. Three models were available, a 9-hp and a 14-hp tonneau and a smaller 7-hp vehicle, all of them fitted with Dumont self-starters.

The Delco self-starter, designed by Charles Kettering of Cadillac in Detroit and first demonstrated on 27 February 1911, has often been described erroneously as the first self-starter on a standard-production model car. Though this is patently not true, the Delco did have a special significance as part of the first completely self-contained electrical system performing the three functions of ignition, starting, and lighting. It was offered as a standard fitting on the 1912 Cadillac.

The first automobile with a key-activated self-starter was the 1914 Inter-State manufactured in Muncie, Ind. Most systems were push-button until Chrysler reintroduced the ignition key in 1949.

THE FIRST AUTOMOBILE INSURANCE

was introduced by the General Accident Co. of London on 2 November 1896, terms of the policies being arranged individually between the company and the insured. The first general quotation was made about a week later by the Scottish Employers' Insurance Co. of Edinburgh, offering coverage at 30s ($7.50) per car outside of London plus 30s per £100 on the sum assured; London rates were 25 percent higher. Damage caused by frightened horses was specifically excluded. **U.S.:** The first policy was taken out by mechanic Gilbert Loomis of Westfield, Mass., who paid a $7.50 premium in 1897 to underwrite a $1,000 risk on his homemade one-cylinder automobile. The policy was one designed for horse-drawn vehicles. The first insurance company to offer a specific policy for automobiles was Travelers Insurance Co. of Hartford, Conn., on 1 February 1898, when Dr. Truman Martin of Buffalo, N.Y., paid $11.25 for $5,000 of liability coverage.

The first country to introduce compulsory liability insurance was Norway in 1912. In the United States liability became compulsory in Massachusetts on 1 January 1927 except for those willing to deposit $5,000 with the Division of Highways. In the first year of operation, opponents of the measure gleefully reported, there were 32,000 accidents involving injury to a third party but 43,000 claims.

THE FIRST AUTOMOBILE MANUFACTURE

of gasoline-powered vehicles was begun in 1888 by the Rheinische Gasmotoren-Fabrik Karl Benz of Mannheim, Germany. Benz had produced the first efficient and commercially practicable *motorwagen* three years earlier (SEE **automobile**), but the first recorded sale was made to Émile Roger of Paris, the invoice being dated 16 March 1888. The 2-hp single-cylinder car, a three-wheeled two-seater, was forwarded to Paris in four packing cases, and when it arrived Roger found he was unable to assemble the parts. He took the vehicle in pieces to the Panhard et Levassor factory to consult with their engineers, but the car remained immobile until May, when Benz himself paid a visit to the firm.

Benz issued its first catalog the same year. Initially the cars were all three-wheelers, but in 1893 two basic four-wheeled models were produced, the Victoria and the Vis-à-vis. Neither of these was standardized, being built according to the customer's specifications. Total sales of Benz vehicles at the end of that year stood at sixty-nine. The first standard model in series production was the Benz Velo, produced in April 1894. Powered by a 1½-hp engine, it had a maximum speed of 12 mph and was priced at 2,200 marks ($550).

Benz's company amalgamated with the Daimler Motoren-Gesellschaft in 1926 to become Daimler-Benz AG, manufacturers of the distinguished Mercedes marque that had been introduced by Daimler in 1901.

Despite the early lead in motor manufacture taken by the German Benz and Daimler enterprises, restrictive traffic laws and some of the worst roads in Europe (in contrast to France, which had the best) hindered the progress of the industry in Germany, and the French soon became recognized as world leaders in the development of the automobile. Production was started in 1891 by Panhard et Levassor and by Peugeot, both firms being aided by the distinction they won in the earliest automobile races (qv). By the end of 1893 cumulative world production stood at around 190 vehicles, Benz leading with 69, followed by Panhard with 60, Peugeot with 58, and Daimler about a dozen. Some two thirds of the Benz output, however, had been exported to France. By 1896, the year in which the Americans and British were taking their first faltering steps in automobile manufacture, French production was 320 completed cars. Two years later it had risen to over 1,500, compared to 232 in America. The first reliable world figures, for 1903, show France producing three times as many cars as her nearest competitor, the United States, and half of the world output of 61,927 vehicles:

France	30,204
United States	11,235
United Kingdom	9,437
Germany	6,904
Belgium	2,839
Italy	1,308

France, however, would not retain her world dominance for long. In 1904 the United States became the major automobile manufacturing nation with 21,692 cars to France's 16,900, a lead it retained until Japan became the leader in 1980.

U.S.: While the Duryea Motor Wagon Co. of Springfield, Mass., is generally acknowledged as the founder of the American automotive industry, it should be noted that there were three other firms that began producing gasoline-engine cars that year, 1895. One was G. Edgar Allen, a carriage builder resident in Englewood, N.J., who established a motor manufactory at 304 West 53rd Street in New York City, which survived until 1900; while elsewhere in the city, on 138th Street, the De La Vergne Refrigerating Co. completed its first four production vehicles, two single-cylinder traps and two twin-cylinder drags, in December. That month the company reported that it had orders from such luminaries of the financial world as John Jacob Astor, William Waldorf Astor, William Rockefeller, George Gould, Edwin Gould, and William Havemeyer, as well as beer barons Jacob Rupert of New York and Fred Pabst of Milwaukee. Building of cars to fulfill these and other orders was subcontracted to Hincks & Johnson of Bridgeport, Conn., and Valentine, Linn & Son of Brooklyn.

Production was abruptly halted on the death of the company founder, John Chester De La Vergne, in May 1896. Meanwhile, in Harvey, Ill., the Chicago Motor Vehicle Co., which despite its name also built horse-drawn carriages, was boasting of its factory capacity for a hundred vehicles weekly (for this figure to be realistic it would have to include the horse buggies). It continued making cars for four years before switching to motor buses and delivery vans. The company went bankrupt in 1904.

The brothers Charles and Frank Duryea of Springfield, Mass., probably deserve their titular honor as fathers of the motor industry in America on the grounds that manufacture was sustained over many years and that unlike most other pioneers their output consisted of a standardized marque, i.e., series production. Their first car had been road-tested in September 1893, and their second, probably the most efficient gasoline-powered vehicle built in the United States up to that time, won the *Chicago Times-Herald* contest in November 1895. By then the brothers were already in business, as evidenced by a letter Frank had addressed to Charles on 10 June concerning the new prototype:

> Everybody pleased with it and Clapp [a partner in the enterprise] is getting actual orders every day. An order received by AM. says book me two carriages to be delivered at earliest possible date . . . Some of the orders state that they do not care how much the wagon costs—send it and draw on our bank. There is no doubt but that the orders are genuine.

Despite the bulging order book, production of Duryea cars in 1895 was only two, with the first sale being made to George H. Morril Jr. of Norwood, Mass., the following February. For the remaining years of the decade annual output scarcely climbed into double figures: 1896, 13; 1897, 6; 1898, 12; 1899, 12. Thereafter it began to rise, peaking at 83 in 1907, then falling year by year until the company's demise in 1917.

Mass-produced gasoline-powered automobile: The first was the curved-dash Oldsmobile, which made its appearance in April 1901. The decision to build this particular model in quantity was prompted by a fire that destroyed the Olds Motor Works in Detroit in March 1901. The only vehicle saved was a prototype curved-dash runabout, and in order to resume production there was no choice but to concentrate on this single experimental vehicle. (It also had the effect of establishing Detroit as the auto capital of America, as Olds had to subcontract production of parts, and many of these small engineering shops then started automobile manufacture on their own account.) Output of the "merry little Oldsmobile" (as it was extolled in a popular song) was 433 by the end of the year, a figure comparable to that of the top French manufacturers, but then rose rapidly to 2,500 in 1902 with Olds' adoption of the assembly line, some twelve years before Henry Ford, and a prodigious 5,508 in 1904. Oldsmobile continued production for another hundred years. The last Olds, an Alero GLS 4-door sedan, rolled out on 29 April 2004. It was signed by every worker on the assembly line. The oldest surviving American marque is now Cadillac, production having started in March 1903.

THE FIRST **AUTOMOBILE RACE**

was organized by M. Fossier, editor of the French cycling magazine *La Vélocipède*, and held on 20 April 1887 over a course from Saint-James in Paris along the Seine to the bridge at Neuilly. The race resulted in a walkover for Georges Bouton, the only competitor, who completed the course in his four-seater steam quadricycle. The first race in which there was more than one competitor was organized by *La Vélocipède* the following year, when Bouton drove a three-wheeled De Dion to victory over his only rival—driving a Serpollet steamer—in a time of 30 minutes for the 12.4-mile course between Neuilly and Versailles.

The first motor race that included gasoline-driven cars and the first long-distance race was arranged by the Automobile Club de France and the French Newspaper *Le Petit Journal* over a course from Paris to Bordeaux and return, 11–14 June 1895. Although Émile Levassor was the first to complete the 732-mile run—in a time of 48¾ hours at an average speed of 15¼ mph—he was disqualified because his 3½ hp Phoenix-engine Panhard et Levassor car was a two-seater, proscribed under the rules of the race. His nearest rival, Koehlin, driving a much slower Peugeot, was declared the winner. Of the twenty-three starters, eight gasoline vehicles and a steamer arrived back in Paris.

U.S.: The first race was held on 2 November 1895 on public roads in Chicago and was sponsored by the *Chicago Times-Herald*. The event had been scheduled for 1 November, but as few of the entrants had their vehicles ready on time it was decided to postpone the main contest until 28 November but hold a preliminary one (a day late) for the four cars declared fit to race. It transpired that in fact none of them was, as there were no finishers. On 28 November the promised main event was duly held. There were six starters: a Duryea, an Electrobat, three American-made copies of the German Benz, and the already fairly historic 1892 Morrison electric. The race was run over a snowbound 55-mile course north to Evanston and back, and the $5,000 first prize went to J. Frank Duryea of Springfield, Mass., in his Duryea Motor Wagon, subsequently the first car in the United States in series production (SEE **automobile manufacture**). Average speed of the winner was 7½ mph. Second across the line, winning its owner $1,500, was the Mueller-Benz, which had started the race with Oscar Mueller at the tiller. An hour later he collapsed from hypothermia, and Charles Brady King, an umpire, volunteered to take over. No other contestant completed the course.

Automobile track race: The first in the world was held as one of the attractions of the Rhode Island State Fair on 7 September 1896 at a dirt track a mile in circumference at Narragansett Park in Cranston. Seven vehicles were entered, a Riker Electric Stanhope, a Morris & Salom Electrobat, and five gasoline-powered Duryeas, of which two were disqualified. There were five heats of a mile each, all of which were won by A. H. Whiting in the Riker, the first at an average speed of 26.8 mph. His average for the series of five was 24 mph. The dominance of one car and the modest speeds attained did not satisfy the crowd, who began chanting "Get a horse!"

THE FIRST **AUTOMOBILE RADIO**

on record was fitted to the passenger door of a Ford Model T by eighteen-year-old George Frost, president of the Radio Club at Lane High School in Chicago, and was in use by May 1922. The first manufacturer's installation was made by the Marconiphone Co., which exhibited a Daimler limousine fitted with a customized radio of its own design at the Olympia Motor Show in London in November 1922 and at the Scottish Motor Show in Glasgow the following January. Although their intention was to exploit car radio commercially, Daimler-Marconi's experiments proved to be premature, and the development program was dropped.

It is claimed that the American-made Rolls-Royce Springfield Sedan of 1924, manufactured by the Rolls-Royce subsidiary in Springfield, Mass., was offered with radio as an optional accessory. Certainly the new model was exhibited with radio at the New York Auto Salon in autumn 1923, but whether it was actually sold with the optional extra has not been possible to verify.

The first car definitely known to have been offered with radio as an optional extra was the 1925 Summit, an Australian-built car produced by Kelly's Motors of Alexandria, New South Wales. The prototype was fitted during 1924. Passengers listened in through headphones, and the aerial was attached to the waterproof canopy. At the end of that year, when the 1925 model of the Summit was launched, there were 38,336 domestic radios in Australia, a figure that grew to 85,000 over the next twelve months. Broadcasting was burgeoning, and there was therefore a market for car radios to tap into, particularly in a country where so much time was spent out of doors. The make of radio is not recorded, but the leading local manufacturer at the time was the joint Marconi/Telefunken New South Wales subsidiary Amalgamated Wireless (Australia) Ltd., so it is possible that it was an adaptation of its popular Radiola set.

The first manufacturer to design and market a purpose-built car radio was the Automobile Radio Corp. of New York, which launched its Transitone receiver in 1927. This had a control head clamped to the steering column, with most of the "doings" located under the hood; automobiles of the period were not designed to admit a receiver in the instrument panel. Transitones were sold direct to manufacturers. During the late '20s the makes that were wired to Transitone specifications were Cadillac, Chrysler, Desoto, Dodge, Franklin, Hupmobile, Jordan, La Salle, Packard, Peerless, Pierce-Arrow, and Studebaker—all of them at the upper end of the market. Radio was

generally offered as optional, though the 1929 model of the Cleveland-built Jordan is said to have had the Transitone fitted as standard. The Automobile Radio Corp. was acquired in 1930 by Philco, which adopted the Transitone brand for a range of domestic receivers as well as car radios. Philco introduced car radio to Europe when the Transitone was offered for sale in Britain at 33 guineas ($115) in the autumn of 1932. The *Autocar* reported in November that "several high-grade coach builders are now fitting them in bodies for Rolls-Royces."

The first receiver that would fit any make of car and could therefore be offered direct to motorists rather than to manufacturers is invariably asserted to have been the Motorola from the Galvin Manufacturing Corp. of Chicago. The initial Motorola—the name is said to have come to founder Paul Galvin, like many such inspirations, while he was shaving and was a combination of "motor" and "victrola"—was the model ST71, launched on 1 September 1930 at $110–$130 including installation. Alas for those who prefer to attribute "firsts" to celebrated brand names, there was already a car radio available for purchase over the counter. The Crosley Roamio could also be fitted to any standard make of car and had been advertised by Crosley Radio of Cincinnati at $75 (not including installation) in the July 1930 issue of *Radio News*. Motorola was to become synonymous with affordable car radio and accounted for a large proportion of the estimated 100,000 automobiles fitted with radio by the deep-Depression year of 1933, but first in the field it was not quite.

Early antennas tended to be festoons of chicken wire; the telescopic rod antenna was introduced by Philco in 1934. Four significant advances emerged from the Delco Radio Division (later Delphi Delco) of General Motors, based at Kokomo, Ind.: the push-button radio in 1938, the signal-seeking set in 1947, the all-transistor receiver in 1957, and the AM/FM combination in 1963. A notable advance from outside the United States was the removable operating panel, one of the most effective security devices against thieves, introduced by Grundig of Nuremberg, Germany, in 1989.

THE FIRST **AUTOMOBILE RENTAL SERVICE**

was instituted by the Paris Automobile Club in January 1896. Six vehicles were stationed outside the clubhouse and were available for immediate hire at 3 francs (60¢) an hour, or 30 francs ($6) a day, with driver.

The Automobile Club's service was instituted principally with the idea of winning converts to the cause of motoring. A strictly commercial car-hire service was started the following month by the Société Anonyme Française des Fiacres Automobiles of 52 rue des Dames, Paris. The brain behind this enterprise was Émile Roger, the agent for Benz cars in France, who in 1888 had been the first person to purchase a commercially manufactured gasoline-driven car (SEE **automobile manufacture**). He undercut the Automobile Club's rates, offering Benz cars for 2 francs (40¢) an hour.

U.S.: W. T. McCullough, proprietor of the Back Bay Cycle & Motor Co. of 122 Massachusetts Avenue, Boston, advertised "motor carriages to rent" in the 1899 edition of the *Boston City Directory*. As this would have been published in advance of the new year, the service was probably in operation during 1898.

Car rental outlet at an airport: The first in the United States was established by Hertz at Chicago Midway in 1932. Hertz failed to capitalize on this pioneering endeavor, the first to establish a network of airport outlets being Avis Airlines Rent-a-Car Co., starting in 1946 at Detroit and Miami.

THE FIRST **AUTOMOBILE SEAT BELTS**

were fitted to vehicles manufactured by Nash Motors of Kenosha, Wisc., and Muntz of Evanston, Ill., in 1952. These were simple two-point straps buckled across the abdomen and, while they improved passenger safety, they did little to protect drivers and passengers from the possibility of head, spinal, and internal injuries. Indeed, Nash Motors did not introduce them as a safety device but as a means of protecting passengers from rolling out of the reclining seats.

The now universal three-point seat belt was designed by Swedish aerospace engineer Nils Bohlin, who was recruited by Volvo to work on seat-belt improvements because of his experience with Saab on aircraft ejector seats. The simple yet elegant solution was introduced on the Volvo PV544 in its home market in 1959, but by 1963 they were standard on Volvos worldwide, and in that same year the design was made freely available to all car makers. In 1966 Volvo issued the *28,000 Accident Report*, which claimed that the use of three-point seat belts reduced the risk of death or injury in automobile accidents by 75 percent. The only significant improvement to Bohlin's original design has been the introduction of the inertia reel, also by Volvo, in 1968.

The first seat-belt legislation was passed in Illinois on 27 June 1955, requiring that cars be fitted with attachments to which the then two-point belts could be fastened. Wisconsin was the first state to require that all new cars be fitted with seat belts, beginning with the 1962 model year. The first mandatory requirement to wear seat belts in the United States went into effect in New York State on 1 January 1985. They are now compulsory in all states except New Hampshire. The first country to legislate nationally for the wearing of seat belts was Czechoslovakia (now Czech Republic) in 1969.

In 1985 the German Patent Office chose the three-point seat belt as one of the eight most significant inventions of the previous hundred years.

THE FIRST **AUTOMOBILE SPEEDOMETER**

was invented by Joseph W. Jones of New York, who built himself a kerosene-burning steam-powered automobile in 1899 in the machine shop where he worked on Houston Street on the Lower East Side. While Jones was taking a drive with his wife, she happened to ask him how fast they were going. When Jones replied that he did not know, she suggested that he create a device for measuring speed. He did so, patented it, and made his fortune. Jones also coined the term "speedometer."

THE FIRST **AUTOMOBILE TOUR**

of any distance in a gasoline-engine car was made in August 1888 by Bertha Benz, wife of the inventor of the practical automobile (qv), Karl Benz, with her sons Eugen, age fifteen, and Richard, age thirteen, from their home at Mannheim in Baden-Württemberg, Germany, to Pforzheim on the northern fringe of the Black Forest, a round-trip of 120 miles.

Although the two boys had been taught to drive, neither was allowed to take the tiller of their father's cars except under his supervision or that of the shop foreman. Their mother having occasion to visit relatives in Pforzheim, Eugen suggested this would be an ideal opportunity to make an extended motor journey on their own. Frau Benz entered into the conspiracy with a readiness not usually associated with Victorian matrons, and the three set off from Mannheim early one morning in the 2-hp three-wheeler car. Karl Benz was unaware of their intentions, though a note was left for him, explaining that they would be coming back and had not deserted him.

Eugen drove, with Frau Benz occupying the seat next to him and Richard perched on the rear over the engine. The first stop was made at Heidelberg, where they ate a meal, and the motorists then continued to Wiesloch. From there the road became steeper, and Frau Benz and Eugen were obliged to dismount and push the vehicle up the hills while Richard took the tiller. Progress downhill afforded unforeseen hazards owing to the inadequacy of the leather brake linings, which soon wore away with pressure. Periodic stops had to be made at cobblers on the way, to obtain more leather for the brake blocks.

Further trouble was experienced when the driving chains became loose. A little later the fuel pipe to the carburetor was found to be blocked, but this was remedied with one of Frau Benz's hatpins. When an ignition wire short-circuited after rubbing against another part of the engine, Frau Benz once more rose to the occasion by taking off her garter and using it to insulate the wire.

Throughout the journey the Benz family was the object of incredulous amazement, and this nearly provoked a fight at an inn in the Black Forest, when two peasants began a violent dispute about whether the car was driven by clockwork or by a supernatural agency. They arrived safely at Pforzheim, and after a five-day stay, the two boys and their mother motored back to Mannheim.

One positive outcome of the trip was that Benz accepted his son Eugen's judgment that the vehicle was underpowered for hill climbing and added an additional gear.

U.S.: Not known. The editor invites nominations.

~~~~~~~~~~~~~~~~~~~~~~~ **B** ~~~~~~~~~~~~~~~~~~~~~~~

THE FIRST **BABY CARRIAGE**

of record was a miniature phaeton built c. 1733 at Chatsworth, the seat of the dukes of Devonshire in Derbyshire, England, by painter, landscape gardener, and architect William Kent on behalf of William Cavendish, the 3rd duke. This elegant little vehicle was fitted with 21-inch wheels at the rear and 16-inch wheels in front and had a body in the shape of a scallop shell with folding hood. Its most bizarre feature was the undercarriage, a framework made up of bronze snakes imitative of the Cavendish snake that forms part of the Devonshire family crest. Shafts and a small collar indicate that it was intended to be drawn by a dog. The most likely occupant was Frederick Cavendish, the duke's fifth child, who went on to become a field marshal, the highest rank in the British Army. It may also have transported his nephew, the physicist Henry Cavendish, after whom Cambridge University's Cavendish Laboratory is named.

The only surviving baby carriage that might possibly be contemporary with the Chatsworth example is a *voiture d'enfant* in the collection of the French Musée National de la Voiture at the Château de Compiègne. This has been claimed by some historians to have been built for Louis XV's infant dauphin (b. 1729), but the director of the museum is of the opinion that it is of German rather than French origin and most likely to date from the second half of the eighteenth century.

Regular manufacture of baby carriages: Two-wheel basswood baby carriages that sold for $1.50 each were being manufactured by Benjamin Potter Crandall in Westerley, R.I., before 1841, the year that he moved his business to Madison Avenue in New York City. There he started producing four-wheelers, and the "oscillating axle" that he developed for these carriages, with independent suspension on each wheel, was many years later adopted by car manufacturers.

It is not known whether these pioneer baby buggies were designed to be pulled or pushed. A pushchair was designed by Charles Burton of New York in 1848, but it appears that Manhattanites, as impatient then as now, made such a fuss about their rapid progress on the sidewalk being impeded by Burton's buggies that he crossed the Atlantic to set up business in the more toddler-tolerant atmosphere of London.

Prior to 1876 nearly all baby carriages were of the pushchair type, designed for children old enough to sit up. In that year a number of firms in both Britain and the United States introduced bassinet models in which a small baby could lie full length. Like a miniature brougham in appearance, they were really the prototype of the modern baby buggy. It must remain one of the mysteries of the trade why such a seemingly obvious development took so long to come to fruition.

Lightweight folding baby stroller: This, the first major advance in baby-carriage development in sixty-five years, was invented in 1942 in Australia by Harold Cornish, founder of Stoway Strollers—so called because his buggies could be stowed under a streetcar seat. The ultra-lightweight aluminum pushchair, patented in Britain on 20 July 1965 by former test pilot Owen Finley Maclaren (designer of the undercarriage of World War II's Spitfire fighter), weighed a mere 7 pounds and was designed to be foldable with one hand while the other held a kicking, sprawling infant.

It is unlikely that any other invention based on so simple a concept as the baby carriage has ever been the subject of so many patents, well over three thousand having been granted since the first in 1853. Some represented genuine advances in design, the majority, however, leaving little imprint on perambulator history. The gasoline-engine model of 1921, which accommodated its driver standing up on a rear platform, has passed into the same limbo as the perambulator that turned into a bath, the garden-roller that turned into a perambulator, and the floating pram shaped like a canoe. Other flights of fancy included a carriage propelled by the baby itself, who was expected to keep the mechanism in motion by alternately rising and sitting.

THE FIRST **BABY FOOD**

processed was Liebig's Soluble Food for Babies, introduced in Germany in 1867 to a formula devised by University of Munich chemist Baron Justus von Liebig. It was claimed that the chemical makeup of the preparation was identical to that of mother's milk. For women of the leisured class who could not or did not want to breast-feed, it meant that they no longer needed to employ wet nurses. The product was an instant success, being introduced in Britain and the United States the following year. Competitors soon began manufacturing their own versions, most notably Farine Lactée Nestlé, produced at Vevey in Switzerland in 1868 and marketed in Germany in opposition to Liebig's.

Liebig's was a mixture of wheat flour, cow's milk, and malt flour cooked with bicarbonate of potash to reduce the flour's acidity. Despite the baron's claims, it did not replicate human milk. The first of the modern infant formulas, a synthetic milk product simulating the fatty acid content of human milk, was developed by Dr. H. I. Gerstenberger and Dr. H. O. Ruh of Tufts–New England Medical Center, who fed their Synthetic Milk Adapted (SMA) formula to three hundred infants in a 1919 test. It was marketed in powdered form as Franklin Infant Food (later Similac) by the Moores & Ross Milk Co., Columbus, Ohio, in 1925.

Canned baby food: The first was Clapp's Vegetable Soup, marketed in 1922 by restaurant manager Harold H. Clapp and his wife Anna of Rochester, N.Y. Large-scale production of canned baby foods was inaugurated by Gerber's of Fremont, Mich., in 1929, but they found sales resistance from mothers sampling the unsalted food and finding it tasteless. Although babies' taste buds are insufficiently developed to tell the difference, Gerber's bowed to matriarchal demand in 1931 and began adding unnecessary salt.

The first processed baby foods in glass jars were marketed in 1931 by the Beech-Nut Packing Co. of Canajoharie, N.Y.

Cereal baby food: The first pre-cooked, vitamin-enriched cereal was Pablum, devised by Canadian pediatrician Dr. Alan Brown and introduced c. 1928 at the Hospital for Sick Children in Toronto. Brown, something of a classicist, took the name from the Latin word for food, *pabulum*. Pablum was first marketed commercially by Mead Johnson, which launched it throughout North America in 1930. Substantial royalties continue to go to the hospital's Pediatric Research Foundation.

THE FIRST **BABY INCUBATOR**

was designed by Odile Martin of Neuilly, France, in response to a request by Stéphanie Tarnier, who had been impressed by Martin's apparatus for the artificial hatching of chickens that she had seen in 1878 on a visit to the Jardin d'Acclimatation. Two years later the prototype was installed by Tarnier at the Paris Maternity Hospital, where the death rate for premature babies of less than 2 kg (4½ pounds) at birth fell from 66 percent to 38 percent.

Far to the south, in Nice, Dr. Alexandre Lion developed an improved version, in which the air in the incubator was purified through a filter and kept constantly fresh by means of a fan ventilator, while the temperature was regulated automatically by a thermostatic control. In 1892 he set up the first special unit for premature babies, the Oeuvre Maternelles Couveuses d'Enfants, and this was followed by similar establishments in Bordeaux, Marseilles, Lyons, and Paris. The Nice clinic was supported partly by charitable contributions and partly by a subsidy from the municipality. In Paris the public was admitted to inspect the incubated babies for 50 centimes (10¢) a head, and this was sufficient to cover the nurses' wages of 60 francs ($12) a month and other expenses.

Dr. Lion claimed a 74-percent success rate, 137 out of the 185 children reared in the incubators at Nice during the first three years surviving infancy. None of the 185, he considered, would have lived in the ordinary course of events. Babies too weak to swallow naturally were fed through the nose with a specially molded spoon, or breast-fed through a tube attached to the nipple of the wet nurse. "Black women often take care of white babies," noted an English reporter in wonder, "and white women take care of black babies, as occasion requires."

U.S.: The first incubator was designed by Dr. Allan M. Thomas and Dr. William C. Denning, pediatricians who headed the maternity ward at State Emigrant Hospital on Ward's Island, New York. The first baby to be reared in the 3' x 3' "hatching cradle," as it was called, was 2-pound 7-ounce Edith Eleanor McLean, born on 7 September 1888. The apparatus was warmed by 15 gallons of water.

THE FIRST BABY SHOW

was held in Springfield, Ohio, on 14 October 1854. There were 127 exhibits, including one five months of age that weighed twenty-seven pounds and another that was a seventeenth child. The winner was the ten-month-old offspring of William Romner of Vienna, Clark County, Ohio, who was awarded a service of silver plate. The prevailing spirit of mutual admiration was marred when one of the judges had the temerity to define a baby as "an alimentary canal with a loud noise at one end and no sense of responsibility at the other."

THE FIRST BAKED BEANS

in popular New England mythology originated as a Native American dish baked in holes in the earth with maple syrup and bear's fat. There is absolutely no evidence that this is an Indian dish any more than is popcorn (qv), though whereas popcorn was not possible in early New England (the strain of corn for popping did not grow there), the Navy beans used in Boston Baked Beans were native to the Massachusetts Bay Colony. It is improbable, though, that it is aboriginal in origin, as there are no references earlier than the mid-eighteenth century. According to Keith Stavely and Kathleen Fitzgerald, authors of *America's Founding Food* (2004), Wright's Tavern in Concord, Mass., was baking the villagers' bean pots in the tavern's ovens in 1747. At this time most domestic cooking, certainly in humbler homes, was done over an open hearth. Baking for those without brick ovens at the side of the fireplace tended to be something indulged in but once a week, with pies, bread, or baked bean pot being carried to a local tavern, or in larger communities a bakehouse, and collected the following day. The usual day for baking was a Saturday, rural New Englanders still abstaining from cooking on the Sabbath. In some towns the "bean feast" was a Saturday-night celebration; elsewhere it followed the Sunday-morning meeting.

The earliest recipe for baked beans appears in 1829, in Lydia Maria Child's *The Frugal Housewife* (Boston). "A pound of pork is enough for a quart of beans," she wrote, "and that is a large dinner for a common family." The only seasoning she recommended was black pepper to render the beans "less unhealthy" (there was a longstanding belief that legumes, one of the most nutritious of foods, were bad for you); tomato sauce and molasses were not added for another half-century. The British, who consume twice the volume of baked beans per capita the Americans do, still eschew molasses, and within recent years their version, customarily served on hot buttered toast or as an accompaniment to a breakfast "fry up," has made its appearance on supermarket shelves in the United States.

Canned baked beans were first produced by the Burnham & Morill Co. of Portland, Me., in 1875 for the benefit of its fishing fleet, the men having expressed a desire to enjoy at sea the same Saturday-night pleasure as on shore. Baked beans in tomato sauce were canned by the Van Camp Packing Co. of Indianapolis in 1891.

THE FIRST BALLET

was the 6-hour *Ballet comique de la reine*, choreographed by Baldassare di Belgioioso, aka Beaujoyeux, court musician and dance master, and staged at the Louvre in Paris, then a royal palace, on 15 October 1581. The production, which had been commissioned by Catherine de Médicis to celebrate the wedding of her daughter-in-law, sister of the queen of France, included song, pantomime, and poetry as well as dance but is generally recognized as the first ballet because of Belgioioso's innovation of extended choreographed steps rather than free motion. It told the story of the escape of Odysseus from the sorceress Circe and drew on French and Italian court dance traditions to achieve what Belgioioso described as the "geometrical arrangement of many persons dancing together under a diverse harmony of instruments." Catherine herself regarded the spectacle as a new art form and promoted it as such throughout the courts of Europe.

The first ballet to rely on mime and gesture to the exclusion of either speech or song was John Weaver's *The Loves of Mars and Venus*, presented at the Theatre Royal, Drury Lane, in London on 22 March 1717 with Louis Dupré dancing the part of Mars, Mrs. Santlow as Venus, and Weaver himself in the role of Vulcan. The music was written by two different composers, Richard Firbank, who was responsible for "the Dancing Airs," and Henry Symonds, a member of the King's Band of Musicians, who was commissioned to compose the "Symphonies." The latter's contribution was intended to reflect "the Passions and Affections of the Characters." The production was mounted on a shoestring budget, because the manager of Drury Lane, Colley Cibber, was reluctant to invest very much in a completely untried form of entertainment (though he later wrote one that was the first ballet performed in America—SEE BELOW). As far as the public was concerned, Weaver's innovation was a considerable success. He himself, having more exacting standards than his audience, admitted that he was not wholly satisfied with the performance of the dancers, who, it seems, were somewhat bewildered by Weaver's avant-garde choreography. "I must confess," he wrote afterward, "that I have in his entertainment too much inclin'd to the Modern Dancing."

Weaver was the first to liberate ballet from opera and give it an independent existence as an art form. Although it may appear an anomaly that England, which won little distinction in the world of dance until the twentieth century, should have been the birthplace of the classical *ballet d'action*, there are some sound historical reasons for this early development. England had established a tradition of popular dramatic entertainment earlier than most Continental countries. Dance in England, too, had a wider currency in the court entertainments of the sixteenth and seventeenth centuries than was general in Europe, though it must

be said that ballet in its primitive form, as an interlude in operas and masques, saw its earliest flowering in France and Italy.

The first *ballet d'action* to be performed on the public stage in Continental Europe was Marie Sallé's *Pygmalion*, which had been premiered at Covent Garden in 1734 and was opened in Paris later the same year by François Riccobini at the Théâtre-Italien. From France the ballet was introduced to Russia, where the Imperial Theatre School was established under the direction of the ballet-master Landé in 1751. It was from this fertile soil that the classical ballet was destined to return to its birthplace, England, when in 1911 the Diaghilev troupe, known as the Ballets Russes, took London by storm, causing a revival of interest in dance that ended a century of stagnation. So barren had the nineteenth century been in the chronicle of English ballet that the term "ballet dancer" had been debased to mean at best a performer in pantomime, and at its worst a euphemism for the kind of harlot who pretended connections with the stage.

U.S.: The first theatrical production to contain a significant element of dance was Colley Cibber's *Flora, or Hob in the Well*, presented on 18 February 1735 by dancing master Henry Holt at the Play-House (which was actually the long room of Shepheard's Tavern) in Charleston, S.C. The ballet sequences comprised "the dance of two Pierrots and the pantomime of Harlequin and Scaramouche."

The earliest recorded American ballet was *Columbus, or the Discovery of America, with Harlequin's Revels*, performed in New York in 1783. As the title suggests this was a harlequinade, as were most ballets produced in the United States in the eighteenth and early nineteenth centuries. What dance historian Lillian Moore has described as "the first *serious* ballet to be given in this country," *La Forêt Noire*, opened at the New Chestnut Street Theater, Philadelphia, in the spring of 1794. Based on a French ballet-pantomime, this had new music specially composed by the theater's orchestra director, Alexander Reinagle. The choreography is believed to have been by the French dancer Quesnet. With a ballet company directed by William Francis, the leading role was taken by the exquisite Madame Gardie, a Creole from Santo Domingo, who was to be tragically murdered by her husband in New York four years later. The ballet was sufficiently successful to be repeated five times during the season (unusual then) and was subsequently presented in Boston and New York.

American-born prima ballerinas: The first two both made their debut in the same production of Auber's *The Maid of Cashmere* at Philadelphia's Chestnut Street Theater on 30 December 1837. Mary Ann Lee, who danced Fatima, had been born in that city in 1822 and had been a child actor before training in ballet. The leading role, Zoloe, was danced by Augusta Maywood, stepdaughter of the manager of the theater, who was twelve at the time and had trained under the same ballet master as Lee, the French dancer and choreographer P. H. Hazard, formerly of the Paris Opéra. Audiences at this and subsequent performances divided into pro-Ann and pro-Augusta factions, each passionate in defense of their juvenile favorite. Augusta was the more talented of the two, but Ann had a winsomeness and appeal that won her an army of admirers. After a successful season in New York, followed by another in Philadelphia, Augusta departed for fresh triumphs in Europe, never to return. Only fourteen years old, she opened at the Paris Opéra, the world's most prestigious fulcrum of the ballet, performing a pas in *Le diable boiteux* on 11 November 1839, the leading critic Gauthier declaring that "her little legs of a wild doe make steps as long as those of Mlle [Marie] Taglioni." Her success with the demanding Parisian audiences was instantaneous, and a theatrical annual for 1840 already listed her, alongside the incomparable Fanny Elssler, as *première ballerine*—the first American dancer to achieve such recognition in Europe. She received the coveted title of *prima ballerina* with her opening in Vienna in *Giselle* in 1845. From 1848, when she debuted at La Scala in Milan, most of her career until retirement was in Italy, where she reigned with Fanny Elssler as *prima ballerina e prima mima assoluta*.

Mary Ann Lee followed in Augusta's footsteps, going to Paris in 1844 to train at the Opéra under Jean Coralli. She decided against a European career, but returned home with much improved technique and formed her own touring company. On 1 January 1846 she danced in the first American production of *Giselle* at the Howard Athenaeum in Boston. Soon after, she began to lose her health and retired in 1847 at the age of twenty-four, having achieved in her own country a distinction only surpassed by the finest foreign talents to tour America.

Choreographer to introduce the use of pointe: The first was Charles Didelot for his ballet *Zéphyr et Flore*, originally presented at London's Theatre Royal, Drury Lane, in 1796. The dancers were enabled to rise on pointe by special machinery, also used to carry them up into the air and away into the wings. *Zéphyr et Flore* is also notable as the first ballet in which the male lead lifts his partner, and for its introduction of the pas de deux as a "conversation" between two dancers. Once it had been established as a graceful and desirable element of the dance, the use of pointe was found to be perfectly feasible without the aid of artificial support. This, though, was by no means immediate. The first ballerina named as dancing en pointe unsupported (in a fellow dancer's later memoir) was Geneviève Gosselin, possibly as early as 1813. The earliest contemporary reference to the practice dates from 1815, a visitor from Scotland to the Opéra describing how the Parisian audience broke out into "extravagant exclamations of astonishment and delight" when "one of the females wheels around on the toes of one foot, folding her other limb nearly in a horizontal position." Nor were those toes sustained by a block in the shoe: Early pointe shoes had no such device, so it is not surprising that the great Fanny Elssler should wear out three pairs in a single performance.

Ballet tutu: The first was designed by A. E. Chalon (or, according to some authorities, the painter Eugène Lami) for Filippo Taglioni's *La Sylphide*, which opened at the Paris Opéra on 12 March 1832 and was presented at Covent Garden on 26 July the same year. In both productions the *première danseuse*, Marie Taglioni, and the corps de ballet were similarly attired in these simple white muslin costumes, with a low décolletage, skirts halfway down the calf, and the arms left bare. This marked a radical departure from the elaborate ballet dress formerly in vogue and remains, with some modification, the standard "neutral" costume for romantic ballet to the present day. Fashion historian James Laver has pointed out that the ballet tutu was in fact but a "slight theatricalization" of the fashionable dress of the 1830s.

The first wheel-shaped tutu was worn by the Italian ballerina Virginia Zucchi when she danced the title role in *La Fille du Pharaon* at the Imperial Theatre in St. Petersburg in 1885.

SEE ALSO **television ballet performance**.

THE FIRST **BALLOON-FRAME BUILDINGS**

transformed the nascent city of Chicago a generation before the Great Fire. Most of the houses of the first two centuries of America's settlement were built according to techniques long hallowed in England: thick beams a foot square joined by mortise (an aperture in one beam) and tenon (a tongue carved at the end of another) and held together with wooden pegs fitted into auger holes. The result was sturdy enough to withstand the travail of centuries but was costly, labor intensive, and demanding of craft skills of a high order. What replaced this method of building in America was the balloon frame, eventually to account for at least three quarters of all houses constructed in the United States. Its pioneer was Augustine Deodat Taylor, an unsung hero whose name seldom makes an appearance in the annals of American progress, not even in specialist histories of American building types. He migrated to Chicago in 1833 from Hartford, Conn., coincidentally the site of the first house designed by a woman in America—on a balloon frame (SEE **woman architect**). Where Taylor got the idea of substituting a light frame of thin sawed timbers, predominantly two-by-fours held together with nails, is not known, but within a month of his arrival he was busy erecting Chicago's first Catholic church, St. Mary's, under the direction of Fr. John St. Cyr. The spindly-looking construction at State and Lake streets measured 36' x 24' and was 12' high, but its strength belied the apparent flimsiness of the frame. "Balloon" had nothing to do with its shape; the term was used by detractors to suggest that it would be tossed about by the first puff of wind. The cost of $400 was about half that of a conventional church of the same dimensions, and it was completed in half the time. Moreover, it was portable. Being so easily dismantled, St. Mary's was moved three times within ten years according to the changing demographic of its Catholic parishioners in the fastest-growing city in America.

The astonishing speed at which Chicago expanded—it was the first city to grow from the size of a village to a million population in its first half century of existence—was in no small measure facilitated by Taylor's remarkable innovation, remarkable not least for the lengthy time it had taken to emerge and then the rapidity with which it was adopted. What historian Daniel J. Boorstin has described as "a common-sense way to meet the urgent housing needs of impatient migratory people" found immediate application elsewhere in the emergent boomtown that was early Chicago. By October 1833 there were some 50 balloon-frame buildings, and the following April 7 new ones went up in the space of a week. A commentator writing in October 1834 said he had counted no fewer than 628, of which 212 were stores.

Other mushroom cities of the Plains were soon to follow Chicago's lead, as the new availability of dimensioned lumber and a rapid fall in the price of nails—from 8¢ a pound in 1828 to 3¢ in 1842—brought ease and economy to wood framing; and while the steel plow, the reaper, and barbed wire have been hailed as the inventions that opened up the rural West, it was Taylor's balloon frame that was to stimulate its urban growth. "A man and a boy," observed one writer, "can now attain the same results, with ease, that twenty men could on an old-fashioned frame." Nor were all the balloon-frame buildings on the small scale of St. Mary's; the huge apartment blocks with plastic cladding that now adorn so many upscale residential communities had their early counterpart in the 3½-story, 180-foot-long Astor House in Gold Rush–era San Francisco, which boasted a hundred rooms and accommodated ten shops in its frontage. It had been prefabricated in New York and shipped around the Horn in the equivalent of today's flat-packs. In a city where craftsmen were at a premium, putting it up did not present a problem. "To erect a balloon-building," Solon Robinson was to assert in 1855, "requires about as much mechanical skill as it does to build a board fence."

THE FIRST **BALLPOINT PEN**

for writing on paper was devised in 1938 by a Hungarian hypnotist, sculptor, and journalist, László Bíró, who at this time happened to be editing a government-sponsored cultural magazine in Budapest. During the course of a visit to the printers of the magazine, Bíró was struck by the advantage of a quick-drying ink for use in pens, and he subsequently constructed the prototype ballpoint to this end. Shortly afterward he escaped from Hungary to Paris in the face of the encroaching Nazi menace, and from thence to Argentina in 1940. Here he continued to work on his idea for a pen that would not blot and patented it on 10 June 1943. About the same time, he met a visiting Englishman, Henry Martin, who had arrived in Buenos Aires on a mission for the British government. Martin was impressed with the invention, which he saw as an answer to the problem experienced by air crews having to make navigational calculations at high altitudes. Fountain pens would not flow, but he found that Biro's ballpoint was in no way affected by changes of air pressure or atmosphere. Accordingly he acquired the British rights, and in 1944 began producing ballpoints for the RAF in a disused aircraft hangar near Reading. His staff of seventeen young women turned out thirty thousand finished pens the first year.

The first commercially produced ballpoint on regular sale was produced under the Bíró patents by the Eterpen Co. of Buenos Aires early in 1945 and marketed at the equivalent of $110.

U.S.: Chicago businessman Milton Reynolds bought a number of the Eterpen ballpoints while on a trip to Buenos Aires in June 1945. On his return home he hired William Huenergardt to replicate the pen, introducing some different design features that enabled him to evade Bíró's U.S. patent of 1943 and apply for one of his own.

Advertised as the "first pen that writes under water," the American version won an immediate response when it went on sale, priced at $12.50, at Gimbel's of New York on 29 October 1945. It was reported that nearly ten thousand had been sold before closing time.

Bíró licensed Eversharp to produce the original version in the United States. By 1949 sales of ballpoints had overtaken fountain pens, though Reynolds was not among the beneficiaries of the "must-have" explosion. His firm folded in 1951, victim of too many defective product returns—in the opinion of some, a well-deserved retribution for his shabby treatment of Bíró.

The first successful "throwaway" ballpoint was manufactured as the Bic by Baron Marcel Bich at his plastics factory near Paris in 1953 and introduced in the United States and Britain in 1958. In Britain during its first year, sales of 53 million averaged more than one for every man, woman, and child in the country. In America, where the Bic was launched at 29¢ with the slogan "Writes first time, every time" (not all ballpoints did, especially Bics), it rapidly captured 50 percent of the entire market for pens of all kinds.

THE FIRST **BANK**

in the United States was the Pennsylvania Bank, which opened on 17 July 1780 on Front Street in Philadelphia. The bank was founded as a temporary war measure, at a time when the Continental currency was fast depreciating in value and the Continental Congress's treasury was empty, to use the credit of patriotic Philadelphia merchants to provide provisions and rum for the Revolutionary army. It remained in operation for eighteen months and was wound up when its objectives had been achieved.

The first permanent bank was the Bank of North America, which opened on 7 January 1782 in the "commodious store" of its cashier, Tench Francis, on the north side of Chestnut Street in Philadelphia. Its first president was Thomas Willing. The government invested $254,000 in the new venture, then promptly borrowed a like amount from the bank. At the beginning of 1791 a change was made in the keeping of the bank's accounts that was to have a far-reaching effect. Pounds, shillings, and pence were abandoned in favor of dollars and cents, and it was suggested in the press that citizens should follow this example. Thus began a process by which the decimal system of currency gradually replaced that of the former colonial power, the merchants of Philadelphia following the banks' example by mutual agreement on 1 January 1801.

Drive-in bank: The first was the Exchange National Bank of Chicago at 130 LaSalle Street, opened on 12 November 1946 with ten bulletproof teller windows and automatic slide-out drawers.

Home or telephone banking began with the Dial-A-Computer system of electronic funds transfer introduced by Seattle–First National Bank in the fall of 1973 using a program devised by Telephone Computing Services Co. Subscribers paying $6.50 per month were allocated one hundred units of computer time monthly, with a printout every two weeks summarizing transactions for the month and year to date. **Computer banking** as such (i.e., transactions activated via the client's PC) was first offered in 1980 by Bank One of Columbus, Ohio, using the British Post Office's Viewdata system. Internet banking was introduced in October 1994 by Stanford Federal Credit Union of Palo Alto, Calif.

THE FIRST **BARBED WIRE**

has a complex genesis. It was first patented in France on 7 July 1860 by Léonce-Eugène Gassin-Baledans, and this was followed by another French patent of 19 April 1865 for what were described as "metallic thorns" by the patentee, Louis-François Jannin. The earliest U.S. patents were taken out on 2 April 1867 by Alphonso Dabb of Elizabethport, N.J., and on 25 June 1867 by Lucien B. Smith of Kent, Ohio, quickly followed by another French patent in August. A claim to earlier priority in the United States, however, was made in 1907 by one Adrian C. Latta, who wrote to *Scientific American* to say that as a boy of "ten summers" in 1861 he had invented barbed wire as a means of keeping the neighbors' hogs off his parents' property. He inserted sharp points between two strands of twisted wire, and though the hogs got through a few times "the barbs had the desired effect, as the owner saw his hogs were getting terribly marked, and kept them home."

The emergence of barbed wire as a practical, inexpensive means of fencing in areas only lightly timbered is further complicated by the fact that the first of the patents to form the basis of manufacturing was not the first barbed wire to be manufactured.

Michael Kelly sold the rights in his 1867 patent to a consortium who established the Thorn Wire Hedge Co. of Chicago and began production in 1876. In the meantime, however, manufacture had started elsewhere in Illinois, by the Barb Fence Co. of DeKalb. This company was founded in 1874 by Isaac Ellwood and Joseph Glidden to exploit the patent granted to the latter on 24 November of that year. At first sales were meager and confined to the vicinity of DeKalb, but once the partners had appointed agents they succeeded in drumming up business as far afield as Texas. Indeed it was the penetration of the Lone Star State, with its vast treeless ranges, that was the key to barbed wire becoming the means of opening up the American West to large-scale cattle ranching. The agent who finally convinced the tough Texan cattle barons that this was not another Yankee ruse to extract tribute from the South was John Warne Gates, a young hardware-store owner from Turner Junction, Ill., who had won the agency for Glidden's barbed-wire fence, otherwise known as "the Winner." Texans were less certain that it was a winner, believing that the barbs would harm their cattle as well as their pockets. Gates built a barbed-wire corral in a San Antonio plaza and stocked it with longhorns that he claimed were the "toughest and wildest in all Texas" (though some assert that he actually chose the most docile beasts available). He challenged the skeptical onlookers to wager against him on the security of the fence. When it became apparent that the cattle were happy to stay put, he engaged a "howling Mexican rider" to charge the herd with flaming brands. Even when they stampeded, the fence held. This legendary episode occurred in late 1876; by 1883 nearly the whole of Texas was crisscrossed with what would soon become known as the "devil's rope" to the free-spirited cowboys who so reviled it.

Barbed wire in warfare was used on a small scale for the first time during the Spanish-American War in Cuba of April–August 1898 and on a much larger scale by the British in the Boer War of 1899–1902, when it was the means of connecting a chain of several thousand blockhouses that proliferated across the open South African veldt and impeded the free movement of the Boer commandos. It was also in this war that camps used for detention were first enclosed with barbed wire. The British forces in South Africa had started bringing in from the veldt Boer women, children, and other noncombatants, partly for their own protection but also to prevent them from succoring the commandos, and concentrating them in unfenced locations for which they chose the unfortunate name of "concentration camps" (thereby facilitating the myth, much propagated by the Nazis, that the forerunners of Dachau and Bergen-Belsen were English). On 11 August 1901 a Boer commando raided the camp at Standerton in the Transvaal and rustled 157 head of cattle. The camp was a large one, housing 3,329 inmates, but the superintendent, Frank Winfield, immediately gave orders that the whole was to be surrounded by two rows of barbed-wire fences with further barbed-wire entanglements sandwiched between them. The task was completed by 29 August. It was the first of the new century's thousands of barbed-wire camps, followed by those that were to house prisoners of war and internees in almost every war to follow, as well as the yet grimmer enclosures of the Nazi Holocaust and the Soviet gulag.

Barbed wire in its more benign agricultural guise is one of the more esoteric subjects of antiquarian pursuit, being much collected in the rural areas of the Southwest (where it is commonly known as "bobbed wire") and in the outback of Australia. More than 1,500 different types of wire have been identified by collectors, who rejoice in the sobriquet "barbarians," and rare examples have been known to fetch as much as $1,000 per 18-inch piece at auction. Museums devoted to diverse but nearly always rusty specimens include the Kansas Barbed Wire Museum in LaCrosse, which bills itself as the "Barbed Wire Capital of the World," the Devil's Rope Museum in McLean, Tex., and the Koppio Smithy Museum near Port Lincoln, South Australia, which houses the fabled Bob Dobbins Collection.

THE FIRST **BARBIE DOLL**

was launched in the United States dressed in a zebra-striped swimsuit by toymaker Mattel, Inc., of Hawthorne, Calif., on 13 February 1959. Barbie was designed by Jack Ryan, five times married, lastly to nine-times-married Zsa Zsa Gabor, and was based on a German novelty doll for adults called Lilli to which Mattel had acquired the American rights. Ryan later designed the Sparrow and Hawk missiles (the real ones, not the toy versions).

The Americanized Lilli was renamed Barbie after Barbara Handler, the seventeen-year-old daughter of Mattel's founder, and boyfriend Ken was named after Ms. Handler's brother. Neither felt much warmth toward their plastic alter egos. As a divorced mother of two, Barbara Handler Segal told the *Los Angeles Times* in 1989, "I am tired of being a Barbie Doll" and Ken, a successful real estate agent, declared, "I really don't like her—she's a bimbo." Small girls the world over do not agree, with sales running at 20 million a year. Nor do collectors, who will pay up to $12,000 for one of the original 1959 Barbies retailed at $2.50. One mystery of Barbie and Ken's relationship has never been satisfactorily explained. The wardrobe for successive incarnations of Barbie has included a wedding dress, but after fifty years she has yet to walk down the aisle with Ken. Perhaps they really are brother and sister?

THE FIRST **BAR CODE**

was devised by Bernard Silver and Norman Woodland, graduate students at the Drexel Institute of Technology, Philadelphia, after Silver had overheard the dean rejecting a request from the CEO of a grocery chain for a means of capturing product information automatically at the checkout. Having filed a patent for the methodology as early as 20 October 1949, they built a prototype in the living room of Woodland's home in Binghamton, N.Y. Remarkably, both the bar code and the scanner were based on antiquated technology: the former derived from Morse Code (1838) and the latter using Lee De Forest's sound-on-film system (1923). Silver died in 1963 before advances in computer technology made their concept feasible on a commercial scale. Woodland joined IBM after leaving Drexel, and it was they who eventually picked up on his and Silver's private R&D and built the first bar-code scanners in regular operation, incorporating state-of-the-art components, lasers, and microchips. The first machine in regular service was introduced at the Marsh Supermarket in Troy, Ohio, where the first bar-coded product to be scanned passed through the checkout at 8:01 A.M. on 26 June 1974. The item was unquestionably Wrigley's chewing gum, but retail historians are still arguing whether it was a 10-pack or a single packet.

THE FIRST **BASEBALL**

is first recorded in print in *A Little Pretty Pocket-Book*, published by John Newbery in London in 1744. A picture book showing various children's games, it contains an illustration of boys playing baseball, and accompanying text uses this name rather than "rounders," a game played with a soft ball from which it may have been derived. Baseball was probably more widespread in eighteenth-century England than is generally supposed, Lady Hervey writing in 1748 that the family of the Prince of Wales "diverted themselves at base ball, a play all who . . . have been schoolboys, are well acquainted with." The eldest son, then ten years old, was to become George III in 1760; it is interesting to reflect that he who lost the American colonies was a practitioner of what was to become the national game. Whether his sisters participated is not recorded, but it is perfectly possible. A diary entry for Easter Monday 1755 by nineteen-year-old William Bray, later a lawyer, documents a game played at Guildford, Surrey: "After dinner, went to Miss Jeale's to play at base ball with her the 3 Miss Whiteheads, Miss Billinghurst, Miss Molly Flutter, Mr. Chandler, Mr. Ford and H. Parsons. Drank tea and stayed til 8." In Jane Austen's *Northanger Abbey*, written in 1798–99 (though published in 1818), the heroine is said to have enjoyed playing baseball as a girl.

U.S.: The earliest contemporary allusion to what may have been baseball dates from 1778, when George Ewing, an American soldier encamped at Valley Forge, Pa., recorded that he and his fellow starved and shivering compatriots had been "playing at base." Baseball historian George Thorn disputes whether this is the same game and cites his own discovery of a 1791 bylaw prohibiting ball games within 80 yards of the New Meeting House at Pittsfield, Mass., as the earliest specific reference to baseball. It is preceded by a reference to students playing "Baste Ball" at Princeton in 1786, which is more likely to be a variant spelling than a different game. There is additional hearsay evidence of baseball being played in America in the eighteenth century. John Montgomery Ward, a pioneer from the early days of organized baseball, recorded in a pamphlet he wrote titled *Base Ball*: "Col. James Lee, elected an honorary member of the Knickerbocker Ball Club in 1846, said that he had often played the game when a boy, and at that time he was a man of sixty or more years." This suggests that the colonel was born in the 1780s, so his boyhood would have been in the closing years of the century.

Baseball separated from the eighteenth-century version of the game when the former practice of throwing the ball at the batter as he ran around the bases, a hit meaning out, was replaced during the 1830s by the device of hurling the ball at the base instead. This meant that there was no longer a need to play with a soft ball, the adoption of a hard ball revolutionizing the game as it hugely increased the velocity. It was this adult version of the pastime that was espoused by the Knickerbocker Ball Club (SEE BELOW), which framed the first rules for it.

Baseball club: The earliest reference to organized play appeared in the *National Advocate* for 25 April 1823. A correspondent reports: "I was last Saturday much pleased in witnessing a company of active young men playing the manly and athletic game of 'base ball' at the Retreat in Broadway. I am informed they are an organized association." In his memoirs the editor and politician Thurlow Weed recalled what may have been an earlier club in his youth (he was born in 1797), which had its games in Mumford's Meadow, outside Rochester, N.Y. "A base-ball club numbering nearly fifty members," he wrote, "met every afternoon during the playing season." In 1832 there were two informal clubs functioning in New York City, one comprising players from the First Ward (Lower Manhattan), the other with players from the Ninth and Fifteenth (Upper Manhattan). The former was known as the New York Base Ball Club, aka the Gothams, by 1837, while the latter became the Washington Club (SEE **interclub game** BELOW).

All this activity was taking place before the inception of what is usually hailed as the first formally constituted club, the Knickerbocker Ball Club of New York, founded on 13 September 1845 under the presidency of D. F. Curry. The founder members appear to have been playing together for at least three years and may well have been members of the Gothams. The earliest known scorecard, for a game played on 6 October 1845, is preserved at the New York Public Library. Early the following year a young surveyor named Alexander Cartwright, who headed a committee deputed to produce an agreed set of rules for interclub play, submitted his fourteen proposals. These were accepted, together with a diagram of the prototype baseball diamond.

An open challenge having been made by the Knickerbocker Ball Club and accepted by a scratch team designated the "New York Nine," the first match played under standardized rules took place at the Elysian Fields, a picnic ground and former cricket pitch in Hoboken, N.J., on 19 June 1846. Much to their chagrin the Knickerbockers were roundly defeated 23–1 in four innings, their only consolation being that one of the Nine, a player called Davis, was fined 6¢ by the umpire for profane language. The Nine dispersed, while the Knickerbockers retired from competition for five years. The only important innovation they made during this period was the adaptation of a uniform on 24 April 1849, essentially the same as worn for cricket at the time, except for straw sailor hats. Their colors were blue and white.

The first **interclub game** proper (the Nine not being a club) was played between the Knickerbockers and the Washington Baseball Club of New York (later renamed the Gothams) at the Red House Grounds on 106th Street and Second Avenue on 3 June 1851. This time the Knickerbockers salvaged their reputation, winning 21–11 in 8 innings, and again by 22–20 in 10 innings when a return match followed two weeks later. **Professional player:** The first was rags-to-riches Albert Reach, born in England in 1840 and brought to America as an infant. He peddled newspapers in the streets of Brooklyn as a boy and later worked in an iron foundry, playing for the amateur Brooklyn Eckfords in his spare time. Despite his diminutive stature, in 1865 he was offered $25 per game "expense money" to join the Philadelphia Athletics. As this was about twice his weekly earnings pouring molten metal in the

foundry to danger of life and limb, it was a lucrative offer. When he retired from baseball he founded the Reach Sporting Goods Co., which rivaled that of the Spalding Brothers and made its owner a millionaire.

The first **professional team** in this or any other sport was the Cincinnati Red Stockings, whose president, A. B. Champion, wanted to end the hypocrisy of a pretense at amateurism from teams who paid their members' expenses. The inaugural professional tour began on 15 March 1869, when the Red Stockings traveled east on the first leg of a 12,000-mile circuit that attracted 200,000 paid admissions. Under the new dispensation the captain, George Wright, earned $1,400 for the season, $200 more than his brother Harry as manager. The other players received from $600 to $1,000 for an eight-month season, which made them a lot better paid than artisans, clerks, or cowboys.

The Red Stockings proved that financial incentives produce results by winning 65 of their matches and tying in one, against the Troy Haymakers, with a total of 2,395 runs versus 574 by their contestants. Amateurism in baseball died a quick death, its governing body, the National Association of Baseball Players, barely surviving the founding of the National Association of Professional Base-ball Players at Collier's on Broadway in New York City on 4 March 1871. This, the first **major league**, initially comprised nine teams: Philadelphia Athletics (winners of the inaugural pennant), Troy Haymakers, Washington Olympics, Boston Red Stockings, Forest City (Rockford), Forest City (Cleveland), Chicago White Stockings, New York Mutuals, and Fort Wayne Kekiongas. Thus baseball was the first team sport in the world to become, at its higher reaches, predominantly a paid occupation. Though unremarked at the time, it signified another transformation of immense historical significance—the beginning of American sporting hegemony, surpassing that of Great Britain, whose dedication to amateurism in all the major sports it had initiated was ultimately to herald its decline as the world's leading sporting nation.

The league expired after five years, principally on account of habitual drunkenness among the players, who were often incapable of taking the field. It was replaced in 1876 by the National League, which remains one of the two professional leagues in American baseball. The first pennant holder was Chicago.

Baseball is the only team game anywhere in the world that is still played in nineteenth-century costume. The modern **baseball uniform** with knickerbockers was adopted by the then still amateur Cincinnati Red Stockings in 1868. (By contrast, the first club to adopt a uniform, the Knickerbockers, failed to live up to their name by wearing cricket trousers.) Shirts, as now, carried a designation of the team, in Cincinnati's case a Gothic capital *C*; numbers on the back did not appear until the New York Yankees adopted them in 1929. Various styles of cap were prevalent in the early days of baseball, including vertically striped pillboxes with peaks and a button in the crown (Philadelphia Athletics) and horizontally striped locomotive engineers' caps (St. Louis Brown Stockings). Cincinnati wore skullcaps with a barely visible recessed peak, mostly with flat crowns. However, the baseball cap as we now know it, a close fitting skullcap with a prominent peak, seems to have preceded the Red Stockings' uniform, as the earliest known group photo of a baseball team, depicting the New York Knickerbockers in 1857, shows headgear barely distinguishable from that article of apparel which was to become universal leisure wear 120 years or so later.

The first **catching glove**, which was unpadded, was devised by Charles G. Waite of Boston in 1875, with padded gloves emerging in 1891. The **catcher's mask** followed shortly after the glove when Fred Thayer, captain of the Harvard team, adapted a fencing mask by cutting eyeholes in the mesh. It was worn for the first time by Thayer's teammate James Tyng for a game against the Lynn Live Oaks Base Ball Club on 11 April 1877. Thayer patented his invention (by this time purpose-designed) on 12 February 1878, by which time it was already on sale from Spalding, the sporting goods manufacturers. The **catcher's chest protector** appeared the same year as Thayer's face mask, 1877, in Hartford, Conn.

The first **batter's helmet** was an inflatable device produced in 1905 by the Reach Sporting Goods Co. and was worn in spring training the following year by Roger Bresnahan of the New York Giants. This pneumatic headgear proved too bulky for league games, however, and it was not until 1952 that any club adopted helmets for all its players, manager Branch Rickey of the Pittsburgh Pirates outfitting his players in a lightweight model with ear flaps.

Black baseball players: The first professional was Bud Fowler, who began appearing for Chelsea Mass., and Lynn Live Oaks in exhibition games in April 1878. First to play in a major league were Moses Fleetwood Walker and his brother Welday Wilberforce Walker, who unusually for professional ballplayers in the nineteenth century were both college graduates (University of Michigan and Oberlin). They had joined the Toledo Blue Stockings in 1883 when the team was playing in the minor Northwest League. The following year the team was promoted to the American Association, and the Walkers made their major-league debut on 1 May 1884. Moses Fleetwood, known as "Fleet," was a catcher and played in forty-one games, hitting .251. Welday Wilberforce, an outfielder, played in only six games and left baseball to go into publishing. Fleet continued playing ball in the high minor leagues for many years after leaving Toledo. No further blacks played in the major leagues before Jackie Robinson was recruited from the Montreal Royals to the Brooklyn Dodgers in 1947.

Woman to play in league baseball: The first was Lizzie Arlington, who pitched in a single game for the Eastern League club of Reading, Pa., in a match against Allentown on 5 July 1898. She was subsequently hired by Atlantic League president Ed Barrow to play in exhibition games. There were no others until seventeen-year-old pitcher Jackie Mitchell was signed for the Southern Association's Chattanooga Lookouts in the spring of 1931. On 2 April of that year she made her debut in an exhibition game against the New York Yankees, pitching to Babe Ruth and Lou Gehrig, who both, amazingly, struck out. The Babe, it was reported, "kicked the dirt, called the umpire a few dirty names, gave his bat a wild heave, and stomped out to the Yanks dugout." When Gehrig followed him, the crowd gave Jackie a standing ovation that lasted several minutes. Only a few days later Baseball Commissioner Kennesaw Mountain Landis banned her from league games on the grounds that they were too strenuous for women.

The Little League was inaugurated in Williamsport, Pa., in 1939 by oil company clerk Peter Stotz, who wanted to provide supervised team competition ball games for his nephews, six and eight, and their neighbors. There were initially three teams, as three dozen was the number of pint-size uniforms Stotz was able to buy from the local discount store for the $37 collected in subscriptions—with $1 over for ongoing expenses. The first match was played on 6 June, Lundy Lumber defeating Lycoming Dairy 23–8. (The third team was Jumbo Pretzel.) The idea spread so rapidly that by 1947 Stotz was able to establish a World Series, albeit for a world bounded initially by Pennsylvania, New York, and New Jersey, though unlike the adult World Series (contested in by the United States and a single team from Canada) it eventually did become worldwide, with Mexico becoming the first foreign champions in 1957. Since 1975, however, teams are no long national, after riots followed an earlier victory by Taiwan in Taipei.

By this time Peter Stotz had long ceased to be head of the organization he founded. It must have seemed to him a good idea in 1949 to seek sponsorship from the U.S. Rubber Co. (Uniroyal), who planned to promote rubber Little League shoes; rather less so when in 1955 he was ousted from his voluntary position in a power struggle with company executive Peter McGovern. Girls were only admitted in 1974 under pressure of lawsuits and accusations of boy chauvinism, though it is alleged that as early as 1950 crop-headed girls had joined Little League clubs in drag.

SEE ALSO **softball**.

THE FIRST **BASKETBALL**

was devised in December 1891 by Canadian physical education instructor James A. Naismith at the International YMCA Training School in Springfield, Mass. During the winter, between the close of the football season and the start of the baseball season, the only athletic activities enjoyed, or rather not enjoyed, by the students were marching, calisthenics, and gymnastics. Aware of their dissatisfaction, Dr. Luther S. Gulich, head of the Physical Education Department, asked Naismith to devise some

other form of exercise. Juvenile games proving insufficiently challenging for the young adult students, and indoor versions of rugby, soccer, and lacrosse too raucous, Naismith determined to devise his own game, within these self-imposed constraints: no running with the ball, as this would involve tackling; no implements to strike the ball; no need for force to propel the ball into goal. He asked janitor "Pop" Stubbins for some 18-inch-square wooden boxes, but as none were available, he opted for peach baskets instead. These were nailed to the base of the gymnasium's gallery, which happened to be 10 feet from the floor, thus setting the regulation height.

The first game, between two scratch teams of Naismith's students, is believed to have been played on 21 December 1891. There were nine players on either side, for no better reason than the fact that there were eighteen men in the class. The score was 1–0, the historic first goal going to William R. Chase of New Bedford, Mass. The original rules of basketball were published in the school journal, the *Triangle*, on 15 January 1892. A rare copy in original wrappers, bought for 10¢ in Boston in 1962, was sold at auction in 2010 for $7,750.

Because the students went back to their hometowns on graduation to become instructors in their local YMCAs, basketball spread faster than any other sport before or since. It took only six years from the original publication of the rules for the setting up of the pro National Basketball League in 1898. Within ten years basketball, the only major sport to have originated in the United States, had spread around the world, reaching Canada, France, and Britain in 1893, India, Australia, and China in 1894, Brazil in 1896, and Japan in 1900.

Naismith's students played with a soccer ball. The first basketballs designed as such (slightly larger than a soccer ball) were produced in 1894 by the Chicopee Overman Wheel Co., bicycle manufacturers, of Fall, Mass. These were brown; the orange ball was only introduced in the late 1950s by Butler University (Indianapolis) coach Tony Hinkle. The first iron hoop with netting (originally wire) was made by the Narragansett Machinery Co. of Providence, R. I. in 1893, though curiously it did not occur to those who made this improvement on the peach basket to leave the bottom of the net open. It remained necessary to poke the ball out with a pole for several years before some unnamed hero had the bright idea of cutting a hole in the bottom. Backboards were adopted in 1895, to prevent partisan spectators in the gallery from interfering with the ball.

Women players: The first were teachers from the Buckingham Grade School in Springfield, which was close to the YMCA Training School. Naismith taught them himself during 1892, later revealing that one of them had called him a son of a bitch when he called a foul on her, or, as he put it more discreetly, "she questioned my ancestry." The first women's match was played on 18 November the same year between the University of California at Berkeley and girls' prep Miss Head's School, Berkeley, the schoolgirls triumphing over the coed collegians 6–5. Separate women's rules, with six players per team, were published in 1895 by Clara Bear of Sophie Newcomb College in New Orleans.

Colleges to adopt basketball: The first were the University of California at Berkeley, Geneva College at Beaver Falls, Pa., and the University of Iowa, all in 1892. Smith College, an all-women's college, played its first game on 23 March 1893 with all the doors locked to prevent the entry of men. The University of California men's team beat the local YMCA 19–11 on 27 January 1894 but did not play against another college until vanquishing Iowa 15–12 on 18 January 1896. In the meantime, however, the first intercollegiate game had been played: On 9 February 1895 the Minnesota State School of Agriculture won 9–3 against Hamline College of St. Paul. On 4 April the following year two collegiate women's teams met for the first time, the University of California playing Stanford. This was the first time that women participated in intercollegiate competition at any sport, though four years later both universities were to ban games against other schools as unladylike.

Professional basketball team: The first was Trenton, N.J., its players being paid $15 a game. They debuted at Masonic Hall, Trenton, against Brooklyn YMCA on 7 November 1896. The first professional leagues, the New England League and the National Basketball League, were formed in 1898, players of the latter earning $150–$250 a month.

The first **black player in pro basketball** was Harry "Bucky" Lew, who made his debut for Lowell vs Marlboro in the New England Basketball League in 1902. The following season he joined Haverhill and played for them until the NEBL disbanded in 1906, but then played another twenty seasons in a team he founded himself.

The first **NBA game** was played on 1 November 1946 at Maple Leaf Garden in Toronto, Canada, where the Toronto Huskies went down 68–66 to the New York Knickerbockers before a crowd of 7,090. The first champions were the Philadelphia Warriors, who beat the Chicago Stags by four games to one in a series played in Philadelphia and Chicago 16–21 April 1947.

The first **black player in an NBA game** was 6' 6" Earl Lloyd of the Washington Capitols, formerly of West Virginia State University, who made his maiden appearance in an away game against the Rochester Royals on 31 October 1950. Despite his scoring six points and grabbing a game-high ten rebounds, Lloyd's debut was not mentioned in sports reporter George Beacon's otherwise detailed report in the *Rochester Democrat & Chronicle*.

THE FIRST BEAUTY PAGEANT

was the Concours de Beauté held at Spa in Belgium on 19 September 1888. The initial judging was done from photographs of the 350 contestants, of whom 21 were chosen to appear at the finals. The contest was conducted with the utmost propriety and discretion. "The finalists were not allowed to be seen by the people," said a Scandinavian journal. "They lived in a separate wing and were driven in closed carriages to the hall, where their charms were judged." First prize of 5,000 francs ($1,000) went to an eighteen-year-old Creole from Guadeloupe called Bertha Soucaret. "It is said," the same paper continued, "that Miss Soucaret will now go on the stage; of course, beauty opens every door."

The first bathing beauty contest was the Miss Venus Quest held in 1911 at the Sydney Stadium in Sydney, New South Wales, Australia. The winner, Miss Millicent Mahy, wore a one-piece bathing suit of a design similar to the one that had caused her fellow Australian, champion swimmer Annette Kellerman, to be arraigned on a charge of indecency in Boston, Mass. It was black with double horizontal white stripes encircling the trunks, which ended some 9 inches above the knee. While Miss Mahy's ample bosom was accentuated by the close-fitting costume, her legs were concealed within black silk stockings. The first prize was a figurine of Venus claimed to be worth £100, and it was reported, without explanation, that the victor failed to collect it. Miss Mahy subsequently modeled for an advertisement for Rexona Skin and Facial Soap, a recently launched local product that went on to become a global brand, but this appears to have been the extent of her life in the public eye, and nothing more is known of her.

U.S.: The history of the beauty pageant in America is bedeviled by a persistent claim that the first was held at Rehoboth Beach in Delaware in 1880, eight years before the event won by Bertha Soucaret in Belgium. One of the judges, it is said, was a tinkerer called Thomas Alva Edison. In fact, on the dates in question the Wizard of Menlo Park was nowhere near Rehoboth Beach; he was indeed tinkering in his laboratory at Menlo Park, N.J. Whoever invented the myth also chose the wrong location—Rehoboth Beach had yet to be developed as a resort in 1880. This was a beauty pageant that never took place.

The first live beauty pageant in the United States (there had been earlier photo competitions) was also the first bathing beauty competition. The Festival of the Sea Bathing Costume Contest was held at Venice Beach, Calif., on 14 July 1912, when 169 contestants paraded their charms before a crowd estimated at 100,000 in a procession that began at Rose Avenue in neighboring Ocean Park. Some were carried in garlanded swings, while others rode on floats, including one in doubtful taste portraying the *Titanic* striking the iceberg that sank it (the disaster had occurred three months earlier). They were competing for prizes worth $200, $100, $50, and two of $25, ostensibly for the most glamorous costume. As all five judges were male, it seems unlikely that their attention was wholly confined to the couture. The winner was Lydia Anderson of 3707 Michigan Avenue, Los Angeles, who wore a white mohair costume trimmed in cerise, matching cerise stockings, white sandals, and a white cap. She had made it herself at a cost, she informed a reporter from the *Los Angeles Examiner*, of $4.50 for cloth, $1 for the shoes, and 50¢ for the cerise trimmings and ribbons for her legs. On receiving the first prize she whispered breathlessly, "It's more than I've ever had in my life," though she had no intention of going on a spree. Asked what she would do with it, Lydia declared, "What every sensible girl should do—put it in the bank."

The first **national beauty pageant**, which began the practice of dubbing the winner Miss [Name-of-Country], was the Miss America contest, first staged at Atlantic City on 7 September 1921. The first Miss America, Margaret Gorman, was only fifteen when she was chosen to enter the pageant as Miss Washington, D.C., and still a pupil at Weston High School in Georgetown. A blue-eyed 5' 1" blonde with a 25-inch waist and weighing 108 pounds, she remains the youngest and shortest winner to date. Sixty years on, contestants were at least 5 inches taller, had waists an average of 3 inches smaller, and were only slightly heavier.

Black beauty pageant contestant: The earliest known was Dorothy Derrick, who gained third place by popular ballot on 4 April 1925 in a pageant organized in Flushing, N.Y., by a local organization of socially prominent women, the Green Twigs. As an honor student and the granddaughter of a Methodist bishop, Miss Derrick was of the utmost respectability, rather more so by the criteria of the Green Twigs than the girl voted into first place, Violet Meyer, the Jewish daughter of a street-corner newspaper vendor. Confronted with the prospect that two out of three who graced the winners' podium would not be of Aryan stock, the good ladies of Flushing canceled the contest. Happily the merchants of Flushing were of a broader mind and resuscitated the contest, with a new round of voting. Miss Meyer having withdrawn from competition, the black contestant, Miss Derrick, secured second place. The *New York Times* headed its report on the unfolding drama with a barely complimentary tribute to Dorothy, "Handsome in her way."

No black contestants competed internationally until 1954, when Evelyn Andrade (who was half Syrian) represented Jamaica in the Miss Universe contest. The first black American to compete in a national final was Corinne Hunt, Miss Ohio 1960, in the Miss USA contest. Another ten years passed before the most prestigious national pageant of all, Miss America, finally removed its color bar and welcomed Cheryl Browne as Miss Iowa. In 1984 a black contestant donned the Miss America crown for the first time in the person of Vanessa Williams, but she was forced to resign after Bob Guccione published revealing pictures of her in *Penthouse* that had been taken when she was a teenager (netting him a windfall profit of $14 million).

THE FIRST **BEER**

brewed in America was being produced by 1629, in which year John Smith, in his history of Virginia, recorded that the colony had two breweries:

> For drink, some malt the Indian corne, others barley, of which they make good Ale, both strong and small, and such plentie thereof, few of the upper Planters drinke any water; but the better sort are well furnished with Sacke, Aquavite, and good English Beere.

Meanwhile the inhabitants of the Plymouth Plantation were relying on imported beer, but with the establishment in 1630 of the Massachusetts Bay Colony, home brewing by the proprietors of "ordinaries" (taverns that also served meals) soon became a local industry. Gov. John Winthrop's letters during the year 1633 frequently refer to shipments of malt from England. In New Netherland a brewery was established in 1632 by the Dutch West India Company on a street that was later to be named after its principal commercial enterprise, becoming Brouwers Streat or Brewers' Street. As early as 1626, the year that New Amsterdam was settled, the Dutch had discovered that the ingredients necessary for making beer could be grown in the New World, so it is possible that its production in New Netherland preceded the introduction of brewing in Virginia. Early farms on Manhattan Island concentrated on raising rye, barley, wheat, oats, and hops, giving them the capacity to distill hard liquor or brew strong beer. During the 1640s these Dutch ales

were exported to Virginia, which suggests either that they were of a quality superior to the English brews or that the Virginian brewhouses were unable to meet demand. Quite possibly the former, as we have it on the authority both of the patroon David de Vries and West India Company councillor Nicasius de Sille that New Amsterdam beer was as good as the beer back home in Holland.

The first brewery known to have produced **bottled beer** in America was an establishment on Front Street in Philadelphia operated by Thomas Freame and partners, which began selling pale ale at 4s 6d a dozen in 1735. Most customers in the eighteenth and nineteenth centuries continued to buy beer in barrels, and it was only after 1870, with the rise of national brands, that bottling became a major element of most breweries' output.

The first **lager** produced in America was produced on a small scale in 1840 by John Wagner behind his house on Philadelphia's St. John Street. Full-scale production was inaugurated soon afterward when George Manger, having acquired some of Wagner's yeast, set up a brewery at Second and New. Lager spread rapidly to other cities with a large German population, so that by 1850 locally produced brews were available in New York, St. Louis, Milwaukee, Cincinnati, St. Paul, Chicago, Detroit, Boston, and Pittsburgh. In the coming decade lager drinking began to make inroads to the general population in these cities, while a number of German breweries were founded that were destined to become household names: Miller (1855), Schlitz (1856), Anheuser-Busch (1857).

It was the latter that first succeeded in pasteurizing lager so that it could be bottled, earlier bottled beers having been of the nonsparkling varieties. In 1872 Anheuser-Busch was shipping bottled lager to various towns in Texas, and in 1876 the company's "St. Louis Lager Beer" was advertised in Denver, Colo., making it the first brewery to expand distribution outside its own region.

As others followed, lager became America's beer of preference, a position entrenched as the big names began to distribute their product not only outside their own regions but throughout the United States, led by Pabst of Milwaukee. In 1892 Pabst became first to achieve sales of one million barrels a year and was generally acknowledged as the first national brand.

Canned beer: The first was Krueger Cream Ale, introduced by the Gottfried Krueger Brewing Co. of Newark, N.J., in tinplate 12-ounce pyramid-topped cans supplied by American Can Co. and test-marketed in Richmond, Va., on 24 January 1935. By the end of that year twenty-three brewers were using cans, with 200 million sold. The first beer packed in aluminum cans was Primo by the Hawaii Brewing Corp. in 1958. The ring-pull all-aluminum can followed in 1962, when Iron City Beer from Pittsburgh, Pa., was test-marketed in Virginia. The idea originated with the singularly named Ermal Cleon Fraze of Dayton, Ohio on a family picnic in 1959 when he had to use the end of a car fender to bash in the top of a beer can because he had forgotten to bring a can opener. The discarded ring-pulls, however, became the bane of friends of the environment, cherished only by teenagers for using in vending machines and avant-garde dress designers who stitched them together to make revealing metallic frocks. The litter problem was only solved in 1975 when the brewers of Falls City Beer of Louisville, Ky., did the world a service by introducing the nondetachable can-opening tab.

THE FIRST **BICYCLE**

has generally been attributed to Scottish blacksmith Kirkpatrick MacMillan of Courthill, Dumfries, said to have built a 57-pound wooden-framed vehicle in 1839 with iron-tired wheels driven by foot-activated cranks attached to the rear axle. The bicycle that accords with this description in London's Science Museum, and sometimes claimed as his, was built by one Thomas McCall of Kilmarnock in 1869. McCall stated that he had earlier made a number of velocipedes patterned on MacMillan's prototype, but not that they had two wheels. He also asserted that his 1869 model was an entirely original design of his own. The famous *Glasgow Herald* report of 10 June 1842 concerning the fining of a velocipede rider who had knocked over a child is the only contemporary reference to what was supposedly MacMillan's machine, though it does not mention him by name, and there

is no indication of the number of wheels. It did state that the apparatus was driven by hand cranks, suggestive of a tricycle.

The other claim for an early bicycle from Scotland centers on the cooper Gavin Dalzell of Hawksland, whose rear-drive machine was said by his son to have been built in 1845. There certainly was a machine, as two repair bills of 1847 attest, but was it a bicycle? David Herlihy, in his magisterial *Bicycle: The History* (2004), suggests that the two-wheeler presented by Dalzell's son to the Transport Museum in Glasgow in 1888 may well have been converted from a tricycle after the early French bicycles became the rage in Britain in the late 1860s. Herlihy is skeptical of the Scottish claims mainly on account of the silence from those notably proud and nationalistic people among the clamor surrounding the latest novelty from France. Surely, he argues, had there been several bicycles on the roads of Scotland within fairly recent memory, someone would have asserted Scottish precedence at the time rather than twenty years later, as was the case with the supporters of MacMillan and Dalzell. In response to Herlihy it should be said that early bicycles were little more than adult toys, ridden by sportsmen and thrillseekers. It may not have seemed important then who was the begetter, whereas after Starley's Rover of 1885 (SEE BELOW) had made cycling a form of mass transportation, the identity of the inventor of the bicycle assumed a new significance.

Scarcely more clarity surrounds the origins of the bicycle in France, where it was first manufactured. The genesis of the industry according to the son of its undoubted founder, Pierre Michaux, was described thus in a letter published in *Le Vélo* in 1893.

In the month of March, 1861 . . . a hat maker, Monsieur Brunel of the Rue de Verneuil, Paris, brought his Vélocifère [hobbyhorse] to my father for the front wheel to be repaired. The same evening my brother Ernest, 19 years of age, took the machine out for a trial on the avenue Montaigne. "I can balance myself alright, but it is quite as tiring to hold my legs up as to give the impulsion on the ground with my feet," he said to my father in my presence on returning home. "Well then," observed my father, "fix two small supports on each side of the front fork of the wheel and once started, as you balance yourself on the machine, you can rest your legs; or, better still, to rest your feet, adopt a cranked axle in the hub of the front wheel, and then you can make the wheel revolve as if you were turning the handle and crank of a grindstone!" My brother put my father's idea into execution and afterwards fitted pedals which were also due to the ingenuity of Pierre Michaux; but it was his son Ernest who carried out the first work.

The prototype models were said to have been produced in 1861, followed by 142 when series production began the following year. Again, however, there is no contemporary evidence to support such early dates. The first advertisements for Michaux bicycles appeared in 1867, and there were no references in the press to cycling before that date. *Le Sport* in July 1867 claimed Michaux's four sons as the world's first cyclists, saying that they had had three years' experience, pointing to 1864 as the year of inception. That is also the year that Anglo-Irish landowner J. Townsend Trench claimed that he had purchased from Michaux the first bicycle to be imported into Britain, riding it in England and at home on his Irish estate, Kenmare. Later on Michaux's backer René Olivier also cited 1864 as the date that the first experimental batch of bicycles was produced in the Michaux workshop.

It is possible that Henri Michaux's apparent backdating was in order to establish precedence over the other main claimant to have been the inventor of the bicycle, Pierre Lallement. As a nineteen-year-old mechanic employed in a workshop in Nancy making baby carriages and children's tricycles, Lallement had watched a man riding a *draisine*, or hobbyhorse, down the street. Rarely seen by then, *draisines* had been popular shortly after the end of the Napoleonic Wars; with the basic configuration of a bicycle but without pedals, they were propelled by pushing on the ground with the feet. Lallement decided to mechanize the means of propulsion by fitting rotary cranks to the hub of the front wheel. Changing jobs, he moved to Paris and began work at Strohmeyer, manufacturer of children's vehicles, where he completed a model in the summer of 1863, which he rode first down the long corridor of the factory, then on the busy Boulevard Saint Martin.

This was a full year before the putative date that Michaux began somewhat hesitant production.

Herlihy believes that Michaux's backers, the brothers René and Aimé Olivier, had seen Lallement's prototype, and probably got to know him personally, but hired Michaux to replicate it as he had the necessary plant. Lallement had tried and failed to get backing to start production on his own account. Certainly Lallement's 1866 U.S. patent (SEE BELOW) depicts a vehicle strikingly similar to Michaux's early models, but the theory does not account for a seeming total absence of any kind of business arrangement between the Oliviers and the young mechanic. It is lent some credence, however, by the fact that after the brothers had fallen out with Michaux and removed the manufacturing operation to Marseilles, René Olivier testified in a court case in 1869 that the inventor was not Michaux but an *ouvrier* whom he did not name.

U.S.: Whether or not it was Pierre Lallement who rode the first bicycle in the world, it was indeed he who rode the first one in America. The young mechanic arrived in the United States in July 1865 with a wrought-iron bicycle frame and settled at Ansonia, Conn. Here he assembled his machine and in the fall was ready to make the first bike trip in the New World, riding from Ansonia to Birmingham (now a suburb of Derby), 10 miles there and back. A co-worker recalled the hilarity his efforts provoked. A longer excursion on 4 April 1866 to New Haven, 12 miles distant, inspired the first press report: "An enterprising individual propelled himself about the Green last evening on a curious frame sustained by two wheels, one before the other, and driven by foot cranks." Lallement applied for a U.S. patent, granted on 20 November 1866, but he made little profit from it himself. After he had returned to France in 1868, having failed once again to interest a manufacturer, he was persuaded to sell his master patent to Calvin Witty, who was already engaged in bicycle manufacture and sought to derive royalties from others in the United States who were similarly engaged.

It was Witty, a carriage maker in Brooklyn, who established bicycle production in the United States in 1868, shortly after a disappointed Lallement left for home. A troupe of acrobats, the Hanlon Brothers, had used imported French bicycles in their act and, believing that there was potential in this strange new means of mobility, had contracted with Witty to manufacture them for sale. Calvin Witty was the first to make his fortune out of the bicycle craze. Armed with Lallement's patent in fall 1868, he demanded $10 from his fellow manufacturers for every machine sold, retrospectively as well as ongoing, and within a few weeks had collected $40,000 in back royalties. By the following April his take had doubled. The scant recognition Pierre Lallement received was the naming of a cycling school in Lynn, Mass., as the Pierre Lallement Rink.

Cycle race: The earliest recorded was an event that took place in Paris on 8 December 1867, about a hundred riders in the accoutrements of jockeys leaving the Champs-Elysées to compete over a 14-mile course to the Château de Versailles. The first long-distance race was organized by Pierre Michaux's backer René Olivier on a 76-mile route from Paris to Rouen. More than four hundred competitors left the Place de l'Étoile in the rain at 7:30 A.M. on Sunday, 7 November 1869, and the winner was English champion James Moore, who completed the course in 10 hours 45 minutes on his French-built rubber-tired Suriray velocipede. A third of the competitors finished, thirty-three of them within 24 hours, including "Miss America," aka Mrs. Rowley B. Turner, the French-born wife of an English bicycle manufacturer, in 29th place, one ahead of her husband.

U.S.: The first race was organized by the newly formed Boston Bicycling Club over a 3-mile course in Beacon Park on 24 May 1878. The winner was Harvard student C. A. Parker in 12 minutes 27 seconds.

Chain-driven safety bicycle: The modern bicycle emerged with the 1886 model of the Rover Safety, designed by John Kemp Starley and manufactured in Coventry, England, by the company that 60 years later produced the Land Rover. This had equal-sized 30-inch chain-driven wheels, a diamond frame, and direct steering—a conception so advanced that it could probably be ridden today without exciting undue attention. Starley's Rover set an established pattern for bicycle design, the basic configuration having undergone no significant modification in a century and a quarter. Probably no other mechanical device has remained essentially unchanged for so long.

U.S.: A specimen Rover Safety was demonstrated at a League of American Wheelmen meet on Martha's Vineyard in the summer of 1886. Despite its winning plaudits from cyclists, the American trade preferred to ignore the upstart, which looked too like an old-fashioned velocipede to them, and go on producing high-bicycles (an enormous direct-drive wheel in front, balanced by a tiny one in the rear). The following year, however, a dealer named George Bidwell was impressed by the safety configuration with its equal-sized wheels and began importing chain-driven Rudge Bicyclettes from England. He made huge profits as the sole supplier in New York, and Boston dealers were quick to follow, importing both the Rover and the Bicyclette. Before the end of 1887 one manufacturer had capitulated, the Overman Wheel Co. of Chicopee Falls, Mass., and others began to do so, too; by the early '90s the high-bicycle was on its way out, the chain-driven safety triumphant. These were the boom years for American bicycle production, as cycling became a standard means of transport rather than a sport and women began to participate on a large scale. The League of American Wheelmen also benefited from having introduced the modern bicycle to America, their number growing from a few thousand to 100,000 by 1895.

Mountain bikes began as rebuilt balloon-tired "clunkers" of the '30s or '40s adapted in the early 1970s for riding the canyons of Marin County in California and particularly for informal races down the 2,600-foot Mount Tamalpais. "Soon," wrote cycling journalist Charlie Kelly in a retrospective of these glory days, "the canyon gangsters were doing such stunts as riding at 40 miles per hour under a gate (with two inches of clearance above the handlebars) to maintain enough speed to launch the bike off a sharp crest for a 40-ft jump." The first purpose-built mountain bike was designed and handmade by bike restorer Joe Breeze, second fastest down Mount Tam with a suicidal 4 minutes 24 seconds, at the suggestion of Charlie Kelly and completed in September 1977. Breeze kept the 38-pound prototype Breezer and then built eight more for sale at $750, the first of which went to Kelly. In 1979 Kelly and racing cyclist Gary Fisher, holder of the course record down Mount Tam at 4 minutes 22 seconds, teamed up with Palo

Alto frame-maker and racer Tom Ritchey to form a company called MountainBikes to manufacture an even lighter, 28-pound "bullnose" handlebar model that retailed at $1,300. The emerging sport and the Ritchey-designed bike were promoted in Kelly's newsletter for Canyonites, *Fat Tire Flyer*. Mountain-Bikes managed to produce 160 units in 1980, but mass production and the breakout from Marin County's canyons came with the 1981 introduction of the $750 Japanese-made Stumpjumper by Michael Sinyard's Specialized Bicycle Components of San Jose. From that point an essentially American and quintessentially Californian product became dominated by Japanese suppliers. By the mid-1990s it was estimated that 95 percent of adult cycles sold in the United States were mountain bikes.

THE FIRST BIKINI

swimsuit to be named as such was designed by French couturier Louis Réard and first modeled by dancer Micheline Bernardi at a Paris fashion show held at the Molitor Pool on 5 July 1946, four days after the Americans had detonated an atomic bomb at Bikini Atoll in the Pacific. The word "bikini" was coined by Réard to convey the idea of something similarly explosive. The prototype bikini was made of cotton printed with a newspaper design. Pictures of Mlle. Bernardi reclining in the new creation were widely circulated, and it was reported that she subsequently received fifty thousand fan letters.

The post-war provenance of the bikini is disputed by British actor John Standing, who has a photograph of his actress mother, Kay Hammond, sporting a skimpy little white costume with polka dots on the beach of Saint-Tropez in the South of France, allegedly in 1936. "On some occasions," Standing states, "she would make bikinis by tying handkerchiefs together." The swimsuit worn by Ms. Hammond in the picture is quite clearly a designer number and has caused Olivier Saillard, curator of Marseille's Musée de la Mode, to question the date attributed to it. Another challenge to Paris as birthplace of the bikini has been made by Peter Middleton of Sydney, Australia, who asserts that he encountered a young

lady wearing one on a beach in Alexandria, Egypt, in July 1943 while serving with the armed forces. She had been fined for indecent exposure the previous week but was determined to go on wearing the skimpy garment.

In the United States the earliest home-grown representation of the bikini appeared in *U.S. Camera* in 1947. It took several years for the bikini to reach out from the photographer's studio to the beach. Not until 1951 did any beauty pageant contestant dare to wear one, and when she did, at the Miss World contest in London, there was such an outcry that the bikini was banned from future competitions. The Miss America Pageant did not finally succumb until 1997, but even then styles considered too revealing were forbidden.

THE FIRST BLACK ACTORS

were the members of the African Theatre, which was inaugurated by West Indian–born former ship's steward and tailor William Brown with a performance of Shakespeare's *Richard III* on 17 September 1821 in a makeshift theater on the upper floor of his house on Thomas Street in New York City. Although on the whole Brown's productions were ignored by the metropolitan press, *Richard III* did receive at least one review in the *National Advocate*. The editor, Mordecai Noah, felt impelled to assure his readers that the presentation of a Shakespeare play by black actors had really happened and that his account of it was not a figment of satirical imagination. Despite this scarcely flattering notice, two of Noah's own plays, *The Fortress of Sorrento* and *She Would Be a Soldier*, were presented by the African Theatre, while other productions included Shakespeare's *Othello*, *Macbeth*, *Julius Caesar*, and *Romeo and Juliet*; Sheridan's *Pizarro*; John Home's *Douglas*; John O'Keefe's comic opera *The Poor Soldier*; the pantomime *Don Juan*; John Fawcett's melodrama *Obi: or, Three-Finger'd Jack*; and William Moncrieff's popular operatic extravaganza *Tom and Jerry: or, Life in London*. Notable also was the first presentation of the first **play by a black playwright**, William Brown's own *The Drama of King Shotaway*, in January 1822. The text has been lost but is believed to have been about the 1795–96 Black Caribs Insurrection on the

Caribbean island of St. Vincent. During the three seasons of the African Theatre's survival, Brown and his players had to put up with frequent harassment from white rowdies and on one occasion a full-scale riot, probably orchestrated by the irascible manager of the Park Theatre, Stephen Price.

The African Theatre comprised some thirty adult actors, male and female, two juveniles, and four musicians. These were part-time thespians other than James Hewlett, a light-skinned mulatto born in Rockaway, Nassau County, N.Y., who took most of the leading roles and was the first **professional black actor**; he continued to perform, often in one-man shows, after the demise of the African Theatre. Far more prominent in the annals of the stage, however, was one of the two juveniles. This was Ira Aldridge, not only the first black person but also the first American to achieve international celebrity on the boards. Aldridge had been educated at the African Free School in New York, where he won prizes for declamation, and joined the company at the age of fifteen. He played Rolla in *Pizarro* and Romeo in *Romeo and Juliet*, as well as getting beaten up in the street by a circus performer called James Bellmont who shortly afterward led the riot alluded to above. When the African Theatre folded, Aldridge emigrated to England, making his debut as the first black actor on the London stage in the Coburg Theatre's production of *The Revolt of Surinam: or, A Slave's Revenge* in October 1825 and, despite *The Times* saying that his lips were so shaped that "it is utterly impossible for him to pronounce English," shortly afterward starred in *Othello* at Brighton. For the next thirty years Aldridge won laurels not only on the stages of Britain and Ireland but throughout Europe and as far afield as Russia and Turkey, playing white as well as black roles to an acclaim (in spite of racist gibes) that helped to win respect for his race and sympathy for the anti-slavery cause. He died at Lodz in Poland in 1867 on the eve of what should have been a triumphant return to the land of his birth.

In the United States it was many years before black actors were able to tread the same boards in leading roles as white actors. A huge number of adaptations of *Uncle Tom's Cabin* appeared from 1853 onward (there being no trans-media copyright to protect Harriet Beecher Stowe's intellectual property), but the principal characters, including the title role, were always played by white actors in blackface. Not until 1878 did the minstrel star Sam Lucas become the first black actor to play a leading role in a white-produced play in America, and he was only cast in the role of Uncle Tom on condition he brought along the diamond he was celebrated for wearing (in case the company needed collateral). Two years later he reprised the role in the first **fully interracial casting on the American stage**, a production of *Uncle Tom's Cabin* at the Gaiety Theatre, Boston, in March 1880 by the black Hyers Sisters Combination in which all black roles were played by blacks and all white roles by whites. Alas for Sam Lucas, the role that gave him credibility on the American stage also to lead to his demise. In 1914, aged seventy-two, he was cast as Uncle Tom in the earliest full-length feature film of the immortal story, the first **black actor to play a leading role in a movie**. Following the shooting of the scene in which he had to leap into the icy Mississippi to save little Eva, he caught pneumonia and died.

The first black actor to star in a full-length straight play on Broadway was Lionel Managas, who opened in Garland Anderson's *Appearances* at the Frolic Theatre on 13 October 1925. Also in the cast of fourteen were black artistes Evelyn Mason and Doe Doe Green. *Appearances* was about a black bellhop falsely accused of the rape of a white woman. What made the production the more remarkable is that Garland Anderson himself was a black bellhop whose education had not passed beyond the fourth grade, the first black playwright to have a full-length straight play produced on Broadway. The play was also the first by a black playwright to run in London's West End, in April 1930. Here the British took such a delight in the antics of comic Doe Doe Green that he was given the principal billing in letters larger than the title.

Black actor to perform on television: The first was former wrestling champion Robert Adams, who played the title role in the BBC's production of Eugene O'Neill's *The Emperor Jones*, transmitted from London on 11 May 1938. Born in British Guiana (now Guyana) c. 1900, Adams was a member of the Unity Theatre, a part of the Workers' Theatre Movement, in

London and went on to found Britain's first professional black theater company, the Negro Arts Theatre Company, some 120 years after the African Theatre had brought black actors to the boards in New York.

U.S.: The first black actors on television were Ethel Waters, Fredi Washington, and Georgette Harvey, in a dramatic sequence from DuBose Heyward's stage play *Mamba's Daughters* performed during NBC's one-off variety show *The Ethel Waters Show*, transmitted on W2XBS New York on 14 June 1939. Philip Loeb and Joey Faye did comedy skits in the same program. *Variety* described the *Mamba's Daughters* excerpt as "deeply stirring drama." Loeb and Faye fared less well in the review: "feeble slapstick comedy." Waters was also the first black actor to play the title role in a drama series, the sitcom *Beulah*, which debuted on CBS on 10 October 1950. In the meantime Amanda Randolph had become the first black actor to play a leading role in a series, the sitcom *The Laytons*, which aired on a local New York City station before being networked by DuMont from August to October 1948. Typically for the period, both Waters's and Randolph's roles were those of the stereotypical comic black domestic who lightens the life of a suburban family.

THE FIRST **BLACK AMERICANS**

were preceded by those who came to these shores involuntarily. The first black people to reside within the present borders of the United States were a hundred male slaves from Santo Domingo working for the five hundred Spanish settlers domiciled at the short-lived settlement of San Miguel de Guadeloupe established on 29 September 1526 by Lúcas Vázquez de Ayllón at Sapelo Sound, Ga. Late in that year, probably November, the slaves rose up in an unsuccessful revolt against their white masters.

The first black people to reside permanently within present U.S. borders were brought to the Spanish colony of St. Augustine, Fla., either with Pedro Menéndez de Avilé's original settlers of 1565 or shortly afterward. Early in the seventeenth century a request was made for more black slave workers, as those then resident had been there some forty years

and were dying off. There were then thirty of these pioneers surviving, of whom nine were women and seven too old to work.

Black people arrived in English-speaking America when twenty were brought to Virginia aboard a Dutch man-o'-war on 31 August 1619. As they had been baptized, they could not, under English law of the time, be held as slaves. Accordingly they were purchased as indentured servants (i.e., they would be freed when their periods of service expired). The growth of the black population was slow: At mid-century there were about three hundred in Virginia, though by 1681 this figure had increased tenfold. In 1708 it stood at twelve thousand out of a population of sixty thousand.

Not all slaves in seventeenth-century Virginia remained so, and some who bought or were granted their freedom became prosperous themselves. There is even an early example of a black man, one Anthony Johnson, who not only received valuable freeholds in return for paying the passage of several immigrants but was himself a slave owner.

THE FIRST **BLACK COLLEGE STUDENT**

in the United States was Revolutionary War veteran John Chavis (born free in Granville County, N.C., in 1763), who grew up in Mecklenburg, Va., and attended Liberty Hall Academy (now Washington and Lee University) in Lexington, Va., between 1795 and 1799 to study for the Presbyterian ministry. The Presbyterian Church required its ministers to be college educated but applied its own examination at the completion of the course of studies. Hence Chavis did not receive a degree, though his examination by Lexington Presbytery in 1799 required him to give exegesis of theological topics in both Latin and Greek. Liberty Hall's records were destroyed in the fire that burned the college, but Chavis's attendance has been confirmed by Washington and Lee's associate professor of history Ted DeLaney by reference to the local court order book for 1802 and the minutes of the Lexington Presbytery detailing his examination. No other Afro-American attended Washington and Lee until 1966. Chavis served as an unpaid circuit-riding missionary in North Carolina, supporting himself by operating his own school in Raleigh. Here he taught the children of both blacks and whites, though in separate classes.

Black student to graduate with a full college degree: The first in the United States was Alexander Lucius Twilight (b. Corinth, Vt., 1795), who was an indentured farm worker until the age of twenty, then attended Randolph Academy preparatory to Middlebury College in Middlebury, Vt., from which he graduated in 1823 aged twenty-eight. He subsequently became a Congregational minister in Browningion, Vt., and principal of Orleans County Grammar School there in 1829. In order to secure funding for the school he stood for the Vermont state legislature in 1832 and was elected for a two-year term, becoming the first black representative in a state legislature. Among his remarkable achievements was building a three-story dormitory for the pupils, who had formerly boarded out locally. Called Athenian Hall, according to local legend it was built by Twilight single-handedly, with only the help of an ox to haul the granite blocks he himself quarried in nearby fields. The building became the headquarters of the Orleans County Historical Society in 1916. Reputed to have been a tough disciplinarian but an inspiring teacher, Twilight died in Brownington in 1857 and was buried in a grave overlooking the school campus.

Black woman to graduate: The first to do so with a full degree anywhere in the world was Mary Jane Patterson (b. Raleigh, N.C., 1840), who received her Bachelor of Arts degree from Oberlin College in Ohio on 27 August 1862. She then taught at the Institute for Colored Youths in Philadelphia before becoming the first principal of Washington, D.C.'s Preparatory High School for Negroes in 1871. She taught at the school until her death in 1894.

This first is often attributed to Lucy Ann Stanton, who graduated from Oberlin on 8 December 1850 as a Bachelor of Literature. Ms. Stanton had taken the special two-year "Ladies' Course," which did not equate to a full college degree course of study. Grace A. Mapps of Philadelphia has been claimed as first to receive a degree from a four-year college in the United States, but her alma mater, the short-lived New York Central College in McGrawville, N.Y., was only opened toward the end of 1849, and Ms. Mapps graduated in 1852.

Black Ph.D.: The first in the United States was Edward Alexander Bouchet, born in New Haven, Conn., in 1852, who on becoming Yale's first black graduate in 1874 returned to his alma mater for graduate studies in physics paid for by Philadelphia philanthropist Alfred Cope. His dissertation on geometrical optics earned him his doctorate on 7 November 1876. Bouchet spent the next twenty-six years teaching chemistry and physics at Philadelphia's only black secondary school, the Institute for Colored Youth, but was fired along with the whole of the teaching staff when the white board of managers, heeding Booker T. Washington's advice that blacks needed vocational training rather than an academic curriculum, replaced them with handicraft instructors. After spells as a hospital manager and a customs official, he became principal of Lincoln High School at Gallipolis, Ohio, in 1908. Bouchet died in 1918.

THE FIRST **BLACK DIPLOMAT**

to represent the United States was Ebenezer Don Carlos Bassett (b. Litchfield, Conn., 1833), formerly principal of Philadelphia's Institute of Colored Youth, appointed minister resident to Haiti on 6 April 1869. This was the first presidential appointment of any black officeholder.

The first **black person to become a career diplomat** was Boston University law graduate Clifton Reginald Wharton (b. Baltimore, 1899), appointed third secretary to Monrovia, Liberia, after he had passed the U.S. Foreign Service examinations in 1924. As minister to Romania, he became the first black to head a U.S. embassy in Europe in 1958 and was the first black *career* diplomat to become an ambassador when he was sworn in on 9 March 1961 as U.S. ambassador to Norway.

Black ambassador: The first was Edward R. Dudley (b. South Boston, Va., 1911), appointed to represent the United States in Liberia as minister in 1948 and as ambassador on 18 March 1949. Prior to this date it was Foreign Service policy to restrict black diplomats to ministerships.

THE FIRST **BLACK DOCTOR**

in the United States was James Durham, aka Derham, who was born into slavery in Philadelphia on 1 May 1762. He served in the Revolutionary War with the Sixteenth British Regiment, acting as an assistant to the surgeon, Dr. George West. Following the war, he is known to have worked as a slave for a physician in New Orleans, but he succeeded in buying his freedom and returned to Philadelphia. By 1789 he had a thriving private practice and was reported to be earning $3,000 a year, making him one of the highest-earning freedmen in America.

The first professionally qualified black doctor to practice in the United States was James McCune Smith (b. New York City, 1813), who, being unable to gain entrance to an American medical school on account of his color, entered Glasgow University Medical School in Scotland in 1832. After receiving his MD in 1837, he served a short internship in Paris, then returned to New York to establish a medical practice and a pharmacy on West Broadway, claimed to have been the first such black-owned outlet in the United States.

First to earn a professional qualification in the United States was David Peck, who graduated from Rush Medical School in Chicago in 1847. He did not practice in the United States but joined a short-lived colony of African Americans in Nicaragua. When this failed he remained in Central America, setting up in private practice. First to earn his professional qualification and practice in the United States was John Van Surly de Grasse, who graduated with an MD from Bowdoin College Medical School in Brunswick, Me., on 19 May 1849. He established a practice in Boston, being admitted to the Massachusetts Medical Society in 1854. During the Civil War De Grasse became the first black physician to serve in the field, the other seven black members of the Union Army's medical establishment holding hospital appointments in Washington, D.C. He was an assistant surgeon with the 35th Regiment of the African Brigade until cashiered in 1864 following charges of unprofessional conduct by a white surgeon. The animosity De Grasse had faced in the army suggests that the allegations were contrived.

THE FIRST
BLACK HEAD OF A PREDOMINANTLY WHITE GOVERNMENT

was the mulatto army surgeon William Fergusson (b. Jamaica, 1795), who served as acting governor of Sierra Leone from September 1841 to January 1842 and was appointed governor and captain-general with effect from 15 July 1845. Fergusson had been the first black officer commissioned into the British Army on 18 February 1813, receiving his medical diploma the same year from the Royal College of Surgeons in Edinburgh. At the time of Wellington's decisive victory over Napoleon at Waterloo, Fergusson was far away serving as a hospital assistant of the Royal African Corps in the West African colony of Sierra Leone, established after the American War of Independence to resettle black Loyalists who had fled the United States rather than be consigned to servitude. Although the principal population of Sierra Leone was black, including large numbers of slaves liberated from Atlantic slave ships by the Royal Navy, the government and military establishment were white. Fergusson was in the unenviable position for a black officer of having to exert his authority over troops who represented little more than a white rabble—many of the rank and file of the Royal African Corps being criminals and deserters from other regiments who had been given the option of penal servitude or service on the so-called Fever Coast. He did so sufficiently effectively, and became so renowned for his dedication to the medical needs of the black civilian population, that he was not only promoted to senior medical officer, but in August 1840 Governor Richard Doherty appointed him to the Council of Government, only the second black so honored. Again he impressed with his devotion to duty and concern for the common people, so that when Doherty was posted to the West Indies the following year Fergusson was made acting governor until the arrival of his replacement. In 1844 Undersecretary of State Sir James Stephen in London appointed William Fergusson as governor and captain-general, the latter status meaning that he was also in command of all land forces. Although his tenure was brief, he won the respect of even those imbued with the commonly racist attitudes of the European hierarchy.

Theodore Poole, the colonial chaplain, said that His Excellency "had the stamp of a superior man," despite the fact that he personally deplored the British government's "marked preference shown to the African over the Englishman" in Sierra Leone. "His manners are perfectly unaffected," Poole observed after their first meeting, but could not resist adding that Fergusson was "a rare exception to the general bearing of Africans and coloured people, when raised over their European neighbours." Sadly Fergusson was already suffering from the "severe digestive disorder," possibly stomach cancer, that was to take his life. Even so, he did much during the following months to put the colony on such a sound commercial footing that when he departed for sick leave to England early the following year the colony's treasury had a greater surplus than ever before. He died at sea aboard the barque *Funchal* in January 1846.

Fergusson was unique in his attainment during the nineteenth century. Although American-born Joseph Roberts, the future president of Liberia, was appointed governor of that territory in 1842, the position was not an official one, his appointment coming from the African Colonization Society in America and not the U.S. government. The first person of black heritage to be elected head of a white government was Cuba's Fulgencio Batista, born in Oriente Province in 1901, the son of peasant laborers, whose mixed ancestry was described as "Negro, White, Indian, and Chinese." An army stenographer with the rank of sergeant, he took control of the government following the "Revolt of the Sergeants" in 1933 but exercised his rule through a succession of puppet presidents until 1940. In that year he stood for election following the implementation of a new constitution and became fourteenth president of Cuba on 10 October. He stood down as required after his first four-year term but staged a coup in 1952 and remained in office until he was ousted by Fidel Castro five years later.

It is hard to describe Batista as a "black president," as he did not define himself as such—nor would many black people wish to identify with such a corrupt and brutal dictator. The first elected head of a traditionally white-led government to assert his black heritage was Hugo Chávez (b. Sabeneta, Venezuela, 1954), who was sworn in as president of Venezuela on

2 February 1999. The degree of his African heritage, like Batista's, remains inconclusive, and he is generally defined as a mestizo, of predominantly Hispanic and Amerindian ancestry. This did not prevent him from claiming, during a 2006 visit to Mali in West Africa, that his father had been as black as Malian president Amadou Touré.

U.S.: The first president defined as black, Barack Obama (b. Honolulu, Hawaii, 1961), was also the first elected head of a predominantly white government anywhere in the world to be generally acknowledged as such. Son of an American mother from Kansas and a Kenyan father (himself born a British subject) of the Luo tribe, Obama is unusual among African Americans in not being descended from slaves. Indeed, at least two of his ancestors were slave owners: The 1850 census record for Nelson County, Ky., shows that his great-great-great grandfather George Washington Overall owned a man of twenty-five and a girl of fifteen, while his great-great-great-great grandmother Mary Duvall owned a man of sixty and a woman of fifty-eight. (Allegations that Obama had slave-trading Arab ancestors on his father's side appear to be conjectural.) The Columbia- and Harvard-educated law lecturer and junior U.S. senator from Illinois was elected on 4 November 2008 with 52.9 percent of the popular vote and with 365 electoral votes against his Republican opponent John McCain's 173. A majority of white voters, 55 percent, voted for the Republican candidate, compared to 58 percent who had voted Republican in the presidential election of 2004—a relatively small decline in view of widespread dissatisfaction with the war in Iraq. The black vote for the Democratic candidate increased from 88 percent in 2004 to 95 percent in 2008, while the Hispanic vote went up from 53 percent to 67 percent. The additional Hispanic vote was the most significant swing of any of the major demographics. Perhaps surprisingly, the gay vote for the Democrat candidate actually declined between the two elections, from 77 percent to 70 percent.

The 44th president of the United States was inaugurated on 20 January 2009, attended by relatives both black and white, among them his eleventh cousin, the outgoing president George W. Bush, and his ninth cousin once removed, outgoing vice president Dick Cheney.

THE FIRST **BLACK LAWYER**

in the United States was Macon B. Allen, born A. Macon Bolling, a free mulatto, in Indiana in 1816 and a schoolmaster before serving an apprenticeship to abolitionist lawyer Samuel Fessenden in Portland, Me., when he was in his mid-twenties. Allen's admission to the bar in Maine was reported in the *Portland American* for 4 September 1844, though the date is not given. He decided to move to Boston the following year since, as he later recorded, "Maine was not a good place for a black man to practice as an attorney." There he opened the first black law office in the United States on State Street on 29 April 1845 in partnership with Robert Morris, formerly of Salem, Mass. Allen was called to the Massachusetts bar a few days later, on 3 May, an event that inspired the following report under the heading THAT COLORED GENTLEMAN in an unidentified Boston newspaper:

> He is of medium height and size, and passably good looking. He is indeed better looking than two or three white members of the Boston bar and it is hardly possible that he can be a worse lawyer than at least six of them that we could name.

Allen's partner Robert Morris was not called to the bar until 1847, but it was he who was the first black lawyer to represent a client in court. He recalled:

> There was something in the courtroom that made me feel like a giant. The courtroom was filled with colored people, and I could see, on the faces of every one of them, a wish that I might win the first case that has ever been tried before a jury by a colored attorney.

Win he did, though sadly Morris vouchsafed no further details other than the fact that his client was a black man suing to recover money owing for services rendered.

In 1848 Macon B. Allen was appointed a justice of the peace for Middlesex County by the governor of Massachusetts, the first judicial appointment filled by a black lawyer. Having moved to South Carolina in 1868, he was elected a judge of the Inferior Court of Charleston in February 1873. He was not, however, the first **black judge** in the United States, an honor accorded to Jonathan J. Wright when he was elected Associate Justice of the South Carolina Supreme Court by the General Assembly on 1 February 1870.

THE FIRST **BLACK LEGISLATOR**

to sit as an elected representative in a predominantly white national legislature was Samuel Jackson Prescod, who was returned as one of two representatives of Bridgetown, capital of Barbados, with 185 votes on 6 June 1843. It was largely owing to Prescod, the son of a white planter and a free woman of color, that free blacks had been admitted to the franchise in 1831, shortly before the emancipation of the slaves in British territories. He subsequently edited the first black newspaper in the colony, the *New Times*. Following his election, Prescod became leader of the Liberal Party, which represented the interests of principally white smallholders, the so-called ten-acre men, and during his twenty years as a member of the House fought to protect the welfare of the underprivileged, including the recently liberated slaves. On his retirement from politics in 1860, Prescod became a judge of the Assistant Court of Appeal, one of the earliest appointments of a black to the judiciary anywhere in the world. On the bench he continued to act as an inflexible champion of liberty and justice, and on his death in 1871 he was eulogized as "the Great Tribune of the People."

The first **black representative to sit in a European legislature** was Mathieu Louisi, a print-worker of Pointe-à-Pitre on the West Indian island of Guadeloupe, who was elected to the French National Assembly representing Guadeloupe on 22 August 1848. His maiden speech, a moderate appeal for more harmonious relations between black and white in the colonies, was received with "loud marks of disapprobation." He lost his seat in the next election.

U.S.: The first **black representative to sit in Congress** was Hiram Rhodes Revels (b. Fayetteville, N.C., 1832), a barber before becoming a Methodist minister, who was elected to the U.S. Senate as a Republican for Mississippi to fill the position vacated by Jefferson Davis some ten years earlier, serving from 25 February 1870 to 4 March 1871. He subsequently became president of Alcorn College.

The first **black representative to sit in the House of Representatives** was former slave Joseph H. Rainey, a barber from Charleston, S.C., who was elected to a vacant seat as a Republican for South Carolina and sworn in on 12 December 1870. He was reelected to the House four times, serving until 1879—the longest-serving black congressman until William L. Dawson in the 1950s.

Black legislator to hold office in an otherwise white government: The first was Cuban-born Severian de Heredia, who became French minister of public works and a member of the Rouvier cabinet in 1888. Besides building some of France's finest highways, he worked for the abolition of slavery in Cuba and Brazil. **U.S.:** The first black to serve in a presidential cabinet was Robert Clifton Weaver (b. Washington, D.C., 1907), formerly administrator of the government's Housing and Home Finance Agency, who served as the first secretary of Housing and Urban Development under President Lyndon Baines Johnson from 18 January 1966 to 18 December 1968.

SEE ALSO **black head of a predominantly white government**.

THE FIRST **BLACK MAYOR**

in the United States was Monroe Baker, elected for the small town of St. Martin, La., on 5 October 1867. First to preside over a city government was Robert H. Wood, elected mayor of Natchez, Miss., in December 1870.

The first **black chief executive of a major city** in the United States was Walter Washington (b. Dawson, Ga., 1915, the son of a factory worker and great-grandson of a slave), who was appointed mayor-commissioner of Washington, D.C., by President Lyndon Baines Johnson on 5 September 1967. (At that time the capital city did not have elected mayors.) Having been twice reappointed as commissioner by President Richard Nixon, in 1974 Washington became the city's first elected mayor in 104 years.

The first **black candidates to be elected mayor of a major city** in the United States were both Democrats, both lawyers, and returned on the same day, 7 November 1967, Carl Stokes for Cleveland, Ohio, and Richard Hatcher for Gary, Ind. Stokes, who won 96 percent of the black vote and 19 percent of the white vote, was first to be inaugurated, on 13 November 1967. Hatcher, who served as mayor of Gary for twenty years, was sworn in on 1 January 1968.

THE FIRST **BLACK MODEL**

was South Carolina–born Ophelia DeVore, who attended modeling school in New York City at age fourteen in the mid-1930s and was a photographic and fashion model for two years c. 1936–38. A light-skinned black woman with both Caucasian and Native American blood, Ophelia passed for white and was usually cast in the roles of Mediterranean types. She subsequently opened a modeling school for blacks, combined with an agency to find them jobs. As a fashion columnist for the *Pittsburgh Courier*, she was able to give many of her students a first chance of exposure by using them to illustrate her articles. The big New York department stores, realizing that an emerging black middle class represented a new market for fashion, lent Ophelia the clothes that adorned her neophyte models.

The first black woman to become a catwalk model, and the first to establish herself in modeling as a full-time professional, was Dorothea Towles from Texarkana, Tex. After training in Los Angeles, she went to Paris on spec and was fortunate enough to capture the attention of legendary Italian couturier Elsa Schiaparelli. In 1949 she was hired as an in-house model at Schiaparelli at a salary of 30,000 francs a month. Although this converted to a fairly modest $100 a month, it was considerably higher than the earnings of most house models. To the color-blind French she was worth more because she possessed the glamour of coming from America; unlike at home, being black was immaterial.

The first black cover girl to adorn a white-oriented magazine was 6' 2" Donyale Luna (b. Peggy Anne Freeman, Detroit, 1945) for the January 1965

Harper's Bazaar. She also became the first to adorn the cover of the world's premier fashion magazine, New York *Vogue*, March 1966. If there was one more river to cross, it was becoming "the face" of a global cosmetics company. The first black woman to achieve that accolade was Veronica Webb for Revlon in 1992.

THE FIRST BLACK NOVELIST

SEE **novel by a black author**.

THE FIRST BLACK PAINTER

in the United States known by name was Baltimore-based Joshua Johnston (1765–1830), who is listed by his avocation in various city directories from 1796 to 1824. He is believed to have been a slave who made sufficient income from painting portraits of the Baltimore gentry to buy his own freedom. Stylistic similarities suggest that he may have learned to paint from Charles Willson Peale or Peale's son Rembrandt or, more probably, Peale's nephew Charles Peale Polk, though Johnston referred to himself in an advertisement in the *Baltimore Intelligencer* (19 December 1798) as "a self-taught genius . . . having experienced many insuperable obstacles in the persuit [*sic*] of his studies." Boston can lay claim to an earlier, unidentified black artist on the evidence of an advertisement appearing in the *Boston News-Letter* for 7 January 1773, seeking commissions for "a Negro man whose extraordinary genius has been assisted by the best masters in London; he takes faces at the lowest rates."

THE FIRST BLACK PLAYWRIGHT

SEE **black actors**.

THE FIRST BLACK POET

to be published in America was African-born Jupiter Hammon (1720–1806), a slave to three generations of the Lloyd family of Queen's Village, Long Island, N.Y., whose eighty-eight-line "An Evening Thought, Salvation by Christ, with Penitential Cries," composed on Christmas Day 1760, appeared in New York on 15 December the following year. Hammon was a devout Wesleyan whose gratitude that slavery had brought him and others like him the blessings of Christianity would be unlikely to find any resonance with African Americans today. His "An Address to Miss Phillis Wheatly" [*sic*] of 1778 was a tribute to the first **black woman poet** to be published. Senegal-born Phillis Wheatley (1753–1784) had been bought by the Wheatley family of Boston at the age of seven and, very unusually for a girl and even more unusually for a slave, had been educated in Latin, translating the Niobe section of Ovid's *Metamorphoses* into English verse while yet in her teens. Her first appearance in print was the poem "On Messrs Hussey and Coffin," which was published in the *Newport Mercury* on 21 December 1767. She was taken to England by the Wheatleys in 1773 in order to improve her failing health, and on 1 September of that year her *Poems on Various Subjects Religious and Moral* were published in London.

The first **American-born black poet** to be published was George Moses Horton (1797–1880) of North Carolina, who unlike Jupiter Hammon felt no misplaced gratitude for his condition of slavery and spent all his adult life trying to secure manumission from his owners, the Horton family, though without success before escaping at the end of the Civil War. He was, however, allowed to hire out his labor by paying a fee of 25¢ (later 50¢) a day to his master, and it was while he was working as a janitor at the University of North Carolina at Chapel Hill in 1829 that his first volume of poetry, *The Hope of Liberty*, was published in Raleigh, N.C. During his Chapel Hill employment he was able to supplement his income by writing love poems for the students to pass off as their own to their sweethearts.

THE FIRST BLACK SOLDIERS

to serve in the forces of America did so in the militias of the Dutch, British, and Spanish North American colonies prior to the Revolutionary War. In 1641 black soldiers were received into the Dutch colonial militia of New Amsterdam (New York City) to help defend the village from the Indians. They were also conscripted for militia training together with whites in Massachusetts from 1652 to 1656 and again in 1660, Maryland in 1658, Rhode Island in 1665, New Jersey in 1668, Connecticut in 1672, and New Plymouth (where one Abraham Pearse, black, was in the reserve in 1643) in 1685. In Spanish Florida there was a unit of black and mulatto men based in St. Augustine, of which the earliest known roster is dated 20 September 1683. These troops saw action shortly after this, probably the first black combat soldiers in North America, when a raiding party of fifty-three men of color (including some Indians) crossed into Carolina to attack the British at Port Royal and Edisto. They also raided the plantations of Gov. Joseph Morton, carrying off money, plate, and thirteen slaves to a total value of £1,500.

Black troops were soon engaged in warfare on behalf of the English-speaking colonies as well. During King William's War of 1690 an unnamed black man from Massachusetts was killed fighting aboard a British ship (it is not apparent whether he was a sailor or a militiaman). In Queen Anne's War (1701–13) black soldiers fought at Fort William Henry in New York in 1702, and there is also record of black militiamen from Massachusetts and New Hampshire on active service. They served in King George's War of 1744–48 and the French and Indian War of 1754–63, in the latter not only as soldiers but also as sailors aboard the sixty ships of the Rhode Island Navy. Five of the thirty-seven crew members of the *Revenge* were black. The soldiers included Samuel Jenkins, serving as a wagoner under Gen. Edward Braddock in 1755. Recorded as a slave belonging to Capt. Breadwater at Fairfax, Va., in 1771, he was the last known survivor of the pre-Revolutionary wars in America when he died in 1849 aged 115. Others fought under Wolfe at the decisive Battle of Quebec of 1759, which resulted in Canada becoming British.

During the Revolution black people fought on both sides, notably for the British in Lord Dunsmore's Ethiopian Regiment of Virginian slave volunteers who were offered their freedom in exchange for service. Gen. George Washington at first excluded "any stroller, Negro, or vagabond" from service but changed his mind when he learned of the large numbers joining the British forces and authorized enlistment of black freedmen (his personal orderly throughout the war, William Lee, was his slave). Eventually eight thousand black men served with the American forces, of whom some five thousand were fully enlisted soldiers.

No black men were allowed to serve in the regular U.S. Army until after the Civil War. The all-black 9th and 10th Cavalry Regiments (the so-called Buffalo Soldiers) were authorized by Congress on 28 July 1866 for service on the western frontier, at the same time as the lesser-known 38th, 39th, 40th, and 41st Infantry Regiments were founded. By 1869 there were approximately 12,500 blacks serving in the regular army.

Black officer: The first known in North America was a West African slave named Francisco Menéndez, who had escaped from the Carolinas to Spanish Florida. He was appointed by Gov. Benavides to command a slave militia in 1726 and was given the rank of captain. Menéndez and his men helped defend St. Augustine against the British in 1728, but it took a further ten years of loyal service to the Spanish crown before he was granted his freedom. The captain then took command of the all-black Spanish garrison at Fort Mose, remaining an officer until Florida was ceded to the British in 1763. He eventually settled in Havana.

Contemporary with Menéndez was a Capt. Simon, commander of a forty-five-strong force of free blacks serving with the French forces that was raised by Sieur Jean-Baptiste Le Moyne de Bienville at Fort Tombecdee, near present-day Epps, Ala., on 23–26 April 1736. They formed part of De Bienville's expeditionary force against the Chickasaw Indians, and in a raid on an enemy village on 25 May Capt. Simon was reported to have performed heroically on two occasions. Other black officers in colonial forces raised in America were three lieutenants and five sublieutenants who served in Gen. Galvez's Gulf Coast Army of 1779–91 and three captains and a lieutenant who commanded black units of the Spanish forces in 1797 as New Orleans came under threat of French attack.

When Louisiana became part of the United States in 1803, the black militia was retained with its officers Capt. Jean-Baptiste Hardy and Louis

Liotant (rank unknown), but the following year the slave war in Haiti caused alarm in the city, and the units were disbanded.

On 17 September 1812 the black militia was reinstated as the Battalion of Free Men of Color, and 2nd Lt. Isidore Honore became the first black to be commissioned by the governor of a state of the United States. The thirty-one black officers of the 1st and 2nd Battalions of Free Men of Color, commanded by 2nd Maj. Vincent Popolus and 2nd Maj. Joseph Savary, respectively, were the first to lead U.S. troops in combat at the Battle of New Orleans, fought against the British between 23 December 1814 and 8 January 1815. Savary, a soldier of fortune from Saint-Domingue (Haiti) and a veteran of the 1803 uprising, was personally commissioned on 19 December 1814 by the commander of the American forces, Maj. Gen. Andrew Jackson, and thus became the first **black officer of the U.S. Army**. In 1816, Savary and many of his men from the 2nd Battalion joined the pirate Jean Lafitte at Galveston, Tex., and became involved in the struggle for Mexican independence. By 1822 he was back in New Orleans, *Paxton's New Orleans Directory* for the year listing him as "Savary, Col. Joseph, 158 Burgundy, cor. Hospital" (interestingly, Andrew Jackson himself referred to Savary as "Colonel" rather than "Major"). According to one authority he died about this time.

Few blacks served in the Mexican War of 1846–47, and none of them as officers. The Civil War, 1861–65, was the first in which black officers were commissioned in relatively large numbers to lead black units or serve as chaplains and surgeons. The highest ranking of a total of 107 was Lt. Col. Alexander Thomas, who headed a hospital in Savannah, Ga.

Black officer commissioned in the regular U.S. Army: The first was Frazier Augustus Boutelle (b. Troy, N.Y., 1840), who, having obtained the rank of 1st lieutenant with the 5th New York Cavalry Regiment in the Civil War, reenlisted as a private in the 1st U.S. Cavalry Regiment in February 1866 (apparently illegally, as blacks were not accepted in the regular army until the creation of the all-black units noted above in November of that year). Following promotion to corporal, sergeant, and sergeant major, he was commissioned as a 2nd lieutenant on 2 January 1869. Having been cited for "gallantry in action" at Lost River, Ore.,

and "conspicuous gallantry" in the Modoc Indian War of 1872–73, Boutelle was promoted to 1st lieutenant on 31 July 1873, becoming adjutant of the 1st U.S. Cavalry exactly two years later. On 24 April 1886 he was further promoted to captain, and on 1 July 1890 became brevet major. He left the regular army in 1890 to enjoy a long and fruitful retirement in Seattle, where he served as adjutant general to the Washington National Guard and subsequently as its commander with the rank of brigadier general (15 June 1895). He died in 1924.

Boutelle's successful career and honored status is in sad contrast to that of the first **black officer commissioned from West Point**, Henry O. Flipper (born into slavery in Thomasville, Ga., 1856). He was the seventh black to enter the academy, which had earned a reputation for mistreatment and discrimination. Flipper's predecessors had either dropped out or been failed. He himself was determined not to allow the negative attitudes of other cadets or members of the faculty to distract him from his studies, in which he was sufficiently assiduous to graduate 50th in a class of 76 on 14 June 1877. On receiving his commission he served first at Fort Sill, Okla., as a lieutenant in the 10th Cavalry, then was posted to Fort Davis in Texas after a liaison with the daughter of a white officer had caused a scandal. In charge of the commissary, he found a shortfall in funds and suspected that this had been engineered to entrap him. Perhaps foolishly, he replaced the funds out of his own pocket rather than report the matter to his commanding officer. This was revealed and he was court-martialed for embezzlement. Although found not guilty of this charge, he was convicted of "conduct unbecoming a gentleman" and dishonorably discharged in December 1881. Nearly a century later the army reopened the case and quashed the conviction. The injustice suffered by Flipper was finally expunged in 1999 when President Bill Clinton granted him a full presidential pardon.

Flipper is often cited as the first black officer in the U.S. Army, which he was not, but he did achieve a little-known first later in life as the first **black editor of an American newspaper with a predominantly white readership**, the *Sunday Herald* of Nogales, Az., in 1889.

THE FIRST BLOOD TRANSFUSION

to a human being was carried out on 12 June 1667 by Jean-Baptiste Denys, professor of philosophy and mathematics at Montpellier University in France and personal physician to Louis XIV. The patient was a boy of fifteen suffering from a severe fever who had already been bled twenty times "to assuage the excessive heat." In order to compensate for this loss of blood, Denys gave him a transfusion of 9 ounces of blood from the carotid artery of a lamb. According to the professor, his patient responded to this extremely dangerous experiment by displaying "a clear and smiling countenance" and eventually recovered. Others were not so fortunate, and after one of Denys's victims had died as a result of receiving animal's blood, the practice was prohibited in France and fell into disrepute elsewhere.

The first transfusion of human blood to be attested at the time was performed on 25 September 1818 by the brilliant twenty-eight-year-old Dr. Thomas Blundell of Guy's Hospital, London. He used a syringe of his own invention to inject some 12–14 ounces of fresh blood from several different donors, but his patient was in a moribund state and already beyond hope of recovery. Blundell continued to give transfusions, though he was not to succeed in saving a life by these means until ten years later, by which time others had preceded him. In 1824 he gave a transfusion of 4 ounces of blood from her husband to a patient with postpartum hemorrhage and it was a report of this procedure in the *Philadelphia Journal of the Medical and Physical Sciences* the following year that provides the only evidence that the first transfusion with human blood may, after all, have been conducted in the United States. A brief two-line note appended to the articles records: "Thirty years ago, the experiment of transfusion of blood under precisely the same circumstances as above, was performed by Dr Physic." In 1795, the date postulated, Dr. Philip Syng Physick was a surgeon at the Pennsylvania Hospital in Philadelphia, and it seems likely that this was where the experiment was conducted. He was a renowned teacher of medicine and at his private practice he attended to such luminaries as Dr. Benjamin Rush, scientist and signatory of the Declaration of Independence, first lady Dolley Madison, and the future president Andrew Jackson, whom he tried to persuade to give up smoking.

The first recorded instance of a patient's life being saved by a blood transfusion occurred in London in 1825, when a Dr. Doubleday gave 14 ounces of blood to a woman suffering from a severe internal hemorrhage. After receiving only 6 ounces she sat up in bed and announced, "I feel as strong as a bull." Her pulse rate subsequently fell from 140 to 104.

Although this case demonstrated that blood transfusion could be effective if carefully regulated, there were still two major obstacles to be overcome before it had any chance of general acceptance. Foremost was ignorance of incompatibility, and not until Karl Landsteimer of Vienna discovered blood groups in 1900 was it possible for doctors to match the donor to the patient. Several years were to pass before this knowledge was applied in a practical manner, but in 1907 the Czech scientist Jan Jansky made the first reliable classification of blood groups, and in 1912 Dr. Reuben Ottenberg of New York instituted the practice of making blood tests before a transfusion.

The other major difficulty was blood clotting, a factor that had probably helped to save some of the unfortunate subjects of those gruesome experiments with animal blood, since it prevented more than a few ounces from entering the bloodstream. The answer to this lay with the chemical sodium citrate, which acts as an anti-coagulant and enables blood to be decanted into bottles ready for use, so that a transfusion can be given without the presence of the donor. The citrate method was discovered by the Belgian surgeon A. Hustin, who performed the first indirect transfusion with blood stored in this way at the Hôpital Saint-Jean in Brussels on 27 March 1914.

Although citrate would prevent clotting, the problem of preserving blood supplies for more than a few hours remained. This was overcome in 1917 by Dr. Oswald Robertson, an American physician serving with the Canadian forces on the Western Front, who conceived the idea of storing blood corpuscles in jars of glucose, in much the same way as jelly is preserved. The blood was collected behind the lines from Group O donors and then brought under refrigeration to the Casualty Clearing Station near Doullens by ambulance. There, under Dr. Robertson's supervision, it was stored in a cool dugout until required, the blood corpuscles needing only the addition of a saline solution to be ready for use.

U.S.: As noted above, a transfusion was later claimed to have been made in 1795 by Dr. Philip Physick in Philadelphia. Another was said to have been performed in the same city on a cholera victim in 1832, but the first contemporary report, in the *New Orleans Medical News and Hospital Gazette*, was of a cholera patient given 10 ounces of blood by syringe at the Charity Hospital in New Orleans in 1854. This was an emergency treatment in extremis, the patient expiring only moments later. The surgeon is not named, but it is believed to have been the editor of the journal himself, Dr. Samuel Choppin. The donor was a nurse on the ward. There were four reported cases of transfusions to Union Army soldiers during the Civil War and in its aftermath the practice became gradually more frequent, though seldom with decisive results. So retarded was the scientific thinking in some medical circles that transfusions were made using milk from cows, goats, or nursing mothers as a substitute for blood. As late as 1890 a transfusion of blood direct from a live lamb was given to a typhoid patient in North Carolina. The successful and ongoing implementation of blood transfusion in the United States can be dated from August 1906, when Dr. George W. Crile performed a transfusion between two brothers named Miller at the St. Alexis Hospital in Cleveland that was instrumental in the recovery of the patient. He published reports of a number of other transfusions the following year.

Blood donors: The first panel was set up in 1921 by Dr. P. L. Oliver, who arranged for four volunteers from the Camberwell Division of the London Branch of the British Red Cross Society to donate their blood at King's College Hospital. This was the beginning of the London Blood Transfusion Service, which provided a register of donors who were prepared to respond to a call for blood from any of the London hospitals in an emergency. At first the demand was small, only twenty-six requests for blood being made in 1924, but five years later the number had increased to 5,333.

U.S.: The first blood donor panel was established in August 1937 by the Augusta, Ga., chapter of the Red Cross, with five hundred volunteers signing on within a few days. In 1941 the American Red Cross began empaneling large numbers of people willing to give blood for American and British frontline forces, the first blood center in a nationwide network opening in New York on 4 February. A total of 12 million units of blood was collected during World War II.

Blood bank: The first was established in 1931 by Prof. Sergei Yudin at the Sklifosovsky Institute, Moscow's central emergency service hospital. Much of the blood used by Yudin came from involuntary donors who had died suddenly, many of them in streetcar accidents (blood from those suffering lingering deaths clotted). By the mid-'30s stored blood was being shipped all over the Soviet Union. The term "blood bank" was coined by Bernard Fantus, who set up America's first centralized depot for the storage of blood at Cook County Hospital in Chicago in 1937.

Pre-natal blood transfusion: The first was performed by Prof. George Green and Sir William Liley on a child born to Mrs. E. McLeod at the National Women's Hospital, Auckland, New Zealand, on 20 September 1963.

THE FIRST **BOOK CLUBS**

were the so-called guilds founded in Germany in 1919 to supply an impoverished population with cheap reprints of classic works of literature on the subscription principle. The most prominent of these was the Volksverband der Bücherfreunde, which specialized in the arts, history, and travel. It was the success of these ventures that inspired Samuel Craig to found the Literary Guild (SEE BELOW) some years later.

U.S.: The first was the Book-of-the-Month Club, founded by Canadian-born former copywriter Harry Scherman, who had given up the advertising business to produce the largely mail-order Little Leather Library. What he wanted to achieve with BOMC was the convenience and low price of mail order combined with a built-in mechanism for repeat sales. The selections were to be chosen by a panel of experts from current books at no more than $3 list price, and Scherman and his partners gave a daring guarantee that they would not seek to influence or interfere in the panel's choices. This may have been rash, as their initial choice nearly sank the venture at the outset. *Holly Willowes* was a mystical work by British writer Sylvia Townsend Warner, scarcely known in America, and when it went out to 4,750 members in April 1926, many copies were immediately returned with stern letters of rebuke. The second month's book, T. S. Stribling's *Teeftallow*, went to 12,500 members, and the third, Esther Forbes's *O Genteel Lady*, to 13,500. From there membership began to climb steeply, boosted by popular selections like John Galsworthy's *Silver Spoon* and Edna Ferba's *Show Boat*, and by the end of the year there were 46,539 members. This success rapidly inspired imitators, and by 1928 the BOMC was competing not only with the Literary Guild but also with the American Booksellers Association Book Selection, the Book League of America, the Catholic Book Religious Book Club, the Free Thought Book of the Month, the Detective Story Club, and the Crime Club. A number of others had already come and gone, including the Junior Book Club for children.

Whereas the BOMC sold its selections at the same price as the bookshops, Samuel Craig's Literary Guild was the first book club to sell below publisher's price, $1.50 for books that cost $2.50 or $3 in a store. Its inaugural selection, for January 1927, was Heywood Brown and Margaret Leech's *The Life of Anthony Comstock*, about the notorious bluenose, distributed to the 8,000 founder members. One pioneer club even did the opposite, selling books above list. This was the highly exclusive Book Club of Texas, limited to only 300 members, founded in late 1928 by department store founder Stanley Marcus to produce fine editions for discriminating collectors.

THE FIRST **BOOK DUST JACKET**

was issued with *The Keepsake, 1833*, an annual published by Longman in London in November 1832. It was pale buff, with a decorative border enclosing the title printed in red, and advertisements for other Longman publications on the back. The spine was plain. This unique book jacket was discovered by the English bibliophile John Carter in 1934 and predated by twenty-eight years the earliest book jacket reported

hitherto. It was lost in 1952 while being taken to the Bodleian Library in Oxford, and no other example has ever been found.

The first pictorial dust wrapper was issued with an edition of Bunyan's *Pilgrim's Progress* published by Longman in 1860. The illustration reproduced on the buff wrapper was a woodcut by Charles Bennett, also contained in the book itself.

The *Keepsake* jacket of 1832 and the *Pilgrim's Progress* jacket of 1860, as well as the half-dozen or so examples known to have been issued between these dates, were all designed to completely enclose the book. The earliest known example of a book jacket of the modern kind (i.e., with flaps folding in between cover and endpapers, leaving the edges of the pages free, and with the title printed on the spine) was issued with Noel Paton's *Poems by a Painter*, published by Blackwood of Edinburgh in 1861. The first on a novel enclosed Thomas Hughes's *Tom Brown's Schooldays*, published by Macmillan in London in 1869.

U.S.: The first was a wrapper enclosing William E. Lord's *Poems*, 1845, and is printed in three colored inks. The only known copy is in the Huntington Library, San Marino, Calif. The earliest known on a novel came with the first American edition of Dickens's *Edwin Drood* of 1871. The first pictorial jacket encased the second edition of Joel Chandler Harris's *Uncle Remus: His Songs and Sayings*, published by D. Appleton & Son, New York City, in 1881, with illustrations from the book reproduced on the front and an advertisement for the *Orthopedist* on the back.

The first publishers known to have used **blurbs** on their book jackets were Harper and Dodd Mead, both of New York. Three examples survive from 1899—Harper's *Admiral George Dewey* by John Barrett and *The Enchanted Typewriter* by J. K. Bangs, and Dodd Mead's *Janice Meredith* by P. L. Ford.

The word *blurb* was coined by American author Gelett Burgess in 1907. At the American Booksellers Association banquet that year he defined the verb "to blurb" as "to make a sound like a publisher" and added, "A blurb is a check drawn on Fame, and it is seldom honored."

THE FIRST BOWLING

as an indoor sport in the United States began with the opening of Knickerbocker's Bowling Alley in New York City in 1840, patrons playing a version derived from the German peasant game of *Kegelspiel*, or nine-pins. Nobody has been able to pinpoint exactly when the tenth pin was added. The most generally touted theory that it was to evade an anti-gambling law of 1841 prohibiting ninepins in Connecticut fails to stand up to scrutiny. In fact, this ordinance prohibited bowling "whether more or less than nine pins are used in such play." The earliest specific reference is the caption of an illustration, "The Ten-Pin Player," which appeared in the *New York Atlas* in 1842. The first multi-lane alley, and probably the first to lift bowling out of the dark and smoky proletarian aura of the saloon, was the six-laner built in 1891 by Joe Thum at Germania Hall in New York City. The march toward suburban respectability had begun.

Automated pin setter: The first was produced by the American Machine and Foundry Co. in 1946 and used at the American Bowling Congress National championship in Buffalo, N.Y., but at two tons it was operationally unpredictable and contrary. It took another five years of refinement before AMF was able to launch the first apparatus that could be operated wholly independently of pinboys, installed in 1952 at the sixteen-lane Farragut Pool Lanes in Brooklyn, N.Y.

THE FIRST BOXING

on an organized basis began with the earliest recorded prizefight, reported in January 1681 by the London newspaper *True Protestant Mercury* in the following brief paragraph:

> Yesterday a match of boxing was performed before his Grace, the Duke of Albemarle, between his butler and his butcher. The latter won the prize, as he hath done many times before, being accounted, though a little man, the best at that exercise in England.

Boxing stadium: The first, which was also the first sports stadium of any kind, was Figg's Amphitheatre, opened in London in 1719 by James Figg "on ye right hand in Oxford Road near Adam and Eve Court" (between present-day Oxford Street and Tottenham Court Road). It was probably financed by the Earl of Peterborough, who had brought Figg to London after witnessing the young fighter display his extraordinary powers on the village green of his native Thame in Oxfordshire. Before opening the Amphitheatre, Figg had won fifteen fights in a row and had been acclaimed champion of England. The stadium was a wooden building seating one thousand spectators around the ring and another two or three hundred in the gallery. The ring itself was a circular stage without ropes measuring about 40 feet in diameter. Figg was reputedly "a great believer in adjourned meetings, so that his patrons might pay at the door twice." He was also the first promoter to run a boxing booth at a fair, putting on exhibitions every September at the Bowling Green in Southwark.

Title fight: The first was fought between James Figg and Ned Sutton of Gravesend for the championship of England at Figg's Amphitheatre on 6 June 1727. Among the spectators were the prime minister, Sir Robert Walpole, *Gulliver's Travels* author Jonathan Swift, soon-to-be poet laureate Colley Cibber, and the bewitching sixteen-year-old Irish beauty Kitty Clive.

The contest was held in three parts, namely broadsword, cudgels, and fisticuffs. To secure the title the challenger had to win all three. There were no rules, and a round only came to an end when one of the men was knocked down. An unscheduled interval occurred in the middle of the fight when some of the sporting fancy in the gallery sent down a footman with a bottle of port, a drink new to England at the time. It took the two opponents only 15 minutes to finish the bottle and resume the fight. The contest ended in the fifth round when Figg knocked Sutton down with a blow to the chest, then held him on the floor until he gave in. The boxing event was followed by the fight with cudgels, which gave Figg an opportunity to consolidate his victory by breaking his opponent's knee.

Rules of boxing: The first, which were also the first recognized rules for any sport, were drawn up by ex-champion Jack Broughton, "approved of by the gentlemen, and agreed to by the pugilists" of Broughton's Amphitheatre in the Haymarket, London, on August

18, 1743. Broughton's Rules remained in force until 1838, when they were superseded by the London Prize Ring Rules, which introduced the requirement for a square ring (formerly a circle of spectators and officials) bounded by ropes. It was to be 24 feet square, still the maximum size for professional fights. (SEE ALSO **Queensberry Rules** BELOW.)

Boxing gloves: The first padded gloves were devised for sparring purposes by Jack Broughton in February 1747 for the use of pupils at his new boxing academy in London's Haymarket. These 10-ounce "mufflers" would, according to Broughton's advertisement in the *Daily Advertiser*, "secure them from the inconvenience of black eyes, broken jaws, and bloody noses." The first prizefight to be fought with gloves was contested between two unnamed Englishmen in Aix-la-Chapelle, France, on 8 October 1818. This was exceptional, because generally gloves were not used for formal contests until a new set of rules was produced in 1867 by John Graham Chambers of Britain's Amateur Athletic Club to govern amateur boxing.

These so-called Queensberry Rules (named in honor of boxing patron the Marquess of Queensberry, who brought about the downfall of Oscar Wilde) also prescribed rounds of a set time of 3 minutes, with a 1-minute interval between them. Formerly a round lasted until one of the contestants was knocked down, whereupon he had 30 seconds to resume the fight. (An exhausted boxer could play for time by lying down each time a new round started and so gaining repeated 30-second periods of recuperation.)

American prizefighter: The first and also the first black professional boxer was the former slave Bill Richmond, who secured his initial victory by defeating Jack Holmes with a knockout in the sixth round at Cricklewood Green, near London, on 8 July 1805. Richmond had been brought to England and set free after the American War of Independence by the Duke of Northumberland. He began his professional boxing career in England in 1804, at a time when there was no organized boxing in the United States.

The first formal boxing match in the United States was a bare-knuckle grudge fight between English-born ex-sailor Tom Beasley of Boston and New York bartender Jacob Hyer for $150 a side on 15 October 1816. Held at Hingham, Mass., in order to evade the notice of the law, the fight continued viciously for over an hour, whereupon Hyer succeeded in breaking Beasley's arm and declared himself champion of America. Since no one was prepared to risk a limb in pursuit of this self-proclaimed title, Hyer never fought again. Jacob Hyer's son Tom contested a couple of fights in the 1840s and also claimed the championship, but generally prizefighting only began to emerge as an organized sport in the United States in the 1850s and 1860s. It was to remain illegal in most states until the twentieth century, the first to legalize boxing, with gloves only, being Louisiana in 1890.

Weight classes were introduced at a London amateur tournament in 1872 and were three in number, light weight (less than 140 pounds), middle weight (140–158 pounds), and heavy class (more than 158 pounds). Bantamweight (113–118 pounds) originated in the United States in 1894. Flyweight (less than 112 pounds) was introduced in England in 1910 and adopted in the United States the same year.

World Heavyweight Championship: The first fought with gloves (i.e., under Queensberry Rules) was contested between John L. Sullivan of Boston and Dominick F. McCaffery of Pittsburgh at Chester Park in Cincinnati on 29 August 1885. Pioneer fight promoter "Biddy" Bishop wrote of the fight: "Billy Tait was the referee. Immediately after the sixth and final round ended, Tait jumped out of the ring, without announcing his decision. He went to Toledo, Ohio. Forty-eight hours after the fight ended, someone in Toledo reminded Billy that he had forgotten to make a decision. So Billy said: 'Sullivan won.'"

Four years later, on 8 July 1889, John L. Sullivan became the last heavyweight champion to fight a bare-knuckle title contest, defeating Jake Kilrain in seventy-five rounds in Richburg, Miss.

THE FIRST **BOY SCOUT**

movement originated in England with an experimental camp held on Brownsea Island, Poole, Dorset, by Lt. Gen. (Sir) Robert Baden-Powell from 29 July to 9 August 1907. Twenty-one boys were invited to try out the new "Game of Scouting," based on ideas the South African War commander had developed from using local boys as military scouts during the Siege of Mafeking (1899) and strongly influenced by the outdoorsman Ernest Thompson Seton, proponent of Native-American lore who had founded the Woodcraft Indians (1902) and who was later to become the first Chief Scout of the Boy Scouts of America. Of these twenty-five, nine were working-class members of the Bournemouth and Poole Boys' Brigade companies, and the remainder were sons of Baden-Powell's upper-middle-class friends. They were formed into four patrols—Curlews, Ravens, Wolves, and Bulls—to carry out a range of activities that included woodcraft, observation, swimming, knot-tying, cooking, calisthenics, boat and fire drill, night patrols, and a game called Harpooning the Whale that consisted of harpooning a floating log from a boat. Although there were no uniforms, at Baden-Powell's direction the boys wore shorts—unusual for the period—and a badge based on the north point of the compass. This last was borrowed from the 5th Dragoon Guards and remains the official insignia of the Scout Movement worldwide.

The continuous development of the movement began with the publication of the first fortnightly 4d part of Baden-Powell's *Scouting for Boys* on 16 January 1908. It was not the author's intention to found a national youth organization, but rather to provide guidance for boys who wanted to train themselves in the frontier skills that he himself had learned while soldiering in various parts of the empire. The movement grew quite spontaneously, boys in all parts of the country—though principally those from middle- and lower-middle-class suburbs—banding themselves into patrols to put into practice the advice imparted by Baden-Powell in his book.

The earliest Scout troop of which there is definitive evidence was the 1st Glasgow, which has in its possession an official registration certificate retrospectively dated to 26 January 1908. This troop was originally founded in September 1907 by Capt. Robert Young as an association of Glasgow schools' Officer Training Corps members who had met and formed friendships at their annual summer camp. Soon afterward Baden-Powell visited Young and persuaded him to introduce the Scouting methods previously tried out at the Brownsea camp. The cadets having

accepted this idea, the association was renamed the 1st Glasgow Scout Troop and formed into four patrols, each of which represented one of the four schools from which membership of the troop was drawn—Hillhead High, Glasgow High, Glasgow Academy, and Kelvinside Academy.

The formal beginning of the Scouts as a national, later international, movement had been instituted before the end of 1908 when Baden-Powell established a permanent headquarters at 116–118 Victoria Street and appointed two full-time Scout Inspectors.

U.S.: As in Britain the first troops were founded informally, sometimes by British immigrants or by Americans who had read Baden-Powell's *Scouting for Boys*. Among the latter was Myra Greeno Bass, whose Eagle troop in the Kentucky mountain town of Burnside was established in the spring of 1908 and is the earliest known. Hiking and, it is believed, camping were early outdoor activities, and when it was wet Mrs. Bass corralled her Scouts in the parlor of her home and read them *Treasure Island*. During the same year troops were founded in Fort Leavenworth, Kan., and Paterson, Montclair, and Weehawken, N.J. City-based troops followed in Buffalo, N.Y., and Chicago the following year, as well as what is now probably the oldest troop in the nation, Troop 2 of Bloomfield, N.J.

The founding of a national organization had nothing to do with these or the many other pioneer troops springing up in mainly small-town America, but was due to an overseas trip taken in late 1909 by a millionaire Chicago publisher named William Dickson Boyce who had never heard of Boy Scouts. He found himself lost in a London pea-souper and unable to orient himself until approached by a boy in khaki shorts and a flat-brimmed pointed hat who timidly saluted and asked if he could be of service. Having been led by his guide safely through the fog to his destination, Boyce offered the boy a shilling (20¢). The youngster responded, "Sir, I am a Scout. A Scout does not accept tips for courtesies and good turns." In answer to Boyce's questions, his benefactor explained about Baden-Powell's youth movement and, when Boyce had completed his business, took him to Scout headquarters to learn more. Boyce arrived back in the United States with a trunkful of Scout literature, insignia, and uniforms and the determination to import the movement to his native country. The Boy Scouts of America was incorporated in the District of Columbia on 8 February 1910. The lad encountered by Boyce in the London fog was never identified, but a painting of the incident by Donald N. Ross adorns a wall at BSA's headquarters. At the Gilwell Scout Training Centre in England stands a bronze buffalo presented by one of the BSA's earliest supporters, George D. Pratt of the Pratt Institute, Brooklyn, inscribed with the testimony: "To the Unknown Scout whose faithfulness in the performance of the 'Daily Good Turn' brought the Scout Movement to the United States of America."

From the beginning, the activities of the Boy Scouts of America were based, as in Britain, on the winning of merit badges for a wide range of attainments, culminating in the Eagle Scout badge for those with twenty-one such merits. The first Eagle Scout was Arthur R. Eldred of Troop 1, Oceanside, N.Y., who received his award on Labor Day 1912. The millionth was thirteen-year-old Alexander Holsinger of Normal, Ill., in 1982. By that date some 70 million Americans had enjoyed the adventure of belonging to what had become, even before World War II, the largest voluntary organization in the United States.

SEE ALSO **Girl Scout**.

THE FIRST **BRASSIERE**

was the breast supporter patented by Luman L. Chapman of Philadelphia on 15 December 1863. There is no evidence that this was ever produced commercially, and the earliest to be advertised for sale was a garment patented by prominent Boston dressmaker Olivia Flynt on 15 February 1876. Mrs. Flynt was a dress reformer, and her breast supporter was specifically designed to free women with large breasts from the constraints of the corset, or, as she expressed it, to enable "beauty of form to be preserved without lacing or otherwise injuriously pressing or binding the body." It was originally sold at her workshop but by 1881 was also available by mail order, as were most of the early breast supporters, catering, as they did, to a niche market of the over-endowed or nursing mothers, pioneers of the

women's movement, and, from the 1880s onward, those daring spirits who indulged in cycling and outdoor sports. (It was alleged that when Lottie Dod won the Wimbledon Championship in 1887 she had an unfair advantage; as a fifteen-year-old, she was the only competitor not obliged to wear corsets.)

Fashionable women, determined to maintain hourglass figures, remained resolutely wedded to their corsets until the second decade of the twentieth century. Nevertheless, progress in design continued to be made before 1900, most notably with the earliest push-up breast supporter, the first to encase the breasts in cups, patented by New Yorker Marie Tucek, on 28 March 1893. With the dawn of the new century, brassieres began a slow but steady penetration of the general market, with J. C. Penney starting over-the-counter sales in 1902, while Sears, Roebuck included them in its mail-order catalog, retail bible of the American heartlands, the following year, with prices ranging from 19¢ to 88¢. The early designs went under a variety of names; besides "breast supporter," they were sold as "bust girdles," "short stays," and, perhaps with a nod to the Grecian-robed "greenery yallery, Grosvenor Gallery" aesthetes, "strophiums." The term "brassiere" was originally coined for such garments by the Charles R. De Bevoise Co. of Newark, N.J., in 1904. It had been used in France since the Middle Ages to denote a child's sleeved vest, though the French themselves did not apply it to the bust supporter, which they called (from at least 1889) as they still do, a *soutien gorge* (literally "throat support"). Within a year other manufacturers, such as Gabrielle Poix of New York, had adopted the name, and from 1907 it began appearing in *Vogue* and other fashion journals.

Considering that the term "brassiere" had been in use for a full decade by the time New York socialite Mary Phelps Jacob took out a patent in 1914, it is surprising that almost every reference work mentioning the garment attributes its invention to her. Writing under the pen name Caresse Crosby, she claimed as much in a 1951 autobiography, describing how, while changing for a ball, she had had her French maid join two handkerchiefs together with pink ribbon. She then sold the skimpy, backless design to the Warner Brothers Corset Co. of Bridgeport, Conn., for a modest $1,500, and, she asserted, they had made a fortune from this "first ever" bra. Apart from the fact that Warner had been manufacturing bras for twelve years at this date, Jane Farrell-Beck and Colleen Gau in the first serious historical study, *Uplift: The Bra in America* (2002), say that they have found no evidence that Jacob's brassiere was ever made by Warner. They suggest that the eagerness to accept her unmerited claim as only begetter may be on account of her social position and the fact that she was a well-known writer of popular fiction.

Warner is also credited with introducing cup sizes in 1935, though in fact the familiar A through D designation had been pioneered by S. H. Camp & Co. of Jackson, Mich., in an advertisement it ran in *Corset and Underwear Review* in February 1933. Exactly one year later, however, Warner did pioneer in one important respect, with a February 1934 advertisement that provided the earliest known use in print of the abbreviation "bra."

"Falsies" entered the American language in 1943, when the *New York Post* explained to its readers that it was "the term for the pads that convert [nightclub chorus girls] from 32s to 34s."

THE FIRST **BREAKFAST CEREAL**

ready-to-eat, was devised by Dr. James Caleb Jackson, proprietor of a water-cure spa at Dansville, N.Y., called variously the Jackson Sanatorium and "Our Home on the Hillside." In 1863 he began producing a breakfast health food branded as Granula and sold by mail order through the Our Home Granula Company. It was made from graham flour (the bran-full primary ingredient of graham crackers) that Jackson mixed with water and baked into briquettes. These were then broken into bite-size knobs and baked again. The resulting breakfast cereal was tough and tasteless and needed to be soaked overnight in milk before it could be properly masticated, but the very fact that it was so unappetizing gave the product an attraction for health faddists, who then, as now, felt that maximum benefit could only be derived from something repugnant.

First of the surviving cereals was Shredded Wheat, patented by Henry D. Perky of Denver, Colo.,

on 1 August 1893. Initially the product was sold locally in Denver and Colorado Springs, the latter a mecca for delicate constitutions, but in 1895 Perky founded the Natural Food Co. and commenced manufacture on a factory scale in Worcester, Mass. A lawyer by profession, Perky was a martyr to dyspepsia, and it was after encountering a fellow sufferer in a Nebraska hotel, a man who ate whole boiled wheat with milk for breakfast, that he was inspired with the Shredded Wheat idea. One of his ventures was a restaurant in Denver at which every dish, from mashed potatoes to ice cream, included Shredded Wheat. Even the after-dinner coffee.

Flaked breakfast cereal: The first was Granose Flakes, prepared from wheat by Dr. John Kellogg of the Battle Creek Sanitarium in Michigan and announced in the February 1895 issue of *Food Health*. They were retailed at 15¢ for a 10-ounce package, enabling Kellogg to sell wheat that cost him 60¢ a bushel for $12 a bushel.

Corn flakes were invented by Dr. John Kellogg and his brother William in 1898 and sold as Sanitas Toasted Corn Flakes in blue packets depicting the Battle Creek Sanitarium. The original flakes suffered from two deficiencies: They rapidly went limp, and they lacked flavor. The crispness problem was largely overcome by 1902, though for many years consumers were advised to freshen the flakes in a hot oven. The other problem was solved in 1905 when William Kellogg, against the entrenched opposition of his brother the doctor, insisted on adding sugar. With the product ready to launch not just as a health food, but as an appetizing and easy substitute for a cooked breakfast, it was first advertised nationally the same year. William Kellogg had worked for his brother at the Battle Creek Sanitarium as a general factotum up to twenty hours a day seven days a week for more than twenty-one years, much of it at a salary of $7 a week. He now seized his chance to put the manufacture of corn flakes on an industrial base, taking them out of the niche health-food market to establish breakfast cereals as an everyday commodity first in American kitchens and eventually worldwide. While it meant a permanent split with his domineering brother, who was forbidden the use of the Kellogg name as a brand by the Michigan Supreme Court in 1920, William was at long last able to demonstrate the business acumen that had always eluded the bullying and overbearing Dr. John. Dying a billionaire at the age of ninety-one (Dr. John died at the same age, a comparatively poor man), William not only had made his own fortune but had inspired many others to seek theirs in the breakfast cereal business. In Battle Creek alone, a modest-sized town, there were no fewer than 108 manufacturers of corn flakes by 1911.

Granula, which had started it all as a health food, became a mainstream breakfast cereal (with slightly different spelling) when Quaker Oats introduced Quaker 100 percent Natural Granola in 1972. Unfortunately for the healthy image, the Center for Science in the Public Interest revealed that it contained more saturated fat than a McDonald's hamburger, though this did not dissuade other major manufactures from following suit: Pet with Heartland Natural, Kellogg's with Country Morning, and General Mills with a brand simply called Granola.

THE FIRST **BRIDGE (CARD GAME)**

probably originated in Turkey, where the first laws of the game were compiled about 1885 by John Collinson, an English visitor to Constantinople. On his return to London he published a pamphlet titled *Biritch or Russian Whist* in February 1886. The Russian origin he ascribed to the game is unsupported by any evidence, and the word *biritch*, while it exists in Russian, means a town crier, not something with any apparent connection to the game.

Writing in 1906, a well-known exponent of the game, William Dalton, suggested that it may have been played in England even earlier than Collinson's return from Turkey.

We have received a letter from a well-known Greek gentleman, now resident in London, in which we are assured that the writer can remember the game of Bridge, very much in its present form, being regularly played among a colony of Greeks, settled in Manchester, of whom his own father was one, as far back as the seventies of the last century. The only important point of difference between the game as it was then played and as it is played now was, that the value of No Trumps was 10 points per trick instead of 12, and that the four aces in one hand counted 80 above the line instead of 100 as at present. Also, the lead of a heart, in answer to a double of No Trumps by the leader's partner, which is commonly supposed to have originated in America, was the general custom.

By 1892 bridge had invaded London's clubland, being played originally at the St. George's Club in Hanover Square, though it was at the Portland Club two years later that the first official laws were drawn up. Meanwhile the game had reached Paris, where a visitor from New York, Henry I. Barbey, encountered it while staying in the city during the winter of 1891–92. Fired with enthusiasm, on his return home in April 1892 he introduced it at the New York Whist Club. He later published his own set of rules and established a bridge club, the first in America.

Auction bridge is traditionally believed to have been the invention of three Anglo-Indian civilians marooned in a remote hill station in 1902 with no fourth man to make up the usual table. The first printed reference to the game is contained in a letter to the *Times* (London) of 16 January 1903 from a Mr. Oswald Crawford, lately returned from India. The following year John Doe published his *Auction Bridge* in Allahabad, and in 1906 the new version of the game was adopted by the Bath Club and regularized for four-handed play.

Contract bridge was adapted from auction bridge and the French game Plafond by the railroad magnate Harold S. Vanderbilt during a voyage aboard the SS *Finland* from San Pedro, Calif., to Havana, Cuba, in October–November 1925. Having taken what he felt were the best features of these two games, he added premiums for slams bid and made, vulnerability, and the decimal system of scoring. He put the finishing touches to his creation as the ship passed through the Panama Canal on 1 November, which may be regarded as the birth date of the new version of the game. On his return to New York, Vanderbilt had his manuscript rules typed up for distribution to his friends and introduced the game at the Knickerbocker Whist Club, where it met some resistance until it was championed by America's leading bridge player, Ely Culbertson. By 1928, the year he donated the Vanderbilt Cup for a contract bridge tournament, it had become the dominant form of the game on both the East and West coasts.

International bridge match: The first was held on 15 September 1930 at Almack's, London, between a British team captained by Lt. Col. Walter Buller and an American team captained by Ely Culbertson. The United States won the match of 200 deals by 4,845 points.

THE FIRST BUGGING SYSTEM, ELECTRONIC

SEE **loudspeaker**.

THE FIRST BUSES

were eight-seater vehicles known as *carrosses à cinq sols*. They were introduced in Paris by a company formed under royal patent in January 1662 by the French philosopher and scientist Blaise Pascal and his friend and chief financial backer the Duc de Roannez. A scheduled service began between the Porte Saint-Antoine and the Porte du Luxembourg on 18 March 1662, four vehicles running in one direction and three in the other at 7- to 8-minute intervals. It was stressed by the *commissaire* at the inauguration ceremony that the *carrosses* would leave punctually whether full or empty, an innovation in itself. The fare was a flat-rate 5 sous for the whole or any part of the journey, though later a circular route was added with intermediate fare stages.

At first the idea of an urban system of public transport was greeted with great enthusiasm, except by the soldiers and peasant classes, who were excluded from using the service under the terms of the patent. Aristocrats were known to leave their carriages at one of the termini, and brave the discomforts of sharing a confined space with seven others of humbler birth, solely for the novelty of the experience. Even the king himself indulged the popular fancy, becoming one of the few reigning monarchs who have ever traveled on a bus.

By 5 July, a further four routes had been opened, but then the craze began to wane, and as the aristocracy reverted to a more conventional mode of travel, the bourgeoisie ceased to ape their superiors and made a virtue of walking to save the fare. When Pascal died in August, a bare five months after the start of the enterprise, the *carrosses* were already running half empty, though the undertaking contrived to stay alive until the aged Duc de Roannez surrendered his monopoly nearly twenty years later. Buses were not reintroduced to Paris, or any other part of the world, until 1819, when Jacques Lafitte began operating a fleet of buses each carrying sixteen to eighteen passengers.

U.S.: The first purpose-built vehicle for localized public transportation was the *Accommodation*, commissioned by Abraham Brower from the New York coach builders Wade & Leverich in 1827 and operated up and down Broadway as far as Bleecker Street for a flat fare of 12½¢ (still called a shilling at that date). This conveyance was based on a stagecoach design, carrying up to twelve passengers in two compartments with vis-à-vis seats each accommodating three people. The sides were open, but there were blinds to roll down in inclement weather. Brower's next vehicle, the *Sociable* of 1829, took a step toward bus design by incorporating a door in the rear, whereas the *Accommodation* was entered by using steps at the side. Conceptually, though, this was still a stagecoach. It was only in the spring of 1831 that he introduced a full-sized omnibus, built for him by John Stephenson. With the word *omnibus* emblazoned in large letters on the side, it ran from the Battery to Bond Street, the shilling fares being collected by a juvenile conductor who stood on the steps at the rear. The larger vehicle was an immediate success, and by 1835 there were more than a hundred elaborately decorated buses operating in the streets of New York. Brower's big bus was not, however, the first of a recognizable bus design to enter service. In the previous year, 1830, long-bodied vehicles probably based on similar omnibuses recently introduced in London began operating in Washington, D.C. They ran on two routes, from Georgetown to the Navy Yard and between the wharves and L Street, and as in New York the flat fare was 12½¢. The buses were single-deck twelve-seaters, passengers facing each other in rows of six. Washingtonians called them "seagoing hacks," the streets being so awash with mud.

Self-propelled omnibus: The first was the ten-seat steam-driven *Infant*, built by Walter Hancock and put into service experimentally "as a means of dissipating . . . prejudices" (it was not licensed to carry paying passengers) in London between Stratford and the City in 1831. The first scheduled service for paying passengers was inaugurated by the London & Paddington Steam Carriage Co. on 22 April 1833, when Hancock's fourteen-seat *Enterprise* began plying between Paddington and the City. During the next three and a half years the company's steam buses carried 12,761 passengers without mishap and traveled 4,200 route miles, but they were finally driven off the road by unnecessarily harsh restrictions on their use.

U.S.: The first self-propelled bus was an electric surrey built in 1891 by William Morrison and powered by a 44-hp DC motor with a Siemens armature. Electricity was supplied by 24 storage batteries weighing 768 pounds in total. The vehicle was purchased in 1892 by J. B. MacDonald, president of the American Battery Co., and it was used by the firm of Harold Sturges and John A. Qualey to carry passengers around the grounds of the 1893 World's Columbian Exhibition in Chicago. Bench-style forward-facing seats provided accommodation for eight passengers.

Gasoline-engined bus: The first was a 5-hp Benz single-deck enclosed landau, which began running on a 9.3-mile route, Siegen–Netphen–Deuz, in the North Rhineland of Germany on 18 March 1895. Operated by a local cooperative, the Netphener Omnibus Co., the bus could seat six to eight passengers inside and another two outside on the driver's box. The driver was Hermann Golze from Netphen. A second, exactly similar bus came into service on 1 July 1895. They maintained an average speed (without stops) of 8.7 mph and took 1 hour 20 minutes for the complete journey. The buses were heated inside for winter comfort, a luxury not afforded by the post-wagon that had previously constituted the sole means of public transport on the route. On the other hand, passengers could be called upon to get out and help push the bus uphill whenever required. High operating costs and frequent breakdowns combined to render the service

uneconomic, and it closed down on 20 December 1895. The two vehicles had carried 10,600 fare-paying passengers during the time they had been on the road.

The first full-size gasoline omnibus with a conventional bus body in regular service was a 16-hp 6-ton single-deck Tenting Omnibus seating eighteen passengers, which was running between Nantes and Vetheuil, France, by March 1898. The first to ply a city route were two steel-tired 12-hp German Daimlers with twenty-six-seat Bayley double-decker bodies, introduced by the Motor Traction Co. on 9 October 1899 on a route from Kennington in South London to Victoria Station via Westminster Bridge.

U.S.: The first motor bus to run on a regular route had a De Dion–Bouton engine and chassis imported from France by the Fifth Avenue Coach Co. of New York and body work by the J. G. Brill Co. of Philadelphia. The single twenty-four-seat double-decker started working the Fifth Avenue route in 1905 at a fare of 10¢, and within two years the company had added another fourteen. In 1908 it put a further twenty motor buses into service and at the same time sold off all its horses at auction.

Inter-city bus service was inaugurated between London and Clacton, Essex, by the London Motor Van & Wagon Co. at the beginning of August 1898. The company ran four vehicles every Friday from Clacton to London and back to Clacton, taking 5½ hours in each direction to cover the 70-mile distance. The service does not appear to have been sustained for more than a few weeks.

U.S.: The first service was established by the Nassau County Motor Coach Co., founded early in 1899 to run coaches between suburban points on Long Island. After this there was little progress until 1905. On 13 April of that year the Gas Engine & Machine Co. of Portland began a service covering the 80-mile route from Shaniko to Bend in Oregon. Journey time was 5 hours.

The first coast-to-coast service was inaugurated on 5 September 1928 by Pioneer Yelloway in a California Transit Co. bus from Los Angeles via Denver, St. Louis, and Pittsburgh to New York. The distance of 3,433 miles was covered in 5 days and 14 hours, 24 hours longer than the average train time but a lot cheaper.

~~~~~~~~~~~~~~~~~~~~~~~~~ C ~~~~~~~~~~~~~~~~~~~~~~~~~~~~~

THE FIRST **CALCULATOR**

was the "calculator-clock" for addition, subtraction, division, and multiplication built by Wilhelm Schickard of Tübingen, Germany, in 1623. The invention is usually attributed to the French polymath Blaise Pascal, who constructed his ingenious "pascaline" in 1642, but the publication in 1957 of Schickard's papers, which had been missing until they were found by German historian Franz Hammer in 1935, provided evidence of his priority. The first to be manufactured was the arithometer, introduced in France in 1820 by Thomas de Colmar.

The first calculator with a keyboard was marketed by Door Felt of Chicago, who sold his first Comptometer to the Equitable Gas, Light & Fuel Co. in January 1888. He then founded the Felt & Tarrant Manufacturing Co., which developed the first recording calculator, the Comptograph. The initial sale was to the Manufacturers' Merchant Bank of Pittsburgh in December 1889.

The first all-transistor calculator was the 55-pound desktop CS-10A Compet produced in 1964 by Japanese electronics giant Sharp. The first handheld electronic calculator was an experimental model built by microchip pioneer Jack Kilby of Texas Instruments together with Jerry Merryman and James van Tassel and presented to the company's executive vice president, P. E. Haggerty, on 29 March 1967. Texas Instruments formed an association with Japan's Canon Business Machines to develop the idea commercially, and the resulting Pocketronic, with printout on thermal paper tape, was launched in Tokyo on 15 April 1970. Despite its name, the Pocketronic weighed 2½ pounds and would have required a capacious pocket. Truly pocket-size electronic calculators bowed on 1 February 1972 with the Hewlett-Packard HP-35, manufactured at the company's Advanced Products Division in Cupertino, Calif.

THE FIRST **CALL GIRLS**

in the literal sense, meaning ladies of easy virtue whose services could be ordered by telephone, were operating in Melbourne, Australia, as early as 1891. Madames of all the leading city brothels agreed to establish a telephone network to enable tired businessmen to book the girl of their choice without the need of a personal visit.

U.S.: New Orleans, at the time the only city in the United States with licensed prostitution, had in the 1890s a publication called the *Blue Book* that listed in alphabetical order more than seven hundred white, mixed-race, and black women whose services were available, together with their addresses and, for the most successful or enterprising, their telephone numbers. New Orleans's most luxurious bordello, the Arlington, which boasted that its walls were graced with "the work of great artists from Europe and America," also operated the call-girl system: the number was MAIN 1888.

THE FIRST **CANNED FOOD**

was based on a technique for preserving perishable foods in sealed containers discovered by Parisian confectioner Nicolas Appert. He developed a commercially practicable process in response to an offer made by the French government in 1795 of a 12,000-franc prize for an improved method of food conservation. Appert himself did not use metal canisters but employed glass bottles. It is generally accepted, however, that the present-day canning industry owes its inception to Appert's pioneer work in the art of preservation. The first independent test of his products was made in 1804, when the minister of marine directed that samples be sent for appraisal to the naval station at Brest. The bottles were kept for three months before opening. The marine prefect then submitted the following report to the Board of Health in Paris: "The broth in bottles was good; the broth included with boiled beef, in a special vessel, good also but weak; the beef itself very edible. The beans and green peas, prepared both with and without meat, have all the freshness and the agreeable flavor of freshly picked vegetables." During the course of the same year Appert established a factory at Massy, just outside Paris, and laid out a market garden on the adjoining land in order to grow his own fruit and vegetables for bottling.

The use of tinplate cans for preserving food on a commercial scale was pioneered by Donkin & Hall, who established the world's first cannery at Blue Anchor Road, Bermondsey, in London in 1812. Appert's principal difficulty had been in sealing the bottles—he used up to five layers of cork cut so that the pores ran horizontally—and it was to solve this problem that Bryan Donkin and John Hall decided to experiment with tin cans. For the sum of £1,000 they acquired the rights to a patent, taken out in 1810 by their associate Peter Durand, that covered the use of "vessels of tin or other metals" for food preservation.

The first consumers of canned goods were Capt. George King and the crew of the *Mary & Susannah* on a round-trip to Jamaica between November 1812 and July 1813, an experiment undertaken at the behest of Peter Durand. On his return Capt. King reported that "the meats and soups I opened during the voyage, were as good as when first put up, and I have no doubt will keep in all climates." He brought back with him four unused tins, one of which was kept by the partners; another was sent to the Prince Regent, and a third was sent to his brother the Duke of Kent (father of Queen Victoria), who responded with a testimonial that its contents "with the addition of a little sauce and vegetables, proved as excellent a dish as any one could desire to have at their table." The fourth tin went to the Commissioners for Victualing His Majesty's Navy and resulted in the first sale of canned goods, the navy ordering canned meat to be carried to both the West Indies and East Indies in trials where it would form part of the diet of sick and convalescent sailors. The navy was to become the cannery's largest customer, particularly after canned food was added to the rations of the healthy seamen (1846), varying

their monotonous diet of salt pork, sauerkraut, cheese, pease, and hardtack.

Encouraged by the navy's positive response, Donkin, Hall & Gamble (as the firm had become) sent sample cans to high-ranking officers of the army. One of these was the illustrious Lord Wellesley, later Duke of Wellington, whose secretary wrote to say that he had found the preserved beef very good. Unfortunately the writer was tactless enough to add that His Lordship could not reply himself as he was indisposed. Favorable reports having been received, the authorities ordered supplies for a number of overseas stations the following year, including St. Helena and the West Indies.

A list of the supplies delivered to the Admiralty Victualing Depot by Donkin, Hall & Gamble between March and December 1818 gives an indication of the range of canned foods then available. The Admiralty order, totaling 23,779 cans, included the following: Mess Beef, Corned Round of Beef, Roasted Beef, Seasoned Beef, Boiled Mutton, Seasoned Mutton, Boiled Veal, Roasted Veal, Veal and Vegetables, Soup and Boulli, Vegetable Soup, Mess Beef and Vegetables, and Concentrated Soup.

Vegetables on their own had made their appearance by 1824, when Capt. W. E. Parry ordered 12,000 pounds of canned carrots and 8,000 pounds of canned parsnips for his second voyage in search of a Northwest Passage. Two cans from his expedition—one a 4-pound tin of Roast Veal, the other a 2-pound tin of Carrots and Gravy—were brought back to England and preserved intact until 1936, when they were opened by scientists of the International Tin Research and Development Council. The contents of the 112-year-old veal tin were fed to young rats and an adult cat without any adverse effects. The carrots had the appearance of freshly cooked vegetables on opening but had a metallic smell and taste.

The cans used by Donkin, Hall & Gamble were filled through a small aperture in the top, which was then sealed with a soldered disk. Manufacture was by hand, and in the 1840s it was recorded that sixty canisters a day was the maximum output of an expert craftsman. The can opener being unknown at this time, directions on the label of the can read, "Cut round on the top near to the outer edge with a chisel and a hammer." This cumbersome method seems to have persisted for many years, the earliest patent on a **can opener** being granted to cutler and surgical instrument maker Robert Yeates of Hackney Road, London, on 13 July 1855. The Yeates can opener was attached to a clasp-knife.

U.S.: English immigrants were the first to produce preserved foods, led by former pickling specialist William Underwood of Boston, who began bottling lobster and salmon by the Appert process in 1819, followed by Thomas Kensett in New York, whose oysters and other seafood also came in glass jars. Both firms started using cans in 1839, by which time Kensett was partnered by Ezra Dragett and had moved operations to Baltimore. It was Underwood's that gave the English language the word "can," first used in that year instead of the British term "tin" by bookkeepers at the Boston cannery as an abbreviation of "canister." Canned goods were adopted by the U.S. Army during the Civil War, the first time they were consumed on a mass scale in America: Armies so provisioned did not have to carry their meat on the hoof or live off the land as they had in previous campaigns. After the war they became a staple of the civilian diet, and by the 1870s America was producing a wider variety of canned food in far greater quantities than any other country.

Although canned goods had become available in English shops in 1830, their exterior appearance remained as starkly utilitarian as the goods supplied on contract, and it was left to the more sales-conscious Americans to realize the need for attractive packaging. The earliest known colored pictorial label was designed for Reckhow & Larne of New York, probably in the 1860s, and depicts a dish of tomatoes in red and green against a sky blue background. The sole surviving example of this label was found on an empty tin can in an old house in Salem, Ind.

SEE ALSO **baked beans**.

THE FIRST
CAPITAL PUNISHMENT, ABOLITION

was enacted by Leopold of Lorraine, Grand Duke of Tuscany, then a sovereign state, under his penal reforms of 30 November 1786. The death penalty was restored after the fall of Napoleon. The nation in which capital punishment has longest been in abeyance is Finland, where the last execution took place in 1824. From 1826 death sentences were automatically commuted for all crimes except treason in Russia and Finland, then under the sovereignty of its powerful neighbor. In Russia the death penalty was restored when the Soviets seized control, but in Finland, which had secured its independence in 1882, the practice of commuting the sentence continued until the death penalty was formally abolished in 1949.

U.S.: The first state to abolish capital punishment, and also the first jurisdiction in the English-speaking world to do so, was Michigan under an act passed by the legislature on 4 May 1846 and effective on 1 January 1847. (No English-speaking nation followed suit until New Zealand in 1936.) In 1972 the U.S. Supreme Court ruled capital punishment unconstitutional in *Furman v. Georgia*, on grounds that those executed were disproportionately black and poor, but this was overturned by *Gregg v. Georgia* in 1976.

Today thirty-eight American states and seventy-four nations retain capital punishment, of which the United States is numerically the fourth most frequent practitioner (after China, Iran, and North Korea). The Democratic Republic of the Congo, Pakistan, Yemen, Saudi Arabia, Nigeria, and Iran retain the death penalty for juveniles, the latter having imposed it on schoolgirls of fourteen for the crime of criticizing the government.

THE FIRST **CARDIAC SURGERY**

involving a suture of the heart itself (SEE NOTE BELOW) was performed by Ludwig Rehn at Frankfurt City Hospital, in Frankfurt, Germany, on 9 September 1896. The patient, a twenty-two-year-old gardener's assistant called Wilhelm Justus, had been stabbed in the heart by an unknown assailant after a tavern brawl. A wound 1.5 cm long was found in the right ventricle, from which there was active bleeding. It was closed with three silk sutures and the blood was removed from the pleural and pericardial cavities; the patient made a complete recovery. Out of the 124 cases of cardiac surgery coming to Rehn's notice during the ensuing ten years, about 40 percent of the patients survived; formerly mortality among victims of heart wounds had been almost 100 percent.

Note: Earlier claims on behalf of such nineteenth-century luminaries as the Catalán Francisco Romero, the French military surgeon Baron Larry, Henry Dalton of St. Louis City Hospital, and the black Chicago surgeon Dr. Daniel Hale Williams were limited to incisions of the pericardium (the tissue sac surrounding the heart), and these operations, notable as they were in their time, are not generally regarded as heart surgery proper.

The first **open-heart surgery** was conduced at the University of Minnesota, Minneapolis, on 2 September 1952 by a team led by Dr. Walton Lillihei and Dr. John Lewis, who lowered five-year-old Jackie Johnson's body temperature to 79°F to slow the flow of blood. After the operation a 40-minute hot bath restored her circulation.

Heart bypass surgery was first carried out at the Albert Einstein College of Medicine–Bronx Municipal Hospital Center by Dr. Robert H. Goetz on 2 May 1960, performing an intima-to-intima anastamosis with the vessels held together with circumferential ligatures. The anastamosis was performed in 17 seconds, and the patient, a cabdriver suffering from angina, survived for thirteen months. It was Dr. Goetz's only bypass, as most members of the cardiac department were vehemently opposed to the technique. The continuous development of bypass surgery, and the first to be carried out using the now standard suture technique, dates from the pioneering work by Dr. Vasilii Kolesov at the First Leningrad Medical Institute in the Soviet Union, with a series of operations beginning on 25 February 1964. He used the mammary artery from inside the chest wall to create a bypass to the coronary artery. Five of his first six patients survived. Bypass surgery was reintroduced in the United States at the Cleveland Clinic by Argentine surgeon René Gerónimo Favaloro, who reported several operations in which he had used the saphenous vein from the leg in May 1967.

Heart transplant: The first was performed by Prof. Christian Barnard at Groote Schuur Hospital, Cape Town, South Africa, on 2 December 1967, when Louis Waskansky, a wholesale grocer suffering from chronic heart disease, received the heart of twenty-five-year-old traffic victim Denise Darvali. The operation took 6 hours, and Prof. Barnard worked with a team of thirty, all of them highly qualified white doctors and nurses except one, a poorly educated black gardener called Hamilton Naki. Employed unofficially as a lab assistant, Naki was so adept at surgical procedures that Barnard insisted that he participate in the groundbreaking operation. Waskansky died of pneumonia eighteen days later owing to the effects of the drugs administered to prevent rejection of the new heart. Subsequent patients of Barnard's achieved a significant extension to what would otherwise have been their very limited life expectancy. The first heart transplant patient to survive for his natural life span was Emmanuel Vitria, who was given a new heart at Salvator Hospital in Marseilles on 28 November 1968 and lived until May 1987.

U.S.: The first was performed at Maimonides Medical Center, Brooklyn, by surgeon Adrian Kantrowitz on 6 December 1967, but the patient, a two-year-old infant, survived only a few hours owing to immunological problems. The first successful operation was by Dr. Denton Cooley on 2 May 1968 at St. Luke's Episcopal Hospital, Houston, Tex. The patient, a forty-seven-year-old man, received the heart of a fifteen-year-old girl who had committed suicide. He survived for 204 days.

THE FIRST **CARTOON**

in America is customarily but incorrectly attributed to Benjamin Franklin, whose "Join or Die" depicting a snake divided in eight pieces (representing the principal colonies) appeared in the *Pennsylvania Gazette* in May 1754. William Murrell of the Whitney Museum of American Art argued persuasively in his *History of American Graphic Humor* (1933) that it was not intended as a cartoon but as a political emblem, endlessly reproduced in other papers supportive of the federalist cause. Franklin, was, however, a prominent figure behind America's first cartoon proper, a 10"x 14" engraving of 1764 entitled *The Paxton Expedition* by Henry Dawkins of Philadelphia. The "Paxton Boys" were frontiersmen who had massacred peaceful

Indians in their area and been denounced by Franklin. When they marched on Philadelphia, the governor called for volunteers, and it is these ragtaggle worthies, shown mustering before the State House, who are exposed to ridicule in the caricature. More than a hundred figures are shown, of whom about twenty have speech balloons emanating from their mouths.

Newspaper cartoon: The first in the United States was titled "Gerrymander," by Elkanah Tisdale, and appeared in the *Boston Weekly Messenger* for 26 March 1812. It depicted a grouping of political wards in Essex County, Mass., in the form of a salamander, and referred to this arbitrary act intended to produce a Democratic majority in elections for Congress. "Gerry," the name of the governor alleged to have fomented this scheme, was attached to the last two syllables of "salamander" (a fabulous bird of evil disposition) to produce a neologism that has survived to this day.

All early cartoons were either political or caricatures of well-known people. The earliest known **joke cartoon** is titled "How to Follow a Prescription" and depicts an exchange between a lodger and a servant in a boardinghouse with some rather lame repartee printed beneath. It is unsigned but may have been by the precocious teenaged Canadian artist Napoleon Sarony. It appeared originally as a print sold by stationers and subsequently as a woodcut in *The Devil's Comical Texas Oldmanick 1837* (New York, 1836). Generally, though, the joke cartoon only took hold with the satirical weeklies published in imitation of Britain's celebrated *Punch* (1841), led by *Yankee Doodle* (New York, 1846) and *John Donkey* (Philadelphia, 1848).

Cartoons in newspapers remained exceptional until the second half of the nineteenth century. The first newspaper to use cartoons on a regular basis was James Gordon Bennett's *Evening Telegram*, which began in New York in 1867 and published a half-page political caricature on its front page every Friday. The most distinguished of its earliest cartoonists was Charles G. Bush. The *New York Daily Graphic*, starting in 1873, ranged more widely in its caricatures, with social satires by Arthur Lumley and by C. Grey-Parker, an English-born cartoonist who specialized in pretty women and fast horses and who has been hailed as a precursor of George Du Maurier in England and Charles Dana Gibson in America. The

work of another contributor, about whom nothing is known, appeared over the signature "Miranda." Could this have been America's first woman cartoonist? (The first woman on record to draw political cartoons for a newspaper was Edwina Dumm for the *Columbus Monitor* in 1916.)

The newspaper cartoon became a strong political force with the advent of daily cartoons drawn by Walt McDougall and Valerian Gribayédoff in Joseph Pulitzer's *New York World* during the presidential campaign of 1884. Combined with the paper's partisan editorializing, they helped to secure the election of Grover Cleveland, first Democratic president since the Civil War.

The **colored cartoon** entered the newspaper sphere with Charles Saalburg's "The Ting-Lings" (a kind of Oriental version of the Brownies; SEE **character merchandising**) in the children's supplement of the *Chicago Inter-Ocean* from 15 May 1894.

Cartoons, however scabrous, are often cherished by their victims, who beg for the originals. Not so, though, in the case of some leading members of the California legislature, who in 1897 promoted a bill banning caricatures of themselves. So derided was this measure that even though it passed into law, it was disregarded by the newspapers it sought to muzzle.

SEE ALSO **comic strip**.

THE FIRST **CCTV SURVEILLANCE**
....
operation was by London's Metropolitan Police, which erected two cameras lent to them by EMI to monitor the crowds in Trafalgar Square on the occasion of the state visit by the king and queen of Thailand, 19–21 July 1960. On 5 November the same year they were again set up in Trafalgar Square to keep an electronic eye on what one assistant commissioner called "the usual Guy Fawkes rabble" (Guy Fawkes Night, commemorating the 1605 attempt to blow up the Houses of Parliament, being Britain's principal occasion for letting off fireworks).

The first use of CCTV as security against criminal activity occurred in Liverpool in 1964, when four cameras were mounted on buildings in the downtown commercial area. "Operation Commando" involved the use of fifty-nine plainclothes officers on the ground who were in touch by walkie-talkie. Although no arrests were made, the Liverpool police claimed that it had been a success because public knowledge of the operation had deterred would-be offenders. The Home Office (responsible for policing in Britain) was more skeptical, asserting that it was more likely that the presence of fifty-nine undercover agents had discouraged the commission of crime. Later the same year the Metropolitan Police made the first CCTV installation resulting in arrests, with hidden cameras in London's jewelry district, Hatton Garden, providing evidence on three occasions of attempted fencing of stolen property.

After a number of other experiments, the first permanent installation of CCTV cameras was made in 1968 following the anti–Vietnam War riot outside the American Embassy in Grosvenor Square in October of that year. Three of what had been intended to be temporary sites were left in situ, and early the following year others were established in London's Whitehall and Parliament Square. All the early CCTV surveillance systems were covert (the Metropolitan Police had been greatly encouraged that none of the fifty or so Council of Civil Liberties observers had noticed the cameras at the Grosvenor Square demonstration). The first permanent and public installation for the control of crime was at the seaside resort of Bournemouth in August 1985, followed by cameras at Edinburgh housing projects two years later. By the early 1990s there were an estimated 1 million surveillance cameras in Britain's inner cities, the highest density in the world.

U.S.: The earliest reports of surveillance cameras in public places appeared in New York newspapers in 1965. CCTV was installed in Times Square in 1973 but was abandoned after eighteen months when there had only been ten arrests directly attributable to the cameras, all for trivial offenses. When they came back a few years later, it was with a vengeance. By 2002 there were 258 cameras, making it the most heavily monitored area in the United States.

THE FIRST **CELLOPHANE**

was developed by Dr. Jacques Brandenberger, a Swiss chemist employed by textile manufacturers Blanchisserie et Teinturerie of Thaon-les-Vosges, France, in an attempt to produce an up-market version of oilcloth by treating fabric with viscose. This idea had been inspired in 1904 by a minor accident in a restaurant when a waiter knocked over a bottle of red wine, saturating the tablecloth. Brandenberger labored for the next nine years in unsuccessful attempts to apply a thin film of cast viscose onto a textile surface. Abandoning the notion of a wipe-clean tablecloth, he went into partnership with France's major producer of viscose, Le Comptoir des Textiles Artificiels, setting up a firm called La Cellophane in November 1913 to manufacture cellophane safety film for cinematography at a small factory in Thaon. Nitrate cinema film was highly inflammable, but unfortunately cellophane was not the answer, being too flimsy and difficult to perforate effectively. After failing to revolutionize the textile and cinema industries, Brandenberger selected a third, which he did indeed succeed in transforming: packaging. At 50 centimes a square meter, the target market was luxury goods. The first product to be wrapped in cellophane was Coty perfume (already packed in a bottle, so the wrapping was purely decorative), followed by Gibbs dentifrice, which came in the form of a round tablet, and gingerbread from an exclusive Paris boulangerie.

The outbreak of World War I interrupted cellophane's progress as the first plastic packaging material, and production at Thaon was placed on a war footing with the manufacture of lenses for gas masks. At the end of hostilities the chemical giant DuPont, anxious to diversify out of munitions, acquired the American rights to viscose from Brandenberger's partner, Le Comptoir des Textiles Artificiels, which suggested that the deal should be extended to include manufacturing rights to cellophane. DuPont agreed, and it was Jacques Brandenberger himself who pulled America's first sheet of cellophane out of the rolling machine at the new viscose plant near Buffalo, N.Y., on 4 April 1924. The first cellophane-wrapped product in the United States was Whitman's Chocolates from Philadelphia. There was, however, a problem.

Cellophane would only be viable for DuPont if it could expand out of the luxury goods market and into high-volume mass-produced goods such as groceries, but Brandenberger's formula had a significant disadvantage: It admitted moisture. The solution was found by twenty-seven-year-old DuPont research chemist William Hale Church, who discovered that a composition of nitrocellulose and wax would act as a barrier, and the first batch of moisture-proof cellophane was rolled in June 1926. As the price dropped from $1.45 per pound in 1927 to 23¢ ten years later, cellophane launched the pre-wrapped foodstuffs revolution that made self-service and the supermarket a practical reality.

THE FIRST **CENTRAL HEATING**

was a steam-pipe system devised by James Watt, the Scottish-born inventor whose steam engine powered the industrial revolution; it was installed in 1784 at the Boulton and Watt Soho Manufactory near Birmingham, England. The Soho Manufactory produced a huge range of metal goods and at that date was the largest hardware factory in the world, employing probably in excess of a thousand men, women, and children. It is doubtful that it was simply benevolence that motivated Watt and his partner, Matthew Boulton, to heat their vast concourse of workshops from a central source; warm workers performed more efficiently than cold ones in the chilly climate of the English Midlands.

At about the same time, Matthew Boulton's private residence, Soho House, is believed to have also been heated by steam, but little is known about this installation, probably the world's first domestic central heating since the Romans' underfloor hypocausts. Rather more is known about the system that replaced it when the house was remodeled and enlarged by the architect brothers James and Samuel Wyatt between 1796 and 1805. Somewhat surprisingly this did not depend on steam. An enclosed coal-fired furnace, or "cockle," in the cellar circulated warm air around the building by convection. Cold-air ducts from outside supplied air to the stove and passed through a heat exchanger, then via a large rectangular duct to subsidiary ducts, which circulated warm air beneath the floors and between the hollow walls. An arrangement of holes in the risers of the staircase allowed warm air to escape to heat the passages. Temperature was regulated by key-operated flaps to open or close off different sections of the ducting.

Whereas the Soho Manufactory has long since ceased to exist, Soho House survives and has recently been restored and opened to the public. Modern engineers have tested the central heating system, and more than two centuries on, it still works.

U.S.: The first system to be adopted in America was developed by Oliver Evans of Philadelphia and illustrated in the 1795 first edition of his *The Young Mill-Wright and Miller's Guide*. As at Soho House, a closed stove in the basement of a building carried hot air through ducts to the various rooms to be heated. From a footnote in the text it is apparent that Evans had actually constructed one of these systems, but he does not say where. The earliest American central heating system of which we have certain knowledge was the work of Evans's fellow Philadelphian Daniel Pettibone, whose "rarifying air stove" of 1808 was installed at the White House in 1813, at the Patapsco Cotton Mill in the Patapsco Valley, Md., in 1815, and in the Hall of Representatives in the Capitol in Washington, D.C., in 1818. The latter remained in use until the late 1850s. Contemporary with these was a hot-air system laid by Jacob Perkins at the Massachusetts Medical College in Boston in 1815. The earliest known domestic installation was made by Reuben Haines III at his Queen Anne mansion Wyck in Philadelphia in November 1820. This was a hot-air system fueled by anthracite.

Early central heating systems used either warm air ducts or steam pipes. The first central heating system to incorporate hot water **radiators** was patented in Britain by Jacob Perkins's American-born son Angier March Perkins on 30 July 1831 and installed at the bookbinding establishment of Robert Caddell in Edinburgh, Scotland, two years later. About the same time, this high-pressure hot water (HPHW) system with coiled radiators was put in service at his father's Adelaide Gallery in London, a showcase for popular science exhibits and "objects blending instruction with amusement," and at the

British Museum Reading Room (now the British Library). Others were installed at the Bank of England, the Elephant House at Regent's Park Zoo, and Mr. Palmer's hothouses at Parson's Green (reported in the *Gardener Magazine* for April 1832). The pipes for Perkins's system were manufactured from surplus rifle barrels produced by Thomas Russell's pipe foundry, and the installations were made by Walker & Sons of Clerkenwell.

A young American from Boston, Joseph Nason, worked for Angier Marsh Perkins in London and on his return to the United States in 1841 introduced coil radiators in the counting room of the Middlesex Mill at Lowell, Mass., and later, in 1846, at the Eastern Exchange Hotel in Boston. Nason-Perkins's coil radiators were placed in the White House in 1853. Joseph Nason is credited with introducing the word *radiator*.

On 30 October 1854 Stephen J. Gould of New Haven, Conn., patented his "mattress radiator," essentially a **panel radiator**, though it is not known whether this went into production. Panel radiators failed to make any marked impact on domestic heating until their reintroduction by Runtal Radiation of Switzerland c. 1950. **Cast-iron radiators** were patented in 1855 by A. D. Pelton of Clifton, Conn., and by Italian-born German citizen Franz SanGalli of St. Petersburg, Russia. The latter's innovation is commemorated by a monument of a cat sleeping in front of a SanGalli radiator, which was unveiled at the Samara power station in 2005.

THE FIRST **CESAREAN SECTION**

in which both mother and baby survived is alleged to have been performed on the wife of Jacob Nufer, a pig gelder of Sigershauffen, Switzerland, in 1500. The operation was carried out by Jacob himself with his pig-gelding instruments. According to François Rosset's text on cesarean section, 1581, Frau Nufer lived to the age of seventy-seven and subsequent to the operation was delivered of a pair of twins and four other children, all by normal delivery. This remarkable postoperative history has caused some authorities to cast doubt on the authenticity of the episode.

The first successful cesarean section to have been authenticated was performed in Charlemont, Ireland, in January 1738 by an illiterate local midwife, Mary Donally, who used a razor to deliver her patient, Alice O'Neal, of a healthy child. The mother had been twelve days in labor at the time of the operation. Having cut through the abdominal wall and opened up the uterus, Mary Donally removed the child, placenta, and membrane, and then held the lips of the incision together with her hands while neighbors went a mile in search of silk and a tailor's needle. The wound was dressed with white of egg after stitching, and Alice made such a rapid recovery that she was able to go about her normal business on the twenty-seventh day after the operation.

The first successful cesarean section to be performed by a qualified medical practitioner took place at Blackburn, Lancashire, in England in 1793, when Dr. James Barlow delivered a child from a patient with a fractured pelvis. It was to be many years before the operation became in any degree routine. According to one medical historian, not a single woman survived cesarean section in Paris between 1787 and 1876. **U.S.:** Performed by Dr. Jesse Bennet of Edom, Va., on his wife Elizabeth on 14 January 1794. Another local doctor was asked to assist, but he refused as he considered the operation too dangerous. Two field hands were drafted to hold the unfortunate patient down on a wooden table during the operation. Mother and baby both survived.

THE FIRST **CHAIN LETTER**

known is in the VanArsdale Chain Letter Archive in Lompoc, Calif., and was sent from Hartford, Vt., with a covering letter from Ella A. Keagen (?) dated 4 September 1888 to Miss Helen E. Wood of Lebanon, N.H. The chain letter itself is signed by a Mrs. George O. Haman and seeks donations for the education of the children of poor whites in the Cumberlands region of Appalachia. "Four of us have agreed each to give ten cents and to write to four friends, asking of each two favors," explains Mrs. Haman. "First that they will wrap a dime in paper enclosed in an envelope and mail to Mrs. Geo. O. Haman, Sherwood,

Tenn.—second that you will send this letter or a copy of it to four of your personal friends, asking of them the same two favors." She concluded, "If you will do this you will receive the Blessing of Him who was ready to die for us" (in marked contrast to modern chain letters, which promise the direst consequences for any who break the chain).

The chain letter promising personal enrichment in a pecuniary sense did not emerge until the dark days of the Depression. What is believed to have been the earliest was started by a person or persons unknown in Denver, Colo., in April 1935 under the name of the Prosperity Club. The letter contained a list of five names and addresses with a request to send a dime to the name at the head of the list. This name was then deleted, the recipient added his or her own to the bottom of the list, and the letter was copied to five friends or acquaintances. In theory, assuming that no one broke the chain, each participant would in course of time receive 15,625 envelopes (5 to the power of 5) containing a dime, a total of $1,562.50 for an outlay of 10¢ plus five 2¢ stamps.

The chain letter craze spread through Denver so rapidly that within two or three weeks the post office was handling up to 165,000 additional pieces of mail a day and had been obliged to hire 100 casual workers to sort them. On 20 April the *Denver Post* declared that nearly every household in the city had received at least one chain letter, though there were no reports of anyone receiving 15,625 envelopes containing dimes.

The chain expanded beyond Denver rapidly, with more than 200 "send a dime" letters addressed to President Franklin D. Roosevelt being received at the White House. New chains based on a $1 or $10 contribution followed, and there was even one with an ante of $100—not surprisingly, this emanated from Hollywood. Variants included the "send a pint" letter with pints of bourbon substituted for cash, a panty chain started in Dallas, and a dating chain at the University of California that was supposed to provide the 6,000 coeds on campus with 26,000 dates each.

THE FIRST **CHARACTER MERCHANDISING**

began in or before 1888 with the production of goods based on Ally Sloper, a comic character originally created by Charles Ross for the London cartoon weekly *Judy* in 1867 and featured in *Ally Sloper's Half-Holiday* from 1884 to 1916. According to G. K. Chesterton, the disreputable bottle-nosed drunkard in the high choker, worn tail coat, and battered top hat was based on Charles Dickens's Mr. Micawber. By the mid-1890s this mischief-maker had evolved into the more genial FoM, or "Friend of Man," and a Brighton journal declared that he had become the most famous fictional character in Britain, which, considering Sherlock Holmes was then at the peak of his popularity, was testimony to his status as a cultural icon.

During the opening decade of the twentieth century W. C. Fields, then a vaudeville artiste, toured the English music halls. It is believed that he based his subsequent stage persona and costume on Ally Sloper, neither needing much adjustment when he played his acclaimed Micawber in the 1935 movie of *David Copperfield*.

The earliest Sloper product that can be dated with certainty is a nickel-plated brass match-safe with the striker beneath Ally's hinged top hat, the dies for which were registered by Frederick Tomkinson of Birmingham on 31 July 1888. Examples are now sufficiently collectable for fakes to have come on the market. It is possible that the silver Ally Sloper watch, which bore his image, may have preceded the matchbox holder. Other products included "Ally Sloper's Favourite Relish," which had a relief portrait of the hero in a state of intoxication; a tobacco humidor in the form of a china Ally Sloper head; a magic lantern together with stereoscopic slides depicting scenes such as the Friend of Man being denounced to a policeman by an outraged housemaid; clay pipes with Ally's head forming the bowl; Sloper's Pills for liver complaints, headaches, and stomach upsets (odd to associate medicine with a character renowned for unreliability); Denby-ware Sloper-head toby jugs; "Ally Sloper Waltz" sheet music; cast-iron doorstops featuring both Mr. and Mrs. Sloper; and cigars labeled Ally Sloper's Torpedoes. There were also bicycles, neckties, postcards, and letterheads. A particularly striking object was a vending machine depicting the Friend of Man that was manufactured by the Interchangeable Co. of London c. 1899. The patron put a penny in a slot in Ally's hat and pulled his bulbous nose, whereupon a novelty was delivered into a tray. Few of these articles are dated, and it is not apparent whether they were licensed or whether Gilbert Dalziel, the proprietor of *Ally Sloper's Half-Holiday*, who had bought the copyright in the character from Charles Ross, was simply gratified at the extra publicity they brought to his paper.

U.S.: The first characters to be merchandised, and possibly the first anywhere under license, were the Brownies, based on the elves of that name in Scottish folklore and featured in magazine stories, books, and plays written and illustrated by Canadian-born Palmer Cox of New York between 1881 and 1925. The earliest known product was the Brownie Blocks, copyrighted by Cox in 1891 and manufactured by New York jigsaw specialist McLaughlin Bros., comprising twenty hollow wooden cubes that would make six different pictures when placed in the right sequence. The following year Cox received a patent on twelve of his Brownies, individually represented as the Red Indian, the Russian ("Brownski"), the Chinaman ("Ah-Brown-Ees"), the Irishman ("O'Brownie"), the Policeman, the Dude, etc. Fortified by this protection, Cox issued a license to the Arnold Print Works of North Adams, Mass., which reproduced the fronts and backs of the figures on muslin sold at 20¢ a yard. These were designed to be cut out, sewn together, and stuffed, the resulting rag dolls being 7 inches high. Over the next twenty years a proliferation of Brownie merchandise followed, ranging from nursery wallpaper and candy molds to (surprisingly) mustache cups and cigar holders.

Probably the best known of all the products was the Box Brownie camera marketed in a Brownie-decorated cardboard box by Eastman Kodak in 1900. Additionally Brownies were used in advertising by Ivory Soap, Armour's Mincemeat, and Upton's Fish Glue and as a trademark on La Grippe cough drops.

Merchandising of screen characters: This started in 1914, though there is uncertainty whether the first was John Bunny or Charlie Chaplin. Both were comedians who played fictionalized versions of themselves, though the outsize, goggle-eyed Bunny was already a "name" by c. 1912, whereas Chaplin was not seen in his Little Tramp persona of derby hat, whangee cane, and outsize boots until *Kit Auto Races in Venice*, made in January 1914. Two different John Bunny dolls were marketed by the Louis Amberg Co. of New York during 1914, and Amberg also had a Chaplin doll, though given that Chaplin did not achieve a comparable celebrity until the following year, it seems likely that this originated in 1915. Bunny, however, died that year, bringing an abrupt end to merchandising opportunities, whereas Chaplin went on to even greater fame and ever increasing use of his screen character as a vehicle for toys and novelties. He was certainly the first character merchandised on an international scale, though it seems likely that many of the European games and toys were unauthorized.

The world's largest and most profitable merchandising enterprise, Disney, began in 1927 with a humble celluloid pin-back button depicting Oswald the Rabbit, who also featured in a stencil set the following year. Mickey Mouse, who made his screen debut in 1928 (SEE **film, animated**), did not become an item of merchandise until 1930 despite the fact that the character had won almost instant worldwide adulation. The first product, to be followed by literally tens of thousands of others from that date to this, was a wooden representation designed by Burton "Bert" Gillett for the George Borgfeldt Corp. of New York. On 1 July 1932 a new profession was born when Kansas City advertising executive Kay Kamen was appointed by Walt Disney (a K.C. native) to handle licensing of his ever-growing pantheon of animal cartoon characters. By 1936 Walt Disney Enterprises had an official merchandise licenser in London, William Banks Levy, who founded and published the full-color gravure *Mickey Mouse Weekly* that year. More than 140 companies held Disney licenses during the 1930s, including many that had helped to make *The Three Little Pigs* of 1933 the first film to return a higher gross in merchandising royalties than it did at the box office.

Generally speaking, merchandising spin-offs from feature films did not emerge on a regular basis until Disney's animated *Snow White and the Seven Dwarfs* of 1937 and scarcely before the 1970s for live action pictures, when the opportunities offered by *Star Wars*, whose merchandising rights were somewhat casually assigned by Twentieth Century Fox to George Lucas in exchange for a smaller cut of the gross, made the fledgling director among the richest men in Hollywood. There had, however, been a few predecessors, including an isolated example from the end of the silent era, when Universal's 1929 part-talkie *Show Boat*, based on the smash-hit Ziegfeld stage musical, stimulated the Arcade Co. of Freeport, Ill., to manufacture a lithographed tin version of the eponymous vessel. An obscure Republic Pictures sci-fi pic of 1954, *Tabor the Great*, resulted in the Ideal Toy Co.'s battery-powered Robert the Robot, an instant bestseller, and MGM's 1959 sword-and-sandal epic *Ben Hur* inspired a 217-piece replica of sets, props, and leading characters, made by Marx & Co. of New York and retailed at $12.98.

Television characters to be merchandised: The first were Howdy Doody in the United States and Muffin the Mule in the United Kingdom, both in 1949. Howdy Doody, a freckle-faced flap-eared dude cowboy who greeted his juvenile TV fans with the unchanging six-day-a-week welcome "Howdy doody, boys and girls" on NBC's *Puppet Playhouse* in 2,343 performances starting 27 December 1947, had his first spin-off in the form of a comic book for which Western Printing offered an unexpectedly high royalty as the show went into its second year. When 10 million copies flew off the newsstands, the producers realized that the future profitability of the program lay with tie-ins that could be promoted on air as part of the script. Best known of the Howdy Doody toys were the marionettes by Peter Puppet Playthings, but there were also bubble pipes by Lido Toy Co., crayons by Milton Bradley Co., plastic figures by Tea-Vea Toys, ukuleles by Emenee Industries, "Doodle" skates by Stickless Corp., plastic inflatables by Kestral Corp., and card games by Russell Manufacturing Co. The first generation of children (now drawing their pensions) to bug their parents into buying products given allure by kids' TV had been beguiled with goods to the value of $25 million when the series ended in 1960, but Howdy Doody merchandise continued on sale right into the 1970s. The savings bank, cookie jar, wristwatch, musical rocking chair, rubber masks, lightbulb cover, bow tie, Christmas stocking, and innumerable other artifacts continue to be traded at prices that can be several hundred times their original retail price (especially in original packaging) by members of the Howdy Doody Memorabilia Collectors Club, few of them alive when their wooden hero rode the electronic range.

On the other side of the Atlantic, Muffin the Mule, a marionette created by Fred Tickner, debuted as early as November 1934 as a then unnamed comic character in a circus-themed show presented by Hogarth Puppets on the BBC's low-definition television service. In 1946 Muffin returned to television, now high-definition, performing on the top of a piano played by Annette Mills (sister of film star Sir John Mills) in the BBC's *For the Children*, always introduced with the words "Here comes Muffin, Muffin the Mule, Dear old Muffin, playing the fool." From 1952 to 1957 he starred in his own BBC show, *Muffin the Mule*, the filmed episodes being syndicated in the United States. The earliest dated product is a Beeju toy television receiver whose box bears the legend "Muffin Syndicate © 1948." While it is possible that this preceded the earliest Howdy Doody products, Muffin the Mule Collectors Club doyenne Adrienne Hasler has found no evidence of it being on sale before 1950. Items that can definitely be dated to 1949, she says, include records, Huntley & Palmer biscuit tins, a song book, slippers, a glove puppet, a card game, a story book by Annette Mills, and a wooden articulated Muffin (possibly unlicensed) sold exclusively by Selfridge's department store. Another sixty or so followed, among them tea sets, mugs, and dishes, a Pin the Tail on Muffin game, lapel buttons, postcards, and a Luntoy Pull-along Muffin. More than seventy years after his original television incarnation, Muffin made another comeback to the small screen in September 2005, this time as a cartoon character, providing a new opportunity for merchandising an old favorite.

THE FIRST **CHARTER FLIGHT**

took place on 28 June 1911, the day that the ocean liner *Olympic* left New York on the return half of her maiden voyage across the Atlantic. Among the *Olympic*'s passengers was a Philadelphia merchant, W. A.

Burpee, who had broken his spectacles shortly before the ship sailed and sent them to Wanamaker's for repair. Just before the *Olympic* left harbor he sent a wireless message to the store asking them to forward the spectacles to London. An executive of Wanamaker's had heard that the celebrated English aviator Tom Sopwith was in New York with his Howard Wright biplane and suggested that the firm charter the aircraft to deliver Burpee's spectacles, which had already been repaired. Sopwith agreed to the terms offered and set off in pursuit of the *Olympic*, then a few miles out to sea. He overtook the vessel and, flying low, dropped the carefully wrapped package onto the deck.

The first regular **air charter company** was Chalk's Flying Service, established by former Illinois farmer A. B. "Poppy" Chalk on the newly formed Watson Island across the causeway from downtown Miami on 1 June 1919. The office consisted of a stand under an umbrella on Flagler Street and the sole aircraft, the first "air taxi," a three-seat Stinson Voyager with floats attached. Most of Chalk's best-paying customers were gangsters, who would charter the plane to fly them to Bimini in the British West Indies during Prohibition. Later, in the 1930s, he piloted Howard Hughes, Errol Flynn, Ernest Hemingway, and none other than the surviving father of aviation himself, Wilbur Wright, on fishing expeditions. In 1936 the name was changed to Chalk's International Airlines; sixty years later, with a change of ownership, it was renamed again as Pan Am Air Bridge. Now once again Chalk's, it continues to operate as the oldest airline in the world, its nearest competitor, Dutch national carrier KLM (founded October 1919), only able to claim to be the oldest *scheduled* airline.

THE FIRST **CHEERLEADERS**

were six male undergraduates at the University of Minnesota organized by first-year med student Johnny Campbell to lead the Gophers' fans in the varsity yell—Rah, Rah, Rah! Sku-v-mar, Hoo-Rah! Hoo-Rah! Varsity! Varsity! Varsity, Minn-e-so-tah!—at the last game of the season, played against Northwestern, on 12 November 1898. Student newspaper *Ariel* reported: "The following were nominated

to lead the Yelling today. Jack [*sic*] Campbell, F. G. Kotlaba, M. J. Luby, Albert Armstrong of the Academics, Wickersham of the Laws, and Litzenverg of the Medics. These men would see to it that everybody leaves the park today breathless and voiceless."

Cheerleading spread rapidly, a Harvard student named Franklin Delano Roosevelt revealing in a letter dated 26 October 1903 that he was a cheerleader for the game with Brown. By 1924 it had become a sufficiently organized activity, and one of increasing importance in the athletic program, for Stanford and Purdue universities to have established formal courses in cheerleading.

Flash cards were used for the first time, though on a moderate scale, at Yale Bowl Dedication Day on 21 November 1914, but they only became an essential element of grandstanding when Lindley Bothwell developed the art during his tenure as Yell King at the University of Southern California from 1920 to 1923. He trained and regimented a uniformed (white shirts, bow ties, pillbox caps) claque of 2,500 flash-carders to create elaborate and striking designs.

The date that **women cheerleaders** first emerged is not recorded (though the editor welcomes any information on this). May Ellen Hanson, in *Go! Fight! Win! Cheerleading in American Culture* (1995), cites Trinity University of San Antonio, Tex., as an early progenitor. In 1923 its thirty-strong pep squad under a male Yell Leader comprised equal numbers of men and women, while two years later women outnumbered men twenty-two to twelve and the Yell Leader, redesignated the Cheer Leader, was a coed. Elsewhere the transition was much slower, the University of Michigan finally succumbing to a mixed squad only in 1975. In that year Randy Neil, founder of the International Cheerleading Foundation, estimated that 95 percent of the five hundred thousand cheerleaders from grade school through college were female.

Cheerleading as pure entertainment emerged with the creation in 1940 of the first **drill team** at Kilgore College in Kilgore, Tex. The dean, Dr. B. E. Masters, a Baptist, formed an all-female dancing, marching, and cheering squad, the Rangerettes, to deter his students from going out for a quick fix of alcohol in the parking lot during halftime. With the girls dressed in short skirts and figure-hugging sweaters, and taught to leap, cavort, and cheer in unison by professional choreographer Miss Gussie Nell Davis, male students rapidly found the lure of the hip flask overtaken by this new form of worldly pleasure.

The first professional sports team supported by a cheerleading squad was the Baltimore Colts in 1954. These were volunteers, as were the thirty high school students comprising the Belles and Beaux whose job it was to lead collegiate-style cheers for the Dallas Cowboys from their founding in 1961. Cowboys manager Al Schramm had wanted to use glamorous models instead but was talked out of the idea. Ten years later it had become apparent that the sweet-as-apple-pie Belles and Beaux did not have what it takes to rouse the hard-boiled fans at the Cotton Bowl, and Schramm finally got his way with the formation of the first **professional cheerleading squad**, the now world-famous Dallas Cowboys Cheerleaders, starting with seven trained dancers under a Broadway choreographer in 1972.

THE FIRST **CHEWING GUM**

commercially produced, was the State of Maine Pure Spruce Gum, manufactured by twenty-one-year-old swamper John Curtis on a Franklin stove in the kitchen of his home in Bangor, Me., in 1848. At two sticks for a penny, he made $5,000 in his first year of trading. He moved to Portland in 1850, opened the world's first chewing gum factory, and began production of paraffin gums under names like Sugar Cream, White Mountain, Four-in-Hand, Biggest and Best, and Licorice Lulu. Curtis & Son (unusually, in this case the "Son" was the founding father) continued in business until 1923. The barely literate John Curtis died a multimillionaire in 1897.

The first chewing gum manufactured from chicle was produced by a Staten Island photographer named Thomas Adams. He was introduced to chicle by Gen. Antonio López de Santa Anna, the Mexican commander who had led the assault on the Alamo. The general, who had settled on Staten Island after eleven terms as president of Mexico, had brought a load of chicle with him into exile in the hope of exploiting it as a material for manufacturing tires. He and Adams formed a partnership to this end. During their many experiments the general was wont to chew on lumps of the chicle, and Adams's son Horatio also acquired the habit. When the attempts to produce synthetic rubber proved fruitless, Adams decided to recoup his outlay on the large quantity of chicle he had acquired by rolling small pieces into balls and selling it as chewing gum. The first batch went on sale at a drugstore in Hoboken, N.J., in February 1871 at 1¢ each. These balls (later replaced by strips) were unflavored. The first flavored chicle gum was Taffy-Tolu, introduced by John Colgan of Louisville, Ky., in 1875. Colgan was a pharmacist, and his flavoring was an aromatic resin from the bark of the South American tree *Myroxylon tolul-ferum*—best known as an ingredient of cough medicine. In spite of this the flavored gum caught on, and Adams countered with a sassafras gum, followed by a licorice-flavored one under the name Black Jack. This is the oldest flavored gum still on sale today.

Another of Adams's flavors, the very popular Tutti-Frutti, was the first gum to be sold from vending machines (qv), the first in America. They were installed on station platforms of the New York Elevated Railroad in 1888.

Although prim and proper Victorian Britain somewhat improbably took to chewing gum with the introduction of Beeman's Pepsin Chewing Gum in 1894 (its advertising targeted, perhaps unwisely, at the upper classes), the introduction of the habit elsewhere in the world had to await the first mass incursion of Americans to Europe in World War I. During 1918 the American Red Cross shipped 4½ million packets "over there," and doughboys were free and easy about distributing the novel treat to the local, mainly juvenile, population. Whether they intended it or not, hearts and minds had been won, and at the conclusion of hostilities massive export orders were received from France, Belgium, and Italy, as well as the United Kingdom, where Wrigley's had been entrenched since 1911 (selling gum from vending machines, as confectionery shops refused to handle anything so vulgarly American). Asia was a more difficult market, not only because of cultural differences but because the mass of the population had insufficient money to buy gum. In the early 1930s William Wrigley met this with ingenuity; he encouraged Chinese shopkeepers to unwrap the packet, cut each stick into two, and sell the half for

1 sen, a fraction of a cent. By 1935 he was selling over $1 million worth of gum a year in China. Whereas "Wrigley's" is synonomous with chewing gum in many countries, in Iran it is still called "Adams."

Bubble gum: The first successful brand was Dubble Bubble, introduced by the Fleer Chewing Gum Co. on 26 December 1928, when it went on sale at a small grocery store on Susquehanna Street in Philadelphia. Many years earlier founder Frank Fleer had attempted to market a brand called Blibber-Blubber, but this failed because it invariably burst before a satisfactory bubble was blown, and the remains could only be removed from the face with turpentine. The unsung hero who achieved the breakthrough to true bubble action was one Walter Diemer, an employee of the Fleer Co. who confessed in later years that he had been working on a quite different gummerial problem and that the bubbles were fortuitous. Unsung, that is, until his death aged 93 in 1998, when he was honored with the lead obituary in the *New York Times*.

The first bubble gum baseball cards were the 240-card *Big League Chewing Gum* set released in 1933 by the Goudey Gum Co. of Allston, Mass.

Non-stick chewing gum: The first was developed by Prof. Terence Cosgrove of Bristol University, England, who founded Revolymer in 2007 to bring it to market. Capable of being flushed off almost any surface with water, it seems poised to eradicate the stigma attached to gum in its disposal mode. It can even be washed out of hair, but Prof. Cosgrove concedes there is still one bridge to cross: the removal of his invention from shoes with leather soles.

THE FIRST **CHILDREN'S BOOK**

printed (other than schoolbooks) was *The book of Curtesye*, issued by England's first printer and publisher, William Caxton, at Westminster in London in either 1477 or 1478. Addressed to "little John," it is a book about good manners and behavior, starting with what to do on getting up: "Comb your head, clean your ears and nose and don't pick it. Wash your hands; don't keep your nails dirt-black or too long" (modern English condensation by Dr. Frederick Furnivall of the Early English Text Society). Other advice is "As you

walk, look pleasantly at folk... don't shy stones at birds or beast, or quarrel with dogs. When you speak to men, look 'em in the face. Keep secret all your hear... and don't run down absent men." Precepts for behavior at table included "Don't blow on your food," "Don't break wind up or down," and "Eat with your lips closed." Picking your teeth with a knife was also a no-no, as was leaving dirt on the towel when washing up after the meal (people ate with their hands, so this was necessary). There was also advice on what to read, with Geoffrey Chaucer given the top recommendation; as *The Book of Curtesye* was the only book specifically for children, by definition a child's reading matter had to be books written for adults. The only extant copy is in the Cambridge (England) Public Library.

Most juvenile literature prior to the mid-eighteenth century was didactic and heavy on moral exhortation. The earliest known book designed to entertain children rather than improve them was *A Booke in Englyssh Metre, of the great Marchante Man called Dives Pragmaticus, very preaty for Children to reade*, printed by Alexander Lacy, London, 1563. A small quarto of eight pages, it contains a series of rhymes, chiefly about the traders or shopkeepers who were invited to purchase stocks from Dives' extensive range of wares:

> *Dripping pans, pot hooks, old cats and kits;*
> *And preaty fine dogs, without fleas or nits.*
> *Axes for butchers, and fine glass for wives:*
> *Medicines for rats to shorten their lives.*

The first **picture book for children** was *Kunst und Lehrbüchlein* ("*Book of Art and Instruction for Young People*"), published by Sigmund Feyerabend of Heidelberg in 1580 with woodcut illustrations by the Nuremberg-based Swiss-born artist Jost Amman. Many of the pictures are charming; one of them shows a bouncing infant slurping milk out of the cat's bowl (the feline looks on crossly), and another is the earliest printed illustration of a child with a doll. The doll's dress is a miniature replica of the child's.

The first publishers to specialize in children's books were both based in London, but one, unusually for the book business at that time, was a woman. Mary Cooper's earliest known imprint is *The Child's*

New Play-Thing: or, Best Amusement: Intended to make the Learning to Read a Diversion instead of a Task of 1743, but as this is the second edition she was presumably publishing for children somewhat earlier. It was promoted by an entirely new idea in merchandising: a free gift or premium in the form of an accompanying cutout. The better-known John Newbery (SEE ALSO **children's fiction; children's magazine**) commenced a thriving business in London in 1744 with the publication of *A Little Pretty Pocket Book Intended for the Instruction and Amusement of Little Master Tommy and Pretty Miss Polly.* Newbery copied Mary Cooper's premium offer, though in this case the "gift" was not free: The little volume on its own cost 6d, but for an extra 2d "Master Tommy" was entitled to a red and black ball to go with it, and "Miss Polly" a red and black pincushion. A letter addressed to the children from Jack the Giant Killer explained that they should stick a pin in the red half of their respective toys for every good deed performed, and a pin in the black side for every act of mischief.

U.S.: Early children's books were deeply religious, produced as they were to keep Puritan children on the straightest and narrowest paths of moral rectitude and prim piety. Most authorities cite *Spiritual Milk for Boston Babes: In either England* as the earliest to emanate from these shores, written by John Cotton of Boston, Mass., formerly of Boston, Lincolnshire (in whose honor New England's Boston was supposedly named). Originally published in London in 1646, it was reissued in its city and country of origin in 1657. It seems likely, however, that there was an earlier book for children both written and published in America. This was a slender volume entitled (in later editions) *A Short Catechism Composed by Mr. James Noyes, Late Teacher of the Church of Christ in Newbury, in New England. For the Use of the Children There.* James Noyes (1606–56) was a native of Wiltshire, England, who emigrated to New England in 1634. According to Wilberforce Eames, in *Early New England Catechisms* (1898), the Newbury Catechism was probably published in 1642, in compliance with a recommendation made by the General Court the previous year. No copies have survived, but if indeed it was issued the publishers would have been Stephen & Mathew Daye of Cambridge, Mass., the only press in America at that date.

For well over a century all books for children, apart from a few school texts, were intended for one thing only: to deter children from sin. The general tone is epitomized by an effusion of 1714 entitled *A Legacy for Children, being some of the Last Expressions, and Dying Sayings, of Hannah Hill, Junr. Of the City of Philadelphia, in the Province of Pennsilvania, in America, Aged Eleven Years and near Three Months.* It was published at the "Ardent Desire of the Deceased," who spent several days dying (an account of which occupies seventeen pages of the thirty-five page book) and occupied the time by giving moral advice to her family and friends: "The Council which she gave to her Dear and only Sister and Cousin Lloyd Zachary, whom she dearly loved, was very grave and Pithy."

So, not much joie de vivre there. The earliest known book published in America purely for the pleasure of its readers was a reprint of an English chapbook (a paper-covered ephemeral publication sold by peddlers) called *The Friar and the Boy: or, The Young Piper's pleasant Pastime. Containing the witty Adventures between the Friar and Boy in relation to his Step Mother, whom he fairly fitted for her unmerciful cruelty.* Published in Boston by A. Barclay in 1767, this exposition of the generation gap is believed to have evolved from an early French folktale originally put into print in English by Wynkyn de Worde as a book for adults c. 1500.

The earliest known children's book originating in America and intended for leisure reading was *The Life of General Washington, Commander in Chief of the American Army during the late War, and present President of the United States. Also of the brave General Montgomery,* published by Jones, Hoff & Derrick of Philadelphia in 1794. No author is named.

Between these two publications Isaiah Thomas of Worcester, Mass., had become the first specialty children's publisher beginning with two adaptations from the French, a play for children based on Madame Leprince de Beaumont's *The Beauty and the Monster* and a biblical story, *Hagar in the Desert,* both published in 1785. From the following year until 1797 most of his output for juveniles consisted of reprints of the highly entertaining little books published by John Newbery (SEE ABOVE) in London, as well as other British-sourced material. While the didactic work of moral self-improvement had far from run its course, from this point onward there was alternative, more cheerful fare issuing from American presses for the delight of the first generation of U.S. citizens.

THE FIRST CHILDREN'S FICTION

was the collection of fairy tales published as *Histoires ou contes du temps passé* in Paris in January 1697 by the poet and critic Charles Perrault. It contained *La Belle au bois dormant* (*Sleeping Beauty*), *Le Petit Chaperon rouge* (*Little Red Riding Hood*), *La Barbe-bleu* (*Bluebeard*), *Le Maître Chat ou le chat botté* (*Puss in Boots*), *Les Fées* (*The Fairies*), *Cendrillon ou la petite pantoufle de verre* (*Cinderella; or, The Little Glass Slipper*), *Riquet à la houppe* (*Rumpelstiltskin*), and *Le Petit Poucet* (*Tom Thumb*). A year after the appearance of Perrault's *Contes*, the first woman writer of children's fiction, Contesse Marie-Catherine d'Aulney, brought out her own collection of fairy tales, *Contes des fées*. This included *The Yellow Dwarf* and *The White Cat*.

The first original work of children's fiction in English was *The Governess; or Little Female Academy: Being the history of Mrs. Teachum and her nine Girls* by Sarah Fielding, sister of Henry Fielding, author of *Joseph Andrews* (1742) and *Tom Jones* (1749). Published by A. Millar in London in 1749, it was, in spite of its main title, set in a school and recounted a minor outbreak of rebellion among the pupils over a basket of apples donated by their teacher, Mrs. Teachum. All the girls want the largest apple, which the head-girl, Jenny Peace, flings over a hedge after the other girls have rejected her offer to divide it. Eventually harmony is restored by Mrs. Teachum, who prevails upon her charges to be "obedient to their Superiors, and gentle, kind and affectionate to each other." Included in the volume were several fairy tales.

U.S.: There is difficulty in establishing the first original work of children's fiction, as so many tales were reprints of English material and seldom acknowledged their source. The earliest known that is explicit about its American provenance is *True Stories Related. By a friend to little children*, published by Samuel Wood, New York, 1814. Ten moral stories are recounted, some biblical but the majority described as "tales of contemporary American Life." Titles included *Wicked and Unmannerly Children*; *Disobedience, Punishment and Repentance*; *Daniel in the Lion's Den*; *The Crane with a Broken Leg* (set in New Rochelle, N.Y.); *The Dangerous effects of fear in the Water* (a story about Long Island); *The Danger and Sad Effects of Gun-Powder*; and *The Sad Effects of Wrestling*. The anonymous author denounces "ridiculous and baneful Stories" in the preface, singling out Tom Thumb, Gulliver, and Sinbad for special disapprobation, along with "Stories of Hobgoblins, Enchanted Castles, Fairies, Sylphs, Magical Wands, Wishing Caps, Etc. Etc, Etc." One doubts that his young readers would have concurred.

Children's novel: The first full-length work of juvenile fiction by an American writer was Catherine Maria Sedgwick's *The Travellers: A Tale Designed for Young People*, published by Cummings, Hilliard & Co. of Boston in 1825. Miss Sedgwick was born in Stockbridge, Mass., the daughter of a largely self-taught lawyer and congressman, Theodore Sedgwick, and a mother whose ancestors came from two prominent New England families, the Dwights and the Williamses. Unusually for a girl at the time, Catherine was given a classical education. She began writing comparatively late with *A New England Tale* in 1822, making her name with the adult novel *Redwood* two years later. Although she continued producing fiction until the late 1850s, Catherine Sedgwick is now principally remembered for her social activism, founding New York's first free school and leading the prison reform movement. Her children's fiction has tended to be overlooked. *The Travellers* has only now been identified as America's first novel for children.

The story related is of a vacation trip taken by Mr. and Mrs. Sackville in 1818 with their children, twelve-year-old Edward and ten-year-old Julia. The children are extremely reluctant to go, as they have been brought up in the city and think that journeying through the countryside will be mindbendingly boring. It seems that the authoress, despite her small-town background, shared something of her protagonists' views, as she several times breaks off a description of scenery with an admonition to herself not to bore her young readers. As soon as they are on the road, the children find that travel is full of enchantment, especially when they arrive at Niagara and spend a week admiring the Falls (we are not told from which city they have come, as Mrs. Sedgwick believes it is better for every reader to imagine it as his or her own). Here they encounter a poverty-stricken, ugly, but virtuous Englishwoman, Mrs. Barton, and her two children and learn how she is looking for the soldier husband she had lost touch with when he was captured in the War of 1812. She is desperate to get to Quebec, where his regiment was originally stationed. The rest of the tale is about how the children assist her in this journey, even sacrificing the $5 that each of them was given by Mr. Sackville to buy Canadian souvenirs, and the adventures that befall them as they travel via Montreal to Quebec. Mr. Sackville thinks the whole exercise misconceived, as the husband's regiment has long since been posted overseas, but Edward succeeds in finding Corporal Barton, who has transferred to another regiment in order to stay and look for his family, and a joyful reunion takes place.

Although didactic and moralistic in places, as almost all children's literature was at the time, *The Travellers* is nonetheless a lively read and particularly interesting as a piece of social history in depicting a family vacation at a time when very few Americans indulged in such pleasures. It has never been reprinted and is so completely forgotten that it is not even listed in the bibliography of her works given in the standard life of Catherine Sedgwick, nor is it mentioned in her own memoirs. Unfortunately it is unlikely ever to be reissued because Mrs. Sedgwick, as was common in the literature of the period, made casually racist remarks about African Americans ("degraded"), the Irish ("dirty"), and Native Americans ("savages") and observes of an Indian maiden that she "would be a perfect beauty, if . . . the olive tinge could be washed out of her skin."

THE FIRST **CHILDREN'S MAGAZINE**

was *The Lilliputian Magazine; or, The Young Gentleman and Lady's Golden Library*, price 3d, a monthly edited by the children's-book publisher John Newbery at the Bible and Sun in St. Paul's Churchyard, London, and probably first issued in June 1751. In accordance with its title, the magazine is truly Lilliputian, measuring only 4" x 2½". It contained short stories, riddles, jokes, songs, and pictures and, unlike its early nineteenth-century successors, was designed solely to entertain, not for moral uplift. The final issue, dated 3 July 1752, contains a list of members of the Lilliputian Society (i.e., the juvenile subscribers), from which it is apparent that the magazine circulated on both sides of the Atlantic, as many of the children resided in Maryland.

U.S.: The first was the *Children's Magazine*, published by Barzillai Hudson and George Goodwin in Hartford, Conn., from January through April 1789, price 6d. Heavily didactic, its "Moral Tales" and sentimental verses failed to find favor with robust American youngsters. The only other eighteenth-century juvenile, New York's *Youth's News Paper*, expired after six weeks. The *Juvenile Magazine* (Philadelphia) of 1802 died after a single issue, as did the *Juvenile Monitor* (New York City) in 1811. The first to survive for any length of time was the *Juvenile Port-Folio* (Philadelphia), 30 October 1812 to 7 December 1816. Remarkably the editor of this publication, Thomas G. Condie Jr., was only thirteen years of age at its inception. Boston's *Juvenile Miscellany* of 1826 managed a respectable run of eight years. Then, the following year, appeared the magazine that still holds the record for the longest duration of any juvenile periodical in the English-speaking world—the venerable *Youth's Companion*, again from Boston, with more than a century of continuous issue from 16 April 1827 to September 1929. By 1885 it had become the largest-circulation magazine in the nation, eclipsing all the mass-circulation adult weeklies. Among its innovations was the first full-page color advertisement in any periodical publication (SEE **advertisement, printed**).

The first gender-specific juvenile magazine in the United States was the *Boys' Monthly Gazette* of Charleston, Mass., which began in May 1857. Girls did not get their own paper until *Girls* began publication in Alexandria, Va., in 1898.

Most juvenile literature, particularly in magazines, is ephemeral. Probably the earliest enduring contribution in an American children's journal appeared in the September 1830 issue of the *Juvenile Miscellany*, Boston—the much-loved, oft-quoted "*Mary Had a Little Lamb*" by Sarah Josepha Hale.

THE FIRST **CHOCOLATE, EATING**

is among those significant innovations about which least is recorded. It is believed that French and Italian confectioners were producing eating chocolate by hand on a very limited scale in the early nineteenth century, the Italian variety generally made in thick rolls and then sliced. The earliest known references to chocolate produced on a factory scale emanate from England, the most industrially advanced nation in the world at the time. In 1826 an advertisement for Fry's Chocolate Lozenges, from the Bristol firm of J. & S. Fry, appeared in *Butler's Medicine Chest Directory*. They were described as "a pleasant and nutritious substitute for food in traveling, or when unusual fasting is causing by irregular periods of meal times." Whether these were pieces of chocolate, or a lozenge formed principally from some other substance and flavored with cocoa essence, is not revealed.

It is claimed in France that the chocolate bar was first manufactured by pharmacist Jean-Antoine Brutus Menier in 1836. The Chocolat Menier archivist concedes that there is no contemporary evidence to support this in their much depleted archives and that the assignation of 1836 is "traditional." The earliest contemporary evidence of such a commodity is in the price list issued in 1842 by John Cadbury of Birmingham, which offers "French Eating Chocolate" at 2s (50¢) a tablet. It is not known whether this was Cadbury's own product, made according to the French style, or imported French chocolate. In 1847 Fry's responded with "chocolate délicieux à manger," which again suggests a French connection, though this could have been simply to imply an exotic provenance for a luxury product. A recent discovery, however, provides circumstantial evidence that eating chocolate was being manufactured in England as early as 1840 and possibly earlier. This is bound up with the introduction of eating chocolate to America, at least a generation earlier than usually stated.

U.S.: The earliest evidence of eating chocolate lies in a letter written on 18 March 1845 to wholesalers Smith & Wood of Dorchester, Mass., by Walter Baker, proprietor of the first chocolate factory in America. The Baker Chocolate Co., also of Dorchester, had been producing drinking chocolate since the previous century, but in this letter Baker invites Smith & Wood to distribute his "chocolate sticks." These, he informed them, already enjoyed a ready sale amongst Boston grocers, who retailed them at 1¢ for a small stick and 2¢ for a large one. They were particularly popular with children and Baker asserted that his chocolate was "much more healthy and suitable for them than candy or sugar plums." He had learned to make them in London, he wrote: "there as in Boston the sticks are piled in the retail shop window across each other, and rather ornament the store."

Two important questions arise: From whom did Baker learn to make them in London, and when? While most English cocoa factories were situated in provincial cities, there were two prominent manufacturers in London, Taylor Brothers and Dunn & Hewett. The latter are known to have been producing chocolate sticks wrapped in silver foil about the middle of the century. They seem the most likely candidate for the visit from Walter Baker that resulted in eating chocolate crossing the Atlantic. Unfortunately we do not know when Baker traveled to London. However, he remarried in 1840 and prosperous Americans had already begun to venture to Europe on honeymoon. It is possible, then, that Baker combined business with pleasure and that he had already been manufacturing his chocolate sticks for the Boston trade for a number of years when he sent his 1845 letter to Smith & Wood.

Whatever the outcome of that letter, eating chocolate does not seem to have spread outside New England until considerably later. William Loft, founder of the Loft Candy Co., opened a store in New York City in 1860 selling bonbons that he molded from chocolate supplies bought in bulk and probably imported. He gradually expanded his retail chain through the states of New York, New Jersey, and Connecticut. On the opposite side of the continent Domingo Ghiradelli and his rival Etienne Guittard, both of San Francisco, were manufacturing for local consumption by the end of the 1860s. Another decade passed before chocolate was available throughout the United States, Maillard of New York City advertising in 1878 that their "celebrated Vanilla chocolates" were available "from grocers everywhere."

Candy bar: The first was Fry's Cream Stick, consisting of fondant enrobed in dark chocolate, originally manufactured by J. & S. Fry of Bristol, England in 1853 and sold for a penny (2¢). The stick became a flat bar in 1866 and as Fry's Chocolate Cream, now manufactured by Kraft, is still one of Britain's most popular candy bars.

U.S.: It is a mystery unexplained by confectionary historians why it took nearly sixty years from the introduction of the first candy bar in Britain for what is now considered an American institution to make its appearance in the United States. Its debut on this side of the Atlantic is claimed to have been in the guise of the Goo Goo Cluster, a mixture of caramel, marshmallow, and fresh roasted peanuts enrobed in milk chocolate, which was launched by the Standard Candy Co. of Nashville, Tenn., in 1912. This is disputed by the National Confectioners Association, which asserts that chocolate-coated marshmallows with peanuts and almond nougat were being sold at baseball stadiums a year earlier.

Boxes of assorted chocolates: "Fancy boxes" are mentioned in a Cadbury's price list issued from its factory in Birmingham, England, in 1861. Chocolate des Délices aux Fruits contained a selection of orange, lemon, raspberry, and almond soft centers, while Cadbury's Flavoured Bonbons included cinnamon, almond, lemon, and spice-flavored chocolates. The earliest-known pictorial chocolate box, an unlabeled Fry's assortment, dates from 1868 and depicts a group of children in a goat-carriage. The real father of "chocolate-box art," though, was Richard Cadbury, who executed the first specially produced commercial design in the fall of the same year. This was a portrait of his doe-eyed six-year-old daughter, reproduced as an oleograph and stuck on the lids of 4-ounce oval boxes of Cadbury's dragées.

Milk chocolate was invented by Daniel Peter in a house in the rue des Bosquets, Vevey, Switzerland, that now has a plaque proclaiming, "Dans cette maison a été créé en 1875 le premier chocolat au lait du monde." He had already tried combining chocolate with milk without success—the water content of milk prevented a stable emulsion with the cocoa butter. The breakthrough occurred because of his daughter Rose's intolerance to mother's milk. Peter had a neighbor at No. 17 rue des Bosquets, a German pharmacist originally from Frankfurt, Henri Nestlé, who had recently begun

manufacturing a powdered milk that he marketed as "milk flour." The new product not only satisfied Rose's need but also provided the solution to Peter's emulsion problem. His patent of 1875 was for a process of making milk drinking chocolate, but a decade later he succeeded in adapting it to eating chocolate, launched in 1886 as Gala Peter with a marketing pitch aimed at establishing its nutritive value (in actuality less than that of dark chocolate) and—possibly a reference to its genesis—as being particularly beneficial to children. Peter Chocolate was absorbed by Nestlé in 1929.

U.S.: The first milk chocolate bar was produced by the Hershey Chocolate Co. of Lancaster, Pa., on 9 February 1900.

THE FIRST **CHORAL SOCIETY**

in America began in Boston, where two distinguished diarists noted its debut performance under the date of 16 March 1721. The Rev. Cotton Mather recorded: "In the Evening I preached unto a large Auditory, where a Society of persons learning to Sing, began a quarterly solemnity." His nephew, the eminent jurist Samuel Sewall, wrote: "At night Dr. Mather preached in the School-House to the young Musicians, from Rev. 14:3. 'No man could learn that song.'—House was full, and the Singing extraordinarily Excellent, such as has hardly been heard before in Boston. Sung four tunes out of Tate & Brady." Tate & Brady was a lyrical and rhythmical paraphrase of the Psalms, which appealed to those who liked to sing for pleasure; it had largely been replaced in Puritan New England by the Bay Psalm Book (SEE **printed book**), which provided an austere, literal translation from the original texts.

THE FIRST **CHRISTMAS CARD**

was designed in 1843 on behalf of (Sir) Henry Cole by Royal Academician John Calcott Horsley, later to become famous for his campaign against the use of nude models by artists, which earned him the nickname "Clothes-Horsley." Cole was a member of the committee that produced the first postage stamps (qv) and went on to establish the first public toilets (qv) and to found the Victoria and Albert Museum. He was also the author of a series of children's books under the imprint of Felix Summerly's Home Treasury that were sold by his friend Joseph Cundall at Summerly's Home Treasury Office, 12 Old Bond Street, in London. It was to Cundall that Cole entrusted the publication of the world's first Christmas card. It depicted three generations of a Victorian family party sitting round the festive board, their glasses raised to the absent guest, otherwise the recipient. This charming and seemingly innocuous little scene gave rise to heated denunciations on the grounds that the card encouraged alcoholism and drunkenness. According to tradition Henry Cole commissioned the card because pressure of business had prevented him from writing to all his friends at Christmas, as was his usual custom. One thousand were printed by Jobbins of Warwick Court in London's Holborn from a lithographic stone, each on a single piece of pasteboard measuring 5" x 3¼", and colored by hand. All those surplus to the requirements of Cole and Horsley were sold by Joseph Cundall at Summerly's Home Treasury Office for 1 shilling (25¢) each.

According to a census conducted by Canadian antiquarian Kenneth Rowe, twenty-five known copies of the Cole-Horsley card survive, including four proofs. Of the twenty-one nonproof examples, the only unused one is in the Hallmark Historical Collection in Kansas City, Mo. Two others are also in American collections, one in Connecticut, the other in New York. The most recent reported sale was in December 2010 when three specimens from the Christmas collection of the late John Elliott were auctioned at Sotheby's New York for $4,250, $7,000, and $10,000, respectively. One of them had been sent by the artist himself, J. C. Horsley, to his "old young friends Emma and Agnes."

Although a few other examples of similar cards are known to have been published in succeeding years, regular commercial production did not start until the London printing firm of Charles Goodall & Sons entered the field. The Christmas card industry, wrote the Victorian artist Luke Limmer (John Leighton),

> began in 1862, the first attempts being the size of the ordinary gentleman's address card, on which

was simply put "A Merry Christmas" and "A Happy New Year"; after that there came to be added robins and holly branches, embossed figures and landscapes. Having made the original designs for these, I have the originals before me now; they were produced by Goodall & Son. Seeing a growing want, and the great sale obtained abroad this house produced [1868] a "Little Red Riding Hood," a "Hermit and his Cell," and many other subjects in which snow and the robin played a part.

The traffic in pasteboard greetings during December had grown to a sufficient volume by 1871 for a leading daily newspaper to complain of people trying to outdo each other in the number they received (dependent, of course, on the number they sent) and a "subsequent delay in legitimate correspondence." Not surprisingly such immoderate enthusiasm by the middle classes soon caused a reaction among their social betters, and in 1873 the first advertisement apologizing for "not sending Christmas cards this year" appeared in the personal column of the *Times*.

U.S.: The earliest known Christmas card is a one-off produced by Richard H. Pease for "Pease's Great Varety [*sic*] Store in the Temple of Fancy" in Albany, N.Y. This is undated but must belong to either 1850, 1851, or 1852, as these were the only three years in which Pease's occupied the building depicted on the card. Although primarily intended to be promotional, it can be considered a legitimate Christmas card rather than simply a seasonal trade card because, as George Buday indicates in the description of the design in his *History of the Christmas Card* (1954), it was clearly intended for conveying Christmas greetings to the well-wisher's friends:

> Above the holly decorated curved display line, carrying Peases's advertisement, the design includes the features of a small, rather elf-type Santa Claus with fur-trimmed cap, sleigh and reindeer. A ballroom with dancers, the building marked "Temple of Fancy", an array of Christmas presents and Christmas dishes and drinks decorate the four corners of the card, while in the center we see a young couple with three children visibly delighted with their presents; behind the family group a black

servant is laying the table for the Christmas dinner. In addition to the central "A Merry Christmas And a Happy New Year" the ornamented lettering includes "To:" and "From:" with spaces to be filled by the sender.

The only known copy of the Pease card is in the collection of the greeting card manufacturers Rust Craft (now Ziff Corporation).

The first Christmas card publisher in the United States was German immigrant Louis Prang (b. Breslau, 1824), whose lithographic color printing company, L. Prang & Co. of Roxbury, Mass., began producing cards for the British market in 1874. He launched them in the United States the following Christmas. During the early years of production these were generally small single (i.e., unfolded) cards measuring 3½" x 2" or 4" x 2½" and the designs consisted most frequently of flowers or a combination of flowers and birds. The first artist to design for Prang was watercolorist Mrs. O. E. Whitney. The most comprehensive collection of Prang cards is contained in seventy volumes held by the American Antiquarian Society in Worcester, Mass.

Charity Christmas card: The earliest known was designed by Harry Payne and printed by Raphael Tuck & Sons for Britain's National Relief Fund in 1914. This was a charity set up under the patronage of the Prince of Wales (later King Edward VIII) soon after the outbreak of World War I to give aid to service families struggling to survive on separation allowance. Unusually the card had pictures inside and out, the cover showing "Defenders of the Empire" and the third page "The Dreadnaught of to-day saluting Nelson's 'Victory' " (*Victory* was Nelson's flagship at the Battle of Trafalgar, 1805). The second page contained lines from Shakespeare, and the fourth details about the NRF. After the war, what seems like an obvious way for charities to raise funds at the season of goodwill failed to take off, the only known example from this period being issued at Norwich, England, by the Norfolk Naturalists Trust in 1930 with a picture of a bearded tit by J. C. Harrison.

It was not until after World War II that a quiet revolution occurred in the greeting card industry on both sides of the Atlantic. The ascendancy of charity cards among the well-intentioned as well as the image conscious, now estimated at 20 percent of the total volume, began with the UNICEF card for Christmas 1949, designed by seven-year-old Jitka Samkova of Rudolfo, Czechoslovakia. Like many other villages in Czechoslovakia, Rudolfo had been devastated in the war, and there was at the time a severe shortage of food, medicines, and other basic necessities. UNICEF helped to feed the hungry population of the village and organized a campaign to fight tuberculosis. In gratitude to the organization, Jitka painted a picture of gaily dressed children dancing around a maypole. She used a sheet of glass to work on as there was no paper available. The scene, she explained, "means joy going round and round." Her teacher entered the painting for a UNICEF competition; winning first prize, it attracted the attention of the director of the organization and was subsequently made into the first mass-produced Christmas card sold for charity.

Personalized photo Christmas card: The earliest known was sent by the Blackton family of Brooklyn, whose head, movie producer James Stuart Blackton, had made the world's first cartoon film (SEE **film, animated**) in 1906. It depicts him, his second wife, the actress Paula Dean, and his three children, Marian, Charles, and Violet, smiling over the gate of Sloane House, the mansion in London's Chelsea they had rented during a two-year sojourn making films in England. The Blacktons spent the Christmases of 1921 and 1922 in London, so the card may have been sent in either of these years.

Electronic Christmas card: The first was devised by Scott Lorenz and Haithem Sarafa of Domino's Farms in Ann Arbor, Mich., in 1995 as a means of promoting the office park's annual charity Christmas light display. Internet users were invited to access the Branch Mail "shopping mall" Web site operated by Jon Zeeff and select one of six designs depicting the festive lights. Some 14,500 were dispatched the first year and 40,000 the next.

THE FIRST CHRISTMAS GIFTS

reference to in America is a German Moravian diary entry made on 25 December 1745 in Bethlehem, Pa.: "Some received scarves, some a handkerchief, some a hat, some neckerchiefs, and some a few apples." Rather more common in colonial America, though by no means widespread, was the bestowal of gifts to celebrate New Year, particularly in Dutch communities.

It is almost certainly to the Dutch that we owe **Christmas stockings**. Although in northern Europe today these are virtually unknown (the equivalent is the rather less capacious shoe), there is evidence of present-filled stockings in a painting of 1686 titled *The Eve of St. Nicholas* by the Haarlem-born artist Cornelius Dusart.

The earliest reference to Christmas stockings in America is a woodcut illustration in a broadside headed *St. Nicholas* by John Pintard, founder of the New-York Historical Society, published in New York in December 1810. This depicts a fireside with a stocking on either side of the mantelpiece, one bulging with gifts for a good child, the other holding a birch-rod for the naughty child. Two weeks later a newspaper published an anonymous poem titled "Knickerbocker Santa Claus" (the earliest known allusion by that name), presumably in response to Pintard's verse offering, in which the saint is adjured:

Oh! Come with our panniers and pockets well stow'd
Our stockings shall help you to lighten your load
As close to the fireside gaily they swing.
While delighted we dream of the presents we bring.

Christmas historian Stephen Missenbaum has postulated that this may have been the work of Clement Moore, Pintard's fellow member of the New-York Historical Society, whose 1822 classic "The Night Before Christmas" also evoked the hanging of stockings by the chimney.

The commercialization of Christmas had advanced sufficiently by 1830, at least in urban centers, for John Pintard to remark on the "endless variety of European Toys that attract the admiration and empty the pockets of parents, friends, and children." These might have been either for Christmas or New Year, as the usual designation in early seasonal advertising by the stores was for "Presents for the Holidays" or "Holiday Gifts." That the toys noted by Pintard are described as European reflects the fact that Germany

was the main source for children's delights, there being little domestic manufacture either in the United States or Britain against the competition of cheap imports.

The earliest reference to **wrapped gifts** in the United States is contained in a short story by Lizzie M'Intyre titled "The Christmas Tree," which appeared in the December 1860 issue of *Godey's Magazine and Lady's Book*. The children's presents are suspended from the Christmas tree unwrapped, but those for the adults are "packages, wrapped in paper" inscribed with the recipient's name. Karal Ann Marling, in *Merry Christmas!* (2000), surmises that these were probably simple white paper packages. Contrary to sentimental belief, the majority of presents in the nineteenth century were store-bought and not hand-wrought at home, and she believes that the purpose of wrapping was to add a personal touch to otherwise mass-produced goods. Increasingly in the 1880s and '90s there are references to gifts done up in white tissue paper and colored ribbons. The chief importer of tissue paper, which came from England, was the Dennison Manufacturing Co. of Framingham, Mass. By 1897 they were offering red and green tissue and in 1908 introduced the earliest known **decorated gift wrap**, somewhat predictably a holly design, available either on tissue or crepe paper. There was no variation on this for ten years. Then, in December 1918, Kansas City stationer Joyce Hall ran out of his stock of holly paper and red, white, and green tissues. His brother went off to find something suitable as a substitute and returned in triumph with sheets of gaily designed polychromatic French paper intended for envelope linings. The take-up at 10¢ a sheet was so insistent that the following year the Halls sold them in packs of three with equal success. When Joyce Hall went on to found Hallmark Cards, among the earliest sidelines to the main greeting card business was gift wrap. Samples from the early 1930s in the Hallmark archives include plaid and checkerboard papers and tissues in saturated tones of cobalt, sienna, purple, yellow, and a reflective silver. Matching sets of wrappings offered paper together with tinsel ribbon and foil seals depicting Christmas icons such as candles, lanterns, and stars and also President Franklin D. Roosevelt's Scottie dog Fala.

The term "gift wrap" is comparatively recent, the philological journal *American Speech* noting early in 1936 that many department stores the previous Christmas had proclaimed, "We Gift-Wrap Here."

THE FIRST CHRISTMAS TREES

on record were firs decorated with paper roses that were erected in the marketplaces of Riga, Latvia, and Reval (now Tallinn), Estonia, on 24 December 1510 and 24 December 1514, respectively. In both instances members of a local guild danced around the tree before setting it on fire as a climax to the celebration. Indoor Christmas trees were known by 1605, when an unidentified visitor to Strasbourg in Alsace-Lorraine (then part of the German Empire) reported: "For Christmas they have fir-trees in their rooms, all decorated with paper roses, apples, sugar, gold and wafers."

It has been suggested that the Christmas tree may have been known in Alsace as early as 1521. Here it was customary on May Day to set up decorated fir trees known as *Maien*. The municipal account books of the small Alsatian town of Schlettstadt indicate that not only was there an upsurge of activity among the local foresters just before May Day during the fifteenth and sixteenth centuries, but also that in three specific years—1521, 1546, and 1556—a similar number of Christmas *Maien* were cut.

The earliest reference to a lighted Christmas tree is contained in a letter written by Liselotte von der Pfalz, Comtesse d'Orléans, in 1660, in which she stated that it was the custom in Hannover to decorate box trees with candles at Christmastide.

U.S.: The earliest representation of a Christmas tree is a drawing by John Lewis Krimmel, which has been dated as either 1812 or 1819. The scene is the parlor of a Pennsylvania German home with a large family gathered around a richly decorated tabletop tree. At the foot of the tree is a fence within which stand a group of model people and animals, including a man on horseback and what appears to be a giraffe.

The earliest recorded public Christmas tree in the United States was the centerpiece of a Christmas Fair held on 24 December 1830 by the Dorcas Society of York, Pa. Admission was 6¼¢, proceeds going to charity. This may also have been the first occasion on which non-Germans were exposed to what continued to be regarded as an essentially German custom until at least the 1850s. The first community Christmas tree was erected in Pasadena, Calif., in 1909.

The Christmas tree became popularized outside the German community in America only after an engraving of Queen Victoria and Prince Albert's decorated tree at Windsor Castle had appeared in the December 1850 issue of *Godey's Magazine and Lady's Book*, doctored for a republican audience by deleting all trappings of royalty from the picture. The same illustration had between reproduced in the *Illustrated London News* two years earlier; in England it had the similar effect of introducing people to a custom that had formerly been known only among German immigrants.

Glass Christmas tree ornaments: The first were silvered *Kugeln*, or balls, produced in Lauscha in the Thuringian Forest, originally manufactured in the early nineteenth century as window or garden ornaments. The earliest known order for Christmas tree *Kugeln* was in 1848. It is probably imports from Lauscha that are referred to in the first American mention of such decorations, an article in *Harper's Bazaar* in 1869 describing a tree dressed with "globes, fruits and flowers of colored glass." They were not manufactured in the United States until 1918, the war having cut off supplies from Germany.

Christmas tree lot: The first in America was established at New York City's Washington Market in 1851 by logger Mark Carr, who hauled two ox-sleds of balsam firs from the Catskill Mountains.

Electrically lit Christmas tree: The first, with 80 red, white, and blue bulbs each about the size of a walnut, was installed at his home in New York in December 1882 by Edward H. Johnson, vice president of Edison Electric. The tree was set on an electrically powered revolving stand, and as it turned the lights blinked on and off in series, making the colors twinkle and dance.

The first commercially produced Christmas tree lamps were manufactured in nine-socket string sets by the Edison General Electric Co. of Harrison, N.J., and advertised for sale in the December 1901 issue of the *Ladies' Home Journal*. Each socket took a miniature 2-candlepower carbon-filament lamp operating on 32 volts.

The first public tree illuminated by electricity was decorated with 250 bulbs and radiated its cheerful glow in front of the Hotel del Coronado, San Diego, Calif., from 24 to 31 December 1904.

Artificial Christmas trees: Introduced in Germany in the 1880s, these were generally made from goose feathers dyed green to look like fir needles and attached to wire branches. The oldest tree on record, however, is made from green rafia. This has been in the same English family since 1886, when it was purchased for 6d (12½¢); present owner Janet Parker of Chippenham, Wiltshire, was given it by her aunt Lou Hicks in the 1940s. Artificial trees were on sale in the United States by 1901, sales outstripping real trees for the first time in 1991. According to Tanya Gulerich in *Encyclopedia of Christmas* (2000), 35 million Americans have a real tree each year but 37 million favor fake.

THE FIRST **CHURCH**

within the present borders of the United States was San Miguel de Gualdape, built at the short-lived Spanish settlement of the same name on Sapelo Sound, Ga., in October 1526. The pastor was Fr. Antonio de Montesinos, who, together with two other Dominican priests, ministered to the six hundred settlers of the colony until it was abandoned soon after, four hundred having perished from disease and hunger. The first church of any permanence was the Mission Nombre de Dios, established by Spanish chaplain Fr. Francisco Lopez de Mendoza Grajales shortly after the settlement of St. Augustine, Fla., in September 1565. Archaeological evidence from other mission sites in Florida suggests that it was probably 50' x 100', made of pine posts and thatched with cypress fronds. The original church was torched by the English raiding party under Sir Francis Drake that attacked and destroyed St. Augustine in 1586. Originally administered as part of the diocese of Santiago de Cuba, the parish survives today as the oldest in the United States.

Protestant church: What was probably the first (but SEE BELOW) was built for Anglican worship in Jamestown during 1607 and described by Capt. John Smith as "a homely thing like a barne, set upon crachets, covered with rafts, sedge and earth." Before this was built,

services were held beneath an awning stretched over three or four trees or, if wet, in "an old rotten tent." With the erection of a more permanent structure, services were held daily, morning and evening, with two sermons on Sundays and communion every three months until the minister died. The original church burned down the following year, and no fewer than four replacements followed between then and 1639. The fifth church was the first to be built of brick, and the ruined tower and porch chamber of this survive. Remnants of the earlier churches have been found by archaeologists and affirm that they stood on a site within the wooden walls of James Fort.

An alternative "first Protestant church" was built at St. George's Fort, Popham Beach, Sagadahoc County, Maine, and is believed to have been extant by 8 October 1607, the date of a pictorial map of the fort drawn by settler John Hunt. The site had been selected on 18 August of that year, which was three months after the settlement at Jamestown, but it is not known whether the church there had been built by then. Hunt's drawing depicts a fairly substantial building with three sets of windows to the left of the door and a tower at one end surmounted by a spire. The church lasted for less than a year, because the settlers had all set sail back for England by May 1608.

What is particularly remarkable about these two structures is that they preceded the first purpose-built Episcopal churches in the country where the denomination had begun. No churches were built in England between the founding of the Anglican Communion (of which America's Episcopal Church is a constituent) in 1534 and the erection of Pear Tree Church in Itchen, Hampshire, in 1620.

The oldest church in the United States is uncertain. Architectural historian James D. Kornwolf (*Architecture and Town Planning in Colonial North America*, 2002) believes that substantial portions of the Roman Catholic mission church at Zia (possibly c. 1614) and Isleta (possibly 1613–17), both in New Mexico, may date from before 1620. San Miguel in Santa Fe has portions predating 1628. The earliest church of more certain provenance to have much of its original fabric intact is San Estevan del Rey at Ácomo Pueblo, N.M., which was begun in 1629 and completed in 1640.

The oldest surviving Protestant church in North America that continues to function as such is Newport Parish Church, Isle of Wight County, Va., traditionally dated 1632 but asserted by architectural historians to have been built between c. 1662 and 1682.

There are nearly 400 surviving churches (some ruined) in the United States that predate federation in 1789, of which 342 are located in the original 13 colonies and are mainly Protestant.

THE FIRST CIGARETTES

originated at an unknown date (probably late eighteenth century) as the hand-rolled *papelotes* of shredded tobacco wrapped in paper that were smoked by the Spanish urban proletariat, including the bare-breasted and nimble-fingered gypsy girls of the *fábrica de tabacos* in Seville who inspired Prosper Mérimée's *Carmen*. Visiting French writers, following in Mérimée's footsteps, enraptured by the sexual connotations of *papelote* smoking by the free-spirited sorority of the *fábrica*, took the habit back to Paris, where this poor relation of the masculine cigar was renamed in feminine form by romantic novelist Théophile Gautier. In his 1833 *Les Jeunes-France*, one of the protagonists is presented "nonchalantly smoking a little Spanish cigarette." The word had passed into the English language by 1842.

The first commercially produced cigarettes were manufactured in France in 1843 by the state-run Manufacture française des tabacs. The initial consignment of 20,000 gold-tipped cigarettes rolled in lithographed paper was sold at a charity bazaar organized by Queen Marie-Amélie in Paris that year. Production was entirely by hand and the output was consequently limited, totaling 6 million in 1845. Only in 1872 did the consumption of cigarettes in France reach the 100 million mark.

The first factory to produce cigarettes by mass-production methods was established in Havana, Cuba, by Don Luis Susini, who abandoned hand-rolling for steam-driven machines in 1853. An alleged production figure of 2,580,000 cigarettes a day is thought to be exaggerated and may represent the monthly total.

U.S.: The earliest cigarette smokers were inhabitants of Mexican or former Mexican territories. A traveler in California in 1834 recorded: "I heartily cursed our guide, while listening to his singing of the *patenara*, and seeing him strike the steel to light his cigarette" (quoted in *California Historical Society Quarterly* 8). In 1838 "Texian" in *Mexico v. Texas* recalled, "[The general] lay himself, half reclining, on his camp bed, smoking a *cigarrito*." An officer of the U.S. Army stationed in Florida in 1841 wrote home that he was tempering the monotony by smoking "a little segar, in paper, called by the Spaniards 'Cigarito', which I can smoke with decided enjoyment, and I think without any detriment," while he could not smoke a whole cigar "without revulsion." Nor were the only smokers men. In 1848 we learn from Byant's *California* that "the cigarita is freely used by the señoras and señoritas, and they puff it with much gusto while treading the mazes of the cotillon or swinging in the waltz." These cigarettes were made from a species of Mexican tobacco called *punche* and hand-rolled in dried corn-husks.

Ready-made cigarettes began to be imported into the United States in small quantities in the 1850s. Manufacture was begun in New York in 1864 by Greek and Turkish migrants, the earliest known by name being Nicholas Coundouris. Some 20 million cigarettes were produced that year, but the inception of the new industry seems to have been premature, as the number had fallen to 2 million by 1869. Smokers of cigarettes were nearly all foreign, notably Mexicans, French, Italians, and Cubans, the only American adherents being those who had lived abroad. The tobacco used was mainly Turkish. The first manufacturers to use American leaf were probably the Bedrossian brothers, Armenians who set up a workshop at 23 Wall Street, New York, in February 1867. At first they used a supply of Turkish tobacco direct from Constantinople but they started production with the golden "bright" tobacco from Virginia and North Carolina later the same year, the homegrown product being cheaper. The first to export American cigarettes was Allen & Ginter, who were the earliest manufacturers in the Virginia-Carolina area when they opened their factory in Richmond to produce the first prepacked cigarettes, Richmond Gems, in 1875. By 1883 they had depots in France, Germany, Switzerland, Belgium, and Australia, as well as a factory in London. The launch of Richmond Gems also marks the point at which cigarettes began to be smoked by native-born Anglo-Americans.

Despite the labor-intensive nature of hand-rolling, some prodigious quantities were produced by individual firms. Bull Durham's total output in 1883 was 14,407,200, but the company was unable to keep up with orders.

Mass production in the United States began after James Buchanan Duke of Durham, N.C., bought a machine invented by eighteen-year-old James Bonsack of Virginia. It had previously been turned down by Allen & Ginter after a short trial, since they believed their customers preferred roll-ups. The Bonsack machines extruded an endless tube of wrapped tobacco, which was cut with a miniature circular saw into 200 cigarettes a minute. On their first full day in use, 30 April 1884, Duke's two Bonsacks produced 120,000 cigarettes in a 10-hour day, equivalent to the work of forty hand-rollers. Faced by such competition, all the major companies agreed to merge under Duke's leadership, and the American Tobacco Co. was born in 1890. The combine made Duke himself a fortune, part of which he used to found Duke University. There he can be seen still, cast in bronze and holding a cigarette, the only statue in the United States with such an appendage. And it stands on a nonsmoking campus.

Women cigarette smokers: A Spanish law of 1802 that sought to protect the tobacco monopoly by banning the smoking of *papelotes* imposed harsh but differing penalties on offenders of both sexes, women who transgressed being sentenced to up to four years in either a convent or a lunatic asylum. This is the earliest specific reference to women smokers, and it is indicative of the fact that the practice was already widespread. The mention of Mexican women in California smoking in 1848, noted above, is contemporaneous with Charles Baudelaire's description in *Les Salons de 1848* of Paris prostitutes in the Ninth Arrondissement puffing on cigarettes "to kill time" between customers. The earliest reference to cigarette smoking by non-Hispanic American women is the shocked reaction of British visitor Dr. R. T. Trall in 1854 to the habits of New Yorkers:

Some of the *ladies* of the refined and fashion-forming metropolis are aping the ways of some pseudo-accomplished foreigners, in smoking tobacco through a weaker and more *feminine* article, which has been most delicately denominated *cigarette.*

Cigarette packs: Early packs were of the paper cup variety. The hull-and-slide cardboard pack was in use by Allen & Ginter of Richmond, Va., by 1885. The company is usually credited with originating the cigarette card, aka tobacco card, but this is not so. The idea came from a stiffener inserted in paper cup packs for Marquis of Lorne cigarettes by the Jos. Koehler Co. of New York in 1879; the card reproduced the illustration on the pack, a portrait of the Marquis of Lorne, governor-general of Canada, but it was not conceived as a collectable or trading card. The following year, however, another New York tobacco company, Thomas H. Hall, invented the tobacco card in the form it is best known, as a series of cards the collecting and trading of which would inspire brand loyalty. The initial series of 1880 were "Actresses" and "Presidential Candidates," issued with their Between the Acts and Bravo brands. The first sporting cards followed the next year with "Athletes," but it was not until Old Judge cigarettes issued their New York Giants set in 1886 that the baseball card emerged.

Three pack firsts originated with the R. J. Reynolds Co. of Winston-Salem, N.C.: the ten-pack carton in 1915; aluminum foil linings, for Camel and other brands from 1926, using an ultra-thin foil developed by R. J.'s nephew R. S. Reynolds; and cellophane wrapping in 1931. In Britain, Craven A had introduced the first cellophane-wrapped pack in May of the same year.

The "push-up" slide pack was replaced by the modern "flip-top" pack with a hinged lid, first introduced by Rothmans for its king-size filters in South Africa in August 1952 and in the United States by Marlboro in 1955 with the distinctive pack designed by Frank Gianninoto, which has scarcely changed to this day.

The first surgeon general's **health warning** on cigarette packs took effect on 1 January 1966. The message read "Caution: Cigarette smoke may be hazardous to your health." "May be" was changed to "is" in 1970.

The first **generic packaging** will be introduced under Australia's Plain Tobacco Packaging (Removing Branding from Cigarette Packs) Act with effect from 1 July 2012. No colors, logos, or images other than those associated with health warnings will be permitted and the brand name must be in small, nondecorative type.

Mentholated cigarettes: The first were Spud, manufactured in Wheeling, W. Va., in 1925 by Lloyd "Spud" Hughes, who sold his premium-price 20-for-20¢ cigarettes door-to-door from his car up and down the Ohio Valley where he lived. After selling out for $90,000 to the Axton-Fisher Tobacco Co. in May 1926, he opened his own airport and staged air races. Within two years the money had been squandered and he was working as a gas pump jockey while scheming to launch another flavored cigarette—mint julep.

Filter-tipped cigarettes: The first major brand was Du Maurier, introduced in 1929 by Peter Jackson Ltd. of London and named after the celebrated actor-manager Sir Gerald Du Maurier (father of Daphne). The first in the United States was Philip Morris's Parliament brand of 1931, which had a filter wad of cotton impregnated with caustic soda. The first brand with cellulose tips was L&M, introduced by Ligget & Myers in 1953. They were advertised as "just what the doctor ordered" in the same year that *Reader's Digest* published the first warning in any consumer publication that smoking causes cancer.

King-size cigarettes: The first were Pall Mall, which were lengthened to 85 mm from the standard 70 mm in 1939 after American Tobacco's chief George W. Hill discovered a little-publicized amendment to U.S. excise regulations that allowed an increase of 17 percent in tobacco content without any added tax.

THE FIRST CINEMA THEATER

was the Cinématographe Lumière at the Salon Indien, a former billiard hall in the Grand Café, 14 boulevard des Capucines, Paris, opened under the management of Clément Maurice on 28 December 1895. The proprietors of the show were Auguste and Louis Lumière, the pioneer cinematographers whose films made up the program. The opening performance included *Le Mur, L'Arrivée d'un train en gare, La sortie des Ouvriers de l'usine Lumière, Le goûter de Bébé, La pêche des poissons rouges, Soldates au manège, M. Lumière et le jongleur Trewey jouant aux cartes, La rue de la République à Lyon, En mer par gros temps, L'Arroseur arrosé,* and *La destruction des mauvaises herbes.* Returns from the box office on the day of opening were disappointingly low, as only thirty-five people had ventured a franc to see the new form of entertainment. This barely covered the rent of 30 francs a day, and the owner of the Grand Café, Monsieur Borgo, doubtless congratulated himself that he had refused Maurice's offer of 20 percent of the receipts in lieu of rent. Later he came to regret his decision, when the Cinématograph Lumière became the sensation of Paris and box-office receipts rose to 2,500 francs a day.

Most historians have assumed that the Cinématographe Lumière at the Grand Café was simply a temporary show, and consequently it has usually been claimed as the first presentation of films before a paying audience (which it was not—SEE **film, commercial presentation**) instead of the first cinema. Although the exact date of its closure is not known, there is contemporary evidence that it was still functioning as late as 1901. The fact that it operated continuously for at least five years should be sufficient to justify any claim based on permanence.

U.S.: The four-hundred-seat Vitascope Hall was opened at the corner of Canal Street and Exchange Place in New Orleans by William T. Rock on 26 June 1896. Admission was 10¢, and patrons were allowed to look in the projection room and see the Edison Vitascope projector for another 10¢. Those possessed of a liberal supply of dimes could also purchase a single frame of discarded film for the same price.

The first projectionist was William Reed. Most of the films were short scenic items, including the first British film to be released in America, Robert Paul's *Waves off Dover.* A major attraction was the film *The May Irwin Kiss,* which may be said to have introduced sex to the American screen. A typical program shown during the fall of 1896 consisted of the following:

The Pickaninnies Dance
The Carnival Scene
The Irish Way of Discussing Politics
Cissy Fitzgerald
The Lynching Scene

Purpose-built cinema: The first was the Cinema Omnia Pathé, Boulevard Montmartre, Paris, opened on 1 December 1906 with *Le Pendu*. The world's first luxury cinema, and the first with an inclined floor so that everyone could see above the heads in front, it was decorated in classical style with columns and Grecian friezes. The 20' x 30' screen was one of the largest installed in any cinema at that time. Admission for the 2-hour show ranged from 50 centimes (10¢) to 3 francs (60¢)—prices at other cinemas were generally in the range of 25 centimes (5¢) to 2 francs (40¢).

The first of the giant picture palaces was the 5,000-seat Gaumont-Palace, formerly the Hippodrome Theater, that opened in Paris in 1910. Back projection had to be used as there was no room for a projection booth behind the auditorium. It was one of the first cinemas to employ the use of two projectors for the continuous showing of multi-reel films. The extraordinary capacity of the Gaumont-Palace at this early date can best be understood by comparison with the largest ever built, the Roxy Theater in New York, which had 6,200 seats.

U.S.: The first purpose-built cinema is not known. Nominations are invited.

Drive-in cinema: The first was the Camden Automobile Theater, opened by Richard Hollingshead on a 10-acre site off Wilson Boulevard in Camden, N.J., on 6 June 1933 with a presentation of *Wife Beware* starring Adolphe Menjou. The giant screen measured 40' x 30', and there was accommodation for four hundred cars. The sound came from high-volume screen speakers provided by RCA Victor.

The expansion of drive-ins began very slowly; twelve years after the opening of the Camden there were still only 60 in the whole country. The growth years were the same as for television, for no clear reason except that parents stayed home and teenagers, freer to roam than ever before, needed somewhere to pair up in the dark. The marquee of a drive-in in Cleveland County, N.C., enticed patrons in 1960 with

the simple declaration "Two features." The manager explained, "People who patronize this drive-in don't care what's playing." In 1949 there were 1,000 drive-ins, and the peak was reached in 1958 with 4,063 against 12,291 hard-tops. There are now 383 in the United States and 39 in Canada. Pennsylvania has more than any other state.

Multiplex: A choice of films at the same cinema was not unknown even before the advent of the multiplex. In 1926 a correspondent for the German film journal *Lichtbühne* reported that he had visited a cinema in Cairo with twin screens in one auditorium showing two different films at the same time. The first cinema with more than one auditorium was the Regal Twins in Manchester, England, opened on 30 September 1930, each of whose auditoria held five hundred seats. The first in the United States was the Alhambra Twin in Alhambra, Calif., in 1939.

These early duplexes were exceptional. The continuous development of the multiplex dates from the opening of the first triplex, the Lougheed Mall Theater in Burnaby, British Columbia, by Taylor Twentieth Century Theaters in 1965. The first quadruplex was the Metro Plaza in Kansas City, opened by the Durwood family (forerunners of the present American Multi-Cinema chain) in 1966. This was followed by a six-plex in 1969.

The first **megaplex** (defined as a cinema with fourteen or more screens) was the fifteen-screen Palads in Copenhagen, Denmark, converted from an existing structure, one of the oldest cinemas in Europe (1918), on 1 September 1978. The first in the United States was AMC's Grand 24, opened in Dallas, Tex., in November 1995.

THE FIRST **CIRCUS**

was established in London by ex–cavalry sergeant major Philip Astley. In 1769 he sold a diamond ring that he had found on Westminster Bridge and, with the £60 obtained (equal to a year's salary for a senior clerk), opened an equestrian ring on Halfpenny Hatch, Lambeth. No admission fee was charged, but in common with other equestrian shows of the time a collection was taken up after every performance.

Evidently the audience responded generously, for the following year Astley moved to a better site close to Westminster Bridge. Here he constructed a roped-off enclosure with stands around the sides, and charged an entrance fee of 1 shilling for a seat and 6d standing. At the same time a drummer-boy was hired to add musical effects.

The precise date at which Astley's became a circus in the modern sense rather than simply a trick-riding display is hard to establish. It is known that he had a strongman, one Signor Colpi, working for him in 1777, and that within the next three years he acquired a clown called Fortunelly, another called Burt (sometimes claimed as the first circus clown), a number of acrobats who performed rope-vaulting tricks "in different attitudes," and an engaging performer known as "The Little Military Learned Horse." The equestrians, the real stars of the show, were three men named Griffin, Jones, and Miller, who performed under the aegis of Astley himself, considered by many the greatest horseman of his age.

Apart from horses, few animals were displayed. A "military monkey" named General Jackoo made his appearance in the ring at Astley's early on, but there is no record of any larger beasts making their circus debut until 1816, when two elephants named Baba and Kiouny went through a routine at Franconi's Circus, Paris, that included catching apples with their trunks, uncorking bottles and drinking the contents, and playing the hurdy-gurdy. Only in 1828 did Astley's follow this lead, when an elephant was hired from Cross's Exeter Change Menagerie. The animal was merely shown to the wondering spectators and was not required to perform. A lion, a tiger, and four zebras, all similarly inactive, appeared at Astley's in 1832. A year earlier the first real wild-beast act had taken place at the Cirque Olympique in Paris, where Henri Martin performed with lions, an elephant, and a boa constrictor.

As a popular medium of entertainment the circus spread rapidly. A Spaniard named Juan Porte established the first in Europe in Vienna in 1780. Two years later Astley himself introduced circus to Paris. Russia also had a circus by 1793. Philip Astley is reputed to have helped found no fewer than nineteen circuses in various countries in Europe, although he was not the first to call his entertainment "circus"; the word was coined by Charles Hughes for his Royal Circus in London in 1782. The original Astley's Amphitheatre continued to function on the same site at the south side of Westminster Bridge until as late as 1893.

U.S.: The first circus performance was presented by John Bill Ricketts, Scottish equestrian, at his purpose-built seven-hundred-seat circus building at 12th and Market streets, Philadelphia, on 3 April 1793. Price of admission was 7s 6d or 3s 9d in the pit. Ricketts himself performed equestrian feats on his horse Cornplanter, which had been trained to leap over the back of another horse. He also astonished the audience by riding two horses at once at full gallop. Other attractions included rope-walkers and tumblers, as well as America's first clown, the British-born Tom Sully. Ricketts's circus in Philadelphia was twice patronized by President George Washington, on 22 and 24 April 1793, ensuring its success with the public. He paid another visit on 24 January 1797 and even sold the showman his horse Jack, which he had ridden during the War of Independence, for the then very substantial sum of $150. The permanent amphitheater Ricketts established in New York was attended by President John Adams on 21 October 1797.

Both Ricketts's permanent circuses were burned down in 1799, and he set sail for England the following year. Alas, he never arrived, as the ship was lost at sea.

The first circus wild-beast act in America was a mixed troupe of lions, tigers, and leopards—a highly risky combination—presented by Isaac Van Amburgh at the Richmond Hill Theater in New York City in 1833.

Big top: The first circus under canvas was the Great North American Circus, inaugurated in Salem, N.Y., in 1826 by Aaron Taylor and brothers Nathan and Seth Howes. It had six wagons and twenty horses and a band of four musicians. Among the staff was a young ticket-seller, who occasionally doubled as a blackface minstrel, called P. T. Barnum.

Flying-trapeze circus act: The first was performed by Jules Léotard at the Cirque Napoléon, Paris, on 12 November 1859. Only twenty-one years of age at the time, Léotard had devised the act while practicing on the ropes and rings suspended above the swimming pool at his father's gymnasium in Toulouse. During the early 1860s he appeared at the Alhambra in London, causing a sensation by flying across the hall from trapeze to trapeze above the heads of the audience sitting at their supper tables. Léotard was immortalized as "That Daring Young Man on the Flying Trapeze" in a popular ditty sung by George Leybourne. He also lent his name to the tight-fitting costume still worn by acrobats and trapeze artistes.

The first **safety net** was introduced by the Spanish acrobatic troupe the Rizarellis at the Holborn Empire in London in 1871. Léotard had relied on the less certain precaution of a pile of mattresses on the floor.

THE FIRST

CITY TO EXCEED 1 MILLION IN POPULATION

was London, which according to the census of 1811 was inhabited by a total of 1,009,546 people. Seventy years later there were still only 7 cities in the world with a population of a million, namely:

London—3,452,350
Paris—2,269,023
Peking—1,648,814
Canton—1,500,000 (estimated)
New York—1,206,299
Vienna—1,103,857
Nanking—1,000,000 (estimated)

The number had grown to 31 by 1925 and is over 430 today. London remained the largest city in the world until 1957, when it was overtaken by Tokyo. The Japanese capital became the first city with a recorded population of 10 million in January 1962, a staggering rise since its wartime decline from 6,779,100 in 1940 to only 2,777,000 in 1945. In 1995 the United Nations Census showed it as the first city to top 20 million, which presumably it had done several years earlier, as the figure given was 27.2 million.

U.S.: The largest cities in America were successively Boston, until the early eighteenth century, then Philadelphia, until overtaken by New York between the census of 1800 and that of 1810. The first with a population of more than a million was New York, the population of the five boroughs* totaling 1,174,779 in the 1860 U.S. Census, up from 696,115 ten years earlier. If the rate of growth was steady, this would imply that New York City attained seven figures in 1856 or 1857.

As of 2009, there are nine cities in the United States with a population of more than a million:

New York City—8,391,881
Los Angeles—3,831,868
Chicago—2,851,268
Houston—2,257,926
Phoenix—1,593,659
Philadelphia—1,547,297
San Antonio—1,373,668
Dallas—1,229,542
San Diego—1,306,300

THE FIRST **CLOCK**

mechanical, was a water-powered astronomical device built by the Chinese Tantric Buddhist monk I-Hsing (d. 727) and set up in front of the Wu Ch'eng Hall of the Imperial Palace in A.D. 725. It did not have hands or a dial, but a bell was rung automatically to sound the hours and a drum beaten to signify the quarters. Five years later candidates for the imperial examinations were required to write an essay on the new marvel. A contemporary text indicates, however, that it failed to remain in working order for long: "Soon afterwards the mechanism of bronze and iron began to corrode and rust, so that the instrument could no longer rotate automatically. It was therefore relegated to the museum of the College of All Sages and went out of use." Presumably the Chinese continued to construct clocks, but the next of which there is record, some 350 years later, was described with diagrams by the Chinese imperial tutor Su Sung in his *Hsin Hsiang Fa Yao* of 1088. Su Sung's clock was a massive machine, 30 feet high,

---

* i.e., present-day New York City. In 1860 only Manhattan was New York City proper. Manhattan achieved a population of 1 million in 1873.

with a water-powered driving wheel and an escapement to control the gear wheels regulating the timekeeping mechanism.

The earliest recorded mechanical clock in Europe was made by the Austin Canons and set up against the roodscreen of Dunstable Priory, Bedfordshire, England, in 1283. This probably had a verge and foliot escapement of the kind common to most medieval clocks.

It is possible that the cathedral in Beauvais, France, had a clock with a bell before 1324. The earliest known European clock that struck the hours with a graduated number of strokes was in use at the Church of St. Gottardo in Milan, Italy, in 1335. This is also believed to have been the first **public clock**.

The earliest record of a clock with a dial in Europe is contained in the Sacrist's Rolls of Norwich Cathedral for 1325. This was an astronomical dial and was set up inside the cathedral. The first clock dial known to have been fixed to the outside of a building was erected on the newly built tower of Magdalen College, Oxford, in 1505. The first illuminated clock dial was that of St. Brides Church, Fleet Street, London, in 1826. It was lit by twelve gas burners.

The oldest surviving mechanical clock in working order in the world is the Salisbury Cathedral clock of 1386. It was found in derelict condition in the cathedral tower by T. R. Robinson in 1929 and has since been restored to its original condition.

Domestic clock: The earliest known is listed in the effects of Charles V of France (d. 1380) as "one clock made all of silver and with no iron, that had belonged to the late King Philip the Fair, with two weights covered with silver and filled with lead." Philip the Fair died in 1314, but during 1299 and 1300 a goldsmith called Petrus Pipelard or Perrotus was on the palace payroll "because he is constructing a clock for the King." It seems probable that this was the same timepiece as the one inherited by Charles V.

Alarm clock: The earliest known is a small German timepiece from Würzburg dating from 1350 to 1380 and designed for hanging against a wall. It is now preserved at the Main-fränkische Museum in Würzburg. Alarm clocks during the Middle Ages were confined almost exclusively to monasteries, where it was necessary to keep the canonical hours.

Clock with a minute hand: The first was made by Swiss watchmaker Jost Bürgi in 1577 for the astronomer Tycho Brahe to use at his Uraniborg observatory on the Danish island of Hveen-in-the-Sound.

Pendulum clock: The first was made by the Dutch scientist Christiaan Huygens at The Hague in December 1658. It was based on the principle of oscillating motion expounded by Galileo some seventy years earlier. Commercial production was undertaken by Huygens's clockmaker, Samuel Coster, from c. 1658.

U.S.: The earliest known clockmaker was William Davis, who arrived in Boston in 1683. As he had small means but a large family, one David Edwards offered an indemnity that he would not become a charge on the town. The only other clockmaker recorded in seventeenth-century America was Everardus Bogardus, active in New York by 1698. The first clock factory (as opposed to a workshop maintained by a master craftsman) was established by Eli Terry in Plymouth, Conn., where he was turning out ten to twenty clocks at a time by 1803. Mass production followed in 1807 when he was contracted by the Rev. Edward Porter and his brother Levi to produce four thousand clocks with wooden movements at $4 apiece, the Porters then selling them at a profit. The order was completed in three years. Following the invention of his celebrated pillar and scroll tall-case clock in 1816, production was increased to twelve thousand a year. Clocks were America's first mass-produced item to achieve deep penetration in overseas markets. In nineteenth-century Britain any cheap timepiece was known as an "American clock."

The first alarm clock in the United States was made by Levi Hutchins of Concord, N.H., in 1787 for his personal use. It had only a single setting—an exemplar of successful American entrepreneurs being early risers, Hutchins fixed his clock to wake him at an inexorable 4:00 A.M.

THE FIRST **CLONE**

....

of an adult mammal was a 14½-pound Finn Dorset lamb born at the Roslin Institute in Roslin, near Edinburgh, Scotland, at 5:00 P.M. on 5 July 1996. She had been created by embryologists Prof. Ian Wilmut, Dr. Keith Campbell, and Bill Ritchie, who fused an udder cell from a six-year-old sheep with an egg of another sheep from which all genetic material had been removed. The result was an identical twin of the donor of the udder cell, and in a whimsical allusion to her genetic source, Wilmut named her Dolly after another mammal who owed her fame to mammaries. The sponsor of the work was PPL Therapeutics Ltd. of Edinburgh, whose aim was to produce cloned sheep that could be genetically engineered to generate specific proteins in their milk for use as drugs in the treatment of diseases such as hemophilia and cystic fibrosis.

Wilmut's achievement, remarkable as it was for the prospects it offered (including, ultimately but most controversially, human cloning), did not achieve an immediate realization of this goal. He and his team had made 276 earlier attempts to clone an udder cell, all of which had failed. Future progress would mean isolating the factor on which success depended. There was also the question of whether the newborn lamb was genetically six years old like its twin and would age prematurely. In fact Dolly failed to live out a full life span, eleven–twelve years, being put down in February 2003 at the age of six and a half. She was suffering from a progressive lung disease with no prospect of recovery. It was not possible to determine conclusively whether the death was due to a genetic disposition to aging or simply natural causes.

U.S.: The first mammal cloned from adult cells was a mouse called Cumulina born at the John A. Burns School of Medicine at the University of Hawaii at Manoa on 3 December 1997, the first of more than fifty identical sisters. The so-called Honolulu Technique used to reproduce the mice was developed by Japanese-born Ryuzo Yanagimachi and his co-workers of "Team Yana," Japan's Teruhiko Wakayama, Italy's Maurizio Zuccotti, American K. R. Johnson, and Britain's Anthony Perry. Cumulina, named because she was made with the DNA of cumulus cells, gave birth to two litters of babies and lived a normal life span, dying in May 2000.

The first **pet animal cloned** from adult cells was CC (carbon copy), a calico cat born at Texas A&M College of Veterinary Surgery at College Station, Tex., on 22 December 2001.

The first pet to be cloned commercially was Little Nicky, a longhaired tabby reproduced from a cat called Nicky that died in Texas aged seventeen in 2003. Her owner, identifying herself only as Julie for fear of persecution, paid Genetic Savings & Clone of Sausalito, Calif., $50,000 to clone her deceased pet. It is believed that the birth took place at Texas A&M, whose cloning work has been partly funded by Genetic Savings & Clone, but the date is not on record.

THE FIRST CLUB

on record founded for social intercourse was a London dining society called La Court de Bone Compagnie, which is known to have been in existence in 1413. Most of the members were drawn from among the gentlemen of the Temple, the center of London's legal profession, including the poet Hoecleve, two of whose ballads relate to the activities of the club. The first is in the form of a letter addressed from the brethren to their fellow member Henry Somer, congratulating him on his appointment as sub-treasurer of the exchequer. The contents indicate that Somer has remonstrated with the Company for lavish expenditure, to which the members reply that they are willing to reduce their expenditure whenever Somer chooses to set an example.

The Court de Bone Compagnie appears to be an isolated example of a medieval club. There are no further recorded examples of any similar association of like spirits until the advent of the "Right Worshipfull Fraternity of Sirenaical Gentlemen," better though anachronistically known as the "Mermaid Club," which began meeting at the Mermaid Tavern at the end of the sixteenth century. This was the club of which Raleigh, Shakespeare, and Ben Jonson were supposed to be members, though on no very reliable authority.

The earliest known use of the word *club* in the sense employed here is contained in Ben Jonson's "Vision on the Muses of His Friend Michael Drayton" of 1627, in which the dramatist declares that it is not his intention to "raise a rhyming club about the town." The first club known to have used the word in its title was the Rota Club, a London debating society founded 1659.

U.S.: The earliest known club for social intercourse was an unnamed organization founded in New York

City in 1668 by the governor of New York, Francis Lovelace, and comprised ten French and Dutch families and six English families who met in each other's houses from 6:00 to 9:00 P.M. twice a week in winter and once a week in summer. Polite conversation in three languages was aided by Madeira wine or rum and brandy punch served in silver tankards and "not compounded or adulterated as in England." The French were Huguenots (Protestants) who had been driven from their native country by the religious persecutions of Louis XIV.

Sports club: The first in America was the Schuylkill Fishing Company of Philadelphia, instituted on 1 May 1732 as the Colony in Schuylkill with a clubhouse called the Castle at the foot of the Schuylkill River falls at Fairmount (recorded by a marker on the present Martin Luther King Drive). The angling club is still in existence, now at the Devon estate on the Delaware River near Andalusia, Pa., and is the oldest sporting club in the world with a continuous existence. It also claims to be the world's oldest social club.

The first club devoted to a ball game in the United States was the Greenwich Cricket Club of New York, functioning in 1779 but about which little else is known. At that time Greenwich Village was literally a village, some 2 miles distant from New York City. For the first clubs devoted to baseball, basketball, bowling, football, golf, hockey, skiing, tennis, and track and field, see under those headings.

THE FIRST **COCHLEAR IMPLANT**

(multi-channel), a speech processor that sends nerve impulses directly to the brain of a deaf person, was developed by Prof. Graeme Clark of the University of Melbourne in Australia and was implanted in the mastoid bone of patient Rod Saunders's inner ear on 1 August 1978. The sound of talking as heard by a bionic ear has been described as like hearing Donald Duck on a transistor radio; it is nevertheless an enormous advance for the totally deaf. The device was produced commercially by Nucleus Ltd. of Sydney, the first implant of a standard fitment being made on 14 September 1982. It was approved for clinical use in the United States by the Food and Drug Administration

in late 1984 together with an alternative multi-channel model developed by Dr. William House and 3M. These were the first freely available implanted devices to substitute for a human sense.

THE FIRST **COCKTAIL**

authentic reference to, is contained in the American periodical *The Balance* for 13 May 1806 in the following terms: "Cocktail is a kind of stimulating liquor, composed of spirits of any kind, sugar, water, and bitters—it is vulgarly called bittered sling and is supposed to be an excellent electioneering potion."

There are numerous stories accounting for the origin of the name. In the version favored by Joseph Nathan Kane, author of *Famous First Facts*, the first so-called cocktail was served by a barmaid named Betsy Flanagan at Halls Corners, Elmsford, N.Y., in 1776. The bar was decorated with tail feathers, and when a drunk called for a glass of "those cocktails" Miss Flanagan responded by giving him a mixed drink decorated with a feather.

This episode probably belongs in *Famous First Fairy Tales*. Betsy Flanagan was a character in James Fenimore Cooper's 1821 novel *The Spy*, set in the Revolutionary War. Although it is partly based on the oral testimony of survivors, there is no evidence that Betsy was a real person. Different versions of the provenance of the word are many and varied and mainly improbable. Least so is the theory that it is a corruption of the French argot *coquetel*, used in the Bordeaux region to signify a mixed drink, which may have been used by French soldiers fighting for the American cause during the Revolution.

Likewise the picturesque tales of the origin of the **dry martini** may be dismissed, like Betsy Flanagan's tail feathers, as fables. The first one was neither shaken nor stirred by Jerry Thomas at the Occidental Hotel in San Francisco in 1862, and there is no mention of it in the celebrated bartender's *How to Mix Drinks; or, The Bon Vivant's Companion* of that year (though it *was* the first cocktail guide). Nor was the martini invented, as alternative versions have it, at Julio's Bar on Ferry Street in Martinez, Calif., by Julio Richelieu, who did not mix one for a gold miner who paid for a bottle of whiskey with a nugget and asked for "something special" in lieu of change. Various recipes for drinks called Martinez and martini were published during the 1880s and 1890s, but these called for *sweet* vermouth as the principal additive to Old Tom gin, also sweet. The earliest recipe for a cocktail composed of *dry* gin and *dry* vermouth appears under the name Marguerite in Thomas Stuart's *Stuart's Fancy Drinks*, published in New York in 1896.

> 1 dash of orange bitters
> ⅔ Plymouth gin
> ⅓ French vermouth

Of course ⅓ vermouth would not accord with surreal film director Luis Buñuel's insistence that the vermouth bottle should be held between the glass of gin and an open window and a shaft of sunlight allowed to pass through it, but the martini's principal historian, Lowell Edmunds, in *The Silver Bullet: The Martini in American Civilization* (1981), believes that despite the name, this was the dry martini proper. He points out that orange bitters often featured in early-twentieth-century recipes for it. Edmunds does not claim Stuart as the inventor of the drink, only as its earliest chronicler. That benefactor of mankind will, it seems, remain ever unknown to posterity.

Cocktail party: The invention of the cocktail party is claimed by Alex Waugh, author and brother of Evelyn, who gave one at the Haverstock Hill studio of painter C. R. W. Nevinson in London on 26 April 1924. Londoners at that date being wholly unaccustomed to drinking at such an early hour as 5:30 P.M., only one guest turned up—described by Waugh as "an obscure middle-aged journalist who did a London gossip column for a provincial newspaper." A more successful venture followed in the autumn of 1925, when Waugh tried subterfuge, inviting thirty guests to tea but serving them potent daiquiris mixed by an American diplomat expert in their concoction. Everyone drank themselves silly, had a wonderful time, and started giving their own cocktail parties.

Barely a year later brother and sister Gaspard and Loelia Ponsonby (later Duchess of Westminster) invented the **bottle party** on an evening in November 1926 when their parents were away shooting grouse.

Despite the fact that they lived in the splendor of a grace-and-favor house within the precincts of St. James's Palace, the young Ponsonbys were hard up. They invited their friends, a group of gilded youth known to the popular press as the Bright Young Things, to attend a party at which the girls were to provide the food and the boys were to bring a bottle. The best-selling novelist Michael Arlen made up for the rather meager offerings of the younger men by producing a dozen bottles of pink champagne. Various guests contributed music by strumming on the piano, and theatrical designer Oliver Messel performed a one-man cabaret with impersonations that Loelia later recalled as being "in dubious taste."

THE FIRST COFFEE

as a beverage is recorded in Abyssinia (now Ethiopia) c. 1000 by the Persian philosopher and physician Avicenna, who called it *bunc*, a word still used in Ethiopia. It only spread northward after 1454, the year in which the mufti of Aden, Sheik Gemaleddin Abou Muhommad Bensaid Aldhabkani, encountered coffee in Abyssinia and sent for some when he became ill after returning to Aden. He sanctioned the use of the drink among the dervishes "that they might spend the night in prayers . . . with more attention and presence of mind." Here, then, was the earliest example of the use of coffee as an anti-soporific, but generally in Arabia and Persia it was used, as Sheik Gemaleddin had done, as a medicine.

Coffee began to be drunk socially in the Arabian Peninsula at Mecca at an uncertain date, probably at the end of the fifteenth century. In 1511 the governor, Kair Bey, attempted (ultimately unsuccessfully) to close down the coffeehouses, seemingly on the grounds that people were enjoying themselves too much. The indictment read in part that "in these places men and women meet and play tambourines, stringed instruments, and other musical devices. There are also people who play chess, mankala, and other similar games, for money; and there are many other things done not according to our sacred law." Despite this portrayal of unbridled vice, coffeehouses acquired the sobriquet *Mekteb-i-irfan*, meaning "schools of the cultured." They appear to have also been schools of desire. Sir George Sandys, who later emigrated to Virginia, described those coffeehouses he saw in Constantinople during a visit in 1610 and the means by which proprietors lured Turkish men, notorious at the time for pederasty, through their doors:

> Although they be destitute of Taverns, yet have they their Coffa-houses, which something resemble them. There sit they chatting most of the day: and sippe of a drinke called Coffa (of the berry that it is made of) in little China dishes as hot as they can suffer it: blacke as soote, and tasting not much unlike it. . . . Which helpeth, as they say, digestion, and procureth alacrity: many of the Coffa-men keeping beautifull boyes, who serve as stales to procure them customers.

It was not until the end of that century that coffee penetrated Europe. An Italian merchant called Mocengio is reputed to have introduced the beans to Venice in the late 1590s, and Anthony Sherley carried some home to England from Persia in 1599 following his unsuccessful attempt to form an alliance between Queen Elizabeth I and Shah Abbas. They sold for £5 an ounce in London, equivalent to a maidservant's wages for a full year, at which price it is hardly surprising coffee failed to replace ale as the national beverage.

What was probably the first coffeehouse in Europe was opened in Oxford in 1650 by a Jew from Lebanon called Jacob or Jacobs "at the Angel in the parish of St. Peter in the East." Here hot chocolate was also sold, and the venture rapidly became a popular resort of the university students. Some Italian authorities assert that a *caffè* had been opened in Venice as early in 1645, but there is no contemporary evidence of such an institution anywhere in Italy before 1683. France was introduced to the coffee-shop concept in 1672 when an Armenian called Pascal opened a booth at the fair of Saint Germain in Paris. He is reputed to have used the first purpose-designed silver coffeepots on this occasion. Germany followed, with a coffeehouse opened by an English merchant in Hamburg in 1679.

It was the custom at all these early cafés to drink the beverage black and unsweetened, as in the Middle East. Milk was first added to coffee by the Dutch ambassador to China, one Nieuhoff, about 1660, and in 1665 Sieur Monin, a celebrated doctor of Grenoble in France, introduced *café au lait*, with the powdered coffee boiled in milk, as a medicament. A polish adventurer called Franz Georg Kolshitzky, who opened a coffeehouse at 30 Haidgasse, Vienna, in 1685, gave coffee with milk and sugar a wider currency. He was also the originator of the style of coffee known as Viennese, straining it to produce a pure liquid without grounds. Sugar as an additive to coffee had been noted earlier by Johann Veslingius, who stated that about 1625 patrons of Cairo's 3,000 coffeehouses "did begin to put sugar in their coffee to correct the bitterness of it."

U.S.: The earliest allusion to the drinking of coffee in America dates from 1668, when New Yorkers were said to imbibe it sweetened either with sugar or with honey and cinnamon. The first known seller of coffee was Dorothy Jones of Boston, who was licensed to purvey "coffee and cuckaletto" (chocolate) in 1670. Coffee at this time was too expensive to be consumed by any but the rich. William Penn wrote in his *Accounts* for 1683 that coffee could sometimes be procured in New York for 18s 9d a pound. The identity of the first coffeehouse is questionable, but it is known that on 20 April 1678 John Parrey petitioned the Suffolk County Court for a license to operate "a publique house for retailing of Coffee and Chocolato" in Boston. The term "public house" implies that the beverages were drunk on the premises.

Tea was the favored hot drink of the American colonists, rivaled by chocolate, with coffee as something of an also-ran except as a breakfast drink, displacing ale and tea about 1750. The eventual supremacy of coffee was principally to do with British government policies in the run-up to the Revolutionary War. A tax was imposed on tea in 1767, along with paint, oils, lead, and glass. When the Americans launched a trade boycott, all were repealed except the tax on tea. The precious commodity was smuggled in from Holland. Consignments of tea sent to the chief American ports from Britain by the East India Company were seized by the colonists and discharged into the harbor, most notably at the 1773 event that came to be known as the Boston Tea Party. War effectively cut off supplies of both tea and coffee except in areas of British occupation; once they were resumed, many of the newly independent Americans opted for coffee as less redolent of what they regarded as British oppression. Nevertheless tea remained an American staple throughout the nineteenth century, particularly among women, and it was only with the introduction of packaged coffee, led by Lewis A. Osborn of New York with his Osborn's Celebrated Prepared Java Coffee in 1863, and the mass immigration of coffee drinkers from Germany, Scandinavia, and Eastern Europe, that America's favorite beverage achieved its undisputed ascendancy.

Decaf: The first brand was Sanka, developed in 1903 after German coffee merchant Ludwig Roselius of Bremen had succeeded in restoring a cargo of coffee that had been contaminated with seawater by extracting the caffeine. It was first sold in the United States by Merck & Co. in 1910 under the brand name Dekafa, later changed for reasons not readily apparent to Dekofa.

Instant coffee: The first soluble (i.e., powdered) coffee was invented in Tokyo by Japanese chemist Dr. Sartori Kato, who brought the process to Chicago in 1899. It was launched commercially as Kato Coffee at the Pan-American Exposition in Buffalo, N. Y., in 1901, attracting the notice of Capt. Baldwin, who placed the first bulk order for use on the Ziegler Arctic Expedition. Numerous other soluble coffees followed, notably Red E in 1910, later called G. Washington's Instant Coffee, and Barrington Hall, introduced by the Baker Importing Co. of Minneapolis c. 1918. Both these brands were included in the reserve ration issued to troops of the U.S. Army serving in France, ¾ of an ounce in an envelope forming a daily ration. These and the brands that followed after the war, such as Blanke's Health Coffee, Hires, and the Soluble Coffee Co.'s Ev-Ry-Da, suffered from impaired flavor and tended to be used on camping expeditions or picnics rather than, as the Soluble Coffee Co. suggested in its choice of brand name, every day.

The first instant coffee to solve the flavor problem and become a global brand was Nescafé, developed by Nestlé of Vevey, Switzerland, in response to a request from the Brazilian Institute of Coffee in 1930 for a product that could compete with ground coffee.

At this time Brazil was suffering such a glut of coffee that it was burned as fuel on steam locomotives. Not for eight years was the task crowned with success. Nescafé was launched in Switzerland on 1 April 1938 and in Britain, Australia, and the United States the following year.

THE FIRST COINS

struck in the United States were the so-called pine tree coinage produced by John Hull and Robert Sanderson at the Boston Mint House in October (?) 1652 for circulation in the Massachusetts Bay Colony. The dies were made by Joseph Jenks at the Iron Foundry in Lynn, Mass. The issue consisted of shillings, sixpences, and threepences, bearing the date, the name of the colony, and the pine tree in the center "as an apt symbol of progressive vigor." It was necessitated by the dearth of silver specie in the colony, nearly all commerce being conducted by barter and taxes paid in kind. Cast from sterling silver, they were by weight "two pence in the shilling of less valew than the English coyne" (i.e., a pine tree shilling was worth five sixths of an English shilling).

The Boston Mint continued to issue these unauthorized coins for over thirty years, all of them dated with the same year, 1652, to hoodwink the English authorities, and they circulated so widely that some were even used as currency in England itself. When shown some of the coins, King Charles II was said to have been extremely angered by such presumption on behalf of his far distant colonial subjects, but he was appeased by the quick thinking of Sir Thomas Temple, who had just returned from New England. The monarch asked what kind of tree was depicted, to which Temple responded that it was the royal oak that had saved His Majesty's life (he hid in it during the Civil War). The king was sufficiently amused or flattered by this that he declared the Americans "a parcel of honest dogs."

The first copper coins, as well as the only other silver coins prior to the Revolution, were issued by Maryland in 1662. Copper halfpennies emanated from Carolina in 1694, followed by pennies and twopences in 1723 and another penny in 1733. Connecticut also issued coppers in 1737 and 1739 and Virginia halfpence in 1773.

United States coins: The first so inscribed were authorized by the Continental Congress and struck in copper by a government order of 6 July 1787 decreeing that they should bear the following:

device A dial, with the hours expressed upon the face, with "fugio" on the left and "1787" on the right. A meridian sun above the dial, and below it the

legend "Mind your Business."

reverse Thirteen circles, linked together, forming a large circle. In the centre of the same a small circle, with "United States." Around it and in the center, "We Are One."

The coins were produced under contract. The first coins issued from the U.S. Mint, established at the seat of government in Philadelphia, were half-dimes struck when the coin presses imported from England were put into operation on or about 1 October 1792. Dimes and cents followed the same year, followed by silver dollars and half-dollars in 1793 and gold eagles and half-eagles in 1795. The purpose-built U.S. Mint, a three-story brick edifice on Seventh Street, was the first building owned by the U.S. government.

The first coin to bear the inscription "In God We Trust" was the bronze 2¢ piece issued on 22 April 1864.

THE FIRST **COLLAPSIBLE TUBE**

was patented by American artist John Rand on 11 September 1841 and first used commercially by the Devoe & Reynolds Co. of Louisville, Ky., for packing oil paints. Rand's lead tubes were one of the first American technological innovations to be introduced on a widespread scale in Europe; within a year or so of their U.S. debut they had been adopted by most of the London artists' colormen.

Toothpaste tube (collapsible metal): The first was introduced in Britain in 1891 for Dr. Zierner's Alexandra Dentifrices, which retailed at 1–2s 6d each (25¢–62½¢). Toothpaste was formerly packed in round Staffordshireware pots. In America the first

toothpaste tubes appeared the following year, when Dr. Washington Wentworth Sheffield of New London, Conn., introduced his Dr. Sheffield's Creme Dentifrice. He founded the Sheffield Tube Corp. to produce collapsible tubes for any product that can be squeezed through an aperture.

Collapsible polyethylene tube: The first was made by the Bradley Container Corp. of Delaware in 1953 for Sea and Ski, a suntan lotion.

THE FIRST **COLLEGE**

in the present United States was founded by an order of the General Court of Massachusetts Bay of 28 October 1636. The as yet unnamed "Colledge" in Cambridge, Mass., opened, probably in July or August 1638, under Nathaniel Eaton in a house on the north side of Braintree Street (now Harvard Street) formerly belonging to Goodman Peyntree. The exact date is uncertain. Eaton and his family are known to have moved into the Peyntree house before 9 June 1638, and a letter written by Edmund Browne of Boston on 7 September records: "Wee have at Cambridge heere, a College erecting, youth lectured, a library, and I suppose there will be a presse this winter." "Youth lectured" implies that instruction of the initial intake of students had already begun by that date.

A week after Browne's letter was written, the man after whom the college was to be named died at the early age of thirty. John Harvard was a native of Southwark in London, where his father was a butcher and owner of the Queen's Head tavern, and came to settle in Charlestown, Mass., in 1637. Only a year later he died there of consumption, leaving his 260 books and half his estate of £1,600 to the college. (All but one of the books was destroyed when the library caught fire in 1764; the survivor had been taken out overnight, illegally, by a student.) The bequest appears to have been the first endowment as well as the first significant act of philanthropy in American history. On 13 March 1639, the General Court "Ordered, that the colledge agreed upon formerly to bee built at Cambridg shalbee called Harvard Colledge."

Life was harsh for the first Harvard freshmen under the choleric and savage Nathaniel Eaton. Several testified that they had been cruelly beaten by Eaton, receiving twenty or thirty stripes before confessing to whatever he had accused them of. There was seldom sufficient to eat, and that little commonly porridge or pudding. Mistress Eaton, in charge of the feeding arrangements, admitted to having deprived them of the beef and beer to which they were entitled, serving them bad fish and also mackerel that still contained the guts, and serving bread made of sour meal, and moreover that there was goat's dung in the hasty pudding. What little bread they had was the crusts left over by "the Moor" (who happened to be the first slave known in New England), which they had to share with the pigs.

All this came to light after Eaton had been arraigned in September 1639 for battering the assistant master, Nathaniel Briscoe, about the head and shoulders with two hundred blows of a stout cudgel while the unhappy man was pinioned by two servants. Eaton was dismissed and fined, also being required to pay damages to the much bruised Briscoe. It was then discovered that he was in debt for £1,000, and circumstantial evidence suggests that he had also plundered the college funds, including part of John Harvard's bequest. It was his replacement, Henry Dunster, who turned the moribund college into the august seat of learning that was to confer so much distinction on emergent American culture.

The first **purpose-built college building** in America was that which later came to be known as Old College, a two-story E-shaped 63' x 900' clapboard structure "very comely within and without," that was completed in September 1642. It was within its "spacious Hall" that the first **graduates of an American college** received their degrees at the commencement held on the 23rd of that month. They were nine in number:

BENJAMIN WOODBRIDGE, b. Highworth, Wiltshire, 1622, traveled to join his brother John at Newbury, Mass., in 1639 after matriculating from Oxford; returned to England to take his MA at Oxford and was for nearly forty years minister of Newbury, Berkshire, where he died in 1684.

GEORGE DOWNING, probably b. London 1625; emigrated to Salem, Mass., 1638; returned to England via Newfoundland and the West Indies in 1645; appointed scoutmaster-general of Cromwell's army in Scotland 1652. Minister to Holland 1657 and subsequently helped to engineer the restoration of Charles II, for which he was knighted; elected MP Member of Parliament Morpeth 1661; organized the seizure of New Amsterdam (New York) from the Dutch 1664; appointed secretary to the Treasury 1667; died 1684 having received at least £80,000 for personal services to the king (equivalent to a present-day purchasing power of not less than $100 million). Whether on this account or not, he was one of the most hated men in England.

JOHN BULKLEY, b. Odell, Bedfordshire, 1619; emigrated to Concord, Mass., 1635; returned to England 1645 and became minister at Fordham, Essex, from which he was ejected under Act of Uniformity 1662 and became a physician in Wapping, London, where he died in 1689.

WILLIAM HUBBARD, b. 1621 probably in London; emigrated to Ipswich, Mass., (his mother was from Ipswich, England) in 1635; minister at Ipswich from 1688 to 1703 and died there in 1704. Hubbard led a tranquil life, except for an episode in 1694 when, aged seventy-five, he married a lady considered by his congregation to be his social inferior.

SAMUEL BELLINGHAM, birth date and place unknown; emigrated in 1634; returned to Europe after graduation, and qualified as doctor of medicine at Leyden. He settled in London and died sometime after 1700.

JOHN WILSON, b. London 1621; emigrated to Boston as a child; became minister at Dorchester, Mass., in 1649; moved in 1651 to Medfield, Mass., where he spent the rest of his life as minister, physician, and schoolmaster; died 1691.

HENRY SALTONSTALL, birth date and place unknown; emigrated to Watertown, Mass., 1630; returned to England 1643; qualified as doctor of medicine at Padua 1649. Date and place of death unknown.

TOBIAS BARNARD. Nothing known except that he returned to England.

NATHANIEL BREWSTER, probably b. London c. 1620 (BUT SEE NOTE UNDER **American-born graduate** BELOW); emigrated to New Haven, Conn. Returned to England shortly after graduating and became minister at Norfolk; emigrated to Boston 1663 and became minister of Brookhaven, Long Island, 1665, where he died in 1690.

It is notable that all of the graduates whose dates of death are known lived to a goodly age, way beyond average life expectancy for the period; but also that only two of them (Hubbard and Wilson) remained the rest of their lives in America. Given that the founders of Harvard had sought to establish an institution for the training of the future leaders of the colony, this may seem unexpected. It was probably on account of the ascendancy of the Puritans in England, which meant that those who had sought freedom from religious persecution by emigrating to America were now able to return home with impunity—and in some cases persecute in turn any who differed in persuasion.

American-born graduate: The first cannot be asserted with certainty, because not all the birthplaces of early scholars are recorded. The first who is definitely known to have been of American birth was Isaac Allerton, born in Plymouth in about 1630, son of the Isaac Allerton who had come over on the *Mayflower* ten years earlier. After graduation from Harvard in 1650 he moved to New Haven and later to Northern Neck, Va. He was known to be alive in 1682, after which there is no further record. It has been claimed that Nathaniel Brewster, class of 1642 (SEE ABOVE), may have been born in Plymouth, but this is probably owing to mistaken parentage (there were several Brewsters on the *Mayflower*). It is more probable that he emigrated from London to New Haven as a child.

Oldest college building: The original college buildings at Harvard were replaced in 1677 by Harvard Hall I, burned down in 1764. Harvard's earliest building extant is Massachusetts Hall of 1718–20.

The oldest college building in America, therefore, is that of the second such institution in the colonies, William & Mary at Williamsburg, Va. (chartered 1693). Most of the original structure was destroyed by fire, but parts of the rebuilding of 1705 survive, as well as some walls dating from 1695.

Remarkably, by the time of the Revolution, the American colonies already had more universities than the mother country—a total of nine: Harvard (1636); William & Mary (1693); Yale (1701); College of New Jersey (1746)—now Princeton; College of Philadelphia (1749)—now the University of Pennsylvania; College of Rhode Island (1764)—now Brown; Queen's (1766)—now Rutgers; and Dartmouth (1769). Britain had seven: Oxford, Cambridge, Saint Andrew's, Edinburgh, Aberdeen, Glasgow, and Trinity College Dublin. By 1800 there were 25 U.S. colleges, then 52 in 1820 and 241 in 1860. The present number is 4,861 (including two-year colleges) with an enrollment of over 18 million.

State university: The first was the University of the State of Pennsylvania, formed when the Revolutionary State Legislature seized the College of Philadelphia from its provost and trustees in 1779 because of suspected Tory sentiments among some of the faculty, including Scottish-born Provost William Smith himself. New trustees were appointed, including state officials. The provost resisted staunchly, refusing to leave his house, the property of the university, until evicted the following year, and took legal action against the state. In 1789 a state legislature committee assigned to examine the merits of the case ruled that the state had no right to hold the College Building, as it was legally the property of the original trustees. The college was restored to its provost and those of the original trustees surviving and resumed the private status which, as the University of Pennsylvania, it retains to this day.

The first to be founded and become operative as a state university was the University of North Carolina at Chapel Hill, formally opened by Governor Richard Dobbs Spaight on 15 January 1795. The first student, Hinton James from New Hanover County, arrived on 12 February and comprised the entire student body for the next two weeks. At that time the university campus boasted a main faculty and dormitory building called the East Building, a student refectory and accommodation at Steward's Hall, and the President's House. The East Building, now called Old East, survives. Students paid 15 pounds North Carolina currency per annum for board and $5 for rent, with tuition gratis. They had to bring their own beds, though bedding was provided, and furnish their own firewood and candles. (It should be noted that the University of Georgia received its charter earlier than North Carolina, in 1785, but did not open until 1801.)

Roman Catholic college: The first in the United States was Jesuit-run Georgetown in Virginia, which opened on 22 November 1791 with one pupil, William Gaston, who was later to represent North Carolina in Congress. Fees were $44 per annum, board $133.

Black college: The first college to admit black students on a regular basis was Oberlin College in Ohio in 1835 (there had been occasional earlier admissions elsewhere—SEE **black college student**).

The first black college was Lincoln University, incorporated on 1 January 1854 as the Ashmun Institute in Chester County, Pa. The first students were accepted on 30 August 1856. It was originally named after the first president of Liberia, but took its present name in honor of the assassinated U.S. president in 1866. Alumni include the first president of Ghana, Kwame Nkrumah, U.S. Supreme Court Justice Thurgood Marshall, and poet Langston Hughes.

Graduate school: The first American university to accept graduate students was Harvard, which instituted an advanced course on comparative philology in 1831. It soon folded, however, for lack of enrollments. The first graduate school is therefore normally said to be the Yale Graduate School of Arts and Sciences, which originated in August 1847 with the establishment of a Department of Philosophy and Arts for Graduate Study, funding and administration being separate from those of the main college. The first Ph.D. was not conferred until 1861, when doctorates were awarded to three graduate students: James Morris Whiton (class of '53), for his six-page dissertation on the Latin proverb "Ars longa, vita brevis," who became a staff editor on the *Outlook*; Eugene Schuyler (class of '59), doctorate in philosophy and psychology, who became a career diplomat; and Arthur Williams Wright (class of '59), doctorate in physics, who became professor of experimental physics at Yale.

University: The American and European definitions of a university differ. In Europe any institution authorized to confer degrees is a university; it does not even have to have any students or lecturers. (London University for many years conferred degrees only on graduates of *other* seats of learning not so empowered.) By this criterion Harvard was a university from its foundation. Some Americans assert that a university must have a professional school, and it is on this basis that William & Mary claims to have been the first in 1779, when its law faculty was established under Prof. George Wythe. The University of Pennsylvania also claims the distinction, citing its medical school founded in 1765. This, however, overlooks the fact that the school was founded in that year as a separate and autonomous institution called the Medical College of Philadelphia and only became the Medical Department of Penn in 1791. According to Webster a university must comprise professional and graduate schools "authorized to confer master's or doctorate degrees." By that definition, Yale would have become the nation's first university in 1861. It is worth noting, though, that Pennsylvania has used the word "university" in its name ever since 1779 when the College of Philadelphia was seized by the state (SEE **state university** ABOVE), well before it acquired a professional school. Harvard University was named as such in the Massachusetts Constitution of 1780.

SEE ALSO **college to admit women**.

THE FIRST **COLLEGE JOURNAL**

on record was the *Telltale*, which was produced in manuscript as a satirical commentary on student life at Harvard in 1721. The editorial collective was known as the Spy Club and included Ebenezer Pemberton, co-founder of Princeton, Isaac Greenwood, who became Harvard's first mathematics professor, and John Lowell, founding father of a Harvard dynasty.

The first printed journal was the *Student*, published at Oxford University in England, with the imprint of the London bookseller and publisher John Newbery (SEE ALSO **children's magazine**), from 31 January 1750 to July 1751. The editor was the poet Christopher Smart, a Fellow of Pembroke Hall, Cambridge, described by one unflattering biographer as a bookseller's hack who "made for some years a hard living betwixt improvidence, dissipation, and a wife and children." The wife was John Newbery's daughter. Smart was later confined to a madhouse, where he wrote his most famous poem—"A Song to David"—using a key to scratch its eighty-six stanzas on the wainscot, writing paper having been denied him. The *Student* ran for nineteen issues and is considered to possess little literary distinction other than a contribution from Dr. Samuel Johnson.

The first printed journal in the United States was the *Literary Miscellany*, published by Harvard's Phi Beta Kappa Society quarterly from July 1804. The first college daily was the *Yale Daily News*, which debuted on 28 January 1878 and has been continuously published ever since. The *Harvard Crimson* claims to be "the oldest continuously published college daily," but while it was founded in 1873 (as the bimonthly *Magenta*) it did not become a daily until 1883.

America's oldest college journal is the *Dartmouth*, dating from 1843.

THE FIRST COLLEGE TO ADMIT WOMEN

was Oberlin Collegiate Institute, Oberlin, Ohio, founded by Theodore Weld and a number of his fellows who withdrew from Lane Theological Seminary in Cincinnati in order to establish a college with neither sex nor color as an entry qualification. It opened on 3 December 1833 with forty-four students, twenty-nine men and fifteen women. Although the declared intention of the college was to fit its women students "for intelligent motherhood and a properly subservient wifehood," Oberlin did in fact become one of the fountainheads of the feminist movement.

For the first few years women were only accepted in the preparatory department, which provided a level of education little different from the numerous female seminaries of the time. In 1837 a special ladies' degree course was instituted with a class of four. By the time three of them graduated as bachelors of arts on 25 August 1841, however, another American college had already conferred a degree on a woman. This was Georgia Female College (now Wesleyan), the world's first college for women only, which opened in Macon on 7 January 1839 under a charter that authorized it to "confer all such honors, degrees, and licenses as are usually conferred in colleges or universities." Among the initial intake was one Catherine Brewer, who became America's first female graduate on 16 July 1840. Her diploma does not state the type of degree, only that she had "passed through a regular course of study. . . embracing all the Sciences which are usually taught at the Colleges of the United States." Subsequent degrees offered at what had by then become Wesleyan (1844) were *Artium Baccalaureus* for graduates of the regular, nonclassical course and *Literarum Baccalaureus* for those adding Latin, so it seems likely that Miss Brewer graduated with an AB degree. Until 1886 all graduates of ten years' standing automatically received an MA, so Catherine would have had hers conferred in 1850. Wesleyan has two other notable firsts in women's collegiate education: the earliest Greek letter sororities, the Aldephean Society (Alpha Delta Pi), founded 15 May 1851, and the Philomathean Society (Phi Mu) of 1852; and the first alumnae society, founded 11 July 1859.

It should be noted that while Mount Holyoke has an earlier date of foundation than Wesleyan, it began life in 1837 as a female seminary, albeit one for mature students of high educational attainments, and did not receive a college charter until 1888. The oldest foundation is Salem College, Winston-Salem, N.C., established as a girls' school in 1772 and designated a college in 1890.

Neither Oberlin nor Georgia Female/Wesleyan conferred degrees that were recognized as comparable to those conferred by the better men's colleges. The first to do so is usually claimed as Elmira Female College, which was founded in the town of Elmira, N.Y., in 1855 and conferred its first seventeen degrees four years later. Comparing Elmira's admission requirements with those of Vassar (opened 1865), the other main contender for the first women's college on a par with men's, Thomas Woody in his magisterial *History of Women's Education in the United States* (1929) concluded that Vassar was marginally ahead on the classics and Elmira superior in history, geography, and the sciences.

The first state college to admit women was Iowa from its opening in March 1856, though originally only as trainee teachers in the normal department. The first private men's college to become co-educational was Boston University in 1869, which three years later would be the first in the world to open all its postgraduate schools to women, Helen Magill becoming America's first female Ph.D. when she earned a doctorate in Greek drama in 1877. Cornell University, usually cited as the first private men's college to go coed, did so in 1870, a year after BU. The first college with a mixed dorm was the University of Oregon, where Friendly Hall accommodated both sexes in 1893.

THE FIRST **COMIC BOOK**

in the current style and format was *Funnies on Parade*, published as a one-off in an edition of 500,000 by the Eastern Color Co. of Waterbury, Conn., in 1933. Its format, 7" x 9", was determined by the size of a standard American newspaper page; four pages were printed to the sheet and folded twice. *Funnies on Parade* was produced in four colors and contained reprints of "Joe Palooka," "Mutt and Jeff," "Hairbreadth Harry," "Keeping Up with the Joneses," and "Connie." It was not sold direct to the public, but issued as a gift premium by such companies as Procter & Gamble and Canada Dry. The first on the news-stands and first to be issued as a periodical was *Famous Funnies*, published by the Dell Publishing Co. at a price of 10¢ in May 1934 (though dated July).

Comic book to contain original material: The first in standard format was *New Comics*, issued by Maj. Malcolm Wheeler Nicholson in December 1935. The accent was on adventure serials, and the first eighty-page issue introduced characters like Homer Fleming's Captain Jim of the Texas Rangers. This led to a new trend in comic-book publishing, the creation of the comic-book heroes, characters who had not previously appeared in newspaper comic strips. The two most enduring figures in this genre debuted within twelve months of each other, Joe Schuster's Superman performing his first deeds of valor in the No. 1 June 1938 issue of *Action Comics*, while Bob Kane's Caped Crusader Batman began his rise to comic-book immortality in the May 1939 issue of *Detective Comics*. An unrestored copy of *Action Comics* No. 1 established a record price of $317,200 in an online auction in March 2009. The vendor had paid 35¢ for it as a

nine-year-old in 1951, and his father had remonstrated with him for paying such an extortionate amount for a used comic that had cost 10¢ new.

THE FIRST **COMIC STRIP**

in a newspaper was Richard Outcault's "Yellow Kid," which first appeared in strip form in the Sunday color supplement of the *New York Journal* on 24 October 1897. This initial episode was entitled "The Yellow Kid Takes a Hand at Golf" and depicted the erratic efforts of its hero to address the ball. The Yellow Kid had originally been featured as a single-panel cartoon in Joseph Pulitzer's *New York World* in February 1896. The central character was a flap-eared, bald-headed child, clad only in a sack-like yellow robe, whose pranks and antics were vigorously chronicled by Outcault against a background of New York slum tenements. The Kid's most distinctive feature, his curious saffron garment, was designed by the artist specially for an experiment in tint-laying. The experiment was successful, with two unexpected results—the entry into English usage of a new phrase, the "yellow press," and the genesis of the newspaper comic strip. This was six weeks before the debut of Rudolph Dirks's "Katzenjammer Kids" in William Randolph Hearst's *New York Journal* on 12 December 1897, often claimed as the first newspaper strip by historians who have assumed that "The Yellow Kid" continued as a single-panel cartoon. The mischievous twins Hans and Fritz of "The Katzenjammer Kids" still wreak havoc weekly in about fifty papers, syndicated by King Features, and it is now the longest-running strip in the world. It remains remarkably faithful to an age in which German American culture was a much more prominent feature of American life, though there has been one significant change: The character called "the King" rules over dusky South Sea Islanders. His subjects used to be black Africans, now way off-limits to cartoonists.

Daily comic strip: The first was "A. Piker Clerk," drawn by Clare Briggs for Hearst's *Chicago American* December 1903–June 1904. A. Piker Clerk was a chinless follower of form whose exploits at the racetrack and efforts to raise loans for "dead certs" enlivened the sports page of the *American* for six months before William Randolph Hearst decreed that Briggs's creation was vulgar and must be dropped forthwith.

The first successful daily cross-strip was Bud Fisher's "Mr. A. Mutt," another luckless gambler, who began to appear on the sports page of the *San Francisco Chronicle* on 15 November 1907. Mutt was joined by Jeff on 29 March 1908, and they have stayed together ever since.

Comic strip superhero: The first comic-strip superhero was the justice fighter the Phantom, drawn by Ray Moore with story and captions by Lee Falk, who made his debut in what was to become regulation superhero tights and mask via King Features Syndicate of Philadelphia on 17 February 1936. Lee Falk, an advertising copywriter in St. Louis when he created the Phantom, continued to write the strip for sixty-three years until his death in 1999. SEE ALSO **comic book**.

THE FIRST **COMPANY**

founded in the present United States was the Company of Undertakers of the Iron Works in New England, chartered by the Massachusetts Bay Colony in 1644 in exchange for an undertaking to sell iron in the province at no more than £26 a ton. Although it was registered as a joint stock company in the City of London, the prime movers in the enterprise were the Bay Colony's Gov. John Winthrop Sr. and his son John Jr., and the majority of the two dozen shareholders were prominent Puritan merchants. There was also significant backing from the General Court of the Massachusetts Bay Colony, without which the venture capital, a substantial £15,000, would not have been forthcoming. The company was granted extensive land and timber holdings, including 3,000 acres at Braintree, and its employees were exempted from militia service and, more remarkably in the Puritan colony, from church attendance. It was also given water power rights for the triphammers, forge, and slitting mill, and tax exemption for ten years.

In December 1644 the company built a furnace at Braintree, but abandoned it in 1647 for lack of an adequate supply of ore. A forge on the site continued to operate. The center of operations was then transferred to the Hammersmith Furnace on the Saugus River at Lynn, Mass., completed by 1650. It would eventually comprise a blast furnace 21 feet high by 26 feet square, two fineries, a chaffery, a water-powered forge hammer, a rolling mill, and a slitting mill, capable of producing seven tons of cast iron a week. This was the first major manufacturing plant as well as the first ironworks in America. It continued to operate until 1676.

The development of companies was slow during the colonial period and the early years of the republic. By 1800 there were only 335 business corporations in total, most of them concerned with transportation and banking. A mere 4 percent were manufacturing or trading companies.

The key to the development of companies in America was incorporation, which freed the stockholders from individual liability for debt. Although the New London Society for Trade and Commerce was granted a corporate charter by the Connecticut General Assembly in May 1732, this was revoked the following February; the first effective incorporation was of the Union Wharf Company of New Haven under a charter of 22 May 1760. Incorporation remained exceptional during the eighteenth century, however, and it was this rather than British restraints on colonial manufacturers that impeded America's progress toward the preeminence it would achieve as workshop of the world in the later nineteenth century. The first significant step in the process of liberating companies was taken by North Carolina in 1795 with an act allowing canal ventures to incorporate without specific legislative provision, followed in 1797 by Massachusetts, which granted the same privilege to water companies. In 1830 Massachusetts extended this to certain categories of business other than public works, while Connecticut went farther in 1837 by allowing nearly all kinds of legitimate business to become incorporated by right.

The oldest company in the United States is the Philadelphia Contributorship for the Insuring of Houses from Loss by Fire, founded as a mutual insurance company in 1752 and incorporated by the Pennsylvania Assembly on 20 February 1768. It is the only colonial business corporation to have survived to the present day.

THE FIRST **COMPUTER, ALL-ELECTRONIC**

was a single-purpose, non-programmable binary calculator weighing 700 pounds with 282 vacuum tubes that was built by Dr. John Atanasoff and his assistant Clifford Berry in the basement of the physics laboratory of Iowa State College at Ames (now Iowa State University). Funded with a grant of $850, it was intended that it should solve simultaneous linear equations for the Iowa State Statistical Laboratory, this being the only process in that institution's process output that had not been automated with IBM punch-card equipment. Work began in December 1939, but there is still controversy over whether the apparatus was in working order by the time Atanasoff was drafted to the Naval Ordnance Laboratory in September 1942. Some observers declare that it was at least operational in prototype form, others that it was not yet fully developed but would have worked, and yet others that it was only a collection of unassembled parts. Iowa State College failed to follow through with patent applications, and the ABC (Atanasoff-Berry Computer), as it was later known, was dismantled in 1948 when the basement was converted into classrooms. Only a single memory drum survives. However, an exact replica constructed at a cost of $350,000 by an Ames Laboratory team in 1997 proves that it would have performed the process for which it was designed, though the output system, which depended on burning minute holes in punch cards, would have limited its practical utility.

In 1973 Honeywell sought a judicial hearing on the patent held by Sperry Rand on J. Presper Eckert and John W. Mauchly's ENIAC (SEE BELOW), generally held to have been the earliest electronic computer (Bletchley Park's Colossus still being secret at the time). Mauchly had met Atanasoff at a conference, where they had exchanged information on their respective development programs, and Mauchly spent a week in Ames in June 1941 to inspect the ABC. The two continued to correspond about their progress. Following exhaustive testimony Judge Earl R. Larson ruled that Eckert and Mauchly "did not themselves first invent the automatic electronic digital computer, but instead derived their subject matter from one Dr. John Vincent Atanasoff."

The first **functional electronic computer**—the earliest in regular use for practical applications—was Colossus I, built in conditions of highest secrecy for the Government Code and Cypher School at Bletchley Park in Buckinghamshire, England. The Nazis' Enigma code had been broken early in World War II at Bletchley Park, but even more formidable was the Lorenz cipher used by Hitler to communicate with his generals. Bletchley mathematician Prof. Max Newman wrote a specification for a way to mechanize the cryptanalysis of these messages, but senior officials deemed the project technically impossible. A Post Office engineer, Tommy Flowers, had suggested that the mechanical switching devices used in existing decoders be replaced by vacuum tubes. This was resisted on the grounds that vacuum tubes were not sufficiently durable, but Flowers knew from experience in electronic telephone systems that vacuum tubes would endure provided they were never switched off. Ignoring the turndown from on high, he determined to go it alone with his team at the Post Office Research Station at Dollis Hill in London, a decision that one eminent German military historian has estimated shortened the war by up to two years. As the project was unfunded, Flowers paid for any parts unavailable from stock out of his own pocket.

Colossus I was built over a period of ten months from February 1943, the one-ton machine with its 1,500 vacuum tubes being constructed by Flowers's team working 12 hours a day, 6½ days a week. A single-purpose computer, it was designed to run through the millions of possible settings for the code wheels on the Lorenz. The first test run at Bletchley Park took place on 8 December 1943, operating at 5,000 characters a second.

Colossus I was not programmable. The first **programmable computers** were the ten 2,400-vacuum-tube Colossi II that followed, after twenty-year-old codebreaker Donald Michie had come up with a technique for breaking wheel-patterns. This would also vastly speed up the process of decrypting, to 25,000 characters a second. The computers included a vital input from the United States: a supply of automatic electric typewriters, which were unavailable in Britain, was used for the printed output. These Colossi were the machines that hastened the end of the war.

The decision to go ahead with the invasion of Europe depended on whether Hitler believed the Allies' disinformation that the invasion would take place in the Pas de Calais rather than Normandy. The first machine became operational on 1 June 1944, just in time to decrypt messages from the German High Command confirming that the deception had worked, thereby ensuring that the panzer divisions that would otherwise have wreaked destruction on the American, British, and Canadian forces were not moved forward. The output from this first programmable computer gave Gen. Dwight D. Eisenhower the intelligence needed to proceed with the invasion of Europe.

At the end of the war all those who had worked on the project were forbidden to speak about it, and Churchill gave orders that the Colossi "be broken into pieces no larger than a man's fist." In fact two were saved, being sent to GCHQ (successor to Britain's codebreaking center at Bletchley) for work on Cold War intelligence traffic. One failed in 1954, the other surviving in operational mode until the 1960s. Meanwhile, at Dollis Hill Tommy Flowers acted on government instructions to incinerate all the original Colossus blueprints in 1960. Only in 1976 did Prof. Brian Randall of Newcastle University reveal one of the best-kept secrets of World War II, the role of computers in ending Nazi dominion in Europe.

U.S.: America's first functional electronic computer, the Electronic Numerical Integrator and Computer (ENIAC), is also claimed, somewhat controversially, as the first general-purpose computer, the ABC and Colossi having been designed to perform specific tasks. ENIAC was built for the U.S. Army Ordnance Department by John Mauchly and J. Presper Eckert at the Moore School of Electrical Engineering at the University of Pennsylvania, starting on 9 April 1943. Weighing 30 tons, the 100' x 10' x 3' machine contained more than 100,000 parts, including 18,000 vacuum tubes, 1,500 relays, 70,000 resistors, 10,000 capacitors, and 6,000 toggle switches. Much of this could have been reduced had Mauchly and Eckert chosen a binary system, like Iowa's ABC, rather than decimal. Although ENIAC was intended for making ballistics calculations, the end of World War II obviated this need, and the first task ENIAC undertook on its completion in December 1945 was an assignment

for the atomic bomb center at Los Alamos. Other functions cited in support of the claim that it was a general-purpose computer included weather prediction, thermal ignition, random number studies, and wind tunnel design. Undoubtedly ENIAC could perform a range of tasks, but it was because these were strictly limited that Mauchly and Eckert, together with project consultant John von Neumann, decided to embark on a stored-program computer.

Stored-program computer: Prior to 1948 all electronic digital computers had to be programmed manually. Stored programs meant that the computer itself automatically switched between programs, vastly enhancing speed, power, and flexibility. Computer historian Christopher Evans has said that "in one conceptual jump, the true power of computers moved from the finite to the potentially infinite." Credit for the concept is usually given to the Hungarian-born mathematician John von Neumann, though it seems fairer to say that the idea originated with J. Presper Eckert and John W. Mauchly while they were working on ENIAC and that Von Neumann developed the architecture. This formed the basis of a project to build a successor to ENIAC, a stored-program computer called EDVAC (Electronic Discrete Variable Automatic Computer). Preliminary design work was carried out during 1944–46 and the final design and construction stage in 1946–52.

In the meantime, however, projects on the other side of the Atlantic to build stored-program computers at Manchester University and Cambridge University came to fruition before the completion of EDVAC. First to actually run programs was a 7' x 28' experimental digital computer called the Baby Mark I built by Prof. Frederick Williams and Tom Kilburn as a test-bed for their more ambitious project, the Manchester University Mark I. The Baby ran a 52-minute program written by Kilburn on 21 June 1948, marking the inception of computer software (for the record, it determined the highest factor of a given number). The Manchester Mark I, with a much enhanced specification, was working by April 1949 and it was this machine that was later manufactured by Ferranti as the first commercially produced computer (SEE BELOW). Less than a month later, on 6 May 1949, Maurice Wilkes's EDSAC (Electronic

Delay Storage Automatic Calculator), sometimes mistakenly described as the first operational stored-program computer, was up and running at Cambridge University. EDVAC was completed at the Moore School of Electrical Engineering in Philadelphia in August 1949 and installed at the BRL Computing Laboratory of the Ordnance Department's Aberdeen Proving Ground in Maryland, but due to problems with marginal circuits, it did not become operational until late 1951. In the same month of August 1949 Eckert and Mauchly had delivered their stored-program BINAC (Binary Automatic Computer) to the Northrop Aircraft Co. of California at a price of $100,000, though it had cost $278,000 to build. Thus America's first two stored-program computers were completed simultaneously, but with BINAC the first to become operational.

Commercially produced electronic computers: The first in series production were developed simultaneously in the United States and Great Britain. In March 1946 John W. Mauchly and J. Presper Eckert resigned from the EDVAC project and founded the world's first computer company, the Electronic Control Co. of Philadelphia. This was taken over by Remington Rand in 1950, and on 31 March 1951 the first Univac I was made over to the U.S. Census Bureau, which operated it in situ at the factory until about a year later, when it was moved to Washington, D.C. It was the subject of an official dedication ceremony on 14 June 1951, often erroneously quoted as the delivery date. In the meantime in England, Ferranti of Hollinwood, Lancashire, had delivered its first Ferranti Mark I, based on Prof. Frederick Williams and Tom Kilburn's Manchester Mark I stored-program computer, to Manchester University in February 1951. Here it was installed by Mary Berners-Lee, mother of World Wide Web creator Tim Berners-Lee (SEE **Internet**), who has proudly proclaimed his parent "the first commercial computer programmer." It was officially dedicated on 9 July of that year.

As to which was first, the Ferranti Mark I was delivered before the Univac I, while the latter was dedicated three weeks before its British rival, which is probably honors even. Univac had the added distinction of being the world's first computer operated with magnetic tape, though this proved disadvantageous in selling to the business community, whose records were more often on punch cards.

Forty-six Univacs were sold between 1951 and 1957, of which the initial six went to government agencies and the armed forces, the price of over $1 million putting it out of reach of universities. After the Census Bureau, customers in order of delivery were the U.S. Air Force, the Army Map Service, the Atomic Energy Authority (two Univacs), and the U.S. Navy. The eight Ferranti Mark I's sold after the first to Manchester University went to the University of Toronto in 1952 (the world's first export order for a computer); Britain's Ministry of Supply in 1953 with a second unit in 1955; Shell Oil's Amsterdam office; A. V. Roe Aircraft of Coventry, England; the Atomic Weapons Establishment at Aldermaston, England, in 1954; the Italian National Institute for Application of Mathematics in Rome; and Armstrong Siddeley Motors of Coventry in 1957.

The United States and Britain were again neck and neck in supplying the first **computers used in business**, though Ferranti failed to take the lead in Britain. Unusually the first business computer was developed by a company with no background in electronics, catering giant Joseph Lyons & Co. of London, celebrated for its cakes and teashops and for feeding six thousand people at a time at the Queen's garden parties at Buckingham Palace. The Lyons Electronic Office (LEO) was the inspiration of executive John Simmons, who had long cherished the dream of eliminating clerical drudgery by the application of high-speed machinery to process data. It was based on Cambridge University's EDSAC (SEE ABOVE) but was built in-house at Cadby Hall, Lyons's headquarters building on Hammersmith Road, under the direction of John Pinkerton. Completed on Christmas Eve 1953, it ran tests through January and early February until ready to go live with payroll for the bakery staff on 12 February 1954. Initially some two thousand staffers had their pay calculated and payslips printed automatically, rising to ten thousand within a few months. The following year LEO was contracted by the Ford Motor Co. to do payroll for the several thousand workers at its Dagenham plant. Meanwhile Leo Computers Ltd. had been set up to market computers to other companies.

The first American business computer was a Remington Rand Univac delivered to General Electric's Appliance Park facility in Louisville, Ky., in January 1954. It took a number of months to become operational, but once it was, it proved adept at producing payroll slips for ten thousand employees, despite the complications of varying hourly rates of pay, piecework, and bonuses. At first it took 44 hours to run the payroll, but this was cut to 20 with experience. When the Univac was given the additional task of inventory control, costs were reduced by $1 million a year (the cost of the computer). By the end of 1954 other Univacs for business use had been sold to insurance companies Metropolitan Life and Franklin Life, as well as to U.S. Steel and DuPont.

Computer with a visual display screen and keyboard: The first, forerunner of the personal computer, was the PDP-1, designed by Kenneth Olsen of the Digital Equipment Corporation of Maynard, Mass., and launched at $130,000 in November 1960. Fifty-one were built, of which a surprising forty-nine survive. PDP stood for Programmable Data Processor, the word "computer" being deliberately avoided as it was widely believed at the time, with some justification, that all computers cost a million dollars or more and needed a computer center and attendant staff for operation. The PDP-1 could be operated by one person.

Microprocessor: The first to be produced commercially was developed in 1969 by Edward Hoff of the Intel Corp. of Santa Clara, Calif., as the central processing unit of a desktop programmable computer. The technology on which it was based, however, had been the subject of a master patent registered the previous year by Gilbert Hyatt of La Palma, Calif., founder of Micro Computer Inc. This was only recognized in 1990 following a long court battle.

All the circuits relating to the main functions of the computer were reduced to a single microchip, instead of the conventional technique of having a number of chips linked together to form the various circuits. Regular production of these one-chip integrated circuits was begun by both Intel and Texas Instruments of Dallas in 1971.

Personal computer: The term "personal computer" was coined by Hewlett-Packard and first appeared in print in an advertisement for its "new Hewlett-Packard

911A personal computer" in *Science*, 4 October 1968. The term only became general, and particularly associated with home computers, after Ed Roberts employed it in advertising for the Altair in 1975.

The first home computer was the Honeywell H316 "Kitchen Computer," advertised at $10,000 complete with chopping board in the 1969 Nieman Marcus catalog. It was designed to store recipes, which people who don't shop at Nieman Marcus usually do in a cigar box. And so, apparently, do Nieman Marcus customers, as there is no record of any examples of this advanced kitchenware being sold. The first to achieve market penetration, albeit on a modest scale, was produced by John V. Blakenbaker of Los Angeles and offered for sale at $750 in *Scientific American* in September 1971 as the Kenbak-1. As this was shortly before the introduction of microprocessors, the machine employed an 8-bit processor built up from standard medium-scale and small-scale integrated circuits. It had 256 bytes of memory. In 1973 the Kenbak Corporation closed down after selling forty of these pioneer PCs.

Microcomputer: The first personal computer based on a microprocessor was the Micral, designed by François Gernelle and Ben Cetrite of the R2E electronics company in Paris. The original machines were built for the French Agricultural Research Institute, which needed a desktop computer with less power but greater economy than standard minicomputers. These were delivered in 1972, and in January the following year the Micral was launched on the open market at 8,450 francs ($1,950). It incorporated the Intel 8008 microprocessor and had 256 bytes of random access memory, which could be expanded to 2K with ROMs and PROMs. The machine evolved rapidly, with later models offering more RAM, floppy disks, hard disks, and a range of standard software. Some 2,500 Micrals were sold in the first three years, but following an unsuccessful attempt to penetrate the U.S. market R2E decided to sell out to French computer giant Bull in 1979.

U.S.: The first micro was the Scelbi-8H, designed by Nate Wadsworth and Bob Findley and advertised as a kit at $565 by Scelbi Computer Consulting of Milford, Conn., in the March 1974 issue of *QST*. Like the Micral it was based on the Intel 8008 microprocessor and had 1K of programmable memory; an additional

15K of RAM could be purchased for $2,760. Some two hundred were sold, each losing the company about $500. According to some reports the Scelbi-8H was also available ready-made, but details are lacking. The Altair 8800, which has gone down in history as the world's first PC, was a kit priced at $397 that did not start shipping until April 1975. It would seem that its fame (and unfounded claim to priority) stems from the fact that the software, Altair 4K Basic, was written by a geek in a baseball cap named William Gates. The Altair users' tendency to pirate the program decided the young entrepreneur to withdraw the license and form a company to take his product directly to market. It was called Microsoft.

Altair did, however, have a claim to priority that has sometimes been overlooked. One of the early hobbyists who bought an Altair was a former TV commercials director from New York named Michael Shrayer, who fitted his instrument with a keyboard and wrote a software program that enabled it to be used for **word processing** (a facility hitherto available only on electronic typewriters—SEE **typewriter**). In December 1976 the program was released commercially for the Altair 8800 as the Electric Pencil by Michael Shrayer Software of Glendale, Calif., and later versions were adapted for over seventy other makes of microcomputers, including the seminal IBM Personal Computer.

Portable computer: The first was the Micro Star (renamed the Small One) designed by James Murez and manufactured in small quantities in 1977 by GM Research of Santa Monica, Calif. Among the earliest customers was the U.S. government. First to be mass-produced was the Osborne I, designed by Lee Felsenstein and launched by Silicon Valley's Osborne Computers in April 1981 at the West Coast Computer Fair. About the size of a compact sewing machine, it weighed in at 24 pounds and was the first computer to come with "bundled" software, including a word processor, spreadsheet, database, and language program. Retailing at $1,795, it was an immediate success, perhaps because of Adam Osborne's uncharacteristically (for Silicon Valley) honest marketing pitch that the machine was "adequate," providing "90 percent of what most people need." Sales peaked at ten thousand units a month, but then Osborne's transparency also proved his downfall. Early in 1983 he announced a

new, much improved model then in development but well in advance of being ready to go into series production. Prospective purchasers of the Osborne I preferred to await the Osborne II. Sales stagnated, and Osborne Computers went bankrupt. "His enthusiasm for the next big thing," lamented a colleague, "meant that Adam couldn't keep a secret."

Computer mouse: Devised in prototype form by Douglas Engelbart and Bill English of the Stanford Research Institute at Menlo Park, Calif., in 1963, the mouse did not achieve commercial application until 1981. On 27 April of that year the Star Information System Xerox 8010 was launched with a mouse designed by Jack Hawley (founder of mouse manufacturer Mouse House) at the National Computer Conference in Chicago, price $16,595. The first mouse-operated PC was the Apple Lisa, brought to market on 19 January 1983.

Laptop computer: The first was the GRiD Compass, designed by Bill Moggridge of London industrial designers Moggridge Associates, for GRiD Systems Corp. of Mountain View, Calif., and introduced in April 1982. It featured an Intel 8086 processor, a 320 x 200 pixel plasma display, a 340K magnetic bubble memory, and a 1,200 bit/s modem. Running on the GriD-oS proprietary operating system, it was not IBM compatible and at a price of $10,000 was targeted at a specialist market, principally the U.S. government. Among the users were the U.S. Special Forces, and NASA sent it into space.

The first laptop designed for the general market was the Kyotronic 85 launched by Kyocera of Kyoto, Japan, early in 1983. Weighing less than 4 pounds, it had 16K of RAM, expandable to 32K, and 40 x 8 character LCD display. Four AA batteries could run it for up to 18 hours, or it could be used with an external power supply. The three built-in applications were Microsoft BASIC, a text processing program, and a telecommunications program. The full-size keyboard, portability, and large legible display ensured the Kyotronic's success, and it was licensed to NEC, Olivetti, and Tandy, all of which produced laptops based on its design. First to be marketed in the United States was the Radio Shack TRS-Model 100 Micro Executive Workstation, launched by the Tandy Corp. of Chicago on 29 March 1983. Two models were available, the 8K at $799 and the 24K at

$999, with memory upgrades available to 32K. With its built-in text editor and facility to plug into almost any telephone in the world, the Model 100 and its successors the 102 and 200 were particularly popular with journalists. Curiously, the brilliantly conceived Kyotronic 85 never sold well in Japan, whereas its U.S. and European clones were highly successful and established the laptop as the sine qua non of globetrotting executives.

Tablet computer: The first was the GriDPad, a handheld touch-screen with a stylus for direct on-screen writing. It was manufactured by Samsung for GriD Systems of Fremont, Calif., and was introduced in September 1989.

The breakthrough for tablet computers was the launch of the **iPad** by Apple on 3 April 2010. A worldwide total of 14.8 million had been sold by the end of that year.

SEE ALSO **Internet.**

THE FIRST **CONCENTRATION CAMP**

was Holmogor, established by the Bolsheviks at Archangel, Russia, in 1921. According to Serbian dissident Milhaljo Mihajlov, this was the first camp "whose sole purpose was the physical destruction of the prisoners." The inmates were captured White Russian officers, Kronstadt sailors (who had mutinied against the Bolsheviks they originally supported), supporters of the Antonoff peasant uprising, any members of the intelligentsia deemed a potential threat to the regime, and members of ethnic minorities such as the Kuban and the Don Cossacks. They were housed in unheated huts in temperatures that fell as low as -58°F, and worked until they dropped on a diet of one potato for breakfast, potato peelings boiled in water for the midday meal, and one potato for supper. Death came from starvation, overwork, and typhus and cholera; there were also mass killings, typically by tying stones around prisoners' necks and casting them into the icy waters of the River Dvina.

Estimates of the numbers who died in Soviet concentration camps between 1921 and 1953 vary, but most authorities agree that it could not have been less than 10 million, and one survey suggests 19 million.

The Stalinist terror reached its peak in 1936–38, when there are believed to have been at least 16 million prisoners in the gulag.

The first Nazi concentration camp was Dachau, near Munich, opened on 22 March 1933—fifty-one days after Hitler had become chancellor. Buchenwald, Sachsenhausen, and Ravensbrück followed the same year. The term "concentration camp" was first used in Spanish Cuba in 1895 and was applied by the British to the civilian internment camps in which they incarcerated Boer women and children during the South African War of 1899–1902 (SEE **barbed wire**). Unlike the Russian and Nazi camps, these were not intended to be punitive.

THE FIRST **CONCERT, PUBLIC**

was held in London on 30 December 1672 at what the organizer, John Banister, described as "the Musick-school," and his contemporary the musicologist Roger North called "a publick room in a nasty hole in White Fryers." Banister was in financial straits at this time, having been dismissed from his position as Leader of the Court Band for impertinence to the king. Accordingly he took a room above a public house behind the Temple and began a series of daily afternoon concerts for which an admission fee of 1 shilling was charged. Seats and small tables were ranged around the side of the room, and the patrons, mainly shopkeepers, were able to call for ale, cakes, and tobacco during the course of the program. The musicians sat on a raised dais and performed behind curtains. The reason for this is obscure. Roger North, to whom we are indebted for the only eyewitness account of Banister's concerts, said merely that modesty required it. Wrote North: "There was very good musick, for Banister found means to procure the best hands in town, and some voices to come and perform there, and there wanted no variety of humour, for Banister himself did wonders upon a flageolett to a thro-base, and the severall masters had their solos."

U.S.: The first on record was "A Concert of Music on Sundry Instruments at Mr. Pelham's Great Room" in Boston, which began at 6:00 P.M. on 30 December 1731 with admission at 5s. Mr. Pelham was the versatile

Peter Pelham, engraver, dancing master, manager of the subscription balls somewhat surprisingly held in Puritan Boston, boarding-school proprietor, instructor in "writing, arithmetic, reading, painting upon glass," and dealer in "the best Virginia tobacco." Though the instrumentalist is unnamed, it is not unreasonable to suppose that a man of such varied accomplishments may have fulfilled the role himself.

Concerts are known to have been given in Charleston, S.C., and New York City during the following year. The latter city quickly became the center of colonial musical activity, the total of forty-six concerts performed there prior to the Revolution far exceeding the number given anywhere else.

O. G. Sonneck, in *Early Concert-Life in America 1731–1800* (1907), advanced the theory that concerts of which no record remains may have taken place in Charleston earlier than in Boston. During the 1732–33 season, the southern city hosted a series of concerts, which suggests that the public presentation of secular music was already an established practice. Second, all information about Charleston's early concert life is drawn from the *South Carolina Gazette*. As this paper only began in January 1732, and there were no others in the city, there would have been no medium in which to record such events.

Concert hall: The first was opened in the York Buildings off the Strand in London in 1685 by a group of musicians who had been accustomed to giving concerts at the Castle Tavern. While most concert groups charged only a shilling for the entertainment, their price of admission was double. Presumably they gave value for money, because sufficient was accrued to rent the room in York Buildings on an ongoing basis and fit it up appropriately. The specialty of the venue was new music, and it opened on 26 November with a concert of works by the baroque German composer August Kühnel. Though attended by the *bon ton*, functions at York Buildings sometimes had a haphazard quality, as a contemporary observer testified:

> *Here was consorts, fuges, solos, lutes,*
> *Hautbois, trumpets, kettledrums, and what Not*
> *But all desjoynted and incoherent for*
> *While ye masters were shuffling*
> *Out and in of places to take their*

> *Parts there was a total cessation,*
> *And None knew what would come next*

U.S.: The first concert hall in America was the Concert Hall opened in Boston in 1754 by King's Chapel organist Gilbert Deblois and his brother, who erected a brick building on the corner of Hanover and Court streets. Their shop, at the sign of the Crown and Comb, was on the first floor and the Concert Hall on the second. The building was demolished in 1869 when Hanover Street was widened.

THE FIRST **CONDOM**

is attributed to Gabriel Fallopius, professor of anatomy at Padua University from 1551 until his death in 1562, and first described in his posthumously published *De Morbo Gallico* in 1564. The linen sheath, which Fallopius claimed to have tried out on 1,100 different men, was designed to be worn over the glans of the penis, and it was necessary to insert it beneath the foreskin to keep it in place. Fallopius intended his invention as a preventive against venereal disease, and its contraceptive properties were incidental. There is no known reference in literature to the use of the sheath other than as a prophylactic until 1655, when an anonymous Parisian publication titled *L'Escole des filles* recommended (unwisely) a linen contraceptive to prevent the passage of the semen.

The earliest known condoms were discovered in the foundations of Dudley Castle in Staffordshire, England, and are believed to date from 1644. In that year the castle was defended by the Cavaliers under the command of Col. Beaumont against Roundhead insurgents, and the five condoms dug up in 1986 were dated by archaeologists from the time of the siege. Made of fish and animal intestines, they were found in a latrine and had been preserved in a moist seventeenth-century brew of feces and urine. It seems likely that they had been taken to England by officers returning from France. If so, this may have been the origin of the term "French letter."

Although by the end of the seventeenth century the use of contraceptive techniques was fairly widespread among the upper classes in France, it was the intrauterine sponge rather than the male sheath that won most favor. Writing to her daughter in 1671, Mme. de Sévigné described the condom as "an armor against enjoyment and a spider web against danger."

Surviving contraceptive sheaths from c. 1800 were made of the dried gut of a sheep and would have required soaking in water before use. It was this kind of condom that Casanova described as an "English overcoat" in his *Memoirs*, adding that they were generally tied at the base with pink ribbon, a necessary precaution, since a wet length of animal intestine would have had limited elasticity. It could also be porous, hence the sound commercial advice given by the "Cundum Warehouse" of St. Martin's Lane in 1744 that it was safer to wear two.

U.S.: The earliest record of condoms in the United States is from a retrospective entry in French refugee Moreau de Saint-Méry's diary dated 31 December 1794 (evidently written some years later). He is writing of the bookselling business that he had opened in Philadelphia three weeks earlier.

> I did not wish to deprive my business of a profitable item, the lack of which in hot climates would not, I think, be without danger. Consequently, when my old colleague and friend, Barrister Geanty, a refugee from Cap François in Baltimore, who had a wide knowledge of medical supplies, offered me a stock of certain small contrivances— ingenious things said to be suggested by the stork—I agreed. I wish to say that I carried a complete assortment of them for four years; and while they were primarily intended for the use of French colonials, they were in great demand among Americans, in spite of the false shame so prevalent among the latter. Thus the use of this medium on the vast American continent dates from this time.

The French connection evidently persisted, as the earliest advertisement for condoms in the United States, published in the *New York Times* in 1861, promoted Dr. Power's French Preventatives. Those without access to manufactured condoms like these had to make their own, though it was not a simple process, as the instructions in *The United States Practical Receipt Book* of 1844 signify:

> Take the caecum of the sheep; soak it first in water, turn it on both sides, then repeat the operation in a weak ley [solution] of soda, which must be changed every four or five hours, for five or six successive times; then remove the mucous membrane with the nail; sulphur, wash in clean water, and then in soap and water; rinse inflate and dry. Next cut it to the required length, and attach a piece of ribbon to the open end.

Even when the manufactured article was available, it was not always easy to find. Under the notorious Comstock bluenose laws of 1873–1938 it was illegal to trade condoms across state borders. Consequently condom production in the United States was localized, with some predominantly agricultural states having no local source of supply at all. Nevertheless, by the mid-1930s Americans were consuming 317 million rubbers a year.

No record of **rubber sheaths** exists before 1858, when New York publisher Gilbert Vale reported in an appendix to an edition he issued of Robert Owen's *Moral Physiology* on "a new article, called 'The French Safe,' made of India rubber and gutta percha . . . It is more durable and less expensive [than other condoms]." Prior to the widespread availability of latex condoms in the 1930s, cost was the principal advantage of rubber. At $5 a dozen, they were about half the cost of the best goldbeater's-skin sheaths, but their comparative thickness limited a man's pleasure. There was also a tendency for early rubbers to break while in use. Latex condoms in the United States were first manufactured by Frederick Killian in 1919 at his plant in Akron, Ohio, using a process developed by the Goodyear Rubber Co.

THE FIRST CONSERVATORY

was a viridarium erected by Daniel Barbaro in the Botanical Gardens at Padua, shortly after they were opened in 1545. The structure was probably brick and stone, without glass, and heated by a brazier or open hearth. Delicate plants were moved into this conservatory when winter set in and replanted outdoors in the spring. Contemporary with this was the stone orangery built at the Villa Reale di Castello by Duke Cosimo de' Medici and his wife Eleanor of Toledo within a few years of their marriage in 1538. In 1815 it was replaced by a larger building, which is extant and contains some four hundred orange trees, some in pots bearing the arms of the Medicis, which means they predate the disintegration of that ruling family in 1730 and were nurtured in the original conservatory.

The earliest known **glasshouse** (i.e., with glass roof and walls) was the Duke of Rutland's grapery at Belvoir Castle in Leicestershire, England. The glazing was completed under the direction of the eminent horticulturalist Stephen Switzer in 1724.

U.S.: The earliest conservatory in America may have been in either Boston or Virginia. In the former, the French Huguenot merchant Andrew Faneuil built a greenhouse in the grounds of the house on Tremont Street he occupied between 1710 and 1735. It is not known when it was erected, only that it was there when Faneuil died in the latter year. The earliest reference to a greenhouse in Virginia is in a letter written by horticulturalist Peter Collinson in London to America's foremost botanist, John Bartram of Philadelphia, in 1738: "I am told that Colonel Byrd has the best garden in Virginia and a pretty greenhouse, well furnished with Orange trees." This was William Byrd II, and the garden was part of the Westover estate on the James River that he had inherited from his father in 1704. Educated in England, he did not return home permanently until 1726, whereupon he set about replacing his father's modest frame house with a mansion appropriate to the estate and began to develop the garden with its greenhouse.

The earliest known hothouses in the United States flanked the magnificent greenhouse built between 1748 and 1755 by Col. John Tayloe II at his Mount Airy estate on the Rappahannock River in the Northern Neck region of Virginia. These are described as "pt [sic] top covered with glass" in one case and having one wall of glass and one of brick in the other. In 1825 a dish of Antwerp raspberries grown in the hothouse was set before Gen. Lafayette when he visited Mount Airy on his triumphal tour of America. The greenhouse and its attendant hothouses were partially destroyed after the Civil War and the materials were used to build tenant farmhouses. What

remains, a high gaunt wall with noble arched apertures and overgrown with vegetation, is now one of the most picturesque ruins in the Old Dominion. The oldest greenhouse in the United States to survive intact is at the Wye estate in Maryland, built originally in 1755 and enlarged twenty-five years later, and is generally rated one of the most beautiful and architecturally distinguished anywhere in the world.

The earliest known glasshouses were the hothouses on either side of the greenhouse at the Elgin Botanic Garden in Manhattan established in 1801 by David Hosack, professor of botany at Columbia University. These were completed in 1803. Hosack could never raise sufficient funds for the garden's maintenance, and after the State of New York took it over in 1811 it fell into decay; only the greenhouse and glasshouses remained by 1817. They were demolished when Columbia University acquired the site for its new campus in 1825.

THE FIRST **COOKBOOK**

in printed form was Bartholomaeus Platina's *De Honesta Voluptate et valitudine* ("On Honorable Pleasure and Health") published in Cividale, Italy, in 1474 and reprinted in 1475 and 1480. None of the first two editions survive, and there are twenty known copies of the 1480 version. Platina was a physician, and his book is about the art of eating healthily. While he advises readers to eat well, he cautions them also to do so frugally. His recipe for *Esicium ex Pulpa*, veal sausages with cheese, egg yolks, and spices, sounds delicious but might not meet with approval in California. Readers stricken with the plague are advised to take cannabis.

The first **cookbook in English** was *A noble bok of festes ryalle and cokery*, author unknown, which was published in London by Richard Pynson in 1500. Only a single copy survives, in the library at the Marquis of Bath's Longleat in Wiltshire, which was valued some years ago at £30,000 ($55,000) and is now probably worth a great deal more. Scribbled notes in the margins in Latin suggest that the recipes were put to practical use by whoever owned it some two and a half centuries before Margaret Harley took it to Longleat upon her marriage to the first Marquis of Bath in 1759. There are, however, no cooking times nor measures of ingredients; skilled cooks were expected to work these out for themselves. The first section records various notable feasts, including one for George Nevill, who became Archbishop of York in 1465, regaled with curlews, gannets, gulls, dotterels, larks, redshanks, peacocks, partridges, woodcocks, knots, and sparrows. The sparrows were minced, probably the only way of making something eatable out of such a small bird. The second section comprised the recipes. "Ledlardes of Thre Colours" is representative of some of the elaborate effects sought. Make three separate portions of scrambled eggs, to which you add *lardons*; color one with spinach, another with saffron, and the third with sandalwood; put each in a muslin cloth and squeeze out the liquid; cut into strips and arrange in green, yellow, and red stripes.

U.S.: The first cookbook known to have come to America was *The English Housewife*, of which a number of copies were dispatched to Jamestown, Va., by the Virginia Company of London in 1620.

The first cookbook published in America was a reprint of Eliza Smith's *Complete Housewife*, issued by William Parks of Williamsburg, Va., in 1742. The book was adapted for American use by omitting recipes "the Ingredients or Materials for which, [were] not to be had in this Country."

The first **American cookbook**, which is to say a cookbook containing recipes indigenous to America as well as using native ingredients, was *American Cooking: or, The Art of Dressing Viands, Fish, Poultry, and Vegetables, and the Best Mode of Making Pastes, Puffs, Pies, Tarts, Puddings, Custards and Preserves, and all Kinds of Cakes, from the Imperial Plumb to Plain Cake. Adapted to this Country, and all Grades of Life. By Amelia Simmons, an American Orphan.* The slender paper-covered volume was published at Hartford, Conn., and contained 147 recipes in its 47 pages, besides a section on choosing meat, fish, and garden produce, and was announced for sale at a price of 2s 3d by Isaac Beers, bookseller of New Haven, in the *Connecticut Journal* of 8 June 1796. Recipes for peculiarly American dishes included several using corn meal, unknown in Britain: three for "Indian Pudding," one for "Johnny Cake or Hoe Cake," and one for "Indian Slapjacks." There were also recipes for "Pumpkin Puddings," "Crookneck, or Winter Squash

Pudding," roast turkey with "cranberry-sauce," "Molasses Gingerbread," and "Spruce Beer." Some of Amelia Simmons's rich concoctions would find little favor with food faddists today. Her baked potato pudding required that a pound of sugar, half a pound of butter, and ten eggs be mixed with a single pound of potatoes; an alternative version used ¾ pound of butter and three gills of cream (equivalent to twenty-four tablespoonfuls) to a pound of potatoes.

Little is known about the author or the circumstances in which she decided to embark on self-publication, a brave venture for one who described herself as "circumscribed in her knowledge." Indeed, it seems she was taken advantage of, for a second impression of the book had an additional page of errata with this explanation: "The author of the American Cookery, not having an education sufficient to prepare the work for the press, the person that was employed by her, and entrusted with the receipts, to prepare them for publication (with a design to impose on her, and injure the sale of the book) did omit several articles very essential in some of the receipts, and placed others in their stead, which were highly injurious to them." Notwithstanding this act of culinary sabotage, numerous editions followed through to 1831, some of them (presumably unauthorized) repeating the errors in the original. Only four copies of the first edition survive.

The first regional American cookbook was Mary Randolph's *The Virginia House-wife: or, Methodical Cook* of 1824, printed by Davis and Force of Washington, D.C., which contained recipes for dishes special to the South such as catfish soup, turnip tops, beaten biscuits, field peas, and okra soup.

THE FIRST **CREDIT CARD**

issued by a third party (cards for individual stores, hotels, and gasoline retailers already existed) was Charg-It, introduced in 1947 by consumer credit specialist John C. Biggins of the Flatbush National Bank of Brooklyn, N.Y. The card was good for purchases at participating outlets in the immediate vicinity of the bank.

The first such credit card usable outside a local area was Diners Club in May 1950. It was conceived during a luncheon the previous year at Major's Cabin Grill next to New York City's Empire State Building, attended by Alfred Bloomingdale (grandson of the founder of Bloomingdale's), his friend Frank McNamara of the not very successful Hamilton Credit Corp., and the latter's attorney, Ralph Schneider. Having hit on the idea of applying the credit principle to restaurant-going as a third-party provider, they called over the proprietor, a Mr. Major, and asked him what commission he would be prepared to pay for new business. Without hesitation he responded 7 percent, which as a result became the credit card industry norm for several decades. As McNamara and Schneider shared an office in the Empire State Building, they launched the venture by the simple expedient of pushing circulars promoting the free cards under the doors of all the other offices in the vast skyscraper. In the first month of operation, two hundred cardholders charged up $2,000 worth of restaurant meals at twenty-seven outlets, generating $140 for the fledgling company at Major's suggested 7 percent. By the fall of 1950, monthly credit had reached $250,000, at which point Diners Club expanded its operation to Los Angeles and Boston. Within the next year or so, the organization began to extend its credit facilities at businesses other than restaurants, including hotels, stores, and, in 1955, its first airline, Western Airlines. In 1953 Diners Club became the first internationally accepted card when businesses in the United Kingdom, Canada, Cuba, and Mexico began signing up.

THE FIRST **CREMATION**

as a substitute for Christian burial took place on 26 September 1769, when the body of Honoretta Pratt, widow of the Hon. John Pratt, Treasurer of Ireland, was burned in her open grave at St. George's Burial Ground in Hanover Square, London. Her monument recorded:

> This worthy woman believing that the vapours arising from graves in the church yards of populous city's [*sic*] must prove hurtful to the inhabitants

and resolving to extend to future times . . . that charity and benevolence which distinguished her through life ordered that her body should be burnt

> in hope that others would follow her example, a thing too hastily censured by those who did not understand her motive.

U.S.: Planter and diplomat Henry Laurens of South Carolina had a rather different motive for choosing cremation. This former president of the Continental Congress had a morbid fear of being buried alive, engendered by an episode when he had nearly consigned his infant daughter Martha to this fate. A victim of smallpox, she was inert and apparently no longer breathing. Only when the child was placed by an open window while a grave was dug did family physician Dr. Moultrie notice that the cool breeze had revived her. Happily she recovered, but Laurens was so horrified by the experience he gave instruction that on his death his body was to be "burnt until it be entirely and wholly consumed." On 9 December 1792, the day after he died, America's first cremation was conducted on a high hill at his principal plantation, Mepkin, and his ashes placed by the grave of eldest son John, killed in the Revolutionary War. This was only the second cremation in the western world and there was only one other in the United States before the opening of the first crematorium.

Crematorium: The first was established in Milan in 1875 by a Swiss, Albert Keller, who did not live to see its fulfillment as it was indeed he who was first to be cremated there on 22 January the following year. America's first crematorium and the second in the world was a private installation for the wealthy Le Moyne family of Washington, Pennsylvania. It was activated on 6 December 1876 when the body of Bavarian nobleman and family friend Baron Joseph Henry Louis de Palm was cremated. He had actually died in New York on 20 May, but the Theosophical Society, of which he was a leading light, had preserved his body in ice blocks until the crematorium was completed. Evidently the Le Moynes were fervent believers in incineration, since no fewer than forty-two of them had passed through its furnace by the end of the century. The first public crematorium in America was opened at Cedar Lawn Cemetery in Lancaster, Pa., on 25 November 1884.

D

THE FIRST **DENTAL DRILL**

was described in 1728 by the Parisian dental surgeon Pierre Fauchard in his book *Le Chirurgien Dentiste*. This was a steel burr specially designed for loosening decayed dental tissue and operated by twisting with the fingers in alternate directions. Fauchard also used a jeweler's bow drill, which had the bowstring wound around a shaft of the drill and was activated when a sawing motion was applied to the bow. This was slow and arduous, but a notable improvement occurred in the United States in 1790 when George Washington's dentist John Greenwood adapted his mother-in-law's treadle-powered spinning wheel to drive a dental drill.

Electric dental drill: The first was a battery-operated device patented by George F. Green of Kalamazoo, Mich., on 26 January 1875. He sold the patent to the Samuel S. White Co. of Philadelphia, who began manufacturing "electro-magnetic dental tools." Dental drills powered from the main electricity supply were not introduced until 1908.

High-speed dental drill: The first was the Dentalair, invented by Stockholm dentist Ivor Norlen and manufactured in Sweden in 1955 by Atlas Copco. Operating at speeds of up to 60,000 rpm, it virtually eliminated the pain and fear from having teeth drilled.

U.S.: The first developed in the United States was the work of Robert J. Nelson of the National Bureau of Standards, Washington, D.C., and was manufactured in 1955 by Bowen & Co. of Bethesda, Md., as the Turbo-Jet. Hydraulically powered, it operated at 61,000 rpm.

THE FIRST **DENTIST**

in America known by name was barber-surgeon William Dinly, who combined the drawing of teeth with blood-letting, purging, and amputating as was customary at the time. Dinly had accompanied two other barber surgeons to New England in 1630. His name is known while theirs is not mainly because he embraced the same eccentric religious beliefs as the Puritan heretic Anne Hutchinson and therefore made himself conspicuous in the nascent city of Boston, where nonconformity was strictly conformist. During a violent storm in the winter of 1638 a Roxbury man suffering from toothache sent for Dinly to come and extract the tooth. Dinly set out together with the maid who had brought the message, but neither of them arrived at their destination. Their frozen bodies were found some days later. Goodwife Dinly was pregnant at the time and when the baby was born she named the child Fathergone Dinly.

New England offered the early physician slender pickings. Giles Firmin, who graduated from Cambridge University in 1629 and subsequently betook himself to America, found the practice of "physick" and dentistry a "meene helpe" in this new land. The lack of opportunity in the dental field may be explained by the lack of teeth. Ned Ward, the London tavern keeper and pamphleteer who voyaged to Boston in 1699 to seek refuge from certain enemies anxious to do him mischief, had little regard for Bostonians, but did help to shed a sidelight on the ravages of dental caries in the colonies. "He that Marrys a New-England Lass at Sixteen," he wrote in *A Trip to New England*, "if she prove a Snappish Gentlewoman, her Husband need not fear she will bite his Nose off; for its ten to one but she hath shed her Teeth, and has done Easting [eating] of Crust, before she arrives to that Maturity."

By 1735, when James Mills of New York advertised his services as a tooth-drawer, there was sufficient demand at least in that city for a practitioner who specialized in this type of surgery. Indeed it may have existed earlier, for Mills declares he had been instructed in the art "by the late James Reading, Deceased, so famed for drawing of teeth."

The first **medically qualified dental surgeon** in America was Dr. John Baker, who arrived in Boston in 1763 having formerly practiced in Ireland (Cork), England, Holland, France "and other principal places in Europe," and in Jamaica. He it was who taught Paul Revere dental surgery and when Baker left Boston for New York in 1768, Revere, better known as a silversmith, took over his practice. It was in that year, in the inaugural announcement of Baker's new practice in New York (*New York Weekly Journal* 28 April), that we find the earliest allusion to gold fillings in America. He continued to be peripatetic, practicing subsequently in Philadelphia, Baltimore, and Williamsburg, Va. It was while residing in the latter place that he acquired his most prestigious patient, the notoriously dentally challenged George Washington. The great man's ledgers record payments varying between 1 shilling 4d and £4 for treatment, the magnitude of the latter suggesting that it was for the fitting of dentures (6 April 1772). During 1773 he paid Baker 1 shilling for dentifrices and 5s for toothbrushes. It is an interesting commentary on the status of a dental surgeon in post-revolutionary but by no means classless America that Baker was invited to dinner with the Father of the Nation in 1785, in the distinguished company of Colonels Fitzgerald and Gilpin. By this time Baker was practicing again in Philadelphia but he is believed to have retired after moving once again to New York, where he bought a 46-acre farm on the outskirts of the city for the considerable sum of £3,600—testimony to his success in his profession.

The earliest professional qualification in the United States was established by the State of Maryland, the Attorney General confirming a resolution of the Medical and Chirurgical Faculty of 3 June 1805 that their existing Examining Board should also license dentists and oculists. Those presenting themselves for examination still had to find an individual preceptor to teach them what they were required to know, but it was also in Maryland that formal dental education in America had its beginnings. Horace H. Hayden, who had been licensed by the Board in 1810, lectured in odontology at the University of Maryland in 1819 and delivered a sustained course of lectures at the University's Medical School from 1823 to 1825. He was a member of the founding faculty of the Baltimore College of Dental Surgery, doubling up as Professor of Pathology and Physiology and also as Professor of Special Dental Anatomy. This was the first **dental school** in the world, Hayden delivering the inaugural lecture on 3 November 1840. Its first graduates with the degree *Chirurgiae Dentium Doctoris* or D.D.S. (Doctor of Dental Surgery) were Robert Arthur and R. Covington Mackall, both of Baltimore, on 9 March 1841, after a course lasting a mere five months, though some students did a two-year course. Dental degrees had, however, already been conferred on members of the American Society of Dental Surgeons, the first national body for the profession (founded in New York City on 18 August 1840), admission being by examination. Appropriately the first to receive a D.D.S. was its president and the man who had done most to elevate dentistry to a profession, Horace H. Hayden.

SEE ALSO **woman dentist**.

THE FIRST **DENTURES**

known, embodying both upper and lower rows of false teeth, were dug up from a field in Switzerland, and are believed to date from the late fifteenth century. The teeth are carved from bone and attached with gut to hinged side-pieces. This set of dentures would probably have been worn as an aid to beauty and would need to have been removed at mealtimes.

The first porcelain dentures were made c. 1770 by Alexis Duchâteau, an apothecary of Saint-Germain-en-Laye, near Paris. After repeated failures—the porcelain contracted under firing, making it extremely difficult to judge how large a mold to use—he at last succeeded in making a pair that fitted so excellently that he was able to wear them for the rest of his life. A Parisian dentist, M. Dubois de Chemant, who had assisted Duchâteau in his experiments, began to manufacture the new dentures. These, the first really satisfactory false teeth to be made available to the toothless public at large, united, said the Paris Faculty of Medicine in a testimonial, the "qualities of beauty, solidity and comfort to the exigencies of hygiene."

U.S.: The earliest reference to dentures is contained in an advertisement placed by Sieur Roquet, a dentist from Paris, in the *Independent Advertiser*, Boston, for 3 July 1749. This contained the claim that: "He cures effectually the most stinking Breaths by drawing out, and eradicating all decayed Teeth and Stumps, and burning the gums to the Jaw Bone, without the least Pain or Confinement; and putting in their stead, an entire Sett of right African Ivory Teeth, set in Rose-colour's Enamel, so nicely fitted to the Jaw, that People of the first Fashion, may eat, drink, swear, talk, Scandal, quarrel, and shew their Teeth, without the least Indecency, Inconvenience or Hesitation whatever."

It is not known whether "an entire Sett" would have comprised both upper and lower fixtures. A full set was made of ivory and fitted for William Walton of New York in 1768 by Robert Woffendale, a surgeon dentist lately arrived from London. On 5 September of the same year the Boston silversmith Paul Revere, who also practiced dentistry, advertised in the *Boston Gazette* that "Persons so unfortunate as to lose their Fore-Teeth by Accident . . . may have them replaced with false ones, that look as well as the Natural, and answers the End of Speaking." Ivory teeth of the kind provided by Woffendale and Revere were liable to go yellow, while real teeth transplanted from others could decay even though no longer live. The ingenious Charles Willson Peale (SEE **art exhibition; art museum**) of Philadelphia set about seeking a substitute. At first he tried organic sources, using horses' and cows' teeth, then he turned to the teeth of hogs, which he found the most durable but usually too small, before finally coming to the same conclusion as the French apothecary Duchâteau and manufacturing America's first porcelain teeth in 1807.

THE FIRST DEPARTMENT STORE

on a criterion of magnitude alone was the Marble Dry Goods Palace opened at 280 Broadway, New York City, by Alexander Turney Stewart on 21 September 1846 with a 90-foot frontage on Broadway itself and a 100-foot frontage on Reade Street. The purpose-built Anglo-Italianate building had four stories and a basement, the two lower floors being used for retail selling and the remaining floors for wholesale and offices. Although on the east side of Broadway, generally shunned by fashionable shoppers, the Marble Palace was an instantaneous success and it was estimated that a thousand customers an hour passed through its stately portals on opening day. Among its attractions were the huge 6' x 11' plateglass windows on the first floor, specially imported from France and the first to adorn any prominent retailing establishment in the United States. The store started with 100 clerks, but as Stewart took leases on adjoining properties to expand the number and size of his departments the staff doubled to 200 (1852), then rose rapidly to 300 (1853). At the outset, the store was rivaled in size by only one other in the world, the Parisian *grand magasin* Ville de Paris, which was employing 150 clerks in 1844, but by 1850, now occupying the entire Broadway frontage between Chambers and Reade Streets, the Marble Palace was preeminent. In 1862, when Stewart moved the retail operation to a new Cast Iron Palace on Tenth Street, he was employing 400 to 500 clerks (according to season) with annual retail sales of $5 million.

Alexander Stewart had been born in Lisburn, Ireland, in 1803 and emigrated to New York in 1818, where he became an usher at $300 a year at Isaac N. Bragg's academy on Roosevelt Street. A timely inheritance in 1822 enabled him to enter the dry-goods business, at which he immediately proved himself adept with such innovations as fixed prices and refunds on demand. At the Marble Palace a particular feature that attracted repeat custom was the absence of high-pressure salesmanship. Customers were free to wander as they pleased, whereas in other stores they were constantly attended by a clerk who would be penalized if no purchase was made.

When income tax was introduced in the United States in 1863, Stewart had the highest reported income of any man in America. In that year he paid tax on earnings of $1,843,637 (at a time when average male earnings in the city were about $600 a year). His wealth may have inspired envy, as he has not enjoyed a good press. An austere and demanding employer, he is said to have paid among the lowest wages in the retail trade and to have imposed a harsh and merciless discipline on his staff, imposing substantial fines for the slightest infraction of rules. He was also accused of doing nothing for the city that had so enriched him. That there was a more charitable side is attested by his public benefactions in Ireland and England and many private donations to individual supplicants in America who sought his help. *Harper's Magazine* related a story of how an affluent young lady of his acquaintance had asked to be allowed to make the first purchase on the Marble Palace's opening day, buying $200 worth of Irish lace. Years later he learned that she had married a fortune hunter who took her to Europe and left her a penniless widow. He sought her out, established her in a comfortable apartment, and settled on her an annuity for life. On Stewart's death in 1876 his bequests included payments ranging from $500 to $5,000 to 3,000 men and women who had served on his staff.

It has been argued, most cogently by Harvard business historian Ralph M. Hower, that a true department store carries a wider range of merchandise than dry goods. On this criterion neither the Marble Palace and its American rivals, nor the *grands magasins* of Paris, would qualify. The first of the big stores to extend its repertoire beyond fabrics and fashion was R. H. Macy & Co., founded by Rowland Hussey Macy in 1858 as a conventional fancy dry-goods emporium at 204–206 Sixth Avenue, New York City. The gradual accretion of non-traditional lines began with the onset of the new decade:

1860   French and German fancy goods including pocketbooks and purses, chinaware, games, dolls, and toys

1861   Soaps and other toilet preparations, perfumes

1864   Costume jewelry, household ornaments

1868   Clocks, silverware

1869   House furnishings, kitchen utensils, brushes, baskets, baby carriages, birdcages

1870   Candy, books, magazines, stationery, soda fountain

1872   Bohemian glassware, ice skates (followed by other sporting goods)

1873   Folding chairs, rocking chairs, ottomans, commodes, rugs, velocipedes, barometers, gardening sets, fancy grocery

1874   Glassware, sewing machines

1875   Paintings, fishing tackle, luggage, archery equipment, birds

1876   Shoes

In May 1878 a Ladies' Lunch Room was opened, the first restaurant in any department store in America (they already existed in Paris). Much of this diversification may be attributed to the talent and vision of the remarkable Margaret Getchell, whom Prof. Hower has suggested may have been the first **woman appointed to an executive position** (as opposed to a woman *proprietor*, which was not uncommon) in any business in America. A former schoolteacher, the pretty and personable twenty-year-old native of Nantucket had been taken on by Rowland Macy as a cashier in 1861, promoted a year or so later to bookkeeper, and rewarded for her financial acumen when she was given the job of Store Superintendent in 1867 at the early age of twenty-six. In this role she was largely responsible not only for expansion into new lines, but also for overall supervision of a staff of 200 and control over sales of some $1 million a year. To her as well as to Rowland Macy must go credit for creating the modern department store. Unlike many women in positions of command, particularly pioneering ones, Margaret Getchell appears to have been universally adored by male and female staff alike, many of whom testified in later years to the unvarying gentleness and kindness with which she treated them. Among those smitten by her charms was chief lace buyer Abiel T. LaForge, who married her and later became Macy's partner.

A. T. Stewart, founder of the first retailing giant, and Rowland Macy, founder of the first diversified department store, died within months of each other in 1876 and 1877 respectively. The firm of A. T. Stewart & Co. went into decline and was eventually absorbed by John Wanamaker in 1896. Macy's continued to expand, overtaking A. T. Stewart & Co. and becoming in the 1920s the largest and probably the most celebrated department store in the world.

THE FIRST **DETECTIVE STORY**

was Edgar Allan Poe's "The Murders in the Rue Morgue," published in *Graham's Magazine*, in Philadelphia in April 1841. The story was set in Paris and Poe's detective was an impoverished chevalier, Auguste Dupin; Dorothy L. Sayers credited Poe with the introduction of "the formula of the eccentric and brilliant private detective whose doings are chronicled by an admiring and thick-headed friend." *The Murders in the Rue Morgue* was reissued as a 12½¢ paperback in 1842, thereby establishing the form in which the majority of detective tales were to be issued in later years. This slender pamphlet is one of the rarest items of Americana and Howard Haycraft has recorded that copies exchanged hands for as much as $25,000 even before World War II. Poe himself never made anything like this sum for the story. As editor of *Graham's Magazine* at a salary of $800 per annum, it is unlikely that he received any additional emolument for his contributions, and none of the re-publications during his lifetime sold well. Dupin reappeared in "The Mystery of Marie Rogêt" (1842–43) and "The Purloined Letter" (1844). Poe wrote two other private-eye stories, "The Gold-Bug" (1843) and "Thou Art the Man" (1850).

The first full-length work of detective fiction to be published as a book was *Recollections of a Detective Police Officer*, a collection of stories formerly appearing in *Chambers's Journal* that was issued by J. & C. Brown of London in a first edition of 5,000 copies in June 1856. By the time a second series came out in 1859 it was claimed that 75,000 copies had been sold. The story was entirely fictional, though it purported to be the autobiography of a real Metropolitan Police detective called Waters. The author, William Russell, was a hack journalist who made a considerable success of this "true recollections" genre, and "Waters" was followed by *Experiences of a French Detective Officer* (1861), *Experiences of a Real Detective* by "Inspector F" (1862), and *The Autobiography of an English Detective* (1863). The original *Recollections* also achieved the distinction of being the first work of detective fiction to be translated into a foreign language, appearing in German as *Erinnerungen eines Kriminal-Polizisten von Waters* (Leipzig, 1857) and in French as *Mémoires d'un Policeman* (Paris, 1868).

Waters was not, however, the first fictional detective to make his appearance in English literature. Charles Dickens, who early took an interest in the nascent detective force and published a series of articles about it in *Household Words* in 1850, created the character of Inspector Bucket, whose investigations occupy fourteen of the sixty-six chapters of *Bleak House* (London, 1853). Bucket is believed to have been based on the real-life Inspector Field of the Metropolitan Police, who was known personally to the author.

There are a number of claims for the first true **detective novel**, of which Charles Felix's *The Notting Hill Mystery*, published in book form in London in 1865 following serialization, is probably the most prominent. While undoubtedly a novel of suspense, the investigative element is incidental, the sensational story being principally about the fashionable preoccupation with mesmerism. Far more deserving of the title is Wilkie Collins's *The Moonstone*, hailed by T. S. Eliot as "the first, the longest, and the best," which was published in three volumes by Tinsley of London in July 1868. The detective, Sergeant Cuff, was based on Jonathan Whicher, who had figured prominently in the controversial Constance Kent or Road Hill House murder case of 1860, from which the plot of the book is partly derived. Here at last were all the principal elements that were to characterize the classic whodunnit: a country-house crime with an "inside job," a cerebral investigator obstructed by bungling local constabulary, false trails, the least likely suspect as perpetrator, a reconstruction of the crime, and a final twist in the tale.

U.S.: While in America, as in Britain, there had been a flurry of fictional "memoirs," the first true detective novelist has long been held to be the redoubtable Anna Katherine Green. Recently, however, a forerunner has been discovered (and republished) by Emory University graduate studies professor and literary sleuth Catherine Ross Nickerson. She was Seeley Register, pen name of Metta Fuller Victor of New York, mother of nine children, abolitionist, temperance advocate, campaigner against Mormon polygamy, and the wife of Orville Victor, publisher of *Beadle's Monthly*. Her thriller *The Dead Letter: An American Romance* was published by Beadle & Co. of

New York as a dime novel probably in 1866 (undated, possibly 1864). Mrs. Victor's gentleman police detective was called Mr. Butler and he spent many hundreds of pages in pursuit of the miscreants the length and breadth of the United States. The denouement breaks one of the cardinal rules of novels of suspense because Mr. Butler cracks the case not by his superior powers of deduction but by calling in his clairvoyant daughter for a resolution.

Despite this pioneering endeavor, Mrs. Victor was principally a writer of romantic fiction and Anna Katharine Green of Buffalo, N.Y., still deserves the accolade of first to specialize in detective novels. Her rotund and rheumatic detective Ebenezer Gryce of the New York Police made his debut in *The Leavenworth Case: A Lawyer's Story*, published by Putnam in 1878. Miss Green, later the wife of a furniture manufacturer, explained her invasion of this male world by saying that she considered the writing of a detective novel to be a suitable preparation for a career as a poetess. *The Leavenworth Case* concerned the death of a millionaire and had as its principal characters two very attractive female cousins who with sighs and heaving bosoms uttered such deathless lines as "My reputation is sullied for ever" and "The finger of suspicion never forgets the direction in which it has once pointed." Miss Green nevertheless understood her craft and the culprit proved to be one of the characters least expected. *The Leavenworth Case*, praised by Wilkie Collins and a cult at Yale Law School, eventually sold over a million copies worldwide. By the time of her death in her ninetieth year in 1935, Anna Katharine Green had written over thirty detective novels, thirty of them featuring the inimitable Inspector Gryce.

THE FIRST **DICTIONARY, ENGLISH**

was *A Table Alphabeticall, containing and teaching the true writing and understanding of hard usuall English words* compiled by Robert Cawdrey, a schoolmaster formerly employed at Oakham and Coventry, and published in London in 1604. In his dedication Cawdrey said that the work "long ago for the most part, was gathered by me, but lately augmented by my sonne Thomas, who now is Schoolmaister in London." It

contained about 3,000 words. The only surviving copy is in the Bodleian Library, University of Oxford.

The first English dictionary to attempt the definition of words in common use, so-called "easy words," was *The New English Dictionary* by "J. K.," published in London in 1702. J. K. has usually been identified as John Kersey. His work contained only "such English words as are genuine and used by Persons of clear Judgment and good Style . . . Omitting such as are obsolete, barbarous, foreign or peculiar . . . and abstruse and uncouth Terms of Art."

Complete English dictionary: The first that was complete in the sense that the lexicographer included all the English words known to him was Nathaniel Bailey's *Universal Etymological English Dictionary*, London, 1721. It was also the first dictionary to give the derivation of words, and so justified the inclusion of such simple terms as *man*, *woman*, *dog*, and *cat*, which would have been superfluous in earlier compilations concerned only with definition. (Indeed Bailey's definition of cat consisted of a curt phrase: "A creature well known.") Used by Samuel Johnson as a basis for his own, better-known dictionary, Bailey's work remained the chief rival to that of the great Doctor during the latter half of the eighteenth century. It continued to be issued until 1802. Of the revised editions, the 1727 version of Bailey is notable as the first dictionary to contain illustrations, and that of 1731 as the first to give some guidance as to the correct pronunciation of words.

Dictionary containing illustrative quotations from literature: The first was *A Dictionary of the English Language*, compiled by Dr. Samuel Johnson for a syndicate of London booksellers and published in two folio volumes on 15 April 1755.

The significance of Johnson's *Dictionary* reaches far beyond his introduction of quotations into lexicography, for it had an immeasurable effect on the standardization of the English language, particularly with regard to spelling. Dr. James Murray of the magisterial *Oxford English Dictionary* pointed out in his Romanes Lecture of 1900 how the word *dispatch*, given by Johnson as *despatch* (the first time the alternative spelling is noted in print, and probably a slip on Johnson's part), came to be commonly spelled with an *e* in Britain during the first half of the nineteenth century, and this on the *Dictionary*'s authority, though it was never spelled so by the Doctor's contemporaries. **Dictionary of the American language:** The first was *A School Dictionary* compiled by Samuel Johnson Jr. of Guilford, Conn., and published at New Haven in 1798. His great-uncle, Dr. Samuel Johnson, sometime president of Columbia University and author of the first text on American grammar (1756), was almost exactly contemporaneous with his celebrated namesake in England, though they were not related. Samuel Johnson Sr. and Jr. were successive headmasters of the Academy on Guilford Green. Both were Tories during the Revolution and it may have been this that actuated the younger Samuel's decision to turn lexicographer, since there was a serious attempt to abandon English as the language of the new Republic. Equally it may have had to do with the tendency of Guilford folk, including their children, to use strange archaisms that had fallen into disuse elsewhere, such as pampoddlers (strangers), pantspound (forest), and furzino ("as far as I know").

A School Dictionary contained some 4,150 words, many of them copied from earlier dictionaries published in England. According to an article by Henry Pynchon Robinson in *The Connecticut Magazine* (October, 1899), "certain Guilford folk, not lovers of language, laughed at the new dictionary." This may have been on account of some rather odd definitions, e.g.,

> **bemused:** overcome with musing
> **chymistry:** act of separating bodies with fire
> **lout:** to bow awkwardly.

Four copies survive: in the British Library, the Library of Congress, and the libraries of Harvard and Yale Universities. The latter had belonged to a schoolgirl called Sally Stanton, who had nibbled its edges, perhaps as a diversion during a dull class.

Johnson, with co-lexicographer the Rev. John Elliott, pastor at East Guilford, also produced America's second dictionary and the first for general adult use. Published at Hartford in two editions during 1800, *A Selected, Pronouncing and Accented Dictionary* had the useful innovation of phonetic spelling in brackets after a word as a guide to pronunciation, for example [*shugar*] after sugar and [*shammy*] after chamois. It contained 10,870 words, 6,000 more than Johnson's *School Dictionary*. It was probably the reverend gentleman who devised the definition *anti-christ:* "one who opposes Christ, the pope." Most notable of the additions, particularly as Elliott had made great play of the fact that no offensive words would be countenanced, was the first appearance of the word *fuck* in print in America. A reviewer in the *American Review and Literary Journal* waxed apoplectic about this, before concluding that the reason it had been inserted was because the lexicographers did not know what it meant; the definition bore no relation to the act of procreation.

The first attempt toward a **dictionary of Americanisms** was John Pickering's *A Vocabulary, or Collection of Words and Phrases Which Have Been Supposed to Be Peculiar to the United States of America*, Boston and Cambridge 1816. The qualification "toward" is used above because at only 520 words, this work could not really be considered a dictionary, nor did Pickering claim it to be. Moreover, only 70 of the words were of American origin. The remainder were vulgarisms or provincialisms normally excluded from dictionaries of English origin. The first comprehensive collection, a true dictionary, was the 439-page *Dictionary of Americanisms* by John Russell Bartlett, New York, 1848. Bartlett had been inspired to compile this while on a canal journey from Utica, N.Y., to visit his father. The book he was reading abounded in the vulgar tongue of the United States and he noted examples in the margins. As he came across many more from other sources he decided to produce a supplement to Pickering, but he soon found that there were sufficient Americanisms, including those of Dutch and Native American derivation, to justify a full-length dictionary. Many were culled from newspapers, which had none of the restraint of their British counterparts when it came to using the blunt and vigorous language of the common people.

Complete American dictionary: The first was the two-volume *American Dictionary of the English Language*, by Noah Webster, New York, 1828. Its 70,000 words were some 12,000 in excess of the number contained in any dictionary of English thitherto, either British or American. It was everywhere well received. "We can have no hesitation," proclaimed the august

Times of London, "in giving it our decided opinion that this is the most elaborate and successful undertaking of the kind which has ever appeared." Through successive revised editions, "Webster," as it came to be known, attained a supremacy among American dictionaries never effectively challenged, reaching an apogee of authority in matters linguistic when the Government Printing Office in Washington, D.C., hung a simple message of command throughout the building: FOLLOW WEBSTER.

THE FIRST DIESEL ENGINE

or high-pressure compression-ignition engine to be commercially developed was patented in Germany by Paris-born Dr. Rudolf Diesel, sales manager of the Linde Ice-Making Machine Co., on 28 February 1892. The following year Diesel secured the cooperation of the Krupp and Maschinenfabrik Augsburg concerns in providing financial backing and workshop facilities, and his prototype engine sprang fitfully to life for the first time at the latter's plant on 10 August 1893. Another four years of research and development ensued before the Diesel engine was ready for commercial exploitation, but by 1897 it was sufficiently advanced for him to dispose of the American rights to German-American brewer Adolphus Busch for one million marks ($250,000). Although it was several years before Busch was able to instigate production in the United States, he did have a single 60-hp Diesel engine built by the St. Louis Iron & Marine Works, and this became the first high-pressure compression-ignition engine in commercial operation anywhere in the world when it was installed at the Anheuser-Busch Brewery on 2nd Street, St. Louis, Mo. in September 1898. It drove a direct-current electric generator. Regular commercial production of Diesel engines was begun in Augsburg in 1899 and by Busch's New York–based Diesel Motor Co. of America a year or so later.

Dr. Diesel boarded a ship in Antwerp on 1 October 1913 to attend a meeting of the Consolidated Diesel Manufacturing Ltd. in London. He was never seen again. His cabin was empty in the morning and no trace of him was ever found (a fate similar to that of the inventor of the motion picture; SEE **film**). Conspiracy theorists believed that Diesel had been killed by German agents to prevent him from cooperating with the British on military applications of his engine.

THE FIRST DISC JOCKEY

was New York spinmeister Martin Block. Although radio presenters had spun discs since the advent of broadcasting, it is Block who has been nominated "the first true recognizable radio DJ" with his mixture of chat and popular music on *The Make-Believe Ballroom*, aired by WNEW New York from 3 February 1935 until 1950. He also made DJ-ing the lucrative profession it is today, earning nearly $2 million in 1948 when he syndicated the program to thirty stations around the country. Walter Winchell is credited with coining the term *disc jockey* in relation to Martin Block, though the earliest reference in print dates from 1941 in showbiz bible *Variety* (preceded, a year earlier, by *record jocky* with no *e*).

THE FIRST DISCOTHEQUE

was held on the top floor of the Belle Vue Road branch of the Loyal Order of Ancient Shepherds in Otley, West Yorkshire, England, one night in 1943. The DJ and promoter was teenager Jimmy Savile, later to become famous as a TV presenter and now Sir James Savile OBE, but at that time recently released from war service in the coal mines after injuring his back in an underground explosion. The amplification system had been cobbled together by a friend from salvaged parts of Marconi radios wired up to a record player. "Installing the equipment was fraught with great dangers," wrote Savile in his memoir *As It Happens*. "It was in several pieces connected by wires. These covered the top of a grand piano, glowed red hot when switched on for longer than five minutes, and charred the top of the noble instrument for the rest of its days. By 9 P.M. we had taken 11 shillings [$2.75], the machine had melted at several soldered points and died quietly, but not before giving a final electric shock to its inventor, causing him to weep openly."

Savile's mother, a veteran music-hall artiste, came to the rescue, performing songs on what remained of the grand piano.

Despite this initial setback, Savile had launched a new form of entertainment. Subsequent events were more successful, leading to a contract from leisure giant Mecca Ballrooms in 1946 to take disco around the country. For his first professional gig in Ilford, a suburb of London, Savile commissioned a purpose-built player-amplifier from Westrex, the first to incorporate that fundamental of all modern disco systems, the twin turntable.

The word *discotheque* (French *discothèque*) dates from about the same time as Savile's pioneering efforts in Otley, being applied to a small bar in the rue Huchette in Paris called La Discothèque where jazz records by black American performers were played to annoy the occupying Nazis. There is no evidence, though, that this enterprise involved the essentials of disco as understood today, a DJ and a sound amplification system. These were, however, features of the Whiskey-A-Go-Go jazz club opened by Paul Pacine in Paris in 1947, the world's first permanent discotheque. First in the United States was Le Club, opened in an underground garage at 416 East 55th Street (Sutton Place), New York City, by former Parisian entrepreneur Olivier Coquelin on 31 December 1960, with sponsorship by the Duke of Bedford and Henry Ford Jr. The DJ of the exclusive club ($150 initiation fee, $35 annual sub) was Slim Hyatt, society bandleader Peter Duchin's black butler. Nothing could have been more remote from disco's humble beginnings in Otley: Coquelin's family owned the Hotel George V in Paris and he based the décor of Le Club on the grand European hunting lodges he had known in his youth.

THE FIRST DISHWASHING MACHINE

to be manufactured commercially was developed over a period of ten years by society hostess Josephine Garis Cochran (aka Cochrane) of Shelbyville, Ill., wife of a local merchant and politician and descendant of steamboat (qv) pioneer John Fitch, and was patented on 28 December 1886. It was the need to prevent the frequent breakages of her best china when the servants did the dishes by hand after smart dinner parties that made her determined to build a dishwasher. Before reaching this resolve, she tried taking over the dishwashing chores herself but abandoned the task as too demeaning for a woman in her position. The prototype was built in Mrs. Cochran's woodshed, which still stands together with a historical marker.

When William Cochran died, leaving his widow only $1,500 and a pile of debts, friends rallied around to enable Mrs. Cochran to complete the project. She designed various models, some for family and others for hotel use, the larger ones being driven by a steam engine. About the time of the patent she set up the Garis-Cochran Dish-Washing Machine Co. to market the product, farming out manufacture to Tait Manufacturing of Decatur, Ill. A contemporary newspaper report stated that the machines were "capable of washing, scalding, rinsing and drying from 5-20 dozen dishes of all shapes and sizes in two minutes." Later she said that for her the hard part had been not so much the transformation from hostess to mechanic, but from hostess to huckster. Thus it was with considerable relief that she licensed the manufacturing and marketing rights to the Crescent Washing Machine Co., which launched a catering version on 1 April 1889. This was adopted for the vast kitchens of the World's Columbian Exhibition of 1893 in Chicago and was also exhibited in the Women's Pavilion, where it took a medal for "best mechanical construction, durability, and adaptation to the line of work."

Mrs. Cochran died in 1913, the same year that the first **electric dishwasher**, which was also the first specifically for home use, was put on the market at a cost of $100 by Walker Brothers of Philadelphia. Crescent followed suit the next year with a deluxe model at $250. Garis-Cochran and Crescent were taken over in 1926 by the Hobart Company, later renowned for its KitchenAid line of dishwashers.

THE FIRST DIVORCE

civil, since the Roman empire, to be fully documented was granted on 2 June 1545 to former playing-card manufacturer and retailer Pierre Ameaux by the

Small Council of Calvin's Protestant state of Geneva, on referral from the Consistory Court. The significance of the judgment given that day was that it entitled Ameaux to remarry, on the grounds that his wife Benoite "was a fornicator and held false opinions and was condemned to perpetual prison." (The ecclesiastical courts of the Roman Catholic Church had been empowered to grant annulments and legal separations, but these were not full divorces with the right to remarry.) Benoite Ameaux, the daughter of a pin maker, was a wealthy widow first married at the age of 18. During the successive trials that dragged through the Consistory Court, the Lieutenant's Court, and the Small Council for a period of two years, Benoite not only maintained that she had a right to sexual relations with anyone she chose (apparently based on the Biblical command to Christians to love one another), claiming among several wild fancies that Adam had consorted with his daughters, but also asserted that any woman not married at eighteen was a whore. Her testimony evidently came across to her judges as that of a woman mentally unbalanced, as prior to the judgment on divorce she was sentenced to be kept chained to a wall, the customary treatment for those believed to be uncontrollable. It was never proved whether she had really committed adultery or whether her confessions of liaisons with schoolmasters and ministers were simply actuated by desire. She herself had counter-petitioned for divorce on the grounds of physical abuse by Pierre. Despite her sentence of life imprisonment for adultery she was soon pardoned and released, which suggests a strong element of doubt about her guilt.

Pierre Ameaux did indeed remarry, but a year later found himself in jail on a charge of slandering John Calvin, Geneva's religious leader and effectually its head of state. He died in 1552, while Benoite survived him by at least a dozen years, disappearing from the written records in 1565. Divorce remained exceptional in the Geneva of the Protestant Reformation, the only grounds being adultery or desertion. Within a few years of the death of John Calvin, who had supported Pierre Ameaux's petition and several others on grounds that matrimony should be godly, divorce had become a chancy enterprise, at least for the man or woman judged to be the guilty party: the penalty was death.

The first civil divorce in the English-speaking world also took place in dramatic, albeit very different, circumstances. Only a year after the Ameaux divorce in Geneva, Britain's Parliament passed an Act in order to make lawful the bigamous marriage of Lady Sadleir of Standon, Hertfordshire. She had formerly been Mrs. Margaret Barr but had married Sir Ralph Sadleir after her previous husband had disappeared and been presumed dead. Mr. Barr having made an unwelcome reappearance, the Ecclesiastical Courts were powerless to confirm Lady Sadleir's second marriage, since they could only nullify a union where it could be proven to have been contracted unlawfully. Because in these peculiar circumstances the unfortunate Lady Sadleir had entered into her second, bigamous marriage in perfect good faith, a Private Bill was introduced into Parliament to dissolve the contract made with her first husband.

Lady Sadleir had been born Margaret Mitchell in humble circumstances and had been employed as a laundress at the time she married Barr. Her second marriage was exceptionally happy, despite the social gulf that separated her from Sir Ralph, one of Henry VIII's most trusted ministers. They were not only blessed with seven children, but with ever-increasing wealth, for when he died in 1587 Sadleir had the reputation of being the richest commoner in England. Lady Sadleir was perhaps even more fortunate than she knew, for hers was the only civil divorce granted to a woman petitioner in Britain before 1801.

U.S.: The earliest known dissolution of marriage was granted in the Massachusetts Bay Colony in December 1639, when an unidentified magistrate found in favor of the wife of James Luxford on grounds of bigamy. He also gave her the protection of the Court of Assistants by sequestering Luxford's property and assigning it to the wronged wife. The justice saw fit to heap other penalties on the wrongdoer. He was not only fined £100 (a prodigious sum equivalent to the value of a substantial dwelling), but also sentenced to "be set in the stocks an hour upon the market day after the lecture" and to be banished to England "by the first opportunity."

It might be argued that this was an annulment rather than a divorce per se, given that the marriage had been unlawful in the first place. Five years later, in

March 1643, there was an unequivocal case of divorce proper when Anne Clarke successfully sued her husband Dennis for a divorce on grounds of desertion and adultery with another woman. (It is possible that there had been an earlier divorce in the Plymouth Plantation. Governor John Winthrop recorded a petition for divorce in 1636, but the outcome is not known.)

The principle of **alimony** was enshrined in a 1641 Massachusetts law granting wronged wives the same privilege as widows, namely the proceeds of one-third of the husband's estate during her lifetime. This could be increased at the discretion of the court. In 1679 Mary Lyndon won two-thirds of her husband's estate together with other assets.

The total number of known American divorces granted in the seventeenth century was 106, all of them in New England except 8 in New York. Divorce was far more prevalent in the Northern American colonies than it was in the mother country. While the British Parliament only granted 325 complete divorces between 1670 and the setting up of the divorce courts in 1857 (and only 4 of these to women), Connecticut alone made nearly a thousand decrees between 1670 and 1799.

Most early divorces were granted for adultery or desertion. Cruelty (physical) was first admitted as grounds for divorce by New Hampshire in 1791, at a time when elsewhere wives were expected to submit without rancor to being whipped for offenses real or imagined. Mental cruelty was admitted first by the Dakota Territory in 1877. In some other states divorce laws were extremely restrictive. South Carolina prohibited divorce within the state, and would not recognise migratory divorces, until 1949. The only grounds for divorce in New York before September 1968 was adultery, which encouraged the use of "divorce mills" like Reno, Nev., or faking the evidence where no adultery had taken place.

No-fault divorce, requiring only the consent of the two parties, had originated with the French revolutionary government's innovative though short-lived divorce law of 20 September 1792. A spouse could also petition unilaterally on grounds of incompatibility without the need for witnesses or affidavits. The effect of allowing such easy dissolution of the bonds of marriage had immediate repercussions: Within three months of the bill becoming law, the number of divorces almost reached the number of marriages. Pastor Timothy Dwight, of New Haven, Conn., writing in 1818, cited the extreme case of a French soldier who boasted of having taken eleven wives in eleven years.

U.S.: The first no-fault divorce law in the United States became effective in California on 1 January 1970, with assets split equally between the parties regardless of who may have been at fault. By 1985 all other states except New York had followed suit and with one in every two marriages failing the United States had, and still has, the highest divorce rate in the world.

THE FIRST **DNA FINGERPRINTING**

was discovered accidentally by Dr. Alec J. Jeffreys of the Department of Genetics, University of Leicester, England, who found that by analyzing sections of DNA a unique genetic identity of each individual could be produced from samples of blood, saliva, or semen. The technique was first described by Dr. Jeffreys and his colleagues Victoria Wilson of University of Leicester and Swee Lay Thein of the John Radcliffe Hospital, Oxford, in a paper published in *Nature* on 7 March 1985.

The first practical application of the new technique was made in May of the same year when Jeffreys carried out a DNA test on Andrew Sarbah, his mother Christina, and his three siblings. British immigration authorities at Heathrow Airport had denied admittance to Andrew, who had been visiting his father in Ghana. They refused to accept that the boy was British-born or that UK–domiciled Christina was his mother, alleging that he was the son of one of her sisters in Ghana and that his passport was a forgery. When Jeffreys was able to prove that Christina was indeed the boy's mother, the immigration authorities quietly dropped the case, characteristically with no apology for the distress they had caused.

The first use of DNA fingerprinting for criminal detection was by Leicestershire Constabulary, who began collecting samples of blood and saliva from 2,000 men aged sixteen to thirty-four in the villages of Enderby, Narborough, and Littlethorpe, near Leicester on 5 January 1987. This was the area where two schoolgirls, Lynda Mann and Dawn Ashworth, had been raped and strangled. Later the tests were extended to 5,500 men, any of whom could have been the killer. Only two people refused. One of them, Colin Pitchfork, finding himself under pressure to consent, bribed a workmate to take the test in his name. When this substitute confessed to the deception, Pitchfork was DNA tested and charged. He was found guilty at Leicester Crown Court on 22 January 1988 and sentenced to two terms of life imprisonment for murder and two terms of ten years for rape, the first murderer in the world convicted on the evidence of genetic fingerprinting.

In the meantime there had been an earlier conviction on DNA evidence. At Bristol Crown Court on 13 November 1987 burglar Robert Melias was found guilty of raping a polio victim when he had broken into her home in Avonmouth. He had been charged several months after the offense when detectives succeeded in matching up a semen sample on the woman's petticoat with his blood.

U.S.: The first use of DNA testing was by Dr. Edward Blake of Forensic Science Associates, Richmond, Calif., in *Pennsylvania v. Pestinikas* in December 1986 to confirm different autopsy samples to be from the same person. The evidence was accepted by the civil court. It was used for the first time in a criminal court the following year, when local warehouse worker Tommy Lee Andrews was arraigned for a series of sexual assaults in Orlando, Fla. A forensic scientist from Lifecodes Corporation of Valhalla, N.Y., and an MIT biologist testified that semen from one of the victims matched Andrews's DNA and that his genetic print would be found in only one in 10 billion people. Andrews was found guilty on 6 November 1987 and sentenced to twenty-two years in jail.

The first conviction to be overturned on account of DNA evidence in the United States was that of mentally impaired Daniel Vasquez, sentenced in 1985 to thirty-five years in prison for raping then hanging a woman in his hometown in Arlington, Va. Three years later DNA fingerprinting identified another man, Timothy Spencer, as perpetrator of similar crimes that the FBI believed must have been committed by the same person as the Arlington murder. Vasquez was exonerated and released on 4 January 1989, while Spencer achieved the unenviable distinction of becoming the first person to be executed on the strength of DNA testing on 27 April 1994. He was not prosecuted for the crime originally attributed to Vasquez, as he had already been sentenced to death.

THE FIRST **DRIVE-IN RESTAURANTS**

originated in the southern United States. The idea of serving refreshments directly to a patron's vehicle began more or less accidentally in Memphis, Tenn., on a summer's evening in 1905 when there was such a crush of patrons at the drug store operated by Harold Fortune that he permitted gentlemen buying sodas for their lady friends to take them outside for consumption in their carriages, buggies, or, in rare cases, automobiles. The innovation proved so popular that Fortune hired extra help to carry the sodas out to waiting customers at the curb—the first carhops. Indeed the service was too popular, because after he moved the business to a new and even busier location in 1914, ever-increasing demand created traffic jams. His idea of flattening the curb in front of the store to allow cars to park halfway onto the sidewalk did not find favor with the commissioner of police, who banned curbside service in the business district. In 1922 this prompted a further move to the outskirts of the city, where Fortune had sufficient space for a parking lot. Here he began serving food as well as sodas, though the first drive-in restaurant had already opened the previous year.

This was on the outskirts of Dallas, the inaugural Pig Stand barbecue opening by the side of the Fort Worth Highway in September 1921. The money for the venture came from prominent Dallas physician Dr. R. W. Jackson, who put up $10,000 to incorporate the Pig Stands Company Inc., but the idea behind it came from his partner J. G. Kirby, who managed the business. "People with cars," he declared, "are so lazy that they don't want to get out of them to eat." His estimate of the target market proved sufficiently prescient for the expansion of Pig Stands throughout Texas and later to Florida and California, though the success of in-car and take-home "Barbecue Pig and Beef Sandwiches, Hamburgers and Ice

Cold Drinks," was probably aided as much by choosing areas with a benevolent climate as by the alleged idleness of motorists.

Female carhops first made their appearance at Montgomery's drive-in in Los Angeles in 1922. When the restaurant changed its name to the Tam O'Shanter, the wife of one of the owners, Henrietta Frank, had the idea of costuming the girls in "jaunty plaid costumes." One-off designs like this, ranging from matelot to Mexican, soon became standard for waitresses at drive-ins.

The first chain with "drive-through" window service was Jack in the Box, which opened its inaugural outlet selling 22¢ hamburgers in San Diego in 1951.

THE FIRST **DRIVER'S LICENSES**

were issued to French motorists under the Paris police ordinance of 14 August 1893 (Rule 1, Paragraph 1), which stated, "No motor vehicle . . . can be used without a regular authorization issued by us on the demand of the owner. This authorization can at all times be canceled by us, at the instigation of the engineers." Applicants were required to pass a driving exam in order to secure authorization to drive. They had to be twenty-one years of age or older and the exam required that they prove their driving ability, their capacity to undertake running repairs, and their knowledge of the components of the engine.

Driver's licenses in card form were required to be carried and shown on demand by every motorist in France under a decree of 10 March 1899 titled "Circulation des Automobiles" and were issued by the Ministère des Travaux Publics from that date. Licenses had to bear the photograph of the holder and there was a space for insertion by the issuing officer of the type of vehicle the holder was authorized to drive. A total of 1,795 licenses had been issued in the Paris area by 1 November 1899. The decree also extended driving exams to all prospective motorists in France, which thus became the first nation with this requirement.

U.S.: On 28 February 1899 the City of Boston Parks Department issued Operator's License No. 1 to Mr. George Neth of the Boston department store R. H. White & Co., allowing him to drive "on the parks or boulevards." There is no record of a driver's examination to qualify for a license.

The City of Chicago passed an ordnance on 6 July of the same year requiring "the examination and licensing" of drivers. Under this enactment a Board of Examiners of Operators of Automobiles was set up and licensing fees of $3 were imposed for the first year; $1 was charged for renewals. The licensing law was later struck down on appeal to the Supreme Court of Illinois, which ruled that only operators of commercial vehicles should be subject to its provisions. In the meantime the City of New York had introduced licensing on examination, one Harold T. Birnie being the first to receive a certificate of competence on 15 May 1900. The District of Columbia followed suit under the police regulations of 7 May 1903.

The first state to issue driver's licenses was Rhode Island, beginning on 1 June 1908. Applicants had to be sixteen years of age and the fees were 50¢ for a license to operate a motorcycle, $1 for all other motor vehicles. The first state driving examination was introduced at the same time, though it does not appear to have been very stringent; during the period January thru September 1909 only two candidates failed.

Massachusetts and Missouri each claim to have introduced driver's licenses before Rhode Island. These were not in fact licenses for *operators* of vehicles, but certificates of registration of the vehicles themselves.

It is not known which state was first to require photographs on licenses, thereby giving them the status of identity cards. The Smithsonian Institution in Washington, D.C., has an example of a license issued by the State of Indiana on 1 May 1925 bearing a circular sepia portrait of the driver, Howard W. Marty.

As late as 1937 four states—Florida, Illinois, Louisiana, and South Dakota—had no licensing system, and a dozen others issued licenses on demand with no requirement for an examination. The last to introduce a driver's examination was South Dakota in 1959.

SEE ALSO **motor vehicle license plates; woman driver.**

~~~~~~~~~~~~~~~~~~~~~~~~~~~ **E** ~~~~~~~~~~~~~~~~~~~~~~~~~~~

THE FIRST EIGHT-HOUR WORKDAY

was achieved by carpenter and joiner Samuel Duncan Parnell, who had left London for New Zealand in 1839 in despair at the failure of the English labor unions to fight for a reduction in the customary workday of twelve to sixteen hours. He and his 166 fellow passengers aboard the sailing ship Duke of Roxburgh were the first group of emigrants to the new colony. Their number included one George Hunter, a merchant later to become the first mayor of New Zealand's present capital of Wellington. When the ship arrived at Britannia (now Petone) on 7 February 1840 after a five-month voyage, Hunter asked Parnell to build him a store at Korokoro in the Hutt Valley. According to his own account, Parnell responded: "I must make this condition, Mr Hunter, that on the job the hours shall be only eight for the day." When Hunter protested, the carpenter insisted, "There are 24 hours per day given us; eight of these should be for work, eight for sleep, and the remaining eight for recreation." As there were only two other carpenters among the settlers, and they already engaged, Hunter reluctantly agreed to a wage of 5s ($1.25) for an eight-hour day.

Parnell's determination that a new country demanded new conditions of labor soon won other adherents, a meeting of workmen in Wellington in October 1840 agreeing that none would work longer than eight hours and that anyone found to be breaking ranks would be ducked in the harbor. The movement spread to other parts of New Zealand and thence to Australia, where the stonemasons of Victoria won the world's first industry-wide eight-hour day on 21 May 1856.

U.S.: It is said that ship's carpenters in Boston secured an eight-hour day in 1842, but contemporary evidence is lacking. The first state to enact an eight-hour provision was Illinois, applying to all workers other than farm labor with effect from 1 May 1867. Lack of enforcement meant that it was easily evaded. On 25 June of the following year President Andrew Johnson signed an act decreeing an eight-hour day for all workers employed by or on behalf of the government of the United States. If Congress wanted to set an example to American industry, it was not going to be followed without a fight. The first trade in the United States to secure a nationwide agreement was the granite cutters on 16 May 1900, but only after the members of their union had been on strike for ten weeks. Even then it was alleged that the employers had only conceded at the insistence of "Copper King" Senator William Andrews Clark, who needed granite cut for work on his thirty-four-room mansion on, appropriately, Granite Street in Butte, Mont.

SEE ALSO **five-day workweek**.

THE FIRST ELECTRIC CHAIR

was used for the execution of convicted murderer William Kemmler at Auburn Prison in Auburn, N.Y., on 6 August 1890. The idea of inflicting capital punishment by electrocution was conceived by one Harold P. Brown, a strange and rather shadowy figure who conducted the initial experiments with equipment placed at his disposal by Thomas Alva Edison, the so-called "wizard of Menlo Park." Assisted by Dr. A. E. Kennelly, Edison's chief electrician, Brown proceeded to electrocute a large number of animals. The Electrical Engineer, which thoroughly disapproved of the whole undertaking, reported in August 1889, "Many unfortunate dogs and other animals were tortured to death by Messrs. Brown and Kennelly, such of them as could not be killed by electricity being, as one of the spectators testified, dispatched by a blow on the head with a brick."

These allegations stirred up a storm of controversy, which became even more heated when it was suggested by certain leading members of the electrical industry that Brown's use of alternating-current Westinghouse generators for the experiments without the authority of that company was a deliberate attempt on behalf of the Edison direct-current interests to discredit their rivals.

A week after Kemmler's execution, which by that time had become a national issue, *The Electrical Engineer* inveighed against the authorities for having allowed him to be used as a guinea pig in what turned out to be a horrifyingly mismanaged attempt to apply science to the judicial act of killing. Said an angry but carefully composed leading article:

> Making due allowance for the sensational reports of the daily Press it is quite certain that the death of the victim at Auburn was not instantaneous, that respiration was resumed some minutes after the application and cessation of the current, that the current was turned on again, this time despatching the convict, but not without burning his flesh at the points of contact with the electrodes, and not till he had exhibited to the spectators meanwhile evidences of the vital struggle not less revolting than those usually seen upon the gallows.

The *New York Times* described it as "an awful spectacle, far worse than hanging." The official report on the execution stated that the death of William Kemmler had taken 8 minutes from the time he entered the room.

Woman to go to the chair: The first was Martha M. Place of Brooklyn, N.Y., convicted on 7 February 1898 of murdering her stepdaughter, Ida. She paid the supreme penalty at Sing Sing Prison, in Ossining, N.Y., on 20 March 1899.

THE FIRST **ELECTRIC HEATING**

system was patented in the United States by Dr. W. Leigh Burton in 1887 and introduced commercially two years later by the Burton Electric Co. of Richmond, Va. A writer in *The Electrician* said:

> The Burton Electric Heater consists of a cast-iron case, enclosing some resistance coils, which are

covered with dry, powdered clay, for the purpose of absorbing the heat from the wires, and thus preventing them from burning out. The current supplied to the heaters has a potential of 80V, and each heater uses about 1½ amp. It has been found that such a current raises the temperature of a heater to about 200°F.

Shaped like a low table, the radiators were 27 inches long and 8 inches wide, and stood on iron legs raising them 4 inches from the floor. To begin with their use was confined to electric tramcars, though they were advertised as suitable for household use. Toward the end of 1891 the Aspen Mining Co. of Aspen, Colo., acquired a quantity of Burton Electric Heaters from the Electric Merchandise Co. in Chicago for use in their motor-stations. These are the first buildings in the U.S. known to have been heated by electricity. The first domestic application of electric heating had been made earlier the same year in Austria. Swiss-born cotton manufacturer Friedrich Schindler introduced electric fire-clay radiators of his own design at the Villa Grünau, his mansion in Kennelbach. They were powered from his own hydroelectric plant.

THE FIRST
ELECTRIC LAMPS, INCANDESCENT

to be produced commercially were developed independently, but at the same time, by Thomas Alva Edison of Menlo Park, N.J., and by (Sir) Joseph Swan of Newcastle upon Tyne, England. In view of the rival claims to priority that emanate from both sides of the Atlantic, the exact chronology assumes some importance. Edison began his experiments in September 1878, achieving a satisfactory result a little over twelve months later. The first Edison bulb to burn for a reasonable length of time was Model No. 9, which had a carbonized cotton filament. Under the date 21 October 1879 he wrote in his notebook, "No. 9 on from 1:30 A.M. till 3 P.M.—13½ hours and was then raised to 3 gas jets for one hour then cracked glass and busted." The lamp was patented on 1 November 1879, but it soon became apparent that carbonized sewing thread, which Edison was using for a filament, was not sufficiently durable for constant burning. Early in 1880, therefore, he switched to carbonized paper filaments, and these proved sufficiently long-lasting to be used in the first commercially produced lamps, manufactured in October (SEE BELOW). On 31 December he put on a spectacular display for the public at Menlo Park, illuminating the laboratory with twenty-five lamps, the offices with eight, and another twenty in neighboring houses and the street to the railroad depot, at which crowds of rubberneckers arrived on special trains.

Joseph Swan made the first public announcement of his incandescent electric lamp at a meeting of the Newcastle upon Tyne Chemical Society on 18 December 1878. In the course of his lecture he displayed a bulb containing a carbon conductor just over an inch long but was unable to show it in operation, as it had already burned out through excessive current being applied in a laboratory test. A similar lamp was shown alight during another lecture that he gave at Sunderland on 18 January 1879. Although this demonstration took place some ten months before Edison's successful laboratory experiment, it cannot be regarded as more than a preliminary stage in the progress toward the production of a marketable electric light bulb. Not until late in 1879 did Swan produce a true filament lamp, employing a carbonized cotton thread similar to that used by Edison, but rather longer lasting. This was the subject of a patent taken out on 27 November 1880, and under which Swan lamps were subsequently manufactured.

Edison began regular manufacture of lightbulbs at Menlo Park on 1 October 1880, the Swan Electric Light Co. following early in 1881 with the opening of a factory at Benwell, outside Newcastle upon Tyne. There were originally some 200 stages in the manufacturing process of each individual Edison bulb, and the fact that most of them had to be performed by hand accounts for the initially high retail cost of $2.50 per lamp.

The first commercial installation of incandescent lightbulbs was made even before regular manufacture began. Once again Edison took the honors, installing 115 lamps aboard the Oregon Railway and Navigation Co.'s steamer *Columbia* at San Francisco on 2 May 1880. This was a few weeks ahead of the first commercial use of Swan lamps on 24 June, also aboard ship, installed on the Orient Line's *Chimborazo* then lying at Gravesend, Kent. Swan, however, preceded Edison with the first building lit with incandescent lightbulbs, armaments manufacturer W. G. Armstrong's mansion Cragside at Rothbury, Northumberland, in December 1880 (operated by hydroelectric power), while Edison lamps were used to illuminate the lithography shop of Hinds, Ketchum & Co. of New York City during the first week in February the following year. A number of other installations of Edison bulbs in factories and industrial plants were made between August and November 1881, most notably at James Harrison's woolen mill in Newburgh, N.Y.; at the Alfred Dolge Felt Mills in Dolgeville, N.Y.; at the U.S. Rolling Stock Co.'s car-building plants in Chicago and Urbana, Ohio; and at the Winona Flour Mills in Winona, Minn. Swan stole a march on his competitor, though, with a number of world firsts for incandescent lamps during 1881, including street lighting (Newcastle upon Tyne, 11 April) and installations in a hotel (Lamb's Temperance Hotel, Dundee, Scotland, in June); coal mine (Earnock Colliery, Hamilton, Scotland, in August); railroad station (Queen Street, Glasgow, in August); railroad car (London–Brighton, 14 October); store (Stephen Tanner, dry goods, Godalming, Surrey, in December); and theater (Savoy, London, 28 December).

The first domestic installations were made by Swan at Cragside in the north of England in December 1880 as noted above and by Edison at Drexel-Morgan banker James Hood Wright's palatial residence in the Fort Washington district of New York City in late 1881. All early applications of incandescent lighting required an independent power source and were therefore confined to dwellings like those large enough to accommodate their own generators, as well as public and commercial buildings. Smaller houses and shops were able to acquire electric lighting from a central source with the opening of the first electric power plants (qv). Distribution of current for incandescent lamps began on a small scale at Godalming in Surrey, England, in September 1881 (Swan Lamps) and on a larger scale in London and New York (Edison Lamps) in 1882.

Neither Edison nor Swan "invented" the incandescent electric lamp, as much of their work was derived from that of earlier experimenters in the same field who failed to achieve their commercial success. Nevertheless each tried to sue the other for patent infringement and each sought to invade the other's home territory. During 1882 Edison reluctantly merged with Swan in Britain to form the Edison & Swan United Electric Light Co., better known by its brand name Ediswan, and also in that year the Swan Incandescent Electric Co. of New York began manufacture in the United States. Curiously both the Edison Electric Light Co. and Swan Electric Light Co. survived to the end of the twentieth century as part of industrial giants with the same name but no other connection—Edison as a component of the General Electric Co. based in Fairfield, Conn., and Swan as a component of the General Electric Co. based in London (since 1999 Marconi plc).

SEE ALSO **electric power plant; electric street lighting; fluorescent lighting**.

THE FIRST **ELECTRIC MOTOR**

capable of practical application was patented by Thomas Davenport of Rutland, Vt., on 25 February 1837. Davenport put two 50-pound motors of his own design to work the same year, one for drilling holes up to ¼ inch diameter in iron and steel, the other for turning hardwood. Each incorporated an electromagnet and operated at a speed of 450 rpm. In 1839 he built a larger motor to drive a rotary printing press, which he used to print the first electrical journal *The Electro-Magnet and Mechanics Intelligencer,* published 18 January 1840.

The industrial application of battery-powered electric motors was severely limited since, as the editor of the *Philosophical Magazine* pointed out in 1850, electric power from this source was about twenty-five times more expensive than steam power. The first use of electricity to provide mechanical power on a considerable scale for industrial purposes was made at the Paris factory of the Société Gramme in, or shortly before, 1873. All the machinery was driven by a motor supplied with current from a Gramme dynamo.

The first miniature electric motors were made by Thomas Alva Edison at Menlo Park, N.J., in 1880 to drive an electric pen he had designed for producing punctured copying stencils. The motor measured 1' x 1½", and operated at approximately 4,000 rpm to drive a vibrating needle in the pen-holder that would prick out letters in punctured dots. It was powered by twin wet-cell batteries. Edison's electric pen provided a successful method of duplicating multiple copies of manuscripts before the typewriter stencil rendered it obsolete. Manufacture was undertaken by the Western Electric Co. and at least sixty thousand miniature motors and pens were sold for use in banks and offices.

THE FIRST **ELECTRIC POWER PLANT**

in the world supplying current centrally for public consumption was not, as most reference works insist, Thomas Edison's celebrated Pearl Street generating station in New York City (SEE BELOW), but the small installation established in San Francisco by the California Electric Light Co., founded by visionary twenty-seven-year-old Canadian broker George W. Row and incorporated on 30 June 1879. A steam engine, boiler, a pair of small Brush dynamos, and a coal pile were placed in a shed consisting of sheet iron nailed to 4" x 4" timber uprights and from these unpromising premises on Fourth and Market streets, generation of sufficient electricity to power twenty-one Brush arc lamps began in September. The tariff was $10 per week per lamp for unlimited supply between sundown and midnight, Sundays and public holidays excluded. Although this equated to the weekly wage of an adult store clerk, the appeal of being able to illuminate their windows and frontages with the brilliant if piercing light of the carbon arcs was such that proprietors of stores rushed to sign up and by the end of the year an additional four dynamos powering a hundred lamps were in operation. Unlike many of the pioneer utilities, the California Electric Light Co. survived the difficult early years when competition from incandescent electric lights lessened the attraction of arc lighting and was eventually absorbed into the present West Coast power supplier Pacific Gas & Electricity Co.

Power plant generating electricity for incandescent lamps: The first was the hydroelectric Central Power Station at Godalming, a small market town with some two thousand population in Surrey, England, which was built by Calder & Barrett at Pullman's Leather Mill on the River Wey and operated by them with effect from 26 September 1881. This was the first central power plant in the world to cater to domestic consumers of electricity, arc lamps being too intense for lighting ordinary households. The generating equipment was supplied by Siemens Bros., who took over the running of the power station the following year. The principal customer was the Godalming Town Council, the instigator of the project, which contracted with Calder & Barrett to light the town for twelve months for £195. Ordinary gas standards were converted for use with electricity and the cables were laid along the gutters of the streets. The town was lit by four 300-candlepower Siemens arc lamps and thirty-five incandescent Swan lights.

Among the private customers was the man who had originally conceived the project, W. R. Pullman, who lit his own house with Swan lamps as well as his tanning factory that housed the plant and its offices. Not a great deal is known about the others. George F. Tanner, who was thirteen in 1881, recalled in a recording made in 1954 that his father's drapery store (i.e., dry goods), Stephen Tanner's of 18 High Street, was lit by Swan lamps, as was the family accommodation above it. The only other named personal consumers were Mr. Ballard, Mr. Burgess, and Mr. Collier. Strangely all five of these known individuals who opted for the new technology went on to become mayors of Godalming. Probably the best known and most distinguished customer was Charterhouse, one of the seven leading boarding schools in Britain, which in 1882 became the first school in the world to be lit by incandescent lamps.

Despite Godalming's pioneering efforts, a much greater community was needed for the effective distribution of an electricity supply for incandescent lamps and it was the world's largest city, London, that first succeeded in lighting up a commercial district. The central generating plant established by the Edison Electric Light Co. at 57 Holborn Viaduct began serving the area between Holborn Circus and the Old Bailey with public power supply for street lighting on 12 January 1882 and domestic current on 12 April. In contrast with the rather lukewarm attitude of Godalming consumers, response from commercial undertakings on the Holborn Viaduct was enthusiastic and immediate. No fewer than thirty buildings were lit up with Edison incandescent bulbs on the first day of supply, including the General Post Office at St. Martin le Grand, and such famous business houses as photographers Negretti & Zambra, the Vaseline Co., tobacco giant W. D. & H. O. Wills, and the sewing machine manufacturers Coventry Machine Co. The London, Chatham & Dover Railway Station also shone forth, as did the City Temple, the first church in Britain illuminated by electricity, and the first two hotels in London to be lit by incandescent bulbs, Spiers & Pond's and the Imperial. Notable also were the first electrically lit pub, the Viaduct Tavern, and the first electrically lit restaurant, Spiers & Pond's, next door to their hotel.

U.S.: The first central power plant servicing incandescent electric lamps was established in Pearl Street, New York City, by the Edison Electric Light Co., covering the heart of the Manhattan business district between City Hall and the East River, and began generating electricity for public consumption at 3 A.M. on 4 September 1882. The massive 27-ton "Jumbo" dynamo, generating 100 kilowatts, could power 1,200 lamps. As well as stores and hotels, customers included bankers Drexel Morgan; brokers Kidder, Peabody & Co.; Continental Bank, the Merchants Bank of Canada, Third National Bank; the New York, Guardian, Great Western, Knickerbocker, National Fire, Continental, and Home Insurance companies; and the offices of the *New York Times*, *New York Truth*, *Mail and Express*, *Sun*, and *Commercial Advertiser*. No charges were made during the first five months of operation, as regular and stable supply could not be guaranteed. The first electricity bill was sent to the Ansonia Brass & Copper Co. on 18 January 1883 and was for $50.44. Pearl Street was decommissioned in 1895.

SEE ALSO **nuclear power plant**.

were advertised by Willing's Electric Signs of King's Cross, London, in *The Electrician* for 31 December 1881, as being "Suitable for signs, fascias, window decorations, novelties, advertisements, etc." On 14 January 1882 Thomas Edison's London representative Major W. J. Hammer displayed the word EDISON, spelled out in Edison bulbs that flashed on and off, above the Great Organ in the Crystal Palace at Sydenham. This was hand-operated but the following year another illuminated EDISON sign appeared over the entrance arch to the International Hygiene Exhibition in Berlin and this time a motor produced the flashing effect automatically. Meanwhile in New York, Miner's Theater became the first to put its name up in lights. The first restaurant to do so was the Boston Oyster House in 1884.

In 1890 the first electric advertising sign in London's Piccadilly Circus, believed to have been for Bovril, was erected on the northeast side. A year later, Broadway was lit up with the legend BUY HOMES ON LONG ISLAND SWEPT BY OCEAN BREEZES, a persuasive electrical message spelled out by the Long Island Rail Road, which stood to gain from the commuter traffic. By 1906 there were three thousand electric signs in Manhattan, most of them bedazzling the denizens of Broadway. G. K. Chesterton commented on the "Great White Way" after visiting New York: "What a glorious garden of wonders this would be, to anyone who was lucky enough to be unable to read."

The first **movie star whose name was up in lights** was Mary Pickford, her employer Adolph Zukor arranging with the manager of the Hamilton Theater in New York City to emblazon his marquee with it when her new picture *Hearts Adrift* opened there on 10 February 1914. She had known nothing about this until he and Mrs. Zukor had taken her to tea at a café opposite the theater, sitting on and making small talk about nothing until it became dark. He then led her out on the sidewalk and displayed his surprise, which Miss Pickford later recalled as "one of the most thrilling sights of my whole career."

The first **strip lighting** capable of being twisted into words was Moore Tubing, developed by D. McFarlan Moore of the Moore Electric Co., London, and originally used for advertising signs in 1905. The earliest practical electric-discharge lamps, Moore Tubes were filled with carbon dioxide or nitrogen and gave a good quality of light, but suffered from being expensive both to install and maintain. They were eventually superseded by neon lighting that was brighter and more economical to run.

Neon lighting was developed by French physicist George Claude and displayed for the first time at the Paris Motor Show on 3 December 1910. Two 45-mm-diameter neon tubes, each 35 meters long, were used to illuminate the peristyle of the Grand-Palais where it was held. The main drawback of neon lighting at this stage of its development was its color—red—and although Claude had originally intended it for ordinary lighting purposes, he was persuaded by an advertising man, Jacques Fonseque, that it could be better utilized for illuminated signs. The rights were acquired by the agency Paz et Silva, for whom Fonseque worked, and in 1912 the first neon sign was erected over a barbershop at 14 boulevard Montmartre. This announced LE PALACE COIFFEUR in large red letters. In the same year the first neon advertising sign, consisting of the single word CINZANO, was displayed on the front of 72 boulevard Haussmann. Claude himself joined the firm of Paz et Silva to continue developments, and soon produced a tube giving a blue light. Other colors were added to the range by introducing powders of the appropriate hue into the glass tube (the one color neon cannot do to this day is brown). By 1914 some 150 signs had been installed on buildings in Paris.

U.S.: The first neon sign was erected on the Packard Showroom at Seventh and Flower streets in Los Angeles in 1922 after proprietor Earle C. Anthony had taken a European vacation and witnessed the neon wonders of the Paris night. It consisted of the Packard logo, with the name in orange-red framed in a blue argon border. Two years later Claude opened a New York office and brought neon to Broadway with another auto-themed sign, for Willys-Knight Overland Motors.

THE FIRST **ELECTRIC STOVE**

was installed at the Hotel Bernina in Samaden, Switzerland, in 1889. No record survives of the inventor, but *The Electrician* reported, in August of that year, that it contained German silver resistance coils, and that it had been found capable of performing all the normal cooking operations. The Hotel Bernina had its own electric power supply generated from a dynamo driven by a waterfall. As a good deal of power was going to waste during the day, the proprietor hit upon the idea of utilizing the current for cooking when it was not required for lighting.

U.S.: An electric griddle was made by self-taught electrician Charles E. Carpenter in 1889 and used for cooking food in the window of the Minneapolis restaurant where he worked as a cashier. Carpenter then went into partnership with a tailor called Nevius, for whom he had made an electric sadiron, and established the Carpenter-Nevius Electric Heating Co. in St. Paul, Minn. There in 1891 he began manufacturing the world's first production-model cooker, as described by the New York trade journal *The Electrical Engineer*:

> The baking oven is 18 ins long, 14 ins high, and 12 ins deep, made of well-seasoned white pine, lined with asbestos felt, and bright tin. There are two sheet-iron shelves in each oven, and also two resistance plates on the bottom and one on the top, connected with a switch on the outside of the oven, so that two temperatures may be obtained. These ovens have a small glass window in each door, so that the baking can be watched. Each resistance plate consumes about five amperes on 110 volts, and it has been found that it only requires from 12-15 minutes, at a maximum temperature, to heat the oven to 250°F. The current can then be turned off and the baking continued.

Early electric cookers were generally black in imitation of the coal- or wood-fired ranges they supplanted. The first white-porcelain enamel stoves were produced by Hotpoint in 1923.

THE FIRST **ELECTRIC STREET LIGHTING**

was installed experimentally at the Quai Conti and the Place de la Concorde in Paris with arc lamps by Deleuil & Archereau in 1841. The first street lit permanently by electricity was the rue Impériale in Lyons, where arc lamps were installed by Lacassagne & Thiers in 1857. Little further progress appears to have been made in France until Paris's avenue de l'Opéra was electrically lit in June 1878.

U.S.: Twelve Brush arc lamps lit the streets enclosing Monumental Park (now Public Square) in Cleveland, Ohio, from 29 April 1879. It was also Brush lamps that made Broadway in New York City into the "Great White Way" when the stretch from 14th Street to 34th Street was illuminated on 20 December 1880.

Town in which electric lighting was the sole outdoor illumination: The first was Wabash, Ind., which was illuminated by four 4,000-candlepower Brush arc lights, each suspended 50 feet above the business quarter, on 31 March 1880.

Incandescent electric street lamps: The first permanent installation was made at Newcastle upon Tyne, England, by Mawson & Swan in 1881. The initial five lamp standards, three in Mosley Street, one in Pilgrim Street, and another in Grey Street, were illuminated on 11 April. The *Newcastle Daily Chronicle* reported enthusiastically, noting that "the shadows generally lurking around the ordinary street lamp-post were palpably absent."

U.S.: Incandescent street lamps were demonstrated by Thomas Edison at Menlo Park, N.J., on 1–2 November 1880. The first permanent installations were made in the downtown business area served by Edison's electric power plant (qv) in Pearl Street, New York City, which became operative on 4 September 1882. About one third of the lower City District was illuminated.

THE FIRST **ELECTRIC TELEGRAPH**

in commercial operation was the system of instant communication patented on 12 June 1837 by William Fothergill Cooke and Prof. Charles Wheatstone of London. On 24 May the following year they contracted with the Great Western Railway for its use between the London terminus at Paddington and West Drayton. The 13-mile five-wire telegraph line was encased in an iron tube that ran along the side of the track above the ground, and the cost of erection, including the five-needle electromagnetic telegraph instruments at either end, was estimated at between £250 and £300 per mile (about $1,500). It was first brought into practical use on 6 April 1839. The telegraph line having been completed the 5 miles as far as Hanwell, Traffic Superintendent Seymour Clarke wrote:

> The Telegraph has been of use today. Mr. Brunel, with whom I fell in at Maidenhead, asked me to stop the 12 o'clock at Hanwell, and after looking at Peto and Grisell's proposal for the Bridge we were waiting at the Hanwell Station and playing on the Telegraph when we found that the *Atlas* [a locomotive] had dropped her fire bars at Bourne farm and stopped the down train at 2 to caution it.

The Mr. Brunel who wanted the 12-o'clock train stopped was the GWR's Chief Engineer, Isambard Kingdom Brunel, celebrated for building the first purpose-built Atlantic steamship, the *Great Western*, and the first screw-driven ocean liner, the *Great Britain*.

The line was completed to West Drayton on 9 July 1839 and for the next ten years was in regular use for conveying the traffic superintendent's orders and reporting breakdowns and other emergencies. In 1843 it was extended on iron telegraph poles to Slough and on 10 January of that year it was agreed at a GWR board meeting that patentee William Cooke should provide the company with a free telegraph service and that in return, he or his licensee should be permitted to open the telegraph line to the public as a commercial undertaking.

The license was acquired from Cooke by Thomas Home for an annual rental of £170 ($850) and on 16 May 1843 the first paid **telegrams** in the world were dispatched by Cooke's new double-needle electromagnetic telegraph over the 20-mile-long wire from Paddington to Slough. The fee per telegram was one shilling (25¢) irrespective of the number of words, and messengers were kept in constant attendance at both ends for delivering the telegrams to any address in London at one end and within Windsor, Eton, Slough, or neighboring districts at the other. Patrons who wanted to try out the new means of communication, but knew nobody in the Slough area, were able to dispatch questions to be answered by the operator at the other end, or alternatively a bell could be rung in the dispatch office to demonstrate that the message had been received. The telegraph office at Paddington was on the arrival platform, while the one at Slough was in a separate building called Telegraph Cottage. Home claimed that "in the list of visitors are the illustrious names of several of the Crowned Heads of Europe, and nearly the whole of the Nobility of England."

The Crowned Heads simply came to gawp at this latest wonder, while most of the paid messages were sent by people ordering post horses to be ready on the arrival of the sender. Tradesmen at Slough and Windsor used the telegraph for ordering supplies, as testified by this telegram which has survived:

> SEND A MESSENGER TO MR HARRIS, DUKE STREET, MANCHESTER SQUARE, AND REQUEST HIM TO SEND 6LB OF WHITEBAIT AND 4LB OF SAUSAGES BY THE DOWN TRAIN TO MR FINCH AT WINDSOR. THEY MUST BE SENT BY THE 5.30 DOWN TRAIN OR NOT AT ALL.

With no limit on the number of words, the truncated language later to be known as *telegraphese* had yet to come into being. (As also the word *telegram*, originally used by the Albany (N.Y.) *Evening Journal* in 1852.)

Two notable innovations occurred during the four and a half years that Home operated this fledgling public service. One was the official announcement of the birth of Prince Alfred to Queen Victoria on 6 August 1844, conveyed from Windsor Castle via the Slough telegraph office to her Cabinet ministers in London. So rapid was the communication that *The Times* of London rushed out an edition containing the joyous news just 40 minutes after the child was delivered. The other occurred later the same month when the police made their first use of the telegraph. The 28 August was Montem Day at Eton College near Windsor, an event that always attracted thieves lured by the prospect of rich pickings from the pockets of young sprigs of the aristocracy. Detectives were positioned at Paddington Station to identify known malefactors and their names and descriptions were wired to Slough. Two of their number, Oliver Martin and "Fiddler Dick," were arrested on arrival, having already purloined the purse of a lady passenger.

Sir Charles Wheatstone and Sir William Cooke were both knighted. Wheatstone had already invented the concertina before his work on the telegraph and he went on to develop the stereoscope and the dynamo. In 1846 Cooke became a founder of the Electric Telegraph Company, he and Wheatstone receiving £168,000 ($840,000) for their patents, and it was this enterprise that succeeded in establishing a national network of telegraphs at the same time as parallel developments were happening in the United States (SEE BELOW). As for Thomas Home, progenitor of the paid telegram, he surrendered his license to Cooke's newly formed Electric Telegraph Co. in 1847 and receded into the obscurity whence he had come. Little is known about his subsequent career, save that he was established as a brick and drainpipe manufacturer at Brill in Buckinghamshire in 1865 and that he died there in 1898.

U.S.: The first electric telegraph to reach practical fruition in America and the first successful **recording telegraph** in the world was developed by the artist and founder of New York's National Academy of Design, Samuel F. B. Morse, at the same time as Cooke and Wheatstone's work in England. It was his misfortune that the instrument that was to become predominant in worldwide telegraphy failed, mainly owing to the vacillation of government, to achieve commercial utility before the British had established a working system, albeit with inferior technology.

Morse conceived the idea for his recording telegraph aboard the ship *Sully* in October–November 1832 as he returned from a three-year sojourn studying art in Europe. This followed a conversation at dinner one night during which Dr. Charles T. Jackson of Boston had observed, apropos recent developments in electrical science, that electricity passed through any known length of wire and that its presence could be observed at any part of the line by breaking the circuit.

Morse later claimed to have responded, "If the presence of electricity can be made visible in any part of the circuit, I see no reason why intelligence may not be transmitted instantaneously by electricity." (While this is often held as a Eureka moment in the inception of the electric telegraph, it should be noted that the same thought had occurred to other men of science and that a number of experimental devices had already been constructed.)

The prototype instrument was built by Morse in a room next to the chapel at New York University in Washington Square shortly after he had been appointed professor of design in 1835. This was completed before the end of the year and demonstrated to some of his friends and colleagues, including Prof. Leonard D. Gale, later a partner in the enterprise, early in the New Year.

A first draft of the **Morse Code** (later amended) but in a recognizable dot-and-dash form was included with the caveat that Morse filed with the Patent Office on 3 October 1837. The design of the Morse Code has often been attributed to Morse's assistant Alfred Vail, though no contemporary evidence of this exists.

The first public demonstration of Morse's telegraph was made at the Vail family's Speedwell Ironworks at Morristown, N.Y., on 11 January 1838, Samuel Morse writing to his brother Sidney two days later:

> The machinery is at last completed and we have shown it to the Morristown people with great éclat. It is the talk of all the people around, and the principal inhabitants of Newark made a special excursion on Friday to see it. The success is complete. We have tried the experiment of sending a pretty full letter, which I set up from the numbers given me, transmitting through two miles of wire and deciphered with but a single unimportant error.

The numbers referred to were a somewhat cumbersome means of transmitting with numerals representing words, soon to be discarded, because on 24 January Morse exhibited the apparatus to a select group of the great and the good at New York University in Washington Square and on this occasion he used the dots and dashes of the Morse Code. The first such message was transmitted in honor of Gen.

Cummings, who had just been appointed to a new command, and read:

ATTENTION THE UNIVERSE, BY KINGDOMS RIGHT WHEEL.

The original transcription is preserved at the Smithsonian Institution.

There followed a long delay before the Morse telegraph came into public use. It was a matter of constant frustration to its inventor that while his system was ready for commercial exploitation at about the same time as Cooke and Wheatstone's in England, in 1838, they were able to secure backing from the Great Western Railway (and subsequently from most other railroad companies in Britain), while in a land celebrated for mercantile opportunity he was unable to secure any substantive support. It was only after a delay of seven years that the U.S. Government—having first invited proposals for a telegraph system as early as 1837, to which Morse had promptly responded—eventually accorded his invention the subvention it so abundantly deserved. This was an appropriation of $30,000 for the building of a telegraph line between Baltimore and Washington, authorized by an Act of Congress of 3 March 1843.

Construction of the line began at 8 A.M. on 21 October. Following Cooke and Wheatstone's example, Morse determined to lay the cables in lead pipes in trenches, unaware that they had already abandoned this system for the extension to Slough in favor of telegraph poles. When the underground system failed in March 1844, Morse also turned to overhead wires and poles, using a method of insulation devised by his mechanical assistant Ezra Cornell, who probably deserves to be known as America's "father of the telegraph pole."

Although the formal opening of the Baltimore–Washington line was scheduled for 24 May 1844, in fact the telegraph had come into practical use more than three weeks earlier. The wires extended 22 miles from Washington to the junction of the Annapolis railroad with the Baltimore and Washington track by 1 May, the date of the Whig National Convention in Baltimore. Morse arranged for Alfred Vail to establish a telegraph office at the junction depot, exactly halfway to Baltimore, with instructions to meet the trains from Baltimore and find out the latest news of the Convention. The first substantive message to be transmitted was THE PASSENGERS IN THE CARS GAVE THREE CHEERS FOR HENRY CLAY (Clay had been nominated for president), followed by a rather less ambiguous message that Mr. Frelinghuysen had been nominated as vice president. This last was received and acknowledged in 2 minutes and 1 second. The news had spread all over Washington, Morse reported, 1 hour and 4 minutes before the train arrived.

The celebrated message WHAT HATH GOD WROUGHT? was not, then, the first wire sent in the United States, though it was the first to be transmitted on the official opening day of the Baltimore–Washington service on 24 May. The quotation, from Numbers 23:23, had been chosen by Annie Ellsworth, teenage daughter of the commissioner of patents, who had brought Morse the original news that the bill authorizing the line had passed the Senate and had been promised the inaugural transmission as a reward. (According to Ellsworth family tradition, Annie had a crush on Morse.)

At 2 P.M. on the following day a reporter in Congress despatched the world's first **press telegram** to the editor of the *Baltimore Patriot*. The rather unexceptional message read: 1 O'CLOCK—THERE HAS BEEN A MOTION IN THE HOUSE TO GO INTO COMMITTEE OF THE WHOLE ON THE OREGON QUESTION. REJECTED. AYES, 79; NOES, 86. The New York *Daily Sun* commented in wonder, "This is indeed the annihilation of space." Rather more dramatic was the announcement over the wires on 29 May that James Polk had received the Democratic nomination for president, news that caused a sensation when it reached Washington as Van Buren had been front runner.

The Washington–Baltimore line was free to users until the postmaster general, seeking to recover some of the government's costs, started charging at the rate of 1¢ per four characters with effect from 1 April 1845—the beginning of paid telegrams in the United States. During the first four days' operation total revenue was 1¢. A man with a $20 bill and a penny had gone into the telegraph office in Washington and asked for a demonstration. Alfred Vail, who was in charge, could not change the twenty, so offered the customer half a cent's worth, transmitting the figure 4 (code for "What time is it?") to Baltimore and receiving the digit 1 ("1 o'clock") in response. The man left without his half-cent change, thereby doubling receipts. Eventually business did pick up somewhat, though revenue in the first three months was only $193.56 against running costs of $1,859.05

Much more successful, and the progenitor of the first telegraph network in the United States, was the New York–Philadelphia line operated by the Magnetic Telegraph Co., a commercial undertaking formed by Morse and journalist Amos Kendall, which opened on 27 January 1846 with a charge of 25¢ for ten words. Despite being more expensive than the postmaster general's line (soon to be handed over to Alfred Vail and his partner Henry J. Rogers), the tally for the first four days was $100 and the treasurer confidently predicted that within a month it would be $50 a day. Success came because both New York and Philadelphia were major centers of trade (so also to a lesser extent was Baltimore, but Washington enjoyed little commerce other than providing services to politicians and civil servants). Bankers and merchants were the principal customers of the 11 lines that radiated out from New York City by 1852. In that year there were already 23,000 miles of line in the United States, with another 10,000 under construction. "No invention of modern times," declared the *Scientific American*, "has extended its influence so rapidly as that of the electric telegraph."

One unlooked-for influence was the ability of unmarried women to make a living for themselves outside factory or school. The telegraph companies were the first large corporations to employ women in white-collar jobs, a social revolution that began with the hiring of Sarah G. Bagley as superintendent of the Lowell, Mass., office of the Magnetic Telegraph Co. on 21 February 1846. Miss Bagley was formerly a factory operative for ten years and it was remarked at the time that the appointment of a woman of her background to a position of responsibility and command marked a new departure in the employment prospects of both her class and her gender.

By mid-1846 the Magnetic Telegraph Co. had united the four principal commercial centers of the Union—New York, Boston, Philadelphia, and Baltimore—and extended to Richmond in the South. In 1847 the lines reached St. Louis in the West and Charleston in the South, followed the next year by Chicago and Milwaukee. Florida was the only state east of the Mississippi to remain unconnected.

In the far west the telegraph took longer to be established, but in 1852 the first Pacific Coast network was inaugurated from San Francisco. For the rest of that decade there remained a vast tract of prairie and plains over which no telegraph wires hummed in the breeze, but on 24 April 1861 the first **transcontinental telegraph** spanning the United States was opened by Western Union with the completion of the line from St. Joseph, Mo., to Sacramento, Calif. Abraham Lincoln had told the company's president, Hiram Sibley, that he considered it "a wild scheme," warning that as soon as Sibley erected his telegraph poles, the Indians would cut them down. Engineering experts predicted that bridging the gap between St. Joseph (where the eastern telegraph lines terminated) and the Pacific would take ten years. In fact it was achieved by heroic endeavor in just three months and twenty days. One casualty of this success was the Pony Express, which shut down after a brief existence of only sixteen months.

The telegraph began its global reach the same year as California went "online," Great Britain being joined to the European network by submarine cable on 13 November 1851. The next major step was to unite Europe with the Americas with a **transatlantic telegraph cable**. Laid by USS *Niagra* and HMS *Agamemnon* via Valentia Island, Ireland, and Newfoundland, this was opened to paid traffic on 16 August 1858, when John Cash of Cash's Woven Nametapes cabled his New York representative from London. As Cash was not a man to waste words at $4 each, the first transatlantic telegram was succinct: GO TO CHICAGO STOP CASH. Only 4,354 words later the service abruptly terminated with the rupture of the cable. It did not resume until July 1866 following the laying of a new cable by the *Great Eastern* (the largest ship afloat, built by the same Isambard Kingdom Brunel at whose behest the inaugural telegraph message had been sent).

Within five years the last of the continents to be brought into this worldwide web, Australia, was connected to other national networks with the completion of the line across the Central Australian Desert from Darwin to Adelaide. The first global system of instant communication was in existence scarcely thirty years after the earliest messages had been transmitted over the few miles from Paddington to Slough.

It is claimed that the longest telegram ever sent was the draft text of the Nevada State Constitution, transmitted from Carson City, the then capital of the territory, to Washington, D.C., at a cost of $3,000 in 1864. The first part, before exhaustion compelled his replacement, was tapped out in Morse Code by Frank Bell. Eventually the telegraph would be superseded by the telephone (qv), invented by his cousin Alexander Graham Bell.

These twin systems of telecommunication were to coexist, however, for well over a century. The peak year for United States domestic telegraph traffic was 1945, with 236 million telegrams dispatched. During the 1950s the cost of a 3-minute telephone call became less than a ten-word telegram and the telegraph system began to go into decline. It survived in the United States, though, for some three decades after Britain, the pioneer of paid telegrams, had phased them out, and the service finally succumbed, well into the era of e-mails, when Western Union closed down its 155-year-old telegraph service on 27 January 2006. In the final year of operation just twenty thousand telegrams had been dispatched.

THE FIRST **ELEVATOR**

....

(passenger) was installed in King Louis XV's private apartments in the Petit Cour du Roi at the Palace of Versailles outside Paris in 1743. The king had provided a suite on the second floor for his mistress, Mme. de Châteauroux, and the elevator was designed to give him access to her from his own apartment on the floor below. It was on the outside of the building, though within the privacy of a courtyard, and was entered by the king via his balcony. The mechanism consisted of a carefully balanced arrangement of weights inside one of the chimneys, so that the "flying chair," as it was known, could be raised or lowered by hand with the minimum of effort.

The first passenger elevator for public use was installed at the Colosseum, a panorama building designed by Decimus Burton and erected in Regent's Park, London, for a Quaker land-surveyor and cartographer called Thomas Hornor. It was opened on 10 January 1829. Panoramas were a popular entertainment in which a vast concave scene, painted on a canvas extending beyond the angle of vision, was given an illusion of depth by the trick effects of light. Hornor's establishment opened with a "View of London from the Top of St. Paul's." Spectators had first to ascend into a replica of the dome of the cathedral, whence they were able to look down in wonder at the majestic city spread before them. That there was an alternative to an arduous climb is known from the *Visitor's Guide to London* published by N. Whittock in 1835. The reader is informed: "Those that wish to ascend to the panorama without the trouble of walking up stairs, may, by paying sixpence, ascend by the moving apartment, which is a small circular room, in which six or eight persons are comfortably seated."

A descriptive booklet of the Colosseum issued some years later gives a further account of the elevator, now enlarged, after the building had been "re-embellished" in 1848. "The Ascending Room, capable of containing 10 or 12 persons . . . is raised by secret machinery to the required elevation. This chamber is now entirely altered, being decorated in the Elizabethan style, and the light admitted through a stained glass ceiling." Although nothing positive is known about the nature of his "secret machinery," it seems probable that it was hydraulic. Harder to account for is why the successful invention of the powered elevator attracted so little attention, despite the fact that the Ascending Room at the Colosseum appears to have continued in service until the show closed down in 1864.

U.S.: The first passenger elevator was supplied by Elisha Graves Otis for the five-story building of the E. V. Haughwout department store on Broadway, in New York City, on 23 March 1857 at a cost of $300. Haughwout's was then the only building in the city that exceeded four stories. Otis was the first manufacturer of passenger elevators, having been previously engaged in the production of freight hoists at his Yonkers, N.Y., elevator plant. While he is often mistakenly credited with the invention of the passenger elevator, it is true that he was the first to devise a safety device to arrest the fall of an elevator if the cable failed. When he first demonstrated his freight hoist at New York's Crystal Palace exhibition hall in 1854 he would sometimes amaze spectators by cutting the cable as he rode up and down.

Hotel elevator: The first was a vertical screw-operated model installed at the six-story Fifth Avenue Hotel in New York City by O. Tuft of Boston on 23 August 1859.

Office block equipped with a passenger elevator: The first was the Equitable Life Assurance Society Building in New York City in 1868.

Group of high-speed passenger elevators: The first was installed at the Boreel Building in New York City by the Otis Elevator Co. in September 1879 and consisted of four units designed to be operated simultaneously. The introduction of high-speed passenger elevators had a profound effect on town planning in the United States and ultimately in most other industrialized nations, as it meant that cities could grow upward rather than simply outward. The building of skyscrapers, which would have been technically feasible many years earlier, was necessarily delayed until elevators could replace stairways.

Electric passenger elevator: The first was built in Germany by Siemens & Halske for service in a 66-foot-high observation tower at the Mannheim Industrial Exposition in 1880. Designed to operate at a speed of ½ meter per second, it carried eight thousand passengers without incident during the month of the exposition.

U.S.: William Baxter Jr. installed the first electric passenger elevator in Baltimore in 1887. It was powered by an electric motor supplied by the Elektron Manufacturing Co. of Brooklyn, N.Y. The first with push-button control were six Sprague-Pratts installed at the Postal Telegraph Building in New York City in 1892. Collective control, by which stops are made in sequence regardless of the order in which the buttons are pushed, made its debut with an installation at St. Luke's Hospital in Chicago by Otis in 1925. The following year the Haughton Elevator Co. of Toledo, Ohio, introduced automatic doors.

Electronically controlled passenger elevators (i.e., a group of elevators in which all traffic patterns are supervised automatically via an electronic data bank): The first was installed by the Otis Elevator Co. at the Universal Pictures Building in New York City in April 1948. A single push-button call would be responded to by whichever of four elevators was best placed to answer it, the attendants being required only to open and shut the doors. A completely automatic electronic system of elevators with self-opening and closing doors was introduced by Otis in 1950 at the Atlantic Refining Building in Dallas, Tex. Since that date similar installations in high-rise buildings throughout the western world have resulted in the demise of a once honorable occupation: elevator operator.

THE FIRST **ELEVATOR MUSIC**

originated not in an elevator but as *Musique d'ameublement* "furniture music"), which debuted at the Galerie Barbazanges in Paris on 8 March 1920, when an arrangement for a piano, three clarinets, and a trombone by Erik Satie was played during the intermission of a play by his friend Max Jacob. According to Rollo H. Myers in his book *Erik Satie* (1948), "the music, which consisted of fragments of popular refrains from *Mignon* and the *Danse Macabre*, and isolated phrases repeated over and over again, like the pattern of wallpaper, was meant strictly to be nothing more than a background and was not intended to attract attention in any way." There are a number of versions to account for Satie's idea, of which the most persuasive has him lunching with painter Fernand Léger in a restaurant whose orchestra played so loudly that the two men could not hear each other speak and were constrained to leave before finishing their meal. Léger later recalled Satie making this declaration once they were out in the street (translation from Alan M. Gillmer, *Erik Satie*, 1988):

> You know, there's a need to create furniture music, that is to say, music that would be a part of the surrounding noises and that would take them into account. I see it as melodious, as masking the clatter of knives and forks without drowning it completely, without imposing itself. It would fill up the awkward silences that occasionally descend

on guests. It would spare them the usual banalities. Moreover, it would neutralize the street noises that indiscreetly force themselves into the picture.

The inaugural performance of furniture music did not have quite the effect Satie had intended. Instead of ignoring it, as he intended, and chattering away *over* the indifferent cadences, the sophisticated Paris audience did as they were accustomed when an orchestra struck up and strained to catch every banal motif. Satie jumped up and down, imploring them to relax, but to no avail.

Satie may have pioneered elevator music conceptually, but it was not being *piped*. This notable advance took place in the United States, where Brig. Gen. George Owen Squier, who had invented multiplexing (the sending of simultaneous messages down one telephone line) in 1910, applied the same technique for the transmission of music into the home and into stores. He sold his patents to the North American Co. of Cleveland, Ohio, which set up Wired Radio Inc. in October 1922 to sell piped music to subscribers. Initial tests were conducted in the appropriately named Ampere (with no grave accent) in New Jersey and on Staten Island, but difficulties with interference meant that the company did not start piping its easy-listening mood music into restaurants and hotel dining rooms until technical advances made this commercially feasible in 1933. A year later the general whose dream it had been would be dead, but not before he had coined a word for the system that would become not only the company's trademarked brand but also, despite its best efforts, a generic for elevator music: Muzak.

THE FIRST **EMPLOYMENT AGENCY**

was the Bureau d'Adresse, opened in Paris by Théophraste Renaudot at the sign of the Grand-Coq in rue de la Calandre on 4 July 1631. A registration fee of 3 sous was charged to employers seeking staff, and likewise to prospective employees seeking engagement, unless they were too poor to pay, in which case the service was free. Renaudot's intention was principally philanthropic and he paid particular attention to the needs of clients up from the country for the first time. In 1639 the Paris police issued an ordinance to the effect that all unemployed strangers arriving in the capital must register with the Bureau d'Adresse within 24 hours on pain of being sent to the galleys for vagabondage. The employment section of the bureau dealt chiefly in vacancies for domestic servants and shop assistants; in addition there were a number of other departments dealing in houses for sale and rent, furniture and effects, traveling arrangements, etc.

A similar enterprise was conducted in London by the apothecary John Houghton (SEE ALSO **weather forecasts**) in the 1690s and his lists of vacancies, which happily survive, provide the only detailed evidence of the kind of jobs offered through a reputable employment agency during the seventeenth century. "I want a Negro man that is a good house carpenter and a good shoemaker," runs one entry, while another says, "I want a pretty boy to wait on a gentleman who will take care of him." Others are for "a good usher's place in a grammar school," "a young man that can read and write, mow and roll a lawn garden, use a gun at a deer, and understand country sports," and for "several curious women that would wait on ladies to be housekeepers." The adjective "curious" in this context meant solicitous.

U.S.: The earliest known example of an employment agency is recorded by the French refugee Moreau de Saint-Méry, who wrote of his sojourn in New York in 1794:

> The difficulty of getting domestics is very great, and they are lazy, demanding, and capricious. Somebody had the clever idea of setting up an office in Maiden Lane where the name of those looking for a place and of those wishing servants could be registered; but this enterprise didn't result in placing more than half a dozen servants a year. The fee for making an application is three sixteenths of a dollar.

An abundant supply of slaves and of indentured servants from Europe probably militated against the success of the venture, and in general employment agencies did not become a fixture of American life until the second half of the nineteenth century.

Employment agency specializing in temporary help: The first was Russell Kelly Office Service (now Kelly Services), founded in Detroit by Russell Kelly in 1946. His original intention had been to provide a service by which office paperwork could be contracted out to his firm, but in response to an urgent call from an accountant needing a short-term typist he sent one of his own female employees over and this focused his attention on the demand for "temps." His "Kelly Girls," as they became known in this pre-PC age, were drawn from his own staff until demand outstripped supply, at which time he started placing women wanting part-time work, mainly mothers with secretarial skills whose children were now in school. The company changed its name to Kelly Girl Service Inc. in 1959; the "Girl" was dropped in the 1960s not in deference to the rising tide of feminism but because Kelly had diversified to provide other talents in the marketing and technical fields.

THE FIRST ENCYCLOPEDIA

titled as such was Paul Scalich's *Encyclopaedia, seu Orbis disciplinarium*, published in Basel in 1559. The literal meaning of the term is "learning within the circle." The first encyclopedia with entries arranged in alphabetical order was Antoine Furetière's *Dictionnaire Universel*, published in Paris in 1690.

Encyclopedia in English: The first was John Harris's *Lexicon Technicum: or, An Universal English Dictionary of Arts and Sciences*, published in London in 1704.

Encyclopedia containing entries from outside contributors: The first, compiled under the direction of specialist editors, was Johann Zelder's monumental 64-volume *Universal-Lexicon*, published in Leipzig from 1731 to 1750. Zelder was a bookseller by trade, without patronage or additional source of income. His vast work was only completed when a lottery was held in Leipzig to provide him with funds. Even then he remained in such straitened circumstances that he was unable to afford a complete set of his own encyclopedia, and was obliged to supervise the later volumes without reference to vols XIII and XIV.

Encyclopaedia Britannica: The first edition was produced by Andrew Bell, Colin Macfarquhar, and William Smellie and published in sixpenny parts at Edinburgh from December 1768 to 1771. One notable entry read: "WOMAN. The female of man. See HOMO." After the celebrated 11th edition of 1911 (now available online for free; SEE BELOW), *Britannica* was sold to Sears, Roebuck and Co. of Chicago, which owned it until 1943. All subsequent editions have been produced in the United States.

U.S.: The first encyclopedia published in America was a reprint of the *Encyclopaedia Britannica* by Thomas Dobson, who carried on his business at the Stone House on Second Street, Philadelphia. The first half volume was issued in 1790 in a run of 1,000 copies, of which 246 had been pre-subscribed. By the time the eighth volume had been put on sale, all copies of the first had been sold and a second impression was put in hand. The 21st and last volume was completed in 1803. As no international copyright then existed, Dobson had no need to remunerate the originators of the work.

The first encyclopedia containing original material was *The Encyclopaedia Americana*, compiled by German-born Francis Lieber and published in 13 volumes by Carey, Lea & Carey of Philadelphia from 1829 to 1833. Although based on the 7th edition of Germany's Brockhaus encyclopaedia, it contained additional material of interest in the United States, including "a copious collection of original articles in American biography."

Online encyclopedia: The first was the 11th edition of the *Encyclopaedia Britannica* (1911), published in ASCII text by Project Gutenberg starting in January 1995 but halted after the first volume following disagreements on methodology. It has since been completed as the *Gutenberg Encyclopedia*. The first online encyclopedia to accept contributions from any volunteer participant, a wholly new concept in the making of encyclopedias, was *Wikipedia*, created by Jimmy Wales and others and based in San Diego, Calif., which went online on 15 January 2001.

THE FIRST ENVELOPES

known, date from 1615 and are preserved at Geneva, Switzerland. In 1675 a French book of etiquette recommended their use as "a mark of respect to one's superiors." The earliest example in Britain, preserved at the Public Record Office, is a diminutive 4½" x 3" enclosure of a letter addressed to the secretary of state, Sir William Turnbull, by Sir James Ogilvie on 16 May 1696. Any pre-nineteenth-century envelope is exceptional, as the usual practice was to fold a letter in three and seal it with a wafer. Prior to the introduction of uniform postage, letters were charged by the number of sheets and an envelope would count as an additional sheet.

These early examples were almost certainly homemade. The first envelopes for sale were produced by booksellers S. K. Brewer in the fashionable English seaside resort of Brighton in 1830. These proved sufficiently popular with the modish Brighton visitors, who apparently did not object to paying double postage, for Brewer to place an order with the London firm of Dobbs and Co. when he was no longer able to meet the demand by his own efforts. Either these or a competitive range were on sale in London by 1837, stationer John Dickinson's daughter Fanny noting in her diary that they could be bought at 209 Regent Street for 2s 6d (62½¢) per 100. They were sold flat and ungummed, the four corners meeting under a seal. A year previously (6 April 1836) Fanny recorded that she had been busy all day making her own envelopes to send out invitations to a party.

U.S.: The first envelopes for sale were manufactured by Edward Maxwell of Louisville, Ken., in 1835. Apparently these did not win wider renown, because when envelopes were imported from France in 1842 they were hailed as "the latest European novelty."

Prepaid envelopes: The first were issued by the New South Wales Post Office in Sydney, Australia, on 1 November 1838. The embossed stamp was an interesting forerunner of adhesive postage stamps, and was the first of the modern methods of indicating prepayment. These envelope-sheets were sold for 1 shilling 3d (31¢) a dozen and were for use within the Sydney district-post. The standard rate was 2d (4.2¢).

U.S.: Buff envelopes with imprinted 3¢ stamps bearing a white silhouette portrait of George Washington against a red background were issued in 1853.

Gummed envelopes were introduced in Britain in 1844, and according to the testimony of a memoir written some forty years later, they provoked a number of affairs of honor precipitated by recipients who asserted that a man who sends his spittle through the post to another must expect to be called upon to give satisfaction in the traditional manner.

Window envelope: The first was patented by Americus F. Callahan of Chicago on 10 June 1902 and issued by the U.S. Envelope Co. of Springfield, Mass., the following month.

Airmail envelope: Issued by the Belgian post office in 1913, this was prestamped and inscribed POSTE AERIENNE. Little is known of its provenance but it may have been used with Belgium's inaugural experimental airmail flown in association with an exhibition at Ghent in May of that year.

THE FIRST **ERASER**

is recorded by Dr. Joseph Priestley, the discoverer of oxygen, in his *Familiar Introduction to the Theory and Practice of Perspective* (London, 1770). In an addendum he wrote:

> Since this work was printed off, I have seen a substance excellently adapted to the purpose of wiping from a paper the marks of a black-lead pencil. It must, therefore, be a singular use to those who practice drawing. It is sold by Mr. Nairne, Mathematical Instrument Maker, opposite the Royal Exchange. He sells a cubical piece of about half an inch for three shillings, and he says it will last for several years.

As well it might, as 3s was more than a day's wage for most workers. Edward Nairne does not appear to have been in any way exceptional in his prices, for five years later stationers were reported to be charging a guinea (more than a week's wage) for one ounce of the rare substance. Although the French term *caoutchouc* persisted in Britain until the 1850s, an encyclopedia of 1778 notes that the device "is popularly called rubber or lead eater." The term *rubber* became the most common usage in England, as it is today, causing ribaldry in the United States when expats ask a colleague for the loan of one.

U.S.: The earliest record of erasers is an advertisement by the New York stationer Peter Goelet in 1786.

THE FIRST **ESCALATOR**

was the Reno Inclined Elevator, patented by Jesse W. Reno of New York on 15 March 1892 and originally installed at the Old Iron Pier on Coney Island in September 1895. The Reno escalator consisted of an inclined endless-belt conveyor made up of wooden slats each 4 inches wide and 2 feet long. The grooved slats had rubber-covered cleats running in a forward direction to give the necessary grip and passed under comb-plates at either end of the belt, as in a modern escalator. An electric motor drove the conveyor and its plush-covered rubber handrails at a speed of about 1½ mph.

The first practical moving staircase (i.e., with steps) was patented in the United States by Charles A. Wheeler on 2 August 1892. This did not have a comb-plate landing device, and passengers had to get on and off via a side entrance. Although Wheeler's escalator was never actually built, his patent was purchased in 1898 by Charles D. Seeberger, who incorporated its flat-step feature into an improved design of his own. Seeberger's prototype model was built by the Otis Elevator Co., with whom he made a manufacturing agreement, and brought into operation at their Yonkers, N.Y., factory on 9 June 1899. The first Seeberger escalator in public use was installed at the Paris Exhibition in 1900. It was brought back to America the following year and re-erected at Gimbel's department store on 8th Street in Philadelphia, where it continued to operate until 1939.

The first step-type escalator with a comb-plate landing device was the Otis "L." Embodying the salient features of both the Reno and Seeberger models, it was introduced commercially in 1921. Since then there has been no radical change in escalator design.

Early users of escalators sometimes needed restoration or reassurance. When a Reno Inclined Elevator was installed at London's foremost department store, Harrods, in November 1898, an attendant was positioned at the top ready to dispense brandy or smelling salts free of charge to those ladies and gentlemen who were overcome by the experience of having ridden up a floor. On the day in October 1911 that London's first subway elevators, two 40-foot Seebergers, opened at Earls Court Underground station, the clerk of works, whose name was "Bumper" Harris and who had only one leg, rode up and down all day to instill confidence into the fainthearted.

THE FIRST **EUTHANASIA, VOLUNTARY**

to be practiced with the cognizance of the legal authorities followed an act passed by the Netherlands parliament on 30 November 1993 granting immunity from prosecution to physicians who reported mercy killing in cases of unbearable pain where the patient lucidly and repeatedly requested termination of life. This stopped short of legalizing the practice and the first jurisdiction where a law fully empowering doctors to end life took effect was the Northern Territory of Australia in July 1996. A terminally ill cancer patient, Bob Dent, became the first to elect for a physician-assisted, legally sanctioned suicide on 22 September of that year, dying by lethal injection administered by computer. The patient himself activated the computer by answering a series of questions, the final one being whether he chose to die. Three more patients ended their lives in this way before the Australian federal government outlawed the practice by quashing the Northern Territory's Rights of the Terminally Ill Act in March 1998. All the assisted suicides had been facilitated by Dr. Philip Nitschke, who later developed a machine for the self-administering of lethal gas and a drink that terminated life painlessly.

U.S.: Although Oregon's Death with Dignity Act was passed in 1994, two years earlier than the Northern Territory enactment, it was inoperative until the Ninth Circuit Court of Appeals lifted the legal injunction against it on 27 October 1997. An attempt by state legislators to have the law repealed was then defeated in a referendum a week later by 60 percent to 40 percent. The act permitted adult Oregon residents who were terminally ill to take an overdose of drugs provided that two doctors confirmed the diagnosis and that the patient was of sound mind. During 1998, the first full year that the act was in effect, fifteen patients died from legally prescribed lethal medications. The first was a woman in her mid-eighties with terminal breast cancer who swallowed a fatal dose of sleeping pills under the supervision of her doctor. The cumulative total had reached some two hundred by January 2006, when the U.S. Supreme Court ruled 6–3 in Gonzales v. Oregon that overturning Oregon's physician-assisted suicide law would contravene the right of states to regulate the actions of doctors. The only other state to have adopted physician-assisted euthanasia is Washington in November 2008.

The Netherlands legalized physician-assisted suicide for the terminally ill in April 2001, followed by Belgium in September 2002. Two countries, Switzerland and Colombia, condone the practice of physician-assisted suicide without having decriminalized it. In Australia, following the repeal of the Northern Territory's enactment, a number of suicide clinics are believed to have operated in Victoria and New South Wales without suppression.

THE FIRST **EXCAVATOR**

was a steam shovel of extraordinarily modern appearance built at Canton, Mass., in 1835–36 to the design of Williams Otis of Philadelphia. He and Elisha Otis, inventor of the safety elevator (SEE **elevator**), were both descended from a John Otis who emigrated to Hingham, Mass., in 1631. The Canton prototype was later used by Charles French on the construction of the Norwich & Worcester Railroad, though in the meantime manufacture of the initial batch of seven production excavators had started in 1837 at locomotive engineers Garrett & Eastwick of Twelfth Street, Philadelphia. Two of these remained in the United States, while five were exported to Russia and Great Britain—an astonishing tribute to American engineering at a time when Britain was hailed as the workshop of the world and the United States was only just emerging from its agricultural hegemony. Of the remaining two, the first powered excavator actually used in construction was the one employed at Springfield, Mass., in 1838 by Carmichael, Fairbanks & Otis, who were building a link of the Western Railroad to Worcester (it may have been used earlier on the Baltimore & Ohio Railroad, but documentary evidence is inconclusive). It was at Springfield that a local newspaper referred to the Otis shovel as "a specimen of what the Irishmen call 'digging by stame.' "

These $7,500 machines were powered by a 15-hp single-cylinder, high-pressure engine that was capable of excavating 1,500 cubic yards of earth in a 12-hour day. This compared so favorably with the 12½ cubic yards of *loosened* earth a laborer could shift in a day that Otis's American Steam Excavator rapidly transformed the construction industry, arriving just in time for the building of a network of railroads that rapidly criss-crossed the Eastern Seaboard, then pushed west beyond the Allegheny Mountains. An excavator, it was estimated, did the work of 120 men, with comparative costs in its favor of 3¢ per cubic yard against 8¢ per cubic yard for manual operations. Some believed the benefits to be moral as well as physical. In 1841 the directors of the American Institute, after visiting the site of steam-shovel excavations at what was to become City Park (now Commodore Barry Park) in Brooklyn, declared: "The masses of unruly men collected on our public works will be dispersed by its use, and compelled to till the land, thereby making them good and quiet citizens." They were wrong. Excavators enabled ever larger construction projects to be undertaken, thereby freeing thousands of laborers from the servitude of agriculture.

Excavator mounted on crawlers: The first was built in prototype form by Leach Bros. of Maumee, Ohio, in 1905 (only a year after Holt had pioneered the crawler tractor (qv)) and subsequently was manufactured to their design by the Bucyrus Foundry at Bucyrus, Ohio. This development led to the demise of railroad-mounted shovels. No longer would the operator who filled his train quickest from a 70C excavator receive a prize of a fine $5 panama hat.

Gasoline-engined excavator: The first was a Chicago-built Page-Monighan dragline powered by a 50-hp Otto engine, supplied to the Mulgrew-Boyce Co. of Dubuque, Iowa, in 1910. Just as the Otis steam shovel had helped build the railroads, it was these highly mobile crawler and gas-engined excavators that built a new road network for the age of the automobile.

~~~~~~~~~~~~~~~~~~~~~ **F** ~~~~~~~~~~~~~~~~~~~~~

THE FIRST **FALSE EYELASHES**

were invented by the great silent-film director D. W. Griffith during the production of his flawed 1916 masterpiece *Intolerance*. The role of Attarea, the Princess Beloved in the Babylonian sequence, was played by twenty-two-year-old blonde newcomer Seena Owen, considered by many Hollywood cameramen of the silent era to have been one of the most striking natural beauties to grace the silver screen. Nevertheless, for the demanding Griffith her natural beauty was not quite sufficient. He wanted her eyelashes to brush her cheeks each time she blinked. Since no normal eyelashes perform to this requirement, he engaged a wigmaker to weave very fine human hair through a strip of gauze. The false eyelashes were then chopped into short lengths and gummed to Miss Owen's eyelids. The scenes in which she wore them were filmed on the massive 90-foot-high-walls-of-Babylon set built opposite Fine Arts Studios, where the interiors were shot, at the intersection of Hollywood and Sunset boulevards. There she met handsome leading man George Walsh. Griffith, an incorrigible romantic from the South, played matchmaker. Whether her appeal to Walsh was enhanced by the compelling effect of the false eyelashes we do not know, but . . . reader, she married him.

For the next thirty years false eyelashes were solely the privilege of those who lived under the klieg lights of Hollywood. It was, however, filmdom that brought them to the shopping mall. Makeup artists David and Eric Aylott were working for British National at Elstree Studios in England in 1946 when they created some false eyelashes for French actress Yvonne Arnaud to wear in *Woman to Woman*. She was so delighted with them that she ordered a dozen pairs for her personal use. Encouraged by this testimony to their inventiveness, the brothers rented a derelict hut in a disused gravel pit at Welwyn Garden City and began commercial production in 1947 with a workforce of four. Under the brand name Eyelure, the new product was launched at the not inconsiderable price of 12s 6d ($2.50). Initially most of the clients were in show business, but soon another, lucrative market emerged: Mayfair hookers. Housewives started to wear them with the appointment of distributors in Belgium, Holland, and Denmark. False eyelashes returned to their country of birth a year or two later when New York cosmetician S. H. Swick acquired the agency for Eyelure in the United States.

THE FIRST **FAN CLUB**

was the Keen Order of Wallerites, founded in London by fans of the popular actor-manager Lewis Waller. It was in existence by 1902 and is thought to have been established a year, or possibly two years, earlier. Members wore a badge showing on one side Waller in powdered wig as Monsieur Beaucaire and, on the other, his favorite flower—somewhat inappropriate for so masculine an actor—a pansy. The club colors were blue and mauve, Waller's racing colors. The behavior of adherents toward Waller himself was strictly controlled by the regulations of the society, which forbade anyone but the secretary to address him personally, but members were expected to gather in force to support their hero on every first night. A rival fan club, the True-to-Trees, was founded to pay honor to Sir Herbert Beerbohm Tree, first actor to star in a Shakespearean film (*King John* 1899).

Members of the Keen Order did not refer to themselves as "fans," since the term was at that time unknown in England. In the United States, however, it had been used as early as 1889, the first recorded appearance in print being a reference to "Kansas City baseball fans" in the 26 March issue of the *Kansas Times and Star*. America also saw the birth of the

movie star fan club, of which the earliest known was the Peggy Snow Club, founded by Miss Kathryn Temple of Northboro, Mass., in the summer of 1914. Peggy aka Marguerite Snow (1889–1958) was the leading lady of the Thanhouser Studios in New Rochelle, N.Y., where she had made her debut in *Baseball and Bloomers* in 1910. She had come second to Florence E. Turner but ahead of Mary Pickford in America's first popularity poll in December 1911 and was thus one of the first movie stars to become a household name. The *Moving Picture World* reported that the club consisted of young ladies of Miss Temple's acquaintance who admired Peggy Snow's work on the screen and "adopt, as far as possible, clothing patterned after the best dressed women in the Movies." Miss Snow promised to send the club a letter of greeting once a month and presented her Northboro fans with a large portrait for display at their monthly meetings.

THE FIRST **FASHION PHOTOGRAPHS**

appeared in the Parisian fashion journal *La Mode Pratique* in December 1891. The photographs were tinted by hand and reproduced by a crude two-color process. There was also a London edition of the magazine, titled *Fashions of Today*. Neither journal can be considered a leader in its field and there was little further development until the founding of *Les Modes* in 1901. Not only did the photography in this magazine show a marked improvement over earlier efforts, but the attitudes of the models, opined fashion historian Doris Langley Moore in her *Fashions Through Fashion Plates*, "show a high degree of professionalism."

The first fashion photographs taken by a photographer of international renown were a series of thirteen studies of Paul Poiret creations by the Luxembourg-born Edward Steichen, who had been urged by Lucien Vogel to make fashion a fine art through photography. These were reproduced in the April 1911 issue of *Art et Décoration*, published in Paris. They mark the point at which fashion photography began to develop into an art in its own right and ceased to be a cheap substitute for engravings.

First to specialize as a full-time fashion photographer was Baron Adolphe De Meyer, who joined *Vogue* magazine in New York at a salary of $100 a week in 1913. His first model was the bohemian society matron Gertrude Vanderbilt Whitney, who was attracted by the daring of exposing herself to public gaze in this way, rather than to monetary reward. Edward Steichen, by now in America, succeeded Meyer at *Vogue* when the latter was poached by William Randolph Hearst (the model for Orson Welles's Citizen Kane) in 1918 for *Vogue*'s chief rival, *Harper's Bazar [sic]*. Steichen went on to take *Vogue*'s first color fashion photograph, of a bathing beauty posed against an azure sky, which was also the fashion bible's first photographic cover (1 July 1932). In that same year De Meyer's career took a sharp decline when he was fired from *Harper's Bazaar* (by then spelled with a double *a*), his rather stiff style of photography now considered passé. *Vogue*'s proprietor Condé Nast said to Steichen, "Every woman De Meyer photographs looks like a model. You make every model look like a woman." The unstable, homosexual De Meyer became increasingly dependent on opium and cocaine and died a broken man in Los Angeles in 1949. Steichen by contrast died aged ninety-three laden with honors, having eventually abandoned fashion to become director of photography at the Museum of Modern Art in New York. In February 2006 one of his early works "The Pond—Moonlight" of 1904, set a new auction record for an American photograph of $2.9 million.

Woman fashion photographer: The first of distinction was New York–based Louise Dahl-Wolf, whose work first appeared in a top fashion magazine with the November 1933 issue of *Vanity Fair*. She joined *Harper's Bazaar* in 1937, the sole woman to operate at the summit of fashion photography and one of the first practitioners to travel to exotic locales for her shoots. No matter how primitive or picturesque her choice of location, though, her ultra-sophisticated and perfectly groomed models always looked as if they had stepped out of a bandbox.

Color fashion photographs: The first were eleven shots of Paris haute couture in the Finlay Direct Color process that appeared in the October 1930 issue of *Ladies' Home Journal*. They depicted offerings from the salons of Jane Régny, Lucien Lelong, Lucile Paray, Callot Soeurs, Worth, Jean Patou, and Chanel, some taken at the salons, others at the nightclub Les

Enfants Terribles and outdoors at the Pavillon Dauphine, in the garden of Laurent's Restaurant, on the Champs-Élysées, and in the Bois de Boulogne. No photographers are credited.

SEE ALSO **photographic model**.

THE FIRST **FASHION SHOW**

was mounted in 1899 by the couturier Lucile (Mrs. James Wallace), sister of the popular novelist Elinor Glyn, at the Maison Lucile, 17 Hanover Square, London. As there were no fashion models in London at that time, Lucile had to recruit and train them from scratch. And since no respectable girl would have deigned to make a spectacle of herself in this way, she sought what she described as "glorious, goddess-like girls" in the mean streets of Bermondsey and Balham. The six working-class girls selected to be adorned in the raiment of the aristocracy were given lessons in hairdressing, style, and deportment; elocution was considered unnecessary as these latter-day Galateas were not expected to speak to their betters. They were also deprived of their own names, Florrie and Ada and Madge becoming the exotics Dolores, Hebe, and Gamela.

Lucile recalled that she sent out the invitations "on dainty little cards, keeping the illusion that I was inviting my friends to some afternoon party rather than to a place of business." The salon in which the show was held was an elegant Adam room with an Angelica Kauffmann ceiling. The models appeared first on a stage, then walked down a short flight of steps and paraded the length of the room and back. Among those in the distinguished audience were Princess Alice of Hesse, actresses Ellen Terry and Lily Langtry, and the energetic Margot Asquith, wife of a future prime minister, referred to by Lucile as "rather noisy."

The first fashion show and the first fashion models were not the only innovations Lucile made on this occasion. She also introduced the idea of giving the creations special names, a practice that survives among leading couturiers today. The show collection was called "Gowns of Emotion" and individual dresses were labeled with rather gushing names that might have been the title of her sister's novels: "Give Me Your Heart," "When Passion's Thrall is O'er" (layers of transparent gray chiffon), and "Do You Love Me?" Lucile's "emotional" frocks were a huge success and the show established her as the most sought-after dressmaker in London. The girls from Balham and Bermondsey also came out of it well. Heralded with newspaper headlines such as "Lucile's mysterious beauties," the silent ones found themselves famous overnight and courted by young sprigs of the aristocracy normally to be found hanging around stage doors. They were founder members of a new and glamorous profession, one destined, as Lucile herself remarked, "to survive as long as there are dressmakers whose purpose it is to lure women into buying more dresses than they can afford."

U.S.: The first show was organized by Edna Woolman Chase, editor of American *Vogue*, and was held in the ballroom of the Ritz-Carlton Hotel in New York City on 4 November 1914 and on two successive afternoons and evenings thereafter. The ostensible object was to showcase American fashion, imports of Parisian couture having been suspended due to the war, though Mrs. Chase admitted in her memoirs to an ulterior motive: with no new designs from Paris, she had nothing with which to fill the pages of *Vogue*. Among the fashion houses represented were Bendel, Mollie O'Hara, Bergdorf-Goodman, Gunther, Tappé, Maison Jacqueline, and Kurzman. The models appeared on a stage, turned left, turned right, descended a short flight of steps, and paraded down the center aisle. The only essential difference between this first New York fashion show and those of today was that the catwalk had yet to be invented.

SEE ALSO **photographic model**.

THE FIRST **FILM**

process was developed by the French-born naturalized American inventor Louis Aimé Augustin Le Prince, who began experimenting with moving photographic images at the Institute for the Deaf in Washington Heights, New York, where his wife was employed as a teacher of art. His daughter, Miss M. Le Prince, claimed to have seen the dim outlines of moving figures projected on a whitewashed wall at the Institute in 1885. In November 1886 Le Prince applied for an American patent for "The successive production by means of a photographic camera of a number of images of the same object or objects in motion and reproducing the same in the order of taking by means of a 'projector'. . . with one or more intermittently operated film drums."

Although the U.S. patent in respect of an "Apparatus for producing Animated Pictures" was granted on 10 January 1888, the part of the specification referring to cameras and projectors with a single lens was disallowed on the questionable grounds that it infringed Dumont's British patent of 1861. In fact this related only to an arrangement of glass plates to form the facets of a prismatic drum, and had nothing to do with the reproduction of moving images on a screen. As it stood, Le Prince's U.S. patent covered only a more complex sixteen-lens device. Consequently, many film historians have discounted his claim to have developed a practical single-lens film camera despite the accumulation of evidence in his favor. The following is a summary of the points made by E. Kilburn Scott in an article published in the May 1931 issue of the *Photographic Journal*:

1. Miss M. Le Prince stated that she had clear recollection of her father working with a single-lens camera-projector at the Institute for the Deaf between 1885 and 1887, when the family moved to Leeds, England. The individual frames of the films taken during this period were about 1½ inches square.

2. Le Prince's British patent, issued on 16 November 1888, covered both a single-lens camera and a single-lens projector.

3. In an affidavit sworn on 21 April 1931, Frederick Mason, a woodworker of Leeds, declared that he had assisted in the construction of a single-lens camera in the summer of 1888, which he described thus:

The camera has two lenses, one being for taking the photograph and the other for the view finder. The gate mechanism behind the lens is constructed to hold the film firmly in position during exposure, and then to momentarily release it while being drawn upward without it being scratched. The intermittent movement consists of a toothed cam which engages with a projection on the side of the top reel, the latter pulling the film through the gate and also winding it up. The handle projecting from the side of the camera operates the mechanism through gear wheels. A brass shutter revolves in front of the lens which has in it an adjustable diaphragm. Turning the handle at the proper rate enables pictures to be taken at the desired speed.

4. Two fragments of film taken with this camera survive, and afford the earliest evidence that Le Prince had succeeded in making motion pictures. The first was taken in the garden of Le Prince's father-in-law, Mr. Joseph Whiteley, at Roundhay, Leeds, and was labeled at a later date by the inventor's son Adolphe: "Portion of a series taken early in October, 1888, by the second one-lens camera. Le Prince's mother-in-law in this picture died October 24, 1888. Le Prince's eldest son is also in the picture, as is his father-in-law. Taken from 10 to 12 a second. There was no trial of speed contemplated here."

The second fragment, taken from the window of Hicks Bros., ironmongers, at the southeast corner of Leeds Bridge, is labeled: "Portion of a series taken by Le Prince with his second one-lens camera in October, 1888. A view of the moving traffic on Leeds Bridge, England, taken at 20 pictures a second in poor light. His eldest son was with him when he took the picture."

5. Commenting on the above film, Le Prince's mechanic James W. Longley indicated that a projector had already been completed at this time:

Leeds Bridge—where the tram horses were seen moving over it and all the other traffic as if you was on the bridge yourself. I could even see the smoke coming out of a man's pipe, who was lounging on the bridge. Mr. Augustin Le Prince was ready for exhibiting the above mentioned machine in public. We had got the machine perfect for delivering the pictures on the screen.

According to the testimony of Adolphe Le Prince two projectors were built, one with three lenses in 1888–89 and a single-lens apparatus in 1889. The former is known from a diagram of Longley's to have incorporated the use of a Maltese cross to secure intermittent picture shift.

The film used by Le Prince for the Roundhay and Leeds Bridge sequences was sensitized paper in rolls 2 1/8 inches wide. In the autumn of 1889 he began using Eastman celluloid roll film, which had just been introduced into Britain. This provided a far more suitable support material and it seems likely that Le Prince was ready to start the commercial development of his motion-picture film process by the beginning of 1890. A new projector was built so that a demonstration could be given before M. Mobisson, the secretary of the Paris Opéra. On 16 September 1890 Le Prince boarded a train at Dijon bound for Paris with his apparatus and films. He never arrived. No trace of his body or his equipment was ever found and after exhaustive inquiries the police were able to offer no rational explanation of his disappearance. The mystery has never been solved.

The first motion-picture film process to be developed commercially is generally attributed to Thomas Alva Edison, who filed a caveat with the U.S. Patent Office on 17 October 1888 for an optical phonograph. In this he proposed an apparatus for viewing in rapid succession a series of micro-photographs wound around a glass cylinder. The idea was not a practical one. In January 1889 Edison assigned William Kennedy Laurie Dickson, an assistant at his laboratories in West Orange, N.J., to work on the development of what was to become the Kinetoscope, a film-viewing machine designed for use in amusement arcades. Dickson, the French-born son of English parents, had early training as a photographer and was better suited to this kind of research than his mentor, who knew little of optics. He abandoned the use of rectangular sheets of celluloid for camera work, and tried the Eastman celluloid roll film. On finding this unsuitable, he substituted 50-foot lengths of film produced by the firm of Merwin Hulbert. These long rolls were first purchased on 18 March 1891, which is the earliest date at which it seems likely that Dickson could have made successful films for viewing in the peep-show Kinetoscope apparatus. There is an oft-quoted claim that a film was projected on a screen in synchronization with a phonograph record for Edison's benefit on his return from visiting the Paris Exhibition in October 1889. This, however, seems highly improbable in view of the lack of any references to the supposed projector in the very complete Edison archives for this period.

Public display of films: The first showing took place at the Edison Laboratories in West Orange on 22 May 1891, when 147 representatives of the National Federation of Women's Clubs, having lunched with Mrs. Edison at Glenmont, were shown her husband's workshops and allowed to view the new Kinetoscope. The *Sun* newspaper reported:

> The surprised and pleased clubwomen saw a small pine box standing on the floor. There were some wheels and belts near the box, and a workman who had them in charge. In the top of the box was a hole perhaps an inch in diameter. As they looked through the hole they saw the picture of a man. It was a most marvelous picture. It bowed and smiled and waved its hands and took off its hat with the most perfect naturalness and grace. Every motion was perfect...

The film used for this demonstration appears to have been taken with a horizontal-feed camera without sprockets. This would have been an imperfect apparatus at best, and it is not until October 1892 that there is evidence that Dickson had built an effective vertical-feed camera using perforated film. In that month the *Phonogram* published an illustration showing sequences from four films evidently taken with such a device. These included pictures of Dickson himself, together with his helper, William Heise, and also shots of fencers engaged in swordplay, and wrestlers. By this date, then, it can be positively asserted that Dickson had overcome all the obstacles that had stood in the way of making films suitable for commercial exhibition. He was to receive little thanks for his work. After Dickson had left West Orange in 1895, following a dispute with his employer, Edison steadfastly refused to concede that anyone but he himself was responsible for bringing the invention to fruition. Most writers were content to accept Edison's own version of events until the appearance in 1961 of a painstaking work of scholarship titled *The Edison Motion Picture Myth*. The author, Gordon Hendricks, demonstrated by reference to thitherto unpublished papers in the Edison archives that all the experimental work on the Kinetoscope had been conducted by Dickson, or under his direction, and that Edison himself can be credited with little more than instigating the research program and providing facilities for carrying it out.

Commercial presentation of films: The first showing took place at Holland Bros. Kinetoscope Parlor, 1155 Broadway, New York City, which opened for business on 14 April 1894. The Edison Kinetoscopes were arranged in two rows of five, and for 25¢ viewers were allowed to watch five films; to see all the films they had to pay double entrance money. The sum of $120 was taken the first day, which suggests that this first "cinema audience" totaled nearly 500. The films, made in the Edison "Black Maria" in West Orange (SEE **film studio**), were entitled: *Sandow, Bertholdi (Mouth Support), Horse Shoeing, Bertholdi (Table Contortion), Barber Shop, Blacksmiths, Cock Fight, Highland Dance, Wrestling*, and *Trapeze*.

The Edison Co. had commenced the making of films for commercial exhibition the previous month, and was thus the first film production company in the world. The earliest subject that can be positively dated is the *Sandow* film which, according to Gordon Hendricks, was made on 7 March 1894. Eugen Sandow was a professional strongman and may have been the first stage performer to appear before the film camera. Other celebrities who made films for Edison during 1894 were Annie Oakley, later to be immortalized by the musical based on her life, *Annie Get Your Gun*, and the legendary Buffalo Bill.

The first catalog of Edison films, issued by distributors Raff & Gammon at the end of 1894, listed fifty-two titles, at prices ranging from $10 for a *Marvelous Lady Contortionist* to $100 for a five-round prizefight shown in full.

Film presented publicly on a screen: The first was a short film titled *La Sortie des ouvriers de l'usine Lumière*, which was shown before the members of the Société d'Encouragement à l'Industrie Nationale by Auguste and Louis Lumière at 44 rue de Rennes in Paris on 22 March 1895. The film, believed to have been taken by the Lumières in August or September 1894, showed workers leaving the Lumière factory at Lyons for their dinner hour. The Lumières began exhibiting films commercially in Paris on 28 December 1895 and this is usually claimed to have been the first such venture in the world. The Lumières undoubtedly attracted huge attention with their very accomplished show (SEE **cinema theater**), but it was not the first before a paying audience.

The first **commercial presentation of a film on a screen** took place in a converted store at 153 Broadway, New York City, on 20 May 1895, when a 4-minute film of a boxing match, specially staged between Australian prizefighter "Young Griffo" and "Battling Charles Barnett," was shown before a paying audience by Major Woodville Latham, founder of the Lambda Co., the first film company in the world to be established as such. The projector, called the Eidoloscope, had been designed for the Lambda Co. by former Edison employee Eugène Lauste (SEE **films, sound**). The show was apparently still running three months later, *The Photographic Times* for September reporting that a film of a horserace was shown as well as the boxing one. At about the same time, beginning 25 August 1895, the Eidoloscope played for a week at the Olympic variety theater in Chicago, billed as "Living Motion Pictures; Life Size of Real Events." This was followed by a week's engagement at Kohl & Middleton's Clark Street Dime Museum, which was sufficiently successful to be held over for a second week. There was then a break before the machine's reappearance at Keith's Bijou Theatre in Philadelphia on 23 December 1895. By the time it reached the Wonderland Theater in Rochester, N.Y. for two weeks commencing 20 January, the subjects included a skirt dance by the Nichols Sisters and a wrestling match between Donald C. Ross and Ernest Roeber, in addition to the well-traveled Griffo–Barnett fight. Next stop was Syracuse, N.Y., for two weeks (21 March 1896) at a store show in South Salina

Street, where it was reported that the show lasted 20 minutes, before a complete change of program at Hammerstein's Olympia in New York on 11 May. Here the films shown were *Whirlpool Rapids, Niagara Falls*; *Fifth Avenue, Easter Sunday Morning*; *Drill of the Engineer Corps*, and *Bull Fight*, "all of which were excellently produced and won storms of applause."

By this time, however, Edison had presented his first on-screen show at Koster & Bial's Music Hall on Broadway (23 April), using Thomas Armat's Vitascope projector, which he claimed as his own after failing to develop a workable machine himself. (Armat was paid to keep his mouth shut.) The occasion has generally been hailed as the first commercial screening of motion pictures in America, most historians having overlooked the pioneering presentations by Woodville Latham's Eidoloscope. This is undoubtedly partly owing to the heroic status of Thomas Edison as America's inventor non-pareil, but George C. Platt, first to chronicle the Eidoloscope's progress in detail (*Image*, Rochester, N.Y., December 1971), has advanced the theory that Latham's Lambda Co. deliberately suppressed widespread publicity for their shows for fear of attracting unwelcome attention from the highly litigious Edison.

After the five-week Olympia engagement, the Eidoloscope continued its nationwide travels. The Lambda Co. pioneered once again when it produced a multi-scene version of *Carmen*, starring Rosabel Morrison. This had the added excitement of a real bull fight, achieved by interpolating the *Bull Fight* subject (filmed in Mexico City on 26 March 1896) shown at the Olympia with the scenes shot in the studio. It is likely that this was the first true **narrative film** made anywhere in the world, earlier dramatic subjects having been either brief single-scene excerpts from stage shows or simple comedy sketches. *Carmen* was a huge success, being shown in no fewer than 19 states between November 1896 and February 1897. In Waco, Tex., the bullfighting scene "brought down the house." But again, Latham and the Lambda Co. seem to have been written out of history, *Carmen* not even being listed in the authoritative *American Film Institute Catalog: Film Beginnings 1893–1910*.

THE FIRST **FILM: ANIMATED CARTOON**

was J. Stuart Blackton's *Humorous Phases of Funny Faces*, produced by the Vitagraph Co. of New York and copyrighted on 6 April 1906. Like nearly all early film cartoonists, Blackton used the technique of showing an artist drawing a still picture which then magically came to life and moved. Most of the illusions were created by means of cardboard cutouts, but a few genuinely animated drawings featured at the beginning of the film, showing a man and a woman rolling their eyes and a gentleman with derby hat and umbrella apparently drawing himself.

The first cartoon films to tell a story and the first to dispense with the live artist technique were Émile Cohl's *Le Cauchemar du fantoche* and *Un Drame chez les fantoches*, released in Paris by Gaumont on 14 September and 7 November 1908 respectively. The former portrayed, as the title indicates, a puppet's nightmare; the latter relates a characteristically French tale of two men pursuing the same woman. Both can be viewed on YouTube.

The first rudimentary narrative cartoons in the United States were produced by Winsor McCay for Vitagraph, of which *Little Nemo* (released 8 April 1911) told a live-action story involving the artist himself with interpolated animated scenes and *The Story of a Mosquito* (January 1912) had a live-action prologue, also introducing the artist. The first standalone cartoons not to show the artist were short comic sequences in a series featuring the Bud Fisher newspaper cartoon characters Mutt and Jeff, which Charles Bowers animated for the "comic supplement" of the *Pathé Weekly* newsreels released between 10 February and 4 December 1913. But it was the French pioneer Émile Cohl who gave America the first true **cartoon series** in the world, based on regular characters and released as self-contained films. Cohl had emigrated to the United States in 1912 to join the U.S. studio of the French production outfit Éclair at Fort Lee, N.J. There he drew *The Newlyweds*, based on George McManus's popular comic strip in the *New York World*. The adventures of a young married couple in the suburbs and their baby Snookums, the series began with the release of *When He Wants a Dog, He Wants a Dog* on 16 March 1913 and continued for fifteen episodes spread over a period of a year. It was an advertisement for this series, appearing in *Moving Picture World* for 15 February 1913, that contained the first use of the term *animated cartoon*. Cohl made about a hundred cartoons between 1908 and 1918 and can thus be regarded as the first professional screen animator.

Animal cartoon character: The first was Old Doc Yak, a tail-coated billy goat in striped pants, who was brought to the screen by *Chicago Tribune* cartoonist Sidney Smith in a Selig Polyscope series starting 8 July 1913. It was the much-loved animal cartoon characters who eventually gave animated films a distinct appeal of their own as suitable entertainment for children. This development can best be dated from the advent of Pat Sullivan's Felix the Cat in 1919, an animal who "kept on walking," and who was the first cartoon character to attain the celebrity of a human star, as well as the first to be merchandised (SEE **character merchandising**).

Color cartoon film: The first was *The Debut of Thomas Kat*, produced by Bray Pictures of New York in the Brewster color process and released on 8 February 1920. Drawings on transparent celluloid were painted on the reverse, then filmed in color. Thomas was an unfortunate kitten taught by his mother to pursue mice, but who inadvertently mistook a rat for the smaller breed of rodent.

Cartoon talkie for theatrical release: The first was Max Fleischer's Song Car-Tune *Come Take a Trip in My Airship*, which opens with a 25-second sequence wherein the animated figure of a woman in a white dress speaks some patter as the lead-in to the song. The sound-on-film synchronization was by De Forest Phonofilm and the sound version (there had been an earlier silent version) was released in January 1925.

All-talking cartoon: The first was Paul Terry's "Aesop's Film Fable" *Dinner Time* of 1928, produced by Van Beuren Enterprises in the RCA Photophone sound system and premiered at the Mark Strand Theatre in New York on 1 September 1928. Walt Disney dismissed it as "a lot of racket and nothing else." His own initial venture in talkies, *Steamboat Willie*, presented at New York's Colony Theater on 18 November 1928, was more auspicious: it marked the debut of the most successful cartoon character of all time, Mickey Mouse.

Color cartoon talkie: The first was a 3-minute sequence in Universal's *The King of Jazz* which opened at the Roxy, in New York City, on 2 May 1930. Made by Walter Lanz in two-color Technicolor, it depicted a cartoon version of bandleader Paul Whiteman on a big-game hunt in Africa. The first complete film was Ub Iwerks's two-color Technicolor *Fiddlesticks*, featuring Flip the Frog, which was released on 16 August 1930. Disney's original color cartoon was not, as often claimed, the world's first but it was the first in a three-color process. A Silly Symphony titled *Flowers and Trees*, the Technicolor short premiered at Grauman's Chinese Theater in Hollywood on 15 July 1932.

Full-length feature cartoon: The first was Don Frederico Valle's 1917 Argentine production *El Apóstol*, a political satire on president Hipólito Irigoyen released on 9 November 1917. A team of five animators under Diógenes Taborda executed 50,000 drawings for the 70-minute film. All known copies of the film were destroyed in a fire at Valle's vaults in 1926. Surprisingly the first full-length cartoon talkie was also from Argentina. Made by Quirino Cristiani in 1931, *Peludópolis* was another satire on President Irigoyen and used the Vitaphone sound system. The first in color was Disney's Technicolor *Snow White and the Seven Dwarfs*, which opened at the Cathay Circle Theater, Los Angeles, on 21 December 1937. Usually cited as the world's first animated feature, it was the first American example but the sixth in the world; besides the Argentine cartoons there had been Lotte Reiniger's 65-minute silhouette-animated German production *The Adventures of Prince Achmed* of 1926 and two stop-motion puppet or claymation features, Wladyslaw Starewicz's 65-minute *Le Roman de Renard* (U.S.: *The Story of the Fox*) of 1930 from France and the 75-minute Russian version of *Gulliver's Travels* titled *Novyi Gulliver* (U.S.: *The New Gulliver*) of 1935.

THE FIRST **FILM ACTORS**

appeared in *The Arrest of a Pickpocket*, made by U.S.-born Birt Acres of Barnet, Hertfordshire, England in April 1895. There were three performers, playing the eponymous pickpocket, a policeman who attempts to apprehend him, and the gallant sailor who succeeds in doing so after the miscreant has slipped out of his jacket to escape. None of these actors has been identified, nor those in Acres' *The Comic Shoeblack* (lost), which followed a few weeks later. The first performer known by name and first to act in a film in the United States was Robert L. Thomae, secretary and treasurer of the Kinetoscope Co., who adopted drag to play the title role in the costume drama *The Execution of Mary, Queen of Scots*, shot by Alfred Clark of Kinetoscope proprietors Raff & Gammon at the Edison studio in West Orange, N.J., on 28 August 1895. After approaching the block and laying his head upon it, Thomae removed himself, the camera was stopped, and a dummy was substituted. The camera was then started again for the decapitation scene. This was the first **special effect** in a film.

The first **actors to appear on screen** (the previously noted films having been made for the Kinetoscope peepshow machine) were a Monsieur Clerc, a gardener employed by Mme. Lumière at Lyons, France, and his fourteen-year-old apprentice Duval. Clerc was cast in the part of the gardener in the Lumière brothers' production *L'Arroseur arrosé*, a film premiered at the Grand Café in Paris on 28 December 1895 (SEE **cinema theater**). He is seen watering flowerbeds with a hose. A mischievous boy, played by Duval, creeps up behind the gardener and places his foot on the hose to stop the flow of water. As the perplexed gardener holds the nozzle up to his eye to see whether there is a blockage, young Duval removes his foot and dances with joy as a burst of water gushes into M. Clerc's face.

Professional actors to perform in a film: The first such appearances took place in the United States and the United Kingdom in April 1896. John Rice and May Irwin performed the first **screen kiss** in a re-enactment of the final scene from the Broadway play *The Widow Jones*, filmed by Raff & Gammon for the Edison Kinetoscope as *The Kiss*. This innocent little production provoked the first review of a film in print, in *The Chap Book*—"absolutely disgusting"—as well as the earliest demand for movie censorship. In London the same month Fred Storey and Julia Seale, who were appearing together in a production at the Alhambra in Leicester Square, played in a short comedy *The Soldier's Courtship* that was made on the theater's roof by R. W. Paul and premiered underneath it. Fred Storey is chiefly remembered for his portrayals of Rip Van Winkle, which was also the forte of the distinguished American thespian Joseph Jefferson. It was Jefferson who top-lined in the only other United States movie in 1896 with a named star, a series of eight scenes from the stage production of *Rip Van Winkle* made by W. K. L. Dickson of the American Mutoscope & Biograph Co. and released in September of that year.

The **star system**, usually thought of as an American invention, in fact had its earliest beginnings in Germany. Here, as in the United States, it was deliberate policy on behalf of filmmakers not to give their lead players any star billing, lest they should over-value their services. From 1907 onward, it was recognized that particular performers could draw the crowds, but they were identified only by such pseudonyms as the Vitagraph Girl "Biograph Girl," or, in the case of the German actress Henny Porten, who made her debut in Oskar Messter's 1907 production of *Lohengrin*, the "Messter Girl." It was Henny Porten who eventually emerged as the first "film star"—the first actress to establish a personal following among moviegoers and have her name promoted as an attraction. This came about through the unprecedented success of a Messter film of 1909 that she had scripted herself and in which she played the romantic lead. Titled *Das Liebesglück der Blinden (The Love of the Blind Girl)*, it was received with such acclaim that Messter was persuaded to reveal his star player's identity. With her name on the credits, Henny then proceeded to justify the filmmakers' worst fears by demanding an increase in salary, from $50 to $56 a month. Messter refused and Henny walked out of the studio. Having failed to call what he thought was her bluff, the director sent an assistant, Kurt Stark, to fetch the girl back with the promise that the raise would be paid. Henny returned to the studio, married Stark, and went on to become Germany's idol of the silent screen.

In the United States, the star system emerged soon after Germany had paved the way. Perhaps fittingly it began with an outrageous publicity stunt, establishing a tradition that has enlivened and bedeviled the American movie business ever since. Early in 1910 Carl Laemmle had succeeded in luring the still-anonymous Florence Lawrence away from Biograph to work for his own company, Independent Moving Pictures (IMP). He then arranged for a story to break in the St. Louis papers that the actress had been killed in a street accident. Public interest in the supposed tragedy having been thoroughly aroused, Lacmmle placed the following advertisement in the same papers on 10 March 1910:

> The blackest and at the same the silliest lie yet circulated by the enemies of IMP was the story foisted on the public of St. Louis last week to the effect that Miss Lawrence, "The Imp Girl," formerly known as "The Biograph Girl," had been killed by a streetcar. It was a black lie so cowardly. We now announce our next film *The Broken Oath*.

Within a year her name was appearing on film posters in larger type than the title and she would remain the movies' biggest box office draw until displaced by her fellow Canadian, Mary Pickford.

Thereafter her career declined and she eventually became a humble extra at the MGM Studios. Sadly America's first named star committed suicide in December 1938.

THE FIRST FILM SHOT FROM AN AIRPLANE

was taken by L. P. Bonvillain, a Pathé cinematographer, piloted by Wilbur Wright at Camp d'Auvours, France, in September 1908. This was more than a year before the first still photograph was taken from an aircraft in flight.

U.S.: The first was taken of the city of Beaumont, Tex., and its neighboring oil wells on 17 December 1911 by R. H. Sexton of the Champion Film Co. Sexton was accompanying aviator Robert G. Fowler during his transcontinental flight from San Francisco to Jacksonville, Fla., in a Wright biplane. "Fowler at times came down to within fifty feet of the housetops," reported the *New York Times*, "and the pictures of the streets clearly show the crowds of people gazing skyward at the airmen." Later during the flight Sexton filmed the Louisiana swamps and while flying from Morgan City to New Iberia, La., they raced the De Luxe Express of the Southern Pacific Railroad. The

train was given a 15-minute start from Morgan City and the film showed it appearing in the distance, then gradually being overtaken by the flying machine.

THE FIRST FILM AWARDS

were made in respect of a festival that began in Monte Carlo on 1 January 1898 and was open to amateurs and professionals alike for the best films shot in Monaco. Organized by the Société des Bains de Mer (which despite its name ran the casino), the festival offered three prizes of 2,000 francs ($386), 1,000 francs ($193), and 500 francs ($98). The jury, which included such well-known figures in the film world as Léon Gaumont, Frédéric Dillaye, and Georges Mareschal, awarded the first prize to the French cinématographer Clément-Maurice for *Monaco vivant par les appareils cinématographique*.

The first awards for feature-length films were made in connection with a special cinema competition held at the International Exhibition in Turin in 1912. The grand prize of 25,000 francs was awarded to the Ambrosio Film Co. for the Italian feature *After Fifty Years*, a historical drama set in the Austro-Italian War of 1859.

Academy Awards: The first were presented by the Academy of Motion Picture Arts and Sciences at the Roosevelt Hotel in Hollywood on 16 May 1929 for films released between 1 August 1927 and 31 July 1928. The winner of the Best Actor Award was the German star Emil Jannings for his performances in *The Way of All Flesh* and *The Last Command*; the Best Actress Award went to Janet Gaynor for her roles in *The Last Command*, *Seventh Heaven*, *Street Angel*, and *Sunrise*. The Award for Best Picture was made to William Wellman's *Wings*, starring Clara Bow. The ceremony was the shortest of any to date, Academy president Douglas Fairbanks handing over the statuettes in just 4 minutes and 22 seconds. Media coverage was rather more than muted: there wasn't any.

The name "Oscar" for the trophy presented to winners was first used in 1931, after Mrs. Herrick, secretary of the Academy, had remarked of the sculpted figure, "He looks like my Uncle Oscar." Formerly it had been known simply as "the Statuette." This was also the year of the first Academy Awards at which the names of the winners were supposed to be kept secret until the night. The atmosphere of suspense was somewhat depleted by the fact that Best Actor winner George Arliss and Best Actress winner Norma Shearer had both posed for photographers with their statuettes two days earlier.

THE FIRST **FILM: CLOSE-UP**

was a scene of Edison employee Fred Ott sneezing, filmed by William K. Dickson at the newly built Edison studio (SEE **film studio**) at West Orange, N.J., on 2 February 1893. *Fred Ott's Sneeze*, which was also the first film to be copyrighted (7 January 1894), was distributed via Edison's Kinetoscope peep-show machines. The first on-screen close-up was of the Bohemian cabaret artist Josef Sváb-Malostransky in a film directed by Prague strudent Jan Krizenecky called *Plác a Smích/Smiles and Tears*, released on 1 October 1898. The persistent claim of D. W. Griffith to have been the only begetter of the close-up—he went so far as to suggest he could have patented the technique—has now been rejected by most film historians, though many still credit him with having been the first to employ the interpolated facial close-up as a dramatic device to register emotion. Even this had been accomplished a year before Griffith entered the film industry. In the American Mutoscape and Biograph Co. release (28 Oct 1907) *The Yale Laundry*, a comedy about students at Yale University playing a jape on their professors, close-ups are used to show surprise on the faces of the victims. It is precisely this technique of advancing the narrative by means of a close-up shot that Griffith was later to claim as his innovation and his alone. There is a certain irony in the fact that it had been used earlier by an uncredited director of the very company with which Griffith was to establish his reputation. The great director also seems to have overlooked the fact that hc himself was the subject of a close-up when he played the part of a clown in *At the French Ball* (1908), a film made shortly before his directorial debut at Biograph.

Despite the pioneering efforts of the Edison Co., AM & B, and the "Brighton school" (in England),

elsewhere the notion that a film should give its audience the same view as a theater audience received of the stage persisted for many years. As late as 1911 the leading production company in Scandinavia, Nordisk Film, was using a 16-foot-long pole attached to the camera as an indication to the actors that they must come no closer. Albert E. Smith recalled that about this period at Vitagraph in New York the actors were always positioned 9 yards in front of the camera. Mary Pickford, who claimed that she had been the subject of the first close-up, in D. W. Griffith's *Friends* (1912), said that the front office at Biograph had vigorously protested the idea on the grounds that audiences were paying to see the whole of the performer, not only the top half.

THE FIRST **FILM: COLOR PROCESS**

that was commercially successful was Kinemacolor, a two-color system using panchromatic film stock developed in 1906 by George Albert Smith of Brighton, England, for the Charles Urban Trading Co., a leading production company of the day. The first natural color film made by this process was taken outside Smith's house at Southwick, Brighton, in July 1906 and showed his two children playing on the lawn, the boy dressed in blue and waving a Union Jack and the girl in white with a pink sash. Kinemacolor was patented in November of that year.

The first commercial production in Kinemacolor for general release was *A Visit to the Seaside*, probably made in the summer of 1908. Taken at Brighton, it showed scenes of the Front, a boat party disembarking, pierrots, children eating ice cream, boaters paddling, bathing belles emerging from bathing machines, and the band of the Cameron Highlanders. This was one of twenty-one Kinemacolor films shown at the first presentation of color movies before a paying audience, which took place at the Palace Theatre in London's Shaftesbury Avenue on 26 February 1909. Other English subjects included sailing at Southwick and various scenes taken at the military garrison of Aldershot, Hampshire; and French subjects included the Water Carnival at Villefranche and the Children's Battle of Flowers at Nice. Kinemacolor's U.S. debut took place on 11 December the same year at Madison Square Garden and included the first film made in America in color, showing 2,000 children in formation as a giant, live Stars and Stripes.

Subsequently the National Color Kinematograph Co. made a speciality of news pictures, the first important event to be filmed in color being the funeral of King Edward VII on 20 May 1910, at which no fewer than nine kings were present. The first dramatic film in color was track shown in September of the same year, a one-reeler title *Checkmated*, directed by Theo Bouwmeester, who also played the lead role of Napoleon.

Full-length color feature film: The first was *The World, the Flesh and the Devil*, a 1-hour 40-minute melodrama produced by the Union Jack Co. in Kinemacolor from the book by Laurence Cowen and trade shown on 4 February 1914. Billed as "A £10,000 Picture Play in Actual Colours" in "four parts and 120 scenes," the film opened at London's Holborn Empire on 9 April 1914. Like most of the Kinemacolor dramas, the acting and direction were execrable, the color impressive.

Kinemacolor brought the American-born Charles Urban an international success, for in addition to the three hundred cinemas and halls that installed Kinemacolor equipment in Britain, Urban was able to dispose of foreign exhibition rights in most major countries of the world. However, the special projection equipment necessary put Kinemacolor beyond the range of the small exhibitor, and the Natural Color Kinematograph Co. was never able to produce enough films to keep a cinema constantly supplied with color programs. Other limitations included the necessity to film in strong sunlight, and the loss of light occasioned by projecting through filters, meant using a smaller screen than customary for black-and-white films.

Three-color process: The first to achieve practical results was Gaumont Chronochrome, exhibited before the French Photographic Society in Paris on 15 November 1912. The films shown were taken with a three-lens camera, each lens having a filter in one of the primary colors. Subjects exhibited at the first demonstration included scenes taken in the Vilmorin-Andrieux Gardens, butterflies, the Deauville beach at the height of the social season, and harvesters and other rural scenes. Chronochrome was shown in London on 16 January 1913, and in June of the same year it was used for America's first color talkies, a number of brief humorous sketches with synchronized dialogue from an Englephone phonograph attachment, which were presented at the 39th Street Theatre in New York City. Although Chronochrome cannot be described as a commercial success, demonstrations of the process were still being given as late as 1920.

Technicolor film: The first was *The Gulf Between*, starring Grace Darmond and Niles Welch and produced by the Technicolor Motion Picture Corporation in a two-color-additive system at Jacksonville, Fla., in February 1917. It was trade shown in New York on 21 September and released on 25 February 1918. This was the third full-length color feature in the world and the first produced in the United States. The process had been developed in Boston by Dr. Herbert Kalmus of the Massachusetts Institute of Technology two years earlier. Kalmus took Technicolor to Hollywood in 1923. Although he had developed a subtractive process the previous year, the double-coated film was given to cupping and scratched more easily than monochrome. To most producers the cost at 27¢ a foot was prohibitive in comparison with an average 8¢ a foot for monochrome stock. Technicolor's breakthrough came with the introduction of the three-color process on 30 July 1932, which made its commercial debut with the Disney cartoon *Flowers and Trees*. The first **feature-length film and the first talking feature in a three-color process** was *Becky Sharp*, starring Miriam Hopkins, directed by Rouben Mamoulian for Pioneer Films and released on 13 June 1935. The actors, according to one critic, looked like "boiled salmon dipped in mayonnaise."

In 1954 for the first time the majority of Hollywood features were in color; by 1970 only a single release was in black and white.

SEE ALSO **film: animated, color cartoon; film: sound, color talking feature.**

THE FIRST FILM, FEATURE

was Charles Tait's *The Story of the Kelly Gang*, a 4,000-foot Australian production with a running time of 60 to 70 minutes. A biopic of Victoria's notorious bushranger Ned Kelly (1855–80), the film was produced by the theatrical company J. & N. Tait of Melbourne and shot on location over a period of about six months at Whitehorse Road, Mitcham (Glenrowan Hotel scenes, including the last stand of the Kelly Gang), at Rosanna (railroad scenes), and on director Charles Tait's property in Heidelberg, Victoria (all other scenes). One of the actual suits of armor worn by the Kelly Gang during the final shootout—a bullet-proof helmet and jerkin fashioned from plowshares—was borrowed from the Victorian Museum and worn by the actor playing Ned, Frank Mills from the Bland Holt touring company, who disappeared before the film was finished. It had to be completed with an extra standing in for him, all these scenes being taken in long shot.

Made on a budget of £450 ($2,250), *The Story of the Kelly Gang* was premiered at the Athenaeum Hall, Melbourne, on 26 December 1906 and recovered its cost within a week, eventually grossing some £25,000 ($125,000), including receipts from the English and New Zealand releases. It was not without controversy, moralists complaining that it glorified crime. As a result the movie was banned in Benalla and Wangaratta and later throughout the state of Victoria.

For a long time it was thought that the film had been totally lost, but a few years ago some fragments were discovered in Melbourne and recently another 11 minutes of footage turned up in England. There is now a total of 17 minutes, which has been edited together and digitally enhanced. The impression is of a vigorous, all-action drama made with imaginative use of outdoor locations—a significant advance on the studio-bound one-reelers being churned out in Europe and America at the time. Its success was such that other Australian filmmakers started to produce full-length features and in 1911 no fewer than sixteen were released, before either the United States or the United Kingdom had begun regular feature production. It also stimulated a series of remakes, in 1910, 1917, 1920, 1923, 1934, 1951, 1960, 1967, 1970 (with Mick Jagger as Ned), 1977, 1993, 2003 (with Heath Ledger), and two in 2004.

U.S.: Two multi-reel movies were released by Vitagraph in 1909, each directed by J. Stuart Blackton but neither shown as a whole because it was believed that American moviegoers were incapable of sitting through a picture lasting an hour or more. The four-reel *Les Misérables*, starring Maurice Costello (great-grandfather of Drew Barrymore) as Jean Valjean, was released in separate one-reel parts between 18 September and 27 November, and the five-reel *The Life of Moses*, with Pat Hartington in the title role, was released in parts from 4 December 1909 through 19 February 1910. The first American production to be released in its entirety was a five-reel *Oliver Twist*, starring Nat C. Goodwin as Fagin and a fifteen-year-old newcomer from Utah called Vinnie Burns as Oliver (it was usual for actresses to take the roles of prepubescent boys at the time). Released on 20 May 1912, it was produced and probably directed by the obscure H. A. Spanuth, who made only one other film (a one-reeler). The innovation did not inspire an immediate changeover to features. There were only four others during 1912, though they included the first based on an original story, *The Adventures of Lieutenant Petrosino*—the first feature-length action movie. Output in 1913 was a modest dozen and it was only in 1914, just as production was starting in Hollywood, that the feature came into its own with 212 full-length releases. That year the United States overtook Germany as the most prolific producer of feature films, with production peaking at 854 in 1921 (the current figure is about a quarter of that). India has topped the feature-film production table every year since 1971.

THE FIRST FILM FESTIVAL

annual, was inaugurated in Venice in an attempt to revive the tourist trade, which had been badly hit by the Depression. It was held at the Hotel Excelsior in association with the International Art Exhibition, 6–12 August 1932. The nations represented were the United States, Great Britain, France, Germany, Italy, and the Soviet Union. There were no awards, but judging took place by popular vote with these results:

Which actress did you like the best?
—Helen Hayes.

Which actor did you like the best?
—Fredric March.

Which director seemed the most convincing?
—Nikolai Ekk (*Road to Life*).

Which film was the most entertaining?
—*À Nous la Liberté*.

Which film moved you the most?
—*The Sin of Madelon Claudet*.

Which film had the most original sense of fantasy?
—*Dr. Jekyll and Mr. Hyde*.

U.S.: The first regular festival was the Columbus Film Festival, founded in 1953 by Ohio State University's Dr. Edgar Dale to promote the use of 16mm documentary and educational films. Still running, it now embraces video as well as film and is international in scope.

The first regular festival of feature films in the United States was the San Francisco International Film Festival, which opened at the Metro Theater on Union Street on 4 December 1957 with a screening of Helmut Käutner's *The Captain from Köpenick*. There were competitive entries from twelve countries, the winners of the inaugural Golden Gate Awards being India's *Pather Panchali* with Best Film and its maker Satyajit Ray for Best Director; Heinz Rühmann as Best Actor in Germany's *The Captain from Köpenick* and Dolores Dorn-Heft as Best Actress in the American entry *Uncle Vanya*. A total of 11,500 attended the festival.

SEE ALSO **film awards**.

THE FIRST **FILM, GAY**

....

was Richard Oswald's *Anders als die Andern*, which opened in Berlin on 14 May 1919 during a short period following the conclusion of World War I when film censorship was in abeyance, though the subject was still proscribed in literature.

Conradt Veidt, himself gay, played a violinist who is loved by two women but loves a young man. He is blackmailed by another man whom he had met years before at a gay ball, is denounced, and is sentenced to prison. He commits suicide and his young lover decides to kill himself too. The homosexual rights activist Dr. Magnus Hirschfeld, playing himself, talks the youth out of this course of action by persuading him to devote his life to the repeal of the penal laws against male-to-male congress.

Only one print survives, discovered in Ukraine in 1979. All others had been destroyed by the Nazis.

U.S.: The first Hollywood film on an overtly gay theme was *Suddenly, Last Summer*, directed by Joseph L. Mankiewicz from Gore Vidal's adaptation of Tennessee Williams's play of the same name. Released in the United States on 22 December 1959, it concerned a homosexual poet whose beautiful cousin (Elizabeth Taylor) suffers an emotional disturbance after having unwittingly lured Italian beach boys for his delectation. He had eventually been cannibalized by them.

Erotic kiss between two men portrayed on screen: The first was bestowed on Murray Head by Peter Finch in *Sunday Bloody Sunday*, John Schlesinger's study of a bisexual love triangle, which premiered in London on 1 July 1971. Originally the intention was to show an embrace in long shot, but the scene developed from there. Schlesinger remarked that the two actors "were considerably less shocked by the kiss than the technicians on the set were." The fiercely hetero Finch, on being asked by a TV interviewer how he had coped with this histrionic challenge, responded with admirable sangfroid: "I did it for England."

THE FIRST **FILM, IN-FLIGHT**

....

was shown during a 7,000-mile, multi-stop demonstration flight by Aeromarine Airways Type 75 Cruiser *Santa Maria* in May 1921, passengers being entertained with a travelog titled *Howdy Chicago!* as they flew at 2,000 feet above the Windy City.

The first in-flight feature film and the first movie shown during a scheduled flight was First National's production of Conan Doyle's *The Lost World*, shown during an Imperial Airways flight from London to the Continent on 6 April 1925.

U.S.: The first show on a scheduled flight comprised a Universal newsreel and a couple of cartoons, one of them a Disney *Oswald the Lucky Rabbit* subject, aboard a transcontinental Air Transport Inc. Ford tri-motor on 8 October 1929.

The first airline to introduce regular in-flight movies was TWA, commencing with the presentation of *By Love Possessed* (Lana Turner, Efrem Zimbalist Jr.) in first class during a flight from New York to Los Angeles on 19 July 1961.

In-flight movies on-demand: The first video system delivering movies to passengers' personal seat-back LCD screens was supplied by the Airvision Co. of Valencia, Calif., to Northwestern Airlines and introduced on their Boeing 747 flights from Detroit to Tokyo on 21 June 1988. The choice of six channels included TV reruns, sports, and news, as well as movies.

THE FIRST **FILM MUSIC**

was composed by Romolo Bacchini for the 1906 Cines productions *Malia dell'Oro* and *Pierrot Innamorato*. Italy was the first country whose major films were regularly supplied with an original score, a practice that did not become widespread elsewhere until the 1920s. The first composition by a major composer was Camille Saint-Saëns's score for the inaugural Film d'Art production *L'Assassinat du Duc de Guise*. The arrangement for this French film released on 17 November 1908 was for piano, two violins, viola, cello, bass violin, and harmonium.

U.S.: The first was Manuel Klein's score for the All Star Corporation's production of *The Jungle*, based on Upton Sinclair's "muckraker" novel of the same title about exploitation in the Chicago stockyards, which opened in New York on 25 May 1914.

Woman film composer: The first was Jaddan Bai, with the score for Chimanlal Luhar's *Talash-e-Huq* of 1935, starring the composer's six-year-old daughter, the future superstar Nargis, in her debut role.

U.S.: Elizabeth Firestone of Akron, Ohio, daughter of tire magnate Harvey Firestone, composed the score for Universal's Robert Montgomery–Ann Blyth comedy *Once More, My Darling*, previewed on 21 July 1949.

THE FIRST **FILM: NEWS-FILM**

(other than sporting subjects—SEE **film of a sporting event**) was made in Germany by British cinematographer Birt Acres on the occasion of the opening of the Kiel Canal by Kaiser Wilhelm II on 20 June 1895. In addition to the arrival of the kaiser at Holtenau aboard his yacht *Hohenzollern*, Acres took footage of the laying of a memorial stone and of a number of other events held as part of the celebrations, including scenes of the kaiser reviewing his troops at Hamburg and leading a procession through the streets of Berlin. He also filmed a charge of Uhlan Lancers at the Tempelhof Feld in Berlin, starting a cameraman's tradition of taking risks in the cause of news-film reportage by arranging with their commander that the horsemen should charge directly at the camera. Seized with the desire to run for his life as the troop thundered toward him with drawn lances, he nevertheless continued to grind the handle of his camera and was afterward congratulated by the commanding officer as "the pluckiest fellow he had ever met." The first public screening of the films took place before the Royal Photographic Society in London on 14 January 1896.

U.S.: The first news films were of the Chinese statesman and general Li Hung-Chang (1823–1901) driving through 4th Street and Broadway during his visit to New York City in 1896, other scenes of him on 5th Avenue and 55th Street, and another paying homage at Grant's Tomb. These were shot on 28, 29, and 30 August 1896 respectively by W. K. L. Dickson, who had designed and built the first American film camera for Thomas Edison in 1891 (SEE **film**), and were released by Dickson's new employer, the American Mutoscope and Biograph Co. Dickson went to Canton, Ohio, the following month and there on 18 September made the first news films of an American politician, showing presidential candidate William McKinley heading a civic procession and receiving a telegram from his secretary on the lawn of his home. The latter was released by AM & B after his election as 25th president on 3 November 1896, with a new and wholly spurious title *William McKinley Receiving Telegram Announcing His Election*: the news film had embraced the art of spin.

THE FIRST **FILM REVIEWS**

(regular) were written by Frank W. Woods for the *New York Dramatic Mirror* commencing with the issue for 1 May 1908. Woods used the pseudonym Spectator, which was to be adopted some twenty-five years later by the world's first television reviewer. The first newspaper to introduce film reviews was *Vilag (World)*, a Budapest daily, which engaged Sándor Kellner as its critic in August 1912. Kellner's sojourn with the paper was brief, since he was determined to get into the production side of the movie business, which he did with conspicuous success as (Sir) Alexander Korda.

U.S.: The first newspaper to introduce regular film reviews was the *Chicago Tribune*, which appointed Jack Lawson as film critic in 1914. Lawson was killed in an accident soon after and his place was taken by Miss Audrie Alspaugh, who wrote under the byline Kitty Kelly. American film historian Terry Ramsaye recalled: "Kitty Kelly could make or break a picture in the Middle West . . . Her column was a large success, and she became the best disliked name in the world of the film studios."

THE FIRST **FILM SCRIPTWRITER**

was New York journalist Roy McCardell, who was hired in 1900 by Henry Marvin of the Biograph Co. to write ten scenarios a week at $15 each. Since most of the films made by Biograph at that time ran for one or two minutes, McCardell found he was able to complete his first week's assignment in a single afternoon.

THE FIRST **FILM: SERIAL**

was the twelve-part *What Happened to Mary* about a foundling (played by Mary Fuller) seeking her lost inheritance, of which the first episode was released to movie theaters in the United States by the Edison Co. on 26 July 1912. When it started running at the local picture house in Haddington, Scotland, the manager put up a poster with the enigmatic statement: WHAT HAPPENED TO MARY TWICE NIGHTLY.

THE FIRST **FILMS, SOUND**

with synchronized accompaniment to be successfully shown before a paying audience were presented at three temporary cinemas operated at the Paris Exposition between 15 April and 31 October 1900. All three used a sound-on-disk system under separate but not totally dissimilar patents. The Phonorama, exhibited by the Compagnie Générale Transatlantique, showed colored scenes of "la vie Parisienne" and "a series of tableaux of the cries of Paris," accompanied by music, singing, and speech. In the rue de Paris, the Phono-Cinéma-Théâtre was bringing major stars to the talking screen for the first time. Presented by Clément-Maurice, the program of seven films included the celebrated comedy actor Coquelin in the role of Cyrano de Bergerac and Sarah Bernhardt playing the duel scene from *Hamlet*. Mme. Bernhardt was thus first to speak the words of Shakespeare from the screen. The other exhibition of talking films, given by Henry Joly at the Théâtre de la Grande Rue, included a short film titled *Lolotte*, the first comedy film with dialogue, and the first talkie to relate some kind of story. The scene takes place in a hotel bedroom and is played by three characters, a newly married couple and the *patron* of the hotel, the latter performed by Joly himself. The script survives.

U.S.: The first commercially successful talking films made in the United States were by the National Cameraphone Co., New York, which began leasing them together with the sound-on-disk synchronization equipment in 1908. The following year they released the first American-made dialogue drama, a short adaptation of Dumas's *The Corsican Brothers*. The actors, as was customary at this date, were not identified, but one reviewer noted that their deep voices "helped the phonograph materially in reproducing the text." While many of the competing sound-on-disk systems produced in the period 1908–14 used comic sketches from vaudeville, the first "real comedy talking picture which tells a story" was claimed to be the Edison Kinetophone production *The Irish Politician*, directed at the company's Bronx studio in 1913 by Allen Amsey and starring Eddie O'Connor.

Sound-on-film process: The first was patented by French-born Eugène Lauste of Brixton, London, on

11 August 1906. Lauste's first successful experiment in recording and reproducing speech on film was made in 1910, with an electrodiamagnetic recorder and string galvanometer. He used a French gramophone record, selected at random, for the initial trial, and by coincidence the first words to be heard in the playback were "J'entends très bien maintenant." (I hear very well now.) A colleague in the business, L. G. Egrot, recalled visiting Lauste about this time:

> He had already started building his camera to take pictures and sound together, the front part of the camera allowing to test the different systems he was experimenting with for sound recording...
> Very often on a Sunday, a bandmaster friend of his, Mr. Norris, would come along with his band and play in the garden of the house where, in 1911, Mr. Lauste had had a wooden building erected as an experimental studio. The machine was taken out, with all leads, some pictures would be made and some sound recorded.

Lauste completed his sound-on-film projector and reproducing apparatus in 1913 and was about to embark on the commercial exploitation of the process when war broke out. In 1916 he went to the United States with the idea of obtaining financial backing, but the entry of America into the war the following year dashed his hopes again.

The first program of sound-on-film productions to be presented in public was shown at the Alhambra cinema in Berlin on 17 September 1922 before an invited audience of a thousand people. The films were made by the Tri-Ergon process developed by Joseph Engl, Joseph Massolle, and Hans Vogt and included the first story film with dialogue recorded on the actual film. Titled *Der Brandstifter* ("The Arsonist"), and taken from Von Heyermann's play of the same name, it had a cast of three with Erwin Baron playing seven of the nine parts. The other films were mainly orchestral with vocal accompaniment. Press reaction was mixed, criticism being leveled not so much against the level of technical achievement, but at the notion of talking films, which it was said would destroy the essential art of the motion picture—mime—and detract from the cinema's international appeal.

The first presentation of sound-on-film productions before a paying audience took place at the Rialto Theater, New York City, on 15 April 1923, when Lee De Forest (SEE **radio broadcast; radio telephone**) showed a number of singing and musical shorts made by his Phonofilm process. The sound films formed a supporting program to the main (silent) feature, *Bella Donna* with Pola Negri. During the following twelve months, thirty-four cinemas in the eastern United States were wired for Phonofilm sound. The films made at the De Forest Studios between 1923 and 1927 included monologue numbers by Eddie Cantor, George Jessel, and Chic Sale; dialogues between Gloria Swanson and Thomas Meighan and Weber and Fields; Folkina's "Swan Dance"; playlets with Raymond Hitchcock; and orchestral subjects featuring Ben Bernie, Paul Specht, and Otto Wolf Kahn. The year 1924 saw three notable sound-on-film "firsts" from Phonofilm: President Calvin Coolidge was filmed delivering a campaign speech on the White House lawn; the first Technicolor film with a sound-track was made, the subject being Balieff's *Chauve-Souris* danced in the open air; and the first commercially released story film, *Love's Old Sweet Song*, a two-reeler directed by J. Searle Dawley with Mary Mayo and Una Merkel in the leading roles. Although the first to exploit sound-on-film commercially, De Forest failed to establish talking pictures as a major entertainment medium and the Phonofilm patents were eventually taken over by William Fox together with those of the Tri-Ergon system.

Full-length feature film with sound (in part): The first was D. W. Griffith's *Dream Street*, produced by United Artists in 1921. Described by one cinema historian as "a dreadful hodgepodge of allegory and symbolism," it was a total failure when originally presented as an all-silent picture at the Central Theater, New York City, in April. After it had closed, Griffith was persuaded by Wendell McMahill of Kellum Talking Pictures to add a sound sequence. On 27 April the star, Ralph Graves, was taken to the Kellum Studios at West 40th treet to record a love song on synchronized disk, and this was included when the film re-opened at the Town Hall civic center on 1 May. Two weeks later a second sound sequence was added, consisting of the shouts and whoops of Porter Strong shooting craps together with other background noises.

Talking feature film: The first was Warner Bros.' *The Jazz Singer*, directed by Alan Crosland and starring Al Jolson, which opened at the Warner Theater on Broadway on 6 October 1927. The film was made with the Vitaphone synchronized disk system and originally it had only been intended to use this for song sequences. Hence there was no script, but Jolson began to ad lib during a scene in a music saloon called Coffee Dan's, where the hero is making his debut as a jazz singer. The opening words, often mistakenly described as the first to be spoken from the screen, but nevertheless of historic significance, follow his rendering of "Dirty Hands, Dirty Face." Amid the applause, Jolson holds up his hands and urges: "Wait a minute. Wait a minute. You ain't heard nothin' yet! Wait a minute, I tell you. You ain't heard nothin'. You wanna hear 'Toot-toot-tootsie'? All right. Hold on." Although there were only two talking sequences in the whole film, and no more than 354 words spoken in total, *The Jazz Singer* achieved the long-awaited breakthrough for sound. The phenomenal reception it received on both sides of the Atlantic marked the beginning of the end of the silent picture.

The first all-talking feature film was Warner Bros.' Vitaphone production *Lights of New York*, which was premiered at the Strand Theater, New York City, on 6 July 1928. Starring Helene Costello, the picture was so determinedly all-talking that the dialogue continued nonstop from opening credits to end title. Warner's billed it as "100 per cent Talking!"; *Variety* commented "100 per cent Crude."

For the better part of a year after the premiere of *The Jazz Singer*, the only sound system used for talking features was synchronized disks. The first sound-on-film dialogue feature, with the sound track optically recorded on the film itself, was the RCA–Photophone part-talkie *The Perfect Crime*. Starring Clive Brook, the film was released with a 15-minute dialogue sequence on 17 June 1928. The first all-talking sound-on-film feature was a Fox Movietone production, Raoul Walsh's *In Old Arizona*, which opened at the Criterion, Los Angeles, on 25 December 1928. This picture enjoyed the added distinction of being the first western talkie (qv).

Full-length color talking feature: The first was Warner Bros.' *On With the Show*, directed by Alan Crosland with Ethel Waters and Joe E. Brown and premiered at the Winter Garden, New York City, on 28 May 1929. It was made in two-color Technicolor with Vitaphone sound.

The talking picture arrived amid predictions of failure on almost every side; within three years of the first successful all-talkie, sound had all but ousted the silent picture—the last major silent, *The White Hell of Pitz Palu*, being made in Germany in 1931. By December 1930, 13,500 out of 21,700 cinemas in the United States had been wired for sound, and at the end of the following year there were scarcely any silent cinemas remaining.

THE FIRST **FILM OF A SPORTING EVENT**

was taken at the Edison Laboratories, West Orange, N.J., on 14 June 1894 and depicted a six-round boxing bout fought between Mike Leonard and Jack Cushing. Leonard, the better-known fighter, was paid $150 for his services and his opponent $50. The ring was only 12 feet square, in order that all the action might be followed by the immobile camera. Having knocked Cushing out in the last round, Leonard summed up after the fight: "I hit him when I liked and where I liked. I'd hit him oftener, only Mr. Edison treated me right and I didn't want to be too quick for his machine. I generally hit 'im in the face, because I felt sorry for his family and thought I would select the only place that couldn't be disfigured." The film was premiered at a Kinetoscope parlor located at 83 Nassau Street, New York, probably at the beginning of August 1894. From a commercial point of view it was not a complete success, as each round was shown in a different Kinetoscope for which a separate charge was made. At 10¢ a round, it cost 60¢ to see the whole film, so most patrons preferred to pay a single dime to see the knock-out round only.

The first film of a regularly scheduled sporting contest was made by American-born Birt Acres of the Oxford and Cambridge Boat Race on the Thames in London on 30 March 1895. It was primarily intended for viewing in the Kinetoscopes manufactured by Acres's partner Robert Paul, but was probably also seen on the screen when Acres became an exhibitor the following year.

THE FIRST **FILM: STEREOPHONIC SOUND**

process was patented by the Parisian filmmakers Abel Gance and André Debrie in 1932. The first film with a stereophonic sound accompaniment was a re-edited version of Gance's 1927 8-hour silent epic *Napoléon Bonaparte*, presented with added dialogue and sound effects at the Paramount Cinema, Paris, in 1935.

The first successful process of stereophonic musical accompaniment was Fantasound, developed by Walt Disney Studios in association with RCA, and first employed for the sound track of Walt Disney's feature-length cartoon *Fantasia*, with music by the Philadelphia Orchestra under the direction of Leopold Stokowski. The picture premiered in New York on 24 November 1940.

The first feature with a complete stereophonic dialogue was Warner Bros.' 3-D horror film *House of Wax*, starring Vincent Price, released in the United States on 25 April 1953.

THE FIRST **FILM STUDIO**

was Thomas Edison's "Black Maria," a frame building covered in black roofing paper, built at the Edison Laboratories in West Orange, N.J., and completed at a cost of $637.67 on 1 February 1893. Here Edison made short vaudeville-act films for use in his Kinetoscope, a peep-show machine designed for use in amusement arcades. The building was so constructed that it could be revolved to face the direction of the sun.

The first studio in which films were made by artificial light was opened by Oskar Messter at 94a Friedrichstrasse, Berlin, in November 1896. For illumination Messter used four Körting & Matthiessen 50-amp arc lamps on portable stands. His earliest productions by artificial light included *From Tears to Laughter* and *Lightning Artist Zigg*. The first artificially lit studio in the United States, the Biograph Studio on East 14th Street, New York City, opened in 1903.

Hollywood studio: The first was established as the result of a toss of a coin. Al Christie, Canadian-born general manager of the Centaur Co., wanted to make westerns in California, since he was tired of having to simulate sagebrush country in New Jersey. Centaur's owner, David Horsley, thought that Florida would be better, but he agreed to abide by a heads-or-tails decision. Christie tossed and won. On the train out west, they met the proprietor of the Blondeau Tavern, a roadhouse on Sunset Boulevard and Gower that was struggling under California's new restrictions on liquor. Christie rented it for $30 a month and converted the building into a studio in October 1911 by the addition of a 40' x 20' wooden stage. As well as the westerns, the Nestor Studio, as it was called, put out a single-reel drama each week and a weekly episode of the *Mutt and Jeff* comedy series. By the end of the following year there were fifteen studios in Hollywood, occupied by production outfits attracted by the year-round sunshine and California's reassuring distance from the litigious Patents Trust. The Nestor Studio was soon taken over by Carl Laemmle, later to establish Hollywood's largest studio (to this day), Universal. The original building on Sunset was demolished in 1936 and the site is now occupied by CBS's Columbia Square television studios.

THE FIRST **FILM MADE FOR TELEVISION**

was a silent short titled *Morgenstunde hat Gold im Munde* ("The Early Bird Catches the Worm"), produced in 1930 by F. Banneitz of Commerz-Film AG, Berlin, for the Reichs-Rundfunkgesellschaft, the German state broadcasting corporation. Intended specially for transmission by low-definition television, the actors' movements were exaggerated for visual emphasis and the costumes were designed for greater contrast than in a normal cinema film.

The first film drama made for high-definition television (i.e., 120 lines or more) was *Wer fuhr IIA 2992?* ("Who was Driving Car Number IIA 2992?"), a thriller scripted by Gerhart W. Göbel of the Reichspost and produced by UFA in Berlin in the summer of 1939. Göbel devised the plot after watching a police announcement on television appealing for help in a murder case. The story centered on a hit-and-run driver, since the Nazi Propaganda Ministry would not allow murder as a theme in films to be shown abroad. The film was first shown during television demonstrations in Bucharest, Romania, and Sofia, Bulgaria, in 1940 and was also used after the war when the German Post Office resumed experimental transmission in 1950.

U.S.: RKO Television Productions, Inc., was founded in Los Angeles in May 1944 to produce news and entertainment shorts exclusively for TV. Its first production was *Talk Fast, Mister*, a one-hour drama filmed at the RKO-Pathé Studios in New York and transmitted by DuMont's New York station in December 1944.

Television series made on film: The first was *Public Prosecutor*, of which seventeen 20-minute episodes were shot by producer Jerry Fairbanks at Paramount Studios in Hollywood during the summer and fall of 1947. The prosecuting attorney was played by John Howard, his assistant by Anne Gwynne, and the police lieutenant by Walter Sande. There is some doubt whether the series was syndicated as Fairbanks intended. According to Vincent Terrace in *Fifty Years of Television* (1991), it was; whereas Michael Ritchie, in *Please Stand By: A Prehistory of Television* (1994), asserts that the emerging networks strongarmed the independent stations into a belief that TV could only be delivered live. The series was picked up by the DuMont network in 1951 and transformed into a 30-minute game show in which a panel of detective-fiction buffs viewed the first 15 minutes of the TV films and had to deduce the identity of the culprit. Then the remainder of the film was shown to reveal the answer.

The first all-film series on network TV was NBC's *Your Show Time*, in which one-act plays filmed in Los Angeles were presented by Arthur Shields. The 30-minute program ran weekly from 21 January 1949. The first filmed western series, which was also the first TV series to play mainly outdoors, was *The Lone Ranger*, with Clayton Moore as the eponymous guy in the white hat and Jay Silverheels as his loyal sidekick Tonto. Starting on ABC on 15 September 1949, the phenomenally successful half-hour show ran until September 1965. (The earlier *Hopalong Cassidy* series was simply a TV rerun of William Boyd's Hollywood B pictures.)

Hollywood's production of filmed TV programs exceeded its output of feature films by 988 hours to 855 hours for the first time in 1950, per an industry survey reported in June 1951. An average of thirty-seven TV programs a week were released to the networks.

Made-for-television movie: The first full-length feature was Hal Roach's production of Alexandre Dumas's *The Three Musketeers*, starring Robert Clarke (d'Artagnan), John Hubbard (Athos), Mel Archer (Portos), and Kristine Miller (Lady de Winter), which premiered on CBS's Magnavox Theater on 24 November 1950. At 60 minutes this just qualifies as a full-length feature film and indeed it was released theatrically under the title *Sword of d'Artagnan* as a supporting feature.

Although there were a few examples of TV movies over the following decade, it was not until the October 1964 transmission of Universal's chase drama *See How They Run*, with John Forsythe and Jane Wyatt, that they became a recognized and continuing genre in television programing.

THE FIRST **FILMS SHOWN ON TELEVISION**

are claimed to have been transmitted by WCFL Chicago from June 1928 and in telecasts sponsored by the *Boston Post* in April and May of that year, but no details survive. The first televised film whose title is known was a short of vaudeville artiste George Robey performing a monologue, *The Blushing Bride*, transmitted from the Baird Studios, Long Acre, London, on 19 August 1929.

The first television station to show films as part of the regular program service was the De Forest Radio Corporation's W2XCD Passaic (N.J.), commencing 1 March 1931. These were mainly documentary and travel shorts, two of the earliest to be aired being *People Who Live in the Desert* and *Lumbering in British Columbia*.

Full-length feature film shown on television: The first was a 1925 dramatic comedy titled *Police Patrol*, which was transmitted in six daily episodes by W2XCD Passaic (N.J.) on 6–11 April 1931. Directed by Burton King for Gotham Productions, it related the story of a New York cop (James Kirkwood) who arrests a girl thief (Edna Murphy) who is the exact double of his sweetheart (also Edna Murphy).

The first feature to be shown without interruption was World Wide Pictures' 1932 production *The Crooked Circle*, starring ZaSu Pitts and Ben Lyon, a comedy about an amateur detective exposing a secretive group of hooded occultists that aired on the 80-line, 15-frames-per-second Don Lee Broadcasting System's station W6XAO Los Angeles on 23 March 1933. Don Lee made a deal with Paramount for the televising of their films and over the next four years, starting in September 1933, transmitted sixty-two features, including *Blonde Venus* (1932), *A Farewell to Arms* (1932), *Duck Soup* (1933), *Alice in Wonderland* (1933), *Little Miss Marker* (1934), and *The Scarlet Empress* (1934), as well as forty-eight Paramount shorts.

Once television was established as a commercially viable medium, Hollywood pulled down the shutters on its upstart rival, so that the only films available were B movies, out-of-copyright or British productions. Not until 1956 did the studios yield to the buying power of the networks, though for the next ten years only pre-1948 pictures were licensed for transmission.

THE FIRST **FILM IN 3-D**

of feature length was Nat Deverich's five-reel melodrama *The Power of Love*, starring Terry O'Neil and Barbara Bedford, premiered at the Ambassador Hotel Theater on 27 September 1922. Produced by Perfect Pictures in an anaglyphic process developed by Harry K. Fairall, it related the adventures of a young sea captain in the California of the 1840s.

Feature-length talkie in 3-D: The first was Sante Bonaldo's *Nozze vagabonde*, starring Leda Gloria and Ermes Zacconi, which was produced in 1936 by the Società Italiana Stereocinematografica at the Cines-Caesar studios in Rome, Italy.

The first in color was Alexander Andreyevsky's *Robinson Crusoe*, starring Pavel Kadochnikov as Crusoe and Y. Lyubimov as Friday. It was a Soyuzdetfilm production filmed at studios in Tbilisi, Georgia in what was then the U.S.S.R. and released in 1947. The Stereokino process used was the first to successfully dispense with anaglyphic spectacles. Developed by S. P. Ivanov, it employed "radial raster stereo-screens"—a corrugated metal screen with "raster" grooves designed to reflect the twin images separately to the left and right eye. The most difficult technical problem encountered during the filming of *Robinson Crusoe* was persuading a wildcat to walk along a thin branch towards the camera. After five nights occupied with this one scene, the cameraman succeeded in getting a satisfactory shot. The effect, it was reported, was riveting, the animal seeming to walk over the heads of the audience and disappear at the far end of the theater.

U.S.: Arch Obeler's Ansocolor *Bwana Devil*, an adventure tale about the building of Kenya's railroad in the 1890s, starred Robert Stack and Barbara Britton and was released on 30 November 1952. The billboards promised "A lion in your lap! A lover in your arms!"—which about sums up the merits of the picture.

THE FIRST **FILM: WAR**

news subject was made during the Greco-Turkish War of 1897. The sole cameraman in the field was British war correspondent and pioneer cinematographer Frederick Villiers, who filmed the Battle of Volo in Thessaly, Greece, in April. He wrote in his memoirs:

> Luckily I was well housed during the fighting in front of Volo, for the British consul insisted on my residing at the consulate. To me it was campaigning in luxury. From the balcony of the residence I could always see of a morning when the Turks opened fire up on Valestino Plateau; then I would drive with my camera outfit to the battlefield, taking my bicycle with me in the carriage. After I had secured a few reels of movies, if the Turks pressed too hard on our lines I would throw my camera into the vehicle and send it out of action, and at nightfall, after the fight, I would trundle back down the hill to dinner.

These first historic war films were destined never to be seen by the public. When he finally arrived back in London, Villiers found to his consternation that Star Film of Paris had already flooded the market with dramatized reconstructions of the campaign and there was no demand for the genuine article. He was equally unlucky during the Sudan campaign the following year when he filmed the Battle of Omdurman from a gunboat on the Nile. As the gunboat's battery opened up, the camera tripod collapsed and Villiers's camera hit the deck; the magazine fell out and the film was exposed to light.

Villiers was not the only cinematographer present at Omdurman. The other one, Old Etonian John "Mad Jack" Bennet-Stanford, succeeded in bringing back footage of the battle and at least one of his films, *Alarming Queens Company of Grenadier Guards at Omdurman*, was exhibited in Britain in November. In the meantime, however, the earliest war footage to be shown publicly had been released in the United States.

U.S.: The fact that so many faked "actualities" of the Spanish-American War of 1898 were produced to satisfy the passionate desire for scenes from the front by a war-frenzied public has given rise to the oft-repeated assertion that no genuine footage of the conflict was ever taken. There appear, however, to have been at least two war cameramen in Cuba. One, unidentified, was supplying the Lubin Co. with short subjects. Claimed by Lubin as "the first life [*sic*] motion picture of the war," *Brave Cubans Firing at Spanish Soldiers* showed a dynamite cannon in action and was said to have been made "in a country town near Havana." Contemporary with this subject was *American Commissary Wagons Landing on Cuban Soil*; both these Lubin releases were noted by the *New York Clipper* on 11 July 1898.

The Selig Polyscope Co.'s *Cavalry Horses Fording a Stream in Santiago de Cuba* also purported to have been shot at the front, but it could have been taken at an embarkation camp in Florida. More likely to be authentic is *U.S. Troops Landing at Daiquiri, Cuba*, shot by William Paley on 22 June 1898 and released, together with three short actualities of ammunition pack mules, by the Edison Co. in August.

The earliest known footage of American troops in action was of a charge by Companies I and K, 3rd Battalion, 13th Infantry on an insurgent stronghold at Daguban in Northern Lozon during the pacification of the Philippines. This was shot by Raymond Ackerman on 30 January 1900 and released by the American Mutoscope & Biograph Co. the following May.

Earlier so-called battle subjects are believed to have been dramatizations.

War films in color: The first were taken by James Scott Brown of Kinemacolor (SEE **film, color**), who accompanied the Greek forces in the Balkan War of 1912–13. He filmed under the supervision of Frederic Villiers (SEE ABOVE) and this time the films did reach the screen, debuting at the Scala Theatre in London on 20 January 1913.

THE FIRST FILM: WESTERNS

were copyrighted by the American Mutoscope & Biograph Co. on 21 September 1903. One was titled *Kit Carson* and related the story of its hero's capture by Indians and subsequent escape through the agency of a beautiful Indian maiden. There were eleven scenes and the film had a running time of 21 minutes. The other film, titled *The Pioneers*, showed the burning of a settler's homestead by Indians, who kill the homesteader and his wife and carry off his daughter. The film ends with the dramatic rescue of the child by frontiersmen who have found the bodies of her parents. Running time was approximately 15 minutes. Both films were released in August 1904. (NB: The more celebrated *The Great Train Robbery*, generally described as the first western and often as the first film to tell a story, was copyrighted by the Edison Co. on 1 December 1903, nearly six weeks after these two films.)

Kit Carson and *The Pioneers* were filmed in the Adirondacks of upstate New York. Film historian William K. Everson has observed, "The American western started in artifice and pantomime in the East, found reality and a rough poetry as the industry moved west, and then deviated into myth and fiction as the star system took over." Despite the enormous popularity of cowboys-and-injuns pictures during the first decade of the twentieth century, the term *western* was not used generically until coined by *The Motion Picture World* in its issue for 20 July 1912. That same year it was reported that the Polynesians of Tahiti were so enraptured with these cinematic tales of derring-do they had taken to wearing cowboy hats.

Western talkie: The first was Fox Movietone's *In Old Arizona*, directed by Raoul Walsh and Irving

Cummings with Edmund Lowe, Warner Baxter, and Dorothy Burgess, and presented at the Fox West Coast Criterion Theater, Los Angeles, on 25 December 1928. Billed as "The First All-Talking Outdoor Picture," it was shot on location in Zion National Park and Bryce Canyon in Utah, in the Mojave Desert, and at the San Fernando Mission in California—almost anywhere except in Old Arizona.

THE FIRST USE OF **FINGERPRINTING**

as a means of identification was initiated on a systematic basis by William Herschel of the Indian Civil Service at Jungipur in 1858. On 28 July of that year he took the palm-print of Rajyadhar Konai, a local contractor from the Bengali village of Nista, on the back of a contract for 2,000 mounds of road metaling. The impress was made with the homemade oil-ink used by Herschel for his official seal, and included clear prints of all the fingers of the right hand. Herschel admitted that his original intention in taking Konai's fingerprints was not so much for the purpose of positive identification as a means of frightening the Bengali out of all thoughts of repudiating the document at a later date, but so pleased was he with the success of the experiment that he determined to pursue it further. Accordingly he inaugurated the first register of fingerprints while serving as magistrate at Arrah, Bengal, in June 1859. At first he contented himself with collecting the prints of his friends and colleagues, but on being transferred to Nuddea the following year he found such an alarming incidence of fraud and forgery that he began to investigate the possibility of enforcing the statutory use of fingerprints on leases and contracts. His proposals, however, were rejected by the Calcutta Secretariat. It was not until appointment to the magistracy of Hooghly in 1877, when he became responsible for both the criminal courts and the Department for the Registration of Deeds, that Herschel was able to introduce the use of fingerprinting for official purposes. In order to prevent Indian Army pensioners from drawing their pensions twice over, he maintained a record of their fingerprints and required them to make an imprint on receipt of money due, for purposes of comparison.

At the same time the system was adopted at Hooghly Gaol as a precaution against the hiring of substitutes to serve sentences—a fairly common practice at the time—and also for the registration of legal documents. Herschel regarded fingerprinting chiefly as a means of preventing impersonation, and did not foresee its use in criminal investigation.

The use of **fingerprints as a means of criminal detection** was first advocated by Henry Faulds, a Scottish physician, who made a number of experiments while employed at the Tsukiji Hospital in Tokyo. He wrote a letter to *Nature*, published in the issue for 28 October 1880:

> When bloody finger-marks or impressions on clay, glass, etc., exist they may lead to scientific investigation of criminals. Already I have had experience in two such cases, and found useful evidence from these marks. In one case greasy finger-marks revealed who had been drinking some rectified spirit. The pattern was unique, and fortunately I had previously obtained a copy of it. They agreed with microscopic fidelity. In another case sooty finger-marks of a person climbing a white wall were of great use as negative evidence.

Faulds's letter brought little immediate result, except the revelation of Herschel's previous researches in the field. Failing to attract the notice of the police commissioners in Britain—nor the many police departments around the world to which he wrote—he spent the rest of his life making vitriolic attacks on Herschel and anyone else who proved unwilling to accept his claim to be the sole pioneer of fingerprinting.

The first police force to adopt the use of fingerprints for criminal investigation was the La Plata Division of the Provincial Police of Buenos Aires. This was done more or less unofficially by Croatian migrant Juan Vecutich, who had been deputed by the chief of police to set up an anthropometrical department and used the opportunity to establish a fingerprint classification based on the system devised by the eminent British scientist Francis Galton. His classification, which he called by the unwieldy name of Icnofalagometrico, came into regular use on 1 September 1891, and on 31 May 1892 he inaugurated the world's first Fingerprint Bureau at San Nicolas, Buenos Aires.

Criminal case solved by fingerprints: The first occurred soon after these events. On 29 June 1892 at Necochea, Buenos Aires Province, a woman called Francisca Rojas had come running out of her house covered in blood, screaming that she had been attacked and her children murdered. She accused a neighbor called Velasquez, a ranch worker who had been pestering her to marry him. He was arrested the same night, beaten up, and then bound and laid by the corpses of the victims as an inducement to confess. When it was revealed that Rojas had a lover who had publicly declared he would marry her but for the children, the police began to entertain doubts, and on 8 July Inspector Eduardo Alvarez was sent from La Plata to search for incriminating evidence. He found it on a doorpost in the woman's hut: a number of bloody fingerprints. Alvarez cut the wood away and sent it to headquarters at La Plata. The prints were compared with those of the suspect and those of the mother of the murdered children, and found to correspond exactly with the latter. Confronted with the evidence, she broke down and confessed the crime. As there was no capital punishment for women in Argentina at that time, she was sentenced to life imprisonment.

As Rojas had confessed, the fingerprint evidence did not need to be presented in court. The first **conviction secured on the presentation of fingerprint evidence in court** was that of Kangali Charan at the Court of Sessions in Jalpaiguri, Bengal, India on 25 May 1898. Charan was indicted on charges of murdering and robbing his former employer, tea-garden manager Hriday Nath Gosh, whom he had robbed previously after being sacked. Despite the fact that fellow prisoners testified that while in jail for that offense he had sworn vengeance on Gosh, the Muslim judge was not prepared to accept the fingerprint evidence—Charan's bloody thumbprint on the cover of a diary—as proof that he had murdered Gosh, but did accept it as proof that he had committed robbery on the same occasion. Accordingly Charan was found guilty only of the lesser charge and sentenced to two years in jail. No charge was ever brought against anyone else for the murder.

The first conviction in a murder trial on the evidence of fingerprints occurred in London, where the Assistant Commissioner of the Metropolitan Police, (Sir) Edward Henry, who had introduced the fingerprinting of criminals in Bengal in 1892, had set up Scotland Yard's Fingerprint Bureau in July 1901. In May 1905 professional burglars Alfred and Albert Stratton, brothers, were found guilty at the Old Bailey of battering to death an elderly couple, Thomas and Ann Farrow, at 34 Deptford High Street, mainly on the evidence of Scotland Yard's Inspector Charles Collins that the thumbprint left on a cash box matched that of Alfred Stratton. Henry Faulds, still bitter at not being lauded as the only begetter of forensic fingerprinting, was on hand as adviser to defense counsel in an unsuccessful attempt to discredit the Yard. Both brothers were hanged.

U.S.: The official use of fingerprints began on 19 December 1902 when one James Johnson, a candidate for the civil service exams, became the first American to have his dabs taken. The background to this innovation was that a scam was being carried on involving the hiring of the highly cerebral by the not-so-clever to take the exams in their name. Particularly scandalous was the case of one Mannix, who revealed that he had taken the exam for no fewer than twelve candidates. Dr. Henry P. DeForest of the New York Civil Service Commission solved the problem by fingerprinting all the applicants, after reading in a newspaper about the work of London's Scotland Yard (probably the case noted above). Johnson, a candidate for fireman, was fingerprinted again by DeForest several decades later to demonstrate that fingerprints do not alter with age.

The use of fingerprints for criminal identification followed on 1 March 1903 when it was adopted by the New York State Bureau of Prisons after security chief Charles K. Baker had obtained a copy of *Classification and Uses of Finger Prints* by Scotland Yard's Edward Henry. Police departments began adopting the technique when John Kenneth Ferrier of Scotland Yard taught it to nine American and Canadian police officers at the St. Louis World's Fair of 1904. He had actually been sent over to guard the Crown Jewels, but he spent most of his time demonstrating Edward Henry's system of fingerprinting, positioning himself next to the New York State Bureau of Prisons exhibit, which did not endear him to those fellow practitioners of the art. Something of a showman, he would leave the hall while one of his audience left a fingerprint on a test surface, then return to identify them. With the police representatives he was more systematic, demonstrating the procedure for taking prints, pattern analysis and classification, file systems, the use of powder to create an image of a print at the scene of the crime, and the technique for matching filed prints with those dusted as evidence. The Henry system would be adopted by police departments all over America, led by the local St. Louis police department.

The first use of **fingerprint evidence** in the United States was effective in securing the conviction of Thomas Jennings of the murder of Clarence B. Hiller at Cook County Criminal Court, Chicago, on 1 February 1911. The five expert witnesses had all been trained by John Ferrier at the St. Louis World's Fair. Jennings was executed on 16 February 1912 following an appeal hearing at which fingerprint evidence had been ruled admissible by the Illinois Supreme Court. While the Jennings case depended on circumstantial evidence supplementary to the presentation of fingerprints, an even more telling demonstration of the system's utility followed soon afterward with the first conviction in an American court on the evidence of fingerprints alone. This was a burglary case brought by the New York Police Department against Carlo Crispi, whose prints were on file because of a similar crime a few years earlier. Although there was a perfect match found with a pane of glass at the scene of the crime, when polled by the judge several jurors indicated that they would not convict on this evidence alone. Judge Rosalsky, determined that such conclusive proof should not be disregarded simply because the technique was so new, next set himself the task of persuading Crispi to confess. This he did by telling him that "it is important to the cause of justice...[and] important to the cause of science to know whether or not the expert testimony is valuable or valueless." Rather remarkably Crispi sacrificed himself to these noble causes and complied. He was convicted on 11 May 1912, the judge rewarding his new-found sense of civic responsibility with the very mild sentence of six months.

The final step to bringing fingerprints to the forefront of police forensics in the United States was the founding of the FBI Fingerprint Section under A. J. Renver by a Congressional Act of 21 June 1924. By the outbreak of WWII it had already overtaken the New York and Buenos Aires police fingerprinting bureaus as the largest in the world.

THE FIRST FIRE ENGINE

was built for the city of Augsburg, Bavaria, by Anthony Blatner, a goldsmith, in 1518. Although few details survive, it appears from the reference in the *Kunstgeschichte der Stadt Augsburg* that it consisted of a large lever-operated squirt mounted on a wheeled carriage.

U.S.: A portable wooden pump was built by ironmaker Joseph Jencks of Lynn, Mass., in 1654 for the town of Boston. It was worked by teams of men raising and lowering the handles and was replenished by a bucket brigade.

Self-propelled fire engine: The first was the Exterminator, completed by Paul Rapsey Hodge at his New York City works on 25 April 1841. The steam-powered vehicle was driven by 9½-inch-diameter horizontal cylinders. Public demonstrations were held in the park adjoining City Hall, after which it was employed on contract by the Pearl Hose Company No. 28 of New York City.

The first self-propelled fire engines powered by a gasoline engine were built in 1898 by Christian Braun's Nürnberger Feuerlöschgeräte of Nuremberg, Germany, and by Cambie et Cie of Lille, France. The latter, a 30-hp four-cylinder machine, introduced two notable innovations: a battery-operated starter and battery-powered floodlights to illuminate the scene of the fire. It was demonstrated at the Heavy Autocar Trials at Versailles, France, in October.

U.S.: The first gasoline-powered fire engine was built by the Waterous Engine Works of St. Paul, Minn., in 1906 and sold to the Radnor Fire Company of Wayne, Pa. Dual engines propelled the vehicle and drove the rear-mounted pump, which was capable of discharging 300 gallons of water per minute.

Motorized fire department: The first metropolitan fire department to use only motor fire engines was Cape Town Fire Brigade, South Africa, which withdrew its last horsedrawn vehicle in 1909.

THE FIRST **FIREFIGHTERS**

as an organized body in the United States were the members of the Union Fire Company, formed in Philadelphia on 7 December 1736 at the instigation of Benjamin Franklin. This was a volunteer fire department comprising thirty members, prominent among them Isaac Paschal, Samuel Powell, William Rawle, and Samuel Syms, who undertook to furnish six leather fire buckets and two stout linen bags at their own expense. The buckets were for dousing the flames with water, the bags for holding possessions recovered from a house on fire to protect them from theft. The members were divided into those who actually fought the fire and those who were detailed to stand guard against looting, an interesting commentary on the morality of the inhabitants of the Quaker City. The fire engine, imported from England, was kept behind a house in Grindstone Alley off Market Street. The social side of volunteer fire companies (of which the phrase "visiting firemen" is a remaining vestige) began with the Union Fire Company, whose members met eight times a year for a convivial supper, with a penalty of one shilling for coming late and four shillings for absence. The price of the supper was three shillings, so it was cheaper to attend.

It has been claimed that the first fire department was founded in New Amsterdam (later New York) when Governor Peter Stuyvesant set up what became known as the "Rattle Watch" in 1659. These good citizens were not, however, firefighters as such, even if they helped to fight fires. Their primary task was to give warning of fires by rotating a wooden rattle, the signal for neighboring households to turn out to man the buckets and ladders that Stuyvesant had imported from Holland. New York was not far behind Philadelphia, however, in setting up a force of volunteer firemen, for in 1737 the General Assembly authorized the recruitment of thirty "strong, able, discreet, honest, and sober men," to fight fires. The oldest active volunteer fire company in the United States is Relief Company No. 1, founded as the Britannia Fire Company at Mount Holly, N.J., in 1752.

Fire department: The first in the United States with paid employees was established by the Cincinnati city council in March 1853. While most of the regular firemen were part-timers at $60 per annum, there were also a number of full-time horsemen and drivers as well as a professional chief engineer and his assistants. The need for a paid fire department had been highlighted by the inefficiency of the volunteer fire companies and their unwillingness to work with steam-driven fire engines. Cincinnati's paid firefighters worked with a 22,000-lb machine built by local mechanical engineers Abel Shawk and Alexander Bonner Latta and capable of discharging no fewer than six 225-foot jets of water at once. Other cities rapidly followed suit in setting up fire departments and acquiring steam fire engines, though some held out for the voluntary companies, notably the forerunners, Philadelphia and New York City. When the city fathers of New York did finally succumb in 1865, it was they who appointed America's first fully professional fire department, employing only full-time firefighters.

THE FIRST **FIVE-DAY WORKWEEK**

was instituted at an unnamed New England cotton spinning mill in 1908, according to Dr. J. J. Rhyne of the University of Oklahoma, in an article published in the *American Economic Review* for September 1930. He explained that the reason for the innovation was that part of the workforce was Jewish; in order to accommodate the religious beliefs of these workers and their Christian counterparts, the proprietor decreed that both Saturdays and Sundays should be holidays. Regrettably Dr. Rhyne omitted to name the factory and its location (nominations are invited). The first workplace with a five-day week that has been identified by name was the Knox Gelatin Co. in Johnstown, N.Y., where Rose M. Knox, widow of the founder, introduced this innovation together with two weeks paid vacation and sick pay—both rare for factory workers at the time—in 1913.

By 1920, according to the Bureau of Labor statistics, there were 32 companies with a five-day week and by 1927 the number had risen to 262. These included the Ford Motor Co. in Dearborn, Mich., where Henry Ford had made the change on 25 September 1926. He was not, as innumerable Web sites state, the progenitor of the five-day working week, though half of the 400,000 American workers enjoying the privilege of a full weekend were employed in his factories. His motive was not only to retain satisfied workers. Ford believed that only with increased leisure would the American people have the time and inclination to spend on nonessentials, including automobiles, and he aimed to set an example to his fellow industrialists. The five-day week became standard in the United States following the implementation of the Labor Standards Act 1938, which legislated for a forty-hour week for the first time. Although this provision applied to only 20 percent of the nation's workforce, and did not prescribe the number of days to be worked, forty hours divided more easily into five working days of eight hours and once the majority of large corporations had made the change, others had to follow if they were to retain key workers. Two years earlier the newly elected Labour government of New Zealand had brought in the world's first statutory five-day workweek as part of a package of measures designed to improve working conditions, but elsewhere half-day Saturday working remained the norm for most workers until after World War II. In West Germany, propelled from devastation to a prosperity unparalleled in Europe by its post-war "economic miracle," the five-day week was not formalized until 1959.

THE FIRST **FLAG**

of what was to become the United States was the Continental Colors, also known as the Flag of the United Colonies and the Grand Union Flag, which was raised for the first time on 3 December 1775 by Lieutenant John Paul Jones aboard the *Alfred*, flagship of the nascent Continental Navy, as she lay in dock at Philadelphia. Made by local milliner Margaret Manny, it bore thirteen alternating red and white stripes to symbolize the unity of the thirteen colonies in rebellion, but with the crosses of Saint George and Saint Andrew (the then Union Jack) in the upper inner quarter seemingly acknowledging some residual respect for the Mother Country. The Grand Union Flag is said to have been raised by order of George Washington at Prospect Hill, Charleston (now

Somerville), outside Boston, on New Year's Day 1776 to mark the birth of the Continental Army, but this is disputed by Peter Ansoff in "The Flag on Prospect Hill" in *Raven: A Journal of Vexillology*. Ansoff believes the evidence points to the flag raised that day having been a standard Union Jack of Great Britain.

Despite its use on the *Alfred*, the Grand Union Flag seems to have been flown chiefly on land. A letter written by John Jay in July 1776 noted that Congress had yet to make any order concerning naval flags and that captains of the armed vessels had "followed their own fancies." Eventually some marine flags were procured, for in May 1777 the Pennsylvania Naval Board made payment "to Elizabeth Ross for fourteen pounds, twelve shillings, and two pence, for making ship's colours." The sum was substantial for a seamstress, being equivalent to some $66 or more than a month's wages for a skilled artisan, but whatever her degree of industry there is no record of Betsy Ross's design, the legend that it was the original Stars and Stripes being a much later invention.

If any one person can be credited with inspiring creation of the Stars and Stripes, it was an American Indian named Thomas Green, who applied to the president of the Continental Congress on 3 June 1777 for an American flag to take to "the chiefs of the nation" and enclosed "three strings of wampum to cover cost." A few days later on 14 June, a set of resolutions published by the Marine Committee included the following: "RESOLVED: that the flag of the United States be made of thirteen stripes, alternate red and white; that the unison be thirteen stars, white in a blue field, representing a new constellation." There is evidence that it was at least partly the work of the New Jersey signatory of the Declaration of Independence Francis Hopkinson, who sent in two invoices to the Continental Congress for a design for the flag of the United States in May and June 1780, the first for a quarter cask of wine, the second for $24. Neither was paid on the grounds that he "had not been the only person consulted" and that in any case he was drawing a public salary; but his involvement was not denied.

Despite the Marine Committee's resolution, there was no standardization of the arrangement of stars, and naval captains seem to have followed their own inclination or that of their suppliers. Nor was the

Stars and Stripes adopted by the Army at the time; indeed it was not until shortly before the Civil War that it became the "national colors" of the U.S. armed forces on land as well as sea. The military standard until then was a blue silk banner embroidered with the eagle and shield of the national arms. (The many representations of the Colors in nineteenth-century paintings of episodes of the Revolutionary War are largely fanciful.) There had, however, been sporadic military use of the Stars and Stripes on land, most notably at the Battle for Fort McHenry in 1814, an event that inspired Francis Scott Key's anthem "The Star-Spangled Banner" and helped to raise what was officially the Marine Flag into the revered patriotic icon it was to become. By the following decade it had come to be recognized generally as the American Flag, an Act of Congress of 4 April 1818 having standardized thirteen stripes for the original colonies and the number of stars determined by the number of States of the Union, as now without distinction for use at sea or for civil purposes ashore.

The "cult of the flag," as it has been labeled by historians, emerged during and following the Civil War, gaining fresh impetus from the patriotic fervor of the Centennial Exhibition at Philadelphia in 1876. This was followed by the holding of the first nationwide, albeit "one-off," Flag Day to celebrate the centenary of the Colors on the 14 June the following year; the distribution of flags to public schools inaugurated by the Grand Army of the Republic veterans' association in 1888; and the introduction of the Pledge of Allegiance (SEE BELOW) in 1892. By 1893, the year of C. H. Weisgerber's immensely popular painting *The Birth of Our National Flag*, hallowing the Betsy Ross myth, the Stars and Stripes had attained the status of a sacred symbol.

The Pledge of Allegiance was first published in the 8 September 1892 issue of *The Youth's Companion* in preparation for patriotic ceremonies the paper was promoting for the celebration by schools of the 400th anniversary of Columbus's discovery of the Americas. The National Columbian Public School Celebration took place throughout the country on 21 October 1892 and thereafter the Pledge became a familiar ritual in the nation's schools, with several states, led by New York in 1898, making it mandatory. The exact phrasing of the Pledge has evolved through the years, with the notable phrase "under God" being added by the attorney Louis A. Bowman in 1954.

State law on desecration of the flag: The first was passed in 1897 by South Dakota, where use of the flag for advertising or party political purposes was restricted. In the second half of the nineteenth century it had been common to print advertising slogans on the flag and as early as 1840 the supporters of William Henry Harrison had his name inscribed on it during the presidential election campaign. By 1907, thirty-one states and territories had enacted laws against desecrating the flag.

Fifty-star U.S. flag: This became official on 4 July 1960 following the admission of Hawaii as a State of the Union. It was raised for the first time at 7:59 A.M. on that day in Auckland, New Zealand. The island nation lies on the other side of the International Date Line from the United States, where it was still 3 July. Some hours later it broke out, for the first time on U.S. soil, over Fort McHenry, Baltimore.

Note on national flags: The Stars and Stripes' forerunner, the Continental Colors of 1776 (SEE ABOVE), was arguably the first national flag of any country, even though several flags later designated as national are older. Possibly the earliest existing flag is that of the principality of Monaco, a red and white bicolor dating from at least 1339 and derived from the arms of the ruling Grimaldi family. It was, however, regarded as a royal standard until adopted as the national flag in 1881. Roughly contemporaneous is Denmark's Danneborg. Originating according to legend in 1219 but first recorded in the reign of King Valdemar IV (1340–75), it was not adopted as the official national flag until 1848. The Netherlands' tricolor (the first such design) was adopted in 1630 as the emblem of the Dutch rebels against Spanish rule, but again was not adopted officially until the nineteenth century. Great Britain's Union Jack, which dates from 1606, was originally a naval flag for royal ships and there is little evidence of its use as a national emblem rather than a royal one before the Act of Union in 1801.

For the first occasion the Stars and Stripes was raised in victory overseas SEE **war—foreign war**.

THE FIRST FLAG FLOWN AT HALF-MAST

(recorded) was on board the *Heartsease* on 22 July 1612, as a mark of respect to Capt. James Hall, leader of an English expedition in quest of the North-West Passage. He had been killed by Eskimos on the west coast of Greenland apparently in an act of revenge for some wrong he had committed, since they did not attempt to attack anyone else. The log of the *Patience*, her sister ship, reported: "When the *Heartsease* joined the *Patience* her flag was hanging down and her ensign was over the poop which signified the death of someone on board."

THE FIRST FLASHLIGHT

was the Ever Ready tubular electric device manufactured under a patent of 10 January 1899 by the American Electrical Novelty and Manufacturing Co. of New York. This enterprise had been founded by Russian immigrant Akiba Horowitz, who changed his name to Conrad Hubert when he began operating a novelty shop on Center Street, New York City. Among the notions he stocked was an "electric flowerpot" invented by one Joshua Lionel Cowen, consisting of a flowerpot containing a battery that lit up an artificial flower. It did not sell particularly well, but Hubert bought the rights in 1896 and, with the help of a scientifically minded assistant, David Misell, converted the useless fake flowerpot into the useful flashlight, which they promoted by giving free samples to the police and using their testimonials in advertisements. The descriptive name *flash light* (originally spelled in two words) was derived from the fact that batteries were insufficiently powerful for sustained lighting, though it was claimed that a single battery would last for 6,000 to 8,000 flashes. As for Joshua Cowen, he went on to greater things than electric flowerpots when he invented the first successful electric train set and founded Lionel Model Trains.

THE FIRST FLUORESCENT LIGHTING

(hot-cathode) was developed by the General Electric Co. at Nela Park in East Cleveland, Ohio, and was first shown publicly at the annual convention of the Illuminating Engineering Society in Cincinnati in September 1935. The tube, 2 feet long, emitted a brilliant green light and was labeled: "The fluorescent lumiline lamp—a laboratory experiment of great promise."

The first practical application of fluorescent lighting was made at a dinner held in Washington, D.C., on 23 November 1936 to celebrate the centenary of the U.S. Patent Office. The banqueting hall was illuminated by GEC fluorescent lamps.

Commercial production of fluorescent lamps was inaugurated by GE and Westinghouse, both companies launching their product on 1 April 1938. The GE lamps came in three sizes—15W, 20W, and 30W—and in lengths of 18, 24 and 36 inches, respectively. The price range was $1.50 to $2.00 and the lamps were available in seven different colors.

THE FIRST FOOTBALL

game of which there is pictorial evidence in America is an 1806 drawing of the yard at Yale University in which a group of students in tail-coats and beaver hats are having a punt-about under the stern and watchful eye of formidable college president Timothy Dwight. Football had, however, been played at Yale in the 1760s. A form of football called "ballown" was recorded at Princeton University in 1820. These rudimentary games preceded the introduction of rugby and soccer in England and, like the English forerunner, probably consisted of a limitless number of players seeking to penetrate the opposite goal without the encumbrance of formal rules, nor restraints on hacking, biting, kicking of shins, and fisticuffs.

Gridiron evolved from rugby football, the handling game that developed from 1841 at Rugby School in England. It cannot be assigned a precise date of birth. Harvard University adopted a predominately kicking game in which handling was permitted, known as "the Boston Game," in 1871, at a time when the other East Coast colleges were beginning to play an Americanized version of soccer. Harvard having played Montreal's McGill University, a rugby playing college, under "Boston Game" rules on 14 May 1874, a return match was played the next day under rugby rules, which the American players then decided to adopt. This decision marked the introduction of the **oval ball** into American football. When the American Intercollegiate Football Association was established in 1876, the rules agreed were essentially those of rugby with some elements of soccer. The first move toward the modern American game followed in 1880 when the number of players on a team was reduced from 15 to 11 and the rugby "scrum" was abandoned in favor of a prototype scrimmage line. Another significant change was made two years later with the rule on "downs" and "yards," viz: "If, on 3 consecutive downs, a team has not advanced ball 5 yards, or lost 10 yards, it must give up ball to other side at the spot where the final down is made." By this time the gridiron had emerged. Sometime at the end of the 1870s the field had been marked off with white lines every five yards by Walter Chauncey Camp, a star halfback of the Yale team from 1876 to 82 (a medical student at Yale after graduation, hence the seven-year run), and this was adopted as a rule by all the handling-game schools in 1882. For this and further innovations Camp earned the title of "Father of American Football"; he also wrote every set of rules until 1925.

At this point American football had almost parted company with its progenitor rugby. The final break came in 1906 when the National Collegiate Athletic Association, set up to revise the rules and eliminate the thuggery that characterized the early game, authorized the **forward pass**. This was fundamental to the game as played today and the historic occasion of its first application occurred in a game between St. Louis University and Carroll College [now Carroll University] at Waukesha, Wis., on 2 October 1906. (The honor is usually claimed for the Wesleyan–Yale game of the same date, but the Midwesterners had kicked off 2 hours earlier.)

Pro football: "Pudge" Heffelfinger of Yale was reputedly paid $500 in 1892 to play for the Allegheny Athletic Association against Pittsburgh Athletic Club. Thus he was able to earn the annual salary of a stenographer in an hour and a half of strenuous but well-rewarded effort. The first game in which a whole team was remunerated was played at Latrobe, Pa., on 31 August 1895, when the local YMCA beat nearby Jeannette 12 to 0, the Latrobe players sharing the gate money among them. The winning team had also paid guest quarterback John Brallier of Indiana Normal and the University of West Virginia an appearance fee of $10 plus expenses.

Pro football, bitterly resented by college coaches, made slow progress in the early years of the twentieth century and it was not until 1920 that the first **transfer fee** is recorded, Columbus paying Akron $300 for Bob Nash. The same year saw the founding of the first **national league**, the American Professional Football Conference (Canton, Ohio, 20 August), which changed its name to the National Football League in 1922.

Football helmets were originally made of leather, as eulogized in George Clooney's film evocation of 1920s football, *Leatherheads* (2008). The earliest known is claimed to be a beehive-shaped helmet worn by the U.S. Naval Academy's Joe Reeves in the 1893 Army–Navy game after doctors warned him that further kicks to his head would render him insane. The modern fiberglass helmet was developed by former math teacher John Riddell Sr., football coach at Evanston High School in Evanston, Ill., and his son John Jr., both of Wheaton, Ill., who filed their patent in 1940.

THE FIRST **FOREIGN-AID PROGRAM**

of the United States was appropriated by Congress in June 1934 to enable the governments of Panama, Honduras, and Guatemala to build three large bridges for the proposed Inter-American Highway to Panama. The U.S. Bureau of Public Roads provided plans and engineering supervision as well as steel and cement and some of the heavy equipment, while the recipient countries supplied labor and local materials. The initial phase of the work, to 1938, cost the U.S. government $680,000, with $710,000 being spent by the recipients. The Pan-American Highway to Panama was not finally completed until April 1963.

The first general-purpose aid program funded by the U.S. was the Marshall Plan, instituted under the Economic Cooperation Act of 2 April 1948 as an emergency measure to stabilize the ravaged economies of war-torn Europe. In the words of its founder, former Army Chief of Staff George C. Marshall, it was designed to fight "hunger, poverty, desperation, and chaos." During the four years of the plan $13 billion was disbursed in aid. The expenditure revitalized Europe and restored economic stability to the western world.

THE FIRST **FROZEN FOOD**

packaged product to go on sale was haddock, retailed in 1-pound packs as Fresh Ice Fillets in Toronto by the Biological Board of Canada in January 1929—an unusual example of a government department going into the food processing business. The technique for freezing the fish was developed by Dr. Archibald Huntsman of the Fisheries Experimental Station in Halifax, Nova Scotia, who had begun work on the project in 1926. The fresh fillets were frozen quickly between metal plates bathed with refrigerated brine, but the brine was never allowed in contact with the fish. Initially 600 pounds of Ice Fillets were shipped to Toronto each week, but this proved insufficient and the order was increased to 1,000 pounds. Even this failed to satisfy demand, despite the fact that the frozen product was about 50 percent more expensive than unfrozen. The premium was judged worthwhile by discerning housewives because the frozen fish tasted much fresher. Other varieties of fish were added to the range, including cod, halibut, russet flounder, gray flounder, mackerel, swordfish, and cusk, and shipments were extended to Halifax, Ottawa, Montreal, Winnipeg, Calgary, and Prince Edward Island. Once the experiment was shown to be a success, the Biological Board began licensing food processors to undertake production on their own account, the first two, in the spring of 1929, being Lunenburg Sea Products and the Lockeport Co.

This pioneering Canadian venture was confined to fish. The man usually credited with founding the frozen-food industry, Clarence Birdseye, was not the first in the field, but it was he who brought a wide range of pre-packaged frozen goods to the domestic ice box and thereby created a culinary revolution. Birdseye had become interested in the possibility of preserving perishable foods by deep freezing while engaged in a U.S. government survey of fish and wildlife in Labrador between 1912 and 1915. "The first winter," he wrote, "I saw natives catching fish in fifty below zero weather, which froze stiff as soon as they were taken out of the water. Months later, when they were thawed out, some of these fish were still alive." While in Labrador Birdseye learned to preserve fresh vegetables by putting them in a tub of water and freezing them solid. In 1924 he established a company at Gloucester, Mass., called General Seafoods Corp., to develop the process commercially; he sold out to the Postum Co. five years later for $22 million. It was agreed that Birdseye's name, split into two words, should be used for brand identification.

The initial range of twenty-seven Birds Eye products were test marketed at 18 grocery stores in Springfield, Mass., starting 6 March 1930 and included peas, spinach, raspberries, loganberries, cherries, fish, and various meats. Sales resistance was high at first, partly because the packets were kept in ice-cream cabinets and were not easily visible, but also because of the relatively high price. One pioneer retailer recalled in later years that "it took about five minutes to fast-talk a reluctant housewife into buying a package of peas at 35¢." By 1933, however, there were 516 frozen-food retail outlets in the United States.

Prepacked frozen meals: The first were chicken fricassee and criss-cross steak, introduced by Birds Eye in 1939. The first complete meals were not, as generally supposed, Swanson's TV Dinners, which only came to market in 1953, but the Strato-Meals developed by W. L. Maxson of Maxson's Food Systems, Long Island City, N.Y., some eight years earlier. Originally these were sold to the U.S. military for use on transport aircraft, but on 20 September 1946 a range of ten different meals served in a three-compartment paperboard platter went on sale at New Jersey's largest department store, L. Bamberger's of Newark. The initial retail Strato-Meals ranged in price from 98¢ for beef goulash with simmered gravy, garden peas, butter sauce, and a potato patty to $1.98 for chicken paprika with French beans and potato patty. These were concocted at a kitchen in Queen's Village presided over by a Swedish chef formerly in the employ of Queen Marie of Romania.

G

on record, purpose-built to house automobiles, appeared in the United States and the United Kingdom about the same time, either in late 1898 or 1899, and both were designed for doctors. The British example was erected for Dr. W. W. Barrett of 29 Park Crescent, Hesketh Park, Southport, in Lancashire. It was joined to his house by a passage for easy access and was equipped with engine-pits and facilities for cleaning his two cars, an 1898 Daimler and an 1898 Knightley Victoria. Dr. Barrett was also distinguished as the first man in England to own a totally enclosed car, and as the inventor of the first practical jack for lifting cars. The garage still exists, now converted into an apartment but preserving much of its exterior.

In the United States a Dr. Zabriskie of 2103 Church Avenue, Brooklyn, N.Y., built a brick garage measuring 18' x 22' for a cost of $1,500. He had purchased his Winton Road-Wagon in September 1898, but it is not known whether his garage was completed before or after Dr. Barrett's.

Contemporary with the two doctors' garages, and possibly earlier, were the "motor stables" built by Sir David Salomons at his house Broomhill in Tunbridge Wells, Kent, England. Sir David, son of the first Jewish Lord Mayor of London, was the third person in Britain to own an automobile, a Peugeot 9 imported from France in 1895. He subsequently bought two De Dion-Bouton motor tricycles and the pair of buff brick garages he built were designed to house the three vehicles.

By December 1899, commercially built wooden garages were being supplied to customers' requirements by F. Jackson & Co. of the Soho Bazaar in London's Oxford Street. Builders, too, were not slow to appreciate that the provision of a garage could enhance the value of a property. The *Autocar* of December 1901 reported that in the select North London suburb of Hampstead "a number of new houses have recently been erected, the appointments of which include a motor stable."

Like traditional stables, these were separate from the dwelling. The first American house to have a garage incorporated in its structure was built in New York in 1906 by architect Ernest Hagg for his own occupancy. Another pioneer of the integrated garage was Frank Lloyd Wright with the dwelling he designed for Frederick C. Robie at 5757 South Woodlawn Avenue in Hyde Park, Ill., in 1908.

The French word *garage* did not find immediate acceptance. Reporting in October 1901, the *Morning Leader* (London) stated that the following terms were in current use by car owners: *motor shed, motable, motor den, motor barn, motorium.* The paper itself favored *the motory.* Correspondents to the *Autocar* suggested *carhome, carrepose, carrest, cardomain, cardom, motories, motostore,* and—the nearest anyone came to the word that was soon to supersede all others—*carage.* Even after *garage* had passed into general currency, it was not until 1925 that the august French Academy was prepared to accept it as a recognized word in the French language.

Perhaps the two most important innovations of twentieth-century garage technology were made by the same man, C. G. Johnson of Detroit. In 1921 he invented the **overhead lifting garage door** and founded the Overhead Door Co. (extant) to manufacture it. Five years later he developed the push-button **electric garage door opener**, produced at Overhead Door's plant in Hartford City, Ind. The first **garage door remote control**, introduced in Britain by G. Brady & Co. of Manchester and in North America by the Montreal-based Brady Shutter Co. of Canada, was being advertised as an optional extra to their roller-shutter doors by 1936. This was a key device, enabling drivers to raise the doors from a pillar without leaving their cars. The in-car push-button remote was pioneered by Genie in 1954.

THE FIRST **GARBAGE BAGS, PLASTIC**

are one of Canada's more notable contributions to western civilization (along with egg cartons and paint rollers), though who made the first one is disputed between Alberta and Ontario. Harry Wasylyk of Winnipeg was a manufacturer of polyethylene packaging for fruit and vegetables and of polyethylene surgical gloves for Winnipeg General Hospital. It was the hospital management who told him in 1950 that they had a problem in disposing of surgical waste, which was simply tipped into garbage cans and could thus cause a health hazard. Wasylyk's solution was a polyethylene garbage bag that could be tied or sealed at the top to forestall contamination. The other contender for "father of the garbage bag" is Larry Hanson of chemical giant Union Carbide, who claimed to have made polyethylene garbage bags for use in the company's plant in Lindsay, Ont., and also for his own use at home. As no date is attributed, it is unclear whether he preceded Wasylyk. However, when Union Carbide bought Wasylyk's business, it was the garbage bags being produced for Winnipeg General and a few industrial plants that attracted most notice. Union Carbide's John Morley had been given the task of finding a use for 11 million tons of polyethylene resin stockpiled at their plant in Montreal. The biggest barrier to promotion of the product for domestic garbage, however, was the fact that most Canadian municipalities banned the use of any kind of container other than the approved garbage can. Eventually in the 1960s he prevailed on the municipality of Etobicoke, which comprises much of western Toronto, to give the bags a trial and helped to ensure its success by personally walking the route before the garbage trucks arrived and using sticky tape to repair any bags with holes caused by pets or rodents. The trial having been declared a success, Union Carbide launched Glad Garbage Bags as a domestic product.

THE FIRST **GAS COOKER**

commercially practicable, was designed by James Sharp, assistant manager of the Northampton Gas Co., and installed in the kitchen of his home in Northampton, England, in 1826. The first commercially produced models were acquired by the Bath Hotel, Leamington, and the Angel Inn, Northampton, in 1834. At the former a special dinner was cooked for a hundred people by gas alone. "Everything was excellently done," said a contemporary report, "and notwithstanding that fish, pudding, fowl, bacon, greens had been steamed in the same steamer, no dish had contracted any unpleasant taste from its neighbor." Despite this success, Sharp was chary about undertaking full-scale manufacture. One day, however, a magnificent four-horse carriage with liveried outriders drew up before his modest house and Earl Spencer (ancestor of Princess Diana) descended to demand a gas-cooked lunch. This mark of approval convinced Sharp that a demand waited to be satisfied. In 1836 he opened a factory in Northampton, employing thirty-five hands, and so established Britain's gas-appliance industry. In the meantime manufacture had already begun in France, where the Merle company began producing a cooker with three compartments for roasting, baking, and heating in 1835.

U.S.: The first gas cooker was Morill's Evaporator Cooking Stove, manufactured in Boston in 1858. Gas was slow to catch on in American kitchens because municipal gas suppliers offered a low-temperature flame suitable for lighting but not for cooking. Maintaining heat at an even temperature was also a problem until the American Store Company of St. Louis, Mo., launched the first gas stoves with thermostat controls in 1915. All early gas stoves were black; the white enamel stove was introduced by Hotpoint in 1923.

THE FIRST **GASOLINE**

was refined from petroleum naphtha by lubricating engineer Joshua Merrill at the Downer Kerosene Oil Co.'s plant in Boston in 1863 and was supplied commercially to the largest manufacturer of air-gas machines. These were lighting installations that produced illuminating gas for large buildings, such as colleges, factories, or country mansions, remote from a centralized gas supplier (which used coal-oil). They had formerly been operated with benzole or naphtha, but gasoline had less tendency to condense and therefore produced a greater illuminating power. Merrill and Samuel Downer began production of gasoline in Corry, Pa., the same year, whence the first shipments were made to the lucrative New York market in 25- and 40-gallon beer barrels. It sold for 30 to 35¢ a gallon. This new branch of the oil industry received a significant boost in 1867 when insurance underwriters sanctioned air-gas machines as a viable risk and by 1872 there were 101 manufacturers, most of them producing machines that consumed gasoline.

In 1899, the first year that automobile production achieved sufficient volume to be included in the *U.S. Census of Manufactures*, the number of barrels of gasoline sold in the United States was 6.2 million. An infinitesimal proportion of this total went toward keeping horseless carriages chugging through the mud of the appalling unmade roads of the day. While the use of gasoline for illumination had declined, new markets had opened for petroleum-based solvents in chemical plants and dry cleaners, with a lesser amount for oil burning stoves and heaters. It was not until 1915–16 that gasoline consumption by automobiles overtook other uses, by which time there were more than 18,000 service stations (qv) dispensing gas.

The first **gasoline tax** was introduced by Oregon on 25 February 1919 at the rate of 1¢ per gallon. By 1932 all states had a fuel tax, ranging from 2¢ to 7¢ per gallon. A federal tax of 1¢ a gallon was imposed the same year, effective 21 June, as a boost to declining highway funds.

The first oil company to sell its product to the public by **octane rating** was Sun Oil Co. in 1931. The rating of Sunoco gasoline was 72 octane, compared with an industry average of 59.2 for regular and 74 for premium.

THE FIRST **GAY MARRIAGE**

was preceded by civil unions, which gave same-sex couples most but not all the rights and privileges of matrimony and required a formal process for termination equivalent to divorce. The first country to legalize such partnerships was Denmark, with effect from 1 October 1989. On that day 11 male couples were joined in union at Copenhagen Town Hall by Mayor Tom Ahlberg. First of the ceremonies was between a Lutheran pastor, the Rev. Ivan Larsen, and child psychologist Ove Carlsen, the father of two children. Afterward, each referred to the other as "my husband" and they explained that they took turns doing the cooking and housework at the rectory in alternating weeks. The only significant difference between Denmark's "registered partnerships" and conventional marriages was that they did not confer rights to adoption or artificial insemination.

U.S.: The first civil unions were legalized in the state of Vermont with effect from 1 July 2000 and gave same-sex couples entering into such unions a greater approximation to marital rights than in most of those countries that had already made enactments, namely Denmark, Norway, Iceland, Sweden, and the Netherlands. First to be joined together in this way were college dean Carolyn Conrad (age twenty-nine) and Kathleen Peterson (age forty-one), employed at a ski resort. At the stroke of midnight on 1 July, Brattleboro town clerk Annette Cappy signed their license and there followed a 10-minute ceremony next to a public fountain presided over by Justice of the Peace T. Hunter Wilson, who declared "By the powers vested in me by the State of Vermont I join you in civil union."

Gay marriage law: The first giving same-sex spouses the same rights and privileges as heterosexuals was enacted in the Netherlands and took effect on 1 April 2001. At midnight Amsterdam's mayor Job Cohen, who had become a registrar in order to perform the first such marriages, presided over a group wedding in which he joined three male couples and a female couple in matrimony. One of the couples had been partners for thirty-six years. The presence of only seven protesters testified to the acceptance by the Dutch people, of whom 75 percent, per poll results, were in favor of the measure.

U.S.: The first state to legalize gay marriage was Massachusetts, though 4,037 marriages of same-sex couples had been licensed by San Francisco's City Hall starting 12 February 2004. The following month these were declared invalid by California's Supreme Court. In Massachusetts the first applications for licenses were issued at Cambridge on the stroke of midnight on Monday 17 May 2004. Tanya McClosky (age fifty-two) and Marcia Kadish (age fifty-six) of Malden, partners for eighteen years, obtained a waiver from the usual three-day waiting period and returned to City Hall in the morning to obtain their license and exchange vows. At 9:15 A.M. Cambridge City Clerk Margaret Doury told the couple, "I now pronounce you married under the laws of the Commonwealth of Massachusetts." The United States thus became the fourth country in which gay couples were able to form full marriage partnerships, after the Netherlands, Belgium (January 2003), and Canada (Ontario, June 2003). Since then Spain (October 2004), Canada (by federal law July 2005), South Africa (2006), Norway (2008), and Sweden (2009) have enacted same-sex marriage laws. In the United States, following Massachusetts' lead in 2004, California legalized same-sex marriage in June 2008, but this was nullified by Proposition 8 in the November election (the marriages performed are still recognized). Connecticut introduced same-sex marriage in 2008; and Iowa, Maine, and Vermont followed suit in 2009.

Canada pioneered with the first officially sanctioned public rite uniting same-sex couples of any mainstream church, inaugurated at St. Margaret's Cedar Cottage, Vancouver, British Columbia, on the authority of the Rt. Rev. Michael Ingham, Anglican Bishop of New Westminster, on 28 May 2003. The couple receiving the new rite of blessing, Michael Kalmuk and Kelly Montfort, had been together for twenty years. The Archbishop of Canterbury, head of the worldwide Anglican Communion, expressed his "sadness" at Bishop Ingham's decision. The first **mainstream church to sanction same-sex church marriages** was the Lutheran Church of Sweden with effect from 1 November 2009.

THE FIRST **GIRL SCOUT**

troops began informally during the eighteen months following the publication of Sir Robert Baden-Powell's *Scouting for Boys* (SEE **boy scout movement**) in Britain in January 1908. The earliest on record was the Cuckoo Patrol of Girl Scouts, which was founded by Glasgow schoolgirl Allison Cargill during the summer of that year. At first the patrol was unsupervised except by Miss Cargill herself, who as instigator of the project was elected patrol leader; but in the autumn of 1909 it was taken under the wing of the 1st Glasgow Troop of Boy Scouts (SEE **boy scout movement**), and William B. Heddow was appointed Scoutmaster. The girls were allowed to wear the Scout belt and badges, as well as the khaki neckerchief of the 1st Glasgow Troop, and were often invited to accompany the Scouts on Saturday afternoon expeditions to Acre Wood at Maryhill, where they joined in the tracking games, fire-lighting exercises, and other activities.

The idea of a female branch of the Scout movement first received official recognition with the publication of "A Scheme for Girl Guides" in *Scout Headquarters Gazette* for November 1909. This had been prompted by the appearance of three members of the 1st Pinkney's Green Girl Scouts at the Crystal Palace Scout Rally in September of the same year, when Baden-Powell was reluctantly forced to take notice of their existence. Originally he had had no intention of extending the movement to include girls, lest it should be subjected to ridicule. By this time, however, there were already more than six thousand female "Boy Scouts" registered in the United Kingdom (most of them having concealed their gender by giving initials instead of Christian names) and there was little choice, short of mass expulsion, but to form them into a separate section with a program of activities suitable to the Edwardian young lady of genteel upbringing. This plan met with some resistance from the girls, who did not want to be relegated to the somewhat domestic role allotted them by Baden-Powell—in his own words "to give them the ability to be better mothers and Guides to the next generation." They were nevertheless obliged to submit to the direction of a committee of ladies formed early in 1910 under the leadership of the founder's sister, Agnes Baden-Powell. The adventurous masculine pursuits described in *Scouting for Boys* had to be abandoned in favor of learning to bandage patients and to make tea (a novel skill to many girls accustomed to servants). At first camping under canvas was vetoed as indecorous, but this prohibition was later relaxed as patrol captains were often in favor of allowing their girls an opportunity to fend for themselves in the open.

U.S.: The first patrol, the White Rose, was organized on 12 March 1912 in Savannah, Ga., by Juliette Gordon Low, who had met Sir Robert Baden-Powell in Britain the previous year and been inspired to transplant his ideas to the United States. Earlier that day she had telephoned a cousin and declared, "I've got something for the girls of Savannah, and all of America, and all the world, and we're going to start it tonight!" The first registered Girl Guide, as members were then designated, was Low's niece Daisy Gordon, though she was not present at the inaugural meeting. The leader of the eight-strong White Rose patrol was Page Wilder Anderson; there was soon a second patrol, Carnation. The original uniform consisted of a dark blue blouse, skirt, and bloomers accompanied by a sky-blue neckerchief. This was kept knotted until the daily good deed had been performed.

The girls met once a week for supper, games, and activities in the stable house of Mrs. Low's property on Lafayette Square. Activities included first aid, homemaking, nature craft, and cooking (mainly making fudge). Mrs. Low was fond of repeating "This will be for all girls in America." Proficiency badges were introduced in 1913, the first to be so honored being Elizabeth Purse.

Whereas in Britain members were originally called Girl Scouts and then became Girl Guides (1910), in America they began as Girl Guides and became Girl Scouts in 1913. The national organization, Girl Scouts of the USA, was established two years later. It would become the largest organization for girls in the world.

Girl Scout cookies had their origin during Girl Scout Week in Philadelphia in 1933. The girls were demonstrating cooking skills in the windowed kitchen of the Philadelphia Gas & Electric Co. and as the mounds of cookies grew, people started entering to inquire if they were for sale. They hadn't been, but they were now. The following year the Philadelphia Girl Scouts started selling cookies packaged in boxes in the shape of their trefoil insignia. The idea soon spread elsewhere and in 1936 the national organization began licensing the name Girl Scout Cookies to bakery companies.

THE FIRST GLIDER

(full-size man-carrying) was designed by English scientist and landowner Sir George Cayley of Brompton Hall, Brompton, Yorkshire, and described in the *Mechanics Magazine* for 15 September 1852. The aircraft was a monoplane with a kite-shaped wing and an adjustable tail-plane and fin. The total wing area is estimated to have been 500 square feet and the weight of the machine 300 pounds. The pilot was carried in a boat-shaped nacelle with tricycle undercarriage; by means of a tiller control, he could operate a second smaller tail-unit that served as both rudder and elevator.

Practical experiments with this glider are believed to have commenced the following year, when Sir George Cayley's coachman was persuaded to make the first true airplane flight in history by piloting the machine across a small valley at Brompton Hall. Mrs. George Thompson, Cayley's granddaughter, a child of ten in 1853, was able to recall the epoch-making event in an eyewitness account written nearly seventy years later: "Everyone was out on the high east side and I saw the start from close to. The coachman went in the machine and landed on the west side at about the same level. The coachman got himself clear, and when the watchers had got across, he shouted, 'Please, Sir George, I wish to give notice, I was hired to drive, not to fly.'" In a letter to J. E. Hodgson dated 2 November 1921, Mrs. Thompson said that she thought the distance covered was about 500 yards and that the coachman "came down with a smash." Although the name of the world's first airplane pilot is not known for certain, research among Sir George Cayley's household papers by *Guinness World Records* founder Norris McWhirter has revealed that he was probably one John Appelby.

U.S.: The first glider flight, which was also the first controlled airplane flight made anywhere in the world, was achieved by John Montgomery, who flew a distance of 200 yards at about 18 mph at Otay Mesa in San Diego, Calif., on 28 August 1883. This was an isolated achievement and he did not succeed in maintaining control in flight on any subsequent occasion. The glider crashed the same year, terminating experiments.

The first **series of controlled flights** was made by Otto Lilienthal in a 44-pound hang-glider of his own design with wing area of 150 square feet. In 1892 a canal was being cut through Grosskreuz, a suburb of Berlin, and the excavated earth was deposited on a level open space in the form of a conical hill. In the summer of the same year Lilienthal began using this mound for a series of more than two thousand jump-off flights, controlling the glider by shifting his body to alter the center of gravity. He was killed on 10 August 1896 after losing control of the aircraft at a height of 25 feet. According to an article by the Wright brothers in the September 1908 issue of the *Century Magazine*, it was the reports of Lilienthal's death that first inspired their interest in flight.

Soaring flight: The first was made on 27 June 1909 in a Weis glider piloted by British schoolboy Gordon England, who attained a lift of nearly 40 feet over a distance of just under a mile at Amberley Mount, near Arundel, Sussex.

The creation of the modern glider—separating the designer of the glider from that of the airplane—is generally credited to Frederick Harth, who built his first machine at Hildenstein, Germany, in 1914. It was designed specifically to obtain lift and not merely to sustain flight. Two years later, Harth succeeded in remaining in the air for 3½ minutes without losing height during a flight in the Rhön Mountains.

Gliding as a sport began with the efforts of some enthusiastic German students who formed the first gliding club in 1909 after a visit to the International Aeronautic Exhibition in Frankfurt. Under the leadership of Hans Gutermuth, the members of the Darmstadt High School Flying Sport Club built their own biplane and monoplane gliders, basing them initially on the designs of Otto Lilienthal. Their first flights were made from an elevation on the Darmstadt Parade Ground known as Chimborazo. During the summer vacation of 1911 and 1912 the students held a camp on the Wasserkuppe in the Rhön Mountains and built about thirty new gliders, in one of which Hans Gutermuth made a 1,000-yard flight of 1 minute and 52 seconds' duration. Five of the ten club members who took part in the Wasserkuppe trials in 1911–12 were killed in action as air force pilots in World War I.

U.S.: The first American to fly gliders for pleasure was William Hawley Bowlus, a fifteen-year-old schoolboy from the San Fernando Valley in California, who built his first sailplane (a word that he coined) in 1911 after visiting the previous year's Los Angeles Air Meet. Bowlus later worked for the first overland passenger airline in the United States, Ryan Airlines (SEE **airline**) and was the production manager in charge of building Charles Lindbergh's *Spirit of St. Louis*. In 1928 he built his sixteenth glider since 1911, the superb high-performance Bowlus SP-1 *Albatross*, and it was in this and subsequent models that he became America's pre-eminent sporting glider pilot, establishing a series of new altitude, duration, and distance records. He also trained nine of the first ten licensed glider pilots in the United States, including Charles Lindbergh and his wife Anne (SEE BELOW). His other achievements included the first all-metal travel trailer, which became the Airstream, and building the prototype of the Lear jet.

Gliding meet: The first was the Intercollegiate Gliding Meet hosted by Harvard University on the college's Squantum Field in Quincy, Mass., on Memorial Day weekend, 28–30 May 1911. There were two classes: "body-control" gliders (i.e., hang-gliders) and "mechanical-control" (i.e., sailplanes), the former being won by MIT, who also contributed the most aircraft and made the most flights, and the latter by Tufts. Cornell won the prize for the best-designed glider. Launching was facilitated by an ingenious swiveling ramp, devised by the Harvard organizers, which could be turned into the wind for takeoff.

The college boys participating in this one-off event were mainly engineering students interested in the infant science of aeronautics but unable to contemplate the expense of powered aircraft. The continuous development of gliding as a sport is usually dated from the celebrated meet held on the Wasserkuppe in Germany in August 1920, the first such annual event. Having been prohibited from using powered civil aircraft in a private capacity under the Treaty of Versailles, the Germans concentrated their attention on gliders and established a commanding lead in the sport that they maintained throughout the inter-war years. In the United States there was little post-war activity until 1928, when J. C. Penney Jr. founded the

American Motorless Aviation Corporation to manufacture sailplanes and invited German glider pilots to set up the first gliding school in the United States at Cape Cod. The first gliding club, the Evans Gliding Club, was founded the same year by Bob Evans of Detroit, and it later became today's Soaring Society of America.

Woman to pilot a glider: The first was Geneve Shaffer, chief rigger of her brother Cleve's Shaffer Aero Manufacturing Co. of San Francisco. She made her first solo flight on 1 August 1909 in Cleve's glider. Such was the public interest in this intrepid bird-woman that Cleve painted two signs with 4-inch-high letters: SHE WILL FLY TODAY and SHE WILL NOT FLY TODAY.

The first woman to qualify as a glider pilot in the United States was Anne Morrow Lindbergh, who won a first-class license on 29 January 1930 after a 6-minute solo flight in a Bowlus sailplane over the Soledad Mountains, San Diego, Calif. Hers was the tenth license issued in the United States. Her husband Charles's had been the ninth.

Paraglider: The first was the Sail Wing designed by NASA engineer David Barish, who made his maiden flight at Bel Air in the Catskill Mountains of New York State in September 1965, with subsequent flights from the slopes of nearby Mount Hunter. Conceived as a recovery vehicle for space capsules, the paraglider was adopted by ski enthusiast Barish as a mean's of "slope soaring" from the piste. Sponsored by *Ski* magazine, he made a tour of American ski resorts during the summer of 1966 promoting the idea of a new out-of-season sport for the slopes. It was an idea before its time, he later admitted, because the resorts were deserted. The continuous development of paragliding as a sport dates from 1978, when it was resurrected in the French Alps. France still has the largest number of paragliders in the world, about five times the number in the United States.

Hang-glider: The first for leisure use was developed in the United States by Australian engineer Bill Moyes while working for NASA. Its maiden flight was on 4 July 1969, when Moyes's fellow Australian Bill Bennett took off on water skis at Staten Island, New York, and flew over the Statue of Liberty in New York Harbor.

THE FIRST GO-KART

was built in a small garage on Echo Park Road, Los Angeles, in August 1956 by Art Ingels, a mechanic at Frank Kurtis's racing car workshops Kurtis Craft, and his friend Lou Borelli. It was powered by a 2½-hp West Bend 750 motor-mower engine, one of eight thousand that had been purchased by the McCulloch Co. for an unsuccessful lawn mower. The kart was test run on Baxter Street, but after failing to carry Art Ingels's 210-pound body weight up a steep hill, was taken back to the workshop for engine modifications. With a much-increased performance, not only in hill climbing but also on the level, the kart attracted the attention of potential buyers, and in October Ingels and Borelli started producing a batch of six to be ready for the Christmas season. This informal partnership was later to develop into a full-scale manufacturing concern under the name of Caretta. The original prototype was taken to Britain after it had been acquired by Alan Burgess, founder of the world's first kart magazine *Karting*.

The first go-karts in regular commercial production were manufactured by the Go Kart Manufacturing Co. of Azusa, Calif., in the spring of 1957. Marketed as kits retailing at $120, the initial series of one hundred were sold inside three weeks and a further one thousand were embarked upon forthwith. The name Go Kart was one of twenty submitted to the proprietors by Lynn Wineland, art director of *Road and Custom*, a magazine that helped to launch karting as a sport.

Kart races: The first were held informally in the parking lot of the Pasadena Rose Bowl in Pasadena, Calif., in March 1957. Organized kart racing under rules began at the Eastland Shopping Center at West Covina in December of the same year. The first purpose-built kart racetrack was opened by the Go Kart Manufacturing Co. at Azusa in December 1958.

THE FIRST GOLD RECORD

awarded to a recording artist in recognition of a million sales was Glenn Miller's "Chattanooga Choo Choo," a novelty song originally heard in the 1941 film

Sun Valley Serenade and recorded by RCA Victor the same year. Sales having reached seven figures within a few months, RCA had a master disk sprayed with gold and presented to Glenn Miller during a Chesterfield broadcast on 10 February 1942.

It cannot be established with certainty which was the first recording to sell a million copies, since audited sales figures are a relatively recent innovation. The performance most often cited in this respect is Enrico Caruso's rendering of the aria "Vesti la Giubba" ("On with the Motley"), from *Pagliacci*, which he originally recorded for the Gramophone Co. of London on 12 November 1902 and remade for Victor with orchestral accompaniment in 1907. The latter version achieved cumulative sales of more than a million during the next forty years or so. In fact it has no claim as "the first disk to sell a million," only a tentative claim to have been the first disk recorded that ultimately topped the million mark, and even that is arguable.

The most likely candidate for the first disk to achieve "golden" status is Victor Talking Machine Co.'s record No. 17081, Al Jolson singing "Ragging the Baby to Sleep," made on 17 April 1912. An instantaneous success, it was reported to have sold 1,069,000 copies within a year or two of issue, and was probably the only record to attain this distinction before World War I. Jolson's claim to precedence is, however, challenged by *Billboard* chart compiler Joel Whitburn, who asserts that Arthur Collins's comic song "The Preacher and the Bear," which he had recorded for six separate labels, achieved the magic million in 1905.

Female vocalist to achieve golden status: The first was Romanian-born soprano Alma Gluck with the 1915 Victor recording of James A. Bland's "Carry Me Back to Old Virginia" (1878) backed with Stephen Foster's Old Black Joe (1860).

Blues recording to sell a million: The first was Bessie Smith's rendering of "Down Hearted Blues," recorded by Columbia on 15 February 1923. It sold 800,000 copies at the premium price of 75¢ before being reissued and going on to even bigger sales. The record's success inspired Columbia to begin its "race series."

Country-and-Western record to sell a million: The first was "The Prisoner's Song" backed by "The Wreck of the Old 97" performed by Vernon Dalhart for Victor Records in 1924. "The Prisoner's Song" was written by ex-jailbird Guy Massey, whom Dalhart later claimed as a cousin and whose name he expropriated, among many, as a recording artist. Dalhart recorded the song for at least twenty-eight labels under his various pseudonyms and the aggregate sales are estimated at some 25 million. The flip side "The Wreck of the Old 97" had been the first country-and-western recording the previous year (SEE **sound recording**) as rendered by Henry Whitter, also claimed to be its author.

Million seller by a vocal group: The first was the Mills Bothers' "Tiger Rag" backed with "Nobody's Sweetheart," released on the Brunswick label in 1930. The first female group to go golden was the Andrews Sisters with "Bei Mir Bist Du Schön," also on Brunswick, released in 1937 as "the new French song." The Yiddish song was in fact by the very non-French team of composer Sholem Secunda and lyricist Jacob Jacobs, who had sold it outright for $30.

Million-selling LP: The first was Decca's 1949 release of Rodgers & Hammerstein's *Oklahoma!* with the original Broadway cast, which had sold 1,750,000 copies by 1956—before any other LP had made the million mark—and 2,500,000 by 1960. The 1955 Capitol LP of the film soundtrack also struck gold.

Million-selling rock-and-roll recordings: The first were "Shake, Rattle and Roll" and "Rock Around the Clock," both recorded by Bill Hayley & His Comets for Decca on 12 April 1954. The latter hit the million mark in 1955. It was also the first disk of any kind to sell a million copies in Britain, and went on to sell an estimated 22 million copies in 140 versions recorded in 25 different languages.

Golden CD: The first was Dire Straits's recording *Brothers in Arms*, first released in Britain on 17 May 1985. It passed the million mark for worldwide sales the following year.

THE FIRST **GOLD STRIKE**

....

of significance in the United States was made by twelve-year-old Conrad Reed, son of a former Revolutionary War soldier John Reed (probably an Anglicization of Johannes Reith), a Hessian mercenary who fought with the British Army and later became a farmer at Stanfield in the lower Piedmont area of

North Carolina. In the spring of 1799 the youngster found a 17-pound nugget in Little Meadow Creek and carried it back to the family farm, where for the next three years it was used as a doorstop. In 1802 the farmer took the yellow rock to a jeweler in Fayetteville, N.C., who, figuring that the barely literate German probably had little knowledge of the value of gold, asked him what he wanted for it. He was delighted to pay Reed's asking price of $3.50; it was actually worth about $3,600, a fortune at the time. When Reed realized his error he decided to start prospecting and in 1804 founded the Reed Gold Mine in Stanfield, N.C., in partnership with neighbors Frederick Kiser, Rev. James Lore, and Martin Phifer Jr. Although they continued farming and mined only in the off-season, their enterprise reaped an early reward when a slave called Peter belonging to Reed found a nugget weighing 28 pounds. This time the farmer knew how to sell it. News of the discovery attracted other fortune hunters to the area and America's first gold rush was under way, with miners traveling from as far as Europe. The original Reed Mine was open cast, but after gold was found in veins of white quartz in 1825, a number of underground operations began in the lower Piedmont. Despite family conflict that resulted in a court injunction closing the mine for ten years, Reed died a rich man in 1845. Within a few years the California Gold Rush had lured away the Piedmont prospectors and America's first goldfield became inactive, though the Reed Gold Mine at Stanfield, with underground tunnels dating from 1831, survives as a tourist attraction owned and administered by the State of North Carolina. During its years of operation it was claimed to have yielded gold to the value of $10 million.

THE FIRST GOLF

earliest reference to, is contained in a decree of the Scottish Parliament dated March 1457 and ordaining that "wapinschawingis be halden be the Lordis and Baronis spirituale and temporale, foure times in the zeir, and that the Fute-ball and Golfe be utterly cryit doune, and nocht usit . . ." All other references to the game as played in Scotland during the fifteenth century are of a prohibitive nature, but an item of expenditure in the accounts of the Lord High Treasurer of Scotland dated 3 February 1503 indicates that golf had already secured royal patronage by this time:

> *Item to the King to play at the golf with the Earle of Bothuile . . . xlij s.*
> *Item to Golf Clubbis and Ballis to the King that he playit with . . . ix s.*

There is no compelling evidence that the game was introduced into Scotland from the Continent as has often been suggested, and golf should not be confused with the Dutch game *Kolf*, the Belgian *Chole*, or the French *Jeu de Mail*, none of which involved driving a ball into a hole.

Golf course: The first is open to dispute, though Perth North Inch in central Scotland has been claimed as the oldest course in the world and may have been in existence at the beginning of the sixteenth century. The earliest written reference to a named course is contained in the *Registrum de Parmure*, which alludes to Sir Robert Maule as a habitué of Barry Links (now Carnoustie) in the year 1527.

Early golf courses were laid out with a purely arbitrary number of holes. Leith, the principal Scottish course in the seventeenth and eighteenth centuries before the ascendancy of Saint Andrews, had only five holes, while Montrose had twenty-five. Saint Andrews originally had twelve holes, laid out in a strip along the shore. A round started with the players teeing off at the first hole, continuing to the twelfth, and then playing back on the reverse direction, making twenty-two holes in all. In 1764 two holes were discarded and the standard golf round became eighteen holes.

Golf "International": The first was played at Leith in 1657 between James, Duke of York (later James II), and John Patersone, shoemaker, representing Scotland, and two visiting English Peers (i.e., members of the House of Lords). Patersone, a poor man, was selected for this honor as he was considered the champion Scottish golfer of his time and his royal partner put up the stakes for both of them. Scotland won and with his half of the prize money Patersone was enabled to build himself a substantial house at 77 Canongate, Edinburgh—known thereafter as the "Golfer's Land."

Golf tournament: The first was played at Leith on 2 April 1744 for a silver club presented for this purpose by the City of Edinburgh to the Gentlemen Golfers. The ten competitors each paid a five-shilling entry fee and the trophy was won by an Edinburgh surgeon, John Rattray, who thereby became "captain of the Goff" (sic) for the ensuing year—an office that entitled him to dispose of the entry fees for such purposes as he saw fit and imposed on him the position of arbiter in disputes between players and the superintendency of the Links.

Golf club: The first was the Honourable Company of Edinburgh Golfers, generally said to have been established with the holding of the first tournament (above) at Leith in 1744. Since the Gentlemen Golfers of Leith, as they were originally known, elected no office bearers, kept no minutes, and solicited no subscription, it is apparent that they acted only in the loosest association and can hardly be described as a club in the proper sense. It is arguable that the Honourable Company only began to function as a club in 1764, when conditions of membership were prescribed for those entering the Silver Club competition. The foundation stone of a clubhouse, the world's first, was laid at the southwest corner of Leith Links on 2 July 1768.

Championship golf tournament: The first was played in club foursomes at St. Andrews, 29–31 July 1857. Eleven clubs competed and the championship was won by George Glennie and Lieut. J. C. Stewart of the Royal Blackheath Golf Club.

Professional golf tournament: The first was held at Prestwick in Scotland over 36 holes on 17 October 1860 and was won by Willie Park of Musselburgh, Scotland, with a score of 174. Golf was thus the first game to become professionalized, the only professional sportsmen hitherto being jockeys and prize fighters.

Although the Prestwick tournament of 1860 is usually described as the first "Open Championship," it was in fact restricted to Scottish players, and it was not until the following year that the contest was opened to the whole world, amateur and professional. Thus what can accurately be described as the British Open was first contested at Prestwick on 26 September 1861, when the championship was won by local professional Tom Morris with a score of 163. One player established a record on this occasion that will probably never be exceeded in championship golf, taking 21 strokes for a single hole. There was no prize money until 1864, when the winner received £6 ($30) in addition to the championship belt.

The first American golfer to win the Open was Jack Hutchinson, who tied with R. H. Wethered in Saint Andrews in 1921. American players won eleven of the twelve subsequent championships.

U.S.: Golf was known in America by 1729, when the inventory of Governor William Burnet of New York included "Nine Gouff Clubs, one iron ditto and seven dozen balls." The prodigious quantity of the latter suggests a propensity for losing them, though the only pictorial representations of the game in colonial America show something resembling miniature golf played in a wooden sided court not unlike a bowling alley. During the British occupation of New York in the War of Independence, golf was evidently one of the pastimes that kept British officers occupied when garrison duties were undemanding, as evidenced by an advertisement in *Rivington's Royal Gazette* for 21 April 1779 addressed "to the golf players" and offering a selection of clubs and "Caledonian balls" for sale.

The earliest reference to a golf club in the United States in an advertisement that appeared in the *City Gazette* of Charleston, S.C., on 13 October 1795:

> Notice—The anniversary of the Golf Club will be held on Saturday next, at the Club House, Harleston's Green, where members are requested to attend at one o-clock.

Further notices appear during the remaining years of the century, some in the name of "the South Carolina Golf Club," yet none concerns the game of golf itself. A similar succession of advertisements ran in the *Daily Republican* of Savannah, Ga., between 1811 and 1820, but the activities related are balls and dinners, not matches or tournaments. Most sports historians have concluded that these so-called golf clubs were social rather than sporting organizations.

The first **golf course** of record in the United States was the 9-hole Oakhurst Links, laid out in 1884 at the White Sulphur Springs estate of Russell

Montague in the foothills of West Virginia's Allegheny Mountains. Montague had learned to play golf at Saint Andrews in 1870 while studying law at London's Lower Temple. He had moved from Boston to White Sulphur Springs for his health and there encountered a group of expatriate Scots: George Donaldson, retired British Army officer George Grant, and gentleman farmers the McLeod brothers, Roderick and Alexander. Together they decided to build a course for the impending visit of Grant's nephew Lionel Torrin, a golfer of some renown. Donaldson, having business to undertake in Britain, was commissioned to procure clubs at Saint Andrews. They were confiscated on his return by an overzealous customs officer, who believed them to be "elongated blackjacks or some other instruments of murder." Eventually the Treasury Department relented and dispatched the clubs to Oakhurst, where play was able to commence. Montague and his Scots friends "were looked upon . . . as victims of an insane fad or folly," wrote West Virginia historian F. F. Flynn in 1913. A neighbor, he declared, "expressed the disgust of the others when he remarked, 'well, I did play marbles when I was a kid, but by gad, this is the first time I have seen men play! It might be a fine game for a canny Scotsman, but no American will ever play except Montague.'" On Christmas Day 1888 this group and others played in America's first golf tournament, the Oakhurst Challenge Medal, and the contest was repeated each 25 December through 1893. Eventually the Scots returned home or were scattered about the Empire and the Oakhurst Links fell into disuse. They were no longer a golf course by 1912 and reverted to pastoral land. During the 1990s the then owner Lewis Keller was inspired by golf champion Sam Snead to restore the course to its original appearance, Montague's son Cary having earlier furnished details of how it was laid out together with contemporary documentation. It has now been reopened as a period public course where for a green fee of $50 visitors, some in costume, can play the game with hickory clubs and gutta-percha balls (made to order by Penfold of Birmingham, England).

Oakhurst Links was a private course used by Russell Montague's personal friends, mainly Scots. The first **golf club** in the United States was Foxburg Golf Club, founded by Joseph Mickle Fox of Philadelphia in 1887 at the 5-hole course he had laid out at his summer home in the village of Foxburg in Clarion County, Pa., two years earlier. Like Montague he had learned to play the game at Saint Andrews and brought back clubs and balls on his return home. Harry R. Harvey was elected secretary and treasurer, offices which he continued to hold for fifty-four years until August 1941; he continued to play on the course well into the 1950s. Foxburg Country Club, as it became, remains the oldest golf club in the United States, though not the oldest in North America, Royal Montreal having been founded by expat Scots in 1873.

By October 1894, when the first **open tournament** was played, there were a scattering of clubs and courses on the East Coast and one in far-off Chicago. The event, "open to the world," was held at a new 9-hole course called Saint Andrew's in Yonkers, Westchester County, N.Y., where Willie Dunn of Long Island's Shinnecock Hills Golf Club beat Willie Campbell two up to win the championship. What is recognized as the inaugural **U.S. Open** followed the founding of golf's first and only governing body, the United States Golf Association, on 22 December 1894, with five constituents: Saint Andrew's Golf Club, Brookline Country Club (Mass.), Newport Golf Club (R.I.), Shinnecock Hills Golf Club (Southampton, Long Island, N.Y.), and Chicago Golf Club. The USGA's first championship was played on 4 October 1895 at Newport, R.I., and was won by Horace Rawlins of the home club with a score of 173 over 36 holes.

The first **professional tournament** in the United States was held by the Professional Golfers' Association of America (founded 17 Jan 1916) on 9–14 October 1916 at Siwanoy Golf Club, Bronxville, N.Y., and was won by Jim Barnes, who beat Jock Hutchison one up.

SEE ALSO **women's golf**.

THE FIRST GREETING CARD

known, for birthdays and other occasions, was designed by W. Harvey and engraved by John Thompson of London in 1829. The design was in the form of an elaborately decorated medallion surrounded by scrollwork and surmounted by the date, together with the words: "To . . . on the ANNIVERSAIRIE of . . . Day. From . . ."

The earliest recorded greeting card for a specific occasion was a New Year card produced in 1841 by Charles Drummond, printer and publisher of Leith, Scotland, from a design by his friend Thomas Sturrock. Engraved by Alexander Aikman of Edinburgh and sold at Drummond's shop at 133 Kirkgate in Leith, it depicted a chubby-cheeked smiling boy and bore the legend "A Gude New Year an' money o' Them." At about this time the decorative **valentine** emerged, following the introduction of universal penny postage in Britain in 1840. No record exists of the earliest publisher. The first Christmas card (qv) was issued in London in 1843, but regular commercial production did not begin until 1862.

U.S.: The earliest known example is a New Year's card containing text only and believed to have been printed in New Orleans in 1848. The card was commissioned by black veteran Jordan B. Noble and presented the compliments of the season to the officers of the regular army and militia under whom he had served as a drummer in the War of 1812 and the Mexican War of 1846–47.

The first regular publisher of greeting cards in the United States was Esther Howland, whose father maintained a large stationery store in Worcester, Mass. Shortly after graduating from Mount Holyoke female seminary at age nineteen in 1847, Miss Howland received a valentine card from one of her father's business associates in England. This inspired her to go into business as a manufacturer of valentines, using paper lace, ribbons, and cutouts sourced from England and New York to achieve highly decorative effects. Her brother took a dozen samples with him on a sales trip for their father. He and his sister had hoped they might achieve $200 worth of sales and Miss Howland was amazed when he returned with $5,000 of advance orders. When she took out her initial advertisement in Worcester's *Daily Spy* on 5 February 1850, some of her more elaborate offerings commanded prices of $5 to $10—roughly the weekly earnings of a female store clerk or factory worker. By the time Miss Howland sold out to George C. Whitney's rival Worcester

valentine company in 1881, the business was worth $100,000 per annum—remarkable for a product only on sale for a very few weeks each year.

Last of the greeting card staples to emerge was the **birthday card**, in spite of the fact that the 1829 *anniversairie* card noted above was probably primarily for such occasions. The earliest known dated American examples are in the Hallmark Collection in Kansas City and were printed at Roxbury, Mass., by Louis Prang (also the first to produce Christmas cards in the United States) in 1875–77. However, there are also a number of cards published by Jonathan King that were attributed to the same decade when they were acquired in the 1950s, but curator Sharman Robertson believes may belong to the late 1860s. This was also the time when birthday cards began to emerge in England and Germany. Nevertheless it took much longer for the birthday card to become established, the earliest appearance in print of the compound noun noted by the *Oxford English Dictionary* being 1902.

THE FIRST **GUIDE DOG**

training on an organized basis is evidenced from a painting executed by Jean-Baptiste Chardin in 1752 depicting blind inmates of the Quinze-Vingts hospital in Paris being guided by dogs. The earliest description of a systematic method of training dogs as guides was published in 1819 by Johann Wilhelm Klein, director of the Institute for the Blind in Vienna. This included the use of a rigid stick running through a loose brace around the body of the dog, so that any sideways movement would be clearly apparent to the guided.

The first permanent center for the systematic training of guide dogs was established by Dr. Gerhard Stalling, president of the German Red Cross Ambulance Association at Oldenburg in what is now Lower Saxony. Here dogs had been trained since 1893 to locate the wounded on battlefields, but it was the huge numbers of servicemen blinded in World War I that inspired Stalling to diversify. The first dog to complete the new form of training was handed over to blind veteran Paul Feyen in October 1916 and within a year there were a hundred dogs in service, including

German shepherds, Dobermans, and Airedales. Classes for blind civilians started in 1922.

U.S.: The first trained guide dog was "Lux of La Sallc," a German shepherd imported from Germany by Minnesota businessman and dog trainer John Sinykin, who after completing the dog's tutelage in the United States handed him over to blind senator Thomas D. Schall of Minnesota. They remained together from 1926 until Lux's death in 1933. Sinykin went on to found the first training center, His Master's Eyes Institute. This was destroyed in a disastrous fire in 1935, and although he continued training under the Master's Eye name the success of Mrs. Dorothy Eustis's Seeing Eye training program has meant that Sinykin's pioneering role has been largely overlooked.

Mrs. Eustis, who bred dogs in Switzerland, had visited the guide-dog training school at Potsdam, Germany, and under the title "The Seeing Eye" (from Proverbs 20:12, "The hearing ear, and the seeing eye, the Lord hath made even both of them") published a laudatory story about it in the 5 November 1927 issue of the *Saturday Evening Post*. It exercised the attention of Morris Frank, a nineteen-year-old blind insurance salesman from Nashville, Tenn., who wrote to Mrs. Eustis to say that he wished to test a dog for himself in America and, if this proved successful, to set up a training center so that others might benefit similarly. She agreed to back him and had him travel to Switzerland to train with two dogs from the Potsdam school. One of these, Kiss, whom Frank renamed Buddy, traveled back with him to the United States in June 1928. Attracting a welter of publicity, Morris Frank and Buddy became so celebrated that they are generally acclaimed as the first master and trained guide dog combination in the United States and Mrs. Eustis as the progenitor of the first such training program. While hers was not the first, she certainly deserves credit for helping to launch the first guide-dog service in France, Italy, Switzerland, and the United Kingdom and also for an essential prerequisite to the spread of the movement internationally, the first training center for instructors, L'Oeil qui Voit (The Seeing Eye) at Vevey, Switzerland (1929).

THE FIRST GUNS

were in use in China by 1128, according to research by the world's leading authority on Chinese scientific history, Dr. Joseph Needham of Cambridge University. While exploring a Buddhist cave in Szechuan in 1986 he discovered a stone carving representing a mythical army surrounding a statue of the Buddha. This included the figure of a soldier carrying what Needham recognized as a bombard. The carving is known to have been executed in 1128, which is about 150 years earlier than the date hitherto assigned to the invention of the gun in China.

The bombard depicted in the Szechuan sculpture is identical in shape to those shown in the earliest illustrations in Europe. A manuscript of 1326 titled *De Officiis Regum* ("On the Duties of the Kings"), compiled by Walter de Milemete for England's boy king Edward III, contains an illustration of a vase-shaped gun mounted on a table and being fired at the touch-hole with a red-hot iron. The projectile is a four-headed arrow and it is probable that the shafts would have been bound around with leather to the same diameter as the bore of the weapon. A manuscript from Holkham Hall in Norfolk, England, dated 1326–27, depicts a much larger gun mounted on stone supports. Neither mentions the guns in the text.

The earliest written evidence of guns is a decree passed by the City of Florence on 11 February 1326 which refers to *"pilas seu palloctas ferreas et conones de metallo"* ("iron bullets and metal canon"). Most of these early guns were designed to destroy masonry rather than men. The first antipersonnel gun was the *ribauldequin*, a kind of primitive machine gun consisting of a line of small-bore barrels each loaded separately, of which the earliest known is recorded at Bruges, Belgium, in 1339.

The claims advanced on behalf of Berthold Schwartz as inventor of the gun should be entertained with caution. This legendary figure may or may not have led an earthly existence. He is variously recorded as having been born in Freiburg, Goslar, Ghent, Mainz, Metz, Cologne, Brunswick, and Prague, as well as being of Danish, Greek, African, and Welsh origin. He is asserted to have been a Franciscan, Augustinian, and Dominican monk and not a monk at all and is variously supposed to have invented the gun in 1250, 1313, 1320, 1354, 1359, and 1380.

Guns used in warfare: The first recorded use occurred at the Siege of Cividale in Italy by German forces in 1331, when *vasi* (artillery) and *sclopi* (handguns) were employed by the defenders to repel the attack. The earliest battle in which the use of artillery was decisive was the Battle of Crécy on 26 August 1346. According to an anonymous Italian manuscript, "The English knights, taking with them the Black Prince, a body of wild Welshmen and many bombards, advanced to meet the French army...they fired all the bombards at once and then the French began to flee." Artillery was used by both sides at the Battle of Kauthal in 1367 between the Muslim forces of Kulbarga and the Hindu empire of Visayanagar in southern India.

The earliest known **rifle** dates from the same century, a 24-bore weapon made for the Emperor Maximilian I, probably in Vienna c. 1495. Rifles remained rare for the next three centuries, though the first in service use had been issued in limited quantities to detachments of the Danish army in 1611. What may have been the first rifles in America were a "Dozen of Refled Barrel Carbines" ordered by the British Army's Quarter Master General Sir John St. Clair 1754 for use in the French and Indian War. Although the Pennsylvania longrifle is claimed to have originated about this time, no dated examples are known until later in the century.

Pistols are generally said to have been named after the town of Pistoia in Italy, where it is claimed that they were first manufactured in the late fifteenth century. In fact what Pistoia manufactured were *pistole*, which meant daggers. The earliest known pistols are in the collection of the Tower of London Armories and date from c. 1520.

The earliest pistol to have survived intact in America is a brass-barreled muzzle-loading snaphaunce (the name refers to the firing mechanism, which preceded the flintlock) probably made in the lowlands of Scotland at the beginning of the seventeenth century and brought to Virginia by the Jamestown settlers in or shortly after this first permanent English-speaking settlement was established in 1607. Dug out of a disused well in 2007, this is one of the oldest European artifacts to have been discovered by archaeologists in America. It can be seen at the newly opened Archaearium at Jamestown.

U.S.: The earliest record of gun manufacture on an industrial scale dates from 1740, when Scots-born shipsmith Hugh Orr established a forge at Bridgewater, Mass., to produce edged tools and muskets as well as ironwork for shipping. In 1748 he delivered 500 stands of muskets to Castle William, the garrison at Boston. It is unlikely that these were wholly manufactured by Orr; they were probably assembled from parts imported from Europe. The few gunsmiths in America prior to the Revolution devoted their attention to repair and maintenance rather than manufacture.

When the incipient nation went to war the main stock of guns consisted of the 20,000 Brown Bess muskets left over from the French and Indian Wars of twenty years earlier, most of which were in disrepair. This was the same weapon as that which equipped the British Army. The priority for the Colonial Assemblies charged with mustering their forces was to establish something that had never happened on American soil before—regular gun manufacture.

It was in Lancaster County, Penn., that the new industry was born. Despite the area boasting more gunsmiths than anywhere else in America, owing to a recent influx of German craftsmen, productivity was hardly impressive. William Henry had been commissioned by the Pennsylvania Committee of Safety in March 1776 to arrange manufacture of 200 muskets; even under the pressure of war it took a whole year to fulfil the order. North Carolina's Public Gun Factory on Black River produced a hundred rifles, the first in series production in America. At the North Furnace Mill in Bridgewater, Mass., Hugh Orr (SEE ABOVE) pioneered again by producing the first artillery pieces cast in America, though in strictly limited quantities. Perhaps the largest gun making establishment of the war was Adam Stephen and Anthony Nobile's factory at Martinsburg, Va., where thirty craftsmen had an output of up to 18 muskets a week; hardly sufficient to equip an army.

So desperate were the former colonies to procure arms that New York even went so far as to send an agent over to Britain to recruit gunsmiths from within the very bosom of the enemy. But this was not the answer either. The war was won with imported guns from France and the Netherlands (the latter was, perhaps surprisingly, Europe's greatest arsenal at the time), no fewer than 100,000 of them, supplemented by consignments smuggled in by Britain's old enemy Spain. When the initial shipments began to arrive in the spring of 1777, Gen. George Washington had just received word that the Continental Congress's armories were empty. It was not, however, until late in 1783, just before the termination of the war, that the Continental Army was, for the first time, fully armed. Only with the Mexican War of 1846–48 would domestic manufacture of firearms become a significant industry in a nation destined, a century later, to become the world's most prolific supplier of armaments.

SEE ALSO **machine gun; revolver**.

~~~~~~~~~~~~~~~~~~~~~~~~~~~~ **H** ~~~~~~~~~~~~~~~~~~~~~~~~~~~~

THE FIRST **HALFTONE**

process of reproducing photographs in printers' ink was developed by William A. Leggo of Montreal and used for the first time for the cover illustration of George-Édouard Desbarats's *Canadian Illustrated News* of 30 October 1869. This was a portrait by photographer William Notman of Prince Arthur, Queen Victoria's seventh child, later Duke of Connaught, who had recently visited the newly independent dominion. Another illustration inside depicted an American Indian lacrosse team arrayed in feathers and finery. Leggotypes, as they were called, continued in the magazine until 1871, when technical problems made Desbarats revert to line engravings. He revised the technique, however, for the first halftone published in the United States (SEE BELOW).

A separate process was developed in Sweden at about the same time by engraver Carl Carleman and used for magazine illustrations in *Nordisk Boktryckeri-Tidnung* (Stockholm) in 1871 and the French weeklies *Le Monde Illustré* and *L'Illustration* in 1874. This was the first **halftone process used for book illustrations**, three studies of Paris in ruins after the great siege of 1870–71 being reproduced in Iwar Haeggström's *Paris' Ruiner*, Stockholm 1871.

The first magazine to use halftones in every issue was the London weekly *Life*, which began using photographic reproductions of portraits of society women from the studio of Swiss artist Fritz Zuber-Buhler in 1880. All these early halftones were either portraits or views. The first action photographs as well as the first photographs of a news event to be reproduced in halftone were two studies of the imperial maneuvers at Hamburg by Ottomar Anschütz, published by the Meisenbach process in the 15 March 1884 issue of *Ilustrierte Zeitung* of Leipzig. Georg Meisenbach of Nuremberg had patented his "autotype" process of halftone reproduction on 9 May 1882; it would later be used for the first advertising photograph (qv).

Newspaper photograph: The first, which was also the first halftone published in the United States, was a view of New York's Steinway Hall reproduced by the Leggotype process on the back page of George-Édouard Desbarats's *New York Daily Graphic* on 2 December 1873. The experiment was not repeated until 4 March 1880, when Stephen Horgan's "A Scene in Shantytown" appeared in the paper. Possibly because Horgan's picture was at once artistic and evocative, while the anonymous architectural study of Steinway Hall was singularly unrevealing, it is the former that is nearly always cited as the first halftone (also ignoring forerunners in Montreal, Stockholm, and Paris). The *Daily Graphic* never used halftones on a regular basis, as they were too costly prior to the process improvements made later in the 1880s by Georg Meisenbach in Nuremberg and Frederick Ives (SEE BELOW) in Philadelphia.

The first newspaper to use halftones with any regularity was *Novoye Vremya* ("New Times") of Saint Petersburg, Russia, in 1887. It was not until ten years later that the *New York Tribune* did so in the United States. Most of the early newspaper halftones were portraits of people in the news, many of them politicians, and were bought in. There were no staff photographers. The first newspaper to carry news photographs taken by their own photographers was Alfred Harmsworth's *Daily Illustrated Mirror* (London), which carried pictures of the state funeral of the Duke of Cambridge on its front page of 23 March 1904. Prime Minister Lord Salisbury observed of Harmsworth's two national dailies, the *Daily Mail* and *Daily Mirror*: "Having invented a newspaper for those who cannot think, Mr. Harmsworth has now invented one for those who cannot read."

Frederick Ives is the person generally credited with the invention of the halftone. Although the various halftone applications enumerated above indicate that this is not so, it was he and the German inventor Georg Meisenbach, working independently of each other, who were eventually to make the halftone process an economically viable way of illustrating mass circulation magazines and later newspapers. He was also the first to introduce the modern form of halftone composed of dots rather than lines (earlier halftones were not unlike an analog TV image on pause), which he patented on 8 February 1881. Its public bow was a photograph reproduced in the *Philadelphia Photographer* for June that year. While the definition and shading were superior to those in previous efforts, the process was a protracted and costly one involving a swelled gelatin print, dotted plaster casts, and a rubber inkpad impression. It took a whole day for Ives and his apprentice to make a single plate. It was, however, used commercially, *Harper's* signing an agreement in January 1883 with Ives's employer the Philadelphia engravers Crosscup & West. The first halftone to appear in an American magazine (unusually, after the first appearance of a halftone in a newspaper) was made from an Ives plate reproducing a rather dull photograph of an Indian drinking vessel illustrating J. L. Kipling's article "Indian Art in Metal and Wood" in *Harper's Magazine* for June 1883.

Ives persevered in simplifying the process and in 1888 was able to announce his crossline screen enabling halftones to be produced optically in the camera itself. It was this technique that heralded the advent of the mass circulation ten-cent general-interest and women's magazines of the 1890s. It also enabled the news weeklies to dispense with wood engravings. Whereas a wood engraving had cost as much as $300 for a full-page illustration in the 1880s, by the mid-90s the price of a similar-size plate of photographs was only $20. By 1893 nearly a third of the pictures in *Century* were halftones, almost half in *Harper's*, two thirds in *Scribner's*, and practically all of them in *Cosmopolitan*.

Color halftone: The first was made by Frederick Ives while under contract to photoengravers Crosscup & West of Philadelphia and exhibited at the Novelties Exhibition held in that city in 1885. The technique does not seem to have been practicable for long runs, but it attracted sufficient interest for Ives to turn his attention to the development of color photography (SEE **photograph in color**), launching the first

commercially available system in London in 1895. This may have been the reason he failed to take the color halftone process to market.

The first color halftones to be published were studies of the newly built Eiffel Tower and the surrounding buildings of the Paris Exposition that appeared on the cover and as a center-page spread of the 6 July 1889 issue of *Paris Illustré*. The color Meisenbach autotype was made by Boussod, Valadon et Cie. The photographer's name is not recorded. The first American example was a still life of fruit on a table made by William Kurtz of New York and published in the German photographic journal *Photographische Mitteilungen* of 1 January 1893. The fact that Kurtz had chosen a foreign publication in which to display America's first color halftone aroused the editorial ire of the *Photographic Times*, which may be why he hastened to reprint the same image in the March 1893 issue of Boston's *Engraver & Printer*. For the first color newspaper photograph SEE **newspapers: newspaper illustration**.

SEE ALSO **advertising photography; fashion photographs; postcard: photographically illustrated; printed book: color-printed plates**.

THE FIRST HAMBURGER

is elusive. The earliest known printed reference to hamburger meat is contained in an 1873 issue of the *New York Times*, which defines a "hamburger steak" as "simply a beefsteak redeemed from its original toughness by being mashed into mincemeat and then formed into a conglomerated mass." Ten years on we find the earliest reference by its present name in the *New York Sun*: "Those flat, brown meat cakes on that dish there are Hamburg steaks; the people call them 'Hamburgers.' They are made from raw meat chopped up with onions and spices, and are very good." A further reference from the same decade comes from *The Union* of Walla Walla, Wash., for 5 January 1889: "You are asked if you will have 'porkchopbeefsteakhamandegghamburgersteak or liverandbacon.'"

Many authorities have attributed to hamburger meat a much earlier inception, based solely on a

Delmonico's menu card that the New-York Historical Society, in whose collection it resides, has erroneously dated 1836. As nothing on the card is priced above 12¢ (the hamburger steak is offered at 10¢) this was clearly not the fabled Delmonico's restaurant that introduced America to fine wining and dining, but a much later "greasy spoon" calling itself after the original as a wry joke. The dating is absurdly wrong. It is readily apparent from the typography that the card belongs to the 1880s or 1890s, the period when references to hamburger meat first appear in print.

The origins of the hamburger sandwich are equally cloudy. Claims are various: that fifteen-year-old Charlie Nagreen of Seymour, Wis., served the first one at the Outagamie County Fair in 1885; that pork sandwich purveyor Frank Menches, who also claimed to be the inventor of the ice cream cone, created the hamburger in Ohio at the 1892 Akron County Fair when his meat supplier ran out of pork and substituted ground beef; or that fry cook Fletcher "Old Dave" Davis from Athens, Tex., introduced hamburger patties between two slices of Texas Toast—a heavy white bread with a crisp brown crust—at the 1904 World's Fair in St. Louis. (Unfortunately for the attempt by the Texas House of Representatives to have Athens declared "Original Home of the Hamburger," Davis is not listed among the concessionaires at the fair.) The town of Hamburg, N.Y., is also insistent that it is the birthplace of the hamburger, but local historians are vague as to details. The Library of Congress favors the claim of Louis' Lunch three-seat diner in New Haven, Conn., where Louis Lassen ground up prime lean beef costing 7 cents per pound, broiled it, and served it between two slices of toast. This was reputedly in 1900, to oblige a customer who had to take lunch on the run.

None of these claims stands up to scrutiny. The only certain knowledge about the inception of the hamburger sandwich is that it happened in or before 1893, the year in which the Reno, Nev., *Evening Gazette* made reference to "Tom Fraker's celebrated Hamburger steak sandwiches." Who was Tom Fraker and when did his sandwiches first achieve this celebrity status? Alas, the Reno City Library's files of the *Gazette* do not extend so far back and they have no local directories of the period. The likelihood, however, is that the hamburger was already known

elsewhere. The following year the *Los Angeles Times* carried an article headed TAMALES CALIENTES: PUSH-CART PURVEYORS WHO FLOURISH AT NIGHT (23 September 1894). These push-cart purveyors catered mainly to drunks and, per the *Times*'s report, the tamales might be supplemented by "trotters, ham, egg and hamburger steak sandwiches."

First to design a hamburger bun and also first to open a dedicated **hamburger joint** was Walter Anderson, a dropout of Baker University in Kansas who had become an itinerant fry cook at Wichita, Kan., in 1916. Anderson refined the burger by making patties thinner than was customary elsewhere and searing them to seal in the juices—something not possible with a thicker patty. The buns he developed were square with a crust dense enough to hold the juices when the patron bit into his sandwich. Having elevated the hamburger to what he believed was a pitch of perfection, Anderson threw in his job as a fry cook, bought a used trolley car with his life savings, and installed it at 800 East Douglas Avenue in Wichita. He stripped out the seats and built a kitchen inside with a griddle of his own design capable of cooking at 500°F, compared to the 350° maximum of standard griddle tops. Five stools at the side completed the arrangements for the pioneer hamburgers-only restaurant. Within four years Anderson was operating two other similar stands in Wichita and was poised to expand into what was to become the first **burger chain**. Teaming up with insurance agent Edgar Waldo Ingram, he formed the White Castle System Inc. in 1921 and began to erect purpose-built outlets to a uniform "fair castle" design with whitewashed crenellated walls (actually based on the exuberantly Gothic Chicago Water Tower, survivor of the Great Fire), opening the first on Douglas Avenue in Wichita in March of that year. The key to the success of this venture was standardization, driven by Ingram as the partner with the vision, energy, and business acumen to work out the principles and implement them.

Whereas hamburgers were often made of the cheapest offcuts of fat-ridden meat and usually dispensed in insalubrious surroundings, the White Castle System imposed the strictest standards in both the quality of its meat and the maintenance of cleanliness and hygiene. The ground beef was never more than

4 or 5 hours from the butcher's shop and rolls were delivered several times daily. The employees, mainly eighteen to twenty-four-year-olds who had graduated from high school, had to pass a physical and were attired in spotless uniforms laundered by the company. In return for absolute obedience to corporate rules on behavior and appearance, and a requirement of unvarying cheerfulness and courtesy to customers, they were paid wages of $18 to $30 per week, higher than average for the catering business, and earned an annual profit-sharing bonus. Salesmanship was also emphasized; if a customer ordered a single 5¢ burger the "operator," as the company called its employees, was to put two on the griddle and then ask the customer if he would like both. As there were only five stools to a counter, most of the business was takeout, White Castle publicity urging "Buy 'em by the sack."

Ingram's other major innovation in mass catering was "vertical integration"; as the chain grew (within ten years there were 115 outlets in 11 states), the company began to butcher its own meat and bake its own rolls. A subsidiary company called Porcelain Steel Buildings was formed to construct new outlets with gleaming white porcelain steel exteriors and interior walls, and another subsidiary called the Paperlynen Co. was created to produce paper hats (introduced in 1930) and aprons, **heat-resistant takeaway cartons** (an industry first in 1931), napkins, and publicity material. Both these enterprises earned huge profits for White Castle by servicing other restaurant chains as well.

White Castle not only set the template for fast-food chains, most of them franchise operations (as White Castle never was), but also achieved a significant shift in the American diet. During the early period hamburgers were proletarian food eaten by male industrial workers: White Castle and its many imitators deliberately sited their stands in factory areas. With the onset of the Depression, it became essential to expand the customer base. Ingram targeted three new markets: women, middle-class families, and college students. In 1932 the virtually all-male company appointed its first woman executive, Ella Louise Agniel, with the sole duty of persuading women to patronize its outlets with their friends and encouraging them to serve White Castle burgers at home instead of cooking. The remarkable success of this exercise in repositioning helped to change the status of hamburgers from a marginal snack of the working-class male to a staple enjoyed by all. So rapid was the shift in image that by 1937 the president of the National Restaurant Association was able to proclaim that the hamburger was truly a "national food," joining only apple pie and coffee on a very short list. In 1939 President Franklin D. Roosevelt served burgers to the king and queen of England.

White Castle's role in establishing the fast-food industry received formal recognition when one of the last pre-war all-metal White Castle outlets extant, located in Minneapolis, was designated by the National Register of Historic Places.

Cheeseburger: The first was created in 1926 by eighteen-year-old Lionel Sternberger at his Boulevard Stop barbecue stand (acquired in exchange for his aged Jordan auto) at the top of Colorado Boulevard hill on the Pasadena side of Glendale, Calif.

Double-decker hamburger: The first was the Big Boy, a fully dressed extravaganza in a triple-decker bun that was introduced in 1937 by Robert C. Wian Jr. at his ten-stool Bob's Pantry, 831 East Colorado Boulevard in Glendale, Calif. (by remarkable coincidence on the same street as the birthplace of the cheeseburger eleven years earlier). A local band, the Chuck Foster Band, frequented the Pantry at the end of their sessions. Reputedly Wian created the behemoth in response to band member Harry Lewis, who protested "Hamburgers! Don't you have anything different?" "Big Boy" was the nickname Wian had conferred on a 90-pound six-year-old, Richard Woodruff, who hung around the stand and was given odd jobs to do in exchange for ice cream and sodas. The double-decker caught on, enabling Wian to expand first to a statewide, then a nationwide chain of Bob's Big Boy Drive-Ins. He began franchising the double-decker concept in 1946, though unusually it was the product itself that was franchised, the outlets using their owner's name combined with the Big Boy logo. The famous larrikin in checked pants, based on the portly Richard Woodruff, started out in 1937 as an obese youngster. By 1988, whether for PC reasons or because the suggestion that Big Boys made their consumers gross was bad for business, the youth had become no more than cuddlesome.

McDonald's: The first was opened on 20 December 1948, when brothers Richard and Maurice McDonald converted their drive-in restaurant on E Street in San Bernardino, Calif., to self-service and introduced the McDonald's merchandising concept of low-cost food (burger 15¢, fries 10¢, shakes 20¢), fast service, and no dishes or cutlery. Their first franchise opened in Phoenix, Ariz., in May 1953 and its original golden arches, proclaiming the McDonald's ethos of standardized quality and service from Arizona to Zanzibar, are preserved at the Henry Ford Museum in Dearborn, Mich., as a monument to this multi-cultural manifestation of the American Way.

THE FIRST **HEARING AID, ELECTRIC**

was the Acousticon, patented by Miller Reese Hutchinson of New York on 15 November 1901 and manufactured by the newly formed Hutchinson Acoustic Co. the following year. It consisted of a large housing for the batteries, about the size of a portable radio, and a telephone-type receiver to hold to the ear. One of the earliest users was Britain's Queen Alexandra, who had been partially deaf since infancy. The queen used the Acousticon aid throughout the coronation ceremony in 1902 and afterward presented the twenty-six-year-old inventor with a medal to mark her appreciation. Among the ninety or so patents granted to Hutchinson during his lifetime was one for the Klaxon, an innovation that caused his friend Mark Twain to remark to him: "You invented the Klaxon horn to make people deaf, so they'd have to use your acoustic device in order to make them hear again!"

Electronic hearing aid: The first was the battery-operated Vactuphone. Invented by Earl Charles Hanson, it had a carbon microphone and incorporated a single Western Electric Type 215 "peanut" vacuum tube. Manufactured by Western Electric of Chicago, the Vactuphone was marketed in October 1921 at $135 by the Globe Phone Co. of Reading, Mass. The first electronic model designed to be worn on the person was the Amplivox, which weighed 2½ pounds and was marketed by A. Edwin Stevens of London in October 1935.

Transistor hearing aid: The first was manufactured by the Sonotone Corp. of Elmsford, N.Y., and marketed at $229.50 on 29 December 1952. This was also the earliest consumer product to incorporate transistors.

Digital hearing aid: The first was the pocket processor Phoenix launched by Nicolet Instrument Corp. of Madison, Wis., in 1987, but it was too large as well as too costly to win commercial success. Fully digital in-ear and behind-ear hearing aids were introduced in April 1996.

SEE ALSO **cochlear implant**.

THE FIRST **HELICOPTER**

capable of full takeoff and forward flight control, as well as being able to maintain stability and fly at a reasonable speed, was the Gyroplane-Laboratoire, designed by Louis Bréguet and René Dorand and first flown on 26 June 1935 by French Army pilot Maurice Claisse. Powered by a 420-hp Hispano-Wright engine, the Gyroplane established a speed record of 67 mph on 22 December 1935, an altitude record of 517 feet on 22 September 1936, and a duration record of more than 1 hour on 24 November 1936. Development continued up to the outbreak of war, when it was stored at Villacoublay Air Base on the outskirts of Paris. The machine was destroyed in an Allied air raid in 1943.

The first helicopter to be registered as an "approved" aircraft and thus the first that can be regarded as truly out of the experimental stage was the Focke-Wulf FW 61, designed by Dr. Heinrich Focke and test-flown in free flight at Bremen, Germany, on 6 June 1936. In June 1937 it broke the Bréguet-Dorand records with a speed of 76 mph, altitude of 7,999 feet, and duration of 1 hour 20 minutes and 30 seconds, as well as a distance record of 50 miles. Registration was secured the same year. The reality of practical helicopter flight was brought to general notice in 1938, when the twenty-five-year-old woman pilot Hanna Reitsch gave a brilliant display of the FW 61's control and maneuverability before a large audience in the Deutschlandhalle, Berlin—one of the few occasions on which an aircraft has been flown indoors.

U.S.: The first practical helicopter was the Vought-Sikorsky VS-300, designed by Ukrainian-born Igor Ivanovich Sikorsky, who had built the first passenger transport plane, the four-engined *Russky-Vityaz*, in Russia in 1913. The VS-300 made its first flight on 13 May 1940 at Stratford, Conn., but it was not until the spring of 1941 that the rebuilt and re-engined machine, now powered by a 100-hp Lycoming engine, was outflying any previous helicopter. This was never intended as a production model; even Charles Lindbergh found it difficult to control. Its significance lies in the fact that it was the first helicopter built in what was to become the more or less standard configuration of single main rotor and tail rotor and that it was the test bed for the much more advanced Sikorsky XR-4, the first American helicopter in series production. The VS-300, having done its job, was donated to the Edison Institute Museum at Dearborn, Mich., in October 1943, where it remains to this day.

Helicopters in series production: The first emerged in Germany and the United States at the same time and were also the first helicopters used in warfare, albeit on a very limited scale. In Germany, the twin-rotor, 1,000-hp BMW Bramo-engined Focke-Achgelis (FA) 223 *Drache* ["Dragon"], originally designed as a six-seater transport for the German airline Deutsche Lufthansa, was adapted to multi-function military use as a supply, rescue, and reconnaissance aircraft armed with an MG15 machine gun and two 551-pound bombs. Capable of speeds up to 110 mph and with a range of 435 miles, it achieved an altitude record of 23,643 feet on 28 October 1940. Production began early in 1942, but the factory was destroyed by Allied bombing in June and manufacture was restarted at Laupheim, where seven production models were built before this factory was also obliterated in an air raid. Two of these were used to supply mountain troops in the Austrian Tirol, flying eighty-three missions during September 1944 and carrying ordnance and other goods to a height of 6,500 feet in 7 minutes—an operation that would have taken twenty men on foot a day and a half. Five of the original seven helicopters were then assigned to Transportstaffel 40 at Ainring, two of which, along with an FA-223 that had been built at Berlin's Tempelhof Airfield, fell into American and Russian hands. The Americans made over one of

theirs to the Royal Air Force for evaluation and this became the first helicopter to fly the English Channel in September 1945.

Owing to the disruption of production by Allied bombing, the FA-223 was not the first **helicopter to enter service**. This distinction went to the Flettner 282 Kolibri, of which the first twenty production models were delivered to the German Navy in 1942 for submarine spotting and escort duty in the Mediterranean. Some of the eventual thirty-two aircraft also served in the Aegean and the Baltic and a number were delivered to the Luftwaffe's Transportstaffel 40 at Ainring, where they were later joined by the remaining FA-223s. Although precise numbers are difficult to verify, it would appear that some forty helicopters were on active service with German forces during World War II, of which six survived—three of each marque.

The first American helicopter in series production and the first to become operational was the Sikorsky R-4, a bigger and more powerful version of the VS-300 (SEE ABOVE), which made its maiden flight on 14 January 1942. During 13–17 May 1942 this prototype made the first cross-country flight by a U.S. helicopter when it was flown 761 miles from the Sikorsky plant at Bridgeport, Conn., to the U.S. Army Air Forces test center at Wright Field in Dayton, Ohio, with sixteen stops for refueling. In December, Sikorsky received an order for 30 R-4s for service testing, three of which went to the Navy and seven to Britain's Royal Air Force. One of the naval helicopters made the first helicopter landing on a vessel of the U.S. Navy on 6 May 1943, Frank Gregory putting it down on the tanker USS *Bunker Hill*.

These were the first American helicopters to become operational, with U.S. Coast Guard, Royal Navy, and Royal Air Force pilots taking turns on escort duty accompanying an Atlantic convoy in 1944. The first battlefield use of helicopters took place on 25–26 April that year, when Lt. Carter Harman USAAF, a music critic and composer in civilian life, flew his R-4 from India across a 5,000-foot-high mountain range to Allied base Aberdeen near Mawlu in Burma and from there mounted a dangerous 60-mile rescue mission behind Japanese lines. He made four return flights to succor three wounded British soldiers and their pilot who had been shot down in the jungle, evacuating them one at a time.

The testing batch having proved their worth, there followed an order for 100 production models of the R-4, of which 35 were assigned to the USAAF, 20 to the U.S. Navy, and 45 to the Royal Air Force and the Royal Navy's Fleet Air Arm. The USAAF and U.S. Navy helicopters served mainly in the Pacific theater and flew dangerous casualty evacuation operations in the Philippines. The RAF R-4s served with 529 Squadron on radar calibration missions, helping to protect beleaguered Britain from the menace of German rocket attacks. Other American helicopters to see active service in World War II were the Sikorsky R-5, of which 65 were built, and the R-6 with 224, of which 40 went to the RAF. With the addition of 10 Bell Model 30s ordered by the U.S. Army, there were about 430 helicopters on the Allied side (including trials models), about ten times the number available to the German forces.

Civil helicopter: The first in series production was the Bell 47, built by the Bell Helicopter Co. of Niagara Falls, N.Y., which received a U.S. civil certificate of airworthiness on 8 March 1946. The first commercial delivery was made at the end of December that year. Production continued until the end of 1973, with a total of 6,263 U.S.-built aircraft. Another 1,700 were built in Italy, Japan, and the United Kingdom under license. The Bell 47 was used for most of the functions now associated with civil helicopters, including air-sea rescue, disaster relief, air taxi services, and TV traffic spotting, but the oddest may have been coyote bounty hunting. In 1947, when the Bell 47 had only just appeared on the market, coyotes were infesting farmlands in the Pacific Northwest, and the State of Washington offered a bounty for their tails. Regular hunting with a rifle was slow and uncertain. Instructor Tommy Hale of Yakima, Wash., and his French student pilot Jacques Filliol found a better and more profitable way. Having sought out their quarry in the Bell 47, they let down a rope which the coyotes would pursue and bite, holding on even as the chopper lifted them in the air. When the coyote was about 100 feet up in the air, Filliol let go of the rope. Another tail was ready to earn its bounty.

Helicopter troop transport: The first was the 120-mph Piasecki HRP-1, powered by a 600-hp Pratt & Whitney R-1340 Wasp engine, of which the first production model was completed at the Piasecki Helicopter Co.'s plant near Philadelphia on 15 August 1947. Designed to carry ten troops, six stretchers, or cargo, the HRP-1, or "Flying Banana" as it was irreverently known for its bent fuselage, was also the first tandem twin-rotor helicopter as well as the first **helicopter ambulance** and **helicopter freighter**. It served with both the U.S. Navy and the U.S. Marine Corps.

THE FIRST **HEROIN**

in its refined sate was synthesized by Felix Hoffmann at the laboratories of the Bayer pharmaceutical company in Wuppertal, Germany, in 1897, two weeks after he had synthesized Aspirin (qv). The project had been initiated by Heinrich Dreser, head of the pharmacological laboratory, who was seeking a nonaddictive substitute for morphine, the principal painkiller of the time and an important palliative for respiratory conditions. Dreser's testing program included dispensing diacetylmorphine (its clinical name) to the workers, some of whom declared that it made them *heroisch* (heroic). This inspired the name. Bayer launched the product as Heroin in November 1898, promoting it to the medical profession as a harmless cough medicine ten times as effective as codeine but with only a tenth of its toxic effects. In order to concentrate the company's efforts on the new wonder drug, from which he was entitled to royalties, Dreser had terminated the development of Aspirin on the grounds it would enfeeble the heart. (He changed his mind when it became apparent how profitable it might be.)

By 1899 Heroin was being exported to the United States as well as twenty-two other countries. With no fewer than a quarter of a million morphine addicts in America, proportionately more than any other country, as well as a highly developed market for patent medicines, it was here that Heroin made its deepest inroads, appearing in the form of lozenges and water-soluble salts and as an elixir in a glycerine solution. As early as 1902 the first reports of addiction were received and by the end of the decade, hospitals in New York and Philadelphia were being swamped by addicts. While some of these patients had taken

Heroin as a substitute for morphine to relieve medical conditions, others were recreational users. These were the original "junkies," so called because one way of feeding a habit was by scavenging for scrap metal to sell to junkyards.

Heroin was restricted to prescription-only in the United States in 1914 and in 1924 it was banned outright. In that year 98 percent of New York's drug addicts were Heroin users. Dreser ultimately failed with Heroin, now the world's most successful illegal drug, but he profited beyond all expectations with Aspirin, the world's most successful legal drug. The simple headache pill made him a multimillionaire, though if persistent rumors at the time of his death were true, it was hastened by his own addiction to that other drug he had proclaimed as safe for all to use.

THE FIRST **HOCKEY ON ICE**

is believed to have originated in Nova Scotia. The earliest reference to a game resembling ice hockey is by the internationally renowned Canadian author Thomas Chandler Haliburton, who recalled playing "hurley on the ice" on the Long Pond at Windsor, N.S., while he was a boy at King's College School between 1806 and 1814. The school was founded in 1788, so it is possible that a rudimentary form of the game had emerged by the end of the eighteenth century. Whether this was actually derived from hurley is open to debate. Hurley or hurling, introduced to Canada by Irish immigrants from Waterford and Kilkenny in the 1780s, is a handling game played with a long handled, flat-faced bat. Rather more probable as the basis for a game on ice is the traditional Scottish game of shinty or shinny, well known in Canada at the time, which is played with a hockey stick. (Informal games of hockey are still called "shinny" in Canada.) An alternative provenance was advanced by the Mi'kmaq Indian historian "Old Joe" Cope, who claimed in a 1943 letter to the *Halifax Herald* that his people had played an ice as well as a field version of a game called Oochamkunukt. When they started playing with white settlers the ice version assumed the name Alchamadyk.

While Nova Scotians are passionate in defense of their province as the birthplace of modern hockey, no evidence has been adduced to suggest that it evolved beyond impromptu, scratch games. Nevertheless it was a Nova Scotian, Dalhousie University graduate George Aylwin Creighton, who arranged the first game in Montreal, marking the beginning of hockey as an organized sport. This was played at the Victoria Skating Rink, Montreal, on 3 March 1875 between Creighton's team and a team put together by F. W. Torrance, using hockey sticks the Nova Scotian had brought with him from Halifax three years earlier. It was also the first hockey game to have been played indoors on a rink.

Creighton, an engineer, subsequently attended McGill University to study law. On 27 February 1877 he published the first rules of ice hockey in the *Montreal Gazette* and the same year established the first **hockey club**, McGill University Hockey Club aka the Redmen, who played their inaugural game on 31 December. Later, having moved to Ottawa, he was one of the Government House set who established the Rideau Hall Rebels, which also included the Gov. Gen. Lord Stanley's sons William and Arthur. Through his friendship with them he enthused Lord Stanley himself with an interest in what had yet to become the national game, inspiring him to establish the Stanley Cup competition as the championship of Canada in 1892.

U.S.: The game was imported from Canada in 1893 in two places, though which has precedence is not known. Tennis players Malcolm G. Chase and Arthur E. Foote introduced it at Yale University after a visit north of the border, while one C. Shearer from Montreal formed a team while he was studying at Johns Hopkins, in Baltimore, and is reputed to have invited a Quebec club to compete against them that year. League play in the United States followed the founding of the American Amateur Hockey League in New York with four teams in November 1896. The first **league game** was played the following month between the St. Nicholas and Brooklyn Skating Clubs. On 19 January 1898 the first **intercollegiate game** was played at Franklin Field, Boston, when Harvard beat Brown 6–0.

Professional hockey team: The first in the world was the Portage Lakers, founded in the small mining town of Houghton, Mich., who won 24 out of their 26 games in their debut year 1903. They had been founded by Houghton dentist J. L. Gibson, who imported his players from north of the border. The following year he established hockey's first professional league, the International Pro Hockey League.

THE FIRST **HORSE RACING**

on an organized basis in America originated at a 1-mile track laid by Col. Richard Nicolls, first colonial governor of New York (1664–68), at Hampstead Plain (near present-day Garden City) on Long Island. The earliest record of a race meeting at the track is a porringer, the oldest known surviving example of American silverware, wrought by Dutch silversmith Pieter van Inburg and inscribed 1668. WUNN ATT. HANSEAD PLANES. The winning owner who received this, probably America's first sporting trophy, has since been identified as English army officer Capt. Sylvester Salisbury. Meetings were held annually in May and it is believed that there had been earlier events, probably starting in 1665. According to Nicolls's successor, Col. Francis Lovelace, who was himself a keen racegoer, they were not designed "for the divertissement of the youth alone" but for "the encouragement of the bettering the breed of horses." In the first account of the province of New York written in English (published in London in 1670), Daniel Denton described the site of the race course, which became known as Newmarket after the principal track in England:

> [There] lieth a plain sixteen miles long and four broad upon which plain grows fine grass ... where you shall find neither stick nor stone to hinder the horse-heels or endanger them in their races, and once a year the best horses in the island are brought hither to try their swiftness, and the swiftest rewarded with a silver cup, two being annually procured for that purpose.

Later known as Hemstead Plain, it was still operating as a racetrack in 1909.

The first **thoroughbred** in America was Bulle Rock, whose sire Darley Arabian was one of the three Arabian desert horses from which all thoroughbreds are descended. The horse was imported to Virginia by merchant mariner James Patton in 1730 and the following year is known to have been in the possession of Samuel Gist of Hanover County. The first thoroughbred bred in America was born to English mare Bay Bolton out of Bulle Rock in 1740.

THE FIRST **HOSPITAL**

in America was a palm-thatched wooden structure called the Soledad built at St. Augustine, Fla., in 1597 at the instigation of King Philip II of Spain, who had directed that a facility should be provided for poor people suffering from non-contagious diseases. This won the support of the newly appointed and go-ahead governor Gonzalo Méndez de Canzo, who also laid out the town plaza and built the first public market, as he believed it would benefit the garrison. It was partly financed by an annual contribution of 12 reals a year from every soldier entitled to its care.

The hospital was built next to the church of Nuestra Señora de la Soledad (Our Lady of Solitude) and care of the sick was in the hands of convicts or the soldier who also served as church sexton. On 23 February 1598 Gov. Canzo wrote a letter to Madrid which said that but for the hospital many soldiers, slaves, and Indians would have died of the fever that had swept the town the previous summer. He also raised the matter of the deficit, clearly linking the utility of the amenity to the shortfall in funds, the cost of construction having gone over budget by 500 ducats. At the same time he asked for an appropriation of 500 ducats a year for running costs and the services of a royal slave, from those already in the colony, to act as hospital orderly. The latter's duties would include cooking for the patients, making the beds, and keeping the hospital clean. The petition was endorsed by the Council of the Indies and King Philip agreed to it.

Before the money could be appropriated, however, the southern part of St. Augustine was devastated by fire, consuming the church and the Franciscan convent. The Franciscans moved into the hospital, which left the town without such a resource until Gov. Canzo built a new hospital dedicated to Santa Barbara and assigned royal slave Maria Joijò as nurse. Opened at the end of 1599, this was financed by deducting 2½ reals from the daily rations of the soldiers admitted, as well as the customary 12 reals annual subscription levied on the troops of the garrison. Medicines were supposed to be free, paid for by the Spanish Crown, but one Juan Nuñez Rioz complained to the king that Canzo made the patients buy them from his cousin Juan Garcia.

Canzo, embroiled in other charges of maladministration, was recalled in 1602. His successor, Gov. Pedro de Ibara, declared Santa Barbara Hospital to be a miserable hole. It was, he declared, "in such a bad state and so small that from six soldiers who would be admitted for cure, three would die and others never get well." Fortunately the convent had been rebuilt by 1605 and the Franciscans vacated Soledad, which was then refurbished and enlarged from donations. Reopened as a hospital, it was claimed that "the soldiers and slaves are cured with much more comfort and care." Support from the royal treasury was not forthcoming, however, and a fund-raising drive included the performance of religious plays on the premises. The amount raised was insufficient and according to the new governor, petitioning Madrid in 1611, there was "great need and discomfort for the ill." By mid-century there were two hospitals in St. Augustine, the Royal Hospital at Soledad for the garrison and another, of which little is known, for the poor.

Hospital in English-speaking America: The first was reported by Robert Johnson in his May 1612 *The New Life of Virginea* (sic) to have been in the course of construction near Henrico, the second settlement of the Virginia colony centered on Jamestown. Given the length of time it took for news to cross the Atlantic, it was probably started shortly after Henrico was settled in September 1611. The facility was planned to have "fourscore lodgings (and beds already sent to furnish them) for the sick and the lame, with keepers to attend them for their comfort and recovery."

That the hospital was indeed opened is confirmed by the Virginia Company's secretary, Raphe Hamor the younger, in *A True Discourse of the Present Estate of Virginia* (London 1615). Hamor located it at a fort named Mount Malado across the James River from Henrico. It was, he said, "a retreat, or guest house, for sick people—a high seat and wholesome air." What call there was for an eighty-bed hospital in so small a

community is questionable; shortly before the hospital was completed in 1612 the minister at Henrico, the Rev. Alexander Whitaker, declared that there were but three sick people in the settlement. Five years later John Rolfe reported that Henrico's population stood at thirty-eight men and boys and it is probable that Anglo-America's pioneer hospital had fallen into disuse by the time Henrico was abandoned after the Indian uprising of 1622.

The hospital most often claimed as America's first, the Pennsylvania Hospital founded by Benjamin Franklin at Philadelphia in 1752, was preceded not only by the St. Augustine and Henrico establishments, but also by a hospital opened by the Dutch West India Company at New Amsterdam (New York) in 1658 and two institutions in New Orleans, the Royal Hospital managed by Ursuline nuns from 1727 and the Charity Hospital, founded in June 1736 and still operative as the nation's oldest hospital. However, the Pennsylvania Hospital can claim two historical distinctions: the oldest hospital building in the United States, being the East Wing of 1757; and the oldest operating theater, dating from June 1804. Of lesser antiquity, but notable perhaps for the longest gestation of a project before its realization, is the Physic Garden. Originally planned in 1769, after more than two hundred years of vacillation and inactivity the hospital authorities finally got around to planting the garden in the southwest corner of the grounds in 1975. Appropriately it features plants used medicinally in the eighteenth century.

THE FIRST HOTEL

depends on definition. The late Sir Nikolaus Pevsner, in his book *A History of Building Types* (1976), elucidates the difference between a hotel and an inn thus: "The hotel is nearly always larger than the inn, especially in its public spaces. The hotel has a number of public rooms, not just a tap room and some tables to eat at." To which might be added that the hotel caters to people needing a place of temporary residence, not just transitory accommodation on the way from and to a destination. On this basis, the earliest recorded hotels as such existed at the Swiss spa town of Baden as early as 1417. A visitor from that year, the Florentine humanist Poggio Bracciolini, wrote to his friend Niccolò Niccoli that magnificent houses for those taking the waters stood around a square at the center of the spa precinct. In 1580, by which time Baden was the seat of a Confederation Diet and thus virtual capital of Switzerland, Montaigne reported that his hotel had two hundred beds and that next door there was an establishment with fifty well-furnished rooms. He also complained about the cost.

The first hostelry in America designed principally for accommodation rather than eating and drinking was the Stadt's Herberg or City Tavern, a handsome stone-built structure of two stories, basement, and high attic erected at New Amsterdam (later New York) by order of Gov. Willem Kieft in 1642. Standing apart from the main settlement, it faced the East River on the north side of what was to become Pearl Street. The licensee was Philip Geraerdy, who paid 300 guilders a year for the lease and undertook to sell only the West India Company's liquor and wines. Gov. Kieft was not only concerned with the West India Company's profits when he decided to erect a hostelry; according to pioneer settler Capt. de Vries, the governor was fed up with having to play host to the numerous English sea captains who stopped at New Amsterdam on their way from New England to Virginia, from whom he "had suffered great annoyance." Thus the first "hotel" in America was founded mainly to accommodate foreign visitors. De Vries remonstrated with Kieft that he had built an inn before New Amsterdam had even a proper church, pointing out that the English in their colonies always built a church as soon as they had erected their dwellings. Kieft turned the tables on his critic by soliciting from De Vries a donation of 100 guilders to start a church building fund. As an inn the Stadt's Herberg was fairly short-lived, being converted into a Stadt Huis or City Hall when New Amsterdam's first municipal government was formed in 1653. The building was declared unsafe in 1697 and subsequently demolished. The site is now occupied by a tower block at 85 Broad Street.

The French word *hôtel* originally meant a substantial town house or major public building, such as *hôtel de ville* or city hall. The earliest citation in the *Oxford English Dictionary* as an English word meaning a place of temporary residence is a quote of 1766 from the novelist Tobias Smollett, who echoed Montaigne when he declared that "The expense of living at a hotel is enormous." Some four years later was established the first hotel in the English-speaking world to be named as such. This was The Hotel in the Cathedral Close at Exeter, capital of the county of Devon, originally built in 1769 by William Mackworth Praed as assembly rooms (i.e., a place of fashionable resort for balls, concerts, routs, etc.). During the following year a French entrepreneur called Pierre Berlon, married to an Englishwoman and living in Devon, became landlord of the establishment and announced in the *Exeter Flying Post* for 7 September 1770 that his "hôtel" was open for the accommodation of visitors. It attracted what Jenkin in his 1806 *History of Exeter* described as "people of the first quality," including England's naval hero Lord Nelson and Queen Victoria's father the Duke of Kent. Interestingly it had at its front that appendage of most modern hotels of any size, a coffee shop. After the Duchess of Clarence, later Queen Adelaide, had honored The Hotel with two visits, the proprietors changed its name to the more grandiose Royal Clarence Hotel. As such, having survived the devastation of Exeter in the bombing raids of World War II, it continues in business to this day.

U.S.: The first establishments to be designated as hotels were Corre's Hotel, founded in New York in 1790, and Oeller's Hotel, on Chestnut Street in Philadelphia, opened by James Oeller the same year in a building that had formerly been the Episcopalian Academy. Corre's is chiefly remembered for the fact that twenty-four merchants met there on 17 May 1792 to found the New York Stock Exchange. Oeller's, described by the émigré Moreau de Saint-Méry as "the most beautiful and comfortable inn in the United States," was the haunt of Congressmen during the decade that Philadelphia was the seat of the federal government. Renowned for glittering occasions like Washington's Birthday Ball, the hotel was burned down in 1799 when a nearby circus building caught fire.

The first purpose-built hotel in the United States, also the first American building with a slate roof, was the opulent redbrick five-story City Hotel in New York, located on the site of Burns's Coffee House on the west side of lower Broadway between

Thomas & Cedar streets and opened in February 1797. Built by a consortium of ten wealthy merchants, it was popular with packet-boat captains as well as society folk, artists, and writers. A correspondent in the *New York Journal*, unimpressed by their exclusivity, characterized the grand opening ceremony as having been attended "particularly by those who are attached to the ancient Colony system of servility and adulation." Among the literati who frequented the City Hotel was James Fenimore Cooper, as a member of the Bread and Cheese Club that met there. It was not to everyone's taste, however. Lt. Fitzgerald of the Royal Navy found it "immense, full of company, but a wretched place . . . the floors without carpets, the beds without curtains. There were neither glass nor cup and a miserable little rag was dignified with the name of a towel." Nevertheless the City was one of the two costliest privately owned buildings in New York at the end of the century and it remained the city's largest hotel until 1813, much used for concerts in the days before concert halls and for the weekly subscription balls organized by "gentlemen of the town." Prior to the introduction of the "European plan" in the 1830s, room and board, the latter comprising four meals a day, cost $2. In the 1840s the City pioneered **room service**, denounced by an ardent upholder of American values as likely to encourage "dangerous blue blood habits . . . a menace to the foundation of the Republic . . . a threat to democracy." It finally closed in 1849 to be replaced with shops and offices.

The first of the grand hotels in the United States was Boston's famed 170-room Tremont House, designed by Isaiah Rogers and built at a cost of $300,000, which opened on 16 October 1829. Not only was this the largest hotel in the world, but it pioneered a number of innovations later to become standard. It was the first with a hotel lobby and desk clerk, other hotels opening on to the barroom; the first with bellboys (though not yet in livery); the first to offer single and double rooms, obviating the need to share as in other hostelries; the first with locks on every bedroom door and to offer free soap for every guest; the first in the world with bathrooms (eight, in the basement) and the first public building in America with water closets (SEE **toilet, flush**), also eight in number; and

the first American hotel to offer French cuisine in its dining room. The handwritten bill of fare from the restaurant's opening night is believed to be the earliest surviving example of a menu in America.

Hotel chain: The first was inaugurated by Paran Stevens (1802–72), proprietor of the Tremont House in Claremont, N.H., who began the chain with the acquisition in 1843 of the New England Coffee House (a major hotel despite its name). Jewel in the chain's crown was the Revere House, also in Boston, which opened in 1847. When he died in New York in 1872 Stevens was reputedly worth $3 million. Hotel chains existed before any other multiple commercial enterprise, though the practice of labeling all the outlets in a group by a single brand name did not emerge until Ellsworth M. Statler, who had begun his working life at age nine earning 50¢ for a 12-hour day, opened the first Hotel Statler at Buffalo, N.Y., on 18 January 1908.

Hotel with baths: As mentioned above, the Tremont House in Boston had eight bathrooms when it opened on 16 October 1829. These are generally claimed as the first, though it should be noted that an advertisement appearing on 1 July 1812 for the Eagle Hotel at Raleigh, N.C., promised that "Bathing Rooms will be constructed by the next season." Whether they were history does not record. The Tremont House bathrooms, all located in the basement, were approached by a separate entrance onto the street. Since the hotel could accommodate 250 guests, this may have helped discourage a long line for their use. The first with private baths was the New York Hotel in 1844, while the first with en suite bathrooms throughout was the 240-room Victoria Hotel in Kansas City, opened by George Holmes on Ninth Street on 14 May 1888.

Hotel with running water in all bedrooms: The first was Boston's New England Coffee House in 1833. Hot and cold running water in all rooms was offered by the Mount Vernon Hotel at Cape May, N.J., in 1853.

Hotel with bridal suite: The first was Irving House, on Broadway in New York City, which offered this attraction when it opened on 20 September 1848.

Centrally heated hotel: The first was the Eastern Exchange Hotel, in Boston, where steam radiators were installed in 1846.

Hotel to employ waitresses: The first was the Delavan House in Albany, N.Y., in May 1853. The celebrated American feminist Amelia Bloomer, promoter of the pantaloon garments named after her, recorded in a letter:

> Stopping overnight in the Delavan House in Albany, we were agreeably surprised on entering the dining-room for supper to see about a dozen young women in attendance on the tables. This was something new. When we visited the house last winter the waiters were all men, as is usual in such places. Now not a man was to be seen in that capacity; but in place of their heavy tread, and awkward motions, was woman's light footfall and easy graceful movements. In a conversation with the proprietor we learned that the change was . . . Entirely satisfactory. . . The only objectors being a few women preferring black men.

Hotel with a safe deposit: The first was the New England Hotel, Boston, in 1866.

Hotel lit with electricity: The first was the Langham in London's Portland Place, which installed arc lamps in the entrance and courtyard in 1879. The first lit with incandescent electric lamps was Lamb's Temperance Hotel in Dundee, Scotland, which was illuminated with Swan lightbulbs in June 1881.

U.S.: The first with arc lighting were the Palmer House Hotel, in Chicago, in time for the Republican Convention in the first week of June 1880 and the Continental Hotel on Ninth and Chestnut in Philadelphia, where Brush arc lamps were installed on the first floor during the same year (date not known). The first with incandescent electric lighting was the Hotel Everett at 84–90 Chatham Street (now Park Row), New York City, which had 101 Edison fixtures installed in the public rooms early in 1882. The first to provide electric lighting in its guest rooms was Sagamore Hotel at Green Island, Lake George, N.Y., where all 172 bedrooms were so equipped in the spring of 1883.

Hotel with telephones in the guest rooms: The first was the Hotel Netherland, New York City, in 1894.

Hotel swimming pool: The first known was a "big cemented pool of soft fresh water, filled from the wonderful springs on the old Emerson homestead" built at the Haleiwa Hotel in Waialua, Oahu, Hawaii in 1899.

Air-conditioned hotel: The first was the Congress Hotel in Chicago, where the Pompeian Room and banquet hall were equipped with a carbon-dioxide fan-coil system in 1907 by Frederick Wittenmeier of Kroeschell Brothers Ice Machine Co. The temperature had to be raised four degrees when diners complained they were too cold. First to be air-conditioned throughout, including the guest rooms, was the Dearborn Inn airport hotel on Oakwood Boulevard, Dearborn, Mich., in 1937.

Bibles in hotel rooms were first distributed by the Gideons at Superior Hotel, Iron Mountain, Mont., on 10 November 1908.

Airport hotel: The first was the Aerodrome Hotel at Croydon Airport in Surrey, England, opened on 2 May 1928. Croydon was the terminal for London. Although the airport has been replaced by Heathrow, the hotel survives under its original name.

U.S.: The Dearborn Inn, a 179-room hotel on Oakwood Boulevard designed by Albert Kahn to serve Ford Airport at Dearborn, Mich. Opened in July 1931, it is usually claimed as the first airport hotel in the world despite the precedence of Croydon's Aerodrome Hotel (SEE ABOVE).

Hotel to install television: The first was the Hotel New Yorker, New York City, in February 1932. The low-definition mechanical sets, supplied by the Freed Television & Radio Corp., were provided in all deluxe suites. Guests were able to tune in to up to 5 hours of entertainment programs daily from the CBS television station W2XAB.

The first hotel with high-definition all-electronic television was the Brent Bridge Hotel in the London suburb of Golders Green, where a set costing 130 guineas ($650) was installed in the Brasserie by the proprietor, Mr. H. Appenrodt, in time for the opening of the BBC television service on 26 August 1936. The first in the United States was the Waldorf-Astoria in New York City, two RCA sets being made available for guests in June 1939. The Park Sheraton became the first hotel with a receiver in every guest room in the fall of 1949.

Hotel with key cards: The first in the United States was the Peachtree Plaza Hotel, Atlanta, Ga., where conventional key-operated locks were replaced by Norwegian VingCard locks in 1979 following a spate of burglaries.

For the first hotel to cook by electricity, SEE **electric stove**; by gas, SEE **gas cooker**. For the first hotel elevator, SEE **elevator**. SEE ALSO **motel**.

THE FIRST **HOUSING PROJECT**

in America to supply low-rental accommodation supported by public funding in peacetime (there had been some emergency housing for war workers provided by the federal government in WWI) was built in the Bronx by the Amalgamated Housing Corporation, a cooperative venture sponsored by the Amalgamated Clothing Workers of America, under the auspices of the State Housing Board of New York established by Gov. Al Smith in July 1926. The subsidy from the state took the form of tax relief on projects developed by limited-dividend corporations and approved by the State Housing Board. Designed by architects Springsteen & Goldhammer, the project had 303 two- to six-room apartments (but mainly three and four rooms) built on 13 acres of vacant land to the southeast of Van Cortlandt Park and north of 200th Street. The first five-story landscaped block to be completed was opened on Christmas Day 1927 and the adjoining one in the late summer of 1928. Total cost was $1,930,000, of which $300,000 had been paid for the land. Rents were from under $25 to $72.50 per month, the majority $30 to $55. About three quarters of the tenants had a family income between $1,500 and $3,500 per annum.

Amenities developed by the tenants themselves (of whom only a minority were garment workers) included a cooperative commissary from which groceries, milk, meat, and ice were distributed on a non-profit-making basis; electricity supply also bought in bulk; and a tearoom in the basement where, according to a contemporary account, the men gathered in the evening to "smoke, talk, and play checkers or other games" (their womenfolk were allowed to do the serving). Profits from the tearoom were used to buy a school bus and provide picnics and excursions. The basement also housed a barber, a cobbler, a library, and an auditorium.

Municipal housing project: America's first was also in New York. First Houses on Third Street and Avenue A comprised 122 three- and four-room apartments built at a cost of $300,000 with free labor supplied by the Public Works Progress Administration and was dedicated by Mayor Fiorello LaGuardia, prime mover in the slum clearance scheme, and First Lady Eleanor Roosevelt on 3 December 1935. They rented for $6.05 per room, about a third less than commercial rates for accomodation of similar size (but poorer standard) in the area. The 3,800 applicant families were carefully screened by the New York Housing Authority, eliminating those who were too rich, too poor, too big, too small, too lazy, or too dirty. Those accepted had at least one member in paid employment as taxi drivers, barbers, garment workers, and the like and by the end of the first year had proved to be model tenants. There were no delinquencies and nobody was on relief. First Houses continue to be occupied, now designated a historic landmark.

THE FIRST **HUNGER STRIKES**

were staged by Russian prisoners during the reign of Tsar Alexander III (1881–94). The earliest definitive evidence of the practice dates from July 1882, when it was reported that some male inmates of Kara prison in the Trans-Baikal region had been forcibly fed.

U.S.: The first was by militant suffragettes Alice Paul and Rose Winslow. Alice had been born to a privileged New Jersey family, but she became attracted to direct action in favor of women's right to vote while studying in England. By contrast Rose, formerly Ruza Wenclawska, was a Polish-born immigrant who had started work in a Pennsylvania textile mill at the age of eleven. Both members of the National Woman's Party, they had begun picketing the White House in January 1917 in what has been claimed as the first act of orchestrated civil disobedience in the United States. In October 1917 they were convicted of obstruction of the public way and taken to serve their seven-month sentences in the Occuquan Workhouse in Fairfax County, Va. When their demand to be acknowledged as political prisoners was refused, they went on hunger strike on 5 November 1917. Efforts to persuade the women to eat by offering them tempting food having failed, Alice Paul was taken to a psychopathic ward at the District of Columbia jail and force-fed thrice daily for three weeks through a tube that was pushed up a nostril, then down her throat. Under similar treatment Rose Winslow vomited and screamed, lying gasping long afterward with her nose bloody and her throat raw. Fifteen other suffragette prisoners joined them in their hunger strike on 16 November. One resister, Lucy Burns, was stripped naked and pinioned to a bed by five warders as a director thrust the tube into her nose. The women's refusal to submit led to their release and subsequently the U.S. Supreme Court ruled that the manner of their sentencing had been unconstitutional. Alice Paul spent most of the remainder of her long life (she died aged ninety-three in 1977) working for women's rights. In 2004 an HBO television movie, *Iron Jawed Angels*, portrayed the women's ordeal, with Hilary Swank portraying Alice Paul.

THE FIRST HYMN BOOK

in the vernacular was published in Prague by Severin for the Hussites of Bohemia on 13 January 1501. It contained eighty-nine hymns in the Czech language, of which twenty-one were by the Bohemian divines Konvaldský, Taborský, and Lucas Pragensis (Lucas of Prague). The name of the hymnal is not known, as the only surviving copy lacks the title page.

The first hymnal containing original matter (i.e., not translations) in English was George Wither's *Hymns and Songs of the Church*, for which Orlando Gibbons provided sixteen of the tunes. On its publication in London in 1623 King James I granted Wither a privilege by which a copy was to be bound up with every Bible printed. This aroused intense opposition from the Stationers' Company and they were able to obtain an order from the Privy Council for the suppression of the hymnal. It is unlikely that Wither's hymn book would have been employed in church worship, as the singing of hymns at services was proscribed by an act of Elizabeth I and remained so until the end of the seventeenth century.

U.S.: The first hymnals were printed in German by Benjamin Franklin at Philadelphia for the German-born religious mystic and commune leader Conrad Beissel: *Göttliche Liebes und Lobes Gethöne* ("Melodies of Love and Praise"; 1730), *Vorspiel der Neuen-Welt* ("*Prelude to the New World*"; 1732), and *Jacobs Kampff*

und Ritter-Platz ("Jacob's Place of Struggle and Elevation"; 1736). These were used at the Ephrata Cloister in Lancaster County, Pa., a Seventh-day Adventist commune of vegans, many of them also sworn to a life of celibacy, that Beissel founded in 1732. During his lifetime he wrote more than a thousand hymns and was the first composer in America whose music was published.

The first English-language hymnal published in America was the Rev. James Lyon's *Urania, or A Choice Collection of Psalm-Tunes, Anthems, and Hymns*, published in Philadelphia in 1761. Besides the wordless psalm tunes, this contained fourteen hymns and twelve anthems, some of them by Lyon himself. The music was printed from plates engraved by English immigrant Henry Dawkins. The first hymnal to contain American hymns only was the *New England Psalm-Singer, or, American Chorister* by William Billings, Boston 1770.

THE FIRST HYPNOTIST

to induce a state of trance was Amand-Marie-Jacques de Chastenet, Marquis de Puységur (1751–1825), a disciple of Anton Mesmer and a practitioner of the latter's therapeutic technique known as "animal magnetism." On 4 May 1784, at his estate at Buzancy near Soissons, the marquis first induced artificial somnabulism in a twenty-three-year-old peasant called Victor Race who was suffering from an inflammatory condition of the lungs. In a manuscript detailing various therapies attempted at Buzancy, Puységur described how after a quarter of an hour of magnetism Race fell into a hypnotic trance and began to talk loudly about his domestic worries. Puységur continued:

> When I thought his ideas might affect him in
> a disagreeable way, I stopped them and tried to
> inspire more cheerful ones; . . . at length I saw
> him content imagining that he was shooting at a
> target, dancing at a festival, and so on. I fostered
> these ideas in him, and . . . forced him to move
> about a good deal on his chair, as though to dance
> to a tune, which I was able to get him to repeat by
> singing in my mind. By this means I produced in

him an abundant sweat. After an hour of crisis, I calmed him down and left the room . . . The following day, being unable to remember my visit of the previous evening, he told me of his improved state of health.

Thereafter Puységur made a practice of placing his patients in a hypnotic trance and it was adopted by other animal magnetists, although it was rejected derisively by their mentor Anton Mesmer. It is Mesmer, however, who is most often cited as the originator of hypnotism rather than his pupil; more properly it should be said that Mesmer's technique of charismatic healing by autosuggestion was a precursor of somnambulistic hypnotism as developed by Puységur. Further confusion has been caused by the use of the word *mesmerism* as a synonym for hypnotism.

The first recorded case of **post-hypnotic suggestion** was reported by the Strasbourg animal magnetist M. de Mouillesaux in 1789. He had instructed a young lady of twenty-two, while in trance, to "visit someone to whose house she never went" at nine o'clock the following morning. Mouillesaux and several others gathered at the house to await the outcome. Shortly before nine the young lady appeared outside the house, passed and repassed it several times, then went into a church. The observers believed the experiment had failed, but as they sat down to breakfast she appeared in the room. "Her embarrassment cannot be described . . . She was soon reassured and told us that ever since she had got up she had had the idea of taking this step, that she even believed she had dreamed it, that . . . an irresistible impulse had made her brush aside all opposition . . ."

The first **stage hypnotist** was the half-Indian, half-Portuguese priest and compulsive gambler José Custódio de Faria, born in Goa in 1756, who gave weekly shows at 49 rue de Clichy, Paris, for a period of three years from 11 August 1813. These demonstrations of *sommeil lucide* (lucid sleep) were attended by some hundreds of people at five francs a head, most of them elegant women. He was able to induce trance in more than half his subjects by simply issuing the command

"sleep . . ." in a deep voice, repeating it once or twice if they did not go under immediately. Those for whom this failed were told to gaze at his open hand, which he then moved forward toward their eyes until their eyes closed.

Although promoted as scientific demonstrations, Faria's shows contained much of the repertoire of modern stage hypnotists and were constructed to maximize entertainment value. For example, a subject would be told that a glass of water was alcohol and would appear to become tipsy. Sensations of heat and cold, taste and smell were artificially induced; subjects were unable to move an arm or a leg; soldiers far from home wept as loved ones seemed to appear before them. The lucrative enterprise ended after an actor called Potier, having volunteered as a subject, feigned lucid sleep, responded to Faria's suggestions, then opened his eyes and denounced the priest to his audience as a charlatan. When Potier appeared in a comedy called *Magnetismomania* in 1816 in a role clearly based on Faria, the hypnotism act rapidly came to an end. The hypnotist became chaplain at a girls' school, not perhaps the most appropriate choice. Today he is remembered, if at all, only as the original of the mad old priest Faria in Alexander Dumas's classic *The Count of Monte Cristo*.

U.S.: Animal magnetism was introduced by Joseph du Commun of Paris on his arrival in New York in 1815. He later claimed to have founded a society for its promotion in that year but nothing else is known about its activities or its scope. Du Commun became a teacher of French at the United States Military Academy at West Point in 1829 and during July and August of that year lectured on the subject at the Hall of Science in New York City. It was only in 1837 that hypnotism became a popular phenomenon in the United States, when another French animal magnetist, Charles Poyen Saint-Sauveur of Providence, R.I., acquired a gifted somnambulist partner in the person of Miss Cynthia Gleason of Pawtucket, R.I. He toured with her throughout New England to mounting acclaim from a press and public hungry for novelty.

~~~~~~~~~~~~~~~~~~~~~~~ **I** ~~~~~~~~~~~~~~~~~~~~~~

THE FIRST ICE CREAM

Few subjects have been more distorted by popular myth than has the history of food and few foods have been as mythologized as has ice cream. Its true origins have been obscured by claims that it was eaten by Alexander the Great, Nero, and the Egyptian pharaohs. These, and other of the ancients, were fond of confections made with, or chilled by, snow, but those dishes were not *frozen* and therefore were not ice cream. Nor is there any evidence that frozen sherberts or sorbets were known in Italy in the sixteenth century; as Elizabeth David has shown in *Harvest of the Cold Months* (1995), a dish called a sorbet may have existed, but not in frozen form.

The available evidence points toward Britain as the birthplace of dairy ice cream, though here again its provenance is clouded by unsubstantiated claims, based on no contemporary record, that King Charles I employed a French chef called Gerald Tissain (or any of twenty other names, depending on which nineteenth-century raconteur is favored) who was given a handsome pension as a reward for its invention. The earliest documented reference to ice cream is contained in Elias Ashmole's *The Institution, Laws and Ceremonies of the Most Noble Order of the Garter* (London, 1672). Ashmole, the first freemason and founder of Oxford's Ashmolean Museum, lists the dishes served at royal banquets celebrating the Toast of Saint George at Windsor Castle on 28 and 29 May 1671. On both occasions, the eve of the feast day and the feast day itself, the top table presided over by King Charles II was served with "One plate of white strawberries and one plate of Ice Cream." Those seated at lesser tables could only look on in envy. Charles II's successor, his brother James II, appears to have been more liberal in sharing the delicacy with his subjects, the accounts of the Lord Steward's department for 1686 itemizing twelve dishes of ice cream at £1 per dish (a prodigious sum) for the refreshment of the monarch and officers of his army, who were in camp on Hounslow Heath. A banquet held at Stockholm by James II for Swedish senators to celebrate the birth of his son James Stuart ("the Old Pretender") in September 1688 shows that ice cream was already being incorporated into elaborate desserts. "After the Meat was taken off," the *London Gazette* reported, "there was served up a very fine Desert, with many great Piramids of dry Sweet–Meets, between which were placed all such Fruits, Iced Creams, and such other Varieties as the Season afforded."

At about this time or possibly earlier, ice cream made its debut in France. It had not been brought to the French court by Florentine confectioners when Catherine de Médicis married the Duke of Orléans in 1533, nor had it been served at the Café Procopio in Paris in the 1660s, both persistent legends briskly dismissed by the redoubtable Miss David. The first certain evidence of ice cream in France, and indeed the earliest known recipe for the delight anywhere, is contained, together with instructions for sorbets or water ices made from fruit juices, in the Parisian confectioner L. Audiger's *La Maison Réglée* of 1692. "Pour faire de la Cresme glacée," as he calls it, Audiger gives these instructions:

> Take a *chopine* (16 ounces) of milk, a half *septier* (8 ounces) of good sweet cream, or else three *poissons* (12 ounces), with six or seven ounces of sugar & a half spoonful of Orange flower water, then put it in a tin or earthenware or other vessel to freeze it.

At first the difficulty and expense of making ice cream confined it to the tables of the great, but it began to penetrate middle-class homes after Mrs. Mary Eales published the earliest known English recipe in her *Receipts* of 1718. This called for 18 to 20 pounds of ice to effect the freezing, which meant that ice cream could only be made in winter unless the household was one affluent enough to boast an ice house. Flavorings included cherry, raspberry, and strawberry. (The recipe concludes with directions for making lemon popsicles, using the same apparatus as for ice cream.)

U.S.: The earliest reference to ice cream in America comes from an entry in the diary of William Black for 19 May 1744 describing a dinner given by the native-born Gov. Thomas Bladen of Maryland in Annapolis. The profusion of delicacies at this repast were, he declared,

> ... plain proof of the Great plenty of the country, a Table in the most Splendent manner set out with Great variety of Dishes, all Serv'd up in the most Elegant way, after which came a Desert no less Curious, among the Rarities of which it was Compos'd was some fine Ice Cream, which with the Straw-berries and Milk, eat most Deliciously.

Thirty years later ice cream was available for sale, according to a series of advertisements that appeared in the *New York Gazette and Weekly Mercury* starting 12 May 1777 in which former London caterer Philip Lenzi (aka Lindsay) offered to provide the delicacy "to the gentry... For ready money." Probably a wise precaution, given the proclivity of the English gentry for extended credit and bearing in mind that New York at this juncture of the War of Independence was under British occupation. Lenzi, probably Italian by birth, claimed to have been selling his ice cream since 1774.

The indulgence became prominent among the pleasures offered at their entertainments by the First Family of the new nation. George and Martha Washington served ice cream both as an after-dinner dessert and at the levees they introduced in imitation of those held at court in London (not every aristocratic notion from the Old Country was abandoned by the Founding Fathers, though these were open, in theory at least, to any citizen suitably dressed). Sen. William Maclay of Pennsylvania recorded the menu at the presidential dinner party he attended in the then capital, Philadelphia, in August 1789: soup, roasted and boiled fish, meats, gammon and fowl, followed by apple pie, pudding, ice cream, jellies, watermelon, musk melon, apples, peaches, and nuts. The levees were afternoon receptions presided over by the president, in which

case they were formal, or by the first lady, informal. The refreshments were equally simple in either case: tea, coffee, lemonade, cake, ice cream. For entertaining on this scale the ice cream was ordered in from a confectioner, but the Washingtons also had the means of making ice cream at home, having acquired "a cream machine for ice" in 1784. Purchased ice cream was a luxury indeed: the president spent $200 on it in only two months during 1790.

Flavors tended to be dictated by which fruits happened to be in season. Thomas Jefferson, to whom many innovations have been fancifully attributed, probably really was responsible for the earliest vanilla ice cream in the United States. While he was serving in Paris he copied down his French chef's recipe for the delicacy and took it home to Monticello in Virginia. This comprised two bottles of "good cream," six egg yolks, half a pound of sugar, and a stick of vanilla. As Secretary of State in 1789 he wrote to the U.S. minister in Paris asking him to send over fifty vanilla pods, as they were unobtainable in Philadelphia.

Choice of flavor was restricted to vanilla and lemon before 1810, when Mr. Ensley introduced strawberry, raspberry, and pineapple ices at his "New and Elegant Columbian Garden" in New York.

Factory-produced ice cream did not emerge until mid-century and America was its birthplace with the introduction of mass-production methods by Baltimore dairyman Jacob Fussell. He ran four milk routes in the city, and found that the irregular demand for cream caused severe wastage. The only person making ice cream in Baltimore at this date was producing a confection of doubtful wholesomeness with boiled milk and sugar and retailing it at 60¢ a quart. Purchasing a quantity of freezers, Fussell set up as an ice-cream wholesaler and started what was in effect the world's first ice-cream factory, delivering his first consignment on 15 June 1851. Bulk production enabled his ice cream to be retailed at 25¢ a quart, an unprecedentedly low price, and he was able to expand his operation elsewhere on the Eastern Seaboard, opening factories in Washington, D.C., in 1856, Boston in 1862, and New York in 1863.

Ice cream sundae: According to the authoritative *Oxford Companion to Food* (1999), this originated at the ice cream parlor of Ed Berners in Two Rivers,

Wis., in 1881 when a customer called George Hallauer asked him to pour some of the chocolate syrup used for sodas over his ice cream. Berners at first said no, then changed his mind and began trying out other flavors each with its own name: the chopped peanuts essential to a modern Sundae came with a version he dubbed the Chocolate Peany. The adoption of the name *sundae*, a corruption of Sunday (still unaccounted for), is reputed to have taken place at another ice cream parlor in nearby Manitowoc, where proprietor George Giffy decided to copy Berners's innovation but only on Sundays (also unexplained). According to local legend a small girl asked for a dish of ice cream "with stuff on it." On being told that he only served the concoction on Sundays, she is said to have responded "Why, then, this must be Sunday, for it's the kind of ice cream I want." Giffy gave in graciously, subsequently adopting the name Sunday before it transmuted into sundae.

Ice cream cone: The earliest reference to an edible cone specifically for ice cream is contained in Agnes B. Marshall's *Mrs. Marshall's Cookery Book*, published in London in 1888. Mrs. Marshall ran The School of Cooking in London's Mortimer Street and it was probably there that the cones were developed. In her later publication *Fancy Ices* (1894) two fillings are described. Christina Cornets were filled with vanilla ice cream mixed with finely diced dried fruits, cinnamon, ginger, and maraschino. The cones were then piped with royal icing around the rim and down the side before being dipped into chopped, blanched pistachios. Margaret Cornets had a combination of ginger-water ice and apple ice cream. Neither of these sophisticated confections was the kind of thing you would eat in the street and unsurprisingly it was the democratic Americans who reinvented the cone as a convenience food, generally eaten al fresco.

Just which democratic American is the subject of heated controversy, obfuscation, and partisanship. The version of the introduction of the ice cream cone to the United States favored by the International Ice Cream Association is that a Syrian immigrant called Ernest Hamwi was finding it difficult to sell hot Persian waffles on a very hot day at the 1904 World's Fair in St. Louis. At the next stall, according to this picturesque legend, one Arno Fornachau was doing a

roaring trade in ice cream until he ran out of plates. The two traders combined their resources, Hamwi rolling his waffles into a cone as a receptacle for the ice cream. There were, however, at least a half-dozen other vendors who claimed to have originated the ice cream cone at the St. Louis World's Fair, including Frank and Charles Menches of Canton, Ohio, who added another twist to the tale with the assertion that they had wound the waffle around a wooden fid used to split tent rope. (Menches also claimed to have invented the hamburger in 1885 together with his brother at a country fair in Hamburg, N.Y.) Moreover there are photographs of children eating ice creams at the fair that depict cones that are clearly machine made, not fashioned by hand around a wooden fid or whatever. These may have been produced by a number of other claimants. Foremost among them is Italo Marchioni, an Italian immigrant who on 23 September 1903 had filed a patent for a mold that could make ten ice cream cups at a time (not strictly cones). Marchioni claimed that he had been selling cones since 1896 (two years after Mrs. Marshall's recipe), but according to his grandson these were made of paper. Cones proper were said to have been produced by Cyrus Pemberton at Fairmont, Ind., in 1904 shortly before the opening of the St. Louis World's Fair. Other "inventors" of the ice cream cone at the fair have been named as Lebanese immigrant Abe Doumar, Syrian immigrants Nick and Albert Kabbaz, and Turkish immigrant David Arayon. North of the border Walter Donelly of Sussex Corner, New Brunswick, claimed that it was he who had created the first cone. Seldom has any invention been claimed by so many only begetters fully sixteen years after the first evidence of its existence in print. Happily there is less controversy about the origin of the **double-dip ice cream cone.** Everyone seems prepared to acknowledge that it emerged perfectly conceived, indeed unchanged to this day, at Cabell's in Dallas, Tex., in 1932.

Eskimo Pie was launched in 1921 by Danish-born Christian K. Nelson of Onawa, Iowa, a teacher who ran a candy store in his spare time. The idea came to him after an eight-year-old boy had come into the shop and could not decide between a chocolate bar and a scoop of ice cream; Nelson decided to combine the two. The original chocolate-covered block of ice cream was marketed as the I-Scream bar, because it was Nelson who had coined the slogan that was set to music and became a hit tune: "*I-scream, you scream. We all scream for ice cream.*" Fearing, however, that once the song lost its popularity so would his ice cream bar, he renamed it Eskimo Pie. When Christian Nelson died at age ninety-nine in the politically correct America of 1992, his concoction was still brand leader despite his resistance to changing the name to Inuit Pie.

Soft-serve ice cream was devised in 1934 by Greek immigrant Thomas Carvelas of Yonkers, N.Y., who borrowed $15 from his fiancée to buy an old truck from which to peddle his "frozen custard." This enterprise burgeoned into the Carvel ice cream parlors that spread throughout the northeastern United States.

THE FIRST **IDENTIKIT**

was used in the identification of a criminal by Sheriff Peter Pitchess of the Los Angeles County police in February 1959. The case involved the armed robbery of a liquor store, the owner of which was able to give the police a sufficiently clear description of the thief for them to build up an Identikit likeness for circulation in the neighborhood. This resulted in the naming of a suspect, who confessed to the crime on being apprehended.

The idea of Identikit was originally conceived by Hugh C. McDonald, a detective in the Los Angeles Identification Bureau, who began working on it shortly after the end of World War II. Some 50,000 photographs were dissected and reduced to 500 master foils, making up a kit comprising 37 noses, 52 chins, 102 pairs of eyes, 40 lips, 130 hairlines, and an assortment of eyebrows, beards, moustaches, spectacles, wrinkles, and headgear. Selections could be composed into a drawing of the suspect.

The Photofit system, which uses photographs rather than drawings of facial features, was devised in Britain by Bristol-born Jacques Penry. It was produced commercially by John Waddington of Kirkstall Ltd., specialists in jigsaw puzzles, and first supplied in 1969 to the West Midlands Police Force in Birmingham, England.

THE FIRST **INCOME TAX**

was the *catastro* introduced in Florence under Lorenzo de' Medici in 1451. It was later replaced by the *scala*, an income tax levied on a progressive basis, but this degenerated into a convenient means of political blackmail and on the overthrow of the Medicis in 1492 it was repealed. There were no further attempts at imposing an income tax until the prime minister of Great Britain, William Pitt the younger, did so as a war measure with effect from 9 January 1799. The tax was repealed following the Peace of Amiens in 1802, by which time the public outcry was so great that Parliament ordered that all documents and records relating to it should be destroyed.

The first modern democratic state to impose an income tax on its citizens in time of peace was the Swiss Canton of Basel in 1840.

U.S.: Income tax was introduced as a war measure by an act of Congress adopted on 5 August 1861. The rate was 3 percent on income of $600 to $10,000 and 5 percent on income above $10,000. Peacetime and permanent federal income tax was introduced under the Sixteenth Amendment to the Constitution, ratified on 25 February 1913. This followed an 1894 Income Tax Act that had been declared unconstitutional. The standard rate was 1 percent on incomes of all persons resident in the United States, Puerto Rico, and the Philippines, with a threshold of $3,000 for single taxpayers and $4,000 for married couples. The president, federal judges, and officers and employees of state governments were exempt. Surtax was applied on incomes exceeding $20,000 at 1 percent to 6 percent (on incomes over $500,000). Corporations paid a flat 1 percent. Revenue in the first full year of the new taxes was $28,263,535.

The first state or territory to introduce income taxes, both personal and corporate, was the territory of Hawaii in 1901; first on the mainland was Wisconsin in 1911.

THE FIRST **INOCULATION**

with human smallpox pustules (variola) was practiced in India, China, Senegal, Tripoli, Tunis, Algiers, Turkey, Circassia, and Persia for a considerable length of time before the earliest accounts were published by Europeans at the beginning of the eighteenth century. The first description in English was published by a Mr. Kennedy, surgeon, in *An Essay on External Remedies*, London, 1715. Kennedy wrote of the method used by the Turks at Constantinople:

> They first take a fresh and kindly pock from someone ill of this distemper, and having made scarifications upon the forehead, wrists and legs, or extremities, the matter of the pock is laid upon the foresaid incision, being bound on there for eight or ten days together; at the end of which time, the usual symptoms begin to appear, and the distemper comes forward as if naturally taken ill, though in a more kindly manner and not near the number of pox . . . I was credibly informed . . . that of the number of two thousand which had then lately undergone that method there was not any more than two that died.

The author went on to say that just before his arrival in Constantinople a Greek physician, Dr. Janoin, had experimented by inoculating his two sisters and was thus the first European doctor known to have conducted the operation.

Inoculation in the western world is believed to have originated in South Wales, where it was also of ancient custom. The earliest instance of which details survive occurred in 1668, when one Margaret Brown, described as twelve or thirteen years of age, was inoculated from the pustules of a midwife called Joan Jones at Haverford West. According to the testimony of William Allen of St. Ishmaels, who was born c. 1642, inoculations had been a common practice when his mother was a child. It would seem likely, therefore, that variola inoculation was known in Wales at the beginning of the seventeenth century.

The first inoculation by a qualified English medical practitioner was made on the son of Lady Mary Wortley Montagu, wife of the British ambassador to the Ottoman Court, by the embassy surgeon, Dr. Charles Maitland, at Pera in March 1717. Lady Mary introduced the practice into England in April 1721, when her infant daughter was inoculated by Dr. Maitland in London. The first adults to be inoculated were seven prisoners in Newgate Gaol, who were promised a free pardon if they survived. The operation was carried out by Maitland on 9 August 1721 and all seven lived to enjoy their liberty.

U.S.: Dr. William Douglas, graduate of Edinburgh University medical school and the only physician in Boston possessed of a medical degree, lent the eminent divine Cotton Mather his copy of the *Philosophical Transactions* of the Royal Society in London describing the new technique. Mather recommended to the physicians of Boston on 6 June 1721 that they adopt it, bringing a messge of support from Dr. Zabdiel Boylston in the *Boston Gazette* of 17 July saying that he had already inoculated one of his children and two of his slaves without harmful effect and offering his services to the public in this capacity. Writing under a pseudonym, Dr. Douglas, who opposed the practice, then launched a vehement attack on Boylston in the rival *Boston News-Letter* which provoked a counterattack on the editor of that paper, John Campbell, from six Congregationalist ministers, including Cotton Mather and his father, Increase, the controversy resulting in a temporary ban on the practice by the Boston selectmen. Though they may have been actuated by the petty squabbles of a self-appointed oligarchy in a small colonial town, there was indeed a sound medical basis to the objections. The principal danger of variolation was that the patient was liable to infect others with a more serious eruption of the disease, and there were a number of instances in which whole towns suffered epidemics spread from someone in the process of being inoculated.

Vaccination (i.e., inoculation with non-variolous matter): This is believed to have been performed for the first time in 1771 on Robert Fooks, a butcher of Bridport in the English county of Dorset, in order to induce cowpox as a prophylactic against smallpox. The vaccination was made with a needle in two or three places on the palm of his hand, which later became inflamed, leaving permanent scars afterward. On recovering from the cowpox he was inoculated with human smallpox by Mr. Downe, surgeon of Bridport, but without effect. Although in after years Fooks was often in contact with members of his own family suffering from smallpox, he never caught the disease himself.

The first physician to make a systematic practice of vaccination and publish the results of his experiments was Dr. Edward Jenner, who had originally been inspired with an interest in the subject while an apprentice at Chipping Sodbury in 1770, when he had heard a dairymaid remark concerning smallpox, "I cannot take the disease, for I have had cowpox." He performed his first vaccination on an eight-year-old boy, James Phipps, at Berkeley, Gloucestershire, on 14 May 1796, using virus from a cowpox pustule on the hand of Sarah Nelmes, a dairymaid who had been infected by her master's cows. On 1 July Jenner inoculated James with variolous smallpox matter which produced no result, thus establishing that the earlier experiment had been effective. He published his *Inquiry into the Causes and Effects of the Variolae Vaccinae* in June 1798, after it had been rejected by the Royal Society the previous year. By 1801, six thousand people had been vaccinated, and the number greatly increased after the opening of thirteen vaccination clinics in London by the Royal Jennerian Society in 1803.

U.S.: Vaccine from Dr. Jenner's stock was received early in July 1800 by Dr. Benjamin Waterhouse, professor of physic at Harvard, from Dr. Haygarth of Bath, England. On the 8th of that month he performed the first vaccination in America on his five-year-old son Daniel, followed by vaccinations on three other of his children and three of his servants. Daniel, as the primary test case, was then variolated at Boston Smallpox Hospital, and his immunity to the normal effects of variolation demonstrated the integrity of the practice. Unlike Jenner, who had freely bestowed the discovery on his fellow medical practitioners for the benefit of mankind, Dr. Waterhouse saw it a source of profit and sought to establish a monopoly in New England. He demanded a royalty of $5 for every vaccination, but he was thwarted when other physicians obtained supplies of vaccine from elsewhere. Most of these came from contacts in England but, according to Jenner's first biographer John Baron, some Americans bought shreds of patients' shirtsleeves stiffened with the purulent discharge from an ulcer following vaccination, then soaked them in water to obtain the life-saving matter.

Over the last two centuries vaccination has proved to be the most powerful engine of preventive medicine, helping to reduce the incidence of innumerable diseases, but it is fitting that smallpox should be the first disease to be wholly eradicated. In 1979 the World Health Organization declared that for the first time in recorded history there were no known cases anywhere in the world.

THE FIRST **INSULIN**

was isolated by Dr. Frederick Banting and his assistant Charles Best at the University of Toronto Medical School in Canada on 27 July 1921 and was applied to a depancreatized dog the same day. Banting's discovery derived from his idea that a "hypothetical hormone" necessary for the utilization of sugar might be extracted from a duct-litigated pancreas. This secretion, later known as insulin, was to prove the ultimate weapon against the scourge of diabetes.

Diabetic patient treated with insulin: The first was fourteen-year-old Leonard Thompson, to whom the drug was administered at Toronto General Hospital by Dr. Walter A. Campbell and Dr. Alma A. Fletcher on 11 January 1922. In an advanced stage of the disease, the boy had little prospect of survival when he was admitted to the hospital. With the aid of the insulin he was afterward able to lead a normal life.

Commercial production of insulin was begun by Eli Lilly and Co. of Indianapolis under an agreement with the University of Toronto on 30 May 1922.

THE FIRST **INTERNAL-COMBUSTION ENGINE**

to be commercially developed was a three-stroke gas engine designed by Eugenio Barsanti and Felice Matteucci of Florence, Italy, in 1853 and patented three years later. The first engine in actual operation was installed at the Maria Antonia Railway Station in Florence in 1856. On 19 October 1860 the Società Anonima del nuovo motore Barsanti e Matteucci was formed to manufacture the engines.

Manufacture also began in France the same year and it is possible that commercial production preceded the Italian venture. J. J. Étienne Lenoir of Paris (SEE ALSO **automobile**) had designed an engine powered by illuminating gas in 1859, receiving French Patent No. 43,624 on 24 January 1860. A company called the Société des Moteurs Lenoir was formed the same year, the actual manufacture of the engines being undertaken by the firm of Gautier et Cie. By December 1864 there were 143 Lenoir gas engines being used for industrial purposes in Paris.

U.S.: The first was a two-stroke compressed kerosene engine patented by George G. Brayton of Boston on 2 April 1872. It was produced commercially in limited numbers, the first practical application being when a Brayton engine was used to power Streetcar No. 13 at Providence, R.I., the same year. In September 1880 a gasoline-driven version was fitted to a government launch in Exeter, N.H. (SEE **motorboat**).

SEE ALSO **diesel engine**.

THE FIRST INTERNET

in its earliest incarnation was the Arpanet, a project for linking computers in different scientific and research institutions so that they could "talk" to each other and benefit from the secure exchange of files. This was inaugurated by the U.S. Department of Defense's Advanced Research Project Agency (ARPA) in 1969. The principal obstacle to development of such a network was the time it would take for lengthy messages to be transmitted from one computer to another and the consequent traffic buildup. The solution was found by Donald Davies of Britain's National Physical Laboratory, who worked out a method of breaking up messages into a number of short pieces that would be transmitted in turn with pieces of other messages. Called packet-switching, it meant that a long program would not unduly delay the execution of a short one. Based on this principle, a network was designed for ARPA, by Elmer Shapiro of California's Stanford Research Institute (SRI), which became one of the first two host computer centers on the "net." The other host center was the University of California at Los Angeles (UCLA), and the world's first packet-switched message was sent from one to the other on 29 October 1969. It was brief.

The first task was to log on and UCLA sent an L, which SRI acknowledged, followed by an O, also received. When the UCLA operator keyed in the G, the system crashed. UCLA's Prof. Leonard Kleinrock recalled ruefully, "So the first message was 'LO,' or, if you will, 'Hello.'" At the second attempt the network was up and running. It was to expand rapidly, the third host being the University of California at Santa Barbara in November, followed by a hookup to the University of Utah in December and three months later another at R & D company Bolt, Beraneck & Newman (BBN) in Cambridge, Mass., who had won the contract to design and build interface message precursors (IMPs) linking each host. By the end of 1970 the net was growing at the rate of about one host a month.

Meanwhile progress was being made on the other side of the Atlantic with networks established by the National Physical Laboratory in London in January 1970 and by the Délégation à l'Informatique in France a year later. As new networks began to proliferate, the search began for a method of linking them together—a network of networks, otherwise known as the Internet. Or to be more precise, a search for how to send data on packet radio networks and how to enable these networks to communicate with the incompatible Arpanet. Starting in June 1973 the primary work on this was done on behalf of ARPA by Vint Cerf and his team at Stanford, who developed a host-to-host protocol for Internet working which they called TCP (Transfer Control Protocol). To this was added an Internet Protocol or IP whose task was routing packets around. The date that Arpanet changed over to TCP/IP working, 1 January 1983, is generally accepted as the birth date of the Internet as we know it today.

E-mail: The first was an internal message to his colleagues sent by Roy Tomlinson of BBN at Cambridge, Mass., who developed a program in 1970 for sending mail from one digital computer to another. The inaugural e-mail, transmitted on an unrecorded date in July of that year, helpfully explained how to use e-mail. It was also Tomlinson who devised the @ form of e-mail address to link the name of the user to the name of the host computer. Within a couple of years the majority of Arpanet Internet transmissions consisted of e-mails and in September 1973 Vint Cerf of Stanford sent the first international e-mail while attending the International Networking Working

Group at the University of Sussex near Brighton, England. At this stage, however, there was no "answer" command to enable the recipient to send an instant reply simply by hitting a key. It was an advance that was to follow in 1975 thanks to the ingenuity of University of Southern California Information Sciences Institute programmer John Vittal, who included it in the e-mail reader of his popular program MSG.

Spam made its unwelcome Internet debut on 1 May 1978 when a DEC-Marlboro representative sent an unsolicited e-mail to every Arpanet address on the West Coast inviting recipients to a presentation of DEC-System 2020 at Hyatt House, near Los Angeles Express Airport on 9 May. For the first spam on the Web, SEE BELOW.

Domain names for Web sites were first issued in 1985 by the Network Information Center of the U.S. Department of Defense, whose RFC (Request for Comments) 920 by John Postel and Joyce Reynolds established the top-level domains: .com, .edu, .gov, .mil, and .org, as well as two-digit country domain names, such as .uk for the United Kingdom (.us exists but is seldom used). First to be registered was symbolics.com on 15 March 1985 by artificial intelligence specialist Symbolics Inc. of Woburn, Mass. It took another fifteen months to register the first hundred names, mainly universities and global corporations. Registration was originally free. When the World Wide Web became a global phenomenon in 1994, reaching far beyond the academic and military communities, the deluge of applications became so great that NIC began charging for the service the following year.

Internet service provider: The first commercial operation offering dial-up access was the World (world.std.com) of Brookline, Mass., in 1990. Compuserve and AOL began to provide World Wide Web access in 1995.

Search engine: The first was Archie (from "archive"), designed in 1990 by Alan Emtage, Bill Heelan, and Peter J. Deutsch, students at McGill University in Montreal. This and other early search engines accessed only by Web-page title. The first to offer full text search was WebCrawler, devised by CSE student Brian Pinkerton at the University of Washington, which went live on 20 April 1994. Google was also created by students, Larry Page and Sergey Brin of Stanford University, who incorporated Google Inc. on 7 September 1998 in a friend's garage in Menlo Park, Calif. It took very few years to bestride the Internet: The verb *to google* entered Merriam-Webster and the Oxford English Dictionary in 2006.

World Wide Web: The outline for the World Wide Web was a paper titled "Information Management: A Proposal" written by Londoner (Sir) Tim Berners-Lee in March 1989 while he was employed at the European Organization for Nuclear Research (CERN) at Geneva, Switzerland. On it his line manager, Mike Sendall, to whom it was addressed, scribbled the words "Vague but exciting . . ." At the end he wrote, "And now?" The answers were several: the Web *client* program that Tim Berners-Lee wrote to allow the creation, browsing, and editing of hypertext pages including the actual hypertext window; a line-mode browser developed by a technical student from England's Leicester Polytechnic, an intern called Nicola Pellow; and a set of protocols, devised by Berners-Lee, that ensured that publicly available information resources on any networked computer in the world could be accessed through the browser. He also created the first **Web server** nxoco1.cern.ch (later info.cern.ch), which was up and running by December 1990. The World Wide Web itself became operative in August 1991 when Berners-Lee released his Web client, the line-made browser, and the server on the Internet for anyone to use freely.

While this may be said to mark the birth of the Web, at its outset it was primarily an information exchange for professionals. The first American Web server was set up just twelve months after CERN's pioneer site, with the launch of the Stanford Linear Accelerator Center's Palo Alto–based http://slarvm.slac.stanford.edu on 12 December 1991, but again this was a facility for physicists. The Web only really began to enter homes and offices two years later with the introduction of a graphics-powered browser called Mosaic. It was the brainchild of University of Illinois at Urbana-Champaign undergraduate and archetypal pizza-chomping geek Marc Andreessen, who was working his way through college in a lowly $6.85-an-hour job at the National Center for Supercomputer Applications. In the free-for-all tradition of the Web's founding father Tim Berners-Lee, Andreessen gave to the world the first browser to offer point-and-click access to the Web and the first to run on simple desktop computers rather than complex workstations. He posted a laconic but nonetheless historic announcement on the Internet dated 23 January 1993:

> By the power vested in me by nobody in particular, alpha/beta version 0.5 of NCA's Motif-based networked information systems and World Wide Web browser, X Mosaic, is hereby released.
> Cheers
> Marc

Users began downloading the software almost immediately and within an hour Andreessen was receiving enthusiastic e-mails from all over the world. When NCSA officially released Mosaic browsers for X-Window, Macintosh, and PC in November, the Information Superhighway rapidly became a reality (though that expression was coined some months later by U.S. vice president Al Gore).

That year marked the breakout of the new communications system. As *American Scientist* reported: "The first components of the system were working by 1991, but the Web did not begin to spread outside the high-energy-physics community until 1993."

While Andreessen had to be content with his $6.85 an hour during the remainder of his time at NCSA, he did become among the first to make a fortune from the Web when he went on to launch the ultrafast Netscape Navigator browser, another quantum leap in the Web's phenomenal expansion. This he also placed in the public domain, but he sold the server software to go with it. From the release of Navigator in December 1994, Netscape's share of the global browser market grew to 75 percent in just four months, which Internet historian John Naughton has declared "must be the fastest growth in market share in the history of capitalism."

Webcam: A video camera linked to a computer was set up in the Trojan Room of the Computer Laboratory at Cambridge University, England, in late 1991, trained on the lab coffee pot. The resulting images were transmitted over the local network shared by the fifteen or so researchers of the Systems Group. They also shared the filter coffee pot, which was too small to serve all at once—first come first served. The images gave members of the group outside the Trojan Room an opportunity to dive for it when the coffee was ready. After the Mosaic browser (SEE ABOVE) had been introduced, with its ability to display images over the World Wide Web, researchers Daniel Gordon and Martyn Johnson made a hookup in November 1993 that enabled anyone anywhere to share the doubtful thrills of the gurgling coffee machine. This was the first webcam. Despite a distinct lack of character development or twists in the plot, the coffee pot saga ran and ran, with hits topping one million in 1996, surpassing the King's College Chapel site, and two million in 1997. When the Computer Laboratory moved in 2001, the world's most visible coffee pot was auctioned on eBay for £3,350 ($5,360). The proceeds went toward a coffee machine capacious enough not to need webcam support.

Weblog or blog: The first of general interest (i.e., not confined to computer matters) was *Justin's Home Page* (later renamed *Links from the Underground*), created by Swarthmore College (Swarthmore, Pa.) student Justin Hall after he had read an article in the *New York Times* in December 1993 explaining how Mosaic had made it possible for non-specialists to traverse the World Wide Web. Justin set up his blog on his Powerbook 180, providing information about life at Swarthmore, a photo of himself with Oliver North, a sound clip of Jane's Addiction's lead singer saying "Well I'm on acid too, and I ain't throwin' shoes at you," and a list of his favorite Web sites. Soon he added a picture of Cary Grant taking acid. The first login from outside the college was on 23 January 1994. The term *weblog* was coined by Jorn Barger with the inception of his "Robot Wisdom Weblog" on 17 December 1997.

Advertising on the World Wide Web began in 1994 with twelve advertisers paying *HotWired*, the online version of *Wired* magazine, $30,000 each for a twelve-week sponsorship. First up with banners on 25 October were AT&T (with an ad created by Modern Media) and Zina soda pop. Other advertisers included MCI, Sprint, Club Med, Coors, IBM, JBL speakers, and Volvo.

The first large-scale distribution of commercial **spam** (unsolicited ads by e-mail) on the Web was also in 1994. Attorneys Laurence Canter and Martha Siegel of Phoenix, a married couple, distributed ads offering non-U.S. citizens assistance (for a fee) in entering a green-card lottery. This went to nearly six thousand Usenet groups from Arizona ISP Internet Digest on 12 April in only 90 minutes. The huge response, in which complaints far exceeded applications, resulted in Internet Direct's servers repeatedly crashing and earned Mr. and Mrs. Canter opprobrium in both the legal and cyberspace communities.

E-commerce: Selling online preceded the World Wide Web, IBM and Sears joining forces to launch Austin, Tex.-based subscription service Prodigy nationwide on 5 September 1990 at $12.95 per month. Besides news/information sites and video games, Prodigy offered electronic shopping for CDs, airline tickets, and other items. There were 500,000 subscribers within a month. Peter Adler of Cape Cod, Mass., began selling sunglasses at shades.com via Compuserve the same year, although whether before or after Prodigy's September launch is not known. Another pioneer online retailer was Computer Literacy Bookshops of Palo Alto, Calif., retailing technical books at clbooks.com in 1991.

E-commerce via the World Wide Web followed the launch of Mosaic in late 1993. In April the following year Silicon Valley-based Internet Shopping Network went live selling computer equipment and software online, their choice of product determined by the fact that at this early stage of the Web's development most of its estimated two million users were computer hobbyists or professionals. Probably the first to offer non-computer related merchandise was Duthrie Books of Vancouver, Canada, in June, with a choice of 50,000 books that could be ordered by e-mail. On 11 August a Swarthmore College grad was the first customer to buy a record on the Web, paying $12.48 plus shipping for a CD of Sting's *Ten Summoner's Tales* from a Web site called NetMarket set up by classmates in Nashua, N.H. A few days later, on 22 August, Pizza Hut became the first household name on the Web when it offered a facility for ordering local delivery in its hometown of Santa Cruz, Calif., before rolling out to other areas. They were shortly followed on to the Web by the first corporation doing global business, FTD (Florists Transworld Delivery). In October 1994 Stanford Federal Credit Union became the first financial institution to offer Internet banking, serving the city with probably the highest concentration of Web users anywhere in the world, Palo Alto, Calif.

The Web started to attract a substantial body of users from outside computer circles during 1995 and e-commerce expanded with this new customer base. On 16 July Amazon.com began operating from Jeff Bezos's garage in Seattle, though its first sale was computer-related: Douglas Hofstadter's *Fluid Concepts and Creative Analogies: Computer Models of the Fundamental Mechanisms of Thought*. eBay was founded on 4 September by Paris-born Iranian-American Pierre Omidyar of San Jose, Calif., as Auction Web—first item sold was a broken laser pointer for $14.83, bought by a self-proclaimed "collector of broken laser pointers." On 11 December, British Midland Airways of Derby, England, became the first airline to peddle its tickets via the Web.

Social network site: The first open to all and offering most of the facilities associated with present-day sites, including member profiles and lists of friends, was SixDegrees.com, started with 150 members by New York City lawyer Andrew Weinreich in January 1997. By October of the following year membership had grown to one million. Doug Bedell of the *Dallas Morning News* explained how the new service operated:

> No-charge bulletin boards, e-mail service, and online messaging are offered to those who fill out a brief information form and list e-mail addresses for 10 friends, relatives, or business associates. They comprise your first degree. The entire SixDegrees network of people is the sixth degree. In between are the circles of associations formed by the friends of friends and the contacts each invites on board.

Or as founder Andrew Weinreich put it more succinctly, "Our free networking services let you find the people you want to know through the people you already know." Weinreich sold out for $125 million shortly before the dotcom crash of 2000 and within a year the SixDegrees network, comprising more than 3 million members in 165 countries, had been closed down.

Broadband: High-speed Internet access was first offered experimentally by a number of providers in 1996, with full commercial service beginning in 1998. At the end of that year there were 375,000 U.S. households with Broadband. By 2000 Korea was leading the world in Broadband with penetration of 9.2 percent of population compared to 2.2 percent (7.1 million homes) in the United States.

Wireless Internet originated as the Wi-Fi system developed by Dutch scientist Vic Hayes of NCR Corp. in Utrecht, Netherlands, in 1997. It began to achieve widespread penetration after Apple had offered Wi-Fi upgrade to its iBook portables in 1999 at a highly competitive $99.

THE FIRST **IQ TEST**

for the measurement of intelligence was developed by the Parisian psychologist Alfred Binet, adapting methods that the English scientist Francis Galton had previously employed for the assessment of sensory perception. In 1896 Binet began his work by examining eighty children, asking them to describe a simple picture, and classifying the descriptions into four or five generic types. After considerable research he devised a scale for registering intelligence quotient and this was published in *L'Année Psychologique* in 1905. The Binet Scale was used by the Paris educational authority for examining children who had been recommended for transfer to a special school for what were then known as mental defectives. This was not, however, the first use of IQ tests in schools, for as early as 1897 the German psychologist Hermann Ebbinghaus introduced his *Kombinations-Methode*, based on Binet's initial researches, for the examination of pupils in certain Silesian schools. Ebbinghaus's tests were mainly concerned with comprehension and imagination, for which he used sections of mutilated prose, the child being required to fill in the missing words.

U.S.: Intelligence testing was introduced in 1912 by Henry Goddard, a psychologist who coined the word *moron*, for prospective immigrants being processed at Ellis Island. The results "proved scientifically" to Goddard's satisfaction that a majority of Russians,

Italians, Hungarians, and Jews of various nationalities were "feebleminded." A few years later the first college to introduce IQ tests, Columbia University in New York City, did so because the president wanted to reduce the number of Jews applying for admission without actually declaring a discriminative policy based on religion or race. Not surprisingly the exercise failed to achieve its objective.

The first use of IQ tests on a mass scale was by the Division of Psychology of the U.S. Army Medical Department, which in October 1917 began using a group test devised originally by A. S. Otis of [Leland] Stanford University and adapted for military use by Robert M. Yerkes. The purpose of the tests was to classify men according to their mental capacity and to assist in selecting them for responsible positions. Although intended as a measure of innate intelligence, the tests demanded factual knowledge of a kind that would have challenged many recent immigrants. Such questions included "Crisco is a (A) patent medicine (B) disinfectant (C) toothpaste (D) food product" and "The forward pass is used in (A) tennis (B) hockey (C) football (D) golf." By the end of World War I, the Army intelligence examination had been applied to 1,726,966 men, of whom 7,800 had been recommended for immediate discharge as being of subnormal mental caliber. Nearly 30 percent of the total were found to be illiterate.

THE FIRST **IRON BRIDGE**

incorporating iron girders in its structure was built over the Rhône River at Lyons by the French engineer M. Garbin in 1755. Originally it was intended to build the whole bridge of iron, but owing to the high cost only one of the three arches, a 25-meter span, was forged in iron, the remainder being completed in wood.

The first wholly iron structure of this kind in the world was a 100-foot span built in England across the River Severn in 1779 between Benthall and Madeley Wood (now the village of Ironbridge), Shropshire, and opened to traffic on 1 January 1781. The height from the baseline to the center was 40 feet. The bridge was designed by John "Iron-Mad" Wilkinson and the 378 tons of iron used in its construction were cast at Coalbrookdale by Abraham Darby the third, grandson of the man who first smelted iron from coke. It took three months to erect and no screws, rivets, nuts, or bolts were used; dovetail joints together with pegs and keys were employed throughout. The structure is extant.

U.S.: The first was an 84-foot single-arch bridge built by Capt. Richard Delafield of the United States Army Corps of Engineers in 1838–39 to carry the National Road across Dunlap's Creek at Brownsville, Pa. Dedicated on 4 July 1839, its total cost was $39,811.63. It remains in use, carrying main-road motor traffic.

THE FIRST **IRON SHIP**

SEE **ocean liners**; **steamboat**.

~~~~~~~~~~~~~~~~~~~~~ J ~~~~~~~~~~~~~~~~~~~~~~~

THE FIRST JAZZ BAND

is claimed to have been formed by black musician Buddy Bolden in New Orleans c. 1900. Besides Bolden on trumpet, it comprised a cornet, clarinet, trombone, violin, guitar, string bass, and drums. According to musician Bud Scott, "Bolden went to church, and that's where he got his idea of jazz music."

In assessing Bolden's claim to have been the originator of jazz, historians can rely only on the testimony of those who knew him and heard him play. However, one very illuminating piece of evidence is a recorded demonstration of his style, made by Bunk Johnson in the 1930s. While owing something to march tunes and ragtime, Bolden's music appears to have had a distinctive rhythm of the kind now associated with pure jazz. His playing may have been only a stage in an evolutionary form; but if it is possible to mark a progression from the earlier forms of minstrel and traditional plantation music, and call it the beginnings of jazz, this was probably it. Bolden's band continued to play in New Orleans until 1907, when its leader went mad and was confined to an asylum.

Jazz orchestration: The first to be published was Ferdinand Joseph "Jelly Roll" Morton's "Jelly Roll Blues," Chicago, 1915—though apparently it had been composed ten years earlier. Morton, self-proclaimed "inventor" of jazz, claimed to have composed his first jazz orchestration in 1902 and called it "New Orleans Blues."

The origin of the word *jazz* itself is obscured by conflicting claims. Morton asserted that he coined the term in 1902 to differentiate his music from ragtime. This has been disputed by historians who believe that the new style of music remained without a distinctive name until its northern awakening in Chicago around 1916. According to band leader George Morrison, however, it was known in Colorado at least five years before this date. Recording his impressions of early jazz on tape for Gunther Schuller at his Denver studio in June 1962, he recalled:

> I first heard the word jazz back around 1911. Yes. When I married, that word was coming in then. I remember it well because in 1911 when I first got married and I played for the dances, it was jazz we played. I had a sign on my little Model-T Ford with a clef sign and lines and notes and everything, in green and gold and black, and on each side of my car I had a sign on the running board: George Morrison and his Jazz Orchestra.

The word *jass* made its first appearance in print in the *Chicago Herald* with reference to Johnny Stein's band on 1 May 1916. In a report of a raid on Schiller's Café by a vigilante temperance group called the Anti-Saloon League, the paper stated that the sixty intrepid women who entered the nightclub found that it was impossible to be heard. "The shriek of women's drunken laughter rivaled the blatant scream of the imported New Orleans Jass Band." The word continued to be spelled in this way until the *New York Times* featured an advertisement for "The Jasz Band" in its issue of 15 January 1917. The remaining *s* was dropped in an advertisement that appeared in the same paper on 2 February 1917 announcing "The First Eastern Appearance of the Famous Original Dixieland JAZZ BAND." The band had been formed the previous June by the members of Stein's Dixie Jass Band after a dispute with their leader.

SEE ALSO **sound recording: jazz**.

THE FIRST JEANS

Strictly speaking jeans should be made of Genoese, since the name of the garment is a contraction of the name of the fabric. Work clothes of Genoese were made in Kentucky and elsewhere in the early nine-teenth century, but the story of "jeans" as understood today starts only in 1870. In December of that year a twenty-nine-year-old former tailor, now a horse-blanket and tent maker, born Jacob Youphes in Riga but since coming to the United States known as Jacob Davis, was approached by a woman neighbor in Reno, Nev., who wanted a pair of outsize and extra-strong pants for her mountainous husband, a laborer who was the victim of dropsy. They agreed a price of $3 and Davis fashioned the garment from the tent fabric he used for his horse blankets, off-white 10-ounce duck twill. One problem he had encountered as a tailor of work clothes was that the seams on the pockets were usually the first to go. On his horse blankets he used rivets and it occurred to him to rivet the pockets of the new pants, which he did front and rear with a hammer. Evidently the large laborer was satisfied, because four orders for riveted pants came from other customers in January 1871, followed by another ten in February and in March Davis was asked for a dozen pairs to outfit a surveying party. As off-white was not the ideal color for work pants, he ordered 9-ounce blue denim from his wholesaler in San Francisco, Levi Strauss & Co.

In the eighteen months after taking his first order for riveted pants, Davis had sold more than two hundred pairs and purchased $350 worth of cloth from Levi Strauss for their manufacture. On 2 July 1872 he wrote to the wholesaler with a proposition. Enclosed was a check for the balance of what was owed, he wrote, and continued:

> I also send you by Express 2 ps. Overall as you will see one blue and one made of 10 oz Duck which I have bought in greate many Peces of you, and have made it up in the Pents, such as the sample.
>
> The secratt of them Pents is the Rivits that I put in those Pockets and I found the demand so large that I cannot make them up fast enough. I charge for the Duck $3.00 an the Blue $2.50 a paer. My nabors are getting yealouse of these success and unless I secure it by Patent Papers it will soon become a general thing. Everybody will make them up and thare will be no money in it.
>
> Tharefore Gentleman, I wish to make you a Proposition That you should take out the Latters

Patent in my name as I am the inventor of it, the expense of it will be about $68, al complit and for these $68 I will give you half the right to sell all such clothing Revited according to the Patent, for all the Pacific States and Teroterious, the balince of the United States and half of the Pacific Coast I resarve for myself.

Levi Strauss agreed to the proposals and the patent, granted to Davis on 20 May 1873, was assigned to him and the company, who invited the inventor to join them as supervisor of the manufac-turing process. By the end of the 1880s he was in charge of 450 factory hands. He continued in the job until retirement in 1906, when he was succeeded by his son Simon.

Levi Strauss's Double X denim jeans, or overalls as they preferred to call them—despite the fact that they ended at the waist—were promoted as "excel-lently adapted to the use of those engaged in manual labor" and sold mainly to cowboys, miners, teamsters, and lumberjacks of the western states, though by the 1880s there were agents in Mexico, Hawaii, Tahiti, and even in faraway New Zealand. Just how and when jeans broke out of their western, workman's confines is still being debated by leisurewear historians. Ed Cray, in his definitive *Levi's* (1978), attributes the move away from workwear to students at the University of Cali-fornia at Berkeley and the University of Oregon at the end of the 1930s. At the former, the company offered lettermen free 501s in return for the prestige they con-ferred on the humble garment. Up in Oregon they succeeded in persuading the governor to issue an edict that the wearing of Levi's (a term just coming in at the time) was a privilege reserved for sophomores at the state university, thereby making them doubly desir-able to every freshman.

There is evidence, however, that jeans had been adopted as a fashion item earlier in the decade and that it was women who spearheaded the trend. The earliest known representation of **females wearing jeans** appeared in *Vogue* for 15 May 1935 and showed two excessively chic and sophisticated Manhattanites improbably dressed as cowgirls. The accompanying text advised:

Your uniform for a dude ranch or a ranch near Reno is simple-but-severe blue jeans or Levi's, turned up at the bottom once, laundered before wearing (to eliminate stiffness), cut straight and tight fitting, worn low on the hips, in the manner of your favorite dude wrangler. With these jeans go a simple tailored flannel or plaid cotton shirt, or possibly a Brooks sweater; a plain silk kerchief knotted loosely; a studded leather belt, high-heeled Western boots; a Stetson hat; and a great free air of bravado.

Away from the great open spaces it appears that girls first took to the blue-denim look on Seven Sisters college campuses. In February 1937 *Life* magazine reported that jeans had become standard wear at Vassar, the highly upmarket but progressive women's college in Poughkeepsie, N.Y. This had started with the free spirits in Mrs. Hallie Flanagan's drama course the previous year, but had then spread throughout the college until even classics majors were wearing them.

The first *fashionista* to give her imprimatur to the new look was the celebrated beauty and London society hostess Lady Diana Cooper, youngest daughter of the 8th Duke of Rutland and wife of a future cabinet minister, who brought a pair back from a trip to America in 1936—the same year that the Vassar drama students abandoned their skirts. It is notable that it was upper-class women who were first to adopt what had originated as work wear for cowboys and miners. Only when jeans became the uniform of teenagers of both sexes in the late 1940s and early '50s did working-class girls, followed much later by their mothers, begin to wear them.

Designer jeans: The first were introduced by London designer and trendsetter Mary Quant in her 1963 collection. Curiously the United States did not pick up on the trend until fifteen years later, when the Nakash brothers launched their Jordache line and Calvin Klein unveiled hip-hugging denims designed to accentuate a woman's figure; formerly jeans had been unisex.

For the first jeans with zippers, SEE **zipper**.

THE FIRST JEWISH INHABITANT OF AMERICA

was Joachim Ganz, aka Dougham Gannes, of Prague in Bohemia, who was one of the original colony of 108 men who temporarily settled on what later became Roanoke Island, N.C., on 31 July 1585. He was the leading metalurgist in the small community, having been involved in the locating and working of copper mines in England, and as such one of the most important colonists as far as the commercial out-turn of Sir Walter Raleigh's venture was concerned. The colony failed to prosper, however, and when Sir Francis Drake visited in June 1586 he found the inhabitants starving. They gratefully accepted his offer to repatriate them.

The first known Jewish immigrant to settle permanently was an Ashkenazi, Jacob bar Simson, who arrived in New Amsterdam from old Amsterdam aboard the *Pereboom* on 2 August 1654 and took up work as a day laborer. It is possible, however, that he was preceded by Solomom Pietersen, America's first Jewish lawyer, who acted for the Sephardic Jews who fell afoul of the authorities shortly after their arrival in September (SEE BELOW). There is no record of his immigration to New Netherland, nor of whence he came, but it is a truth universally acknowledged that "no Jew is ever the first Jew to arrive anywhere, there has always been one before him."

The first congregation of Jews were twenty-seven men, women, and children under the leadership of Abraham D'Lucena who had fled Brazil when the Dutch West India Company had surrendered its colonies there to the Portuguese and came via Curaçao to New Amsterdam in September 1654. They arrived about two weeks after bar Simson and on 12–13 September held services for Rosh Hashanah, the first Jewish festival to be celebrated in America.

In leaving Brazil on the resumption of Portuguese rule, the emigrants sought what they hoped would be greater tolerance by the Dutch in New Netherland. Toleration of their religious practice was about the most that they received. The richer among the arrivals had pledged the passage money of the poorer, but before they had had an opportunity to discharge the debt, their goods were seized and sold at auction, while two of their number were held as hostages. Although the church came forward to relieve their needs, one leading pastor, Domine Megapolensis, urged that these "godless rascals" be banished and supported Gov. Peter Stuyvesant in petitioning the Dutch West India Company, proprietors of the province, to forbid all Jews to "infest New Netherland." He explained that his congregation rejected them because they had no God other than "the unrighteous Mammon" and aimed "to get possession of Christian property."

The Dutch West India Company was more magnanimous than their principal representative in New Amsterdam. They responded to Stuyvesant that the Jews were free to remain provided they took care of their own poor and reproved him for his recommendation that the Jews should be denied the right to open shops or to be employed in the public service. They insisted that the new arrivals were to be allowed to hold real estate, trade within the city (though not externally), and "exercise in all quietness their religion within their houses." Before this encouraging response had been received, however, several of the Jews had become so disheartened by the hostility they had encountered that they left the city and sought refuge in Rhode Island, traditionally the least repressive of any of the English colonies, and established a Jewish community at Newport—the beginning of the diaspora within North America.

Those who remained formed themselves into the congregation of Shearith Israel (SEE **synagogue** BELOW). For a while they continued to be reviled, the citizens expressing "disgust and unwillingness" to associate with them in the burgher guard, which meant that for the Jews to be exempted from service they were obliged to pay a commutation tax. In 1657 when burgher rights were established in New Amsterdam, several Jews wanted to purchase the civic privileges of the Small Burgher Right. The burgomasters rejected their applications but were overruled by the Governor in Council on the basis that Jews were eligible in Holland.

This appears to be a turning point in the Jews' relationship with their fellow New Yorkers–to–be, because from this point, as far as the record shows, there were few further protests about their presence in the community. Indeed their leader Abraham D'Lucena was to become a highly successful and respected merchant of the city, which by then had become New York. Although Jews did not have the right to worship publicly (which an act of the Assembly restricted to Christians), they began to start occupying public positions when one of their number was elected as a constable of the city in 1686. That same year a Jew was naturalized for the first time, and two years later two were admitted to the roll of Freemen of New York. The Jews, initially rejected, had by the closing years of the seventeenth century begun to make an impact on the life of the city that would become increasingly evident in the years that followed.

Synagogue in America: The first was Shearith Israel, built in 1730 in Mill Street, New York City, by the community of Sephardic Jews discussed above. The oldest is Touro Synagogue, Newport, R.I., founded by Dr. Isaac de Abraham Touro formerly of Amsterdam, of which the cornerstone was laid in 1759 and the building dedicated in 1763.

The Jewish population of America remained insignificant for nearly two centuries, numbering only 6,000 in 1826. The first large influx of Jewish immigrants followed the failure of the European revolutions of 1848, with mainly German refugees swelling the Jewish population in the United States to 150,000 by 1860. Another two million had arrived by 1924. Today the United States has the largest population of Jews in the world at 5.9 million (out of a total of 13.3 million), compared to 5.6 million in Israel.

THE FIRST JIGSAW PUZZLE

was also the first invention by a woman still in general use today. The unresolved question is which woman. The earliest surviving jigsaws are sixteen "dissected maps" in a wooden cabinet that were used by Lady Charlotte Finch to teach geography to the children of King George III, including the future King George IV and King William IV, at their home in Kew Palace. Lady Charlotte was appointed royal governess in 1762, but she is believed to have started making the puzzles two years before. Initially she drew them by hand in pen and ink on pasteboard and cut them into as many as seventy shapes designed to be reassembled into a complete map. The surviving puzzles include a number of these and others with a wooden backing made from printed maps, some of French origin and others the work of Thomas Jeffreys, official geographer to George III. In 2007 the cabinet was purchased from Lady Charlotte's descendants for £120,000 ($230,000) and donated to Kew Palace and London's Museum of Childhood at Bethnal Green, where they are displayed alternately.

Lady Charlotte's puzzles, however, may not have been the first. Jill Shefrin, author of *Such Constant Affectionate Care: Lady Charlotte Finch—Royal Governess & the Children of George III* (2003), believes that she borrowed the idea from another governess, Jeanne-Marie Le Prince de Beaumont, employed to tutor the children of Charlotte's sister Sophie. Born in Rouen in 1711, Mme. Le Prince de Beaumont was a successful novelist and writer of fairy tales for children, but she fled to London in 1746 after an unhappy marriage had been annulled. There is some evidence that it was she who conceived the dissected map idea during the 1750s and may even have produced them for sale earlier than John Spilsbury, the man generally credited with the introduction of the commercially produced jigsaw.

Spilsbury had been apprentice to cartographer Thomas Jeffreys, from whom Lady Charlotte had obtained some of her maps. He appears to have been selling jigsaws by 1763, the year that he was listed in *The Universal Director* as "Engraver and Map Dissector in Wood, in order to facilitate the Teaching of Geography." His range comprised about thirty different dissected maps, the usual price being 10s 6d in a chip box, or 12s in a square box. Spilsbury continued in this business for twenty years, giving it up on becoming drawing-master at Harrow School in 1783.

The Anglo-French provenance of the jigsaw has been challenged in *Stukje Voor Stukje* (Amsterdam, 1988), by Betsy and Geert Bekkering, who have discovered eighteenth-century Dutch puzzles representing maps printed by Covens & Mortier of Amsterdam in 1725. There is, however, no evidence that they were cut at such an early date or indeed before Lady Charlotte's and John Spilsbury's puzzles. The Bekkerings counter that outdated maps would have been rejected by the literate, cultured classes at whom such puzzles were aimed.

Pictorial jigsaws had made their appearance before the end of the century. Examples dating from the 1790s in the Hannas Collection in London include an oval engraving of John Gilpin's famous ride, derived from Cowper's comic poem of 1782; a series of six woodcuts illustrating the fortunes of Hogarth's Industrious Apprentice; views of the Bastille, exterior and interior, complete with rats; a hand-colored engraving of soldiers drilling at Warley, Essex; and another of a milkmaid offering a jug of fresh milk to her swain. Some of these puzzles had interlocking frames, but fully interlocking puzzles only emerged in the 1840s when puzzle cutting became a widespread industry in Germany, France, and the Netherlands.

U.S.: The earliest known puzzle is the off-puttingly titled *Geographical Analysis of the State of New York*, produced by Samuel McLeary and John Pierce of New York City. This is undated but is thought to be contemporary with their 1849 patent for a method of die-cutting map puzzles. It came with testimonials of its educative value from Emma Willard of Troy Female Academy and New York governor Hamilton Fish.

It was not until 1909 that puzzles were first named after the type of tool, a jigsaw, used for cutting the pieces. This was a French invention consisting of a wafer-thin .007-inch blade powered either by a treadle or, later, by electricity. It was exhibited at the Philadelphia Centennial Exposition in 1876 and used shortly thereafter for cutting interlocking jigsaw puzzles by Philadelphia manufacturer the Rev. Charles Jeffreys.

THE FIRST JUKEBOX

was installed at the Palais Royal Saloon, San Francisco, by Louis Glass, general manager of the Pacific Phonograph Co., on 23 November 1889. It consisted of an electrically operated Edison phonograph with four listening tubes, each controled by a separate nickel-in-the slot device.

Pre-selective jukebox: The first was the Multiphone, invented by John C. Dunton of Grand Rapids, Mich., in 1905. Standing 7 feet high, it comprised a lyre-shaped, glass-fronted wooden cabinet containing an Edison spring-motor phonograph and a hand-cranked rotary-selector mechanism that gave the listener a choice of twenty-four cylinder recordings. The cylinders, visible through the glass panel, were numbered, and an accompanying chart listed the titles.

The first disk-playing pre-selective jukebox was the John Gabel Automatic Entertainer, manufactured by the Automatic Machine & Tool Co. of Chicago in 1906. The 5-foot cabinet was glassed in on three sides, and a 3½-foot horn protruded out of the top. It held twenty-four 10-inch disks.

After going into a decline from about 1910, the industry revived with the introduction of the first all-electric jukeboxes by the Automatic Musical Instrument Co. of Grand Rapids, Mich., and by the Seeburg Co. of Chicago in 1927. The addition of electrostatic speakers gave the jukebox the raucous effect that was to endear it to teenage patrons the world over. After a temporary setback during the early Depression years, large-scale mass-production began c. 1934, and by 1939 there were 350,000 jukeboxes in the United States. It was only in that year, however, that the term *jukebox* was used in print for the first time. An article in *Time* magazine reported that "Glenn Miller attributes his crescendo to the 'jukebox' which retails recorded music at 5 cents a shot in bars." "Juke" is Southern black slang for dancing.

THE FIRST JUVENILE COURT

was established in April 1890 in a room of the State Children's Department, Flinders Street, Adelaide, South Australia. It was instigated by social reformer Miss Caroline Clark. The police magistrate or two justices of the peace attended to try cases and only the parents and witnesses were allowed to be present. Under an act of 1896 it became mandatory to try offenders under eighteen at the Children's Court in the city and suburbs and in the magistrate's room in the country. According to a report a few years later, a large proportion of misdemeanors tried were "breaking windows, obstructing or endangering the streets by playing games in the public thoroughfares, and so on. Offences like these against city by-laws of course have to be repressed, but they do not necessarily indicate the beginning of a criminal record. Hence the danger that this should be the case is minimized by the operation of a Court which does not have any criminal taint behind it."

U.S.: The juvenile court widely proclaimed as the first in the world was established in Chicago nearly a decade after Adelaide's. The state of Illinois's *Act to Regulate the Treatment and Control of Dependent, Neglected and Delinquent Children* created the Cook County Juvenile Court, in which a circuit court judge would try defendants of sixteen years or under. At the time this reform was proposed in 1898 there were 575 children incarcerated alongside hardened criminals in the Chicago House of Corrections, some as young as seven. The new approach to juvenile delinquency was illustrated by the outcome of the first case held at Cook County Juvenile Court on the day it opened, 3 July 1899, Judge Richard Tuthill presiding. "Henry Campbell, 11 years old, living with his parents at 84 Hudson Avenue, was arrested last week on the complaint of his mother, Mrs. Lena Campbell, she charging him with larceny," reported the *Chicago Tribune*. Judge Tuthill, the paper went on to say, "left the group of probation officers with whom he had been in consultation and in an informal way disposed of the case."

~~~~~~~~~~~~~~~~~~~~~~ **L** ~~~~~~~~~~~~~~~~~~~~~~~~

THE FIRST **LABOR UNION**

in America, albeit short-lived, was composed of twenty-three coopers of New York who, according to the minutes of the Governor's Council of 1680, "subscribed a paper of combination" not to sell casks other than at rates they themselves had agreed "under fifty shillings penalty to the poor." As it turned out, they each had to pay precisely that sum, having been found guilty of a breach of the Combination Acts current in England, the fines to go "to the church or pious uses." Furthermore those who were in the employ of government were dismissed and the nascent trade union collapsed within a month of its founding.

The first successful strike was called by the Typographical Society of Philadelphia in 1786. The twenty-six strikers agreed "to support such of our brethren as shall be thrown out of employment on account of their refusing to work for less than six dollars per week."

THE FIRST **LAUNDROMAT**

was the Washateria opened in Forth Worth, Tex., by J. F. Cantrell on 18 April 1934. It contained four electric washing machines that were charged for by the hour, the money being handed to an attendant. The first coin-operated laundromat was the infelicitously named Launder-Ur-Own Station opened in Buffalo, N.Y., by Easy Washing Machine dealer Lars Edstrom in 1936. He had been inspired by a Depression-era practice by which salesmen of domestic appliances such as washing machines sold them for a small down payment to cash-strapped homemakers with coin-op meter machines attached. Every time the lady of the house did the washing, she contributed toward paying off the amount outstanding. Edstrom concluded that there was even greater potential in the housewife not having to buy the machine in the first place and

he thereby created what was to become a new worldwide service industry—or, more precisely, self-service industry.

The first unattended 24-hour laundromat was opened in 1949 by Nelson Puett on North Loop in Austin, Tex.

SEE ALSO **washing machine**.

THE FIRST **LAWN MOWER**

was invented by Edwin Budding of Stroud in Gloucestershire, England, who on 18 May 1830 signed an agreement with John Ferrabee of the local Phoenix Iron Works for the manufacture of "machinery for the purpose of cropping or shearing the vegetable surface of lawns." Budding was employed at Lister's textile mill and is said to have been inspired with the idea of the lawn mower from using a machine designed to shear the nap off cloth. The first recorded customer was Mr. Curtis, head gardener of Regent's Park Zoo in London, who bought a Ferrabee machine in 1831, paying 10 guineas ($55) for the large model. A smaller mower at 7 guineas ($36.25) was available for the use of country gentlemen who, said Budding, "will find in my machine an amusing, useful, and healthful exercise." Just how amusing the country gentlemen found the heavy and inefficiently geared machine is open to doubt, but it was clearly an improvement on cutting the lawn with scythes, which could only be done effectively when the grass was wet. The growth of the new industry was slow, only two firms exhibiting at the Great Exhibition in 1851, but the advent of croquet in the 1860s and lawn tennis in the 1870s brought a big influx of light side-wheel models into suburban back-gardens all over games-loving Victorian England.

U.S.: The first was a reel model built by Thomas Coldwell at Newburgh, N.Y., while he was in the employ of W. H. Swift. This was in production by 1856 at a plant Swift established in Wicopee, near Beacon, N.Y., and is said to have been patterned after English models. In 1868 Coldwell established his own manufacturing concern in Newburgh and this eventually became the Coldwell Lawn Mower Co., responsible for the introduction of the first motor mower in the United States and the first electric mower in the world (SEE BELOW). Thomas Coldwell was an inventive genius who believed that innovation could be cultivated and to this end established what is reputed to have been the earliest staff suggestions scheme in any American company. His son William followed in his father's footsteps, designing and patenting the first gang mower. Consisting of several mowers connected in line on a rigid frame and driven by a tractor, these huge machines were produced by the Coldwell Lawn Mower Co. in 1915 for use on golf courses and sports grounds.

Gas-engined mower: Experimental machines were made by the Benz Co. of Stuttgart, Germany, and the Coldwell Lawn Mower Co. in 1897, but it was in Britain that the first commercially produced model was manufactured for sale. This was designed by James Edward Ransome and marketed by Ransomes, Sims & Jeffries at Ipswich, Suffolk, in 1902. The first model sold, a 42-inch machine with a 6-hp four-stroke Sims engine and driver's seat, went to a Mr. Prescott Westcar to help in the upkeep of the landscaped parkland at his Italianate mansion Strode Park at Herne Bay, Kent. Early models cost as much as a small house, the 1906 catalogue offering a choice of three ranging in price from £75 ($365) to £150 ($730). Production prior to World War I ran at about eighty a year, customers including the Royal & Ancient Golf Club at Saint Andrews, Scotland; the Hurlingham Club at Buenos Aires; Government House in Calcutta; Flemington Racecourse in Melbourne and others as far flung as Shanghai, Port of Spain, and Rio de Janeiro. One notable customer was King Edward VII, who ordered a Ransomes mower for Buckingham Palace in 1906 after he had staged a contest between a lumbering, snorting, steam-driven behemoth and the nimbler, smooth-running gas-engined interloper.

U.S.: The first gasoline-powered mower was introduced by the Coldwell Lawn Mower Co. of Newburgh,

N.Y., in 1903. This, like its Ransomes antecedent, was designed to be ridden. William Coldwell designed America's first push-type motor mower in 1914.

Electric mower: The first was invented by Alwin Smith, who applied for a U.S. patent in August 1925. Rights were assigned to the Coldwell Lawn Mower Co. of Newburgh, N.Y., whose 21-inch five-bladed model, powered by a ½-hp General Electric universal motor, was reported in September 1925 to have been launched "recently." The 157-pound machine was said to consume about the same amount of electricity as an iron and had a cutting capacity of a ¼ acre per hour. A reel of 150 feet of cable was attached to the mower and driven by the motor.

Rotary mower: The first was the electric Pioneer, manufactured by the Louisville Electric Manufacturing Co. under a patent applied for by Josephus Miller of Louisville, Ky., on 19 October 1928. The first hover rotary was invented by Swedish engineer Karl Dahlman and marketed as the Flymo in 1963 in Sweden and Britain.

THE FIRST LAWN TENNIS

was played in varying and separate forms at a number of places in Britain during the 1860s. Rival claims to its invention were discussed in the letters column of the *Field* during the closing months of 1874, when the game was first beginning to attract widespread attention. The results of these deliberations were inconclusive but may be briefly summarized as follows:

Mr. R. A. Fitzgerald, secretary of the Marylebone Cricket Club, stated that there was "authority for its existence in Paris upwards of 30 years ago" (i.e., in the 1840s). He produced no evidence of the authority.

Another correspondent asserted that lawn tennis had been played "more than ten years ago at Ancrum, Sir William Scott's place, in Roxburghshire."

A writer signing himself G. C. C. said that lawn tennis had been played at Layton, Essex, in 1868.

Mr. J. H. Hale of Germains, Chesham (a large country house in Buckinghamshire) described how he had devised his Germains Lawn Tennis as a game suitable for women, when enthusiasm for croquet had begun to decline. He did not state when this had been.

Germains Lawn Tennis was one of three versions that reached commercial development, special equipment being sold by John Wisden & Co. at 5 guineas ($26) a set immediately following the publication of the rules on 24 October 1874.

The most popular of the early versions, the barely pronounceable Sphairistike, was invented by Maj. Walter Clopton Wingfield and first played at Lansdowne House, Berkeley Square, London, in 1869 by Lord Lansdowne, Walter Long (then a Harrow schoolboy), the twenty-one-year-old future prime minister Arthur Balfour, and Maj. Wingfield himself. Lord Lansdowne recorded: "We four played the first game of lawn tennis on my lawn, over a net about two feet wide hung on sloping posts kept erect with strings attached to pegs. We found it good exercise and quite interesting, even with the crooked racquets and plain uncovered balls of that day." Wingfield's first book of rules was issued in December 1873 and contained an advertisement stating that the necessary equipment could be obtained from Messrs. French & Co. of Churton Street, price 5 guineas ($26) a set. He was granted a patent for a "New and Improved Court for Playing the Ancient Game of Tennis" on 24 July 1874. ("Ancient" referred to Real or "Royal" Tennis played in an indoor court.) In fact Wingfield's court was retrogressive in its design, being of an hour-glass shape with a narrow 4-foot-high net spanning the neck and totally superfluous wing-nets on either side. Nevertheless it was Sphairistike that achieved the biggest early success on the superannuated croquet lawns of England's country houses, and that instigated the correspondence in the *Field* concerning possible predecessors.

The remaining contender among the *Field's* claimants to the honor of originating lawn tennis was Mr. J. B. Perera, who said that he had "first introduced the game fifteen years ago." Perera was a Spanish merchant living in the large manufacturing city of Birmingham, and he called his version of tennis after the quite dissimilar Spanish game of Pelota. The date he advances for its invention, 1859, seems improbably early, and Lord Aberdare states in his *Story of Tennis* that Pelota was first played on the lawn of Perera's house, Fairlight, in Ampton Road in the select Birmingham suburb of Edgbaston in 1866.

Associated with him in its development was Maj. T. H. Gem, and it was when both men moved to Leamington Spa in the fall of 1872 that they introduced the game to a wider public. According to an obituary of Maj. Gem published in the *Leamington Spa Courier* for 31 December 1881, he and Perera, together with Dr. A. Wellesley Tomkins and Dr. F. H. Haynes, founded that same year the first **lawn tennis club** in the world on land in Avenue Road adjacent to the Manor House Hotel. The original laws, drawn up by Maj. Gem in 1875 to govern the club game, show that by this time they were already calling the game Lawn Tennis. They also indicate that both the method of play and the layout of the court, a rectangle measuring 90' x 36' with a 4' 1"–high net, approximated more closely the conditions under which the modern game is conducted than had Maj. Winfield's Sphairistike. (The present court is 78' x 36' with a net 3' 6" high at the sides, 3' in the center.)

In his *Royal Leamington Spa: a Century's Growth and Development*, H. G. Clark wrote, "The first match to be played by the Leamington Club against another combination was at Oxford University, where they were defeated owing to the damp ground and consequent heaviness of the ball, for at home they were always accustomed to more lively conditions." No contemporary record of this historic match has been found, and it seems probable that Clark was told about it by one of the participants.

The Perera-Gem version of lawn tennis was played with a 1½-ounce ball "of India-rubber or other substance answering the purpose, punctured or not, as may be agreed upon..." The manufacturers of Sphairistike offered plain rubber balls imported from Germany and priced 5s ($1.25) a dozen. The **cloth-covered ball** was invented by Mr. J. M. Heathcote of Conington Castle, Huntingdonshire, and the prototype, fashioned by Mrs. Heathcote, was used for the first time in 1874. By the following year its use had become general.

The first attempt to standardize the game was made in 1875 by a committee of the Marylebone Cricket Club (MCC, the governing body of English cricket) resulting in an agreed set of rules combining various features derived from Sphairistike, Germains Lawn Tennis, and Pelota–Lawn Tennis. Scoring was up to 15, a system common to all three versions, and the court followed the dimensions and hourglass shape of Sphairistike. When the All England Croquet Club took up the sport at Wimbledon two years later they determined on a rectangular court of the kind favored by Perera and at the same time introduced a system of scoring based on the one used in Real Tennis, still standard today.

U.S.: There are two principal claims for the introduction of lawn tennis to the United States. According to one, the game had its American genesis in late August 1874 when two schoolboys, Fred R. Sears, grandson of David Sears who had been left "the largest fortune ever inherited in New England," and his friend James Dwight, later the prime mover behind the Davis Cup, came across a boxed set of Maj. Clopton Wingfield's Sphairistike at the summer residence of their parents' friend William Appleton at Nahant, Mass. Appleton's son-in-law, J. Arthur Beebe, had recently brought the tennis set with him from London as a gift for the Appletons, but the two young men intercepted it and marked out a court by the side of the house. There they played the inaugural game, donning raincoats and rubber boots when it began to pour with rain, and continuing their match on a sodden court until each had won a set.

The other claim for the introduction of lawn tennis to America attributes it to Mary Outerbridge, said to have acquired a set of Sphairistike in Bermuda which she brought to New York aboard the SS *Canima* on 2 February 1874. Miss Outerbridge learned the game at Clermont in Bermuda, whence it had been imported by a fellow officer of Maj. Wingfield who is said to have played it with him at a Christmas 1873 house party before being posted to the island. Given the fact that he would not have sailed until the new year, the timetable for the game to become established at Clermont and for Mary Outerbridge to have learned the game and brought the anonymous army officer's Sphairistike set to New York by the beginning of February seems improbably tight. Certainly, Miss Outerbridge did sail on the *Canima* but she was a frequent visitor to the colony and some authorities believe that her encounter with the new game there took place the following year. She was, however, instrumental in popularizing the game in the United States, as she set up court at the Staten Island Cricket and Baseball Club (which thus became America's pioneer tennis club), the first at any public venue, in the summer of 1875. Not that the game was welcomed unequivocally. "It will no doubt furnish quite a good deal of amusement to Staten Islanders," remarked the *Richmond County Sentinel* loftily, "to see able-bodied men playing this silly game."

Lawn tennis tournament: The first in America was played on the Appletons' court at Nahant, Mass. (SEE ABOVE), thirteen competitors meeting on an indeterminate date in August 1876. Serving was as for rackets. James Dwight and Fred R. Sears, the progenitors of the game in America, met each other in the final, the former winning 12–15, 15–7, 15–13.

The first **open tournament** and the first **championship**, now the world's oldest, was organized by the All England Croquet and Lawn Tennis Club at Wimbledon, South London, from 9 to 19 July 1877. Two hundred spectators paid a shilling each (25¢) to watch twenty-two players (all male) compete for a Silver Challenge Cup, valued at 25 guineas ($130), presented by the *Field*. It was won by twenty-seven-year-old Spencer Gore, who had been captain of cricket at Harrow School, and who wrote about this time:

> That anyone who has really played well at cricket, tennis [meaning Real Tennis], or even rackets, will ever seriously give his attention to lawn tennis, beyond showing himself to be a promising player, is extremely doubtful; for in all probability the monotony of the game as compared with others would choke him off before he had time to excel in it.

Despite excelling in it, Gore was sufficiently "choked off" to abandon the game after defending his title unsuccessfully at the 1878 Wimbledon tournament.

The first Americans to compete at Wimbledon were James Dwight; Richard (Dick) Sears, the younger brother of Fred Sears (SEE ABOVE); and Al Rives in 1884. Together with South Africa's E. L. Williams they were also the first overseas competitors.

The first U.S. national championship was played under that name (it later became the U.S. Open) on 31 August 1881 at the Newport Casino in Newport, R.I., now the site of the Tennis Hall of Fame. The singles champion was Dick Sears, who was to repeat this victory on no fewer than six subsequent occasions.

Women's championship: The first was played on the covered asphalt court at the Fitzwilliam Club, Dublin, in 1879, and won by Miss M. Langrishe 6–2, 0–6, 8–6, who at fourteen was the youngest competitor. The first **mixed-doubles championship** was contested on the same occasion, Mr. E. Elliott and Miss Costello beating Mr. C. Barry and Miss Langrishe in the final. Tennis was the first ball game at which women competed in tournaments, the mixed sport of croquet having been occasion for little more than decorous flirtation between the sexes on rectory lawns.

U.S.: The first women's championship was inaugurated in 1887 at the Philadelphia Cricket Club as a competition that was to become the U.S. Open and won by a seventeen-year-old local girl, Ellen Hansell, 6–1, 6–0.

Seeding was authorized by the U.S. Lawn Tennis Association in 1922 as a means of avoiding leading contenders meeting in the early rounds of a tournament. It was first adopted at the U.S. National Championships played at the Germantown Cricket Cub in Philadelphia that year and for the Wimbledon Championships in 1924.

Professional tennis players: The first (other than coaches) were recruited in 1926 by sports promoter Charles C. Pyle to provide support for his star attraction, French champion Suzanne Lenglen, who was probably the only player at the time who could attract a paying audience to a non-championship event. Pyle offered her the sensational sum of $50,000 to tour the United States and, as he needed someone for her to compete against, made a rather less generous offer to American player Mary K. Browne, though sufficient at $25,000 to persuade her to abandon her amateur status. Four men were added as ballast, Americans Vincent Richards at $35,000; Howard O. Kinsey at $20,000; Harry Snodgrass at $12,000; and Frenchman Paul Peret at $10,000. The tour opened at Madison Square Garden on 9 October 1926 and by its end Pyle had attracted so many eager fans that after all expenses had been paid, and even more largesse heaped on Mlle. Lenglen with a $25,000 bonus, he had still cleared $80,000 for

himself. Vincent Richards and H. O. Kinsey formed the U.S. Professional Lawn Tennis Association in 1927, Richards becoming the first U.S. professional champion the same year.

THE FIRST **LAWYER**

in what is now the United States was Miguel Delgado, resident at St. Augustine, Fla., who was married to Maria, daughter of tailor and taverner Alonso de Almos. The Almos family moved from Florida's "second city," St. Elena, to St. Augustine in 1576 and Miguel and his bride had a house in their compound. It seems doubtful that he could have earned a regular living as a lawyer in what was then principally a military garrison, but he may have been employed as a scrivener by the authorities of the nascent Spanish colony.

The first lawyer in English-speaking America was Thomas Morton, who sailed to Massachusetts with Capt. Wollaston in 1624 or 1625 and settled in what is now Quincy. He was held in the same low regard as most of the others of his profession in seventeenth-century America. Gov. William Bradford called him "a kind of pettie-fogger of Furnewells Inne," though on the title page of his *New British Canaan* (London, 1637), Morton declared himself "of Clifford's Inn Gent" (Furnevall's Inn and Clifford's Inn were Inns of Chancery and were deemed inferior to the Inns of Court, where barristers—counsel able to plead in court—received their training). According to Gov. Thomas Dudley he was "a proud, insolvent man" who had been "an attorney in the West Countries while he lived in England." Certainly Morton seems to have gone out of his way to cause the maximum offense to his stern Puritan neighbors. At his property, which he named Merry Mount, he was said to have opened "a school of Atheism, set up a maypole and did quaff strong waters as they had anew revived and celebrated the feast of ye Roman Goddess Flora or the beastly products of ye madd Bacchanalians." Such scandalous and profane conduct was not to be tolerated and Morton was thrown into jail before being deported whence he had come.

It is not apparent whether this scapegrace ever practiced law in New England, though the odds seem against it. The first known to have been active was Thomas Lechford "of Clement's Inn in the County of Middlesex, Gentleman," who arrived in Boston in 1637 or 1638 and like Morton before him seems to have lost little time in upsetting the authorities. Despite the fact that for three years he was, according to Emory Washburn in *Judicial History of Massachusetts* (1840), "the Embodied Bar of Massachusetts Bay," he found it difficult to make a living from his avocation and what little fee income he earned was mainly as a scrivener "writing petty things." Nevertheless, it was at his instigation that a law was passed in 1639 in order that the records "bee of good use for president [*precedent*] to posterity . . . every judgement with all the evidence bee recorded in a book, to bee kept to posterity." He came into conflict with the judiciary in September 1639 when at a Quarter Court he was "admonished not to presume to meddle beyond what he shall be called to by the court." The following year the records of the same court report that Lechford "acknowledged he had overshot himself, and was sorry for it, promised to attend to his calling, and not to meddle with controversies . . . " He returned to England in disgust and published his *Plain Dealing or News from New England* (London, 1642) in which he explained that these upsets had been caused by the fact that he had been trying to assert the English Common Law whereas Puritan leaders of the colony, in seeking to establish a theocracy, were aiming to bring it under Mosaic Law, especially in criminal cases (not unlike the adoption of *sharia* law today in countries whose governments come under the control of Muslim fundamentalists).

The first public prosecutor—or **district attorney** in modern parlance—and probably the first person to practice law successfully as a full-time occupation in America was Adrian van der Donck, a graduate in politics and jurisprudence of the University of Leiden, who was appointed in 1641 by the absentee *patroon* Kilaen van Rensselaer as *schout* (an office combining the duties of law enforcer and public prosecutor) of his semi-autonomous fiefdom of Rensselaerswyck. This was a vast territory administered from Fort Orange on the site of what is now North Albany, N.Y. His activities there included suppressing the illegal grain trade, prosecuting settlers who contravened van Rensselaer's monopoly of the beaver pelt trade,

and pursuing indentured servants who moved away before their contracted time. One such was a pregnant servant girl who had fled to New Amsterdam (New York), where on being discovered by van der Donck she was arraigned before the court at Fort Amsterdam. A humane man, though he demanded her return to fulfill her contract, the lawyer agreed to allow her to remain in the capital of New Netherland until she had given birth and the baby was old enough to travel. For this magnanimity he was reprimanded from across the Atlantic by his stern and unbending master van Rensselaer, ever jealous of his own interests. Directed to collect outstanding rents, van der Donck quietly ignored the instruction when he found the tenants were too poor to pay.

Van Rensselaer's increasing resentment of his brilliant young protégé meant that van der Donck's contract was not renewed on its expiry and in 1644 he moved to New Amsterdam. There he became the legal adviser to the Dutch West India Company and as an expert on Native American lore and custom was largely responsible for arranging the treaty with the Lenape of Manhattan and adjacent lands, ending a long period of conflict. His private practice involved representing merchants, sea captains, property-owning widows, and *patroons* in court. For his services to the Company, van der Donck was rewarded with a 24,000-acre estate stretching from the present-day Bronx to Yonkers. The latter town takes its name from him, as in his new capacity as landowner, the honorific "Yoncker" or "young squire" was conferred on him by tenants and neighbors. Like many lawyers he turned to politics, becoming a noted and formidable opponent of Gov. Peter Stuyvesant's dictatorial rule. For one who had always been a staunch friend and defender of the Native American tribes, his eventual fate was particularly cruel: he was murdered at the age of thirty-seven in the Indian uprising of 1655–56 known as the Peach War.

Outside the Dutch colony, for most of the seventeenth century the practice of law in New England and Virginia was distinguished only by the lowly calling and lack of qualifications that marked those who presumed to call themselves attorneys, mainly men engaged in mercantile activities who would undertake to represent litigants in court for a meager consideration. With the dawning of a new century it began to emerge as a regular profession, originally through the statutory requirement in Massachusetts for an oath of adherence to what would now be called a code of conduct. Almost identical provisions were prescribed in Connecticut in 1708, Pennsylvania in 1726, and Virginia in 1732. In his *History of the American Bar* (1911), Charles Warren cited as the first American-born lawyer of distinction the Harvard-educated John Read. Admitted to the bar in Connecticut in 1708, during his forty years of practice Read became "the greatest common lawyer that ever lived in New England"; by that time English Common Law, for which Thomas Lechford had striven in vain a century earlier, had indeed been asserted.

Bar association: The first was founded in New York in 1748. Admission to the bar was originally by apprenticeship to an established lawyer and sponsorship for approval by the senior members of the bar. The first formal qualification was introduced in 1761 by the bar association founded in Massachusetts that year. A seven-year probation had to be served, with three years of preliminary study, two of practice as an attorney in the Interior Court, and two of practice as an attorney in the Superior Court. Many Americans from prosperous families went to London to train at the Inns of Court, which exempted them from such requirements. After the Revolution, however, American law, while still largely based on English Common Law, went its own way.

SEE ALSO **black lawyer; woman lawyer.**

THE FIRST **LEGISLATURE, REPRESENTATIVE**

in America was the Virginia General Assembly, first convened on 20 July 1619 at Jamestown following **elections** in which all the freemen of the colony were entitled to vote. The General Assembly comprised twenty-two elected representatives or burgesses, two from each constituency, and six ex-officio members in addition to the governor of Virginia, George Yeardley. The Speaker, John Poxy, had been a Member of Parliament in England; consequently procedure followed that of the House of Commons. He recorded that "The most convenient place we could find to sitt was the quire of the Churche." The General Assembly sat annually, the first session lasting only six days because of "the intemperature of the Weather, & the falling sicke of diverse of Burgesses." It was, nevertheless, extraordinarily productive, with a wide range of laws regulating tradesmen; servants; travel; cultivation of silk, flax, hemp, vines, and mulberry trees (every landowner was required to plant a minimum of six a year); the price of the main cash crop, tobacco (3s per pound for best grade); injury to Indians; and idleness, drunkenness, and gambling ("both winners and losers shall forfaite ten shilling a man"). Anyone failing to attend divine service on Sundays had to pay a fine of 3s to the church, except servants—who were whipped. This was considerably more liberal, though, than the martial law that had preceded the introduction of democracy to America. Formerly everyone had to attend church services twice daily on penalty of a day's allowance for the first offense, a whipping for the second, and six months as a drudge for the third.

The first purpose-built legislature was the statehouse erected at Jamestown in 1632. It served for only a few years, being succeeded by four other statehouses, the last of which burned to the ground in 1698, thereby precipitating the removal of the capital of Virginia and its legislature to Williamsburg. There may be found the oldest surviving legislature building, the Old Town House of 1712–13. (The oldest in current use is Maryland's State House of 1772 in Annapolis.)

Legislature with paid members: The first was the Pennsylvania Assembly in Philadelphia. Members were paid 6s per diem while attending, plus three pence mileage, beginning with the session starting 14 October 1706.

THE FIRST **LIFE INSURANCE POLICY**

recorded, was taken out in London on 18 June 1583 by Ald. Richard Martin, who paid a group of merchant underwriters a premium of £30 13s 4d to insure the life of one William Gibbons for the sum of £383 6s 8d. The contract stipulated that this benefit should only be paid if the insured died within a year and ended hopefully "God send William Gibbons health and long life." Eleven months later Gibbons died and the underwriters then sought to evade payment by the dubious argument that he had not died within "the full twelve months accounting 28 days to each month." The case having been brought to court, it was ruled that "the month is to be accounted according to the Kalendar" and Martin received the money due to him.

Life insurance company: The first was the Amicable Society for a Perpetual Assurance Office, established in London by Sir Thomas Allen and the Bishop of Oxford in 1706. Insurers paid an annual fixed-rate premium in multiples of £6 4s (maximum £18 12s) and the company put £5 of each share toward a fund that was divided annually among the nominees of deceased insurers. The insured person had to be between the ages of fifteen and forty-five, though no account was taken of his or her state of health. A limit of two thousand was put on the number of £6 4s–shares issued. This was reached by 1770, when the company claimed that it had already paid a total of £378,184 to 3,643 claimants and boasted capital assets of £33,000.

A remarkable feature of early life insurance was the propensity of speculators to take out insurance on the lives of well-known persons, particularly those with hazardous occupations, such as highwaymen. Among those who were the object of this form of gambling—it was little else—were the prime minister, Sir Robert Walpole; King George II (when he fought at Dettingen); and the Young Pretender, Prince Charles Edward Stuart, during the Rebellion of 1745. This practice continued until made illegal by the Life Assurance Act 1774.

The first life insurance company to base its premiums upon a scientific calculation of life expectancy and grade them according to age at entry—the fundamental principles of modern life insurance—was the Society for Equitable Assurances on Lives and Survivorships. It was established in London on 7 September 1762 according to a plan proposed some six years earlier by James Dodson, master of the Royal Mathematical School at Christ's Hospital, who had died in the meantime. The society's actuary, the first employed by a life insurance company, was Mr. William Mosdell (who died in 1764). The term *actuary* (from the Latin *actuarius*, a recorder of state papers) was coined by one of the founders of the Equitable,

Edward Rowe Mores, to denote one who interprets bills of mortality, population figures, and other relevant figures in terms of insurance risk.

U.S.: The first policy was written by the Corporation for the Relief of Poor and Distressed Widows and Children of Presbyterian Widows, in Philadelphia, on 22 May 1761 on behalf of Francis Alison. Despite a name that sounded more like a charity, this was in fact a well-regulated mutual enterprise that was to become the Presbyterian Annuity and Life Assurance Co. Premiums of £2 to £7 per annum would pay out annual pensions of £10 to £35 to beneficiaries.

Early life insurance companies in America used British actuarial tables, as there was a lack of reliable bills of mortality at home. Hence it was some time before the profession of actuary emerged. The first was the self-educated mathematical genius and mariner Nathaniel Bowditch (born in Salem, Mass., in 1773), who was appointed actuary to the Massachusetts Hospital Life Insurance Co. of Boston in 1804, serving with distinction for fifteen years and earning an honorary doctor of laws from Harvard.

Insurance salesman: The first in the United States was Israel Whelan of New York City, appointed as an agent of the London-based Phoenix Fire Office Insurance Co. in 1804. In 1807 he began selling life insurance on behalf of the Pelican Life Insurance Co. of London.

THE FIRST **LIGHTNING CONDUCTOR**

designed for the protection of buildings was attached by Benjamin Franklin to his house on the north side of Market Street, Philadelphia, in September 1752. The upper end of the steel-pointed iron rod projected 7 or 8 feet above the roof, while the lower end was thrust 5 feet into the ground. Less than a year and a half earlier Franklin had been the first to publicly propound the theory that lightning was composed of electricity. The ideas expounded in his *New Experiments and Observations in Electricity* were put to the test by a French amateur scientist, M. Dalibard, who had an experimental lightning rod erected in the grounds of his country house at Marly-la-Ville, 18 miles out of Paris. On 10 May 1752 lightning struck the 80-foot-high iron rod, and phenomena were observed that established beyond doubt that Franklin's hypothesis was correct. Before the results could be communicated to America, Franklin had made his famous kite experiment (4 July 1752) and proved the soundness of the theory for himself.

After fixing a lightning conductor on his own house, Franklin arranged for similar rods to be erected on the State House (Independence Hall) and the Academy Building in Philadelphia, also in September 1752. These were the first public buildings in the world to be so protected. He made no attempt to patent his invention, but gave it freely to the world, publishing a full description in his own *Poor Richard's Almanac* in November of the same year. The idea spread rapidly through the American colonies, except in parts of New England, where it was denounced as a means of obstructing the will of God. In Europe its development was retarded by the equally shortsighted pronouncements of a celebrated French scientist, the Abbé Noller, who began by declaring Franklin himself a fiction, and on the worthy American's existence being proved, went on to assert that lightning conductors would suck the lightning down from the clouds and so cause the destruction of the very buildings they were supposed to preserve. Unfortunately he was widely believed, with the result that no lightning conductor was erected on a public building in continental Europe until 1769, when one was fixed to the Church of Saint Jacob in Hamburg, Germany.

THE FIRST **LIMERICK**

appeared in *The Midwife, or Old Woman's Magazine* in 1752 and referred to locales in London. Titled "On Jollity," it began

> *There was a jovial butcher,*
> *Who liv'd at Northern-fall-gate,*
> *He kept a stall*
> *At Leadenhall*
> *And got drunk at the Boy at Aldgate . . .*

Various scholars have sought to establish that the earliest examples of the verse form originated from the Irish town of Limerick, but the evidence is tenuous at best. Since the word is not known in print until nearly 150 years after the earliest dated example, when J. H. Murray defined the limerick in *Notes & Queries* in 1898 as an "indecent nonsense verse," the Irish provenance seems improbable. As for limericks about Limerick, they are among the hardest to compose because of the difficulty of finding a rhyme for the name of the city. (It is claimed that the only English word in common parlance for which there is no rhyme is *oblige*, but many place names are unrhymable.) Probably the only Limerick limerick to get anywhere close is this:

> *There was a young farmer of Limerick*
> *Who started one day to trim a rick,*
> *The Fates gave a frown,*
> *The rick tumbled down,*
> *And killed him—I don't know a grimmer trick.*

The first collection of bawdy limericks was the twelve-page *A New Book of Nonsense* (London, 1868), which is noted in the Campbell-Reddie manuscript bibliography of nineteenth-century erotica but of which no copy is known to survive. Alfred, Lord Tennyson is alleged to have been an early exponent of the bawdy limerick, but all such verses from his pen were destroyed shortly after his death. The earliest surviving examples from a poet of repute were the work of the somewhat disturbed Algernon Charles Swinburne, whose classic tribute to the young girl of Aberystwyth is believed to date from the 1870s:

> *There was a young girl of Aberystwyth,*
> *Who took grain to the mill to get grist with.*
> *The miller's son Jack*
> *Laid her flat on her back*
> *And united the organs they pissed with.*

U.S.: The verse form first became popular in March 1903 when numerous newspapers began publishing variations of what was dubbed the Nantucket limerick. The original ran:

> *There once was a man from Nantucket*
> *Who kept all his cash in a bucket;*
> *But his daughter, named Nan,*

Ran away with a man,
And as for the bucket, Nantucket.

Reputedy the limerick is the only original verse form in the English langauge.

THE FIRST **LIP-READING**

originated in Spain. The first deaf and mute person known to lip-read was Luis de Velasco, younger brother of the Constable of Castile, who was taught the art by Manuel Ramérez de Carrión, c. 1615–1620. Sir Kenelm Digby, who accompanied the Prince of Wales (later Charles I) on a visit to Madrid in 1623, described an encounter with Velasco in his book *On the Nature of Bodies*:

> The Spanish lord was born deaf—so deaf that if a gun were shot off close to his ear he could not hear it—and consequently he was dumb. To remedy this unhappy accident physicians and surgeons had long employed their skill, but all in vain. At last there was a priest who undertook the teaching him to understand others when they spoke, and to speak himself that others might understand him; for which attempt at first he was laughed at, yet after some years he was looked upon as if he had wrought a miracle.

Digby went on to say that he had witnessed Velasco lip-reading some Welsh speakers who had accompanied the prince's party and that Velasco had perfectly caught the pronunciation. (Digby was wrong in describing Carrión as a priest.)

U.S.: Lip-reading came to America late. The first person to teach the art was Bernard Engelsman, formerly of Deutsch's Jewish School in Vienna, who began teaching a pupil by the oral method shortly after his arrival in New York in 1864. He started his own class of mainly German and Jewish pupils and this became the New York Institution for the Improved Instruction of Deaf Mutes, which opened at 134 West 27th Street on 1 March 1867 as the first deaf school in America to rely wholly on oral methods. During the same year Harriet Burbank Rogers began to teach lip-reading at the newly established Clarke Institution for Deaf Mutes, first in Chelmsford, near Boston, and shortly afterward at its new site in Northampton, Mass. Before these initiatives nearly all instruction of the deaf had been in sign language and little attempt had been made to teach any but the partially hearing to speak.

THE FIRST **LOUDSPEAKER**

electrically operated was developed in 1906 by Miller Reese Hutchinson (SEE ALSO **hearing aid**) and Kelly Turner of the Hutchinson Acoustic Co. of Jamaica, N.Y. Their Dictograph loudspeaker wired to a Metrophone microphone was marketed the following year as part of the first **intercom system**. The company adapted a miniaturized version as the Detective Dictograph in 1911 and this was the first **bugging system** for clandestine eavesdropping. The Chicago-based Burns Detective Agency used it to secure convictions in a number of cases. (SEE ALSO **radio-microphone** BELOW.)

The first public use of electrical loudspeakers took place in September 1912, when the Bell Telephone Co. cooperated with Western Electric in installing two water-cooled loudspeaking transmitters, an induction coil, and ten loudspeaker receivers at the Olympic Theater in Chicago. These were used not for amplifying speech from the stage, but to transmit sound-effects from backstage to the auditorium, including cheers and applause from a supposed nearby baseball stadium.

Public address system: The first occasion that loudspeakers were used as part of a PA system was early in 1913, when the governor of Oklahoma, Lee Cruce, spoke over a 122-mile open-wire circuit from Oklahoma City to an audience of 345 people assembled in a hotel in Tulsa. The first open-air public address demonstration was conducted by Bell Telephone on Staten Island, N.Y., on 30 June 1916. Following these experiments, public address by loudspeaker was used to reach a large audience (i.e., beyond range of the un-amplified human voice) for the first time on the occasion of the National Educational Association Convention at Madison Square Garden in New York from 3 to 8 July 1916. The idea of speechmakers talking into a microphone made its breakthrough into general use after Woodrow Wilson had become the first U.S. president to be "wired for sound," speaking about the League of Nations over Magnavox loudspeakers to a crowd of 50,000 on 19 September 1919 at San Diego's City Stadium.

Radio-microphone: The so-called "neck-mike" was developed by electrical engineer, unicyclist, and fire-eater Reg Moores and first used for the ice show *Aladdin* at Brighton Sports Stadium in Sussex, England, in September 1949. It was worn by George Stevens in the role of the wicked wizard Abanazer, stitched inside his cloak. Moores did not patent the invention, as he was using radio frequencies illegally.

U.S.: The first radio-microphone was devised by John F. Stephens of the U.S. Navy for a musical show put on at Milligan Naval Base, Memphis, Tenn., in March 1951, each performer having a personal mike housed in an aluminum cigarette case. It was later adapted by the Secret Service as a bugging device.

The first neck-mike in series production was the cordless Vagabond system manufactured by Shure Inc. of Chicago in 1953 and priced at $800. Among the first artists to use it in performance was Frank Sinatra at Las Vegas.

~~~~~~~~~~~~~~~~~~~~~~ **M** ~~~~~~~~~~~~~~~~~~~~~~~

THE FIRST **MACHINE GUN**

was patented by London lawyer James Puckle on 15 May 1718 and demonstrated before the British Army's Ordnance Board at Woolwich about this time. The gun was mounted on a tripod and had a fixed barrel of brass that was served by a circular multi-cylinder chamber on the revolver principle. A crank handle at the rear controlled the action of the chamber. According to the patent specification round bullets were used for firing at Christians and square for Muslims (a practical impossibility).

In 1721 Puckle formed a company to exploit his invention and established a factory in White Cross Alley, Middle Moorfields, London. By the following March production was under way and a demonstration was given at the Artillery Ground. Despite foul weather, the gun proved itself capable of firing sixty-three shots in 7 minutes, clearly a considerable improvement on the muzzle loaders of the time.

The number of sales is not recorded, but it is known that Capt. Nathaniel Uring took two Puckle machine guns with him on an expedition to the West Indies in 1727. Three examples survive, two in the Tower of London and one in the Tøjhusmuseet in Copenhagen. One of the Tower guns is made of iron and appears to have been an early experimental model. The other two are brass having a bore of 1.2 inches and 1.3 inches respectively and each is fitted with a nine-cylinder chamber.

U.S.: The first machine gun was a 9½-pound breechloader advertised for sale by its maker John Cookson in the *Boston Gazette* of 12 April 1756. It was described as "having a Place convenient to hold 9 Bullets, and Powder for 9 Charges and Primings; the said Gun will fire 9 Times distinctly, as quick, or as slow as you please, with one turn of the Handle of the said Gun, it doeth charge the Gun with Powder and Bullet, and doth prime and shut the pan, and cock the Gun. All these Motions are performed immediately at once, by one turn of the said Handle."

Machine gun used in warfare: The first was the Ager Gun, also known as the Union Repeating Gun, designed by Wilson Ager, of which the only ten models then in existence were purchased by President Abraham Lincoln for the Union Army at $1,300 each on 16 October 1861. Later that year Gen. McClennan ordered fifty at $735, while Gen. Butler and Gen. Fremont each purchased two. Nicknamed the "Coffee Mill," it was reputed to be the first machine gun to kill a man in battle, though generally it was used to guard bridges or narrow passes. It made its debut at Lee's Mill during the Warwick–Yorktown siege of April–May 1862.

The Gatling gun, first machine gun to be adopted as army ordnance in quantity, was patented by Richard Gatling on 4 November 1862 but was not adopted by the U.S. Army until 1866, a year after the Russian army had placed its initial order for twenty. It was manufactured by the Cooper Firearms Manufacturing Co. of Philadelphia. Firing two hundred rounds a minute, the Gatling was adopted by the armies of every major nation in the world, including Britain and Japan in 1867, Turkey in 1870, and by the Spanish for use in their colony of Cuba in 1873. The Russians were the first to use it with decisive effect in warfare in their campaigns in Central Asia, breaking up the Turkish cavalry charge at Khiva in 1870.

Gatling, a doctor, believed that his gun would save lives by allowing warfare to be prosecuted by smaller armies. Certainly it saved lives on the side with the machine guns, as at Omdurman in the Sudan in 1898 when the British and Egyptian forces sustained only five hundred casualties against fifteen thousand by the Dervishes. Where both sides were so equipped, mortality was higher than ever before, as the killing fields of Flanders were to demonstrate so grimly.

The Gatling and its several successors were operated by turning a crank handle. The first **fully automatic machine gun** was the Maxim that used the force of recoil to operate the ejection, loading, and firing mechanisms. Hiram Maxim, an American domiciled in London, reported that he had been inspired to make this improvement when an American Jew he encountered in Vienna in 1882 advised, "Hang your chemistry and electricity! If you want to make a pile of money, invent something that will enable these Europeans to cut each other's throats with greater facility." The Austrian army placed the first order for 160 in 1884, after Maxim had demonstrated his own skill as well as the prowess of the gun by spelling out the emperor's initials with bullet holes.

THE FIRST **MAGAZINE**

in the sense of a general-interest miscellany was the *Mercure Galant*, established by Jean Donneau de Vise and first published in Paris in March 1672. Concerned principally with the gossip of the town, it enjoyed a considerable success in fashionable circles.

The first magazine in English was *The Gentleman's Journal: or, the Monthly Miscellany, by way of a letter to a gentleman in the Country, consisting of News, History, Philosophy, Poetry, Musick, Translations, Etc.*, an octavo published monthly from January 1692 by R. Baldwin "near the Oxford Arms in Warwick Lane" in London. The editor was Peter Anthony Motteaux, a Huguenot refugee, who seems to have written most of each sixty-four-page issue himself, though there were verses contributed by Matthew Prior, Sir Charles Sedley, and other poets of repute. Perhaps the most notable feature was an original composition by Henry Purcell every month. Another interesting innovation was the magazine short story, which made its first appearance in the issue for March 1692. The *Gentleman's Journal* continued for thirty-three numbers.

The term *magazine* was first employed to signify a periodical miscellany by Edward Cave, who, as "Sylvanus Urban, Gent.," started the *Gentleman's Magazine*—the first to use the word in its title—in January 1731. The word rapidly entered general currency and

was used in the title of the first English-language magazines to be published in North America.

U.S.: *Der Hoch Deutsch Pennsuylvanische Geschichty Schreiber, oder Sammlung Wachtiger Nachrichten aus dem Natur und Kirchen Reich* ("The High German Pennsylvania Historiographer, or Collection of Important Intelligence from the Realm of Nature and the Church"), a quarterly, was first published by Christopher Saur at Germantown, Pa., on 20 August 1739. It also had the distinction of being the first publication printed from type cast in America, Saur not only operating his own type foundry but also manufacturing his own ink. The magazine soon became a monthly, then in 1744 a weekly under the title *Der Germantauner Zeitung*. At this stage it can be said to have metamorphosed into a newspaper, as it continued to be until the War of Independence, which is probably why the *American Magazine* is invariably credited as the first magazine in America.

The first two **magazines in English** in the United States were both dated January 1741 and each emanated from Philadelphia, then the largest English-speaking city outside London. Neither, however, was actually published until the following month (the reverse of the present practice of monthlies appearing in the month preceding their cover date), and in the event Andrew Bradford's *American Magazine; or, A Monthly View of the Political State of the British Colonies*, came out first, on 13 February, three days prior to Benjamin Franklin's *General Magazine, and Historical Chronicle, For All the British Plantations in America*, much to the chagrin of that eminent innovator who was thus deprived of achieving yet another American "first." Franklin, however, was able to deal the opposition what may have been a mortal blow by exercising his prerogative, as postmaster of Philadelphia, to refuse the rival publication carriage in the mails. Curiously, despite his control of the mails, he did not offer his own magazine on subscription; it could only be bought by the issue, at a cost of 9d sterling, slightly more than the *American Magazine*'s cover price of 8d.

The two proprietors were already rival newspaper owners and enjoyed attacking each other with vituperation and bitter invective in their respective organs. Relations were not improved by the fact that the *American Magazine*'s editor, John Webbe, was

Franklin's lawyer and had been the latter's choice as his own editor. The self-serving Webbe, with all the cunning of his profession, had sought out Bradford and offered to edit a magazine for him instead, provided he was paid more.

Veniality apart, Webbe was probably not the ideal choice of editor, given the leaden prose and heavy subject matter that adorned the *American Magazine*. Most of the articles were about colonial politics, including lengthy accounts of the proceedings of the Pennsylvania, New Jersey, New York, and Maryland legislatures and animadversions on excessive land grants. The only literary content was lifted from the *London Magazine*. Franklin is believed to have acted as his own editor, but the content of the *General Magazine* was not much livelier. He was much preoccupied at the time with the paper currency question and exercised an editor's privilege of using his paper as a platform, perhaps without regard to the fact that his readers may not have felt as passionate on the issue. Bradford's pioneering venture expired after only three months, while Franklin's struggled on for six.

A total of ninety-nine magazines were published in America during the eighteenth century, few of which survived more than two or three years. The most published at one time was seven toward the end of the century. Prior to 1786 there had never been more than three. Within the total were the first specialist women's, children's, medical, agricultural, military, musical, and theatrical journals. One factor contributing to the short existence of many eighteenth- and early nineteenth-century magazines was that editors were not accustomed to paying for articles and their parsimony was reflected in the paucity of well-written pieces. It was only in 1819 that the *Christian Spectator* of New Haven, Conn., became the first American magazine to adopt a policy of paying for all published contributions, though at the rate of $1 a page no budding author was likely to grow rich on the proceeds. Circulation was commensurately modest. It is doubtful whether any eighteenth-century magazine attained the two thousand subscribers achieved by the acclaimed *Port Folio* of Philadelphia in 1801.

Illustrated magazine: The first was *Memoirs for the Curious: or an account of what occurs that's rare, secret, extraordinary, prodigious and miraculous through the world, whether in Nature, Art, Learning*, a monthly printed by R. Janeway for A. Baldwin in London in January 1701. Although eighteenth-century miscellanies carried occasional plates, illustrations in the text remained exceptional until the advent of the *Penny Magazine* in 1832.

U.S.: The first magazine illustration, apart from cover embellishments, was a crude engraving of a fowling scene in Norway, artist unknown, that appeared in the February 1769 issue of the *American Magazine: or General Repository* of Philadelphia. The first with regular illustrations was the *Royal American Magazine*, which was published in Boston first by Isaiah Thomas and later by Joseph Greenleaf, January 1774–March 1775. The total of twenty-two illustrations in fifteen issues included engravings by Paul Revere designed to cast the British in an unfavorable light.

The first **color illustration** printed in an American magazine was a lithotint titled "Grandpapa's Pet" in *Miss Leslie's Magazine*, Philadelphia, April 1843. The world's first magazine with regular color was the *Colored News*, issued weekly from London from 4 August to 29 September 1855, price 2d (4¢). Its color was produced from wood blocks. The only known set (incomplete) is in the British Library. This was an idea ahead of its time; in general color was to remain the preserve of Christmas and special promotional issues until the January 1876 inception of New York's *Frank Leslie's Popular Monthly* (SEE ALSO **full-color advertisement**), which published a chromolitho frontispiece in every issue.

Magazine to publish a photograph: The first was the *Art Union*, London, June 1846. Some seven thousand Calotype positive prints were supplied by William Henry Fox Talbot (SEE ALSO **photograph**), the specimens being used to illustrate an article on the Calotype process. The photographic historian Helmut Gernsheim said that of the eight copies of this issue of the *Art Union* in his collection, each accompanying photograph depicts a different subject. First to be regularly illustrated with photographs was the *Stereoscopic Magazine*, which was published monthly from 1 July 1858 to February 1865. Each number contained three stereoscopic studies.

U.S.: A portrait of photographer Edward Anthony of Washington, D.C., appeared as a frontispiece in the April 1853 issue of the *Photographic Art Journal.* In general few photographs were used in magazines until the widespread adoption of the halftone (qv) in the 1890s.

SEE ALSO **advertising photography; cartoon; children's magazine; fashion photographs; halftone; women's magazine**.

THE FIRST **MAGICIAN**

to have performed in America was Miles Burroughs, probably an English immigrant, who demonstrated the "Art of Legerdemain and Subtle Craft" at Newton, Mass., in 1712. When this came to the ears of the Assemblymen, the unfortunate Burroughs was run out of town. Rather more enduring was the show advertised by the German magician Joseph Broome in the *New York Weekly Journal* of 18 March 1734, performing nightly "Wonders of the World of Dexterity of Hand" at the house of Charles Sleigh on Duke Street until well into April.

The first American-born stage magician, who adopted the name Philadelphus Philadelphia after his natal city, never performed in America. Born Jacob Meyer in 1734, his parents were Jewish immigrants from Polish Galicia. At an early age he traveled to England, where he became the protégé of the notorious Duke of Cumberland, known as "Butcher" Cumberland for his ruthless treatment of the surviving Jacobites after the Stuart uprising of 1745. Evidently the Duke had a kindlier side, for he arranged for the lad to perform his tricks at court. After his patron's death in 1765, Meyer toured Ireland, Portugal, Spain, and Central Europe before giving a command performance in Russia for Catherine the Great in 1771 and for Sultan Mustafa III of Turkey the following year.

Many of Meyer's illusions involved elaborate apparatus. One was an automaton attired as an Egyptian that gave answers to arithmetical questions and identified numbers and suits of playing cards. A figure of Bacchus held a small barrel of water that he changed to wine at will. A pen dipped into a pot of black ink wrote in different colors. The act for which he was most celebrated was the production of

phantasmagoria, luminous ghostly shadows that materialized in smoke on the darkened stage (by agency of a hidden magic lantern). Among those who saw his performances were the two giants of German literature, Schiller and Goethe, and it is believed that the latter's masterpiece *Faust* may have been partly inspired by Meyer's invocations of the apparently supernatural.

All the eighteenth-century magical performers in America were visitors or immigrants, as were most entertainers. The first American-born magician to establish a reputation in his own country was Richard Potter, born on the estate of Sir Charles Henry Frankland at Hopkinton, Mass., in 1783 to a slave called Dinah. His father was a local white man called George Simpson and it is not known how Potter acquired the name. At the age of ten he signed on as a cabin boy with a Captain Skinner, friend of the Frankland family, but finding the sea life was not for him was paid off at Liverpool. Shortly afterward he encountered a Scottish magician and ventriloquist called John Rannie at a country fair and was taken on as his assistant. The pair toured Europe before Rannie decided to travel to America in 1800. During the ensuing decade they made sufficient money on the road for Rannie to be able to retire to Scotland, having taught his assistant enough of the trade for Potter to have his own act.

The mulatto magician made his debut as an independent performer at the Exchange Coffee House in Boston on 2 November 1811 with his wife, Sally, a Penobscot Indian, as his assistant. Subsequently most of his Boston appearances were at the Columbian Museum, but he also performed from time to time at the Concert Hall and Julien Hall as well as the Exchange Coffee House. The act featured ventriloquism and "one hundred curious experiments with money, eggs, cards, and the like." Among these tricks was one in which he burned a $100 bill in a candle flame before restoring it whole, and another in which he seemed to cut off the finger of someone in the audience and then reattach it to the hand. Also popular was turning water into wine and tossing into the air a cat that promptly disappeared. One of the most spectacular was appearing to swallow molton lead, which he then spat out as nuggets. When a member of the audience was invited to pick them up, they would be too hot to touch. A variation of this was described in Potter's advertisement for a performance at the Columbian Museum on 8 August 1818:

> Mr. Potter will perform the part of the anti-combustible Man Salamander and will pass a red hot bar over his tongue, draw it through his hands repeatedly and afterwards bend it into various shapes with his naked feet, as a smith would on an anvil. He will also immerse his hands and feet in molten lead, and pass his naked feet and arms over a large body of fire.

The Potters prospered, buying a 200-acre farm in Andover, N.H. They often performed in New York as well as Boston and also went on tour, even venturing into the deep South, an extraordinarily courageous or possibly foolhardy thing for a non-white couple to do at a time when recent slave uprisings had added fear and distrust to the usual racial contempt. In Mobile, Ala., they had to flee for their lives after patrons of a tavern where the Potters were performing discovered that they had also the temerity to stay there.

After Potter's death in 1835 he was largely forgotten and even now, with the emphasis given to reclaiming black history, his name is seldom recorded in books on African-American achievements. That he is known at all today is probably owing to an advertisement placed by the master escapologist Harry Houdini in the *Conjurer's Magazine* in 1906 seeking information on "old-time magicians." An elderly magician called G. Dana Taylor, whose family had been neighbors of the Potters, wrote in with his recollections, including a description of what may have been the earliest American version of the Indian Rope Trick:

> Before a score of people and in the open air, free from trees, houses, or mechanisms, he threw up a ball of yarn and he and his wife climbed upon it and vanished in the air. A person coming up the road asked what the people were gazing at, and being told, said he met them going down the road.

This helped to prevent Potter's name falling into total obscurity. Jim Haskins and Kathleen Benson in *Conjure Times: Black Magicians in America* (2001), have recorded that in 1965 the Manchester, N.H., chapter (or "ring") of the International Brotherhood of Musicians renamed itself the Black Richard Ring in his honor and that shortly afterward a white entertainer called Robert Olson began presenting a show at the Old Sturbridge Village open-air museum in Massachusetts in which he impersonated the pioneer magician. It is a testimony to Potter's extraordinary achievement as one of the only black performers in an age of entrenched prejudice that not for another half-century would another black American achieve fame as a magician.

THE FIRST **MAGNETIC RECORDER**

was the Telegraphone, patented by Valdemar Poulsen, a Danish engineer employed by the Copenhagen Telephone Co., on 1 December 1898. It was demonstrated publicly for the first time at the Paris exposition of 1900, where the earliest surviving magnetic recording was made by the Emperor Franz Josef of Austria. The Telegraphone used magnetized piano wire running between spools at 7 feet a second, and recordings could be erased at will. Commercial production was undertaken by the American Telegraphone Co. of Washington, D.C., in 1903, the machine being promoted as an office dictation apparatus and also as an automatic telephone-message recorder. An improved model with direct current bias was employed by Prof. Lee De Forest in 1913 for talking-film experiments he made at the Biograph Studios in New York. The Telegraphone suffered from a number of drawbacks that made its appearance as a commercial product somewhat premature, chiefly poor amplification—reception was via earphones—and its unwieldy bulk, which made it unsuitable for home or office use. Its failure, though, had to do more with inept company management than anything radically wrong with Poulson's recording sytem, which was not only sound in principle, but provided the basis on which later inventors in the field developed commercially successful apparatus.

Tape recorder (i.e., a magnetic recorder using tape instead of wire): The first was the Blattnerphone, publicly demonstrated in London on 10 October 1929 when a recording by Shakespearean actor Henry Ainley was played. Designed by film producer Louis Blattner, it was based on the patents of German sound engineer Dr. Kurt Stille and was also the first successful magnetic recorder with electronic amplification. The machine was originally used for adding synchronized sound to the films made at Blattner Colour & Sound Studios, Elstree. The first commercially produced Blattnerphone was acquired by the BBC in 1931.

The first radio program made up entirely of taped items was *Pieces of Tape*, recorded in 1932. King George V's Christmas speech was recorded on the Blattnerphone the same year, and early in 1933 the BBC set up a special Recorded Programmes Section. The Blattnerphone used steel tape on large reels and was extremely bulky, so that it was generally necessary to carry the voice to the machine (via wire relay) rather than the machine to the voice.

U.S.: The first was the Millertape developed from 1930 by James Arthur Miller of Forest Hills, N.Y., founder of the Viktavox Co., and subsequently manufactured under license by the Philips Electrical Co. of Einthoven, Netherlands. It was adopted by Radio Luxembourg, an English-language station broadcasting to Britain at a time when commercial broadcasting was illegal in that country. The Millertape made its U.S. debut with the broadcast of a half-hour program recorded on 2,000 feet of steel tape by WXQR New York at 6:30 P.M. on 26 August 1938.

Tape recorder using plastic tape: The first was the Magnetophon, demonstrated by AEG at the Berlin Radio Fair on 16 August 1935. The tape speed was 30 inches a second, and though the performance of earlier models was inferior to that of the Blatterphone, the running cost of only 25¢ a minute compared favorably with the latter's $1.62 a minute. The oxidized cellulose acetate tape had been developed by BASF of Ludwigshaven, Germany, and the first public recording was made at the BASF concert hall in the town on 19 November 1936 of Sir Thomas Beecham conducting the London Philharmonic Orchestra. Magnetophons were adopted by the Reich-Rundfunk Gesellschaft, Germany's state radio, in January 1938. Among the earliest customers when the improved Magnetophon came on the market was Adolf Hitler, who was able to pass off his pre-recorded, taped speeches on radio as live owing to the absence of background noise on the plastic tape.

While magnetic-recording technology remained relatively static in Britain and the United States during the war years, in Germany it made a number of major advances, of which the most important was the application of a high-frequency bias to the oxide-coated tape of the Magnetophon by H. J. von Braunmühl and W. Weber in 1940. This enabled AEG to develop an efficient stereo recorder by 1943 (SEE BELOW). At the end of the war eighteen complete Magnetophons (out of a total production run of more than nine hundred) were recovered by the Allies from the AEG plant in Berlin and portioned out among the British, French, and U.S. occupation authorities. In addition, U.S. Signal Corps technician Jack T. Mullin retrieved two working Magnetophon recorders and fifty plastic tapes from a radio station at Bad Neuheim near Frankfurt that he took back to the United States. These were acquired by Bing Crosby Enterprises and enabled the Old Groaner to be heard crooning on the *Philco Show* in 1947 when he was actually on the golf course. No other means of recording was good enough at that time to be indistinguishable from a live broadcast.

The first U.S. tape recorders to use plastic tape were launched by Rangertone of Newark, N.J., in late 1947 or early 1948 and by Ampex of San Carlos, Calif., in April 1948. These and every tape recorder developed since can be regarded as a lineal descendant of the captured German Magnetophons.

Tape recorder produced for home use: The first was the Soundmirror, marketed by the Brush Development Co. of Cleveland, Ohio, in 1947. The tapes used with this machine had 30-minute playing time and cost $2.50.

Pre-recorded tapes were first offered for sale by Recording Associates, New York, N.Y., in 1950. Their catalog listed eight recordings on plastic tape, of which No. 001 was titled "Cocktail Time" and featured eleven popular songs.

Stereophonic tape recorder: The first to be commercially produced was the Magnecord, which was demonstrated at the U.S. Audio Fair of 1949 by the Magnecord Co. of Chicago. It was developed in response to a request from General Motors for a binaural recorder suitable for analyzing engine noise, monaural machines having failed to give the sound perspective required. The first home stereo outfit was produced by Livingston Electronics of New York, N.Y., in 1954 and the same company issued a catalog of pre-recorded stereophonic tapes in May of the same year. The first of these Audiosphere recordings, No. BN701, was Schubert's "Unfinished" Symphony together with Sibelius's *Finlandia* and was issued on a 7-inch reel at $10. Stereo tapes preceded stereo disks (SEE **sound recording: stereophonic**) by nearly four years.

Cassette tape recorder: The first was introduced in the United States by RCA Victor in June 1958 together with a selection of pre-recorded musical cassettes. These were simply standard-size tape reels enclosed in a fairly large plastic box. The present compact cassette, one-sixteenth of the size of its predecessor, was the C60 launched at the Berlin Radio Show of September 1963 by Dutch electronics giant Philips. Their compact-cassette recorder, the battery-operated Model 150 Carry-Corder, came on the market the following year. Philips licensed the innovation without charge in order to ensure that it became the industry standard.

In-car tape deck: The first was the Stereo-Pak four-track cartridge player introduced in 1962 by Earl "Madman" Muntz of Los Angeles. Among the first to have one installed in his car was Frank Sinatra. The first in-car cassette player was available as an optional extra with 1965 Ford models.

Personal stereo: The first was the Walkman launched in Japan by Sony on 1 July 1979 at a price of ¥33,000 ($165). Its development followed a failed attempt to adapt the monaural Sony Pressman to stereo. Sony engineers succeeded in converting it to stereo playback, but only at the expense of its recording function. With a tape recorder that could not record, Sony's Tape Recorder Division was ready to abandon the project. The idea of adding lightweight headphones came from Sony's founder, Masaru Ibuku, as did the stimulus to develop a product that no one else in the company believed in except chairman Akio Morita, who saw it as a means of gratifying teenagers' constant need for loud music. (Legend has it that Morito was fed up with the racket from his own children's hi-fi.) In fact it failed to catch on with teenagers at

the outset; the initial market for the Walkman was young affluent professionals for whom recorded music had been a pervasive influence all their lives. It was introduced in the United States in December 1979 as the Soundabout and to the United Kingdom in February 1980 as the Stowaway. The name changes were because Sony had been told by their overseas marketing advisers that the name "Walkman" did not work in English. Tourists who imported the machines from Japan brought the original name with them, causing confusion in the U.S. and UK markets; by mid-1980 it had been decided that the Walkman was the Walkman worldwide.

The inception of the Walkman has become a classic case history of product development and marketing. It was a product for which there was no apparent demand. It filled no perceived gap in the market. And it embodied no innovative technology. Moreover the target market did not buy it. The Walkman was simply a concept—one that has enjoyed a success scarcely rivaled in the history of consumer durables.

THE FIRST **MAILBOXES**

for the receipt of letters for transmission were erected in Paris by Jean-Jacques Renouard, Seigneur de Velayer for his Petite Poste in 1653. Nothing is known about their appearance, but they probably consisted of no more than a locked wooden box with an aperture on the top, fixed either to the walls of buildings or inside taverns and other places of public resort. Although it is recorded that they were sufficiently plentiful for no house in Paris to be far distant from one, they did not remain in service for very long as the *savoyards* (messengers), fearful for their livelihood, put mice in the boxes to destroy the mail. No further attempt to install letter boxes in the French capital was made until 1758, by which time they had been in use in Germany for more than half a century.

The first freestanding, outdoor mailboxes were introduced in Belgium and were certainly in use by 1850, the year that the Parisian postal authorities adopted what was known as the "Brussels-style box." Although the date 1848 has been assigned to them by some postal historians, it is more probable that they made their first appearance on the streets of Brussels after the introduction of adhesive postage stamps in Belgium on 1 July 1849. Made of cast iron, these first pillar boxes resembled an up-ended cannon with a decorated top. The horizontal aperture was protected from the rain by a projecting capital and the whole was richly ornamented.

U.S.: The early history of the outdoor mailbox in America is inadequately documented. The first official pronouncement on the topic dates from 1825, when the postmaster of New York City was instructed to "provide a suitable box for the reception of letters in the upper part of the City... and at any other places in any quarter of the City which shall appear likely to promote the public convenience." It is not known whether these were ever installed. When the privately run New-York City Despatch Post was established on 1 February 1842 (SEE ALSO **postage stamp**), a circular announced: "Letter boxes are placed throughout every part of the City in conspicuous places, and all letters deposited therein not exceeding three ounces in weight will be punctually delivered three times a day at 9, 1 and 4 o'clock, at three cents each." According to Carl Wilhelm Ernst, assistant postmaster of Boston 1891–93 and author of *Postal Services in Boston, 1639–1893*, the first official Post Office street mailboxes were installed in that city on 4 June 1857, though he says nothing about their design. Boxes attached to lampposts were erected in Boston and New York in August the following year. The free-standing bin with the curved top now standard for the U.S. Postal Service was introduced in 1924. There has been little alteration in the basic design since.

THE FIRST **MAIL ORDER**

was pioneered by the Paris-based Petit Saint-Thomas, a dry-goods store whose earliest surviving catalog (of which a single copy is known to survive, in the Bibliothèque Nationale in Paris) was issued in 1844. In this the mail-order side of the business is said to have been only recently introduced by the firm. The Petit Saint-Thomas was known for its innovations, among them no obligation to buy, refunds on demand, fixed prices, and (by the end of the 1840s) annual sales. While most

stores at the time demanded that their salesmen seek the highest price the customer was prepared to pay, Petit Saint-Thomas bought in bulk at a deep discount and passed the savings on to their customers, a policy that would have been an attractive feature of buying by mail for provincial homemakers on restricted budgets.

U.S.: The first mail-order business in America was also started by an established dry-goods merchant, Irish-born Alexander T. Stewart (SEE **department store**) of New York City. During the mid-nineteenth century it was customary for any merchant receiving requests for goods to be sent by mail to consign them to the wastepaper basket. About 1868 Stewart decided not only to respond positively to such requests, but to advertise in newspapers throughout the United States that he would do so. Within a short time the volume of orders received by mail was sufficient to justify appointing a sales clerk to handle them full time, but when it was found that he was overwhelmed by the ever-increasing number, three more clerks were assigned to mail-order duties. By 1876 the number had grown to twenty and in that year they handled $500,000 worth of business, well in excess of the total amount of trade done by the majority of dry-goods merchants. Like the Petit Saint-Thomas, Stewart defied customary practice by selling at the lowest possible price, with the result that even when postage was factored in, many out-of-town customers found it was cheaper to buy from A. T. Stewart & Co. than locally.

The first retail business run exclusively by mail order was established in a single room at 825 North Clark Street, Chicago, in 1872 by Aaron Montgomery Ward. His first price list consisted of a single sheet of paper measuring 12" x 8", which he mailed out to forty "Grangers," members of farmers' association the National Grange. A thirty-two-page catalog followed in the spring of 1874; by the fall issue it had grown to a hundred larger pages as the business became known to isolated farmers' wives. The 1883 catalog listed more than ten thousand items. The biggest earner in the formative years was sewing machines, which Montgomery Ward sold for $26 (with instructions in German as well as English) against $50 for the cheapest competing models.

Prior to parcel post, packages under 4 pounds could be mailed for 1¢ an ounce. Larger articles were sent by rail express, neighbors often banding together as a "club" to offset freight charges for bulk consignments. The price advantage of mail, though, was such that when a parcel containing perhaps a men's overcoat weighed over 4 and under 8 pounds, the garment was cut in two and shipped as two parcels—together with free needle and thread. (When the U.S. Post Office honored Montgomery Ward with its "100th Anniversary of Mail Order" stamp in 1972, the illustration was erroneous: it showed a rural postmaster handing a farmer a large parcel considerably over 4 pounds in weight.)

In 1904 no fewer than three million copies of the catalog were dispatched, to every state in the Union. For most of the twentieth century mail-order in America was dominated by two names, Montgomery Ward and Sears, Roebuck, whose catalogs offered the abundance of the city to rural heartlands. As America became a predominantly urban nation in mid-century, and as the automobile and out-of-town shopping centers (qv) gave country dwellers the means to shop in person, mail order went into decline. Both market leaders began to diversify into retail stores and Montgomery Ward, faced with rising costs, discontinued its catalog in 1985. The company struggled on until December 2000, when it went out of business with the loss of 37,000 jobs. Mail order survives, but increasingly with customers placing their orders not by mail but with the click of a computer mouse (SEE **Internet: e-commerce**).

THE FIRST **MAIL SERVICE**

regular, within America was inaugurated by Gov. Francis Lovelace of New York between New York City and Boston on 22 January 1673, "consonant to the demands laid upon by his sacred majesty, who strictly enjoins all his American subjects to enter into a close correspondence with each other." Despite this laudable sentiment, the service was only open to official correspondence. Traveling what was to become the Boston Post Road, the mail riders took an average of three weeks for the journey in either direction. In the same month Massachusetts passed an act giving mounted messengers a fixed fee of 3d a mile from the public treasury, though this did not mean a regular

service over set routes. Connecticut passed an act in 1674 that not only allowed for carriers to be paid from the public purse but established twenty-four routes, though as with the New York City–Boston service and with Massachusetts' provision of public riders, the amenity was confined to mail on government business. Moreover, Lovelace's interstate service soon fell victim to the disruption of communications occasioned by the Indian and Dutch wars.

The first mail service available to the general public followed the appointment of John Hayward, "the Scrivener," as Boston's postmaster on 27 December 1677. This was in response to a petition to the General Court "to depute some mete person to take in and convey letters according to direction" and to "sett the prices on letters." There do not appear to have been regular routes or a timetable and it is likely that most of the mail handled by Hayward was for dispatch overseas, principally to England, for the burden of the merchants' complaint had been the mishandling of transatlantic letters.

It would appear that it is to Pennsylvania that we need to look for the inception of fixed routes, fixed postage, and regularity. Under postmaster Henry Waldy, a weekly service open to all was started in July 1683 on a route from Philadelphia to Maryland via New Castle and the Delaware Falls. Rates of postage were from 3d to 9d according to distance.

The first comprehensive postal service covering (at least in intent) all of British North America, as well as the first international service available from anywhere within its provinces, was instituted with the appointment on 4 April 1692 of Andrew Hamilton, governor of New Jersey, as representative of the London-based Thomas Neale, who had been granted a private monopoly of the service for twenty-one years. Several of the colonies passed acts to provide the legislative framework for the new network and it was under the New York laws that the first dedicated **post office** was established later in 1692 (earlier postmasters having operated from their own homes or places of business). Post offices in Boston and Philadelphia followed soon thereafter. Postal rates quoted in Hamilton's first report to the postmaster general in London in 1698 were as follows (d = pence):

	d
Not over 80 miles	4½
Boston to New York	12
Boston to Jersey	15
Boston to Philadelphia	15
Boston to Maryland	24
Boston to Virginia	24
New York to Maryland	12
New York to Virginia	12

While it is difficult to give modern values to these sums, suffice to say that 12d would have probably represented a day's pay for a journeyman. A fixed rate for transatlantic mail was introduced in 1711, letters being carried between London and New York for 12d (rates within America having been reduced). Speed of delivery was not an attribute expected or received by colonial correspondents. In 1777 it was recorded that "advices from Boston unto Williamsburg in Virginia" took four weeks during the summer months and double that in winter.

This mail service is particularly notable as being the earliest example of what would now be described as a federal institution, being under the command of an office holder, the Postmaster General in America, whose area of responsibility covered all the otherwise separate jurisdictions. The U.S. Post Office was effectively born with the election of Benjamin Franklin as postmaster general by the Continental Congress on 26 July 1775, a date that marks the independence of the American postal administration from the British Post Office. With the advent of federation in 1789, this first department of government boasted 75 post offices and 1,875 miles of post road serving a population of some 3 million Americans. The number of letters carried in 1790 (the first year of statistical returns) was 265,545.

Household delivery within cities was authorized in 1794, though it remained very patchy until the mid-nineteenth century owing largely to the additional fee of 2¢ payable to the otherwise unremunerated mailman. Even by 1825 six mailmen were sufficient to cover the whole of New York City, the majority of customers preferring to collect their mail personally from their private boxes at the post office. Free city delivery service was introduced first in Cleveland, Ohio, in 1862 at the instigation of postal employee Joseph Briggs, who had been moved by the sight of soldiers' wives and mothers waiting outside the post office in freezing weather to collect letters from their loved ones. At the same time he designed the first mailman's uniform for the men taken on to do the deliveries. The postal authorities in Washington, D.C., moved with uncharacteristic promptitude to extend household delivery to another 48 large cities of the Union, with a total of 449 mailmen, on 1 July 1863.

This may be regarded as one of the few blessings of the Civil War, as it was the withdrawal of U.S. mail services in the South, which had always tended to be uneconomic, that enabled the change to free delivery to be made. It was not until 1887, however, when the system was extended to cities of 10,000 population, with discretion to include even smaller towns, that the majority of the urban population enjoyed the privilege of household delivery. Rural free delivery began on 1 October 1896 on five 20-mile routes centered on Charles Town, W.Va. It was extended nationally during the early years of the twentieth century, with the unforeseen effect of a huge improvement in the roads servicing rural areas—crucial to the growth of inter-urban motor traffic.

Postage rates by weight instead of per sheet were introduced at 5¢ per half ounce for under 300 miles and 10¢ for 300 miles or over plus 2¢ carrier fee by an act of Congress of 3 March 1845. A **uniform postage rate** regardless of distance followed on 1 July 1863 at 3¢ per half ounce.

ZIP codes: The first were two-digit numbers assigned to postal zones of Pittsburgh, Pa., by the U.S. Post Office on 1 May 1943. This was soon followed by assignment of ZIP codes to the nation's 125 busiest postal areas. The first national system was introduced on 1 July 1963 with the inception of the five-digit ZIP, the first two numbers signifying a large postal area and the last three a local delivery area. (ZIP is an acronym for Zone Improvement Plan.)

SEE ALSO **airmail; postage stamps.**

THE FIRST **MAIL TRUCK**

in the United States was a two-cylinder gasoline-powered enclosed vehicle built in 1898 by Frank Edson and Louis Greenough in a blacksmith's shop at Pierre, S.D. Although designed primarily as a passenger vehicle it performed so reliably that the Pierre post office contracted with Frank Edson for him to carry the mail to Fort Sully. The first in regular city use and the first operated by the U.S. Post Office were two Columbia trucks placed in service on 1 October 1906 by the Baltimore Post Office to make collections from street mailboxes. By 1918 there were 1,004 mail trucks operating in 12 cities. The last horse-drawn mail wagon was withdrawn from use in Philadelphia on 31 January 1955.

THE FIRST **MAN-MADE FIBER**

in commercial production was artificial silk made by a process of extrusion of nitro-cellulose in 1885 by Comte Hilaire de Chardonnet, who established the world's first factory for the manufacture of man-made fiber at Besançon, France, in 1892. Chardonnet's *soie artificielle* was satisfactory for braids, tassels, fringes, and the like, but inadequate for woven goods. Eventually the French government banned the manufacture of artificial silk owing to its flammability. A contemporary un-PC joke was that the best present for a mother-in-law was a Chardonnet silk dress and a box of matches.

Man-made textile yarn: The first capable of being woven and dyed was viscose rayon, developed by C. H. Stearn and C. S. Cross at a pilot plant set up at Kew, Surrey, England, in 1898. The earliest surviving sample of the product, now in London's Science Museum, is dated 30 August of that year. Viscose filament had been patented about that time by Stearn, while viscose itself, a substance obtained by treating wood pulp with caustic soda and other chemicals, was the subject of a master patent taken out by Cross in 1892. British rights to the process were acquired by Samuel Courtauld & Co. for £25,000 ($125,000), and commercial production began at a specially built factory outside Coventry in July 1905. Manufacture of

rayon by the purchasers of the French and German patent rights was started in their respective countries the same year. It was in Germany that the first stockings made from synthetic fiber were produced at the J. P. Bemberg AG rayon factory of Barmen in 1910.

U.S.: Manufacture by the American Viscose Co. began at Marcus Hook, Pa., on 19 December 1910. The firm eventually became the largest rayon manufacturer in the world.

Nylon was discovered in 1930 by recent MIT graduate Julian Hill at the laboratories of the Wilmington, Del., chemical company E. I. DuPont de Nemours and developed by a research team under the direction of Dr. Wallace Carothers. It was patented on 16 February 1937. The first commercially produced nylon product was toothbrush bristles, manufactured at DuPont's Arlington, N.J., plant on 24 February 1938. The first experimental nylon stockings were knitted the same month and were displayed at the San Francisco and New York world's fairs. DuPont employees were allowed to purchase two pairs each of the initial batch at $1.15. They went on sale to the local ladies of Wilmington on 24 October with a limit of three pairs per customer. Four thousand pairs flew out of the stores in only 3 hours.

Mass production of nylon yarn began at DuPont's factory in Seaford, Del., on 15 December 1939 and it was made up into stockings by various hosiery manufacturers. By mutual agreement within the trade, the competing brands of nylon stockings were launched throughout the United States simultaneously on 15 May 1940. During the first year 160 million pairs were sold, at least two for every female in America. By 1949 nylon had grabbed 85 percent of the ladies' hosiery market.

Other uses were found for nylon even before DuPont closed down civilian production after Pearl Harbor, most notably nylon sportswear in the form of football pants in 1941. Its main contribution to the war effort was in the form of parachute fabric (SEE **parachute: nylon**).

Polyester or PET: The first was Terylene (in the United States called Dacron), a polyester fiber extruded by J. R. Whinfield and J. T. Dickson in 1941 in the laboratories of the Calico Printers Association in Accrington, Lancashire, England. World manufacturing rights were sold to Britain's chemical giant ICI, which began commercial production of Terylene fabric at Wilton, Teesside, in 1951. American rights had been acquired in 1945 by DuPont, which began production under the name of Dacron at a pilot plant at Seaford, Del., the same year. The first suit made of the machine-washable material was worn by a DuPont employee for sixty-seven days without pressing, including two fully clothed immersions in a swimming pool.

The first commercially produced garments made of polyester fiber in the United States were men's suits made from 55 percent Dacron fabric (45 percent worsted) woven by Deering Milliken Co. in New York City and made up by Hart, Schaffner & Marx Co. of Chicago. These went on sale on 8 May 1951. The first drip-dry shirts followed soon after when Brooks Brothers introduced a 60-percent polyester/40-percent cotton combination garment that was an immediate success with traveling salesmen cut off from regular laundry services.

THE FIRST MAP

printed in the United States was *A Map of New-England, being the first that ever here was cut*, executed as a woodcut by John Foster, a schoolmaster of Dorchester, Mass., who seven years earlier had made the first printed illustration in America. It was published in William Hubbard's *The Present State of New-England, Being a Narrative of the Troubles with the Indians. . .* in Boston in 1677.

Street map: The first of an American city depicted Boston and was drawn by John Bonner and engraved by Francis Dewing in 1722. It delineated forty-two streets, thirty-six lanes, and twenty-two alleys, with a total complement, according to the legend inscribed on the map, of three thousand houses, one thousand of these being constructed of brick. The other two most important cities in eighteenth-century America, New York and Philadelphia, had their first street maps in 1731 and 1752, respectively.

Road map: The first in the United States was a *Specimen, of an Intended travelling Map of the Roads of South Carolina* dated 1 September 1787, which shows the "Road to Watboo Bridge from Charleston, by Goose Creek Bridge and Strawberry Ferry." At a scale of one inch to a mile, it included all "Gentlemen's houses," churches, taverns, private as well as public roads, causeways, rivers, creeks and gullies, and county and parish lines. It was intended as a sample of a road atlas for the whole state to be published by Scots immigrants Thomas Walker and Thomas Abernethie in three volumes, each containing 2,000 miles of roads, but this ambitious project came to naught. Two copies of the *Specimen* survive, one in the collection of the South Carolina Historical Society and the other in the Library of Congress.

The first **American road atlas** was published as *The Survey of the Roads of the United States of America* by Dublin-born engineer Christopher Colles of New York from 1789 to '92 as separate plates to be bound by the subscriber. The total of eighty-three, with two or three strip maps on each, illustrated about a thousand miles of roads from Williamsburg, Va., in the south to Albany, N.Y., in the north. The scale was 1:110,000. Although a number of prominent people subscribed to the *Survey*, including George Washington and Thomas Jefferson, the general uptake was disappointing. The reason seems to be that Colles had misjudged his market. In Britain, whence he came, there was a proportionately small but numerically quite large sector of the population affluent enough to maintain their own carriages and therefore to have a need for road maps. There was certainly a lot of movement in post-revolutionary America, but in a population that made a virtue of a modest lifestyle it was mainly by public transport, generally stage coaches and river craft. The need for road maps would not become sufficiently pressing to constitute a market opportunity for another generation at least.

Colles was a visionary whose enthusiasms tended to fall short of expectation. He built the first steam engines in the United States, for a Philadelphia brewery in 1783, but the boiler had insufficient capacity for efficient working; and in 1816 he established the first telegraph system in the United States, a semaphore to alert the merchants of New York City to the arrival of ships in which they had an interest. None of his enterprises brought him prosperity and when he died in October 1816 he had just been appointed doorkeeper for the New York Academy of Fine Arts. There are twenty-three known copies of the *Survey* extant, of which nine are incomplete.

The first commercially produced **road map for motorists** in the United States was Rand McNally's 1904 *New Automobile Road Map of New York and Vicinity*. The first free promotional maps issued by an oil company were of Allegheny County, Pa., and were mailed by Gulf Refining Co. of Pittsburgh in 1914 to all of the 10,000 motorists registered in the county. The following year Gulf distributed 9" x 12" state maps for Texas, Pennsylvania, New Jersey, and New York, together with regional maps of New England, the Middle West, and the South, through its chain of seven gas stations. By the end of World War I the company had distributed no fewer than 16 million road maps. During the period up to 1973, when the oil crisis all but extinguished the promo map, it has been estimated that 8 billion were given away by gas, oil, and tire companies, motels, and eateries.

THE FIRST **MARGARINE**

was patented in France by Hippolyte Mège-Mouriès of Paris on 15 July 1869 and was the only entry in a prize competition organized by Napoleon III for "a suitable substance to replace butter for the Navy and the less prosperous classes."

Mège-Mouriès had begun his experiments at the Ferme Impériale de la Faisanderie in Vincennes two years earlier, and he is said to have outraged the villagers by underfeeding his cows in the cause of science. The conclusion he drew from this exercise was that the natural fat in a cow's body is the agency that produces milk, and that it could also provide a substitute for butter. The final result of his researches took the form of a compound of suet, skim milk, pig's stomach, cow's udder, and bicarbonate of soda. At one stage of the process it had the appearance of "a cascade of pearls," so the inventor called it "margarine"—from the Greek *margarites*, meaning "a pearl."

Although a factory was established at Poissy to undertake manufacture of margarine, the Franco-Prussian War broke out before production was under way. Two enterprising Dutch butter-merchants, Jan and Anton Jurgens, acquired the rights for 60,000 francs a year and in 1871 opened the world's first fully operative margarine factory at Oss in Holland.

U.S.: Commercial production was inaugurated in New York City by the Oleo Margarine Manufacturing Co. at an uncertain date between 1874 and 1876. By 1886 there were thirty-seven American manufacturers, but demand remained low while a law against adding coloring matter was enforced. Few people wanted to spread their bread with something that looked like lard. Even when this was rescinded, a federal tax on colored margarines was introduced in 1902. It was only with the rationing of butter during World War II that margarine became, at least temporarily, an acceptable substitute. To avoid the tax, manufacturers included yellow coloring matter in a separate packet for consumers to add to the unappetizing block of white vegetable fat. Once the tax was repealed in 1950, sales began to take off at half the price of butter. Total consumption exceeded that of butter for the first time in 1957 by 8.6 pounds to 8.3 pounds per capita; by 1970 it was double.

Low-fat spread: Becel was introduced in the Netherlands by Unilever in 1960 as a margarine low in saturated fat and with no trans fats. Developed in response to a request from the medical profession for a cholesterol-reducing spread, it was originally available only from pharmacies, but in 1963 Becel was repositioned as a diet margarine and became available in supermarkets. It was launched in the United States under the brand name Promise.

THE FIRST **MARKET RESEARCH**

as a systematic approach to advertising strategy began with two studies conducted in the United States in 1911. The Campbell Soup Co. of Camden, N.J., carried out research at the behest of its vice president, John T. Dorrance, to determine whether there was a relationship between household income and consumption of canned soups. The results demonstrated that canned soups suffered from no class stigma, which assured Dorrance that he could gainfully target upper-middle-class housewives. The other study was a comprehensive analysis of the market for agricultural instruments conducted by Charles Coolidge Parkin for the advertising department of the Curtis Publishing Co. of Philadelphia, publishers of *Tribune and Farmer* as well as the two leading weeklies in the women's and general-interest fields, *Ladies' Home Journal* and the *Saturday Evening Post*. Parkin followed this up the next year with a survey of department store lines.

The first **advertising agency to establish a market research department** was J. Walter Thompson (JWT) of Chicago and New York, whose initial foray into the new science was a readership profile of forty-four magazines conducted in 1923 in Cincinnati, considered an archetypal metropolitan area. Readers were classified according to marital status, income, and occupation, the latter divided into categories: Group 1, executives, professionals, merchants, commercial travelers; Group 2, clerical workers and skilled workmen; Group 3, unskilled workers, domestics, teamsters, etc. JWT's clients were thus able to match their products to the socio-economic groups they were targeting, a notion sufficiently revolutionary in 1923 to win that year's Harvard Advertising Award. This and subsequent studies, including the earliest consumer surveys, were conducted under JWT research director Paul T. Cherington, formerly Harvard Business School's first professor of marketing, who brought on board behavioral psychologist John B. Watson to assess consumer motivation and convert that knowledge into creative briefs. "Excessive scientific advertising takes undue advantage of the public," deplored sociologist Gordon B. Hancock in 1926, which was exactly what Cherington, Watson, and their cohorts in the JWT Research Department intended.

Consumer preference research was first introduced by William Burnett Benton at Chicago's Lord & Thomas agency in 1928. This was a speculative venture for use in trying to win the Colgate-Palmolive account after the two giant toiletries manufacturers had merged. Lord & Thomas CEO Albert Lasker told Benton it did not matter what was researched just so long as it could be claimed as the largest market survey ever conducted. Traditionally such research concentrated on general market data, but Benton decided to focus on the consumer and spent two months working night and day to tabulate housewives' preferences for the products of each company. In the event Lord & Thomas landed the unified account before the survey was completed, but Benton's pioneering study was used in planning the initial Colgate-Palmolive campaign.

After cofounding Benton & Bowles the following year with just one client, General Foods, William Benton and Chester Bowles and their wives would conduct door-to-door motivational research themselves, checking with housewives what would stimulate them to buy General Foods' Certo jelly preservative.

Focus groups: The first were conducted in New York City by Philadelphia-born sociologist Robert Merton in 1941 for CBS and Columbia University's Office of Radio Research. The purpose of what Merton originally called "focused interviews" was to determine what made members of the group choose particular radio shows. He would later apply the technique to assessment of training and morale films on behalf of the U.S. Army. It was Robert Merton who coined the terms "role model" and "self-fulfilling prophecy."

THE FIRST **MARRIAGE**

according to the Christian rite within the boundaries of the present-day United States of which there is record was solemnized between Catalina de Valdes and Gabriel Hernandez, a soldier garrisoned at the Presidio of Saint Augustine, in Florida, by the chaplain Fr. Diego Escobar de Sambrana on 2 February 1594. The page from the parish register recording the marriage in Fr. de Sambrana'a own hand is the oldest written document in the United States to have originated within the present boundaries of the nation. It can be seen at the Museum of the Mission de Nombres in St. Augustine, on the actual site where the marriage took place.

The first Protestant marriage and the first in English-speaking America took place in November 1608 at Jamestown, Va., where Anne Burras was married to John Laydon, variously identified as a laborer or a carpenter. Anne herself had arrived in Jamestown with the first supply expedition the previous month as the twelve-year-old "maide to Mistress Forrest," but she is believed to have been just thirteen when the wedding ceremony was performed in America's earliest Episcopal church by the Rev. Robert Hunt. Unlike so many of the early colonists of Virginia the couple survived and are recorded in 1625 as living in Elizabeth City Corporation (now Hampton) with their four daughters.

Civil marriage: The first was performed at Plymouth Plantation "according to the laudable custom of the Low Countries," as Gov. William Bradford put it, on 12 May 1621. The Pilgrims believed that nowhere in scripture were ministers empowered to conduct marriages and did not regard the conjoining of husband and wife as a sacrament (besides which there was the practical consideration that the settlement was without a pastor). The couple were both *Mayflower* Pilgrims who had lost their spouses during the "Starving Time" of the previous winter, he a former printer of London and Leyden called Edward Winslow (born in Droitwich in 1595), she Susannah, widow of William White. The ceremony was performed by a magistrate. Winslow himself became a magistrate and solemnized marriages, informing the Archbishop of Canterbury of this during a hearing before the Lords Commissioners for the Plantations in America that he attended in London 1635, so arousing the ire of the Primate of the Church of England that the unfortunate American found himself languishing in the dank and dreadful Fleet Gaol for a period of seventeen weeks. Winslow returned home to become governor of the colony. His portrait, which may be seen at Pilgrim Hall in Plymouth, is the only one of a Pilgrim Father.

Seventeenth-century civil marriages in New England were generally contracted at the home of the bride's family and there is no indication of any set form of words. It would appear that magistrates were free to perform the ceremony in any way they thought fit.

SEE ALSO **divorce; gay marriage; woman minister of religion: marriage solemnized by**.

THE FIRST **MATCH**

(friction) was invented in England in 1826 by John Walker, a pharmacist of 59 High Street, Stockton-on-Tees, County Durham. The discovery was accidental, as Walker's original intention was to produce a readily combustible material for fowling-pieces. His first match was a stick that he had been using to stir a mixture of potash and antimony; it burst into flame when he scraped it against the stone floor to remove the blob on the end.

The earliest recorded purchaser of a box of matches was a Mr. Hixon, a Stockton attorney, and the transaction is entered in Walker's daybook for 7 April 1827. The price was 9d (19¢) for 100 matches plus 2d (4¢) for the tin tube in which they were packed. Walker's matches were originally made of cardboard, like modern book-matches, but he soon adopted flat wooden splints, which were cut by hand by the inmates of the Stockton almshouses. He attempted to tap another source of cheap labor by employing boys from the local grammar school, paying them 6d (12½¢) for 100, but the arrangement was terminated after one enterprising youth had tried his hand at mass production by using a jack-plane to cut the splints. Although this brought a sharp rise in productivity, the matches were curved and would not lie flat in the box, with the result that Walker lost his temper and the boys lost their job.

By this time he had abandoned the tube in favor of a pasteboard box supplied to him by local bookbinder John Ellis at 1½d (3¢) each. A strip of sandpaper was enclosed inside the box. Most of Walker's sales were to local people, but the fame of his matches spread far wider, and soon after he began production other chemists started to manufacture friction matches on their own account.

For Walker, match-making always remained a sideline to his pharmacy business. When urged by Michael Faraday to take out a patent, he had rejoined: "Oh, no! I doubt not that it will be a benefit to the public, so let them have it."

U.S.: Matches were first manufactured by Alonzo Phillips of New York City under a patent of 24 October 1836. These were sold as *loco facos*, both the name and the chemical composition being derived from a self-igniting cigar that had been launched two years earlier but failed to catch on. By 1850 New York, center of the match industry, had sixty factories devoted to their manufacture.

Safety matches were invented by Johan Edvard Lundström of Jönköping, Sweden, in 1855 and manufactured by the Jönköpings Tandstricksfabrik the same year.

Book matches were patented by American attorney Joshua Pusey of Lima, Pa., on 26 September 1892 and manufactured in 1896 by the Diamond Match Co. of Barberton, Ohio, which had bought the patent rights for $4,000. Two years later they produced the first advertising matchbook, promoting "America's Youngest Operatic Comedian Thomas Lowden and the Mendelson Opera Co."

THE FIRST MEDALS

awarded to members of the American armed forces were three special one-off presentations to senior officers: Gen. George Washington as commander in chief by an order of the Continental Congress of 25 March 1776; Gen. Horatio Gates for the defeat of Gen. John Burgoyne at Saratoga, N.Y., approved 25 November 1777; and Henry "Light-Horse Harry" Lee, father of Robert E. Lee, for his attack on the British at Paulus Hook, N.J., in July 1779, when 160 enemy were captured without American losses, approved 24 September 1779. These were medals for display in a cabinet. The first designed to be worn as a decoration were the three André Medals awarded in 1780 to militiamen John Paulding, Isaac Van Warr, and David Williams for apprehending British intelligence officer Major John André en route to New York City from West Point. Two of the medals are in the collection of the New-York Historical Society.

The original **Purple Heart**, formally known as the Badge of Military Merit, was inaugurated by Gen. Washington on 7 August 1782 for enlisted men or non-commissioned officers and was in recognition of "any singularly meritorious Action." This has been claimed as the first general award for those below the rank of officer in any country. The war being then in its latter stages, only three of these badges were awarded: to former carpenter Sgt. Elijah Churchill of Enfield, Conn., and Sgt. William Brown of Stamford, Conn., at Washington's headquarters in Newburgh, N.Y., on 3 May 1783 and to Sgt. David Bissell of East Windsor, Conn., on 10 June 1783. The recipients were entitled to pass guards and sentinels without challenge.

The Purple Heart was revived at the instigation of Gen. Douglas MacArthur to commemorate the bicentennial of the birth of George Washington and promulgated by General Order No. 3 of 22 February 1932. It was awarded to Army personnel (later extended to other services) who had received wounds or been killed in the line of meritorious service and was retroactive. There is no record of the first recipient.

The first awards of the **Medal of Honor** were to six survivors of the nineteen Union Army volunteers who had captured the locomotive *General* at Big Shanty, Ga., 200 miles into enemy territory, but had been captured after the 90-mile "Great Locomotive Chase." After parole from a Confederate prison, they arrived in Washington, D.C., on 25 March 1863 and were presented with their medals by Secretary of War Edwin Stanton. The remaining members of the party were subsequently invested, including eight who had been executed and were the first posthumous recipients.

Campaign medal: The first was struck by a resolution of the Chamber of Commerce of the State of New York of 6 June 1861 for "the execution of a series of medals of proper character" for the defenders of Fort Sumter and Fort Pickens at the outset of the Civil War. The first authorized by Congress, on 3 June 1898, was awarded to the officers and men of the six U.S. Navy cruisers that had defeated the Spanish at the Battle of Manila Bay off the Philippines on 1 May.

Woman to receive a medal for war service: The first was Dr. Mary Walker, whose award of the Medal of Honor on 11 November 1865 was in respect of her work as a contract surgeon during the Civil War in charge of female prisoners at Louisville, Ky., and of her privations while in Confederate captivity. It was rescinded in 1917 together with nine hundred other Medals of Honor but was restored posthumously by President Jimmy Carter on 10 June 1977. She remains the only woman to have received the Medal of Honor.

All medals awarded for gallantry to women during the first and second world wars and other conflicts of the twentieth century were in respect of nurses protecting or evacuating patients under fire. The first woman combat soldier honored for gallantry in action was Sgt. Leigh Ann Hester of the National Guard's 617th Military Police Company, based in Richmond, Ky., who led an assault on Iraqi trenches on 20 March 2005 when the convoy she was traveling in was attacked by enemy insurgents. She personally shot three of the twenty-seven enemy dead with her rifle. Sergeant Hester received the Silver Star at Camp Liberty, Iraq, on 16 June 2005.

THE FIRST **MICROWAVE OVEN**

was patented on 8 October 1945 by Percy LeBaron Spencer of the Raytheon Co., Waltham, Mass., who had conceived the idea when he stopped in front of a magnetron, the power tube that drives radar, and found that when he put his hand in his pocket there was a gooey brown mess where formerly there had been a candy bar. The following day he put an egg in a kettle with a hole cut in the side and placed it next to a magnetron. A passing engineer took the lid off the kettle to inquire within and was rewarded with a faceful of half-cooked egg, the shell having been exploded by the steam pressure. Since the oven developed by Spencer was essentially a radar set adapted to cookery, Raytheon marketed it in 1947 as the Radar Range. Early models, designed for the catering trade, hospitals, and army canteens, weighed 750 pounds, stood 5 feet 6 inches high, and cost $3,000. A prototype had been installed in the kitchen of Raytheon director Charles Adams, whose Irish cook declared it was black magic and gave in her notice.

The first domestic microwave was launched at Mansfield, Ohio, in 1955 by Tappan at $1,295. The size of a refrigerator, the 220-volt machine required an electrician to wire it in and a plumber to plumb in the water-cooled power tube. Even with these impediments, the pioneer home microwave might have sold better but for one salient fact: the only thing it could not cook was what every red-blooded American man wanted for dinner—a big, thick, juicy steak. From 1953 to 1967 fewer than 11,000 microwaves were sold in the United States, including catering units.

As with many domestic appliances, the touchstone of success was miniaturization. It was only with the introduction of the first countertop model, the $495 Radarange, by Raytheon subsidiary Amana Refrigeration Inc. of Amana, Iowa, in August 1967 that microwaves began to penetrate American kitchens in significant numbers.

Elsewhere, and at about the same time, the breakthrough occurred in Japan, where the microwave was ideal for rapid heating of two staples, rice and sake. When the Japanese National Railroad decided to install 2,500 Toshiba microwave ovens in its dining cars, a culinary revolution was under way.

THE FIRST **MILITARY MOTOR VEHICLE**

was a three-wheel Duryea on which Col. Royal P. Davidson, professor of military tactics at Northwestern Military and Naval Academy, Lake Geneva, Wis., mounted a .45-caliber Colt Model 1895 automatic machine gun and armor plate in 1895. This proved unreliable and was replaced the following year by a more stable four-wheel Duryea carrying the same gun mounted on a swivel. Both vehicles were intended for use as scout cars.

Davidson's pioneering effort was unofficial. The first motor vehicles in service with any army were an electric staff car and two light 3½-hp electric trucks purchased from the Woods Motor Vehicle Co. of Chicago in 1899 for the use of the U.S. Army Signal Corps in the Philippines. The delivery vans, painted olive green and inscribed SIGNAL CORPS US ARMY below the headlamps, were powered by forty batteries capable of propelling the vehicles for 30 miles at speeds of up to 10 mph. The purpose was "to furnish electrical power in the field for use of telegraphy, telephony, signal lights etc." One was used for carrying instruments and materials, the other for personnel. Both vehicles were equipped with electric headlamps and electric lighting inside. The four-seater staff car, like the vans, had tiller steering.

Heavy truck used for military purposes: The first was a curious vehicle fabricated at Johannesburg in the Transvaal Republic in 1898 or '99 and powered by an American-made gasoline-powered marine engine, which was mounted on the chassis unenclosed. There were no seats and the driver stood up to steer. In 1900, soon after the outbreak of the Anglo-Boer War in South Africa, the truck was seized by a Boer Commando operating in the Transvaal and used for transporting ammunition and stores until it ran out of fuel, when they abandoned it.

During the same year two 27-hp steam-driven Scotte Tracteurs were acquired by the French army, the first heavy trucks on the regular strength of any military force. Although designed primarily for hauling trailers, the tractor unit had its own load platform capable of carrying four tons of freight. M. Scotte himself had been nothing more military than a hatter by trade before he turned his attention to putting the French army on wheels. Also in 1900 the Swiss army used an Orion truck built by Huber-Zürcher of Zurich on maneuvers; and the German Naval Union sent a benzine-powered Marienfelder transport truck fitted with a Slaby-Arco radio set out to China for use by the allied forces engaged in suppressing the Boxer Rebellion in and around Pekin (now Beijing).

U.S.: A 1½-ton 24-hp "motor field forge" built by the U.S. Long Distance Automobile Co. of New York was service tested at Fort Leavenworth, Kan., in 1902. The vehicle had two engines, the second for operating a generator, lathe, and grindstone.

Gasoline-powered military vehicles: The first in use with regular forces were purchased for the French army in 1900 after the government had voted 35,000 francs for the purpose. Besides the steam-driven Scotte Tracteurs noted above, the initial acquisitions included two Panhard et Levassor troop carriers (the first such vehicles intended for an infantry role), two De Dietrich medical vans, and two De Dion-Bouton tricars for carrying dispatches. The German army took delivery of the first gasoline-driven trucks, nine Daimlers, in December 1901.

U.S.: The first gasoline-powered U.S. Army vehicles (also the first military vehicles in regular service on U.S. soil) were two eight-seater Winton staff cars equipped with radio and a half-ton two-cylinder "automobile telegraph car," which was assigned to the Signal Corps at Fort Omaha, Neb., in 1904. Generally the U.S. Army continued to rely on horses, long after the European powers had taken to mechanized transport in their armies. Few military motor vehicles were assigned to units of the U.S. Army other than the Signal Corps until the second decade of the twentieth century, the first gasoline-powered vehicle to serve with any other unit being a 20-hp Hupmobile Runabout allocated to the 26th Infantry in 1911.

Armored cars: The first in regular military service were the 35-hp Austro Daimler in 1904 and the French-built Charron of the same year. The Daimler, built for the Austro-Hungarian army, was a four-wheel-drive vehicle with armored hull and a revolving dome-shaped turret mounting a Maxim machine gun. It had a top speed of 28 mph. The front seat could be raised so that the driver and the commander could see over the front armor when not in the line of fire. At the autumn maneuvers at Tulln, Austria, in 1905 the Austro-Hungarian army was also using a 14-hp Bock and Hollander armored car and a 14-hp Opel-Darracq.

The 30-hp Automitrailleuse Charron, manufactured by the Société Charron, Girardot et Voigt of Puteaux, France, was armed with a single Hotchkiss machine gun. One model was acquired by the imperial Russian government in 1904 and became the first armored car to be used in action when riots broke out in St. Petersburg in January 1905. Subsequently the Russians ordered ten of the improved 1906 35-hp model and nine of these had been delivered by the outbreak of World War I.

The first armored cars used in warfare were an Automitragliatrice Isotta-Franchini and an Autoblindata Fiat that served with the Italian forces in Tripoli during the Italo-Turkish war in 1912. Both vehicles were fitted with Maxim quick-firing guns.

U.S.: The first was Armored Car No. 1, built on a Jeffrey Quad chassis in 1915 and in service with Pershing's expeditionary force on the Mexican border the following year. Powered by a 40-hp Buda cylinder engine, the vehicle had both four-wheel drive and four-wheel steering with two driving positions, front and rear. While the rear driver could steer and stop, speed and gear changing was under the control of his co-driver forward.

Mechanized war: The first was the Italian campaign against the Turks in Tripoli fought in 1911–12, which saw not only the use of armored cars (SEE ABOVE) but also aircraft (SEE **aerial warfare**), motorized troop transport, and motor ambulances (qv). The first vehicles to arrive were two light trucks soon after the beginning of thc war in September 1911. These were followed by a consignment of thirty Fiat trucks, and further deliveries during the course of 1912 brought the total vehicle fleet up to two hundred.

The first extensive use of motor transport in battle was by the Lequio Division of the Italian army in Tripoli at the Battle of Zanzur fought on 8 June 1912. Capt. Corazzi was placed in command of the transport section, which consisted of a total of fifty-four vehicles divided into four columns. Lt. Milani and Lt. Bosio's columns were charged with transporting spades, shovels, barbed wire, netting, and sandbags; Lt. Marocco was in command of fourteen trucks carrying the pioneers' tools and explosives, while the remaining column consisted of ten ambulances belonging to the Medical Corps.

At the end of the war in October 1912 a Tripoli newspaper commented on the mobility of the victorious Italian army.

> The motor was ubiquitous . . . It transported ammunition or succored the wounded, fetched fodder for the horses and other animals, or money for the troops and for the Arabs; it brought new boots for the soldiers or delivered urgent messages, as well as being used for the transport of troops from the various bases right up to the first fighting line in battle. Only the advent of the automobile rendered possible many of the daring moves of the war, as it solved the difficulties of desert transport.

SEE ALSO **tank**.

THE FIRST **MOBILE HOMES**

providing living accommodation were probably used by European showmen at the beginning of the nineteenth century. Few records of their use have come down to us, but it is known that an elaborate *voiture nomade* containing a kitchen, dining room, and bedroom was built in Paris for the circus proprietor Antoine Franconi during the early 1830s.

The first tour for pleasure in a recreational vehicle was made by the African explorer Sir Samuel White Baker, the discoverer of Lake Albert, who purchased a gypsy wagon in London in 1878 to take with him to Cyprus on a holiday and fact-finding trip. Before leaving England he had it painted, varnished, and fitted out by Messrs. Glover of Dean Street, Soho, London. "This van," Baker wrote, "was furnished with a permanent bed; shelves or wardrobe beneath; a chest of drawers; table to fold against the wall when not in use; lockers for glass and crockery; stove and chimney; and in fact resembled a ship's cabin, nine feet six inches long, by five feet eight inches wide." Accompanied by his wife, half a dozen servants, and three spaniels, Sir Samuel left Larnaca for a six months' tour of the island on 29 January 1879. As the caravan had to be drawn by oxen, progress was naturally exceedingly slow, but the comfort he and Lady Baker were able to enjoy at night compensated for some of the frustrations of the day. At their first overnight halt he noted, "The gypsy van presented such a picture of luxury that if the world were girded by a good road instead of a useless equator, I should like to be perpetually circumvanning it."

Purpose-built recreational vehicle: The first was the 12-foot-long 2-ton *Wanderer*, designed for his own use by Scottish ex-naval surgeon Dr. Gordon Stables, prolific author of boys' adventure stories, and delivered by the Bristol Wagon Co. in the spring of 1885. This contained two compartments, a kitchen fitted with a Rippingille cooking-range; and a living room furnished with a sofa upholstered in strong blue railway rep fabric, bunk, lockers, table, chiffonier, piano stool, gilt candle-brackets, Persian rug, music rack, and a small harmonium. The Stableses occupied the bunk, while his valet Foley used to make up a bed on the floor. The coachman John slept in a tent outside. Foley's principal job during their 1,300-mile tour of Britain in 1885 was to travel in advance of the caravan on a tricycle and warn other road users of its approach. *Wanderer* survives in the collection of Britain's Caravan Club and is periodically displayed as an attraction at trailer rallies.

Motor recreational vehicle: The first was a 25-hp gasoline-driven vehicle built in 1901–2 by Panhard et Levassor of Paris at a cost of $15,000 for Dr. E. E. Lehwass, a German who hoped to become the first man to drive around the world. The canary-yellow *Passe-Partout* set out on this expedition from London in April 1902, and traveled across Europe, via Paris, Berlin, Warsaw, and St. Petersburg. Disaster struck in the form of cracked cylinders at a place near Nizhny Novgorod (Gorki), and the vehicle was abandoned in a snowdrift, having completed one fifth of its projected journey.

U.S.: The earliest known motor vehicle with sleeping accommodation (earlier designs, probably never built, are reported) was constructed by Boston electrician Roy A. Faye and electrical engineer Freeman N. Young of Arlington, Mass., who installed a hardwood-and-iron box body on an automobile chassis in 1905. This held four bunks in twin tiers with pneumatic mattresses, designed to be folded up during the day; a kind of internal kennel for dogs; and an icebox. Faye and Young were keen hunters and the camper van was used each summer from 1905 until 1908 for an expedition to the Maine woods with fellow sportsmen.

A much more sophisticated camper, probably the first to contain furniture and cooking facilities, and the first recreational vehicle purpose-built from the chassis up, was constructed by mining engineer Henry W. Larsson of Los Angeles for his own use in 1908. Measuring 13½' x 5½' and 7' high, the 33-hp RV had a fully enclosed body with plate glass on three sides, rear access, and a center side door. The interior was furnished with twin berths, chairs, table, lamp, cooking stove, kitchen cabinet, a chemically cooled water tank, and electric heating and lighting. There was also an ore crusher powered from the engine, doubtless used for prospecting when Larssen and his wife took off for their first expedition, to Death Valley, in December 1909. The solid tires were replaced with pneumatics in 1911.

The first RV in the world to be manufactured commercially was the ultra-luxurious six-cylinder Pierce-Arrow Touring Landau, manufactured in Buffalo, N.Y., and launched at the Madison Square Garden Automobile Show in New York City in 1910. Priced at $8,250, at a time when a Model T Ford could be had for $950, the high-roofed chauffeur-driven vehicle had a cordovan leather passenger seat that could be extended as a bed. It also boasted a toilet and a folding washbasin. Presumably the chauffeur slept in a tent or perhaps under the car, and it is doubtful that he would have been invited to share the toilet facilities with his betters. Among the wealthy elite who pioneered this form of independent travel was breakfast cereal magnate Charles W. Post, whose custom-built Pierce-Arrow even had hot and cold running water.

The Pierce-Arrow and the various other, usually one-off, camper vehicles that followed it in the early teens of the twentieth century were seldom more than automobiles adaptable to rudimentary sleeping arrangements. Probably the first American house car, i.e., a fully furnished mobile dwelling, was the Gypsy Van built by Roland R. Conklin of the Gas-Electric Motor Bus Co. of New York in order to make an extended trip across America to the 1915 Panama–Pacific International Exposition in San Francisco. With a bus body and ash cladding, this 8-ton 25-foot vehicle had no fewer than forty-four windows with awnings and an interior with all the comforts of home, including a fitted kitchen. The main living room, decorated to reflect the traditional English furnishings of the Conklins' mansion at Huntington, N.Y., boasted a sofa and two armchairs that converted to beds, besides four Pullman-type upper berths that were folded into the ceiling by day. Intimate touches included a folding desk, concealed bookcase, and phonograph. The roof had a canvas attachment that allowed it to be used as a covered outdoor sitting area and also accommodated the water tank. Above the driver's cabin was a flagpole, from which Old Glory proclaimed the Conklin family's do-anything, go-anywhere spirit.

While numerous custom-built house cars were recorded in the period 1915–20, it was not until 1921 that series production, albeit in modest numbers, began. Two were offered for sale in that year: the Norrington Auto-Home, built on a Dodge chassis by British-born William Norrington of San Francisco in both "Rough and Ready" and more elaborate "Pullman" models (the latter providing the luxury of heating, electric lighting, and a shower); and the Lamsteed Kampkar from St. Louis, Mo., which was designed to fit a Model T chassis and could be purchased (minus the Model T), for $735 including all the culinary utensils and tableware.

The **Winnebago**, the world's most popular motor home, originated as the 19-foot, $5,995 Life-Time

Premier, built under contract by Winnebago Industries of Forest City, Iowa, for Life-Time Industries of San Jose, Calif., in 1966. Later the same year Winnebago began selling a similar model under its own name. In 1992 they rolled out their 250,000th motor home.

Motor trailer: The first was built in 1897 by Jeantaud of Paris for Prince Oldenburg, uncle of the tsar of Russia. The two-wheel trailer, in which he proposed touring the Caucasus, was drawn by a 30-hp De Dion steam-tractor, and the whole massive combination, nearly 30 feet long, was claimed to be capable of speeds up to 19 mph. The double folding doors let on to a side corridor, in imitation of European railroad cars. The most luxurious living vehicle ever built up to that time, it contained a number of striking and novel features, such as running water in the kitchen, an up-to-date water closet, a cage for dogs slung underneath the wagon, and a promenade deck on the roof furnished with chairs for sitting out. The roof also accommodated a reservoir and a coke burner carrying fuel sufficient for a run of 500 km. The outside was painted pale green and the inside was paneled with polished mahogany. Cost of the tractor and trailer together was $6,000.

U.S.: The earliest known is the Earl Travel Trailer, which was custom-built by an unidentified coachbuilder in Los Angeles for a Mr. Earl in 1913. Designed to be hauled by a Model T Ford, the two-wheeler had an 8-foot-long laminated wood body, a rear door, and picture windows on either side with exterior roller blinds. It slept two. Nothing is known about Mr. Earl or his motives for commissioning the trailer, which is preserved at the RV/MH Heritage Foundation at Elkhart, Ind.

Series production began in Britain, where the first (one-off) trailer, an extraordinarily advanced design with a streamlined body shaped like a ham can, had been built for Frederick Alcock of Birmingham in 1914. The outbreak of World War I had suspended any further progress on private trailers but in 1919 a number of veterans put skills learned in the services to practical use by manufacturing trailers for touring. The inspiration for these in many cases was the wartime Red Cross trailer units and the War Department mobile headquarters used by staff officers. At least one entrepreneur converted these war-surplus vehicles for recreational use, but probably the first manufacturer was Richard St. Barbe Baker, who had the right pedigree, being descended from Sir Samuel White Baker, first to tour in a mobile home in 1879 (SEE ABOVE). He formed the Navarac Caravan Co. while reading for a degree in forestry at Cambridge University, employing experienced aircraft fitters to build the four-wheel, lantern-roofed trailers. Baker emigrated to Kenya the following year, but in the meantime Eccles Motor Transport of Birmingham had become the first manufacturer to achieve sustained production. They remain a brand leader over ninety years later.

Manufacture in the United States was initiated by aeronautical pioneer Glenn Curtiss (SEE **airplane manufacturing company**) of Hammondsport, N.Y., who had designed his prototype two-wheeled trailer in 1917. Of canvas and plywood construction, this housed two stretcher-type tilt-out beds on either side. The framework was a wire-braced skeleton of aircraft spruce, akin to the fuselage structure of Curtiss's most celebrated aircraft, the World War I "Jenny." The Curtiss Motor Bungalow was produced in limited quantities between 1920 and 1922 but its price put it beyond the range of most of the "Tin Canners," as motor campers were dubbed. No further attempts at trailer manufacture were made in the United States until Curtiss resumed production in 1928 with his ultra-luxurious Aerocar Land Yacht. Custom-built at prices ranging between $3,000 to $25,000, the larger models of 30 feet or more had an observation desk, chauffeur's quarters at the rear, two or three bathrooms, Pullman furnishings and fittings throughout, hot and cold running water, a rudimentary system of air-conditioning, and telephonic communication between trailer and auto. There was even an altimeter, a nice aeronautical touch, for those who wanted to know how far above sea level they were.

Trailers for the average Joe emerged when bacteriologist Arthur Scherman of Detroit launched his two-berth 9' x 6' Covered Wagon at the Detroit Auto Show in January 1929. By 1936 Sherman was turning out a thousand Covered Wagons a month and had been joined in the new industry by an estimated 800 other manufacturers, 85 of them in Los Angeles alone.

Hard to account for is the fact that Britain, known for its uncertain weather and with far fewer cars, was able to sustain a flourishing trailer industry throughout the 1920s, whereas in the United States, with the exception of Curtiss's upscale venture, the business only emerged with the onset of the Depression. Economic hardship may have favored inexpensive vacations, but why the Tin Can Tourists of the 1920s, estimated at 100,000 strong, had been content to travel with tents for so long remains unexplained. Once Sherman and his competitors had shown the way, the Tin Canners took to the trailer with alacrity, those unable to afford an "off-the-peg" vehicle building their own. In 1936 it was estimated that two thirds of the trailers on the road were homemade. Not all were used for touring. That same year the *New York Times* reported what it regarded as a new phenomenon: people living in their trailers year-round, 300 of them in Omaha, Neb., alone. A survey of the time indicated that trailer-dwellers were middle-income former city-based Mid-westerners with an above-average education and one child to every two couples.

In fact it was not so new. As early as 1920 a group of about eight or ten families, the bread-winners unskilled and low-paid factory workers, had settled in a suburb of Detroit in crude, homemade trailers, a kind of Hooverville on wheels. This was the first known **trailer park**. Until ready-made trailers became widely available in the 1930s, trailer dwelling remained exceptional. Nonetheless there were four trailer parks in Detroit by 1930, the year that regular manufacture of popularly priced trailers began, and by 1935 nine with a total population of 250, a year before the *New York Times* took notice. While the abusive term *trailer trash* had yet to be coined, many city fathers took the view that these denizens within their municipal boundaries were tax-dodging vagabonds rather than the well-educated bourgeois folk identified in the survey quoted. Oakland, Calif., voted to ban them in September 1936; Detroit, cradle of the trailer industry as well as the trailer park, followed suit the following summer.

Ironically it was at that very moment in time, September 1937, that Detroit-based Covered Wagon decided to launch its $750 Residential Model, the first **trailer specifically designed for permanent habitation**. The first commercially built 8-foot-wide trailer (the standard was 6 feet), it boasted a living room, kitchen, bathroom, and bedroom in its 20-foot length. The Residential was ahead of its time, not only owing to the growing official opposition to trailer dwelling but because its all-weather boxlike, square-cornered construction, however practical, was derided by an auto and trailer press preoccupied with streamlining. The fall of 1937 also saw the start of a new recession, which halted the burgeoning trailer industry in its tracks. The residential trailer or mobile home was only to come into its own with the need for temporary housing as the nation transferred its industrial base to a war footing.

An answer to the need for temporary wartime living space lay in the sectional mobile home, later to be called **manufactured housing**, which had its earliest manifestation in a pitch-roofed, 25' 8" x 13' 6" one-bedroom dwelling designed by Carroll A. Towne to accommodate workers for the Tennessee Valley Authority (TVA). Built by Schult Trailers of Elkhart, Ind., in 1940, it was constructed of stressed-skin plywood panels and comprised two sections of equal size that could be dismounted from their wheelboxes. In 1941 the TVA modular house was adopted by the Federal Works Administration to provide temporary homes for employees in the vastly expanded defense industry as the nation confronted the prospect of war. Hundreds of thousands of migrant workers were to take up temporary residence in them over the next four years and many of them, by now accustomed to living in a limited space, found mobile homes to be the solution to the housing shortages of the post-war boom years. The trailer park had become an American institution.

THE FIRST MODEL AGENCY

SEE **photographic model**.

THE FIRST MONOPOLY

board game was invented, or more properly reinvented, by unemployed heating engineer Charles Darrow of Germantown, Pa., who eked out a living after losing his job in 1931 by mending electric irons and walking his neighbors' dogs. At night he spent his time inventing toys and games, none of which attracted any attention until he and his wife Esther were introduced to a handmade game brought along for an evening's entertainment by their friends Jeff Raiford and Charles Todd. The guests had copied it from a set belonging to a lady from Atlantic City called Ruth Hoskins. She in turn had adapted it from the "Landlord's Game," originally devised in 1903 by a Quaker lady, Elizabeth Magie, who had created it to show how unfair rents could be imposed by unscrupulous landlords. Ruth Hoskins's version used streets from her new home city of Atlantic City but as she had only recently moved from Indianapolis she misspelled Marven Gardens as Marvin Gardens.

Darrow was captivated by the Landlord's Game and made his own set, carving houses and hotels out of scraps of wood from a lumber yard and using charms from his wife's bracelet as counters. He also replicated the misspelling Marvin Gardens. This persists on the Monopoly board today, but it was a telling factor when the rights in the game were successfully challenged in the courts half a century later.

On completing the game Darrow offered it to America's leading games manufacturers, Parker Brothers of Salem, Mass., but they rejected it on the grounds that it had fifty-two fundamental errors. An internal report summarized: "It takes too long to play, there's no winning post, no finishing line, the rules are too complicated and the players just keep going round and round." In 1934 Darrow had five thousand sets privately printed in Philadelphia and at $2.50 a set the game—labeled simply "The Game"—caught on sufficiently with local people for Parker Brothers to reconsider. They launched it nationally for Christmas 1935 and at first it showed no signs of having any unusual popularity. Not until Christmas was over did Monopoly-mania suddenly sweep America. "In January 1936," the head of the company is on record as saying, "it became the hottest fad the game field has ever known." It went on to become the largest-selling board game of all time, with current figures standing at 260 million sets sold. There are versions in twenty-six languages licensed in eighty-one countries. This does not include Cuba, where Fidel Castro ordered all existing Monopoly sets to be seized, doubtless unaware that the game had originated as a means of illustrating the evils of capitalism.

THE FIRST MOTEL

built to a recognizable motel plan, though without the name, was Atkins' Cottage Camp in the copper mining town of Douglas, Ariz. This was opened in the pre-motoring era at the start of the twentieth century and had become Atkins' Tourist Court by c. 1910. It comprised rows of cabins each containing a bedroom, kitchenette, and parlor, for which the nightly charge was 50¢ and an extra quarter if you wanted a bucket of coal on chilly Arizona nights. In the 1920s an additional six cabins with garages were built and the name changed again to Atkins' Auto Court.

First to be called a motel was the Milestone Mo-Tel (later the Motel Inn) at 2223 Monterey Street, San Luis Obispo, Calif., opened under the management of Harry Elliott by Hamilton Hotels on 12 December 1925. It was designed in the California Spanish Revival style by Arthur Heinman, who originated the name *motel* in 1924, though the word did not enter any dictionary until 1950. The Motel Inn had accommodation for 160 guests, and each chalet had its own bathroom, telephone, and garage. A number were equipped with kitchenettes and there was also a central dining room. The Hamilton chain of hotels stretched from San Diego to San Francisco on one of the busiest motor routes in the United States, Route 101, and this undoubtedly contributed to the initial success of the venture.

The original Mo-Tel buildings survive, standing in the grounds of another motel, not named as such, the Apple Farm Inn.

THE FIRST MOTOR AMBULANCE

SEE **ambulance.**

THE FIRST MOTORBOAT

powered by an internal-combustion engine was a small illuminating gas-driven 2-hp craft built in Paris by J. J. Étienne Lenoir (SEE **automobile**), consulting engineer to the firm of Gautier et Cie, and launched on the Seine in 1864. By Lenoir's own account this boat performed indifferently, but the following year he built a larger 12-meter launch with a 6-hp motor for M. Dalloz, editor of the Parisian newspaper *Le Moniteur Universel*. The inventor complained that it was too slow and used up too much fuel, but his customer seems to have been better satisfied, for he continued to use it on the Seine for two years and made a number of successful trips from the center of Paris to the outlying suburb of Charenton-le-Pont, at the junction of the Marne.

Lenoir built a third motorboat, which he demonstrated at the Maritime Exposition held at Le Havre in 1878. Despite a carburetor that was described in Gallic terms as being "as capricious as a pretty girl," the craft performed relatively successfully until some mysterious and unrecorded disaster struck. Nothing more was heard of it until ten years later, when some workmen dredging Le Havre harbor recovered the submerged remains. These were sent to Charles Tellier's in Paris for restoration, and the great engineer's son Alphonse, then only a schoolboy, spent his weekend putting it in order. With a skill remarkable in one so young, he was eventually able to make the motor work again and drive the boat himself on the Seine.

U.S.: The first was a government launch fitted with a Brayton gasoline engine at the Exeter Machine Works in Exeter, N.H., in September 1880. The Brayton motor had been patented in 1872 by George G. Brayton of Boston and was the first practical internal-combustion engine (qv) made in the United States.

Motorboat in series production: The first was a 20-foot naphtha expansion-engined launch designed by F. W. Ofeldt in 1885 and manufactured by the Gas Engine & Power Co. of New York. Within three years the firm had established an export trade with Europe, with thirty boats going to an agent in Britain.

The prototype of the first gasoline-powered boat in series production was built by Gottlieb Daimler (SEE **automobile**; **motorcycle**) in Cannstatt,

Germany, and launched on the River Neckar in August 1886. Since gasoline engines at that time were thought likely to explode, Daimler adopted the subterfuge of festooning the vessel with insulators and wires in order to give the impression that it was powered by electricity. Commercial production began in Hamburg in 1890, and Daimler launches were in use by the Hamburg harbor police before the end of the year. Another early customer was the former chancellor of Germany, Prince Otto von Bismarck.

Motorboat races: The earliest recorded (there may have been prior, informal events) were three races hosted by the Columbia Yacht Club of New York City over a 12-mile course on 26 June 1902. The "electric class" was won by C. A. Starbuck's *Carmen*, the "green class" by Harry S. Elliott's *Alpha*, and the "checkered class" by collectively owned *Ardea*. ("Green" and "checkered" classes referred to engine power.)

The first international powerboat race was the Harmsworth Cup Competition, held over an 8½-mile course from the headquarters of the Royal Cork Yacht Club to Glanmire, County Cork, Ireland, on 11 July 1903. The cup was won by Campbell Muir representing Great Britain in S. F. Edge's 75-hp Napier launch, a 40-foot vessel with a steel hull. The Harmsworth Cup is the oldest annual powerboat race in the world. It was first won by the United States in 1907.

Motorboat in scheduled commercial service: The first was a gasoline-driven passenger and cargo vessel that began operating on the River Niger between Timbuktu (Tombouctou) and Kulikoro in the French Sudan (now Mali) at the end of 1904.

THE FIRST MOTORCYCLE

was built by Gottlieb Daimler at Cannstatt, Germany, and patented on 29 August 1885. It was powered by a single-cylinder four-stroke engine developing 700 rpm and incorporated internal flywheels, fan-cooling, a mechanically operated exhaust valve, and an automatically operated inlet valve.

The first motorcyclist was Paul Daimler, Gottlieb's son, who drove the machine from Cannstatt to Untertürkheim and back, a round trip of 6 miles, on 10 November 1885. Daimler did not intend the vehicle as a commercial proposition, but as a test-bed for his newly developed gasoline engine. It was destroyed by fire in 1903.

Commercially produced motorcycle: The first was the 2½-hp Motorrad, manufactured at the Munich works of Heinrich and Wilhelm Hildebrand and Alois Wolfmüller in 1894. It was powered by a water-cooled 760-cc single-cylinder engine developing 600 rpm, and was capable of 24 mph. The first batch of fifty was delivered in November 1894 and more than a thousand were produced during the next two years. Alexandre Darracq commenced manufacture of the Millet motorcycle in France the same year.

U.S.: M. M. M. Slattery, chief electrician of the Fort Wayne, Ind., Electric Light Co., built an electrically driven tricycle in 1887. The first gasoline-powered motorcycle was built in 1896 by E. S. Pennington of Cleveland, Ohio, a somewhat dubious character who made extravagant claims for his various vehicles, which included a tandem, a four-seat tricycle, and a quadricycle on which he later mounted a machine gun. The two-wheeler had a twin-cylinder horizontal four-stroke engine that drove directly onto cranks attached to the rear wheel hub. Although capable of impressive speeds under demonstration conditions, it was underpowered and erratic in performance. Pennington exhibited the machine at various cycle shows, then took it to England, where he managed to create sufficient publicity to attract numerous orders. None of these was fulfilled and instead Pennington disposed of his useless patents for a reputed £100,000 ($500,000).

The first American motorcycle to go into production was the Orient-Aster, manufactured at Eltham, Mass., in 1899 using a French-made copy of the De Dion-Bouton engine. The following year E. R. Thomas of Buffalo, N.Y., began manufacturing the Auto-Bi with an American-made engine. Production continued until 1912 and in 1905 W. C. Chardeayne rode an Auto-Bi to a new transcontinental record of forty-eight days. First of the classic marques, the Indian, was launched by George M. Hendee of Springfield, Mass., in 1901. Hendee introduced the twist-grip throttle in the United States in 1904.

Motorcycling fatality: The first in America was Frank A. Elwell of Portland, Maine, who had organized the earliest group bicycle tours in Maine, Quebec, and Europe in the 1880s and 1890s. He was killed in 1902 when the front forks of his motorcycle collapsed at high speed.

THE FIRST **MOTOR HEARSE**

was used for a funeral that took place in Buffalo, N.Y., in May 1900, when a cortege of fourteen electric vehicles was led by a Pope-Columbia omnibus bearing the coffin. The occupant of the coffin has not been identified, nor has the reason for the large turnout of electric motor vehicles in a city that had no motor industry and had yet to see its first gasoline automobile. A photograph of the funeral procession exists, but the background to the occasion remains elusive.

The first purpose-built motor hearses appeared in France, Britain, and the United States during the same year, 1905. The French example was a 24-hp De Dion used by a firm of funeral directors in Paris, while the British hearse used a 12-hp Wolseley engine and a Wolseley chassis and went into service with Reuben Thompson of the Yorkshire steelmaking town of Sheffield. The American hearse was built in their own livery by Stevens & Bean Undertakers of Fresno, Calif., on a Rambler Surrey Type 1 chassis with a receptacle for the casket on the left and two seats, one behind the other, on the right.

The Thomas A. McPherson Collection of automobilia contains a photograph of a highly ornamented electric hearse in an unidentified German city which McPherson believes may predate the examples cited above. All these pioneer vehicles, and the several that followed in the next three or four years, were one-offs built to order. The first auto hearse in series production was a 30-hp chain-driven four-cylinder gasoline-powered truck introduced to the trade on 15 June 1909 by the Crane & Breed Manufacturing Co. of Cincinnati. It was capable of speeds of up to 30 mph, which was "fifteen miles-per-hour faster than any hearse should have to go" according to the makers, who went on to explain: "People who continuously ride in automobiles object to the long and (to them) uncomfortably close and slow carriage ride. They want speed—a smooth glide to the cemetery, same as downtown or anywhere else—and especially in the larger cities." Above the casket chamber, which was flanked by Grecian columns, was a somewhat grotesque replica of Scipio's tomb.

THE FIRST **MOTOR ROAD**

was built by French engineers over the 140-mile route from the port of Tamatave, on the east coast of Madagascar, to Antananarivo, the capital of the island, and opened on 1 January 1901. The curious anomaly of the pioneer motor road being constructed in such a remote part of the world is paralleled by the development of airlines in underdeveloped countries of Africa and South America in the 1920s. As the nineteenth century drew to a close, Tamatave and Antananarivo had yet to be served by a railroad link, and the French decided on the daring experiment of building a motor road to carry supplies by truck from the principal port to the capital.

The enterprise was conceived by the energetic and far-sighted governor of Madagascar, Gen. Joseph S. Gallieni, who deserves to be remembered for this in addition to his more celebrated act of rushing the French troops from Paris to the front in taxicabs at the beginning of World War I. He was himself an enthusiastic motorist and kept a Panhard et Levassor while serving on the island. The building of the road was a direct outcome of the abolition of slavery in Madagascar in June 1896. In order to implement this decree, no mean task, Gallieni ordered that all male persons between the ages of sixteen and sixty must show evidence of paid employment. Those who could not establish this—i.e., the genuine unemployed, and slaves who had not been freed by their masters in accordance with the law—were "arrested" and put to work on road building for fifty days at set rates of pay. On expiry of this "sentence," they were free to remain with the road gang if they wished. Many did remain rather than risk recapture by their former masters. In this way, Gallieni obtained a large and willing labor force of ex-slaves to assist him in his plan for bringing motor transport to the island.

The building of this first motor road was a considerable feat of engineering, as it had to be laid through dense tropical rain forests and made two precipitous descents, one of about 1,950 feet into the valley of the Mangoro and the other of 2,275 feet to sea level at Tamatave. At first motor vehicles were considerably outnumbered by carts, most of them drawn by hand, using three men for a ton of freight; but in 1903 Gen. Gallieni established a motorized *correspondance* and *messageries* service over the whole route. A long-distance motor-coach service was begun the same year. The cost of goods haulage, which stood at 1,100 francs per ton in 1895, had fallen dramatically to only 250 francs per ton by 1904. The motor road remained the only link between the chief port and the capital until 1913, when a railroad was completed.

Remarkably, there were two motor roads in African countries before any existed elsewhere in the world, the other being built in 1902 between Songololo and the Kwango River in the Belgian Congo (now the Democratic Republic of the Congo). The first in Europe was opened between Ostend in Belgium and the channel port of Dunkerque, France, in the summer of 1903. Built at the instigation of King Leopold II of Belgium, a keen motorist himself, the road was intended to divert traffic arriving from England to the Belgian coast resorts—one of the earliest instances of official backing for its tourist industry by any country.

U.S.: The first road designed specifically for motor traffic, the Long Island Motor Parkway, was also the world's first **freeway**, having controlled access and no grade crossings or stop signs. It was built by millionaire motor-racing enthusiast William K. Vanderbilt after a spectator had been killed in the 1906 Vanderbilt Cup Race and was intended foremost as a racetrack. In order to recoup some of the $2 million cost, however, it was also to be opened to private motorists as a toll road. Eventually the Parkway would run 46 miles from Flushing to Ronkonkoma, but the first 10-mile stretch was opened to traffic probably on 25 October 1908, the day after the Vanderbilt Cup Race for that year. Originally it was 16 feet wide (later widened to 22 feet) and had a reinforced concrete paving with banking at corners for speed. There were sixty-five reinforced-concrete and steel bridges to carry the Parkway over other roads or rail tracks and twelve toll booths. The toll of $2, later reduced to $1.50, would have deterred all but the most affluent and this is reflected in the traffic counts. Peak year before the Parkway closed in 1938 was 1929 with 175,000 cars, or fewer than 480 a day. By contrast its successor, the Long Island Expressway, was carrying 750,000 vehicles a day by 1987.

The Long Island Motor Parkway and the other parkways built in the 1920s and 1930s were designed for recreational motoring in places of natural beauty and commercial vehicles were banned. In Europe the first **inter-urban freeway**, with no such restrictions on commercial traffic, was Italy's 30-mile Milan–Varese Autostrada, opened 21 September 1924. By 1932, the year that the Bonn–Köln Autobahn became Germany's first inter-urban freeway, Italy already had eight *autostrade* totaling 330 miles. It was the German *autobahnen*, however, that added another feature considered essential to the modern freeway: the divided highway. In 1939, the year before America's first divided freeway opened, the *autobahnen* already crisscrossed Germany for 2,300 miles.

America's first inter-urban freeway open to commercial as well as private traffic, and therefore comparable to the freeways of Europe, was the Pennsylvania Turnpike. This ran for 160 miles from just west of Harrisburg to just east of Pittsburgh and opened on 1 October 1940. It was later extended a further 200 miles west to the Ohio border. During the first year of operation it carried 2.4 million motorists willing to pay $1.50 to halve the 5 hours it had taken to drive the same route on the old Lincoln Highway. The four-lane road, separated by a 10-foot grassy meridian, carried traffic at up to 90 mph, but with drivers complaining of the lethargy induced by the straight and largely featureless highway before them, a 70-mph limit was imposed within a year of opening. With its cloverleaf intersections, on- and off-ramps, and service areas, it was the prototype of the super-highways connecting every major city of America today. Apart from Italy and Germany the only countries that had preceded the United States with public freeways were Canada, where the 60-mile Queen Elizabeth Way opened between Toronto and Hamilton in 1939, and the Netherlands, which had 70 miles of freeway open to traffic that year.

Urban freeway: The first, and also the first **divided highway**, was the AVUS (Automobil-Verkehrs- und Übungs-Strasse) Autobahn running 6¼ miles from the Grünewald in Berlin to the suburb of Wannsee, which opened to traffic on 24 September 1921. Like William K. Vanderbilt (SEE ABOVE), the instigator of the project, Karl Friedrich Fritsch, was a motor-racing enthusiast and his idea was that the freeway should double as a racetrack and proving ground. For this reason it was designed with a loop at either end, so that in its sporting capacity the road would provide the means of racing back and forth without stopping. On completion it had two tarred-surface 26-foot-wide carriageways on either side of a 26-foot meridian planted with grass, ten ferro-concrete flyovers, and a number of underpasses. The AVUS now forms part of the A115 Autobahn and is the oldest freeway in the world.

U.S.: The 8-mile Arroyo Seco Parkway in Los Angeles opened on 30 December 1940, just three months after America's first inter-urban freeway. Unlike Berlin's AVUS, patronized principally by motorists who wanted to check out just how fast their cars could go, this was intended for the use of commuters, shoppers, and business users in a city notoriously difficult to negotiate by public transport. Its original name was very soon changed to the Pasadena Freeway, the first use of the term *freeway*, which was coined by a lawyer named E. M. Bassett to distinguish between the older and newer versions of controlled-access highways.

Interchange between freeways: The first in the United States (claimed by the Michigan Department of Transportation as the first in the world) connected I-94 (Edsel Ford Expressway) and M-10 (John Lodge Expressway) on the outskirts of Detroit and opened to traffic 18 January 1955.

Interstate highways: This network, planned on the personal initiative of President Dwight D. Eisenhower, was inaugurated under the Highway Act of 1956 that imposed a gasoline and diesel tax hike of 1¢ per gallon (to 3¢) toward the 90 percent of the cost of the program to be paid from federal funds. The Missouri State Highway Commission completed the first section of Interstate in the United States, an 8-mile stretch of Interstate 70 near Eisenhower's hometown of Abilene, on 26 September 1956. The first transcontinental route, the 2,907-mile Interstate 80, linked the Atlantic and Pacific without an intervening traffic signal on 22 August 1986. The Interstate system, which regenerated the domestic economy of the United States, was deemed completed with the conclusion of Boston's "Big Dig" in 2006. It then comprised 46,677 miles of restricted-access highway linking forty-four of the forty-eight contiguous U.S. state capitals (exceptions Dover, Del., Jefferson, Mo., Carson City Nev., and Pierre, S.D.) with 54,663 bridges and 104 tunnels. The realization of Eisenhower's dream had, in the words of the president himself, changed the face of America.

THE FIRST **MOTOR TRUCK**

in the sense of a practical self-propelled goods wagon capable of carrying (as opposed to drawing) freight was built by John Yule in 1870 for transporting large marine boilers from his works at Rutherglen Loan, Glasgow, Scotland, to the Glasgow docks, a distance of 2 miles. The vehicle was powered by a 250-rpm twin-cylinder steam engine mounted on a 26-foot chassis of red pine, and fully loaded it was capable of moving at ¾ mph.

Even at this slow speed Yule considered his six-wheeled steam wagon an economic proposition. The cost of employing four hundred men to drag a 40-ton marine boiler to the docks worked out at about £60 ($300); a single journey by the wagon incurred a fuel bill of £10 ($50)—a carriage rate of 2s 6d (60¢) per ton mile.

Delivery wagon: The first was a steam-driven van with a Serpollet engine built by M. Le Blanc of 19 rue Lord Byron, Paris, in 1892 for the celebrated Paris department store La Belle Jardinière. The bodywork by Châtelet David was finished in the store's livery and bore the inscription LIVRAISON À DOMICILE ("Deliveries to the Home"). The van remained in service for about three years.

The first motor company to undertake the manufacture of gasoline-powered delivery vehicles was the French firm of Peugeot Frères, which completed its initial production model in December 1895. Powered by a 4-hp Daimler motor, the van was claimed to be able to carry a load of about 1,000 pounds at 9½ mph, and about 650 pounds at 12 mph. The Grands

Magasins du Louvre put in an order for eighteen Peugeot vans for carrying parcels, the first of which was delivered on Christmas Day.

Gasoline-powered truck: The first for hauling freight was the chain-driven Panhard et Levassor *Chariot à plate-forme*, which was built at the Panhard works at 19 avenue d'Ivory, Paris, from a design dated 13 October 1894. The overall length of the vehicle was 9½ feet and it had an open platform at the rear 5 feet long. The Panhard truck was driven for the first time by M. Mayade, the chief engineer of the firm, on 10 February 1895, but did not go into production.

The first commercially manufactured gasoline truck was produced by the Daimler Co. of Cannstatt, Germany, in 1896. Development had begun as early as 1891, but it is not clear whether a prototype had been built in the intervening period. A catalog of September 1896 offered the Daimler-Güterwagen in four models: 4-hp designed to carry a 1,500-kilo load; 6-hp with 2,500-kilo capacity; 8-hp with 3,750-kilo capacity; and 10-hp with 5,000-kilo capacity. The vehicles were powered by twin-cylinder Phoenix engines mounted at the rear and were capable of speeds of up to 12 kph. The catalog offered as an optional extra a heating arrangement, consisting of hot water circulating in tubes, that could be mounted on the driver's box. This may have afforded some scant comfort in cold weather as the driver's box was unenclosed.

The first Daimler truck to be sold was acquired by the Speditions Firma Paul von Maur of Stuttgart in the spring of 1897. The second, the first mechanized **brewer's dray**, went to Böhmisches Brauhaus in Berlin.

U.S.: Two Roger-Benz delivery vans imported from France by R. H. Macy & Co. of New York City in 1895 were used on a limited scale for deliveries, though as managing partner Isidor Straus conceded, they were "more for advertising purposes than practical use." One of these vans participated in America's first motor race, from Jackson Park, Ill., to Evanston and back, on Thanksgiving Day 1895 and was one of only three vehicles to finish in appalling weather conditions.

What was probably the first powered road vehicle in the United States for hauling freight was a heavy truck with 100-pound rear wheels built the same year by piano manufacturer George Schleicher of Stamford, Conn., for the company's own use. Little is known about this; it was probably steam-driven.

Early in 1896 chocolate manufacturer Milton Hershey of Lancaster, Pa., bought a Riker-Electric delivery wagon for $2,000 at the New York Automobile Show. Like the Macy vans, this was used chiefly for promotion. Several other light trucks emerged during the year. About the same time as Hershey acquired his vehicle, Montgomery Ward & Co. acquired one of the earliest delivery wagons produced by the American Electric Vehicle Co. of Chicago, a go-ahead outfit that was to make its name with electric hansoms (SEE **taxicabs**). They also sold two wagons to local silk merchants Charles A. Stevens & Bros., who were so pleased with their purchase that they bought four more the following year. A steam wagon designed by L. F. N. Baldwin and built by the Cruikshank Steam Engine Works of Providence, R.I., went into service with local department store Shephard & Co. Two gasoline-powered commercial vehicles also appeared during 1896, one by old established engine manufacturers L. J. Wing & Co., the other by the Langert Co. of Philadelphia, who entered it in the Cosmopolitan Memorial Day Race from New York City to Irvington-on-the-Hudson and return.

The Wing vehicle was intended as a demonstration model only and there is no evidence that the Langert ever went into commercial service either. It seems that the first gasoline-powered delivery wagons to be successfully manufactured in America for sale were those produced by the Winton Motor Carriage Co. of Cleveland, Ohio, who received an order for a fleet of vehicles from the Dr. Pierce Medical Co. of Buffalo, N.Y., in 1898. Eight had been completed by the end of the year.

America's earliest heavy trucks were introduced in 1899. The Riker-Electric Motor Co. of Elizabeth, N.J., produced a 6-ton vehicle powered by twin 10-hp motors with a platform 14 feet long by 6 feet wide, capable of 5 mph fully loaded. Heavier still but speedier, with a maximum of 8 mph, was the Chicago-based Fischer Equipment Co.'s execution of a design by another Chicago firm, the Patton Motor Vehicle Co. This had a vertical three-cylinder engine made by the American Petroleum Co. which

drove an 8-kw Crocker-Wheeling dynamo, in turn powering a 7½-hp motor on each rear wheel. The first gasoline-powered heavy truck in the United States was probably the Sturgis operated by W. H. Manchester; SEE BELOW.

Trucking company: The first contractor to employ trucks for general freight-work was M. Felix Dubois, who inaugurated a long-distance service over a 400-km route between Kayes and Bamako in the French Sudan (now Mali) in the fall of 1899. The vehicles were 9½-hp De Dietrich gasoline-powered wagons built to the design of Amédée Bollée at Lunéville, France. Dubois employed Chinese coolies to drive them. There were said to be sixty trucks and omnibuses at work by the early part of 1900, but this figure was probably exaggerated. The service lasted only a few months. Owing to the absence of made-up roads the working parts soon became choked with sand and the enterprise had to be abandoned. (Even today the road from Bamako to Kayes is virtually impassable.)

U.S.: The first contractor was W. H. Manchester, who operated a freight route from Los Angeles to Pomona, Calif., starting in 1900. The vehicle used was a 5-ton gasoline-powered 40-hp truck built by S. D. Sturgis & Bros. of Los Angeles and bought by Manchester for $4,000. It was designed to haul a trailer with an additional 5-ton load, making 10 tons in all. Speeds over the 25-mile route were 1¼ to 6 mph. This service was sustained with the same truck for several years.

SEE ALSO **mail truck**.

THE FIRST **MOTOR VEHICLE LICENSE PLATES**
....
were introduced in the Department of the Seine under the Paris Police Ordinance of 14 August 1893, which stated:

> Each motor vehicle shall bear on a metal plate
> and in legible writing the name and address of
> its owner, also the distinctive number used in the
> application for authorization. This plate shall be
> placed at the left-hand side of the vehicle—it shall
> never be hidden.

The requirement for motor vehicles to carry number plates was extended to the rest of France under a decree of 30 September 1901 and applied to any vehicle capable of exceeding 30 kph. By this date registration plates were already mandatory in the Netherlands, which in 1898 became the first country with a nationwide system, and in Belgium. The latter also had a novel requirement: The number at the rear of the vehicle had to be illuminated. (Massachusetts followed suit in 1923.)

U.S.: The first state to require registration of motor vehicles was New York under an enactment of 25 April 1901 that required drivers to pay a $1 registration fee and display their initials on the car in letters at least 3 inches high. Although this is usually held to be the origin of the license plate, there is in fact nothing in the regulations requiring a *plate* as such. Painted letters would presumably have sufficed. As the number of vehicles increased, the sets of duplicate initials multiplied and from 15 May 1905 drivers were issued with a number on a circular tag. It was permissible to carry the tag in your pocket provided the number was also displayed on the vehicle, so again New York system fell rather short of what would be recognized today as a license plate.

The first state to issue license plates was Massachusetts. These were of blue porcelain-enameled iron with white numerals and No. 1 went to Frederick Tudor of 17 Regent Circle, Brookline, on 1 September 1903. Three days later he collided with the car bearing license plate No. 2. The original plate remains in the Tudor family. (It is not, however, the oldest plate in the world; this belongs to the descendants of a Herr Beissbarth, whose Warburg car was registered as No. 1 in Bavaria by the Munich Police Department on 14 April 1899.) The first 99 plates were square; only with the addition of a third digit did they expand into the present rectangular shape. The first annual dated plate was issued by Pennsylvania for the year starting 1 January 1906. By 1915 every state had a registration requirement, but not until 1921 was annual registration mandatory in all states.

Slogans on license plates: These were introduced by the Canadian province of Prince Edward Island, which boasted of its SEED POTATOES AND FOXES in 1928. The first U.S. state to adopt the practice was

South Carolina with the even less compelling IODINE in 1930.

The first personalized or "vanity" plates were issued in 1937 to Connecticut drivers with clean licenses, who were able to buy four-letter combinations of their own choice, though "four letter words" were disallowed.

THE FIRST **MUSEUM**

public, was the Statuario Pubblico in the *antisala* of the Liberia di San Marco, Venice, established by the Venetian Republic in 1596. The exhibits were some two hundred classical sculptures originally assembled by Cardinal Domenico Grimani, who had left his collection to the state on his death in 1523, and his nephew Giovanni Grimani, patriarch of Aquileia, who made a similar bequest sixty years later. The museum continued to be open to the public until its closure in 1797. The statues were eventually put on public display again at the National Archaeological Museum in Venice, where they may still be seen.

The first purpose-built museum was the Ashmolean Museum in Broad Street, Oxford, England, opened on 6 June 1683. This was also the first public museum anywhere in the English-speaking world and is now the world's oldest. The nucleus of the Ashmolean's collection was John Tradescant's "cabinet of rarities," which had been formed earlier in the century at Lambeth and eventually willed to the antiquary Elias Ashmole. He in turn presented the collection to the University of Oxford. The exhibits, dispatched to Oxford in twelve carts, fell into two basic categories, "Natural" and "Artificial." The former comprised stuffed animals and birds (including a specimen of the dodo), shellfish, insects, minerals, and plants; the latter a caseful of weapons from all nations, armor, costumes, household goods, coins, and general curiosities. The first curator was Robert Plot. Admission charges were in the form of an exit rather than an entrance fee, since the amount was calculated in accordance with the length of time a visitor had spent in looking at the exhibits.

U.S.: The first museum was established by a committee of the Library Society of Charleston, S.C., which met on 12 January 1773 to discuss a proposal that the members form a scientific collection for mutual study. A few months later another committee was appointed by the president of the Library Society, Lt. Gov. William Bull II, to organize donation of exhibits. Principally relating to natural history, these were put on display at the society's rented rooms in Kinlock Court, a cul-de-sac running out of the northern part of Union (now State) Street. Sadly the museum had a short life, many of the exhibits being destroyed in a fire that ravaged the library in 1778. Those remaining were put into storage until after the founding of the College of Charleston in 1790, when they formed the nucleus of the college's museum. This was opened to the public in 1824. In 1907 Paul Rea persuaded the college and the city authorities to separate the museum from the college and reconstitute it as the Charleston Museum, of which he became the first curator.

The Charleston Museum claims to be "the first museum in America." As the foregoing indicates, its connection with the short-lived Library Society Museum is tenuous. A rather stronger claim, for "oldest continuously operating museum in America," is that of the Peabody Essex Museum in Salem, Mass., founded in 1799 by the East India Marine Society as a repository for the "natural and artificial curiosities" brought back to the seaport by its members, local mariners and merchants. The East India Marine Museum (which became the Peabody following a bequest in 1867) was formally opened to the public in 1824 with the appointment of Dr. Seth Bass as first full-time curator. This was the same year that the College of Charleston Museum opened its doors to the public. So either the Peabody or the Charleston Museum (since exact dates of opening remain elusive) might claim the title of oldest public museum in the United States. Peabody Essex has a further claim to fame, however, that has not been acknowledged hitherto. When East India Marine Hall (extant) was dedicated on 14 October 1825 in the presence of President John Quincy Adams, the collection of mainly Asian artifacts was housed in the first purpose-built museum (other than those dedicated exclusively to fine art) in America.

SEE ALSO **art museum; preservation movement: historic house museum**.

THE FIRST **MUSICAL COMPOSITIONS**

originating in America were by German-born Conrad Beissel, who wrote scores for the hymns and chorals performed by the sisters for the Ephrata Cloister near Philadelphia in the early years of the eighteenth century. The first edition of the Ephrata hymn collections, printed in Philadelphia by Benjamin Franklin in 1730, contained more than a thousand hymns that have been attributed to Beissel (SEE **hymn book**).

The earliest known music by American-born composers were two pieces composed in 1759: a setting for Thomas Parnell's poem "My Days Have Been So Wondrous Free" by twenty-two-year-old Francis Hopkinson of Philadelphia, who was the first graduate of the University of Pennsylvania and later a signatory of the Declaration of Independence; and an ode written and set to music by student James Lyon, a native of Newark, N.J., for Princeton College's graduation ceremony that year. Hopkinson's composition is not known to have been performed, though a musical ode of his, "sacred to the memory of our late Gracious Sovereign George II," was performed at the University of Pennsylvania's 1761 Commencement, together with an anthem by the Rev. James Lyon. The latter was the first American composer whose work was published, in his compilation *Urania, or A Choice Collection of Psalm-Tunes, Anthems, and Hymns*, published in Philadelphia in 1762. Although the 198 pages of music in this volume were mainly English, there were also six of Lyon's original American works.

Piano compositions: The first in America were also by Francis Hopkinson (SEE ABOVE) and contained in his mistitled *Seven Songs for the Harpsichord or Forte Piano* (there were actually eight songs). Published in Philadelphia in 1788, the songs were intended for "young practitioners on . . . the forte piano" and dedicated to music lover George Washington, who responded with the modest disclaimer that he could not "raise a single note on any instrument to convince the unbelieving."

Orchestral music: The first composed and published in the United States was German-born Hans Gram's *The Death Song of an Indian Chief*, scored for strings, two clarinets, and two E-horns, which appeared on a flyleaf in the *Massachusetts Magazine* for March

1791. Gram was organist at Brattle Square Church in Boston.

Symphony: The first by a native-born composer was Philadelphia-born William Henry Fry's *Santa Claus*, premiered by the Louis Julien Orchestra in New York on 24 December 1853.

American woman to compose orchestral music: The first was Amy Marcy Cheney Beach, whose choral *Mass in E-Flat* was presented by the Handel and Haydn Society at the Boston Music Hall in February 1892. She also composed the first symphony by an American woman, the *Gaelic Symphony* premiered by the Boston Symphony Orchestra on 30 October 1896 and performed the same year in Buffalo and Brooklyn, followed by a rendering the next year by the Chicago Symphony Orchestra under Theodore Thomas. The comparative lateness of women composers of orchestral music has much to do with the fact that it was considered improper for ladies to play stringed instruments before the 1870s.

SEE ALSO **ballet; opera.**

N

THE FIRST **NAVAL ACTION**

involving an American ship was an engagement between an unnamed armed merchant vessel from Cambridge, Mass., on her maiden voyage in 1645 to the Canary Islands and a Barbary rover intent on plunder. The New England vessel, with a crew of thirty men and fourteen guns, fought an all-day action against the more heavily armed rover, which had twenty guns manned by a crew of seventy. Eventually the Americans succeeded in hitting the rudder of the rover and made good their escape.

The first **naval war fought by American vessels** was that of the United Colonies against the Acadians of Canada, following attacks on Maine and New Hampshire in early 1690 by the French commander Frontenac. Massachusetts mounted the inaugural naval expedition in late April of that year, when a frigate and half a dozen smaller vessels under the command of Sir William Phips, ex–Royal Navy and formerly the colony's agent in England, sailed from Boston. They sacked the French post at Port Royal, Nova Scotia, took sixty prisoners, and returned south within the month laden with booty. This success encouraged a larger expedition, this time of more than thirty vessels from Massachusetts and Plymouth Colony that set sail from Boston on 9 August 1690 under Phips's command to attack the French at Quebec. Manned by 2,200 sailors, the fleet reached Quebec on 5 October, but bombardment and a land attack both proved fruitless, with many of the ships damaged by heavy cannonades from the fort. Dysentery and smallpox broke out and provisions ran short. Phips's force limped back to Boston in November, having achieved little more than the burning of a French post on Anticosti Island and the interception of a few French supply ships, but at a cost of the loss of a number of his own ships and of nearly half his men from disease, cold, and drowning. Much more successful was the infant navy of New York, consisting

of a single twenty-gun man-of-war, a brigantine, and a Bermuda sloop, which sailed for Canada shortly after Phips's second expedition under the command of Capt. Mason. They devastated Port Royal, burned eighty French fishing boats along the coast, and returned to New York with no fewer than six prizes, including one of 150 tons and another of 200 tons. It was the first great feat of American arms, precursor of a naval tradition that would reach fulfillment in the early years of the nineteenth century when the U.S. Navy acquired a reputation quite disproportionate to the modest status of the fledgling republic.

For the first naval action by a steamship, SEE **steamboat: steam naval vessel**; for the first action fought by the U.S. Navy, SEE **war–foreign war**.

THE FIRST **NEWSPAPERS**

in the sense of printed journals of news appearing at frequent intervals under the same imprint were two German publications that began life more or less simultaneously in the middle of January 1609. *Aviso Relation oder Zeitung* was published weekly, commencing 15 January. Recently it has been proved beyond doubt that the paper was published at Wolfenbüttel in Lower Saxony, and it is now believed that the printer and publisher was Julius Adolph von Söhne, keeper of the royal press. The *Aviso* continued to be issued until 1616, when there was a gap of four years before it was restarted by Elias Holwein. It was still in existence in 1624, but no copies are known after that date.

The other paper, *Relation: Aller Fürnemmen und Gedenckwürdigen Historien*, was published weekly at Strasbourg, numbered but not dated. The publisher was Johann Carolus and the paper lasted until at least 1622. The 37th number, issued in September 1609, contains a report of Galileo's telescope.

English-language newspaper: The first was the *Corrant out of Italy, Germany, Etc.*, of which 11 numbers survive bearing dates from 2 December 1620 to 18 September 1621. It was printed at Amsterdam by George Veseler and "soulde by Petrus Keerius, dwelling in the Calverstreete, in the uncertaine time." The first issue bears no title at all, while some of the later numbers have a slightly varying title, not unusual in the early days of newspaper publishing. The lead story in the first issue, dateline "Weenen, the 6 November" relates: "The French ambassadour hath caused the Earle of Dampier to be buried stately at Presburg."

Peter van den Keere, the publisher, was a map engraver who had lived and worked in England. The political climate of the time made it safer for any printed news for English consumption to be printed abroad, and a number of other English-language corantos were produced at Amsterdam and The Hague during 1621, much to the annoyance of England's King James I, who took vigorous action to have them suppressed.

U.S.: The first was a one-off reprint of the *London Gazette* of 9 February 1685, published in Boston by Samuel Green Jr. in mid-April of that year. This reported the death of Charles II and the accession of his Roman Catholic brother James II, portentous and unwelcome news for Bostonians. The first American newspaper, also a one-off but not intended as such, was bookseller and former London newspaper writer Benjamin Harris's unauthorized three-page *Publick Occurrences Both Forreign and Domestick*, issued in Boston on 25 September 1690 with the declaration that it would be "furnished once a moneth (or if any Glut of Occurrences happen, oftener)." Remarkably this preceded the publication of provincial newspapers in England by a full decade; indeed the only newspapers serving cities outside London in the whole of the English-speaking world were a short-lived *Edinburgh Gazette* of 1680 and Dublin's *News-Letter*, which began in 1685. *Publick Occurrences* was notable also for the fact that it dealt principally with local affairs, whereas the staple of the newspapers of Harris's native London was foreign news. The single issue contained reports of a Boston suicide; a disastrous fire in the city, the second in only a few weeks; the state of the harvest; a thanksgiving ceremony by Indian converts to Christianity; the decline in deaths from smallpox following a violent epidemic; and "news from the front" in King William's War, in which New England forces had joined with loyal Indian tribes to attack the French in Canada. It was probably the reporting of this last that provoked the suppression of the paper by Gov. Simon Bradstreet and his council four days after publication. Harris had cast doubt on the reliability of the New Englanders' Mohawk allies, describing them as "miserable Salvages" [*sic*] for their barbarous treatment of prisoners of war, an insult to a coalition partner that could not be countenanced by the authorities. Henceforth, it was decreed, nothing further could be printed without a license from government. Harris returned to London and became a purveyor of quack medicines. The only surviving copy of *Publick Occurrences* is held at Britain's Public Record Office.

The first sustained American newspaper was the *Boston News-Letter*, of which No. 1 was published by the city's postmaster, John Campbell, on 24 April 1704, price 2d or 12 shillings a year delivered. By virtue of his office Campbell was among the first to receive news from Europe via ships' captains who brought not only the public prints from London but also their own personal accounts of news learned in coffeehouses or taverns. Moreover he was already himself a disseminator of news, as the author of a handwritten news dispatch that, like his father (Boston's previous postmaster) before him, he had been accustomed to sending to Gov. Winthrop of Connecticut. Just as this news was of the tide of affairs in Europe, so also did the *Boston News-Letter* recount matters of moment on the other side of the Atlantic, with scant attention to New England happenings. Charles E. Clerk, author of *The Public Prints: The Newspaper in Anglo-American Culture 1665–1740* (1994), accounts for this by virtue of the fact that both old England and New England were at war with the French and that statecraft, dynastic change, and military adventures in Europe, however distant, could have a more direct bearing on the safety and livelihood of the citizens of the New World than on the inhabitants of the mother country, whose island fortress secured them from depredation. There was also sporadic news from the West Indies; but mainland American reports were largely confined to shipping movements and official pronouncements of the governor of the colony.

The original *News-Letter* consisted of a single sheet measuring 12" x 15", was printed front and back in twin columns, and was issued weekly with a circulation of some 250 to 300 at a time when Boston had a population of 7,000. (Though a significant number were distributed farther afield; the *News-Letter* enjoyed the privilege of free postage.) It remained the only newspaper in the American colonies until the debut of William Brooker's *Boston Gazette* on 21 December 1719, a single day before the emanation of the third, Andrew Bradford's *American Weekly Mercury* in Philadelphia. It was only once there were a number of colonial newspapers that American news began to be featured to any extent—each newspaper copying reports from the others.

Daily newspaper: The first was *Einkommenden Zeitungen*, published by Timotheus Ritzsch at Leipzig between July and September 1650. The paper was numbered but not dated, although there are grounds for believing it was first issued on 1 July. The only surviving examples are 68 issues from No. 6 to No. 83 (some are missing), preserved at Uppsala University in Sweden.

U.S.: Benjamin Towne's *Pennsylvania Evening Post, and Daily Advertiser* changed to daily publication on 30 May 1783. It lasted for a further seventeen months, a difficult time for Towne as he was under indictment for treason. He had started the *Post* in Philadelphia in 1775 as a staunchly patriotic organ, the first newspaper to publish the Declaration of Independence (6 July 1776), but when the British occupied the city Towne switched his allegiance and became a Tory, only to turn his coat a second time when the occupiers evacuated. In some weeks the "daily" appeared only five times, possibly because the editor not only did all the work of writing copy, setting type, and printing by himself, but even hawked it in the street with the cry "All the news for two coppers." By the time the paper succumbed, a much more successful paper in the same city, the *Pennsylvania Packet*, had become a daily (21 September 1784), and barely three months later there were two dailies in New York. It was a remarkable achievement for these cities, each with a population of about 25,000, to sustain daily newspaper publication;

in England no city outside London had a daily before 1855. As early as 1794 Philadelphia even had a foreign-language daily, *Le Courier Français*, catering to the many refugees from the French Revolution residing in the city.

Sunday newspaper: The earliest American attempt, Philip Edwards's *Sunday Monitor*, of Baltimore, did not survive beyond its first issue on 18 December 1796. The following month, however, another Baltimore publisher launched the *Weekly Museum* as a Sunday paper and this ran for five months. The first daily to publish seven days a week was a *Boston Globe* (not the present paper of that title) of 1832–33.

Newspaper illustration: Early newspapers were not generally illustrated but there were occasional exceptions. The first such illustration in America appeared in the *Boston News-Letter* as early as 26 January 1707 and depicted the change in design of the Union Jack after the union with Scotland. It was copied from a woodcut in the *London Gazette*.

The first newspaper with illustrations in every issue was the Canadian-owned 5¢ *New York Daily Graphic*, founded in New York by George-Édouard Desbarats of Montreal on 4 March 1873. Most of the illustrations, which appeared in four pages of each issue's eight, were printed from photo-lithographic electroplates, though the *Daily Graphic* was also the pioneer of **newspaper photographs**. The earliest of these, a world first, was a study of New York's Steinway Hall that appeared on the paper's back page on 2 December 1873 (SEE ALSO **halftone**).

Early newspaper photographs tended to be static, usually portraits of distinguished men (seldom women). The earliest known live coverage of an unscheduled news event appeared in the *Christchurch Press* in New Zealand on 7 June 1902 and depicted the rescue by the Sumner lifeboat of one John Frances, whose small rowing boat had collapsed. The photo was taken with an Underwood camera by seventeen-year-old Havelock Williams, who had just opened his own photographic studio in Christchurch.

The first newspaper with **color illustrations** was the *Chicago Inter-Ocean,* where a four-color rotary press was installed by Walter Scott & Co. in May 1892. The following month the paper carried red and blue illustrations in its weekend supplement to celebrate the Democratic convention. By 22 October it was able to print in the full range of colors. During 1893 most of the color news pictures were of the World's Columbian Exposition at Chicago, but these were also color cartoons by Thomas Nast and Art Young. After the Exposition closed in October the color supplement became a Children's Extra.

Color began to be adopted for advertising (qv) using four-color run-of-paper machines in the early 1930s. The first **color news photograph** was a four-column 9¼-inch study in natural colors of the winners of a six-day bicycle race the previous day that appeared on the front page of the *Minneapolis Journal* on 27 February 1936. Some forty to fifty U.S. newspapers were estimated to be running photographs in full color by 1958.

SEE ALSO **advertisement: newspaper; cartoon: newspaper; college journal; comic strip; electric telegraph: press telegram; film review: newspaper; newspaper: horoscope; Sudoku; war correspondent; weather forecast; woman editor; woman journalist.**

THE FIRST **NEWSPAPER HEADLINE**

only emerged some 150 years after the birth of the newspaper. Early newspapers prefaced their news reports with a dateline and sometimes a place name, but eschewed any other heading. The earliest recorded headline appeared across a single column of the *Maryland Gazette* of Annapolis in 21 October 1762 and announced in eighteen-point great primer type, GREAT JOY TO THE NATION! A PRINCE OF WALES IS BORN. GOD SAVE THE KING. The infant was to become the spendthrift, scandal-ridden obese popinjay George IV, sometime Prince Regent during his father George III's bouts of madness, who reigned on his own account between 1820 and 1830, dying largely unlamented by his subjects.

The earliest known headline across multiple columns, at a date when any heading was still the exception rather than the rule, announced GLORIOUS TRIUMPH in the *United States Telegraph* of 22 October 1828. The triumph in question was Gen. Andrew Jackson's election as U.S. President. In general, though,

headlines only became commonplace with the Mexican War of 1846–48, the drama of eyewitness accounts of battles (SEE **war correspondent**) demanding strident assertions in large bold type, often stacked six or seven high across a single column.

Banner headline: The first appeared on the front page of London evening the *Star* on Wednesday 16 July 1890 and read somewhat enigmatically MANY HAPPY RETURNS OF THE DAY—WEDDING OF PROFESSOR STUART MP. This was a one-off and there were no further examples in the London press until the Matabele War of 1896 in what is now Zimbabwe. The *Evening News* for 9 July that year wrung its editorial hands with MATTERS IN RHODESIA GROW WORSE INSTEAD OF BETTER.

U.S.: The *Chicago Times* began using banner headlines in the fall of 1893, but originally these were editorial exhortations rather than proclamations of the main news story. One such declared LET CONGRESS STOP TALKING AND ACT; THEN BUSINESS CONDITIONS WILL SOON IMPROVE. By the following summer the paper was occasionally using a banner headline to herald a news story, but it was in New York that the banner came into its own for exclusive news stories. On 24 December 1895 Joseph Pulitzer's *New York World* signaled MESSAGES OF PEACE, COMMON SENSE AND HUMANITY TO THE PEOPLE OF THE UNITED STATES. Anodyne as this appears, it was in fact a call to avert a major war. A boundary dispute between Venezuela and British Guiana threatened to embroil Britain and the United States in armed conflict over what President Grover Cleveland alleged was a breach of the Monroe Doctrine. While most of the press took a belligerent attitude in support of the president, the *World* declared Cleveland's stand to be a wholly false application of the Monroe Doctrine; it would be a "colossal crime" if the two greatest English-speaking nations fought a war over it.

The headline had been engendered by Pulitzer's action in cabling various notables of church and state in England seeking their views on the issue. These were unanimous in their opposition to war, the most influential being elder statesman William Gladstone's calming message that "Only common sense is required." Even then the vindictive U.S. secretary of state Richard Olney, the most vociferous and bellicose of the saber-rattlers, tried to have Pulitzer prosecuted under a long-moribund statute of 1799 that prescribed heavy penalties for any citizen who communicated with a foreign power "in relation to any controversy with the United States." Eventually the lead given by the *World* and the rightness of its cause persuaded others and for one of the first times in history a government was deterred from a course of action by the force of public opinion as molded by the media. And in this case a headline was instrumental in the outcome.

While the first significant banner headline helped to prevent war with a European power, the next paper to adopt the technique did so in the cause of starting one. During 1897 William Randolph Hearst, the larger-than-life model for *Citizen Kane* and proprietor of the *New York Morning Journal*, began to stir up public revulsion at Spanish oppression in their colony Cuba with stories trumpeted by the first regular and systematic use of banners. This began on 22 February when pages one, two, and three each had a banner headline, the one on the front page reading SHERMAN FOR WAR WITH SPAIN FOR MURDERING AMERICANS. Subsequent banners proclaimed a typically Hearstian episode when he arranged for beautiful teenage agitator Evangelina Cisneros to be spirited out of a Cuban jail, followed by the blowing up of the battleship USS *Maine* in Havana harbor in February 1898, and then on 25 April the U.S. declaration of war against Spain itself.

In the run-up to war Pulitzer's *World* had allied itself with Hearst's *Journal*, resuscitating its use of banner headlines to urge the U.S. government to take on the colonial oppressor. It was of this conflict that Hearst memorably told illustrator Frederic Remington, "You furnish the pictures and I'll furnish the war," a remark that might have been more accurate had he said that he and Pulitzer would furnish the war together. In marked contrast to the Venezuelan affair, on this occasion banner headlines fed the fervor for war, the successful prosecution of which was to initiate the United States as a world power and usher in the "American Century."

One other irony is that Pulitzer, though he introduced banner headlines to mainstream journalism, actually disliked their use, which he had sanctioned on a regular basis only in order to compete with Hearst's flamboyant and bombastic *Journal*. After the war he sought to eliminate them altogether by ordering that all the *World*'s large headline type be melted down.

THE FIRST **NEWSPAPER HOROSCOPES**

were published in the *Sunday Express*, London, on 24 August 1930. The editor had been looking for a novelty feature to celebrate the birth of Princess Margaret Rose earlier that week and commissioned astrologer R. H. Naylor to cast a horoscope for the new addition to the royal family. With remarkable prescience Naylor forecast the princess's marital difficulties, at a time when the first family in the land were not expected to have any. He also prophesied "events of tremendous importance to the Royal Family and the nation will come about near her seventh year." That year was 1936, which would see Edward VIII's abdication to marry Mrs. Wallis Simpson. To round the feature off he added a few "what the stars foretell" notes for readers with birthdays coming up the following week. It was this afterthought that brought a wholly unexpected response from other readers eager to know what the future had in store for them too. Bowing to popular demand the editor engaged Naylor to do a weekly column of horoscopes. Almost immediately the innovation crossed the Atlantic and it was in 1936 that the *New York Post* introduced the now standard practice of running the horoscopes under the twelve signs of the Zodiac. Today all of Britain's tabloids and some 90 percent of America's 1,600 daily newspapers feature horoscopes, while there are some forty magazines in the United States devoted to star signs.

THE FIRST **NOVEL BY AN AMERICAN**

was *The Female Quixote: or, the Adventures of Arabella* by New York–born Charlotte Ramsay Lennox, published in London, where she was then living, in 1752. The book is partly set in her native country and she later adapted it as a play, the first by an American woman playwright (qv). She wrote a number of other romances, of which *Euphemia* (1790) was also part American in setting.

Novel by an American-born writer to be published in the United States: The first was *The Power of Sympathy*, written by the Boston-born son of a clockmaker William Hill Brown "to represent the specious Causes, and to Express the fatal Consequences of Seduction" and published anonymously in Boston in 1789. It was derivative of Samuel Richardson's *Pamela*, often claimed as the first English novel and also the first to be published in America (1744), being epistolary in form and concerned with seduction as a principal element. In this case, however, the seduction was a real one, for Brown based his fiction on a true-life case in which the Harvard-educated patriot and politician Perez Morton had effected the ruin of his wife's sister, Fanny Apthorp, an act not only adulterous but also incestuous according to the law as it then applied. Thus American fiction began as it was destined to continue, once nineteenth-century reticence was no more, embracing one theme above all other: sex.

Novel by an American-born woman to be published in the United States: The first is usually cited as Hannah Foster's *Coquette*, another sex scandal fiction-based-on-fact, which she published anonymously in Boston in 1797. However, this overlooks two earlier novels that attracted less attention. *The History of Maria Kittle*, in which the eponymous heroine is captured by Indians during the French and Indian War, was originally written by New York–born Ann Eliza Bleecker as a very lengthy letter to her half-sister Susan Ten Eyck. It was serialized together with an unfinished novel *The History of Henry and Ann* in the *New-York Magazine* 1790–91 and published in book form under the title *Posthumous Works of Ann Eliza Bleecker* in New York in 1793. *The History of Maria Kittle* was sufficiently popular to be twice republished on its own, in Hartford, Conn., in 1797 and 1802. Possibly the reason it has been expunged from orthodox literary history was that it portrayed Native Americans as ignoble bloodthirsty savages. The other pre-*Coquette* female novel appeared the same year as *Maria Kittle*. This was *The Hapless Orphan: or, Innocent Victim of Revenge*, published anonymously "By an American Lady" in Boston in two volumes. Her identity is not known.

The year 1794 saw the U.S. publication of what has been described as "America's first best seller," *Charlotte Temple*, about a sweet innocent English girl brought to America by a rogue who deserts her. This was by Susanna Rawson, who was born in England, brought up in America, returned to England after the Revolutionary War, but came back in 1793 and settled permanently in Philadelphia, where the first American edition appeared (it had been published earlier in London). It was to go through eighty-four American editions by 1850 and though not by an American-born writer, it may be perceived as an American novel by virtue of the fact that it was American themed and the work of one who was to become American by adoption.

Professional novelist: The first in America was Charles Brockden Brown, who abandoned the practice of law in his native Philadelphia to pursue his literary muse in New York, starting with the now lost *Sky-Walk* (1797) followed by *Alcuin: A Dialogue*, a plea for women's rights published in 1798. During the same year he published the Gothic horror story *Wieland*, a heady mixture of religious murder and ventriloquism in Pennsylvania. In 1799 he produced no fewer than three novels: *Arthur Merryn*, about the 1793 plague in Philadelphia; *Ormond*, another Philadelphia tale replete with the perils of yellow fever, suicide, rape, and murder; and *Edgar Huntley*, a melodramatic frontier tale of a sleepwalker and a homicidal maniac. *Jane Talbot* came out in 1801 as well as *Clara Howard*, the first American novel to be reissued overseas (in London, re-titled *Philip Stanley*). After this prodigious output, Brown went into business, though also editing the *Monthly Magazine & American Review* and the *Literary Magazine & American Register*. The former serialized his unfinished *Memoir of Carawin, the Biloquist*, a prequel to *Wieland*, in which the hero develops the power of ventriloquism but falls under the malign influence of an Irish rogue.

Brown's second novel, *Ormond*, is noted for the first lesbian passage in American literature, wherein the narrator Sophia Westwyn, a week after her marriage in Europe, rushes back to the United States on learning that her best friend Constantia has been left destitute and spends three days in her company "lost within the impetuosities of a master passion." (Interestingly this was written within a year of the earliest known reference to lesbianism in the United States, by Philadelphia-based French immigrant Moreau de Saint-Méry.)

Altogether 28 American novels, including several by British-born Susanna Rawson, were published in the United States by the end of the eighteenth century. During the same period some 350 fiction titles by overseas authors were published by American presses, greatly encouraged by the fact that they did not need to pay for copyright. Against this competition only 25 American novels appeared in 1800–09 and 28 in 1810–19. The 1820s saw a spurt, with a total of 128, a figure more than doubled to 290 in the 1830s and vastly increased again to 767 in the 1840s.

SEE ALSO **children's fiction: novel; detective story: novel; book dust jacket; paperback book**.

······································

THE FIRST **NOVEL BY A BLACK AUTHOR**

······································

was *Clotel*, by William Wells Brown, born in March 1815 as a slave on the farm of Dr. John Young of Lexington, Ky., whose half-brother was Brown's father; his mother was a field hand. He escaped to Cleveland, Ohio, in 1834, throwing himself on the mercy of a Quaker called Wells Brown when he was starving and suffering from exposure; he later assumed his rescuer's name in tribute. His novel *Clotel; or the President's Daughter* is the story of a slave girl of that name in Richmond, Va., of her mother, Currer, who is separated from her and sold in Natchez; and of her sister Althesa, who is also lost to her when she is sold in New Orleans. Brown wrote it in London, whence he had been persuaded he would be safer than as a fugitive slave in America, and the novel was published there by Partridge & Oakey on 27 July 1853. It seems to have been at least partly inspired by a contemporary allegation that the mulatto daughter of President Thomas Jefferson had recently been sold for $1,000 in the New Orleans slave market, hence the subtitle of the novel. A revised version under the title *Clotelle: A Tale of the Southern States* was published in Boston in 1864 as a 10¢ paperback by James Redpath & Co. and in this the heroine had shed her distinctive lineage. **Novel by a black American woman/Novel by a black writer published in the United States:** The first was

Our Nig: or Sketches from the Life of a Free Black by Harriet E. Wilson, which was privately published in Boston on 5 September 1859. A fictionalized version of her own life, Harriet Wilson's novel recounts the childhood of a free indentured mulatto servant girl growing up in the household of a tyrannical white woman who frequently whips her, clothes and feeds her inadequately, and breaks her health from overwork. The significance of the work was its depiction of a life of servitude and later destitution of a black in the free North that was little or no improvement on the condition of slavery in the South.

After an upbringing that paralleled that of "Our Nig" (the racist diminutive with which the protagonist of the novel was dubbed by the family she served), Harriet Wilson became a seamstress in Boston and married a free black who deserted her while she was pregnant. Destitute and unable due to ill health to earn her own living, she wrote the novel in order to make sufficient money to support her infant son. It is not apparent how she was able to have the book printed by George C. Rand & Avery of Boston, who were not commercial publishers, though possibly they had a profit-sharing arrangement. Whether there were any profits is doubtful and its message that the abolitionist Northern states were as morally bankrupt in their treatment of blacks as were the slave-holding Southern states was unlikely to have met with a receptive audience.

The book is so obscure that it is omitted from several otherwise comprehensive bibliographies of African-American literature and only thirteen extant copies had been identified when the novel was republished for the first time in a scholarly edition in 1983. Harriet's child, George Mason Wilson, died in February 1860 and she herself is believed to have expired the same year.

Another novel by a black woman was also published in 1859, *Ursula* by Brazilian free black Maria F. dos Reis. It is not known which appeared first.

NOVEL BY AN AMERICAN ON AN EXPLICITLY GAY THEME

was *The Young and Evil* by Charles Henri Ford and Parker Tyler, published by Obelisk Press in Paris in 1933 after the authors had failed to find a publisher in the United States ("Life is short and the jails are uncomfortable," as one of them tersely remarked). Ford was principally a poet and his lover Tyler a critic. The novel explored the adventures of their alter egos Julian and Karel in the high-camp homosexual underworld of New York's Greenwich Village, cruising the parks and all-night "coffeepots" while evading the attentions of New York's notoriously homophobic police, and attending drag balls in Harlem begowned and made up to the nines. It was not only the moral majority who were disgusted by these goings-on. Avant-garde English poet Edith Sitwell described the novel as "entirely without soul, like a dead fish stinking in hell" and threw it in the fireplace, declaring that in earlier times she would have had Ford's skin made into a bath mat. (Relations were not improved when later Sitwell nursed an obsessive passion for Ford's new lover, the Russian Pavlick Tchelitchew.) Gertrude Stein, on the other hand, was mad about the book. When Ford died in 2002 at the age of ninety-four the London *Daily Telegraph* felt able to conclude a lengthy and appreciative obituary without its customary formulaic sign-off for deceased bachelors: "He never married."

THE FIRST **NUCLEAR POWER PLANT**

was a small establishment built at Obninsk, 55 miles from Moscow, which began producing electrical current for industrial and agricultural purposes on 27 June 1954. It had a useful capacity of 5,000 kW.

The first full-scale nuclear station in the world was Britain's Calder Hall (now Sellafield), Cumberland, which began generating on 20 August 1956, the date on which the first turbine was brought into operation. It was formally opened by Queen Elizabeth II on 7 October 1956, when power was first fed into the grid of the Central Electricity Authority. The 90,000-kW plant comprised four graphite-moderated, gas-cooled

reactors with their associated heat exchangers, two turbine halls, and four cooling towers.

U.S.: The first American nuclear power plant was built on a similarly small scale to the world's first at Obninsk. Its modest output of 5,000 kW probably accounts for the fact that the Vallecitos Boiling Water Reactor (VBWR) at Pleasanton, Calif., is almost always overlooked as the pioneer in favor of the much larger Shippingport (SEE BELOW). The VBWR was designed by Samuel Untermyer of the General Electric Co. and built by GE and the Pacific Gas & Electric Co. It began delivering power to the Pacific Gas & Electric Co. grid for public consumption on 21 October 1957.

The first full-scale nuclear power plant in the United States was the 90,000-kW Shippingport Atomic Power Station on the Ohio River in Pennsylvania, built as a collaborative project of the Department of Energy and the Duquesne Light Co. Curiously the project had begun as a light-water reactor designed to power a nuclear aircraft carrier until re-directed into public electricity supply. Shippingport started generating power for the greater Pittsburgh area on 18 December 1957. When President Dwight D. Eisenhower formally dedicated the plant the following May, he was keen to declare it to be the first nuclear power plant in the world. After he was advised that Calder Hall was already generating on the same scale, the speech was rewritten to say that it was the "first in the world devoted solely to peaceful purposes," the British plant using some of its waste to produce plutonium for nuclear weaponry. The priority of the Obninsk and Vallecitos reactors according to this definition was conveniently forgotten.

THE FIRST **NUDIST CAMP**

was the *Freilichtpark* ("free-light park") founded in 1903 by Paul Zimmermann at Lingsberg near Lübeck on Germany's Baltic coast. Zimmermann's *Nacktkultur* ("naked culture") was a deeply earnest philosophy—its founder was a disciple of Nietzsche—and fun and frolic was almost wholly absent from a regime in which each morning began with 2 hours of vigorous gymnastics. Only vegetarian food was allowed and alcohol and tobacco were prohibited. Not all the adherents of the cult embraced its rigors as wholeheartedly as did Zimmermann himself. When a young American couple, Mason and Frances Merrill, stayed at the camp in the late 1920s they found that many of the naturists gathered after meals on the porch of Zimmermann's home for a smoke. Dropping in at the local hostelry for a surreptitious drink, they found that most of the campers had preceded them.

U.S.: Social nudism was introduced to the United States by German immigrant Kurt Barthel, who joined with three German couples of his acquaintance on Labor Day 1929 for a picnic in the buff at Hudson Mountain near Peekskill, N.Y. On 7 December that year he founded the American League for Physical Culture and this had about fifty members when their first camp was established at Spring Valley, in Rockland County, N.Y., on 21 June 1930. During the winter members met at a gym in New York City, initially without being molested, but during the following winter they were arrested by police. On 9 December 1931 the New York Court of General Sessions dismissed the case, declaring that disrobing at a members-only gathering was not a public act and that nakedness in this context did not constitute indecency. Emboldened by the vindication of their recreational rights, Barthel and his members, now some two hundred strong, proceeded to establish America's first permanent camp, Sky Farm, at Liberty Corners, N.J., on 15 May 1932. Still flourishing, it is believed to be the world's oldest nudist camp. The earlier German camps had been forced to close during the Third Reich.

THE FIRST **NURSES, TRAINED**

were Sisters of the Institution of Deaconesses at Kaisersworth in north Germany, founded in 1836 under the direction of Friederike Fliedner. Previous to this time, apart from the religious orders in Catholic countries, hospital nurses were generally uneducated and notoriously drunken members of the lowest social order. The first nursing sister and first matron at Kaisersworth was Gertrude Reichardt (1788–1869),

the daughter and sister of physicians and herself an experienced and highly responsible nurse—an exception to the generality—who arrived at Kaisersworth on 20 October 1836. A substantial house in the village had already been purchased for conversion into a hospital. Here, together with Frau Fliedner, she began the training of the initial intake of deaconesses, Sisters Beata, Johanna, Helena, Franziska, Catharina, and Carolina. They were given theoretical and clinical instruction under Dr. Thönissen and also studied for the state examination in pharmacy. By 1840 student nurses were being sent from France and Switzerland to be trained at Kaisersworth. Among its innovations was that of district nurses, with the first appointments being made to the parishes of Bielefeld and Cleve in 1844. Five years later the United States received its first trained nurses from Kaisersworth, when several sisters were sent to Pittsburgh, Pa., in response to a plea from Pastor Passavant for help in containing the typhus and cholera epidemics sweeping the city. Although a training school in Pittsburgh was planned, only a single probationer applied for admission.

The Kaisersworth Institution, which also ran orphanages, homes for the aged, and asylums for the blind, was a religious foundation under the overall supervision of a Protestant pastor, but there were no vows and deaconesses were free to return home or to marry after five years' service. Kaisersworth nursing was not an occupation for the faint-hearted. The working day began at 5 A.M. and ended at 9 P.M. and for this there was no payment, only board and lodging. The institution earned money by charging a fee for the services of trained nurses sent out to serve in other hospitals.

The first wholly secular training school for nurses was organized by the Nurse Society of Philadelphia, established 5 March 1839. This was a charitable institution concerned with the provision of trained private nurses to look after maternity cases at home. The training scheme was under the direction of Dr. Joseph Warrington and probationers attended lectures together with male medical students, a mannequin being used to demonstrate obstetrical procedures (though it was stressed that the nurses were not being trained as midwives). After attending six "live" cases satisfactorily they were granted a certificate and the entitlement to a wage of $2.50 per week from the society while they were employed. By 1850 some fifty trained nurses had been certified, of whom "only four" were dismissed for drunkenness; evidently there was still some way to go before nurses threw off their old reputation for addiction to the bottle.

The first **secular school for the training of hospital nurses** was the Nightingale School for Nurses, established at St. Thomas's Hospital, London, under the superintendence of Mrs. S. E. Wardroper with the first intake of fifteen probationers on 9 June 1860. It was financed from the Nightingale Fund, set up in tribute to the work of Florence Nightingale and her band of nurses in reforming the military hospitals of the Crimean War. Miss Nightingale had visited Kaisersworth in 1850 and readily acknowledged the debt that she, usually accorded the title of founder of trained nursing, owed to her predecessors at the institute. In contrast to Kaisersworth, however, where no social distinctions obtained, the Nightingale School graded inmates as "lady nurses," "lady probationers" (who paid fees and were not required to do any laborious work), and "servant class." Nevertheless even the latter could, by application, aspire to the status of "lady," an appellation that would have been granted them in few other avocations at the time. The formidable Mrs. Wardroper was indeed a lady born and bred (she always wore black kid gloves on duty), but it was she who instituted, over a period of thirty-three years, most of the basic practices of modern nursing. Florence Nightingale, who has tended to be given (not of her own volition) much of the credit for Mrs. Wardroper's work, said of her:

Her whole heart and mind, her whole life and strength were in the work she had undertaken. She never went a-pleasuring, seldom into society. Yet she was one of the wittiest people one could hear on a summer's day, and had gone a good deal into society in her young unmarried life. She was left a widow at 42 with a young family. She had never had any training in hospital life. There was none to be had. Her force of character was extraordinary. Her word was law.

So was Miss Nightingale's, making it all the more remarkable that the two architects of professional nursing enjoyed such apparent harmony.

U.S.: The first training school for hospital nurses was established under Dr. Susan Dimock and Dr. Marie Zakrzewska at the New England Hospital for Women and Children at Roxbury, Mass., where the first member of the initial intake of five probationers, Linda Richards, began her course of instruction on 21 January 1873. She was also the first to graduate, going on to Bellevue Hospital in New York City as night superintendent in October 1873. She thereafter bore the proud title of "the First Trained Nurse in the United States." Later she became superintendent of nurses at Massachusetts General Hospital, went to England to study the training methods at St. Thomas's and met Florence Nightingale, and organized the training schools at Boston City Hospital, Philadelphia's Methodist Hospital and University Hospital, the Homeopathic Hospital of Brooklyn, (N.Y.) and Hartford (Conn.) Hospital, eventually returning, after twenty years, to her alma mater as superintendent.

THE FIRST **OCEAN CRUISE**

was a four-month voyage around the Mediterranean organized by Peninsular & Oriental (P&O) Steam Navigation Co., starting from Southampton, England, on 26 July 1844. Three ships were employed: the *Lady Mary Wood* (553 tons), taking passengers to Vigo, Lisbon, Cadiz, and Gibraltar; the larger *Tagus* (782 tons), taking them on to Constantinople via Athens; and the *Iberia* (516 tons), completing the outward trip as far as Jerusalem and Cairo. The return journey was made by the same ships and by the same route. This particular excursion was chronicled by the novelist William Makepeace Thackeray, who was offered a free passage by the company in order to popularize the idea of cruising as a pastime.

Thackeray published a full account of his cruise as *Notes of a Journey from Cornhill to Grand Cairo* in 1846. In the preface to this work he makes it clearly apparent that he was one of a party of cruise passengers, even though the ship did carry a number of other people with more orthodox reasons for traveling. Despite the fact that he was prodigiously seasick for much of the cruise, Thackeray seems to have enjoyed the novelty of voyaging for pleasure and entered into shipboard life with nautical gusto. His published description tends to concentrate on the shore excursions, but he does give some account of impromptu saloon concerts and the joy of sitting on deck beneath a star-studded sky at night, as well as the feeding arrangements. These varied according to the ship. In the *Lady Mary Wood*, Thackeray and his fellow passengers suffered the ministrations of "a cook, with tattooed arms, sweating away among the saucepans in the gallery, who used (with a touching affection) to send us locks of his hair in the soup." Aboard the *Iberia*, however, the dinners so excelled that he reproduces the bill of fare for 12 October as they approached Alexandria:

Mulligatawny Soup

Salt Fish and Egg Sauce

Roast Haunch of Mutton
Boiled Shoulder and Onion Sauce
Boiled Beef
Roast fowls
Pillow ditto

Ham
Curry and Rice

Cabbage; French Beans;
Boiled Potatoes; Baked ditto

Damson Tart
Currant ditto
Rice Puddings
Currant Fritters

The directors of the P&O had every cause to be satisfied with Thackeray's response to their generous gesture in offering him a free cruise, for in his book he recommended "all persons who have time and means to make a similar journey"—notwithstanding the fact that several incredulous friends refused to believe he had been abroad at all, insisting that he had concocted the whole thing in the safe seclusion of his home in the London suburb of Putney.

U.S.: The first ocean cruise from America and also the first by a ship chartered solely for this purpose, the *Quaker City*, was organized in 1867 by Capt. Charles C. Duncan of New York and advertised as "An Excursion to the Holy Land, Egypt, the Crimea, Greece, and intermediate points of interest." The original instigator of the scheme was the noted divine Henry Ward Beecher, who was planning to write a biography of Jesus Christ and wanted to do some field study in

Palestine. Why he should have considered it necessary to take several hundred companions with him remains obscure, but in the event he decided not to go. Those who did paid $1,200 for the trip, excluding the $5 a day in gold that they were advised to take for shore expenses, and were only accepted as passengers after a careful screening by a selection committee. Not only were they expected to be of an acceptable social standing, but they also had to display a fitting degree of moral earnestness.

The humorist Mark Twain applied for a berth so that he could write a series of articles for the *Daily Alta Californian*. He prejudiced his chances by presenting himself before Capt. Duncan exuding "fumes of bad whisky," but scraped by as the organizer was under the mistaken impression that he was a Baptist minister. Twain had high hopes of "a royal holiday beyond the broad ocean" and the chance to "dance, and promenade, and smoke, and sing, and make love, and search the skies for constellations . . ." He was doomed to disappointment. Although his book, *Innocents Abroad*, gives a lighthearted account of this first large group of American tourists to Europe, he expressed his true feelings in a critical letter to the *New York Herald*: "Three fourths of the Quaker City's passengers were between forty and seventy years of age. The pleasure ship was a synagogue, and the pleasure trip was a funeral excursion without a corpse . . . Such was our daily life on board ship—solemnity, decorum, dinner, dominoes, devotions, slander."

THE FIRST OCEAN LINERS

belonged to the first shipping line to sail to a fixed schedule and specialize in the transport of passengers, established in November 1783 by Capt. Cornic de Moulin of the Breton seaport l'Orient (aka Lorient). They comprised five fast sailing packets: *le Courier de l'Europe*, *le Courier de l'Amérique*, *le Courier de New-York*, *le Courier de l'Orient*, and *l'Alligator*. Each sailed monthly between l'Orient and New York City on fixed dates every other month. First to arrive in New York was *le Courier de l'Orient* on 18 November 1783. On her return voyage, leaving New York on 18 December, she carried a number of officers of the recently

defeated British army in America. Such as these would have been privileged to use the "noble cabin," which accommodated forty at the captain's table, for a fare of 500 livres ($100). Lesser folk content with "ship's rations" paid 200 livres ($40). The average time to cross the Atlantic was thirty-four days.

U.S.: The first liners were the 424-ton sailing packets *James Monroe* and *Courier* owned by the Black Ball Line of New York City, founded by a group of Quaker merchants under the leadership of Jeremiah Thomson to maintain a fixed schedule of sailings between the home port and England's major seaport Liverpool. The *Courier* left Liverpool on 1 January 1818. The *James Monroe* sailed from Pier 23 on the East River on 5 January and arrived at Liverpool on 2 February after a "downhill" transatlantic run of twenty-eight days. She carried eight passengers. The appointments of the ship far surpassed those of any other passenger-carrying vessels of the time, including a commodious saloon richly furnished in mahogany, and satinwood-panelled staterooms with marble pillars flanking the doors. A small "farm" of cows, pigs, sheep, and hens was maintained on deck so that the voyagers could be supplied with fresh meat, milk, and eggs. Bread was baked daily. Despite the religious propensities of its founders, the Black Ball Line was notorious for brutal treatment of its seamen.

Steamship in regular transatlantic passenger service: The first was the *Great Western*, designed by Isambard Kingdom Brunel for the Great Western Steamship Co. and launched at Patterson's Yard, Bristol, England, on 19 July 1837. Leaving Bristol under the command of Capt. James Hosken on 8 April 1838, she made her maiden voyage to New York in 15 days 5 hours at an average speed of 8.8 knots, just failing to beat the smaller *Sirius* for the accolade of first British steamship to cross the Atlantic. Like the *James Monroe* before her, the 1,320-ton *Great Western* set new standards of passenger comfort, her magnificent 75-foot saloon eclipsing any that had ever been seen on a sailing vessel. Accommodation was provided for 120 first-class passengers, 20 second-class and 100 steerage.

The *Great Western* was celebrated at the time as the vessel that the learned scientist Dr. Dionysius Lardner conclusively proved could not possibly cross the Atlantic under steam; and then proved the contrary when he took passage in her to elope with somebody else's wife.

U.S.: The first was the Ocean Steam Navigation Co.'s 1,640-ton wooden paddle-steamer *Washington*, built by Westervelt & Mackay of New York, which sailed from New York City on 1 June 1847 and reached Southampton, England, two weeks later. She and her sister ship *Herman* maintained a service on the New York–Bremen route via the English Channel for ten years, but they were withdrawn when the $200,000-per-annum U.S. Mail contract expired.

Iron steamship operated as an Atlantic liner: The first and also the first **liner fitted with a screw propeller** was the *Great Britain*, built by Patterson's to Brunel's design for the Great Western Steamship Co. and launched by the Prince Consort at Bristol, England, on 19 July 1843. She left Liverpool for her maiden voyage on 26 July 1845 with sixty passengers and 600 tons of cargo and arrived in New York after a voyage of 14 days 21 hours. The largest and most technically innovative ship of her day, the *Great Britain* was devastated by a hurricane off Cape Horn in 1886 and abandoned at Port Stanley in the Falkland Islands, where she became a hulk for storing coal and wool. In 1970 she was brought back to her home port of Bristol, where she was restored and opened to the public.

U.S.: The first American liner with a propeller was the wooden-hulled 770-ton auxiliary (i.e., a sailing ship with engine) SS *Massachusetts*, which made her maiden voyage across the Atlantic in September–October 1845. The propeller could be lifted out of the water when under sail. America's first iron-hulled screw-propeller liner was the Union Steam Ship Co.'s SS *Mississippi*, in service as a troop carrier in 1862 and as a passenger liner four years later.

The last shipping line to operate a fleet of passenger liners was Union Castle, withdrawing its UK–South Africa service in 1977 just seven years after the advent of the jumbo jet had made long-haul airliners too competitive for ocean liners to survive. The last passenger liner in the world to ply a regular route is the Saint Helena government's RMS *St. Helena*, carrying passengers from Britain and South Africa to the mid-Atlantic island that has now become the sole country in the world accessible only by sea. The RMS, as she is known to crew and passengers alike, is due to be retired with the opening of Saint Helena's planned airport in 2012.

THE FIRST **OFFICE BUILDING**

purpose-built as such was the Palazzo degli Uffizi (Palace of the Offices), designed by Giorgio Vasari for Duke Cosimo I de' Medici to house the administrative and judicial offices of his city-state of Florence (then comprising most of Tuscany) and completed in 1571. Three years later it began to assume the role for which it is now far better known when the Medici collections were accommodated on the top floor. The Uffizi became a public art museum in 1769.

The first purpose-built office building for commercial use was the Oost-Indisch Huis in Amsterdam, built for the Dutch East India Company in 1606 next to the Bushuis armory on the Kloveniersbugwal canal, the building formerly used as the company's headquarters. The Dutch East India Company had been formed four years earlier to engage in the Malukan spice trade and was the first in the world to issue tradeable shares (20 March 1602). The Oost-Indisch Huis is a vast building in classical Amsterdam Renaissance style that was extended in the 1660s by the addition of western and northern wings to enclose an inner courtyard. The original mansion-block, which contains the now restored Meeting Room of the Seventeen Regents (the boardroom of the company), is believed to have been the work of the distinguished Utrecht-born sculptor and architect Hendrick de Keyser. The Dutch East India Company continued to occupy the building until bankruptcy forced its dissolution in 1800. The Oost-Indisch Huis is now part of the premises of the University of Amsterdam and has been declared a national monument.

Apart from the buildings erected for the great trading companies of northern Europe, there were very few purpose-built office buildings before the nineteenth century, when banks and insurance companies began to house themselves in headquarters designed to impress potential as well as existing clients with their solidity and worth. The first office building designed for multiple occupancy by a number of companies was built in 1823 by architect Annesley Voysey at the Lombard Street end of Clement's Lane in the City of London.

U.S.: Not known. The editor invites nominations.

Open-plan office: The first office designed on the open landscape concept that eliminated any permanent barriers between management and staff was created in 1960 for the Boehringer Mannheim Pharmaceuticals Corporation of Mannheim in Baden-Württemberg, Germany, by the Hamburg-based Quickborner Team für Planning und Organization. In 1967 Quickborner also designed the first open-landscape office in the United States, a department of the DuPont Corporation at its headquarters in Wilmington, Del.

THE FIRST **OLD-AGE PENSIONS**

were introduced in Germany by the chancellor, Prince Otto von Bismarck, under the Old Age Insurance Act of June 1889, which came into operation on 1 January 1891. The contributory scheme was compulsory for persons over sixteen years of age who were in full employment and earning less than 2,000 marks per annum (then equivalent to approximately $500). The pension became payable at the age of seventy after premiums had been paid for a minimum of thirty years (or at a lesser rate until the scheme had been going that long). Contributions were graduated according to income, starting at 7 pfennigs a week for those whose annual wage did not exceed 30 marks. The employer contributed an equal amount. As in Germany today, the amount of the pension depended on the rate of contributions. During 1891, the first year of the scheme, the sum of 15,299,004 marks was paid out to 132,926 pensioners—an average per capita of 115 marks ($28.77).

The pension was not sufficient to live on, because it was paid only to those of seventy or over still capable of working and was intended as a subsidy to their earnings; those incapable of further labor (of whatever age) were entitled to disability benefits, amounting to roughly half as much again.

The old-age pension intended to cover the cost of the necessities of life, and therefore the forerunner of most modern pension schemes, was introduced by New Zealand under the Old Age Pensions Act passed on 1 November 1898. The scheme was non-contributory and provided for an annual pension of £18 ($90) for those with an annual income of £34 ($170) or less, diminishing by £1($5) for every £1 of income in excess of this sum. Applicants had to be sixty-five years of age if male and sixty if female, of good moral character, and at least twenty-five years resident in the colony. The first payments were made in March 1899 and were made retroactive to 1 January of that year. A total of 4,699 pensions were granted during the first full year of operation, including one of only £1 per annum ($5) to an applicant in Otago.

U.S.: The first old-age pensions paid in the United States were by Alaska under an enactment of the territorial government passed in 1915. Most payments were in the $7 to $10 per month range; as in 1890s Germany they were not designed for subsistence. At most payment might cover the rent. A number of states attempted to introduce old-age pensions, including Arizona in 1914 and Nevada and Pennsylvania in 1923, but their legislative provisions were ruled unconstitutional on grounds of public money being diverted to "charitable" ends. Montana's act of 5 March 1923 was the first to be upheld, though it was not statewide in operation: counties could choose whether or not to implement it for their residents. When Kentucky passed a similar act in 1926 not a single county elected to pay out pensions to their elderly and in Maryland the following year only the city and county of Baltimore did so. Nevertheless, by 1935 there were thirty states that offered some form of old-age assistance, meager as it might be at the height of the Depression.

America's first nationwide system of pensions provision was introduced under the Social Security Act that President Franklin D. Roosevelt signed into law on 14 August 1935. State agencies were set up to administer the program, with the federal government paying half of local grants provided the total did not exceed $30 a month. This started to become operative on 1 January 1937, when workers and their employers in states with approved schemes became subject to a 1-percent tax on wages of up to $3,000. By September 1938 all states were participating, though initially only lump-sum payments were made to eligible contributors, called Old Age Assistance. Monthly benefit payments began on 31 January 1940, with Ida Fuller of Brattleboro, Vt., being issued check number 000-000-001 for the sum of $22.54. She had contributed $24.75 in payments on her $2,484-per-annum income between 1937 and 1939. Her last check was issued in 1974 when she was one hundred years old, by which time she had received $20,944 in monthly benefits.

THE FIRST **ONE-WAY STREETS**

were introduced in London by an act of Common Council passed in August 1617 to regulate "the disorder and rude behaviour of Carmen, Draymen and others usinge Cartes." The traffic order embraced seventeen narrow and congested lanes into Thames Street, including Pudding Lane, where the Great Fire of London began in 1667. It remained in force for the following two centuries.

Between then and the motor age there is only one recorded example of a one-way traffic restriction. This was in January 1800 and was caused by the popularity of American physicist Count Rumford's newly opened scientific lecture hall known as the Royal Institution, which became all the rage with the fashionable ladies of the town. Such was the congestion in Albermarle Street that the only solution was to restrict the carriages of the beau monde to entering at one end and leaving at the other.

U.S.: The first was the 7-foot-wide Pierce's Alley (later Change Avenue) in Boston in 1639. As in Britain, a long while passed without any further such measures before Columbus Circle and part of Times Square in New York City were designated one-way in 1905. By 1916 there were twenty-seven one-way streets in Manhattan, mainly narrow thoroughfares unable to accommodate the crush of automobile traffic.

THE FIRST **OPERA**

was *Dafne*, with libretto by Ottavio Rinuccini and music by Jacopo Peri, originally performed at the Palazzo Corsi in Florence during the Carnival early in 1597 (exact date unrecorded). None of the music survives except for some brief passages interpolated by Corsi himself. The story was founded on the legend of Daphne and Apollo.

The earliest opera of which both text and music survive is Rinuccini and Peri's *Euridice*, which was performed for the first time at the Palazzo Pitti in Florence on 6 October 1600. The orchestra on this occasion consisted of a clavecin, a chitarrone, viol, and great lute.

U.S.: The earliest known operatic performance was of Colley Cibber's ballad farce *Flora, or Hob in the Well*, which opened in the "long room" of Shepheard's Tavern in Charleston, S.C., on 18 February 1735. This was also the first theatrical performance in America to contain a ballet (qv) sequence.

Opera composed by an American: The first was Andrew Barton's *The Disappointment or the Force of Credulity*, scheduled to be performed by the Douglass Company of Philadelphia in April 1767 but canceled due to opposition from local bluenoses. The identity of Andrew Barton, a pseudonym, is not known for certain, but is believed to have been prominent Philadelphia businessman and legislator Thomas Forrest. The story is typical of ballad opera, a farce centering on the hunt for the pirate Blackbeard's buried treasure on the banks of the Delaware, but is notable for being wholly American in theme. The work was published in New York in 1767 and Philadelphia in 1796 but was not performed until the 1930s.

The first opera by an American to be performed and America's first grand opera was *Leonora* by William Henry Fry, based on Bulwer-Lytton's play *The Lady of Lyons*, which premiered at the Chestnut Street Theater, Philadelphia on 4 June 1845. First on an American theme was Brooklyn-born George F. Bristow's *Rip Van Winkle*, set in upstate New York, which opened at Niblo's Garden on Broadway, New York City, on 27 September 1855.

Italian opera in the United States: The first season opened at the Park Theater in New York on 29 November 1825 with a performance of Rossini's *Il Barbiere di Siviglia* that starred Manuel Garcia and his seventeen-year-old daughter Maria (later a celebrated singer known as Malibran). A distinguished audience included Joseph Bonaparte, ex-king of Spain;

novelist James Fenimore Cooper; and Mozart's librettist Lorenzo da Ponte. The box office took $2,980 and librettos were sold at the theater for 37¾¢. The season continued to 30 September 1826.

American-based opera company: The first was established by Paris-born John Davis at the Orleans Theater in New Orleans in 1822 with singers imported from France. Most of the repertoire was French, with the occasional incursion into Italian and German opera. The star performer was Madame Alexandre, who became the toast of the young bucks of New Orleans. Between 1827 and 1833 the company mounted a series of extensive tours of northern cities, including Boston, Philadelphia, Baltimore, and New York. James Caldwell's Virginia Company, based at the Orleans Theater from 1820 and at the Camp Street Theater in New Orleans from 1824, also performed opera in competition with Davis's troupe, but it was not exclusively an opera company since the repertoire comprised a good deal of spoken drama as well.

Opera house: The first theater in the United States designated as such was the Southwark Opera House in Philadelphia, opened in 1766. The largest theater in colonial America, it also played host to spoken drama. The first devoted wholly to opera and built for that purpose was the Italian Opera House in New York City, built at a cost of $150,000 by eighty-four-year-old Lorenzo da Ponte, who had been Mozart's librettist and poet to the Imperial Hapsburg Court, and opened with a season of Rossini on 18 November 1834. Da Ponte, despite his distinguished background in Europe, had not fared so well in America, at one point making a meager living as a hat salesman in Elizabethtown, N.J., and at an even lower point peddling sausages from "L. da Ponte's Wagon." The money for the opera house was raised from wealthy subscribers eager for a share of the reflected glory that a specially reserved seat at this temple of European culture and sophistication would confer on them. Alas, support from those in the unreserved seats was insufficient to maintain the ambitious venture and after two seasons of Italian opera the opera house was sold to new and less elevated proprietors to become an ordinary theater. The oldest functioning opera house in the United States is the Academy of Music, Philadelphia, known as the "Grand Old Lady of Broad Street,"

which opened with the American premiere of Verdi's *Il Trovatore* on 25 February 1857.

SEE ALSO **radio broadcast: opera**; **sound recording: operatic recording**.

THE FIRST **ORAL CONTRACEPTIVE**

was a form of the hormone progesterone formulated at the Syntex research laboratories in Mexico City on 15 October 1951 by Carl Djerassi. What this twenty-eight-year-old Austrian-born son of a Bulgarian father was actually seeking was an oral progestational compound that could be used to treat some kinds of infertility and menstrual disorders. In the meantime, however, Dr. Gregory Pincus of the Worcester Foundation for Experimental Biology of Shrewsbury, Mass., had been invited by the Planned Parenthood Movement to devise an ideal contraceptive, defined as "harmless, entirely reliable, simple, practical, universally applicable, and aesthetically satisfactory to both husband and wife." When Djerassi's compound was sent to the Worcester Foundation for testing, Pincus discovered that it could inhibit ovulation and so be used as a contraceptive. He and co-worker Dr. John Rock proceeded to develop progestin and estrogen compounds with this end in view, clinical tests beginning in 1954. The work was funded with a donation of $2 million by McCormick reaper heiress Katherine McCormick.

Djerassi was paid $1 by Syntex for the patent to his discovery, but he was also given shares in the company that were then worth $2 each. By 1993 the shares stood at $8,000 each.

The first large-scale oral contraceptive tests on human beings with "the Pill" were initiated in 1956 at San Juan, Puerto Rico, where 1,308 women being rehoused from a favela volunteered to participate. Of this number 811 were put on Conovid and 497 on Uvulen. At the end of the three-year trial, out of the 830 women remaining in the test group, only seventeen had become pregnant.

Following approval by the Food and Drug Administration, the first commercially produced oral contraceptive, Enovid 10, was marketed by the G. D. Searle Drug Co. of Skokie, Ill., on 18 August 1960.

P

PAINTING

THE FIRST PAINTBALL

was devised in the late 1970s by American Stock Exchange broker Hayes Noel and his outdoorsman friend Charles Gaines, who lived in the New Hampshire wilderness. Following a succession of discussions about survival skills, in which Gaines as the experienced hunter challenged Noel's assertion that as a survivor of the Wall Street jungle he could hold his own in any jungle, they decided to devise a means of testing the practiced hunter versus the urban predator. Nothing seemed very effective until they found an advertisement for the Splatmaster paint gun, used by cattlemen to mark cows, in an agricultural catalog. They sent for two guns and staged a duel, which resulted in victory for Gaines when he shot Noel in the butt. Convinced that they had the makings of a real test of survival skills, they proceeded to devise rules for what they termed the National Survival Game and invited a group of friends, including a wild-turkey hunter from Alabama, two Vietnam War long-range patrol leaders, a Chicago doctor, an L.A. movie producer, some lawyers, and a *Sports Illustrated* journalist, to join them for the first organized paintball game, to be played in an 80-acre cross-country ski area of New Hampshire. It took place near Henniker on 27 June 1980 and was won by a local lumberman and deer hunter, Richard White. Noel subsequently made a deal with the providers of the paint guns, the Nelson Paint Co. in Michigan, to supply them exclusively to him and his partners, other than to cattlemen. In the first year of operation Noel and Gaines sold some 7,000 to 8,000, mainly to people wanting to organize a paintball franchise and rent out the guns, and within six months the fledgling enterprise was in profit. It grew to an $800 million industry, but satisfied with having made his imprint on the leisure business, Noel moved to Santa Cruz, Calif., and continued trading stocks.

THE FIRST PAINTING

surviving, of an American subject by an artist who had visited America was *René de Laudonnière and Chief Athore*, a watercolor on parchment painted by Jacques le Moyne de Morgues, probably in 1566 on his return to France from Florida. Le Moyne, originally from Dieppe, had served as cartographer and official artist on René de Laudonnière's expedition to reinforce the French Huguenot colony established by Jean Ribault at the mouth of St. John's River (now Jacksonville). By the time Laudonnière arrived in 1564, little of Ribault's settlement survived, but Chief Athore was able to show him the stone column that Ribault had erected as proof of France's claim over Florida and that had become an object of veneration to the Indians. This is the scene depicted by Le Moyne, not only the first known eyewitness representation of a scene within the present United States, but one of the earliest paintings anywhere of a contemporary event. Its documentary value is enhanced by the fact that strewn around the column are foods and domestic utensils of the Indians as well as a sheath of arrows. Laudonnière gathered together the remnants of the colony and removed it to the south bank of St. John's River, where he established Fort Caroline. This, however, was short lived; it was attacked and destroyed by a Spanish expedition from St. Augustine and Le Moyne was fortunate to be among the survivors who fled back to France. Also fortunate for posterity was the fact that he was able to escape with his drawings, from one of which his only surviving American painting was executed. There is record of one other painting, a watercolor of a palisaded Timucuan village with palm-thatched houses and sentry posts at its narrow entrance; it is believed to have been painted in 1564 and is known from the engraving based on it in Theodore de Bruy's *Historia Americae* (Frankfurt, 1634).

Professional painter: The first known to have practiced in what is now the United States was Hendrick

Couturier, who is recorded as a member of the Leiden guild of painters in 1648 and emigrated to the Dutch settlement of New Amstel on the Delaware River in about 1661. There he made a living as a trader and a public official, but he also spent time in New Amsterdam, where he painted a number of portraits. He acquired the status and rights of a burgher of the fledgling city in 1663 as a reward for painting a portrait of the governor, Peter Stuyvesant, and executing a number of drawings of Stuyvesant's sons. This is probably the "Peter Stuyvesant" in the collection of the New-York Historical Society. The society's 1666 portrait of the governor's seventeen-year-old son, "Nicholas William Stuyvesant" is also attributed to Couturier, as is the Metropolitan Museum of Art's "Jacobus G. Strycker." The artist settled in England in 1674, dying there ten years later.

Painting in New England probably emerged a little later than in New Netherland, though the sailor-artist Capt. Thomas Smith had emigrated from Bermuda as early as 1650. His surviving works (or those attributed to him, as all are unsigned) include a "Self-Portrait" (Worcester Art Museum, Worcester, Mass.) as well as portraits of his daughter, "Maria Catharine Smith" (American Antiquarian Society, Worcester, Mass.), of Captain George Curwin (Peabody & Essex Museum, Salem, Mass.) and of Major Thomas Savage (Henry L. Shattuck Collection, Harvard University), none of which is dated. The earliest record of Smith as a professional painter is from 1680, when Harvard College paid him 4 guineas for a portrait, now lost, of the Rev. William Ames. It is likely that his surviving works were painted later than Couturier's in New Amsterdam, although Smith had arrived in America at least ten years earlier. The earliest dated New England portraits, by at least two different unknown artists, are inscribed 1670.

The earliest known **woman painter** in the United States was Irish-born portraitist Henrietta Johnson, wife of a clergyman, who emigrated to Charleston, S.C., from England in 1708. She worked in pastels and at least thirty of her works have survived.

The **earliest native-born** American artist with surviving works of certain provenance is Nathaniel Emmons, born in Boston in 1703 and active during the 1720s and '30s, three of whose undated portraits

survive. According to his 1740 obituary in the *New England Journal*, he also painted "rural scenes." If so he would be one of the first artists in America to have painted landscapes.

Art historian E. P. Richardson believes that there were native-born artists of Dutch descent operating in the Hudson River Valley as early as the first decade of the eighteenth century. He cites the portraits "Pieter Schuyler" (City Hall, Albany), "Ariaantje Coegmans," "Gerardus Beekman," and "David Davidse Schuyler" (all at the Albany Institute of History and Art), all of which are undated; the style of dress dates them from c. 1700–10. The painter has not been identified, but Richardson asserts that they were not the work of a European artist.

A perhaps more substantive claim can be made for Gerret Duychinck, born in New Amsterdam in 1660 and the son of Evert Duychinck, a former professional soldier turned painter. Three portraits— "Self-Portrait," "The Artist's Wife," and "Mrs. Augustus Jay," all in the collection of the New-York Historical Society and painted c. 1700, have been attributed to the younger Duychinck. By profession he was a glazier, a craft that involved painting, such as when he decorated the windows for a new church at Hysophus. He also taught drawing in the infant metropolis, where his son and grandson also became craftsmen-artists.

THE FIRST **PANTYHOSE**

were developed in 1959 by Allen Gant of North Carolina's Glen Raven Mills, at the request of his pregnant wife. She found stockings uncomfortable to wear in her condition because of the need to attach them to a constrictive garter belt. Gant assigned his workforce at a mill in Altamahaw, N.C., to work on a prototype, which they developed from the 70-denier stretch leotards that were then fashionable. The new garment used 40-denier nylon in the panty part and 15- or 20-denier nylon in the legs, which had a seam up the back. It was launched the same year under the brand name Panti-legs. Allen Gant wanted to call it Panty-Hose, but another North Carolina hosiery company had already applied for the name.

Among the earliest customers was the celebrated dancer Sally Rand, famed in the 1920s and 1930s as one of America's first stage nudes and particularly for a dance she performed in 1933–34 at the Chicago "Century of Progress" world's fair in a pair of shoes and three balloons. Still performing as the 1960s dawned, she was attracted to the idea of the new tights for their warmth on drafty stages, but the seam would have betrayed the fact that she was at least partly clothed. At her insistence Allen Gant went back to the drawing board and by 1961 Glen Raven Mills were ready to start production of seamless fine-denier tights. There was still the problem of the waistband, but Miss Rand cut this off and inserted transparent tape to hold the garment to her body. It was a testimony to the quality of the product that even from the front row of the stalls, audiences were unaware of her innocent deception.

THE FIRST **PAPERBACK BOOK**

series emerged in Germany and the United States the same year, 1841. In Leipzig Christian Bernhard Tauchnitz launched his "Collection of British Authors" with *Pelham* by Edward Bulwer-Lytton (chiefly remembered today for penning the opening line "It was a dark and stormy night"). Other early Tauchnitz authors included Charles Dickens, Sir Walter Scott, William Makepeace Thackeray, Capt. Marryat, Thomas Carlyle, and George Eliot. The books were all printed in English and were intended for the use of the English and American tourists who were traveling on the Continent in ever-increasing numbers with the advent of rail networks. Tauchnitz secured the rights to publish English works in all non-English-speaking countries, one of the terms of his contracts being that the purchasers would be instructed that the books must be discarded when finished, and not taken into an English-speaking country. Hence Tauchnitz introduced a new formula into publishing that still pertains to paperbacks today—the idea of the disposable book. He was also a pioneer in another respect, for his scrupulously drafted agreements between author and publisher were the precursor of modern international copyright. Until that time, authors had seldom been paid royalties on books published abroad, nor would they be on the early American paperbacks.

In 1860 Tauchnitz was raised to the rank of Freiherr with the title of Baron for his services to publishing, and he was elevated to the Saxon First Chamber (equivalent to the Senate). England made him an honorary consul-general and he became a very close personal friend of Queen Victoria. Tauchnitz died in 1895, but the series was continued by his heirs until 1933, by which time it comprised 5,097 titles by 525 different authors. It was subsequently taken over by another firm of Leipzig publishers, and since 1960 has been published in Stuttgart.

U.S.: The first series of paperbacks began with the publication of full-length novels as an "extra" to the New York magazine *New World*, starting with the first volume of Charles Lever's *Charles O'Malley*, separately priced at 50¢ and issued in July 1841. The second paperback in the United States was also Volume 1 of *Charles O'Malley*, because *New World*'s principal rival, *Brother Jonathan*, promptly brought out the same work at only 25¢. They were sold in bright colored covers by street vendors and were also available, without covers, by mail order. The absence of covers enabled the publishers to maintain the fiction that these books were periodicals and benefit from cheaper postage. The Boston *Nation*, New York *Sun*, New York *Mirror*, and Philadelphia *Public Ledger* soon followed their example, driving the price down to 12½¢ at a time when the cheapest hardcover novels sold at $1 to $2. First of the book publishers to succumb to this competition was Harper's in 1843, with a series of popular British reprints at a quarter. Nearly all the paperback novels were of British authorship as there was no need, prior to international copyright, to pay royalties. The price war between the various competitors reached the point where separate imprints of Bulwer-Lytton's *Zanoni* were available from the *New World*, from *Brother Jonathan*, and from *Harper's* for as little as 6¢. The U.S. Post Office put an end to the "extras" the same year when they ruled that the publications must be carried at the rate for book post, but by this time public demand for cheap literature was such that the paperback, as a legitimate field of conventional trade publishing, had become an ongoing institution.

Paperback series continued to proliferate during the remainder of the nineteenth century, with no fewer than fourteen different imprints in 1877 and twenty by 1887. Most were of the dime novel variety, specializing in adventure, or romance novelettes. The first quality paperbacks in a recognizably modern format were Paper Books, founded in New York by Charles Boni in 1929, of which the first was Takaski Ohta and Margaret Sperry's *The Golden Wind* on 25 September, followed by Margaret Goldsmith's *Frederick the Great* on 22 October, L. A. G. Strong's *Dewer Rides* on 25 November, and Stuart Chase's *Prosperity: Fact or Myth* on 26 December—the answer to the latter proposition being already apparent since Wall Street had crashed as the book was going to press. Paper Books were sold by subscription at $5 for twelve monthly books or singly at 75¢ (later 50¢) a copy. With one exception, all the covers of Paper Books and their successor series Bonibooks (sold in bookshops) were designed by Rockwell Kent, the quality of his designs reflecting the high standard of literature that Charles Boni espoused. The venture became a victim of the Depression in 1932.

The so called "paperback revolution" occurred first in Britain with the founding of Penguin Books by Allen Lane in July 1935 and subsequently in America with Robert F. de Graff's launch of the first ten Pocket Books at 25¢ each in New York on 19 June 1939. The best seller of the original Pocket Books list was Emily Brontë's *Wuthering Heights*, doubtless stimulated by the recent movie version, and the one attracting fewest purchases was *Five Great Tragedies* by William Shakespeare.

THE FIRST **PAPER CLIP**

is most frequently attributed to the Norwegian Johan Vaaler, who took out a patent in 1900 for a model that never went into production. Norway being less than liberally endowed with significant "firsts," Vaaler has become a national hero. Indeed during the Nazi occupation of Norway in World War II patriotic citizens took to wearing paper clips in their lapels as a small act of defiance. More recently a monument in the form of a giant paper clip has been erected outside Oslo. This takes the form of the standard double loop Gem type, though Vaaler's patent shows a triangular design. Alas for Norwegian pride, his bent-wire fastener was neither the first nor was it of any significance in paper-clip development.

The first paper clip known to have been manufactured was patented in the United States by Erlman J. Wright in 1877. The patent stated that it was designed for "fastening together loose leaves of papers, documents, periodicals, newspapers." It was advertised for sale the same year, specifically for holding newspaper pages together, probably one of the few paper fastening functions *not* performed by paper clips today.

The Erlman J. Wright paper clip had a single loop and an extended "tail." The origin of the most common type of paper clip in use today, the double loop with rounded ends known generically as the Gem, is open to question. Prof. Henry Petroski of Duke University, in *The Evolution of Useful Things* (1993), points to the United Kingdom as its place of origin but has been unable to locate any British references earlier than 1907. The Wikipedia article "Paper Clips" is more categoric, saying it was first manufactured in England by the Gem Manufacturing Co. in 1890. We have been unable to trace a nineteenth-century British company of that name and the earliest definitive evidence is American, an advertisement of September 1898 by Cushman & Denison of Ninth Avenue, New York City, offering Gem paper clips by that name at 15¢ for a box of one hundred.

Finally it is perhaps worthy of mention that according to a 1958 study, probably as valid now as then, made by Howard Sufrin of the Pittsburgh firm of Steel City Gem Paper Clips, three of every ten paper clips were lost and only one in ten was ever used to hold papers together. Collections of historic paper clips are held at the Smithsonian Institution, Washington, D.C. (Emmanuel Fritz Paper Clip Collection) and at the virtual Early Office Museum—Early Paper Clips Gallery (OfficeMuseum.com).

THE FIRST **PAPER MONEY**

is believed to have been issued at I-Chou, China, between 935 and 954. According to the Chinese historian Ma Tuan-lin:

The people of the state of Shu had made paper money without the knowledge of the government, because their iron money was so heavy. They had called this paper money chiao-tzu or bills of exchange. Because these bills of exchange were convenient in trade, sixteen wealthy families had united together to manage the issue. But when the wealth of these families gradually diminished, and they were no longer able to redeem their pledges, many quarrels and lawsuits ensued. Certain persons advised the prohibition and cancelation of the bills. As this however would paralyze trade, it was suggested to establish an office for the issue of paper money on behalf of the government and to prohibit people from making it privately. According to this proposal, a decree was enacted to establish a bank for the issue of bills of exchange at I-Chou. (Vissering translation).

I-Chou was a famous publishing center, so it is almost certain these bank notes would have been printed.

Treasury notes: The first known to have been legal tender were issued in China in February 1024, when the government of the Song Dynasty took over the banks of Cheng tu, Szechwan, in an attempt to rectify the devaluation of paper currency. Certificates of deposit issued by the thitherto private banks then became government backed and recognized as legal tender. In 1107 the Chinese government began printing currency in six colors, using a series of printing blocks for different elements of the design.

The earliest record of forgery dates from 1068, when a quantity of counterfeit notes were issued and a law was enacted that the offense should carry the same penalty as forging seals of state. Over-reliance on paper money led to disastrous inflation in China, and its use was discontinued altogether from the beginning of the fifteenth century until 1851.

The first European paper currency was issued in Sweden by the Stockholms Banco on 16 July 1661. No specimens of the first year's issue have survived, but eleven examples from the years 1662 and 1663 are known to exist, the earliest being one for five dalers dated 6 December 1662. The idea of issuing paper currency originated with the founder of the bank, Johan Palmstruck, in order to stave off a panic caused by the depreciation of Swedish coinage.

U.S.: The earliest paper currency was also the first to be issued by a government anywhere in the western world. In order to prosecute the war between the United Colonies and Canada (SEE **naval action**), the General Court of Massachusetts authorized the emission of £7,000 in Old Charter Bills on 10 December 1690. There were four denominations: 5 shillings, 10 shillings, 30 shillings, and £5 (20 shillings equaling £1) and the bills were printed from engraved copper plates. They bore a seal depicting an Indian with a speech balloon containing the words COME OVER AND HELP US. Each note was personally signed by three members of the Committee of Issuance. There were further emissions for a total of £40,000, on 3 February and 21 May 1691.

Although Spanish and other dollars were common currency in the American colonies, most colonial paper money was denominated in sterling before the Revolution. Rare examples of bills denominated in dollars (spelled out, as the $ sign was not used in print until 1797) were issued by New York on 1 November 1709 for 4, 8, 16, and 20 Lyon or Lion dollars (a Dutch currency) and by Massachusetts in 1750 for "One Sixteenth of a Dollar, Or, Four Pence Half-Penny" (this referred to the Spanish dollar).

Federal currency: The first was the so-called Continental Currency (whence the dismissive "not worth a Continental"), of which an emission of $3 million denominated in Spanish milled dollars was authorized by the Continental Congress in session at Philadelphia on 22–23 June and 25 July 1775 and put into circulation in August of that year. The purpose was to pay for the Revolutionary War, but as Congress had no authority to raise taxes, the emission was to be redeemed with taxes raised on a quota basis by the 13 United Colonies. There were ten denominations, $1 thru $8, $20, and $30, printed by Hall & Sellers of Philadelphia, all except for the $20 bill on thick rag blue-tinted paper made at Ivy Mills, Chester County, Pa., while the $20 was on thin white paper furnished by Benjamin Franklin. It was also he who provided the source for the decorative emblems on the bills, from books in his extensive library.

Other emissions followed, as did the depreciation of the currency, so that by 1780 $40 in Continentals would buy only $1 worth of goods. "A wagon load of money" bemoaned commander-in-chief Gen. George Washington, "will scarcely purchase a wagon load of provisions." Among the first to refuse to accept the new bills were the Quakers of Philadelphia, on the grounds that pacifists could not aid and abet the financing of the war. A certain amount of humble pie was eaten when it was drawn to their attention that no such scruples had prevented their acceptance of Pennsylvania currency issued to support the war against the French. Congress took a stern line, passing a resolution in January 1776 deploring those "lost to all virtue and regard for this country." The wording was significant, for while citizens of all the colonies were generically "Americans," never before had the colonies been designated collectively as one "country." A cogent reason for refusing Continentals was that the British counterfeited them in order to undermine the American monetary system, the first time but by no means the last that this particular form of economic warfare was waged. Thomas Paine wrote in one of his *Crisis* letters to the British commander-in-chief Gen. Howe, 21 March 1778: "You, sir, have the honor of adding a new vice to the military catalogue; and the reason, perhaps, why the invention was reserved for you, is because no general before was mean enough even to think of it."

U.S. Treasury paper currency: The first was also a war measure. An emission of $150 million was issued on 17 March 1862, followed by a second tranche of $150 million six months later and a third the following year. The second included the first U.S. **one-dollar bills**. Between the creation of the U.S. government in 1789 and the outbreak of the Civil War in 1861 all the paper currency was issued by banks or, occasionally, mercantile companies. Like the former Continental currency, the new "greenbacks" that helped to pay for the Union Army soon suffered depreciation, so that by the end of the war a paper dollar had only half the purchasing power of a gold one. Not until 1878 did its value reach par.

The introduction of the greenback also brought women into government employ for the first time. Seventy of them were employed by the Currency Bureau of the Treasury in Washington, D.C., where the notes were printed, to examine the sheets for errors, cut them into separate bills with shears, and then stack them in piles of $1,000. They were, according to Spencer Morton Clark, the engineer in charge of production, neater in their work than men and less boisterous. In fact he had rather baser reasons for giving them jobs, as became apparent when an eighteen-year-old employee called Ella Jackson revealed under questioning that she slept with her boss for money. Nor was she the only one who did so and as word spread around the highly scandal-prone city of Washington, the term *Treasury woman* accompanied by a wink or a nudge soon became synonymous with hooker.

THE FIRST PARACHUTE

descent by an aeronaut was made over the Parc Monceau, Paris, on 22 October 1797 by André-Jacques Garnerin, who was released from a balloon at the height of 2,230 feet. Garnerin rode in a gondola fixed to the lines of a 23-foot-diameter parachute, which was supported by a rigid pole and had its thirty-two white canvas gores folded like a closed umbrella. Above the parachute his brother rode in another gondola, suspended beneath the balloon, and cut the holding rope with a knife to precipitate descent. Since there was no vent in the apex of the parachute, Garnerin came down to earth with the most violent oscillations, earning the added distinction of becoming the first man ever to suffer from airsickness. For his second jump he had a hole made in the top of the canvas hemisphere.

U.S.: The first descent was made by former circus trapeze artist Thomas Baldwin from a balloon over Golden Gate Park, San Francisco, on 30 January 1885. Baldwin released himself at an altitude of 200 feet, having arranged with the park manager a fee of $1 per foot up to that maximum.

Emergency parachute jump: The first was made by Jordaki Kurapento when his Montgolfier balloon caught fire over Warsaw, Poland, on 24 July 1808. This is the only recorded instance of an aeronaut "bailing out" prior to the advent of powered aircraft.

Parachute descent from an airplane: The first was made by "Captain" Albert Berry from a Benoist biplane flying at 1,500 feet over Jefferson Barracks, St. Louis, Mo., on 1 March 1912. The parachute was stowed in a conical container fixed beneath the mainplane. Piloted by Anthony Jannus (SEE **airline**), the aircraft took off from the Benoist Flying School at Kinloch Park at 2:30 P.M. and arrived at the jump zone half an hour later. According to the report in *Flight*, Berry fell some 400 feet before his canopy opened. He landed safely on the parade ground and immediately reported to the office of the commandant, Col. W. T. Wood, where he delivered a dispatch warning that "the enemy has routed the left flank of the Kinloch Army, wounding the commanding officer, and is rapidly closing in on the remaining forces." Despite the military nature of his exploit, "Captain" Berry's rank was an assumed one, used in his professional role as a stunt parachute jumper. As far as aviators were concerned, the chief importance of his achievement lay in the fact that it proved the ability of an aircraft to remain stable after dropping a passenger. Its military implications were ignored.

Woman to make a parachute descent from an airplane: The first was Mrs. Georgia Thompson of Henderson, N.C., who had joined the Charles Broadwick stunt parachute team as a fifteen-year-old wife and mother in 1908 and made her first aircraft jump from Glenn Martin's home-built biplane over Griffith Park, Los Angeles, on 21 June 1913. At San Diego on 4 July 1914 "Tiny" Broadwick, as she was known professionally, made the first descent from an aircraft using a manually operated **parachute with a ripcord**. It is claimed that another American parachutist, H. Leo Stevens, had introduced a ripcord the previous year, but this was intended as a secondary safety device for use in cases where the static line failed to open the parachute, and there is no evidence of its earlier use in the air.

Service pilots issued with parachutes: The first were members of the German Army Air Service, some of whom are known to have been flying with Heinecke cushion-type parachutes by the spring of 1918. On 1 April of that year Vizefeldwebel Weimer of Jasta 56 became the first pilot to bail out in an emergency when his Albatross DVa was shot down over the British lines. He landed safely and was taken prisoner. Allied pilots were not issued with parachutes during World War I because the authorities thought that it would encourage them to abandon a crippled aircraft rather than attempt a landing.

U.S.: The first order for parachutes placed by the U.S. Army Air Corps was for 300 freefall Irvin A-types in June 1919. Leslie Leroy "Ski-Hi" Irvin had developed the manually operated A-type together with veteran pilot Floyd Smith and first tested it himself in a descent from a DH4 biplane over McCook Flying Field at Dayton, Ohio, on 19 April 1919. Although a descent by a manually operated parachute had been made by woman parachutist "Tiny" Broadwick (SEE ABOVE) nearly five years earlier, the significance of this innovation had been largely ignored at the time and Irvin's A-type became the first parachute operated by a ripcord to go into regular production, rapidly superseding escape parachutes attached to the aircraft by a static line. The success of the Irvin was assured when the Royal Air Force, a much larger service than America's under-resourced Air Corps, ordered 2,261 of the ripcord parachutes in March 1925.

The first emergency descent by an American pilot occurred on 18 February 1921 when Lt. Carroll "Mickey" Eversole of the U.S. Airmail Service made a descent from a DH4 flying from Minneapolis to Chicago using a parachute of his own design. According to Eversole the plane had lost its propeller and gone into a dive and spin some 3 miles south of Mendota, Minn. At the subsequent inquiry it was alleged that Eversole had engineered the loss of the aircraft himself in order to publicize his parachute and he was dismissed from the service. The pilot countered that the allegations against him had been brought because of his complaints about conditions at Chicago's Checkerboard Field, including habitual drunkenness among the maintenance mechanics.

Parachutist to make a delayed freefall descent: The first was St. Sgt. Randall Bose of the U.S. Army, who jumped from a height of 4,500 feet over Mitchel Field, Long Island, N.Y., on 17 April 1925 and deliberately delayed pulling his ripcord until he had fallen for 1,800 feet. The experiment was made to win a bet from a friend that he would not be able to drop for 1,000 feet and still open his parachute.

The first freefall parachutist to use the spread-eagle **skydiving** position to control his descent was American Ephraim "Spud" Manning of Pico, Calif., who pioneered the technique in 1931 with a jump from 15,000 feet. The following year he performed aerobatics in the course of a descent. Modern skydiving as a sport originated in France c. 1946.

Sport parachuting club: The first was formed at Tushiro Aerodrome, Moscow, in 1933. Russia had pioneered sport parachuting three years earlier with the holding of the first Soviet Parachute Sport Festival, participants competing to land on or nearest a target on the ground. During the course of the 1930s hundreds of local clubs were formed and practice-jump platforms erected in most of the public parks, a development that enabled Russia to maintain a world lead in the training of parachutists.

Nylon parachutes: The first were manufactured by the Pioneer Parachute Co. of Manchester, Conn. The first descent with a nylon canopy was made by parachute rigger Adeline Gray over Brainard Field, Hartford, Conn., on 6 June 1942.

THE FIRST **PARATROOPERS**

....

to participate in a collective drop on a known date (but SEE **U.S.** BELOW) were a group of specially trained volunteers of the Italian Army who made a descent from CA 73 transports of the Regia Aeronautica over Cinisello, near Milan, on 6 November 1927. The parachutes employed were of the Salvator type, which opened automatically by the static-line method. The first paratroop fatality occurred the following year when Gen. Guidoni was killed after his parachute failed to open.

The first **use of paratroopers for an offensive operation** took place in 1931 during the Soviet campaign against Basmachi insurgents led by Ibrahim-Bey of Turkestan in Central Asia. Fifteen parachutists of the Red Army equipped with a machine gun landed in the rear of a force of Basmachi and successfully engaged the enemy.

Russia's first paratroop units had been formed the previous year by the Soviet airmen Maschkovski and Monayev, using TB1, Ant 9, and R5 transport aircraft of the Red Air Force. They gave their first official demonstration at the 1930 military maneuvers at Voronezh, a lieutenant and eight men jumping behind "enemy" lines and taking a corps commander prisoner.

By 1935 the Russians had progressed to the stage where they could drop a whole battalion of paratroopers from their giant four-engine TB3 transports. The parachutes used by the Russians were of the Irvin ripcord type and as Maurice Tugwell has pointed out in his book *Airborne to Battle* (1971), the style of parachuting was rather less sophisticated than the static-line procedure used by the Italians nearly nine years earlier. A film taken at the Kiev maneuvers of 1935, when a thousand fully equipped paratroops took part in a mass drop, shows the men climbing out of a hatch on the top of the aircraft's fuselage, then rather laboriously clambering down onto the wings, there to remain hanging on grimly until given a signal to jump. Nevertheless, Commissar of War K. Y. Voroshilov was able to advance a legitimate claim in a speech to the All-Union Congress of Stakhanovite Shock Workers the same year that "parachuting is one phase in the field of aviation that has become a monopoly of the Soviet Union."

The first large-scale parachute assault and the first to meet with armed opposition was undertaken by the 1st Battalion of the 1st Parachute Regiment of the Wehrmacht under the command of Hauptmann Erich Walter during the German invasion of Norway and Denmark on 9 April 1940. Number 3 Company jumped over Sola airfield, near Stavanger in Norway, to clear the area preparatory to airborne infantry landings. The paratroopers descended from their Ju 52 transports at a height of 400 feet and were met by Norwegian machine-gun fire, but within half an hour the paratroopers had complete control of the landing zone. One platoon of No. 4 Company secured two airfields at Aalborg in Denmark without encountering opposition, and the remainder captured the Falster-Seeland bridge leading to Copenhagen. The other companies of No. 1 Battalion had been detailed to attack Fornebu airport, Oslo, but were forced to turn back before reaching their objective due to poor visibility. Six Me 110 fighters having landed at Fornebu, the paratroopers were recalled and succeeded in holding the airfield until relieved by the 324th Infantry Regiment. The role of the paratroopers in capturing these strategic airfields is considered to have been a vital element in the success of the German invasion.

U.S.: The first airborne troops to participate in a collective drop were twelve battle-ready Marines who successfully parachuted from a Marine Corps transport in 14 seconds at Anacostia Naval Support Facility in Washington, D.C., on an uncertain date during 1927. Soon afterward they made another drop over the Potomac River with rubber rafts, which they inflated during their descent. Of more certain date was an exercise on 19 October of the following year when a six-man machine-gun crew parachuted on to Brooks Field in San Antonio, Tex., from a formation of six aircraft.

The first airborne unit in the U.S. Armed Forces was the Parachute Test Platoon, formed on 1 July 1940 at Fort Benning, Ga., which comprised forty-eight of the two hundred volunteers of the 29th Infantry Regiment who had sought selection. They made their initial jumps from a Douglas B-18 on 16 August followed by the first mass jump on 22 August. It was on this latter occasion that 6' 8" private Aubrey Eberhardt, who had been taunted that he would be too scared to open his mouth, proved to the contrary by emitting the first "Geronimo" yell (he had recently watched a western portraying the Indian chief). These pioneers and their successors were to become the 501st Parachute Battalion. Remarkably all the original forty-eight survived World War II.

The first combat operation by U.S. airborne troops took place on 8 November 1942 when the 509th Parachute Infantry Battalion flew from their base in Britain to Oran, Algeria, as the spearhead of Operation Torch, the Allied invasion of North Africa. The operation did not achieve all its objectives, most of the force being scattered over an area ranging from Gibraltar to Tunis, but they did succeed in seizing Tafarquay Airport from the enemy. On that day Lt. Dave Kunkle became the first U.S. paratrooper to be killed in combat.

THE FIRST **PARK, PUBLIC**

was the Bowling Green, New York City, a military parade ground that was redesignated as a public park by the Common Council on 12 March 1733. The oval plot was leased for one peppercorn a year (a "peppercorn rent") on condition that it be landscaped "for the beauty and ornament of the said street as well as for the recreation and delight of the inhabitants of this City." Bowling Green Park survives as the oldest of the New York City parks and its claim to be the first public park lies in the fact that, unlike earlier public open spaces in cities, such as Boston Common, it was established for recreation rather than for grazing or other utilitarian purposes, and that it was landscaped. It also had the distinction of being the site of the first public statue (qv) in America, erected in 1770 in honor of King George III. (The statue was torn down by disconsolate colonists in 1776.) Present-day Bowling Green Park, now the world's oldest municipal park, plays host to Arturo di Modica's magnificent sculpture *Charging Bull*.

Gotham was far in advance of its metropolitan neighbors in the provision of such an amenity. Philadelphia, the largest city in America for much of the eighteenth century, did not establish a public park until 1812. The city's Fairmont Park, however, which dates from a plan of 1869, was the first of the really extensive metropolitan parks. It remains America's largest, comprising 8,579 acres on either side of the Schuylkill River, with museums, historic houses, horticultural centers, and several miles of scenic drives.

The first public park in the United States to contain a **children's playground** was Washington Park, in Chicago, in 1876, also the site of the first **public baseball diamond** in 1887. First with **public tennis courts** was Prospect Park, Brooklyn, N.Y., in 1885, while the first with a **public golf course** was Van Cortlandt Park in the Bronx, N.Y., in 1895.

THE FIRST **PARKING GARAGE**

recorded in the United States was opened as part of a larger automobile servicing and repair depot, the Back Bay Cycle & Motor Co., by W. T. McCullough of Boston on 24 May 1899. This may have been preceded by any of the six storage-repair garages in New York City reported in 1901 by the *Horseless Age*. The most prominent of these was the depot of the Winton Motor Carriage Co. (SEE **automobile manufacture**), where there were thirty-three parked cars at the time

Horseless Age's reporter visited. By the following year there were twenty-four garages offering parking in New York City and six in Chicago.

Parking deck with ramps: The first was a five-story redbrick edifice with a spiral ramp designed by Holabird & Roche in 1918 as part of the Hotel La Salle complex in Chicago. The hotel was demolished in 1976 but the garage continued in use. The first open-deck parking garage was the Cage Garage built in Boston by office building manager Sam Elliot in 1933. The first public underground garage was built in Union Square, San Francisco, by the Union Square Garage Corporation and completed in September 1942. Its four levels of parking accommodated 1,700 cars.

THE FIRST **PARKING LOT**

emerged informally c. 1910 when Detroit police began impounding illegally parked cars and depositing them in Cadillac Square (now Kennedy Square). Drivers in Motown took to parking there anyway in preference to getting towed. Within a few years the parking arrangements had been formalized to accommodate twin double ranks of cars extending for the length of two blocks, some three hundred in all.

The first parking lot to be operated commercially was opened by Herman R. Schmitt of the Duquesne Parking & Automobile Co. at the corner of Cecil and Duquesne ways in downtown Pittsburgh in June 1914. The first municipal lot opened ten years later in Flint, Mich.

THE FIRST **PARKING METER**

was devised by Carlton Magee, editor of the *Oklahoma City News*, who was appointed chairman of a Businessmen's Traffic Committee set up in 1933 to inquire into methods of imposing stricter parking controls in the town. Magee established the Dual Parking Meter Co., so called because the meters were designed to serve the dual purpose of regulation and revenue. The Oklahoma City Traffic Authority gave the company an initial order for 150 units and the first

parking meters, costing 5¢ an hour, came into service on 16 July 1935.

Despite Magee's declared intention of raising revenue, the primary impetus for the introduction of parking meters seems to have been the rather more altruistic one that people occupying a parking place for hours on end prevent other people from parking. Or perhaps not wholly altruistic, because the storekeepers of Oklahoma City were concerned that someone hogging a parking place too long was a constraint on prospective trade, as evidenced by Magee's survey that showed four out of every five vehicles parked in the city center stayed there all day. These were not shoppers, but people who had driven in to work.

However worthy the motivation of the Traffic Committee, the citizenry saw otherwise. On that first day of what was to become a universal form of traffic regulation, the National Guard had to be called out to suppress the heated emotions of those who saw 5¢ an hour for parking as an infringement on personal liberty. It was not until the following month that the authorities had the temerity to actually book a driver for non-payment, the first miscreant to fall afoul of the law and incur a fine being the otherwise saintly Rev. C. H. North of Oklahoma City's Third Pentecostal Holiness Church.

When the legality of parking meters was challenged the following year (1936) following proposals to introduce them in Miami, the Florida Supreme Court in a landmark decision ruled that parking on the public highway was a "privilege and not a right." By August of that year 11 cities had installed meters and by the time of America's entry in World War II there were 320 cities using meters. After the war the number climbed rapidly, reaching 800 in 1949 and 2,800 in 1953. By that time there were more than a million meters, each generating an average annual revenue of $70.

The first "meter maids" were introduced by New York City mayor Robert Wagner on 1 June 1960.

THE FIRST **PENCILS**

reference to, is contained in a treatise on fossils published in 1565 by Konrad Gesner, professor of natural philosophy at Zurich University, Switzerland. The work contains an illustration of a pencil, its lead protected by a wooden sheath. This was unusual, as most early pencils consisted only of the writing substance. Gesner described his pencils as being made of "stimmi Anglicanum," which was probably graphite. At the top end was a knob to allow the pencil to be attached to a notebook by a length of string.

The earliest reference to the use of pencils for drawing is found in *Il Riposo di Rafaello Borghini*, Florence, 1584. These Italian pencils were known as *stiles* and were a compound of lead and tin. Markings or writing made with them could be erased—prior to the introduction of India rubber (SEE **eraser**)—with crumbs of bread.

Production of pencils on a commercial scale began in England with the opening of the Borrowdale graphite pits in Cumberland in 1584. According to legend the graphite had originally been used by local shepherds for marking sheep. It then occurred to someone that if graphite would mark a fleece, it would also mark paper. At first the sticks of graphite were sold uncovered, but as this soiled the hand, it became customary to provide a string coiled around the lead. As the lead wore down the string was unwound. Pencils with a wooden sheath of deal or cedar are first recorded in England by J. Pettus in his *Fleta Minor* of 1685, though the existence of a "pencil maker," one Friedrich Staedtler, in Nuremberg in 1662 suggests that regular production of wood-sheathed pencils may have originated in Germany. Until the early nineteenth century it was usual for the lead to terminate an inch or so from the end of the sheath, reflecting the scarcity of graphite: there was no point in extending it into what would become a useless pencil stub, too short to hold. Hence the reference in Jane Austen's *Emma* (1815) to "the end of an old pencil—the part without any lead."

Writing in 1831, Samuel Lewis noted Borrowdale's former importance in his *Topographical Dictionary:*

Owing to the abundant produce . . . the mine was formerly opened only once in five years, and that but for a short space of time; of late, however it has been less productive, and the demand has greatly increased, so that about eight miners have been engaged for several successive years in working it.

The lead is found lying in lumps, or nodules, varying in weight from an ounce to fifty pounds, in the clefts of the rock. The finer sort is packed in barrels, sent to London, and deposited in the warehouse belonging to the proprietors of the mine, where it is exposed for sale to the pencil-makers on the first Monday in every month . . . To protect the interests of the proprietors, an act was passed in 1752, whereby persons stealing, or receiving this article, knowing it to be stolen, are subjected to the same punishment as felons. A house has been built over the entrance where the workmen undress and are examined, every time they leave the mine.

During the seventeenth and eighteenth centuries nearly all the pencils sold in Europe and America came from the Borrowdale mine. Its decline toward the end of the eighteenth century posed a serious threat to pencil production until N. J. Conté of Paris devised a compound of graphite and clays in 1795—a formula that laid the foundation of modern pencil manufacture.

U.S.: The earliest allusion to pencils in America is by the diarist Judge Samuel Sewall of Boston, one of the magistrates presiding over the Salem witch trials, who possessed a pencil in the 1690s. He used it to write parts of the diary he kept between 1673 and 1729.

In 1740 pencils were available from Boston booksellers for 3d apiece and could be had with either black or red lead. Alice Morse Earle, in *Child Life in Colonial Days* (1899), observed that pencils were not in common use even in city schools until well into the nineteenth century, all the early arithmetic or "sum-books" she had inspected being done in ink. She quotes, however, a letter from John Ten Broeck who wrote from his school in Stamford, Conn., to his father in Albany, N.Y., on 13 October 1752 requesting a host of supplies including "Wall Nutts, smoke befe, a pare of indin's Schuse," and "som pensals."

The identity of the first manufacturer of pencils in the United States remains unknown, as neither of the two authorities who have written about her give her a name, though both agree that she was a Massachusetts schoolgirl. Horace Hosmer, writing in 1880 when he was fifty years old, recorded:

Before 1800, there was a school for young ladies kept in the ancient town of Medford, and one of the pupils was from Concord, Mass. Besides learning to sketch, paint, embroider, etc., she learned to utilize the bits and ends of Borrowdale lead used in drawing, by pounding them fine and mixing a solution of gum arabic or glue. The cases were made from twigs of elder, the pith being removed with a knitting needle. So far as the writer knows, this was the first pencil-making establishment in the country. Forty years ago [1840], the writer, then a boy of 10 years, helped the same lady to make similar pencils from plumbago and English red chalk.

Writing in 1946 Charles Nichols Jr. of the Joseph Dixon Crucible Co., reputedly the first to mass-produce pencils in the United States, agreed about the Borrowdale source for the graphite and the hollowed-out elder twigs, but he placed the enterprising anonymous schoolgirl in Danvers, Mass. She then, he says, went into partnership with a man called Joseph W. Wade to inaugurate manufacture.

Letters for the grading of pencil leads were probably originated by Brookman's of London early in the nineteenth century, H standing for "hard" and B for "black," the number of successive Hs and Bs signifying the degree of hardness and blackness.

Pencil with an eraser attached to the end: The first was patented on 30 March 1858 by Hyman L. Lipman of Philadelphia, who later produced the first postcards (qv). Lipman's eraser was inserted in a groove at the tip. The eraser encircled by a metal crown, a more practical arrangement, was introduced by the Eagle Pencil Co. of New York in 1872.

Varnished pencils, including the latterly ubiquitous yellow pencil, were being produced at Keswick in England's Lake District by 1854. Yellow only became the color of choice after the Czech-manufactured Koh-I-Noor made an indelible impact at the World's Columbian Exposition in Chicago in 1893. Prof. Henry Petroski, author of *The Pencil* (1990), notes that a Texan who collected used pencils had received thirty-one from state governors, of which twenty-nine were yellow.

There is no reliable evidence when pencils were first made to a standard length. In the William Koch Collection in Des Moines, Iowa, there are 15,000 different pencils from all parts of the world and nearly every one is 7 inches long, including the oldest, which dates from c. 1750. The U.S. Pencil Manufacturers' Association has failed to account for this phenomenon, but proffers instead the information that an average 7-inch pencil can be sharpened 17 times, write 45,000 words, and draw a line 35 miles long.

The oldest pencil in the world and the only surviving seventeenth-century example was purchased for the Faber-Castell archive in Stein near Nuremberg, Germany, in 1994.

THE FIRST **PENICILLIN**

was discovered by Dr. Alexander Fleming at St. Mary's Hospital, Paddington, London, in September 1928. Having been absent on holiday since the previous month, Fleming had left a pile of culture plates in a corner of the laboratory beyond the reach of the sun. These were about to be submerged in antiseptic when he took some plates off the pile in order to demonstrate a point to research scholar D. M. Pryce. One of the plates displayed unusual characteristics, as there was an absence of staphylococcal colonies in the vicinity of the mold. Following an intensive study of the phenomenon, Fleming made his initial findings known when he read a paper, "Cultures of a Penicillium," to the Medical Research Club on 13 February 1929. Audience reaction was nil, no questions being asked at the end whereas questions were customary when a theory or new discovery had excited the members' interest.

Clinical application of penicillin: The first was made at St. Mary's on 9 January 1929, when Fleming treated his assistant, Stuart Craddock, for an infected antrum by washing out the sinus with diluted crude penicillin broth and succeeded in destroying most of the staphylococci. Rather more effective use of the drug was made in 1931 at the Royal Infirmary, Sheffield. Here Dr. C. G. Paine successfully relieved two cases of gonococcal ophthalmitis in children (gonorrhea contracted from their mothers at birth) and one of an adult suffering from severe pneumococcal infection of the eye. The latter was a colliery manager who had been injured at the coalface when a small piece of stone had lodged behind the pupil of the right eye. Penicillin cleared the infection, enabling an operation to be carried out to remove the stone. The patient subsequently recovered his normal vision. These were probably the first cases in which ordinary hospital patients were successfully treated with penicillin, though no attempt was made to establish the possibility of effective chemotherapy of the common bacterial infections. There was little further development during the remainder of the decade.

Purified penicillin was first prepared at the Sir William Dunn School of Pathology in Oxford, England, during the summer of 1940 by Prof. Howard Florey of Adelaide, South Australia, and Prof. Ernst Chain, a German-born Jewish refugee. Florey announced the results of their research in a paper titled "Penicillin as a Chemotherapeutic Agent," which appeared in the *Lancet* for 24 August 1940. The first clinical application of the purified antibiotic took place at the Radcliffe Infirmary, Oxford, on 12 February 1941, the patient being a policeman suffering from generalized blood poisoning from a small sore at the corner of his mouth. A striking improvement was made in his condition after 800 mg of penicillin had been administered in 24 hours, but within five days Florey's team had exhausted the entire world supply of the drug and on 15 March the patient died.

The first completely successful treatment with purified penicillin began at the Radcliffe Infirmary on 3 May 1941, when a patient suffering from a 4-inch carbuncle was administered the drug intravenously by Florey's assistant Charles Fletcher. Within four days the infected area was already healing and on 15 May the patient was discharged from the hospital.

The first plant for the regular production of penicillin was constructed by Normal Heatley at the Sir William Dunn School of Pathology at Oxford under the direction of Prof. Chain in the summer of 1941. Seven hundred vessels for fermenting "mold juice" were looked after by six technicians, dubbed the "penicillin girls,"and Heatley developed an automatic extraction plant that had as its free-standing base an oak bookcase somehow spirited out of Oxford University's celebrated Bodleian Library. The juice was filtered through parachute silk. The first commercial firm to undertake production of penicillin was Kemball, Bishop & Co. of Bromley-by-Bow, East London, which delivered its initial consignment of twenty 10-gallon churns of penicillin brew to the School of Pathology "as a free gift in the interest of science" on 11 September 1942.

Most of the penicillin produced in Britain during World War II was reserved for military use. It was first made widely available to civilians in Prof. Florey's native Australia, where the Commonwealth Serum Laboratories in Melbourne started production in 1943.

Sir Alexander Fleming, Sir Howard Florey, and Dr. Ernst Chain were jointly awarded the Nobel Prize in Physiology or Medicine in October 1945 for their work on penicillin.

U.S.: Prof. Florey and Norman Heatley flew to New York on 26 June 1941 in a blacked-out Pan American Clipper to seek cooperation from American pharmaceutical companies and the U.S. government, Heatley spending a year working with government scientists to produce America's first penicillin at the Northern Regional Research Laboratory at Peoria, Ill. Here they developed a new strain of the bacterium that had been found growing on a moldy melon, pushing up yields twenty-fold.

The first American patient to be treated with penicillin was Anne Shaefe Miller, wife of the Yale University athletic director, at New Haven Hospital, in Connecticut, on 14 March 1942. Suffering from a life-threatening streptococcal infection, she had been treated by conventional means for twenty-seven days without improvement and was expected to die when a small dose of penicillin was made available by Merck Laboratories of New Jersey. Within one day her temperature had dropped to near normal; the historic temperature chart is now enshrined at the Smithsonian Institution. So scarce was the precious drug that Mrs. Miller's urine was sent back to Merck so that the antibiotic could be extracted and reused. She survived for another fifty-seven years, dying in 1999 at the age of ninety.

By late 1943 mass production of the drug for military use had started in America, using a "deep tank" process that proved far more practical for volume fermentation than the makeshift arrangements with flasks or bottles that had been used at Oxford. It was to prove crucial in saving the lives of battle casualties during the later stages of the Pacific War and the liberation of Europe.

THE FIRST PERMANENT WAVING

was introduced by Karl Ludwig Nessler, who was born at Todtnau in Germany's Black Forest in 1872, the same year as Paris stylist Marcel Grateau devised his Marcel Wave. The son of a poor shoemaker, Nessler would have been apprenticed to his father's trade but for defective eyesight. Instead he became a hairdresser, first in Switzerland, then in Paris, where he learned the art of Marcel waving. By the time he arrived in London in 1902 he was already experimenting with a device of his own, designed to make Marcel's *ondulations* longer lasting. One day he tried it out on a client, but he was detected by his employer and instantly dismissed. Fortunately he had sufficient savings to open a salon of his own in Great Castle Street and to develop his machine. On the evening of 8 October 1906, the permanent wave was publicly demonstrated for the first time before an audience of hairstylists invited by Nessler to his latest salon at 245 Oxford Street. The system was effective, but the trade was not enthusiastic. The machine was large and cumbersome, the client was obliged to wear a dozen brass curlers each weighing 1¾ pounds, and the whole difficult process took more than 6 hours to complete. It was also expensive, and it is not surprising that at 10 guineas ($52.50) per application customers for his Nessler permanent waving averaged scarcely seventy a year. With the outbreak of World War I Nessler emigrated to New York rather than face internment as an alien. It was a fortuitous move, for in 1915 the celebrated exhibition ballroom dancer Irene Castle introduced the "bobbed" hairstyle to America and permanent waving became the rage. Nessler opened a successful salon on East 49th Street, subsequently establishing branches in Chicago, Detroit, Palm Beach, and Philadelphia.

The modern **cold wave** perm process was developed in 1945 by Eugène Schueller of L'Oréal, in Paris, by combining the action of thioglycolic acid with hydrogen peroxide.

THE FIRST PHOTOCOPIER

was marketed by the Rectigraph Co. of Rochester, N.Y., in 1907. The patentee was George C. Beidler, who had conceived the idea four years earlier while working in an Oklahoma City land-claim office. The need for constant duplication of legal documents led him to search for a better means than retyping or laborious copying by hand, his initial experiments being made with an ordinary dry-plate camera. The prototype Rectigraph photocopier followed and was patented in 1906. The earliest known surviving photocopies date from 1909 and are of graphs in the DuPont Archives at Wilmington, Del. These are believed to be Rectigraphs, though DuPont also acquired a Photostat (manufactured by an associate of Eastman-Kodak) in 1912.

Dry copier: The first was the Xerox Model A, an oversize 600-pound machine developed by Chester Carlson and known to its detractors as the Ox Box. It was unveiled at the Optical Society of America meeting in Detroit on 22 October 1948 by the Haloid Corporation of Rochester, N.Y., successors to the Rectigraph Co. This was ten years to the day since Carlson had made his first successful Xerocopy. The apparatus was too expensive and too complicated—it required thirty-nine different manual operations—to compete successfully with wet copiers. The breakthrough came with the first automatic office copier to use plain paper, the Xerox 914—so called because it copied on standard 9" x 14" typing paper—which was demonstrated in New York on 16 September 1959. This had cost $12.5 million to develop, more than the Haloid Co.'s total earnings for the whole of the 1950s, but *Fortune* magazine was later to call it "the most successful product ever marketed in America." The first production model was shipped to the Pressed Steel Co. of Boston on 1 March 1960. Within eight years sales had topped $1 billion.

Color photocopier: The first was the Color-in-Color launched by 3M of St. Paul, Minn., in 1969. The first using plain paper was introduced by Canon in Japan in 1973.

THE FIRST **PHOTOGRAPH**

....

was a 6" x 4" heliograph of a drawing depicting a boy leading a horse taken by Nicéphore Niépce in 1825. It was sold at Sotheby's in 2002 to the Bibliothèque Nationale in France for $392,000. The first of a "live" scene was made by Niépce from an upper-story window at his house at Gras, near Chalon-sur-Saône, France, probably in the spring or summer of 1827, and represents a view of the courtyard with a pigeon-house on the left; a pear tree, bakehouse, and barn in the center; and another wing of the house to the right of the picture. It was made in a camera obscura obtained from Paris opticians Chevalier et fils in January of the same year. A pewter plate was rendered light-sensitive with a solution of bitumen of Judea and exposed in the camera for about 8 hours. The latent image was then developed by washing the plate with a mixture of oil of lavender and white petroleum, a process that dissolved away those parts of the bitumen that had not been hardened by light. The resulting picture was a permanent direct positive.

During the following year, while on a visit to his brother at Kew outside London, Niépce presented this photograph to the English naturalist Francis Baur. It was lost in 1898 and only recovered in 1952, when it was found in a trunk that had been stored unopened in an English country house since 1917. The pewter plate was then presented by the owner to the photographic historian Helmut Gernsheim, who had been instrumental in locating it. A halftone of the original made by the Kodak research laboratory was reproduced in the *Times* of London for 15 April 1952, the first occasion the photograph had been seen publicly since it was taken 126 years earlier. It is now in the Gernsheim Collection at the University of Texas. Niépce died in 1833 before his process was sufficiently developed for commercial exploitation (SEE BELOW). Most of his energies during the 19 years he spent in research were concentrated on photographic art reproduction, and only one other surviving fixed image from nature is known. This was a still life made on glass in 1829, which shows a table laid for a meal. The original plate was smashed by a madman in 1909, but a rather poor halftone made in 1891 indicates the progress made by Niépce in 3 years. In contrast with the impressionistic 1826 view at Gras, every object in the still-life study is almost perfectly defined.

Photograph on paper: The first was made by English amateur chemist William Henry Fox Talbot of a central leaded window in the South Gallery of Lacock Abbey, his Wiltshire home, and labeled by him on the back: "Latticed window (with camera obscura), August 1835. When first made the squares of glass, about 200 in number, could be counted with the help of a lens." Fox Talbot used ordinary writing paper sensitized with silver chloride, which he exposed for 30 minutes in the several miniature camera obscuras made for him by the local carpenter at Lacock. He wrote in *The Pencil of Nature* (1844):

> With these I obtained very perfect but extremely small pictures, such as . . . might be supposed to be the work of some Lilliputian artist . . . In the summer of 1835 I made in this way a great number of representations of my house in the country, which is well suited to the purpose, from its ancient and remarkable architecture.

Fox Talbot had been inspired to invent a means of fixing the camera's image by his own inability to draw accurately. The original latticed-window negative is preserved in the Science Museum Collection in London. This and other studies of Lacock he exhibited for the first time at the Royal Institution on 25 January 1839—two and a half weeks after the Frenchman Louis-Jacques-Mandé Daguerre (SEE BELOW) had announced success in the same field. Up until this time Fox Talbot had been working solely with negatives. His major contribution to photography, the **negative-positive process**, was described in the 2 February 1839 issue of the *Literary Gazette*. Helmut Gernsheim has written that in this single brief paragraph Fox Talbot "laid the foundations of modern photography; a negative which can be used for the production of an unlimited number of positive copies."

Commercially successful photographic process: The first was introduced in August 1839 by Daguerre, proprietor of the Diorama in Paris, who had formed a partnership with Nicéphore Niépce ten years earlier for the improvement of the latter's system of "heliography." Daguerre's advances in technique enabled the exposure time for a photograph to be reduced from about 8 hours to only 15 to 30 minutes. His results were published for the first time in a report made by the distinguished astronomer Dominique-François Arago to the French Academy of Sciences on 7 January 1839. In response to Arago's urging, the government acquired the rights from Daguerre and Isidore Niépce, Nicéphore's heir, and made the method public property for all the world to use on 19 August 1839. (It was not known then that Daguerre had patented the process in England five days earlier.) Details of the process were announced at the same time and caused an immediate sensation in Paris. "An hour later," wrote Ludwig Pfau, a German living in Paris at the time,

> all the opticians' shops were besieged, but could not rake together enough instruments to satisfy the onrushing army of would-be daguerreo-typists; a few days later you could see in all the squares of Paris three-legged dark-boxes planted in front of churches and palaces.

These would have been standard camera obscura of the kind used by artists as an aid to drawing. Photographic cameras manufactured to Daguerre's specifications went on sale the following month.

U.S.: The first photograph was a daguerreotype of New York's St. Paul's Church and its surrounding houses on Broadway and Fulton taken by English immigrant D. W. Seager on 27 September 1839. The exposure was 8 to 10 minutes and the result, described as "the size of a miniature painting," was exhibited at Dr. James R. Chilton's drugstore at 263 Broadway, where it was viewed with wonder and amazement. Seager made this view before news of Daguerre's photographic process reached America, which it did four days later when the *British Queen* docked in New York carrying English newspapers reporting the technique. What enabled Seager to do so was that just as the packet boat bringing him to New York had cast off from the London docks, a friend had rushed up bearing one of the first Daguerreian manuals to reach London from Paris and flung it across the water onto the deck for Seager to retrieve. Seager is also notable for having compiled the first exposure table in the world, published in the pioneering American photographic manual that went on sale at Dr. Chilton's shop in March 1840. Seager's view of St. Paul's has been lost; the earliest surviving photograph taken in the United States is the study of the Philadelphia Arsenal and the cupola of the city's Central High School made by Joseph Saxton, an engineer at the U.S. Mint in Philadelphia, on 16 October 1839 and preserved at the Historical Society of Pennsylvania. What ultimately happened to America's first photographer is not known. None of Seager's daguerreotypes survives and the last heard of him was in 1867 as economic advisor to the Mexican government, a post he had held for ten years previously. He had long since abandoned photography.

Photograph of a living person: The first was a view of the boulevard du Temple in Paris by Daguerre taken either in late 1838 or early 1839. Although the exposure time meant that the traffic and pedestrians in the busy street do not appear, in the foreground can be seen the figure of a man having his boots blacked by a shoeshine boy. The static nature of the activity meant that their images were accidentally captured on the light-sensitive metal plate. The first **portrait photograph** was made on paper by English schoolmaster the Rev. Joseph Bancroft Reade in the spring of 1839 of his gardener leaning against the greenhouse in the grounds of the school he ran at Peckham, Surrey.

U.S.: The first, a profile portrait of New York dental supplies manufacturer John Johnson, was taken by his partner Alexander S. Wolcott on 7 October 1839. It measured a mere 9 mm square. The partners opened the world's first photographic portrait studio (qv) the following March. The earliest surviving living likeness is a 2¾" x 3¼" self-portrait of metalworker Robert Cornelius, made in the yard of his Philadelphia home probably in April 1840.

Photograph of a topical event: The first were fourteen daguerreotypes taken in 1841 by Reisser of Vienna depicting the presentation of new colors to a regiment of the Austro-Hungarian Army in Linz. The first in the United States and the earliest known news photograph of an unscheduled event anywhere was taken at Philadelphia on 9 May 1844 and showed the military occupation of the city center under Girard Bank following anti-Catholic riots in the area. For the first to be published SEE **halftone**; for the first of an unscheduled news event to be published SEE **newspaper: photographs**.

SEE ALSO **magazine: photograph; printed book: American book illustrated with a photograph**.

THE FIRST PHOTOGRAPH IN COLOR

was a transparency of a tartan ribbon bow taken against a black velvet background by Thomas Sutton of Jersey (Channel Islands) under the direction of the Scottish physicist James Clerk Maxwell and shown for the first time at the Royal Institution in London on 17 May 1861. Clerk Maxwell had the ribbon photographed three times, using color filters consisting of bottles of green and blue liquids that were placed between the camera and the subject. Glass positives from the collodion negatives were then projected in register on a screen by three separate lanterns, each lantern being fitted with a filter to correspond with its transparency. Although the process was only of scientific value, in 1939 modern techniques were employed to make a color print from the original negatives and a reproduction in the following year's *Penrose Annual* indicates that Clerk Maxwell had obtained an amazingly naturalistic effect.

Color print: The first was a picture of the spectrum, displayed before the Société Française de Photographie by Louis Ducos du Hauron on 17 March 1869. The inventor had patented his subtractive method of color photography on 23 February of the same year. Du Hauron's earliest surviving color prints are "Still Life with Butterfly," c. 1875, and a view of Angoulême taken in 1877, showing the red-roofed Romanesque cathedral rising above honey-colored houses and the greenish waters of the Charente river in the foreground.

In 1883 Du Hauron set up a three-color printing plant to produce book illustrations in Toulouse with a collotype printer, André Quinsac, as partner. Regrettably it was destroyed by fire within a year or so, but not before the partners had become the first to reproduce color photographs by photomechanical means.

Systems of color photography to be developed commercially: The first were both introduced in London in 1895, though neither originated there. Frederick Ives (SEE ALSO **halftone**) had developed his process in Philadelphia, where he took out patents in 1890 and 1892. Ives's Kromskop camera was fitted with two reflective mirrors by which three negatives of the same image might be obtained simultaneously through orange, green, and blue-violet filters. The positive transparencies were combined in a special viewer, the Photochromoscope, and illuminated by red, green, and blue-violet light respectively. The resulting single image appeared in natural color. In 1895 Ives organized the Photochromoscope Syndicate Ltd. of Clapham Common, London, to produce viewers and lanterns for use with his Kromogram color slides, as well as the Kromskop camera. The Kromograms were available in 3-D (stereoscopic) versions.

The other process was developed in Dublin by Prof. John Joly, who used additive screen-plates with a screen of red, green, and blue-violet lines ruled on a gelatine-coated glass plate. It was introduced commercially by Newman & Guardia Ltd. of London at a cost of 5 guineas ($26.25) for a complete kit, including a dozen plates. Ready-made three-dimensional transparencies made by the process could be had for 5s to 10s 6d each ($1.25 to $2.62½) and at double these prices for stereoscopic slides. Both Ives's and Joly's system suffered from low sensitivity, making them suitable chiefly for well-illuminated still lifes.

U.S.: While Ives was in London, lens maker Robert D. Gray used a similar process in a demonstration at Clickering Hall in New York City on 10 January 1894. This became the first commercially developed system available in the United States, his Natural Color Triple Stereopticon being manufactured by J. B. Colt & Co. of New York and on sale by July 1896. The Ives Komskop was manufactured in the United States in 1899.

The first single-plate color process and the first suitable for use by amateur photographers was introduced commercially by Sanger-Shepherd & Co. of Red Lion Street, London, in 1904. This was priced at £8 14s ($48.50) for the camera attachment and development/printing outfit in the 8" x 3½" plate size and £12 5s ($61.25) for the 9¾" x 4¼" plate size. Within the next two years some four or five competing systems of color photography came on the market, but it was not until the introduction of the Lumière Brothers'

Autochrome color plates in 1907 that photography in natural colors can be said to have moved beyond the experimental stage.

Although Autochromes were transparencies, they could be used to produce prints with a multilayer bleach-out paper called Utocolor by anyone with sufficient patience: Owing to low sensitivity it took 20 minutes to make a single print even in strong sunlight. Developed in Zurich in 1904, Utocolor was commercially available in France, the United Kingdom, and the United States.

Color roll film: The first was invented by Robert Krayn and launched in Germany in 1910 by the Neue Photographische Gesellschaft. This had only a brief life and no further roll films appeared on the market until Lignose Natural Color Film, another German development, in 1924. Lignose was the first color roll film available in Britain, introduced in 1926 at 2s 9d for three exposures, as well as the first in America. It was manufactured in the United States under license from the British concern Color Snapshots (Foreign) Ltd. by Agfa-Ansco of Binghamton, N.Y., under the name of Colorol and launched in 1929 at $2 for six exposures including developing. Amateurs had to wait until 1936 for successful three-color film in the form of 35-mm Kodachrome in the United States, Agfacolor in Germany, and Dufaycolor in Britain. Initially Kodachrome transparencies would be returned from the processors in the form of a film strip, but from 1938 the modern system of individual card mounts was adopted. "Minicolor" prints on paper could be made from the transparencies from 1941. The following year Kodacolor was introduced expressly for prints.

SEE ALSO **fashion photographs: color; halftone: color; newspapers: color news photograph; postcard: photographically illustrated (color); printed book: American book illustrated with a photograph (color).**

THE FIRST PHOTOGRAPHIC CAMERA

manufactured for sale was marketed by Alphonse Giroux of Paris in September 1839, at a price of 400 francs ($80). A manufacturing agreement between Giroux and the inventor, Louis Daguerre (SEE **photograph**), had been signed on 22 June of the same year. The wooden camera measured 10½" x 12¼" x 14½" closed, and was fitted with an achromatic lens by Charles Chevalier of Paris. The firm of Giroux et Cie were the first photographic dealers in the world, supplying all the equipment necessary for daguerreotypy from their shop at 7 rue du Coq-Saint-Honoré.

U.S.: George W. Prosch, a scientific instrument maker occupying the basement of the Morse Building at Nassau and Beekman streets, New York City, made the first recorded American camera for telegraph pioneer Samuel F. B. Morse, whose laboratories occupied the same building, probably in October 1839. He began selling a range of cameras the following March.

Snapshot camera: The first camera designed for amateurs with no technical interest in photography was the fixed-focus Kodak No. 1 launched by George Eastman of Rochester, N.Y., at $25 in June 1888. It used paper roll film already loaded in the camera, giving 100 circular pictures of 2½-inch diameter. The camera had to be mailed to the Eastman factory to be unloaded and processed and it was returned reloaded together with the hundred prints. Formerly enthusiastic amateurs using cameras designed principally for professional use had to do their own developing and printing. Eastman's advertising slogan for the camera summed up the ease and simplicity of his idea: "You press the button, we do the rest." The name Kodak was chosen because it was pronounceable and without specific meaning in any language; Eastman already knew that snapshot photography would girdle the Earth. While it was an immediate success—within a year the Eastman Co. was processing 7,500 prints a day—the very ease with which instantaneous snaps could be taken presented its own problems. In England in 1893 the *Weekly Times & Echo* reported:

> Several young men, I hear, are forming a Vigilance Association for the purpose of thrashing the cads with cameras who go about at seaside places taking snapshots at ladies emerging from the deep in the mournful garments peculiar to the British female bather.

Digital camera: The first was a Nikon F-3 adapted by Kodak with a 1.3-megapixel sensor and marketed for professional use by photojournalists in 1991. The first for amateur use was the Apple QuickTake 100 developed by the Apple Advanced Technology Group at Cupertino, Calif., and launched at the Tokyo Mac-World Expo on 17 February 1994. This was designed for use with a home PC via a serial cable and had a 640 x 480 pixel resolution. It was marketed in May 1994 at $750. Sales of digital cameras in the United States at 12½ million exceeded sales of roll-film cameras for the first time in 2003. The following year Kodak announced that they were ceasing production of the latter in the United States and Europe.

THE FIRST PHOTOGRAPHIC MODEL

specializing in commercial work is noted as early as 1895, though it was a precarious existence as this anonymous practitioner vouchsafed to a reporter from the *Chicago Tribune* during an interview at a local photographer's studio:

> I've done a great deal of it and make as much as $30 a week during the busy season. One can't make a living at this business, though, because the season's so short, and the people get tired at seeing the same old face every time, and the old model has to step out and a new one step in. I know a girl who made enough last year to send her mother to Virginia for two months. Although that girl is just as pretty as ever she was no one wants her this year, and she's taking lessons in bookkeeping. I am regularly employed as a "cloak model" in an establishment on State Street and what I earn here is extra. I am called a professional model because I am not an amateur. No, I never posed for anything but advertising pictures. Compensation? Well, this man pays $2 an hour, and that is the maximum price, I think.

This compared favorably with the fixed fee for artist's models of 50¢ an hour. The new profession had emerged extraordinarily rapidly, because the first photographically illustrated advertisements (SEE

advertising photography) had only started appearing in American magazines some two years earlier and most of these tended to be pack-shots of the product.

Model agency: The first was established in 1903 by Tonnensen Sisters, Inc., a commercial studio on Michigan Avenue in Chicago that had been founded in the previous decade by Beatrice and Clare Tonnensen. The sisters used large numbers of models, principally women and children, whom they featured on calendars as well as for advertising and catalogs. The "Famous Tonnensen Models," as they were known, were hired out to other studios for an agency fee.

The creation of the model agency is usually attributed to John Robert Powers, ignoring Chicago's considerably earlier claim. His was, though, the first independent agency (i.e., unconnected to a studio), the first in what was to become the world center for modeling, Manhattan, and the first to specialize in fashion.

Powers was a failed New York actor and part-time model who began representing other out-of-work actors for modeling assignments after *Harper's Bazaar*'s chief fashion photographer, Baron Adolphe De Meyer (SEE fashion photographs), asked him to round up eight men for an ensemble picture. This was in about 1921. Thereafter Powers began recording the details of the many unemployed film extras who, like him, hung around the Fort Lee, N.J., studios waiting for work. Photographers for whom he had worked found it easier to call Powers than to advertise for models. This, however, was on a casual basis and the agency was not formally established until his wife, Alice Hathaway Burton, prompted him to turn a sideline into a paying business. With backing from British theatrical elder statesman Sir Herbert Beerbohm Tree (SEE fan club), the Powerses began operating out of their apartment above a speakeasy at 19 West 46th Street in 1923. There they published the first modeling directory, the inaugural issue containing some forty prospects with their photographs. At the beginning these were all actors, but after Powers had been offered new premises at the fashionable address of 247 Park Avenue he began attracting mannequins from the fashion houses keen to earn $5 per 90-minute photo session. There was a further development after the 1929 stock-market crash, when high-born debutantes whose fathers had been wiped out clamored to display their charms to the camera. While the business had started with film actors who became models, in time the process went into reverse and many Powers models graduated to stardom in Hollywood, among them Fredric March, Henry Fonda, Tyrone Power, Jennifer Jones, Barbara Stanwyck, Jean Arthur, Ava Gardner, Lauren Bacall, and Rosalind Russell.

THE FIRST **PIANOFORTE**

was built in 1709 by Bartolomeo Cristofori, who was a repairer and tuner of harpsichords in the service of Ferdinand de' Medici, Grand Duke of Tuscany, and keeper of his instruments. The earliest description of Cristofori's pianos was written by Scipione Maffei and published in the *Giornale de'Letterati d'Italia* (Venice) in 1711. By this time he had completed three examples of his new instrument. Maffei explained how it differed from the familiar harpsichord:

> Instead of the jacks that produce sound by quills, there is a little row of hammers that strike the string from below, the tops of which are covered with leather. Every hammer has the end inserted into a circular butt that renders it movable; these butts are partially embedded and strung together in a receiver. Near the butt, and under the stem of the hammer, there is a projecting part or support that, receiving the blow from beneath raises the hammer and causes it to strike the string with whatever degree of force is given by the hand of the performer; hence the sound produced can be greater or less, at the pleasure of the player.

Cristofori's own name for the instrument was *gravicembalo col piano e forte* ("harpsichord with soft and loud"). The English, French, and Portuguese adopted the last two adjectives, strung them together, and made the word pianoforte. The Germans preferred to call it the *Hammerklavier* ("keyboard instrument with hammers"), but subsequently abbreviated this to *klavier*.

The earliest surviving example of a Cristofori piano dates from 1720 and is preserved at the Kraus Museum in Florence. The inventor made few instruments, finding little profit in it, and was eventually obliged to return to making and repairing harpsichords.

The first instrument maker to manufacture pianos on a commercial scale was Gottfried Silbermann of Kleinbobritzsch, Saxony, in 1726.

U.S.: The earliest record of a piano dates from 1773 when the German violinist Hermann Zedwitz gave a concert in New York at "Hull's Assembly Rooms at the sign of the Golden Spade." A reviewer remarked that "the accompaniment of Mr. Hulett on the pianoforte was very chaste . . ." This was William C. Hulett, who was later to achieve prominence as a pianist. In 1780 the visiting Marquis de Chastellux, evidently expecting to find America a wilderness peopled by savages, expressed astonishment at the many pianofortes he encountered in Boston and Philadelphia, and was further surprised that the ladies of those two cities should display such a keen appreciation of good music.

The first piano built in America was by woodworker and joiner John Behrent Jr., at his workshop at Third and Brown streets, Philadelphia, in 1775. He advertised that he had "just finished an extraordinary instrument by the name of piano-forte, of mahogany, in the manner of harpsichord, with hammers and several changes." In general, manufacture of pianos in the United States was slow to emerge. When a Boston newspaper reported in 1791 that there were twenty-seven pianos in the city, it was noted that all of them had been imported from London. In Philadelphia, however, the story was different. Although Behrent seems to have abandoned piano making with the onset of the Revolutionary War, by 1783 James Juhan of Franklin and Arch streets was manufacturing "the great *American pianoforte* of his own invention." What is believed to be the oldest piano of American make is also from Philadelphia, a 1789 model by Charles Albrecht, now in the collection of the Pennsylvania Historical Society.

Upright piano: All early pianofortes were grands. Although some uprights had appeared in Europe during the eighteenth century, these were essentially grand or square pianos set on end with the keyboard moved accordingly. The prototype of the modern upright, formerly known as the cottage piano, was invented by a British immigrant to Philadelphia called John I. Hawkins in 1799 and patented in Britain and the United States the following year. The U.S. patent was granted 12 February 1800. Hawkins was a civil engineer, not an instrument maker, so it seems probable that the instruments were made to his design by one of Philadelphia's established manufacturers, possibly Charles Albrecht or the Scotsman Charles Taws.

By 1853 there were 204 piano manufacturers in the United States, ranging from large factories like those of Chickering & Sons and Albert Weber to small workshops turning out a handful of instruments a year. That year they were joined by a family of recent immigrants from Brunswick (Braunschweig) in Germany called the Steinwegs, who chose to anglicize their name to what was to become the best-known name in the business: Steinway. In the space of scarcely six years Heinrich Steinweg Jr., son of the founder, had made a series of improvements that created the modern piano, enumerated thus by Richard K. Lieberman in his magisterial study *Steinway & Sons* (1995):

> a cast-iron plate with a downward projecting flange, longer and heavier overstrung bass strings fanning out over the center of the soundboard, a vibrant soundboard with the bridges closer to the center, and a responsive action that gave performers more control over the new power at their fingertips.

Not all these ideas were original; it was the way Heinrich combined them that made the 1859 Steinway the finest concert grand that had ever been built. There have been few changes of major significance since, making the piano a rare example of a mechanical device essentially the same today as it was in the second half of the nineteenth century (the safety bicycle and the Yale lock being the only other ones of prominence).

At this time the English-made Broadwood was generally considered the world leader. International recognition for the upstart German-Americans came at the 1867 Paris Exposition, at which Steinway pianos were placed first in the official medal list. America, hitherto regarded as world beaters only in agricultural

machinery and small arms, was now recognized as producing the best pianos in the world, a reputation that neither the nation nor the Steinway company has ever lost.

THE FIRST PLASTIC

was Parkesine, a thermoplastic material produced in 1861 from nitrocellulose, camphor, and alcohol by Alexander Parkes of Birmingham, England, and originally manufactured by the Parkesine Co. of Hackney Wick, London, in April 1866. It was, the inventor said, a "beautiful substance for the Arts, suitable for the production of medallions, salvers, hollowware, cubes, buttons, combs, knife handles, pierced and fretwork, inlaid work, book binding, card cases, boxes, and pen holders." A number of these carved and press-molded articles, and also plastic doorknobs and hand mirrors, had been exhibited at the International Exhibition in London of 1862. Parkes sold his patent rights in 1869 to the newly formed Xylonite Co., which manufactured plastic billiard balls, napkin rings, knife handles, photo frames, imitation coral, and other articles, totaling 330 tons in volume in 1888. The main drawback to these products was that they were highly flammable.

U.S.: As were the products produced by John Wesley Hyatt of Albany, N.Y., who patented a similar but more durable thermoplastic on 15 June 1869 to which he gave the name *celluloid*. His purpose was to find a substitute for ivory, which was becoming scarce as elephants were slaughtered in their thousands so that the tusks could be used for making billiard balls. Those manufactured by his Albany Billiard Ball Co. were coated with a film of cellulose nitrate, otherwise known as gun cotton. Hyatt observed somewhat ruefully in an unpublished memoir:

> Consequently a lighted cigar applied would at once result in a serious flame and occasionally the violent contact of the balls would produce a mild explosion like a percussion guncap. We had a letter from a billiard saloon proprietor in Colorado, mentioning this fact saying he did not care so much about it but that instantly every man in the room pulled a gun.

Scarcely less hazardous were the dentures produced by the Albany Dental Plate Co. that Hyatt set up in 1870, as cigar smokers complained of explosions when they lit up. Nevertheless he expanded into a wide range of plastic goods after changing the name to the Celluloid Manufacturing Co. in 1872. Among the most successful were celluloid collars, cuffs, and shirt bosoms, which could be cleaned with a lump of stale bread, thus saving on laundry bills for ill-paid clerks requiring a clean collar every day. These were also the last celluloid products produced at the company's factory in Newark, N.J., before it closed down in 1949, since detachable collars and cuffs were, it seems, still de rigueur in certain circles in Texas and Oklahoma—together with one other item, dice, as it seems crapshooters were of a conservative disposition and would brook no change to the agency of their fortunes.

The first **wholly synthetic plastic** was the phenolic resinoid known as Bakelite, developed by Belgian-born Dr. Leo H. Baekeland of Yonkers, N.Y., in 1906 in response to a request by the Loando Hard Rubber Co. of Boonton, N.J., for a resin that could take the place of rubber in molded electrical insulation compounds. W. Seabury, then manager of Loando, recalled:

> The first molded Bakelite parts, some with asbestos and some with wood flour, were made by me in 1907. Dr. Baekeland brought the resin from his Yonkers laboratory, and I made the molding powders and molded parts in our molds and presses. My first customer for this new "Bakelite" material was the Western Instrument Corporation of Newark, New Jersey.

Baekeland patented his process on 14 July 1907 and, after the initial production at Loando, manufacture was undertaken by the General Bakelite Co. of Perth Amboy, N.J.

Polystyrene was originally produced commercially in 1929 by BASF in Germany and first injection-molded the following year. Dow Chemical and the renamed Bakelite Corporation pioneered manufacture in the United States in 1937, the former with Styron and the latter with Bakelite Polystyrene. Early polystyrene was a rigid substance, first used in 1942 for buoyancy in a six-man life raft for the U.S. Marines. Styrene foam or Styrofoam, thirty times lighter than regular polystyrene, was developed in 1954 by Dow Chemical's Ray McIntire, originally as a flexible electrical insulator; but later it was both championed and reviled as the fast-food packaging discarded on sidewalks.

PVC (polyvinyl chloride) was developed by Waldo Lonsbury Semon as a waterproof, fireproof fabric after watching his wife Marjorie make a set of new shower curtains out of rubberized cotton. It was manufactured in 1929 by his employers B.F. Goodrich at their vinyl plant in Louisville, Ky. Early uses of PVC were mainly as a substitute for rubber and it came into its own during World War II as a fireproof upholstery in naval vessels. After the war it was used increasingly for clothes, particularly the "plastic raincoats" of the 1940s and '50s and more glamorously the couture offerings of Mary Quant, Courrèges, and others in the '60s. In the form of vinyl it replaced shellac for phonograph records (SEE **sound recording: record on vinylite**); and as rigid unplasticized PVC (UPVC) it manifested itself in plastic guttering and other outdoor applications demanding lightness and durability.

Polyethylene was discovered accidentally by British research chemists E. W. Fawcett and R. O. Gibson at Imperial Chemical Industries' (ICI's) Winnington Research Laboratories on 26 March 1933 after pumping 24 cc of benzaldehyde-ethylene gas mixture into a high-pressure reaction vessel that then sprang a leak. The reduction in pressure resulted in what Gibson noted as "Waxy solid found in reaction tube." The effect was not replicated until December 1935 and after further intensive development the first practical application of polyethylene was made in June 1939 when a mile of coaxial cable sheathed in the material was laid between the mainland and the Isle of Wight by the British Submarine Cable Co. Regular production began 1 September that year.

U.S.: In 1942 ICI licensed DuPont to have free use of their patents in respect to polyethylene for military purposes for the duration of the war.

Plexiglas: The first commercially produced transparent hard plastic or acrylic was developed independently in Britain and Germany, with research programs beginning in both countries in 1931. In Darmstadt it was fashioned from polymethyl metharulite by organic chemist Otto Röhm, whose research laboratory Röhm & Haas sold manufacturing rights to Germany chemical giant I.G. Farben. From 1934 they used Plexiglas for making cockpit canopies for Luftwaffe bombers (secretly and in contravention of the Treaty of Versailles). Röhm & Haas themselves produced consumer goods in Plexiglas including transparent rules, set squares, and other drafting equipment for architects.

An exactly similar acrylic had been developed in the meantime by ICI, which registered the name Perspex (as it is still known in Britain) on 16 November 1934. When commercial production began that year, the drying room for Perspex was kept at a constant 104 degrees Fahrenheit. Every week the workers were weighed for weight loss, having lost their appetite for anything other than tinned fruit. The first products manufactured in this new material were vases and candlesticks exhibited at Burlington House in London on 4 January 1935. As in Germany, though, the principal uses found for Perspex in the run-up to war were military, most notably cockpit covers for the Royal Air Force's Spitfire fighters that won the Battle of Britain in 1940.

U.S.: Similarly in America, where the Philadelphia-based Otto Haas of Röhm & Haas had the development rights to Otto Röhm's process and sent his staff chemist Dr. Donald Frederick to Darmstadt to learn the techniques of production. On Frederick's return, Haas secured the interest of the Army Air Corps. While the first Plexiglas constructs seen by the American public were two of the most popular exhibits at the 1939 New York World's Fair—General Motors's transparent Pontiac and RCA's transparent TV receiver—once again primary production comprised aircraft nose cones, canopies, and gun turrets, DuPont alone producing 370,000 units. After the war it became the material of choice for automobile taillights.

Biodegradable plastic: The first practical and fully biodegradable plastic was Biopal, manufactured by ICI at Billingham, Cleveland, England, from minute soil microbes. The first product packed in Biopal was Wella shampoo in Germany in May 1990. In 1993 the Kai Corporation of Japan launched a biodegradable razor made of Biopal that would break down completely into water and carbon dioxide within two or three years of being buried in the earth or submerged in the ocean. Conventional plastic takes from fifty to a hundred years to degrade. Biopal is also recyclable.

SEE ALSO **man-made fiber: nylon**.

THE FIRST **PLAY**

performed in what is now the United States was an un-named Spanish *comedia* by Marcos Farfán de los Godos performed by Spanish troops of Juan de Oñate's expedition near the present site of El Paso, Tex., on 30 April 1598. The subject, appropriately, was a military expedition. Another play, titled *Moros y los Cristianos* ("Moors and Christians"), was performed by the same actors on 10 July.

The first play in English known to have been presented in America was the anonymous *Ye Bare and Ye Cubb* performed at Accomac, Va., on 27 August 1665, probably at Cowles Tavern. Three of the actors were arraigned for their participation, despite the fact that Virginia, unlike most of the other colonies, had no law forbidding stage performances.

Play written in America: The first was *Cornelia* by Sir William Berkeley, who was governor of Virginia at Jamestown when he penned it in 1641. By the time he returned to England the playhouses had been banned by Cromwellian zealots and it was not until the Restoration that the play was eventually performed in London in 1662.

Play set in America: The first was written in London by Mrs. Aphra Behn, the first woman playwright (qv), and titled *The Widow Ranter, or Bacon in Virginia*, the subject of which was Bacon's Rebellion in 1676 when Jamestown was burned by insurgents. It was performed in 1689 and published in 1690.

Play written by an American: The first was *Gustavus Vasa*, about the Swedish patriot who freed his nation from Danish rule and became king, which was the work of Boston-born Benjamin Colman. He was only seventeen when his play was performed by fellow students at Harvard College in 1690. Colman subsequently became pastor of Medford, Mass., he was captured by a French privateer and became a prisoner of war while on a voyage to England in 1695. He was eventually exchanged and became a successful preacher in London before returning to America to spend the rest of his life as minister of Brattle Street Church in Boston.

The first American play to be published was *Androboros*, co-written by Gov. Robert Hunter of New York and Chief Justice Lewis Morris, a native New Yorker, and printed by William Bradford in New York City in 1714. It was a satire on the meddling of Trinity Parish officials in the affairs of the colony. Only one copy survives, in the collection of the Huntington Library in San Marino, Calif.

The first play by an American-born playwright to be performed on the professional stage in the United States was the tragedy *The Prince of Parthia* written by the twenty-one-year-old Thomas Godfrey Jr. of Philadelphia while living in North Carolina in 1759. He died in 1763 but the play was presented posthumously as a one-off by David Douglass' American Company on 24 April 1767 at the Southwark Theatre, Philadelphia.

Play set in America to be performed in the United States: The first was Le Blanc de Villeneuve's French-language *Le Père Indien*, staged in New Orleans in 1753. This seems to have been about relationships within the Native American community rather than about Indians and settlers.

The first English-language play set in America to be performed here was a farce titled *The Blockade of Boston* exposing patriot Americans to ridicule and attributed to the pen of Gen. John Burgoyne himself. It was performed by his officers at Faneuil Hall in Boston on 6 January 1776 and inspired another American-set play, *The Blockheads: or, the Affrighted Officers*, by an anonymous patriot (wrongly identified as Mrs. Warren), which was about the performance of *The Blockade of Boston*. Schoolteacher Hugh Henry Brackenridge's *The Battle of Bunkers-Hill* (published in Philadelphia in 1776) was probably performed by his pupils at an academy in Somerset County in Maryland.

Professional performance of a play set in America by an American: The first was *The Contrast* by Boston lawyer Royall Tyler, which was premiered at the John Street Theater in New York City by the American Company on 16 April 1787. He was inspired to write it after seeing a production of Richard Brinsley Sheridan's *The School for Scandal* in New York and produced a comedy of American manners in which he contrasted (hence the title) the corrupt and frivolous world of fashion with the sturdier, more vigorous types of American manhood. Despite being called the American Company, the cast espousing these native virtues was English to a man and woman.

American to become a playwright by profession: The first was William Dunlop, born in 1776, who was filled with ambition to be a dramatist after hearing plaudits for Royall Tyler's *The Contrast*. At the time he began writing plays in 1787 he was living at the home of his father, a china dealer in New York, and trying to make a living as a portrait painter, having studied in London under the great expatriate artist Benjamin West. In that year he wrote *The Modest Soldier, or Love in New York*, but it was turned down by the choleric John Henry's American Company because, as Dunlop later learned, he had neglected to insert a sufficiently prominent female role for Mrs. Henry. Success came with another comedy, *The Father, or American Shandyism*, which opened at the John Street Theater in New York on 7 September 1789 with Mrs. Henry in the female lead as Carolina. Subsequently he wrote another fifty-eight plays, of which *Darby's Return* (1789) was a favorite piece of that indefatigable playgoer George Washington. Dunlop died in 1839, six years after the publication of his theatrical history, America's first, titled *History of the American Theater*.

THE FIRST PLAYING CARDS

were Chinese sheet dice, believed to have originated in the tenth century A.D., made to reproduce the notation of dice on paper. Others were derived from Chinese paper money, and it is thought that some of the earliest card games were played with actual bank notes. The *T'u-shu-chi-ch'eng Encyclopaedia*, Book 807, folio 6, contains the following passage:

> According to the History of the Liao Dynasty, the Emperor Muy Tsung, in the 19th year of the period Ying-li [A.D. 969] . . . made reference to the game

of cards when he said to his ministers, "Games of cards were played in the house of Duke Ch'ien, and in that very year in the second month he was killed by Siao-ho, ruler and subjects became victims of barbarity, and misfortune followed misfortune. Yet such unlucky objects are now held in the hand daily by scholars and officials. Is that not the following of an evil example?"

A Chinese playing card believed to be the oldest surviving example in the world was found in 1905 by Dr. A. von Le Coq together with fragments of manuscript dating from the Uighur period, in the Sangim Valley near Turfan, Chinese Turkestan. This card, which corresponds to the Red Flower of the modern Chinese pack, probably dates from the eleventh century. It forms a narrow rectangle in shape, about three times as long as it is broad, and bears the figure of a man bordered by a thick black line. Characters inscribed at the top and bottom of the card denote the name of the maker.

The origin of playing cards in Europe is obscure. The earliest reference in literature appears in an Italian manuscript by Pipozzo di Sandro titled *Trattato del governo della famiglia*, believed to date from 1299. This work contains a sentence that reads: "If he play for money in this manner, or at cards, you must facilitate the means of his doing so." (*Se guichera di denari a cosi o alle carte, gli apparuchierai de vie.*)

The earliest known surviving examples of European playing cards came from France. Charles Poupart, treasurer to Charles VI, made the following entry in the accounts of the Royal Household for 1392: "Paid to Jacquemin Gringonneur, painter, for three packs of cards [*ieux de cartes*] in gold and colors of divers devices, to present to the said lord the king for his amusement, 60 sols parisis." These cards were intended to humor the monarch during his recurrent bouts of madness. Seventeen cards of this period from a tarot pack, almost certainly dating from the last quarter of the fourteenth century, are preserved at the Bibliothèque Nationale in Paris and are thought to be examples of the actual cards painted by Gringonneur.

The earliest known playing cards printed in Europe, and the earliest to bear the four suits of the modern pack, were found in 1841 by the French antiquarian M. Henin in the cover of an old book he purchased in Lyon. These ten cards had been used as stiffeners in the binding. All are court cards and the pictures on them are wood engravings printed with a pale ink of brownish tint and afterward colored with a stencil. They are thought to date from c. 1440 and to have been made in Provence. They would doubtless have been used for playing Piquet, the earliest known game played with the conventional (as opposed to tarot) pack. Eight of the cards are preserved in the British Museum and two, the knave of clubs and the knave of spades, are in the collection of the United States Playing Card Co., in Cincinnati.

U.S.: Although Jazaniah Ford of Milton, Mass., is widely hailed as the first manufacturer of playing cards, there seems to be little consensus about the date he started the business. Most authorities plump for c. 1785 and 1790 and the difference assumes a greater significance in the light of playing-card historian Catherine Perry Hargrave's discovery of an advertisement in the *Federal Gazette* (Philadelphia) for 19 February 1790 offering "Ryves and Ashmead's Super-fine American manufactured playing Cards." Ford was not so forthcoming about the provenance of his cards, which were imprinted "London" with an illusory address, even though the watermarked cardstock came from the Tikston & Hollingsworth Paper Mill at neighboring Mattapan. Whether or not he was the first card master, he was the first to issue a commemorative pack, the highly prized *Decatur* of 1814, which extolled the naval hero Stephen Decatur's feats of derring-do against the British in the War of 1812 and his earlier feats of arms against the Bey of Tripoli. This was reissued ten years later to commemorate the visit of Gen. Lafayette to the United States to celebrate the fiftieth anniversary of the Revolution, the sea battle depicted on the ace of spades being replaced with a portrait of the dashing Marquis. It is now regarded as one of the most collectible of all American packs.

Advertising playing cards: These were first issued in 1700 by Thomas Tuttle, scientific and mathematical instrument maker of London, and reproduced his trade card on the back.

Double-head court cards: The earliest known belong to a German pack issued in 1813 to celebrate the Battle of Leipzig. The kings are represented as the monarchs of the four allied countries on the victorious side, the knaves by portraits of the marshals commanding the armies in the battle; and the queens are personified as Pomona, Flora, Diana, and Ceres. Double-head court cards remained rare until the middle of the nineteenth century.

Joker: The earliest known is contained in a London Club pack issued by Samuel Hart & Co. of 222–228 West 14th Street, New York City, in 1857.

THE FIRST **PNEUMATIC TIRES**

were patented by civil engineer R. W. Thompson of London on 10 December 1845 as an "Improvement in Carriage Wheels which is also applicable to other rolling bodies." They were demonstrated publicly for the first time the following summer. The *Mechanic's Magazine* for 22 August 1846 reported:

> The interest of the visitors to the parks this week has been much excited by the appearance among the crowd of gay equipages of a brougham with silent wheels, so silent as to suggest a practical inconsistency of a most startling character between the name and quality of the thing. The tyres of the wheels consist of elastic tubular rings, made, we believe, of caoutchouc enclosed in leather cases and inflated with air to any degree of tightness desired.
>
> The motion of the carriage is exceedingly easy. We are informed that it is now gone about a hundred miles over roads of all sorts, even some which are newly macadamised, and that the outer leather casing is (contrary to what might have been expected) as sound and entire as at first, not exhibiting in any part of it the slightest tendency to rupture.

The tires were subsequently tested on a number of heavy wagons and demonstrated an improvement in tractive effort of 60 percent over iron tires when used on smooth roads and over 30 percent on rough roads.

In the spring of 1847 the *Mechanic's Magazine* announced that Whitehurst & Co. had secured a license to fit Thompson's Ariel wheels to any type of carriage and that a demonstration model was on view at their Oxford Street showroom. The first recorded sale of pneumatic tires was made to Lord Loraine of Albury Park, Guildford, Surrey, who had them fitted to his brougham by a local firm, May & Jacobs, on 1 October 1847. The price paid was £44 2s ($220.50) for a set of four. In 1895 these same tires were found rotting in a barn and sold to the Dunlop Pneumatic Tyre Co. for $2,500.

Demand, however, was limited and as the tires had to be made by hand they were correspondingly expensive. More than seventy bolts were used to fasten them to the wheel, so they were not easily detachable. This may have been the reason they failed to catch on and had been completely forgotten by the time Dunlop reinvented the pneumatic tire forty years on.

Pneumatic bicycle tire: The first was made by John Boyd Dunlop, a prosperous Belfast veterinary surgeon who had gained experience in working with rubber while devising various appliances for use in connection with his profession. He had never ridden a bicycle in his life.

Dunlop's attention was originally drawn to the need for an improved cycle tire one day in October 1887 as he stood watching his ten-year-old son Johnny riding his solid-tired tricycle around the garden and leaving deep tracks in the turf. The precursor of all Dunlop tires was fashioned from a length of garden hose and filled not with air, but with water. Happily the Dunlops' family doctor, Sir John Fagan, was looking on and he, having had considerable experience of inflatable cushions and mattresses for the sick, suggested blowing the tire up with air. This time Dunlop used sheet-rubber for the tube, which he attached to a wooden disk with a linen cover tacked on to the sides and inflated with a football pump.

Dunlop's first pair of cycle tires were fitted to the rear wheels of Johnny's Edlin Quadrant tricycle on the night of 28 February 1888 and ridden on by the boy that same evening. In June 1888 Dunlop purchased a bicycle from Edlin & Co., and fitted it with pneumatic tires covered with finest Gents' Yacht sailcloth from Arbroath. The success of this full-size machine encouraged Edlin's to enter into an agreement with the veterinary surgeon for the manufacture of racing safety-bicycles fitted with his tires and on 19 December 1888 this historic advertisement in the *Irish Cyclist* announced the birth of a new industry: "Look out for the new Pneumatic Safety. Vibration impossible. Sole makers—W. Edlin and Co., Garfield Street, Belfast."

The front forks of the Pneumatic Safety were specially widened to a breadth of 2 inches to allow for the swollen girth of Dunlop's tire, which was covered by two layers of canvas stuck together with rubber solution, the overlapping ends of the outer layer being bound around the rim of the wheel. Only cycles equipped with pneumatics were sold—about fifty during the first year of manufacture—and the tires could not be purchased separately. The success of his tire on the racetrack encouraged Dunlop to undertake manufacture on his own account. The Pneumatic Tyre and Booth's Cycle Agency Ltd. issued its first prospectus on 18 November 1889 and a small manufacturing plant was established in Dublin early in the New Year. By April 1891 it was turning out three thousand tires a week.

U.S.: A number of cycle manufacturers began fitting pneumatics in 1890. The first has not been positively identified.

Pneumatic automobile tires: The first were fitted to a 4-hp Peugeot by the Paris cycle-tire manufacturer Édouard Michelin, who drove the car in the Paris–Bordeaux Race of 11 June 1895. Although twenty-two tire changes were necessary over the 1,200-km there-and-back route, Michelin succeeded in finishing ninth out of nineteen entrants, achieving speeds of up to 25 kph on the level. Each tire was screwed to the wheel with twenty nuts and bolts. The first automobile to have pneumatics fitted as standard was the 1896 Bolée Voiturette.

U.S.: Two two-seater Kane-Pennington Victorias built by the Racine Motor Vehicle Co. of Racine, Wis., were fitted with pneumatic tires in anticipation of the *Chicago Times-Herald* contest in Chicago of 28 November 1895. The vehicles, extremely unreliable—their designer, Edward Joel Pennington, was a confidence trickster—did not compete in the contest but were demonstrated over short distances. Typically Pennington claimed that his tires were "impuncturable."

One other automobile with pneumatic tires is recorded from 1895. This was a steamer built by John B. West of Rochester, N.Y., which had bicycle wheels and tires in the front and balloon tires in the rear. The vehicle was considerably more efficient than Pennington's dismal effort, as he ran it for at least three years.

The first automobile tires manufactured for sale were a set of 36" x 4" double tube clinchers made by B.F. Goodrich Co. of Akron, Ohio, for the Winton Motor Carriage Co. of Cleveland and delivered in December 1896. By 1904 the value of automobile tires sold in the United States was almost double that of bicycle tires.

Bus with pneumatic tires: The first was a 2¼-ton De Dion-Bouton steam omnibus built in Paris and fitted with 4½-inch Michelin tires late in 1900. This was the first motor vehicle of substantial weight to be run on pneumatics.

Truck to be fitted with pneumatic tires: The first was a 1½-ton 8-hp Daimler of German manufacture, supplied to the Dunlop Pneumatic Tyre Co. in July 1902 and used daily for delivering stocks of tires from Dunlop's Clerkenwell Road depot in London. Few heavy goods vehicles were driven on pneumatic tires until the 1920s.

Aircraft to be fitted with pneumatic tires: The first was the Vuia I built by the Romanian-born aviator Trajan Vuia, and first tested at Montesson, France, on 3 March 1906. The tires were of some practical service, as the Vuia I covered a greater distance on the ground than it ever did in the air. Although five "flights" were made in the aircraft, the longest, and last, was for a length of only 24 meters, terminating in a crash landing.

Tubeless tires: The first to prove commercially successful were manufactured by the B.F. Goodrich Co. of Akron, Ohio, which began test-marketing the puncture-proof tires in Indiana, Ohio, Kentucky, and West Virginia on 11 May 1947.

THE FIRST **POETRY**

of American provenance to appear in print was composed by the rapscallion lawyer and adventurer Thomas Morton of Merrymont, a trading colony established by Captain Wollaston c. 1624 at what is now Quincy, Mass. Morton aroused the ire of the Pilgrims at nearby Plymouth by erecting a maypole and leading his friends in dancing around it in the company of their Indian girlfriends, as well as what Gov. William Bradford referred to darkly as "worse practices" (presumably involving the same wanton women). They also, according to the censorious Bradford, drank to excess, on one occasion consuming wine and strong liquor to the value of £10 (a servant's wage for a year) in the course of a single morning. "Morton," wrote the Governor, "...to show his poetry composed sundry rhymes and verses, some tending to lasciviousness, and others to the detraction and scandal of some persons, which he fixed to this idle or idol maypole." A selection of these appeared in Morton's *New English Canaan*, Amsterdam, 1637, which he wrote to spite his Puritan detractors. Among them is the earliest known American lyric, a drinking song for performance in taverns or elsewhere in all-male company, of which one verse goes:

> *Give to the Nymph that's free from scorn*
> *No Irish stuff nor Scotch over-worn.*
> *Lasses in beaver coats, come away,*
> *Ye shall be welcome to us night and day.*
> > *Then drink and be merry, merry, merry boys*
> > *Let all your delight by in Hymen's joys*
> > *Io! To Hymen, now the day is come,*
> > *About the merry Maypole take a room.*

"Irish stuff" and "Scotch" were not whiskey but woolens. It is interesting to observe that "Yo!" (as "Io!" was pronounced) was a salutation some 350 years before it was adopted by African Americans.

The first **poetry by a woman living in America** to be published was *The Tenth Muse Lately Spring Up in America . . . by a Gentlewoman in Those Parts*, published by Stephen Bowtell in London in 1650. The "Gentlewoman" was Anne Bradstreet, originally from Boston, Lincolnshire, England, and latterly of Merrimack (now North Andover), Mass., the mother of eight children and ancestor of Oliver Wendell Holmes. The poems were published without her knowledge, her brother-in-law John Woodbridge having taken a manuscript copy with him to England in 1647. The opening lines acknowledge the hostility to be expected by a woman daring to assert herself in verse:

> *I am obnoxious to each carping tongue*
> *Who says my hand a needle better fits.*
> *A poet's pen all scorn I should thus wrong,*
> *For such despite they cast on female wits:*
> *If what I do prove well, it won'd advance,*
> *They'll say it's stol'n, or else it was by chance.*

Mistress Bradstreet was also the first American woman to be published in America, with the posthumous publication in 1678 of *Several Poems*, from the press of John Foster of Boston. As well as the poems in *The Tenth Muse* this "was enlarged by an Addition of several other Poems found among her Papers after her Death."

Poetry by an American-based poet to be published in America: The first was *The Day of Doom*, by Yorkshire-born Michael Wigglesworth, pastor at Malden, Mass., for fifty years, which was published at Cambridge, Mass., in 1662; its purpose was to awaken readers to their spiritual destiny. The poem became the first American bestseller, with 1,800 copies sold in the first year of publication and another four editions during the remainder of the seventeenth century and six in the eighteenth century. It has been estimated that during Wigglesworth's own lifetime there was one copy for every thirty-five people in New England, which, given the size of the average family at the time, suggests that every third or fourth household must have possessed a copy.

Poetry by an American-born poet to be published: The first was *New Englands Crisis: or, a Brief of New Englands Lamentable Estate at present, compar'd with the former (but few) years of Prosperity* by Benjamin Tompson, published by John Foster of Boston in 1676. Tompson, born in Braintree, Mass., was former master of the Boston Latin School, though during King Philip's War, the conflict between the colonists and tribes of the Algonquian Confederation that was the subject of his poem, he was practicing as a physician. The work is important as history as well as poetry, being an eyewitness account of the first major war between settlers and Native Americans. It was of sufficient interest outside New England to become the first American publication to be reissued overseas, appearing the same year in London initially in a pirated edition titled *Sad and Deplorable News from*

New England . . . and then in an official version, with revisions and additions by Tompson, as *New Englands Tears for her Present Miseries*. Tompson was lauded as "the Renouned Poet of New England," but he produced only occasional poems thereafter, of which some thirty survive. He was content to return to Braintree as master of the local grammar school, raising eight children and serving also as physician and town clerk.

THE FIRST POKER

reference to by that name is contained in *Dragoon Campaign of the Rocky Mountains: Being a History of the Enlistment, Organization, and First Campaigns of the Regiment of United States Dragoons*. According to the anonymous author of this 1836 publication, the game was already popular in the South and West. Two later literary references push the date back a few years farther. In a book published in 1843, *The Exposure of the Arts and Miseries of Gambling*, reformed gambler Jonathan Green mentions a game of twenty-card poker that was played on a Mississippi riverboat headed for New Orleans in February 1833, while the stage comedian Joe Cowell's 1844 memoir *Thirty Years Passed Among the Players in England and America* ("Players" here referring to thespians, not gamblers) describes a game aboard another steamboat, the *Helen M'Gregor*, in which he traveled from Louisville to New Orleans in December 1829. He records:

> Close by us was a party playing poker. The aces were the highest denomination, then the kings, queens, jacks, and tens. The smaller cards were not used; those I have named are dealt out, and carefully concealed by the players from one another; old players pack them in their hands, and peep at them as if they were afraid to trust even themselves to look.

Here then is a further reference to the twenty-card game, which the indefatigable collector of pokerana Judge Oliver P. Carriere of New Orleans believed had originated in his native city, born of two foreign imports, *poque* and *As-Nas*. *Poque* is first described in the *Académie Universelle des Jeux*, published in Paris in 1718, coincidentally the year that New Orleans was settled, and was a game in which the hands with value were confined to single pairs, threes, and four of a kind. The Persian game *As-Nas*, which was probably brought to Louisiana by Frenchmen who had served in Persia, had two types of hand not existing in the French game, two pairs and the full house. When the two games became amalgamated, the French not surprisingly preferred to retain the name of their own game. At some point after 1800 *poque* morphed into *poker*, while the twenty-card deck seems to have been largely abandoned in favor of a full fifty-two-card deck by the 1845 edition of the card-players bible *Hoyle's Games* (though Carriere notes that a twenty-card deck was still played in New York as late as 1857).

The next major development was the addition of the draw, recorded in *Bohn's New Handbook of Games* of 1850. The straight and the straight flush had emerged by 1864, when they are noted in *American Hoyle*, which also made the earliest reference to stud poker, a game originated by cowpokes in the West.

Carriere says that jackpots are reputed to have originated in Toledo, Ohio, c. 1870, but there is no corroboration of this; he cites the first printed reference as appearing in the New York sporting journal *The Spirit of the Times* in 1874. Their purpose was a cure for cautiousness, which was beginning to afflict the game as serious players took to calculating the odds in relation to the size of the pot. Jackpots caught on in most parts of America except the Southern states, where gentlemen who cherished tradition considered it to be a game for wimps. It was in Texas that Hold 'Em, a game definitely not for the fainthearted, originated in the 1890s. A resolution of the Texas State Legislature of 11 May 2007 accords official recognition to Robstown, Tex., as its birthplace. With the rise of the World Poker Championship and the huge popularity of televised poker, Hold 'Em has become the game of choice for everyone from Friday-night nickel-and-dime players to the giants of the game, including a disproportionate number of Texans, who continue to dominate the tables at World Series of Poker tournaments in Las Vegas.

THE FIRST POLICE CAR

was an electric paddy wagon capable of speeds up to 16 mph that was built in 1899 by brothers Frank and C. H. Loomis for the Akron Police Department in Akron, Ohio. The original crew were George Wilson and Dick Bradbier, who had formerly driven Akron's two-horse wagon. It was Patrolman John Durkin, however, who had the distinction of making the world's first motorized arrest. This was of a drunk picked up on the corner of Exchange and Main streets for being a public nuisance. He appeared so delighted with the experience of riding to jail in an automobile that it dawned on the police that they had been deliberately set up. The vehicle remained in service for six years, surviving the great Akron riot of 1900 when a jeering mob hijacked the car, packed it to capacity, including the roof, and drove it recklessly around the downtown area before pushing it into the canal.

Pursuit car: The first occasion on which an automobile was used by police in a chase situation occurred in April 1899, when Sgt. McLeod of England's Northamptonshire County Police borrowed a Benz vehicle belonging to Jack Harrison to pursue a man on a bicycle who was selling forged tickets for the Barnum & Bailey Circus in Northampton. The chase continued up the Weedon Road until the fugitive was apprehended between Harpole and Fore. Referring to the mandatory speed limit, the *Autocar* drily commented. "We are not told if twelve miles an hour was exceeded at any part of the chase."

U.S.: A traffic squad was already in operation at St. Louis, Mo., by June 1905, when it was reported in the *Automobile* that the force was in need of faster and more powerful machines in order to overtake speed-limit violators.

Patrol car: The first was a Packard purchased in 1909 for $350 from his own pocket by Detroit police commissioner Frank Croul, after he had failed to dislodge the money from a parsimonious city treasurer. It began patrols on 1 December of that year and responded to 2,235 police calls in the next seven months. Detroit was the pioneer again with America's first radio-cars (SEE BELOW).

Radio-cars: The first were two ex-Royal Air Force Crossley tenders fitted with radio in 1921 by Scotland Yard's Flying Squad, the motorized arm of the Criminal Investigation Department of London's Metropolitan Police. Fitted with large rooftop aerials mounted on adjustable arms, they were known to the criminal fraternity as the "Flying Bedsteads." The Flying Squad took elaborate measures to disguise their conspicuous outline. The vehicles would appear in a different disguise daily, sometimes as milk trucks or railway lorries, sometimes as newspaper wagons or Post Office vans. A house code for street names and districts was devised in case of the interception of the message by similarly up-to-date radio-equipped criminals.

U.S.: The first were Detroit Police Department patrol cars equipped with radio at the direction of Commissioner William P. Rutledge in 1922. The transmitter was licensed as a regular radio station with the call letters KOP. Several times the Federal Communications Comission refused to renew the license, demanding on one occasion that the police department broadcast "entertainment during regular hours, with police calls interspersed." An exasperated Rutledge rejoined, "Do we have to play a violin solo before we dispatch the police to catch a criminal?" Communication was originally one-way only, from headquarters to car. Two-way radio patrol cars were introduced by the Bayonne Police Department of New Jersey in March 1933.

THE FIRST POLICE DEPARTMENT

functioning independently of the judiciary was established in Paris by a royal edict of March 1667, separating the judicial and police responsibilities of the Royal Watch. For the first time a lieutenant of police was appointed and charged with the security of the city. This post was filled for the next thirty years by Gabriel-Nicholas de la Reynie, who commanded a paramilitary force of 554 policemen, of whom 144 were mounted.

Originally the Paris Police Force was operated exclusively from the Châtelet, but in 1698 La Reynie's successor, the Marquis d'Argenson, established a police post at the Pont-Neuf, the first office to correspond to a station house.

The Paris police became a uniformed force by an ordinance of the prefect, Louis-Marie Debelleyme, dated 12 March 1829. This stated: "The purpose of uniform will be to constantly keep in the public's mind the presence of policemen at points where they will be of service; at the same time to compel them to intervene and restore order instead of vanishing into the crowd for fear of being noticed as often happens."

The uniforms were military in appearance and Paris police officers carried cavalry sabers. The prototype of modern police departments, civilian in organization, outlook, and uniform type, was London's Metropolitan Police, which held its initial parade on 26 September 1829. The uniforms consisted of a blue frock coat with brass buttons and a top hat reinforced with an interior framework of metal, intended to protect the wearer from violent assault but also to allow the wearer to stand on his hat to see over walls or reach high windows. Just how civilian the new guardians of the law felt themselves to be was illustrated by the fact that a number turned up for the inaugural muster carrying umbrellas. (A prohibitive order was issued the same evening that still remains in force.) It was London's "Met" on which the earliest police departments of the United States were modeled, despite the low caliber of many of its recruits: of the initial 2,800, no fewer than 2,238 were subsequently dismissed, 1,790 of them for being drunk on duty.

U.S.: The first police department was New York's Municipal Police (forerunner of the NYPD), established with an original strength of 800 on 2 June 1845. Unlike the Paris and London forces, however, there were no uniforms, as the wearing of such was considered demeaning for proud citizens of the young republic. When blue frock coats similar to London's were eventually adopted in 1853, several policemen were dismissed for refusing to wear them.

All appointments were political, with a requirement that the men live in the wards they patrolled (hence the Irish policed the Irish) and a maximum tenure of two years. The pay of $500 per annum was better than that of an unskilled worker, but the hours were intolerably long: 36 of every 48 hours were spent on duty and the policemen could be summoned for extra duties at processions, fires, or riots even during their meager time off. No training was given and the men were not armed until 1853, when a 22-inch nightstick was issued for urgent self-defense. As

in London, many of the early policemen were ill-disciplined and slovenly, commonly smoking cigars on duty. Before 1853 there was no literacy requirement; even then the test consisted of reading the title of a major newspaper. The captains were not much better; Mike Murray of the First Ward was a former saloon keeper notorious for having bitten off half of Paudeen McLaughlin's nose in a barroom brawl. Corruption, then and later, as in all the metropolitan departments, was endemic.

Police detective: The first was former professional criminal, convict, and informer Eugène François Vidocq (SEE ALSO **private detective agency**), appointed head of the French Sûreté in 1812. Detectives were first appointed in the United States by Boston's police chief Francis Tukey in 1851. The NYPD had its initial 20 detectives in 1857 and Chicago created its Detective Force in 1860.

THE FIRST

POLICE SWAT (SPECIAL WEAPONS AND TACTICS) TEAMS

were formed at the instigation of officer John Nelson of the Los Angeles Police Department in 1969 in response to a spate of sniping incidents directed at both police officers and the public. The original Platoon D, as the unit was designated, comprised fifteen teams of four men each. The first SWAT operation took place on 9 December 1969 when a 4-hour confrontation with members of the Black Panthers ended with three casualties on each side. It was the LAPD's SWAT team that engaged in one of the most highly publicized of such operations, the siege of the house at East 54th Street and Compton Avenue occupied by the revolutionary group the Symbionese Liberation Army on 17 May 1974. The SLA defied twenty-six appeals to surrender and fired 3,772 shots at the besiegers before the building caught fire, resulting in the death of six of their number.

THE FIRST **POLICEWOMAN**

was Lola Baldwin, formerly director of the YMCA's Traveler's Aid in Portland, Ore., who was sworn in as a detective of the Portland Police Department on 1 April 1908. Her official title was Superintendent of the Women's Auxiliary to the Police Department for the Protection of Girls and as a divisional head she was awarded the salary of a captain, which at $150 per month meant that she was paid $35 more than male detectives (an unusual inversion of the then-standard practice of paying women less for equal work). In her first monthly report she wrote that her division's "chief aim and purpose is to *prevent* downfall and crime among women and girls." Samuel Walker, author of *A Critical History of Police Reform* (1977), has observed that this represented "a distinct departure from the traditional police role" in adding a preventive role in what was more generally a retributive profession. However liberal Baldwin's approach may sound to socially sensitive modern ears, in practice her fulfilment of it could be heavy-handed. Born before the Civil War, she embodied the attitudes of an earlier generation and her prescription for preventing indelicate behavior between the sexes was to keep them apart as much as possible. To this end she waged a vigorous campaign against most of the recreational venues frequented by the working-class young, especially carnivals and shooting alleys, dance halls, vaudeville theaters, and movie houses. She strove to have women barred from saloons, contrived to have singer Sophie Tucker banned from performing, railed against girls riding pillion on motorcycles and joyriding in taxis, closed down fortune-tellers and clairvoyants, prosecuted cross-dressers, cleared the streets of disabled people selling merchandise, eliminated marriage agencies, and prevented mixed bathing at swimming pools and the wearing of one-piece bathing costumes.

All this whirlwind of suppressive activity, however, was subordinate to Baldwin's continuous and relentless campaign against prostitution. Her proselytizing seems to have been influential in changing public perceptions, not only in Portland but far beyond, of prostitutes from victims to be treated with a degree of compassion to criminals willfully spreading venereal disease. Largely at her behest the city's judges stopped fining and releasing them and started sentencing them instead to detention, often for indeterminate periods. At times Baldwin behaved as if she was above the law, detaining young girls without charge in breach of habeas corpus and abrogating the right of the juvenile court to determine whether there was a case to answer.

In her defense, it must be said that Baldwin had the full support of successive mayors and police chiefs and most of the judiciary. Venereal disease was one of the major health scourges of the time and her efforts to prevent young girls from losing their virginity, and to ensure that afflicted women were locked away and treated, probably did achieve a diminution of the disease. Her most fulfilling role was as a federal agent during World War I, when as supervisor of the law enforcement division set up to cover the whole Pacific coast and Arizona, with four hundred policewomen under her command, she was able to employ similar measures to prevent the spread of venereal disease among troops in training camps and to do so with the full backing of martial law. Although she returned to the Portland Police Department after the war, she found less support for her essentially nineteenth-century views on morality as society's norms changed with the advent of the roaring twenties. She retired in 1922 to run a bakery and campaign from the sidelines against such depravities as women smoking and prom nights at high schools.

Lola Baldwin's legacy was to have established a new profession for middle-class women (seventeen police departments had women officers by 1913, largely owing to her considerable powers of persuasion), even though in the process she blocked avenues of employment for their working-class sisters. "Her neo-Victorian moral judgmentalism and protective social control ordinances," wrote her biographer Gloria E. Myers, in *A Municipal Mother* (1995), "eliminated female access to a variety of urban amusement jobs because of potential ties to the vice trade."

While Lola Baldwin was designated a detective, her division was separate from the Portland Police Department's detective bureau and her work, like that of other pioneer policewomen, was largely confined to matters concerning women and children. The first woman detective employed in a detective bureau on general investigative duties was former NYPD police matron Isabella Goodwin, who was promoted to Acting Detective Sergeant First Grade on 1 March 1912 after having spent some two years on undercover work. Her promotion and new status as a full member of the Detective Bureau, paid at the male yearly rate of $2,250, followed a spectacular success when she solved the Trinity Place robbery. The thieves had made off with $25,000 and Detective Sergeant Goodwin, forty-seven-year-old mother of four, disguised herself as a domestic to get a live-in job with two women she suspected of being connected to the main suspects. The information she gleaned while working in the house confirmed that the suspects had indeed done the robbery and she was able to discover where they were hiding out, leading to their arrest. Goodwin's status was a rare one, then and for many years to come; generally, as Josephine Nelson wrote in the mid-1930s, "the American policewoman is a social worker with police powers." Goodwin was privileged in her rank, as there were no other women sergeants in the NYPD until 1965 and then only after a lawsuit forced equality of opportunity. Nowhere in the United States were policewomen eligible to take the promotion exams open to their male colleagues.

Uniformed policewomen: The first were Mary Allen and E. F. Harburn of Britain's Women's Police Volunteers. Members of this privately sponsored body, raised at the outset of World War I to provide policing services wherever the exigencies of war created abnormal social pressures, wore a dark blue tunic with shoulder straps bearing the letters wpv in silver, a flat cap with silver braid for officers and a hard hat in blue felt for other ranks. The uniform, designed by WPV officer Henrietta Robley-Brown, was one of two that had been submitted to Queen Mary for selection on 16 November 1914. Her choice was then sanctioned by the Metropolitan Police commissioner, Sir Edward Henry. Ten days later Miss Allen and Miss Harburn were the first WPV recruits to assume active duty on completion of their training, reporting to the Provost-Marshal at Grantham, Lincolnshire, on 27 November. Their principal task lay in controlling the effects on local civilians of a new army camp containing 18,000 men, the population of the town itself being only 20,000. Up to that point the WPV had operated with

the blessing of the Metropolitan Police commissioner but had enjoyed no official standing. The date that Miss Allen and Miss Harburn arrived at Grantham, in response to a formal request by the military authorities, can be regarded as marking the real entry of women into uniformed police work.

In December 1915, having been posted to Hull, Miss Allen and Miss Harburn became the first women sworn in as police constables. Working directly under the chief constable, they were now vested with full powers of arrest and subject to the rules and discipline of Hull Police Force. In 1919 Mary Allen became commandant of what had been renamed the Women's Police Service and continued in that role for more than twenty years, traveling widely and advising foreign governments on the introduction of women police. She had the unusual distinction for a police officer of having served two terms of imprisonment in her younger days: As a militant suffragette she had on one occasion tried to force her way into the Houses of Parliament and on another had smashed the windows of the Home Office (the executive department responsible for policing).

U.S.: Whereas in Britain nearly all policewomen, including those in London's prestigious Metropolitan Police (from 1919), were uniformed from the outset, in the United States the reluctance of police chiefs to put them into uniform reflected the ambivalent attitude toward women in the force. Probably the first police department to prescribe a uniform was the NYPD in 1935, though significantly the women had to pay for it themselves and it was not for regular wear. The only occasions they wore it was when patrolling places like beaches, where visitors unfamiliar with policewomen needed something more than a badge to help them recognize them as official guardians of the law.

Even when women did win the right to wear uniforms in the 1940s and '50s, their status was still lower than that of male colleagues, mainly because they were confined to duties that did not require physical strength or the use of firearms and were discouraged from making arrests (a male colleague being summoned to assist). A breakthrough in the quest for equality was made in the late 1960s by two officers of the Indianapolis Police Department, Elizabeth Coffal and Betty Blankenship, who petitioned for more than a year to be allowed to go on patrol-car duty. Finally in September 1968 the police chief grudgingly relented, despite what he called "departmental hostility." They were given 24 hours' notice and no training and were sent out together rather than each being teamed with an experienced patrolman. Assigned to patrol car 47, they were given all the worst jobs by the male dispatchers, including handling long-dead corpses. "Instead of hurting us, it was beneficial because we got the worst at the beginning," recalled Coffal. Overcoming all the obstacles placed in their way, the team in car 47 proved they could cope in a traditionally male role and by so doing helped to bring about the change in attitude that finally allowed women to move into regular, non-gender-specific police work.

Portland, Ore., where women policing had begun in 1908, pioneered again when Penny Orazetti Harrington was sworn in as the first **woman police chief** of a metropolitan city in the United States on 24 January 1985.

THE FIRST **POLISH IMMIGRANTS**

to America were five skilled glassmakers who arrived at the Jamestown Colony, in latter-day Virginia, together with three "Dutchmen" (probably Germans) aboard the supply ship *Mary and Margaret* on 1 October 1608. Their identity remains uncertain, as they are referred to in contemporary records only as "Robert, a Polonian," "Matthew, a Polander," "Molasco, the Polander." Karl Wachtl, in *Polonia w Ameryce* (1927), purports to give their full names, as Zbigniew Stafanski, Jan Mata, Stanislav Sadowski, Karol Zrenica, and Jan Bogdan, citing as his source a broadside *Wiesci Polskie* ("Polish News") he states was published in London in 1631. No trace of this fugitive document has been found.

The Poles established the first manufactory in America, a glasshouse built about a mile from the settlement (qv) at Jamestown, and about the same time inaugurated the production of other primary wares. Thus we learn that when the *Mary and Margaret* returned to England in December 1608 she carried with her the first American exports, described as "tryals of Pitch, Tarre, Glasse, Frankincense, Sope

Ashes with Clapboard and Waynscot." Capt. John Smith, president of the Jamestown Colony, recorded that their output also included resin, cordage, masts, and yards. He also noted that it was only the Poles and the "Dutchmen" and "some dozen other" who did any hard work in the nascent colony, "for all the rest were poore Gentlemen, Tradsmcn [*sic*], Servingmen, libertines, and such like." Certainly he had cause for gratitude to at least one of their members, "Robert the Polonian," who saved his life during an assault by Indians. Sadly Robert was himself killed by Indians during the attack on Jamestown in 1622.

By 1619, when America's first legislature (qv) was established, there were about fifty Poles working in the colony. When it was declared that they would not be enfranchised, they downed tools. This has sometimes been called the first strike in America, but as the Poles were self-employed it is probably more apt to describe it as an act of civil disobedience. Such was the value of their industry to the colony, it rapidly brought the outcome desired. Not only were they granted full civil rights, but by the same order of the court of 21 July 1619 it was decreed "that some young men shall be put unto them to learn their skill and knowledge therein for the benefits of the country hereafter." Thus began the apprenticeship system in America, cornerstone of crafts and manufactures for three and a half centuries to come.

THE FIRST **POPCORN**

was not, as legend has it, introduced to the Pilgrim Fathers by friendly Native Americans. Popcorn is one of six major maize types (the others being pod corn, sweet corn, flour corn, dent corn, and flint corn) and was unknown on the Eastern Seaboard of America in colonial times. It therefore follows that popcorn was not known to the indigenous tribes of New England, nor was it served to the starving Pilgrims of Plymouth Plantation at the "first Thanksgiving" in 1621, a picturesque myth propagated in American grade schools to conform to modern orthodoxies about the ingenuity as well as the humanity of the people no longer called Indians. The only eyewitness account of the Thanksgiving at Plymouth, by Edward Winslow, records but two types of food: fowl and deer. Indeed, as Andrew F. Smith has observed in his scholarly treatise *Popped Culture* (1999), the elevation of Native Americans from ignoble savage to spiritual being in harmony with nature only began once white Americans had finished killing them off. He might also have mentioned that the source of the Plymouth popcorn legend, Jane Adams's *Standish of Standish: A Story of the Pilgrims*, happened to be published in the same year, 1889, as the last major battle between U.S. forces and the native population.

Corn had certainly been popped by Indians in pre-Columbian times, but not by North American Indians: Archaeological evidence shows that it was prevalent among the Amerindians of Central America and known to the Aztecs. Early Spanish accounts refer to it being ground into flour after popping, so it does not appear to have been eaten in the form in which it is best known today.

Popcorn was probably introduced to the United States by American sailors returning from Chile, since it became known here as Valparaiso corn, and by the mid-1820s it was being sold by seedsmen. The earliest known reference to popped corn in print is from the *Yale Literary Magazine* of January 1843, though it seems likely that popping would have begun almost as soon as the strain was cultivated some twenty years earlier. The first recipe was appended to Daniel Jay Browne's *The Hasty-Pudding: A Poem, with a Memoir of Maize, or Indian Corn* (New York, 1847): "Take a gill, a half pint, or more of Valparaiso or Pop Corn, and put in a frying-pan, slightly buttered, or rubbed with lard. Hold the pan over a fire so as constantly to shir or shake the corn within, and in a few minutes each kernel will *pop*, or turn inside out." He concluded by saying that as soon as the popcorn was ready, sugar or salt could be added.

Two claims were advanced for the first corn popper, though neither until many years later. One was that the earliest were made by the Bromwell Brush Wire Goods Co. that had been founded in Cincinnati in 1819; no date is assigned to "earliest." The other was that one Francis P. Knowlton of Hopkinton, N.H., had fashioned his poppers from wire netting he obtained from hardware retailer Amos Kelly in 1838. His mesh box with a wire handle had the distinct advantage over fry-pans that the exploding corn would not fly about the room, but Knowlton lacked the salesman's gift and it was not until Kelly and his son took over that the product became a success. Certainly the date seems about right, just as corn popping was beginning to emerge as a popular family recreation. Browne mentioned corn poppers as "a very ingenious contrivance" nine years later.

Considering that ready-made popcorn had been sold on the streets since the 1840s, it took a curiously long time to invade what most people consider to be its natural habitat, the movie theater. Not until 1928 did David Wallerstein, manager of one of the Chicago chain of Balaban & Katz theaters, think of this way of vastly increasing profits. According to King Vidor, Hollywood's most durable director (sixty-seven years from first to last film), audiences at silent movies were too engrossed to do anything but gaze enraptured at the silver screen. "Popcorn and necking only came into pictures with the talkies," he asserted.

THE FIRST POP GROUP

of the current vocal and instrumental genre was the band Gene Vincent and His Blue Caps, a five-man group from Nashville, Tenn., comprising Dickie Harrell (drums), Jack Neal (string bass), Willie Williams (rhythm guitar), Cliff Gallup (lead guitar), and lead singer Gene Vincent. Their first recordings, "Be-Bop-a-Lula" and "Woman Love," were recorded by Capitol Records on 4 May 1956 and released the following month. While the former climbed rapidly into the American charts, "Woman Love" achieved almost equal distinction by being banned by the BBC in Britain. An LP album, *Bluejean Bop*, came out later the same year. The group disbanded at the end of 1956 but re-formed early in 1957 with Johnny Meeks, Bill Mack, and Tommy "Bubba" Facenda replacing Neal, Williams, and Gallup. They split up again in 1959, having released sixteen singles, thirteen EPs, and five LPs.

THE FIRST **POP MUSIC CHART**

based on record sales was published in *Billboard* (New York) for 4 January 1936. There were separate listings for the 10 bestsellers of the three leading record companies. Chart toppers for the week ended 30 December 1935 were "Stop, Look and Listen" by Joe Venuti and Orchestra (Columbia); "Quicker Than You Can Say" by Ozzie Nelson and Orchestra (Brunswick); and "The Music Goes Round" by Tommy Dorsey and Orchestra (RCA-Victor). The lists were consolidated as the Top 10 from 20 July 1940, producing the first all-out No. 1: "I'll Never Smile Again" by Tommy Dorsey with vocals by Frank Sinatra.

The Billboard chart subsequently expanded to Top 15 (7 November 1947), Top 30 (4 June 1948), and top 100 (10 August 1955), becoming the "Hot 100" on 10 August 1958.

Album chart: The first was published by *Billboard* on 15 March 1940, when the chart topper was *King Cole Trio* with Nat King Cole.

THE FIRST **POPSICLE**

reference to, is contained in *Mrs Mary Eales's Receipts*, published in London in 1718. In this she gives the first recipe in English for ice cream, which concludes with advice for making popsicles in the same freezing receptacle using a mixture of lemon, spring water, and sugar. As Mrs. Eales had formerly been court confectioner to Queen Anne (reigned 1702–14), it is possible that lemon popsicles had been enjoyed by the sovereign herself, though she is better known for clandestine consumption of gin from a silver teapot.

It was over two hundred years before the popsicle became a branded product as the Epsicle. An eleven-year-old San Francisco schoolboy named Frank Emmerson had mixed himself a lemonade from powder one exceptionally cold day in the winter of 1905, forgot to drink it, and left it on the porch overnight with the spoon standing in the glass. Come morning he tugged on the spoon and lifted a perfect popsicle from the glass. Emmerson became a realtor in neighboring Oakland and in 1922 he introduced his ice lollipop at a local fireman's ball, where it was received

with such acclamation that he decided to launch it commercially. This he did at a concession on Neptune Beach in Alameda, Calif., the following year, offering seven flavors of what he billed as "the drink on a stick." He was granted a patent on 19 August 1924 and the description indicates that Emmerson made his popsicles in test tubes, a shape that they still retain today. The name change from Epsicle was made at the suggestion of his children. Conditions in the real estate business, though, were unfavorable, and sales of the drink on a stick were not sufficient to keep the family going. In 1925 Emmerson sold his rights in the product to the Joe Lowe food company of New York. "I was flat and had to liquidate all my assets," he explained later, adding ruefully, "I haven't been the same since."

THE FIRST **POSTAGE METER**

authorized for the franking of business mail and other bulk mail was devised by Charles A. Kahrs and installed in the lobby of the General Post Office at Christiania (now Oslo), Norway, for public use on 24 August 1900. It was withdrawn as unsatisfactory in December, but a fresh attempt at metered mail was made with a machine invented by Karl Uckermann and manufactured in 1903 by Krag Maskinfabrik of Christiania. The frank-dies were supplied to licensed users of the machines by the Norwegian postal authorities and covered the value, town of origin, and date. The first machines came into use on 15 June 1903 and the system continued in operation until January 1905. During that time three machines were in use by private firms and four by the Norwegian Post Office.

The first country to adopt metered mail on an ongoing basis was New Zealand, where in 1909 the postal authorities accepted for public use a machine patented five years earlier by Ernest Moss of Christchurch, founder of the Automatic Stamping Co. Ltd.

U.S.: The first meter in actual use was patented on 14 October 1902 by Arthur Hill Pitney, who formed the Pitney Postal Machine Co., later the Pitney-Bowes Postage Meter Co., the same year. Pitney's third, improved model was used for franking mail despatched from the office of the third assistant postmaster general in Washington, D.C., between November 1903 and March 1904. As a result of this test, permit imprints, which meant franking without cancellation, were authorized in lieu of adhesive stamps from 1 October 1904, but applied only to third- and fourth-class mail (mainly circulars and catalogs). The use of meters for first-class letter mail, which required a postmarking as well as a stamping element, was authorized by Congress in 1920. On 16 November of that year the first American business to meter its general correspondence was the Pitney-Bowes Co. itself, forwarding the franked and canceled mail via the local Stamford, Conn., post office. Advertising slogans and meter tape for packages too big to pass through the meter were introduced in 1929. By 1959 revenue from metered mail exceeded that of postage stamps and pre-stamped postal stationary.

THE FIRST **POSTAGE STAMPS**

were struck on the *Billets de port payé* used by Jean-Jacques Velayer's Petite Poste that operated in Paris from 8 August 1653. No examples of the *billets* survive, but they are believed to have consisted of bands of paper bearing a printed device indicating postage paid. They sold for 5 centimes each. At this time prepayment was exceptional for general posts, the more usual practice being for the receiver of the letter to pay for the postage fee. (SEE ALSO **mailboxes**.)

Adhesive postage stamps: The first were the Penny Blacks and Twopenny Blues officially issued by the British Post Office on 6 May 1840. A few had been sent through the post during the preceding days, and the earliest surviving example of a used Penny Black is on a letter addressed to Peckham (a suburb of London) and postmarked Bath, 2 May 1840. This was sold at Harmers Auctions in Lugano, Switzerland, in 1991 for the world-record price for a postage stamp of £1,350,000 ($2,370,000). The stamps were designed by William Wyon and Henry Corbould, engraved by Charles & Frederick Heath, and printed by Perkins, Bacon & Co. They did not state the country of issue as the portrait of Queen Victoria was considered sufficient identification, and the United Kingdom remains the only stamp issuer to retain this anonymity. The original suggestion for adhesive postage stamps had been made by Postmaster General Rowland Hill in a pamphlet on postal reform published in 1837.

U.S.: The first were rectangular 3¢ recess-printed blacks issued by the New York City Dispatch Post on 1 February 1842. They bore a portrait of George Washington in an oval vignette containing the name of the postal service and the denomination (a later issue incorporated UNITED STATES in the inscription). The stamps, and the local postal service in Manhattan for which they represented prepayment, were the idea of Henry Thomas Windsor of Hoboken, N.J. At this time the U.S. Post Office charged extra for household deliveries, so local carriers in most large cities seized the opportunity to undercut it.

When uniform postage rates by weight were introduced by the U.S. Post Office in March 1845 (SEE **mail service**), postmasters began issuing their own stamps to signify prepayment. The first of these Postmasters' Provisionals was issued in New York City, the earliest known postmarked example being dated 15 July. Others were issued at St. Louis, Mo., in November and the following year at Alexandria, Va.; Annapolis, Md.; Boscawen, N.H.; Brattleboro, Vt.; Lockport, N.Y.; Millbury, Mass.; and Providence, R.I. A cover with its provisional from Alexandria became the first philatelic item to sell for $1 million at an auction in Geneva, Switzerland, on 8 May 1981.

The first official U.S. Post Office stamps were the 5¢ orange, brown, and red-orange Benjamin Franklin and the 10¢ dark brown George Washington, both imperforate and issued on 1 July 1847. They were inscribed POST OFFICE above the oval vignette containing the portrait and UNITED STATES below it.

Pictorial postage stamp: The first stamps to illustrate something other than portraits were the 1d, 2d, and 3d "Sydney Views" issued by the New South Wales Post Office on 1 January 1850. They were designed and engraved by Robert Clayton.

U.S.: The first pictorial stamps without a presidential or Franklin portrait were the 2¢ Post Horse and Rider and 3¢ Locomotive issued on 27 March 1869, followed in the next few weeks by the 10¢ Shield and Eagle, 12¢ *Adriatic* (a ship), 15¢ Columbus landing, 24¢ Declaration of Independence, and 30¢ Shield, Eagle, and

Flags. For the world's first pictorial series (i.e., all on the same theme) SEE **commemorative stamp, U.S.,** BELOW.

Perforated stamp: The first was Britain's Penny Red issued on 28 January 1854. The originator of the idea, Henry Archer, had constructed his first perforating apparatus in 1847, but this only made slits along the sides of the stamps. By the end of the following year, however, he had adapted it so that a succession of small holes was punched in the paper.

U.S: The 1¢ blue Franklin; the 3¢ Washington in various hues of rose, red, claret, and carmine; the 5¢ Jefferson in various hues of red and brown; and the 10¢ green Washington were all issued on 6 February 1857.

Commemorative stamp: The first was the 2-pfennig green and carmine pictorial, issued by the Frankfurt-am-Main Privat-Brief-Verkehr (District Post) to commemorate the 25th anniversary of the German Federal and Jubilee Shooting Contest, Frankfurt, July 1887.

The first commemorative stamp issued by any national postal service was the New South Wales 1 shilling Centenary Issue of January 1888, marking 100 years of European settlement.

U.S.: A set of sixteen pictorials ranging in value from 1¢ to $5 and illustrating the life and voyages of Christipher Columbus was produced to celebrate the World's Columbian Exposition of 1893, which itself commemorated the 500th anniversary (a year late) of Columbus's discovery of the New World. They were issued on 2 January 1893 and were also the world's first pictorial series on a single theme.

Christmas stamp: The first was a 2¢ pictorial bearing a map of the world, issued by the Canadian Post Office on 7 December 1898 and originally designed only to mark the advent of Imperial Penny Postage. According to Sir John Henniker Heaton, then postmaster general, it had been intended to introduce Imperial Penny Postage on 9 November, the Prince of Wales's birthday. When Sir John explained the new scheme to the Queen, she inquired when it was to come into force. "We think of introducing it on the Prince's birthday," he replied. The Queen, never too enamored of the philandering Prince of Wales, asked coldly, "And what Prince?" The postmaster general responded without hesitation, "The Prince of Peace, Your Majesty." The Canadian stamp, which had

already been designed to include the date, was thereupon changed to read "Xmas 1898."

U.S.: A 4¢ green and red Wreath and Candles was issued 1 November 1962.

Stamp machines: These were devised by the Stamp Distribution Syndicate and fixed on pillar boxes in London by special arrangement with the British Post Office in May 1891. The machine supplied penny postage stamps (the ordinary rate for an inland letter), which were slotted into the back of a memo book containing sixty-four pages of notes, a number of full-page advertisements, and a calendar for 1891. There was no charge for the book, the cost of which was covered by advertising revenue. The stamps had the initials SDS punctured through Queen Victoria's neck.

The first Post Office stamp vending machine was invented by New Zealand mail clerk Robert J. Dickie and installed at Wellington Head Post Office on 15 June 1905. It sold 3,902 stamps before a customer figured out that the machine was unable to distinguish between a penny and a lead disk. Dickie returned to the drawing board to produce a new, tamper-proof version that was eventually sold worldwide.

U.S.: The stamp vending machine was introduced at the General Post Office in New York City on 6 May 1948.

Stamp books: The first were issued by the Luxembourg Post Office in 1895.

U.S.: The 1894 George Washington 2¢ stamp was issued in booklets of 25¢, 49¢, and 97¢ at one cent over face value on 16 April 1900.

Airmail stamps: The first official issue was by the Italian Post Office in 1917, when 200,000 25¢ Express Letter stamps were overprinted with the words ESPERIMENTO POSTA AEREA—MAGGIO 1917—TORINO-ROMA ROMA-TORINO for the experimental airmail service operated between Rome and Turin in May of that year.

U.S.: The 24¢ airmail stamp introduced by the U.S. Post Office on 13 May 1918 was also the world's first airmail definitive stamp. It featured a Curtiss Jenny biplane as used by the Air Mail Service. This was printed upside down on some sheets, now among the most celebrated philatelic errors.

Self-adhesive postage stamps: The first were the circular "gold coins" issued by Tonga on 17 June 1963.

U.S.: The imperforate pre-canceled Christmas special 10¢ Dove Weather Vane Atop Mount Vernon, inscribed PEACE ON EARTH and issued on 15 November 1974, was the first self-adhesive postage stamp issued by the U.S. Post Office.

Freeform stamps: The first were self-adhesives issued in fourteen denominations each with a different irregular shape by Sierra Leone on 10 February 1964.

U.S.: Die-cut imperforate 55¢ and 33¢ Love Stamps, each depicting a different heart-shaped garland, were issued on 20 and 28 January 1999, respectively.

SEE ALSO **stamp collector**.

THE FIRST **POSTCARD**

was issued by the Austrian Post Office on 1 October 1869, following a suggestion by Dr. Emmanuel Herrmann of the Wiener Neustadt Military Academy that had been published in the *Neue Freie Presse* the previous January. The straw-colored official prepaid cards were imprinted with a 2-kreuzer stamp. During the first two months of issue no fewer than 2,930,000 cards were sold, part of the attraction being that no extra charge was made beyond the cost of the stamp.

U.S.: The first privately issued postcard was copyrighted by John P. Charlton of Philadelphia on 17 December 1861. The rights were acquired by Philadelphia stationer Hyman L. Lipman, who issued the cards printed with a decorative border pattern and the words LIPMAN'S POSTAL CARD, PATENT APPLIED FOR. It has generally been assumed that these preceded the Austrian Post Office's official issue of 1869, but the Metropolitan Postcard Club of New York says there is no record of the Lipman cards having been placed on the market before then. The earliest known postally used example is postmarked Richmond, Ind., 25 October 1870. The Lipman cards remained on sale until the introduction of the first U.S. Post Office official prestamped postcard on 13 May 1873.

Picture postcard: The first was engraved by twenty-one-year-old Franz Rorich of Nuremberg and published in Zürich by J. H. Locher in 1872. It showed six small views of Zürich and was followed by two other cards each with three views of the city. During the same year Rorich and Locher produced view cards of Geneva, Basel, Schaffhausen, Rorschach, and Neuchâtel, all Swiss towns, and of Lindau and Nuremberg in Germany. Rorich's 1872 Nuremberg card, which shows the city from the Mohrentor Gate, is the oldest surviving view card in the world. Collectors have identified earlier examples of official post office cards bearing pictorial advertisements and decorated field postcards of the Franco-Prussian War, but these cannot be regarded as true picture postcards.

U.S.: The earliest known postally used, dated card is a view of Buffalo, N.Y., one of a set of seven published by Matthews Northrup Co., engravers of that city, and postmarked 27 January 1893. Viewcards were also being produced in 1893 by the Souvenir Postal Card Co. of Albany, N.Y. Three of their views of Pike's Peak, "Summit of Pike's Peak" in red and black, "From Summit House" in red, and a colored multiview also labeled "From Summit House," are known to date from that year. Two sets of official souvenir cards of the World's Columbian Exposition printed by the American Lithographic Co. of New York for Charles W. Goldsmith of Chicago, agent for the cards, bear a printed date 1892. As official cards it seems unlikely that they would have been on sale before the Exposition opened on 1 May 1893, but four "pre-official" postcards are known to have been sold by Goldsmith from vending machines at 5¢ for two before the opening; how much earlier is not recorded. These are full-color lithograph artist's renderings in wash of the Fisheries Building, the Women's Building, the Agricultural Building, and the model of the battleship *Illinois* at the U.S. Navy exhibit. The likelihood is that production of picture postcards in the United States began in 1892, probably by both the Matthews Northrup Co. and the American Lithograph Co. (and possibly the Souvenir Postal Card Co.), but there is no hard evidence that they were on sale until early in the following year.

Photographically illustrated picture postcard: The earliest known is a German *Gruss aus* ("Greetings from") view of the lake at Schwarzwald, posted on 6 July 1889. The monochrome photograph measures 3" x 2" and is reproduced by the halftone process. The first in natural colors were issued in Germany by the Rotophot Co. of Berlin in Prof. Miethe's

Naturfarbenphotographie process. The earliest known example is a view of an unidentified village and is postmarked Hamburg, 16 October 1904.

Picture postcard art reproductions: These are believed to have been issued first in Italy c. 1889. The earliest surviving dated example is a card published in Florence in 1891, showing Raphael's *Madonna della Seggiola*.

THE FIRST **POST-IT NOTES**

were launched nationwide by 3M of St. Paul, Minn., in 1979. The special gum that enables the ubiquitous little yellow paper rectangles to "stick without sticking" had been created by chance in 1970 when 3M's Dr. Spencer Sylver was researching a completely different product. Although he sent samples of the adhesive to other research labs in the 3M group, no one saw its potential and several years were to pass before another company researcher, Arthur Fry, found a means of putting it to purely personal use. As a member of a local choir, Fry needed to find a way to hold page markers temporarily in place in his music book without sticking them down. He applied a thin streak of Dr. Sylver's unwanted gum to the markers, attached them to the pages to be marked, and was later able to pull them off without leaving any soiling. What worked for marking music books would later find hundreds of different uses in offices and homes throughout the world.

The idea might not have progressed farther, however, but for 3M's enlightened policy of "bootlegging." This meant that all its research scientists were allowed, and had been since the 1920s, to spend up to 15 percent of their time on personal projects. Fry says that this creates a culture of creativity, amply demonstrated in his own case. At first he thought of the notelets solely as bookmarks. It was only when one day he needed to comment briefly on a report and wrote a note on a Post-It, stuck it on the report, and received his boss's reply on the same Post-It, that he realized their real use was for short written comments, annotations, or reminders. Using his "bootlegging" time, Fry was able to iron out the various development problems, but when the product was test-marketed as "Peel and Press Studs" in 1977 the public remained unimpressed.

Not only a change of name was needed but also an explanatory brochure detailing the many uses for Post-It notes before success was assured, with 90 percent of users saying they would buy the product again.

Even then you could only buy them in one noncolor, white. It took a woman's touch to bring in the pastel hues favored today by most aficionados of Post-It notes. Following her purchase of Britain's stationery chain Ryman in 1981, entrepreneur Jennifer d'Abo happened upon the somewhat dull white stickers at a Frankfurt trade fair and agreed to introduce Post-Its to the United Kingdom provided they could be produced in pink, blue, and the now ubiquitous yellow.

THE FIRST **POTATO CHIPS**

as we know them today are described by Louis XVI's chef Louis Eustache Ude in *The French Cook*, published in London in 1813. The recipe is for potatoes cut in "the shape of large corks" and cut into slices "as thick as two-penny pieces." These are to be fried either in clarified butter or, preferably, in goose fat, until "a fine brown colour, and crisp," drained on a towel and sprinkled with salt. The telling features of this recipe, separating it from recipes for French fries, are the shape (large cork) and thickness (that of a twopenny piece). This is where culinary scholarship joins hands with numismatics. The twopenny piece, a copper coin first minted in 1797, was about 2 millimeters thick in depth. Ude would have encountered them when he fled revolutionary France and took employment in England with the Earl of Sefton. The thickness is precisely right for a good crunchy chip, especially one deep-fried in goose fat.

U.S.: Culinary historians have been unable to agree whether the recipe given in Mary Randolph's *Virginia House-wife* (Washington, D.C., 1825) is for French fries or potato chips. Contrarily she directs that large potatoes should be sliced "a quarter of an inch thick, or cut . . . in shavings round and round, as you would peal [*sic*] a lemon." Slices a quarter of an inch thick are not potato chips as dunked in dip; on the other hand shavings could constitute a genuine American-style chip. Or was this neither, but a recipe for sautéed potatoes?

Historians of popular culture, unlike their culinary counterparts, have no such uncertainties. The potato chip, they assert, was invented by chef George Crum, African American according to some sources, Native American according to others (or both, per multi-culturalists), at Montgomery Hall in Saratoga Springs, N.Y., or, if you prefer, at Moon Lake House in the same resort town. All seem agreed on the year, 1853, but only one provides a precise date, 24 August. According to legend on this or some other day either Cdre. Cornelius Vanderbilt, or an unnamed guest of lesser celebrity, sent back an order of French fries to the kitchen because they were cut too thick. Displaying the temperament for which chefs are notorious, Crum then sliced some potatoes ridiculously thin and fried them, the idea being to expose Vanderbilt or whoever to ridicule when he attempted to spear them with a fork. But, so says the story, he picked them up in his fingers and pronounced them delicious.

There is no contemporary evidence to support this picturesque version of the origin of potato chips, but George Crum undoubtedly existed and a portrait photograph survives. Most sources agree on his irascible nature and several refer to five (simultaneous) wives with whom he set up a restaurant called Crumbs House at the south end of Moon Lake after quitting whichever hotel he had or hadn't invented chips at. Here he is said to have placed a basket of chips, which he dubbed "potato crunchies," on every table. One other piece of hard evidence lends some credibility to Crum's involvement in the creation of what some have castigated as America's original junk food. This is a carton labeled Saratoga Chips, dating from around the end of the nineteenth century, illustrating Crumbs House on its lid. So it would seem that he or his successors did produce potato chips for sale through retail outlets.

It is not known whether this predated 1895, the year in which William Tappendon of Cleveland, Ohio, began making them in his kitchen and packing them for sale in local stores, later converting a barn at the back of his house into a "chip factory." These, together with the produce of subsequent manufacturers, were dispensed in bulk from barrels or glass display cases. First in the United States to package chips in bags, originally of waxed paper, was Laura Scudder of Monterey Park, Calif., in 1926. The waxed paper was ironed to shape it into bags, filled by hand, and ironed again to seal. Chips in bags were already a major seller in Britain by this date, having been introduced by Carter's Crisps of London in 1913. (Carter had first encountered chips in France, which lends credence to their Gallic provenance.) The oldest surviving bag of chips, a Smith's Crisps glassine package dating from the 1930s, still containing its original contents (including a twist of salt in blue waxed paper), is preserved in the Robert Opie Collection at the Museum of Brands, Packaging & Advertising in London.

In the United States chips did not match the popularity they had won in England until after World War II, the catalyst being the invention of California Dip in 1954. This was an amalgam of Lipton's dehydrated onion soup mix and sour cream and its appeal to the newly prosperous denizens of 1950s suburbia as the party snack à la mode was that serving it with potato chips as miniature scoops did away with the need for plates or cutlery. It was also the period when television penetration in the United States reached saturation point; couch potatoes and potato chips soon found they were made for each other.

THE FIRST PREP SCHOOL

in the United States was the Phillips School (later Phillips Academy) in Andover, N.H., founded by twenty-six-year-old Samuel Phillips and opened on 30 April 1778 with thirteen pupils, of whom the first name on the register was thirteen-year-old Thomas Payson of Boston. Phillips bases its claim as the first prep school not on its being a private foundation, for there were many such in America already, nor on its being a boarding school, but because it was clearly established at its foundation that the school was to serve the populace as a whole, not just that of the locality as other schools did. For this reason the original articles prescribed that the majority of trustees must not be inhabitants of Andover. It was also the first school in the United States to be incorporated, on 4 October 1780, the older Dummer School (1763), Samuel Phillips's alma mater, following suit in 1782.

By the end of the first year the roll had increased to fifty-one pupils of whom the eldest, James

Anderson of Londonderry, N.H., was nearly thirty and the youngest, Josiah Quincy, who sat next to him in class, was six. The latter was to become the second mayor of Boston, succeeding his schoolmate John Phillips, the first mayor, in 1823. Quincy went on to become president of Harvard in 1829.

The school day comprised 4 hours of mainly classical studies in the morning and another 4 hours in the afternoon. Two days of the week held in particular dread were Mondays, when the pupils had to recite as much as they could of the previous day's sermon, and Saturdays, when floggings were administered, those who had failed Monday's exercise having had five days in which to anticipate their nemesis. The birch was wielded by the formidable and ferocious principal, Eliphalet Pearson, known to the boys, though not in his hearing, as "Elephant." Josiah Quincy declared that he had "no recollection of his ever having shown any consideration for my childhood. Fear was the only impression I received from his treatment of myself and others." A remarkable scholar himself, Pearson was not always capable of nurturing the scholastic talents of others. He told Josiah Quincy's mother that the boy was too dull for university, advice fortunately ignored as the future president of Harvard became valedictorian of his class. Like Quincy, most of the early Phillips alumni were destined for Harvard, attended by seventy-six out of the eighty-nine boys who went on to college during Pearson's tenure of office. Subsequent early alumni included Samuel Morse of electric telegraph (qv) fame and Oliver Wendell Holmes Sr., and later graduates included father-and-son presidents George H. W. Bush and George W. Bush. Jack Lemmon added thespian luster, but actor Humphrey Bogart was expelled.

Phillips Exeter Academy at Exeter, N.H., was founded by Samuel Phillips's uncle, Dr. John Phillips, in 1783; it was he who had purchased the land for Phillips Academy at Andover and he was its major benefactor, not only endowing it in his own lifetime but leaving the school a third of his fortune on his death, the other two thirds going to Phillips Exeter. Despite the fact that Exeter was only 30 miles from Andover, there appears to have been no intercourse between the two schools until football matches began in 1878—now the oldest annual game between schools in the sporting calendar.

Other surviving prep schools that followed the model of the two Phillips academies are Bristol Academy, Taunton, Mass. (1792); Fryeburg Academy, Fryeburg, Me. (1792); Groton (now Lawrence) Academy, Groton, Mass. (1793); Cheshire Academy, Cheshire, Conn. (1794); Deerfield Academy, Deerfield, Mass. (1797); Milton Academy, Milton, Mass. (1798); and Wilbraham & Monson Academy, Wilbraham, Mass. (1804).

The oldest boarding school in America (predating prep schools per se) is West Nottingham Academy in Colora, Md., founded in 1744. The oldest girls' boarding school is Linden Hall, in Lititz, Pa., founded in 1746.

THE FIRST PRESERVATION MOVEMENT

began with what are now called house museums. The first historic building to be acquired for preservation in the United States was the Dutch Colonial house built by Jonathan Hasbrouck at Newburgh, N.Y., in 1750 and which served as Gen. George Washington's headquarters during 1782–1783. It was here that the American commander in chief learned of the cessation of hostilities and was invited to become "King" of the newly liberated nation, a notion the future president rejected in a famous letter of rebuke.

Here also the Order of the Purple Heart (SEE **medals**) was established by a decree Washington issued from the house. The property was acquired by the State of New York from the Hasbrouck family in 1849 at a cost of $2,391.02 and was opened to the public on 4 July 1850 as America's first **historic house museum**.

Several years passed before there were any other preserved buildings. In 1856 the State of Tennessee bought Andrew Jackson's 1819 property called The Hermitage at Nashville and a year later Carpenter's Hall in Philadelphia, site of the first meeting of the Continental Congress, was opened to the public. In 1858 the first **preservation society**, the Ladies' Association of Mount Vernon (chartered 17 March 1856), acquired the Washington family's 1735 farmhouse, to which the Father of the Nation had moved as a child of three and which he later enlarged into the "great house" we know and cherish today. The association had been founded by Miss Ann Pamela Cunningham after the State of Virginia and the federal government had failed to muster the $200,000 demanded by owner John A. Washington, a figure probably well above market value, as the price for ensuring the preservation of America's most celebrated dwelling.

The first preservation society founded to save historical sites and structures in general rather than one particular building was the Association for the Preservation of Virginia Antiquities (APVA), founded at Williamsburg on 4 January 1890 by Mary J. Galt and Cynthia Coleman after the collapse of an old brick ruin known as Powhatan's Chimney. Their first acquisition was the 1715 Powder Magazine in Williamsburg, followed by the cottage of Washington's mother Mary at Fredericksburg, bought for $4,500. Three years later they purchased the remains of the late seventeenth-century church at Jamestown, then acquired the whole site of what had been the first permanent English settlement (qv) in North America.

The APVA was founded at a time when the Southern states were still suffering from the consequences of their defeat in the Civil War, both economically and in terms of identity. The agenda of its well-meaning ladies (who made up most of the membership) was focused more on stimulating patriotism and local pride than on the more academic side of conservation and restoration. Essentially enthusiastic amateurs, they imbued their properties with a warm glow of romantic myth. One of their members, Boston antiquary William Sumner Appleton, dissented from this approach. In 1910, having successfully saved and restored to its original appearance the oldest house in Boston, the c. 1685 Paul Revere House, he established the Society for the Preservation of New England Antiquities (SPNEA). This is generally recognized as the first such organization to bring professionalism and scholarship to the task of preservation. Appleton's chief interest was identifying and preserving the few remaining seventeenth-century dwellings in New England, whose numbers were being steadily depleted through ignorance and indifference. The SPNEA developed a program to acquire domestic buildings, preferably with an endowment; restore them as nearly as possible to their original state; and

rent them to tenants "under wise restrictions." By the end of its second year the society owned its first two houses, and by the time Appleton died in 1943 it was custodian of fifty-one.

The first preservation society to focus on a single city was Charleston's Society for the Preservation of Old Dwellings (now the Preservation Society of Charleston), founded by unorthodox realtor Susan Pringle Fox in 1920 to save the 1803 Joseph Manigault House from demolition. Charleston was in particular need of an organized preservation movement because its wealth of Colonial- and Federal-era buildings was subject to two particular threats: acquisition by Standard Oil, which was trying to build up a chain of gas stations in a city with a paucity of vacant lots; and the depredations of antiques dealers, who stripped historic houses of their architectural features, interior and exterior, to sell in other parts of the United States less richly endowed.

In October 1931 the City of Charleston became the first in the United States to give **legislative protection to historic buildings** when it adopted a planning and zoning ordinance establishing the Old and Historic District preserving four hundred residential properties in a twenty-three-block area south of Broad Street. Mayor Thomas P. Stoney won approval of the measure following public outrage generated by Standard Oil's action in demolishing three historic residences on Meeting Street (which the company tried to deflect by building the gas station in Colonial Revival style, thereby adding insult to injury). The protected area was tripled in size in 1966 following the destruction of the landmark Charleston Hotel, taking in Ansonborough, Charleston Village, and other areas between Broad and Calhoun Streets.

Other cities followed Charleston's lead, starting with New Orleans in 1937, and by the 1970s more than 200 American cities had local laws preserving historically and architecturally significant private property. Twenty years later the number had risen to more than 1,800.

THE FIRST **PRINTED BOOK**

known is a copy of the *Mugu chŏnggwang tae dharani-gyŏng*, also called by its short title the *Dharani Sutra*, printed in Korea from woodblocks on a scroll 8 centimeters by 630 centimeters and believed to date from no later than A.D. 704. It was discovered in the foundations of the Pulguk Sa pagoda in what is now Gyeongju, South Korea, on 14 October 1966 and predates what was until then the earliest known printed book, the Buddhist scripture known as the *Diamond Sutra* from Turkestan, by at least 164 years. The scroll is now in the collection of the National Museum of Korea, designated National Treasure No. 123.

Book printed from movable metal type: The earliest known is the *Songjŏng yemun* or "Compendium of Rites and Rituals," a work in fifty chapters of which twenty-eight copies were published in Korea in 1234. The type was fashioned by sand-casting in iron from clay model-types. This process was based on a sand-molding technique developed in 1102 for casting coins.

The earliest tangible evidence of a book printed from movable type in Europe is two leaves of a twenty-seven-line *Donatus Latin Grammar* that were found in the binding of an account book dated 1451. The type is believed to be the same as that used by Johannes Gutenberg of Mainz for the printing of his forty-two-line-per-page Bible in Mainz three or four years later.

The earliest dated book printed from movable type in Europe and the first in a vernacular tongue is *Eyn manung der Christenheit widder die durken* ("Appeal of Christianity Against the Turks"), believed to have been printed by Gutenberg in Mainz in 1454. The only existing copy contains six leaves, with nine pages of German text, including a calendar.

Printed Bible: The first, and the earliest known full-length work printed from movable type in Europe, was Gutenberg's forty-two-line Bible believed to have been printed in Mainz between 1454 and 1456. Of the forty-eight copies known to survive, thirty-six are on paper and twelve on vellum. The copy preserved at the Bibliothèque Nationale in Paris, is in two folio volumes with a total of 643 leaves. It contains a manuscript colophon at the end that reads in translation, "This book was illuminated, bound, and perfected by Henry Cremer, vicar of the Collegiate Church of Saint Stephen in Mainz, on the Feast of the Assumption of the Blessed Virgin [15 August] in the year of Our Lord 1456. Thanks be to God. Hallelujah." Other copies may have been printed earlier, possibly in 1454 or 1455.

Book printed in the English language: The first was *The Recuyell of the Histories of Troye*, a translation from the original French published by William Caxton at Bruges in 1474. Caxton prefaced the work with the explanation, "It is not wreton with penne and ynke as other bokes ben . . . for all bokes of this storye . . . were begonne in oon day, and also fynysshid in oon day."

U.S.: *The Whole Book of Psalms Faithfully Translated into English Meter*, with a preface by Puritan divine John Cotton, was published in 1640 by Stephen Daye and his son Matthew at their press in Cambridge, Mass. The *Bay Psalm Book*, as it is usually known, was intended as a replacement for the 1562 translation of the psalms by Sternhold and Hopkins, which offended Puritan susceptibilities because it was a loose, literary rendering of the sacred texts. The American version, edited by Richard Mather, was intended as a faithful translation of the words of David from the Hebrew, without regard for poetic form or facility to the ear. It was deliberately unliterary. The first edition of the 148-page quarto volume numbered 1,700 copies and James D. Hart, in *The Popular Book* (1950), has speculated whether the market could have borne so many. In 1640 there were some 3,500 families in the northern colonies and as the separatists in Plymouth and Puritans in some of the outlying plantations would have had none of this work, he argues, there were "probably only as many families amenable to the Bay Psalm Book as there were copies in the first printing." Nevertheless there were many printings to come. At least fifty-one editions were published in New England, old England, and Scotland in the next century and a quarter. Only eleven copies of the first edition survive, of which five are in the original binding.

Surviving books and pamphlets published at the Cambridge Press by Stephen and Matthew Daye before Matthew's death in 1649 were: Harvard theses for 1643; pamphlet on Narragansett Indians, 1645;

almanacs for 1646, 1647, and 1648; and second-edition Bay Psalm Book, 1647. With no known copies surviving are an almanac for 1639; Harvard theses for 1642; the Newbury Catechism c. 1642; a book of capital law from 1643; a spelling book from 1644; a book of laws and liberties from 1648; and a Salem Catechism c. 1648. Between 1639 and 1670 a total of 157 publications emanated from the Cambridge Press, of which 63 were religious, 8 were history or biography, 4 were secular poetry, and the remainder were schoolbooks, official publications, almanacs, Harvard theses, and books in the Algonquian language (also religious).

American book to contain a pictorial illustration: The first was Increase Mather's *Blessed Hope*, published in Boston in 1701, some copies of which had a portrait of the author by local artist Thomas Emmes as a frontispiece. The same portrait appeared in Mather's *Ichabod* the following year.

The first **American book with color-printed plates** was Jacob Bigelow's *American Medical Botany*, published in multiple volumes in Boston from 1817 to 1820. Some of the engraved plates in Volume I had been hand colored, but Bigelow's engravers William Annin and George Smith adopted a new printing technique from France by which colored inks *à la poupée* were applied to the aquatint engraved copper. The process was slow and costly but gave excellent color reproduction.

The first **American book illustrated with a photograph** was *Homes of American Statesmen*, published in New York in 1854, which has a calotype frontispiece by an unidentified photographer of John Hancock's house in Boston. The first with natural color photographs was *An Illustrated and Descriptive Album Art Collection of America's New Possessions* containing more than one hundred three-color photos of U.S. military action in the Philippines taken by F. Tennyson Neely, published in 1901 at $2.50 by the International View Co., Chicago. The pictures include several of Gen. Arthur MacArthur, father of Douglas. It is remarkable that at this very early stage in the development of color photography it was possible to make photomechanical halftone reproductions from transparencies for publication in magazines or books, while there was still no process for making a straightforward one-off color print (SEE **photograph**

in color). The Art Institute of Chicago has one of the few surviving copies.

SEE ALSO **children's book; children's fiction; novel; paperback book; poetry.**

THE FIRST **PRINTED WORK**

in North America was a half-sheet broadside of 222 words entitled *The Oath of a Freeman* printed on Stephen and Matthew Daye's press at Cambridge, Mass., early in 1639. The text was the pledge taken when an adult received the right to vote in the Massachusetts Bay Colony. The Cambridge printing press, the first in America, had been brought from England by the Rev. Jose Glover, but he died at sea. His widow established a printery, however, employing her husband's former apprentice Stephen Daye and his son Matthew to operate it. Their second publication was more substantial than the first: *An Almanac Calculated for New England by Mr. Pierce, Mariner*. No copy survives. The third, *The Whole Book of Psalms*, was the first printed book (qv) published in America.

THE FIRST **PRISON**

in the United States to which offenders were sentenced to terms of imprisonment—earlier jails were for holding prisoners pending trial—were opened in Connecticut and Pennsylvania in the same year, 1773. One was Newgate, named after the notorious London jail, which was established by order of the Connecticut General Assembly in a disused copper mine at East Granby, near Simsbury, and received its first inmates in November of that year. It was intended for robbers, burglars, forgers, counterfeiters, and horse thieves, who received sentences of from two years to life, served, as one of these desperadoes described it, in "a dungeon with continually dripping water and foul air." In fact none of the original inmates served even as much as two years. Within three weeks the first escapee had made it to freedom and by the end of six months all the other prisoners had emulated his example. Newgate continued in use, however, and was officially designated a state prison in 1790. The first prison riot in the United States took place there the following year as a result of "violence, poor management, escapes, assaults, orgies, and demoralisation." A Boston lady poet who put her feelings into verse after a visit in 1797 called Simsbury "a living tomb."

Philadelphia's original Walnut Street Jail of 1773 was designed by Robert Smith to give an air of "solitude and fitness." It comprised a central building with eight arched rooms and twin two-story wings each containing five rooms. When it was rebuilt in 1790, Walnut Street became, in a literal sense, America's first penitentiary or correctional institution, i.e., its purpose was "reformation through reflection and penitence," based on the system instituted at England's Wymondham Gaol. It was also the first in the United States to employ solitary confinement, a practice originating in Louis XIV's jails a century earlier. About 5 percent of inmates, prisoners who would formerly have received the death penalty, served between one twelfth and half of their sentences in solitary. There were sixteen solitary cells, each measuring 6' x 8' x 9', from which the prisoners were never allowed out during that part of their sentence. Furthermore they were served but a single dish, an unappetizing pudding of maize and molasses. For the other inmates, though, there was a new privilege. Well-behaved cons were allowed visits from close family members for 15 minutes every three months. Visitor and visited spoke through two grilles under the scrutiny of a guard.

Women's prison: The first was Mount Pleasant Female Prison, established as an adjunct to the notorious Sing Sing at Ossining, N.Y., in 1835. The first wholly separate establishment was Indiana Reformatory Institution for Women and Girls at Indianapolis, opened under Superintendent Sarah Smith in 1873.

Military prison: The first in the United States was the U.S. Army Disciplinary Barracks, unfondly known as "the Castle," opened on 15 May 1875 at Fort Leavenworth, Kansas. It is now the only maximum-security jail of the United States Military.

Prison to operate the parole system: The first was Elmira Reformatory in New York State a year after it had opened in July 1876 to receive first-time offenders aged between sixteen and thirty. Parole was instituted by visionary young warden Zebulon R. Brockway as an appendage to his system of merits and demerits that conferred privileges on the compliant and withdrew them from troublemakers. Sentences were for a stated maximum period but otherwise indeterminate. After a minimum of twelve months, those in the top grade were eligible for parole on condition that they had a promise of employment. On release they were required to report to a "guardian" on the first day of each month and could be returned to Elmira if their conduct was considered unsatisfactory.

Federal penitentiaries: The first were opened under the Three Prisons Act of 1891 and located in Fort Leavenworth, Kan.; McNeil Island in Washington State; and Atlanta, Ga. The first of these to open was Fort Leavenworth in the former military prison (SEE ABOVE), transferred to the Department of Justice on 1 July 1895; this was replaced by a purpose-built civilian jail in 1906. It was the largest maximum-security federal prison until regraded medium security in 2005.

The first **federal prison for women** was the Federal Industrial Institution for Women (now Alderson Federal Prison Camp or, to the media, "Camp Cupcake") opened in Alderson, W.Va., under Superintendent Mary Belle Harris on 30 April 1927 with accommodation for five hundred inmates. It was based on a boarding-school concept and was exceptionally liberal, with no armed guards and self-government by the inmates. Alumnae include Billie Holiday, Tokyo Rose, Lynette "Squeaky" Fromme, and Martha Stewart.

Prison gang: The earliest known was the so-called Gypsy Jokers Motorcycle Club at Walla Walla, the Washington State Penitentiary, who were terrorizing their fellow inmates by 1950.

Private prison: The first fully privatized was Marion Adjustment Center, opened by the Corrections Corporation of America at St. Mary, Ky., on 6 January 1986.

THE FIRST **PRIVATE DETECTIVE AGENCY**

was the Bureau des Renseignements au Service des Intérêts Privets, established in Paris by the ex-chief of the Sûreté, Eugène François Vidocq (SEE **police** department: police detective), in 1833. The agency suffered a setback when Vidocq was charged with assaulting one of his employees and fined 50 francs plus 60 francs damages. After a few years it was closed down under government pressure, some of Vidocq's more spectacular successes having proved embarrassing in high places. A former criminal himself, it was Vidocq who coined the phrase "set a thief to catch a thief."

U.S.: The earliest recorded agency was founded by George Relyea and two partners at 48 Center Street, New York City, in 1845. Their announcement in the *National Police Gazette* of 16 October of that year offered to conduct "both Criminal and Civil business [to find] all kinds of property... obtained by False Pretenses, Forgery, Burglary, or any other dishonest means" and declared that its agents were "always ready, at a moment's warning, to travel to any parts of the United States." This last reflected the fact that the jurisdiction of New York's Municipal Police, the sole police force in the United States at that time, extended only as far as the city limits.

The Pinkerton National Detective Agency, founded by Glasgow-born Allan Pinkerton in Chicago in 1850, gave the English-speaking world the term *private eye*. It was derived from the ever-open eye used in the Pinkerton logo with the slogan "We never sleep."

Female private eye: The first was Mrs. Kate Warne, a twenty-three-year-old widow, who was hired by the Pinkerton Detective Agency in Chicago in 1856 after she had convinced Allan Pinkerton that she could "worm out secrets in many places to which it was impossible for male detectives to gain access." She so amply fulfilled this promise that by 1860 Pinkerton had hired a number of other women, with Kate at their head, whom he referred to as "my Female Detective Bureau." She died at the early age of thirty-five, extolled by her employer as "the greatest female detective who ever brought a case to a successful conclusion," and her grave lies next to that of Allan Pinkerton at the Graceland Cemetery in Chicago.

THE FIRST **PROFIT-SHARING SCHEME**

was announced on 15 February 1842 to the skeptical house-painters in the employ of Edmé-Jean LeClair of Paris, who declared his belief that it would "create by the common effort, in view of the division of profit, and with the energy this provokes, an increased return, sufficient not only to pay the workman's dividend, but even enlarge that of the master." Not only did LeClair have to convince his truculent *ouvriers*, but he also had to withstand the opposition of the police (notorious in France for interference in the affairs of private citizens) who objected that it constituted an "unfair competitive practice." LeClair resorted to a theatrical gesture when the day of the first distribution came on 12 February 1843, staggering into the paint shop under the weight of a bag containing 12,266 francs in gold. Each of forty-four eligible employees received a dividend proportionate to his earnings, with an average of 278 francs ($70). The effect on morale was immediate and much to his delight, changes in working practices vindicated LeClair's commitment to his revolutionary ideas. "Abandoning the system of organized waste of time, which was thought an excellent expedient for thwarting the master under the old system, they work with self-sustained energy during the hours of labor," he observed. The quality of the work also improved, the workmen having a vested interest in attracting new and repeat customers. Lest all this should seem a little too good to be true, let it be said that the profit-sharing scheme initiated by Maison LeClair, which was eventually to become Laurent, Fournier et Cie, is still operating today.

U.S.: The first scheme was instituted by the Bay State Shoe & Leather Co. of Worcester, Mass., in 1867, with the intention that 25 percent of net profits should be distributed to employees. This did not enjoy the same success as its French forebear. The shoemakers and tanners went on strike in 1869 and management–worker relations steadily worsened until the company head decided to wind up the scheme, noting despairingly that as soon as the men received their bonuses they went off to the saloon, often to spend the lot. Successful schemes did develop elsewhere, albeit slowly. There were thirty-five in all in the United States by 1889, including the earliest still operative, started by Procter & Gamble in 1887.

THE FIRST **PUBLIC ADDRESS SYSTEM**

SEE **loudspeaker**.

THE FIRST **PUBLIC LIBRARY**

in the United States was established in the Town House on King Street, Boston, in 1658 and was variously known as the Public Library of Boston and the Town Library. Both the Town House, which was used for various municipal and social functions, and the library within it were the result of a bequest by Capt. Robert Keayne, the first commandant of the Ancient and Honorable Artillery Company, as well as merchant, amateur divine, and extortioner. The original collection of books came from his private library of religious works that, unusually for the day, were entirely in English rather than Latin or Greek. This was augmented from time to time by other gifts or bequests. Little is known about the usage of the library, nor its administration, though it is probably safe to assume that its patrons would have been confined to the clergy and perhaps the occasional lay scholar. The Town House and the library were destroyed by a mighty conflagration in 1747, only one volume surviving. This was a copy of Samuel Mather's *A Testimony from the Scripture Against Idolatory and Superstition,* published in Cambridge, Mass. c. 1670, which is inscribed "ffor the publike Library at Boston, 1674." It is now in the Boston Athenaeum, though there is no record of how it got there.

There is no evidence that the Boston Public Library received financial support from the municipality, a practice that did not emerge until the nineteenth century (SEE BELOW), nor that the books could be borrowed. The earliest American lending library of which there is record, albeit scant, is the collection of books maintained by the town of Concord, Mass. The date that this was established is not known, but in 1672 the selectmen were enjoined "that ceare be taken of the bookes of marters [martyrs] and other bookes that belong to the Towne, that they may be kept from abeuceive vesage and not to be lent to any person more than one month at one time." The only other public library established in the seventeenth century was the Charles Towne (Charleston, S.C.) Public Library, founded in 1698 with a bequest of books from the Rev. S. C. Bray.

The first secular rather than theological library in America and also the first subscription library was established by Benjamin Franklin's Library Company of Philadelphia, which was founded in 1731 with fifty subscribers (later increased to a hundred) who put up 40 shillings each as seed money and undertook to pay an annual subscription of 10 shillings. An order for books to the value of £45 was placed with the London bookseller Peter Collinson on 31 March 1732 and these arrived in Philadelphia at the end of October, being placed in the library premises at Robert Grace's home in Jones' Alley (later Pewter Platter Alley). The library was then open to its members and to the public, the hours being from 2 to 3 P.M. on Wednesdays and 10 A.M. to 4 P.M. on Saturdays. Although only members could take books out, any "civil gentleman" could peruse the books in the reading room. Nothing was said about civil ladies.

The first librarian, probably the first salaried librarian in America, albeit part time, was Louis Timottiée (aka Lewis Timothee). The first printed catalog, also an American first, was produced by Benjamin Franklin, himself a printer by trade, in August 1741. A single copy of the fifty-six-page volume is known to survive, in the possession of the library.

The first **purpose-built library** in America was a neo-classical structure supported by doric columns designed by Peter Harrison, one of only two trained architects in the colonies and reputedly a pupil of Sir John Vanbrugh, and erected in 1750 to house the Redwood Library at Newport, R.I. This was a library established by philanthropist Abraham Redwood, a prominent citizen and landowner of the town and heir to extensive sugar plantations in Antigua. Like Franklin's foundation, the Redwood was a social library and its first catalog, issued in 1764, shows that only 13 percent of the seven hundred books were theological, exceeded by literature and the arts (33 percent), science (19 percent), and history (16 percent). The library survives in its original building, one of the oldest public library buildings in the world.

Fiction hardly impinged on the "social libraries" of the eighteenth century; their promoters, the clergy or men of affairs, usually dwelled on loftier planes. The Social Library established at Abington, Conn., in 1793 was so much biased toward theology that those in the town who sought to read for entertainment rather than spiritual elevation set up a Junior Library in 1804 that included novels as well as works of general interest. Women may well have been among the most active supporters, as this was a period noted for frequent denunciations by the high-minded of the female predilection for sentimental fiction.

Library to receive municipal support: The first was the Bingham Library for Youth, established by a gift of books to his birthplace, the town of Salisbury, Conn., by the Boston bookseller Caleb Bingham. On 4 January 1803 he wrote to his brother David, who lived in the town:

> I well remember, when I was a boy, how ardently I longed for the opportunity of reading, but had no access to a library. It is more than probable that there are, at the present time, in my native town, many children who possess the same desire, and who are in the like unhappy predicament. This desire, I think I have it in my power, in a small degree to satisfy...

Accompanying the letter was the gift of 150 titles, which formed the first **children's library** anywhere in the world. Municipal support for the collection began with a vote passed at the town meeting of 9 April 1810 to appropriate $100 for augmenting it. Further grants for the library, which was later absorbed into the Scoville Memorial Library, were made in 1821 ($20), 1826 ($50), and 1836 ($50).

Library established by a municipality: The first in the world was founded at Peterborough, N.H., by a vote of the town meeting on 9 April 1833. A committee was set up under the Rev. Abiel Abbot, the original proposer of the scheme, and the following April they reported that $67 had been appropriated for the purchase of books. A further $130 had been received from the local Bible Society for the acquisition of books "relating to Moral and Religious Subjects" and with a total fund of $197 the committee purchased 370 volumes. They had, they explained, avoided buying any expensive titles "in order that every family in

Town might have access to the Library." Additionally, the town's Juvenile Library (1829), which operated by subscription and contained some 200 books, most of them "considerably worn," was absorbed into the Town Library. The collection was placed in the Peterborough Post Office and the postmaster, Riley Goodrich, was appointed librarian. A manuscript catalog dated 1834 shows that history and biography predominated at 40 percent, followed by theology at 33 percent (which suggests that not all the Bible Society's funding went to religious works). Fiction at only 2 percent comprised works by Maria Edgeworth, Washington Irving, Daniel Defoe, and Cervantes. The library continues to flourish, based now in a modern purpose-designed building.

Peterborough was a small town of some 2,000 inhabitants. The first metropolitan city in the United States to establish a fully fledged public library was Boston, founded under an enabling act of the State of Massachusetts and opened to readers on 20 March 1854 and to borrowers on 2 May following. There were originally 12,000 volumes, rising to 16,553 by the end of the year. Aggregate borrowings in the first six months totalled 40,000. The Boston Public Library was the first library in the United States to employ women, originally as library clerks.

Access to the books was restricted in all the early metropolitan libraries. The first to adopt an open-shelf policy was Cleveland, Ohio, in 1886.

The first state to pass legislation enabling municipalities to devote public funds to public libraries was New Hampshire in 1849.

Children's section: The first was established in 1877 at Pawtucket Public Library in Rhode Island by librarian Minerva Saunders.

Branch library network: The first was established by Enoch Pratt Free Library in Baltimore in 1886.

Audio section: The first was inaugurated in 1914 at St. Paul City Library, St. Paul, Minn., following the gift of 25 records from a local women's club. By 1919 it had a stock of nearly 600 recordings of the classics, patriotic music, and folk songs, and circulation for that year, to schools and clubs (individuals were not eligible), was 3,505.

Video/DVD section: Not known. The editor invites nominations.

THE FIRST **PUBLIC-OPINION POLL**

was conducted in Wilmington, Del., to determine voters' intentions in the 1824 U.S. presidential election. The result of the poll, based on a random sample of 532 electors, was published in the *Harrington Pennsylvanian* on 24 July 1824. It showed a clear lead for Andrew Jackson over John Quincy Adams and two other candidates. The following month the *Raleigh Star* polled 4,256 voters at political meetings in North Carolina and confirmed Jackson's supremacy. Jackson carried North Carolina in November.

The first opinion poll on an issue (as opposed to voting intentions) was carried out by the *Chicago Journal* between 18 and 29 March 1907, and put the question whether the privately run Chicago tramways should be taken over by the municipality. The poll indicated that 59 percent of the people were in favor of the proposal. In the official referendum held to vote on the ordinance the corresponding figure was 55 percent.

The first nationwide public-opinion poll was organized by *Farm Journal* in an attempt to predict the result of the 1912 U.S. presidential election.

The modern representative-sampling method of conducting public-opinion polls was developed independently by Dr. George H. Gallup of the American Institute of Public Opinion, Elmo Roper of the Fortune Survey, and Archibald Crossley of the Crossley Poll. All three began publishing results in 1935, though Roper's July poll on automobile ownership is believed to have been the first in print. This included the question, "Do you regard an automobile as a luxury or a necessity?" to which 75.5 percent of male respondents said it was a necessity. Representative sampling was the first scientifically calculated method of polling, since it ensured that respondents were selected from age, sex, class, and other interest groups in correct proportion.

The validity of the new techniques was demonstrated by the results of the 1936 presidential election. One of America's foremost mass-circulation magazines, the *Literary Digest*, had been conducting polls for each presidential election since 1920 with what was claimed as 100-percent accuracy and had won huge public acclaim for its apparent ability to predict national voting intentions. With Franklin D. Roosevelt up for reelection after his first term of office, *Literary Digest* polled 10 million voters by mail. They were selected mainly from telephone directories and car registrations and 2.4 million responded, showing a landslide victory for Republican candidate Alf Landon with 57 percent of the vote. In the event he received 38.5 percent Gallup, Roper, and Crossley used a small but scientifically selected sample and each correctly predicted Roosevelt's overwhelming victory. Telephone subscribers and car owners were not representative; they were predominately white, older, affluent, and Republican. The *Literary Digest*, already struggling financially, lost public confidence and soon after ceased publication.

Roosevelt himself was the first politician to use polling as a policy-making tool. Before agreeing to Prime Minister Winston Churchill's request for destroyers for the British war effort in 1940, he engaged Gallup and Roper to submit the lend-lease deal to the court of American public opinion. Satisfied that the people were overwhelmingly in favor of cooperation with Britain and that isolationists constituted a relatively small minority, he told the prime minister yes. A contrary result could have given the Nazis victory.

THE FIRST **PUBLIC RELATIONS**

as a recognized technique of business management originated with Ivy Ledbetter Lee, a former financial correspondent who set himself up as a public relations consultant in partnership with experienced journalist George Parker as the Parker & Lee Co. in New York in 1903. Early clients included a number of politicians, a circus, a group of bankers, and the unpopular tobacco baron Thomas Fortune Ryan. At first Lee's approach to the art of public persuasion differed little from that of other press agents, one of whom wrote in 1905 that this business was "not the dissemination of truth, but the avoidance of its inopportune discovery." The emergence of modern public relations can really be dated from 1906, when Ivy Lee was called in by the proprietors of anthracite coal mines during the major miners' strike of that year. Before Lee was hired, their proprietors' leader George F. Baer had refused to talk to either the press or the president of the United States, the latter having attempted to arbitrate in the dispute. In contrast, the miners' leader, John Mitchell, had won over both by his charm, forthrightness, and evident desire to supply all the facts for which he was asked. While the miners' cause was acclaimed by the press, Baer and his colleagues were almost universally condemned.

Lee's first act was to issue a press notice signed by Baer and the other leading proprietors. It began: "The anthracite coal operators, realizing the general public interest [in] conditions in the mining regions, have arranged to supply the press with all possible information . . ." This was followed by a notice setting out Lee's own "Declaration of Principles," which was in the nature of a charter for public relations as a business activity separate from press agentry on the one hand and advertising on the other.

Following the coal strike, Lee was retained by the Pennsylvania Railroad Co. to handle press relations after a major rail disaster. Reversing the usual practice of suppression of facts when accidents were likely to tarnish the reputation of a railway company, Lee gave full facilities to the press to view the disaster scene for themselves and released all available information. The result justified what seemed to the more conservative-minded railway directors to be reckless indiscretion. The Pennsylvania Railroad received fairer press comment than had ever been its experience previously after a serious accident.

One of Lee's most notable successes was as public relations adviser to John D. Rockefeller, who had an unenviable reputation as a hard-faced capitalist oppressor. Lee succeeded in transforming this image by a skillful projection of the more attractive traits of his client's personality. One device he used was filling the old man's pockets with dimes for distribution among urchins in the street, an activity that provided press and public with visible evidence of what was in fact a genuinely kindly nature.

Lee was less successful in his efforts on behalf of Rockefeller's behemoth Standard Oil, which was excoriated for rapaciousness and lack of scruple in seeking control of the United States oil industry. He represented Rockefeller's interests after the infamous Ludlow Massacre of 1914, in which fourteen striking mineworkers, wives, and children had been slaughtered by company goons in Colorado. Lee asserted

Rockefeller had not been involved; it became apparent he had been. Hauled before the U.S. Commission on Industrial Relations in January 1915, Lee put a broad interpretation on what truth meant in PR terms: It was, he declared, "the truth as the operators saw it." For this, and for similar accommodations with the *actualité*, Ivy Lee acquired the sobriquet "Poison Ivy."

The year 1906, which saw the emergence of public-relations consultancy, also witnessed the start of public-relations departments within corporations, led by United States Steel and Standard Oil and followed soon after by telecommunications colossus AT&T. All three were perceived, in an oft-quoted aphorism of the time, as "soulless corporations" and each succeeded, over a period of decades, in transforming itself into an icon of American enterprise, know-how, and public service. It is worthy of note that 1906 was also the year of publication of Upton Sinclair's novel *The Jungle*, in which he castigated the Chicago meatpackers in what must surely be the most damaging attack on capitalism unrelieved by social responsibility in the whole canon of English literature. It was against this volatile background that America invented "spin."

THE FIRST PUBLIC TOILET

containing flush lavatories was a men's room opened at 95 Fleet Street, London, by the Society of Arts on 2 February 1852. One for ladies, situated at 51 Bedford Street, off the Strand, was opened on 11 February. The two principal instigators of the scheme were (Sir) Samuel Morton Peto, the building contractor who erected Nelson's Column in Trafalgar Square, and (Sir) Henry Cole, father of the Christmas card (qv) as well as one of the principal promoters of the first world's fair, held at the Crystal Palace in Hyde Park the previous year. It was the success of the toilets provided at the Crystal Palace that had inspired the Society of Arts to promote the idea of installing public conveniences in the principal thoroughfares of London. Not only would this high-minded endeavor answer an urgent public need, argued Cole and Peto, but it was also likely to be a paying proposition. The Crystal Palace restroom had reaped a net profit of £1,790 ($8,950) in only twenty-three weeks.

The arrangements made for fitting out and operating what the Society of Arts euphemistically dubbed "Public Waiting Rooms" were admirable. Peto personally supervised the installation of handsome water closets set in box-frames of polished wood and each convenience was placed in the charge of a superintendent and two attendants. That these facilities were intended for the benefit of the middle classes is evidenced by the price charged: 2d (4¢) for the use of the basic amenities and another 2d or 3d for "washing hands, clothes brushes, etc." It evidently occurred to the society, though, that not all the bourgeoisie were as respectable in their habits as might be wished, for a request was made to the Metropolitan Police Commissioners that their men on the beat should make periodic visits.

The first mechanism for toilet doors indicating whether the cubicle was occupied was patented by Arthur Ashwell of West Dulwich, a suburb of London, on 17 February 1882. Ten years later London-based magician John Nevil Maskelyne patented the coin-operated lavatory lock.

U.S.: According to the scurrilous London pamphleteer Ned Ward, author of *A Trip to New England* (London, 1699), in late seventeenth-century Boston even women were wont to defecate in the street. Alas, we are unable to reveal when such desperate measures ceased to be necessary. Our search for the first restroom has remained elusive and nominations are invited. Meanwhile it is claimed that the first coin-operated public toilet was installed at the Terre Haute, Ind., railroad depot in 1910 by a zealous stationmaster wanting to discourage the use of the facilities by the non-traveling townsfolk. The nickel-in-the-slot mechanisms were supplied by the Nik-o-lok Co. of Indianapolis.

R

THE FIRST RADAR

as a working apparatus was developed by Dr. Rudolph Kühnold, chief of the German Navy's Signals Research Department, during the summer and autumn of 1933 and consisted of a 700-W transmitter working on a frequency of 600 megacycles, a receiver, and disk reflectors. The first practical tests with this equipment were conducted at Kiel Harbor on 20 March 1934, when Kühnold succeeded in receiving echo signals from the battleship *Hesse* as she lay at anchor 600 yards distant from the transmitter. An experimental installation was then made at the Naval Research Establishment at Pelzerhaken, near Lübeck, and in a demonstration before high-ranking naval officers in October 1934 echoes were picked up from a ship 7 miles away. By chance, signals were also received from a seaplane flying through the beam. Following this achievement the German authorities allocated the sum of 70,000 Reichsmarks for the setting up of a continuous development program.

In the meantime, practical trials of **airplane detection by radar** had been carried out in the Soviet Union by the Leningrad Electro-Physics Institute. On 10 and 11 July 1934 aircraft at heights of up to 3,300 feet and within 2 miles of the receiver were detected, while further tests on 9–10 August demonstrated that ranges of up to 50 miles were achievable.

It was in Britain that radar progressed most rapidly in the run-up to war. The program had its start in January 1935 when (Sir) Robert Watson-Watt, superintendent of the Radio Research Laboratory at Ditton Park, was asked by the newly formed Committee for the Scientific Survey of Air Defence to investigate the possibility of devising a "death ray." He replied that in the present state of scientific knowledge death rays were out of the question, but he presented instead a paper titled "Detection and Location of Aircraft by Radio Methods." A practical demonstration of aircraft detection by electromagnetic waves was held by Watson-Watt and his junior colleague A. F. Wilkins at Daventry before the secretary of the committee on 26 February 1935. A Heyford bomber, flying through the short-wave radiations of the BBC's Empire Station at Daventry at a height of 6,000 feet, was identified at a distance of 8 miles on a cathode-ray oscilloscope display housed in the back of a Morris van.

This initial experiment, using only readily available laboratory equipment, was followed by the setting up of a purpose-built installation at Orfordness, Suffolk, where in mid-June an aircraft was tracked by radar for a distance of 17 miles, a performance improved to 40 miles the following month. These tests were particularly significant for the fact that the observers were able to take continuous measurements of the range of the aircraft.

The encouraging results achieved at Orfordness, and later at Bawdsey Manor, near Felixstowe, prompted a government decision in December 1935 to build five permanent air-defense radar stations covering the approach to London via the Thames Estuary. The first of these, at Bawdsey Manor, was handed over to the Royal Air Force in May 1937. By August a further decision had been made to provide an apron of radar stations protecting the whole east coast of England. The complete chain of twenty stations, stretching from Ventnor in the Isle of Wight to the Firth of Tay in Scotland, went on continuous watch starting on Good Friday, 7 April 1939.

At the outbreak of World War II, Germany had eight similar coastal radar stations guarding the narrow approach between the Dutch and Danish borders. Bearing in mind how conspicuous high-masted radar stations are, it is an extraordinary fact that neither country was aware that the other had discovered radio detection and developed it for air defense.

It is clear that Britain derived greater benefit from radar during the early part of the war than did her opponent, whose progress had been hampered by Hitler's edict that work was to be halted on all research projects that could not show a tangible result within a few months. Prof. P. M. S. Blackett, one of the original members of the Air Defence Committee, is on record as saying that without radar "the Battle of Britain in 1940—a near thing at best—might have been lost, with incalculable historic consequences."

Radar is not, strictly speaking, an invention nor can any one nation claim credit for originating it, since the technique used by Watson-Watt and others for measuring the distances of electrically charged layers in the upper atmosphere was known several years before its inception. For this reason it is not surprising that radar was evolved independently by a number of other countries—France, Japan, Italy, the Soviet Union, and the United States—concurrently with developments in Britain and Germany. In assessing relative achievements, however, it is worthy of note that although Germany was the first country to produce a working radar-detection system, only in September 1935 did her scientists adopt the use of pulse transmissions for calculating range, some three months after this essential prerequisite to the effective use of radar had been accomplished in Britain. None of the pre-war pioneers called radio detection by the name *radar* (RAdio Detection And Ranging); that was coined by Cdr. S. M. Tucker of the U.S. Navy in November 1940.

U.S.: Work on radar was begun by the Naval Research Laboratory at Anacostia, Washington, D.C., as early as January 1934, though progress by a nation not under the immediate threat of war was inevitably slower than in an unsettled Europe. The first detection apparatus was built between 1934 and 1936 by Albert Taylor and Robert Page with a transmitter in one building and receiver in another, linked to rooftop antennas. The first test was carried out on 26 April 1936 when it detected the passage of a small aircraft flying through the beam, but the power was insufficient to distinguish it on the screen until well within visual distance. Further trials on 6 May were more successful with aircraft detected from up to 17 miles away.

Although research by the Navy and the Signal Corps (starting in 1937) continued, U.S. radar research only became a high priority in the fall of 1940 after

Sir Henry Tizard's scientific mission to Washington, D.C., had made American physicists privy to radar's most significant wartime development, the microwave or cavity magnetron. This device, which was later adapted rather more mundanely as the microwave oven (qv), had been invented by Henry Boot and John Randall at Birmingham University in England and first demonstrated on 21 February 1940. Its 10-centimeter transmissions ran a mere fifteenth of standard airborne radar and were powerful enough to enable aircraft detection in darkness and heavy cloud cover for the first time. James Phinney Baxter III, official historian of the Office of Scientific Research & Development, said of the magnetron that "when the members of the Tizard Mission brought one to America in 1940, they carried the most valuable cargo ever brought to our shores." A team of physicists under Vennevar Bush was assembled at MIT's newly established Radiation Laboratory in Cambridge, Mass., and, within barely three months, America's first **airborne radar** had been installed in an Army B-18 and flown from East Boston Airport. The exact date is variously reported as 7 March and 10 March 1941. The difference of three days is significant. If it was the former, the United States had achieved the first use of microwave radar air-to-air detection in the world; if the latter, they tied with Great Britain, who carried out their initial such trials at the Telecommunication Research Establishment, near Swanage, Dorset, on the same date. A few weeks later on 27 March, the same B-18 did undoubtedly score a world first with the detection of submarines as it flew over Long Island Sound.

The first use, or sadly misuse, of radar by the United States in wartime occurred on Oahu in Hawaii on that day of destiny 7 December 1941. Three of the five radar stations on Oahu, America's first permanent ground installations, picked up faint signals from the Japanese invaders at 6:45 A.M., but no alarm had been raised when the stations were stood down as was customary at 7 A.M. Only one remained live. At Opana, Pvt. George E. Elliott asked the more experienced Pvt. Joseph L. Lockard for additional instruction time and the two men picked up increasingly strong signals that seemed to indicate a massive concentration of aircraft. The information was relayed to duty officer Lt. Kermit Tyler, who dismissed the warning in the belief that the aircraft detected were U.S. bombers returning to base. At 7:53 A.M. Lt. Cdr. Mitsuo Fuchida, leading the attack force, radioed the Japanese Navy with the signal "*Tora! Tora! Tora!*" which signified that the U.S. Pacific fleet had been attacked unawares.

Ship to be fitted with radar: The first was the 500-ton German naval-trials vessel *Welle* at Pelzerhaken in September 1935. Transmitting pulses on 600 megacycles, the radar installation was capable of detecting and ranging coastlines at a distance of 12 miles and other ships at 5 miles.

The first warship to carry radar as part of her regular equipment was the German pocket battleship *Graf Spee*, which was fitted with a 355-megacycle Seetakt gun-ranging set during the summer of 1936.

U.S.: Tests of a 200-megahertz pulse radar set developed by Robert Page of the U.S. Naval Research Laboratory were carried out aboard the destroyer USS *Leary* in April 1937, when ranges of up to 20 miles against aircraft were obtained. The first permanent installations were of the 20 CXAM sets built for the Navy by RCA, of which the battleship *California* had the inaugural one in May 1940, followed by battleships *Texas*, *Pennsylvania*, *West Virginia*, *North Carolina*, and *Washington*; the aircraft carriers *Yorktown*, *Lexington*, *Saratoga*, *Ranger*, *Enterprise*, and *Wasp*; seven cruisers; and the seaplane tender *Curtis*. *California* was sunk at Pearl Harbor, but the radar installation was salvaged for shore use at Oakee radar training school.

Radar bombing: The first raid detecting invisible targets by radar took place on 30 January 1943, when six Pathfinders left RAF Wyton near Huntingdon, England, under the command of Australian Donald Bennett for an attack on Germany. Equipped with H$_2$S radar, the Pathfinders successfully detected the target at 20 miles distance, then marked it for a raid by one hundred Lancaster bombers.

THE FIRST RADIO

system of signaling by, was described by Mahlon Loomis of Washington, D.C., in a paper dated 21 July 1866. During October of the same year Loomis succeeded in conveying messages over a distance of 14 miles between Catochin Ridge and Bear's Den in Loudon County, Virginia. The experiment was witnessed by U.S. senator Samuel C. Pomeroy of Kansas and U.S. representative John A. Bingham of Ohio. The inventor gave the following account of the method by which he achieved radio telegraphy:

> From two mountain peaks of the Blue Ridge in Virginia which are only about two thousand feet above tide water, two kites were let up—one from each summit... These kites had each a small piece of fine copper-wire gauze about fifteen inches square attached to their underside and connected also with the wire six hundred feet in length which held the kites when they were up... Good connection was made with the ground by laying in a wet place a coil of wire one end of which was secured to the binding post of a galvanometer. The equipments and apparatus at both stations are exactly alike. The time pieces of both parties having been set exactly alike, it was arranged that at precisely such an hour and minute the galvanometer at one station should be attached, or be in circuit with the ground and kit wires. At the opposite station the ground wire being already fast to the galvanometer, three separate and deliberate half-minute connections were made with the kite wire and instruments. This deflected, or moved, the needle at the other station with the same vigor and precision as if it had been attached to an ordinary battery.

After this initial demonstration, Loomis erected a pair of permanent steel radio masts to continue his experimental work. On 20 July 1872 he was granted the world's first wireless patent for an "Improvement in Telegraphing." In January of the following year Congress passed a bill incorporating the Loomis Aerial Telegraph Co. with the right to sell stock to the value of $2 million, but in a period of severe financial blight the necessary funds were not forthcoming and

Loomis was obliged to struggle on with his research without capital until his death in 1886.

Commercially practicable method of radio communication: The first was devised by Guglielmo Marconi of Bologna, Italy, who conducted his initial laboratory experiments at his father's country house, the Villa Griffone at Pontecchio, 11 miles from Bologna, in 1894. He began experimenting out of doors toward the end of September 1895, his brother Alfonso carrying the receiving set while Guglielmo himself worked the Morse key of the transmitter. Successful transmission across an open space was acknowledged by Alfonso with a white flag, but Guglielmo considered that the real test of the effectiveness of his apparatus was whether he could transmit signals over such natural obstacles as hills and mountains. Accordingly Alfonso discarded the flag and took the receiving set and a hunting rifle to the far side of the hill behind the Villa Griffone. After a while Guglielmo began to signal from a room in the house, and a few minutes later a shot from the rifle announced that he had achieved what Sir William Preece was later to describe as a "new system of telegraphy that will reach places hitherto inaccessible . . ."

Following his successful demonstrations at the Villa Griffone, Guglielmo Marconi offered his invention to the Italian Ministry of Posts and Telegraphs. On receiving a letter of rejection, he decided to take his apparatus to England, which was then the foremost naval power in the world and the most likely to appreciate the potentiality of radio signaling. Arriving in February 1896, he received an initial setback when his radio equipment was broken beyond repair by aggressive customs inspectors, who suspected that it was some "infernal machine" and its owner, being Italian, an anarchist. Guglielmo took rooms at 71 Hereford Road, Bayswater, together with his mother, who had accompanied him, and on 2 June 1896 he applied for a patent for a method by which "electrical actions or manifestations are transmitted through the air, earth or water by means of electrical oscillations of high frequency." Shortly afterward, he secured an introduction to Sir William Preece, chief engineer of the Post Office, who took an immediate interest in the twenty-one-year-old Italian and his remarkable achievement and did much to further his cause in scientific circles. On 12 December 1896 the first public demonstration of radio was given under his auspices at Toynbee Hall in London. The following July Marconi formed the Wireless Telegraph & Signal Co. Ltd. for the manufacture of radio equipment and maintenance of radio stations.

Radio station: The first was the experimental Royal Needles Hotel Wireless Station at Alum Bay, Isle of Wight, established by the Wireless Telegraph & Signal Co. Ltd. with a 120-foot-high radio mast and operative on 6 December 1897. The company's first order was received from Lloyd's of London, which ordered transmitters and receivers for the Rathlin Island Lighthouse and a shore station in Ballycastle, County Antrim, in Ireland. The initial messages from the lighthouse, reporting ten ships, were received on 26 August 1898. Subsequently all Lloyd's signal stations were equipped with radio.

U.S.: Marconi arrived in the United States in September 1899 to supervise the wireless relay of messages reporting the America's Cup races between Sir Thomas Lipton's *Shamrock* and the New York Yacht Club's *Columbia*. The contest began off New York on 3 October, with reports transmitted from wireless installations aboard the steamships *Ponce* and *Grande Duchesse* to shore stations in the Navesink Highlands in New Jersey and on 34th Street in Manhattan. From there they were sent by cable to Europe and across North America. The Navesink and Manhattan terminals were the first permanent radio stations in the United States, continuing to be operated for experimental work by the newly established Marconi Wireless Telegraph Co. of America after Marconi himself had returned to Britain.

Commercial radio service: The first in the world open to the paying public was inaugurated in Hawaii by the Inter-Island Telegraph Co. on 2 March 1901. Back on the American mainland, the Marconi Wireless Telegraph Co. of America received its first order from the *New York Herald* in August of the same year for radio installations at Siasconset on Nantucket Island and on *Nantucket Lightship No. 66*, stationed some 40 miles offshore in the South Shoals. As Nantucket was often the first point of contact for American-bound ships, this enabled the *Herald* to steal a march on its rivals with the arrival times of transatlantic liners bearing the great and the good. Under the terms of the contract, Marconi also reported arrivals to the steamship companies at a rate of $5 per vessel.

Regular commercial service on or from the American mainland was inaugurated in 1902 by the American Wireless Telephone & Telegraph Co. between radio stations established at Los Angeles and Avalon, Santa Catalina Island, divided by 22 miles of Pacific coastal waters. The first substantive message sent between the two stations was the result of the Bob Fitzsimmons and Jim Jeffries title fight in San Francisco on 25 July, reporting that the American heavyweight Jeffries had knocked out the Cornishman in the eighth round. Curiously the American Wireless Telephone & Telegraph Co. was almost entirely fraudulent, having been set up by its dubious backers to milk a public enchanted by the wonder of wireless. The Pacific concession, however, was in the hands of a capable young man of integrity called Robert H. Marriott, who abandoned the worthless patents held by the parent company in favor of equipment of his own devising. Another "first" followed on quickly from the fight result, when two men who had failed to pay their tab for a heavy drinking session at Santa Catalina's Metropole Hotel were apprehended as they docked in Los Angeles. A radio message sent by Marriott's operator on the island to the Los Angeles Police Department had resulted in the earliest instance of criminals being arrested through the agency of radio, eight years before the much more celebrated case, normally cited as the first, of the murderer Dr. Crippen's arrest after fleeing across the Atlantic. Santa Catalina pioneered once again in radio history when the world's first public radio telephone service (SEE **radio telephone**) was established in 1920.

THE FIRST **RADIO BROADCAST**

is generally claimed to have been presented by Canadian-born Prof. Reginald Aubrey Fessenden (SEE ALSO **radio telephone**) via the 420-foot-high radio mast of the National Electric Signaling Co.'s radio station at Brant Rock, Mass., on 24 December 1906. The program, Fessenden's widow was later to record in her 1940 biography of him, opened with the inventor himself playing "O, Holy Night" on the violin, after which he sang and then recited some verses from the Gospel of Saint Luke. The next item was a recording of Handel's "Largo," and the transmission concluded with a Christmas greeting from Fessenden to his listeners. The broadcast was said to have been picked up by a number of ships' radio operators within a 5-mile range of the radio station. A second broadcast, Helen Fessenden wrote, was made on New Year's Eve with much more favorable atmospheric conditions, reception being reported from as far away as the West Indies.

The veracity of the story, which has been written into every standard history of radio, has been disputed by radio historian James O'Neal. Writing for *Radio World* (25 October 2006), O'Neal points out that the claim was originally made by Prof. Fessenden twenty-five years after the fact and that there is no contemporary record of it. Nor did anyone recall hearing either broadcast in later years. The only available daily radio log surviving from the period, kept by a wireless buff named Francis Hart located within easy range of Brant Rock, makes no mention of them. Moreover in a 1925 article for *Radio News* Prof. Fessenden gave the year of his first broadcast as 1907. When Lee De Forest claimed to have made the first broadcast in February 1907 (SEE BELOW), Fessenden did not challenge him.

The first regular experimental broadcasts—or, if James O'Neal's findings are accepted, the first of any kind—were transmitted from a studio on the top floor of the Parker Building on Fourth Avenue, New York City, in February 1907 by the De Forest Radio Telephone Co. (SEE **radio telephone**). Lee De Forest wrote in his diary, "My present task (happy one) is to distribute sweet melody broadcast over the city and sea so that in time even the mariner far out across the silent waves may hear the music of his homeland . . ." To start with the programs consisted solely of Columbia phonograph records; the first live performer—and the first **professional artiste to broadcast**—was the Swedish soprano Eugenia Farrar, who sang "I Love You Truly" and "Just a Wearyin' for You" in a broadcast from the USS *Connecticut* at Brooklyn Navy Yard on 16 December 1907.

Although he concentrated on musical presentations, in 1909 De Forest brought his well-known mother-in-law, Harriet Stanton Black, to the studio to give the world's first broadcast talk, her subject being the topical one of women's suffrage. Other notable "firsts" included the first "remote" in January 1910, when listeners were able to hear Italian tenor Enrico Caruso live from the Metropolitan Opera House in New York City (SEE **radio broadcast: opera**), and the first studio broadcast by an artiste of international repute, given by the prima donna Mme. Mariette Mazarin the following month.

The De Forest transmissions are believed to have ceased in 1911, when the fortunes of the De Forest Radio Telephone Co. were at a low ebb. Other early broadcasting services were offered by Thomas E. Clark of the Clark Wireless Telegraph & Telephone Co., Detroit, who began transmitting phonograph record programs in 1907 for the benefit of the Great Lakes steamers; and by Charles D. Herrold, with broadcasts from his School of Radio at the Garden City Bank Building in San José, Calif., starting in January 1909. The exact date when daily broadcasting was initiated is not known, but a number of pioneer amateur radio operators in the San José area signed affidavits to the effect that they were listening to the Herrold station every weekday as early as 1910. The Herrold station was assigned the call letters SJN in 1912, was reclassified as KQW in 1921, and became KCBS in 1949. As such, it is generally acknowledged to be the oldest broadcasting station in the world. A plaque, now adorning the American Trust Co. Building in San José, asserts that this was where the "world's First Regular Broadcasting Station" had its beginning, a claim that must rest on whatever definition of "regular" is accepted in this context.

Rival claimants to the honor are far from few, though all but one are North American. De Forest's 1907 station had been "regular" in the sense that it continued broadcasting for four years without any long intervals off the air. The station started up again in 1916 with the installation of a transmitter on the roof of his laboratories at High Beach in the Bronx, N.Y., and broadcast phonograph record concerts five nights a week until America's entry into the First World War put a stop to all nonessential use of radio telephony. It reopened as Station 2XG in 1919, taking an important step toward the realization of radio as a real entertainment medium by the appointment of **announcers** (Bill Gowen and Bill Garity) as well as the first **program director** known to history, Richard Klein.

Early in 1920, 2XG came to a premature end when De Forest decided to move the station from High Beach to the World's Tower Building on 46th Street and Broadway. In doing so, however, he unwittingly broke the law by transferring his transmitter from the Bronx, where it was licensed, to Manhattan, where it was not. The New York Federal Radio Inspector not only notified De Forest that he must cease broadcasting forthwith, but at the same time ruled that "there is no room on the ether for entertainment."

Thus 2XG represented the halfway stage between purely experimental broadcasting and fully fledged entertainment service. De Forest himself credited Station WWJ Detroit with having initiated the modern era of broadcasting, describing it as "the first commercial radio station in America to broadcast regular daily programs." Originating as 8MK Detroit, the station began transmitting experimentally from the *Detroit News* office early in 1920. Regular scheduled broadcasts, consisting of record concerts, were advertised in the *News* from 20 August 1920—the first time that **daily program listings** had appeared in any newspaper. From that date there were also **news broadcasts**, compiled from news agency wire service reports supplied by the *Detroit News*. The newscaster is unidentified.

On 31 August it was announced that returns from the Michigan county, state, and congressional primaries would be aired that evening. The 4-hour program was the first occasion on which **broadcast election results** were heard. Unlike KDKA Pittsburgh (SEE BELOW), WWJ made no attempt to sell radio receivers in conjunction with the new service. At that time there were about 300 "radio hams" able to pick up the transmissions within the approximately 100-mile range of the transmitter.

Until December 1921 the programs consisted mainly of news reports and phonograph records, but that month there was a considerable expansion of the service. By this time the WWJ's radio department comprised three full-time staff, a program manager and two engineers. Six months later when the staff had grown to eight, the manager reported that phonograph recitals now occupied "an incidental place on the daily schedule, and the programmes are filled by stage celebrities, prominent clergymen, musicians, and public figures of various sorts, many with national reputations." Finzel's Orchestra had been engaged on a regular basis and it was "common for Detroit families to hold parties in their homes and dance to the music played by their favorite orchestra." The audience had also expanded, with reports from listeners coming in from as far afield as Wyoming, Alaska, Saskatchewan and Alberta in Canada, Cuba, and Honduras.

The other principal American contender to the title of "first full-service broadcasting station" (i.e., not experimental) is KDKA Pittsburgh. A comparison between the claims of WWJ and KDKA is made below.

KDKA owes its origin to an advertisement placed in the *Pittsburgh Sun* by the Joseph Horne Department Store on 29 September 1920. Headed AIR CONCERT PICKED UP BY RADIO HERE, it described how programs broadcast by Dr. Frank Conrad's amateur station 8XK could be heard "on the wireless receiving station which was recently installed here for patrons interested in wireless experiments." Similar receivers, stated the advertisement, were then on sale in the West Basement at prices of $10 upward.

Dr. Conrad was a radio engineer employed by the Westinghouse Co., whose vice president, H. P. Davis, was among those who saw the Joseph Horne advertisement. The next day Davis suggested that Westinghouse erect a station at East Pittsburgh and operate it on a daily schedule "so that people would acquire the habit of listening to it just as they do of reading a newspaper."

The station was licensed by the Department of Commerce and assigned the call letters KDKA on 27 October 1920. Westinghouse had already begun manufacturing a special home receiver in sufficient quantity to ensure that everyone who wanted one would be able to listen in to the opening broadcast on 2 November. These can reasonably be regarded as the first American **radio sets** designed solely for listening to broadcasts rather than for conducting radio experiments.

At the time that KDKA came on the air under the direction of Frank Conrad, Detroit's 8MK was still being run as an amateur experimental staion

personally financed by William Scripps, publisher of the *Detroit News*. It was not owned by the newspaper, and despite Lee De Forest's generous tribute, it was not at this stage in any sense commercially operated. KDKA's claim to priority, as the earliest non-experimental broadcasting station, is based on the fact that it was founded as a commercial enterprise whose only object would be to provide a *program service sufficiently entertaining and informative to induce prospective listeners to buy radio sets*. In this important respect it differed from 8MK, which still referred to its listeners as "radio operators," seeing them as fellow experimenters, while Westinghouse aimed to reach the family circle rather than just the radio ham.

A challenge to KDKA comes from north of the border, where Marconi's XWA Montreal had been licensed in September 1919. This has been countered on the grounds that XWA's initial transmissions were spasmodic and experimental. The key date, however, is 21 May 1920, when XWA began regular scheduled programming—more than five months ahead of KDKA. As the Marconi Co. was the pioneer manufacturer of radio components, they clearly had an interest in promoting the sale of receivers. But there is an even earlier claim to priority from Europe, based on the fact that the service, like KDKA's, was intended to promote the sale of radio sets for entertainment. This was the Dutch station PCGG Hague, which began regular scheduled transmissions from the Philips Co. premises on 5 November 1919. The broadcasts were organized by the impressively named Hanso Hericus Schotanus à Steringa Idzerda, whose radio manufacturing company Nederlandse Radio-Industrie obtained its valves from Philips. The *Nieuwe Rotterdamse Courante* wrote of the inaugural concert: "Everybody who possesses a simple radio receiver may listen to music in the comfort of his own home. With the aid of amplifiers it can be made audible across the entire room."

At first the programs were weekly and from December 1919 twice a week. Starting on 29 April 1920 a special "Dutch Concert" for English and French listeners was broadcast on Sunday afternoons between 3 and 5:40 with announcements in three languages. This was occasionally interrupted for London listeners by air traffic control from Croydon Aerodrome, but elsewhere in Britain good reception was reported from Dumfries in Scotland to Honiton in Devon.

PCGG remained on air until October 1924 and was undoubtedly broadcasting scheduled entertainment programs, designed to cater to purchasers of radio sets, earlier than WWJ Detroit, KDKA Pittsburgh, or XWA Montreal. By a sad irony Idzerda, who has some claim to the title of "father of full-service broadcasting," was executed by the Nazis in World War II for listening in to an illegal Allied broadcast.

.

THE FIRST **RADIO BROADCAST ANNOUNCER**

full-time, was Harold Arlin, who was appointed by KDKA Pittsburgh with effect from 1 January 1921. He was also the first to do a baseball commentary—Pittsburg Pirates vs Philadelphia Phillies on 5 August 1921—and a football commentary, University of Pittsburg vs University of West Virginia on 8 October 1921. Arlin's KDKA broadcasts were heard on both sides of the Atlantic. When he gave up broadcasting in 1925 to rejoin KDKA's parent company Western Electric, the *Times* of London said that his was "the best-known American voice in Europe."

THE FIRST
RADIO BROADCAST: COMMERCIAL

is usually attributed to WEAF New York, but nearly four months earlier, on 4 May 1922, IXE (later WGI) of Medford, Mass., aired an advertisement for a local auto dealer.

WEAF (now WNBC) was the first radio station to broadcast commercials, or more precisely, **sponsored programs**, with any regularity, starting on 28 August 1922 with a 10-minute talk by the Queensboro Corporation promoting Hawthorne Court, a new cooperative apartment house in Jackson Heights, New York City. It was scripted and performed by Queensboro's sales manager Maxwell Blackwell. The sponsor paid $250 for five successive daily airings and was later able to report that two apartments had been sold in response to the advertisement. Shortly after this the station manager of WEAF New York

rejected an ad for toothpaste on the grounds that "care of the teeth" was too delicate a subject to be mentioned on air. WEAF's service was described by the owners of the station, the American Telephone & Telegraph Co., as "toll broadcasting." The station itself provided no program material at all, but anyone could come in and give his or her message to the world, commercial or otherwise, or demonstrate his own particular talents, for a set fee of so much per minute of airtime. Within a year WEAF had twenty-five advertisers, including Macy's, Greeting Card Association, American Hard Rubber Co., the Bedford YMCA, National Surety Co., Metropolitan Insurance Co., and Haynes Automobile Co. These sponsors were forbidden to mention anything about their products or services. All they were allowed to do was attach their names to general-interest programs that they either made themselves or had made by their advertising agencies. Some advertisers found ways to overcome these restrictions. The National Carbon Co.'s *Eveready Hour*, which debuted on WEAF on 4 December 1923 and became the first **network sponsored program** the following 12 February, succeeded in maximizing mentions of the brand by introducing flame-haired topliner Wesley Hall every time he came on by one of a number of different sobriquets: "The Eveready Redhead," "Eveready Red," the "Eveready Entertainer," and "The Eveready Red-headed Music Maker."

Other stations did permit spot commercials, but they were read live by the presenter of the sponsored program. The modern concept of the radio commercial, as a pre-recorded product plug produced within an advertising agency and using outside talent, was pioneered in 1933 by Boston agency Kasper-Gorden Inc. In 1935 Cecil Widdifield of the Schwimmer & Scott Advertising Agency took this concept farther with spots transmitted nationally. These were designed for insertion in the 20-second interval between programs that was standard in the 1930s. According to E. P. J. Shurick in *The First Quarter-Century of American Broadcasting* (Kansas City, 1946), the first artiste to star in a series of commercials was the Omaha-born comedian George Girot, known as "the Greek Ambassador of Goodwill" (he played an immigrant who mangled the English language). This was around 1936 but Shurick does not identity the name of the client.

SEE ALSO **advertising jingle; television commercials**.

THE FIRST **RADIO BROADCAST: OPERA**

was transmitted from the Metropolitan Opera House, New York City, on 13 January 1910 by the De Forest Radio Telephone Co. This occasion was also notable as the first "remote broadcast" in history. The operas heard were *Cavalleria Rusticana* and *I Pagliacci*, with Italian tenor Enrico Caruso singing the role of Canio in the latter. The female leads were sung by Mme. Emmy Destinn and Bella Alten, respectively. The acoustical microphone was placed in the footlights, though for the first aria—"La Siciliana" from *Cavalleria Rusticana*, sung by Riccardo Martin from behind the curtain—a microphone was placed on a table in front of him. Receiving sets were installed at the opera house itself and at the Park Avenue laboratory of the De Forest Radio Telephone Co., the Metropolitan Life Building, and the Hotel Breslin near Times Square. In addition, the broadcast was picked up by radio operators at the Brooklyn Navy Yard and by a number of ships in New York Harbor, including RMS *Avon*, whose Captain had invited 260 guests on board to listen.

The first full opera presentation by a regular radio station was of an amateur performance of *Martha* from the Denver Auditorium by 9ZAF Denver on 19 May 1921. The first performance by professional singers followed on 15 March 1922, when WJZ New York presented Mozart's *The Impresario* with Tom McGranahan and Hazel Huntingdon.

THE FIRST **RADIO BROADCAST: ORCHESTRAL**

was an hour-long performance of the California Theater Orchestra of San Francisco under Herman Heller, transmitted by Lee De Forest (SEE ALSO **radio broadcast; radio telephone**) via a transmitter on the Humboldt Bank Building adjoining the theater in April 1920. These Heller concerts were continued on a regular basis for some months and attracted an appreciative audience of music lovers as well as radio hams. "In one isolated community far back in the Coast Range," wrote De Forest in his *Autobiography*, "an opulent rancher installed a receiver and loud-speaker, and for miles around, his neighbors would journey each Sunday to hear that marvel coming out of the air from 'Frisco.'"

THE FIRST **RADIO BROADCAST: PLAY**

was the Broadway production *The Perfect Fool*, presented by WJZ from its New York studio on 19 February 1922. It starred Ed Wynn, who also toplined in the stage version. Discomforted by the lack of an audience, he "froze" before the microphone. When he later became a regular radio performer, Wynn always insisted on a studio audience.

The first regular drama series on radio began in September 1922 with the inception of the WGY Players, who presented a play every Friday night from the General Electric station WGY in Schenectady, New York. The scripts were typed on paper "especially selected for its freedom from crackling sound." At first the Players gave their services gratis, but by 1924 Rosaline Greene, America's "first leading lady of radio," was being paid $5 a performance.

Play written for radio: The first was *The Truth About Father Christmas*, a Christmas play for children by Phyllis M. Twigg, broadcast by the BBC from its Marconi House studios in London on 24 December 1922.

U.S.: *When Love Wakens* (note initial letters) by WLW Cincinnati program director Fred Smith, presented on 3 April 1923, was the first play written for radio in the United States.

The first **soap opera** was *The Smith Family*, a lighthearted serial detailing the triumphs and tribulations of an upper-crust family. Mr. and Mrs. Smith were played by vaudeville team Jim and Marion Jordan, later to become celebrated as Fibber McGee and Molly. It debuted on WENR Chicago on 7 June 1929 and from March 1930 was sponsored by the National Tea Company. Most of the daytime soaps, targeted at stay-at-home housewives, were sponsored by the hugely competitive soap companies such as Procter & Gamble, Colgate-Palmolive, and Lever Brothers, hence the term. It is probably derived from "horse opera" (a B-movie western), an expression first noted in 1927, whereas "soap opera" first appeared in print in 1939. The abbreviation "soap" was in use by 1943.

THE FIRST

RADIO BROADCAST: REQUEST PROGRAM

was inaugurated by WDAF Kansas City, whose late-night broadcasts by the Coon-Sanders Novelty Orchestra from the Plantation Grill at the Hotel Muehlebach began on 5 December 1922. Soon afterward the band changed its name to the Coon-Sanders Original Nighthawks Orchestra and began inviting listeners to phone in their requests. These were played immediately and as the transmission was made "in the clear" they could be picked up anywhere in the United States. The program was renamed *Nighthawk Follies* and a fan club formed, believed to have been the first associated with broadcasting. Within two years it had attracted 37,000 members.

THE FIRST

RADIO BROADCAST: SPORTS COMMENTARY

is problematic. It is claimed in innumerable sources (probably copied from each other) that the Jack Dempsey–Billy Fiske prizefight in Benton Harbor, Mich., on 6 September 1920 was broadcast live by WWJ Detroit. No source names the commentator. WWJ, which was then 8MK, had started daily broadcasting three weeks earlier, but it seems unlikely that they would have had the resources or the know-how to mount a remote broadcast from 250 miles distant. More tellingly, a detailed article in *Radio Broadcast* in June 1922 on WWJ's achievements to that date makes no mention of any such transmission. The station was, however, broadcasting news reports on a regular basis and it seems likely that a straightforward report on the fight has been conflated into a play-by-play.

KDKA Pittsburg broadcast Johnny Ray's fight against Johnny Dundee at the Motor Square in Pittsburgh on 11 April 1921. The commentator was Florent Gibson of the *Pittsburgh Star*, but he was not heard on air. He telephoned his commentary to the KDKA studio, where announcer Harold Arlin (SEE **radio broadcast announcer**) repeated it into the microphone. Arlin became a sports commentator himself with the first baseball broadcast on 5 August 1921, when he reported a game between the Pittsburgh Pirates and the Philadelphia Phillies from Forbes Field, the home team winning 8 to 5. On 5 November of that year he also became the first to do the commentary for a football game, University of Pittsburgh defeating University of West Virginia 21 to 13.

In the meantime the first major sports event to be broadcast live had been the heavyweight title fight between Jack Dempsey and France's Georges Carpentier on 2 July 1921 at Boyle's Thirty Acres in Jersey City, N.J., for which David Sarnoff of RCA set up a temporary broadcasting station, WJY Hoboken, with a one-day license. The commentator was wireless enthusiast and amateur boxer Maj. J. Andrew White, whose breathless report of the action was heard by an estimated audience of 300,000 and judged a triumph for the infant medium of broadcasting. It could, however, have been a disaster. Seconds after he had described Georges Carpentier being counted out in the fourth round, the transmission came to an abrupt halt when the transmitter at Hoboken crashed.

The first specialist **sportscaster** hired to fulfill that role rather than general announcing was Hal Totten, who had played baseball for Northwestern University in Evanston, Ill., and had been sports editor of the *Daily Northwestern* before joining the *Chicago Daily News* as a sportswriter. In 1924 he switched to WMAQ Chicago, reporting the University of Chicago football games and Chicago Clubs baseball from Wrigley Field.

THE FIRST **RADIO BROADCAST: TALK RADIO**

was pioneered by WRA of Richmond, Va., in 1937. The 30-minute program was called *Telephone Interviews* and was presented by Irv Abeloff on Wednesday and Friday evenings. *Variety* reported that the station had "taken the man off the street and put him on the telephone." Calls had to be recorded before being put on air, due to telephone company regulations against broadcasting live calls.

THE FIRST
RADIO BROADCAST: VOX POP INTERVIEWS

were conducted on 27 June 1932 by Ted Husing of CBS, who carried a lapel microphone around the lobby of the Congress Hotel in Chicago where the delegates to the Democratic Convention were gathered. Husing asked bystanders spot questions about the prospect of Franklin D. Roosevelt's nomination for the presidency. The first regular interview program of this nature was *The Man Passing By*, which debuted on KRTH Houston on 7 November 1932. Presenters Parks Johnson and Jerry Belcher suspended a microphone out of the window of KRTH's studio in the Rice Hotel and asked passersby who they thought would win the following day's presidential election. This received such a positive response from audiences that the experiment was repeated the following week with a program devoted to Houstonians' views on Prohibition and again the next week with who should be next mayor of Houston. After that it was apparent that *The Man Passing By* had become a regular feature of the schedule, though for some time many of the interviewees refused to believe that they were live on radio. The show was networked by NBC in June 1935 as *Sidewalk Interviews*, which began with broadcasts from the lobby of the Hotel New Yorker, in New York City, by Parks Johnson. It became *Vox Pop* in 1938 and under this title was moved to CBS.

THE FIRST **RADIO DISTRESS SIGNAL**

was transmitted from the *East Goodwin Lightship* on 17 March 1899 when the merchant vessel *Elbe* ran aground on the Goodwin Sands in the English Channel. The message was received by the radio operator on duty at the South Foreland Lighthouse, who was able to summon the aid of the Ramsgate lifeboat. The *East Goodwin Lightship* became the first vessel to send a radio signal of its own distress on 28 April 1899 when it was rammed by SS *R.F. Matthews.*

Prior to the introduction of SOS, the recognized call sign for ships in distress was CQD. The signal, devised by the Marconi Co. and effective from 1 February 1904, was intended to mean "All Stations—Urgent," but was popularly misinterpreted as "Come Quick—Danger." SOS (which does *not* stand for Save Our Souls or anything else) was established as an international distress signal by an agreement made between the British Marconi Society and the German Telefunken organization at the Berlin Radio Conference on 3 October 1906. It was formally introduced on 1 July 1908.

The first occasion on which the SOS signal was transmitted in an emergency occurred on 10 June 1909, when the Cunard liner SS *Slavonia* was wrecked off the Azores. Two steamers received her signals and went to the rescue.

U.S.: The first SOS signal was transmitted by Theodore D. Haubner from the American liner *Arapahoe*, off Cape Hatteras, N.C., on 11 August 1909 following the rupture of a propeller shaft. The signal was received by wireless operator R. J. Vosburg at station HA, Cape Hatteras.

SOS remained the standard distress signal until Morse Code was officially retired as a means of maritime communication in 1999. It has been replaced by the satellite-relayed Global Maritime Distress and Safety System.

Mayday signal: This internationally recognized vocal signal for use over radio telephones was originated in 1923 for aircraft in distress by Frederick Mockford, senior radio operator at Croydon Aerodrome near London. He had been asked to come up with a phrase that would be readily understood by pilots and ground staff in any language. Since much of Croydon's traffic was with Paris, Mockford proposed "Mayday" as a transliteration of the French *m'aidez* or "help me." In neither language does this phrase carry a sense of extreme urgency, though repeated three times, as is customary, and usually in tones of strangulated terror, it does. Mayday was adopted for other emergencies, not only those in the air, and is frequently used by yachts in danger of sinking.

THE FIRST **RADIO-MICROPHONE**

SEE **loudspeaker**.

THE FIRST **RADIO TELEPHONE**

capable of reproducing articulate speech was the Radiophone devised by Charles Sumner Tainter and Alexander Graham Bell and successfully demonstrated for the first time on 15 February 1880. The transmitter was located on top of the Franklin School on 13th Street, Washington, D.C., and Tainter spoke into in the words: "Mr. Bell! Mr. Bell! If you hear me, come to the window and wave your hat!" A moment later Bell appeared at the window of his laboratory on 14th Street, hat in hand.

The great telephone pioneer gave credit for the invention to A. C. Brown of the Eastern Telegraph Co., who had come to him two years earlier with a plan for telephony without wires. This was based on the action of a ray of light falling on selenium connected to a battery, with a telephone receiver in the circuit. The variations in the beam of light, actuated by the voice, were picked up at the receiving end by a wafer-thin mirror in the shape of a telephone diaphragm. The method was only effective across an open space with no obstructions to the light beam, and so its practical application was limited, though successful tests were carried out over a distance of 1½ miles between the Franklin School and the Virginia Hills. It was subsequently developed by the American Telephone & Telegraph Co., and was employed under the trade name Photophone during the early 1900s by the German Government for lighthouse-to-shore communication and also by the U.S. Army Signal Corps. The system had one remarkable advantage over conventional methods of radio telephony in that the conversation could not be tapped.

The first conventional system of radio telephony (i.e., capable of relaying speech through the ether regardless of any barriers between transmitter and receiver) was developed by the Canadian electrical scientist Prof. Reginald Aubrey Fessenden and demonstrated for the first time over a distance of approximately 1 mile at Cobb Point, Md., on 23 December 1900. He

recorded in his diary: "This afternoon, here at Cobb Island intelligible speech by electromagnetic waves for the first time in the world's history has been transmitted." The inaugural message hardly lived up to this sense of occasion. Fessenden asked his assistant "Is it snowing there, Mr. Thiessen? If it is, telegraph me back."

Transatlantic speech transmission by radio telephone was first made unintentionally by Prof. Fessenden in mid-November 1906, when a conversation being transmitted between the National Electric Signaling Co.'s station at Brant Rock, Mass., and a receiver at Plymouth, Mass., was picked up by radio operators at Machrihanish, Scotland. The voice was of a Brant Rock operator, Mr. Stein, telling Plymouth how to run their dynamo.

The first direct transatlantic speech relay by radio telephone was made by the American Telephone & Telegraph Co. from Arlington, Va., to Paris on 21 October 1915. Mr. B. B. Webb spoke to Lt. Col. Ferrie, representing the French government, who was operating a receiver installed at the Eiffel Tower Radio Station by the Bell Telephone System.

Commercial radio telephone installation: The first was made in the spring of 1907 by the De Forest Radio Telephone Co. on behalf of the Lackawanna Railroad Co. Two land stations were erected, one on the banks of the Hudson River at Hoboken, N.J., and the other at the company's offices on 23rd Street in Manhattan. A third transmitter, and the first radio-telephone apparatus to be operated from a ship, was installed on the Lackawanna ferryboat *Bergen*.

The first public service available to telephone subscribers was inaugurated between Long Beach, Calif., and Avalon, Santa Catalina Island, off the California mainland, by the Southern California Telephone Co. on 16 July 1920. The distance was 30 miles, and Avalon subscribers could be connected to callers anywhere else in the United States via the land-lines that terminated at Long Beach. The project was engineered by the American Telephone and Telegraph Co. and by the Western Electric Co. It was abandoned after three years of operation owing to tapping by other radio operators.

Military use of radio telephone: Japan's forces acquired radio telephone equipment during the Russo-Japanese War and it was used to decisive effect at the Battle of Mukden in Manchuria (now the city of Shenyang, China), the last major campaign of the war, which was fought between 20 February and 10 March 1905. The commander of the five armies, Field Marshal Oyama Iwao, was able to transmit orders to his generals from headquarters 12 miles behind the front line.

U.S.: The first use of radio telephone was made by the U.S. Army Signal Corps, which conducted a series of experiments in 1908 over the 18-mile distance between Sandy Hook and Bedloes Island, off Bridgeport, Conn. The German-made Telefunken set was fitted with carbon microphones and worked on a 550v direct current supplied from 10 electric arcs.

Naval vessels to be equipped with radio-telephone apparatus: The first were the USS *Virginia* and USS *Connecticut*, in which installations were made by the De Forest Radio Telephone Co. in September 1907. Tests were conducted off Cape Cod, Mass., in the same month and articulate speech was received at distances of up to 21 miles. As a result of the experiments the De Forest Co. was commissioned by the U.S. Navy to install radio-telephone equipment in all twenty-four vessels of Adm. Evans's fleet, which was then about to start on a round-the-world voyage.

Walkie-Talkie: The first portable radio telephone pack-set or walkie-talkie for military use was produced at the U.S. Army Signal Corps Engineering Laboratories at Fort Monmouth, N.J., in 1933. On 14 September of the same year the first handheld radio telephones, a 3½-pound one-valve model manufactured by the British electronics firm Plessey, were issued to the Brighton Police Force in Sussex, England. The first handheld instrument in the United States was patented by Canadian-born Al Gross of Cleveland, Ohio, in 1938. It was developed during World War II for the U.S. Office of Strategic Services as a two-way air-to-ground communication system, the 3½-pound transceiver being small enough for use behind enemy lines. In the meantime test models of the 5-pound Motorola AM SCR-536 "Handie-Talkie" had been used for the first time by police and secret-servicemen at President Franklin D. Roosevelt's third inauguration in Washington, D.C., on 20 January 1941. The president was sufficiently impressed to write to the Defense Department asking about their potential for military use. With this backing they were rushed into production and from July 1941 some 40,000 were issued to the armed forces, seeing service in every theater of war.

THE FIRST RAILROAD ACCIDENT

happened on the Middleton Colliery Railway near Leeds, England, on 5 December 1821. Carpenter David Brook was killed by a Blenkinsop-Murray locomotive as he walked home from Leeds along the railroad track in a blinding sleet. The first on a public railway occurred at the foot of Simpasture on the Stockton & Darlington Railway in County Durham, England, on 19 March 1828, when driver John Gillespie was killed as the result of a boiler explosion. A second accident of similar nature took place at Aycliffe watering station on 1 July, resulting in the death of driver John Cree. Both fatalities were due to the carelessness of the men involved in not allowing the weights of the safety valves, fixed down during the journey, to remain down while their engines were stationary.

The first accident involving a passenger took place at the opening of the Liverpool & Manchester Railway on 15 September 1830, when Britain's former treasury secretary the Rt. Hon. William Huskisson MP was run down by the *Rocket* locomotive as he stood on the track at Parkside. According to eyewitness Samuel Smiles:

> The "Northumbrian" engine with the carriage containing the Duke of Wellington was drawn up on one line in order that the whole of the train might pass in review before him and his party on the other. Mr. Huskisson had alighted from the carriage, and was standing on the road, along which the "Rocket" engine was observed rapidly coming up. At this moment the Duke of Wellington, between whom and Mr. Huskisson some coolness had existed, made a sign of recognition and held out his hand. A hurried and friendly grasp was given, and before it was loosed, there was a general cry from the bystanders, "Get in! Get in!" Flurried and confused, Mr. Huskisson endeavored to get around the open door of the carriage, which

projected over the opposite rail, but in so doing he was struck down by the "Rocket." His first words on being raised were, "I have met my death."

Huskisson was conveyed to Eccles in a critical condition by the *Northumbrian*, which in the emergency covered the 15-mile distance in a record 25 minutes, but he died at the rectory the same night.

U.S.: The first fatality was caused by the fireman of America's first passenger-train locomotive, the South Carolina Railroad's *The Best Friend of Charleston*, tying down the safety valve while the locomotive stood stationary on the turntable at Forks of the Road, near Charleston, on 17 June 1831. He did so, according to the engineer, Nicholas W. Darrell, because he was tired of listening to its whistling sound. The result was that the boiler exploded, killing the African-American fireman and injuring Darrell and another man. The locomotive was destroyed beyond repair.

The first accident in the United States involving the deaths of passengers and the world's first **derailment** occurred on the Camden & Amboy line between Spotswood and Heightstown, N.J., on 8 November 1833, when two people were killed and twelve passengers injured out of a total of twenty-four as a broken axle caused the car to overturn. Among the injured were future "railroad king" Cornelius Vanderbilt and former president John Quincy Adams.

THE FIRST **RAILROAD DINING CAR**

took the form of a self-service buffet car put into service on the Philadelphia, Wilmington & Baltimore Railroad in 1863. Two day-coaches were divided in the center, one side being designated a "smoker" and the other a "buffet." The food was cooked at the terminus and kept hot in steam-boxes. There were no seats in the buffet section, and passengers either ate standing up at the counter or took their food back into the smoker.

The first dining car to serve full-course meals prepared by a chef on the train was the *President*, a sleeping-car-cum-diner designed by George M. Pullman and put into service by the Great Western Railroad of Canada in 1867. W. F. Rae, who traveled on the Great Central route in September 1869, recorded an impression of Pullman's innovation in his *Westward by Rail*:

> The choice is by no means small. Five different kinds of bread, four sorts of cold meat, six hot dishes, to say nothing of eggs cooked in seven different ways and all the seasonable vegetables and fruit . . . The meal is served on a table temporarily fixed to the side of the car and removed when no longer required. To breakfast, dine, and sup in this style while the train is speeding at the rate of nearby thirty miles an hour is a sensation of which the novelty is not greater than the comfort.

These so-called "hotel cars" were only open to persons who had reserved a sleeping berth. The first full-service diner open to all and the first railroad dining car in the United States was the *Delmonico*, placed in service by Pullman on the Chicago & Alton in 1868.

THE FIRST **RAILROAD LOCOMOTIVE**

was built by Cornish engineer Richard Trevithick and ran for the first time on the Penydarren Railway, near Merthyr Tydfil in Wales, on 13 February 1804. The engine had been constructed as a stationary unit for driving a steam-hammer; it was converted into a locomotive by mounting it on a wagon chassis and connecting the wheels. The first passengers to travel in a train drawn by steam locomotion were Samuel Homfray and Richard Drawshay, ironmasters, and a visiting government engineer, Anthony Hill, who were drawn over the 9¼-mile line from Penydarren to Abercynon Wharf on 21 February 1804. Their coach was an ordinary road vehicle, having axels the same width as those of the locomotive; the rails were flanged. Two days later Homfray won a 500-guinea wager (the value of a substantial town house) from Anthony Hill when Trevithick's locomotive succeeded in drawing a 10-ton load of bar-iron in five wagons over the full length of the track. On this occasion the general public also availed itself of rail passenger transport for the first time, seventy of the spectators climbing unbidden onto the wagons to enjoy the ride.

The first locomotive in regular service on a public railroad (i.e., one providing service to paying customers) was George Stephenson's *Locomotion*, which inaugurated traffic on the 27-mile Stockton & Darlington Railway in County Durham, England, on 27 September 1825. The 15-ton engine, which had a top speed of 15 mph, was designed for hauling freight, the company's rolling stock comprising 150 wagons. Most of the freight consisted of coal; on opening day the twelve wagons of coal (there was one of flour) were distributed to the poor on arrival at Darlington. *Locomotion* remained in service until 1841 and in 1876 was displayed at the Philadelphia Centennial Exposition. It is now on exhibition at the Darlington Railway Centre Museum.

U.S.: A small experimental locomotive was built in February 1825 by Col. John Stevens, who had been trying to promote railroads in America since 1815, and operated by him on a half-mile circular track he built at his estate in Hoboken, N.J. Propelled by a central toothed rack, it had four flat-tired wheels guided by four vertical rollers running against the inside of the rails. The first full-size locomotive and the first to run on a commercially operated track was the 8-ton *Stourbridge Lion*, so called because it was imported from Foster, Rastrich & Co. of Stourbridge in England, which was test-driven on the Delaware & Hudson Railroad by the chief engineer's assistant, Horatio Allen, on 8 August 1829. It proved too heavy for the iron-plated wooden rails and the railroad was subsequently operated by gravity. The *Stourbridge Lion* was dismantled in 1845 and the surviving parts are in the Smithsonian Institution.

The first full-size American-built locomotive was Peter Cooper's experimental *Tom Thumb*, built in Baltimore with boiler tubes fashioned from rifle barrels and tested on the Baltimore & Ohio Railroad on 25 August 1830. The first in regular service was the South Carolina Railroad's *Best Friend of Charleston* (SEE **railroad accident; railroad, passenger**), built at the West Point Foundry in Cold Spring, N.Y. It made its inaugural run on 25 December 1830.

Electric railroad: The first permanent electrification was the 5-mile passenger "Daisy Line," as it was popularly called, from Louisville, Ky., across the Ohio River to New Albany, Ind. Operated by the Kentucky & Indiana Bridge Co., it was originally a steam line, but electric cars replaced steam locomotives on 25 August 1893. Current was obtained via trolley poles to an overhead wire.

The first mainline electrification was carried out by the Baltimore & Ohio Railroad in 1894 over a 3.6-mile-stretch of track, above and below ground (10 tunnels), passing through the City of Baltimore. The innovation was made at the direction of the city authorities in order to obviate the smoke nuisance of steam trains, the locomotives used being 1,080-hp GEC B-Bs each capable of drawing a 1,870-ton load. Current was drawn from a rigid overhead conductor line. Electric working for freight trains began on 4 August 1894 and for passenger trains on 1 May 1895.

The first electrification of a commuter service was by the Long Island Rail Road on 29 August 1905.

Diesel-electric: The first in commercial service was an eight-wheeled 75-hp Atlas railcar with accommodation for fifty-one passengers operated on the Mellersta-Sodermanlands line in Sweden in 1913. The first diesel-electric locomotive in service was a Swedish-built meter-gauge B-B put into operation by Tunisian Railways in 1921.

U.S.: Originally diesel-electrics were used only as switchers in freight yards. The first mainline diesel-electrics for passenger service were introduced by the Union Pacific Railroad and the Chicago, Burlington & Quincy Railroad in 1934. Both had a three-car body. Union Pacific's 600-hp M-10000 Streamliner *City of Salina*, capable of speeds up to 90 mph, was built by the Pullman Company and embarked on a twenty-two-state tour in February. CB&Q's 600-hp *Pioneer Zephyr*, also a Streamliner, was built by the Budd Co. of Philadelphia and entered service between Denver and Chicago on 26 May 1934, covering the 1,015 miles at an average speed of 77.6 mph and with a fuel cost of under $15. A revolution had begun that was to mark the end of steam locomotion in America. Diesel overtook steam in 1952, when there were 19,082 diesel locomotives and 18,489 steam. By 1961 steam had dwindled to 110, with 28,150 diesel units.

was the Oystermouth Railway in South Wales established under an Act of Parliament of 29 June 1804. Horse-drawn goods traffic was inaugurated on the 7½-mile route from Swansea to Oystermouth in April 1806. The passenger service was arranged by contract between the railroad company and Benjamin French, who undertook to run "a wagon for the conveyance of passengers" for a year commencing 25 March 1807 and to pay £30 in tolls for the privilege. (In fact the service continued, with some interruptions and by various means of traction, until 1960.) The train ran twice a day in summer and the fare was 1 shilling (25¢) single. There were no stations as such, but check-gates were erected at the Brewery Yard and at Hughes's Forge. Richard Ayton, writing in 1813, described the passenger wagon thus:

> It is a very long carriage, supported on four low iron wheels, carries sixteen persons, exclusive of the driver, is drawn by one horse, and rolls along over an iron railroad, at the rate of five miles an hour, and with the noise of twenty sledge hammers in full play. The passage is only five miles, but it is quite sufficient to make one reel from the car at the journey's end, in a state of dizziness and confusion of the senses that it is well if he recovers in a week.

Railroad station: The first was completed at České Budějovice in Bohemia (now Czech Republic) in 1828 as the terminal of the 27-km horse-drawn railroad that ran from there to Velešín via Kaplice. Remarkably it has survived the vicissitudes of Czech history, the oldest station in the world. For U.S., SEE BELOW.

Passenger service by steam-traction: The first regular service was inaugurated in Britain by the Canterbury & Whitstable Railway on 6 May 1830, the day after the opening of the line. Trains were hauled by a stationary engine over 4 miles of the route, owing to steep gradients, and by George Stephenson's 0-4-0 *Invicta* locomotive for the other 2 miles. The fare was 9d (18¢), later reduced to 6d (12½¢), the duration of the journey was 35 to 40 minutes, and there were ten trains a day. Passengers rode in open wagons until the introduction of closed carriages in 1834.

The first passenger railroad operated solely by steam locomotives, and the first to introduce first- and second-class carriages, was the Liverpool & Manchester Railway, which opened on 15 September 1830. Regular scheduled passenger service began on 4 October with four trains of first-class carriages a day and two of second class. Fares for the 31-mile journey were 7s ($1.75) for first class, 4s ($1) for second class. The first-class carriages comprised three compartments constructed on the stagecoach principle, except that they had side windows in addition to those set in the doors. Thus the railway compartment survived in Britain, with few structural changes, from the first year of locomotive-drawn passenger traffic until the 1980s. The second-class accommodation consisted of open wagons with awnings.

U.S.: The first passenger railroad was the horse-drawn Baltimore & Ohio, opened on 24 May 1830 on a 14-mile track between Baltimore and Ellicott's Mills, Md. Fare-paying passengers had been carried from Pratt Street, Baltimore, on an excursion to the Carrolton Viaduct on 7 January. Once the scheduled service began, there were three trips a day taking about one and a half hours each, extended to four trips in July. The wagons were horse-drawn until the introduction of steam locomotives on a permanent basis in July 1834. In the meantime, however, Peter Cooper's *Tom Thumb* locomotive had made a number of experimental runs on the track, the first on 25 August 1830. Three days later it carried eighteen (non-paying) passengers over 14 miles of track, the first time a locomotive had been used for this purpose in the United States.

There was no station at the Baltimore end, only a ticket booth at the start of the track at West Pratt Street near Parkin. (Mount Clare Station, often erroneously said to date from the opening of the B & O, was not built until five years later.) The first **station** was built at Ellicott's Mills (which became Ellicott City) in the fall of 1831 and is now a living-history museum, having closed in 1973. As in Britain the early passenger cars were based on stagecoach design, the one that led the procession on the official day of inauguration (22 May 1830) being the four-wheel *Pioneer*, which had a body designed by coachbuilder Richard Imlay mounted on friction wheels by Ross Winans. It was Winans who developed the prototype of the modern American railroad car with eight wheels mounted on trucks, transverse seating, and a center aisle, adopted by the B & O in 1838.

The first American railroad worked by locomotives was the South Carolina Railroad, which opened on a 6-mile track out of Charleston on 25 December 1830. The locomotive, the first in regular service in the United States, was *The Best Friend of Charleston*, built at the West Point Foundry in Cold Spring, N.Y. The daring decision to go for steam traction was made by the South Carolina Canal and Railroad Co.'s chief engineer, Horatio Allen—he who had imported and test-driven the *Stourbridge Lion* (SEE **railroad locomotive**) on the Delaware & Hudson Railroad. The driver, America's first locomotive engineer, was Nicholas W. Darrell. Passengers were carried in two high-sided covered cars and sat on bare wooden cross-benches. After only a few months the *Best Friend* was destroyed by an explosion (SEE **railroad accident**). Fortunately Horatio Allen had a backup locomotive ready, the *West Point* from the same foundry, and passenger service continued uninterrupted. On 1 October 1833 the South Carolina Railroad was completed for its full distance of 136 miles to Hamburg. Built by the Army Corps of Engineers, it was then the largest line under single management anywhere in the world. In the meantime in November 1831 it had become the first railroad to carry the U.S. Mail.

Britain and America were far in advance of continental Europe in the building of railroad networks. No fewer than fourteen states in the United States had railroads operating before the first European line was opened from Brussels to Malines, Belgium, in May 1835. Other countries (present-day names) adopted locomotive traction as follows: 1835 Germany; 1836 Ireland; 1837 Russia and Austria; 1839 Denmark; 1848 Guyana and Spain; 1851 Chile; 1853 India; 1854 Australia, Brazil, and Norway; 1855 Panama; 1856 Portugal and Sweden; 1860 South Africa; 1861 Pakistan; 1862 Algeria and New Zealand; 1865 Sri Lanka; 1869 Greece and Romania; 1872 Japan; 1876 China; 1877 Burma; 1884 Serbia.

Transcontinental railroad: The first in North America is usually said to have been completed with the driving of the famous golden spike, uniting the Central Pacific and Union Pacific railroads, at Promontory Point, Utah, on 10 May 1869. In fact the Central Pacific line only ran as far as Sacramento, Calif., so the tracks did not span the Continent until an extension was built for the 92 miles to the Pacific Coast at Oakland. This was opened on 8 November 1869 and for the first time passengers could ride the rails from coast to coast. The first through train from the Atlantic to the Pacific was operated for a "Transcontinental Excursion" from Boston to Oakland sponsored by the Boston Board of Trade in May 1870. The train, comprised of luxurious Pullman Hotel Cars, took eight days to cross America and passengers could read about their progress in a daily newspaper published on board. There was no regular through-service until 31 March 1946, as prior to that passengers had to change at Chicago or St. Louis.

THE FIRST **RAILROAD SLEEPING CAR**

was the *Chambersburg*, built in Philadelphia and introduced by the Cumberland Valley Railroad on its Harrisburg–Chambersburg, Pa., route in the spring of 1839. The car was divided into three sleeping compartments, two for men each with six 18-inch-wide bunks arranged in two tiers and one for ladies with two 36-inch-wide bunks. A coverlet and pillow were provided and most travelers wrapped themselves in shawls and slept with their boots on. The charge for a berth was 25¢.

Pullman sleeping cars: The first were adapted from two day-coaches by George Mortimer Pullman and placed in service with the Chicago & Alton Railroad between Bloomington, Ill., and Chicago on 1 September 1859. The first Pullman car conductor, unlike most of his successors for the next hundred years, was a white man, twenty-two-year-old J. L. Barnes. He recalled in old age that the pioneer Pullman was "a primitive thing" lighted only with candles and having no carpet on the floor nor sheets on the beds. There were four upper and four lower berths. The latter were seats by day and when passengers wanted to retire, the conductor unhinged the back to lay it flat and placed a mattress and pillow on the resulting couch. Barnes wrote: "I remember on the first night I had to compel the passengers to take their boots off before they got into the berths. They wanted to keep them on—seemed afraid to take them off." The first purpose-built Pullman, the most luxurious railroad car ever seen at that date, was the *Pioneer* commissioned by the Chicago & Alton at a cost of $20,178.14. It made its debut attached to the funeral train that carried the body of President Abraham Lincoln from Chicago to his hometown of Springfield, Ill., on 2 May 1865. The car was occupied by Mary Todd Lincoln, who had traveled in the cortège from Washington, D.C., and by that time was in a state of collapse. The attendant publicity, however tragic the circumstances, stimulated enormous interest in this latest mode of traveling by night. Pullman cars were eventually to achieve a monopoly of sleepers on American railroads that the company sustained until 1947. The last one, the *George M. Pullman*, was built for Amtrak at the Chicago workshops in 1981.

THE FIRST **RAILROAD, TROOP TRAIN**

ran on the Baltimore & Ohio Railroad on 30 June 1831 to carry the 1st Division of the Maryland Guards under Brig. Gen. George H. Steward from Baltimore to Ellicott's Mills, a distance of 14 miles. There the troops quelled a riot of railroad builders, who were striking for back-pay due to them.

The first use of rail transport for the strategic deployment of a large fighting force occurred in March 1846, when the Prussian Sixth Army Corps was moved by the Upper Silesian and Freiburg/Schweidnitz–Breslau lines to the frontier of the Cracow Free State, then in a state of revolt. A total of more than 12,000 men, 300 horses, 16 heavy guns, 15 ammunition trucks, and 30 supply wagons were transported in trains carrying up to 766 men, the whole operation being carried out without interrupting normal civilian traffic on those parts of the railroad affected.

THE FIRST **RAINCOAT**

was made by François Fresnau, chief engineer at Cayenne, French Guiana, who discovered rubber trees growing at Aprouage in 1747 and waterproofed an old overcoat by smearing it all over with latex.

The first raincoat manufactured for sale was Fox's Aquatic Gambroon Cloak, marketed in London by G. Fox of 28 King Street, Covent Garden in 1821 and "warranted never to get wet when properly made up." Gambroon was a type of twill material containing mohair, but nothing is known about the waterproofing process.

At about the same time, Charles Macintosh of Glasgow was producing a waterproof fabric that consisted of two lengths of cloth stuck together with a solution of india rubber dissolved in naphtha. Although this was perfectly weatherproof, it was impossible to tailor such a sandwich. It was not until James Syme, a young medical student from Edinburgh University, discovered a more practical way of dissolving rubber, using a property extracted from coal-tar, that Macintosh, obtaining the rights and patenting the process in 1823, began to produce the waterproofs that were to make his name a generic word (raincoats are still called macintoshes or macs in Britain and Ireland). The first important commission won by the firm of Charles Macintosh & Co. was the outfitting of Sir John Franklin's expedition to the Arctic in 1824. Macintosh continued to sell only the patent cloth, to be made up by individual tailors, until his amalgamation with the Manchester rubber-goods manufacturer Thomas Hancock in 1830. Their initial success in producing ready-to-wear raincoats was offset by the coming of the railways, for travelers who had previously braved the elements on top of a stagecoach now rode enclosed. There was a growing prejudice too against the ungainly appearance of the garments, and also the peculiar smell they emitted, a fact commented on by the *Gentleman's Magazine of Fashion* in 1839: "A Macintosh is now become a troublesome thing in town from the difficulty of their being admitted into an omnibus on account of the offensive smell." Another disadvantage, the tendency of the rubber to melt in hot weather, was overcome by Hancock's patent on the vulcanization process in 1843. The problem of the smell was eliminated c. 1850 by a Lancashire manufacturer called Joseph Mandelberg, who produced a garment advertised as "F.F.O.": Free from Odor.

For the first thirty years of their existence, waterproofs were something to be donned only in extremity. "Some resemble a sack—others an ill made smock-coat," remarked one critic. The first shower-proof material capable of being styled according to the prevailing mode was patented in 1851 by the London firm Bax & Co. of Regent Street, which dispensed with impregnated rubber altogether and produced a chemically treated wool fabric they called by the name of Aquascutum—compounded from two Latin words meaning "water-shield." The Aquascutum raincoat won a considerable reputation during the winter campaign of 1854–55 in the Crimean War, and one distinguished soldier, Gen. Goodlake, owed not only his comfort but his liberty to the coat. During a skirmish with the Russians, he and a British sergeant found themselves cut off. Having disposed of the nearest enemy in hand-to-hand combat, they took refuge in a ravine, only to find themselves completely surrounded. To their surprise, the enemy paid them no attention; because of their gray Aquascutums, the general and the sergeant had been mistaken for Russians. When the Russian troops formed up to march back to the lines, the two Englishmen fell in with them, finally making a dash for freedom when they came within sight of the British encampment. The original raincoat worn by Gen. Goodlake on this occasion is preserved at Newstead Abbey in Nottinghamshire.

U.S.: The first waterproof cloth was produced in the early 1830s by E. M. Chaffee of Boston, foreman of a patent leather factory, in an attempt to produce a substance that could substitute for patent leather. He appears to have been unaware of developments on the other side of the Atlantic and to have arrived at his process of laminating cloth with rubber solution by trial and error over several months. The formula he eventually applied commercially involved dissolving caoutchouc in spirits of turpentine to a ratio of 1 pound of gum to 3 quarts of spirit, to which he added lamp black. The mixture was spread evenly on heavy cloth and dried in the sun to produce a smooth, flexible shiny black surface to the material. In February 1833 Chaffee organized the Roxbury India Rubber Co., capitalized at $30,000, later increased to $400,000. Rainwear appears to have been a prominent product line from the output, as a report from

the first year of operation refers to rubberized jackets and capes.

The products having been launched in winter, all went well for the business until the advent of hot weather. Then the problem that had bedeviled the English and Scots rainwear pioneers, even in their chilly climate, now became even more apparent in the oppressive New England summer when the garments started to stink and their shiny surface lost its luster as the rubber solution became tacky. Retailers made vociferous complaint and returned the rainwear they still had in stock, demanding refunds. It was at this low ebb in the Roxbury India Rubber Co.'s fortunes, during summer 1834, that a young man of ingenuity named Charles Goodyear purchased an inflatable rubber life-ring at the Roxbury retail store in New York City. Deciding the valve could be improved, he invented one and showed it to Chaffee. The despairing rubber manufacturer took scant interest in the valve but told Goodyear that he was in the market for a process that would produce a hardened rubber impervious to temperature change. Goodyear's eventual discovery of vulcanization came too late to save Chaffee's business, but it was to restore the rubber and rainwear industry (SEE **rubber**).

Trenchcoat: The first was introduced as the Tielocken by Burberry of London in 1910. It acquired its present name when a special version for army officers with rings on the belt for hanging grenades was produced in World War I, which was characterized by trench warfare. The famous Burberry check was first used as a lining for the trenchcoat in 1924.

Lightweight tailored rainwear: The classic modern light raincoat is made of proofed poplin, originally produced by the English textile company P. Frankenstein the subsidiary of which, Paul Blanche of Manchester (reputedly the wettest city in Britain), began making it up into high-fashion rainwear in 1950.

THE FIRST REFRIGERATION PROCESS

by chemical action was developed in Rome during the 1540s and consisted basically of dissolving saltpeter in water. An account of this method of cooling was published by Blasius Villafranca under the title of *Methodus refrigerandi* in Rome in 1550. The author asserted that all the wine and water drunk at the tables of the nobility in Rome was cooled in this way, and he claimed to have been the first to make the discovery public. Levinus Lemnius, writing in 1559, said that wine cooled by Villafranca's process was so cold "that the teeth can scarcely endure it." The process spread widely, the notorious eighteenth-century philanderer William Hickey describing how he obtained chilled wine for his ailing mistress Charlotte Barry in Bengal in 1783.

U.S.: The first practical application of refrigeration was made by Dr. John Gorrie at the Hospital for Tropical Fevers in Apalachicola, Fla., an infirmary mainly for mariners afflicted with malaria and yellow fever. Gorrie's interest in refrigeration was for the comfort and well-being of his patients and he devised a machine that created cold by compressing atmospheric air in an open-cycle system. According to a report in the *Apalachicola Advertiser* in 1844, he had already installed air-cooling systems in two hospital wards and in his own house. Gorrie's description in the newspaper even foresaw frozen food: ".. . animals and fruit, when divested of life, may be preserved entirely with all of their juices in a low temperature. The principal . . . might be made instrumental in preserving organic matter an indefinite time and thus become accessory to the extension of commerce." Not everyone was impressed by Gorrie's innovation. The *New York Globe* sneered, "There is a crank down in Apalachicola, Florida, that thinks he can make ice by his machine as good as God Almighty." A Boston financier of philanthropic bent, however, put up the money for a full-size plant for the hospital to be built at New Orleans. A second plant was bought by the engineering company Siemens and shipped to London, where a favorable report was published in the *Proceedings of the Institute of Civil Engineers*. Despite this encouragement, and the granting of British and U.S. patents in 1850 and 1851, respectively, Gorrie did not find the path to commercial development a straight one and after various financial reverses, including the untimely death of his principal backer, he died in 1855 a broken and disappointed man.

Commercially operated freezer plants: These were developed simultaneously in Australia and the United States in 1850. America's pioneer was Alexander Catlin Twining, who began experimenting in 1848 to determine whether ether vapor could be condensed rapidly enough to produce refrigeration. Two years later he had achieved sufficient success to install a commercial refrigeration plant at the Cuyahoga locomotive works in Cleveland, Ohio. The plant consisted of ten freezing cisterns of cast iron, using ethyl ether, with a production capacity of up to 2,000 pounds of ice a day.

In Australia the editor of the *Geelong Advertiser*, Scottish-born James Harrison, established his first mechanical ice-making plant at Rodey Point on the Barwon River in Victoria at a cost of £1,000 ($5,000). This operated on the absorption system of refrigeration by the evaporation of ammonia. The principle on which it was based became apparent to Harrison when he found that the ether he used for cleaning type in his printing operations had a chilling effect on the metal. The following year, in 1851, Harrison made his first sale of refrigerating equipment to the Bendigo brewery Glasgow & Co. Regular manufacture of Harrison freezers was undertaken by P. N. Russell of Sydney in 1859 and at least two installations were made in Britain. Manufactured under Harrison's patents by Siebe & Gorman in 1861, one went to Young, Meldrum & Binney, paraffin refiners of Bathgate in West Lothian, Scotland, and the other went to a brewery.

Cold store: The first was opened by Thomas Mort at Darling Harbour, Sydney, Australia, for the preservation of livestock, poultry, game, fish, milk, butter, and fruit. It incorporated a freezing chamber, devised by E. D. Nicolle, which was wrapped around with 5 miles of iron tubing for keeping liquid ammonia in constant circulation.

On the occasion of the opening on 2 September 1875, Mr. Mort conveyed his guests, including the premier of New South Wales, by special train from the cold store at Darling Harbour to his stockyards in the Lithgow Valley. Here they were treated to a repast prepared wholly from frozen foods—the first such meal anywhere in the world. In his address to the company, Mr. Mort declared, "There shall be no more waste." He continued, "The time is not far distant, when the various portions of the earth will give forth their products for the use of each and all; that the over-abundance of one country shall make up for the deficiency of another." He made good this promise, though posthumously, when two years after his death in 1878 the first consignment of frozen beef from Australia arrived in London aboard the SS *Strathleven*.

Refrigerated meat: The first cargo of frozen meat aboard a refrigerator ship to arrive at its destination wholly intact was 5,500 carcasses of mutton sent on the French vessel *Paraguay*, equipped with a refrigeration plant designed by Ferdinand Carré, from Buenos Aires, Argentina, to France, arriving at Le Havre on 7 May 1878. A shipment from Buenos Aires aboard the *Frigorifique* the previous year had arrived at Le Havre partially intact. First from the United States was a cargo of beef that arrived in Britain from New York City aboard the Anchor Line's *Circassia* in the spring of 1879. The refrigeration plant was a Bell-Coleman dense-air machine.

SEE ALSO **frozen food**.

THE FIRST REFRIGERATOR, DOMESTIC

installed in a private house was not, strictly speaking, a domestic model as the property was the largest in America at 250 rooms (with 43 bathrooms) and the 5 refrigerators in the basement and subbasement of the Biltmore mansion near Asheville, N.C., were on a heroic, indeed industrial, scale. Biltmore was designed for George Washington Vanderbilt by Richard Morris Hunt, known as the "Vanderbilt architect" because he had built so many mansions for this, the richest family in America; it was erected over seven years, opening on Christmas Eve of 1895. Hunt had specified that the fridges must be capable of chilling 50 gallons of liquids and 500 pounds of meat and vegetables at any one time. An ammonia-compression central plant in the subbasement circulated chilled brine into the refrigerators through pipes insulated with horsehair; this was then carried back through the compressor to be chilled again and recirculated. The largest of the five refrigerators was a walk-in affair measuring 10' x 13' in area and 7' 6" high.

The first commercially produced domestic refrigerators appeared in France and the United States in 1904. At the World's Fair of 1904 at St. Louis, the Brunswick Manufacturing Co. of New Brunswick,

N.J., exhibited an ammonia-compression machine designed both for household use and for butcher's shops. The French model had been developed originally as a wine cooler for his Cistercian monks by the Abbé Marcel Audiffren of Grasse in 1889 and patented six years later. As well as a man of God, the Abbé had the benefit of being a teacher of physics. The model placed on the market was an electrically powered sulfur dioxide compressor refrigerator manufactured by A. Singrun Cie and launched as the Audiffren.

The Audiffren made its U.S. debut in 1911 with a model manufactured for the American Audiffren Refrigerating Machine Co. at General Electric's plant in Fort Wayne, Ind., and retailed by the H. W. Johns Manville Co. of New York at $1,000. The domestic model (there were three larger models for institutional use) weighed in at one fifth of a ton and made 11 pounds of ice in an hour. At this size and price—double the cost of a Model T Ford—demand restricted output to 100 to 150 a year. Rather more practical for the suburban household was the Domelre (DOMestic ELectric REfrigerator) designed by Fred Wolf Jr. and manufactured in Chicago in 1913. This was a unit designed to be mounted on an icebox, but at $900 it was still beyond the reach of all but the affluent. On top of the purchase price was the not inconsiderable running cost, since the compressor had to be run continuously unless manually controlled. This problem was overcome with the introduction of a fully automatic model by Kelvinator of Detroit in 1918. Sales of home refrigerators began to climb and by 1924, the year that they first went on sale in Britain, there were already 23,000 in the United States. Some 80 percent of this market was held by Kelvinator. It was not until 1930, however, that refrigerator sales, by then a massive 850,000 a year, exceeded the sale of iceboxes. Today penetration of American homes is higher than for any other domestic appliance at 99.5 percent.

THE FIRST RESTAURANT

to be described as such was Roze's established in Paris in 1766 by Mathurin Roze de Chantoiseau, proprietor of an employment and general information exchange called the Bureau Général d'Indication. It was originally sited in the rue des Poulies, but this proved an unfavorable locale for the new venture and it was soon transferred to the Hôtel d'Aligre in the rue Saint-Honoré. Unlike existing eating establishments, which offered a fixed-price meal at a communal table at a set time (table d'hôte style), Roze's was open at all hours of the day and evening and the dishes were individually priced (à la carte). Unusually, too, ladies were admitted. The cost of a meal was 3 to 6 livres per head, which restaurant historian Rebecca L. Spang has calculated to approximate the cost of 7 to 15 4-pound loaves of bread ($21 to $45 at modern equivalent rates). The establishment had as its slogan a Latin couplet:

> *Hic sapidi titillant juscula blanda palatum,*
> Here are tasty sauces to titillate your bland palate,
>
> *Hic datur effaetis pectoribusque salus.*
> Here the effete find healthy chests.

These words reflected the fact that early restaurants catered specifically to those with delicate appetites, the word *restaurant* having been in use for at least a century to signify a dense meat broth suitable for invalids and those needing to be "restored" (the derivation of the word). Roze himself defined the new trade in these words: "Restaurateurs are those who have the skill of making true consommés, called restaurants or the prince's bouillons, and who have the right to sell all sorts of creams, rice and vermicelli soups, fresh eggs and macaroni, stewed capons, confitures, compotes, and other delicate and salutary dishes." When Roze retired from the restaurant business in 1769 to concentrate on the publication of a commercial directory, the business was taken over by an unmarried woman, Anne Bellot, who was probably the first female restaurant proprietor.

U.S.: The first restaurants are believed to have been opened in New Orleans, then part of the Spanish possessions in America, by French émigrés fleeing the revolution of 1789. Further information is invited. The first in what was then the United States was Julien's Restarator at the corner of Congress and Milk streets in Boston, opened by Jean-Baptiste Julien in 1794. Julien became known as "the prince of soups" among Boston gourmets, soup of any kind being something of a novelty to Americans and seldom served in taverns or ordinaries. One specialty was the eponymous *consommé Julien* and he also introduced New Englanders to cheese fondue and truffles from Périgord. In addition to its main dining room, Julien's offered a number of small rooms for private hire, often by dining clubs such as the one called "Our Club."

New York City's first restaurant was established some five or six years later by émigré Francis Guerin at Broadway, Pine, and Cedar streets, directly opposite the City Hotel.

The French cuisine offered by these pioneer establishments was for the well-traveled or those who wanted to appear to be. Thurlow Weed recorded in his posthumous autobiography that among down-home Americans there was little taste for "fancy French cookin'" and Owen Wister had the titular hero of his novel *The Virginian* declare that "it would give an outraged stomach to a plain-raised man." Among the relatively small coterie of sophisticated Americans, the cult of the restaurant can be dated from the opening of Delmonico's (SEE **restaurant menus**) in New York City in 1827 and the adoption of *la cuisine française* by Boston's Tremont House hotel (SEE **hotel**), which opened two years later. This was also the first hotel in America to offer an à la carte menu.

Nearly all early restaurants in the United States and United Kingdom aspired to French cuisine, Italian only taking root in Anglophone countries (and Argentina) following the mass emigration to New York, London, and Buenos Aires that started in the 1880s. The earliest restaurant offering "ethnic" or Asian cuisine in the western world was the Hindostanee Coffee House opened by Indian immigrant Dean Mohamet at 34 George Street, Portman Square, in London in 1809. Despite the designation of "coffee house," the Hindostanee was not a nineteenth-century Starbucks; it did not even serve coffee. Rather it was a high-class restaurant specializing in curries and the hookah "for the entertainment of Indian gentlemen," which meant English officers and merchants who had retired after serving in India. The Hindostanee was exceptional. No other Indian restaurants catering to a non-Indian clientele opened in London until 1911 and in the United States restaurants specializing in Asian cuisine other than Chinese were unknown before the 1960s.

Chinese restaurant: The first catering to non-Chinese in the western world is believed to have been the Macao and Woosung, opened by stovepipe-hat-wearing Norman Asing in San Francisco in 1849. A precursor of the all-you-can-eat buffet, the restaurant offered a table of delicacies at an all-in price of a dollar—probably the only effective means of catering to Occidentals who would not have understood a Chinese menu.

Restaurant chain: The first comprised the station buffets operated by Spiers & Pond on London's Metropolitan Railway (SEE **subway**) from 1867. Christopher Pond and Felix Spiers, formerly caterers in Melbourne, Australia, had earlier inaugurated the idea of sports sponsorship when they put up the money for the England cricket team's first tour of Australia in 1861–62. On their return to England they were shocked by the low standard of railroad catering and determined to raise standards. Their company later expanded its chain of buffets when they won the contracts for the London, Chatham & Dover Railway and the London & South Western Railway. They also ran the Criterion Restaurant in Piccadilly Circus, the Gaiety Theatre Restaurant, and the refreshment rooms at the London Zoo.

U.S.: The earliest is believed to have been the Vienna Model Bakery & Café, which the brothers Charles, Maximillian, and Louis Fleischmann began rolling out from 1877 with branches in San Francisco, Philadelphia, New York City, St. Louis, and Chicago. They were modeled on continental cafés with superb coffee and newspapers to read and, unusually for the time, they welcomed unaccompanied women seeking somewhere to relax during shopping expeditions. (SEE ALSO **franchised food outlets** BELOW.)

Self-service restaurant: The first was the Exchange Buffet on New Street, New York City, which opened to male patrons only on 4 September 1885. Customers ate standing up. The first for women customers was opened on 15 December 1891 at the YMCA in Kansas City, Mo. The first self-service eatery open to both sexes, and the first to be styled a "cafeteria" (from the Spanish for coffee shop), was operated by John Kruger at the World's Columbian Exposition in Chicago in 1893.

Franchised food outlets: The first such operation was A & W, inaugurated by Roy W. Allen of Sacramento, Calif., in 1925. These small root-beer and hot-dog stands, some of them seasonal only, were franchised for fees of approximately $50 to $100, A & W deriving its main income from selling root-beer syrup to its franchisees. One of the first entrepreneurs to take up an A & W license was J. Willard Marriott, founder of the eponymous hotel and restaurant chain, who opened a roadside stand in Washington, D.C., in 1927. By the mid-1930s there were some two hundred outlets bearing the company's "bull's-eye and arrow" logo.

The first franchised chain of restaurants serving sit-down meals was inaugurated about this time by Howard D. Johnson, who had entered the fast-food business in 1925 when he took over a failing drugstore in Wollaston, Mass., and converted it into a soda fountain with a loan of $500. He subsequently opened a number of other outlets at his own expense, mainly in downtown areas. By 1935, with the burgeoning automobile population and a growing network of fast motor roads, he decided the future lay in siting his restaurants on highways. The problem was capital, but he persuaded a friend to finance the construction and operation of a Howard Johnson's at Orleans, Mass., in return for franchise rights. By the start of the 1936 tourist season there were a further four franchised roadside outlets, each housed in identical faux–New England colonial buildings with orange-tiled roofs and white cupolas. By the outbreak of World War II, the franchise chain had grown to 150 restaurants, most of them 50 percent owned by Johnson, who controlled the menu and sold the raw foodstuffs to his franchisees—principally ice cream ("Howard Johnson's 28 Flavors"), chicken, clams, and hot dogs. In the 1960s, however, the chain began to suffer from the competition of better-managed and more innovative franchises and in 1985 it was acquired by the Marriott Corporation for conversion into Big Boy restaurants.

SEE ALSO **hamburger: burger chain.**

THE FIRST RESTAURANT MENUS

reference to, is contained in the 1769 Paris-based play *Arlequin, Restaurateur*, which contains a scene in which a menu is read out. It begins with soups and *restaurants* (meat reduced to a dense broth) and continues with *chapons au gros sel* and spinach. Printed menus, which became customary at some Paris restaurants in the 1770s, distinguished the à la carte restaurant from the table d'hôte that had preceded it, both remaining in competition well into the next century. These latter, offered by the *traiteurs* (cook-caterers), consisted of a selection of different dishes all set out on the communal dining table at once and partaken of by self-serve customers (usually regulars) who dined at a fixed hour and at a fixed price. It was only with the rise of the restaurant (qv), offering a choice of dishes prepared to the customer's order, that a bill of fare became necessary. Early menus were notable for their vast size and range of dishes. The English traveler Francis Blagdon noted of a Paris restaurant's menu in 1803: "Good heavens! the bill of fare is a printed sheet of double folio, of the size of an English newspaper. It will require at least half an hour to con over this important catalogue." What was described on the copious menu, however, was not always what the diner was served, as the notorious Bezoni trial of 1838 attested: "For rabbit read cat."

The earliest surviving examples of restaurant menus bear out Blagdon's observations. These were discovered in an attic at a house near Salisbury in England in 1996 and are believed to date from the 1780s. Both were from Paris restaurants, the Beauvilliers at 26 rue Richelieu, near the Palais Royal, and the Café Bussière, location unknown. The vast sheets offer no fewer than 275 soups, hors d'oeuvres, entrées, vegetables, and desserts at Beauvilliers and 230 at the Bussière. The upmarket Beauvilliers had *boeuf d'Hambourg* at 1 franc (if this was hamburger, it is the earliest reference to what became America's national dish); salmon, quail, veal, and venison at 1.50 francs; and various chicken dishes—*Poulet Normand, Capilotade volaille, majonaise de volaille*, and *Blanc de volaille aux concombres*—at 3 francs upward. The most expensive dishes were gray partridge stuffed with truffles at 5.10 francs and a whole chicken also with truffles at a prodigious 15 francs. However, contrary to the "Let them eat cake" perception of the ancien régime, the restaurant also catered to the blue-collar worker, who could partake of a robust meal of bread soup at 0.12 francs, *boeuf au naturel* at the same price, and *fromage de Neufchâtel* at 0.04 francs, washed down by a *Bière française* at 0.10 francs. The *ouvrier* would have been ill advised to ask for the dark beer from England called Porter, which cost a budget-busting 3 francs.

U.S.: The earliest surviving American menu is a 12-page à la carte listing of 371 dishes offered at the Restaurant Français des Frères Delmonico at Beaver and South William streets in New York in 1838. Not all the dishes were available, as many were seasonal; those that were had the price set against them in shillings and pence (a reminder of how long it took for the dollar to become almighty; Horatio Alger novels of the 1860s and '70s were still using *shilling* to signify half a quarter). The list starts with 12 soups and 32 hors d'oeuvres, then entrées: 46 of veal, 28 of beef, 20 of mutton and lamb, 47 of chicken, 22 of game, 20 roasts, 48 fish; accompanied by 51 kinds of vegetables and various egg dishes and ending with 19 pastries or cakes and 26 desserts. The game dishes include Welsh Rabbit, which the menu compiler presumably did not know meant toasted cheese. Names of dishes are given in both French and English (with Welsh Rabbit's translation appearing as *Fromage de gibier*: "game cheese"), as few Americans spoke anything except their own language; a generation later menus in sophisticated restaurants would be entirely in French, which probably says more about the pretensions of the rich than about improvements in bilingual education.

Delmonico's was among the first restaurants in America to offer à la carte service: Patrons paid for each dish as a separate item. As in Paris the general practice at "ordinaries" (where most employed people would have lunched) was for meals to be at set times at set prices and for all the dishes to be placed on the table at once, regardless of courses. Another menu of the same year as the Delmonico's one survives, not in its original form, but as transcribed by the English writer Capt. Marryat in his *Diary in America* (1839) to prove that American food was not as vile as it had been declared to be by American writer James Fenimore Cooper. This is an interesting contrast to the Delmonico menu as it lists the table d'hôte menu at the Astor House for 21 March 1838 (Marryat mentions that it was printed every day). There is but one soup (vermicelli), followed by 7 boiled entrées, 12 roasts including game, and various miscellaneous dishes, such as oyster pie, *macaroni au Parmesan*, *Salade de Volaille*, *Compote de Pigeon*, veal cutlets, and *Casserole de Pomme de Terre garnie*, concluding with Queen Pudding, mince pie, cream puffs, and *dessert* (meaning, as it does still in Europe, fresh fruit). There is no mention of vegetables (a later Astor House menu of 1849 lists 13). The difference in prices between the Astor House and Delmonico's is particularly striking, given that the Astor House was probably the most luxurious hotel in America. The room rate of $2 a day included four full meals, so the table d'hôte dinner might be assessed at somewhere between 25¢ and 50¢ as an element of this. A dinner at Delmonico's averaged about $1.25 without wine.

THE FIRST **REVOLVER**

single-barreled in series production, was the flintlock cylinder firearm for which the American inventor Elisha Haydon Collier secured English Patent No. 4315 on 24 November 1818. Collier's system of rotating cylinders was embodied in carbines, pistols, rifles, and shotguns assembled by the firm he had established in Fountain Court, the Strand, London, by 1822. The parts were made separately by outside contractors, the barrels and cylinders by John Evans & Son, Engine Lathe and Tool Manufacturers of Wardour Street; the remaining parts and the making-up by an unidentified gunmaker, possibly W. and J. Rigby of London and Dublin.

During the first year of production a total of 400 Collier weapons were produced, half of them pistols and the remainder muskets. The pistol revolvers generally had five chambers, and one grateful client wrote to Collier in 1824 saying that the first time he tried his new weapon he had succeeded in putting four out of five balls through the mark in the space of 20 seconds.

Although the patent covered mechanical rotation of the cylinders, in practice Collier found his spring mechanism imperfect and most of his firearms were hand rotated. The first practical mechanically

rotated single-barrel revolver and the first revolver manufactured in the United States was designed by the sixteen-year-old Samuel Colt while employed as a merchant seaman aboard the SS *Carlo* in 1830, bound for London and Calcutta. The basic pattern for the revolver was whittled out of wood with a penknife. Having obtained an English patent on 22 October 1835, Colt set up the Patent Arms Manufacturing Co. at Paterson, N.J., the following month to produce the five-shot Colt .34 "Texas" revolver, so called because his principal market was the Texas Rangers in what was then an independent republic. An order was also received in December 1837 from Col. William S. Harney, then fighting the Seminoles in the Florida Everglades. The U.S. Army ordered another hundred at $40 apiece, but these consignments were insufficient to keep the factory going and it closed in 1842. Colt's fortunes revived when 1,000 heavy .44 holster arms, the first six-shooters, were ordered by Gen. Zachary Taylor in 1847 for use in the Mexican War. The weapons were built to Colt's specification by Eli Whitney's Armory at Whitneyville, Conn. He subsequently revived production on his own account at Hartford, Conn., and in 1853 became the first American manufacturer of any product to open an overseas branch factory. This establishment in London delivered more than 18,000 revolvers to the British Army and Royal Navy for use in the Crimean War of 1854–56.

THE FIRST **ROLLER SKATES**

were worn by Joseph Merlin, a musical-instrument maker from Huy, near Liège, Belgium, on the occasion of the celebrated Mrs. Cornelly's masquerade at Carlisle House, Soho Square, in London, in 1760. Mounted on his skates, Merlin came sailing into the ballroom playing a violin. Being quite unable to change direction or retard his velocity, he impelled himself against a large mirror valued at more than £500, smashed it to atoms, broke his instrument, and wounded himself severely.

After this inauspicious introduction nothing further is heard of roller skates until 1823, when Robert John Tyers, a fruiterer in London's Piccadilly, demonstrated his Volitos at the tennis court in nearby Windmill Street. These had five small wheels arranged in a single line and were patented on 22 April of that year as an "apparatus to be attached to boots . . . for the purpose of traveling or pleasure." A somewhat similar skate was used for a simulated ice-skating scene in Meyerbeer's opera *La Prophète* when it was performed in Paris on 16 April 1849.

U.S.: The first were four-wheeled skates patented by James L. Plimpton of New York on 6 January 1863. With their small boxwood wheels arranged in pairs and cushioned by rubber pads, it was possible not only to maintain a proper balance but also to execute quite intricate figures. Their introduction heralded the craze for roller skating that swept first America and then Europe in the late 1860s and 1870s, spearheaded by Plimpton's opening of the first public rink at Atlantic House, Newport, R.I., in 1866.

Rollerblades: Robert Tyers's idea of in-line skates was revived by thirty-year-old Canadian hockey player Scott Olson and his sixteen-year-old brother Brennan for out-of-season training. By using polyurethane wheels they produced a high-speed roller skate capable of up to 45 mph. In 1980 Scott founded Rollerblade Inc. at Minneapolis to put the new skates into production.

THE FIRST **RUBBER**

earliest reference to, is made by Spanish writer Pietro Martyre d'Anhiera in his *De Orbo Novo* (Alcala, 1530), describing an Aztec game played with balls "made of the juice of a certain herbe . . . [which] being stricken upon the ground but softly" rebounded "incredibly into the ayer." A more detailed description of rubber balls as used by the Arawaks of the Greater Antilles for the game of Batey is given by the Spanish historian Gonzalo Fernández de Oviedo in his *Historia General y Natural de las Indias* (Seville, 1535). These balls weighed about 12 pounds and were made from a mixture of grass, tree roots, and other fibrous substances, bound together with a rubber paste and smoked hard. According to Tordesillas, writing at the beginning of the seventeenth century, Columbus saw the natives of Haiti playing games with rubber balls during his second Atlantic voyage of 1493–96.

The first satisfactory solvent for rubber was discovered by François Fresnau, who succeeded in dissolving raw rubber in turpentine at his home in Marennes, France, in 1762 and thus laid the foundations of the modern rubber industry.

Manufacture of rubber goods on a small scale was begun by J. N. Reithoffer at Vienna in 1811, but the range of products remained severely limited until a means could be found of rendering the raw rubber sufficiently pliable to be rolled or beaten into the required shape. This problem was overcome in 1820, when Thomas Hancock of London developed a machine that he called the "pickle," consisting of a revolving drum containing numerous sharp prongs that masticated the rubber and reduced it to a workable plastic mass. Hancock took out a patent on 29 April 1820 for "application of a certain material to render various parts of dress and other articles more elastic." The following year he established a factory at Goswell Mews off London's Goswell Street and installed several large-scale masticators and iron rollers that were driven by a horse-mill.

The first rubber products manufactured by Hancock were made by cutting strips of rubber from a prepared block. These were used for garters, suspenders, trouser-straps (pants were just coming into fashion and were worn strapped under the foot), waistbands, kneecaps, etc., and "for a variety of surgical and other purposes." Generally the application was made by coating cloth or other material with rubber solution and sticking on the strip of rubber. In the case of garters, suspenders, and similar elastic goods the rubber was enveloped in a linen sheath. Another of the early products was rubber gloves, but as they were made with a leather lining, they were only suitable for heavy outdoor or industrial work requiring little manual dexterity. Probably the only one of Hancock's manufactures that was not a "first" for rubber was the eraser (qv), which had already been in use in Britain for half a century.

Sheet rubber: This was first made by Thomas Hancock in 1822, using an ingenious process of his own devising to overcome the limitations of his iron rollers. Thin layers of rubber were sliced from a block measuring 8" x 4" x 2", the largest Hancock could make at that time. The strips were then heat-welded together to form a sheet "so thin as to be semi transparent."

The first commercial application of sheet rubber was a covering for corks to make stoppers for bottles. Why it was necessary to cover the corks at all remains a mystery. Rubber sheets for hospital and other sanitary use were manufactured by Thomas Hancock's brother John at his factory in Fulham on the outskirts of London in 1824.

U.S.: The first patent for a rubber process was granted to Jacob Hammel of Philadelphia in 1813 for his "elastic gum to render water proof shoes."

The first manufacturer in the United States was the Roxbury India Rubber Co., established near Boston in 1833. The architect and engineer Robert Mills visited the factory soon after its opening and reported that its output included boots and shoes, waterproof jackets, pants, vests, aprons, caps, capes, inflatable pillows, life preservers, fire hose, and flexible rubber piping. Unfortunately for the Roxbury Co. and the many other rubber manufactories that opened elsewhere in the Boston area, and also in New York, Pennsylvania, and New Jersey, the extremes of climate in the United States made rubber goods far more volatile than in the more stable, albeit damp climate of Great Britain. In 1836 the Roxbury India Rubber Co. had to make refunds on capes, life preservers, shoes, and wagon covers that had congealed into a shapeless mass in the summer heat and the company folded a year or so later. In harsh American winters rubber-coated clothing would become brittle and crack. The public rapidly became disillusioned with defective rubber goods and the industry faced crisis. Its salvation would be vulcanization.

Vulcanization is claimed, as with a number of other significant inventions (cf computers, electric light, television), to have been developed simultaneously in both America and Britain, the proponents of the former citing the name of Charles Goodyear and of the latter that of Thomas Hancock, each of whom received master patents in their respective countries. Regardless of the dates of the relevant patents, the title of "father of vulcanization" belongs rightly to the American.

Goodyear was living hand to mouth as a not very successful rubber-goods manufacturer in Staten Island, N.Y., his family camping out in the waterside factory and subsisting mainly on fish they caught outside, while he carried out his experiments to make raw rubber impervious to temperature change. Among the additions Goodyear tried were quicklime, nitric acid, salt, sugar, castor oil, ink, soap, and cottage cheese, some of these tests being carried out in the kitchens of the various debtors' prisons he was in and out of. An acquaintance observed at this time: "If you meet a man who has on an India-rubber cap, stock, coat, vest, and shoes, with an India-rubber purse, without a cent of money in it, it is he."

In 1837 Goodyear paid a visit to the manager of the Eagle Rubber Co., Nathaniel Hayward, in Woburn, Mass. There his nose was assaulted by the acrid smell of sulfur. In response to Goodyear's question, Hayward revealed that sulfur dissolved in turpentine, mixed with rubber, and then exposed to sunlight would lose its stickiness. The following year, having bought Hayward's company, Goodyear is said to have been showing off a sample of this improved technique in a general store in Woburn, when a quantity of the gummy substance accidentally fell on a hot stove. Although it charred, it did not melt. This is one version of the story of the accidental discovery that was to revolutionize an industry. In the alternative version it took place at home, as his daughter later recalled:

> As I was passing in and out of the room, I casually observed the little piece of gum which he was holding near the fire, and I noticed also that he was unusually animated by some discovery which he had made. He nailed the piece of gum outside the kitchen door in the intense cold. In the morning, he brought it in, holding it up exultingly. He had found it perfectly flexible, as it was when he put it out.

After a lengthy period of experimentation Goodyear determined the optimal temperature and duration of heating to stabilize rubber and patented the process on 15 June 1844. Prior to the granting of the patent, however, Goodyear had sent a sample of the improved product to the Scottish waterproof manufacturer Charles Macintosh (SEE **raincoat**). This was seen by Thomas Hancock, the pioneer of sheet rubber, who recognized from its yellow tinge that the key ingredient was sulfur. Just as Goodyear had derived the secret from another, Hancock borrowed it from the American and by trial and error discovered vulcanization (a word that he coined) for himself a great deal faster. Hancock patented the process on 21 November 1843, more than six months before his unwitting mentor was granted his American patent. Hancock, who got there second, made a huge fortune. Goodyear, who fought thirty-two cases for patent infringement, including one against Hancock that he lost, died in 1860 with debts of nearly $200,000.

Foam rubber was first produced in an electric mixer of the ordinary domestic variety at the Dunlop Latex Development laboratories in Birmingham, England, in 1929. The idea of beating latex into foam with an egg whisk originated with E. A. Murphy. Using a gelling process perfected by his colleague W. H. Chapman, the Dunlop team succeeded in producing a rubber foam capable of being set in molds.

The first foam-rubber products to be marketed were Dunlopillo motorcycle pillion seats, produced in limited quantities in 1931. The following year Dunlop provided foam-rubber seats for three hundred London buses and the new Shakespeare Memorial Theatre at Stratford-upon-Avon. Manufacture of Dunlopillo mattresses began in 1935 and foam-rubber carpet underlays followed in 1937.

THE FIRST **RUBBER BALLOONS**

were made by Prof. Michael Faraday in 1824 for use in his experiments with hydrogen made at the Royal Institution in London. "The caoutchouc is exceedingly elastic," he wrote in the *Quarterly Journal of Science* the same year. "Bags made of it . . . have been expanded by having air forced into them, until the caoutchouc was quite transparent, and when expanded by hydrogen they were so light as to form balloons with considerable ascending power . . ." Faraday made his balloons by cutting around two sheets of rubber laid one on the other, rubbing the inner sufaces with flour to prevent joining, and pressing the edges together. The tacky rubber welded automatically at the edges, and the inside of the balloon was prepared for inflation.

Toy balloons were introduced by pioneer rubber manufacturer Thomas Hancock (SEE **rubber**) the following year in the form of a do-it-yourself kit consisting of a bottle of rubber solution and a condensing syringe. Vulcanized toy balloons, which unlike the earlier kind were unaffected by changes in temperature, were first manufactured by J. G. Ingram of London in 1847 and can be regarded as the prototype of modern festive balloons.

U.S.: The Montgomery Ward catalog for 1889 listed "red rubber balloons with trumpet ends" at 4¢ each or 40¢ a dozen. These are believed to have been imported from Belgium and it was only in 1907 that the Anderson Rubber Co. of Akron, Ohio, began manufacture of balloons in the U.S. Two notable advances in balloon technology originated in America. One was the sausage balloon, also known as the cigar balloon, introduced by Harry Ross Gill of National Latex Rubber Products of Ashland, Ohio, in 1912. The other is first novelty shaped balloon, which was also the first latex balloon and came in the form of a cat's head with projecting ears and a printed face. It was fashioned by Tillotson Rubber Co. founder Neil Tillotson of Watertown, Mass., in his kitchen using a cardboard pattern cut out with scissors. The first order, fifteen gross for display at Boston's annual Patriots Day Parade on 19 April 1931, was delivered just in time after Tillotson's whole family had joined the production line.

Balloon sculpture, the twisting of very slender balloons into animal and other shapes, originated with an act put on at the Pittsburgh Magicians' Convention by H. J. Bonnert of Scranton, Pa., in 1938.

S

THE FIRST **SAFETY PIN**

was patented by Walter Hunt of New York City on 10 April 1849 and is credibly claimed to be the fastest invention from conception to prototype. Hunt was a prolific inventor and depended on draftsmen brothers William and John Richardson for patent drawings. Confronted by them for an outstanding fee of $15, at a time when, like many inventors, he had a cash-flow problem, Hunt agreed to an unusual deal. The Richardsons gave him a long piece of wire, with the challenge to come up with a useful invention fashioned from it. If they considered it marketable, they would pay him $400 for the rights. Hunt took 3 hours to devise the safety pin, discharged his debt to the Richardsons, and came home with $385. The entrepreneurial draftsmen took Hunt's piece of bent wire and converted it into a fortune.

THE FIRST **SAFETY RAZOR**

designed for use with disposable blades was patented by King Camp Gillette on 2 December 1901. The original inspiration had come from his employer, William Painter, inventor of the disposable crown cork, who suggested, "Why don't you invent something which will be used once and thrown away? Then the customer will come back for more." Gillette acted on this good advice in 1895; the idea came to him as he stood before the shaving mirror one day and considered how little of his razor blade was actually used for the business of shaving—no more than the edge. His plan was to produce a sharp edge with as little superfluous steel backing as possible.

The problem of producing a blade thin enough, flat enough, sharp enough, and cheap enough, which steel manufacturers told him was impossible, was finally solved by an inventive mechanic called

William Nickerson, the only employee—on a half-time basis—of the nascent American Safety Razor Co. that Gillette had formed in Boston on 28 September 1901. Production began in 1903, though by the end of the year the sales figures were hardly indicative of the death of the cut-throat razor, the 51 purchasers of a Gillette Safety Razor having disposed of a nationwide total of 168 blades. Gillette's great idea may have seemed an ill-timed disaster; in fact he was on the threshold of triumph. A year later no fewer than 90,000 Americans had taken to the safety-razor habit and consumed between them nearly 12½ million disposable razor blades.

Gillette's razor had two significant social effects. Men took to self-shaving, whereas it had been common practice thitherto to visit a barbershop once or twice a week for a close shave (stubble prevailed for the other days). And the hirsute look of beards and whiskers and "moustachios" gave way to the clean-shaven look, stimulated and exemplified by the early heroes of the new mass-entertainment medium, the movies: Film drama happened to be born in 1903, the same year as the safety razor.

Long-life stainless-steel razor blades, a contradiction of Gillette's "use-once-and-throw-away" principle, were first introduced by the British firm of Wilkinson Sword in 1956.

Disposable razors were introduced in France by Bic in 1974 and in the United States by Bic and Gillette in 1976.

THE FIRST **SCHOOL**

in America was the Franciscan seminary established at St. Augustine, Fla., in 1605. Although intended for the preparation of those planning to take Holy Orders, the school would have given a broad general education as the Franciscans believed that religion should permeate every subject taught rather than that the curriculum should be confined to religious subjects. The first graduates were ordained during his visit to St. Augustine by the Bishop of Havana, Juan de las Cabezas de Altamirano, on Easter Saturday 1606. The seminary seems to have flourished, as it is recorded in 1634 that there were twenty-five padres on the staff. (It is possible that this improbably high number included resident missionaries.) Among its students at about this time was a young man who later became one of the school's most celebrated alumnus, the Jesuit theologian Fr. Francisco de Florencia, author of *La Estrella del Norte*. Born at St. Augustine in 1619, he was the first priest born within the present boundaries of the United States who is known by name.

The first secular school and the first in English-speaking America was the Boston Latin School, founded by a resolution of a general meeting of the citizens of Boston on 13 April 1635 at which it was agreed that "brother Mr. Philemon Pormort shalbe intreated to become scholemaster for the teaching and nurturing of children with us." On 12 August of the following year the "richer inhabitants" subscribed the sum of nearly £50 "towards the maintenance of the free school master...Mr. Danyel Maud being now also chosen thereunto." The cryptic "also" may signify that Maud was appointed assistant teacher to Pormont, or alternatively that he succeeded him. Nothing in the early record signifies the curriculum of the school, but if it was based on that of English grammar schools, as is reasonable to suppose, then the teaching of Latin and Greek would have been supplemented by the elementary subjects of reading, writing, "cyphering," and spelling. The school accepted boys as young as six or seven and some stayed until as late as nineteen, so it clearly functioned as both a primary and a secondary school. It was also the principal feeder for Harvard College, founded a year after the Boston Latin School. Of those pupils who entered the school at or soon after its inception, two notable names have come down to us: John Hull, the Boston mint-master who struck Colonial America's first coins (qv) in 1652, and Sir John Leverett, governor of the Province of Massachusetts in 1673–79. Other distinguished alumni include Cotton Mather, author of 382 works and America's first literary figure

of substance; Benjamin Franklin, scientist and statesman; and Ralph Waldo Emerson, philosopher and essayist. The school is extant.

In its early years the Boston Latin School was housed in the master's own dwelling. The first known **schoolhouse** was already in existence in Hartford, Conn., in 1642, when it is recorded that it was also used for storage of "two large guns, and carriages and other things belonging to the town." It was evidently a small building, because by 1648 it was no longer sufficient for its purpose and funds were voted for a new schoolhouse, with a condition, perhaps influenced by the guns and carriages, that it should not be used for any other purpose without consent. The oldest school building extant is the clapboard Voorlezer House on Arthur Kill Road in Historic Richmond Town, Staten Island, N.Y., which was built as such in 1696 and operated as a school between then and 1701.

School attendance by girls: It seems likely that the school maintained in New Amsterdam by the Dutch West India Company, functioning by 1642, would have admitted girls, as this was the general practice for elementary schools in the Netherlands. In New England during the seventeenth century the town of Waterton in Massachusetts voted in 1650 that the schoolmaster Richard should "attend" any maiden with "a desire to learn to write," which sounds more like private tuition than school attendance. Elsewhere there are occasional references to the admission of girls to town schools, but the practice seems to have been exceptional.

The first known **girls' school** was a privately run establishment advertised by Mary Turfrey in the *Boston News Letter* of 9 September 1706. A small private **boarding school for girls** was opened in Boston by James Ives in 1714 but the first run corporately and on a significant scale was the Ursuline Convent at New Orleans, which began accepting pupils soon after the arrival of the nuns from Rouen, France, on 7 August 1727. By May of the following year there were 20 boarders under the direction of Sister Marguerite Judde, the eldest being about fifteen (the normal age of marriage in Louisiana). It was said of the nuns that they "enlightened the youth of Louisiana, and ameliorated the lot of the savage, the slave...," a statement that tends to skate over the fact that the convent was itself staffed by slaves. By 1803 the number of pupils had grown to 170 and it was reported that "most of the ladies of the colony were educated at the Ursuline Convent," few being sent to France for their schooling after its foundation.

Public high school: The first was the English Classical School, in Boston, authorized by the town on 15 January 1821 and opened the same year with 102 boys under the mastership of George Barrell Emerson. It occupied the upper floor of the new Derne Street Grammar School until 1824, when a purpose-built school was erected on Pinkney Street and the name was changed to Boston High School. From 1844 it shared premises with the Boston Latin School, both schools moving to Warren Avenue in 1881.

The first **public high school for girls** was established in Worcester, Mass., not later than June 1824. This was the result of a proposal to open the town's Latin Grammar School to girls being defeated. It was decided instead to establish a school "composed of the scholars most advanced from all other female schools." Although similar establishments were opened in New York, Boston, and Bridgeport, Conn., in 1826, there were few others until after the Civil War. Bridgeport's was the first **co-ed high school**, though girls and boys were taught in separate departments.

First with integrated classes, as well as first to admit black pupils, was Lowell H.S., Mass., in December 1831.

SEE ALSO **prep school**.

THE FIRST

SCHOOL EXAMINATION AND GRADES SYSTEM

references are contained in a letter written by Dr. Samuel Butler, headmaster of the English boarding school Shrewsbury School, to one of his assistant masters on 10 October 1818:

> I feel myself . . . under the necessity of requesting that you will be more particular with regard to your marks. I lay great stress upon them, being the only clue I have to understand the merits of the different boys, except what I can pick up from the monthly examinations, and I observe that your marks are greatly at variance with mine on these occasions.

The marks or grading system referred to in the above passage was explained by the headmaster's grandson, the celebrated author of *The Way of All Flesh*, Samuel Butler, who was himself a pupil at the school. In his biography of Dr. Butler he wrote:

> There were two sets of marks, one for viva-voce lessons, and the other for exercises—the object being to show at a glance which class of work the marks referred to. For lessons the marks were V (very good), W (well), w (pretty well), t (tolerable), i (idle), and b (bad).

Dr. Weldon of Tonbridge School, who had been an assistant master under Dr. Butler, confirmed that the custom of holding half-yearly examinations had first been introduced at Shrewsbury, and that thitherto the only method of assessing the boys' progress had been for visiting dignitaries to come at set periods to hear them at their lessons. In this respect Shrewsbury resembled most other schools of the pre-examination era. Promotion from one form (i.e., grade) to another was by seniority and unaffected by academic merit; once in the sixth form (the twelfth grade) the principal stimulus to scholarship provided at lower levels—fear of the birch—was removed, and there was little incentive for the boy who lacked the love of learning for its own sake.

The half-yearly examinations were written tests held in the first week of the semester. Nicholas Carlisle, in his *Endowed Grammar Schools in England and Wales* (1818), lists the exams taken by 130 pupils from 3 to 8 February 1817.

Monday: English Theme; English translated into Latin; English translated into Greek

Tuesday: History; Latin Theme

Wednesday: Geography; Latin Verses; Philology

Thursday: Latin translated into English; Algebra

Friday: Greek translated into English; Greek Metres and Greek Chorus

Saturday: Religion

These are the earliest recorded written school exams. Each lasted between 1½ hours and 2 hours and the first exam of the day was held before breakfast. The boys were not told the subject of each paper before it was distributed. The examinations were presided over by the formidable Dr. Butler in person, who, Carlisle notes, "never quits the room." After breakfast on the Saturday prizes were awarded and boys who had done well were promoted to a higher form or grade.

U.S.: Written tests in public schools were instituted by the Boston School Board in 1845. Nominations are invited for any private school with a written examination and grading system prior to this date.

The first **external examinations** in the United States were developed by psychologist Carl Brigham for the College Entrance Examination Board, set up by the presidents of 12 leading colleges in order to standardize admission procedures. The first College Entrance Examination was held at 67 test centers in the United States and two overseas on 17 June 1901. A total of 973 college applicants sat the test, overwhelmingly from private schools (though Brigham had designed it to overcome bias due to socio-economic differences), of whom 60 percent had applied for Columbia University in New York City. Subjects covered were English, French, German, Latin, Greek, history, math, chemistry, and physics, and grading was Excellent, Good, Doubtful, Poor, and Very Poor. The examination was changed in 1923 to the Scholastic Aptitude Test (SAT), in which 315 questions had to be answered in 90 minutes. The first **SATs** were taken by 8,000 students at 300 test centers on 23 June of that year. In 1990 SAT was redefined as the Scholastic Assessment Test. It became just SAT in 1994, the letters no longer forming an acronym, and since 2004 has been officially known as the SAT Reasoning Test.

THE FIRST **SCHOOL MAGAZINE/NEWSPAPER**

was a handwritten sheet edited by George Foster and Caspar Wistar, pupils of the Philadelphia Latin School (now the William Penn Charter School) and first published on 27 July 1774. Its title is not recorded and no copies are known to survive. The *Gentleman's Magazine*, described as "a half sheet published every ten days by Robinson," succeeded it and ran for three issues. In the next three years, six more titles made their appearance. The last of these, *The Students Gazette* (1777), resembled some of the more anti-authoritarian high-school papers of today, its hand-written columns often containing scurrilous remarks about the teachers and school governors. No other school magazine in America is known before 1822 and at the Philadelphia Latin School the pupils' journalistic aspirations lay dormant for 110 years before another, ninth paper was started in 1888.

The first printed school magazine was *The Microcosm: A Periodical Work by Gregory Griffin of the College of Eton*, published weekly by C. Knight of Castle Street, Windsor, from 6 November 1786 to 30 July 1787. Eton then, as now, was the leading boarding school in England. The name Gregory Griffin cloaked the identity of an editorial collective comprising George Canning, John and Robert "Bobus" Smith, and the future diplomat John Hookham Frere. In the opening number they stated an editorial objective fitting to the time and place: "He, who hereafter may sing the glories of Britain, must first celebrate at Eton the smaller glories of this college." This they did in a compilation of essays, letters, and poems, one of the most notable contributions being an article by Canning, "The Slavery of Greece"—an early intimation of the interest that was to influence his policy as minister for foreign affairs (1820–27) and assist the liberation of Greece from the Ottoman Empire. Prime minister for six months prior to his death in 1827, Canning was the first of many British premiers whose earliest experience of "public affairs" has been in editing a school magazine. *The Microcosm* enjoyed a wide circulation outside the school, one of its readers being the Queen, who was sent copies by the novelist and diarist Fanny Burney. It lasted for forty issues.

High school daily: The first was the *Shortridge Daily Echo* produced at Shortridge High School, Indianapolis, Ind., from 26 September 1898. The first editor was Fletcher Bernard Wagner.

THE FIRST **SCRABBLE**

was devised by architect Alfred Mosher Butts of Rhinebeck, N.Y., in 1931 while unemployed during the Depression. He determined the value of the letters by counting the number of times they were used on a single front page of the *New York Times*. This has never been changed, except for foreign-language editions.

Butts produced handmade versions of the game that he began selling for $1.50 in 1933. An improved version called Criss-Cross Words, featuring a board and letter racks for the first time, followed in 1938. None of the games manufacturers evinced any interest in either version, turning it down as too dull. The name Scrabble was adopted in 1948 after Butts had teamed up with retired government official James Brunot, who took over manufacture and gave another tweak to the rules, giving us those used today for the classic version of the game. Production in an abandoned schoolhouse in Doddington, Conn., totaled 2,400 in 1949 and Brunot lost $450. Demand for the game only took off in 1952 after the chairman of Macy's, Jack Straus, who had played it with his family, expressed dismay on finding that the store did not stock it. The very large order placed by Macy's encouraged other retailers to do the same. The Brunot assembly operation (by this time manufacture of the constituent elements was farmed out) was rapidly overwhelmed and he decided to assign the North American rights to Selchow & Righter. More than a million sets were sold in 1953 and 3.8 million the following year. Butts received a royalty of 5¢ per set, which gave him an income averaging $50,000 per annum before his copyright expired in 1974. Meticulous as ever, he calculated that the total earnings from his invention had been $1,066,500.

THE FIRST **SECRET BALLOT**

as it exists today in most democracies, with printed unmarked ballot papers containing the names of all candidates and issued only by government-appointed electoral officers, originated in nineteenth-century Australia. Voting by ballot, with varying degrees of secrecy, is however of ancient lineage. It was known to the Italian communes of the thirteenth century and was used for borough elections in England in the sixteenth and seventeenth centuries. The American colonies were its most vigorous proponents, the General Court of Massachusetts electing governors by ballot after 1634 and the Province of Pennsylvania requiring in 1682 "[that] all the elections of Members or Representatives of the People . . . shall be resolved and determined by ballot." The latter provision may have allowed for secrecy in casting the vote, but such protection was often lost in practice when sheriffs were instructed that on opening the ballot boxes they were to read out who had voted for whom so that illiterates would have confirmation that they had voted as intended.

During the eighteenth century most of the colonies had a secret ballot of some sort, often operated in conjunction with the alternative system of viva voce voting, which many claimed was the more open and accountable process. After the Declaration of Independence, all the states but one enshrined the ballot in their constitutions. The form that ballot papers should take, however, was not prescribed. Some voters wrote the name of their chosen candidate on a piece of scrap paper, but more common was the use of printed ballot papers issued by the parties contesting the election and containing only the names of their own candidates—the so called "ticket."

It was the desire to prevent the manipulation and intimidation such party control of the electoral machinery allowed that caused three of the Australian colonies to adopt a different system when they were granted responsible government by Britain in 1856. First with an electoral act governing the conduct of the secret ballot was Tasmania, the governor signing his assent on 7 February 1856, followed by Victoria on 19 March and South Australia on 2 April. All three directed that ballot papers were to be issued only by government and were to contain the names of every candidate. Victoria, however, decreed that ballot papers should be numbered, intended as a security device but open to abuse. Because what is known in the United States as the "Australian Ballot" has been of such significance in electoral reform worldwide, and because Victoria is credited with the innovation in nearly every reference source, it is worth recording who did what and when.

Victoria was the first to hold an election with government-issued ballot papers containing the names of all candidates, though numbered. This took place on 27 August 1856 with voting for the colony's inaugural Legislative Council under responsible government and was also notable for the first use of **polling booths** anywhere in the world, the idea of Melbourne lawyer Henry Chapman. Tasmania held the first election with *unnumbered* government-issued all-candidate ballot papers when voting was held for the Legislative Assembly on 8 September 1856. Since the island colony had also been first to enact its electoral law, Tasmania was undoubtedly the progenitor of the full Australian Ballot system. South Australia, which also claims paternity, did not hold elections under the new law until March 1857, but was later responsible for another significant innovation. While Tasmanian and Victorian voters struck out of the names of candidates they did not want elected, in 1858 South Australia introduced ballot papers with the name of each candidate next to a box, selection being made with a cross. This system, later to become standard internationally, was devised by the colony's Returning Officer W. R. Boothby, whose aim it appears was not so much to bring clarity and simplicity to the act of voting, but the rather less lofty aim of saving ink provided at taxpayers' expense.

The Australian Secret Ballot was adopted in Britain in 1872, in Canada in 1874, and in the United States by the City of Louisville, Ky., where it was first used for elections in February 1888, and by the Commonwealth of Massachusetts the same year. The first election of a U.S. president held under the system was that of Grover Cleveland in 1892. Coincidentally the same year also saw the earliest use of an instrument that would, a century later, supersede the Australian Ballot in many parts of America: the voting machine.

THE FIRST SEEDS IN PACKETS

were produced by the Shaker community of Union Village near Lebanon, Ohio in 1816. The Shakers, religious zealots who lived a simple way of life known as "concentrated labor," had formed America's second seed company in New Lebanon, N.Y., c. 1800. It is from there that the world's oldest surviving seed packet emanates, produced, it may be assumed, in imitation of the bags used by their brethren in Ohio. This is a 4¾" x 3¾" bag of brown waxy stiff paper printed with the words BEANS. LARGE LIMA. 6 CTS. D.M. According to Shaker historian Dr. M. Stephen Miller, the bag dates from the 1820s and the initials stand for David Meacham, the first trustee of New Lebanon (i.e., an elder appointed to conduct the community's dealings with the outside world).

The packets of seed, which from the 1830s had printed instructions, were sold from boxes of soft pine made by the Shaker Brothers and packed by the Sisters. Distributed by wagon to country stores in the spring, the boxes were collected again at the end of summer. The storekeeper handed over the proceeds less 25 to 40 percent commission and the unsold packets were then destroyed in fulfillment of the Shaker promise of "fresh seeds" every year.

Seed catalog: The first was issued by Scottish-born Grant Thorburn of Newark, N.J., in 1822. Thorburn was the first to mass-produce seeds in the United States. He had fled to America at the age of twenty-one after jumping bail while on a charge of sedition. He set up a hardware store and on finding that his best-selling line was potted plants, decided to specialize in selling seeds. His catalog was one of the first for any product to contain illustrations. The Shakers of New Lebanon issued their first catalog in 1836, Brother Charles F. Crossman printing 16,000 copies.

THE FIRST SERVICE STATION

was established by A. Borol at 41 rue Sainte-Claire, Bordeaux, France, in December 1895. The motoring journal *La Locomotion Automobile* reported that Borol's establishment had facilities for travelers to park their cars overnight. "Additionally there is a workshop for the maintenance, repair, and cleaning of all automobiles," the paper continued. "One can be sure of always finding 680° motor spirit and special oil for motors at this depot. Also, of considerable advantage to tourists, A. Borol sends off onto the road motor spirit, oil, and spare parts to whoever asks him for them." As Borol was also the Bordeaux agent for Peugeot cars, he appears to have fulfilled every important function of a modern dealership-cum-service station.

U.S.: Earle C. Anthony, a Packard dealer who introduced neon signs (SEE **electric signs**) to America, claimed that he and his father established the first bulk-storage service station (i.e., dispensing gasoline from pumps) in the world, called the Red and White Filling Station, in Los Angeles late in 1903 or early 1904. Anthony was rich and had just graduated from the University of California, so this is perfectly possible though contemporary evidence is lacking. The main element of doubt concerns the name: according to Jakle and Sculle in *The Gas Station in America* (1994), the term filling station did not emerge until c. 1915. A rival claim comes from St. Louis, Mo., where Harry Grenner and Clem Laessing established the Automobile Gasoline Co. at 412 St. Theresa Avenue in 1905, dispensing gasoline through a garden hose attached to a curbside gravity-feed tank. The first drive-in with a forecourt and projecting canopy, albeit rudimentary, was opened by John McClean of Standard Oil of California's sales plant in Seattle, Wash., at Holgate Street and Western Avenue in 1907. The canopy was made of canvas and the forecourt made up of planks, with gasoline dispensed from a converted 30-gallon water heater.

Purpose-built service station: The first was built by the Central Oil Co. of Flint, Mich., in 1910. It consisted of two driveways beneath a large canopy, separated by a single hand-operated pump. The first chain of standardized service stations comprised thirty-four outlets operated by Standard Oil of California and erected in 1914. The canopied stations were located on fenced, landscaped sites and each cost between $500 and $1500 to build.

Self-service filling station: The first was opened early in 1930 by the Peoples' Nugas Self Service Co., Cambridge City, Ind., followed soon after by a chain of nineteen others. The motorist paid before filling up and the cashier then pushed a button that not only released the pump but regulated the amount of fuel to be delivered. They were eventually quashed by the state fire marshal and it was only in the 1960s and '70s that most states authorized self-service.

The first self-service pumps activated by credit card were trialed in Los Angeles in 1973 by a partnership of Docutel and card issuer Atlantic Richfield, working with technology devised by British company Revenue Systems Ltd.

THE FIRST SETTLEMENT

(permanent European) in what is now the United States was St. Augustine, Fla., established by Spanish military commander Pedro Menendez de Avilés and 800 followers on 8 September 1565. Of this number 500 were soldiers, 200 mariners, and "the other hundred being of useless people," as Menendez called them, being composed of "married men, women, children, and officials." Many of the soldiers combined civilian skills with their military ones, including 21 who were tailors, 15 who were carpenters, and 10 who were shoemakers. Others were millers, masons, silversmiths, gardeners, and barbers and there was even a hat maker, a brewer, and a silk weaver—altogether 38 trades represented by 137 of the soldiers. Among Menendez's "useless people" were 27 married women and their children and 7 priests.

The site of the new settlement was already occupied by the Indian village of Selooe, whose chief made the Spanish the gift of a "mansion" or council-house standing on the banks of the River of Dolphins. Menendez's engineers immediately created an earthwork entrenchment and ditch surrounding the house, with a sloped approach made of earth and fascines. This fortress was guarded by 80 large cannons from the ships, for protection against the French Huguenots at nearby Fort Caroline, which Menendez subsequently attacked and occupied. One of the commander's first acts was the setting up of a **government**, composed of both civil and military officials, and a **court**, the first in America. The settlement was moved to a more advantageous position in May 1566.

Although established as a military garrison from which the Spanish could extend their control of Florida, St. Augustine fairly rapidly developed into what was recognizably a town. The earliest representation was made in England following Sir Francis Drake's attack on the settlement in 1586. It then consisted of three blocks lengthwise and four in width, with gardens on the west side. There was a newly constructed octagonal wooden fort between two streams, half a mile from the town, and in the town itself a church, a hall of justice, a Franciscan mission, and a lookout tower. There were also buildings and cultivated fields on Anastasia Island in the bay. All the early buildings were described as being constructed of timber (but SEE BELOW) and thatched with palm leaves. The earliest masonry building was the powder magazine in the fort, noted by shipwreck survivor Father Andrés on his arrival at St. Augustine in May 1595 (the fort was built 1586, but the magazine was added later).

Fr. Andrés said that all the town's citizens were soldiers, most of them unmarried. They lived in comrade groups of four, the one with whom the castaway stayed comprising a sergeant, a corporal, and "two honest soldiers."

The strength of the garrison in 1598 was 225 soldiers based at the fort and 400 others, including 1 Englishman and 6 Germans. There were then 120 houses in the town. In 1600 there were 57 married couples of whom 37 were parents of 107 children (7 was the most in any one family). Male children were inducted into the service as soon as they were strong enough to fire a harquebus. Earlier in the 1570s an anonymous visitor said that there were 13 married civilian settlers, each of whom cultivated as much land as a medium-size garden. The reason that proper farms could not be developed was that the only crops known to grow in this climate were maize (corn) and squash. Grinding maize was so laborious that it took half the day and it was a task that had to be performed daily, as the cornmeal would not keep. Hence only as much maize was grown as could be processed on this basis. Cattle, sheep, and hogs had been introduced as early as 1567, but there was insufficient feed to fatten them for meat. There were chickens that lived mainly on molluscs and hence tasted fishy. (It is a mystery why maize was not grown as cattle and chicken feed, as this would not have needed grinding.) Fr. Andrés, however, writing twenty years later, described an abundance of melons "and other garden stuff," with sufficient onions for an export trade with Havana to have developed.

Recent archaeological digs in the Plaza de la Constitución suggest that the earliest buildings were of adobe construction. A hundred years and more after settlement, in 1677, Governor Pablo de Hita y Salazar described St. Augustine's thatched wooden houses as "flimsy," and Quaker traveler Jonathan Dickinson, visiting the town in 1696, declared its dwellings to be old and half-occupied. When English raiders from South Carolina sacked it in 1702, burning all but 20 or 30 houses out of a total of about 170, the only stone dwelling, then under construction, was the Governor's House. Apart from the fortress, the Castillo de San Marcos (1672–95), there are no buildings surviving in St. Augustine that date from earlier than 1706.

St. Augustine came under British rule in 1763 when Spain ceded Florida by treaty. At that time the population, including a garrison of 2,500, was 5,700 and the number of houses estimated at 900. The town became Spanish again from 1784 until 1821, when the United States purchased the whole of Florida for $5 million. Most of the civilian Spanish stayed on, together with the descendants of the large number of Minorcan orange growers who had settled in the town in 1777. By the 1840s about one third of the population was Anglo-American, but following a brief period of prosperity during the Seminole Wars of the 1830s it sank into decay and 50 years later the population had declined to 3,000. The revival of St. Augustine dates from 1888 with the opening of the Hotel Ponce de Leon, one of the largest and most luxurious resort hotels anywhere in the world. Others soon followed and by the turn of the century St. Augustine had become the foremost winter resort in North America.

There is at least one extended family of European descent in St. Augustine that can trace their American ancestry to the sixteenth century. The many Solonas still residing in the city are descended from the union of Vicente Solona and Maria Viscente at the Mission Nombre de Dios on 5 July 1594.

English-speaking settlement, permanent in the U.S.: The first was Jamestown, Va., established with the swearing in of a six-man resid.ent council under the presidency of Edward Maria Wingfield on 13 May 1607. The 105 settlers had voyaged to Virginia under the auspices of the London Company, chartered by King James I to colonize the southeastern seaboard of America and promote trade. Their number included more than 50 "gentlemen," a clergyman (the Rev.

Robert Hunt), 4 carpenters, 12 laborers, 2 bricklayers, a blacksmith, a mason, a tailor, a surgeon, a sailmaker, a drummer, and 4 boys, together with "divers others." Of these only 38 survived the first year of settlement, the others succumbing to disease, starvation, and attacks from Indians. Among the survivors was Capt. John Smith, who was captured by Indians but whose life was spared, according to later accounts that may be apocryphal, at the intercession of the twelve-year-old princess Pocahontas. The first women settlers, Mrs. Thomas Forrest and her maid Ann Burras (SEE **marriage**), arrived with the third influx of immigrants, 70 in number, in October 1608. This group also included 3 German and 5 Polish immigrants (qv), all skilled artisans, and a Swiss laborer—the inception of the American "melting pot." These men established the first manufactories in the United States: pitch, tar, soap, and glass works. French vintners followed with Baron de la Warr's expedition in July 1610 and planted America's first vineyard (SEE **wine**).

Jamestown, ill-supplied with the necessities of life and ravaged by disease, peopled by indolent and largely unskilled colonists, and under constant threat from the local Indian tribes, took some years to acquire a semblance of permanence. That the colony survived at all was due mainly to two factors: the appointment of a strong-willed and determined governor, Sir Thomas Dale, and the cultivation of tobacco, pioneered by John Rolfe, husband of Pocahontas, in 1611. By 1614 the town comprised "two faire rowes of houses, all of framed Timber, two stories, and an upper Garret, or Corne loft," as well as some substantial storehouses, a fort, and a parish church (qv)—the second purpose-built Episcopalian church anywhere in the world.

Jamestown was the capital of Virginia from 1607 until 1699. It was constantly rebuilt after the many fires that destroyed it (most notably during Bacon's Rebellion in 1676), but never succeeded in becoming a city and could scarcely by called a proper town—there is, for example, no record of shops. After the removal of the seat of government to Williamsburg, it fell into decay. The Huguenot John Fontaine described its remains in 1716: "The town chiefly consists in a church, a Court House, and three or four brick houses . . . It was fortified with a small rampart with embrasures, but now all is gone to ruin."

The site of Jamestown was designated an "historic area" in 1893. Much of it has been excavated by archaeologists and by 1956 a total of 140 seventeenth-century structures had been identified, of which the only one above ground is the church tower (SEE **church**). More than half a million historical artifacts are preserved at the Colonial National Historical Park.

The oldest continuously occupied English-speaking settlement in the United States is Hampton, Virginia on the north shore of Hampton Roads, straddling Hampton Creek. Settled in 1610, its name was originally Southampton, after the major seaport on the south coast of England. Hampton's first church was built in 1624 and the town was incorporated in 1705. Its present population is 146,000.

THE FIRST **SEWING MACHINE**

was patented by Thomas Saint, cabinetmaker of Greenhill Rents, in the parish of St. Sepulchre, London, on 17 July 1790. The specification, which lay buried among other patents of Saint's relating to boots and shoes until discovered by Newton Wilson in 1874, was remarkable for its anticipation of so many features that later became basic in commercially developed machines. These included the perpendicular action, patented later by Isaac Singer; the eye-pierced needle and the pressing surfaces designed to hold the cloth taut, pioneered by Walter Hunt and patented by Elias Howe; and the overhanging arm that constitutes a basic characteristic of most modern sewing machines. The apparatus was apparently intended for sewing leather, but there is no record of whether it was built.

The first sewing machine to be produced commercially was constructed in prototype form by Frenchman Barthélmy Thimonnier, a poor tailor of Amplepuis, a Rhône village, in 1829. On 17 July 1830 he received a patent and proceeded, with the backing of a number of rich investors, to form the Société Germain Petit & Cie to manufacture the machines. Production was under way when the company's factory in the rue de Sèvres in Paris was attacked by a mob of two hundred tailors fearful of being put out of work. All but one of the machines already completed were destroyed and Thimonnier had to flee for his life. The single surviving model he carried back to Amplepuis, walking all the way and exhibiting the machine as a sideshow curiosity to earn a few sous.

For the next few years Thimonnier eked out a precarious existence by selling handmade wooden sewing machines for 50 francs each. In 1845 success seemed within his grasp again, a M. Magnin offering to put his latest model into regular series production. Built entirely of metal, the machines turned out by the Magnin workshops were capable of two hundred stitches a minute and had every prospect of finding a secure market, given time to overcome innate French conservatism. Three years later, though, the mob intervened again, this time on a larger scale, and the infant sewing-machine industry was swept away in the Revolution 1848.

Thimonnier's surviving sewing machines, including the 1829 prototype, are preserved at the Thimonnier Museum in Lyon.

U.S.: The first American sewing machine to abandon the misguided attempts to simulate the action of the human arm sewing (all such devices were doomed to failure) was a lock-stitch device with pointed eye-pierced needle constructed between 1832 and 1834 by Walter Hunt of New York City, better known as the inventor of the safety pin (qv). This machine had practical limitations, as it could not sew continuously without the operator removing and adjusting the cloth, nor could it do angular or curved sewing. Hunt did not develop it commercially and he failed, much to his later regret, to patent the crucial lock-stitch mechanism. First to secure a patent on the lock-stitch, farmer and mechanic Elias Howe of Cambridge, Mass., who is generally hailed as the "inventor" of the sewing machine, was granted his patent on 10 September 1846, but his apparatus did not go into commercial production until long after and then in a much modified state. It suffered from the same imperfections as Hunt's forerunner, as it could sew only short, straight lengths.

By the end of the 1840s so many inventors were working on sewing-machine improvements that it is difficult to establish who was the first to put a machine on the market in the United States, but the earliest of whom there is definite evidence were Charles Morey and Joseph B. Johnson, applicants for a patent on a single-thread chain-stitch industrial machine (granted February 1849) that was already on sale in 1848. It was manufactured for the inventors by Safford & Williams of Boston and was priced at $135.

The two names that loom largest in sewing-machine history are Elias Howe and Isaac Merritt Singer. Howe owes his place in the pantheon of great inventors to an 1854 court decision that backed his somewhat dubious claim to hold the master patent. As a consequence of this, all the pioneer manufacturers had to pay Howe royalties. Singer can no more be described as the "inventor" of the sewing machine than can half a dozen other pioneers, but *Sewing Machine Times* (10 January 1896) was probably right in its assessment when they declared that it was his machine that was the first to operate routinely and reliably with an automatic stitch mechanism, an automatic cloth-feeding device, and an automatically driven needle. Whether Singer's initial model, manufactured in Boston toward the end of 1850, was also the first domestic sewing machine, as is sometimes claimed, is open to question. Frank P. Godfrey, in *An International History of the Sewing Machine* (1982), points to the early use of illustrations in promotional material showing it being operated by what is clearly a housewife (rather than a seamstress) as evidence that it was so intended. At a price of $125, however, the domestic market would have been limited to the very affluent. The 1858 model was designed specifically for family use, but the rival Wheeler & Wilson of Watertown, Conn., had been selling a lightweight machine (22 pounds against the original Singer's 55 pounds) suitable for home use since 1854. Wheeler & Wilson were probably also responsible for another innovation usually attributed to Singer, the selling of domestic appliances on the installment plan, which they are believed to have initiated in the mid-1850s. The Connecticut company dominated the sewing-machine market throughout the 1850s and into the 1860s, until it was overtaken by the I. M. Singer Co., with which it eventually merged. Credit for introducing what is generally hailed as the first labor-saving device for the home to find a mass market belongs to both these pioneering companies. In one respect, however, the I. M. Singer Co. of New York (later the Singer Manufacturing Co.) does stand alone: It was to become the world's first global corporation, starting with the franchising of manufacture in France in 1856 and achieving before the end of the century a network of 60,000 sales personnel in almost every country in the world, with subsidiary companies operating in all the larger markets of Europe, as well as South America, Russia, the Far East, and Australasia.

THE FIRST **SEX CHANGE**

was conducted on the Danish artist Einar Wegener, an effeminate but heterosexual man who began crossdressing in the 1920s in order to act as a female model for his wife and fellow painter, Gerda. He began attending costume balls in Copenhagen in the character of a girl called Lili Elbe and when the couple moved to Paris, Wegener spent his time increasingly in women's clothes. Gradually he found himself assuming the identity of Lili and the contours of his body changing to the female form. Even when conventionally attired, people thought he was a woman dressed in men's clothes. Wegener became preoccupied that he was both a man and a woman in one body and his health deteriorated. Doctors he consulted considered he was suffering from delusions or hysteria.

Emotionally in despair, Einar Wegener decided in May 1927 that if within a year he could not find a doctor who could help him, he would commit suicide. Two months before his deadline he met Prof. Warnekros, head of the Women's Clinic in Dresden, who examined him and found that he had incipient ovaries in his abdomen. Warnekros proposed that he should have his male sex organs removed and a transplant of ovarian tissue from a healthy young woman.

The first operation under the supervision of Dr. Magnus Hirschfeld (SEE **sex survey**) in Berlin on 5 March 1930 altered Einar/Lili's voice from a tenor to soprano and the handwriting of the patient became markedly feminine. The second was performed at the Women's Clinic in Dresden a few weeks later when Prof. Warnekros implanted the ovaries of a twenty-six-year-old woman and on 29 April Lili Elbe received a new passport from the Danish Embassy in Berlin

in her female identity. A third operation completed the transformation on 26 May and Lili and Gerda returned to Copenhagen.

In October the marriage was amicably dissolved. Gerda married one of their mutual friends and the following spring Lili became engaged to a Frenchman she had known in Paris. She then went back to Dresden for an operation that it was wrongly claimed would enable her to have children. She grew progressively weaker over the following two months, dying of heart failure on 12 September 1931. She was buried, as she wished, in the cemetery close to the Women's Clinic where she felt she had been reborn.

U.S.: The first American to receive a sex-change operation was Carl/Carla Van Crist (pseudonym), a former female impersonator born of an American father and a German mother and brought up in Berlin and San Francisco. In 1929 he was referred by New York sexologist Dr. Henry Benjamin to Dr. Magnus Hirschfeld of the Institute of Sexual Science in Berlin. Hirschfeld in turn arranged for "Carl" to be genitally changed by Prof. Warnekros at the Women's Clinic in Dresden, where Einar Wegener had been transformed into Lili Elbe. The date is not recorded, but seems to have been in the latter half of 1930.

"Carla" eventually returned to New York, where she coached young actors in English diction and appeared in off-Broadway shows. At least one other American went to Europe for a sex change in the early '30s. In a letter Carla Van Crist wrote in late 1952 to the parents of Christine Jorgensen (often but erroneously claimed as the subject of the first surgical sex change) she referred to an "American boy who had been a female impersonator" undergoing an operation in Germany shortly after her own.

The earliest record of female-to-male sex changes were reports in 1934 that twenty-year old Clara Schreckengost of rural Pennsylvania and sixteen-year-old Henriette Acces of Lens, near Lille in France, were undergoing surgery for this purpose. Clara became Clarence following a series of operations at Western Pennsylvania Hospital in Pittsburgh that were completed in October. Henriette became Henri after Dr. Robert Minne had carried out fourteen operations to release and enhance imperfectly formed male organs concealed in the abdomen.

The first male-to-female sex change carried out in the United States was performed at the Gender Identity Clinic of Johns Hopkins University Hospital, Baltimore, where Phillip Wilson became the first patient in September 1966, emerging as Phyllis Wilson. This marked the inception of a regular and sustained program of gender transformation in the United States.

Woman-to-man to marry a wife: The first was prominent Olympic athlete Mary Weston, who set British women's records for shot putting between 1924 and 1930 and in 1927 for javelin. Dr. L. R. Broster performed two sex-change operations on her in June 1936 and two months later, now Mark Weston, he was married at Plymouth to Alberta Bray, delicately described in a contemporary report as "the girl who had been his closest friend during the days of his girlhood."

THE FIRST SEX EDUCATION

course as part of a school curriculum was introduced in England at the private Abbotsholme School in Derbyshire by its progressive headmaster, Cecil Reddie, during the semester beginning 1 October 1889. Reddie gave two main reasons for his innovation: "to prevent mental illusions due to false ideas from within; to prevent false teaching from other fellows." He had drawn up a memorandum on the subject, dated 30 December 1888, as a guide for the future work of sex education at Abbotsholme. In it he grouped the boys according to three age classifications. The first group, labeled "Pre-Pubity" [sic], were boys from ten to thirteen years old, who were to be taught "the true facts of their origin, of their life development, and of the dangers that surround them . . ." "During Pubity" (age thirteen–sixteen) the boys were to be taught "the laws of the feelings they now experience . . . it is best at this period that they should think as little as possible about these matters." The "After Pubity" group (sixteen–twenty) were to be instructed in "the laws of later life, so that they will enter the world equipped on this point." Reddie was a lone voice in the wilderness as far as England was concerned. He had few, if any, imitators at the time though, perhaps surprisingly, he seems to have attracted little active opposition from professional moralists.

The first officially backed scheme for introducing sex education into the curriculum of public schools was introduced c. 1900 at Breslau, Prussia, where the central school authorities requested Dr. Martin Chotzen to deliver a course of lectures on sexual hygiene in education to 150 teachers. The lectures covered the anatomy of the sexual organs, the development of the sexual instinct, its chief perversions, venereal diseases, and "the importance of the cultivation of self-control."

U.S.: Sex education in public schools was first introduced in Chicago, a city notorious for vice where it was estimated in 1911 that 1 in every 200 women was a professional prostitute. The initiative originated with the unlikely figure of schools superintendent Ella Flagg Young, an elderly spinster lady of rigid Presbyterian background who nonetheless recognized the need for children to be better informed about the peril of promiscuity. Her program of three lectures to be delivered by male physicians to boys and female physicians to girls began when the pupils of the twenty-one Chicago high schools returned after the summer vacation of 1913. The first lecture was about the physiology of the reproductive organs, the second concerned "personal sexual hygiene" and "problems of sex instincts," and the last concluded with some stark facts about venereal disease. Some 20,000 pupils attended the lectures and a survey among them indicated "an almost universal demand for more plain facts," particularly about the relationship between the sexes.

Opposition to the program came not from parents, fewer than 8 percent of whom exercised their right to withdraw their children from the lectures, but from religious leaders, politicians, the press, and organized labor. "Smut smutches" bellowed the *Chicago Citizen*, declaring that it was no less dangerous in the classroom than in the street. The U.S. Attorney General ruled that circulars containing innocuous excerpts from the lectures were obscene and could not be sent through the mails. The powerful Chicago archdiocese of the Catholic Church roundly condemned the innovation and when conservative members of the Board of Education warned Ella Flagg Young that persisting with the program would lose her their support on other reforms, she was forced to terminate it at the end of the school year. The high profile of the crusading venture and controversy over funding to pay the physicians had been its undoing. Henceforth the introduction of sex education in American schools would be accomplished with the maximum of discretion and the minimum of proclamation.

THE FIRST **SEX SURVEY**

was conducted by Berlin physician Dr. Magnus Hirschfeld (SEE **sex change**) to ascertain what proportion of the male population of Berlin was homosexual or bisexual. The first part of the study was undertaken in 1903 when Dr. Hirschfeld sent questionnaires to 3,000 male college-age students at Charlottenburg Technical High School. Among these respondents, 1.5 percent had a sexual preference for other men, while another 4.5 percent were attracted to both sexes. In the following year he followed this up with a similar questionnaire to 5,000 metal workers at a factory, yielding lower percentages at 1.15 percent and 3.19 percent, respectively. Interestingly these percentages are much closer to modern scientific estimates of the proportion of the male population who are gay than the rather wild figure of 10 percent that tends to be bandied about by the uninformed. Like most pioneers in the field of sexual studies, Hirschfeld aroused fierce opposition. Six students took him to court on a charge of disseminating obscene material and seeking to deprave the young. He was found guilty and fined. **U.S.:** The first published survey was conducted by Katharine Bement Davis, general secretary of the Bureau of Social Hygiene, New York, and issued in 1929 as *Factors in the Sex Life of Twenty-two Hundred Women*. The respondents were selected from the membership lists of women's clubs and college alumnae groups and were, therefore, middle class by definition; they were also mainly middle aged. The main findings were that few had experienced premarital sex—hardly surprising in an age group that became sexually mature around the turn of the century; that most of the married women used contraceptives and had a positive attitude toward sex (though it is likely that those with more negative attitudes would have been reluctant to be interviewed); and perhaps most strikingly that 50 percent of the unmarried women

and 30 percent of the married women had experienced "intense emotional relationships" with other women and that 20 percent had indulged in physical relationships with their own sex.

THE FIRST **SHOPPING BAGS, DISPOSABLE**

were red-and-white checkerboard bags promoting Ralston Wheat Cereal that were distributed free to visitors to the World's Fair of 1904 in St. Louis after the locally based Ralston Purina Co. had received a consignment of wrong-size paper flour sacks. Company president Will Danforth had the notion of attaching handles so that they could be used for shopping.

The first plastic disposable shopping bags were produced on 20 August 1960 by the Swedish firm of Akerlund & Rausing and featured advertisements for Strom shoe stores and a hotel. They were the idea of William Hamilton of Svalov, to whom Mr. Strom had complained that paper shopping bags tended to collapse when used to carry his sturdy Swedish shoes. Hamilton, a shoe-polish salesman and a Swede despite his name, came up with the solution but failed to reap any personal benefit as the innovation was not patentable. The original bags differed in one respect from modern ones: They had string handles, threaded by pensioners.

Sweden, normally regarded as among the most socially responsible of nations, may come to regret this innovation, as resistance to plastic bags on environmental grounds gathers momentum around the world. The first city to impose an outright ban was Mumbai (Bombay) in 2001, followed the next year by the first country to do so, Bangladesh. In the United States the first ban was introduced by San Francisco on 27 March 2007.

THE FIRST **SHOPPING CENTER**

to be so called was the Roland Park Shopping Center, a modest development of six stores established in Baltimore by local businessman Edward H. Bouton in 1907. It was set back slightly from the thoroughfare to allow for parking. This was, however, only the shopping center in embryo. The first planned shopping center on a fairly large scale, and recognized as the progenitor by the National Register of Historic Places, was Market Square in Lake Forest, Ill., built in 1916 at a cost of $750,000. The prime mover in the enterprise was Arthur T. Aldis, who declared that he was seeking something "sound, sanitary, and picturesque" in contrast to the decaying buildings that then characterized Lake Forest's downtown shopping area. His aim was fulfilled by architect Howard Van Doren Shaw, who laid out a green sward surrounded by elegant rows and arcades, surmounted by two Tyrolean towers and with an Italian Renaissance central building. There were twenty-eight stores, eight offices, and thirty apartments in the landscaped 400' x 250' area off Western Avenue.

The concept was taken a step farther by the first to be planned as an out-of-town shopping center and more importantly the first designed specifically for a motoring clientele. This was Country Club Plaza, initiated by Kansas City property developer J. C. Nichols to service his pioneering upscale residential development Country Club District. Nichols was the first to recognize the importance of convenient parking for shoppers in the new age of the automobile and, while elsewhere cars were consigned to vacant dirt lots, Country Club Plaza had an abundance of off-street paved and landscaped parking areas. These were recessed below the surrounding sidewalk to ensure an uninterrupted view of the shops. It opened for business in March 1923, when the Marinello Beauty Shop moved into the Suydam Building (now the Mill Creek Building), shortly to be joined by portrait photographer E. Blanche Reincke, Mrs. M. C. Chisholm's smart millinery and sportswear shop, the Lu-France Baby Shop, Hunter Brothers Drug Store, and the eponymous Suydam Decorating Co., featuring European antiques.

As well as pioneering in planned parking facilities, Country Club Plaza was responsible for another innovation that was soon to spread throughout America: outdoor Christmas lighting. This annual display began in 1925 when head of maintenance Charles "Pete" Pitrat hung several strings of colored lights over the doorway of the Suydam Building. As the Plaza expanded, so did the quantity and quality of the illuminations, inspiring local residents in the Country Club District to festoon their homes in colored lights.

Country Club Plaza took some six years to complete, culminating in the grand opening of the Plaza Theater on 9 October 1928. In the meantime construction had begun of other out-of-town centers, notably Dallas's Highland Park, Houston's River Oaks, Cleveland's Shaker Heights, and Grandview Avenue in Columbus, Ohio. The latter was the first shopping center with supermarkets, a Piggly Wiggly, A&P, Kroger, and Polumbo's being among its twenty-four stores when it opened in 1928. Highland Park Shopping Village in Dallas, completed in 1931, marked another significant step in the evolution of the modern shopping center as the first to be totally separated from the street. (Country Club Plaza was off the main highway but had its own streets accessible to automobiles.) Here, also for the first time, the shops were turned inward from the road, facing each other across a pedestrian-only zone.

Enclosed shopping mall: The first of the modern era was the two-level 800,000-square-foot Southdale Center Mall, built at a cost of $20 million at Edina, Minn., and opened on 8 October 1956. Austrian-born architect Victor Gruen had to confront the fact that Minnesota was freezing cold in winter but burning hot in summer and his response was to make the entire complex climate-controlled, maintaining a constant temperature of 72° Fahrenheit. The 95-acre lot had parking for 5,200 cars and among the seventy-two stores, for the first time in any shopping center, there were two competing department stores, Donaldson's and Dayton's. Gruen sought to counter the sterility of suburban living by including an auditorium for community meetings, artworks and aviaries, and for the children, a playroom, a zoo, and a carousel. *Architectural Forum* commented that it provided "all kinds of things that ought to be [downtown] if downtown weren't so noisy and dirty and chaotic—sidewalk cafés, art, islands of plantings, pretty paving." But all these amenities were dedicated to bringing families together for one primary purpose, encapsulated in a new term coined by novelist Aldous Huxley the year that Southdale opened: the *shopping spree.*

THE FIRST SKI

earliest reference to in literature, is by the sixth-century Greek historian Prokopius, who mentions the peculiar gliding action of the Lapps on snow—the term used is *Skrid Finner*, literally "gliding Finns"—in comparison to the clumsier movement of other Finnish snow travelers, who appear to have been mounted on snowshoes.

The earliest reference to skiing as a sport is contained in Archbishop Claus Magnus's *Historia de Gentibus Septentrionalibus*, published in Rome in 1555. The first English translation, published in 1658, reads: "Two sorts of men are found in these places, that run Races for Wagers most swiftly . . . The first is the Wild or Laplander, because upon crooked Stilts, or long Stakes fastened to the soles of his feet, he transports himself upon the Snow in Dales and Mountains, in a dangerous way, by a winding and arbitrary motion." (The second sort being the ice-running Lapps, not on skis.)

Ski meeting: The first was a Langlauf (cross-country) event held at Tromsö in Northern Norway in 1843.

U.S.: The first was organized by the Alturas Snowshoe Club (SEE BELOW) at La Porte, Calif., in February 1867 and consisted of downhill ski races.

Ski club: The first was the Trysil Skytter og Skilöberforening (Trysil Shooting and Skiing Club) established at Trysil, near Hamar in Eastern Norway, on 20 May 1861 with forty-seven members.

U.S.: The Alturas Snowshoe Club ("Snowshoe" was then the commonly used term for skis), was established in 1867 at La Porte, Calif., by Isaac Steward, a bearded Yankee from Skowhegan, Maine. The members were miners of the Sierras who sought this outlet for their energies during the enforced idleness of winter. Steward was not only the founder of their club but also its champion skier, winning most of the informal races and obstacle challenges held in the early years.

Speed record: The first in the United States was established on 22 February 1863 on the "Big Hill" at Onion Valley, Calif., by William Metcalf, who traveled 880 yards in 25 seconds at an average speed of 71.5 mph.

Downhill ski races: The first were held near Christiania, Norway, on 16 March 1866 at the instigation of Elling Baekken of Hönefoss, who challenged the skiers of Christiania to a race down the Iverslökken over a series of small jumps. Baekken himself ran the course three times with and without sticks and was declared the winner. All the other competitors except one fell over.

Ski-jumping in its modern form, whereby the jumper lands on a slope rather than level snow, was first practiced at Mogedal, Telemark, in 1840 by Sondre Nordheim. The first ski-jumping contest was held by the Christiania Ski Club at Huseby Hill, near Christiania, on 12 February 1879 and was won by the Telemarken Torjus Hemmestvedt with a leap of 76 feet.

U.S.: The first ski-jumpers in the United States were Norwegian brothers Torjus and Mikkel Hemmestvedt in Red Wing, Minn., in 1880. The first organized tournament was held in Red Wing by the Aurora Ski Club on 8 February 1887. The championship was won by Mikkel Hemmestvedt.

Ski lift: The first was introduced by Robert Winterhalder, proprietor of the Kurhau Schneckenhof at Schollzach in Germany's Black Forest, and opened for business on 14 February 1908. It consisted of a 280-meter-long continuous-loop cable with hooks; the passenger could either hang on to these or attach a toboggan. Winterhalder offered ten rides for 1 mark (24¢).

U.S.: The first was a 900-foot five-person T-bar ski tow powered by an old Model T Ford engine that began operating at Bob and Betty Royce's White Cupboard Inn Ski Lodge in Woodstock, Vt., on 28 January 1934.

THE FIRST SLICED BREAD

was the invention of jewelry store owner Otto Friedrich Rohwedder, who started working on a slicing machine at St. Joseph, Mo., in 1912. He gave up work in 1915 when his doctor told him he had only a year to live and two years later, still alive, lost his prototype bread slicer and all his tools and equipment in a disastrous fire. In 1922, having secured financial backing, Rohwedder resumed work on his machine, persevering in the face of discouragement from the bakery trade who asserted that sliced bread would dry out too fast. In order to hold the slices together, he designed a machine to impale them on sterile hatpins, but the pins invariably fell out. His next idea was to pack the slices in shallow boxes lined with greaseproof paper. Eventually he hit on the solution that was to make sliced bread a success: a machine that cut the bread and then sealed it in a wrapper. This was in January 1928, by which time he had moved to Battle Creek, Mich.

The first Rohwedder slicer to be sold went into service with Frank Bench's Chillicothe Baking Co. on First and Elm streets in Chillicothe, Mo., on 6 July 1928, producing sliced Kleen Maid in waxed paper wrappers. The anniversary of this event is celebrated annually as Sliced Bread Day by the 9,000 citizens of the small town.

In the same year the Continental Bakery Co. of New York had introduced the first nationally distributed wrapped loaf under the name Wonder Bread and the big breakthrough came in 1930 when the company bought Rohwedder machines and began pre-cutting the loaves. Within three years 80 percent of all the bread sold in America was pre-cut. Notwithstanding this spectacular success, it was another twenty-one years before Rohwedder's invention is known to have appeared in print as a metaphor, the Lowell, Mass., *Sun* of 12 March 1951 quoting columnist Dorothy Kilgallen to the effect that British actor Stewart Granger was "the greatest thing since sliced bread."

THE FIRST SNEAKERS

SEE **sports shoes**.

THE FIRST SOCIAL SECURITY

SEE **old-age pensions**.

THE FIRST SODA POP

to be produced commercially was Mephitic Julep, a beverage produced by Thomas Henry in 1767 at his apothecary shop in Manchester, England. This was made to a recipe devised by Richard Bewley of Great Massingham, Norfolk, who mixed bicarbonate with carbonated water, claiming it as a sovereign remedy for fever, scurvy, dysentery, bilious vomiting, and other stomach disorders. Imbibers were advised to take it with a draught of lemonade or a mixture of vinegar and water.

First to produce artificial mineral water on an industrial scale was German-born Jacob Schweppe in Geneva in 1790 and he may thus be regarded as the father of the soft drinks industry. Schweppe moved to London in 1792, where the firm has had its headquarters ever since. He also pioneered the use of specially designed mineral-water bottles, rival soda waters being sold from crocks or other bulk containers. As early as 1789 he had commissioned a design for a stoneware bottle, but the earliest evidence of the use of such a receptacle was in 1794 when the great engineer Matthew Boulton (SEE **central heating**) recommended Schweppes Mineral Waters to Erasmus Darwin (father of Charles), mentioning that they were sold in Strong Stone Bottles at 6s 6d a dozen. The date at which Schweppes started using glass bottles is not known, though rival manufacturer William Francis Hamilton was using them "in long ovate form" (i.e., like an elongated egg) by 1809. Schweppes appears to have coined the term *soda* for carbonated soft drinks, their advertising using it for the first time in 1798, though an earlier use is recorded from 23 April 1796 in the notebook of Sir Joseph Andrews of Newbury, Berkshire, a satisfied customer.

U.S.: Carbonated soft drinks were produced by three entrepreneurs in 1807: Joseph Hawkins and his partner Abraham Cohen of Philadelphia; apothecary Townsend Speakman of the same city, who has been claimed as the first to add fruit flavorings; and Benjamin Silliman, head of Yale University's chemistry department, who had tried and failed to bottle his beverages (the bottles would self-destruct, to the dismay of customers) and fell back on importing used Schweppes bottles from England. In March 1807 Silliman opened a "Soda Water Concern" in New Haven, Conn., with a Mr. Twining as partner to dispense his bottled product. Joseph Hawkins also used bottles. After dissolving his partnership with Abraham Cohen he opened the first **soda fountain** with a new partner, named Shaw, at 98 Chestnut Street,

Philadelphia. While the fountain dispensed sodas at 6¢ a glass, or in a novel marketing initiative at $1.50 a month for a regular daily glass, the bottled versions, sold under the brand names Pyrmont and Ballston, were available at $1 a dozen standard size or $2 a dozen large.

Sodas were originally sold as a medicinal drink, a substitute for natural mineral waters. Although Townsend Speakman has been credited with flavoring his sodas with fruit juices, there is no contemporary authority for this. Certainly it did not catch on elsewhere in the early years of the nineteenth century. The earliest definitive evidence dates from 1830, when the use of syrups for flavoring effervescent waters was reported by the *Journal of Health* in Philadelphia. Early flavors included sarsaparilla, lemon, ginger, strawberry, and raspberry. It is known that the Smith & Hodgson drugstore in Philadelphia was selling flavored sodas by 1835.

The first of the nationally distributed brands was Hires Root Beer, which debuted at the Philadelphia Centennial Exposition of 1876. This, however, was not a bottled drink (until 1893) but a powdered extract for making up at soda fountains or at home. It was nationally advertised in weekly magazines from 1884. In the meantime Cliquot Club ginger ale had started production at Millis, Mass., in 1881; by 1907 it was being advertised in twenty-five national magazines. It was followed in 1885 by Moxie, distributed in bottles by the Moxie Nerve Food Co. of Boston, but both Dr. Pepper (Waco, Tex.), which emerged the same year, and Coca-Cola (Atlanta, Ga.), which began its extraordinary rise in the next, were originally sold only at fountains. Bottling of the former started in 1888 and of the latter, by Joseph A. Biedenharn of Vicksburg, Miss., in 1894. What was originally produced as Brad's drink (after proprietor Caleb D. Bradham) at New Bern, N.C., in 1896 changed its name to Pepsi-Cola in 1901 when it was franchised to other bottlers.

Soda vending machine: The first was introduced by H. S. & Bert Mills of Chicago in 1906, dispensing ten different flavors from five-gallon bottles mounted in a row. Cracked ice was placed on top of the bottles when they were refilled, but the soda pop grew warmer as the ice melted. The first refrigerated machines were the Sodamats installed at Coney Island, Ashbury

Park, and other amusement parks in Atlantic City and New York in 1926. These were ranged in batteries in a wall serviced by a common compressor, carbonator, and pump. The earliest self-contained coin-operated soft-drink dispenser was the Vendrink developed in 1934 by Leslie Arnett; and after a test run at Chicago's Lincoln Park Zoo and design improvements, the first permanent installation was made at Chicago's W. F. Monroe Cigar Store in April 1935.

Soda sold in cans: The first was Cliquot Club ginger ale in 1936, but the experiment was premature and was abandoned after a year. Cans were reintroduced by Pepsi for overseas shipment in 1948. By 1956, forty brands of soft drinks were available in cans.

Diet sodas: The first were NoCal, launched by Kirsch Beverages of College Point, N.Y., and Diet-Rite from Royal Crown Cola of Columbus, Ga., both in 1952. Diet Coke did not emerge until thirty years later.

Soda sold in plastic bottles: The first was Pepsi in 1976, after polymer engineer Nathaniel Wyeth (brother of artist Andrew) of DuPont had produced a bottle material called PET strong enough to withstand the pressure.

THE FIRST **SOFTBALL**

originated at the Farragut Boat Club in Chicago on Thanksgiving Day 1887 when a number of oarsmen were wiling away the time until news of the result of the Harvard–Yale football game would come over the wire. Someone threw an old boxing glove to another, who struck it with a broomstick. One George Hancock then seized the glove and tied it into a sphere with the laces, declaring "Let's play ball!." That evening he drafted the rules of a game he called Indoor Baseball. Once it was warm enough to play the new game out of doors, it became Indoor-Outdoor, though known to its detractors as "kitten ball" or "mush ball." The rules were formally codified in Minneapolis in 1895, but it was not until 1926 that the name Softball was adopted at a meeting of the National Recreation Congress.

THE FIRST **SOUND RECORDING**

apparatus was the Phonograph, designed by Thomas Alva Edison in 1877. The prototype was completed by his mechanic John Kruesi and Edison's British-born technical assistant Charles Batchelor at West Orange, N.J., on 6 December. The first recording, of Edison reciting "Mary Had a Little Lamb," was made the same day. An account of this latest miracle of science appeared in the *Scientific American* for 22 December 1877:

> Mr. Thomas A. Edison recently came into this office, placed a little machine on our desk, turned a crank, and the machine inquired as to our health, asked as how we liked the phonograph, informed us that it was very well, and bids us a cordial good-night. These remarks were not only perfectly audible to ourselves, but to a dozen or more persons gathered around.

Commercial production was commenced by the Edison Speaking Phonograph Co., 2093 Broadway, New York City, formed 24 April 1878. Initially the machines were leased out with a quantity of blank tin-foil cylinders to traveling showmen, who exhibited them to paying audiences and returned a percentage of the receipts to the company. It was at one of these demonstrations in New York during the early months of the enterprise that the first known musical recording was made by Jules Levy, playing "Yankee Doodle" on a cornet. The first instrument for domestic use, and the first to be sold outright, was the Edison Parlor Speaking Phonograph, marketed at $10 in 1878. After the initial novelty of the phonograph had faded, its obvious deficiencies—poor reproduction, the brevity of the tin-foil cylinder, and difficulty of operation—became apparent, and the public lost interest. Edison himself was busily engaged in the development of his incandescent lamp, and it was not until Bell and Tainter produced their improved Graphophone (SEE BELOW) that he returned to the problem of sound reproduction.

Sound recording apparatus capable of reproducing music: The first with any degree of fidelity (the 1878 experiment noted above can have been little more than a cacophony of sound) was the wax-cylinder Graphophone, developed by Chichester Bell (cousin of Alexander Graham Bell) and Charles Sumner Tainter at the Volta Laboratory, Washington, D.C., between 1881 and 1885 and was granted a U.S. patent on 4 May 1886. Manufacture was by the Columbia Phonograph Co. in 1888, the same year that Edison, spurred on by his rivals' progress, brought out his own wax-cylinder Improved Phonograph. Edison and Columbia tried to promote their apparatus as office dictating machines, but the price of phonographs compared unfavorably with the low wages of stenographers, and there was little response except by some government departments in Washington and a few blind typists. The real future of the phonograph lay in entertainment, and this was demonstrated when the first recording by a recognized musician was made by the eleven-year-old Polish piano prodigy Josef Hofmann at the Edison Laboratories in West Orange, N.J., either late in 1887 or early 1888.

The first **recording of a public performance**, the first **choral recording**, and the first **orchestral recording** were made on 29 June 1888, when Edison recording equipment was set up in the press gallery of the Crystal Palace at Sydenham, South London, on the occasion of the Handel Festival. An *Illustrated London News* reporter wrote:

> The phonograph reported with perfect accuracy the sublime strains, vocal and instrumental, of the "Israel in Egypt", received by a large horn projecting over the balustrade in the vast concert-room in the north transept. The machine was worked by Mr De Courcy Hamilton, one of Mr. Edison's assistants, who had brought it from America. The "phonograms" being sent to Mr Edison, all the Handel choruses, as sung here by four thousand voices, will be heard in New York and other American cities.

The following year Edison recorded an orchestral concert at the Metropolitan Opera House in New York City conducted by Hans von Bülow. Four phonographs were employed for the experiment, and the works recorded were Beethoven's "Eroica," a Haydn symphony in B-flat major, and the prelude to

Wagner's *Die Meistersinger*. This was the first orchestral recording in the United States.

Commercially produced recordings: The first were made on 24 May 1889 at the North American Phonograph Co.'s studios on Broadway, in New York City, where instrumentalist Frank Goede performed four piccolo solos and four flute solos. The former were Gilmore's "22nd Regiment March," "The Warbler," "Liliput Polka," and "Birds Festival Waltz." The latter were a two-part selection titled "Marquis," the waltzes "Abandon" and "La Source," and Scharwenka's "Polish Dance." In all Mr. Goede recorded seventy-five Edison wax cylinders at this session, each one unique as there was no method of duplicating before 1892. They retailed at 90¢ each. (For commercial disk recordings SEE BELOW.)

Record catalog: The first, a ten-page listing of 194 items, was issued by the Columbia Phonograph Co. of Washington, D.C., in 1891. It included 27 marches, 13 polkas, 10 waltzes, 36 recordings by Whistling John Atlee (the first "recording star"), 13 selections for clarinet and piano, 32 vocals (divided into "Topical," "Sentimental," "Irish," "Comic," and "Negro"), 20 spoken records (principally comic monologues), 9 cornet and piano selections, and 34 miscellaneous, including an operatic arrangement from *Il Trovatore*. Most records were sold by mail order, and worn recordings could be returned in part exchange for new. Worn cylinders were consigned to the proprietors of nickelodeons, the jukeboxes of the day.

Disk record-player: The first was the Gramophone, invented by Emile Berliner, a German immigrant living in Washington, D.C., who applied for a patent on 26 September 1887 and demonstrated his apparatus before the Franklin Institute in Philadelphia on 16 May 1888.

Following a visit by Berliner to Germany, commercial manufacture of the Gramophone was begun by Kämmerer & Rheinhardt of Waltershausen in 1889. These hand-cranked machines were intended chiefly as toys and played a 5-inch vulcanized-rubber disk at a speed of approximately 70 rpm. The first disk catalog was issued in 1892 by Parkins & Gotto of London, importers of the German machines. While many of the fifty-four records listed were nursery rhymes and other juvenilia, there was also some adult fare: nine of them English music-hall (i.e., vaudeville) or patriotic songs; two French and six German vocal offerings, including *Deutschland über Alles*; twelve recordings of brass; two piano solos; a clarinet and a street-organ solo; a bass duet; a reading of The Lord's Prayer (in English but in Berliner's guttural German accent) and of Byron's poem *Manfred*; and an extraordinarily poorly rendered *Farmyard Imitations*. The records cost one shilling (25¢) each. The first full-size, electrically operated machines were produced by the United States Gramophone Co., Washington, D.C., in 1894. These played 7-inch records; 10-inch records were introduced in 1900, and 12-inch in 1903.

The earliest known commercial recording on disk in the United States was by George J. Gaskin (known as "The Boy Tenor" but actually a man in his thirties) singing "I Don't Want to Play in Your Yard," made on 29 October 1895. The first American disk catalog was issued by Berliner the same year, listing mainly marches and dance music by John Philip Sousa's band, with ragtime and other light music from Haley's Concert Band of Washington, D.C., and the Metropolitan Orchestra. The first commercial studio for disk recording and the first record store were opened in adjoining buildings on Chestnut Street in Philadelphia by the Berliner Gramophone Co. in 1897. Alfred Clark presided behind the counter of the latter.

Berliner's disks not only played longer than cylinders, making them far more suitable for orchestral recordings, but were capable of being reproduced from pressing molds (SEE BELOW). No satisfactory method of making multiple copies of cylinder recordings was found until after disks had already established their place in the market.

The first factory to be operated solely for the manufacture of disk records was established by the Gramophone Co. at Hannover, Germany, in 1898 to produce disk recordings for the English market. It was equipped with fourteen record presses for the mass production of 7-inch shellac records—an innovation that proved a turning-point in the record industry. Previously the only method of duplication had been to set up a bank of six or more horns, and the artiste was required to repeat the song over and over again until a sufficient number of multiples of six had been made to satisfy consumer demand. The new presses worked with a copper matrix made from a wax master and could reproduce a limitless number of recordings at a correspondingly cheaper price.

In the earliest years of recording, the record player's status as little more than a toy was matched by the contempt with which it was regarded by established artistes. Only those with no reputation to lose, or at the vulgar end of the world of entertainment, were prepared to risk a fall in status among their peers by recording. The first recording artistes of international repute were those whose reputations were unassailable, led by diva Dame Clara Butt, who performed Goring Thomas's "Night Hymn at Sea" for the Gramophone Co. in London on 26 January 1899. Less than three weeks later, on 18 March, at the same studio, the first American of comparable stature to record, soprano Ellen Beach Yaw, rendered "O dolce contento" from Mozart's *The Magic Flute*. Others followed: Caruso (1902), Calvé (1902), Melba (1904), Patti (1905), Chaliapin (1907), Tetrazzini (1907), all for the Gramophone Co. (now EMI), which had early asserted its position as the world's foremost recording company. In the United States the records were issued by the Gramophone Co.'s affiliate the Victor Talking Machine Co., which from April 1903 issued its own celebrity recordings under the Red Seal label, starting with Australian contralto Ada Crossley. A few weeks earlier in Washington, D.C., the Columbia Phonograph Co. had initiated its Grand Opera Series with locally recorded offerings by baritones Giuseppe Campanari and Antonio Scotti, soprano Suzanne Adams, and bass Edouard de Reszke.

Operatic recording: The first was made in New York City in April 1878 when the French soprano Marie Rôze "warbled an aria *entire scena*" from Gounod's *Faust* into an Edison tin-foil cylinder recording machine. The first commercial releases were made on disk by Ferruccio Giannini, who recorded "La Donna è Mobile" and "Questa o Quella" from *Rigoletto* for Berliner's United States Gramophone Co. of Washington, D.C., on 21 January 1896.

Complete opera on disk: The first was Verdi's *Ernani*, released by the Italian Gramophone Co. on forty single-sided disks in 1903.

U.S.: Verdi's *Aïda* on thirteen disks issued by the Zonophone Co. of Camden, N.J., in 1906.

Commercial orchestral recordings: The first were made by Ed Issler's Orchestra at the North American Phonograph Co.'s studios on Broadway in New York City on 6 December 1890. Fourteen titles were recorded, including the march "New York at Night," selections from *The Mikado* and *Ermine*, and a polka "From Vienna to Berlin." The orchestra consisted of Ed Issler on piano, A. T. van Winkle on xylophone, a widower named von der Heide on violin, D. B. Dana on cornet, and George Schweinfest on flute.

Recording of a complete symphony: The first was of Beethoven's Fifth by the Berlin Philharmonic Orchestra under Arthur Nikisch, released by HMV in the United Kingdom on eight single-sided disks in 1914.

Royalties on recordings: The first recording artiste to receive royalties was the Italian tenor Francesco Tamagno on the operatic disks he made for the Gramophone Co. of London in 1902. Royalties were paid at the rate of 10 percent of the retail price, with an advance of £2,000 ($10,000)—a very substantial sum, sufficient in those days to buy a large house. Despite this liberality, Tamagno was not an easy client to deal with. Apart from insisting that all the recording equipment be brought to his home, he also demanded that each record have a separate serial number on it so that he could keep tabs on his royalties.

Jazz record: The first was "The Dixie Jazz Band One Step," backed by "Livery Stable Blues," recorded by Nick LaRocca's Original Dixieland Jazz Band for the Victor Co., Camden, N.J., and released on 7 March 1917. The *Victor Record Review* for that date cautioned prospective purchasers that "a Jass band is a Jass band, and not a Victor organization gone crazy." Although "Livery Stable Blues" was on the B side of the disk, its popularity far outweighed that of "One Step": A clarinet imitation of a rooster crowing, a cornet whinnying like a horse, and a trombone simulating the bray of a donkey doubtless helped to boost the record's sales to more than a million.

Blues record: The first was made by Mamie Smith and her Jazz Hounds, who recorded Perry Bradford's "Crazy Blues" for the Okey Co. in New York City on 10 August 1920. Neither Bradford, whose idea the recording was, nor Smith had any money at the time and the singer had no suitable clothes to go to the studio. Bradford persuaded the jazz violinist George Morrison to lend her $150 and to assemble a black "session" orchestra (the "Jazz Hounds") to accompany her on promise of payment deferred. Over one million copies of the record were sold within six months.

Country and western recording: The first was of fiddle tunes "Sallie Goodin" and "The Arkansas Traveler" by Eck Robertson and Henry Gilliand, made in New York City for the Victor Co. on 30 June 1922.

Electrical recording process: The first was developed by Lionel Guest and H. O. Merriman of London, who made a full-length experimental recording of the burial service of the Unknown Warrior at Westminster Abbey on 11 November 1920. The Abbey recording demonstrated that it was possible to substitute a microphone for the studio horn, and so record on location and at a distance from the sound source. It was issued on 17 December 1920 at 7s 6d ($1.87), available either from the *Times* newspaper or direct from Westminster Abbey. The process was not developed commercially and the first electrical recordings made by a record company for retail distribution were issued in the United States on the Autograph label by Marsh Recording Laboratories of Chicago at $1.50 each in late 1924. These included performances by Jelly Roll Morton, King Oliver, Willard Robison, Merritt Brunies and his Friars Inn Orchestra, and Jesse Crawford playing the Wurlitzer organ.

33⅓-RPM long-playing records: These were first launched by RCA-Victor with a demonstration held at the Savoy Plaza Hotel in New York City on 17 September 1931. Their first release, in November 1931, was of Beethoven's Fifth Symphony performed by the Philadelphia Orchestra under Leopold Stokowski, and this was the first time a complete orchestral piece had been issued on a single record. The 33⅓-rpm record-players were all combined with radios and ranged from $247.50 to $559, a high price bracket in the midst of the Depression that doubtless contributed to the failure of the venture.

The "long-player revolution" that was finally to oust the 78-rpm record forever began at a sales convention for Columbia representatives held at Atlantic City on 21 June 1948. Here Columbia unveiled the first really successful 33⅓-rpm microgroove records, made by a process developed by Dr. Peter Goldmark. These were vinylite disks with a 23-minute playing time on each side, and with 224 to 300 grooves to the inch. The initial releases included Mendelssohn's Violin Concerto, Tchaikovsky's Fourth Symphony, and the Broadway show *South Pacific*, average price $4.85. The success of Columbia's 1948 venture in comparison to RCA-Victor's attempt of 1931 can be attributed to an improved recording technique and longer-lasting records, cheaper record-players (an attachment for a standard player could be bought for as little as $29.95), and, not least, a healthier economic climate in which to launch the enterprise.

Album cover: Originally albums consisted of three or four 78-rpm records contained in separate paper sleeves between thick pasteboard covers. The muted brown, gray, or green covers in their leatherette bindings would be inscribed with the title and the artiste's name but were otherwise unadorned. The first pictorial covers were designed by Brooklyn-born Alex Steinweiss, art director for Columbia Records at their Bridgeport, Conn., headquarters, starting with a Rodgers and Hart collection of 1939 titled *Smash Song Hits* for which he used a photograph of a theater marquee on which the album's title and artistes' names appeared in lights. Although Columbia had turned down Steinweiss's initial proposal for illustrated covers on cost grounds, when he was given a reluctant go-ahead the experiment proved that the young graphic designer's instincts had been sound. An early cover for a reissue of Beethoven's Ninth Symphony produced an 894-percent increase in sales over the previous issue in a plain gray "tombstone" jacket. In 1948 Steinweiss designed the first LP cover, also for Columbia.

High-fidelity recordings: The first were issued by London-based Decca Records in December 1944. The first Hi-Fi record-player was the Decca Piccadilly, with a frequency range of 50–14,000 cps (cycles per second), introduced the following year.

Record on vinylite: The first was the 45-rpm *Till Eulenspiegel* from RCA-Victor in October 1945, premium priced at $3.50. This was the first really practical unbreakable record since Berliner had ceased using vulcanized rubber half a century earlier.

Stereophonic disk recordings: The first were made by Arthur Keller of Bell Telephone Laboratories in March 1932 and consisted of a number of orchestral works performed by the Philadelphia Orchestra under Leopold Stokowski at the Academy of Music in Philadelphia. Twin microphones were used and the recordings were made on wax masters at 78 rpm with two parallel vertically cut tracks. These records were not released commercially but were demonstrated at the Chicago World's Fair the following year.

The first commercial stereo disks were made by Emory Cork of Stamford, Conn., in 1957. The stereo tracks were carried in two separate grooves and a double pick-up head was used for playback. The earliest 45/45 stereo disks, i.e., with both tracks in one groove, were marketed by Audio Fidelity in April 1958.

Compact discs: The first were developed in the Netherlands by Philips over a period of fifteen years and demonstrated at the Salzburg Festival in April 1980 by Herbert von Karajan, who declared that "all else is gaslight." The grooveless miniature 12-cm discs, playing time 75 minutes, use a laser beam to "read" digitally encoded information, a system that eliminates all extraneous noise and enables them to be played indefinitely. Philips entered into an agreement with Sony, which launched the first compact disc player, the CDP-101, on 1 October 1982 in Japan together with a choice of 112 recordings. Its European debut followed on 1 March 1983.

U.S.: Early in March 1983 the first disc preceded the first players with the go-ahead Capitol Record Shop in Hartford, Conn., offering a choice of 24 titles imported from Japan and Europe at a price of $24.95. *Billboard* for 12 March ran an interview with the proprietor, who reported total sales of one. Regular imports began in June, by which time the players were for sale. American sales by the end of 1983 totaled 30,000 players and 800,000 discs. Pressing in the United States did not start until the opening of Sony subsidiary Digital Audio Disc Corporation's plant at Terre Haute, Ind., where Bruce Springsteen's *Born in the USA* became the first American CD on 21 September 1984. CDs began to take off during the 1985 Christmas season and within five years the vinyl market was no more than a specialty niche.

MP3, a compression format that shrinks audio files without discernible loss of sound quality, was originally developed at the Fraunhofer Institute in Germany as a project to see how music could be fed down a phone line. It was patented in Germany in April 1989 and in the United States on 24 November 1996 and all developers of MP3 encoders and decoders pay licensing fees to Fraunhofer-Gesellschaft.

The first handheld player was the MPMan F10 developed by SaeHan Information Systems of Seoul, South Korea, and launched locally in March 1998. In the United States it was marketed by Eiger Labs, Inc. of Newark, Calif., in August of the same year at $250. With 32 megabytes of memory, it could store about eight 4-minute songs. The "personal jukebox" concept was pioneered by South Korea's Remote Solutions, whose $799 PJB-100 launched at the end of 1999 with 4.8 gigabytes of storage, sufficient for 1,200 songs. The high capacity, however, meant that the PJB-100 was too large and too heavy to run around with. The pocket portable with capacious storage emerged with Apple's phenomenally successful iPod in late 2001. Designed by London-born Jonathan Ive at Apple in Cupertino, Calif., the iPod was the size of a cigarette pack and weighed only 6½ ounces. The 5-gigabyte hard drive held 66 hours of music, equivalent to 1,300 songs or 130 albums.

SEE ALSO **magnetic recorder**.

THE FIRST **SPACE FLIGHT**

successful, took place on 14 June 1949, when a monkey with the code name Albert 2 was launched into the stratosphere in a V-2 rocket from White Sands testing grounds in Alamogordo, New Mexico. The purpose was to assess the effects of radiation exposure at high altitudes. The test, known as Operation Albert, was kept secret for fear of objections from animal lovers. The original Albert 1 had failed to survive a mission flown four months earlier. Albert 2 would have survived but for the failure of the parachute intended to bring the capsule to a soft landing. He died on impact.

The first animal to go into orbit round the Earth was the dog Laika, launched in the Russian Sputnik II satellite on 3 November 1957. Although the authorities claimed that the dog expired painlessly after a week in orbit, following the fall of the Soviet Union it was revealed that Laika had succumbed to overheating and panic within a few hours of the launch.

Manned space flight: The first is alleged to have been made by a Russian named Alexis Ledovski in 1957. According to reports of the U.S. House of Representatives Space Committee and the U.S. Air Force Air Research and Development Command, Ledovski was launched from the Soviet missile test center 60 miles southeast of Stalingrad and reached a height of more than 200 miles before all communication with him ceased. The spacecraft could either have been carried beyond the pull of the Earth's gravity into outer space, or could have been burned up on re-entering the Earth's atmosphere. Other astronauts reputed to have lost their lives in unsuccessful space shots prior to 1961 have been named as Serentsy Schiborin (1958), Andrei Mitkov (1959), and Ivan Kachur (1960).

Successful manned space flight: The first was made by twenty-seven-year-old Flight-Major Yuri Alexeyevich Gagarin, who was launched from Baikonur, Kazakhstan, in the Russian spacecraft *Vostok I* at 9:07 A.M. Moscow time on 12 April 1961 and landed 108 minutes later at the village of Smelovka, near Engels in the Saratov region of the Soviet Union. The 6.17-ton carrier rocket contained a 2.4-ton capsule that was released when the speed of the spacecraft reached orbital velocity, about 7.8 km a sec. Gagarin then made a single orbit of the Earth at a maximum height of 203 miles and a maximum speed of 28,000 kph (17,398 mph). The first astronaut to return safely to earth, Maj. Gagarin was killed in an aircraft crash near Moscow on 27 March 1968. Not until many years after his death was it revealed that Gagarin had not actually piloted the spacecraft; it had been controlled wholly from the ground.

U.S.: The first American astronaut was New Hampshire-born Alan B. Shepard Jr., who rode in the Mercury capsule *Freedom 7* in a suborbital trajectory to a height of 116 miles on 5 May 1961. During the 15-minute 22-second flight he was weightless for nearly 5 minutes. First to orbit the Earth was John Glenn on 20 February 1962, completing three orbits in 4 hours 55 minutes aboard the Mercury capsule *Friendship 7.* He was launched from Cape Canaveral, Fla., by an Atlas booster and made a safe touchdown

in the Atlantic Ocean. The flight was witnessed live on television by an estimated 60 million Americans.

Woman astronaut: the first was Soviet cotton mill worker Valentina Nikolayeva Tereshkova, who made forty-eight orbits of the Earth in *Vostok VI* in 71 hours from 16 to 19 June 1963.

U.S.: Los Angeles-born Sally K. Ride was launched into space aboard the space shuttle *Challenger* on 18 June 1983 as one of the first five-person crew to operate in space. As part of the six-day mission STS-7 she participated in retrieving a satellite, the first time this had been accomplished by a manned (or personnel) spacecraft.

Space walk: The first was made by Lt. Col. Aleksey Arkhipovich Leonov, who left the Soviet spacecraft *Voskhod II* at approximately 8:30 A.M. Greenwich Mean Time on 18 March 1965 and spent 12 minutes 9 seconds floating in space connected to the satellite by a nylon cord 16 feet long. During this time he traveled about 3,000 miles at a speed of 17,500 mph.

U.S.: Edward H. White II spent 20 minutes outside the *Gemini 4* capsule on 3 June 1965. He was tethered by a 25-foot tube that provided oxygen and ventilation and used a handheld maneuvering device to control his movements.

The first untethered space walk was made by Bruce McCandless II, who left the U.S. space shuttle *Challenger* on 3 February 1984 to propel himself freely into space with a MMU (manned maneuvering unit) propulsive backpack.

Astronauts to land on the surface of the moon: The first were Neil Armstrong, mission commander of Apollo XI, and Col. Edwin Aldrin, pilot of the lunar module Eagle, who touched down on the Sea of Tranquility at 20:17 UST on 20 July 1969.

Neil Armstrong stepped on to the lunar surface at 2:56 UST on 21 July. As he did so he said: "That's one small step for [a] man, but a giant leap for mankind." (He omitted the crucial "a" before "man.") Aldrin followed him out of the module twenty minutes later, and the two astronauts spent a further hour and forty-four minutes carrying out their assigned tasks, which included collecting soil and rock samples, installing a special laser-beam reflector, planting the U.S. flag, and unveiling a plaque. The words on the plaque were read aloud by Armstrong, and heard by an estimated radio and television audience of five hundred million people: "Here men from the planet Earth first set foot on the Moon 1969 AD. We came in peace for all mankind."

THE FIRST SPECTACLES

authentic reference to, dates from 1289 and is contained in Sandro di Popozo's manuscript work *Traité de Conduite de la Famille.* He wrote, "I am so debilitated by age that without the glasses known as spectacles, I would no longer be able to read or write. These have recently been invented for the benefit of poor old people whose sight has become weak." Richard Corson in his *Fashions in Eyeglasses* (1967) gives Italy 1287 as the probable place and date of the invention. There are various claims as to the identity of the inventor, but none has been substantiated. The earliest pictorial representation is a fresco of 1352 at Treviso, Italy, by Tomaso da Modena and depicts bespectacled Cardinal Ugone of Provence.

Spectacles with concave lenses for myopia are first depicted in a portrait of Pope Leo X painted by Raphael in 1517. The pope is said to have used them most frequently when hunting.

Until the seventeenth century, lenses were generally selected at random from the spectacle-marker's stock according to the whim of the customer. The first attempt to grade spectacle lenses systematically was made by Daza de Valdés in Seville and the technique was described by him in a book of 1623.

Spectacles were only available in America as imports until 1833, when jeweller William Beecher began manufacturing them in Southbridge, Mass. This enterprise grew into the giant American Optical Co.

Temple spectacles: The first spectacles with rigid side pieces (temple spectacles) were manufactured by the London optician Edward Scarlett in 1727. The side pieces terminated in a scroll. Temple spectacles were known in French as *lunettes à temps permettant de respirer à l'aise*—since it was possible to breathe without the spectacles falling off one's nose. Previously the only method of retaining the spectacles against the sides of the head had been with thin cords that looped around the ears. The first with hinged side pieces was the invention of London scientific instrument maker James Ayscough in 1752.

Bifocals: The first are described by Benjamin Franklin, the American Minister Plenipotentiary to France, in a letter to Philadelphia optician George Whateley dated Passy, 23 May 1785:

> I imagine it will be found pretty generally true, that the same convexity of glass, through which a man sees clearest and best for reading at the distance proper, is not the best for greater distances. I therefore had formerly two pairs of spectacles, which I shifted occasionally, as in traveling I sometimes read, and often wanted to regard the prospects. Finding this change troublesome, and not always sufficient ready, I had the glasses cut and half of each kind associated in the same circle. By this means, as I wear my own spectacles constantly, I have only to move my eyes up or down, as I want to see distantly far or near, the proper glasses being always ready.
>
> This I find more particularly convenient since my being in France the glasses that serve me best at table to see what I eat not being the best to see the faces of those on the other side of the table who speak to me; and when one's ears are not well accustomed to the language, a sight of the movements in the features of him that speaks helps to explain; so that I understand French better by the help of my spectacles.

From the foregoing remarks it would appear that Franklin had his first pair of bifocals made before leaving Philadelphia for Paris in 1776. One-piece bifocals were first produced by the Zeiss Co. of Jena, Germany, in 1910. Varifocals were launched as Varilux by the French Society of Opticians in 1959.

Contact lenses: In 1888 Swiss physician A. Eugen Fick of Zurich, Paris optician Edouard Kalt, and August Müller of Kiel, Germany, each reported using contact lenses to correct optical defects. Fick coined the term *contact lens*. The first in the United States were made by New York optometrist William Feinbloom in 1936. The breakthrough to general use came with the introduction of plastic contact lenses by Kevin Tushy of San Francisco in 1948. Soft contact lenses were invented in December 1961 at the Institute for Macromolecular Chemistry in Prague by Otto Wichterle, who cast them in an apparatus fashioned from a children's building set powered by a bicycle dynamo. They were manufactured in Czechoslovakia (now Czech Republic) in 1964 and were introduced in the United States by Bausch & Lomb in 1971. Disposable soft contact lenses followed in 1987.

Plastic spectacle lenses: The first for conventional spectacles (for contacts SEE ABOVE) were manufactured in Adelaide, South Australia, in 1960 from CR39 resin—used in the United States for aircraft windshields—by Scientific Optical Laboratories of Australia (SOLA). By the mid-1980s SOLA had become the world's most prolific lens maker.

THE FIRST SPEED BUMPS

were introduced in the small town of Chatham, N.J., as "speed reducers," 5-inch-high mounds of taprock and clay, on 23 April 1906. Several hundred citizens gathered to watch the impact (in both senses) they made on traffic and were well rewarded when the first car to negotiate them did what millions of others would do over the next hundred years and failed to slow down sufficiently. The *New York Times* reported with ill-concealed relish:

> There were several persons in the machine, and when the heavy rubber tires struck the elevation there was a palpitation of the machinery and the car shot up several feet in the air. Goggles, hats, and monkey wrench, sidecombs, hairpins, and other articles flew in all directions. The crowd gave a cheer and decided the borough's plan was effective.

Effective it undoubtedly was, so it is curious that this was a successful American innovation that failed to stimulate imitation abroad until long after speeding traffic had become a major hazard. There were no speed bumps in Europe before 1970, when the town of Delft in the Netherlands installed them, and the British remained free of what they called speed humps or sleeping policemen until 1984.

THE FIRST SPIRITUALIST MEDIUMS

were Margaretta and Kate Fox, aged fourteen and eleven respectively, who made what has been claimed as the first direct communication with the spirit world at their Canadian immigrant parents' homestead in Hydesville, New York, on the night of 31 March 1848. For some weeks previous to this date the Fox family had been troubled by inexplicable rapping noises coming from all parts of the house, until on the evening in question Kate Fox challenged the unseen instigator of the sounds to repeat the snapping of her fingers. This being instantly responded to, Mrs. Fox began to direct questions to the supposed spirit in such a way that they could be answered either by a rap, signifying "Yes," a silence for "No," or for more complex replies, a rap in answer to particular letters as the alphabet was called over. In this manner the spirit was identified as one Charles B. Rosma, a peddler who allegedly had been murdered in the house some five years earlier and whose body was said to be buried beneath the floor of the cellar. The following day the Fox family and their neighbors dug up the cellar and found fragments of bone and human hair; the remainder of the skeleton was not recovered until fifty-six years later, when it was found behind the cellar wall.

The first public demonstration of mediumship was made by Margaretta Fox and her elder married sister Leah Fox Fish at the Corinthian Hall, Rochester, N.Y., on 14 November 1849. Two weeks later Leah started to accept clients for private séances, becoming the first professional medium, and the following April Margaretta and Kate were placed under contract by the great American showman P. T. Barnum, giving public séances at Barnum's Hotel and Barnum's Museum, as well as private sittings in the homes of rich and eminent persons. The two younger sisters continued their career for the next thirty years, during which time both became incurable alcoholics. Margaretta confessed in 1888 that the whole business of the raps had been artificially contrived and actually gave a demonstration of how she could make loud cracking noises with the bones of her foot. She later retracted this statement, claiming she had been paid to make it by enemies of the spiritualist movement.

THE FIRST **SPORTS SHOES**

known were a pair of football boots made for England's King Henry VIII in 1525 by cordwainer (shoemaker) Cornelius Johnson. They were among a large order comprising ten pairs of leather walking and riding boots, forty-five pairs of velvet shoes for indoor wear, and "one pair *sotular* for football"—sotular being a latinized Saxon word for shoe. The list was only discovered in 2004 by Maria Hayward, head of studies at Southampton University's textile conservation center, thereby giving shoes specially designed for sport a far greater antiquity than had thitherto been believed. Not that Henry's apparent enthusiasm for football did the game any good. In 1548 he banned it because players and spectators at the often violent games of a hundred or so men on each side had a tendency to riot.

No further allusions to special footwear for sporting events occur until cricket became an organized game in England in the mid-eighteenth century, the first team game played on a club basis and to agreed rules. Most early cricketers played in the normal buckled shoes commonly worn by men of all stations in life, but in 1764 there is a reference to boys from the ancient boarding school at Winchester playing "in slippers red." In a portrait titled *Miss Wicket* by John Collett c. 1770, the woman cricketer depicted also sports red shoes, though as they had high heels they would scarcely have aided her in running between wickets. In 1845 the cricket writer who signed himself "Felix at the bat" recommended that players should have spikes fitted to their shoes.

U.S.: Two types of sports shoe emerged in the year 1868. Amateur sprinter William B. Curtis had the first pair of spiked running shoes made to his own design and wore them at the inaugural indoor track and field meeting held in the United States, organized by the New York Athletics Club at the Empire Skating Rink on 11 November 1868. As they were the only pair, he lent them to his friends and the shoes were worn by four different competitors in seven separate events. (For women's spikes SEE **women's track and field**.)

The first shoes to be manufactured specially for sporting use made their debut that year in the Peck & Snyder Sporting Goods Catalog. Selling at $6 a pair, these were "croquet sandals" with canvas uppers

and vulcanized-rubber soles produced by the Candee Manufacturing Co. of New Haven, Conn. By 1887 they had earned the sobriquet "sneaker," as they made no sound. As croquet and lawn tennis became the rage on suburban lawns wherever English-speaking people were settled, so the new footwear became universal. While they were **sneakers** in the United States and Canada, they became plimsolls in Britain and Ireland, sandshoes in Australia and New Zealand, takkies in South Africa and Rhodesia, and keds (regardless of make) in India and Ceylon—possibly the only English words which is different on every continent. By 1900 they had been adopted as beachwear (hence the Australasian cognomen) and within a few years had become general leisure wear, particularly for children. Following the introduction of the enormously popular Keds brand by the U.S. Rubber Co. in 1916, they also became the first shoes that it was considered seemly for girls and young women to wear without stockings. Boys tended to favor the high-top sneakers originally introduced as basketball boots by Marquis M. Converse of Malden, Mass., in 1917; these became the first celebrity-endorsed sportswear in 1923 with the launch of the Chuck Taylor Converse All-Star. In 1963 it was reported that white sneakers had replaced saddle shoes as the American teenage girl's footwear of choice.

What are called "trainers" in most British Commonwealth countries and might best be dubbed "designer sneakers" in North America originated as running shoes to which Adolf Dassler, founder of Addas (later Adidas) of Herzogenaurach near Nuremberg in Germany, added a distinctive triple stripe in 1949. As there was no leather available in devastated post-war Germany, Dassler fashioned the uppers of the shoes from the canvas of disused army tents and the soles from recycled rubber fuel tanks. Gradually these types of sports shoe became more elaborate in construction and fanciful in design, Dassler alone securing more than seven hundred patents for improvements.

The first American brand within the genre was Tracksters, launched in 1962 by New Balance of Boston with a rippled sole and cushioned heel containing a shock absorber. Nike broke into the market in 1966, when University of Oregon track coach Bill Bowerman and miler Phil Knight, also from Oregon, founded what was originally called Blue Ribbon Sports to manufacture the Cortez, a running shoe with a wedge-shaped heel designed to relieve pressure on the Achilles tendon and absorb shock. It was Bowerman who famously experimented with his wife's waffle iron in 1971 to produce the high-traction sole that was to help propel Nike to brand leadership. He also replaced canvas uppers with lightweight nylon mesh, made from the "Swoosh" fiber after which the world's most recognized logo, the Nike "checkmark," was named. (The work of University of Oregon student Carolyn Davidson, who was paid $35 for it.) By this time in the early 1970s designer sneakers had already begun to effect a transformation in leisurewear as people in all walks of life took to wearing them for everyday activities, even to work, joining T-shirts and jeans (qv) as icons of later twentieth-century street fashion.

THE FIRST STAMP COLLECTOR

was Dr. John Edward Gray of the British Museum in London, who bought a block of Penny Blacks, the world's first adhesive postage stamp (qv), on 1 May 1840—five days before official issue. He intended to keep these as a souvenir of Uniform Penny Postage, a reform in which he had been keenly interested, but as other issues came on stream, and other countries began issuing stamps, he decided to form a collection. In 1863 Gray published one of the earliest stamp catalogs.

By 1842 the new hobby had taken off sufficiently to earn a squib from the choleric Member of Parliament Col. Sibthorpe in the satirical weekly *Punch*:

> *When was a folly so pestilent hit upon*
> *As folks running mad to collect every spit upon*
> *Post-office stamp that's been soil'd and been writ upon?*
> *Oh for Swift? Such a subject his spleen to emit upon.*

U.S.: The first collector, per New York's *Metropolitan Philatelist* in 1918, was William H. Faber of Charleston, S.C., who claimed to have taken up the hobby as a boy in 1855. Within five years it had become sufficiently widespread to be the subject of an article in the Boston *Daily Advertiser*, which noted that

the stamps of Mauritius and Hawaii (then an independent monarchy) were considered the rarest. "The elegant and curious 'mania,'" the paper reported, "is now chiefly indulged by young ladies, but we cannot tell how soon it may take possession of the more mature portion of mankind."

Not long was the answer. Already in Europe the Brussels bookseller Jean Baptiste Constant Moëns had begun dealing in stamps at his shop in the Galerie Bortier, in the Marché de la Madeleine, in 1855. The earliest dealer in the United States is disputed. William P. Brown, who began trading in New York City in 1860, is usually credited as the first, but Alvin F. Harlow in *Paper Chase* (1940) quotes him as saying that John Bailey was already a dealer when he opened his business.

Most of the further developments in the world of philately took place in Paris, including the earliest use of the word itself (by George Herpin in the philatelic journal *Collectionneur de Timbre-Post*, 3 November 1864). The first commercially produced **stamp catalog** was compiled by Alfred Potiquet and published by Edard [*sic*] de Laplante and Eugène Lacroix in Paris in December 1861. Within months the first to be published in the United States followed: *The Stamp Collector's Manual*, compiled and issued in 1862 by A. C. Kline of Walnut Street, Philadelphia. It listed 1,500 American and foreign stamps. The first **stamp album** was published by Lallier of Paris in 1862 in French, English, and German editions. First in America was *Scott's American Album*, published by John Walter Scott of New York City at $2.50 in July 1868.

The first **stamp auction** was of the stock of a deceased dealer by the name of Elb and took place in Paris on 29 December 1865. It raised a total of 800 francs. The first in the United States was held in New York City by John Walter Scott at the Clinton Hall Book Sale Rooms and Art Galleries on 28 May 1870 and realized about $500.

First day cover: The first to be purpose-designed was a black bordered envelope with a five-line cachet produced by philatelic publisher George Linn of Columbus, Ohio, for the Warren G. Harding memorial stamp issued on 1 September 1923. The print run was two hundred and surviving examples are valued at $800.

THE FIRST STAPLER, OFFICE

patent was issued in 1877, while the earliest examples of staplers manufactured for sale preserved at the Early Office Museum (www.officemuseum.com) all date from 1879: McGill's Staple Press, produced by Holmes, Booth, and Haydens, New York City; Brown's Single-Blow Staple Driver produced by William J. Brown Jr., of Philadelphia; Victor Paper Fastener and Check Canceller produced by A. A. Weeks of New York City. Each of these could only be loaded with one staple at a time. Magazine staplers emerged about the same date, the first being patented by C. H. Gould of Birmingham, England, on 5 March 1868; prior to this magazines were sewn or occasionally pinned together. Other models formed staples from wire loaded on a spool (1882), cut staples from a strip of metal fed into the machine (1894), or formed the staple from a straight pin (1897). The earliest hard evidence of "frozen wire" staples (a strip of individual staples glued together, as is universal today) was a January 1927 advertisement for Parrot Speed Fasteners. However, the company history of the Boston Wire Stitcher Co. (now Bostitch) claims that they pioneered frozen-wire staples "probably" in 1924 (elsewhere said to be 1923). There has been little change in fundamental stapler design since Speed Products introduced the top-loading (or open channel–loading) magazine with its 1938 Swingline Speed Fastener.

Early staplers were nearly all called "fasteners." The earliest use of "stapler" was in respect of the 1901 Century Pin Paper Stapler. The **staple remover** was patented by William G. Pankonin of Chicago on 3 March 1936.

THE FIRST STATUES

in the United States were effigies of King George III and statesman William Pitt, Earl of Chatham, by the London-based sculptor Joseph Wilton, one of the founders of the Royal Academy, erected in New York on Bowling Green (SEE **park, public**) and at the intersection of Wall and William streets, respectively, in 1770—the statue of the king on 21 April, of Pitt about the same time. These had been commissioned by the City of New York, the citizens wishing to mark their appreciation of William Pitt's efforts on their behalf in obtaining the repeal of the 1765 Stamp Act. As it was considered that honoring one of the king's ministers in this way might be regarded as an act of lèse-majesté, it was decided to commission a statue of the sovereign as well. Further to emphasize their respect for the throne, the statue of George III was to be an equestrian one and was paid for at double the rate of the figure of Pitt—£1,000 for the one, £500 for the other.

Within a very few years New Yorkers had come to regret this mark of submission to royal authority, and in a fit of revolutionary fervor tore down the horse and its rider. All that seemed to have survived was the king's head, the horse's tail, the bridle, and the cap of the pedestal after the 4,000-pound lead statue had been melted down to cast bullets for the rebels' muskets. The head was smuggled to England by Tory supporters and has never been located since. The other fragments repose in the collection of the New-York Historical Society. It transpired, however, that not the whole statue was melted down and various other pieces have been recovered over the years from a swamp in Wilton, Conn., where the statue had been taken. The empty marble pedestal was eventually (1802) to serve as the plinth for another statue, this time to the Father of the Nation, George Washington. The statue of Pitt is also in the New-York Historical Society's museum, less the head and an arm that were broken off by drunken Scottish soldiers of the occupation forces in New York on St. Andrew's Day 1777. These depredations left only one complete statue in America, another William Pitt that had been dedicated in Charleston, S.C., on 5 July 1770.

Statue of an American: The first was commissioned by Lord Le Despencer from John Bacon the elder and depicted William Penn, founder of Pennsylvania and the City of Philadelphia. Completed in 1774, the 6-foot lead figure was erected on the top of the Le Despencer family seat, Wycombe in Buckinghamshire, England. It was removed to nearby Stoke Poges after 1788 by John Penn, grandson of the Proprietor, and thence was taken in September 1804 to Philadelphia, where it was re-erected in the yard of the Pennsylvania Hospital.

The first full-length statue of an American in America (there had been earlier portrait busts) was Lazzarini's 8' 2" Carrara marble effigy of Benjamin Franklin, commissioned at a fee of 500 guineas by Philadelphia's reputedly wealthiest citizen William Bingham and erected in a niche over the main entrance of the Library Company of Philadelphia's building on Fifth Street in 1792. The right hand rested on a pile of books, aptly for the founder of the Library Company (SEE **public library**), and the left held a scepter upside down to signify Franklin's distaste for the institution of monarchy. Much worn by weather, the statue is now protected from the elements inside the Library Company's present building.

Although this was the first such statue erected in America, Jean-Antoine Houdon's celebrated marble statue of George Washington had been completed earlier, in 1788. It remained in Paris, however, for eight years while the capitol in Richmond, Va., was completed and then was erected in the rotunda there in 1796.

Statue of a woman: The first, unveiled on 25 November 1879, was erected in Grand Army of the Republic Park at Haverhill, Mass., in honor of native daughter Hannah Emerson Duston, who had made a daring escape from Indians in 1697. While Haverhill continues to cherish her memory, elsewhere her reputation has been tarnished among white liberals by virtue of the fact that she tomahawked and scalped two Native American men, two women, and six children in the course of liberating herself from her captors. The 6-foot bronze statue, executed by local sculptor Calvin H. Weeks, depicts an angry and determined Hannah Duston striding forth with a tomahawk in one hand, the other hand with a finger pointing accusingly at ... the Politically Correct?

The first woman to be honored with a statue for what today would be called "lifetime achievement" was Irish-born Margaret Gaffrey Haughery, who came to Baltimore at the age of five and settled in New Orleans when she was twenty-one after marrying Charles Haughery. When he and their only child died in the 1835 yellow fever epidemic, she decided to devote her life to orphans. Working first in a laundry, then in a dairy, she saved from her wages and solicited funds to establish Saint Theresa's Asylum on Camp Street in

1840. She went into business, running a highly successful bakery among other enterprises, and made a fortune sufficient to fund the founding of Saint Vincent Infant Asylum, the Female Orphan Asylum, and Saint Elizabeth's Asylum. When Margaret Haughery died in 1882 the proceeds of the sale of her business went to Catholic, Protestant, and Jewish orphanages. The will was signed with an X; she had never learned to read or write. Her statue was sculpted by Alexander Doyle and erected in a small triangular park bounded by Camp, Prytania, and Clio streets in New Orleans in 1884. It shows a seated lady of ample bosom and kindly visage, her arm around a small orphan girl. The inscription simply says MARGARET.

America has more statues to women than any other country, reflecting the greater opportunities that existed for them earlier than in other societies. Most honored is the Shoshone guide Sacajawea, who accompanied the Lewis and Clark Expedition, with five statues.

THE FIRST **STEAMBOAT**

practical, was the 138-foot-long paddle-wheeler *Pyroscaphe*, a 182-ton wooden craft built at Écully, near Lyons, France, by the Marquis Claude-François-Dorothée de Jouffroy d'Abbans. The trial run took place on the River Saône from Lyons to the Isle Barbe on 15 July 1783. This was the first time a vessel had moved against the current under its own power. The engine, constructed by Frèrejean et Cie of Lyons, had a horizontal double-acting 25.6-inch-diameter cylinder enclosed within the boiler, rotary motion being transmitted by a double-ratchet mechanism connected to the piston rod.

Commercial steamboat service: The first was inaugurated on the Delaware River by John Fitch following an announcement in the *Federal Gazette and Philadelphia Daily Advertiser* for 26 July 1790: "The Steamboat is now ready to take passengers and is intended to set off from Arch Street Ferry in Philadelphia every Monday, Wednesday, and Friday for Burlington, Bristol, Bordentown, and Trenton and to return on the following days. Price 2s 6d to Burlington and Bristol, 3s 9d to Bordentown, 5s to Trenton."

As 26 July was a Monday, it is likely that the service actually started on that day. The vessel, designed by Fitch, was a stern paddle-wheeler driven by a beam-engine with a single 18-inch-diameter cylinder. He was joined in the venture by a German watchmaker, Johann Voigt, who was responsible for the working of the engine and boiler, and can thus be regarded as the first ship's engineer. Although the service continued until the end of the summer, Fitch had chosen a route already well serviced with stagecoaches and passenger receipts were correspondingly low. While the average speed of the boat was 7 mph, the coaches were evidently faster, as they could accomplish the journey from Philadelphia to Burlington in 1½ hours less time. After the discontinuance of Fitch's service, there were no other ventures of this kind, either in America or elsewhere, until Robert Fulton began running his famous *Clermont* on the Hudson River between New York and Albany in 1807. This has often been wrongly described as the first commercially operated passenger steamboat, though it would be fair to say that it was the first to maintain sustained regular service.

Steamboat successfully fitted with screw propellers: The first was the 5-ton 25-foot-long *Little Juliana*, demonstrated at Hoboken, N.J., by nineteen-year-old John Stevens (SEE **yachts**) in May 1804. She had twin four-bladed propellers of 18-inch diameter and achieved speeds of up to 8 mph.

The first large seagoing steam vessel driven by a screw propeller was the 237-ton *Archimedes*, built at Poplar, London, by H. Wimshurst for the Ship Propeller Co.—a company formed to exploit Francis Pettit Smith's propeller patent—and launched on 18 October 1838. (SEE ALSO **ocean liners**.)

Steamboat navigated in open sea: The first was John Stevens's 95-ton *Phoenix*, which made the voyage from New York City to Philadelphia in thirteen days under the command of Capt. Moses Rogers on 10–23 June 1809. The *Phoenix* was designed, however, as a river craft and after her arrival in Philadelphia operated on the Delaware. First intended for use in open water was the coastal steamer *Fulton*, designed in 1813 by Robert Fulton and built by Adam and Noah Brown for Cadwallader Colden. She made her maiden seagoing voyage into Long Island Sound on 25 March 1815 under Capt. E. S. Bunker and from March 1817,

together with the SS *Connecticut*, operated a successful passenger service from New York City to New Haven and New London, both in Connecticut. These were also the first steam vessels with covered passenger accommodation, those who traveled on river steamers doing so on deck and exposed to the elements.

Steamship to cross the Atlantic: The first was the 320-ton paddle-wheeler *Savannah*, which left Savannah, Ga., under the command of Capt. Moses Rogers on 24 May 1819 and arrived at Liverpool under sail after a voyage of 27 days 11 hours on 20 June, having run out of fuel off the coast of Ireland. She carried no passengers, as no one could be persuaded to buy a ticket for what promised to be such a hazardous voyage. In fact the danger of a boiler explosion—not uncommon at this stage of steamship development—was minimized by the fact that the *Savannah* spent only about 85 out of her 663 hours at sea under steam. No other American steamship made the crossing until 1845.

The first steamship to cross the Atlantic wholly under power (with brief intervals for boiler-scraping) was the Quebec and Halifax Steam Navigation Co.'s *Royal William*, built in 1831 by Black & Campbell of Quebec with twin side-lever engines by Bennet & Henderson of Montreal. She sailed from Pictou, Nova Scotia, on 17 August 1833 with seven passengers and a cargo of six spars, a harp, and a box of stuffed birds and arrived at Cowes, Isle of Wight, on 4 September.

Steam naval vessel: The first was Robert Fulton's *Demalogos* aka *Fulton*, armed with thirty 32-pounders, which was launched at New York Navy Yard on 29 October 1814. She was, however, never commissioned, being too underpowered to serve as a warship at sea. Employed at the Navy Yard as a receiving ship, she was destroyed in an explosion on 4 June 1829.

The first naval warship commissioned in the U.S. Navy was also one of the first two steamships in the world to be engaged in a naval action, each in March 1824. She was an ex–river steamer called the *Enterprise* that was bought by the U.S. Navy in December 1822, renamed the *Sea Gull*, and fitted out for service with Cdre. David Porter's West Indies Squadron to subdue the pirates rife in the Caribbean. On 30 March 1824, under the command of Lt. Ralph Voorhees, she recaptured the schooner *Pacification* with minimal resistance. She was more actively engaged in combat in the following March, when she joined three Royal Navy vessels in an attack on a pirate lair east of Matanzas, Cuba, capturing two of their schooners with eight pirates killed and nineteen captured. This was the first time that America and Britain participated in a combat operation as allies.

In the meantime, on the other side of the world, a steamer had gone to war. The *Diana* had been built on the Hooghly River in Bengal in 1823 with twin 16-hp Maudslay engines and used as a tug until the following year when the Burma War broke out and she was acquired by the Bengal government. Equipped with Congreve rockets, she joined the British fleet assembling off the Irrawaddy delta and was active in the bombardment of the Burmese capital Rangoon, which fell on 10 March 1824. Other towns on the coast and on the Irrawaddy were then invested, the tiny *Diana* winning a fearsome reputation among the enemy as "the fire ship," her rockets being dubbed "the Devil's sticks."

The first naval steamship to sink another naval vessel was the Greek navy's *Karteria*, under the command of ex–Royal Naval officer Capt. F. A. Hastings, which destroyed Turkish sailing sloops in the Bay of Salona off the Gulf of Corinth in September 1827. The weaponry was also novel, as Hastings had equipped his steamer with four 68-pound deck cannons adapted to fire red-hot shells. Generally paddle steamers were of limited use in battle because the space occupied both by the paddles and the engines severely limited the number of guns in a broadside. With the adoption of screw propellers the steam warship came into its own; SEE BELOW.

The first steamships of the U.S. Navy to engage in warfare were *Scorpion*, *Scourge*, *Spitfire*, and *Vixen*, part of Cdre. Matthew Perry's Gulf Squadron during the Mexican War of 1846–48. On 14 June 1847 these steamers, towing forty barges, passed the bar of the Tabasco River and continued inland to capture the town of Frontera.

Iron steamship: The first was the 116-ton *Aaron Manby*, laid down in 1821 by Aaron Manby, proprietor of the Horsley Ironworks at Tipton, Staffordshire, England. The hull was cast at Tipton from ¼-inch-thick plates and transported in sections for assembly at Rotherhithe, London, where the vessel was completed on 30 April 1822. Following trials on the Thames in May, she made her maiden voyage across the English Channel with a cargo of linseed and, appropriately, iron, arriving in Paris on 10 June 1822.

U.S.: The first iron boat of any kind in America was the 8-hp 5-ton steamboat *Codonus*, built by Quaker John Elgar at York, Pa., and first tested on the Susquehanna River on 14 November 1825.

Steel steamship: The first was the launch *Ma Robert*, constructed in John Laird's shipyard at Birkenhead, England, for the use of David Livingstone in his expedition up the Zambezi River and delivered on 6 March 1858. The vessel was taken out to Africa in sections aboard the sloop *Pearl* and was assembled and launched on the Kongone tributary in May of that year. By the time the expedition had reached Kebrabasa Rapids the unfortunate *Ma Robert* had already been renamed the *Asthmatic*, "from the puffing and groaning with which she managed her six or seven miles an hour, being easily passed by the native canoes." Her steel plates constantly leaked, but with continuous repairs she was kept afloat until 20 December 1860, when she met her end on a sandbank above Senna.

U.S: The first steel ship to operate in American waters, later to become the first **steel warship** in the world, was the paddle-steamer *Banshee*, built by Jones, Quiggin & Co. at Liverpool, England, in 1862 for the Anglo-Confederate Trading Co. as a blockade runner. Her maiden voyage in April 1863 was the first **Atlantic crossing by a steel ship**. *Banshee* made eight successful round trips between Nassau in the Bahamas and Wilmington, N.C., carrying guns, metals, chemicals, and clothing to America and cotton back to the Bahamas for onward shipment to Liverpool, before being captured by the USS *Grand Gulf* in November 1863. She was then converted into a gunboat and, in a classic case of poacher turned gamekeeper, was commissioned in the U.S. Navy in June 1864 for service with the North Atlantic Blockading Squadron.

The first steel ship built in the U.S. was the SS *Chattachoochee*, launched by James Rees & Sons of Pittsburgh in 1881 for the People's Line of Columbus, Ga., whose directors had demanded "the finest vessel ever to wet the Apalachicola-Chattachoochee."

Screw-propelled warship: The first to be commissioned was the 164-foot sloop USN *Princeton* on 9 September 1843, having been launched at the Philadelphia Navy Yard only four days earlier. The six-blade propeller had been designed by Capt. John Ericsson. The Royal Navy's screw-propelled sloop HMS *Rattler* had been launched earlier, on 12 April 1843, but was not commissioned until 12 December 1844.

SEE ALSO **ocean liners; yachts: steam yacht.**

THE FIRST
STORE WITH PLATEGLASS WINDOWS

without sash bars (i.e., the whole window glazed with a single pane) were installed at 16 Charing Cross Road in London, at a former print shop converted into a tailoring establishment by Francis Place and reopened on 8 April 1801. Although this innovation was condemned on all sides as reckless extravagance, Place wrote in his memoirs that he "sold from the window more goods . . . than paid journeymen's wages and the expenses of housekeeping."

U.S.: The earliest record of large panes of plate glass in the United States comes from the unlikely source of Hawaii's *The Polynesian* for 21 December 1844: "Petit's Shawl store in Boston has plate glass windows of but one pane each containing 48 square feet, while A. T. Stewart's store located on Broadway between Chambers and [Reade] had French plate glass seven feet wide by eleven feet two inches high." Both these examples used imported plate glass. The first panes manufactured in the United States were by James N. Richmond of Cheshire, Mass., in 1853.

THE FIRST **STORM WINDOWS**

were installed at the front of 45 Brompton Row (later 168 Brompton Road) in London's Knightsbridge by Benjamin Thompson, Count Rumford, American-born scientist and philanthropist and founder of the Royal Institution. This improvement to conserve heat was part of the refurbishing of the house undertaken with the assistance of the architect of the Royal Institution, Thomas Webster. It was in place by June 1801, when the Swiss scientist M. A. Pictet stayed with Rumford and wrote a detailed description of the house. He recorded that each of the windows was framed with a three-sided glass case in which plants could be placed. Count Rumford left for Paris in May 1802 and the house was rented. The double glazing was probably removed when it was substantially remodeled about 1831. There is no record of double glazing elsewhere in Britain until an installation was made at Cranfield Court in Bedfordshire in 1874.

U.S.: The earliest known storm window is the double-paned pedimented window on the southwest wall of the dining room of Thomas Jefferson's Virginia mansion Monticello. The window has two sets of triple sashes, one inside and one out, designed to act as insulators during the winter. The inner set, unusually, is about 12 inches wider than the outer one. The woodwork of the window frames was executed by James Dinsmore, though it is not known whether he was also responsible for the double glazing. A drawing by Jefferson himself for the frieze and cornice adorning the window, now in the Coolidge Collection of Thomas Jefferson manuscripts of the Massachusetts Historical Society, is believed to date from 1803, which may also be the year the installation was made.

THE FIRST **STREETCARS**

were two thirty-seat horse-drawn vehicles built by John Stephenson of New York (who had also built New York's first bus) and operated by the New York & Haerlem [*sic*] Railroad Co. on a route running down Fourth Avenue and the Bowery from Harlem to Walker Street. The first 1-mile stretch of double track between Prince and Fourteenth streets was opened on 26 November 1832, when both cars set off in procession on the same track. The leading car was driven by highly experienced stagecoach driver "Lank" Odell and contained city bigwigs; the second, in the much less capable hands of a local hackney driver, carried the company officials. Unfortunately this jehu forgot to apply the brakes and the car ran into the one in front, occasioning the passengers considerable alarm and the spectators huge delight.

Electric streetcars: The first operated commercially in the United States were designed by Edward M. Bentley and Walter H. Knight for the East Cleveland [Ohio] Street Railway, using a third rail in an underground conduit to supply the current. The service was inaugurated on 26 July 1884 and continued for about a year. Few other cities chose to follow Cleveland's example in adopting a system not only costly to install but also prone to short-circuiting if rain or snow failed to drain from the conduits.

The first **overhead electric streetcars** in the United States were former mule-driven vehicles adapted by the Belgian sculptor and electrical engineer Charles J. Van Depoele for the Capital City Street Railway of Montgomery, Ala., that began running on the Court Street line on 15 April 1886. The cars had a single motor mounted on the front platform and drew power from an overhead cable. The Court Street line was so successful that all the mule-cars in the city were replaced by electric cars operating on 15 miles of track. Montgomery therefore became first in the world with a citywide system of electrical transportation, European cities running them side by side with horse-drawn means of conveyance.

The number of passenger journeys by bus overtook the number for streetcars for the first time in 1940. At one time streetcars were so ubiquitous that it was possible to travel from Boston to New York by this means alone, never needing to walk more than a mile or so from the outer terminus of one system to the nearside terminus of another.

THE FIRST STREET DIRECTORIES

in the United States were *McPherson's Directory for the City and Suburbs of Philadelphia* and *The Philadelphia Directory* pubished by Francis White, both in November 1785. White's contained a mere 3,569 names whereas the one-armed Scottish sea captain John McPherson, who had made his fortune through privateering, managed to garner no fewer than 6,250. Not that this represented all the dwellings in Philadelphia, then the second most populous city (40,000) in the English-speaking world. He had attempted to list all the inhabitants alphabetically by name and also

by street number, but not all those who answered the door were willing to cooperate. The directory contains many entries that explain the absence of a name, such as "I won't tell you" and "cross woman." While McPherson's invention of a bed that would ward off the depredations of mosquitoes and other insects—an infliction in Philadelphia in the summer months—failed to secure his name in the roster of significant innovators, his street directory deserves to. The only larger anglophone city at that time, London, did not have its first street directory until 1792.

THE FIRST STREETS, PAVED

in America were laid in the flourishing fishing village of Pemaquid, Maine, in 1625. About half a mile of the settlement's streets were paved with flat stones hauled from the beach, large ones on the outer sides and smaller for the crowned center. The streets, paved to facilitate the transport of cod by ox-cart from the wharves to the drying areas behind the town, were 11½ feet wide and flanked by stone gutters. Boston became the first American city with paved streets in 1654. Exactly half a century later the existence of **sidewalks**, together with curbs and gutters, is noted in Boston.

THE FIRST STRIPTEASE

originated as a result of an incident that occurred at the Bal des Quartz Arts held at the Moulin Rouge in Paris on 9 February 1893, when two dancers in oriental costume, Manon Lavalle and Sarah Brown, stripped for the edification of the Paris students. Their subsequent prosecution and fine of 100 francs provoked a riot in the Latin Quarter, and troops had to be called out when the students laid siege to the Prefecture of Police.

The publicity attracted by the girls' action and its consequences inspired the world's first theatrical striptease act, which took place at the Divan Fayouau Music Hall, rue des Martyrs, in Paris on 13 March 1894. The act was titled "Le Coucher d'Yvette" and consisted of a girl stripping to go to bed. The stripper was one Blanche Cavelli, of whom little else is known. She walked onstage to piano music, dressed in outdoor clothes, removing first her gloves, her hat, and a corsage that she threw on to a chair. Then she stepped out of her shoes and her shirt, took off her petticoat and corset, and began peeling off her stockings. Last to go was the chemise, which did not leave her naked as the audience hoped, but wearing a nightgown. How this was effected is not recorded; most likely she divested herself of the chemise behind a screen and threw it over provocatively, to emerge attired for bed. Tame as this may sound, the sight of Mlle. Cavelli's bare legs alone would have electrified an audience that had never before seen unclad limbs onstage, or indeed in public. Certainly her act was sufficiently titillating to inspire some thirty imitations. Variations were presented under such titles as "Liane chez le Médecin" (a girl undressing for the doctor), "Le Bain de Maid" (a girl undressing for her bath), "Suzanne et la Grande Chaleur" (a girl undressing in a heat wave), and "La Puce" (in which the girl removed her garments one by one to rid herself of a flea). The original "Le Coucher d'Yvette" was even made into one of the earliest stag films, by the same name, by Gaumont in 1897.

U.S.: Disrobing onstage made its debut in Florenz Ziegfeld's production of the Parisian divorce farce *The Turtle*, which opened at the Manhattan Theater on Broadway on 3 September 1898. The heroine, played by Sadie Martinot, has left her husband because he is too old-fashioned. On the eve of his marriage to another woman, she sneaks into his bedroom and performs her undressing act.

Undressing to music was brought to burlesque, its natural home, by the scandal-ridden Cincinnati cooch dancer Millie De Leon starting about 1903, but stripping also flourished on the legitimate stage. In November 1915 *New York Times* critic John Corbin complained that "no piece is complete without the undressing or disrobing scene." These antecedents, though, were not striptease as such, according to Rachel Shteir in the only scholarly work so far on the phenomenon, *Striptease* (2004). Striptease as it was to emerge in modern burlesque, she opines, "involved women undressing more fully, more quickly, and more frequently" than the tamer pre–World War I variety.

The surprisingly extensive literature of the striptease invariably goes to the same source for "the night they invented striptease." "They" in this case are the Minsky brothers and the source is Morton Minsky's *Minskys' Burlesque* (1948). In this picaresque memoir, "Mort" recounts how the brothers lured red-headed dancer Mae Dix from Manhattan's Union Square Theater in 1917 to perform at their National Winter Garden roof theater. Her costume for the act comprised a short black dress with detachable collars and cuffs. To save on laundry bills, according to Mort's account, she would discard the collar before giving an encore. One night the audience, misunderstanding the gesture, roared for more, so she threw off the cuffs into the wings as well. When the crowd cheered, she started undoing the buttons of her bodice as she left the stage. The stage manager fined her $10 for bringing unauthorized "business" into the act, but Billy Minsky, who had hired her, reimbursed the $10 and insisted she incorporate the collar and cuffs and bodice routine into the act thereafter. So, as legend has it, striptease was born. Apart from the fact that this seems a lot more restrained than the strip poker and other divertissements on the legitimate stage that John Corbin had denounced, there are certain lacunae in casting Mae Dix in the role of first stripper. Rachel Shteir has searched *Variety* and *Billboard* but found no reference to her performing at the National Winter Garden during that decade. *Variety* in 1920 reported that she had come out of retirement for an engagement at the Union Square Theater.

While stripping and teasing evolved as separate routines between the time that Mae Dix was supposed to be getting her kit off at Minsky's and the early days of Prohibition, Shteir believes that the marriage of the two took place not in New York but in the Midwest and that its progenitor was "Blonde Bombshell" Hinda Wassau, the place Chicago, the year probably 1927. Details are few, though it is said to have occurred during a shimmy contest either at the Haymarket Theater or the State-Congress. Legend has it that Wassau wore a regular chorus-girl costume over a short, beaded fringed dress and that when it was her turn to exit and remove the outer costume so that she could go on again in the fringed frock, the chorus costume got caught on something backstage. Wassau reputedly ran back on with it half on and half off, then climaxed her number by pulling it off altogether. (There are numerous other stories of the birth of striptease, all of them involving some accidental circumstance. One wonders why it could not have just been thought up by a showman who knew what tired businessmen will pay good money for.) Whatever Wassau's role in combining stripping and teasing in one act, she certainly made a good living out of it for the next twentysomething years. And the date seems right given that the word itself was shortly to be minted. *Billboard*, reviewing *Nite Life in Paris* in its issue for 1 September 1928, wrote of headliner Mae Brown, "Sex seductive stripteaser stops the show." The Oxford English Dictionary's earliest citation for *striptease* is 1929. Which also happened to be the year that nudity's first diva, the one stripper everyone can name, Gypsy Rose Lee, began taking it all off in Kansas City.

The evolution of striptease into **lap dancing**, originally known as table dancing, dates from 1977 when impresario Michael J. Peter bought a topless bar called the Red Lion on Orange Blossom Trail in Orlando, Fla., and renamed it the Dollhouse. There he introduced scantily clad dancers who would gyrate and disrobe at a customer's table astride his lap, then opened similar venues in South Florida before being charged with mail fraud and serving two years in a federal jail. In 1996 Mr. Peter, who subsequently founded the highly successful Pure Platinum and Spearmint Rhino chain of lap-dancing clubs, was technical advisor on the Demi Moore movie *Striptease*. **Pole dancing** is said to have originated in Vancouver strip clubs in the late '80s.

Striptease has latterly acquired a new status as art—at least in Norway. In 2005, when the Norwegian authorities tried to tax entry fees to the Diamond Go Go Bar in Oslo, the outraged proprietor went to court. The judge ruled that stripping was an art that should enjoy the same exemption from tax as opera and ballet.

THE FIRST **SUBMARINE**

was built in London by the Dutch physicist Cornelius Drebbel in 1624. The craft was constructed from a wooden framework covered in a greased-leather skin and was manned by twelve rowers whose oars protruded through sealed ports. Drebbel and his crew are reported to have navigated under the surface of the Thames for 7 hours during a demonstration before King James I. One of the most remarkable aspects of his achievement was the breathing arrangement that made such a feat possible, described by Robert Boyle as "a composition of a liquid that would speedily restore to the troubled air such a proportion of vital parts as would make it again for a good while fit for respiration." It is now believed that Drebbel had devised a means of producing oxygen, a century and a half before its official discovery by Joseph Priestley. Though the submersible was intended for naval use, the Admiralty advised against its adoption.

The first submersible vessel to be used as an offensive weapon in warfare was the *American Turtle*, designed by David Bushnell of Saybrook, Conn., as a colonial answer to the might of the Royal Navy during the American War of Independence. Manned by Sgt. Ezra Lee, the one-man midget submarine launched an attack on Adm. Howe's flagship, HMS *Eagle*, as she lay at anchor in New York Harbor on 7 September 1776. The attempt to blow her up failed as the mine that Lee attached to the *Eagle*'s hull drifted away before exploding harmlessly. Nevertheless, the *Turtle* has another claim to distinction as the world's first screw propeller–driven vessel, the motive power being supplied by hand.

The first successful submarine attack was by Robert Fulton's *Nautilus*. Fulton, the American marine engineer chiefly associated with the steamship (qv), went to London in 1804 to try to interest the British Admiralty in his hand-propelled submersible after the French, who had financed its development, withdrew their support. He offered to blow up the French fleet assembling at Boulogne for an invasion of England. On 2 October one of his torpedoes destroyed a French pinnace, drowning its crew of twenty-two. The French kept this humiliation secret, and the success of Fulton's venture being unknown to either him or his prospective paymasters, the Admiralty declined to take up his invention.

The first effective attack by a submarine in American warfare took place in South Carolina on 17 February 1864, when the hand-crank–propelled

Confederate vessel *H.L. Hunley*, armed with a ram torpedo, slipped into Charleston Harbor and sank the newly commissioned Federal corvette *Housatonic*. The *Hurley* failed to return after the successful attack, for reasons that have never been satisfactorily explained, and her crew of eight men were lost at sea. The *H.L. Hunley* was one of a number of submersibles built by the firm of Hunley, McClintock & Watson at Mobile, Ala., for the Confederate Navy during 1863–64. These small hand-propelled screw-driven craft were known as "Davids," as they were designed to do battle with "Goliath"—the Union Navy. The *H.L. Hunley* was recovered in 2000, having been almost perfectly preserved in silt.

Self-propelled submarine: The first was *Le Plongeur*, a 140-foot-long 420-ton vessel driven by an 80-hp compressed-air engine and launched at Rochefort on 18 May 1863. Its range and speed proved too limited for naval use.

Submarines in regular naval service: The first in peacetime were fifty manually operated Drzewiecki submarines ordered by the Russian government in 1879. Designed by Polish engineer Stefan Drzewiecki, they were intended for coastal defense only and could hardly be described as seagoing, but they did have the distinction of being the first submarines equipped with **periscopes**. Construction started at St. Petersburg in 1881.

The first full-size, self-propelled seagoing submarine in naval service was the Swedish-built *Nordenfelt*, based on a design by the Rev. George Garrett of Manchester, England, and built at Landskrona in 1883. Acquired by the Greek government in 1886, the *Nordenfelt* was a steam-driven vessel of 60 tons displacement and had a surface speed of 9 knots. It was also the first submarine to be armed with locomotive torpedoes and the first fitted with a mounted gun, the *Nordenfelt* 1½-inch quick firer. The vessel arrived at Piraeus harbor on 13 January and began sea trials under Greek naval command on 14 March.

U.S.: The first powered submarine of the U.S. Navy was the *Holland* (SS1) built by the Electric Boat Co. of Groton, Conn., at a cost of $120,000 and commissioned on 12 October 1900. She was 53′ 10″ long and 11′ diameter, powered by a pair of four-cylinder engines on the surface and an electric motor when submerged.

The designer was Irish Fenian John P. Holland, who originally intended it as a weapon to be employed against the British in the cause of Home Rule for Ireland. His early experimental models were built in the United States but the work was financed by the revolutionary Fenian movement. In 1898 he produced his celebrated Holland No. 9, which proved far superior to any other existing submarine in rapid diving and general mobility; it was this model, designated SS1, that was acquired by the U.S. Navy in 1900 and, ironically in view of Holland's motivation, by the Royal Navy a year later.

The first U.S. Navy submarine to be sunk was F-4, lost off Honolulu with the loss of 21 lives on 25 March 1915.

Nuclear submarine: The first was the U.S. submarine *Nautilus*, built by the Electric Boat Co. at Groton, Conn., and launched on the River Thames [Connecticut] on 21 January 1954. The vessel, 324 feet long, was designed by Adm. Hyman G. Rickover and was powered by one Westinghouse S2W reactor. The vessel had a maximum speed of 20 knots, and a displacement of 3,747 tons submerged. She carried a crew of eleven officers and eighty-five ratings. Under the command of Eugene Parks Wilkinson, USN *Nautilus* sent the signal "under way on nuclear power" on the occasion of her first sea trial on 17 January 1955. She was refueled for the first time over two years later, after voyaging 69,138 miles.

THE FIRST SUBWAY

was London's 4-mile-long Metropolitan Railway, opened to fare-paying passengers at 6 A.M. on 10 January 1863. There were seven stations, with termini at Farringdon Street and Paddington, and the journey took 33 minutes overall. Passenger compartments were lit with gas which, according to the *Daily Telegraph*, "in some instances was turned on so strong in the first-class carriages . . . that newspapers might be read with ease." On the opening day, six engines each drawing four carriages left at 15-minute intervals and made a total of 120 journeys in both directions, carrying more than 30,000 passengers. It is now part of the Metropolitan Line of the London Underground.

Subway system to be electrified: The first was the City & South London Railway (now the City branch of the London Underground's Northern Line), officially opened on Tuesday, 4 November 1890, when the Prince of Wales made the first royal progress by Underground from King William Street to the Oval. Passenger service commenced on 18 December 1890 with a flat-rate fare of 2d for any distance. There were no tickets, fares being paid at a turnstile. Fourteen four-wheel 12-ton electric locomotives, built by Mather & Platt of Manchester, each drew three carriages at an average speed of 11½ mph. The carriages came to be known as "padded cells" to the traveling public, as they were fitted with 5-foot-high upholstered seats for the full length of the car, reaching up to a narrow, horizontal slit of window at eye level. They were, however, the first carriages on the London Underground to be lit by electric light.

U.S.: New York had a short-lived pneumatic subway (the single cylindrical car fitted the tubular tunnel so that it could be propelled by suction) that ran for three years from Warren Street to Murray Street starting 26 February 1870, but with a tunnel only 312 feet long this was hardly more than an amusement ride. The first proper transportation system built underground in the United States was the Tremont Street Subway, in Boston, a line 1⅔-mile-long that was built at a cost of $4,350,000 and the first section of which was opened on 1 September 1897. When the second section opened on 3 September 1898 the subway had five stations in all: Boylston Street, Park Street, Scollay Square, Adams Square, and Haymarket Square. With two hundred cars an hour in each direction in off-peak and four hundred in rush hour, the subway did much to relieve congestion on Tremont Street, where it was said that at peak traffic time you could just about walk from Scollay Square to Boylston Street on the streetcar roofs. Putting trains below ground had been suggested as a solution to downtown Boston's traffic problems only after a proposal to put them over the ground, on an elevated railway to run across Boston Common, had aroused protests from around the nation. Boston's was the sixth subway in the world, after the three by then operating in London and one each in Glasgow (1896) and Budapest (1896). Others in the United States are New York (1904), Philadelphia (1908), Chicago (1943), Cleveland (1956), San Francisco (1972), Washington, D.C. (1976), Atlanta (1979), Baltimore (1983), Miami (1984), and Los Angeles (1993).

THE FIRST SUDOKU

despite its name did not originate in Japan. The prototype was conceived by the blind Swiss mathematical genius Leonhard Euler, professor of physics at the St. Petersburg Academy in Russia, who claimed that the loss of his second eye in 1771 had enhanced his powers of logic. He improved on the ancient puzzle known as magic squares by the creation of a 9-line by 9-line grid in which Greek or Roman symbols must not recur in each row or column. His so-called Graeco-Roman Squares first appeared in *Verhandelingen uitgegeven door het zeeuwsch Genootschap der Wetenschappen te Vlissingen 9*, published at Middleburg in the Netherlands in 1782. It is believed, though, that this dissertation was first delivered as a lecture at the St. Petersburg Academy on 17 October 1776.

Among the vast welter of academic treatises produced by Euler during his lifetime, the Graeco-Roman Square attracted little attention. It was more than a century before Sudoku emerged in its modern form, the work of an unsung Parisian puzzle-maker called M. B. Meyniel, who divided the 81-square grid into nine 3 x 3 sub-boxes each containing all the numbers from 1 thru 9. This appeared in the *Divertissements Quotidiens* ("Daily Brainteasers") section of *La France* on 6 July 1895 and sparked off a craze comparable to today's that persisted until World War I, when French newspaper readers had more pressing concerns.

What is remarkable is that the reappearance of this version sixty-five years on is attributable to an American who had never heard of Meyniel nor seen any of the French puzzles. A freelance puzzle-maker, Howard Garnes, also divided Euler's 81-square grid into nine 3 x 3 boxes each containing all the numbers from 1 to 9. This he sold to Dell Puzzle Magazines of New York, who first published it in 1979 in either *Math Puzzles and Logic Problems* or, according to other authorities, *Dell Pencil Puzzles and Word Games.*

Garnes named his puzzles "Number Place" and Dell continued to publish them in various of their magazines, where they were spotted by the leading Japanese puzzle-producing company Nikoli. With a couple of small variations on Garnes's original, their version debuted in the April 1984 issue of *Monthly Nikolist* under the less-than-catchy title *Suuji Wa Dokushin Ni Kagiru*, which loosely translates as "the number must only appear once" (actually rather more descriptive than Number Place). It was Nikoli president Kaji Maki who decided, a couple of years later, that the name needed shortening and combined the Su from *Suuji* (numbers) to Doku from *Dokushin* (single) to make Sudoku. He was not responsible for the picturesque legend now prevalent that Sudoku originated in fifth-century Japan as a means of sharpening the wits of Samurai warriors. Westerners remain eager to believe that anything with a Japanese name that is not a car or a video game must have an ancient provenance.

The Sudoku developed by Nikoli became big in Japan, where the alphabet does not lend itself to crosswords, but some twenty years were to pass before it expanded elsewhere. It was a New Zealand judge based in Hong Kong who was to make Sudoku into a global phenomenon. Shopping in Tokyo in March 1997, Wayne Gould picked up a Sudoku puzzle magazine in a bookstore and was instantly captivated. Over the next six years he developed a computer program for making up Sudoku puzzles on the spot. The judge's wife worked in New Hampshire and the first newspaper to buy the program and start a Sudoku feature was the local *Conway Daily Sun* in September 2004. The real breakthrough came two months later when Gould persuaded London's august *Times* to do the same. Within six months every national newspaper in Britain was running Sudoku and American metropolitan dailies duly followed suit. By the end of the year Sudoku had spread worldwide, reaching even the world's most remote country, the Napoleonic isle of St. Helena. Gould's only regret was that his wife was able to complete his computer-generated puzzles in half the time it took their creator.

THE FIRST SUICIDE BOMBING

in a terrorist context was carried out by the unidentified driver of a car packed with explosives that sped through machine-gun fire into the compound of the Iraqi embassy in Beirut, Lebanon, on 15 January 1981. There were two explosions on impact, destroying the embassy and damaging other neighboring buildings. At least sixty-one people were killed, including Iraqi ambassador Abdul Razzak Lafta, and more than a hundred were injured. Although the attack has generally been attributed to al Dawa, an Iraqi Muslim fundamentalist group, two other organizations also claimed responsibility: the Army for the Liberation of Kurdistan (not heard of previously or subsequently) and the Iraqi Liberation Army. The Iraqi government blamed Syrian intelligence agents.

The first **suicide-bomb attack against Americans** was by the Shi'ite terrorist group Hezbollah on 18 April 1983, when a pickup truck carrying almost 2,000 pounds of explosives was crashed through the lobby door of the U.S. embassy in Beirut. "Even by Beirut standards it was an enormous blast..." wrote former CIA agent Robert Baer. "The USS *Guadalcanal*, anchored five miles off the coast, shuddered from the tremors. At ground zero, the center of the seven-story embassy lifted hundreds of feet into the air, remained suspended for what seemed an eternity, and then collapsed in a cloud of dust, people, splintered furniture, and paper." The total of sixty-three dead included seventeen Americans, among whom were all six members of the CIA Beirut station and the visiting CIA national intelligence officer for the Middle East, Robert Ames, whose hand, with its wedding ring, was found floating a mile offshore.

THE FIRST SUMMER CAMP

(sustained) was the North Mountain School of Physical Culture opened as a non-profit venture in 1876 by Joseph Trimble Rothnack at North Mountain in Luzerne County, Pa., to improve the health of "weakly boys." The cost for four months residence was $200, most of the boys coming from nearby Wilkes-Barre and Philadelphia.

The Rev. George Hinckley of Hartford, Conn., ran the first church-sponsored camp near Wakefield, R.I., in the summers of 1880 and 1881.

The first commercially run summer camp was Camp Chocorua, organized by Ernest Balch at Asquam Lake, N.H., from 1881 to 1889. Balch was a Dartmouth undergraduate who wanted to offer twelve- to sixteen-year-old boys from wealthy families a healthier alternative to lazing around in luxurious summer resorts. The presence of the lake enabled Balch to teach the boys how to make their own boats. At first they lived in tents but by the mid-1880s the camp had permanent wooden cabins. Another innovation, not destined like the cabins to be copied by subsequent camps, was a system of artificial money designed to teach the boys about modern commerce.

Camp to admit girls: The first was Cape Arey at Wayne, N.Y., a natural-science camp run by Prof. Albert L. Arey of the Rochester Free School, with girls allowed for a four-week session in 1892. The first all-girls' camp was Redcroft, established on Nofound Lake at Hebron, N.Y., by Mrs. Oscar Holt in 1900. This only operated until 1902, but it was in that year that three summer camps for girls opened that were to put the concept of backwoods adventuring for the future mothers of America on a permanent basis: Wyonegonic at Denmark, Maine; Kelonka at Wolfeboro, N.H.; and Pinelands at Center Harbor, Maine.

The early girls' camps had in common that most were situated in the northeast, that they were founded by progressive educators who believed in girls having the same opportunity as boys to enjoy the freedom of the wilderness, and that they usually had faux Indian names. They also had much the same uniform in common, baggy bloomers worn with high-laced boots and either sailor blouses or, as at Wyonegonic, a white blouse with cowboy-style neckerchief and broad-brimmed hat. Only in the early 1930s did the bloomers give way to almost equally baggy shorts, succeeded in the '40s by slimmer and shorter shorts and in the rock-and-roll '50s by blue jeans and T-shirts.

There are at present some 8,500 mainly co-ed summer camps in the United States, of which the oldest is Camp Dudley, now on Lake Champlain, founded by Sumner F. Dudley in 1886 on Orange Lake in Newburgh, N.Y.

THE FIRST SUPERMARKET

The earliest recorded self-service grocery stores were two independent enterprises established in California in 1912, the Alpha Beta Food Market at Pomona, and Ward's Groceteria in Ocean Park. At approximately the same period a chain of self-service groceries known as Humpty Dumpty Stores was started in California by the Bay Cities Mercantile Co. It is doubtful whether these ventures were large enough to be described as supermarkets, and the customer still paid for her goods at a counter. The next significant advance toward the supermarket proper was made by Clarence Saunders, who introduced a turnstile entrance and regular checkout system at his Piggly Wiggly self-service grocery that he opened at 79 Jefferson Street, Memphis, Tenn., on 6 September 1916. When he was quizzed about the unusual name, Saunders would habitually respond, "So people will ask." The four aisles were so arranged that the customer had to traverse each of them to reach the checkout counter, thereby ensuring exposure to the full range of merchandise. Wicker baskets were provided for the goods selected. Every individual item was price-tagged, another innovation in American merchandising. Saunders's concept proved so successful that seven years later he had built up a chain of 2,800 Piggly Wigglies throughout the United States, most of them franchise operations; in that year, 1923, the first overseas self-service store was opened in Brisbane, Queensland, Australia, by Claude A. Fraser after he had read about Saunders's retail network. There are about 600 Piggly Wigglies surviving, mainly in the deep South. Saunders's mansion in Memphis, preserved as the Pink House Museum, contains a replica of his first supermarket.

The first supermarkets that had a shopping area large enough to satisfy the modern definition of the term *supermarket* (i.e., at least 12,000 square feet) were the King Kullen food stores, started by Michael Cullen with the opening of his first outlet on 171st Street and Jamaica Avenue in Queens, N.Y. on 2 August 1930. Cullen responded to the Depression's low housekeeping budgets by offering the ultimate in cut-price merchandising; up to 300 separate items were sold at cost price only. Typical prices were potatoes at 10 pounds for 15¢, cabbage at 2¢ per pound, lettuce at 3 heads for 10¢, oranges at 15 for 10¢, chuck steak at 12½¢ per pound, round roast for 17¢ per pound, and chicken for 18¢ per pound. In 1932, possibly the worst year of the Depression, the 8 King Kullen supermarkets sold $6 million of groceries alone, besides dry goods.

By 1936 there were some 1,200 supermarkets in the United States. These retailing pioneers, with their range of choice, ease of selection, ample parking, and low prices, raised the average price spent in-store from 35¢ per customer for corner groceries and 60¢ for chain stores, to $1.50 to $2.00 at the vast outlets run by the likes of Cullen and his principal competitor, Big Bear.

The term supermarket was already in use by this date, though at first it appears to have been employed to connote any large cut-price grocery store, not necessarily self-service. The first grocery operators to adopt the word *supermarket* as part of their trade name were Albers Super Markets Inc., who opened their first store in November 1933.

Shopping cart: The first is usually attributed to Sylvan N. Goldman of Oklahoma City, Okla., in 1937, but nearly twenty years earlier Joe Weingarten of Weingarten's Big Food Markets in Houston, Tex., had asked an employee with a mechanical bent, Ellis D. Turnham, if he could come up with a device for customers to haul their groceries around the store. Turnham's first attempt consisted of an adapted child's wagon with a basket mounted on it. This was improved at the second attempt and resembled the single-basket cart of today except that it did not have a hinged back for nesting. Goldman, manager of the Standard Stores and Humpty Dumpty Stores in Oklahoma City, came up with the same idea independently and he also engaged an employee, maintenance man Fred Young, to build a prototype. This was contrived from a folding chair mounted on wheels with two wire baskets mounted one above the other. The new cart was introduced at five Standard Stores on 4 June 1937, but customers steadfastly refused to use them until Goldman hired some unemployed people to pose as shoppers gleefully piling their carts high with groceries. Once they had been persuaded, it became apparent that people would buy far more than they could carry in a basket.

What Goldman did which Weingarten had not was to set up a company to manufacture the carts for sale to other supermarket chains at $7 apiece, introducing them at the inaugural gathering of the Super Market Institute at the Astor Hotel, New York City, in September 1937. Goldman's Folding Basket Carrier Co. went on to produce the first shopping cart with a built-in baby seat in 1940 and the first airport luggage cart in 1956 (SEE **airport: luggage carts**). They also introduced a nesting cart in 1947, but whether this was the first cart to have a hinged back so that it could be pushed into other parked carts is still the subject of heated debate among historians of in-store haulage. Midwesterners favor the claim of Orla Watson of the Western Machine Co. in Kansas City, whose Telescopic Cart debuted at Floyd Day's Super Market the same year. Litigation between the two contenders was settled out of court in 1949.

Goldman may or may not be the "inventor" of the shopping cart, and he may or may not have been first with the nesting device, but it is his original design of 1937 that is preserved in tribute to supermarket mobility at the "nation's attic," the Smithsonian Institution in Washington, D.C. By the time of his death in 1984 the humble cart had earned him a fortune estimated at $200 million and there were some 25 million of them in use worldwide.

Supermarket to introduce unit pricing: Comparative shopping was introduced by Safeway at four Washington, D.C., outlets on 8 December 1969. Gummed labels below each brand displayed the price per pound, per pint, or per other unit of measurement.

Self-service checkout: The system was patented by Dr. Howard Schneider of Montreal, Canada, on 8 December 1992 and manufactured by his company, Optimal Robotics. The first operative units had already been installed that year at the Price Chopper in Clifton Park, N.Y.

SEE ALSO **bar code**.

THE FIRST SURFBOARDING

....

originated in Hawaii as part of ancient religious ritual. The earliest eyewitness account of what the Hawaiians called *he'enalu* or wave-riding was written by Lt. James King during Capt. James Cook's third and final voyage to the Pacific. At Kealakekua Bay, on the island of Hawaii, in January 1779 he recorded of the Hawaiians:

> Where there is a very great sea and surf breaking on the shore, they lay themselves upon an oval piece of plank. They wait the time of the greatest swell and push forward with their arms. It sends them in with a most astonishing velocity, and the great art is to guide the plank so as always to keep it in a proper direction on top of the swell. The boldness and address with which we saw them perform these difficult and dangerous maneuvers was altogether astonishing and scarcely to be credited.

With the arrival of Calvinist missionaries from New England in 1821, surfboarding was suppressed. Evidently the practice survived away from their prying eyes: The oldest surviving surfboard in the world, 14½ feet long and weighing 148 pounds, which is preserved at the Bishop Museum in Honolulu, is known to have belonged to High Chief Abner Paki in the 1830s. One of the first Europeans to "hang five" was Mark Twain, who visited Hawaii in 1866 and declared that surfing was not dead yet but quickly declining. Despite the missionaries' vigorous attempts to destroy the traditional Hawaiian way of life, though, this aspect of it not only endured but metamorphosed from a religious ritual into a leisure pursuit that was to be eagerly embraced in California and Australia early in the twentieth century.

The earliest report of surfboarding in mainland America is with regard to three Hawaiian princes, nephews of King Kalakaua, who were attending St. Matthew's Military School at San Mateo, south of San Francisco, in 1885. Their names were Jonah Kuhio Kalaniana'ole, David Kawananakoa, and Edward Keli'iahonui (the three were brothers, the last names honoring distinguished ancestors). Off-duty weekends were sometimes spent at the home of Mrs.

Lyman Swan, whose mother came from Hawaii, and the trio would surf off the mouth of the San Lorenzo River. The appropriately titled *Santa Cruz Daily Surf* reported in its "Beach Breezes" column on 20 July: "The young Hawaiian princes were in the water enjoying it immensely and giving interesting exhibitions of surfboard swimming as practiced in their native land."

Californians did not adopt the sport until the visit in 1907 of Hawaiian surfer George Freeth, who was sponsored by the Redondo–Los Angeles Railroad Co. as part of a campaign to promote water sports and consequently travel to the Pacific coast. He gave public demonstrations and taught classes in surf riding. In Hawaii itself white Americans began surfing on an organized basis in 1908 when journalist Alexander Hume Ford founded the Outrigger Canoe Cub at Waikiki, so that (as well as canoeing) "men and boys could ride upright on the crest of waves." The Outrigger was also responsible for another first: beach volleyball (SEE **volleyball**). Surfing arrived at its other "natural home," Australia, that same year of 1908 with Solomon Islander Alick Wickham, who had introduced the crawl stroke into competitive swimming at age ten, riding a board at Curl Curl Beach north of Sydney and brothers Frank and Charlie Bell quite independently trying out their homemade surfboard at Sydney's Freshwater Beach.

Competitive surfing dates from 1928, when Wisconsin-born Tom Blake organized the first annual Pacific Coast Surfriding Championships at Corona del Mar, Calif.

THE FIRST SWIMMING POOL

....

known in the modern era was the Fellows' Pool in the Fellows' Garden at Emmanuel College, Cambridge University, in England. The earliest reference to it is a rounded outline illustrated in David Loggan's *Cantabrigia Illustrata* of 1690, but it is possible that it was created up to sixty years earlier when the college was furnished with a regular piped water supply from Hobson's Brook. By 1747 the Fellows' Pool had become rectangular, the shape it retains today. The brickwork lining the tank dates from 1855. Prior to filtration, the pool's waters were so dark and murky that during the 1920s Professor of Aeronautical Engineering Bennett Melvill Jones requested a white line along the floor of the tank to guide him as he swam his customary lengths underwater.

Public swimming pool: The first was opened in London on 28 May 1742. The *Daily Advertiser* announced:

> The Day is opened, at the Bagnio in Lemon St., Goodman's Fields: The Pleasure or Swimming Bath which is more than forty-three feet in length. It will be kept warm and fresh every Day and is convenient to swim or learn to swim in. There are Waiters attend daily to teach or assist Gentlemen in the said Swimming Bath if required. There is also a good Cold Bath. Subscribers may have the use of both for a Guinea.

The first **open-air public pool** designed as such was Peerless (originally Perilous) Pool, which was converted from an existing pond at Old Street, London, in 1743. It measured 170' x 180' and was equipped with an arcade and stalls for dressing, as well as a screen of trees to protect bathers from the gaze of vulgar persons. Subscribers paid an annual subscription of £1 10s, and casual patrons 1 shilling. The proprietor, local jeweler William Kent, also had an artificial stream cut from the pool, and this was stocked with fish for anglers who cared to pay a small fee.

U.S.: The first was the Wigwam Baths, opened by John Coyle in 1791 on the banks of the Schuylkill River at the bottom of Race Street in Philadelphia. To the pleasures of the "plunging-bath" and two shower baths were added other, post-bathing amenities, including a bowling green, a tavern, and a tea garden.

Private house with swimming pool: The first was, perhaps surprisingly, in Dutch South Africa. What was to become the magnificent mansion of Groot Constantia near Cape Town was originally built in 1691 as a country residence for Simon van der Stel, governor of the Cape. In 1778 it was bought by winemaker Hendrik Cloete, who employed the fashionable Parisian architect Louis Thibault to enlarge and extend the property. It is possible that it was Thibault who designed the oval swimming pool that Cloete commissioned in 1795, though architectural historian

Hans Fransen loftily declares that "the quaint structure" is not of the same class as the reconstructed fascia of the house itself. G. E. Pearse, in *Eighteenth Century Buildings in South Africa* (1935), describes its construction:

> The swimming-bath consists of an elliptical bath constructed of stone and plastered with a flight of step leading down into the bath on one side. At one end is a niche in which is placed a modelled Triton through whose horn flows the water from a clear mountain stream. It is probable that this figure, which is of teak, was originally a ship's figure-head, more particularly as the pipe through which the water flows in the bath has obviously been inserted into a hole drilled through the figure. The niche is enclosed by a slightly projecting frame of fluted plasters with a curved pediment above, flanked by simple scrolls. Above the niche is modelled a scallop shell and in the pediment is a star. On either side of this composition simple curved brick and plaster seats are placed.

It is remarkable that only one other pool in a private property is noted in the next hundred years and that it was also in Cape Town, believed to have been built for Maria Johanna Ross after her father bought her the Mount Nelson estate in 1843. The scene then shifted to America.

U.S.: The first private house with a swimming pool was George Washington Vanderbilt's summer villa Pointe d'Acadie at Bar Harbor, Maine, where landscape architect Frederick Law Olmsted designed a 150' x 70' outdoor pool (only a little below present Olympic size) that was completed on 15 July 1891. It was filled from the ocean and as the natural embankment was insufficient to withstand the tidewater, a masonry dam was constructed through which a pipe conveyed the saltwater. A bathing house stood on the southern side and the approach to the pool was a natural depression in the bank sheltered by a thick growth of alders and birches, leading to a flight of stone steps. On one occasion Vanderbilt got into difficulties while bathing and had to be rescued by a young lady. Reputedly the richest man in America, he rewarded her with a bunch of sweet peas. Vanderbilt went on to build Biltmore, a 250-bedroom replica of a Loire Valley château near Asheville, N.C. Here he installed America's first **private indoor pool**. Designed by Richard Morris Hunt, the white tiled pool was located in a crypt at the core of the house and was windowless. It was ready for use when the house was first occupied on Christmas Eve 1895.

The first **freeform pools** originated in California, the state that was to dominate pool design in the twentieth century. Two were constructed in 1920, one an enormous 100-foot-long banana-shaped tank built for Douglas Fairbanks and Mary Pickford at their Beverly Hills mansion Pickfair, with a sandy beach along one side; the other was designed for early movie mogul Thomas Ince by Pascal Paddock and was planted with various kinds of foliage to give the appearance of a natural pond. He was not to enjoy it for long, dying in mysterious circumstances aboard William Randolph Hearst's yacht in 1924.

Early pools required replenishing whenever the water became too dirty for swimming. Private outdoor pools became more common in Los Angeles after 1925 when former chemical engineer John Mudge set up a pool-supply business and developed a recirculating system, enabling installation of pools in areas where there was no natural supply of fresh water. The first pool cleaning service also began in Los Angeles, founded in 1929 by Dave Cavanah, whose first client, Jack Dempsey, used to join him in diving for sunken leaves.

Notwithstanding these advances, *Beach & Pool* magazine estimated in 1950 that there were only about 2,500 domestic pools in the United States, most of them in California. During 1952–55 numbers rose quite substantially, with an average of 7,000 new installations a year. They were, however, still costly: When a Long Island developer offered backyard pools as an optional extra in 1954 it added $4,500 to the $40,000 list price of the property. It was only in 1956 that improved construction techniques brought the price down to a level that brought the private pool within the price range of middle America, while a change of policy by the banks on loans for home improvements enabled homeowners to buy on credit. In 1957 30,500 pools were installed, half of them by families with annual incomes between $7,000 and $12,000. By 1965 there was a total of 570,000 pools throughout the nation, a figure that was to rise to 4 million by the end of the century.

SEE ALSO **hotel: swimming pool**.

~~~~~~~~~~~~~~~~~~~~~~~ **T** ~~~~~~~~~~~~~~~~~~~~~~~

THE FIRST **TABLE TENNIS**

sets were manufactured by John Jaques & Son Ltd. and marketed in 1898 by the London toys and games retailer Hamley Bros. of Regent Street under the name Gossima. The inventor of the game was a Croydon engineer called James Gibb, a distinguished athlete who had won the 4-mile English Championship while a Cambridge undergraduate in the 1870s, and who was one of the founders of the Amateur Athletic Association (1880). The date he originally devised Gossima is uncertain, though 1889 is sometimes quoted. It began as an impromptu wet-weather pastime played on the Gibb family's dining room table with cigar-box lids for bats and balls fashioned from champagne corks. The latter were too irregular and Gibb next tried using small India-rubber balls covered with cigarette paper to make them white. These proved too heavy for fast play and he decided to try hollow celluloid balls, sending to America to have them specially made. Celluloid answered admirably and Gibb felt ready to launch the game commercially. The manufacturer he approached first, Jeffries & Co., turned it down, but John Jaques & Son were enthusiastic. As Gossima the game was slow to catch on, and Jaques decided to change the name to the onomatopoeic Ping-Pong. It immediately became immensely popular, sweeping the country during the course of 1901 to become the first of a succession of Edwardian crazes. In other countries, including the United States, the game enjoyed a similar phenomenal success. The French, however, held aloof, one Parisian newspaper asserting it to be a proof of England's moral degradation that so much attention could be paid to Ping-Pong while her soldiers were dying in South Africa.

Table tennis bats were originally either of plain wood or in the form of vellum-covered battledores. The first with a studded rubber surface was Bryan's Atropos Patent Ping-Pong Bat, announced in the September 1902 Army and Navy Stores catalog with a price of 2s 8d (65¢).

U.S.: Hamley Bros. of London registered their "Ping-Pong" trademark with the U.S. Patent Office on 6 August 1901 and exported sets manufactured by John Jaques & Son for distribution by Parker Bros. of Salem, Mass. Within a very short while at least seven manufacturers in the United States were producing their own versions, most of them labeled "Table Tennis" to avoid infringement of the Ping-Pong trademark. Despite this Americans refused to call the game anything but Ping-Pong, as evidenced by *A Little Book of Ping-Pong Verse* (San Francisco, 1902) and the fact that no fewer than eighteen pieces of sheet music were deposited with the Library of Congress during 1901–03 containing "Ping-Pong" in their titles.

THE FIRST **TANK**

was the Tritton Machine, better known as "Little Willie" after the German Crown Prince, commissioned by the British government's Admiralty Landships Committee on 29 July 1915 and built by William Foster & Co. of Lincoln to the design of William Tritton. Fitted with "Creeping Grip" tracks manufactured by the Bullock Tractor Co. of Chicago and powered by a 105-hp Daimler six-cylinder engine, the Tritton Machine was completed on 8 September 1915, but was unable to meet the Admiralty's specification requiring that it be able to cross a 5-foot trench. It was rebuilt with improved tracks and is now preserved at the Royal Armoured Corps Tank Museum at Bovington, Dorset.

Sir William Tritton, as he became, later told a friend how the name *tank* came to be adopted. On the early drawings the secret "landships" were identified, for security reasons, as "water transporters for mesopotamia" (i.e., Iraq). The down-to-earth Lincoln workers found this too much of a mouthful and spoke of "them bloody tanks." The name, without the qualifying adjective, stuck. While no one person can be credited with the invention of the tank, the most crucial component, its tracks, originated in the United States. Their use was proposed to the Landships Committee on 19 January 1915 by Lt. Col. E. D. Swinton of the Royal Engineers in the words, "So far as the carriage is concerned, there seems to be only one principle which can be employed, namely, that the carriage should lay its own road-bed on the principle of the Hornsby-Akroyd caterpillar type, which has subsequently been improved upon in the Holt caterpillar." The Holt Manufacturing Co., first to produce a practical crawler tractor (qv), was based in Stockton, Calif.

The first successful tank was the HMLS (His Majesty's Land Ship) *Centipede*, also known as "Mother" and "Big Willie," built by William Foster & Co. and test-run on 16 January 1916. "Mother" was designed by Lt. W. G. Wilson and was powered by the same engines as its forerunner "Little Willie." The main armament consisted of two naval 6-pounder guns carried in half-turrets on either side of the hull. Trials were held at Hatfield Park, Hertfordshire, starting 29 January and the tank succeeded in fulfilling War Office requirements by crossing a 5-foot trench, climbing a 4-foot 6-inch parapet, and negotiating barbed-wire entanglements.

The first tank in series production was the Mark I, based on the "Mother" prototype, of which 100 were ordered on 12 February 1916. Twenty-five of these were built by William Foster & Co. and 75 by the Metropolitan Carriage, Wagon and Finance Co. of Wednesbury, Staffordshire. Initial deliveries were made in June.

Following the order for the 100 Mark Is, Col. Swinton was put in charge of the personnel selected to man the new tanks, a unit originally called the Tank Detachment and later attached to the Machine-Gun Corps. Based at Siberia Camp, Bisley, the new arm was organized into six companies with a total of 184 officers and 1,610 other ranks. Training took place on a 15-square-mile area near Thetford, Norfolk, which was landscaped to resemble ground conditions on the Western Front. During August and September 1916, A, C, and D Companies of the Heavy Branch, Machine-Gun Corps left for the front.

Battle involving the use of tanks: The first was the Battle of Flers-Courcellette, which opened on the Western Front in France 15 September 1916, when 36 tanks of the Heavy Branch, Machine-Gun Corps engaged the enemy in the course of an infantry assault by the German Fourth Army. The first tank to be employed as an offensive weapon in the history of warfare was moved forward at 5:15 A.M. supported by two companies of the King's Own Yorkshire Light Infantry. Manned by crew D1 under the command of Capt. H. W. Mortimore, its task was to clear a small pocket of the enemy positioned in the British front between Ginchy and Delville Wood. The infantry operation was successful, although the tank was knocked out by a shell that destroyed its steering gear. The main tank force went into battle shortly before 6 A.M., the secrecy which had been maintained ever since the formation of the Landships Committee proving well justified by the consternation their appearance caused among the enemy ranks. Still they were too few to have any real strategic importance, the lesson of this first essay in tank warfare being that tanks to be effective had to be deployed not as a mere auxiliary weapon but tactically in large numbers. Nevertheless, one tank allotted to the 41st Division, D17, succeeded in entering Flers and was immortalized in a press telegram that read: A TANK IS WALKING UP THE HIGH STREET OF FLERS WITH THE BRITISH ARMY CHEERING BEHIND.

The first **tank versus tank action** in warfare took place at Villers-Bretonneux on 24 April 1918, when thirteen German A.7.1 Vs were met by a section of three British Mark IV tanks commanded by Capt. F. C. Brown of the 1st Battalion, Tank Corps. Two of the Mark IVs were damaged by gunfire from the German tanks and forced to withdraw, but the third, No. 1 Tank of No. 1 Section of a Company under Lt. F. Mitchell, forced the leading German machine against a steep bank, causing it to overturn. It then went on to engage two others, with the result that one of them was abandoned by its crew, who fled.

U.S.: The first tank to be designed as such (as opposed to agricultural tractor adaptations) was the Holt Tractor Co.'s 56,000-pound 16½-foot-long Gas-Electric Tank, test-run at Stockton, Calif., in April 1917. It was powered by a 90-hp gasoline engine driving an electric generator that in turn fueled twin electric motors powering each track, giving a maximum speed of 6 mph. Armament consisted of a 75-mm British-built Vickers mountain howitzer in the nose and Vickers machine guns in side sponsons. Strictly experimental, it did not go into series production.

The U.S. Expeditionary Force's Tank Corps, assembled from 26 January 1918, was originally equipped with British Mk V heavy tanks and French Renault FT light tanks. It was with 144 of the latter that the 344th and 345th Light Tank Battalions, commanded by Lt. Col. George S. Patton, engaged in America's first tank operation on 12 September 1918 when they supported the assault on the Saint-Mihiel salient by the 1st and 42nd divisions of the Australian Expeditionary Force. Heavy rainfall the night before produced muddy conditions in which many of the slow-moving 7-ton Renaults got bogged down or broke down. Casualties were 4 officers wounded, 5 enlisted men killed, and 15 wounded. Five tanks were destroyed by artillery fire.

Heavy tanks were first used by American troops when the 301st Heavy Tank Battalion took their 40 32-ton Mark Vs and 37-ton Mark V Stars into combat with eight-man crews at the Battle of Le Catelet-Bonny on 29 September in support of the Australian infantry offensive. Eighteen tanks were destroyed and there were 115 casualties.

The first **tank to go into series production in the United States** was the 6-ton M1917, a reengineered version of the Renault FT built by government contractors Van Dorn of Cleveland, Maxwell Motor Co. of Detroit, and C. L. Best Co. of Elmhurst, Calif. Powered by a 42-hp Buda gasoline engine giving a maximum speed of 5½ mph, it was armed with either a 0.3-inch machine gun or a 37-mm gun. The first completed tank came off the production line in October 1918 and 64 had been delivered by the armistice on 11 November. A total of 950 of these vehicles served with the armored units of the post-war U.S. Army (the Tank Corps having been wound up) to the end of the 1930s.

The first heavy tank built in the United States and the first with American design input (it was a joint Anglo-American project) was the 35-ton Mark VIII liberty, of which a hundred were completed at Rock Island Arsenal, Ill., by June 1920. They were armed with seven machine guns and two 6-pounder cannon in retractable sponsons.

No further U.S. tanks went into production until October 1939 when orders were placed for 375 11½-ton M2A4 tanks. Developed at Rock Island Arsenal, this was the first all-American-designed tank in regular service. Armed with a 37-mm turret-mounted gun, it was to prove effective in combat as the Japanese did not possess an anti-tank gun capable of penetrating its armor, which was unusually thick for a light tank.

American tank used in warfare: The first was the light M3 of which 108 were taken into battle against the Japanese in the Philippines by the 192nd and 194th Tank Battalions in April 1942. They participated in the withdrawal to Bataan, where, tragically the entire armed force was annihilated, the tanks destroyed and their crews either killed or captured. The successor to the M3, but essentially the same tank with design improvements, was the 33-ton M4 of 1941, better known by its British designation of Sherman. First of the classic American tanks, it was the workhorse of the war, used in almost every theater and in every armored capacity: for anti-tank attack and as infantry support, light cavalry, auxiliary artillery, and as the spearhead of armored assaults.

THE FIRST **TAP DANCING**

evolved in the United States out of Irish step dancing, English clog dancing, African-American buck and wing dancing, and the various adaptations of black traditional dance devised for minstrel shows (whites in blackface). It was in one of these that the term *tap* was first applied to percussive show dancing. The coiner of the term was dance director Ned Wayburn and the show, which toured for eleven months in 1902–03, was called *Ned Wayburn's Minstrel Misses.* The eponymous Misses were sixteen well-built white chorus girls who opened the show by marching on stage dressed as men, half of them in a white satin version of evening dress, complete with tail-coats and cutaway vests, the other half attired as military bandsmen. Then they sat themselves at tables at the back of the stage and made themselves up in blackface in full view of the audience, a piece of "business" that took just 90 seconds and never failed to bring down the house. They were now ready to launch into the tap routine, which was performed in light clogs with split wooden soles. Ned Wayburn not only named and gave focus to a new art form, but was also responsible for the career choice of one of its greatest exponents when he persuaded a student at his New York school of dance to abandon ballet and become a tap dancer. The young man's name was Fred Astaire.

THE FIRST **TAPE RECORDER**

SEE **magnetic recorder**.

THE FIRST **TAXICABS**

to ply for hire were two Benz Kraftdroschkes purchased for 8,000 marks ($1,905) each in the spring of 1896 by "Droschkenbesitzer" Deutz of Stuttgart, and operated by him in that city. Stuttgart had the distinction of having two cab companies running gasoline-driven taxis before any other city, with the exception of Paris, had even one. In May 1897 Friedrich Greiner started a rival service, and according to a contemporary report in *Der Motorwagen*, his cabs averaged a creditable 70 kilometers (44 miles) a day. In a literal sense Greiner's were the first true "taxis," as they were the first motor cabs fitted with taximeters. The Paris taxicab service—a single Roger-Benz operated by the Société Anglo-Française—had been started in November 1896 but does not appear to have survived more than a few months.

U.S.: Robert H. Cloughley built the first steam car west of the Mississippi in 1896 and used it as a taxi in his hometown of Cherryvale, Kan. The fare to anywhere in town was 25¢, but there were few takers. This may have had something to do with the fact that the boiler was under the rear seat and could make for an uncomfortably warm ride in summer.

In November of the same year the Electrobat, a vehicle resembling a four-wheeled hansom cab, was put into service on the streets of Manhattan by its makers, mechanical engineer Henry G. Morris and

electrician Pedro G. Salmon of the Electric Carriage & Wagon Co. of New York. Within a few months there were 13 in operation. The vehicles used 44 chloride lead acid cells generating 88 volts and had a range of about 25 miles between charges. The batteries weighed 1,200 pounds, which gave the cabs reassuring stability but a modest speed of some 8 to 9 mph. By 1898 the fleet had grown to 62 and in 1899 to 100 and during these years company fleets also took to the streets of Chicago, Boston, and Philadelphia. The New York fleet numbered no fewer than 750 in 1907, but in that year 300 were destroyed in a garage fire and the company went out of business soon after.

America's first gasoline-powered taxis were 50 French-made Darracqs introduced in New York by Harry Allen of the New Taxicab Co. on 1 October 1907. These were also the first cabs in the United States with taximeters for automatically recording fares—hence the name of the company. New York came late to gasoline taxicabs, which were already well established in Paris, London, and Berlin. Once on the streets, it took little time for them to relegate horse-cabs to a sightseeing role for tourists and by 1913 they dominated the motor traffic of Manhattan. Ten years later 15,000 cruising cabs were not only making the streets of the city unsafe, per the *New York Times*, but causing gridlocks all over downtown.

THE FIRST **TEDDY BEAR**

is claimed to have been originated by two separate manufacturers, one in the United States and one in Germany, both quoting the same year, 1902, for the innovation, each asserting precedence over the other, and neither being able to provide documentary evidence in support of its claim.

The only proven fact in either version is that on 18 November 1902 the *Washington Evening Star* carried a cartoon by Clifford Berryman titled "Drawing the Line in Mississippi," showing President Theodore "Teddy" Roosevelt refusing to shoot a captive bear cub. At that time the president was visiting Mississippi to intervene in a border dispute the state had with neighboring Louisiana. Berryman's cartoon was founded on an actual incident during a presidential bear hunt. It was reproduced in a number of other newspapers and among those struck by the artist's engaging, cuddly little bear was a Russian immigrant called Morris Mitchom, proprietor of a small candy store in Brooklyn that also sold toys, many of them handmade by Mitchom and his wife.

At this point oral tradition takes over. According to his son Benjamin, Morris Mitchom immediately conceived the idea of re-creating the Berryman bear cub in three-dimensional form. Cut out of brown plush, and with movable arms and legs, the prototype toy animal was placed in the sweetshop window next to a clipping of the cartoon and with a label proclaiming "Teddy's Bear."

Having come from an authoritarian country, Morris Mitchom was concerned about the propriety of using the president's name to promote the sale of his new toy. He plucked up courage to write to the White House asking Mr. Roosevelt if he minded. The reply, in the president's own hand, granted permission in these words: "I don't think my name is worth much to the toy bear cub business, but you are welcome to use it."

This document, which if it could be produced would establish the Mitchom claim beyond doubt, was supposed to be in the procession of Morris's eldest son, Joseph Mitchom, but could not be found among his effects when he died in 1951.

In 1903, according to Benjamin Mitchom, the wholesale firm of Butler Bros. took his father's entire output of Teddy Bears, guaranteeing him credit with the suppliers of plush. Between 1907 and 1938 the business was styled the Ideal Novelty and Toy Co., growing to become the largest manufacturer of dolls and soft animals in the world as Ideal Toy Co. until absorbed by CBS Toy Co. in 1982.

Germany credits the invention of the teddy bear to the Steiff Co., which was begun at Giengen in Swabia in 1880 by a crippled seamstress, Margarete Steiff, as a home workshop producing felt elephants. By 1902 the business was manufacturing a wide range of soft toys, including cats, dogs, pink porkers, donkeys, horses, and camels, but not until then a teddy bear—although there had been some earlier dancing bears, as early as 1892, but these were modeled on real, rather fearsome brown bears and did not have the anthropomorphic qualities of the classic teddy. The breakthrough, which heralded the metamorphosis into cuddliness, was the introduction of jointed limbs, based on Margarete's cousin Richard Steiff's sketches of a bear family at Stuttgart Zoo. The prototype jointed bear, with the uncuddly designation of Bear 55 PB (55 signified 55 centimeters or 21½ inches tall, the P for "plush" and B for *beweglich*, meaning jointed), came off the production line in late 1902 and the first export consignment of three dozen arrived in New York in mid-February 1903. The wholesale price was 48 marks or $11 per dozen, which turned out to be too high for the American market and Steiff's U.S. representative, Richard's brother Paul, had to confess failure: The bear "was severely criticized and did not sell," he wrote home disconsolately. All this is documented. The evidence then becomes secondary sourced, from Steiff's official history. We learn that there was no better response from the German trade when Bear 55 PB went on show at the Leipzig Toy Fair in March 1903. With the fair about to close, the order book was empty. Just as Richard Steiff was nailing down the crates of rejected merchandise, a particularly grumpy buyer called Hermann Berg, who represented Borgfeldt & Co. of New York, came stomping along to complain that he had been looking for a soft and cuddly new toy without success and then asked Richard whether he could design one for him. Richard prized open one of the crates and produced No. 55. Berg was captivated and ordered 3,000 to be shipped across the Atlantic for the delight of American children.

There would be no reason to doubt this story of triumph in adversity but for one slightly disconcerting element. Not one of the supposed consignment of 3,000 bears has survived to lend it veracity (nor, surprisingly, is there one in the Steiff Museum, though documentary and photographic evidence definitely establishes that 55 PB existed). The earliest Steiffs located in America have been Bear 35 PBs, introduced at the 1904 World's Fair at St. Louis, where Margarete and Richard Steiff were each awarded individual gold medals as well as the grand prix going to Steiff GmbH, and at which no fewer than 12,000 teddies were sold.

Although the Steiff concern was undoubtedly one of the earliest to enter the plush-bear business, they have undermined belief in their claims by propagating a wholly unfounded story to explain the acquisition of the name "Teddy." This was to the effect that the table decorations at Alice Roosevelt's wedding in 1906 consisted of Steiff bear-ware, and that when her father, the president, was asked what variety they were, he responded, "a new species called Teddy bears." The use of Steiff products on this occasion has been categorically denied by the Roosevelt Association and by Archibald Roosevelt, the bride's brother.

The late actor Peter Bull, doyen of teddy bear aficionados and arctophilia's first historian, believed that the Mitchom version of the naming was probably accurate, while allowing the possibility that the Steiff prototype could have been made at a marginally earlier date. Finally it should be said that nowhere has the term "Teddy bear" been found in print before September 1906, when it was reported in the trade journal *Playthings* that there was a new craze for having them as car mascots. Bears were already sweeping America at this date, under a variety of names, and soon became such a cult that one Michigan minister roundly declared that the teddy was destroying maternal instincts and leading the nation to race suicide.

THE FIRST **TELEMARKETING**

is shrouded in the obscurity it deserves, but was already arousing the ire of telephone subscribers in 1909 when a lady in Rochester, N.Y., wrote the following to her local newspaper:

> My telephone is far more of a nuisance to me than it is a convenience and I think I will have it removed, if I am called upon as much in the future as I have been during the past week by theater agents, and business firms, who abuse the telephone privilege, using it as a means of advertising. My hands were busy molding bread yesterday morning, when I heard the bell ring, and upon responding was told by a woman just gone into business in a Main Street building, that she had a fine line of curtains, and other hangings, which she would like me to see. Shortly afterward an employee of a firm making extracts, solicited my

patronage in the same way, and though I told him that I did not wish to be annoyed again . . . the afternoon brought another call from the same firm. Last week a number of my friends and I heard over the telephone of a Shakespearean actor who was to fill a long engagement here, and we were asked by an attaché of the theater to please get our seats early, as there would undoubtedly be a rush for tickets. These are samples of a telephone annoyance that I would like to be freed from.

Call center: The earliest known customer contact operations in which calls were routed to dedicated agents by an Automatic Call Distributor (ACD) were established in or about 1965 in the United States by New York City-based American Airlines using a Bell Systems ACD and in the United Kingdom at the Birmingham Post & Mail building in Colmore Circus, Birmingham, with a General Electric Co. ACD. Automated routing of calls obviated the need for operators, enabling customer contact to be carried out on a scale and at a speed that would lead, in the 1980s, to the setting up of companies whose business was conducted solely by telephone.

THE FIRST **TELEPHONE**

capable of sustained articulate speech was patented by Scottish-born Alexander Graham Bell on 9 March 1876. The earliest coherent message was transmitted at 5 Exeter Place, Boston, on 10 March 1876 by Bell to his assistant Thomas Watson and consisted of the words, "Come here, Watson, I want you." This seemingly prosaic first telephone utterance was in fact delivered with pressing urgency: Bell had just spilled battery acid on his pants.

Bell's original telephone was publicly displayed at the Centennial Exhibition in Philadelphia on 25 June 1876. It attracted little attention at first, and would probably have been ignored by the judges then had it not been for the interest of the emperor of Brazil, who opened the first royal telephone conversation with the words, "My God—it talks!"

Two weeks later, on 10 August, Bell proved the utility of the telephone as a means of communication over extended distances when he received the first **inter-city telephone call** at Paris, Ontario, from his father and uncle in Brantford, Ontario. Speech was transmitted one way over 76 miles of telegraph lines. (SEE ALSO **toll line** BELOW.)

Permanent installation of a telephone: The first for private use was made by Charles Williams Jr. at his home in Somerville, Mass., and also at his office at 109 Court Street in Boston, on 4 April 1877. Williams, an electrical engineer, commenced manufacture of Bell's Box Telephone the same month. The first telephone subscriber (i.e., who paid rental) was banker Roswell C. Downer, whose home at 170 Central St., Somerville, was connected to his bank, Stone & Downer, at 28 State Street in Boston on 1 May 1877. The first corporate subscriber followed the same month when the offices of the Cambridge, Mass., Board of Waterworks were connected with their works at Fresh Pond. The rental fee for business phones was $40 per annum, twice that of private installations.

Telephone for government business: The first was a "hotline" from the office of the prime minister of Canada, Alexander Mackenzie, to Rideau Hall, the residence of Gov. Gen. the Earl of Dufferin, installed on 21 September 1877. Rental was $42.50 a year, the prime minister and the governor general being the first subscribers in Canada.

U.S.: On 1 December 1878 the White House was connected to the new Washington exchange as Washington 1; the Capitol was 2 and the Treasury Department 3. The incumbent of the White House was Rutherford B. Hayes, who made the first presidential phone call, to Alexander Graham Bell 13 miles away. His first words to the great inventor were "Please speak more slowly." Most presidents of the period hated the phone (Woodrow Wilson so much so that he refused to receive calls) and it was not until 1928 that Herbert Hoover became the first to have one on his desk.

Telephone switchboard: The first was installed at the Holmes Burglar Alarm Co., 342 Washington Street, Boston, by the proprietor, Edwin Holmes, and brought into operation on 17 May 1877. Five of Holmes's clients (Brewster, Basset & Co., bankers; the Shoe and Leather Bank; the National Exchange Bank; the Hide & Leather Bank; and Charles Williams, electrical engineers) were interconnected over the existing burglar-alarm lines. The switchboard was operated during the day only, the lines reverting to their regular function at night. No fee was charged for the service.

Telephone exchange: The first was established by Isaac D. Smith, agent for the New England Telephone Co., at the Capitol Avenue Drug Store, Hartford, Conn., following an announcement in the *Hartford Courant* for 17 August 1877:

> At the regular meeting of the allopathic physicians on Monday evening experiments were successfully tried with telephones, and it was proposed to have a system of inter-communication between the doctors established by means of the new invention so that by reporting to a central office of the Capitol Avenue Drug Store they can readily exchange views between office and office.

On 8 October 1877 Smith advertised the exchange as a commercial venture, and by the following month there were seventeen subscribers.

Full-time telephone operator: The first was George Willard Coy, who began operating the District Telephone Co.'s exchange at New Haven, Conn., on 28 January 1878. At first his usual call signal was "Ahoy! Ahoy!," but this was abandoned for "Hallo," probably at the instigation of those who liked to address the operator by name. The first woman telephone operator was Miss Emma Nutt, who began working for Edwin Holmes's Telephone Dispatch Co. exchange at Boston at $3 a day on 1 September 1878. By the mid-1880s most exchanges employed women; boys were found to be too quarrelsome for the work.

Toll line: The first for public use was opened by the District Telephone Co. between Springfield and Holyoke, Mass., on 15 June 1878, while the first interstate line connected Boston and Providence, R.I., a distance of 45 miles, on 12 January 1881.

Automatic telephone exchange: The first was patented by Kansas City undertaker Almon B. Strowger on 12 March 1889. According to the prevailing story, Strowger was inspired to invent the automatic switchboard because his principal business rival's wife, who was an operator on the Kansas City exchange, used to put his clients through to her husband. The original prototype of the switching device was worked out with the aid of a collar box and a quantity of spent matches. The first Strowger automatic exchange was opened at La Porte, Ind., on 3 November 1892 and soon came to be known in the vernacular as "the girl-less, cussless telephone." Strowger's early system did not incorporate dial telephones but was operated by a series of three keys, one representing single figures, another units of ten, and the other units of a hundred. To call a number the subscriber depressed each key the number of times required to make up the sequence. La Porte had 75 subscribers; most early automatic exchanges were located in rural communities too small to justify a manual operator.

The first automatic exchange with a trunking system (i.e., able to connect with other exchanges) was a Strowger installation made at New Bedford, Mass., and opened in November 1900. It had 3,600 lines.

Dial telephones: The first were connected to the Private Automatic Exchange (PAX) at City Hall in Milwaukee in 1896. The dial was rotated by means of projecting vanes, finger holes following with the Strowger upright of 1905.

Phone numbers were first assigned to the two hundred subscribers in Lowell, Mass., in 1879 during a measles epidemic, a precaution recommended by local doctor Moses Greeley Parker, who feared that if any of the four operators fell sick their substitutes would be unable to remember subscribers' names. (As late as the 1960s operators in Belize were expected to memorize the list of subscribers for the whole country.)

Pay phone: The first is generally said to have been established by the Connecticut Telephone Co. in their office at New Haven, Conn., with service starting on 1 June 1880. The 10¢ fee was handed to an attendant. It has, however, been claimed (in *Connecticut Pioneers in Telephony*) that Thomas B. Dolittle was operating pay stations in Bridgeport and Black Rock, Conn., as early as 1878.

The first coin-operated pay phone was installed at the Hartford Bank in Hartford, Conn., by the Southern New England Telephone Co. in 1889. The inventor of the coin-fed mechanism was William Gray, who had been inspired to do so when neighbors had refused him permission to use their phone to make an emergency call to the doctor. (Heartless this may have been, but early leases limited use of the phone to the subscriber's family.) In 1891 Gray founded the Telephone Pay Station Co. to rent out coin-operated pay phones to store keepers. (SEE ALSO **telephone card**.)

The first outdoor pay phone was installed in a hexagonal wooden booth with clerestory roof at the foot of Kyobaski Bridge in Tokyo, Japan, in October 1900. The call charge was 15 (7½) sen for 5 minutes. The first in the United States was erected in Cincinnati by the City & Suburban Telegraph Co. in 1905.

Directory assistance: Originally called simply "Information," the inaugural service was launched in New York City on 1 January 1906.

Emergency number: The first combined fire-police-ambulance number was 999, adopted by Britain's General Post Office on 8 July 1937. The first call was made by Mrs. J. Stanley Beard of 33 Elsworthy Road, Hampstead, London, to report an intruder, resulting in the arrest of Thomas Duffy for attempted burglary.

U.S.: At the urging of the Federal Communications Commission (FCC) and inspired by the Canadian city of Winnipeg's adoption of a single emergency number in 1959, AT&T announced on 15 January 1968 that 9-1-1 would be adopted nationwide for emergency calls. Determined to steal a march on its competitors, the Alabama Telephone Co. instituted a crash program to install the necessary equipment and the first 9-1-1 service was inaugurated at Haleyville, Ala., on 16 February 1968.

Color telephones: The first in the United States were Western Electronic model 202, produced in limited quantities in 1937. Ten years later, with black still prevailing in the home and in the office, another experiment in pastel hues was made with the model 302. This also met with public indifference, although on the other side of the Atlantic during the 1930s Britain's General Post Office was already offering desktop phones in pillar-box red, while in Italy white telephones became so fashionable among trendsetters that movies about the rich and stylish became known as "white-telephone films." In the United States it was not until 11 June 1954 that Bell Telephone began mass-marketing color phones in eight different shades.

Direct dialing was introduced on 18 January 1950 at Englewood and Teaneck, N.J., which received the first area code 201, with service to New York City. On 10 November 1951 long-distance direct dialing followed when area code 201 was connected with 12 major conurbations. By 1956 11 million Bell subscribers were able to direct dial to nearby cities and 2.7 million could reach 20 million other phones throughout the United States. International direct dialing was established between London and Paris on 8 March 1963 and between New York and London on 1 March 1970.

Push-button telephone: The first was Bell Telephone's Touch-Tone, market tested in Findley, Ohio, starting 1 November 1960. It became available on a regular commercial basis in Carnegie and Greensburg, Pa., on 18 November 1963. Within a few years the push-button telephone had all but ousted the dial telephone. Dials, however, made an unexpected return in call boxes in some areas of New York in 1993 as part of the fight against crime. Drug dealers were wont to page customers on electronic voice mail, for which a push-button phone was necessary. The older technology simply did not work in the new age of high-tech crime and so dials made their comeback, much to the displeasure of the most impatient citizenry on Earth.

Toll-free numbers: The first in the United States were introduced by AT&T on 2 May 1967. The first subscriber to sign up was Sheraton Hotels (800-325-3535), enabling prospective patrons stranded away from home to book rooms even if they did not have the coins for a pay phone.

Premium rate pay-call service was first offered on the occasion of the Jimmy Carter-Ronald Reagan presidential campaign debate held in Cleveland on 28 October 1980. Those of the 80 million TV audience who weren't brewing coffee when the debate concluded were invited to call a 900 number to vote for whom they thought had bested the other. No fewer than 700,000 viewers were prepared to pay the 50¢ toll to register their opinion (of whom 67 percent reckoned Reagan had the edge).

Cell phones: The handheld cell phone was developed by Motorola research director Martin Cooper, who used the prototype to make the first such call on 3 April 1973 while standing on a corner by the Manhattan Hilton in New York City. Carried via the cell base on the roof of the Burlington Consolidated Tower, the call was to his opposite number at competitor Bell Laboratories, Joel Engel, who was discomforted to learn the means by which it had been made. While the technology existed to usher in the cellular age, progress could not be made until the FCC authorized commercial cell-net service, which it delayed doing until 1982. In the meantime commercial cell-phone service had been inaugurated in Bahrain in May 1978 by Batelco with equipment from Matsushita and on a larger scale in Tokyo by Nippon Telegraph & Telephone in December 1979. These, though, and the commercial services launched in various European countries in 1981, were for car phones only.

The world's first commercially available handheld cell phone, the Motorola DynaTac 800X, was launched on 6 March 1983. Initially the 10-inch-long "brick," as it soon came to be known, weighed in at 40 ounces and cost $3,995. Analog handhelds remained unwieldly and costly throughout the 1980s and reception was often poor over networks designed for car phones; at the end of the decade there were barely a million users in the United States (primarily financiers, admen, and moviemakers). The breakthrough to mass use came in Europe, where all the major countries had agreed to adopt a GSM digital platform compatible between networks, meaning that cell-phone calls could be made internationally. The first such call was made on Finland's Radiolinja network on 1 July 1991. GSM was launched commercially in Denmark, Italy, Finland, France, Germany, Portugal, and Sweden with the 1011 handset on 10 November 1992, just as a new generation of digital cell phones came on the market that were light enough and small enough to fit into the pocket. Australia extended GSM outside Europe the following year and in November 1995 American Personal Communications launched the first service in the United States. GSM also took off in China, which in 2002 overtook America to become the largest user of cell phones in the world with 160 million subscribers.

The first cell phone with e-mail, fax, and Internet connection, billed as the world's first **smartphone**, was the Finnish-made GSM digital Nokia 9000 Communicator, launched in London on 15 August 1996. Equipped with a QWERTY keyboard, it also incorporated a personal organizer, an everlasting calendar, a world clock, and a calculator. The Nokia 9000 bowed in the United States on 14 October 1997.

The first **camera phone** was the Kyocera VP-210 Visual Phone available on the PHS Network in Japan and unveiled at the Tokyo Business Show on 18 May 1999. This combined video and still imaging, though there was no facility for downloading to a computer. This followed with the J-SH04, which had an integrated 110,000-pixel CMOS image sensor for taking digital photos, introduced by Sharp and J-Phone in Japan in November 2000. J-Phone launched "sha-mail" for transmitting pictures to other cell-phone users or to personal computers (PCs) a month later.

SIM card: The first Subscriber Identity Modules (SIM) were produced in Munich, Germany by smart card manufacturer Giesecke & Devrient. The initial batch of 300 were supplied to Finnish GSM operator Radiolinja in 1991.

Text message: The first SMS was "Merry Christmas," sent on 3 December 1992 by test engineer Neil Papworth of the Sema Group from his PC to the Orbitel 901 cell phone of business associate Richard Jarvis of Vodafone, who was at a Christmas party in Newbury, Berkshire, England. This was a one-off between techies. Texting had its commercial beginnings when it was introduced by Sweden's largest mobile operator Telia in 1993 with a system provided by British communications specialist Logica. Texting was first offered in the United States by BellSouth Mobility of Atlanta and Nextel of Reston, Va., early in 1997, but uptake was very limited owing to the fact that messages could only be sent one way, for example from a PC or corporate messaging center to a cell phone, but the cell-phone user could not respond. Nor could text messages be exchanged between networks, a problem first overcome in the United Kingdom in April 1999 with the result that the British rapidly became the heaviest users of SMS anywhere in the world. (By October of the same year BBC Online had published the first text message glossary, a combination of standard stenographers' abbreviations and teenage argot.) Stateside, SMS began to take off with the first two-way service, facilitated by InfoXchange of Chantilly, Va., in late 2000; and with the first inter-network service, introduced by AT&T Wireless via InfoMatch on 19 November 2001.

Ring tones: The first cell phone with an identifiable musical ring tone was a Nokia model of 1991 that played a bar of Francisco Tárrega's "Gran Vals" for classical guitar. Customized ring tones were first offered by Finnish cell-phone operator Radiolinja in the fall of 1996, enabling hip young Finns to download songs like "Smoke on the Water" and the less hip to have their calls prefaced with the Finnish national anthem, "Maamme." The idea had not originated with Radiolinja, which rejected it out of hand when first doorstepped by a twentysomething technology officer called Veska Paanenen. This young visionary had experienced his eureka moment nearly a year earlier after being awoken by the insistent howl of his Nokia 6110 at an unwelcome hour following what he confessed had been a night of overindulgence in Koskenkorva vodka and beer. "I didn't want to hear 'de de de de deeeee,'" Paanenen later recounted. "I wanted to hear Van Halen's 'Jump,' and I was willing to pay for it." Despite the fact that Finland prides itself on its cutting-edge position in the cell-phone industry, nobody wanted to know—until he persuaded the reluctant suits at Radiolinja that personalized ring tones could enable workers in open-plan offices to distinguish their calls from those of their colleagues. Like many compelling ideas, particularly ones that originate in Finland, the ring tone expanded only sluggishly at first, with under three million downloads worldwide in 2001. Then, mainly owing to an insatiable demand from Generation X in Japan and Great Britain, few of whom had ever seen an open-plan office, the number of downloads grew in 2003 to 2.6 billion worth more than $3 billion worldwide, or double the value of all sales of CD singles. By 2008, fueled by an unusually belated embrace of a teen phenomenon by the United States, the market had burgeoned to an estimated 4.2 billion downloads per annum worth $6.5 billion.

THE FIRST

TELEPHONE ANSWERING MACHINE

was the Telegraphone, a wire recorder (SEE **magnetic recorder**) invented by Danish telephone engineer Valdemar Poulsen and manufactured by the American Telegraphone Co. of Springfield, Mass., in 1903. The machine was limited in its application because it could either give a message or receive one, but not both at once. In his 1899 patent Poulsen actually proposed the words to be used for the recorded message to callers: "I am not at home and shall not return till three o'clock. Call me again at that time." Callers could only record a message if the apparatus had been previously set up to do this, in which case there was no outgoing message.

Poulsen is a largely unsung hero of twentieth-century progress, but it is worthy of note that the technology he developed to build a telephone answering machine—way ahead of its time—is the basis of all recording on tape, whether sound or video.

The first answering machine capable of giving and receiving messages was designed by Buhrle & Co. of Oerlikon, Switzerland, in 1943 and subsequently manufactured as the Ipsophone. Like the Telegraphone it used reels of steel wire rather than tape, and it weighed more than 300 pounds, standing 38 inches high and 28 inches wide. One of its most advanced features was that the subscriber, when away from home or office, could call up to hear his messages, but only after proving his identity by recognizing a preselected pair of digits out of the set 0 to 9 spoken by the machine. Among the early customers were wholesale pharmacists, so that they could provide an after-hours ordering facility for drugstores and deliver as soon as they reopened. Although most of the early subscribers were companies, a number of machines were rented to Orthodox Jews for use at home. The machine enabled them to receive messages on the Sabbath without activating electricity.

U.S.: The Swiss Ipsophone (SEE ABOVE) was introduced in 1946. The first American-designed machine was the Electronic Secretary, the brainchild of Joseph L. Zimmerman, an engineer who could not afford a secretary and decided to build a mechanical substitute. The nearly 80-pound contraption, which used a lever to lift the phone receiver, was manufactured in 1949 by the Electric Secretary Co. that Zimmerman and his business partner George W. Danner established in Milwaukee. There were 6,000 in use by 1957 when the partners sold out to the General Telephone Co.

The first compact machine designed specifically for domestic use was the Gray Manufacturing Co.'s disk-operated Peatrophone, marketed through AT&T in 1951.

Voice mail: The first system was patented by Gordon Matthews, founder of VMX Co., Dallas, Tex., which sold it to 3M in 1979. The inaugural greeting was recorded by Matthews's wife, Monica. Voice mail for the home was introduced in 1988 by Bell Cellular for its subscribers in Ontario and Quebec.

Digital answering machine: The first was ADAM (All-Digital Answering Machine), which stored messages on a silicon chip instead of a tape. It was launched by PhoneMate of Torrance, Calif., in 1990.

THE FIRST TELEPHONE CARD

was developed by Italian vending machine company SIDA as a palliative to the shortage of coins in circulation in Italy in the 1970s and the associated problem of vandalism to public pay phones. The original cards were manufactured by Pikopp for use with SIP (now Telecom Italia) pay phones in the Oriolo Romano district of Rome in May 1976. They had no face value but had carrying units valued at 50 lire on the reverse. The cards turned out to be too thin and repeatedly jammed the pay-phone machines designed for SIP by SIDA.

The first phone cards available nationally were issued by the Belgian telecommunications network RTT in March 1979. The orange and silver optical cards were produced by Landis & Gyr and came in denominations of 20 units for 200 Belgian francs and 105 units for 1,000 Belgian francs.

U.S.: The first was introduced by Phone Line, Inc., in December 1980.

THE FIRST TELEPHONE DIRECTORY

was a single sheet published by the New Haven District Telephone Co. of 219 Chapel Street, New Haven, Conn., on 21 February 1878 and listed 50 names (no numbers) under the headings Residences (11), Physicians (3), Dentists (2), Stores, Factories etc (20), Meat and Fish Markets (4), Hack and Boarding Stables (2) and Miscellaneous (8). The latter included the police department and post office, the Mercantile and Quinnipeac clubs (doubtless the first to deny that the caller's husband was in), and the *Yale News*. The only known copy is preserved at the University of Connecticut's Thomas Dodd Research Center at Storrs, Conn. The New Haven District Telephone Co. brought out the first telephone *book* proper in November. This was 40 pages, contained 371 names, and had a handy metal ring in the top left corner so that it could be hung from a hook. The only surviving copy was sold at Christie's in New York City in June 2008 for $170,500.

The first classified telephone directory was published by the Boston Telephone Dispatch Co. the same year and listed 67 business subscribers under their particular trade or commodity from Agricultural to Woollens. **Yellow pages** in a literal sense followed in 1883 when a printer in Cheyenne, Wyo., ran out of white paper.

From the mid-1880s until 1897 there was a telephone directory for the whole United States. It was withdrawn when it reached 1¼ inches thick.

THE FIRST **TELESCOPE**

was a Newtonian reflector built by mathematician, astronomer, and member of Parliament Thomas Digges of Wallingford, Berkshire, England in 1576 to observe "the orbe of stars fixed infinitely." The invention was classified as a state secret because of its utility for sighting hostile Spanish ships.

The first telescope to be made public was submitted to the States General of the Netherlands on 2 October 1608 by Hans Lippershey, spectacle maker of Middleburg, in support of his application for a patent. Two days later a committee tested the instrument and on October 6 agreed to give Lippershey 900 florins for it. The request for a patent was turned down on the grounds that "the means of seeing at a distance" was already known to others. It is not apparent whether this was because of knowledge of Digges's forerunner or whether the committee was simply referring to the magnifying power of lenses.

The first astronomical discovery of importance to be made with the aid of a telescope was the identification of the satellites of Jupiter by Galileo Galilei on 10 January 1610. The Italian astronomer employed a telescope of his own devising, making his observations

from the tenement house where he lived in the Borgo dei Vignali in Padua.

U.S.: The first was a 3½-foot-long instrument with several attachments, which was taken to Hartford, Conn., in 1663 by Governor John Winthrop (1606–76), father of American astronomy and "chief correspondent of the Royal Society in the west" (the Royal Society was England's premier scientific institution). He used it the following year to make the earliest systematic astronomical observations in America, including the passage of a comet that was probably not visible on the other side of the Atlantic. When his sight began to fail in 1672, Winthrop donated his telescope to Harvard.

Radio telescope: The first dish radio telescope was built from discarded lumber and rafters and old car parts by amateur astronomer Grote Reber in his backyard at Wheaton, Ill., in 1937 and connected to a 31-foot-diameter sheet-metal parabolic antenna. Reber achieved his first substantial result with the device in 1939 when the chart graph recorded radio emissions at a wavelength of 1.87 meters and he went on to make a sky survey in the radio frequencies.

Notes on Television Terminology in the Following Entries

Early television was **low-definition** (i.e., the screen image was composed of under 120 lines) and mechanical, meaning that both the camera and the receiver had moving parts that needed to be in synchronization. The development of all-electronic systems with no moving parts led to **high-definition** television, used by the first full-service stations inaugurated in Britain in 1936 (405 lines) and the United States in 1939 (441 lines). This should not be confused with digital HDTV introduced in the 1990s and often referred to simply as "high definition," which operates on 1,041 lines to give a motion-picture clarity of image.

The term **full-service** is used in these entries to mean a regular, permanent service of high-definition programs to viewers in their own homes. The alternative term "public-service," generally employed in this context in Europe, has been avoided since in the United States it tends to connote not-for-profit.

THE FIRST **TELEVISION**

....

transmission of a moving image with gradations of light and shade was made by Scottish inventor John Logie Baird in his attic workroom at 22 Frith Street, London, on 30 October 1925. Baird had recently removed from Hastings, where he had built a crude apparatus comprising a tea chest, an empty cracker box for the lamphouse, Nipkow scanning disks made from hat boxes, darning needles, cycle-lamp lenses, discarded electric motors, piano wire, glue, string, and sealing wax to a total value of under $4. With this primitive machine he had succeeded in transmitting the shadow of a Maltese cross over a distance of about 10 feet in February 1924. He was later evicted from his laboratory at 8 Queen's Arcade after an explosion caused by his electrical supply, which consisted of several hundred flashlight batteries wired together to provide a 2,000 V power source.

In a broadcast made in America six years later, Baird described the events of the last Friday in October 1925 at 22 Frith Street when the dummy's head he had been using for test purposes suddenly showed up on the screen "not as a mere smudge of black and white, but as a real image with details. . ." His first thought was to obtain a living subject and he rushed down to the floor below, occupied by Cross Pictures Ltd. Here the first person he encountered was a fifteen-year-old office boy, William Taynton, whom he seized and hustled upstairs.

> I placed him before the transmitter and went into the next room to see what the screen would show. The screen was entirely blank, and no effort of tuning would produce any result. Puzzled, and very disappointed, I went back to the transmitter, and there the cause of the failure became at once evident. The boy, scared by the intense white light, had backed away from the transmitter. In the excitement of the moment I gave him half a crown [70¢], and this time he kept his head in the right position. Going again into the next room I saw his head on the screen quite clearly. It is curious that the first person in the world to be seen by television should be required a bribe to accept the distinction!

Baird gave his first demonstration of true television to the press on 7 January 1926, when the *Evening Standard* representative saw the face of Capt. O. G. Hutchinson on the screen. On 27 January he gave a public demonstration for some 40 members of the Royal Institution, followed by a series of displays for the technical and scientific press. Dr. Alexander Russell, principal of Faraday House, wrote a special account of Baird's achievement for *Nature* of 3 July 1926.

> We saw the transmission by television of living human faces, the proper gradation of light and shade, and all movement of the head, of the lips and mouth, and of a cigarette, and its smoke were faithfully portrayed on a screen in the theatre. The transmitter being in a room at the top of the building. Naturally, the results are far from perfect. The image cannot be compared with that produced by a good kinematograph film. The likeness, however, was unmistakable, and all the motions are reproduced with absolute fidelity. This is the first time we have seen real television and . . . Mr Baird is the first to have accomplished this marvellous feat.

Baird's system of television employed a mechanical scanner in both the transmitting apparatus and the receiver, and although he was eventually persuaded to develop an electronic receiver, by that time he had already been overtaken by Marconi-EMI (SEE BELOW) in technical quality.

U.S.: A low-definition mechanical television system similar to Baird's but engineered to a higher standard—48 lines as opposed to 30—was built by Dr. H. E. Ives and his research team at AT&T's newly formed Bell Telephone Laboratories in New York City and successfully used for the transmission of motion-picture film in 1925. The earliest record of its use with live subjects was a demonstration held on 10 March 1926 at the conclusion of the ceremonies held for the fiftieth anniversary of Alexander Graham Bell's invention of the telephone, when AT&T's president, F. B. Jewett, spoke over a telephone circuit in the telephone laboratory to executive vice president E. B. Craft and they were able to see as well as hear each other. (Presumably there had been earlier, unrecorded tests featuring anonymous technicians on screen.)

This represented true television akin to Baird's four months earlier, unlike the experiments of C. Francis Jenkins, often heralded as the first to transmit television in the United States, who had succeeded only in sending moving silhouette images without gradations of light and shade.

The first public transmission in the United States was made on 7 April 1927 from the AT&T laboratories in Whippany, N.J., to their headquarters in New York. The transmission began with a hookup between AT&T president Walter Gifford in New York and Gen. J. J. Carty in Washington, D.C. After an exchange of pleasantries, Secretary of Commerce Herbert Hoover was introduced, who thus became the first politician and the first (future) U.S. president to exploit what was to become the most potent method of mass communication the world has known. The initial appearance of the great man on screen, however, was not auspicious, as he was leaning forward in such a way that his forehead occupied most of the picture while the rest of his face was effectively blotted out by the candlestick telephone he was holding in front of it. This was rectified when a technician prodded him into a better position. After his 2-minute speech, Mrs. Hoover became the first woman to be publicly televised in the United States, talking over the phone to Gifford in New York. The demonstration concluded with a further "first" when Irish-American comedian A. Dolan provided TV's inaugural attempt at entertainment (SEE **television performer**).

Although AT&T was the first to present a professional artiste on television, the company had no interest in the use of the medium for broadcasting; their research was directed solely toward developing television telephones. Shortly after startling America with what they chauvinistically claimed as the world's first demonstration of seeing by wireless, they abandoned what proved to be, over the subsequent eighty years, a blind alley commercially—at least until the advent of the video cell phone.

Electronic television system: The first was developed starting in May 1926 by nineteen-year-old Philo T. Farnsworth originally in the dining room of his apartment in 1339 North New Hampshire Street, Hollywood and, from December of that year, in a loft above the Crocker Laboratories at 202 Green Street,

San Francisco. Although he filed a patent on 7 January 1927, it was only on 7 September that Farnsworth succeeded in achieving an image and then only of a black triangle painted on a glass slide. Unlike Baird's and AT&T's mechanical systems, this one contained no moving parts at all; it incorporated a camera employing a dissector tube, a vacuum tube scanning and pulse generator, and a magnetically focused high-vacuum cathode ray viewing tube in the receiver. This was demonstrated publicly for the first time on 2 September 1928 using film and silhouette images, which were received on a screen measuring 1¼" x 1½". At this stage the system was not true television, which demands the capacity to transmit live action, but it was a significant step toward it. When Don Lee Television's W6XAO Los Angeles Station began regular transmissions at 80-line definition on 10 March 1933, it was with cameras and receivers developed by Philo Farnsworth—the first all-electronic station in the world, albeit using low definition and transmitting only film. It was not until the summer of 1934 that Farnsworth was able to transmit live action successfully.

In the meantime a more advanced system had been developed by Russian-born Vladimir Zworykin of Westinghouse, using his revolutionary Kinescope cathode-ray tube that he built into seven domestic television receivers in November 1929. One of these he demonstrated to the Eastern Great Lakes Convention of the Institute of Radio Engineers on the 18th of that month. In 1930 Zworykin moved to RCA to head up television research at their Camden, N.J., laboratories. It was here in 1933 that he developed the Iconoscope camera tube, which became the basis of the system employed by RCA six years later for the first full-service television station in America, W2XBS New York (SEE **television service**), and which was licensed to nearly every subsequent operator in the United States and many others overseas.

This was, not, however the first all-electronic high-definition system to be brought into use for a permanent service to viewers in their own homes. A research team gathered together by EMI began experiments at Hayes, near London, under the direction of Russian-born Isaac Schoenberg in 1931. The demonstration of the EMI system, before the chief engineer of the BBC on 6 December 1932, was also the first time high-definition television had been witnessed in Britain. A film of the Changing of the Guard at Buckingham Palace was viewed on a 130-line cathode-ray receiver with a 5" x 5" screen. The more difficult problem of electronic scanning was solved with the development of the Emitron camera, successfully demonstrated by Dr. J. D. McGee on 29 January 1934. Early the following year Schoenberg decided on 405 lines as the standard of definition, and on 2 November 1936 the Marconi-EMI system, by then the most advanced in the world, came into regular operation with the inauguration of the BBC television service from Alexandra Palace, London (SEE **television service**).

Sir Isaac Schoenberg, as he became, was not only a master scientist, but also a prophet and wit. After the first successful demonstration of the Emitron camera, he turned to his team and said: "Well, gentlemen, you have invented the biggest time waster of all time. Use it well."

THE FIRST

TELEVISION BALLET PERFORMANCE

was rendered by Alisa Bridgewater on 12 December 1930 in a transmission from the Baird Studios in Long Acre, London. Miss Bridgewater wrote of the experience some years later:

Owing to the fact that a full-length picture was then impossible, after a short introductory speech I mounted the stage, which was more in the form of a table than anything else, and commenced to show the rudiments of ballet technique within the carefully marked out space . . . From the moment when the red light showed suddenly and brightly, and the immediate "all quiet please" came from the announcer, an indescribable feeling of romance inevitably pervaded the next half hour. Despite a certain amount of natural nervousness at facing both the microphone and the television, to a far greater extent was the thrill and realization that this was the foundation of new means of presenting the art of dancing to the public.

Although only one other ballet performance is recorded before 1933, in that year the prima ballerina Adeline Genée made dance history when she chose to make her world farewell by the infant medium of television. The importance of this presentation cannot be overestimated at a time when the BBC's television service was being denigrated by its opponents as nothing more than a series of laboratory experiments. On 15 March 1933, eleven days after she had given her farewell theater performance at the Coliseum, Mme. Genée performed opposite Anton Dolin in *The Love Song*, a short ballet in which two eighteenth-century lovers dance round a spinet. The transmission, from the BBC television studio in Broadcasting House, was received by Adeline Genée's compatriots in Copenhagen.

The first complete ballet with full cast performed on television was *The Gods Go a-Begging*, with Lydia Sokolova, Stanislas Idzikowski, and a corps de ballet comprised of pupils from Mme. Sokolova's school, presented by the BBC on 26 June 1934.

U.S.: The first was a pas de deux danced by Tanaquil LeClercq and Francisco Moncion, leading soloists of George Balanchine's American Ballet Company, performed on NBC W2XBS New York probably late in 1938. Balanchine had befriended the young Edward Padula, who had been hired straight from Yale's graduate school of drama by NBC as one of its first producers, and the neophyte was quick to realize that ballet of Balanchine's caliber would bring a distinction to NBC's somewhat lackluster schedule that any number of performing dogs and ventriloquists would fail to match.

The first complete ballet adapted for television in the United States was *Ballet for Americans*, transmitted by WRGB Schenectady, N.Y., on 2 December 1942. Information about the composer, choreographer, and performers is sought.

The first presentation of **ballet televised in color** was of Sol Hurok's New York City Ballet arranged by George Balanchine, transmitted by CBS in its inaugural color program *Premier* on 25 June 1951. First of a full-length ballet was NBC's *Sleeping Beauty* on 12 December 1955.

SEE **television: pay TV**.

THE FIRST **TELEVISION, CABLE**

THE FIRST **TELEVISION CARTOONS**

made for TV were *Crusader Rabbit*, a series of 5-minute films produced at a cost of $350 per episode by Jay Ward and Alex Anderson in a studio above the latter's garage in Berkeley, Calif., between 1949 and 1951. Anderson had trained at Terrytoons, the animation studio founded by his uncle Paul Terry. When he decided to go into TV, his uncle warned him against ever admitting the relationship. Ward was a real estate agent who was hit by a truck immediately after setting up his own business and spent two years in the hospital having his shattered legs mended. It was while hospitalized that he began work on *Crusader Rabbit*. Learning animation from scratch was not without its hazards. The first *Crusader Rabbit* film was animated upside down. Ward later became celebrated for one of the most successful American TV cartoon series, *Rocky and Bullwinkle*.

Crusader Rabbit was syndicated to TV stations (i.e., it was not a network show), debuting on KNBH Los Angeles on 1 August 1950. The voice of Crusader Rabbit was Lucille Bliss, who had worked on Tom & Jerry and Droopy Dog cartoons but was prepared to take a pay cut to $5 per episode as she was working her way through college. The recordings were done between 9 P.M. and 4 A.M. to save money on sound-studio hire. Although the show was aimed at children, Alex Anderson recalled that nearly all the fan mail came from college students.

The initial series was 195 episodes. A second series of 260 episodes made by Capital Enterprises at Creston Studios in Los Angeles in 1957–58 was the first **color TV cartoon** series.

Network cartoon series: The first was Paul Terry's *Mighty Mouse Playhouse*, which bowed on CBS as a Saturday morning offering on 10 December 1955. This was made up of theatrical shorts. The first "made for" network show was Hanna-Barbera's *The Ruff & Reddy Show* about a dumb pooch and a smart feline

fighting for truth, justice, and the American Way, which debuted on NBC on 14 December 1957. It was produced in color from 1959.

THE FIRST **TELEVISION CHILDREN'S PROGRAM**

was a presentation of Bernard H. Paul's Company of Marionettes on W3XK Wheaton, Md., on 6 November 1931.

According to *The First Quarter Century of American Broadcasting*, published in Kansas City in 1946, a children's program was televised by WIP Philadelphia in 1934, but no details are vouchsafed. WIP had a regular children's radio program sponsored by Gimbel's department store called *Uncle WIP's Children's Hour*. There was an experimental TV station, W3XE, run by Philco in Philadelphia. In 1946 its successor WPTZ televised the Uncle WIP show from Gimbel's and it is possible that this was a repetition of something first tried experimentally twelve years earlier.

Children's TV series: The first was *For the Children*, which premiered on the BBC's London Service at 3 P.M. on Saturday, 24 April 1937, with a performance by Zenora the Clown. The series continued as a weekly 10-minute program until the termination of BBC transmission at the outbreak of war, but it returned on 7 July 1946 in a 20-minute slot on Sundays, continuing until 1950. The rescheduling caused problems for the BBC because it was alleged that children were bunking off Sunday school to watch the program. It was on the revived *For the Children* that the first TV character to be merchandised, Muffin the Mule (SEE **character merchandising**), made his debut on 30 October 1946.

U.S.: By March 1940 NBC's W2XBS New York was offering a Saturday afternoon program *Children's Matinee*, which went out at 3:30 P.M. for half an hour, later extended to an hour. The program was divided into three equal segments: ex-Australian Army veteran, explorer, and philatelist Captain Tim Healy spinning yarns; Marion Bishop's Marionettes; and storytelling or pet features. *Paul Wing's Spelling Bee* with child contestants was also running on the channel prior to the start of commercial TV in July 1941. WRGB

Schenectady began targeting youngsters in 1942 with *Children's Story*, *Stories for the Nursery*, and *The Children's Hour*, breaking new ground the following year with the first program for teenagers, *Youth Night*. At that time there were 300 receiving sets in private homes in the Albany/Troy/Schenectady receiving area.

The first **networked children's show** was DuMont's *The Small Fry Club*, with "Big Brother" Bob Emery as the host and producer of a 30-minute program aired at 6 P.M. Monday to Friday consisting of stories, contests, magic, audience participation, and other fun things for pre-teens. It was networked from 11 March 1947 to 15 June 1951. In the first two years 160,000 "small fries" accepted Big Brother's invitation to join his club. Saturday morning network programming for kids began on 19 August 1950 with ABC's *Animal Clinic*, presented by Dr. Wesley Young, and Western circus drama *Acrobat Ranch*.

Drama series: The first for children and also the first sci-fi series was *Captain Video and His Video Rangers*, starring Richard Coogan, which began its six-year run on the DuMont network on 27 June 1949. Made on a budget so small as to be scarcely visible, the total allocation for props was $25—for five episodes a week. Much of the high-tech equipment used by the Video Rangers was simply painted on the studio wall. It was also a nursery for aspiring Hollywood actors. Among those who made their screen debut in *Captain Video* before heading for the Coast were Jack Klugman, Tony Randall, and Ernest Borgnine.

Children's series in color: The first was *My Friend Flicka*, boy-and-horse adventures set in Montana but shot in Wyoming, with Johnny Washbrook as juvenile hero Ken. It debuted on CBS on 10 February 1956 and moved to ABC three years later.

THE FIRST **TELEVISION, COLOR**

transmission was made by John Logie Baird at the Baird Studios, 133 Long Acre, London, on 3 July 1928 and showed red and blue scarves, a policeman's helmet, a man putting his tongue out, the glowing end of a cigarette, and a bunch of red roses. *Nature* reported of a demonstration: "Delphiniums and carnations appeared in their natural colors and a basket of strawberries showed the red fruit very clearly." Baird's low-definition color-television system employed a Nipkow scanning disk with red, blue, and green filters.

U.S.: Color was first publicly demonstrated by Dr. H. E. Ives at the Bell Telephone Laboratories in New York City on 27 June 1929. Ives was the son of F. E. Ives, inventor of the first commercially practicable system of color photography (SEE **photograph in color**). The journal *Telephony* reported that the transmission "opened with the American flag fluttering on a screen about the size of a postage stamp. The colors reproduced perfectly. Then the Union Jack was flashed on the screen and was easily recognized by its colored bars. The man at the transmitter picked up a piece of watermelon, and there could be no mistake in identifying what he was eating. The red of the melon, the black seeds, and the green rind were true to nature, as were the red of his lips, the natural color of his skin, and his black hair..." There was also Technicolor film footage of Al Jolson singing "Sonny Boy" and a live model in a multi-colored dress and a festive paper hat who held up flowers before the scanner.

High-definition color television: The first public demonstration was made by John Logie Baird, whose 120-line system was used to transmit color films on a 9' x 12' screen at the Dominion Theatre, Tottenham Court Road, London, on 4 February 1938. The first live demonstration was made from the Baird Studios at Crystal Palace on 17 February 1938. Baird employed a mirror-drum scanning system, and though the color quality was reported to be of a high standard in controlled experiments, his refusal to consider electronic rather than mechanical means of transmission limited the possibilities of commercial development.

By January 1941 Baird had produced a 600-line 2' x 2½' large-screen color Tele-Radiogram that could also be used for BBC 405-line black-and-white transmissions. At the end of the war he formed a company, John Logie Baird Ltd., to produce these giant sets. Within a few months Baird was dead, however, and with him died his dream of large-screen electromechanical color television.

U.S.: The first all-electronic color system was demonstrated secretly to the FCC by RCA at Camden, N.J., on 5 February 1940. Dr. P. C. Goldmark (SEE ALSO sound recording: 33⅓-RPM long-playing records) of CBS demonstrated a mechanically scanned frame sequential color system based on Baird's (SEE ABOVE) to the FCC on 28 August 1940. Definition was 343 lines. This was capable of transmitting film only, but on 12 November Goldmark was able to show live action in color using an orthicon camera tube.

Color television service: The first scheduled experimental service was commenced by CBS from WCBW New York on 1 June 1941 with daily transmissions by Goldmark's electro-mechanical system.

Regular, commercial color transmissions were inaugurated by CBS from its Color Studio 57 in New York City on 25 June 1951. The first sponsored color show was a variety performance titled *Premiere* featuring Ed Sullivan, Arthur Godfrey, and Faye Emerson, which went on the air at 4:35 P.M. It was produced and directed by Frances Buss, who had become America's first female television producer (qv) nearly seven years earlier. The first color series, Ivan T. Sanderson's natural history documentary *The World is Yours*, began the following day.

CBS bought a manufacturer of television receivers, Air-King, when the trade proved unwilling to commit themselves to a product for which there was uncertain demand. The CBS color system was not compatible with monochrome systems of transmission and therefore purchasers of an Air-King set could only receive the single CBS color channel. When it became apparent that sales were not going to justify maintenance of the service, CBS persuaded the government to make a formal request that they cease manufacture to conserve vital war materials while the Korean War continued. This enabled them to also close down programing on "patriotic" grounds.

Color returned to the small screen after the FCC approved RCA-developed standards for a compatible system, both CBS and NBC starting regular transmissions on 17 December 1953.

Color was slow to penetrate the home, most of the early sets being in bars. With such small takeup, the price of receivers (qv) remained high and the networks, with the exception of NBC, cut back on color transmissions. Between 1958 and 1964 only NBC maintained a regular color schedule and it was not until the 1966–67 season that the three networks offered all

prime-time programing in color. Set prices dropped and color was, for the first time, predominant. NBC scored another first by becoming the first network to switch to color-only transmissions on 7 November 1966. Color viewing households, a negligible 200,000 in 1960, rose a hundredfold to 20 million by 1970.

THE FIRST **TELEVISION COMMERCIALS**

were seen when the initial, hesitant steps at selling off the small screen were taken on both sides of the Atlantic in 1930. In America the first advertiser was Libby's canned goods, whose president, Edward G. McDougal, was interviewed live on W9XAP Chicago on 11 August by the well-known radio announcer Bill Hay. The rest of the program was a variety show headed by comedian Ken Murray, who did the pitch for Libby's, and also featured singers, instrumentalists, and a comedy double act. The program could be viewed on two hundred TV sets specially installed in the windows of Chicago radio stores and was also picked up by numerous amateur TV "hams" on their own home-built low-definition receivers, reports coming in from as far away as Pittsburgh. Libby also sponsored a boxing match telecast (SEE BELOW **television: sport**) on 27 August.

In Britain the first to make use of television for promotional purposes was coiffeur Eugène Ltd. of Dover Street, London. Demonstrations of the "Eugène Method" of permanent waving were transmitted via closed-circuit Baird television at the Hairdressing Fair of Fashion at London's Olympia from 5 to 13 November 1930. According to an advertisement in *Television*, viewers would "learn how the patented Eugène Sachet coaxes the hair into soft, lovely natural waves."

The first commercials aired on regular, full-service television anywhere in the world were delivered by the presenters of NBC's *Vox Pop*, Parks Johnson and Wally Butterworth, which was broadcast from the site of the New York World's Fair via W2XBS during the summer of 1939, starting 30 April. The sponsor, who under FCC rules could not pay for the plugs but could "contribute to costs," was Kentucky Pipe Tobacco. *Vox Pop* was a daily 15-minute show, adapted from a radio program of the same name, in which Johnson and Butterworth talked to fair-goers. Despite the appearance of spontaneity, the guests were pre-selected and the interviews carefully scripted. As were the commercials, with the interviewers constantly refilling and lighting their pipes with exclamations of delight at the fragrant mellowness of Kentucky Pipe Tobacco. At about the same time Andrew Geller's shoe store was sponsoring W2XBS's *Show-Biz Interviews* with George Rois.

Other advertisers were given the opportunity to try out the new medium during the baseball game between the Cincinnati Reds and the Brooklyn Dodgers televised from Ebbets Field, Brooklyn, by W2XBC on 26 August 1939. The commercials were presented live by the commentator, Walter J. "Red" Barber, and were for three companies: the Socony Vacuum Oil Co. (later to become Mobil), the food producers General Mills, and Procter & Gamble, promoting Ivory soap. They were presented impromptu, without scripts, Barber recalled: "For the gasoline sponsor, I put on a filling station man's hat and spieled about gas. For the breakfast cereal spot, I poured some of the stuff into a bowl. There wasn't much I could do for the soap sponsor. I just held up a soap bar and extolled its virtues."

During the first eight months of public service no fewer than seventy-three advertisers sponsored programs, representing 12 percent of airtime.

Commercial television station: The first was the National Broadcasting Company's WNBT New York, whose first commercial was transmitted at 2:29:50 P.M. on 1 July 1941. It showed a Bulova watch with the second hand moving toward the half-hour mark and was accompanied by a voiceover intoning, "America runs on Bulova time," emanating from Studio F at Radio City in New York. The charge for the 10-second spot was $9. The earliest rate card, issued on 27 June, shows that the cost to an advertiser buying time for a fully sponsored program was $120 an hour, plus studio and production costs. Among the advertisers willing to pay this comparatively high rate to reach a maximum of 4,700 television sets were Ivory soap, Sun Oil, Adam Hats, Lever Bros, and Botany Worsted. It was the latter who commissioned the first **animated commercial**, produced by Douglas Leigh and directed by Otto Messmer (co-creator of Felix the Cat) in 1941 to promote men's ties. At the end of each "important announcement from our sponsor" a cartoon lamb would peer through a telescope and predict the next day's weather.

Initially all commercials were integral to sponsored programs. The first station to offer a choice of program sponsorship or buying spots in unsponsored programs was WPTZ Philadelphia. Returned war veteran Robert Jawer believes he was the first TV ad salesman in the world when he was hired in 1946. His first sale of a spot commercial was to Jawer's Auto Supply, 20 seconds for $30, possibly facilitated by the fact that the proprietor was Robert's dad. The practice only became general when former ad executive turned NBC vice president Pat Weaver (father of Sigourney) created the *Today Show* in January 1952.

The first year in which television expenditure registered on the annual survey of U.S. ad spending conducted by McCann-Erickson was 1949 at $58 million. By the end of the century it had risen more than a thousandfold to $59.2 billion (*Advertising Age Survey*), nearly a quarter of total advertising spent. Nevertheless the proportion of advertising budgets spent on TV in 2000 in the United States was lower than in most other advanced nations: In the United Kingdom and France it was 34 to 35 percent, in Japan and Italy 45 percent, and in Brazil (noted for the excellence of its prize-winning commercials) 60 percent.

Color commercials: The first were broadcast live from an unidentified theater for interspersing with CBS's inaugural color program, a variety show titled *Premiere*, on 25 June 1951, which was transmitted separately from CBS Color Studio 57. There were sixteen sponsors, including General Mills, Pabst, Wrigley's, Revlon, Quaker Oats, and Pepsi, and the commercials were directed by Frances Buss. They were received on the small number of color receivers within the five-station CBS color network: New York, Boston, Philadelphia, Baltimore, and Washington, D.C.

TV commercial to feature a black character: The first in the United States to depict an African American in a non-stereotypical role was for All detergent in 1961 and featured actress Gail Fisher as a happy housewife. Its special significance lay in the fact that it was clearly targeted at housewives generally without distinction of race.

For the first jingle in a TV commercial SEE **advertising jingle**. For the first commercial in HDTV SEE **television HDTV**.

was X. Marcel Boulestin, who also has some claim to have been the first celebrity chef of the modern media era. Having started out as personal secretary to the monstrous Monsieur Willy, paramour of the Parisienne novelist Colette, the young Marcel escaped to London to find his true vocation as an interpreter of fine French cuisine for the culinarily challenged British. In 1926 he opened his celebrated Restaurant Boulestin in Covent Garden, London's principal fruit and vegetable market, from which he was able to source seasonal ingredients. There he began offering cookery courses in haute cuisine. A succession of books, starting with *Simple French Cooking for English Homes* (1923), introduced the English to the art of cooking the Continental way a generation before Elizabeth David's crusade against overcooked vegetables and lumpy brown gravy. It was on 21 January 1937 that Marcel Boulestin inaugurated a new series on BBC television called *Cook's Night Out*. As the title indicated, it was assumed that television viewers would employ full-time cooks and only need to fend for themselves on one evening a week. The opening program demonstrated how to make an omelet without the consistency of shoe leather. Each subsequent episode in the series of five showed the aspiring home chef how to prepare the next course of a five-course dinner, culminating in crêpes flambées; clearly viewers were not expected to be watching their waistlines. **U.S.:** The first cookery show was somewhat similar in intention to Boulestin's forerunner. Titled *Sunday Evening Supper*, it was produced by Edward Padula for NBC's W2XBS New York in 1940 and presented by Manhattan socialite Elsie de Wolfe, aka Lady Mendl, celebrated for her lesbian affairs and as the first woman with blue-rinsed hair, as well as for coining the phrase "Never complain, never explain." Uninterested in the money, of which there was scarcely any in the meager budget, she agreed to do the series live every Sunday provided a limousine was sent to collect her and her guests from the St. Regis Hotel. The guests were personal friends, members of New York's 400 and visiting aristocrats from England. A dining room was replicated in Studio 3H, with the cutlery, napery, crockery, glassware, and wines were supplied free by companies who were pleased to do so as product placement—more for the luster thrown on their products by association with Elsie de Wolfe than for any distinction lent by the upstart medium of television. Each week a different chef from one of New York's top restaurants would cook the meal and talk about the recipes while the blue-coiffed Mrs. de Wolfe presided in white gloves and diamonds, the only one of the assembled company melting under the fierce heat of the arc lamps who never broke a sweat. The single occasion on which her sangfroid was momentarily lost was when a chef tossing a salad in a basket lost the lid and deposited the leaves into Mrs. de Wolfe's ample bosom.

Networked TV cookery show: The first also involved Elsie de Wolfe in *Elsie Presents—James Beard in "I Love to Eat,"* which debuted on NBC on 30 August 1946. It was produced by twenty-two-year-old Patricia Kennedy, in between campaigning for her brother John in his first run for Congress.

was an illustrated lecture on art pottery by C. Geoffrey Holme, editor of the monthly art magazine *Studio*, that was transmitted from the Baird Studios at Long Acre, London, in November 1928. Holme brought various exhibits to the studio and held them up before the scanner as he described their points of interest. This was the first occasion on which a scheduled program was transmitted for home viewers in Britain, though the audience was confined to the handful of enthusiastic amateurs who had built their own mechanical, low-definition television receivers.

During the first year of the regular Baird sound-and-vision experimental service (1930) program material was confined almost exclusively to variety acts and instrumentalists, but in the spring of 1931 Mrs. Stackpool O'Dell presented an illustrated talk on phrenology and Mrs. Rhoda Flanders a program about dogs.

U.S.: Documentary TV was pioneered by W2XAB, the CBS station in New York, beginning with a display of oil paintings in November 1931 and followed the next month by a program about the contrasting ways of life in Norway and India. An ambitious 25-minute documentary to celebrate the George Washington Bicentennial was presented on 7 August 1932, followed three days later by another biographical feature on prizefight champion John L. Sullivan. On 16 September 1932, W2XAB broke new ground with the start of the first **documentary series**, which covered the American aviation industry.

With the arrival of high-definition service to the viewing public in 1939, RCA's station W2XBS (later WNBJ) filled its schedule with a plethora of documentary films but little original factual programing other than a topical roundup titled *NBC Tele-Topics*. The real pioneer of features programming once all-electronic sets were available for home viewing was W2XB and its successor WRGB Schenectady, which turned increasingly to the live documentary as an inexpensive and comparatively easy-to-stage form of "infotainment." One of the earliest, presented on 20 September 1940, was not dissimilar to the first-ever documentary twelve years earlier (SEE ABOVE): Julius Pardi presenting *The Ancient Art of Pottery*.

The first **networked documentary series** was Time-Life's *Crusade in Europe*, a study of World War II based on the book of the same name by Gen. Dwight D. Eisenhower, aired by ABC in twenty-six episodes starting on 5 May 1949.

Reality television: This has two distinct meanings. It may be either *cinéma vérité*, a true-to-life observation of unfolding events, or almost the opposite, a kind of knock-out popularity contest in which a group of volunteers in an isolated environment are stimulated to interact in various contrived situations.

The first "fly-on-the-wall" or *cinéma vérité* documentary was Robert Drew's groundbreaking 53-minute *Primary*, which followed presidential hopefuls John F. Kennedy and Hubert Humphrey on the stump during the 1960 Wisconsin primary. The commentary-free film was made for Time-Life Broadcasting using a hand-held camera to chronicle the action uninterrupted and without apparent directorial intervention. Cinematographer Richard Leacock recalled: "On the first day Bob Drew, [cameraman] Al Maysles and I walked into the photo studio where Kennedy was having his portrait taken and just shot what happened—they ignored us."

The first competitive reality TV show was *Big Brother*, created by John de Mol and made by his Amsterdam-based company Endemol. It debuted on the Veronica Channel in the Netherlands to ever mounting audiences, culminating in the victory of Bart Spring in't Veldt on 30 September 1999. Like many subsequent winners, he found the pressures of instant fame hard to handle, suffering five breakdowns and condemning the show as "that mindless monster," adding "*Big Brother* took away the need to make inspiring programs and replaced them with mindless chatter." John de Mol had no such compunctions, licensing the format to nearly seventy countries, including the United States, where reality TV bowed on CBS the following summer. The victor at the end of *Big Brother*'s first American season on 5 July 2000, wheelchair-bound amputee Eddie McGee, fared better than his Dutch predecessor, becoming an actor despite his disability and founding production company Tripod Pictures.

THE FIRST **TELEVISION DRAMA**

was *The Queen's Messenger* by J. Hartley Manners, adapted and produced by Mortimer Stewart and presented by the General Electric Co.'s WGY Schenectady, N.Y., on 11 September 1928. Izotta Jewell played the lady and Maurice Randall the messenger, while Joyce E. Rector and William J. Toniski doubled for hands, holding various props in front of the scanner, including cigarettes, glasses, keys, and a briefcase. Three cameras were used, one for these effects, and one each for the two performers. The play was transmitted on the 24-line low-definition system developed by Dr. Ernst Alexanderson with two live 40-minute performances at 1:30 P.M. and 11:30 P.M., which meant a long and demanding day for the actors as paranoid producer Mortimer Stewart had locked them in the studio at 4 A.M. to start rehearsals. Reception reports came from viewers as far west as the Pacific Coast. Playwright J. Hartley Manners had died that year without ever knowing that his 1899 play was destined to inaugurate a new medium for drama.

The first **television comedy** followed two months later. This was John Maddison Morton's Victorian farce *Box and Cox*, produced by Gordon Sherry with Laurence Bascomb as Box, Vivienne Chatterton as Mrs. Bouncer, and Stanley Vivien as Cox, and presented by the Baird Co. from their studios at 133 Long Acre, London, on 15 December 1928. The fourth member of the cast, a cat, was the first animal performer to appear on television. Although no commercial receivers were available at the time, a number of amateur constructors had already made their own sets from directions published in *Television*, so it is possible that the production was seen by several dozen viewers in addition to the Baird staff. The dialogue could be picked up on an ordinary radio set, and at least one listener was inspired to make his own television receiver after hearing the broadcast.

Drama written for TV: The first was *The Wrong Door*, starring Joan Dare and John Rorke, transmitted by the Baird Co. from their London studios on 19 November 1930. Produced by Harold Bradley, it was scripted by Ruth Maschwitz, who was secretary to the Baird Co.'s director of programs Sydney Moseley. Ms. Maschwitz had another short play, *Great Expectations*, performed the following week and in this one she also starred. What is believed to have been America's earliest written-for-television drama was a musical comedy called *Their Television Honeymoon* transmitted from Chicago by Western Television Co.'s W9XAO and the *Chicago Daily News*'s W9XAP in January 1931. The scriptwriter is unknown.

The first play written specially for electronic high-definition television was *The Love Nest*, commissioned by RCA from Eddie Albert, who also starred opposite Grace Bradt. Transmitted from NBC's Studio 3H in Rockefeller Center's Radio City on 21 September 1936, the 30-minute drama was strictly experimental, both in the sense that it could only be viewed by the fifty or so people involved in NBC's fledgling TV operation on the half-dozen sets available in the RCA building and also that it was designed as a "test-bed" for sponsored programs. The

prospective sponsor in this case was General Foods and the play, first of a series of half-hour domestic dramas starring Albert and Bradt, was intended as a vehicle for product placement. Although there was a director, his name is lost to history as nearly sixty years on Eddie Albert remembered him only as "a guy in a suit who emerged from a back room" and seemed indifferent to the whole undertaking. "It was becoming clear," Albert said in an interview with TV historian Michael Ritchie, "that Grace and I were expected to direct ourselves." For self-directing, acting, and for Eddie Albert's script, the pair received a fee for $10 to divide between them.

When the BBC established the world's first full-service electronic high-definition TV station in London the same year, drama was a staple of the schedule from the outset. During the three years of the pre-World War II BBC television service, there were 362 dramatic productions starting with Scottish comedy *Marigold*, starring Sophie Stewart, on 6 November 1936. Many of these were West End shows transported to the studios at Alexandra Palace with their original casts. Others were scripted for television, the first being J. Bissell Thomas's *The Underground Murder Mystery*, set on the London Underground (subway) and presented with Lance Lister and Nancy Poulteney in the lead roles on 19 January 1937. Agatha Christie's *The Wasp's Nest*, transmitted by the BBC on 18 July 1937, was the only one of her stories she adapted for TV. Starring Francis L. Sullivan, it was notable for the first appearance of the television private eye and in the person of no less a luminary of his profession than everyone's favorite Belgian, master sleuth Hercule Poirot.

In the United States, drama was an important element of Don Lee Telvision's W6XOA Los Angeles live output from April 1938, drawing on the services of the Pasadena Playhouse, Max Reinhardt's theatrical workshop in Los Angeles, and the station's own Teletheater Guild Unit, one of whose more ambitious productions was a forerunner of the miniseries, a three-part *Alice in Wonderland*. An acclaimed *Macbeth* starred the legendary Shakespearean actor Fritz Leiber. The station also produced the world's first continuous drama series to appear on high-definition TV, *Vine Street* (SEE BELOW). On the other coast

RCA launched its drama program with a presentation of *Susan and God* starring Gertrude Lawrence from Radio City on 7 June 1938 and, when the service went public the following spring, aired twice-weekly plays starting with Aaron Hoffman's *The Unexpected* on 3 May 1939. When NBC reduced its programing to 4 hours a week following the attack on Pearl Harbor, the torch of television drama was kept alight by WRGB Schenectady, whose many wartime productions included a notable adaptation of *Uncle Tom's Cabin* by Robert B. Stone.

Television drama series: The first was *The Wide World Review*, presented by CBS Television from W2XAB New York on Monday evenings from 15 August to 12 December 1932. Described by the *New York Sun* as "a musical drama with a fast-moving script," the series starred a well-known English actor and broadcaster, Jack Fleming, who had made his name in the BBC radio feature *London Crime Club*. The first 25-minute episode was set in Shanghai.

This was the only known dramatic series transmitted in any country during the period of low-definition experimental television broadcasting. The first drama series on electronic high-definition TV was *Vine Street*, a sophisticated light comedy scripted and produced by Wilfred Pettit about a girl breaking into movies. Starring John Barkeley and Shirley Thomas, the serial was aired by the Don Lee Television station W6XAO Los Angeles every Tuesday and Friday from 15 April 1938 and ran for 52 episodes. Each was introduced with television drama's first **theme tune**, Duke Ellington's "Sophisticated Lady."

Crime series: The first was *Take the Witness*, presented by CBS from the Columbia Music Box Theater in Los Angeles and transmitted locally by Don Lee Television's W6XAO in 1938. The first on full-service television was the BBC's *Telecrime*, which debuted with *The Back-Stage Murder* by Mileson Horton and H. T. Hopkinson on 10 August 1938. Five episodes were broadcast before the service shut down for the duration of World War II and twelve after it was resumed in 1946.

The first police detective series debuted in Chicago in 1947 as a local production, *Chicagoland Mystery Players*, with Gordon Urquhart as criminologist Jeffrey Hunter and Bob Smith as faithful sidekick Sgt.

Holland. "Whodunnit?" was not revealed in the show, but viewers (and readers) could find out the following day in the *Chicago Tribune*, the station's owner. On 18 September 1949 the show became a networked series with DuMont. ABC had preceded its rival earlier in the year with the first networked police series, *Stand By for Crime*, starting 22 January 1949, with a different sleuth in each episode.

The first private-eye series was *Martin Kane, Private Eye*, with William Gargan as a New York private investigator who achieves his results through determination and force of character. Produced by Edward C. Kahan, it ran on NBC from 11 September to 20 August 1953.

Situation comedy: The first was *Pinwright's Progress* written by Rodney Hobson and transmitted by BBC London in ten episodes from 29 November 1946. It starred well-known movie character actor James Hayter as proprietor of Macgillygally's Stores whose rivalry with the enemy store across the street, and attempts by his staff to be helpful, including the messenger boy Ralph (eighty and deaf), cause him a predictably fraught working life.

U.S.: *Mary Kay and Johnny*, about the fictitious marital misadventures of real-life married couple Mary Kay Stearns and Johnny Stearns, was produced by Ernest Walling and aired in 30-minute episodes by the DuMont network from 18 November 1947 to 24 August 1948 and subsequently by NBC (October 1948–February 1949), CBS (February–June 1949), and NBC again thru March 1950.

Soap opera: The first dramatic serial to conform to the accepted soap-opera format of overblown emotions, family jealousies, scandal, unbelievable situations, and rapturous romance was the DuMont network's *Faraway Hill*, a half-hour show aired in New York City and Washington, D.C., on Wednesdays starting on 2 October 1946. It starred Broadway actress Flora Campbell as Karen St. John, a rich New York widow who goes to live with relatives on a farm and has an affair with the hired hand (Mel Brandt). Unfortunately he is already promised to the farmer's blue-eyed daughter and much overwrought passion ensues. The show was performed live by its cast of sixteen and each episode was made on a budget of $500. When it became apparent that the budget would not be extended beyond the first ten episodes, writer-producer David P. Lewis decided to kill off Karen St. John in the final one. Much to his surprise, there was an outcry from many of the 400 regular viewers, an early indication of the importance soaps would assume in people's everyday lives.

Daily soaps began with Irna Phillips's NBC production *These Are My Children*, live from Chicago on 31 January 1949, starring Alma Platts as Irish widow Mrs. Henehan who runs a boarding house at the same time as she struggles to bring up three children. Blackboards were used by the performers to read their lines from, as there was seldom time to learn them. This gave the cast that unmistakable soap opera look of intensity as they strained to see the words. Despite this attribute, critics were not impressed. Declared *Television World*, "A blank screen is preferable."

Drama series with a black central character: The first was CBS's *Beulah*, the title role being played originally by Ethel Waters, later by Hattie McDaniel and Louise Beavers, in which the protagonist was a much put-upon but ever resourceful black "Mammy" who looked after the upper-crust WASP Henderson family. All the black characters were stereotypes: Beulah rotund and sassy, her boyfriend Bill (Percy Harris) shiftless, and her best friend Oriole (Butterfly McQueen) scatterbrained. *Beulah* ran from 10 October 1950 to September 1953 and was enormously popular with its almost exclusively white audience.

Dramatic series in color: The first was NBC's family sitcom *The Marriage*, produced by Hume Cronyn, about the close-knit Marriott family headed by attorney Ben (Hume Cronyn), wife Liz (English actress, later oldest Oscar winner Jessica Tandy, who was Cronyn's wife in real life), and daughter Emily (Susan Strasberg, daughter of Actors' Studio head Lee Strasberg). It ran 8 July to 19 August 1954.

Miniseries: The first was Lorimar Productions' *The Blue Knight*, from the novel by Joseph Wambaugh, which was aired in one-hour segments by NBC on four consecutive nights, 13–16 November 1973. It won an Emmy for William Holden as Bumper Morgan, veteran Los Angeles Police Department cop a few days off retirement. Lee Remick received a nomination for her role as Bumper's ever-patient girlfriend Cassie Walters.

SEE ALSO **television children's program: drama series; film made for television**.

THE FIRST
TELEVISION, EDUCATIONAL STATION

was the University of Iowa's experimental, low-definition W9XK, which began transmitting educational television programs on a regular schedule from Iowa City on 25 January 1933. The opening telecast comprised an introductory lecture on the university by Dr. E. B. Kurtz, director of the station and head of the Department of Electrical Engineering; a violin solo by a student, Irene Ruppert; a lesson in freehand drawing by the Art Department lecturer Aden Arnold; and a scene from the play *The First Mrs. Fraser*, presented by members of the Speech Department.

During the 1933–34 season instruction was given by University of Iowa lecturers in oral hygiene, botany (identifying trees), engineering (reading architectural drawings), shorthand, French pronunciation, astronomy, drawing, natural history, and a number of other subjects. Programs were aired at 7:30 P.M. on Mondays and Wednesday and included a musical item and dramatic sketch or recitation in addition to the lecture. A total of 389 educational programs were broadcast during the six years that the station continued in operation. A regular body of viewers quite unconnected with the university was built up over this period, and reception was reported at distances of up to 600 miles from Iowa City. Some of these "television students" used home-built receiving apparatus, others purchased the $80 commercially produced 45-line Echophone TV set recommended as suitable by Dr. Kurtz. The largest catchment area was Chicago, where there were estimated to be 1,000 home-based sets in operation by 1934. A "large-screen" set was installed in the Iowa Memorial Union for the benefit of students.

The first electronic high-definition educational station was KUHT Houston, bowing on 25 May 1953. This was the beginning of non-commercial television aimed at the general public in the United States and stemmed from the Federal Communications Commission's allocation of 242 channels for such stations, and the setting up of National Educational Television (NET) as a resource center. What was originally known as ETV (Educational Television) was changed to PTV (Public Television) in 1967 and three years later, under a centralized authority—the Corporation for Public Broadcasting—became PBS (Public Broadcasting Service). PBS transmissions were inaugurated on 5 October 1970, taking over the non-commercial functions of the NET programing facility.

THE FIRST TELEVISION EVANGELIST

was traveling preacher Rex Humbard, luminary of the Gospel Big Top Revue, who rented a movie theater in Akron, Ohio, in 1953 to put out a revivalist show shot live with a single TV camera. He had been inspired with the idea after seeing the rapt attention of a sidewalk crowd outside Akron department store O'Neill's watching a baseball game on a TV in the window. The power of the small screen to apparently mesmerize an audience could be harnessed, he reasoned, in the service of the Lord. Humbard built his own studio complex in 1958, naming it the Cathedral of Tomorrow. Its most striking feature was a giant cross suspended from the roof of the "nave" which was illuminated with 4,700 red, white, and blue lights. In 1970 he built the tallest building in Ohio, with a rotating restaurant and a 750-foot transmitting tower. By 1980 Humbard could be seen or heard via 207 broadcasting stations worldwide.

THE FIRST TELEVISION GAME SHOW

was a six-aside *Spelling Bee* hosted by question master Freddie Grisewood and presented by the BBC from Alexandra Palace, London, on 31 May 1938. This was followed by a number of rather more inventive quiz games, including a *General Knowledge Bee* with A. G. Street (15 October 1938), a *Tactile Bee* with John Betjeman and Christopher Stone (20 December 1938), a *Tasting Bee* with the first television cook (qv) Marcel Boulestin (10 July 1939), and a *Musical Bee* (15 August 1939).

U.S.: The first game show was *The Game*, a contest based on charades presented by Mike Stokey at 8 P.M.

on Saturdays on Don Lee Television's W6XAO Los Angeles for two months in 1939. Stokey was a student at Los Angeles City College and a keen participant in the Radio Club, whose members passed the time in playing charades between rehearsals. It was their version of charades, with rules and a scoring system, that Stokey adapted for television. Two teams of three, drawn from the Radio Club, competed against each other. A more sophisticated version of *The Game* was revived by Stokey as *The Pantomime Quiz* on CBS in 1949, for which he won the first Emmy presented for a game show.

One-off video presentations of radio game shows *Truth or Consequences* and *Uncle Jim's Question Bee* on NBC's WNBT were transmitted on the opening day of commercial television in the United States, 1 July 1941. The first game show series on commercial TV, which began the following day, was *The CBS Television Quiz*, which Gil Fates hosted weekly for a year.

THE FIRST TELEVISION HDTV

began with 17 days of satellite transmissions from the Seoul Olympics by Japan's public broadcaster NHK starting 17 September 1988. Some 3.72 million viewers watched the programs on analog Hi-Vision sets with screens of 1,125 scanning lines (compared to the 525 lines of conventional United States sets) that had been set up in 81 locations throughout Japan. Experimental transmissions on NHK's B5-2 channel for one hour daily followed on 3 June 1989. Regular Hi-Vision broadcasting was begun in November 1991 by a consortium of NHK, commercial broadcasters, and electronics manufacturers called the Hi-Vision Promotion Association. The original 36-inch Hi-Vision receivers cost 3.5 to 4.5 million yen ($18,325 to $23,560), way beyond the resources of even an affluent family, but by 1993 a 32-inch set was available for under 1 million yen ($5,000). When the Nagano Winter Olympics were broadcast in 1998, there were 739,000 sets in use in Japan. HDTV in Japan became **digital** in 2000, digital standard-definition TV having been launched on 1 October 1996.

U.S.: HDTV and digital terrestrial television (DTV) were launched in the United States as a package.

The first transmission by a regular TV station was a one-off made on 23 July 1996 by WRAL Raleigh, N.C., of a baseball game to a single 46-inch Panasonic HDTV receiver at a local Dallas Circuit City store. Full-service HDTV digital broadcasting was due to begin on 1 November 1998, but the flight of Sen. John Glenn aboard the space shuttle *Discovery* 36 years after his inaugural voyage into space provided an irresistible opportunity for a public preview. Produced and broadcast by the Harris Corporation, a 70-minute live program showing the launch was transmitted from Kennedy Space Center in Florida, with support from WRAL-HD Raleigh and Japan's NHK Broadcasting Corporation on 29 October 1998 to network affiliates of CBS, ABC, NBC, Fox, and PBS. It was received in 18 cities across the nation and at Kennedy Space Center itself. Although there were scarcely any HDTV receivers in private hands at the time, viewing facilities were provided at stores, museums, TV stations, NASA headquarters, and the National Press Club in Washington, D.C. One of the outlets was Procter & Gamble headquarters in Cincinnati, the first HDTV commercials being broadcast during the show for P&G products such as Tide, Scope, Pampers, Head & Shoulders, and Bounty. Four days later some 40 stations throughout the United States began transmitting digital HDTV signals.

THE FIRST

TELEVISION: INTERNATIONAL TRANSMISSION BY SATELLITE

as part of the regular program schedule was made via *Telstar* from and to the United States on 23 July 1962 and was viewed by 200 million people in 16 countries. As *Telstar* was in line of sight from both sides of the Atlantic for only about 18 minutes in each 2½-hour orbit, it was divided into two 18-minute segments. The North American contribution comprised baseball from Chicago, a presidential press conference from Washington, D.C., scenes from a performance of *Macbeth* in Ontario, the Seattle World's Fair, the United Nations building in New York and Niagara. On the next orbit pictures from nine European capitals were beamed to the United States and Canada.

These magazine-style programs could just as effectively have been sent "down the line" or transmitted from film, but with orbital satellites only allowing for fairly brief transmissions at certain hours they were not generally practicable for live news or sports. There was, however, at least one notable news event transmitted via orbital satellites, when *Telstar*s I and II were used simultaneously to broadcast coverage of U.S. astronaut Gordon Cooper in Mercury *Faith 7* on 15 May 1963 and his rescue from the Pacific Ocean the following day after he had made an emergency landing. Continuous live international programming only became a reality the following year with the launch of the geostationary satellite *Syncom III*, which reached its station over the International Date Line just in time to transmit the opening of the Tokyo Olympics to the United States on 10 October 1964.

THE FIRST **TELEVISION NEWS**

appeared on the very small screens of mechanical receivers in the pre-electronic era. The earliest evidence of general news reporting on TV comes from a program schedule for radio station WAAQ Chicago for 22 April 1931 which indicates that a 12-minute roundup of news by S. W. Lincoln was simulcast on television via sister station W9XAP. Both stations were owned by the *Chicago Daily News*. Perhaps typically for Chicago, sports news was given more airtime than general news, a 15-minute program anchored by Hal Totten being televised at 6:30 P.M. daily. Other news simulcasts of the pre-1939 era before full-service include a 5-minute daily bulletin at 11 P.M. daily from the Montreal Television Co.'s VE9EC Montreal (jointly owned by radio station CKAC) starting 19 July 1932 and John Cameron Swayze's daily radio (KMBC) and television (W9XAC) *Journal Post News Flashes* from Kansas City between 24 January 1933 and c. 1937.

Out on the West Coast, Don Lee Television's W6XAO became the first television station to transmit specially filmed reports of a news event the day after the Los Angeles earthquake of 10 March 1933. These continued for three days following the disaster and those outside the tiny cadre of TV "hams" with their own, in most cases home-built, receivers could view the scenes of search and rescue among the devastation at either of the two department stores that happened to be giving TV demonstrations at the time. Shortly after this W6XAO was also the first TV station to start airing regular cinema newsreels, *Pathé Newsreel* being shown twice weekly from 4 April 1933 and additionally *Paramount News* twice weekly starting 1 September.

W6XAO had been the first TV station in America to transmit high-definition live programming on a regular schedule in 1936 (SEE BELOW **television service**). At an uncertain date in 1938 it became the first all-electronic station in the world to offer a nightly newscast. Titled *World News*, this was presented by Bob Young, Hugh Brundage, Norman Nesbitt, and James Doyle based on wire-service reports received from Transradio Press and International News Service. Thirty years on Bob Young was the ABC *Evening News* anchor at the time of the assassination of Dr. Martin Luther King Jr. Brundage stayed in Los Angeles to head the newsroom at KMPC Radio and became news anchor at KTLA Television. Norman Nesbitt played a newsreader in Republic Pictures's 1944 serial *Captain America* and an announcer in the 1949 Maureen O'Hara starrer *A Woman's Secret* before joining KRIZ Phoenix as a presenter.

When full-service high-definition television programing in the United States began in April 1939 on NBC's W2XBS, Lowell Thomas's news broadcasts on the NBC radio network were also carried on television nightly at 6:45 for 15 minutes. On occasions when Thomas could not be bothered to come to the studio and instead read the radio news by land-line from his home, announcer Ray Forrest would stand in for him as TV news anchor. Unlike the radio newscasters, with their forceful, rapid-fire style of presentation, Forrest adopted a relaxed, informal manner that suited someone who had, in effect, been invited into the viewer's living room. He was one of the earliest performers on television to realize that the medium demanded a different style of presentation. Indeed, so much did viewers feel an affinity with him that he frequently received invitations from viewers to drop in for dinner if he was passing by.

From 3 May 1939 W2XBS carried a regular 10-minute local-interest newsreel entitled *NBC Tele-Topics*, specially filmed for television, that aired on Saturday afternoons at 3:20. In October of that year the Philco television station W3XE Philadelphia began a regular high-definition program service and, according to a progress report written by program manager E. N. Alexander early in 1941, there were "News Programs, with world-famed war correspondent and Philco News Commentator, Frasier Hunt." It is not clear whether this consisted of straight news reporting or commentary. If the former, then Frasier Hunt would probably have some claim to have been the world's first TV news presenter to be engaged as such, as opposed to the practice elsewhere of televising radio newscasters as they read the news for a primarily radio audience.

Nevertheless NBC's nightly television news was still radio-led and there was no attempt to adapt the material for a viewing audience. The pioneer in this respect was rival CBS's station WCBW, which was the first (with the possible exception of W3XE) to hire a dedicated news team, in the persons of two young men in their early twenties of limited broadcasting experience but boundless enthusiasm. Copyboy Robert Skedgell was promoted to the post of scriptwriter for television news, the first such post at any station, while Richard Hubbell became what was probably the world's first full-time news anchor. Hubbell was one of the original TV team at CBS who had been involved in sporadic experimental telecasts prior to the launch of WNBT on 1 July 1941, but had never been required to perform live on camera before. Together the two produced the twice-daily show at 2:30 P.M. and 8 P.M., their principal visual aids being three 3' x 3' maps showing the principal theaters of war. These could be rotated to show larger-scale maps of battle areas, with silhouettes of tanks, planes, and ships to illustrate strength and arrows to indicate advances or retreats. About 90 percent of news coverage was of the war. The regular cameraman was Edward Anhalt, who was also assigned the task of shooting local news. In an interview with television historian Jeff Kisseloff in *The Box* (1999), Anhalt recalled his good fortune in happening to be at a bank when it was raided by the Esposito brothers. He was able to film the shooting followed by the arrest and have it on air that night. When he filmed the burning of the liner *Normandie* (9 February 1942) he was less fortunate, as Naval Intelligence agents confiscated his film and it was only several days later that CBS was able to transmit the heavily censored remaining footage after its release. Some of the assignments were hazardous. On one occasion Anhalt was instructed to dive into the Hudson River in a diving suit to film an area of Dyckman Street that was pouring raw sewage into the river. He got his scoop but not without the attentions of a colony of rats that crawled all over him.

Nightly network television news: The first was *News from Washington*, which began on the DuMont network on 16 June 1947 with Walter Compton as anchor. It ran for 11 months.

News in color: The first was NBC's *Camel News Caravan*, with 16mm color film inserts, on 16 February 1954.

SEE ALSO **war correspondent: television**.

THE FIRST **TELEVISION: PAY TV**

was inaugurated with 300 subscribers as Phonevision by the Zenith Radio Corporation in Chicago on 1 January 1951. Programming of this cable service consisted of up-to-date feature films, with three on the first day: *April Showers* with Jack Carson at 4 P.M.; *Welcome Stranger* with Bing Crosby at 7 P.M.; and *Homecoming* with Clark Gable and Lana Turner at 9 P.M. Cost per film was $1. Scrambled signals were unscrambled via the telephone circuit. Much of the appeal of the service was that the films were new, whereas regular TV stations were only able to offer movies at least seven years old and these were often poor-quality prints.

Satellite TV service: The first was launched in the United States by Home Box Office, a division of the Time Warner Entertainment Co., on 30 September 1975, transmitting via the Satcom satellite to their existing cable network. The first presentation was the heavyweight championship fight in Manila between Muhammad Ali and Joe Frazier. Within five years the opportunity to see major movies within months of their first-run release had proved so popular that the number of subscribers had grown from 300,000 to 6 million. By 1983 it had doubled to 12 million.

Direct satellite broadcasting (DBS) via dish decoders fixed to the roof of the subscriber was launched in Japan by NHK on its new BS-1 channel via the BS-2a satellite on 12 May 1984 with 18 hours of mainly news and sports programming a day. Satellite dishes and decoders had been placed on the market by Toshiba two months earlier, priced at ¥110,000 and ¥130,000, respectively. BS-2 followed in December 1986 with movies, concerts, and drama.

U.S.: The first DBS service was Primestar, started by a consortium of nine cable companies and satellite operator GE American in July 1991 in 38 communities not served by traditional cable. Primestar offered a choice of seven superstations and three pay-per-view channels. By the latter part of 1993 there were 60,000 subscribers.

THE FIRST **TELEVISION PERFORMER**

(professional artiste) in the United States, and possibly the world (but SEE BELOW), was Irish-American comedian A. Dolan, engaged by the American Telephone & Telegraph Co. to provide a "short act of monologue and song" during an experimental transmission from the AT&T wireless station in Whippany, N.J., to the Bell Telephone Laboratories in New York City on 7 April 1927. This was the first public demonstration of television in the United States, and arguably the first occasion on which television had been used as an entertainment medium anywhere in the world. It was viewed by an invited audience in New York City, 22 miles from the transmitting station, on a large-screen grid receiver giving an image measuring 2' x 2½'. The head and shoulders of the artiste were seen approximately life-size. Interest in the technical achievement eclipsed any attention that Dolan's performance may have deserved, the few facts about it on record being that he wore an Irish costume and side-whiskers, and that the broken clay pipe in his mouth was clearly discernible on the television screen.

After his "oirish" act, Dolan disappeared for a quick change, then returned to the screen "black-faced with a new line of jokes in Negro dialect." He concluded with "a short humorous dialect talk." Nothing is known about Dolan, not even his first name. The editor would like to hear from anyone with biographical information.

At about this time the Welsh-born ventriloquist Arthur Price performed at the Baird laboratories at Motograph House in London. Price was then the best-known ventriloquist in Britain and one of the highest paid entertainers on the variety circuit. He demonstrated his skills in front of the scanner accompanied by his dummy Sailor Jim, an able seaman who played foil to Price's characterization of a naval officer. Whether he performed his most famous piece of business, in which Sailor Jim sang while Price quaffed a glass of ale, is not recorded. In October 1928 the *Windsor Magazine* published a photograph of Price and Sailor Jim in the studio with a caption saying that the occasion was "one of the early experimental transmissions." As "early" could hardly be the same year, this suggests 1926 or 1927—whether before or after Dolan's performance will probably never be known.

The first performer to appear regularly on television was vocalist Lulu Stanley, who made her debut on Baird Television in London on 30 September 1929 singing "He's Tall, Dark and Handsome" and "Grandma's Proverbs." Seven years later, after frequent appearances on the Baird and subsequent BBC low-definition service, she made the transition to high-definition full-service television when she performed on BBC Television from Alexandra Palace, London, in November 1936.

Artiste under exclusive contract for television appearances: The first was Natalie Towers, a recent graduate of Wellesley College in Massachusetts, who was introduced to viewers of CBS station W2XAB New York by Mayor Jimmy Walker on 21 July 1931. According to the *Wellesley Magazine* for April 1931, their now celebrated alumnus had been living on 10¢ a day, "then was offered a $500 a week job which she gave up for the regular broadcasting work." Miss Towers's father, who had wanted her to become a doctor, was shocked by her declared intention of becoming an actress, but he was mollified when he heard that she was going into the more "respectable" medium of television. Only after she had been hired did CBS reveal to her that she would be presenting *The Natalie Towers Show* three times a week and that she would have

to script it herself. On one occasion she appeared on camera wearing $660,000 worth of jewels for a publicity stunt and guarded by ten of New York's finest.

Black performer on television: The first was the South Carolina–born actress-singer Nina Mae McKinney, transmitted in a BBC variety program from Studio BB Portland Place, London, on 17 February 1933. Josephine Baker, then resident in Paris, performed for the BBC low-definition TV service on 4 October the same year.

The first black performers on high-definition television were song-and-dance team Buck and Bubbles, otherwise Ford Lee "Buck" Washington and John William "Bubbles" Sublett, both from Louisville, Ky., who appeared in the opening show from the world's first full-service television station, BBC Alexandra Palace, London, on 2 November 1936. Four days later the first black performers on American television made their debut when the Ink Spots close-harmony quartet (Indianapolis natives Hoppy Jones, Deek Watson, Bill Kenny, and Charlie Fuqua) appeared in a 40-minute variety show staged by NBC in New York for their inaugural demonstration to the press of all-electronic, high-definition TV.

Television star: The first artiste to be referred to as such was CBS's Grant Kimball by the *New York Sun* in its issue for 12 November 1932. Previous to this date, however, the *New York World Telegram* had said on 2 May 1931: "A regular Saturday evening feature over W2XCD, Alice Remsen has built a television public for herself distinct from her radio fans." Alice Remsen was an English actress and singer who also appeared in the weekly WOR radio program *Footlight Echoes*.

The first performer to achieve celebrity solely for television appearances was Canadian-born Joan Miller, the "switchboard girl" who introduced the guests on the BBC's flagship series *Picture Page* from its debut on 8 October 1936 until the outbreak of war in 1939. She also appeared in eight television dramas during this period. The first in the United States was Helen Parrish, a pretty young actress chosen to co-host NBC's *Hour Glass*, a weekly variety show that ran from 14 June 1946 to 6 March 1947. As the first TV show to be adequately budgeted, *Hour Glass* benefited from the fact that the talent Ms. Parrish presented were household names. Soon hers became one too, not only in the 20,000 households in New York City that boasted a TV set and the numerous TV-equipped bars with their half-million-strong audience, but also among non-viewers, owing to the amount of press coverage the show attracted.

THE FIRST TELEVISION PRODUCER

was Harold Bradly, appointed by the Baird Co. as studio director in charge of production for the program service transmitted from the company's Long Acre studios in London commencing 30 September 1929. Sydney Moseley was appointed director of television programs.

The first producers making programs for electronic, high-definition television were appointed by the BBC Television Service that started full-service transmissions to the general public from Alexandra Palace, London, on 2 November 1936. Headed by programs organizer Cecil Madden, who also produced the variety programs, they were Cecil Lewis (talks), George More O'Ferrall (drama), Stephen Thomas (music and ballet), and Dallas Bower (opera and film). On 5 January 1937 Cecil Lewis was succeeded by the first **woman TV producer**, Mary Adams. She brought an idiosyncratic flair to the job; when the director of the National Gallery, Kenneth Clark, gave a talk on the Surrealists she had the studio filled with gas cookers wrapped in bicycle tires.
U.S.: The first producer of electronic high-definition programs was Thomas H. Hutchinson, appointed program director for RCA's W2XBS New York in 1937. He had been an actor and theater director before joining NBC radio in 1928. Six producers with Hutchinson at their head comprised the team when RCA's program service went public in April 1939. Together with John Porterfield he had already produced more than 200 programs for nine months of audience reaction tests starting in July 1938.

The first woman producer in the United States was Francis Buss, who made her debut with the CBS game show *Missus Goes A-Shopping*, televised from various New York City supermarkets starting 3 August 1944. Nearly seven years later she would produce and direct the world's first color program (SEE **television, color**).

THE FIRST TELEVISION: PUBLIC BROADCASTING SERVICE (PBS)

SEE **television, educational station**.

THE FIRST TELEVISION RECEIVER

commercially produced, was manufactured by Waldo Saul for reception of low-definition transmissions from WIXAY in Lexington, Mass. The mechanical set operated with a Nipkow scanning disk to give a square image of 48 lines at 15 frames per second. Saul advertised components for sale in the 11 June 1928 issue of the *Boston Post*, owners of WIXAY, though the set was also available ready-made. Programs were transmitted nightly for 30 minutes, mainly simulcasts from the *Post*'s radio station WLEX.

Probably produced the same month was a receiver advertised for sale at $75 by the Daven Corporation of Newark, N.J., in the July 1928 issue of *Television* (New York). These sets were adjustable to receive 24-, 36-, or 48-line transmissions. Construction kits were offered for sale at the same time. There was no television service operating in New York City at this time, though a very rudimentary series of experimental transmissions on a scheduled basis had already begun in Schenectady, N.Y. (SEE **television service**). Also in 1928 the Pilot Electrical Co. of Brooklyn launched its mechanical receiver, a free-standing model with cabriole legs designed by Theodore Nakken. These "televisors," as they were described, were designed for viewing the television images transmitted for 5 minutes in every hour by Hugo Gernsback's New York radio station WRNY starting in August 1928.

In August 1931, the New York correspondent of the London *Observer* reported that there were an estimated 9,000 television sets in New York City and approximately 30,000 elsewhere in the United States. Prices of the half-dozen different models available, which included the Hollis Baird, the Western Electric Visionette, and the Jenkins Universal, ranged from $80 to $160 for a ready-made set and $36 for a construction kit. The following year W.C. Rawls & Co. of Norfolk, Va., put on the market a luxury, large-screen set in fumed oak at $295. "Large screen" in this case meant 11.3 inches square, but this was considerably in advance of previous image sizes.

The first commercially produced **electronic TV receiver** (i.e., with no moving parts) was placed on the market in January 1935 by Gillavision Television of 23 Chilworth Street, London, priced at 55 guineas ($288). A 4-foot-high free-standing cabinet model with a 5-inch-diameter circular screen, it was designed to receive BBC 30-line transmission of 261 meters, though the manufacturers claimed it could be "easily converted to any other definition and wavelength."

High-definition television receivers: The first to be produced commercially were exhibited at the Radiolympia exhibition in London in August 1936, when the public were offered a choice of 17 models by 10 different manufacturers at prices ranging from 85 guineas ($446) to 120 guineas ($630). According to Sydney Moseley, in *Television Today and Tomorrow* (1940), the first of these sets on the market was the Baird T5, a mirror-top model with a 12" x 9" screen. Full public service having begun on 2 November, sales figures totaled a disappointing 280 by the end of the year. It was thought that most potential buyers were waiting to see if the prices would come down, and in February 1937 the manufacturers felt forced to comply, EMI and HMV reducing their 98-guinea ($515) set to 60 guineas ($315) and Baird cutting the 85-guinea ($446) model to 55 guineas ($288). Further reductions followed in August and sales began to pick up. One purchaser that year was a Sussex farmhand who had never been to London in his life and, having invested his life savings in a set, said that now he would never need to, as he could sit and watch what was going on "up there" by his own fireside. By the outbreak of war in September 1939, there were an estimated 20,000 receivers in use, all within a 50- to 60-mile radius of London, with a probable viewing audience of 100,000.

U.S.: The first high-definition electronic sets available to the public were two models manufactured by Communicating Systems Inc. that went on sale at Piser's Furniture Store in the Bronx, N.Y., in April 1938. The announcement of "Television's here!" brought a crowd of 4,000 rubberneckers who jammed the store to marvel at the $125 version with its 3-inch screen and the deluxe $250 one with its massive 5-inch screen.

Shortly afterward the receivers also went on sale at Bloomingdale's in Manhattan and Abraham Strauss in Brooklyn. Purchasers were able to pick up RCA's sporadic experimental high-definition transmissions from W2XBS before the start of regular service in April 1939.

It is generally recorded that the first high-definition sets in America went on sale at Macy's on 1 May 1939, the day after W2XBS began full-service transmissions. However, not only were the Communications Systems sets already on sale, but a 5-inch receiver from Andrea priced at $189.50 was advertised for sale at Bloomingdale's in the *New York Times* for 30 March 1939. DuMont also launched its 180 table model at $325 several weeks in advance of RCA's regular service. Allen B. DuMont had visited England in 1936–37 and brought back a 1936 Cossor Model-137T on which he based the design of the 180, launched at the Davega City Radio Store, Madison Square Garden. The sets that went on sale at Macy's on 1 May included the Andrea and DuMont models (though not their predecessors from Communications Systems) as well as a 5-inch Westinghouse receiver priced at $199.50 and 5-inch, 9, and 12-inch sets from General Electric at $175 to $600 and RCA models of the same dimensions costing $199.50 to $600. Uptake was modest; 800 sets had been sold by the end of December, while another 4,000 or so remained on dealers' shelves. As in Britain three years earlier, the public was prepared to wait for price reductions. The first sets to go on sale outside New York were from Philco in conjunction with the inception of its W3XE station in Philadelphia in October 1939 and in Los Angeles, where Gilfillan Inc. advertised its G12 model in the *Los Angeles Times* for 10 December 1939 for viewing the long-established program service from Don Lee's station W6XAO.

Elsewhere in the world, Soviet Russia had a 7-inch table model 17TH-1 and a 9-inch mirror lid console TK-1 that were manufactured from 1938 to '40 for reception from the Moscow and Leningrad stations. (Presumably these were for the nomenclatura rather than the general public.) In Germany high-definition receivers were not available to the public until 1939. The German radio manufacturers had been ready to start production of 180-line sets as early as 1935, when 20 different models from 7 firms were exhibited at the Berlin Radio Exhibition. The Nazi authorities, however, were determined that television should not be a preserve of the rich and ordered that production should be halted until the Post Office and the radio manufacturers had succeeded in designing a "People's Television Set" that could be sold for about $60. This venture suffered much the same fate as the Volkswagen, which had been inspired by the same motives. The set was put on sale in Berlin on 28 July 1939, but by the outbreak of war a month later only 50 out of a proposed initial production series of 10,000 were in use.

Estimates vary for the number of television receivers produced in the United States before manufacture was suspended in late 1941. One source quotes 7,000; another 20,000 with about half that number sold. The British figure was 19,800 when BBC Television was suspended on the outbreak of war in Europe in September 1939. A surprising number of pre-war American and British sets survive. According to a count by the Early Television Museum of Columbus, Ohio, they know of 147 sets in Britain but believe there are many more unlisted; and they know of 214 American models, including prototypes and those made from construction kits. One of the surviving U.S. examples is an 8-inch General Electric model, provenance unknown, preserved at President Franklin D. Roosevelt's family home Hyde Park, N.Y. But in the Roosevelt Archives there is a letter from the president dated 30 August 1939 thanking NBC's Carlton D. Smith for installing at Hyde Park a 12-inch RCA receiver. Was FDR the first American with sets in different rooms?

The point at which TV became a significant medium in the United States was 1949–50 when the number of receivers rose from 940,000 (2.3 percent of households) to 3,870,000 (9 percent). The 50 percent mark for TV households was passed in 1953–54. It reached 80 percent in 1957–58, 90 percent in 1962, and 95 percent in 1969. Saturation was attained in 1981 at more than 98 percent, and the figure has remained constant since then.

Color receiver: The first manufactured for sale was the CBS Columbia Air-King Model 12CC2, production of which had begun on 20 September 1951. The first advertisement for it was run by Davega and Gimbels Department Store in the *New York Times* for 28 September, price $499.95. The Air-King was withdrawn from sale on 19 October, the day before CBS closed its fledgling color service; all unsold sets were recalled and destroyed. Production figures differ: CBS claimed 400 produced, 300 shipped; rival DuMont declared the total produced to have been 200, with 100 sold.

Color only returned to American TV screens three years later with the introduction of the first compatible service (SEE **television, color**), meaning that a color set could also receive black-and-white channels. The first receiver to go on sale in anticipation of a permanent color service was the Admiral Corp.'s 17-inch Model C1617A on 30 December 1953 priced at $1,175. A single unit is known to survive, in the hands of collector Bruce Buchanan. RCA's own CT-100 sets followed at $1,000 in the spring of 1954. Only 5,000 had been sold by the end of the year and it was not until 1960, after spending $130 million in development and marketing, that RCA recorded its first profit from color TV. As with the inception of black-and-white television, the core market was bars. Sales began to take off in 1965, when they were double that of the previous year, but it was not until 1968 that color receivers outsold monochrome for the first time. The 50-50 mark for color TV households was reached in 1971–72 and saturation (over 98 percent) in 1991.

LCD receiver: Japanese manufacturer Sharp launched a 3-inch color TFT LCD set in 1987 with the world's highest resolution. The first full-size set was the 14-inch thin-profile, high-definition Sharp TFT LCD of 1988. Sharp offered the first **flat-screen set**, a 3-inch-deep receiver with an 8.6-inch-high LCD screen, in 1991 at approx $4,000.

Widescreen receiver: The first available in the United States was Thomson Consumer Electronics' analog Cinema Screen of 1993.

Plasma receiver: The first was a 21-inch model introduced by Fujitsu at $10,000 in 1993. The company followed this with the first plasma TV manufactured in significant quantities, the 4-inch deep 42-inch-wide Image Site unveiled at the Olympic Games in Atlanta in August 1996. Series production began at Fujitsu's factory at Miyazaki, Japan, in October and the first sets on sale in the United States were available by the spring of 1997 at $20,000.

Digital/HDTV receiver: The first in the United States was RCA's DCT100, launched in August 1998 at $649 in anticipation of the launch of terrestrial digital broadcasting on 1 November 1998. (SEE ALSO **television, HDTV**.)

3-D receiver: The first was the Korean-made 46-inch Hyundai E465 with LCD display that went on sale at 23 Tokyo stores for $4,980 on 12 April 2008. Three-D programs were already being broadcast by Nippon BS Broadcasting Corporation, which had begun transmitting for 30 minutes daily on Japan's Channel 11 on 1 December 2007.

U.S.: Panasonic's 50-inch TC-P50VT20 launched at Best Buy in Manhattan on 10 March 2010 with a $2,499 price tag. Regular programming in 3-D began with the launch of sports, entertainment, and movie channels by DirecTV three months later.

THE FIRST
TELEVISION RECEIVER REMOTE CONTROL

was the Zenith Electronics "Lazy Bones" of 1950, which connected a push-button control to the set by wire. This was succeeded in 1955 by their Flash-Matic, which dispensed with wires and operated by directing a beam of light to photocells at each corner of the screen. It was less than ideal, since the cell could also be activated by sunbeams or other stray light sources. The radio wave system that followed had a tendency to change the channel on next door's TV, while an ultrasonic version might be triggered by a ringing phone or even a clanking dog chain. The remote in its present form, operated by ultrasonic radio, was another Zenith innovation, devised by Dr. Robert Adler and launched in 1956 as an adjunct to the Zenith Space Command 400 receiver. Principal drawback was cost, adding about $100 to the price of a set, and the remote only became a living room icon (and the item in it most frequently mislaid) after TV tuners had become all-electronic in the 1970s.

Dr. Adler recalled that the Zenith CEO's motivation in developing remote control was to eliminate commercials, which he felt were destroying television.

THE FIRST **TELEVISION RECORDING**

system was Phonovision, developed by John Logie Baird at his laboratories at Motograph House in Upper Saint Martin's Lane, London, and first publicly demonstrated at Leeds University on 6 September 1927. It allowed for low-frequency signals to be reproduced on conventional wax disks, using much the same technique as in stereo audio recording. The intention was to record programs that could be purchased by the viewing public and played back by means of a simple attachment to a Baird low-definition Televisor. In practice, it was not possible to play the visual signals back other than in audio form. At least, not until the 1980s, when a computer buff called Donald F. McLean went searching for the very few surviving examples of the original recorded images. These number six in total, dated from 20 September 1927 to 28 March 1928, most bearing the label of the Columbia Graphophone Co. (the British-owned company that established CBS in the United States). Using modern techniques McLean was able to restore the vision, which includes two recognizable human faces identified as Baird's young assistant Wally Fowlkes and his secretary Mabel Pounsford. These recordings can be viewed on tape at the National Media Museum in Bradford, Yorkshire.

A small number of enthusiastic amateurs among the several thousand who tuned in to the Baird and later BBC 30-line broadcasts in the early 1930s made their own video recordings, despite the disability of not being able to play them back. Four of these, from two different sources, have survived and are the only recordings of actual program material (as opposed to lab tests) from the mechanical era of low-definition television. The earliest was made on a standard Silvatone aluminum disk designed for home audio recording and can be precisely dated, as Donald F. McLean's 1994 restoration reveals a 4-minute video clip of a dance troupe called the Paramount Astoria Girls performing high kicks in bathing costumes. This was one of the acts in the BBC program *Looking In*, billed as "the world's first ever television review [*sic*]" and aired from 11:12 P.M. to 11:53 P.M. on 21 April 1933. The other disks were also aluminum, without trade labels, but one of them bears the scrawled inscription

WOMAN LARGE HEAD. While two of the recordings show a female popular singer and a male opera singer whom it has not proved possible to identify, the woman described unflatteringly as having a "large head" was eventually tracked down by McLean. She was Betty Bolton, an extraordinarily versatile singing star of vaudeville, theater, dance bands, radio, records, the movies, and early television. Already a veteran of the earlier Baird Co. public transmissions, she was also the very first performer to appear on the BBC's low-definition TV service when it began on 22 August 1932. Because of the frequency of her performances, it has not been possible to date the recording, but McLean believes it was made in 1934 or 1935. Happily Miss Bolton was still alive to see the restored video clip; in the inaugural program of the BBC's digital widescreen television service in 1998 she was shown watching her 30-line recorded image. By then, sixty-eight years after her TV debut, there were no lines, only pixels.

All the pioneer recordings noted above are described with full technical background in Donald F. McLean's *Restoring Baird's Image*, published by the Institution of Electrical Engineers, London, in 2000.

U.S.: In February 1929 Dr. Frank Gray of the Bell Telephone Laboratories announced a system of directly recording TV images of 50 lines onto 35mm film at 18 pictures per second. General Electric's WGY Schenectady adopted a similar method of telerecording the following year. Both these scanning techniques gave results superior to Phonovision and had the merit of not having to wait sixty years for playback. None of the recordings have been located.

The earliest recording known high-definition telerecording in the United States is a 4-minute silent clip of a BBC transmission from London picked up at the Frequency Measuring Laboratory, Riverhead, N.Y., in 1938 with an antenna 800 feet long by 150 feet wide. The 16mm film recording was located in 1999 by British early-TV buff Andy Emmerson after a five-year search. The fuzzy images show presenter Jasmine Bligh and an excerpt from an unidentified costume drama or possibly operetta.

The earliest recording of an American program is a 5-minute home movie, taken direct from the television screen, of edited highlights of NBC's 31 August 1939 transmission of Dion Boucicault's melodrama *The Streets of New York*, directed by Anthony Mann and featuring Jennifer Jones. The silent footage is preserved at New York's Museum of Television & Radio as Program No. 005494. There is nothing in the catalog to indicate its significance, but as television historian Michael Ritchie has observed, "for anyone researching the history of television, it is like the Dead Sea Scrolls."

Telerecording to be broadcast: The first was made in London on 9 November 1947 by Philip Dorté, BBC Television Outside Broadcasts supervisor. He filmed the Remembrance Day Ceremony at the Cenotaph in London's Whitehall direct from the TV monitor screen at Alexandra Palace, using a specially synchronized camera developed after twelve months of experiment. The ceremony having been seen live by viewers in the morning, it was repeated when the recording was transmitted the same evening.

The system was also used for the first telerecording to be shown in the United States. This was the BBC coverage of the wedding of Princess Elizabeth and Prince Philip, which was transmitted live in Britain on 20 November 1947 and in New York by NBC in the recorded version 32 hours later. It was seen by viewers before the first newsreel film of the event had reached theaters.

U.S.: The first recording system put into practical use was the Eastman Television Recorder, announced in January 1948 by Eastman Kodak, which had developed it in association with NBC and the Allen B. DuMont Studios. It was designed for making "kinescopes" of programs of up to 30 minutes' length for rebroadcasting by network stations yet to be linked by magnetic relay or cable. The first program series to be regularly pre-recorded was *The Ed Wynn Show*, shot on kinescope at the CBS studios in Los Angeles and networked from 6 October 1949 to 4 July 1950. Kinescopes were superseded in the late 1950s by the video recorder (qv).

TELEVISION REMOTE TRANSMISSION

as well as the first telecast of a news event was made by GEC's station WGY Schenectady, N.Y., on 22 August 1928 and showed Gov. Al Smith, Democratic candidate for president, delivering his acceptance speech for the nomination at Albany, N.Y. The tripod-mounted camera, a 24-hole scanning disk unit, was set up about 3 feet from the subject and there were banks of photoelectric cells on either side at a distance of 18 inches from Smith's face. From the hall the signals were sent 18 miles by landline to WGY for amplification and broadcasting within the area. While the rehearsals were very successful, the actual live transmission was marred owing to the powerful arc lights of the newsreel cameras. Nevertheless a report by an AT&T observer noted that "the first appearance of television pick-up outside the laboratory is forerunner of the day when such apparatus will be as familiar as the present microphone, and it may sometime be expected to find its place at all great public functions, at athletics events, etc..." These predictions would indeed be fulfilled, but not during the era of low-definition mechanical television.

High-definition remote: The first followed the opening of the Berlin television station of Germany's Reichs Rundfunk on 22 March 1935. From there on the world's first mobile television unit, the 3½-ton Mercedes-Benz Fernseh-Aufnahmewagen, was sent out on the streets daily to gather contributions for a program called *Spiegel des Tages* ("Mirror of the Day") that was transmitted in the evenings. The first major event to be televised to the viewing public (Al Smith's nomination telecast having been for the benefit of the press and the General Electric Co.'s technicians) was the Berlin Olympics of 1–16 August 1936, the output of four Farnsworth-system electronic cameras being seen by 150,000 viewers at the 28 public viewing rooms in Berlin, Potsdam, and Leipzig.

On 12 May of the following year BBC Television transmitted coverage of the Coronation Procession of King George VI and Queen Elizabeth through the streets of London. This was the first major remote to be received by viewers in their own homes, the television audience being estimated at 50,000. It was a triumph for the infant BBC television service and the more so because the driving rain and darkening sky that rendered the newsreel cameras unusable failed to shut down the upstart TV cameras. The king had been primed in advance to look directly at them and rewarded loyal viewing subjects with his most winning smile.

U.S.: America's first high-definition remote was rather more mundane than Jesse Owens angering Hitler at the Olympics or the King of England playing to the camera, consisting of an exercise by the local fire department in Camden, N.J., televised by RCA in an experimental transmission on 24 April 1936. Thereafter any remotes were constrained by the length of a cable until RCA acquired two mobile units shortly before Christmas 1937. Starting 12 December these telemobiles were able to roam the New York area within 25 miles of the W2XBS transmitter atop the Empire State Building, sending back reports of fires and other newsworthy events and making the earliest attempts at broadcasting boxing and wrestling outside the studio. When full service began in April 1939, the first transmission was of President Franklin D. Roosevelt opening the New York World's Fair, followed over the next year by remotes of virtually every significant sporting activity (SEE BELOW **television: sport**).

Color remotes: Transmission began on 1 January 1954 when NBC's New York station WNBT introduced the world's first color mobile unit.

Telecopter: The first helicopter adapted for TV remotes was a Bell 47 that went into service with KTLA Los Angeles on 4 July 1958 to cover the congested city both for traffic news and action on the streets. It helped KTLA to earn a Peabody Award for their copter coverage of the Watts Riots in August 1965.

THE FIRST **TELEVISION SERVICE**

scheduled, was inaugurated by the General Electric Co.'s Station WGY, Schenectady, N.Y., on 10 May 1928. Transmissions were presented from 1:30 to 2 P.M. on Tuesdays, Thursdays, and Fridays using a low-definition system of mechanical scanning developed by Dr. Ernst Alexanderson. *Television* reported: "Only the faces of men talking, laughing or smoking will be broadcast; no elaborate effects are planned at this stage." The only structured regular program appears to have been WGY's director of programs Kolin Hager presenting the farm news and weather three times a week. There were also two "specials," mainly designed to attract press publicity, one of which was the world's first remote transmission (SEE **television remote transmission**): Gov. Al Smith's acceptance of the Democratic nomination for the presidency from Albany on 22 August 1928; and the world's first television drama (qv), *The Queen's Messenger*, on 11 September the same year. By this time the first commercially produced, albeit primitive, mechanical television receivers (qv) were on the market and enthusiastic radio hams were constructing their own sets. Reception could be had at considerable distances. In late 1928 Murry [*sic*] Mercier, who ran a radio service outlet in Columbus, Ohio, and his son of the same name built their own receiver that was able to pick up the WGY transmissions. On 28 November 1928 they sent a telegram saying that they had viewed a 15-minute transmission in which they had seen block letters, probably GE, from the upper left to the lower right of the screen, followed by a man's head turning from left to right. Such was the state of programming at the birth of regular television service.

The earliest attempt to provide entertainment on a regular basis took place on the other side of the Atlantic the same year. At midnight on 4 December 1928 the Baird Co. in London put on the first of a twice-weekly series of programs via 2TV London that could be received by the radio hams who had been licensed by John Logie Baird to build their own sets under his patents—reportedly 2,600 of them by the end of the year. The inaugural program was produced by studio manager A. F. Birch and consisted of vocal numbers by talented Baird Co. secretaries Dora Caffrey and Annie King, accompanied on the piano by Philip Hobson, who later recalled, "No extra pay, of course, let alone overtime, but it didn't matter and we all enjoyed doing it." Following this a Baird Concert Party was formed from the available talent, prominent among whom were baritone A. Calkin and Reginald Shaw, who specialized in minstrel songs. It is possible that matinee idol Jack Buchanan may have performed,

as he was a close friend of Baird's and a frequent visitor to the specially equipped **television studio**—the first in the world—at 133 Long Acre, London. It was also from here that the first comedy program (SEE **television drama: comedy**) was aired on 15 December 1928. Nowhere do these pioneer telecasts appear in the standard histories of television. Baird had been refused a license for public transmissions and, unusually for such an accomplished self-publicist, elected to maintain the lowest of profiles before he was authorized to start transmitting via a BBC transmitter in September 1929.

The first stations in the United States to offer regular entertainment programs were both located in Chicago: Western Television's W9XAO and the *Chicago Daily News*'s W9XAP. The former began its service at an uncertain date in 1930, though probably before W9XAP in August as it had the earlier call letter. By the following year the station is known to have been transmitting on a regular weekday schedule for about 3 hours a day. The programs included boxing, dancing, musical variety, and **live interviews**, including two notable ones with visiting Hollywood stars, cowboy hero Tom Mix and blonde venus Jean Harlow. On 12 January 1931 W9XAO presented a musical comedy entitled *Their Television Honeymoon*, arguably the first dramatic work written for the new medium (SEE **television drama**). During the fall of that year another first was achieved with the televising of several Saturday afternoon football games. Service continued until May 1933, when the FRC withdrew the frequency on which the audio outlet for the programs was being broadcast.

W9XAP Chicago began broadcasting on 27 August 1930 from studios in the *Daily News* building at 400 Madison Street with an opening program of vaudeville acts presented by Bill Hay, who was later renowned as the announcer for *Amos 'n' Andy*. Performers were drawn from the nearby Palace Theater, including Ransom Miles Sherman of *The Three Doctors* radio comedy team and Ken Murray, who twenty years later would host *The Ken Murray Show* on CBS. The station's inaugural play, staged on 7 January 1931, was Oliphant Down's one-act fantasy-melodrama *The Maker of Dreams*, starring Irene Walker, which was further distinguished by the fact that Max Factor of

Hollywood created the first **TV makeup** especially for it. The programs were seen by viewers from at least eighteen states, reports coming in from as far away as Richmond, Va., and Los Angeles.

There was a remarkable degree of cooperation between the two Chicago stations, which did not regard themselves as in competition with each other but rather as a partnership to further the development of television. Programs from each station were scheduled in order not to overlap each other and the same artists would appear on both. Technical resources were shared and Western Television engineers from W9XAO were known to help out in the studios of W9XAP.

W9CAP changed hands in November 1931 in a deal with NBC involving a half-share in radio station WMAQ. NBC continued to offer a program service until March 1933, when the decision was made to drop all work on mechanical TV in order to concentrate wholly on the development of an electronic system.

Other regular entertainment program services (as opposed to lab tests) were offered by W2XCR Jersey City from the fall of 1930 (earlier transmission of "radio movies" by the Jenkins Television system had been of silhouettes only); CBS's W2XB New York starting 21 July 1931; W1XG Boston from October 1931; W9XG Purdue University, which broadcast film only, mainly newsreels, from December 1931; W9XAC Kansas City and the Kansas State College of Agriculture's W9XAK, both late 1932; Don Lee's WX6 Los Angeles from December 1932; and W9XK at the University of Iowa (SEE **television, educational station**), which debuted on 25 January 1933. Of these by far the most sophisticated, imaginative, and varied programs were broadcast by CBS over W2XB New York. This was the first station to put a TV presenter under contract, "Miss Television" Natalie Towers (SEE **television performer**), other stations relying usually on the part-time services of announcers from affiliated radio stations. The usual television fare of vaudeville acts was leavened with fashion shows, boxing, baseball scores, live football, ballroom dancing, piano and bridge lessons, art shows, documentaries about Norway and India, a series on the aviation industry, a historical program for the George Washington Bicentennial, the first political ad (on behalf of the Democrats), and

the world's first TV drama series (qv). There was also a *Television Beauty Review* and a mystery series with special effects, *The Television Ghost—Murder Stories as Told by the Ghost of the Murdered*. CBS also pioneered (21 July 1932) with the transmission of video and audio on the same channel, other TV stations being video only with the sound broadcast through a separate radio channel. Broadcasting on a daily 8 to 11 P.M. schedule, with test transmissions between 2 and 6 in the afternoons, continued until 20 February 1933.

Elsewhere in the world at this time the BBC in London was offering four half-hour programs a week, principally vaudeville acts and illustrated talks, while other stations transmitting live action were also operating in Berlin, Paris, Rome, Montreal, Tokyo, Moscow, and Leningrad. Others aired only films.

High-definition television service: The first was officially inaugurated by the director-general of German Broadcasting, Herr Hadamovsky, on 22 March 1935, though in fact 180-line experimental transmissions on a regular schedule had been in progress for about six months. The scanning system was mechanical, but the receivers were all-electronic cathode-ray-tube models. Initially the programs were broadcast three times a week from 8:30 P.M. to 10 P.M., and the material consisted chiefly of film, including an excerpt from a main feature. There was a change of program once a week. No television sets were available to the general public, but there were 11 public viewing rooms in Berlin and one in Potsdam, each seating 30 people. There was also a Telecinema with a 4' x 3' screen in Berlin's Leipzigerstrasse with 100 seats. Free tickets were obtainable in advance from post offices, where most of the viewing rooms were situated. A contemporary report said that viewing rooms in the poorer areas were always well attended, particularly in the colder weather; those in residential areas were seldom full.

On 19 August 1935 a fire at the Berlin Radio Exhibition destroyed the two ultra-short-wave transmitters then in use, but new ones were quickly completed, and on 15 January 1936 the service reopened with a daily program from 8 P.M. to 9 P.M., repeated from 9 to 10 P.M. For the first time, live entertainment transmitted from studios in the Rognizstrasse supplemented filmed material. The first artiste to make her debut on a public high-definition (180-line) service was the soprano Inge Vesten. At this state of development only head-and-shoulder images were possible, though on 7 November a play titled *The Rocking Horse* was transmitted, one day after the BBC's first high-definition television play. A typical program, seen on Saturday, 24 October 1936, consisted of the following:

Newsreel

Theres Crones (extracts from the feature film of that name)

Streets Without Obstacles (educational film)

In the intervals between films violinist Erna Hohberg played the Czárdás by Monti; Carl Sollner sang and accompanied himself on a lute.

A higher definition of 441-lines was adopted on 1 November 1938. After the outbreak of war, the Reichs-Rundfunk-Gesellschaft continued transmitting on an increased schedule of up to 6 hours a day, principally for the benefit of hospitals and barracks, where receivers were installed for their morale and propaganda value. The service finally closed down on 23 November 1943, when the Berlin transmitter at Witzleben was destroyed by Allied bombing. German-controlled programs from the Paris Eiffel Tower transmitter continued until 16 August 1944, a week before Liberation.

U.S.: The first high-definition service was inaugurated by Don Lee Television's W6XAO Los Angeles on 15 June 1936 with 4 hours of film-only programming a day on 340 lines using all-electronic equipment (believed to be a world first; Germany went electronic the following month). Live programming began in April 1938 with a weekly schedule of four nights of studio-based productions, mainly using talent from the Mutual Don Lee radio network, and two nights of film, principally newsreels and educational features and the occasional feature movie (SEE **film on television**). Outside talent was recruited for plays and the first drama series on high-definition television (SEE **television drama**). The service was experimental and TV receivers were not available to the general public in association with the program output until December 1939.

Full-service television was inaugurated by the BBC from Alexandra Palace in London on 2 November 1936.

The claim that this was the first fully public service in the world is based on the fact that high-definition television receivers (qv) were on general sale, and that the service was recognized by the government, the Post Office, and the BBC as a permanent entertainment medium. Only one aspect of the transmissions can be described as experimental. Initially, the programs were broadcast by two separate systems on alternate days. The Baird system employed mechanical scanning and transmission on 240 lines, while the Marconi-EMI system used electronic Emitron cameras and gave a picture with 405-line definition. From 5 February 1937 the latter system alone was used, and it remained the standard definition until the introduction of an alternative BBC channel in 1964.

The opening program of the service at 3:30 P.M. featured performances by singer Adele Dixon and two African-American dancer-comedians, Buck and Bubbles (SEE **television performer**). The evening program consisted of a special BBC film, *Television Comes to London*, and the second edition of the first **series** on full-service televison, *Picture Page*, a topical magazine program produced by Cecil Madden, the inaugural program having been aired from Radiolympia (8 October). Among those appearing were the record-breaking pilot Jim Mollison, the Pearly King and Queen of Blackfriars, ghost-story writer Algernon Blackwood, and the Lord Mayor's coachman. The day's transmissions ended with *British Movietone News*.

Originally the BBC television service broadcast on weekdays only for one hour in the afternoon and one hour in the evening. By the autumn of 1939 there were about 4 hours of programs on weekdays and 90 minutes on Sundays. The service closed down on 1 September 1939 for the duration of the war. There was no closing announcement, and the last words heard by viewers were from Mickey Mouse saying, in imitation of Greta Garbo, "Ah tink ah go home."

When the service resumed in 1946 one of the original announcers, Jasmine Bligh, reappeared on screen and said, "Sorry for the interruption of our program service. Our next presentation is . . ." Then they repeated the Disney cartoon Herr Hitler had interrupted.

U.S.: RCA's W3XBC New York became the first all-electronic high-definition station to go public, in the sense that television receivers (qv) could be bought in the shops, with an inaugural transmission of the opening of the New York World's Fair by President Franklin D. Roosevelt on 30 April 1939. Produced by Burke Crotty with a single camera, the program could be seen on the 200 sets already existing in New York City (mainly owned by TV executives and engineers and by prospective sponsors) and 12 special receivers for public viewing in the RCA Pavilion at the World's Fair. Throughout the fair an RCA mobile transmitting van was stationed at the Pavilion to do live vox pop programs. For the first four days the only programs transmitted were these interviews with visitors to the fair. The first program of general entertainment was presented by Helen Lewis on Wednesday 3 May from 8 P.M. to 9:30 P.M:

Newsreel specially filmed for television (SEE **television news**)

Fred Waring's Orchestra

Richard Rodgers, composer, and Marcy Wescott performing songs from Broadway musical *The Boys from Syracuse*

Bill Farren (NBC announcer) interviewing visitors to World's Fair

The Three Swifts vaudeville act

Donald Duck in *Donald's Cousin Gus*

Earl Larimore and Marjorie Clarke in Aaron Hoffman's playlet *The Unexpected*

Lowell Thomas in New York Port Authority information film

Billboard TV critic "Franken" was not impressed, remarking that the selection showed that "television has a long way to go to solve its programming, production, and talent problems" and opining that after several years of experimental transmissions NBC had failed to progress beyond the standards of a "kindergarten play." NBC officials were honest enough to admit that "the subject matter will be found repetitive."

Generally programming tended toward the cheap and cheerful with a heavy concentration on boxing and wrestling, which were comparatively easy to bring to air. Trickier was coverage of team sports (SEE **television: sport**), but by the end of the year NBC had racked up an impressive list of "firsts" with the inaugural American TV transmissions of baseball, prizefighting, football, basketball, and hockey. RCA's mobile television trucks brought remotes (qv) of the stars attending the New York premiere of *Gone With the Wind* (19 December 1939) and coverage of the Republican National Convention in Philadelphia (June 1940).

Owing to the hostility of the Hollywood studios, most of the films available for airing were shorts and documentaries, with the odd British import or "poverty row" movie, most frequently a Hoot Gibson B western. Scenes from Broadway plays were transmitted from Radio City on Sundays (when the actors were available) and there were 75-minute studio dramas on Wednesdays and Fridays. News was the radio news with the presenter in vision. Other studio programs consisted principally of game shows (qv), cooking demonstrations (SEE **television cook**), fashion shows, and lots of variety acts, featuring young unknowns prepared to work for almost nothing like the twenty-two-year-old pianist Leonard Bernstein.

An analysis of program genres (May 1939–Jan 1940) by *Electronics* in March 1940 showed that news and sports led with 35.7 percent, followed by drama (29.3 percent), educational (15.7 percent), variety (12.4 percent), and music (3.3 percent). Audience reaction, rated on a scale of 0 (poor), 1 (fair), 2 (good), and 3 (excellent), had an overall average of 2. Highest rated were "studio features," lowest were "film varieties" (which probably meant educational shorts rather than chorus girls).

A choice of channels became a reality with the return of CBS's former mechanical station W2XAB in all-electronic format on 29 October 1939 and a third station, DuMont's W2XWV, began operating in October 1940. Elsewhere there were stations transmitting a regular schedule of local programs in Chicago; Washington, D.C.; Philadelphia; Los Angeles; and Schenectady, N.Y. W2XBS pioneered once again when it secured the first commercial license and transformed itself into WNBT, going on air on 1 July 1941 with a program slate that differed little from what had been aired before except that the shows could now be officially sponsored (SEE **television commercials**).

Network television was born on 15 April 1946 with the official link-up of DuMont's New York and Washington stations. The NBC and CBS networks soon followed and thenceforth television can be said to have emerged from its long gestation and was set to become, after many further trials and tribulations, America's and the world's most dominant medium of communication.

THE FIRST **TELEVISION: SPORT**
....
telecast was an exhibition bout between boxers Tuffy Griffith and Stanley Harris staged for the opening program transmitted by W9XAP Chicago on 27 August 1930. The program was sponsored by Libby's canned goods.

The first sports remote and the first **telecast of a team game** took place on 17 February 1931, when a baseball game played by new members of the Waseda University Baseball club at the Tozuka Baseball Ground, Tokyo, was transmitted by closed circuit to the Electrical Laboratory at Waseda University. The experiment was conducted under the direction of Dr. Yamamoto Tadaoki and the 60-line low-definition pictures received on a screen 3 feet square. On 27 September 1931 Waseda University presented a public telecast from the Tozuka Baseball Ground in association with the Nippon Broadcasting Corporation. This 40-minute transmission of a match between the Ushigome and Awazi Shichiku Higher Elementary Schools was the world's first telecast of a team game to be watched by viewers in their own homes. The size of the picture on the sets available for domestic use was 8" x 5". The commentator was a Mr. Matsuuchi, Nippon Broadcasting Corporation announcer.

U.S.: The first attempts at transmitting a team game took place in Boston at about the same time as the Japanese transmissions, though the date is not recorded. Hollis Baird's experimental TV station WIXAB backed on to Fenway Park, and his assistant Loyd Sigman recalled that they would take the camera onto the roof and shoot the ball games. CBS's W2XAB New York televised a football game with portable transmitting equipment from 2 P.M. to 5:30 P.M. on Saturday 7 November 1931. W9XAO Chicago, according to its quarterly report of December 1931, had already transmitted several Saturday afternoon football games, though details remain elusive. In 1933 Dr. Vladimir Zworykin of RCA made high-definition, electronic transmissions from the Braves Field in Boston and stills were published in the *Proceedings of the Institute of Radio Engineers* for December of that year. He also transmitted scenes from a football game at about the same time.

Other sports telecasts of the low-definition mechanical era include the first of a **horse race** on 3 June 1931, transmitted by the Baird Co. of the Derby from Epsom via cable to the London studio and thence via the BBC national transmitter at Brookman's Park to the small number of home viewers. The first telecast of **hockey** was a NHL match between the Canadiens and the Maroons from the Montreal Stadium by the Montreal Television Co.'s VE9EC in 1933. On 28 January 1934 Don Lee's W6XAO Los Angeles presented **motorcycle racing** live from Los Angeles Coliseum.

The first public sports telecasts in high definition were transmitted from the Berlin Olympics by four all-electronic Farnsworth-system cameras from 1 to 17 August by the Reichs-Rundfunk-Gesellschaft. The highly successful programs were viewed by 160,000 members of the public at viewing rooms around the city and a 100-seat Telecinema. The first remote of a **soccer game** followed on 15 November, Germany vs Italy from Berlin.

Full-service television sports coverage: Following the inauguration of the world's first full-service TV station by the BBC in November 1936, the following sports were broadcast for the first time in high definition to viewers in their own homes:

Boxing: England v Ireland amateur contest, Alexandra Palace, London, 4 February 1937 (middle-weight amateur champion Henry Mallin first commentator on full-service TV).

Table Tennis: Exhibition replay of English Open Championships, London, 16 February 1937.

Tennis: Bunny Austin v George Rogers, Wimbledon, 21 June 1937.

Motor racing: Imperial Trophy Heats, Crystal Palace, 7 October 1937.

Hockey (field): England v Wales Women's International, Kennington Oval, London, 5 March 1938.

Track and Field: Oxford and Cambridge Intervarsity Sports, White City, London, 12 March 1938.

Rugby: England v Scotland for the Calcutta Cup, Twickenham, London, 19 March 1938.

Soccer: Wembley Cup Final, Preston North End v Huddersfield, 30 April 1938.

Polo: Whitney Cup Final, Hurlingham, London, 14 May 1938.

Horse racing: Epsom Derby (won by *Bois Roussell*), 1 June 1938.

Golf: Tournament at Roehampton, Surrey, 15 July 1938.

Cricket: Second Test v Australians, Lord's, 24 July 1938.

Swimming: European Championships, Wembley Pool, London, 8 August 1938.

Hockey (ice): Haringey Racers v Streatham, Haringey Arena, 29 October 1938.

Rowing: Oxford v Cambridge Boat Race, London, 1 April 1939.

U.S.: The first full-service station, RCA's W2XBS New York, began its regular programming to home viewers in April 1939. As the only station with mobile television units, it was well placed to include a substantial amount of sports (news and sports occupied 35.7 percent of air time). All the following full-service sports "firsts" were aired by W2XBS:

Baseball: second game of doubleheader, Princeton beat Columbia 2–1, Baker Field New York (commentator Bill Stern), 11 May 1939.

Boxing: Max Baer v Lou Nova (Baer knocked out in 11th) with commentator Ed Herlihy, Yankee Stadium, 1 June 1939.

Football: Fordham beat Waynesburg State 34–7, 30 September 1939; pro football: Brooklyn Dodgers beat Philadelphia Eagles 23–14, Ebbets Field, Brooklyn, 22 October, 1939.

Cycle racing: 6-day race from Madison Square Garden 15–21 May 1939.

Tennis: Eastern Court Championship, Westchester Country Club, Rye, New York, 9 August 1939.

Hockey: New York Rangers beat Montreal Canadiens 6–2, Madison Square Garden, 25 February 1940.

Basketball: University of Pittsburgh beat Fordham 50–37, Madison Square Garden, 28 February 1940.

Track and Field: 19th Intercollegiate AAAA Championships, won by New York University, Madison Square Garden, 2 March 1940.

As television began to emerge out of its experimental phase, the bodies representing professional sports were ambivalent about the new medium, believing that it could affect the all-important wickets; it probably occurred to no one that the day would come when the TV rights would far exceed ticket sales. First to concede the value of a television audience was the National Football League, which did a deal with ABC for rights to the Saturday afternoon pro football games. The initial game of these regular weekly contests resulted in a 41–10 victory for the Washington Redskins over the New York Giants on 3 October 1948, with Joe Hasal doing the play-by-play. Major-league baseball did not follow until well into the next decade, again with ABC presenting a Saturday afternoon "game of the week," starting on 30 May 1953 when the Cleveland Indians beat home team Chicago White Sox 7–2. Dizzy Dean and Buddy Blattner were in the commentary box.

Regular TV sports program: The first was the BBC's monthly *Sports Review*, a mixture of interviews and film of sports events normally presented by Howard Marshall who was, unfortunately, indisposed for the initial show on 30 April l937.

U.S.: The first was *The Dennis James Sports Parade*, a weekly half-hour show aired from DuMont's W2XVT Passaic, N.J., starting in September 1938. James, the first American to make a career as a television presenter, used to interview a sportsman, then partake of the sport. He recalled an occasion when his interviewee was wrestler Bibber McCoy. Bibber put a chokehold on him and James passed out on the air.

The first network sports show was *The Gillette Cavalcade of Sport*, which ran weekly on Friday nights on the NBC stations in New York, Philadelphia, and Schenectady from 29 September 1944. Initially hosted by Steve Ellis, the announcer for the Gillette Razor Co.'s radio sportscasts, the highly successful program ran for sixteen years.

Instant replay: The first was aired on an unknown date in 1955 when CBC producer George Retzlaff made a kinescope recording of a goal during a *Hockey Night in Canada* broadcast in Toronto and transmitted it less than 30 seconds later. This was a one-off and instant replays only became a regular feature of sports programming following the episode below.

U.S.: The first was during the Army–Navy football game at Philadelphia on 7 December 1963. It repeated a short touchdown run by Army quarterback Rollie Stichweh. "This is not live!" screamed commentator Lindsey Nelson, "Ladies and gentlemen, Army did not score again."

Satellite sports transmission: The first was unscheduled. The opening transmission from the first telecommunications satellite *Telstar* on 23 July 1962 was supposed to have been an address by President John F. Kennedy, but the signal came through before he was ready. To fill in time a short sequence of a major-league baseball game between the Philadelphia Phillies and the Chicago Cubs was aired from Wrigley Field, including a dramatic moment when Tony Taylor was seen flying out to rightfielder George Altman.

SEE ALSO **television, color.**

THE FIRST **TELEVISION, STADIUM**

or large-screen television system for mass outdoor viewing was inaugurated at Goodman's DuMont Television Stadium, next to the Goodman furniture and appliances store at 830 Bergen Avenue, Jersey City, N.J., on 18 July 1947. With what Goodman's and Allen B. DuMont Laboratories claimed as the world's largest television screen, the opening presentation was of the Charley Fusari vs Eddie Giosa prizefight from Madison Square Garden. The public was admitted free, as the object was to persuade viewers that what could be viewed outdoors in summer could also be viewed in comfort indoors the year round. Stadium TV came into its own as various entrepreneurs adopted large-screen for remote, one-off sports specials, charging premium prices for admission. Following the triumph of satellite and cable, which killed off the pay-remote, it found its present use: for screening to a mass audience at rock festivals and big sporting events like the Olympics where the live action may not be sufficiently visible from the bleachers.

THE FIRST **TELEVISION TALK SHOW**

and one of the earliest regular program series on TV was New York photographer Harold Stein's weekly gabfest *People I Have Shot*, which debuted on W2XCD Passaic, N.J., on 21 June 1931. His first guest was Dorothy Stone, star of Broadway musicals.

The first talk show on high-definition TV was presented in September 1942 by Franklin Lacey, described as "a lanky young writer," on Paramount's W6XYZ Los Angeles. Each show lasted an hour and showcased just one guest. Despite the nil budget and minimal audience, the novelty of the format attracted such show-business luminaries as Beatrice Lillie to face the camera. It was not unknown for Lacey and his guest to receive an invitation to dinner after the show from appreciative viewers. Many years later he was to achieve wider fame as author of Broadway hit and subsequent movie *The Music Man*. The TV talk show had no precedent on radio, but it still took a long time to become an established feature of the small screen. It was not until eight years later that the concept became a fixture with the first networked talk show, NBC's *Broadway Open House*, hosted by Jerry Lester, Morey Amsterdam, and Jack E. Leonard from 22 May 1950 to 24 August 1951. Also the first late-night talk show, it aired from 11 to midnight Monday through Friday.

THE FIRST TELEVISION: 3-D

SEE **television receiver: 3-D**.

THE FIRST THANKSGIVING

was decreed by the charter of "The Town and Hundred of Berkeley" in Virginia, in which it was declared that the day of the settlers' arrival "shall be yearly and perpetually kept holy as a day of thanksgiving to Almighty God." The settlers did give thanks by kneeling and praying on their safe arrival on 4 December 1619, but as Thanksgiving is regarded as a commemorative ritual, the "first Thanksgiving" is more properly that of 4 December 1620. After the Jamestown Massacre of 1622, when the Indians killed and routed hundreds of settlers in an attempt to cease European settlement, the celebration fell into abeyance, but it has been revived in present-day Berkeley.

The more celebrated occasion at Plymouth Plantation in 1621, generally cited as "the first Thanksgiving," took place on a date unrecorded. The only account of it is contained in a letter from Edward Winslow (SEE **marriage**) of 11 December 1621 and described a feast to celebrate the bringing in of the harvest; it was therefore a harvest home, of ancient custom in Britain, and only in the nineteenth century did historians decide to dub the event a "thanksgiving." Where it differed from English practice, though, was that the harvest was of Indian corn, not wheat; that the junketing continued for three days; and that the participants included ninety Indians led by their chief, Massasoit. Gov. William Bradford had sent four men out fowling to provide for the feast; the hunters brought back waterfowl, probably ducks and geese. The Indians for their part supplied five deer.

There was no popcorn (qv); the strain of corn raised by the Indians was not the popping kind (the popcorn legend originated in a nineteenth-century children's novel). Although there were many Thanksgivings in the seventeenth century, these were religious events consisting of services in church. The only recorded commemoration that might have involved feasting was in New England in 1636 when after the service there was "making merry." The whole of the eighteenth century yields but two documented occasions when "Thanksgiving" was associated with food. One was a day of thanksgiving for the American victory in the Battle of Saratoga, proclaimed for 18 December 1777. A soldier recorded that the troops were issued with rice and a spoonful of vinegar in celebration—a somewhat frugal feast. The other was in 1784, but the occasion is unclear; whatever was being thanked for involved a banquet of roast meats and fowl.

Although President George Washington assigned 26 November 1789 as the first national Day of Thanksgiving, followed by another in 1795, there was no annual observance throughout the country until President Abraham Lincoln's Thanksgiving Day Proclamation of 3 October 1863. In the meantime, however, New York State had pioneered with an annual Thanksgiving holiday as early as 1817 and by 1859 thirty states were holding their Thanksgiving Festival on the same day, the last Thursday in November. The adoption of a uniform day was largely owing to the crusading zeal of Boston's Mrs. Sarah Josepha Hale (author of "Mary Had a Little Lamb"), who used her *Ladies' Magazine* to mount a campaign in its favor starting in 1827 and culminating in Lincoln's proclamation, following a personal interview with the persuasive lady, thirty-six years later. The only change to the holiday since then has been the moving of the date from the *last* Thursday in November to the *fourth* by a Congressional Joint Resolution of 1941. The purpose was to allow retailers a week longer, in years when there were five Thursdays in November, to prepare for the post-Thanksgiving, pre-Christmas rush.

THE FIRST THEATER

in America was the Levingston Playhouse, believed to have been built between 1716 and 1718 on the east side of the Palace Green at Williamsburg, the then capital of Virginia. It was owned by the merchant William Levingston, who signed a contract at Yorktown on 11 July 1716 agreeing with Charles and Mary Stagg, actors, to build a theater at Williamsburg and to provide other actors, scenery, and music from England for the presentation of comedies and tragedies. The Staggs were to be managers of the enterprise. On 21 November 1716 Levingston purchased three half-acre lots and proceeded to build a dwelling with a stable, a bowling alley, and the theater.

Levingston was so in debt by 1723 that the mortgagee of the theater and his house adjoining it, Dr. Archibald Blair, foreclosed. Whether the Staggs continued running it is not known. Levingston died in 1735 and his wife then made her living by running "dancing assemblies." Subsequently the theater was being used for amateur productions by the students of William and Mary College and also by the "young Gentlemen and Ladies of the country." Who these were is not known, but their performances in September 1736 of Susanna Centlivre's *The Busybody*, Farquhar's *The Recruiting Officer*, and the same playwright's *The Beaux Stratagem*, together with a presentation by "the young gentlemen of the College of the tragedy *Cato*," are the earliest productions at Williamsburg's theater that we know by name. Nor are any other recorded before the playhouse was bought by a number of prominent men in the colony in 1745 and presented to the citizens of Williamsburg as a Court of Hustings (i.e., a corporation court).

An advertisement in the *Virginia Gazette* of that year inviting tenders for its conversion provides the only contemporary evidence of how the building was constructed: that it was of weatherboarding and had a roof of shingles. Archaeological excavations at Williamsburg indicate that the Levingston Playhouse stood on a brick foundation 30'2" wide and 86'6" long, with the narrow side facing Palace Green.

It was not apparent whether the earlier unnamed productions at Williamsburg were professional or amateur. In the meantime, however, the New Theater at Pearl Street and Maiden Lane in New York had opened on 6 December 1732 with a performance of *The Recruiting Officer* in which Thomas Heady, formerly barber and peruke maker to the acting governor Rip Van Dam, played the part of Worthy. Van Dam owned the building in which the theater operated. While some historians have cited this as evidence that it was an amateur performance, T. Allston Brown in his *History of the New York Stage* (1903) asserted, without quoting an authority, that the players belonged to "a company of professional actors from London." He wrote: "They continued their performance for one month, acting three times a week. Early in December of the same year they resumed, having made several additions to their company. This company continued until February 1734; it then disbanded." An advertisement for the theater in the *New York Gazette* cites the repertoire of the company as *Cato*, *The Recruiting Officer*, *The Beaux Stratagem*, and *The Busybody*, exactly the same as the plays presented at the playhouse in Williamsburg in 1736. Arthur Hornblow, in his *History of the Theatre in America* (1919), has postulated that the New York company may not have disbanded but simply taken their thespian wares south.

The first professional company known by name was the Murray & Kean Company under the management of Walter Murray and Thomas Kean, which began a tour of the Eastern Seaboard with a season at Plumstead's warehouse on the waterfront at Philadelphia in 1749. Thomas Kean, an actor-manager, took most of the male leads, while the female leads generally went to Miss Nancy George and Miss Osbourne. In 1834 an aged black man, one Robert Venable, told John F. Watson, author of *The Annals of Philadelphia* (1857), that he had attended the very first performance at Plumstead's warehouse and that "many fell out" with Nancy George, presumably because in the Quaker City, suspicious as its citizens were of plays and players generally, the appearance of a woman on a public stage was considered scandalous.

The identity of the first **American-born actor** is in doubt. According to the nineteenth-century theatrical historian George O. Seilhamer, *History of the American Theatre* (1888–91), the honor belongs to a Mr. Goodman, who had trained as a lawyer in Philadelphia before joining David Douglass's American Company in 1769 and was said to have been born in that city. J. Allston Brown, however, states that Goodman was born in London, which would accord the distinction to the somewhat later John E.

Martin. Born in New York City, Martin made his theatrical debut with the American Company on 13 March 1790 when he appeared as Young Norval in Horne's tragedy *Douglas* at the Southwark Theater, Philadelphia. Like Goodman, he had been educated for the bar, but "induced by habits of idleness and the applause bestowed upon his recitations by his idle companions, he abandoned law for the stage." The pioneer playwright and theatrical manager William Dunlap, author of his own *History of the American Theatre* (1832), who saw Martin perform, wrote that he "continued for some years a useful though not a brilliant actor, lived poor and died young"; which, the sage observed, was the fate of all actors not endowed with exceptional gifts.

No American-born actress is recorded until c. 1800, when a Mrs. Wheatley, a native of New York, was a member of the company based at the city's Park Theater. The other actresses in the company were English, but in the opinion of early-nineteenth-century English comedian Joe Cowell, she was "a much better actress than all of them put together."

SEE ALSO **black actors**.

THE FIRST **TOILET, FLUSH**

....

was designed by the Elizabethan poet Sir John Harington and installed at his country seat, Kelston, near Bath, England, in 1589, by a local craftsman known to the history of sanitation only by his initials, T. C. In 1596 Harington described his invention in a book called *The Metamorphosis of Ajax* (a pun on *jakes*, the slang word then used for toilet), which itemized the materials necessary for its construction together with their price—30s 6d for the complete installation—and included diagrams to show how it worked. Water was drawn from a cistern—depicted with fish swimming in it—into the pan of the bowl and was flushed into a cesspool when a handle in the seat was pulled to release a valve. Harington's water closet resembled a modern flush toilet in all important respects, having a reservoir of water constantly in the bowl to prevent foul air rising from the pipe, and a discharge that flushed down all the inside walls.

Despite the practical instructions given in his book, only two Harington water closets are known to have been built, the Kelston one for his own use, and another at Richmond Palace, installed at the express command of Queen Elizabeth, who was Harington's godmother. Both courtier and queen were noted in their time for a singular attention to hygiene. The queen was considered by the rest of the court to be uncommonly fastidious about her own person, taking a bath once a month "whether she need it or no." Harington went farther, and had a bath every day, a habit considered by his friends to be a mark of the most eccentric behavior.

The fact that the royal example was not followed by any other of her subjects is a reflection not on the worth of Harington's innovation, but of the total indifference of the majority of Elizabethans to dirt and its attendant odors. There was, however, a practical consideration that made the installation of flush lavatories difficult. The absence of drains or sewers meant that unless a pipe could be run from the water closet to a river or stream, the effluent would have to be discharged into a pit which constituted little improvement over the common midden. The water supply was also extremely limited. The majority of householders relied on a communal pump for their water, drawing it in buckets. Those fortunate enough to have piped water were obliged to refill their tanks by turning on the tap from the main during the 2 to 3 hours that the water was pumped from the waterworks on three days of the week. Until the introduction of ball valves in 1748, this supply depended on the householder or his servants remembering to turn on the tap at the right time, and even more important, to turn it off again. Water being regarded as a precious commodity, the water companies resented any subscriber using more than his fair share. When a Mr. Melmouth of Bath installed a flush toilet in his house in 1770, the company cut off his supply until he consented to remove it again.

The first manufacturer to undertake quantity production of flush toilets was London cabinetmaker Joseph Bramah, who sold some 6,000 units between 1778—the year of his patent—and 1797, "despite the not inconsiderable cost of £11" (half a year's wages for an agricultural worker). The social commentator

Henry Mayhew said that Bramah's valve closet was "brought into general use" about the late 1820s, reflecting the rising prosperity of the new middle class. Bramah closets continued to be manufactured until c. 1890.

U.S.: The first flush toilet was erected in its own semi-octagonal building as an adjunct to the bedroom pavilion on the west side of Whitehall, the classical mansion built in 1764–67 by the governor of Maryland, Col. Horatio Sharpe, at his 1,000-acre plantation of the same name on the River Severn in Anne Arundel County. Some 7 miles from the capital of the colony Annapolis, the great house as well as the diminutive house-of-ease were designed by an architect called Anderson. The early Maryland historian Thomas W. Griffith refers to him as William Anderson, but Charles Scarlett Jr., in "Governor Horatio Sharpe's Whitehall," *Maryland Historical Magazine* 1951, has postulated that he was in fact Joseph Horatio Anderson, the most prominent of early Maryland architects and believed to have been the designer of the statehouse. The water closet at Whitehall was fed by a cistern supplied by rainwater from the roofs and discharged into a cesspool below. The floor was of marble and Scarlett suggests that the walls were of English Delft tile, based on the fact that tiles found at Whitehall after the destruction of the lavatory building are identical to those that graced the water closet at Epsom, the Surrey seat of Frederick Lord Baltimore, proprietor of Maryland.

The mechanics of America's first flush lavatory almost certainly derived from an English model. Glenn Brown in the earliest cloacal history, *Water Closets: A Historical, Mechanical, and Sanitary Treatise* (New York, 1884), noted that the water-seal water closet at Whitehall was identical to one installed at Osterley Park, the mansion at Isleworth, near London, remodeled by Robert Adam between 1763 and 1767. As these dates are almost exactly conterminous with the building of Whitehall, there is a clear inference that either the source of the mechanism was the same or at least that Anderson was familiar with the latest plumbing techniques in London.

The toilet bowls were two in number, carved from solid blocks of marble and set as a pair side by side. Were they, in an age of more robust manners,

intended as "his" and "hers"? According to tradition, the forty-five-year-old bachelor governor had nursed an unrequited passion for the young daughter of former governor Samuel Ogle and had built Whitehall in the hope that they would share his seat together—or possibly seats, in the case of the twin toilets. Alas it was not to be, for she married instead the governor's secretary and best friend, John Ridout. In such circumstances there might have been a falling-out between the First Gentleman of Maryland and his subordinate, but happily Horatio Sharpe was not a man to bear a grudge. His recall to Britain and abandonment of his beloved Whitehall had indeed to do with sexual shenanigans, but not of his or his faithful secretary's making. The absentee proprietor of Maryland, Lord Baltimore, had become enamored of a winsome milliner, Miss Sarah Woodcock, and found himself charged with what today would be termed date-rape. Although acquitted of the charge, he chose to remove himself to the more tolerant climes of Italy and relinquish the proprietorship. Col. Sharpe was commanded to return to London to oversee the transfer of Maryland to the Crown. He hoped to return to the colony he had served so well, but he was prevented by the outbreak of the Revolutionary War. When he died in 1790, Sharpe left Whitehall to his friend John Ridout. So it is possible that Mrs. Ridout did ascend the cloacal throne her lover had intended for her. However, between 1791 and 1798 Ridout took down the various extensions to the house, including the water closet, in order to provide materials for the raising of the roof. All that remained were the twin marble toilet bowls. They survive to this day at Horatio Sharpe's Whitehall.

The first public building in the United States furnished with flush lavatories was Boston's Tremont House hotel (qv) that opened on 16 October 1829 with eight such conveniences.

Most early toilets had boxed wooden surrounds enclosing a metal bowl. The first **ceramic pedestal toilet** of the kind now standard in the United States, United Kingdom, and most of the western world, was the Unitas manufactured by Thomas Twyford of Hanley, Staffordshire, England, in the late 1870s. The exact date of its introduction is not recorded, but the revolutionary new design was advertised as "the perfection of CLEANLINESS, UTILITY AND SIMPLICITY" by Twyford's U.S. agent, E. Aspinall of Pearl Street, New York City, in every issue of the American journal *Plumber and Sanitary Engineer* during the year 1880.

Only one further step was needed to give us the toilet of today: the oval "picture-frame" toilet seat. This first adorned Jennings's Pedestal Vase of 1884 and, if credence be lent to nineteenth-century legend, was actually used as a handsome surround for family portraits by some of his less sophisticated customers. The plastic toilet seat was introduced by the Kohler Co. of Sheboygan, Wis., in 1929. By this date one third of American homes had indoor flush toilets, up from a fifth only ten years earlier.

Railroad car to contain flush toilets: The first was George Mortimer Pullman's "Old No. 9," a sleeping car with a lavatory at either end that was put into service on the Chicago & Alton Railroad on 1 September 1859.

Airplane fitted with a toilet: The first was the giant Russian passenger transport *Russky Vitiaz*, designed by Igor Sikorsky (SEE **helicopter**) and test-flown at Petrograd (now St. Petersburg) on 13 May 1913. Whether this was a water closet proper is doubtful, as it seems unlikely that Sikorsky would have increased the load by carrying unnecessary supplies of water. It is nevertheless recorded here as a tribute to the first man who concerned himself with the problem of high-altitude sanitation.

The first civil airliner in regular passenger service to contain a toilet was the Handley Page W.8., introduced on the London–Paris route on 21 October 1921. Until the end of the 1930s all airliner toilets discharged directly through the fuselage, which could be a draughty experience. Prototype of the modern aerial flush toilet were those on the Boeing Clippers that entered transatlantic service with Pan Am on 28 June 1939. These discharged into a drum mechanism that turned over when the passenger put the lid down, depositing the contents into the ocean below.

Down on the ground, the needs of motorists were first met by Texaco, which began installing restrooms in service stations in 1917. The company claims, somewhat tendentiously, that this feature distinguishes between a "filling station" and a "service station."

Two museums cater to the interests of coprophiliacs: the Sulabh International Museum of Toilets in New Delhi, India, and the International Museum of Toilet Paper in Madison, Wis.

SEE ALSO **public toilet**.

THE FIRST **TOOTHBRUSH**

is claimed in the Chinese encyclopaedia *Lei shu san ts'ai t'u hui* (1609), with somewhat improbably exactitude, to have been invented on 25 June 1498. The illustration given shows what was probably either a wooden or ivory handle with bristles set at right angles. The only difference between this and a modern toothbrush is that the bristles extended nearly half the length of the handle.

In Europe toothbrushes are known to have existed by 1649. In that year a friend wrote to Sir Ralph Verney asking him to purchase, during a forthcoming trip to Paris, some of those "little brushes for making cleane of the teeth, most covered with sylver and some few with gold and sylver twiste, together with some petits bourettes to put them in."

For how long after this it was necessary to send to Paris for a new toothbrush is not known, though the diary of Anthony à Wood for 1690 records that they could be bought in London from one J. Barret, who also sold shirts and sewing thread. According to Messrs. Floris of Jermyn Street, it was their custom in the eighteenth century to sell toothbrushes in sets containing five or six different sizes, though the reason remains obscure. They were supplied to Floris by the firm of William Addis, founded 1780, who claim to have been the first toothbrush manufacturers on a factory scale.

U.S.: Toothbrushes were supplied to George Washington in 1773 by John Baker, the first medically qualified dentist to practice in America. Baker emigrated from Ireland via Britain in 1763, and it seems likely that he would have brought a supply of toothbrushes and dentifrices to sell to his patients. Prior to this time the only dental practitioners were the so-called tooth-drawers, and they had little incentive to help people keep their teeth healthy. The first to manufacture toothbrushes in the United States was probably the ivory turner and umbrella manufacturer Isaac Greenwood of Boston, who began practicing dentistry in addition to his other avocations in 1778, taking over Paul Revere's practice. By 1788 he was advertising "brushes that are suitable for the teeth," but it is likely that he started making them when he began dentistry. His specialty was fitting dentures that he made himself from ivory, compared to which turning handles for toothbrushes would have been a simple operation. Greenwood's toothbrushes were of a novel design. His handbills and newspaper advertisements used as a logotype a pair of crossed toothbrushes with a pot of dentifrice in each of the four segments. The brushes each had two heads of bristles, a long one at the top end and a short one on the opposite side of the handle at the bottom end.

Nylon toothbrush: The first was Dr. West's Miracle-Tuft Toothbrush, the bristles of which were the first commercial application of nylon (see **man-made fiber**), manufactured by DuPont and test-marketed in Arlington, N.J., in September 1938.

Electric toothbrush: The first was an oscillating-motor model invented by Dr. Philippe-Guy Woog of Geneva in 1954 and launched by Broxo in Switzerland two years later. It was introduced in the United States under license to Squibb Pharmaceutical as the Broxodent in 1960. The first rotary-action electric toothbrush was the Interplak marketed at $99 in 1987.

In 2003 the toothbrush was voted by Americans responding to a poll conducted by the Lemelson–MIT Index as the most indispensable invention in their everyday lives, beating the car, personal computer, cell phone, and microwave oven. This is the more remarkable since most Americans only began brushing their teeth at the time of World War II, when the U.S. armed forces promoted a vigorous campaign introducing the troops to elementary dental hygiene.

THE FIRST **TRACK AND FIELD MEET**

of modern times was organized at Shrewsbury, Shropshire, England, by the Royal Shrewsbury School Hunt in 1840. The only positive information on this meeting is contained in a series of letters written nearly sixty years later by C. T. Robinson, who was a boy at the school from 1838 to 1841. The field where it was held was the site of the Shrewsbury cattle market and was used by the boys on non-market days for playing rounders (an early form of baseball), quoits, and "Prisoners' Bars." Members of the Hunt competing in the races were given the names of horses and assigned to "owners." Robinson himself ran as Mr. Kenyon's "Capt'n Pops," which was the name of a real racehorse of the day. The only event mentioned is a "Derby," won by a boy called "Nigger" Kearsley, but it seems reasonable to suppose that this was a full-scale meeting on the evidence of an account of the RSS Hunt Races held in February 1843. The events on this later occasion—most probably the fourth in a series of annual meetings—comprised five foot-races of varying distances, and a hurdle-race over eight 3-foot hurdles. Two of the races were open events, while the others were restricted to "horses" under a certain height, e.g., "The Severn Stakes of 4d each for horses under 5ft 6ins. Twice round and a distance. Second horse to save his stake."

While such lighthearted sport cannot be said to have been more than a track meet in embryo, it clearly had more in common with modern athletics than the rural games held at village fairs and wakes, or the races between running footmen or professional walkers that had been popular during the eighteenth century. The 1840 Shrewsbury meeting is the earliest recorded occasion on which trained runners came together to compete in a number of prearranged races held on the same day. Shrewsbury was followed by Eton College, which instituted annual sprint, hurdle-races, and a steeplechase in 1845. The Royal Military Academy, Woolwich, had its first sports day in 1849, and annual athletics meetings were begun at Kensington Grammar School in 1852 and at boarding schools Harrow and Cheltenham in 1853, Rugby in 1856, and Winchester College in 1857.

The first university meeting was held by Exeter College, Oxford, in the autumn of 1850, and, like the school sports preceding it, was confined to track events. The following year's meeting, however, is believed to have been the first to have included a high-jump and a long-jump competition.

Track and field began to be put on an organized basis with the founding of the Mincing Lane Athletic Club (later London Athletic Club) by a group of City of London businessmen in June 1863. Their first meet was held at the West London Rowing Club grounds at Kensington on 9 April 1864. A rival arose in the form of the Amateur Athletic Club, who sought to become the governing body of the sport, and it was they who opened the first purpose-built **running track** at Lillie Bridge, West Kensington, on 18 March 1869. **U.S.:** The first meet was organized by the New York Athletic Club (NYCA), founded on 17 June 1866 by William B. Curtis, Henry E. Buermeyer, and John C. Babcock, inventor of the sliding seat for racing boats. It was held at the Empire Skating Rink, 63rd Street and 3rd Avenue, on 11 November 1868 and was the first **indoor meet** in the world. Founder member William B. Curtis introduced the first and only pair of **spiked running shoes** on this occasion and four competitors shared them in seven different events. In all there were thirteen events, all won either by members of the NYAC or the Caledonian Club except for the high jump, won by a member of Ward's Gymnasium at 5' 2". The other principal results, which established the first track and field records for the United States, were: 220 yard, 28 seconds; 440 yard, 62 seconds; 880 yard, 2 minutes 26 seconds; broad jump, 17 feet; shot put, 35 feet 5 inches; hammer, 73 feet; pole vault, 8 feet 3 inches.

There were no outdoor meets until 1876. On 20–21 July of that year the first **intercollegiate track and field meet** in the United States was held at Saratoga, N.Y., by the Intercollegiate Athletes of America, with competitors (winning events in brackets) from Amherst, Bowdoin, Brown, City College of New York, Columbia (high jump, pole vault), Cornell, Dartmouth (1 mile), Harvard, Pennsylvania (broad jump, 880 yards, shot put), Princeton, Wesley, Williams (100 yards, 440 yards), and Yale (120-yard hurdles). The New York Athletic Club also organized an outdoor event that year.

Relay race: the first was run experimentally at Berkeley, Calif., on 17 November 1883, when a demonstration team clocked a time of 9 minutes 51 seconds over four half-mile laps. It was not until 12 May 1892 that the first competitive relay race was contested between teams from the University of Pennsylvania and Princeton, resulting in victory for the latter. The annual Penn Relays were instituted on 21 April 1895, the inaugural event introducing the baton for the first time.

SEE ALSO **women's track and field.**

THE FIRST **TRACTOR, AGRICULTURAL**

gasoline-driven, was the Burger, built in 1889 by the Charter Engine Co. of Chicago, who coupled a single-cylinder Charter gasoline engine to the running gear of a Rumely steam-traction engine. The fire-box, boiler, and smokestack, which constituted the frame of the steam engine, were replaced by a chassis, and a reverse gear was added. This first tractor, which was also the first gasoline-engined vehicle in North America, was sold to a wheat farm near Madison, S.D., the same year. It performed sufficiently well for the Charter Engine Co. to build six more, all of which were subsequently employed on wheat farms in the Dakotas.

The pioneering role of the United States in tractor development is in sharp contrast to her belated acceptance of the gasoline engine generally, several years behind the leading European nations. Steam traction, however, had been developed on a fairly extensive scale on the prairies of the West. The flat terrain and dry climate, combined with a shortage of manpower, made steam cultivation a practical and relatively economic proposition. Fuel, however, was in short supply and was bulky and expensive to transport. With the development of an efficient internal-combustion engine, the substitution of gasoline for steam was an obvious step toward effective farm mechanization.

The first production model to be advertised for sale was the Sterling Tractor, produced by the Charter Engine Co. in 1893 and marketed by a Mr. Hockett with financial backing from the farmers of Sterling, Kan. It is not known how many models were sold, but by this date there were already rivals appearing in the field. William Deering & Co. had brought out a prototype in 1891, followed a year later by the Case Co. of Wisconsin and by John Froelich of Froelich, Iowa, who formed the Waterloo Gasoline Traction Engine Co. in 1893. One of the most successful of these pioneer tractors was the Otto, of which fourteen models were sold between 1894 and 1896. Another model of the same period, produced by the Ohio Manufacturing Co., was notable as the first with a chassis specially designed to incorporate a gasoline engine. There is no evidence, though, to suggest that any of these tractors was produced in a quantity large enough to be considered other than experimental until the advent of the Huber (prototype 1894), of which thirty were manufactured at Marion, Ohio, in 1898.

Pneumatic-tired tractor: The first was the 17-hp French Latil tractor, demonstrated at the World Tractor Trials held at Wallingford, Berkshire, in England in June 1930. Charles Cawood has written, "With the pneumatic tyre, the tractor became, at last [the] universally useful farm machine; it could, for the first time in its life, do everything a horse could do and do it better and faster."

U.S.: The first was the Allis-Chalmers Model U of 1932, the same year that Firestone in the United States and Dunlop in Britain began manufacturing the first purpose-designed pneumatic tractor tires. Farmers resisted the idea, so Allis-Chalmers hired a racing driver to take the Model U around a track at the state fair in Milwaukee at 35 mph. They then engaged a team to race the tractors at other state fairs. To top this, they staged a world speed record bid at the Utah salt flats, with racing driver Al Jenkins achieving a speed of 67 mph (a record that still stands). The stunts paid off. Amost half of America's tractors were rubber shod by 1937.

Diesel-engined tractors: These were first produced in a number of countries almost simultaneously in 1930. Examples shown at the World Tractor Trials of that year included the Munktell from Sweden, the Mercedes-Benz from Germany, and the Hungarian Hofherr-Schrantz. The British examples were the Marshall, the McLaren, the Aveling & Porter, and the Blackstone. The first American diesel-engined tractor was produced the same year by the Cummins Engine Co. of Columbia, Ind.

THE FIRST **TRACTOR, CRAWLER**

commercially practical, was the Holt Steam Traction Engine No. 77, built by the Holt Manufacturing Co. of Stockton, Calif., and tested for the first time on 24 November 1904. This machine was fitted with an endless track made up of wooden slats mounted on a linked steel chain. The first production model was sold to the Golden Meadow Developing Co. for $5,500 in 1906

for use in Louisiana delta land. The same year saw the appearance in prototype form of the first gasoline-engined crawler tractor, also by the Holt Co., and in 1908 the first production model went to work on the Los Angeles Aqueduct. It was this machine that inspired the creation of the first tank (qv).

Bulldozer: The first was built in 1923 in Morrowville, Kan., by farmer James Cummings and draughtsman Earl McLeod from a Model T frame to which they added windmill springs, various bits and pieces picked up from a junkyard, and a wooden blade; it was patented on 18 December that year. Having secured a contact from Sinclair Oil Co., they used the device to fill in a pipeline trench running from Deshler, Neb., to Freeman, S.D.

THE FIRST **TRADE SHOW**

was a small exhibition organized in Geneva in 1789. It was followed by similar shows in Hamburg the following year and in Prague in 1791. The first national show, and the first exhibition of any kind to be held in a purpose-built exhibition hall, opened at the Temple of Industry erected on the Champ de Mars on the banks of the Seine in Paris on 17 September 1798. Organized by M. de Neufchâteau, Minister of the Interior, the four-day show displayed the wares of 110 exhibitors, including watches, ceramics and glassware, textiles, chemical products, leatherware, furniture, military and sporting weapons, printing, and scientific and surgical instruments. Characteristically the purpose of the show was not only the glorification of French industry but the discomfiture of France's traditional enemy: in his official report De Neufchâteau declared that it was "a first campaign against English industry." He promised that in subsequent exhibitions special recognition would be given to French manufacturers who could compete successfully against the most important branches of British manufacture and "thereby strike the most effective blows against it."

U.S.: An exhibition of domestic manufactures was held in the rotunda of the Capitol at Washington, D.C., in 1825. The impetus for the show came from a meeting of manufacturers in Philadelphia the previous year.

International trade show or **world's fair:** The first was the Great Exhibition that opened at the Crystal Palace, a vast edifice of glass 1,950 feet in length and 110 feet tall, in London's Hyde Park on 1 May 1851. It was seen by 6.2 million visitors, many of them on their first trip to London, including the first substantial body of American tourists to venture across the Atlantic—5,048 of them.

U.S.: The first was the Exhibition of the Industry of All Nations which opened at the Crystal Palace in Reservoir Square (the present site of the New York Public Library) on 14 July 1853 with 5,272 exhibitors from 24 nations. Although the Crystal Palace was built in imitation of Sir Joseph Paxton's edifice at London's Great Exhibition, it earned rather less acclaim. The roof leaked so badly that exhibits and visitors were drenched. American know-how had yet to assert pre-eminence; the whole vast enterprise was so poorly organized that visitor numbers dwindled and the fair closed at a considerable loss. Both Crystal Palaces were destroyed by fire, New York's in 1857 and London's in 1936.

THE FIRST TRAFFIC SIGNAL

was erected on a 22-foot-high cast-iron pillar at the corner of Bridge Street and New Palace Yard off Parliament Square, London, and came into operation on 10 December 1868. The installation was made at the direction of Metropolitan Commissioner of Police Richard Mayne and was intended principally for the benefit of members of Parliament wishing to gain access to the Houses of Parliament. Manufactured by Saxby & Farmer, the traffic signal was surmounted by a revolving lantern with red and green signals. Red indicated Stop and green Caution. The lantern, illuminated by gas, was turned by means of a lever at the base of the standard so that the appropriate light faced the oncoming traffic. Manning the lever was not without its hazards. The unfortunate constable assigned to this duty on 2 January 1869 was badly injured when the gas apparatus exploded and blew gravel into his eye. The signal was unpopular with the general public, one hansom-cab driver complaining that it was "another of them fakements to wex poor cabbies." It remained the only traffic light in London,

and after it was removed in 1872 there were no similar experiments for more than half a century.

Electric traffic signals were first installed on Main and South Second streets in Salt Lake City, Utah, in 1912. The device, invented by a police detective called Lester Wire, was described as "a wooden box with a slanted roof," with red and green Mazda lights. This was mounted on a pole and the wires were attached to the overhead trolley and light wires. It was operated manually by a policeman. When the signal was decommissioned in the early 1920s, it was moved to Liberty Park and used as a birdhouse.

The first electrically interconnected traffic signals designed to allow an uninterrupted flow of traffic followed in Salt Lake City in 1917, three on Main Street and three on adjacent State Street. Designed by Charles Reading, an electrician who had assisted Wire with his pioneering installation, the system was actuated by a single switch, changing to green for traffic traveling between the two sets of lights at a constant 20 mph.

The first traffic signal to incorporate red, amber, and green lights was developed by William L. Potts of the Detroit Police Department and installed at the intersection of Woodward Avenue and Fort Street in October 1920. Traffic-actuated signals, invented by Charles Adler Jr., debuted on 22 February 1928 at the Belvedere Avenue and Falls Road intersection in Baltimore and within three years were in use in more than 150 cities. Adler also designed the first pedestrian push-button signal, introduced in Baltimore on 4 February 1929 at the intersection of Charles Street and Old Spring Lane.

The first computer-controlled system bowed in Detroit in 1952, one of the earliest applications of computers to have an impact directly on the general public.

THE FIRST TRAFFIC SIGNS

in America were inscribed under a Maryland statute of 1704 that required roads leading to a ferry, courthouse, or church to have directional markers cut into the bark of trees on either side. For a courthouse these comprised two notches close together and one higher up; for a ferry three notches evenly spaced; and for churches a "slipe cutt down the face of the tree near the ground." (A slipe was the mark left by peeling bark from a tree.)

The first signs indicating distance were stone markers erected at 2-mile intervals on the 100-mile main highway from New York to Philadelphia in 1743. The first road required to have signs to towns and villages was the Lancaster Turnpike, opened between Philadelphia and Lancaster County (Pennsylvania) in 1796. Ironically anyone trying to travel from Lancaster County to the City of Brotherly Love today will find an almost total absence of signs indicating the direction of Philadelphia.

The first statewide route signs began to be erected by the Wisconsin State Highway Department in 1918. Standardization of signing and marking started with proposals advanced at the annual meeting of the American Association of State Highway Officials in Chicago in January 1923 and formally adopted two years later. The designs for rural use were codified with the issue of AASHO's *Manual and Specification for the Manufacture, Display, and Erection of U.S. Standard Road Markers and Signs* of 1927, and those for urban use with the National Conference on Street and Highway Safety's own manual, which incorporated AASHO sign standards, in 1929.

U.S. highway shields were introduced under the auspices of the Joint Board on Interstate Highways in 1926. The first to be erected is not recorded, but the oldest surviving example dates from that year and was found by collector Jim Ross on a scrap-metal heap. It marked US 66 and stood in Chandler, Okla.

THE FIRST **TRAVEL AGENCY**

to engage in the tourist trade was established by Thomas Cook of Leicester, England, as an outcome of the cheap railway excursions for temperance galas he had been organizing since 1841. The real beginnings of organized tourism can best be dated from Cook's first vacation excursion to Liverpool and North Wales in 1845, a forerunner of the modern vacation package (qv). The brochure announced: "The Train will leave Leicester at Five o'clock in the Morning on Monday, August the 4th... Parties will have to be wide awake at an early hour, or they will be disappointed.

Promptitude on the part of the Railway Company calls for the same from passengers." Later Cook wrote: "The advertisement of the trip created such a sensation, that at Leicester the tickets issued at fifteen shillings [$3.75] first class, and ten shillings [$2.50] second, were in many instances resold at double those rates."

The tourists could choose between spending the four-day vacation in Liverpool, probably at one of the seven Temperance Hotels recommended in the brochure, or they could stay overnight and proceed to Caernarvon at 8 A.M. by the specially chartered packet boat *Eclipse*. The boat returned from Caernarvon on Wednesday morning, the 350 vacationers having enjoyed in the meantime the opportunity of visiting Snowdon and "beholding from its summit the opening dawn and the rising sun." For this part of the trip Thomas Cook secured the services of the only English-speaking Welshman he could find in Caernarvon to act as guide. Those who were disinclined to spend a night on the bare mountain were assured by their mentor that there were several passable inns at its foot. The indefatigable Mr. Cook himself, however, was among those who climbed to the summit, from which point he wrote afterward, he "looked toward Ben Lomond and Ben Nevis, and determined to get to Scotland the next year, or know the reason why." This decision set the course of his life and established tourism as an industry.

The following year Cook established a booking office at 26 Granby Street, Leicester, an indication that his activities as an excursionist were becoming more than just a sideline to his main business of printing and publishing temperance tracts. The first of the Scottish tours began on 25 June 1846, when a party of 350 excursionists departed from Leicester and Derby for five days in Edinburgh, Glasgow, and the Burns country. On arrival at Glasgow they were conducted to the Town Hall behind a brass band, and there entertained to a series of morally uplifting speeches, including one on "The Natural, Moral, and Political Effects of Temperance" that lasted a full hour. The inhabitants of Edinburgh treated them to more speeches, lightened on this occasion by the addition of "appropriate tunes on the pianoforte" by the Misses Blake. For the rest of the vacation they were free to enjoy themselves.

Cook's initial overseas tour was organized in 1855, the first of two parties of about 50 tourists leaving Harwich for Antwerp on 4 July. They were personally conducted by Mr. Cook to Brussels, the Field of Waterloo, Aix-la-Chapelle, Cologne, up the Rhine to Mainz and Mannheim, thence to Frankfurt, Heidelberg, Baden-Baden, Strasbourg, and Paris. Cook wrote afterward a trifle wistfully, "These were charming Tours, but denuded of much of their enjoyment by pecuniary losses." He was considerably cheered, however, on receiving a letter of gratitude from

> A working man—a model for his order—who having carefully husbanded his surplus earnings, first paid £6 [$30] for a ticket for the long route, and with about £4 [$20] additional managed to enjoy a treat . . . Many a working man who spends £20 [$100] a year in "drink and bacca" would stand appalled at the idea of appropriating half that sum to a trip on the Continent.

By 1865, when he opened his first London office, Cook was offering regular tours to France, Switzerland, Italy, Belgium, the Netherlands, Germany, and Austria and was soon to venture much farther afield, including the United States (1866) and the Middle East (1868). For the next twenty-five years he enjoyed a virtual monopoly of the vacation travel business and the phrase "Cook's tour," used colloquially of any circuitous journey, passed into the everyday currency of the English language.

U.S.: The first agency was Cook, Son & Jenkins, established in the summer of 1872 at 262 Broadway, New York City, by Thomas Cook and E. M. Jenkins, a bank cashier from Allegheny, Pa. Cook was entranced by the United States, partly because Americans were beginning to venture across the Atlantic in significant numbers, but mainly for ideological reasons: Very few of them drank alcohol (or at least not the high-minded ones Cook encountered) and he considered them an exemplar to the bibulous Old World. His new partner Jenkins had been a client, leading a party of Knights Templar on a trip to Europe.

Among the earliest tourists to book with Cook, Son & Jenkins was a party of 150 schoolteachers who made the grand tour of Europe escorted by E. M. Jenkins himself, an indication that travel was no longer the preserve of the rich and privileged. Palestine and the Middle East were a popular destination for church groups. At home Jenkins visited all the most popular tourist destinations, including Niagara, Monmouth Cave, the White Mountains, Colorado, the Grand Canyon, Yosemite, and the Rockies, to check out the best places to stay and make advantageous arrangements for travel; within five years Cook, Son & Jenkins had contracts with 150 railroad and steamship companies enabling them to offer tickets at discount prices. Branch offices were opened in Boston, Philadelphia, and Washington, D.C. Overseas travel for those unable to vacation in Europe was offered to the West Indies and Bermuda in the Atlantic and to Hawaii and Polynesia in the Pacific. Clients included the eminent, the company making all the arrangements for the emperor of Brazil's visit to the Centennial Exposition at Philadelphia in 1876 and his subsequent tour of the United States. Nor were all clients tourists. Before the end of the century Cook's was transporting shiploads of bearded men in fustian with the gleam of gold in their eyes to the Klondike.

The first travel agency that was American-owned and -operated was Raymond & Whitcomb, founded in Boston in 1879 by Walter Raymond, son of a railroad agent, and Irvine Whitcomb, a passenger agent for the Boston, Concord & Montreal Railroad. Their earliest tours were to the White Mountains and Washington, D.C., but with the growth of interest in the Wild West they started offering excursions to Yellowstone Park, the Rockies, and California in 1881. These were the first tours of Yellowstone. The partners also pioneered dining-car service on transcontinental railroads and ran the first all-Pullman trains to the West. So popular were these trips to what sophisticated Easterners regarded as untamed territory, that by 1886 they were able to build the palatial Raymond Hotel in Pasadena to accommodate the intrepid tourists. (Interestingly these tour parties are never depicted in Western movies.) By 1891, when the itinerary had extended to New Orleans and Mexico, Raymond & Whitcomb had already replicated Thomas Cook's concept of the prepaid vacation package (qv).

THE FIRST **TRIVIAL PURSUIT**

was devised in a single evening in Montreal, Canada, on 15 December 1979 by Chris Haney, picture editor of the Montreal *Gazette*, and his best friend and lodger Scott Abbott, a sportswriter. Haney recalled, "We'd had a few beers and decided to play Scrabble for a few dollars' side bet. I got out our set but found that there were lots of letters missing so I had to go out to buy a new one. When I got back we worked out that we must have gotten through six Scrabble sets over the years, and figured 'Jeez, there's a lot of money to be made out of board games.'" The idea for Trivial Pursuit came to them at 5:15 P.M. and, according to Haney, "We had it all wrapped up by about six. It just sprang out of one burst of creative energy."

Haney was going to call the game Trivia Pursuit, but his wife, Sarah, suggested they add an "l" as "it rolls off the tongue better." The original questions and answers were mainly devised in England by Haney's brother John, toiling at the task for weeks in the public library at Weymouth, Dorset. The Haney brothers, Scott Abbott, and lawyer friend Ed Werner founded a company called Horn Abbot and began marketing a test-run of the game, selling 1,200 sets in Canada during late 1980. These cost $75 each to manufacture but sold to retailers for $15. Nevertheless, encouraged by what seemed a signal of success, they took the game to the Montreal and New York trade shows early in 1981. There their hopes were dashed, with orders for only 144 sets at the Montreal show and fewer than 300 in New York. Like the inventors of Monopoly (qv) and Scrabble (qv) before them, they could find no one who shared their belief in the game. Their money ran out and Chris Haney suffered a breakdown from overwork.

The breakthrough came when three executives of American games manufacturers Selchow & Righter played the game and were enraptured with it. This happened to be the company that had first mass-produced Scrabble, the game that had inspired Haney and Abbott with the idea of making their fortune with an equally engrossing pastime. The contract that they and their partners signed with Selchow & Righter on 10 October 1982 is estimated to have earned them nearly $200 million by 2008, the year that the two inventors sold the rights to Hasbro for a further $80 million (the inventor of Scrabble made a little over $1 million). Cumulative sales of sets in twenty languages in fifty countries are estimated at 88 million.

THE FIRST **TRUCK**

SEE **motor truck**.

THE FIRST **TUXEDO**

was designed by Pierre Lorillard V, heir to the Lorillard tobacco fortune, and was worn by his son Griswold on the occasion of the Autumn Ball held at the Tuxedo Park Country Club at Tuxedo, New York, on 10 October 1886. Lorillard's "tux" consisted of a short black coat with scarlet satin lapels and was modeled on the English smoking jacket then in vogue. His temerity in appearing before mixed company without a tailcoat raised a number of eyebrows, for not until World War I would such casual evening wear be considered acceptable in the company of ladies. The society journal *Town Topics* sniffed that Griswold had looked "for all the world like a royal footman" and declared that he and his friends who wore the coats "ought to have been put in straight jackets long ago."

Quite why father and son decided to launch a new and controversial fashion is hard to fathom, especially at a place which Emily Post, daughter of the architect who had built Tuxedo, pronounced to be the most formal in the world. "I've always heard," recalled Griswold's great-grandson Louis, "they just got tired of sitting around on their tails, so they cut them off." In England, where the short jackets were introduced in 1888, they were originally called "dress lounge" until this term was superseded by "dinner jacket" ten years later. Curiously this seems to have gained some currency in the land of the tuxedo's birth. As late as 1952 social commentator Cleveland Amory was able to report: "Even today in Society the word 'tuxedo' is itself considered taboo, the use of 'dinner jacket' being as mandatory as the Society patois which insists on 'to-ma-to' for 'to-may-to' and 'my-on-aise' for 'may-on-aise.'"

THE FIRST **TYPEWRITER**

of practical utility was built in 1800 by Hungarian polymath Wolfgang Kempelen, poet, artist, architect, linguist (he spoke nine languages), and superintendent of the salt mines. It was described in the October 1912 issue of *Office Appliances*:

> Kempelen had successfully experimented with the box shape, with hidden key levers. Under the patronage of a favorite of the Empress Maria Theresa, he continued his researches, and at length brought out a machine which wrote the German alphabet in large, clear type—about the size of modern large primer—several specimens of which are still exhibited in a Vienna museum. This machine also came into active use with the beginning of the nineteenth century. It spaced accurately, punctuated amply and typed clear, firm impressions of each letter. In fact, apart from its still clumsy construction the typewriter had now become a really practical business convenience, and among the limited number of commercial houses which could afford its purchase, was so regarded and used.

U.S.: The first was the Typographer, constructed by blacksmith, postmaster, and county surveyor William Austin Burt in the log cabin he inhabited in the backwoods of Michigan and patented on 23 July 1829. The instrument comprised a rectangular wooden box in which type mounted on a semi-circular frame was brought to the surface of the paper by turning a wheel on the front of the box, the character required being depressed by a small lever. The type came from the offices of the *Michigan Gazette*, whose editor John Sheldon wrote America's first typed letter from Detroit on 25 May 1829. Commending the machine, despite "some inaccuracies in the situation of the letters," it was addressed to Senator (later President) Martin van Buren. A letter from William Burt to his wife Phoebe dated New York, 13 March 1830, is the earliest surviving specimen of typewriting in America. Burt did not develop his Typographer commercially and it was indeed too slow in operation for regular correspondence.

Typewriter in regular series production: The first was the Danish *Skrivekugle* ("Writing Ball"), invented by Pastor Malling Hansen and manufactured by the Jürgens Mekaniske Establissement of Copenhagen in October 1870. Constructed of brass and steel, the flat-bed Hansen machine weighed 165 pounds and worked on the radial-plunger principle. Its fifty-two keys were angled in a hemispherical mounting in such a way that each, when depressed, would extend to a common printing point. The paper lay in a flat-bed case that moved laterally along guide rails one character space at a time. The price of the machine was £100 ($500) when it was marketed in Britain in 1872, though later versions sold for as little as £12 ($60). The Hansen typewriter was sold all over Europe and America and many models were still in use at the time of World War I.

Keyboard typewriter: The first produced commercially was developed by Christopher Latham Sholes and originally manufactured by his financial backer, James Densmore, in a Milwaukee wheelwright's shop in June 1872. To begin with there was no standardized model, each machine incorporating the latest ideas of its promoters.

Although the keys were originally arranged in alphabetical order, Sholes and Densmore decided on a new arrangement based on the order of type in a printer's case. The first machine incorporating the "universal" QWERTY keyboard still in use for word processors was completed by 8 November 1872, when Densmore wrote a letter to his son on it saying that "the change was better to be made than not." (This is open to doubt. Although marketed as a "scientific" arrangement, it is claimed that almost any haphazard ordering of the alphabet would be ergonomically preferable. A simplified keyboard would probably increase average typing speed by as much as 35 percent.)

Nearly all Sholes's output during the first year of production was sold to telegraphers, shorthand-reporters, lawyers, and other professional men; scarcely any to commercial firms, and only one sale to a government office is recorded. One of the 1872 models was sold to Allan Pinkerton, founder of the private detective agency that bears his name, and a number of machines were ordered by James O. Clephane, who set up the first commercial typewriting service the same year with offices in Washington, D.C., and New York.

In the winter of 1873 James Densmore opened the first typewriter shop at 4 Hanover Street, New York City, where Sholes's machine, now standardized for series production, was retailed at a price of $125. The basic design features of this model were similar to those of late twentieth-century typewriters with three important exceptions: It printed only in capital letters, the text was not visible to the operator while typing, and there was no back space.

Meanwhile the two partners, Sholes and Densmore, had signed a contract on 1 March 1873 for the mass production of their machine by the Remington Small Arms Co. of Ilion, N.Y. The Remington model was marketed as the Sholes & Glidden Type-Writer (Carlo Glidden had assisted Sholes at various states of development) on 1 July 1874. Mechanically, this typewriter (renamed the Remington No. 1 in 1876) followed the design of the Milwaukee machines almost exactly, the only significant difference being in the casing, metal having replaced wood. The price remained unchanged at $125.

Of the 400 customers who purchased Remington typewriters during the remaining months of 1874, the most notable was undoubtedly Mark Twain, who saw a model displayed in a store window in Boston while out for a walk one day with his friend and fellow humorist Petroleum V. Nasby. The two men were unable to agree on what purpose the machine was intended to serve, so they went inside to ask. The salesman explained, adding that it could write at a speed of fifty-seven words a minute. Twain replied that this was quite impossible. A "lady typewriter" was summoned and began to operate the machine while Twain and Nasby stood by with watches in their hands. At the end of a minute she had written exactly fifty-seven words. Twain said it was a fluke, so she did it again. The rest of the afternoon was happily passed in further demonstrations, the two spectators stuffing the typewritten pages into their pockets as fast as they came off the typewriter, to keep as souvenirs. It was only on returning to their hotel that they looked at the papers closely enough to see that they all contained the same sentence, repeated over and over again, but if Twain felt he had been duped, it was too late to alter the fact that he had already become the first author to possess a typewriter. Initially Mark Twain used his typewriter

only for correspondence, but in 1883 he submitted to his publishers the world's first **book in typescript:** his memoir of riverboat piloting, *Life on the Mississippi.*

During the first ten years of production, sales of the Remington typewriter were disappointingly small. One of the main reasons for sluggish sales was the use of aniline inks for typewriter ribbons. This retarded the adoption of typewriters by government departments and other institutions requiring permanent records, as the typescript was liable to fade. The breakthrough came in 1885 with the introduction of permanent inks, which was soon to have the effect (coupled with other improvements) of making the typewriter an essential item of office equipment, rather than a novelty or status symbol. A year later the *Scientific American* estimated that there were approximately 50,000 typewriters of all makes in use in the United States, and by 1890 there were thirty manufacturers competing for custom.

Typewriter incorporating a shift key: The first capable of inscribing text in both capital and lower-case letters was the Remington No. 2. of 1878.

"Bar" typewriter: The first model designed so that the writing was visible to the typist was the Horton, manufactured in Toronto, Canada, in 1883.

Portable typewriter: The first of practical utility was designed by George C. Blickensderfer of Erie, Pa., and produced by Blickensderfer Manufacturing Co. of Stamford, Conn., in 1897 as the Blick No. 7. Although lightweight typewriters had been produced earlier, some of them, such as the 7-pound Hall of 1883–84, actually described as portables, the Blick was the first that folded neatly into a carrying case for easy handling.

Electric typewriter: The first in commercial production was a typebar machine designed by Dr. Thaddeus Cahill of Washington, D.C., and manufactured by the Cahill Writing Machine Co. in 1901. Only forty units were built at a development cost of $157,000 before the enterprise was abandoned.

The first successful electric typewriter was the Blickensderfer Electric of 1902, a type-wheel machine operating on the same principle as "golf-ball" electrics of the 1960s. Very sophisticated technically, it would probably have gained greater recognition had more offices had main electricity. The electric typewriter only came into its own with the launch of the IBM Electric Model 01 of 1935.

Word processor: The first was the IBM Magnetic Selectric Typewriter, launched in the United States on 29 June 1964. This was capable of automatic adjustments of text, enabling a relatively unskilled operator to compose clean copy free of errors. With the many improvements made over the next twenty years, what developed into the all-electronic word processor, and was eventually incorporated into the desktop computer, superseded the mechanical typewriter. SEE **computer: word processor**.

Once the PC was established in office and home, the changeover was rapid. The last typewriter manufacturer, Godrej & Boyce of Pune, India, whose output in the 1990s was 50,000 machines a year, closed down production in 2009. In 2011 they announced that stocks remaining stood at just 500.

THE FIRST TYPISTS

The earliest record of female office workers being recruited as typists is contained in an advertisement placed in the New York City paper *The Nation* for 15 December 1875 by the Remington agents Locke, Yost & Bates Ltd. "Mere girls," it ran, "are now earning from $10 to $20 a week with the 'Type-Writer,' and we can secure good situations for one hundred expert writers on it in counting-rooms in this City."

These wages were abnormally high for female workers of the period and probably reflect the scarcity of competent typists only a year after full-scale production of typewriters had been initiated by the Remington Co. By the following decade the beginner's rate had fallen appreciably, but it was still favorable compared to that of female shop assistants. Speaking before a women's club in New Orleans in 1888, a typewriter salesman called Harry Hodgson said that a typist would start at $6 a week if reasonably proficient, and might eventually earn as much as $20 if she proved her worth. A shopgirl could only expect $6 as a top salary. Moreover the typist only worked from 8:30 A.M. to 5:30 P.M. and was given a full half hour off for lunch; the counter clerk might be on her feet for 12 hours or more a day.

The effect of the typewriter in liberating young women of the lower middle class from the bondage of the home was immeasurable. According to the U.S. Census, in 1870 only 1,893 women were employed in offices, representing 2.5 percent of the office workforce. With the advent of the typewriter, and soon afterward the telephone (qv), women began to take their place in offices, not as a rare, privileged exception, but in order to fulfill tasks that in general they were more accomplished at than their male colleagues. The English satirist G. K. Chesterton, however, had a different take on the dawn of these women's liberation: "Twenty million young women rose to their feet and said 'We will not be dictated to' and immediately became shorthand typists."

Training course for office typists: The first was offered in 1877 by the Central Branch of the YWCA in New York City. The eight pioneer girl students were chosen for physique rather than aptitude, as it was claimed that the arduous six months' course was beyond the capacity of female minds and constitutions. All eight girls survived the course and secured immediate employment on graduation. The YWCA was then inundated with requests for more trained typists and was able to establish the course on a more permanent footing.

Touch typist: The first was Frank McGurrin, official stenographer at the Salt Lake City Federal Court, who demonstrated his prowess in public for the first time in a speed-typing contest held at Cincinnati on 25 July 1888. McGurrin used ten fingers to operate his Remington and never looked at the keyboard; his opponent, typing-instructor Louis Taub, was a four-finger typist and kept his eyes on the keyboard of his Caligraph typewriter all the time. Taub lost not only his $550 stake but also his reputation as a speed typist, while the challenger won a victory for his own system of typing that was to have a profound effect on the methods used to train typists all over the world.

As late as 1990 more women in the western world earned their living by typing than any other occupation. This has almost certainly been superseded in the twenty-first century by data processing or call-center employment.

U

THE FIRST UMBRELLAS

(waterproof) are listed in an inventory of the movable effects of King Louis XIII of France made in 1637. The entry refers to: "Eleven sunshades in various colors, made of taffeta. Three umbrellas of oiled cloth trimmed underneath with gold and silver lace." This is the earliest known instance of the sunshade, used by ancient civilizations, being distinguished from its counterpart, the waterproof umbrella. Neither the king nor any of his male courtiers is likely to have carried one of these decorative trimmed umbrellas, but it is quite probable that Louis's beautiful queen, Anne of Austria, went abroad under a protective canopy of oiled silk, setting a style that was to be followed assiduously by the women of France.

The prejudice against the use of the umbrella by men was probably dissipated earlier in France than in any other European country. When the Parisian manufacturer Marius produced the first folding pocket umbrella with a collapsible shaft in 1715, he advertised his wares by means of an illustrated poster that shows a decorative model being carried by a lady of fashion, while a plain, unadorned masculine style of umbrella is held aloft by a man in a tricorn hat.

In Britain a strong prejudice against men using umbrellas persisted throughout the eighteenth century. Umbrellas were commonly kept at coffeehouses to protect the customers as they left to enter their carriages, but for a man to be actually seen carrying one was to invite the kind of ridicule implied in the following advertisement, which appeared in the *Female Tatler* on 12 December 1709: "The young gentleman belonging to the Custom House, that for fear of the rain borrowed the umbrella at Will's coffee house, in Cornhill, of the mistress, is hereby advertised that to be dry from the head to foot on the like occasion, he shall be welcome to the maid's pattens."

Umbrellas in the eighteenth century were expensive and often held as common property, to be lent out from coffeehouse, club, or church porch when the weather demanded. Cambridge University in the 1730s maintained one umbrella for the use of all of the undergraduates, booking being well in advance.

U.S.: The first person known to have used an umbrella was Edward Shippen, a Quaker merchant of Philadelphia, who imported one from England aboard the *Constantine* in 1738 at a cost of 9 shillings (about a week's wage for a laborer). Two years later there is record of a woman in Windsor, Conn., who had brought one with her from the West Indies, being mocked by neighbors who strutted about holding aloft colanders balanced on broom handles. The earliest advertisements for umbrellas appeared in the Boston press in 1762, but as in Britain they were regarded as suitable protection for women only. In 1771 a Philadelphia newspaper ridiculed "those effeminate individuals" who used them as protection from the fierce rays of a June sun. The medical profession, however, stoutly defended the practice and to prove their good faith Dr. Chancellor, Dr. Morgan, and the Rev. Mr. Duché braved the derision of the mob by promenading the streets beneath umbrellas at midday, a demonstration that apparently silenced the opposition. Jacob Duché, who was assistant rector of Philadelphia's Christ Church, also bore his brolly on the day he performed the opening prayers at the First Continental Congress on 5 September 1771. On this occasion he was roundly denounced for toting such a "new-fangled European affectation."

All umbrellas in the United States were imported before 1828, when they were first manufactured by William Beehler at Baltimore.

~~~~~~~~~~~~~~~~~~~~~~~ V ~~~~~~~~~~~~~~~~~~~~~~~

THE FIRST VACATION PACKAGE

was a sixteen-day tour of Switzerland via France by stage coach organized by Mr. B. Emery of Cockspur Street, Charing Cross in London. The earliest advertisement for the prepaid vacations that has been traced appeared in Johann Gottfried Ebel's guide book *The Traveller's Guide Through Switzerland*, published in 1818. Sir John Wraight, former British Ambassador to Switzerland who was the first to identify Emery's pioneering role in the travel industry, believes that the tours could have begun two years earlier in 1816, when there was a big surge of English visitors to Switzerland following the end of the Napoleonic Wars.

Emery's tours started from the White Bear Inn in Piccadilly, which also acted as booking agents. Two days were spent in Paris and the remainder traveling to and around Switzerland and home again, stopping each night in a different place. The number of excursionists was limited to six per tour and baggage allowance was 112 pounds. Inclusive price of the tours was 20 guineas ($105) until 1835, when it was reduced to £20 ($100). Little is known about Emery except that he was the son of a prominent Swiss watchmaker, Josias Emery, who had settled in London.

The first package tour aimed at the mass market was a "Whitsuntide Working Men's Excursion" to Paris, organized by the Committee of Working Men under the presidency of Sir Joseph Paxton, MP, with travel arrangements made by Thomas Cook. The first party of tourists left London Bridge Station at 10:15 A.M. on Friday, 17 May 1861.

Cook departed from his normal tour arrangements (SEE **travel agency**) in that he was prepared to issue coupons for pre-paid hotel accommodation at a cost of 5s to 6s ($1.25) a day, inclusive of meals. Formerly his tourists could pay only their fares in advance and were expected to meet all other expenses on the way as they arose. The innovation meant that

the thrifty working man could pay his 20s ($5) for the journey in a third-class covered carriage, 25s ($6.25) lodging at "a good second-class hotel," and 1 shilling (25¢) registration fee all at once, in effect a 46s ($11.25) package deal for his six-day vacation.

A choice of thirteen hotels was offered, including Austin's Railway Hotel in the rue d'Amsterdam, where those venturing forth from their native shores for the first time (the majority) were assured of a "substantial English dinner." A total of 1,700 working men and their families crossed the Channel on this great adventure.

The idea of letting loose such a large number of the humbler classes on a foreign capital all at once was controversial. "To many the title of the excursion is offensive," it was reported, "especially as it conveys the idea of some great attempt of fraternization of English workmen with French *ouvriers*." However, these fears proved groundless, and Cook was able to write with satisfaction afterward:

> I heard . . . that at a dinner party at which several of the [French] Ministers were present, the Excursion was the subject of conversation, and great pleasure was expressed at the behaviour of the visitors. Up to the latest period it was reported by the police authorities, that not a single case of misbehaviour had come under the argus eyes of one of the most vigilant police systems ever established.

By 1866 Thomas Cook was advertising regular all-in package vacations in Paris throughout the season at an inclusive charge of £3 13s ($18.25) for seven days with third-class travel, £4 1s ($20.25) for second class, and £4 15s ($23.75) for first class. Cook's early package tours ranged in price to embrace most income levels of Victorian middle-class society and on occasion were priced to suit the pockets of the better-paid workers. At one end of the scale was the four-day trip to Paris for the 1867 Exposition for 36s ($9) inclusive, at the other a twelve-week tour with first-class hotels and travel to Egypt, Syria, Palestine, Turkey, Greece, the Ionian Islands, Austria, Italy, Switzerland, and France, offered at 103 guineas ($540.85) in 1868.

U.S.: The first inclusive pre-paid vacations were offered by the Raymond & Whitcomb Travel Agency of Boston (SEE **travel agency**), which was offering packages to Yellowstone, the Rockies, California, and New Orleans, as well as the first foreign tours to Mexico, by 1891. Transportation was by railroad with transfers by stagecoach and customers knew "at the outset precisely what the excursion is to cost, inasmuch as every needed incidental is included in the general ticket—transportation, hotels, meals, baggage checks and insurance, tips, and letters of credit and circulating notes."

Motor coach tour: The first was a six-day Continental excursion from Paris to Aix-les-Bains that began on 11 July 1898. Organized jointly by the Compagnie Nationale d'Automobiles and Thomas Cook & Son, the tour cost 180 francs (about $45) and took the coach party on a route that passed through Fontainebleau, Sens, Auxerre, Avallon, Semur, Dijon, Dôle, Salins, Saint-Laurent, Geneva, and Annecy. The vehicle was a De Dion steam omnibus with seats arranged in six tiers, four facing forward and two backward. The sides of the coach were open, but there was a glazed partition separating the passengers from the driver and also a glass window at the rear. Average speed on a level surface was 10 mph, and the schedule allowed for 6 hours a day to be spent "in actual autocaring." There was a baggage limit of 44 pounds per passenger, as this had to be carried on the roof.

U.S.: Prepaid motor tours were inaugurated by Arthur Tauck of Westport, Conn., a traveling salesman who sold aluminum coin trays to banks throughout New England. His "eureka" moment happened in the fall of 1924 while lunching at the Wigwam Restaurant on the Mohawk Trail, just east of the Berkshire Mountains. All the other patrons of the restaurant were fellow traveling salesmen and it occurred to him that the reason there were no tourists enjoying the splendors of the New England fall was that they needed to be shown the way with an experienced guide—and preferably in a way that took all the business of booking such a tour out of their hands. His initial tour the following year was simply an adjunct to one of his sales

trips. He took four passengers in a rented Studebaker on a tour of the Berkshires and the Adirondacks, upstate New York, Vermont, and Canada, 900 miles of which was on dirt roads in the backcountry. They drove in the mornings and the excursionists relaxed in the afternoon at resorts and scenic attractions while Tauck called on his customers. In 1926 he took a tour to Great Smoky Mountains National Park on the borders of Tennessee and North Carolina and by 1929 he was operating a full-scale travel company, Tauck Tours, with motor coaches. The company he founded continues today as Tauck World Discovery, offering tours worldwide, with granddaughter Robin as CEO.

Vacation by air: Vacation packages by airplane were inaugurated by Pan-American Airways in 1929 with a "20 Day All Luxury Cruise of Adventure" that took a select company of very rich, and perhaps reckless, travelers by train from either New York, Chicago, or St. Louis to Miami, then by Ford Tri-Motor airliner to Havana, Cuba, and on to Haiti and the Dominic Republic, thence to San Juan, Puerto Rico, and eventually home by Puerto Rico Line steamship to New York. By 1936 the even more intrepid and seriously wealthy could take a nineteen-day Flying Clipper Cruise to Rio de Janeiro via Trinidad. In the meantime the Polytechnic Touring Association of London had inaugurated the first European air packages when they chartered a Heracles airliner from Imperial Airways in 1932, carrying a total of 900 vacationists either to Switzerland or on a tour of seven capital cities. The first ski vacation packages by air followed in 1937, KLM (Royal Dutch Airlines) and Deutsche Lufthansa forming a partnership to fly winter sports addicts to the Italian Alps.

THE FIRST **VACUUM CLEANER**

power operated, was devised by English bridge engineer Hubert Cecil Booth in 1901, after watching at the Empire Music Hall in London's Leicester Square a demonstration of an American invention for the removal of dust by blowing it away with compressed air. This technique created clouds of dust, but as there was no way of removing it the dirt simply settled again. Booth asked the inventor why he did not use suction, but the man became heated, declaring it was impossible, and walked away. A few days later Booth was in a restaurant in Victoria Street, where he tried out the principle of vacuum cleaning by holding a handkerchief over the back of the plush seat and sucking hard. Although he nearly choked, a ring of black spots on the handkerchief showed that the idea was sound. A prototype machine was built and on 25 February 1902 Cecil Booth issued a prospectus for his newly formed Vacuum Cleaner Co. Ltd.

Since few houses were served with electricity, and the apparatus was expensive and cumbersome, it was decided not to sell cleaners outright but to provide a cleaning service on demand. A powerful vacuum pump, driven by either gasoline or an electric motor, was mounted on a four-wheel horse-drawn van and stationed by the curbside outside a customer's house. The dust was then sucked out of carpets and soft furnishings through 800-foot-long hoses that passed through the first-floor windows and thence to any part that needed cleaning. Booth later recalled that so atrocious was the noise of the machine that he was frequently sued for allegedly frightening passing horses, cab proprietors being particularly hostile. When finally a test case was taken to appeal, the Lord Chief Justice upheld Booth's right to operate the machines in the street.

One of the earliest successes of the Vacuum Cleaner Co. occurred in connection with the Coronation of King Edward VII in 1902. When all the other preparations in Westminster Abbey were complete, it was found that the deep-pile blue carpets under the twin thrones were in a deplorable state, and by this time it was too late to remove them for cleaning by conventional means. Booth heard of the predicament and approached the Board of Works with an offer of assistance. Within hours a machine was standing in the Cloister Quadrangle and the hoses were being let into the abbey. The king was delighted with the story and commanded a demonstration at Buckingham Palace, which both he and Queen Alexandra watched. Booth was obliged to make an exception to his "no sales" policy when an order was received for two complete vacuum cleaners, one for the palace and the other for Windsor Castle.

As a result of this royal patronage, vacuum cleaners won rapid favor with society hostesses, not only for their practical utility, but as a tea-party attraction.

Soirées were held at which the guests were entertained by a team of Vacuum Cleaner operatives going to work on the carpets and upholstery. As an added novelty Booth provided visible inspection tubes so that the audience could watch the dirt as it was sucked into the machine outside.

Portable electric vacuum cleaner: The first for domestic use was a 92-pound trolley-mounted model marketed by Chapman & Skinner of San Francisco in 1905.

The prototype of the modern, upright vacuum cleaner with dust bag attached to the handle was built in 1907 by J. Murray Spangler, janitor at the Folwell Building in Canton, Ohio, the bottom stories of which housed a department store, Zollinger's. One of Spangler's duties was to clean the rugs on the floor of the store, using a carpet sweeper that created clouds of dust and gave the put-upon janitor an asthmatic cough. Crudely fashioned out of wood and tin, Spangler's machine was fitted with a broom handle, an old pillowcase begged from his wife for a dust bag, and a roller brush made of goat bristles.

Spangler began manufacturing the machines at the rate of two or three a week in his basement. One of these he took to neighboring New Berlin in the hope of selling it to his cousin Susan, married to one William H. Hoover, who was a saddler by trade. Hoover's business had been hit by the advent of the automobile and he was seeking to diversify. He agreed to finance a new company, the Electric Suction Sweeper Co., appoint Murray Spangler in charge of production, and provide factory space at the W. H. Hoover Co. saddling workshops. Sales were the responsibility of general manager Herbert W. Hoover, William Hoover's eldest son, who placed a small double-column 2-inch advertisement in the *Saturday Evening Post* for 5 December 1908 at a cost of $207.90. Hoover's marketing plan was masterly. Housewives were offered a free ten-day trial. He wrote to those who responded saying that the machine could be picked up from the local hardware store in their hometown. Then he wrote to the store that he was delivering a vacuum cleaner and would pay commission on the $70 purchase price if the housewife kept it; if she did not, the merchant could keep it as a free sample.

Bagless vacuum cleaner: The first was the Dyson G-Force, patented by English inventor James Dyson on 14 April 1979 after he had discovered, when cleaning his new home, Sycamore House at Bath, Somerset, that vacuum cleaners with dust bags lose 70 percent of their suction as soon as the bag becomes clogged with dust. After building no fewer than 5,127 designs (believed to be a record for prototypes) he perfected the concept of the Cyclon, which caught dust by centrifugal force at speeds of more than 200 mph. The original G-Force, manufactured by hand at Sycamore House, was sold in very small quantities door-to-door in Britain in 1983 while Dyson sought, without success, to interest European and American manufacturers. It was only when he took his invention to Japan that it was recognized as a revolutionary design far exceeding all dust-bag cleaners in power and performance. Manufactured under license by Apex as the S-Force and launched in March 1986, it became a lifestyle item for design-conscious Japanese happy to shell out $1,765 for the ultimate domestic status symbol. A later model, the Dyson DC01, of 1993, became the biggest-selling vacuum cleaner of all time, outselling all others by nine to one. Unlike most lone inventors, Dyson reaped a rich reward, enabling him in 2003 to buy the fifty-one-bedroom Gloucestershire mansion complex Dodington Park for £50 million ($80 million).

U.S.: The first bagless vacuum cleaner was the Clear Trak produced by Amway of Ada, Mich., in 1987 and retailed in $899. Dyson sued for patent infringement and Amway withdrew from the U.S. market when he launched the DC01 on this side of the Atlantic in 2002.

Robotic cleaner: The first capable of finding its way safely around the cleaning area without human intervention was an industrial model introduced by Electrolux in the United States in 1991 for use in hospitals and airports. The first domestic model was the bagless Dyson DC06, marketed in Britain at £2,500 ($4,125) early in 2000.

THE FIRST VELCRO

fastening was invented by Swiss aristocrat George de Mestral of Saint-Saphorin-sur-Morges, Vaud, as the result of an unfortunate accident that ruined an evening out in 1948. The zipper on his wife's dress jammed and refused to un-jam. De Mestral determined to find a better method of fastening and the solution came to him one day a few months later when he was out shooting with his dog. The dog's ears became covered in burrs from brushing against burdock weed. Examining the burrs under a microscope he found that they bristled with tiny hooks. He realized the principle of a foolproof fastening lay in this bequest of nature and all that was needed was a method of applying it to textiles. Nonetheless nine years of research was required to bring it to a form in which it could be produced commercially and in 1957 De Mestral opened the Velcrotex factory at Aubonne, Switzerland, to manufacture the first Velcro fasteners, the name being a contraction of the French *velours croché*, meaning hooked velvet. Manufacture in the United States began the same year when license holder American Velcro Inc. opened a factory in Manchester, N.H. Americans took to Velcro immediately and by the end of the decade the Manchester looms were turning out 60 million yards a year. Among its users were the first astronauts on the Moon, who used it on their spacesuits and also to fix objects on the cabin walls that would otherwise have floated in weightless space.

THE FIRST VENDING MACHINES

operating on the coin-in-the slot principle were the so-called "honesty" tobacco boxes, which are known to have made their appearance in English taverns by 1615. Insertion of a penny in the slot would release the lock on the lid of the box, enabling the customer to take out a pipeful of tobacco. A strong element of trust entered into this method of vending, relying as it did on the purchaser taking no more than the permissible pipeful, and on his shutting the lid again, though it is unlikely the box was ever allowed out of the publican's range of vision. These primitive vending machines remained in use until well into the nineteenth century. One notable example, which may or may not have been automatic in operation, was installed at his London bookshop the Temple of Reason by radical publisher Richard Carlile in 1822. Most of Carlile's stock, including such inflammatory works as Thomas Paine's *The Age of Reason*, was considered seditious by the authorities and he was in constant danger of arrest. He had the notion, however, that as the police needed to actually catch someone in the act of selling a seditious book in order to make the charge stick, rather than merely stocking it for sale, then books sold by a machine would be outside the remit of law. Nothing is known of the construction of the machine, or indeed who made it, but the fact that it was put into operation is testified by this announcement in Carlile's scurrilous weekly *The Republican*:

> Perhaps it will amuse you to be informed that in the new Temple of Reason my publications are sold by clockwork! In the shop is the dial on which is written every publication for sale. The purchaser enters and turns the hands of the dial to the publication he wants, when, on depositing his money, the publication drops down before him.

It transpired that Carlile was wrong in his interpretation of the law and one of his assistants was convicted of selling blasphemous literature through the device. Whether this was because he had been the one to stock up the vending machine, or whether the apparatus could not dispense books without some third party intervention, the court records do not disclose.

Automatic vending-machine: The first known to have been put into commercial operation was a postcard machine designed by Percival Everitt and set up on the platform of Mansion House Underground Station, London, in April 1883. The Victorian public, it would appear, were no better behaved when confronted with slot machines than the vandals of a later generation. "It has been found in practice," said Everitt in his American patent application of 1886, "that although the apparatus is perfectly successful when not designedly misused, articles such as paper, orange-peel, and other rubbish have been maliciously placed in the slit provided for the admission of the coin..." Notwithstanding this discouraging setback, he pressed ahead with development and on 25 November 1887 the Sweetmeat Automatic Delivery Co. was organized to exploit the machines on a nationwide basis. The range of goods sold was not as restricted as the title suggests, for within a year or two, commodities available at the drop of a coin in the slot included cigarettes, eggs, quinine, cookies, scent, handkerchiefs, condensed milk, towels, cough lozenges, sugar, and accident insurance.

U.S.: The first machines were installed on station platforms of New York's Elevated Railroad in 1888 by Thomas Adams of the Adams Gum Co. (SEE **chewing gum**) to sell his popular new Tutti-Frutti brand. Americans were particularly imaginative in the range of products obtainable by inserting coins in a slot and lost no time in adapting the vending principle for everything from postage stamps to gambling. By the mid-1890s the citizens of Corinne, Utah, were able to obtain divorce papers automatically from a machine that proffered this service in exchange for two silver dollars in one slot and one half dollar in another. The Germans were equally inventive, pioneering the automat or coin-operated restaurant in 1895, and reaching what may have been the ultimate in bizarre slot-salesmanship in 1924, when a Berlin newspaper reported that a machine had just come into operation that would dispense a valid American doctorate for the equivalent of $1.

SEE ALSO **soda pop: vending machine**.

THE FIRST **VIBRATOR, ELECTRIC**

was employed in the treatment of hysterical women (in the clinical sense of disorders stemming from the uterus) at the Salpêtrière in Paris by Auguste Vigouroux in 1875, probably by application to the vulva. Nothing is known of the physical properties of this device, and the earliest electromechanical vibrator of which there is a full description was manufactured by the London surgical instrument manufacturer Weiss for neurologist Joseph Mortimer Granville. This was in use by 1883, the year Granville published a book about the clinical use of vibrators, of which he considered himself the inventor. It was powered by an electric battery about the size of a modern car battery and the vibrator itself could accommodate vibratodes of varying speeds. The purpose of the procedure was to increase the blood supply to the area treated. In men this was often the rectum.

Vibrators were soon to move beyond the clinic to beauty salons and into the home, the earliest example of a domestic model noted by Rachel P. Maines in her pioneering study *The Technology of Orgasm* (Johns Hopkins, 1999) being the Vibratile advertised in the March 1899 issue of *McClure's Magazine*. While this was recommended as a remedy for "Neuralgia, Headache, Wrinkles," it seems likely that Edwardian women would have found another, more sensual use for the many similar home devices offered by mail-order suppliers at prices ranging from $5.95. A 1909 medical catalog observed disapprovingly that "most of the vibrators sold by dealers and hawked about the country are mere trinkets which accomplish little more than titillation of the tissues." Titillation by "30,000 thrilling, invigorating, penetrating, revitalizing vibrations per minute" (Swedish Vibrator Co., Chicago, 1913) was precisely what some customers wanted, especially "penetrating." While the date at which the vibrator came into use as a sex aid must remain conjectural, it was probably long before its appearance in a c. 1924 porn film, *Widows Delight*, in this capacity.

The most comprehensive collection of vibrators is held by the Bakken Museum of Electricity in Life in Minneapolis.

THE FIRST **VIDEO GAME**

was built in 1958 by physicist Willy Higinbotham at Brookhaven National Laboratory, Upton, Long Island, N.Y. It consisted of a tennis match played on a 5-inch circular video screen and each player had a box with a button and a knob. The button served the ball and the knob controlled its elevation. If you hit it into the net, it bounced back along the ground toward your end in a realistic manner. The apparatus was set up in the laboratory's gym, where long lines of visitors queued up to play. The following year Higinbotham built a version with a larger screen that gave contestants the choice of playing on the Moon with very low gravity or on Jupiter with very intense gravity. After two years of fun with the machine he dismantled it, never considering that it might have commercial possibilities. Reproached by his children in later years for lack of foresight, he pointed out that if he had

patented the idea he would not have made a dime; working as he did for a government research installation, the patent would have belonged to Uncle Sam.

The first commercially produced video game was *Computer Space*, devised by Nolan Bushnell of the University of Utah in 1971. He had been inspired by an experimental computer game called *Space War* created by MIT student Steve Russell ten years earlier on a PDP-1 computer, one of the earliest to have a screen monitor. Bushnell, then a young research engineer with Ampex, spent all his spare time over the next few years trying to fit the required technology into a box small enough to be installed in public places. The breakthrough came with the invention of the microprocessor. Nevertheless *Computer Space*, although it simulated an exciting battle between spacecraft and flying saucers, was slow in capturing the public imagination and only 2,000 units were sold. Bushnell persevered with a new game called Pong, based on table tennis, and in November 1972 the first model was installed at Andy Capp's Tavern in Sunnyvale, Calif. This was such an immediate success that the machine seized up after a few hours, completely jammed with coins. He founded a company called Atari (after a term used in the game of Go) to produce and market the game and when he eventually sold out to Warner in 1982 his personal profit from the deal was $15 million.

Home video game: The first was the *Odyssey*, devised by engineer Ralph Baer of Sanders Associates, Nashua, N.H., and launched by licensee Magnavox at $99.95 in May 1972. This involved a handheld console connected to a TV antenna terminal and could play a dozen variations of games based on tennis, Ping-Pong, and hockey. Despite the fact that it was in black-and-white and soundless, some 100,000 units had been sold by Christmas of 1972, spawning a host of imitators. By 1975 there were thirty companies producing similar game consoles and it was in the same year Magnavox pioneered again by adding sound to its *Odyssey 200* system. In August 1976 Fairchild Camera & Instrument introduced the first programmable home video system with its Channel F, retailed at $150 and operated with $20 cartridges or "video-carts" of which the initial offerings were *Tic-Tac-Toe*, *Shooting Gallery*, and a tank warfare game with sound effects called *Space Quadra Doodle*. Atari trumped Fairchild in 1978 by introducing paddle and joystick controllers with the VCS (2600), a bestseller despite an awesome price tag of $200 before purchase of the cartridges.

The first **video game with animated characters** was *Space Invaders*, released by Tokyo-based Taito on 16 June 1978, which featured six horizontal rows of the eponymous aliens, a total of forty-eight. The first built around a central character was Namco's 1980 *Pac-Man*, which had started life in Japan as *Puck-Man*. Unfortunately when this was released in the United States, it soon became apparent how easy it was for adolescent boys with magic markers to change the P to an F. The design of the character was derived from a pizza with a slice removed, which may not sound all that inspiring but proved very appealing to school-age girls, who liked the fact that he was nonviolent. For this reason *Pac-Man* became the first video game with an ancillary life in merchandising, the cutesy face appearing on gift wrap, pillowcases, lunch boxes, backpacks, and Hallmark greetings cards. The first human character was Mario the Italian plumber, hero of Shigeru Miyamoto's 1981 Nintendo game *Donkey Kong*. This was also the first computer game to be adapted as a movie, *Super Mario Brothers* (1993) starring Bob Hoskins, who knew how to play a plumber: He worked as one before becoming an actor.

Handheld video-game console: The first self-contained (i.e., unconnected to a TV receiver) was Nintendo's Game and Watch, developed by the company's master designer Gumpri Yokoi and launched on 28 April 1980. Each console contained a single game. Nintendo set a sales target of 100,000 units. It actually sold more than 45 million, wiping out the company's massive debts and putting it into profit. Yokoi also designed the 1989 Game Boy that exceeded Game and Watch's prodigious sales by 5 million, with 200 million individual games sold. The most successful games console of all, Sony's PlayStation, was the first designed to be operated with games encoded on CDs. It was launched on 3 December 1994 in Japan and on 9 September 1995 in the United States, price $299, and went on to become to first games console to sell more than 100 million units.

THE FIRST **VIDEO RECORDER**

was a monochrome machine demonstrated by John Mullin and Wayne Johnson at the Bing Crosby Enterprises laboratories in Beverly Hills, Calif., on 11 November 1952. Bing Crosby Enterprises also showed the first color video in September 1953, though neither was developed commercially. Mullin had brought two of the first plastic-tape recorders (SEE **magnetic recorder**) back from Germany after World War II and the Crosby machine was derived from these.

The first commercially produced video recorder was demonstrated to CBS by Ampex of Redwood City, Calif., on 14 April 1956. CBS acquired the initial production model, the VR-1000, for $75,000 and on 23 October 1956 aired the first video recording on TV, a short clip of guest singer Dorothy Collins used in *The Jonathan Winters Show*. This was an experiment to see whether viewers could tell the difference (they could not). It was followed on 30 November by the first taped program, *Douglas Edwards with the News*, from CBS Television City, Hollywood. The program had been broadcast live in New York 3 hours earlier. The first videoed program to be aired nationally was NBC's recording of the inauguration of President Dwight D. Eisenhower on 21 January 1957.

Domestic video recorder: The first was the German-made Loewe Optacord 500, exhibited at the Berlin Radio Show on 25 August 1961. The size of most professional units, it used 2-inch monochrome tape on open reels advancing at 19 cm (7.48 inches) per second.

U.S.: The first was the open-reel monochrome Sony CV-2000 Portapack, launched at $995 on 6 July 1965. Tapes cost $60 for one hour of recording. Sony produced the first domestic color VR in February 1966.

Video cassette recorder: The first was the Sony U-matic for professional use, launched in Japan by Sony at $2,500 in March 1972.

The first domestic VCR was the Avco Cartrivision, which went on sale at $1,600 at eighteen Sears stores in the Chicago area in June 1972. It incorporated a color TV set and could record off air as well as play pre-recorded tapes (SEE BELOW). These came in square cassettes and the half-inch tape gave nearly 2 hours of vision, long enough for most feature films. Cartrivision was given substantial backing by its parent company Avco but after two years it was apparent that the grand vision of persuading Japanese manufacturers to adopt the same technical standards, enabling Avco to make its profits from the software, was not going to be realized and the enterprise folded.

VCRs were relaunched in the United States with the one-hour-tape-capacity $2,295 Sony Betamax on 29 May 1975, but the real breakthrough for home video lay with the VHS format. This was unveiled in the United States when Japan's JVC presented the HR-3000 with 2-hour tape capacity and Matsushita the Panasonic with 4-hour capacity at the International Tape Association seminar held at Hilton Head Island, S.C., on 4–6 April 1977. Both were put on the market in the fall, the Panasonic being sold under RCA's Selecta Vision label at $1,000. The longer playing time proved crucial in the Betamax–VHS conflict, the 4-hour capacity of the Panasonic/Selectavision enabling sports fans to record football games in their entirety. By mid-1979 VHS was outselling the technically superior Beta by two to one in the U.S. market.

Camcorder: The first was the $350 Portapack camera introduced by Sony together with its open-reel domestic video recorder (SEE ABOVE) on 6 July 1965. Uptake was limited by the fact that the camera, despite its name, was large and heavy, that it only recorded in black-and-white, and that the tape was difficult to edit. The first cassette camcorder was announced by JVC of Tokyo on 19 September 1976 for use with the VHS tape deck it launched in Japan early the following year and in the United States in the fall (SEE ABOVE). The first for amateurs was announced by JVC of Tokyo on 19 September 1976. It was for use with the VHS tape deck introduced by JVC of the same time (SEE ABOVE). First in the United States was the Sony black-and-white Betamax offered by Sears, Roebuck at $297.50 in 1979.

Pre-recorded tapes: The first for home use were offered through Sears, Roebuck in the Chicago area in the spring of 1972 for use in the Avco Cartrivison VCR (SEE ABOVE). There were two hundred feature movies for hire at $3 to $6 each, including *Casablanca*, *It Happened One Night*, *Red River*, and *Dr. Strangelove*. In order to persuade the copyright holders to release the films on tape, Avco had to agree that the cassettes should be unrewindable at home (a special machine in the store rewound them on return), the rather mean-spirited purpose of this being to limit rental to a single viewing. The catalog of tapes for sale listed III titles, mainly of an informative nature such as *Fishing with Gadabout Gaddis*, *Rembrandt and the Bible*, and *Erica Wilson's Basic Crewel*. The only drama, the first shot expressly for video release, was a version of Checkhov's *The Swan Song*.

Cartrivision was an idea ahead of its time and the rebirth of pre-recorded tapes had to await the introduction of the VHS format in 1977. In July of that year André Blay of the small Michigan-based company Magnetic Video of Farmington Hills acquired the video rights to fifty movies owned by Fox. He started retailing them by mail order for $50 each in October. The titles, issued in both VHS and Beta formats, included *Patton*, *Hello, Dolly!*, *M*A*S*H*, *The Sound of Music*, and *Beneath the Planet of the Apes*.

Although there were fewer than 200,000 VCRs in the whole country, Blay succeeded in signing up 9,000 of them for his Video Club of America in response to a single $65,000 ad in *TV Guide*. Since he charged a $10 membership for the privilege of buying tapes, the whole cost of the ad was more than covered before he had sold a single one. The most popular titles proved to be *M*A*S*H* and *The French Connection*, though one early customer, a veterinarian from North Carolina, was less discriminating; he bought the entire catalog.

He was not the only one to do so. Among Blay's customers was Shanghai-born Anglo-Russian immigrant George Anderson, who ran a small shop on Wilshire Boulevard in West Los Angeles renting out 8mm projectors and old cartoon films for children's parties. He bought all fifty titles in both Beta and VHS formats and established the world's first **video rental outlet**. Even with an annual membership subscription of $50 and a rental charge of $10 a night, business was so good that Anderson was able to open a second store in Pasadena in April 1978 and then to start franchising. Blay also did well. Only a year after buying the rights to the movies at a knockdown price he sold them back to Fox for $7.2 million in cash.

In the meantime the copyright owners of American films released on video were attempting to strangle the rental trade at birth, even though there was little retail trade at the time. Some rental outlets devised an ingenious scheme by which the customer "bought" the tape, then got most of the money back on returning it. Because of the difficulty of obtaining mainstream Hollywood movies, early rental videos tended to be Hollywood B movies, British films, porn, or black-and-white oldies in the public domain. Warner was the next after Fox to license movies for video release with *Superman*, *The Exorcist*, and *The Searchers* among the initial twenty-five titles, followed in the summer of 1981 by Disney, Paramount, Columbia, and MGM. Even then the rental outlets had to buy through intermediaries, as Anderson had done when he bought the Blay offerings, and trust to luck that the studios would not take legal action against them. Only in late 1981 did Hollywood come to the belated realization that video rental was here to stay and it would pay them to accommodate it, first Warner Home Video, then Fox and MGM announcing schemes to legitimize the business.

DVD player: The first was the Toshiba SD-3000, launched in Japan at ¥77,000 on 1 November 1996. The first Hollywood movies available on DVD were released in Japan by Time Warner on 20 December 1996.

U.S.: Matsushita launched their Panasonic DVD player 31 March 1997. At the same time the first U.S.-produced disks were released by the Panasonic Disc Services of Torrance, Calif., starting with *Twister* and a number of other Warner Bros. titles. DVD players had the fastest uptake of any electronic product in history, sales of 437,000 in the first year easily surpassing VCR and CD player sales during the first twelve months those products were available. DVD rentals overtook VHS in the United States for the first time during the week ending 16 March 2003, by $80 million to $78 million.

DVR (Digital Video Recorder) or Personal Video Recorder: The first digital recorders recording on hard disk were developed simultaneously by Japan's Panasonic and Netherlands-based Philips and exhibited at the Consumer Electronics Show in Las Vegas by ReplayTV of Santa Clara, Calif., and TiVo of Alviso, Calif., respectively, in January 1999. Before the end of the month ReplayTV was first to market with the Panasonic model, followed by TiVo at the end of March. Although ReplayTV had won "Best in Show," it was TiVo whose recorder achieved higher commercial uptake.

Blu-ray Disc: The first recorder was the Sony BBZ-577 launched in Japan at the equivalent of $3,800 on 10 April 2003. Owing to difficulties in agreeing technical standards, movies on Blu-ray were delayed until 2006. On 20 June of that year, MGM released *The Terminator* and Sony o *First Dates*, *The Fifth Element*, *Hitch*, *House of Flying Daggers*, *Underworld Evolution*, and *xXx*. The first player sold in the United States was the Samsung P1000, available 25 June 2006 at $999.99.

THE FIRST VIOLIN MAKER

in America was a notorious convict and desperado called Geoffrey Stafford, a "lute and fiddle-maker" by trade, who was transported from England to Boston together with two hundred other felons in 1691. Once there he resumed his legitimate trade (his illegitimate one in London being unrecorded) until recruited with some of his fellow roughs by the unstable Gov. Fletcher of New York as vigilantes to protect the populace from the depredations of the French to the north and their allies, the Indian tribes. Once armed, many took off to become pirates. The gang of which Stafford was a member turned inland and began to terrorize the citizenry around Albany, occasionally breaking off from these activities to pursue Mohawks. Having destroyed several Indian settlements, Stafford came to the favorable notice of Gov. Fletcher, who summoned him to New York City to confer on campaign tactics. Stafford carried with him a violin he had made at Albany and so enraptured the governor with his playing that he was granted a regular military commission and a place in the executive household. The ill-famed governor and his new favorite were wont to get drunk together and on one occasion when both were in their cups Stafford killed Fletcher's personal manservant with his sword, seemingly on a whim. The governor treated this outrage with levity until Stafford began to prod the gubernatorial paunch with the tip of his sword. This appears to have terminated their relationship, Stafford returning to violin making interspersed with occasional highway robbery. Both activities came to a premature end when a Dutchman who had been relieved of his property managed to overcome his assailant and, summoning help, applied instant justice by hanging him from a tree. He left a family, some of whose descendants rewrote history with the assertion that their forbears had come over on the *Mayflower*.

THE FIRST **VOLLEYBALL**

was played formally at Springfield College in Springfield, Mass., on 7 July 1896 and is the only team game originated in America by an American (basketball [qv] had been invented at the college four years earlier, but by a Canadian). It had been developed that year at the YMCA in Holyoke, Mass., by physical training instructor William G. Morgan under the name *mintonette*. Springfield College professor Alfred T. Halstead suggested that the rather more masculine name of volley ball should be adopted (originally in two words) after he observed players volleying the ball back and forth over the net. Volleyball was first recognized internationally when it was included in the 1913 Far Eastern Games in Manila. It was also in the Philippines, three years later, that an offensive style of passing the ball in a high trajectory to be struck by another player (the set and spike) was introduced.

Volleyball was the first women's team sport played in the Olympics, starting at the Tokyo Olympiad of 1964. The gold medal was taken by the Japanese team, ten of whose twelve members worked at the same Kaizuko spinning mill and trained six hours a day, seven days a week.

Beach volleyball was introduced at the Outrigger Canoe Club at Waikiki, Hawaii, by George David "Dad" Center, probably in 1915. A photograph of the game being played toward the end of that year proves the Hawaiian provenance, though many reference works place its origin in Southern California in the early 1920s. It is the only sport in which women professionals, who are required by regulation to wear bikinis, earn more in sponsorship and endorsements than men.

THE FIRST **VOTES AT EIGHTEEN**

were granted to free male citizens, except "those of African descent," under the constitution adopted by a national convention of the Cherokee Republic in Georgia in 1826. This autonomous "nation" had been established in 1817 with its own congress and a senate. With a population of 15,000, and a capital city, New Echota (near what is now Chatsworth, Ga.), it was divided into eight congressional districts, each with a police force, courts, and powers to raise taxes, pay salaries, and collect debts. The first elections in which eighteen-year-olds were able to vote were held in the summer of 1828. The republic was dissolved under the Treaty of New Echota of 1835.

Voting at eighteen appears to have appealed to "nations within nations," because the next judiciary to grant the right was the remote Welsh colony of Chubut in northern Patagonia in 1865—lost when it was incorporated into Argentina ten years later.

The first U.S. state to lower the voting age to eighteen was Georgia under the state constitution ratified on 7 August 1945. The first sovereign nation to do so was Czechoslovakia in 1946, preparatory to the general election held on 26 May that year. The electorate returned 114 communists to the 300-seat parliament, more than any other party. Two years later the Communist Party established one-party rule and there were no further democratic elections until the collapse of the Soviet empire in 1989–90.

In the United States the 26th Amendment of the Constitution in 1971 gave all citizens of eighteen the right to vote, effective 1 January 1972. The change was stimulated by the participation of so many under-twenty-one-year-olds in the Vietnam War; as expressed in the song "Eve of Destruction" by Barry McGuire, "You're old enough to kill, but not for voting" (though even after the amendment, resident foreign nationals could still be drafted without the right to vote). In the first year that the new age qualification was in operation, only half the under-twenty-one-year-olds eligible to vote exercised the privilege.

The first electorate with a voting age to sixteen was Nicaragua in November 1984, since which Brazil, Cuba, and the Isle of Man have also extended the suffrage to sixteen-year-olds. The lowest voting age was fifteen, in Iran, but this was revised to eighteen in 2007. The highest is twenty-five, in Uzbekistan.

~~~~~~~~~~~~~~~~~~~~~~~~~~ **W** ~~~~~~~~~~~~~~~~~~~~~~~~~

THE FIRST WALLPAPER

known, was uncovered at the Master's Lodgings of Christ's College at Cambridge University during the course of restoration in 1911 and is believed to date from 1509. The black-and-white design was an imitation of oriental velvet or brocade, with a central motif consisting of a pinecone surrounded by strapwork and foliage. A Lombardic "H" appears halfway up on the left-hand side, and opposite this the image of a bird. These two variations from the otherwise symmetrical pattern indicate that it was almost certainly the work of the printer Hugo Goes, who employed the mark of an "H" and a goose as a form of signature. Originally from Beverley, Yorkshire, in 1509 Goes was carrying on his printing business at Steengate, York.

The paper itself consisted of discarded printed documents, the design being printed on the reverse from a woodblock 16" x 11". These documents include a poem on the death of Henry VII (21 April 1509), a proclamation issued on the accession of Henry VIII, and an indulgence of about the same time embellished with the della Rovere arms. The dating accords with the fact that the building of the Master's Lodgings was completed toward the end of 1509.

Although China has often been credited with the invention of wallpaper, the earliest known Chinese examples date from the mid-sixteenth century. These were usually presented to their foreign customers by Chinese merchants as gifts. There is no evidence that the Chinese used wallpaper in their own homes, which were generally decorated with hand-painted silken wall hangings. A considerable export trade in wallpaper developed in the eighteenth century and the Chinese designs were widely imitated in Europe. **U.S.:** The earliest reference to wallpaper is in a 1700 inventory of the goods of Boston stationer Michael Perry that lists "three quires of painted paper and seven reams of printed paper."

Like all early wallpaper in America, this would have been imported. J. Leander Bishop, in *A History of American Manufacturers from 1608 to 1860* (1861), states that the earliest advertisement for imported wallpaper appeared about 1737, but does not state his source. When the Swedish traveler Prof. Kalm visited New York in 1748, he remarked on the absence of wallpaper, saying that interiors were generally whitewashed.

The first record of American production of wallpaper is an advertisement in the *New York Mercury* for 13 December 1756 in which silk-dyer John Hickey, formerly of Dublin, announces that he "stamps and prints paper in the English manner and hangs it so as to harbor no worms."

THE FIRST WAR CORRESPONDENT

was John Bell, the Yorkshire-born proprietor of the London newspaper *The Oracle or Bell's New World*. This was a paper that he had founded in June 1789 as a vehicle for hurling abuse at his former business partner, the fashionable rake Capt. Edward Topham. In February 1793, the month that France declared war on Great Britain, Bell was called to judgment for libeling the Foot Guards. When he failed to appear in court, his goods were seized and sold by public auction. Describing this turn of events as "misfortune succeeding injustice," the proprietor of the *Oracle* decided that the only means of restoring his fortunes was to boost the circulation of the newspaper that represented his sole remaining possession. This he proposed to do with on-the-spot accounts of the fighting between the French and British in the Low Countries. His decision to march with the enemy forces rather than with the Duke of York's army may have been made either out of perversity, or from an instinctive flair for the best news angle.

The usual editorial practice at this time was to copy the war news from the foreign press most closely concerned. A few papers received exclusive reports direct from whichever capital lay nearest the fighting, but at best this was a system founded on rumor and hearsay. The readers of the *Oracle*, by contrast, knew at first hand the true nature of the war's progress. They were able to follow Bell in what he described as his "perilous excursion through Flanders" and read his accounts of the British victories at Le Cateau-Cambrésis, Villiers-en-Cauche, and Troixelle, followed by the disheartening report of a major defeat at Tournay at the hands of Marshal Pichegru.

The Times, chagrined no doubt that its thunder had been stolen, described the adventurer as "a bloody satellite of Robespierre and a promoter of Jacobite [*sic*] heresies." Though there was no foundation for these conflicting accusations, it is an interesting sidelight on eighteenth-century warfare that Bell, as a civilian, was able to mingle freely with the enemy and go unmolested.

When the terrible winter retreat of 1794–95 began, John Bell felt it was time to return to the security of the editorial chair. The precedent he had established was followed in future by other papers, notably his chief critic, the *Times*, which commissioned Henry Crabb Robinson in 1808 to cover the Peninsular War. It was a later representative of the *Times*, William Howard Russell, who was accorded the fanciful inscription "The First and Greatest of War Correspondents" on his memorial in Saint Paul's Cathedral. Russell, whose reports from the Crimea in 1854–55 won him national celebrity, was indeed the first to telegraph his dispatches from the battle zone, but this was the extent of his role as innovator. That Bell should have been overlooked is not inexplicable; he died in such obscurity in 1831 that not one of the five newspapers of which he had been at some time proprietor published an obituary notice.

U.S: First journalist to send reports from the front was James M. Bradford, albeit as a combatant, who had enlisted in Gen. Andrew Jackson's army in 1814 shortly before the battle of New Orleans that concluded the War of 1812. Bradford had established the *Time Piece* of St. Francisville, La., shortly before the outbreak of war with Britain and sent a series of dispatches back to his paper.

The first occasion in warfare that a press corps reported from the field was the Mexican War of 1846–48. A large body of journalists accompanied the American forces as they crossed the Rio Grande into Mexico on 18 May 1846, many of them actually serving in volunteer companies as well as filing reports to their newspapers. Perhaps the most celebrated of these pioneer war correspondents was George Wilkins Kendall of the New Orleans *Picayune*, who joined the Texas Rangers and participated in the battles of Chapultepec, Monterrey, Cerro Gordo, and Churubusco as well as reporting them. Most of the full-time reporters were also representing New Orleans papers, but the *New York Herald* fielded no fewer than five correspondents, boasting that they "had more talent than those of any other paper," while the New York *Sun* had the distinction of the world's first **woman war correspondent**, Jane McManus Storm. A year earlier, it had been she who had coined the term Manifest Destiny in respect to the United States' divine right to other nations' lands. Writing under the penname Cora Montgomery, she was the only journalist to report from behind enemy lines. Even braver was her criticism of the U.S. Army's performance, perhaps only surpassed in heroism by her caustic comments on the male correspondents.

War correspondent to telephone his report: The first was *The Times*' representative at the Battle of Ahmed Khel, fought during the Second Afghan War on 19 April 1880. He was able to phone the story of Gen. Sir Donald Stewart's defeat of the Ghilzais to a heliograph station outside the battle area; from there it was flashed to a field telegraph, and then by commercial cable to London, where it was published the next morning.

War correspondent to radio his reports: The first was *The Times* of London reporter Capt. Lionel James, who contracted with Lee De Forest, American pioneer of radio broadcasting (qv) and talking films (qv), to establish a wireless station at the British concessionary port of Wei-hai-wei on the China coast for the reception of his reports of the Russo-Japanese War (1904–05) from a chartered steamship the *Haimun*. James was warned that the Japanese would sink the vessel, but he was enabled to report back to London the naval engagements in the Yellow Sea between March and June 1904 after reaching agreement with their naval minister that he would supply intelligence gained from intercepting Russian wireless messages. This, the earliest known example of espionage by bugging, proved highly beneficial to the victors when he informed the Japanese of the position of a Russian naval station, which was promptly attacked and disabled.

War correspondent to broadcast from a field of battle: The first was Harvard-educated CBS reporter H. V. Kaltenborn, who spoke live for 15 minutes from the Battle of Irun, one of the earliest conflicts of the Spanish Civil War, on 3 September 1936. Listeners were able to hear the sounds of shot and shell, yet remarkably Kaltenborn was not in Spain. A thin finger of French territory protruded into the battle area and the intrepid correspondent had persuaded a French radio engineer to run a cable to a farmhouse and also to a haystack in the line of fire. It took three unsuccessful attempts before the transmission, via Bordeaux to New York, was able to go ahead. The first two were thwarted when the telephone line broke and the third, after the cable had been spliced under fire at great personal risk to the engineer, failed only because the operator of the relay transmitter in Bordeaux had gone out for a drink. Kaltenborn's hazardous enterprise was rewarded with the customary CBS fee of $50.

Television war correspondents: The first were twenty-four-year-old twins Eugene and Charlie Jones, who represented NBC during the Korean War from the start of American military operations in July 1950. The pay was $100 a week each, no expenses and no compensation for death or injury. Concentrating on the U.S. troops in combat, the Jones brothers filmed with a 16mm sound camera taking 3-minute reels and sent the film back from the front line aboard the Piper Cubs the Air Force used as observation planes. From the rear it would be taken by jeep to the nearest airfield handling international flights and airlifted to Tokyo. The bureau chief would then forward the film to San Francisco, where it would change planes for the last leg to New York. From filming to airing took an average of three to four days. The Jones brothers shot some 300 to 500 feet of film every five days, sufficient for 10 minutes of airtime. Eugene Jones recalled: "It seemed we were perpetually under fire. You would be talking to a man beside you when suddenly his face would be drilled with bullets." He

was severely wounded accompanying the Marines' assault on Inchon in September 1950, though he was rescued from the sea still clutching the camera with the film of the action intact. Charlie was himself wounded covering the attack on Seoul, but later both brothers parachuted 88 miles into North Korea on a POW rescue mission. They left Korea in the fall of 1951 having been reassigned to Europe as TV's first foreign correspondents.

SEE ALSO **war photographer**.

THE FIRST **WAR–FOREIGN WAR**

....

fought by the forces of the United States (as opposed to colonial forces; SEE **naval action**) was the Naval War against France, which was never formally declared but can be said to have begun with President John Adams's direction to the fledgling U.S. Navy (scarcely a year old) of 28 May 1798 to capture any French ships preying on American merchantmen. The war was fought entirely at sea, ranging across several oceans. The initial action was the taking of the French privateer *Croyable* by the USS *Delaware* (20 guns) off Egg Harbor, N.J., on 7 July 1798; renamed the USS *Retaliation*, she was recaptured by the French in the Caribbean the following February. On 9 February the first encounter between warships of the opposing navies took place off Nevis when USS *Constitution* defeated the 36-gun *Insurgente* with seventy French casualties to only three American. Many other actions followed, mainly in the Caribbean, and mostly involving U.S. Marines as well as sailors of the U.S. Navy. Hostilities concluded with the capture of the 20-gun *Deux Anges* and the 24-gun *Berceau* by the frigate USS *Boston* on 12 October 1800.

Land battle fought by U.S. troops overseas: The first took place during the 1804–05 Barbary war against Tripolitania (now a province of Libya) provoked by piracy against American shipping. This was the attack on the port city of Derna on 25 April 1805 by seven U.S. Marines and a U.S. Navy midshipman under the Virginian Lt. Presley Neville O'Bannon, part of a force that also comprised some 300 Arabs led by Prince Hamet and a mercenary army raised by American naval agent and self-styled "General" William Eaton, as well as a raggle-taggle body of 38 Greek foot soldiers, 25 cannoneers of mixed nationalities, and but one small gun (borrowed from the U.S. Navy). This extraordinary group of adventurers left Alexandria in Egypt to cross over 500 miles of inhospitable desert and attack Derna from the rear while the American fleet bombarded it from the harbor side. Significantly outnumbered by the defenders, the small force was exposed to heavy fire with no cover for their protection. They lost their sole artillery piece and several Marines were hit. Whereas a real general might have ordered a tactical withdrawal, "General" Eaton ordered his men to charge the strongly fortified castle. The defense wavered and broke. Lt. O'Bannon ran down the Tripolitanian flag and raised the Stars and Stripes, the first time it flew over a foreign stronghold. American casualties were one Marine killed and three wounded (one mortally), including Eaton himself, struck by a ball that shattered his left wrist.

Anglo-American land action: Britain and America, having fought two major wars against each other, first went into battle as allies at the Battle of Muddy Flat on 4 April 1854, when a 90-strong U.S. Navy brigade and a 150-strong Royal Navy brigade, accompanied by the Shanghai Volunteers (mainly British and American civilians) under Capt. Tronson of the Second Bengal Fusiliers, engaged and routed Chinese Imperial troops at Shanghai. American casualties were two killed and four wounded.

THE FIRST WAR MEMORIAL

was erected on the village green at Lexington by the Commonwealth of Massachusetts and completed on 4 July 1799 to commemorate the eight American Minutemen who died in the first conflict of the Revolutionary War. It was here that the opening shots of the struggle for independence were fired at 5 A.M. on 19 April 1775. The memorial is dedicated to those "who fell on this field, the first victims to the sword of British tyranny and oppression...They nobly dared to be free!" It records the names of the following fallen: Ensign Robert Munroe, Isaac Muzzey, Caleb Harrington, Jonas Parker, Samuel Masey, Jonathan Harrington, John Brown—all of Lexington—and Ishael Porter of Woburn. Their bodies were disinterred from the Old Cemetery and re-interred on the site of the memorial on 20 April 1935. The monument at Lexington is believed to be the earliest war memorial commemorating the fallen by name anywhere in the world. The editor would like to hear of any claims elsewhere.

America's first **memorial to the fallen of a foreign war** was the Tripoli Monument erected inside the main gate of the Washington Navy Yard in 1808. The 30-foot-high white Carrara marble monument, topped by an American eagle (copied from the image on a naval officer's coat button), was sculpted in Rome by Giovanni Micali to the order of Captain David Porter (USN). Porter had been captured during the Barbary War of 1804–05 against Tripolitania (SEE **war—foreign war**) and he conceived the monument, Washington's first, as a tribute to the six officers of the U.S. Navy who failed to return. The cost of some $1,200 was paid by a levy on Porter's brother officers of the Mediterranean Squadron, captains being asked to donate $20, lieutenants $10, and midshipmen $5. The inscription on the memorial reads: "Erected to the memory of Captain Richard Somers, Lieutenants James Caldwell, James Decatur, Henry Wadsworth, Joseph Israel, and John S. Dorsey, who fell in various attacks, that were made on the City of Tripoli in the year of our Lord 1804." In 1831 the Tripoli Monument was moved to the base of the Capitol and in 1860 to its present site at the Annapolis Naval Academy.

The first **Civil War memorial** commemorating hometown fallen was dedicated at Berlin, Conn., on 28 July 1863. A quarter of those approached for funding declined because they believed the South had a right to secede.

The first **war memorial to the dead of world wars I and II** in the United States is Stonehenge, a replica of Britain's ancient stone circle of that name, erected near Maryhill, Washington State, by local entrepreneur and Quaker pacifist Sam Hill. Dedicated on 4 July 1918, it commemorates the fallen of Klickitat County and now also includes those who made the supreme sacrifice in World War II, Korea, and Vietnam. At the time of dedication three soldiers of Klickitat County had died and nine more names would be added before the Armistice.

THE FIRST **WAR PHOTOGRAPHER**

was an unidentified American apparently working in and around Saltillo during the Mexican War in 1846–48, probably between the time of the battle of Buena Vista in February 1847 and the end of the American occupation in June 1848. Two caches of daguerreotypes, believed to be by the same photographer, have been discovered. One is of a dozen sixth-plate images in handmade walnut cases acquired c. 1927 by H. Armour Smith for his personal collection. Ten were taken during the American occupation of Saltillo, the other two are of St. Augustine, Fla., which was on the route taken by many of the troops embarked for Mexico. The most evocative of these in terms of military activity is a study of Gen. J. E. Wool and his staff riding down the Calle Real in Saltillo. This and the other daguerreotypes are now in the Beinecke Rare Book and Manuscript Library at Yale University.

No further Mexican War photographs came to light until 1981. How these came into the custody of the Amon Carter Museum at Fort Worth, Tex., was recounted by Martha A. Sandweiss and Rick Steward in their *Eyewitness to War: Prints and Daguerreotypes and the Mexican War, 1846–1848*, published by the museum in association with the Smithsonian Institution on the occasion of the first comprehensive display of the images in 1989:

> The Museum received a call from a bookseller who reported that a much larger group of images had surfaced and had been offered to a military museum that was about to turn down their acquisition. Within the next few hours they might again be available for sale. The Museum's long-standing interest in prints of the Mexican War and its large collection of American photographs, combined with the great scarcity of Mexican War daguerreotypes, made the rumor tantalizing. By late afternoon, the dealer handling the daguerreotypes had been traced, and a week later a brown paper grocery bag containing the photographs was handed over to a museum curator in the waiting room at Dulles Airport in suburban Washington, D.C. The bag was filled with wads of rough paper towels, each wad concealing a naked daguerreotype,

unprotected by the customary presentation case that kept its fragile surface free from dust, abrasions, and fingerprints. Every time the paper bag moved, the towels rubbed a bit more information off the surface of the world's first photographs of war. A quick examination of the plates revealed that they included not only portraits of identified military figures, but scenes of towns and troops in Mexico and, most surprising of all, variations of some of the known Yale views of American soldiers in and around the Mexican city of Saltillo. Soon after, the collection of daguerreotypes was acquired for the Museum.

These sixth and quarter-plates comprised thirteen military portraits, two portraits of Mexicans, two of unidentified civilians, two views of Durango and one of Parras, a harbor view of sailing ships, a photograph of the coffin of, presumably, a dead warrior, two studies of graves, four depicting troops of the occupation forces, and various scenes of Saltillo. Seven are related photographs made in the United States and eight have deteriorated too badly for the subject matter to be discernible. Evidence that these were the output of the same photographer as the Yale pictures is reinforced by the fact they include a photograph of Gen. Wool and his staff in the Calle Real evidently taken only moments after the one in the Yale collection. Among the most arresting of the new finds were the two images of volunteer infantry, one on parade in Saltillo, another of them stood down; these are the earliest photographs that clearly illustrate the common soldier in time of war.

It is doubtful whether these few anonymous images of the Mexican War were taken by a war photographer as such. The first photographers whose coverage of a conflict was sufficiently systematic to be worthy of the title were Surgeon John McCosh, who was serving with the British Army when he made forty-eight studies of the Second Burmese War of 1852–53; and the Hungarian-born artist Károly Pap Szathmári of Bucharest, who photographed camp scenes in November 1853 after Turkey had declared war on Russia and shortly afterward of the initial fighting in the Danube Valley of what was to develop into the Crimean War.

A major conflict involving the great powers when Britain and France declared war on Russia in defense of Turkey in March 1854, the Crimean War was the first war to be extensively chronicled by various cameramen. Szathmári himself assembled an album of 200 pictures from the war zone. This was displayed at the Universal Exhibition in Paris in 1855 and copies were presented to various European statesmen and rulers, though none are known to survive. Best known of the photographers accompanying the British forces was Roger Fenton, who was extraordinarily prolific during his brief sojourn in the Crimea between March and June 1855, though James Robertson, chief engraver of the Imperial Mint at Constantinople, was there for much longer, from the summer of 1854 to the end of the following year, and therefore left a more comprehensive record. Their work constitutes the main surviving images of the war, Fenton's 350 photographs forming the basis of many of the engravings that appeared in European and American illustrated weeklies, with a selection appearing in albums published in London by Thomas Agnew. Two serving soldiers, Maj. Halkett of the 4th Light Dragoons and a Capt. Ponsonby, took cameras with them, but Halkett was killed at the Battle of Balaklava on 25 October 1854 and no pictures from either photographer are known to survive. Nor has any of the output of the first **official war photographers**, Richard Nicklin, appointed by the War Office, and his two soldier assistants. They reached Varna in the summer of 1854, but all pictures were destroyed when the three of them were drowned in the great storm that swept over Balaklava harbor that November. A few months later the War Office sent out the first army photographers, ensigns Brandon and Dawson of the Royal Engineers, but their coverage is also lost.

The Crimean War photographers were discreet in their portrayal of battlefields; theirs is a sanitized view of conflict and no dead bodies appear. Many such were featured in the much more reality-focused pictures of the American Civil War of 1861–65 by such masters of documentary reportage as Mathew Brady, Alexander Gardner, and Timothy H. O'Sullivan. This was not the first war, though, in which photographers revealed the fallen. The Franco-Austrian war fought in Italy in 1859 had even generated stereo views for general sale that showed battlefields bestrewn with dead soldiers. The following year, when the British attacked Peking, Felice Beato was criticized for insisting that a pile of corpses not be moved until he had photographed them.

War photographers representing the media: The first accompanied the American expeditionary forces to Cuba and the Philippines in 1898–99. Most prominent of their number was Jimmy Hare of *Leslie's Weekly*. The Spanish-American War was the first fought between western nations since the widespread introduction of halftone photographs (qv) in the illustrated weeklies.

SEE ALSO **war film**.

THE FIRST **WASHING MACHINE**

power operated, was a steam-driven apparatus designed by the English hosiery manufacturer William Strutt in 1796 and installed at the Derbyshire General Infirmary opened in Derby on 4 June 1810. It consisted of a perforated cylinder divided into four compartments and enclosed in a watertight box. A 6-hp steam engine located in the basement drove the machine by means of a horizontal shaft. This also provided steam to heat the water.

A further installation of Strutt's washing machine was made at the Pauper Lunatic Asylum of Wakefield, Yorkshire, and here the mangle was also driven by steam, doubtless to the relief of the mentally challenged laundry ladies.

U.S.: Steam-powered washing machines on a concentric cylinder system similar to Strutt's were offered for sale by J. T. King of Baltimore in 1855. They were advertised as suitable for "large hotels, laundries, and public institutions." King provided everything necessary for laundry work, including the soap solution or "magnetic washing liquid," which was mild enough, he assured prospective users, to be drinkable in small doses.

Electric washing machines: The first were introduced in 1908 by the Automatic Electric Washing Machine Co. of Newton, Iowa, and the Hurley Machine Corp.

of Chicago. Both had been designed the previous year, the Automatic Electric by Skow Brothers Foundry in Newton, who produced five units a day for selling at $60 each. The Hurley Corp.'s machine was designed by Alva J. Fisher and was marketed as the Thor, a brand name still in existence.

Despite its name, the Automatic Electric still needed a human hand at the controls. The first **fully automatic washing machine** working to a preordained cycle was the Bendix Model A manufactured by Bendix Home Appliances of South Bend, Ind., and launched at the Louisiana State Fair in 1937. General Electric introduced the first top-loading automatic in 1947.

SEE ALSO **laundromat**.

THE FIRST **WATER, PIPED**

in America was brought to New York by Aaron Burr's Manhattan Company, following a yellow-fever epidemic in 1798 so virulent that coffins had been sold on street corners by itinerant vendors. Allegedly the formation of the company on 2 April 1799 was a front to enable Burr to found a bank under the same articles of incorporation to compete with the Bank of New York, one of whose backers was his arch-enemy Alexander Hamilton. Be that as it may, the company did actually perform the function for which it was ostensibly founded, although on a modest scale. Some 2,000 prosperous households were able to have water piped from a reservoir near City Hall Park, which in turn was fed by a pipeline to springs on the city's outskirts. Some 25 miles of pipes made from hollowed-out logs were laid beneath the city streets and modern construction crews still come across them when digging in the older parts of Manhattan. Examples can be seen at the South Street Seaport Museum and the Museum of the City of New York. Rather more remains of the bank founded under the same charter as the waterworks: it is now Chase.

Municipal water supply: The first was provided by the city of Philadelphia, where the first pipes were laid on 18 June 1799. Chief engineer Benjamin Latrobe designed the Fairmount Water Works for pumping water from the Schuylkill River between Market and Chestnut streets to Centre House in Centre Square, whence it was distributed by steam-power to householders and also to the first **street hydrants** in the United States. The system became operative on 21 January 1801.

The first large-scale piped water system began serving the city of New York on 4 July 1842 on completion of the Croton Aqueduct, which brought a huge volume of water from the Croton Reservoir in Westchester County. This made indoor plumbing feasible, over the succeeding two or three decades, for all but the poorest New Yorkers and also necessitated the building of America's first city-wide network of sewers to dispose of the waste. It transformed daily life for an urban population accustomed to outdoor privies and to the toil and inconvenience of bringing all the water needed for drinking, washing, cooking, and laundry in receptacles from standpipes or wells, a major household task in an era of large families. One thing it did not transform, however hopeful leaders of the temperance movement may have been, was New Yorkers' propensity for strong liquors; a former major of New York, Philip Hone, optimistically expressed his hope that the city's moral tone would be improved by the adoption of water as the drink of preference. It was not to be.

THE FIRST **WATER SKIS**

were ridden in 1922 by eighteen-year-old Ralph Samuelson on Lake Peppin at his hometown of Lake City, Minn. He had already tried aquaplaning, a sport that had originated some ten years earlier and consisted of riding a flat board towed by a power boat. A single board, however, allowed little opportunity for control or maneuver and the daring teenager decided to try staying upright on twin barrel staves, with predictably disastrous results. His next attempt was with conventional 7-foot snow skis, but these proved too narrow and too short to sustain his weight on water. Samuelson then went to a lumberyard and bought two pine boards for a dollar each which he cut down to an 8-foot 9-inch length. He curved the front ends by steaming them for 3 hours in his mother's copper boiler. He made the fatal mistake, though, of failing to lift the tips from the water and after two weeks of duckings he had to abandon his prototype skis when they broke under the strain. Following a further trip to the lumberyard, a new and improved pair of skis emerged with rubber foot-treads, with the straps set farther forward to distribute his weight more evenly, and with iron reinforcements at the curved front ends. Yet success still did not come immediately. "It took me at least three weeks and 25 tries before I mastered it," he recalled. "Everyone, of course, thought I was completely nuts." His contemporary Ben Simons, one of many "young punks" of Lake City who went to watch and jeer, confirmed this. "Everyone in town thought it was a kind of joke . . . Because we all thought the idea was so impossible, it was really a thrill when he did get up and go."

During the next few years Samuelson demonstrated the new sport throughout Michigan and Minnesota in the summer and in Florida during the winter. It was in Florida in 1924 that he scored another water-skiing first, albeit unintentionally, when one of his ski straps broke and he managed to stay upright on a single ski. The following year he made a further innovation, this time purposely. He reckoned that if he weighted one end of a floating dock, so that it stood at an angle in the water, he might be able to ski-jump from it. Unfortunately it did not occur to him that the surface of the dock would need to be wet to inhibit friction and on the first attempt his skis parted company with his feet. For the next, he had an inspiration—not the obvious solution, water, but a pound of pig's grease.

Ralph Samuelson never accepted a fee for his daring exhibitions other than gas money for the towboat. Nor did he consider patenting or manufacturing his new water skis. That was accomplished by the prolific inventor (including Cinerama) Fred Waller of Huntington, Long Island, N.Y., who had never heard of Samuelson's Midwestern and Floridian exploits but came up with the same concept independently and applied for a patent on his aquaplane skis on 22 August 1925. They were marketed through marine sales agency William H. Young & Co. of New York as Dolphin Akwa Skis. These were the skis used by the five competitors in the first water-ski contest, held on Lake Howard in Winter Haven, Fla., in 1929 and won by Marilyn Mores Hughes—one of the earliest

occasions on which a woman won a sporting contest against male competition.

The first water-ski jump competition in the United States was held at part of the aquaplaning meet at Massapequa, N.Y., in 1936 and was won by New Yorker Jack Andresen, who rode one and two skis and jumped over a 3-foot 6-inch ramp. Andresen pioneered turnarounds on short double-ended skis in 1940.

The first U.S. National Championship took place at the Marine Stadium at Jones Beach, Long Island, N.Y., on 22 July 1939 and comprised competitions for Slalom, Jumping, and Tricks. The male and female overall champions were Bruce Parker and Esther Yates.

THE FIRST **WEATHER FORECASTS**

had their earliest forerunner in the reports carried by John Houghton's London weekly newspaper *A Collection for the Improvement of Husbandry and Trade*. The issue for 14 May 1692 introduced the subject with the words: "Twould be a great use to have a true history of the weather, from which it is likeliest to draw prognostications." Appended was a seven-day table, recording pressure and wind readings for the comparable dates of the previous year. These, Houghton explained, had been obtained from Henry Hunt of Gresham College and were taken from the "barascope or Quicksilver Weather Glass." The feature continued weekly, readers being expected to make their own forecast from the data supplied.

Unscientific as it was, Houghton's idea soon found a number of imitators, culminating in 1711 in a journal called the *Monthly Weather Paper* devoted exclusively to meteorological predictions. Long-range forecasting of this kind was generally compounded of a mixture of astrology, guesswork, and a very little science and could seldom produce correct prophecies other than by chance.

Accurate and scientific "state of the weather" reports were first published by Charles Dickens's newspaper the *Daily News*, commencing 31 August 1848. At 9 o'clock every morning, observations were made on a uniform plan at a number of meteorological stations and telegraphed to London, where they were then analyzed by James Glaisher of the Royal Greenwich Observatory for inclusion in the following day's issue of the paper. This was a major step forward, but it still fell short of true weather forecasting, as readers were left to draw their own conclusions.

In 1860 Christoph Buys Ballot of Utrecht, who had founded the Netherlands Meteorological Institute six years earlier, began issuing storm warnings for the benefit of ships putting to sea. These covered only a small region of the Netherlands and used data from just four observing stations. That same year Adm. Robert Fitzroy, superintendent of Britain's Meteorological Office, was establishing meteorological stations around the coast of Great Britain. Following several months of testing, from 6 February 1861 he begin issuing official storm warnings for naval and merchant shipping operating from ports in the English Channel, North Sea, Irish Sea, and Atlantic. At the same time he coined the term "weather forecast," believing that this smacked less of the soothsayer than did "prophecy" or "prognostication." Shortly afterward the admiral extended the service offered by the Meteorological Office to include an official daily forecast for public consumption. The first of these was published in the *Times* of London for 1 August 1861. It optimistically predicted fine weather throughout the country.

U.S.: A national system of weather reports, relayed by electric telegraph from some 150 volunteers, was established in 1848–49 by Joseph Henry, secretary of the Smithsonian Institution at Washington, D.C. In 1850 he started displaying daily weather maps in the main hall of the Smithsonian for the benefit of the public. There was, however, no attempt at forecasting as such. This was pioneered by Prof. Cleveland Abbe of the Cincinnati Astronomical Observatory, who persuaded the local chamber of commerce to underwrite the cost of producing local weather reports daily for a trial period of three months. He began publishing his *Weather Bulletin* on 1 September 1869 and it was this publication, available to the public, that contained America's first weather forecast three weeks later. It read: "Wednesday, September 22, morning cloudy and warm; afternoon not so oppressive; evening clear and cool. Thursday, September 23,

morning cloudy and warm; afternoon clear; evening clear and cool; Friday, September 24, morning clear and warm; afternoon hot."

Abbe subsequently joined the Weather Bureau established by the meteorological division of the U.S. Army's Signal Corps in 1870. On 19 February 1871 he began issuing thrice-daily forecasts, including storm warnings, and two years later they were distributed to thousands of rural post offices by telegraph for display as "Farmers' Bulletins." These were the first official weather forecasts in the United States. The first regular weather map in a newspaper in the United States was drawn by Stephen Horgan (SEE **halftone**) for the *New York Daily Graphic* starting 9 May 1879.

Broadcast weather forecasts: The first were transmitted in Morse Code by the University of North Dakota radio station at Grand Forks in January 1914. These were relayed on to farmers out of range by nine dispersed radio hams. The first vocal weather forecasts were broadcast by the University of Wisconsin's Station 9XM at Madison commencing 3 January 1921. The first to be aired on television was read by WGY Schenectady, N.Y., studio manager Kolin Hager on 10 May 1928.

Telephone weather forecast service: The first was introduced in New York City by the U.S. Weather Bureau on 8 April 1939. Calls to WE6-1212 that day totalled 38,310. The equipment was engineered to handle 150 calls at a time.

THE FIRST **WHEELCHAIRS**

appeared in Spain and Bavaria in the same year, 1588. One was built by Jehan L'hermite for King Philip II of Spain with hinged movable arm- and foot-rests and an adjustable back operated by a rack-and-pinion. The other was designed by Balthasar Hacker of Nuremberg and was convertible into a bed. Both of these needed to be pushed by an attendant.

Self-propelled wheelchair: The first also emanated from Nuremberg. This was a tricycle carriage used by paraplegic watchmaker Stephan Farfler in 1655. It was operated by hand-cranks driving an internally toothed front wheel, and it is believed to have been built by Johann Haustach, who had already designed a manumotive vehicle for his own use some ten years earlier. Farfler's invalid carriage was to be seen every Sunday morning standing outside the Lorenze Kirche, waiting for its disabled owner to propel himself home after divine service.

The first push-rim manually operated wheelchair was built by French cabinetmaker Jean-François Oeben in 1760 for the Duc de Bourgogne. This was a one-off and the self-propelled chair did not become common until the reintroduction of push-rims in 1881.

The first lightweight, folding wheelchair was a push-rim model designed in 1932 by Harry Jennings of Los Angeles for Herbert A. Everest, a mining engineer who had broken his back in a mine accident in 1919 and wanted a chair that could go into his car. The two teamed up to found Everest & Jennings, now the world's largest manufacturer of wheelchairs.

Powered wheelchair: The first was the electric Britannia Bath Chair manufactured in 1896 by John Ward of London. The first powered by a gasoline motor was the Coventry Chair, which had a French-built De Dion engine and was manufactured by the Rudge Cycle Co. of Coventry, England, in 1899. Strangely enough this preceded the introduction of the first hand-propelled, chain-driven invalid carriage, which only appeared the following year. Electric wheelchairs reappeared in London in 1916, produced for the many World War I amputees being discharged from the army. The earliest known American example, like the first British marque of nearly thirty years earlier, was an electric bath chair. It was illustrated in the October 1924 issue of *Popular Mechanics* and was said to be commercially available, though no manufacturer is cited. The first mass-produced electric wheelchair in the United States was manufactured by Everest & Jennings of Los Angeles in 1956. The motorized shopping cart or electric four-wheel scooter for the elderly and infirm was designed in prototype in 1968 at Bridgeport, Mich., by Al Thieme, who founded Amigo Mobility International to manufacture it.

Wheelchair athletics: The earliest known event took place at the Royal Star & Garter Home for disabled veterans in Richmond, Surrey, England, in 1923 and comprised a lawn-bowls tournament, a zigzag obstacle race in lever-powered tricycle-chairs, and a race in push-rim wheelchairs. The first team sport to be played in wheelchairs was basketball at the Veteran's Administration (VA) Hospital in Framingham, Mass., and the Corona Naval Hospital in Corona, Calif., in 1945. Athletes from the latter played in a game against Birmingham VA Hospital in Van Nuys, Calif., the first "inter-club" event on record, probably in 1946. By the following year wheelchair basketball had spread beyond the VA hospitals with the founding of the Brooklyn Whirlaways, comprised mainly of disabled students from New Utrecht High School.

At about the same time that wheelchair basketball began in the United States, German-born Dr. Ludwig Guttman introduced wheelchair polo at the spinal injuries unit of Stoke Mandeville Rehabilitation Hospital in Buckinghamshire, England, soon followed by wheelchair netball (a game similar to outdoor basketball). On 28 July 1948 Dr. Guttman organized the first annual wheelchair athletics meeting, the National Stoke Mandeville Games for the Paralysed, at which sixteen athletes from Stoke Mandeville and the Royal Star & Garter Home competed at archery. In subsequent years lawn bowls, table tennis, javelin, shot put, club throwing, fencing, snooker, swimming, netball, and weightlifting were added. The first Paralympics, held in Rome 18–25 September 1960, were in fact the ninth Stoke Mandeville Games; thereafter the Paralympics were held (usually) in the host country of the Olympic Games, whereas the Stoke Mandeville event continued as the World Wheelchair Games.

Wheelchair racing does not seem to have developed beyond the kind of informal competition that had begun at the Royal Star & Garter Home in 1923 until it was included in the 1964 Paralympics at Tokyo. Ten years later Toledo, Ohio, held the first National Wheelchair Marathon; it was won by Bob Hall, who was to become wheelchair athletics' first household name when he competed in the Boston Marathon in 1975.

THE FIRST **WINDSHIELD WIPER**

was a hand-operated rubber wiper devised in 1907 by the editor of *La Vie Automobile* (Paris), Paul Ravigneaux, who published a description in his journal. As Ravigneaux was also chief engineer of De

Dion-Bouton, it seems likely that the wiper would have been fitted, at least experimentally, to some of the firm's vehicles. The earliest certain report of an operative windshield wiper is of another manual instrument invented by no less a personage than Prince Henry of Prussia, grandson of Queen Victoria and brother of Kaiser Wilhelm. It was fitted to a Benz automobile in which he left Hamburg for England on 5 July 1911. The Prince was noted for his interest in technology and has also been credited with the invention of the car horn. The earliest surviving windshield wiper dates from the same year. This was a rubber squeegee fixed to a sliding wooden bar that was patented by English photographer Gladstone Adams of Whitley Bay, Yorkshire. The model used by Adams on his own car is on display at the Discovery Museum in Newcastle-upon-Tyne.

The first windshield wiper manufactured for sale, the pivoted "Gabriel" operated by pulling a string, was advertised in the 1912 catalog of London auto-parts dealer Brown Bro. at 15s ($3.60).

U.S: The introduction of windshield wipers in the United States has been obscured by the fact that their invention has often been attributed to an Alabama lady of leisure called Mary Anderson—not to be confused with the labor leader or the silent-screen star of the same name—who patented a manual device for cleaning snow from the front windows of streetcars in 1905. According to numerous Web sites, this device was then adapted for automobile use and had become standard on all makes of car by 1913. In fact Miss Anderson's patent was never commercially exploited and her invention was used on neither streetcars nor any other vehicles. It is claimed that the first manual windshield wipers were fitted to Willys-Knight coupes and limousines manufactured in Toledo, Ohio, in 1916, but this is subject to verification. A manual wiper called the Rain Rubber was manufactured by Tri-Co of Buffalo, N.Y., in 1917 and retailed at $1.50.

Automatic windshield wiper: Two electric devices were invented in 1917, one by Honolulu dentist Dr. Ormand Wall and the other by ex-vaudeville performer Charlotte Bridgwood of New York. Dr. Wall's wiper was powered by an electric motor mounted on the top of the windshield, the blade describing an inverted rainbow arc. It is not known whether it was ever produced commercially. Charlotte Bridgwood was the mother of Florence Lawrence, the first film star in America to become a celebrity (SEE **film actors**). Mother and daughter had developed the first electric turn signal for automobiles as early as 1913. The wiper, called the Electric Storm Windshield Cleaner, did not have blades but was a roller that passed horizontally back and forth. As Charlotte Bridgwood was proprietor of the Bridgwood Manufacturing Co. of New York, it seems likely that this was manufactured, though it seems to have had a limited takeup. A bladed instrument operated by a vacuum motor was introduced by Folberth Brothers of Cleveland, Ohio, c. 1920 and an electrically powered blade, the Berkshire, in or before 1923. This latter was probably the first to attain any significant market penetration, as it was successful enough to be sold under license in Britain.

Intermittent windshield wiper: The first wiper to operate at varying speeds was the subject of patents by Robert Kearns, associate professor of engineering at Wayne State University, Detroit, in 1964 and 1967. He was unable to interest a manufacturer, but Ford adopted a similar device in 1969, followed by Chrysler. After a fourteen-year patent suit, Ford settled out of court for $10.2 million and Chrysler was ordered to pay Kearns $18.7 million back royalties plus interest.

THE FIRST WINE

in America has been claimed to have been made from wild vines growing at Fort Caroline, the French Huguenot colony established on the St. John's River in Florida in 1564. When the starving inhabitants were relieved by Capt. John Hawkins the following year he noted with disapproval that, though they had failed to grow any food, "in the time the Frenchmen were there, they made 20 hogsheads of wine." According to the colonists' own testimony, however, the only wine they had was the supply they had brought with them. If winemaking was attempted in any of the other failed European settlements of the sixteenth century, or by the Spanish at St. Augustine, no record of it has come down to us. The earliest evidence of winemaking from wild grapes is a report by Robert Johnson, one of the promoters of the Virginia Company, that the Jamestown settlers had sent some of their wine to London before 1609. William Strachey, who spent the year 1610–11 in Jamestown, provided the name of the first known winemaker in America, saying that he had "drunk often of the rath [young] wine, which Doctor Bohoune and other of our people have made full as good as your French–British wine, 20 gallons at a time have been sometimes made without any other help; than by crushing the grape with the hand, which letting to settle 5 or 6 days hath in the drawing forth proved strong and steady." Dr. Laurence Bohoune later became the physician general to the colony; he died in a sea battle with the Spanish while returning to Virginia from a trip to England.

Vineyard: The first in America was planted at Jamestown in 1619 using vines brought from England that year by the governor, Sir George Yeardley. That year also saw the arrival of eight *vignerons* from Languedoc, brought out by the Virginia Company, who settled at Kecoughtan (now part of Hampton) in Elizabeth City County. They probably planted their French vines the following year; in 1621 there is a report of a vineyard with 10,000 vines, though it is not specified whether these were wild vines or the imported plants. None of these early attempts, or others that followed in Virginia, was attended by success; the lure of quick riches from tobacco cultivation meant that there was little incentive for the colonists to produce wine in any quantity beyond their immediate needs, and even wine for personal consumption was mostly imported.

Probably the first vineyard in English-speaking America that can be regarded as moderately successful was Beverley Park, the seat of Robert Beverley of King and Queen County, some 30 miles north of modern Richmond, which was planted in the first decade of the eighteenth century. In 1715 his skeptical neighbors, doubtless goaded by Beverley's bragging of the prospects of his vineyard, offered him odds of 10 to 2 that he could not produce 700 gallons of wine at one vintage within seven years. Beverley wagered 100 guineas (about five years' wages for a laborer) on these terms and in 1722 reported that he had succeeded in producing 750 gallons in a year. These appear to have been both of red and white wines.

The first commercially successful vineyard was the somewhat confusingly named Second Vineyard, established by the Swiss viticulturist Jean-Jacques Dufour in New Switzerland (now Switzerland County), Ind., in 1802. Dufour had read as a boy of fourteen of the scarcity of wine in America and had thereupon decided that it should be his life's work to correct the situation. He came to America at the age of thirty-three, having studied viticulture in his native country, and set up his First Vineyard, so called, in Kentucky. Despite early indications of success, ultimately this failed to sustain durable vines and Dufour sent his extended family, numbering seventeen brothers, sisters, wives, husbands, and children, to cultivate Second Vineyard. The first vintage of Cape vines was harvested in either 1806 or 1807 and production rose from 800 gallons in 1808 to 2,400 gallons in 1810, 3,200 gallons in 1812, and a peak of 12,000 gallons in 1820. The extent of the vineyard in the latter year was some 45 to 50 acres. Vevay vine, as it was called after the neighboring town founded by the Swiss immigrants, was being advertised in Cincinnati in 1813 as "superior to the common Bordeaux claret" and sold for $2 a gallon. Despite such puffery, the quality of the wine was much inferior to the imported product and according to one report was used chiefly for making sangria, fruit juice and nutmeg disguising the tart acidity.

White wine: The first produced in commercial quantities in America was a sweet Catawba emanating from the Vineyard in Georgetown, Va., in 1823. It was the product of Maj. John Adlum, known as the "father of American viticulture," who had established his vineyard on the south slope of a hill running down to Rock Creek, now part of Rock Creek Park. The Catawba grape was a native hybrid of uncertain origin and quickly spread to other parts of the eastern United States, yielding the first domestic wine of palatable quality (though Adlum himself laced his wine, which he marketed as a tokay, with an excess of sugar). Adlum's place in the hierarchy of American viticulturists is assured more for the fact that he provided vines to other growers who succeeded in making wines of a quality superior to his and also for the propaganda effect of his publications on the cultivation of the grape.

American wine to be exported: The first was a sparkling Catawba produced by Nicholas Longworth at his Cincinnati vineyard. Commercial production of this, the first **sparkling wine** made in America, had begun in 1848 and two years later production was running at 60,000 bottles a year. It was exhibited at the Great Exhibition in London in 1851 and the first small shipment for sale overseas, also to that city, then the trading hub of the world, followed in 1855.

California wine originated at the San Juan Capistrano mission, where grapes were planted by Franciscan missionaries in 1778 or 1779, with the first vintage probably in 1782. Commercial production outside the missions was begun by the aptly named Jean-Louis Vignes, an immigrant from Bordeaux, who planted a vineyard at what is now Aliso Street in Los Angeles in 1833. When American forces entered Los Angeles in 1847, Lt. Emory reported on 14 January, "We drank today the wine of the country, manufactured by Don Luis Vignes, a Frenchman. It was truly delicious, resembling more the best description of the Hock than any other wine." Shipment of California wines to other parts of the United States was started some ten years after annexation, i.e., around 1857 or 1858, by the firm of Kohler & Frohling. An export trade began modestly in 1862 with a consignment of twenty-five cases to Japan by the Lake Vineyard of San Gabriel Valley. Exports on an economic scale only started in the 1880s when blight afflicting French vineyards caused a scarcity of the traditional sources of supply. By 1895 California wines were even stocked by London's elegant Knightsbridge emporium Harrods.

THE FIRST **WOMAN AMBASSADOR**

or head of a diplomatic mission was the Hungarian pacifist and feminist Rosike Schwimmer, who was appointed minister to Switzerland by the president of the newly proclaimed republic, Count Michael Karolvi, on 25 November 1918. She resigned the following year when Béla Kun came to power in Hungary and in 1920, under the Horthy dictatorship, had to flee for her life. Smuggled out in a boat down the Danube, she made her way to the United States, where she was denounced as a Bolshevik spy.

The first woman to attain ambassadorial rank probably was indeed a Bolshevik spy. Alexandra Kollontai had served in the Soviet Politburo in 1917–18 (SEE **woman to achieve a cabinet-level position in government**) but by 1922 had become such an outspoken critic of the government as a member of the Workers' Opposition that it was decided to send her out of harm's way by posting her abroad. She served in various diplomatic posts in Norway (1922–25 and 1927–30), Mexico (1926), and Sweden from 1930. In 1943 she was appointed Ambassador to Sweden and served until the end of World War II. During these years Germany, the tide of war turning against the Nazis, attempted to promote peace proposals to the Soviet Union via neutral Stockholm. It was Kollontai's task to resist any such overtures, but Stalin, who had no regard for women's abilities, sent a male minder to ensure that no communication from Berlin would reach Moscow. Her major diplomatic achievement was in concluding the armistice negotiations with Finland in 1944. Another remarkable distinction was to survive Stalin's purges, the only member of the Workers' Opposition to do so.

U.S.: The first woman to serve as a U.S. minister was Ruth Bryan Owen, daughter of famed lawyer and three-time presidential candidate Williams Jennings Bryan and herself a member of Congress from April 1929 to March 1933, who was appointed by President Franklin D. Roosevelt on 13 April 1933 as U.S. envoy to Denmark. She served until relinquishing her U.S. citizenship to marry a Dane, Capt. Börge Rohde, three years later.

The first woman to head a U.S. embassy was Eugenie Anderson Adair, appointed ambassador to Denmark by President Harry Truman on 12 October 1949. She became the first woman to sign an international treaty on behalf of the United States after negotiating a commercial and navigational agreement with the Danes in 1951. She also served as U.S. ambassador to Bulgaria in 1962–64. The first **woman ambassador to the United States**, Vijava Lakshmi Pandit of India, sister of Prime Minister Jawaharlal Nehru and formerly ambassador to the Soviet Union, was appointed in 1949.

THE FIRST **WOMAN ARCHITECT**

to design buildings without input from male associates was Sarah Losh of Wreay, near Carlisle in what is now the English county of Cumbria. Her achievements were extolled by the poet-painter Dante Gabriel Rossetti in a letter to his mother following a visit to Wreay in 1869:

> I saw in the neighbourhood some remarkable architectural works by a . . . Miss Losh, who was the head of the family about the year 1830. She must have really been a great genius, and should be better known. She built a church in the byzantine style, which is full of beauty and imaginative detail, though extremely severe and simple. Also . . . a Pompeian house for the schoolmaster, a parsonage, and a most interesting cemetery-chapel attached to a cemetery which she presented to the parish before such things were instituted by law. The chapel is an exact reproduction of one which was found buried in the sands in Cornwall, and excited a good deal of controversy at the time under the name of "The Lost Church"! She also built a large addition to the family mansion at Woodside in the Tudor style. All these things were real works of genius, but especially the church at Wreay, a most beautiful thing. She was entirely without systematic study as an architect, but her practical as well as inventive powers were extraordinary.

Sarah Losh was heiress to a fortune made by her father in the chemical industry and was unusually well educated for a woman of her period, noted both as a classical scholar and a mathematician. A friend recorded how she was able to translate aloud from Latin text without her listeners being aware that she was not reading an English translation.

The church to which Rossetti refers, the romanesque Saint Mary's at Wreay, was consecrated on 1 December 1842. Considered her masterpiece, it is included in the top hundred churches enumerated in Simon Jenkins's *England's Thousand Best Churches* (1999). Her earliest work, undertaken c. 1825 in collaboration with her sister Katharine (who died early), was the restoration and enlargement of the family

mansion Woodside. Miss Losh then built two schools, one for infants c. 1828 and a village school in 1830. Contemporary with the latter was a house for the schoolmaster known as the Pompeian Cottage, since it was based on an excavated Roman house she had seen at Pompeii. This is the earliest known complete dwelling designed solely by a woman. The schools and cottage survive, though with various alterations. She later built a sexton's cottage (c. 1835), which is probably the "parsonage" referred to by Rossetti. The "Lost Church" in Cornwall mentioned by the poet was the tenth-century chapel of Saint Perran, which Sarah Losh recreated as an oratory in the walled cemetery she designed when the village churchyard became full. Cemetery and chapel were consecrated on 12 May 1842. All these buildings their architect had erected mainly or wholly at her own expense.

Sarah Losh's works, designed to meet the needs of a small village, were spasmodic. The first **woman to practice architecture on a regular basis** was self-taught Sophy Gray, whose husband, the Rev. Robert Gray, was appointed first Bishop of Cape Town in South Africa in 1847. One of the most pressing problems of the new diocese, which covered the whole of the Cape Colony and Natal, was the absence of Anglican churches outside Cape Town itself. The infrequent Church of England services were held in schoolrooms, courthouses, or even stores. Recognizing that the erection of churches would be one of her husband's priorities, Sophy Gray acquired copies of the three-volume *Glossary of Architecture*, Rickman's *Architecture*, and Bloxham's *Gothic Architecture* and proceeded to teach herself. After arriving in Cape Town in 1848, she and her husband set off on a three-month visitation of the vast diocese and together they cajoled local congregations into establishing building funds. On their return the indefatigable Sophy began designing churches suitable to the scattered and distant parishes of South Africa. By the end of 1849 there were twenty-one churches planned or under construction, most of which she had designed herself. The first to be consecrated, on 7 December 1850, was the handsome neo-Gothic Saint Mark's at George Town, now elevated to cathedral status. Also in progress were Saint John's at Rondebosch, its namesake at Port Elizabeth, Saint James's at Graaff Reinet, with others at Colesberg, Beaufort West, and Knysna. The latter, the largely unaltered Holy Trinity dating from 1851–53, is now a South African National Monument. The *Cape of Good Hope Observer* duly remarked: "The English Churches now building in various parts of the Colony, we are informed, will be such as to call out generally a better taste in the erection of Colonial places of worship." Their designs, where they were not altered and debased by local building committees, as all too frequently happened, were indeed both pleasing and practical, though no credit was given to, nor sought by, their anonymous female architect.

Sophy Gray continued to act as diocesan architect for twenty years until her death in 1871. Among the more notable of the forty or so churches she designed or adapted were those at Swellendam, Schoonberg—the charmingly named Saint John's in the Wilderness—Somerset East, Worcester, Riversdale, Robertson, Montagu, Saint Helena Bay, and Oudtshoorn. Not all her buildings were churches. She also built schools, such as the one at Ceres; estate cottages at Newlands; and parsonages, including one at Caledon of local blue-gray slate that left her aghast when she saw how her own designs had been interpreted. It looked, she recorded, "like an old fortress." One of the few building she was able to supervise personally was Saint Saviour's in her local village of Claremont. Not only was she on site to ensure the integrity of her design, but she laid the tiles around the altar with her own hands as well as completing other detailed work.

Sadly Sophy Gray is an almost forgotten name today, whether in South Africa itself or among architectural historians, or even in women's studies. She is commemorated in a stained-glass window above the great high altar at Saint George's Cathedral in Cape Town, but her real memorial is the surviving churches that she designed, albeit few who worship in them or visit are aware that they are the work of the first woman to practice as an architect.

The first **large dwelling of historical importance to be designed by a woman** also emanated from the British colonies. The original Duntroon House at Canberra in what is now the Australian Capital Territory was a modest square stone Georgian bungalow with only three bedrooms. In 1861 its owners, George

and Marianne Campbell, decided to rebuild on a grander scale and it was Marianne who drew the plans for the capacious two-story Victorian Gothic Revival extension to the original property. Completed the following year, the new wing was of brick with sandstone quoins with four bedrooms and a night nursery on the upper floor, while the first floor had a breakfast room, library, morning room, study, and spare room. The old detached kitchen block behind the new wing was considerably enlarged, with additional bedrooms and a large servants' hall. In the meantime Marianne Campbell was busying herself with designs for an array of dwellings to house the outdoor staff and tenants. These included a twin-gabled manager's house, a gardener's cottage, a pair of semi-detached houses, and a row of three, as well as a number of detached cottages each with four rooms. The ground plans and elevations for these houses, as well as for the Duntroon House extensions, survive in a household book still owned by Marianne's descendants. Although few of her cottages survive in bustling modern Canberra, the enlarged Duntroon House does. Seven years after Marianne Campbell's death at age seventy-six in 1903, Canberra was selected as the site for the new capital of the recently federated Australian nation. The estate was compulsorily purchased by the government and the mansion was subsequently converted into an officers' mess for the newly established Royal Military College Duntroon. It still serves that purpose today.

U.S.: There may well have been women who designed their own houses earlier than Harriet Beecher Stowe, but if so their names have not been recorded. In 1860 the author of *Uncle Tom's Cabin*, the best-selling American book up to that time, disbursed some of the proceeds in buying a 4½-acre oak grove on the banks of the Park River in Hartford, Conn. It was there that she had been to school at the Female Seminary. The grove had been a refuge from her demanding sister Catherine Beecher, headmistress of the Seminary, and when she escaped into it with her closest friends Georgina May and Catherine Cogswell the three girls used to plan how one day they would build houses there. In 1862 she began to make the childhood fantasy a reality when she designed an eight-gabled three-story Victorian Gothic mansion and laid plans to move her family from their present home in Andover. It seems that it was the formidable Catherine who had originally stimulated Harriet's interest in architecture. As early as 1841 Catherine Beecher had published the earliest architectural plans by an American woman when she included her designs for "a Greek Revival dwelling" and "a Gothick [sic] cottage" in *A Treatise on Domestic Economy, For the Use of Young Ladies at Home and at School*. Many years later the sisters were to collaborate on a range of floor plans and elevations in *The American Woman's Home*.

The house was called Oakholm. Trees in the grove were cut down for the paneling of the rooms and there was a wide entrance hall looking out onto a two-story conservatory with a fountain in between. She and Prof. Stowe each had their own studies and it should have been idyllic. In fact it was not. Her husband had been reluctant to leave Andover and when they moved into Oakholm in May 1863 it was still a year away from completion. The professor was not pleased when water pipes burst over his head; moreover the house was never warm enough in winter. It also proved much more expensive to build and maintain than expected, so that Harriet was forced to do hack work for magazines to pay off the bills, while the professor attempted to perform what would now be called do-it-yourself, which usually ended with him repairing to bed in despair. Moreover the wondrous riverbank site proved less than so as the industrial sector of Hartford began to encroach. Within a few years Oakholm had become surrounded by factories. By 1870 the childhood dream was a nightmare and the Stowes sold up, rootless for many years before buying a ready-made house in Forest Street, Hartford, where they would shortly have Mark Twain as next-door neighbor. The fate of Oakholm was not a happy one. It became first a tenement house for factory workers and was then bought by the Hartford Cycle Works for use as a warehouse.

In 1864, the year that Oakholm was completed, Harriet Beecher Stowe had written, doubtless inspired by her own efforts in this direction, that "one of the greatest reforms that could be, in these reforming days, would be to have women architects. The mischief with houses built to rent is that they are all mere male contrivances." She observed that "when women plan dwelling-houses ... [they] will be built with more reference to the real wants of their inmates." This consummation so to be desired was shortly to come about in the United States, probably for the first time in the world, but frustratingly we do not know the name of the first woman to practice architecture as a profession. What we do know is that in the 1870 U.S. Census, under "occupations—architects" there was enumerated below "female" a digit: 1. There is record that Harriet Irwin of Charlotte, N.C., was granted a patent on a design for a hexagonal house on 24 August 1869 and that subsequently several were built, the first on West Fifth Street in Charlotte. She may have been the solitary "female."

The first woman to qualify as an architect was Margaret Hicks, who received her degree in architecture from Cornell University in 1880. While still a student she had already had a design for a workman's cottage published in *American Architect and Building News*, which architectural historian Judith Paine has described as "the first published project by an American woman architect." She died only three years after graduating and is not known to have practiced. Louise Blanchard Bethune is generally credited as America's first **female professional architect** and certainly she is the first known by name. She trained at the office of Richard A. Waite of Buffalo, N.Y., before setting up her own practice in Buffalo in October 1881 in partnership with Robert Bethune, whom she married a month later. Most of her buildings were industrial, commercial, and school buildings, few of which survive. She designed eighteen schools in western New York State, including the romanesque Lockport Union High School, a $30,000 brick and stone apartment block in Bridgeport, Conn., a block of stores for Michael Newall, the Iroquois Door Co.'s plant on Buffalo's Exchange Street, an Episcopal Chapel in Kensington, and the Denton, Cottier & Daniels music store. This last was notable as one of the earliest buildings with a steel frame construction and walls of poured concrete slabs to resist fire. The building for which she is chiefly remembered is Buffalo's Hotel Lafayette of 1904, a $1 million commission that she designed in the French Renaissance style. In 1888 Louise Bethune had become the first female associate of the American Institute of Architects.

THE FIRST WOMEN IN THE ARMED FORCES

were those who disguised themselves as men, of which there have been numerous examples over the centuries, but women accepted in the military in their own gender is relatively new. The first woman to serve in a regularly constituted army as a woman was Virginia-born Sally Louisa Tompkins, a wealthy twenty-eight-year-old widow who established Robertson Hospital at the house vacated by Judge Robertson in Richmond, Va., shortly after the outbreak of the Civil War. This she ran at her own expense until an order from the Confederate High Command that all military hospitals were to be run by army personnel. Mrs. Tompkins appealed directly to Confederate president Jefferson Davis, who was so impressed by the efficiency of Robertson Hospital that in order to circumvent the order that he had himself endorsed, he decided to commission her within the Confederate States Army. Accordingly on 9 September 1861 she assumed the rank of a captain of cavalry and was entitled to draw on military supplies, though she refused to accept an officer's pay. Capt. Tompkins continued to run Robertson until the end of the war and despite receiving some of the worst casualties, owing to her obsession with cleanliness and order it had the lowest mortality rate of any military hospital of the Confederacy. Of a total of 1,333 patients, only 73 died. On her own death in 1916 Capt. Tompkins was buried with full military honors.

It has sometimes been claimed that Dr. Mary Walker held a commission in the Union Army, an impression enhanced by the fact that she wore a military uniform (which Capt. Tompkins did not) and that she was invested with the Medal of Honor. In fact she served as an assistant surgeon under contract to the Army and as such retained her civilian status. The uniform she designed herself and wore without authority. (Her Medal of Honor, the first military decoration ever awarded to a woman, was later rescinded but restored by President Jimmy Carter in 1977.)

Capt. Tompkins was, therefore, the only woman to serve as such in the armed forces of either side in the Civil War. There was, however, a women's volunteer unit in Washington, D.C., that wore uniforms and bore arms. Nothing is known about it except for an unlabeled photograph in the National Archives depicting twenty-four ladies in plaid skirts, military tunics, and blue Union Army–style kepis. Each holds a musket in the "stand easy" position. Washington came under threat of attack by the Confederates during 1861–62 and it is possible that these ladies trained in musketry in order to defend the city should it be besieged. Any information about them would be welcome.

The later nineteenth century provides at least three examples of volunteer units of uniformed women at colleges and universities. In 1889 a Ladies Battalion was added to the Cadet Force at Cornell College in Mount Vernon, Iowa (no connection with Cornell University in Ithaca, N.Y.), under the command of a West Point graduate and serving army officer appointed by the secretary of war. It appears that co-eds at Cornell had drilled in uniform as early as 1874, though presumably as a less formally constituted military unit. A year or two after the founding of Cornell's Ladies Battalion, Company Q of the University of Minnesota Cadets was founded for women students wanting to train in the military sciences. An article in *Alumni Weekly* in 1922 recalled that the young women who composed it were considered alarmingly "advanced"—indeed almost "queer." They represented the most active and prominent members of each class, however, and therefore won respect. A contemporary photograph depicts thirty-three ladies attired in long skirts and jackets, in gray except for two in the front who wore dark jackets and were presumably officers or NCOs. At about the same time Louise Pound of the University of Nebraska (class of 1892) helped found a corps of female cadets there.

Uniformed women to serve in the armed forces: The first were four Canadian nurses under the command of Lt. Georgina Fane Pope of Charlottetown, Prince Edward Island, who arrived with the Canadian Expeditionary Force at Cape Town on 30 November 1899, shortly after the outbreak of the Anglo-Boer War. There was nothing new about female nurses serving with the military; they had done so in numerous campaigns since the Revolutionary War (SEE **army nurses**), but in every instance as civilian auxiliaries. During the Boer War there were more than a thousand military nurses from Britain and her colonies, but only the Canadian contingent, supplemented by a second draft of four in February 1900, held commissions in the army. They were ranked as lieutenants, were paid as such, and had all the rights and responsibilities of that rank. They served at hospitals in Wynberg, Rondebosch, Kronstadt, and Pretoria. Following their war service they were transferred to the reserve of Canada's Militia Army Medical Staff Service.

The first women to serve in the armed forces full time in time of peace were South Africa veterans Georgina Fane Pope and Nova Scotia–born Margaret MacDonald, who were appointed to what had now become the Canadian Army Medical Corps on 6 October and 22 November 1906, respectively. Once again they held commissions as lieutenants, earning equal pay and with power of command over male subordinates. They wore military dress uniforms when not on the wards, originally khaki, later blue. Both served at the Garrison Military Hospital in Halifax and on 1 April 1908 Pope was promoted to Nursing Matron with the rank of captain. It was MacDonald, though, as a considerably younger woman, who was chosen to take command of Canada's nursing services during World War I and she became the first woman to attain the rank of major in November 1914. Though the full-time women's nursing service never exceeded 5 prior to the war, a total of 3,100 female officers had served under Maj. MacDonald's command by the time of the Armistice in 1918, of whom 38 died on active service. She continued to serve until 1923.

It was also in the First World War that significant numbers of **women combat soldiers** served without the necessity of masquerading as men. Probably the first unit of women fighters was Serbia's *Legia Smirti* or "League of Death," founded on the outbreak of war by the sixty-two-year-old widow of a Serbian officer who had died in the war against Turkey in 1876. Stationed initially at Kragujevac, the unit was eventually to number 2,400 well-trained female combatants. In Russia in mid-1915 it was reported that there were some 400 women bearing arms, and some 50 had been killed or wounded. The Sixth Regiment of Ural Cossacks, of whose complement about a quarter were women, was commanded by Col. Alexandra Koudasheva, who in her civilian life had been a noted poet and musician. The Don Cossacks also recruited

substantial numbers of women and their unit as a whole was under the command of a soldier's widow, Alexandra Ephimovna Lagareva. After the Revolution, Russia's Legion of Death became the most celebrated of the early women's battalions.

On the opposite side the Germans did not officially recruit women as combat soldiers, though in one battle Russian forces reported that the soldiers they had captured included five uniformed women. The Austro-Hungarian Army was more favorable to women volunteers and its Ukrainian and Polish legions both attracted significant numbers. The Ukrainian Legion is believed to have had about 30 women combatants in 1915–16 and the Polish Legion some 200. A number of women volunteers also joined the main Austro-Hungarian Army, initially as medical staff but within a few months some had succeeded in transferring to combat units. Among their number were Sophie Haletscheko and Olana Stepanovna, who both received the silver medal for bravery second class.

U.S.: The first women to be ranked and uniformed in the U.S. armed forces, as well as the first **female naval personnel** in the world, were the yeomen enrolled in the Naval Reserve under an order of the Navy Department of 19 March 1917. First to enlist was a civilian clerk at the Philadelphia Navy recruiting center, Loretta Perfectus Walsh, who became a chief yeoman at the local naval home for disabled veterans on 21 March 1917. By the time the United States declared war on Germany on 6 April, there were 201 women in the Naval Reserve.

Known to their male counterparts as "yeomanettes," 11,880 women served in the Navy during World War I as clerks, draftsmen, translators, camouflage designers, recruiters, chemists and pharmacists, radio technicians, and telephone operators. There were four ranks: chief yeoman and yeoman first, second, and third class, their rates of pay being $60, $40, $35, and $30 per month, respectively. As all naval personnel had to belong to a ship, but as the Navy regulations forbade women at sea, the yeomanettes found themselves assigned as crews aboard tugs that had long since sunk to the bottom of the Potomac River. Their uniforms, by contrast with the becoming apparel worn by servicewomen in World War II, seem to have been designed with the purpose of making them look as dowdy as possible, their long skirts, jackets drooping below the hips, and flat straw hats giving them the look of nautical Salvation Army lassies.

Opha M. Johnson was the first **woman Marine**, joining at Washington, D.C., on 13 August 1918 and serving as a clerk in the Quartermaster Corps headquarters. A total of 305 "marinettes" performed mainly clerical duties in order to release combat-ready male Marine clerks for overseas duty. It had been estimated that it would require three women to do the work of two men; the actuality proved exactly the reverse.

The first **women to serve with the U.S. Army** (apart from nurses), and the only ones recruited during World War I, were 223 telephone operators posted overseas in March and June 1918 to England and France to work ostensibly as auxiliaries of the Signal Corps. Initially fluent French was required, later dropped in favor of switchboard experience. These "Hallo Girls" manned switchboards at the U.S. Army center in Paris, at Gen. John J. Pershing's headquarters in Chaumont, and in seventy-five other French towns, billeted in separate quarters run for them by the YMCA. Operators received $60 per month, supervisors $80, and chief operators $100 to $125. Some were located within a few miles of the front line and suffered occasional shelling and bombing. As auxiliaries, the surviving women of the Signal Corps Women's Telephone Units were not accorded veteran status until 1978. The veterans long disputed that their status had been that of auxiliaries. They claimed that they had been sworn in as full members of the Signal Corps, had worn the Corps uniform, and had been subject to all Army regulations and could have been court-martialed for infractions of them. If this is so, they were the first women in the U.S. Army.

In World War II the Women's Army Auxiliary Corps (WAAC), formed in May 1942, did not have military status. The first women formally acknowledged as serving in the U.S. Army were members of the Women's Army Corps (WAC), founded with the appointment of Oveta Culp Hobby as director on 5 July 1943; WAACs had the option of transferring if they wished. For the first time women in large numbers served overseas; at the peak of the war 17,000 WACs were stationed in Europe, North Africa,

Australia, and the Pacific. Not without a struggle for acceptance: Gen. Dwight D. Eisenhower had been opposed to women in the military until he saw how well British servicewomen performed their duties. Then he requested Army women to serve at his headquarters in North Africa.

Air Force women: Some 40,000 "Air-WACs" were posted to U.S. Army Air Force bases all over the world during World War II. The USAAF built a reputation as the most women-friendly of the services, opening the doors of all its schools to them, other than those for flying and combat training. Following the passage of the Women's Armed Services Act of 1948, which allowed for the recruitment of women in peacetime, the newly independent U.S. Air Force, no longer a unit of the Army, became the first of the regular services to integrate women rather than brigade them as a separate corps (the Marines did not integrate until 1977 and the Army in 1978). Although the acronym WAF, adopted with the appointment of Col. Geraldine P. May as director on 16 June 1948, was often thought to stand for Women's Air Force, it did not: it signified Women *in* the Air Force. At the end of June the Air Force's female strength stood at 168 officers and 1,433 enlisted women, all of them transferred from the Women's Army Corps. Civilian recruitment began in September, with the first 16 graduates of Officer Cadet School becoming second lieutenants in July 1949. For the first women pilots of the U.S. armed forces SEE **woman pilot**.

Women of the U.S. Navy to serve at sea: The first were 53 enlisted women who came aboard the non-combatant hospital ship *Sanctuary* on 8 September 1972, followed soon after by Lt. Ann Kerr, Ensign Rosemary Nelson of the Supply Corps, and 12 Nurse Corps officers. After sea trials, *Sanctuary* set forth on the 2½-month Project Handclasp mission to Colombia and Haiti. Before she was decommissioned in 1975, 23 officers and 97 enlisted had participated in this experiment to ascertain whether women could handle the same shipboard tasks as men. The conclusion of the captain was that they displayed just as much skill and dedication to duty. Although other women served on inshore craft during this period, it was only in 1978 that a structured plan was introduced to allow women to serve on any ship in peacetime.

Woman member of the U.S. armed services in combat: The first was Capt. Linda Bray, one of 800 women who served in America's brief two-week war with Panama following the invasion of 20 December 1989. On that day Capt. Bray commanded 30 male soldiers of the 988th Military Police Company in a 3-hour firefight after crashing through the gates of a Panamanian military camp in a jeep armed with a .50-caliber machine gun. At this juncture servicewomen had not been authorized for combat duties and Capt. Bray's unit was in any case officially non-combatant.

At the time of Operation Desert Storm, America's and Britain's forty-two-day war in 1990 to recover Kuwait from Saddam Hussein's Iraq, women of the U.S. Air Force and U.S. Navy were prohibited by law from any aircraft or ships engaged in combat, whereas the U.S. Army had no such prohibition but a policy of not exposing women to planned or anticipated combat situations. Nevertheless this proved the first war in which American women in significant numbers—33,300 served out of total U.S. forces of 697,000—operated in combat areas, carried arms, and were exposed to enemy fire. Three of them became the first **American enlisted women killed in action**: Specialist Beverly Clark, 23, and Specialist Christine Mayes, 22, both of Pennsylvania, and Specialist Adrienne L. Mitchell, 20, of California died when a Scud missile hit the reserve barracks in Dhahran on 25 February 1991. Ten other military women died during the campaign.

SEE ALSO **woman pilot: military**.

THE FIRST **WOMAN AUTHOR**

to have a volume of prose published in America was English immigrant Mary White Rowlandson, whose *Narrative of the Captivity and Restoration of Mrs. Mary Rowlandson* was published at Cambridge, Mass., in 1682. The author had been captured with three of her children when Narragansett Indians attacked the settlement at Lancaster, Mass., on 10 February 1676. With twenty other hostages she was held captive for eighty-three days before being ransomed.

The first professional woman writer in America was Hannah Adams, born at Medfield, Mass., in 1755

and a distant cousin of President John Adams. Her father, Thomas, had inherited a comfortable fortune but squandered it in failed ventures as a farmer and later bookseller. Hannah had not attended school due to ill health, but she was home-tutored by her erudite father. Following the financial collapse, Thomas Adams started taking rusticated students from Harvard for tutoring and Hannah shared in this educational process, eventually teaching them herself. It was by one of these students that she was lent a copy of Thomas Broughton's *An Historical Dictionary of All Religions*. Since this was equally skeptical about most religious belief, it distressed the pious Hannah and in 1778 she decided to attempt to revive the family fortunes by compiling a new reference work giving no preference to one sect over another, but presenting the arguments in favor of each according to their adherents' beliefs. This was published in 1784 as *An Alphabetical Compendium of the Various Sects Which Have Appeared from the Beginning of the Christian Era to the Present Day*. It was followed by a number of other works on religion, an autobiography, and the first work of American history by a woman, *A Summary History of New England* (1799), also adapted as a school textbook under the title *An Abridgement of the History of New England* (1801). While never achieving more than a modest competence from her pen, Hannah Adams became a literary celebrity in the Boston area and enjoyed the status, in the words of a modern biographer, of "a dinner and house-party star."

SEE ALSO **black poet: black woman poet; children's fiction; novel: by an American woman; poetry: poetry by a woman; woman playwright**.

THE FIRST

WOMAN TO ACHIEVE A CABINET-LEVEL POSITION IN GOVERNMENT

was Alexandra Kollontai, appointed People's Commissar of Social Welfare in the revolutionary Bolshevik government formed by Lenin on 8 November 1917 (27 October old style).

Born of an aristocratic family, Mme. Kollontai had rejected her own class to embrace the socialist cause in 1899 and subsequently spent many years in exile, returning to Russia immediately after the February Revolution. During her six months' tenure of office as People's Commissar she was responsible for disabled veterans, hospitals, pensions, leper colonies, orphanages, female education, and the administration of playing-card factories (already a state monopoly). Her first act as People's Commissar was to compensate an aggrieved peasant for his requisitioned horse. This was not a responsibility of her office, she explained in her autobiography, but the fellow had somehow secured an audience with Lenin, who had sent him around to Mme. Kollontai with a scribbled note requesting that she settle the matter somehow, as the Social Welfare Commissariat was the only one with any cash at its disposal.

Other accomplishments included the abolition of religious education, the transfer of priests to the civil service, the introduction of pupil participation in the running of girls' schools, and the setting up of a committee of medical men to plan a public health service. She considered her most important achievement to have been the founding of the Central Office for Maternity and Infant Welfare in January 1918.

Mme. Kollontai resigned from the government in March of that year "on the ground of total disagreement with the current policy." Always outspoken and independent, from this time forward she became an increasing liability to the Party and in 1922 she was sent out of harm's way as an envoy with the Russian Legation to Norway, later serving in Sweden as the world's first woman ambassador (qv).

U.S.: The first cabinet member was Boston-born Democrat Frances Perkins, formerly Industrial Commissioner for New York State, appointed Secretary of the Department of Labor by President Franklin D. Roosevelt on 4 March 1933. As such she became the first woman to enter the presidential line of succession. Ms. Perkins served for twelve years, introducing Social Security (SEE **old-age pensions**) in 1935. She and Secretary of the Interior Harold L. Ickes were the only two members of FDR's cabinet to hold their posts throughout his presidency.

Cabinet to contain a majority of female appointments: The first was sworn into office in the new socialist government of Spanish prime minister José Luis Rodriguez Zapatero on 14 April 2008. Among the nine ladies assuming office (to eight men) was Spain's first woman defense minister, seven-months-pregnant Carme Chacón, and a newly created minister of equality, Bibiana Aído.

THE FIRST WOMAN CIVIL SERVANT

was former teacher Clara Harlowe Barton, who was interviewed by Commissioner of Patents Charles Mason in Washington, D.C., as a prospective governess for his daughter and so impressed him with her conversational powers and political acumen that he appointed her a recording clerk at the Patent Office. She took up her new post in July 1854 at an annual salary of $1,400, equal to a man in the same job, which compared favorably with the $250 she had been receiving as principal of a public school in New Jersey. Miss Harlowe aroused the jealousy of her male colleagues, however, who behaved, according to an official history of the Patent Office, insultingly. In 1855 Secretary of the Interior Robert McClelland took advantage of Judge Mason's temporary absence to dismiss her. On his return the commissioner reinstated his protogé, but he was only able to do so in the post of copyist, laborious and dull work paid at the rate of 10¢ per hundred words. She lost her job on the change of government in 1857 but came back to the Patent Office with the accession of President Abraham Lincoln in 1860. When the Civil War broke out the following year Clara Barton resigned to become a volunteer nurse, eventually appointed superintendent of nursing by President Lincoln. She went on to found the American Red Cross and served as a nurse in the Spanish-American War of 1898 at the age of seventy-seven.

No other women served in government departments until 1862, when the departure of male clerks to the colors encouraged Secretary of the Treasury Salmon P. Chase to authorize their recruitment. Seven clerks were appointed to the copyist grade at $900 per annum under Superintendent Jennie Douglas on 9 October 1862: Mrs. Abbie C. Harris, Libbie Stoner, Belle C. Tracy, Mary Burke, Fannic L. Halsted, Jennie L. Wall, and Annie York. They owed their good fortune and a salary double that of a store clerk to the treasurer, Gen. Francis Spinner, who persuaded Secretary Chase that women were "capable of doing certain kinds of clerical work more rapidly and better than it was done by men." Of the seven clerks, three died in office, two married, and two, Libbie Stoner and Belle Tracy, were still employed at the Treasury thirty years later.

The first woman to occupy a position in the federal government sufficiently senior to require Senate ratification was Estelle Reel, who took office as National Superintendent of Indian Schools in the Office of Indian Affairs on 20 June 1898. In her Washington post, which she held until 1910, Estelle Reel had responsibility for 250 schools and 2,000 teachers scattered across the continent from Carlisle, Pa., to Salem, Ore. Over the course of the next three years she traveled 65,900 miles by train, wagon, horse, and foot. While her energy and enterprise were widely acknowledged, she is now a controversial figure for her policy of replacing academic instruction with vocational training, believing as she did that few Native Americans had capabilities beyond manual labor.

Woman to head an executive department: The first was Julia Lathrop, a member of the Hull House settlement in Chicago, who was appointed to run the Children's Bureau of the Department of Commerce (later moved to the Department of Labor) on 15 April 1912. She served until 1921.

THE FIRST **WOMAN DENTIST**

in America was Emeline Roberts Jones of Danielsville, Conn., who began practicing in 1859 after receiving instruction from her dentist husband. At first he had refused to teach her, believing women to be lacking either the stamina or dexterity needed. She persuaded him of her aptitude by secreting the teeth he had extracted and filling them, not revealing to him what she was doing until convinced of her own competence. She practiced for more than fifty years after her husband's premature death in 1864, her professional standing being recognized by election to the Connecticut State Dental Society.

The first professionally qualified woman dental surgeon anywhere in the world was Lucy Beaman Hobbs of McGregor, Iowa, who graduated from the Ohio College of Dental Surgery, Cincinnati, with a doctorate of dental surgery on 21 February 1866. She had already been twice refused admission to the college, but her persistence eventually wore down the dean of admissions and his colleagues. In 1859 Lucy Hobbs had served a three-month apprenticeship with Ohio College of Dentistry graduate Samuel Wardle, supporting herself by taking in sewing while she did so, and she opened her own practice in Cincinnati in March 1861. Because of her several years of experience, she was only required to serve a single semester at the college. After graduation she opened an office at 93 Washington Street, Chicago, moving to Lawrence, Kan., in search of a better climate after marrying James Taylor in 1867. She taught her husband dentistry and they practiced together until his death in 1886. Lucy continued what had already become the most lucrative practice in Kansas until her own death in 1910.

THE FIRST **WOMAN DOCTOR**

with a full medical degree was Dr. Dorothea Christina Leporin-Erxleben, who graduated from the University of Halle in the Prussian province of Brandenburg on 12 June 1754 at the age of thirty-nine. Dorothea Erxleben was the daughter of a physician in Quedlinburg who allowed her as a child to listen in to the lessons he gave her brother; it transpired that she was the more apt pupil. When Frederick the Great visited Halle in 1741 she sought his permission to attend the university with her brother, to which he assented because of the soundness of her home education. Shortly after starting at the medical school, though, her father died and she had to return to Quedlinburg. There she married a minister, a widower with four children, and proceeded to have four of her own. According to some sources she continued her medical studies while raising eight children. After her husband's premature death she returned to Halle and wrote her doctoral thesis on the curative effect of medicines pleasant to the taste (*Quod nimis cite ac jucunde curare saepius fiat causa minus tutae curationis*). Her graduation ceremony attracted huge crowds of spectators, the occasion being considered sufficiently notable for the king himself to present her with her degree. Dr. Erxleben practiced medicine for eight years, before succumbing to breast cancer in 1762 when she was forty-seven years old.

It is something of a mystery why history has passed over Dorothea Erxleben in favor of nineteenth-century women pioneers of medicine. This may be partly because she left no writings, other than an essay on university studies for women in 1742, and also because there has been no biography. Most reference works accord Dr. Elizabeth Blackwell the accolade of "first woman doctor," despite the fact that there were several predecessors. Dr. Jeanne Wyttenbach received her medical degree in 1773 from the University of Marburg. Dr. Maria Pettracini and her daughter Zaffira both received medical degrees from the University of Florence in 1780 and 1800, respectively, and each practiced in Ferrara. Dr. Maria delle Donne graduated from Bologna medical school on 19 December 1799 and subsequently taught obstetrics there. Dr. Charlotte von Siebold received her degree at Giessen in 1817 and was called to London to attend the German-born Duchess of Kent in 1819 for the birth of the princess who would become Queen Victoria. Indeed Elizabeth Blackwell was not even the first woman doctor in the Americas. That honor went to Dr. Marie Durocher, who received the first diploma granted by the Rio de Janeiro Medical School in 1834. She practiced medicine for nearly sixty years until her death in 1893. The case of Dr. James Barry is rather better known than these other pioneers; she studied at Edinburgh Medical School during the 1820s in the guise of a man and had a long and distinguished career as an army surgeon. Her gender was not discovered until she died. Elizabeth Blackwell even had a predecessor of the same name who, though not a medical doctor, was a noted physician in eighteenth-century Scotland. The earlier Elizabeth Blackwell lived from 1712 to 1770, studying anatomy under Dr. James Douglas and her husband, Alexander Blackwell, and obstetrics under Dr. William Smellie. Elizabeth Blackwell the later (no relation) acknowledged her namesake as a "physician-accoucheur worthy of all praise."

U.S.: The first professionally qualified woman doctor was Elizabeth Blackwell, who was originally encouraged to make medicine her career when a friend, dying of cancer, told her that she would have been spared many of her worst sufferings had she been attended by a female medical practitioner. Born in Bristol, England, in 1821, Elizabeth emigrated to New York with her family when she was eleven years old. Her initial attempts to enter a recognized medical school proved unsuccessful. She was refused admittance in Philadelphia and New York, and the only encouragement she received was from a professor who said he would allow her to attend his classes if she was prepared to disguise herself as a man. When she applied to the Medical Institute of the small University of Geneva (now Hobart) in New York State, the Dean, Dr. Lee, turned the decision over to the student body, confident that they would return a negative reply. On 20 October 1847 he replied to her letter, enclosing a copy of the students' resolution:

> Resolved—That one of the radical principles of a Republican Government is the universal education of both sexes: that to every branch of scientific education the door should be opened equally to all; that the application of Elizabeth Blackwell to become a member of our class meets our entire approval; and that in extending our unanimous invitation we pledge ourselves that no conduct of ours shall cause her to regret her attendance at this Institution.

Elizabeth Blackwell entered the Geneva Medical Institute and gained her clinical experience during the summer vacation in 1848 at the Blockley Almshouses in Philadelphia, where she found herself caring for the victims of a typhus epidemic. She graduated at the top of her class on 23 January 1849.

After further training at La Maternité in Paris, Dr. Blackwell returned to New York, and on failing to obtain a hospital appointment she embarked on private practice in March 1852, most of her early patients being women of the Quaker persuasion. Together with Marie Zakrzewska, a Polish woman doctor, she established the New York Infirmary for Women and Children in May 1857. Settling in England in 1874, she was appointed to the chair of gynecology at the newly founded London School of Medicine for Women.

The first American-born woman and the second of her sex to receive a medical degree in the United States was Nantucket-born Dr. Lydia Fowler, who graduated from Rochester, N.Y., Elective Medical College in 1850. She then became a "demonstrator of anatomy" at the college and in 1851 was appointed professor of midwifery and women's and children's diseases, the first woman professor at a medical school (and possibly of any college?) in America.

Woman surgeon: The first to perform major surgery was Elizabeth Blackwell's sister Emily, who had studied under Sir James Simpson in Edinburgh after graduating from Cleveland Medical School. Together with her sister and Marie Zakrzewska she established the New York Infirmary, opened on 12 May 1857—a date chosen because it was Florence Nightingale's birthday. It was there that she became the first practicing woman surgeon of modern times, withstanding not only the hostility of those gentlefolk who considered her avocation improper, but also the more active opposition of angry mobs who stormed the hospital after patients had died following surgery.

THE FIRST **WOMAN DRIVER**

of an automobile was Louise Levassor, wife of one of the partners in the Paris motor-manufacturing concern Panhard et Levassor, but better known by her former name of Mme. Sarazin. Prior to her second marriage, and after the death of her first husband, Mme. Sarazin had acquired the French and Belgian rights of manufacture for the Daimler gasoline engine. The following year, in 1890, she married Émile Levassor, and the patent rights passed to her new husband's firm. They began manufacturing automobiles under their own name in 1891, and it seems likely that this was the year Mme. Levassor learned to drive, though the earliest evidence of her becoming a *chauffeuse* is a photograph showing her at the tiller of a Panhard car and dated 1893. Although the pioneer woman car driver, Louise Levassor was not the first member of her sex to take to the highway in a gasoline-engined vehicle; this distinction was earned by Mrs. Edward

Butler, who rode her husband's motorcycle (qv) at Erith, Kent, England, in 1889.

Woman to pass the driver's exam: The first was the Duchesse d'Uzès, who secured her brevet as a *conducteur d'automobile* in Paris in May 1898 after satisfying the examiner of her ability to brave the hazards of the busy Bois de Boulogne.

Woman owner-driver: The earliest known was Philadelphia-born actress Minnie Palmer, who had a French-built Rougemont motor carriage delivered to her by the Daimler Co. while she was on tour at Aberdeen, Scotland, in September 1897.

U.S.: The first woman driver on record was New York socialite Daisy Post, a niece of Frederick Vanderbilt, who was observed in a car of unidentified make by a reporter in 1898. However, when thirteen-year-old Jeanette Lindstrom of New York received her license to drive in 1900 it was said that she had already been driving for two years, which would make her debut behind the wheel (or tiller) at age eleven contemporaneous with Daisy Post's. The first American woman to pass a driver's exam and receive a license was Mrs. John Howell Phillips of Chicago in 1899.

THE FIRST **WOMAN EXECUTED IN THE ELECTRIC CHAIR**

SEE **electric chair**.

THE FIRST **WOMAN EXECUTIVE**

SEE **department store**.

THE FIRST **WOMAN FILM DIRECTOR**

was Alice Guy, who was hired as his secretary by Léon Gaumont in Paris in 1894 when he was working for Felix Richard's photographic company. The following year Gaumont and Guy witnessed the first on-screen presentation of films by the Lumière brothers at the Société d'encouragement à l'industrie nationale. Inspired by this, Gaumont founded the Gaumont

Co. in 1896 to manufacture the Demenÿ film camera. Now the oldest production company in the world, it began producing films for commercial release in 1897. These were actualities of parades, railroad stations, etc, which Alice Guy considered monumentally dull. Having performed in amateur theatricals, she timidly suggested to her employer that she should direct some films, simple dramatic subjects featuring her friends, who would not require payment. Gaumont rather grudgingly conceded, provided it did not interfere with her secretarial duties.

There is no doubt that Alice Guy was the world's first woman film director. What is rather more open to question is the title and date of her debut movie. According to her autobiography it was a fantasy called *La Fée aux choux*, filmed on an unused terrace with an asphalt floor at the Gaumont photo laboratories at Belleville with a backdrop painted by a local decorator of fans, rows of wooden cabbages cut out by a carpenter, and "costumes rented here and there around the Porte Saint-Martin." Featuring her friends Yvonne and Germain Serand, the 60-second drama told the story of a young couple walking in the country who encounter a fairy in a cabbage patch and are presented with a baby (based on French folklore about the provenance of babies). It is possible that Guy herself played the husband, as she did in a remake a few years later.

La Fée au choux was No. 370 in the Gaumont catalog and it is on this basis that Francis Lacassin's filmography of Guy places it as having been made in August or September 1900, whereas Guy's daughter and her biographer Alison McMahon favor the 1896 attribution. Lacassin is also concerned that *La Fée* was presented at the Paris Exposition of 1900, which as a showcase for the latest of everything seems a doubtful environment in which to present a four-year-old film. The first entry in his filmography of her work is the 16½-meter (54-foot) *Le pêcheur dans le torrent* of April 1897, described in the Gaumont catalog as "comique et très movementé." It was about this time that Guy became head of production at Gaumont, making in all, per McMahon, no fewer than 2,242 short narrative films during the years 1897–1907, of which 562 were Chronophone sound films (songs, excerpts from opera, and comic scenes) made in 1905–06.

Alice Guy was the first to separate the functions of director and cameraman. Her feminist biographer Alison McMahon agonizes over the reasons for this without coming to the obvious conclusion: early ciné-cameras were far too heavy for a Victorian lady of genteel upbringing to carry.

U.S.: Shortly after marrying the chief cameraman at Gaumont, Herbert Blaché, Alice Guy relocated to the United States in 1907 to promote the Gaumont Chronophone. As Alice Guy-Blaché she established the Solax Film Co. at Fort Lee, N.J., in partnership with her husband and with Gaumont as distributor. Per McMahon she made 338 short films (under 4 reels) over the next three years, including the first American film known to have been directed by a woman (but SEE BELOW): *A Child's Sacrifice*, starring child star Magda Foy in her debut role, released on 21 October 1910. Three years later she made the first **feature film directed by a woman**. A four-reel thriller titled *The Rogues of Paris* starring Vinnie Burns, it was about a girl detective rescuing an heiress from the machinations of the rascally rogues of the title. Filmed at Lake Hopatcong and at a castle on the Russell Sage Estate in New Jersey, it was released on 24 October 1913. Between then and 1920 she made another 45 feature films before returning to France following the breakup of her marriage. By this time her early work in her home country had been forgotten and she was unable to return to filmmaking, eking out a living adapting film scenarios as short stories for pulp magazines. She went back to the United States in 1927 in the hope of finding studio work, but the year was inauspicious for a pioneer director of silents: The sound revolution was at hand. She never worked in films again and so totally erased from movie history was she when she died aged ninety-five in 1968 that there was not a single obituary.

The first **American woman to direct** may also have made the first film to be helmed by a woman in the United States, but contemporary evidence is lacking. She was Lois Weber, a former street-corner evangelist who was hired as an actress by Alice Guy's husband Herbert Blaché at the Gaumont Co.'s studios in New York City. Here she is said to have directed as well as scripted and acted in a number of Chronophone short sound subjects, but if so their titles are lost to history. She herself claimed that her first directorial assignment was on a 1908 film called *Mum's the Word* of which there is no record. Weber's sojourn at Gaumont was brief and she moved to Reliance, then on to Rex, where she codirected her first film whose title is known to us together with her husband Phillips Smalley, *A Heroine of '76*, released on 18 February 1911 and in which they costarred. After several more collaborations with Smalley, she earned her first solo directorial credit for *The Power of Thought* in 1912. She codirected again with Smalley for her first feature film, *The Merchant of Venice* (Universal, February 1914), in which she also played Portia opposite her husband's Shylock.

Two years later Weber made her best-remembered film, again for Universal, the highly controversial *Where Are My Children?* on the theme of birth control. The subject matter, at the time when Margaret Sanger was making waves with her attempts to open America's first birth-control clinic, gave it an added luster and Weber was catapulted into the ranks of America's highest-paid directors, reputedly earning $5,000 a week at Universal. She set up her own production company and had one more box office success with *The Blot* (1921), but thereafter her fortunes took a downturn as she divorced the alcoholic Smalley and suffered a nervous breakdown. As her films became increasingly provocative, she had difficulty in obtaining distribution. Her last picture, *White Heat* (1934), about miscegenation on a sugar plantation, aroused the ire of racial segregationists and feminists in equal parts, but it did have the distinction of being one of the first films shown on full-service television when it was aired by W2XBS New York on 21 June 1940.

Sound feature film directed by a woman: The first was former film editor Dorothy Arzner's *Manhattan Cocktail*, starring Nancy Carroll and Richard Arlen, released by Paramount on 24 November 1928. A backstage song-and-dance confection with songs and sound effects but no dialogue, it is now a totally lost film of which only production stills survive. It was followed by Arzner's *The Wild Party* (released 6 April 1929), the first talkie directed by a woman, which starred Clara Bow doing what she did best, getting into trouble at a wild party.

San Francisco–born Arzner, whose directorial career had started with the 1927 silent *Fashions for Women*, the first motion picture by a woman to win a top award (first prize at the International Festival of Women's Films, London, 1928), was the only one of at least thirty-six women directors of silent movies to successfully make the transition to sound. She was the first woman member of the Directors Guild of America and at the height of her career in the mid-1930s was listed as one of Hollywood's top ten directors.

Woman to win the Academy Award for Best Director: The first was California-born Kathryn Bigelow for *The Hurt Locker*, about a bomb disposal team in the Iraq War, for which she was honored on 7 March 2010. Competing against her in the Best Director category was her ex-husband James Cameron, nominated for *Avatar* and favorite to win. Ms. Bigelow was the fourth woman to be nominated for Best Director, after Italy's Lina Wertmuller for her 1975 *Seven Beauties*, New Zealand's Jane Campion for her 1993 *The Piano*, and New Yorker Sofia Coppola for her 2003 *Lost in Translation*. Bigelow's *Hurt Locker* also won Best Picture.

THE FIRST

WOMAN HEAD OF STATE/GOVERNMENT

It should be noted that in many countries, with the United States being a notable exception, the offices of head of state and head of government are separated. In republics where the president is head of state but not the chief executive, the prime minister (or equivalent) is normally the head of government.

The first female head of state of a republic was Khertek Anchimaa, who became her country's titular leader on appointment as chairman of the Little Khural (the executive committee of the Great Khural or parliament) of the People's Republic of Tuva in Central Asia in 1940. Tuva, now part of the Russian Federation, was under Mongol control from 1207 to 1757, then was ruled by China until 1911, when it became the Urjanchai Republic. It was a Russian protectorate from 1914, but Tuvan Bolsheviks declared independence with Soviet support in 1921. Anchimaa was born of a poor peasant family in 1912 during Tuva's first brief independence. She joined the communist youth organization Revsomol at the age of eighteen in 1935 and was one of eleven Tuvans to graduate from Moscow's Communist University of the Toilers of the East. On her return home she was appointed head of the agitprop section of Revsomol and was engaged in settling the nomadic herdsmen of the plains into collectives. Anchimaa is also believed to have been active in the secret police and is alleged to have been responsible for the execution of Prime Minister Chunnit Dazhy and other apparatchiks accused of spying. Her zeal in the Bolshevik cause propelled her to the position of head of state at the age of only twenty-eight and in the same year she married the head of government, Prime Minister Salchak Toka. During the war Anchimaa lent unstinted support to the Soviet Union and in 1944 helped to engineer its annexation of her country. Unlike most of those who gave their loyalty to Stalin, she survived his rule and continued to be active in government until her retirement in 1973. She died in 2008.

Woman head of government: The first and the first female national leader to be elected was Sirimavro Bandaranaike, who had been chosen head of the Sri Lanka Freedom Party following the assassination of her husband, its founder. She led the party to power in the general election of July 1960, taking office as prime minister on the 21st of that month. Having served until March 1965, she returned as prime minister from 1970 until 1977 and from 1994 to 2000. On the third occasion it was as successor to her daughter Chandrika Kunaratunga, who assumed the presidency.

Woman president: The woman first to bear the title of president was former nightclub dancer María Estela Perón, aka Isabel Martínez Perón, sworn in as president of Argentina at Buenos Aires on 29 June 1974 following her husband Juan Perón's death in office. She was deposed on 24 March 1976 and arrested in 2007 for decrees she had signed for the suppression of "subversives" during her period of office. First to be elected was Vigdis Finnbogadóttir, director of the Reykjavik Theater Company, who assumed office as president of Iceland on 1 August 1980. Nicaragua became the first country with a woman president and vice president

when Julia Meña Rivera was appointed vice president by President Violetta Barrios de Chamorro on 22 October 1995.

SEE ALSO **woman candidate for president of the United States**.

THE FIRST WOMAN JOCKEY

to ride in an open race against male competition was fourteen-year-old Dorothy Tyler, who rode her horse Blackman to victory in a quarter-mile race held in 1907 at her hometown of Joplin, Miss.

Woman jockey licensed to ride as a professional: The first was English-born Judy Johnson, who made her debut riding Lone Gallant in a steeplechase at Pimlico Racetrack, Baltimore, on 27 April 1943. She finished 10th out of a field of 11 horses. Her mount was beaten by 30 lengths, though this was an improvement on a previous performance under a male jockey, when it had come in 400 lengths behind the winner. Miss Johnson had first applied to the Maryland Jockey Club for a license in 1927 but had been turned down on the grounds that no woman had been issued with one before. Her renewed application was accepted because of the shortage of jockeys due to enlistment. After riding in a few more races she reverted to her former occupation of trainer.

The first professional to win a race in the United States was Barbara Jo Rubin on Cohesion at Charles Town, W.V., on 22 February 1969. First to win one of the Triple Crown classics was Julia Krone aboard Colonial Affair in the Belmont Stakes on 5 June 1993.

THE FIRST WOMAN JOURNALIST

While a surprising number of women had served as newspaper editors (usually of journals inherited from their proprietor husbands) since as early as the 1730s, first on the staff of an American newspaper was Margaret Fuller, formerly editor of the feminist journal *The Dial*, who was hired by Horace Greeley of the New York *Tribune* as literary editor commencing 1 December 1844. This involved the production of three articles a week, two on literary topics and one on social issues. In furtherance of the latter she did on-the-spot research at Sing Sing prison, Blackwell's Island prison, the Bloomingdale Asylum, and Bellevue Hospital. The literary contributions included both commentary and reviews, with a judicious balance between the giants of the old world and the vigorous and outspoken writers of the new. In July 1846 Fuller gave up her staff job to accompany her wealthy socialist friends on an expedition to England to investigate social conditions in what was then at once the richest nation on Earth and, as the first fully industrialized nation, the one with the most acute social problems. She continued to write for the *Tribune*, but as a freelancer at $10 an article. She has sometimes been cited as the first **female foreign correspondent**, which would be true in a literal sense, though normally a foreign correspondent is a staff appointment and its holder focuses rather more on political and diplomatic issues than the kind of colorful essays on pit ponies and getting lost on Ben Lomond with which Fuller leavened her polemics on poverty. When she moved to Paris in 1847, however, her contributions began to concentrate more on affairs of state, one of her main sources being a fellow woman journalist, the cross-dressing George Sand, who wrote for *Le Figaro*. Fuller next moved on to Rome where she became pregnant by the Marchese d'Ossoli and subsequently married him. She came into her own as a true foreign correspondent with her reports of the revolution that swept Italy during 1848–49. On her return to America, she and Ossoli and the baby were drowned on 19 July 1850 when the barque *Elizabeth* was shipwrecked off Fire Island, New York.

The 1880 U.S. Census was the first to record numbers of women journalists, when there were 288. Ten years later the figure had increased by 600. In 1900 there were no fewer than 2,193, or 7.3 percent of the profession. Recognition of their influence in the world of newspapers came in the form of an issue of *The Journalist*, 26 January 1889, which was wholly devoted to profiles of 50 prominent women editors and reporters, of whom, remarkably, ten were black.

SEE ALSO **war correspondent, woman; woman newspaper editor**.

WOMAN MEMBER OF THE JUDICIARY

was Mrs. Esther Morris, described as "a large, plain-spoken, warmly witty shopkeeper's wife," who was appointed justice of the peace for South Pass, Wyo., on 17 February 1870. South Pass was a roistering gold-mining town that had grown from nothing to become the largest city in the territory of Wyoming. Mrs. Morris, who has been credited with securing the passage of the women's suffrage bill in the territory the previous year, tried twenty-six cases during her eight-and-a-half months in office. The fact that none was referred to a higher court on appeal is held as testimony to her sagacious handling of them. She resigned on separating from her husband, whom she charged with assault and battery.

Woman judge: The first was Alice Jamieson, appointed to preside over the juvenile court at Calgary, Alberta, Canada, in 1913. The first to preside over a general court was Emily Murphy, appointed police magistrate in Edmonton, Alberta, in 1916 with the honorific of "Judge." When she tried her first case on 1 July of that year, the defense counsel challenged her right to pass sentence on the grounds that as a woman she was not a "person" under British and Canadian law. Judge Alice Jamieson was appointed a police magistrate at Calgary a few months later and was subjected to a similar challenge, but the provincial supreme court rejected the argument. This confirmed the right of women to become members of the judiciary in Alberta, but their status in other provinces and at a federal level remained ambiguous before a decision by the Privy Council in 1929 overturned the Supreme Court's ruling the previous year that "women, children, animals, and idiots" were not legally "persons."

U.S.: The first judge was Kathryn Sellers, formerly the first woman district attorney, who was appointed to the juvenile court of Washington, D.C., in September 1918. The first to preside over a general court was Florence Ellinwood Allen, descendant of Ethan Allen, who was elected to the Court of Common Pleas of Cuyahoga County, Ohio (comprising much of Greater Cleveland), on 6 November 1920. Judge Allen achieved further distinctions as the first woman to become a justice of a supreme court (Ohio, November

1922) and the first federal judge of a general jurisdiction when she was appointed by President Franklin D. Roosevelt to the bench of the U.S. Circuit Court of Appeals in Cincinnati on 21 March 1934. She retained her seat for twenty-five years, retiring as chief judge.

The first female federal judge had been appointed in 1928, when Genevieve Rose Cline, formerly an appraiser of foreign merchandise for the U.S. Customs Service, was assigned to the U.S. Customs Court in New York City.

Woman appointed to the U.S. Supreme Court: The first was Texas-born Sandra Day O'Connor, appointed by President Ronald Reagan and sworn in on 25 September 1981. She retired in 2006, two years after *Forbes* magazine had named her as the sixth most powerful woman in the world.

THE FIRST **WOMAN JURORS**

in the world sat on an all-female jury convened for the trial of Judith Catchpole, accused of murdering her infant child, at the General Provisional Court held at Patuxent, Md., on 22 September 1656. The jury accepted the defendant's plea that far from murdering her child she had never had one, and returned a verdict of not guilty.

A mixed jury of six men and six women is recorded at Albany, N.Y., in 1701.

The first legal provision for women to serve on juries was made by an act of the Legislative Council of the Territory of Wyoming passed on 10 December 1869. Chief Justice J. H. Howe, who empaneled the first women to serve on the juries of the supreme court at Cheyenne, wrote in 1872: "After the grand jury had been in session two days the dance-house keepers, gamblers, and demi-monde fled out of the State in dismay to escape the indictment of women jurors."

THE FIRST **WOMAN LAWYER**

was Arabella "Belle" Mansfield of Mount Pleasant, Iowa, who was apprenticed in a law office after graduating from Iowa Wesleyan University. Although she passed the bar examination with high honors, when she applied for admission, Miss Mansfield was at first refused as the code prescribed "any white male person" as eligible. Later the same day Judge Francis Springer, known as a champion of women's rights, found a means of circumventing the code by statutory interpretation of the wording to mean that "the affirmative declaration [for male persons] is not a denial of the right of females" and she was admitted on 15 June 1869. Belle Mansfield subsequently obtained a bachelor of laws degree from Iowa Wesleyan and then undertook further law studies in London and Paris, including courses on Hindu and Islamic law. She did not practice, but returned to Iowa Wesleyan as a law teacher, later moving to the law faculty of Indiana Ashbury University (now DePauw University).

The first **woman to practice law**, albeit briefly, was Brooklyn-born Lemma Barkaloo, also the first woman to attend law school. Having been refused entry to the law school of her alma mater Columbia, she was also rejected by Harvard Law School before gaining acceptance at St. Louis Law School (later Washington University Law School), where she began her studies in the fall of 1869. Despite the fact that "she seemed to enjoy the embarrassment of the young men very much" (according to one of her professors), Lemma decided to quit school after only a few months and presented herself for the Missouri bar exams, passing in March 1870. The fact that she practiced in St. Louis is testified by Ellen A. Martin in an article in the *Chicago Law Times* in 1887 in which she claimed that Lemma Barkaloo was the first woman to appear as counsel in court, but she provided no details about the historic occasion nor the date it occurred. Sadly Lemma died in the St. Louis typhoid epidemic of September 1870.

The first **woman to graduate from law school** was Ada Kepley at the Union College of Law of Chicago University (now Northwestern) on 30 June 1870, but she was unable to practice until the State of Illinois rescinded its law barring women from the learned professions in 1881.

THE FIRST **WOMEN TO SIT IN A LEGISLATURE**

anywhere in the world did so in the Colorado General Assembly. Clara Cressingham and Frances Klock were elected as Republican representatives for Denver and Carrie C. Holly, also a Republican, for Vineland, in Pueblo County, on 6 November 1894. They were sworn in on 2 January 1895. The first state senator was Welsh-born Martha "Mattie" Hughes Cannon, fourth wife of a Mormon polygamist, elected to the Utah State Senate for Salt Lake County on 3 November 1896. She served two terms and made her mark on public health issues.

Women members of a national legislature: The first were elected in Finland on 15–17 March 1907, when nineteen constituencies returned women members to the Diet. Nine were members of the ruling Social Democrat Party, including a journalist, a dressmaker, a schoolteacher, a weaver, and a women's rights agitator. Of the other nine, six were elected for the Old Finnish Party, the majority being teachers, though there was also a restaurant proprietor and a clergyman's wife among their number. The lady members took their seats at Helsingfors on 23 May and appeared, remarked the *Times* correspondent patronizingly, "quite at their ease."

U.S.: The first woman to sit in the House of Representatives was Jeanette Rankin, elected as a Republican for one of the two seats from Montana on 7 November 1916. She sat until early 1919, during which time she was the only member of the House to vote against America's entry into World War I. After two decades as a lobbyist, she was reelected in 1940, in time to cast her vote against America's entry into World War II, again the only member to do so.

The first **U.S. woman senator** was eighty-seven-year-old Rebecca Latimer Felton, widow of a senator from Georgia, who served for 24 hours on 21–22 November 1922 as a Democrat representing Georgia to fill a vacancy following the death of the incumbent. A successor having been elected, she immediately stepped down. The first to be elected was Hattie Wyatt Caraway as a Democrat from Arkansas, appointed by Gov. Harvey Parnell in November 1931 to succeed her late husband and confirmed by a special election on 12 January 1932. Despite the fact that she never spoke from the floor, she was reelected later in 1932 and again in 1938, serving until 1945.

National legislature with a majority of women members: The first was the Chamber of Deputies of the Central African nation of Rwanda following the general election of 16 September 2008. Women won forty-four seats out of a total of eighty.

SEE ALSO **woman head of state/government**.

THE FIRST **WOMAN MAYOR**

was twenty-seven-year-old Susanna Medora Salter, who was elected in Argonia, Kan. (population 500) by a two-thirds majority on 4 April 1887. She herself was unaware that she had been nominated until the day of the poll. Mrs. Salter was a member of the Women's Christian Temperance Union, an organization determined to enforce the prohibition laws recently and controversially enacted in the state of Kansas. Some opponents of Prohibition placed her on the ballot clandestinely with the intention that a resounding defeat would discredit the WCTU position. On polling day the chairman of the local Republican Party discovered the ruse and went to inform Mrs. Salter, who was engaged in the family washing. He told her that if she would accept office were she to be elected, he would get out the vote. When she consented, he declared "All right, we will elect you and just show those fellows who framed up this deal a thing or two." Somewhat to her chagrin, she found that three of the five members of the council who were also elected were among the pranksters. Mrs. Salter exercised a becoming tact on calling her first meeting of the council to order. "Gentlemen, what is your pleasure?" she enquired disarmingly. "You are the duly elected officials of this town. I am merely your presiding officer." Their pleasure, it transpired, was masterful inactivity. During her year in office, the only measures impinging on the sedate life of the small Quaker town were the arrest of two draymen for refusing to buy licenses and a warning to some urchins who had thrown stones at a vacant house. Nevertheless the mayor maintained the dignity of her office. A representative of the *New York Sun*, one of many who descended on Argonia to witness this first manifestation of petticoat government, reported that she was adept at bringing the debate back to the point when her male colleagues showed an inclination to digress.

Susanna Salter did not offer herself for reelection at the termination of her year in office. She and her lawyer husband became pioneer settlers in Oklahoma when the territory was opened up in 1893. There she remained until her death in 1961 at the age of 101, having seen in the meantime almost every significant role in public life achieved by members of her sex.

Woman mayor of a metropolitan city: The first was Bertha Knight Landes, elected Mayor of Seattle on 9 March 1926 on a platform of "municipal housekeeping" and a promise to end corruption in city government. She called on citizens to report bootleggers and offered a $7-per-annum retainer to those pledging to write down the numbers of reckless drivers. After serving a two-year term, Landes was defeated by an unknown on seeking reelection.

THE FIRST WOMAN MINISTER OF RELIGION

was the Rev. Antoinette Brown, who entered Ohio's Oberlin College Theological Seminary as the first female divinity student and preached her first sermon in New York City in 1848 before she had graduated. She was ordained minister of the South Butler Congregational Church in N.Y., at a salary of $300 per annum on 15 September 1853 and two months later officiated at the **first marriage solemnized by a woman**, that of the daughter of fellow women's-rights activist Rhoda deGarmo. Although accepted in her parish, reaction outside was not always favorable and the *New York Independent* denounced her as an infidel. On one occasion when she was sent as a delegate to a temperance convention she was greeted with hoots and jeers. Later she became a Universalist and married Samuel C. Blackwell, through whom she was sister-in-law of both suffrage pioneer Lucy Stone (her classmate at Oberlin) and America's first woman doctor (qv) Elizabeth Blackwell. Antoinette Brown had six daughters, wrote ten books, and in her seventies went to Palestine to draw water from the River Jordan with which to baptize her grandchildren, subsequently

setting out for Alaska as a missionary. She was still preaching at All Soul's Church, Elizabeth, N.J., in 1912. On her death at age ninety-six in 1921, it was estimated that there were then 3,000 female clergy in the United States.

Anglican/Episcopal woman minister: The first was the Rev. Florence Tim-Oi Lee of Macao, who was ordained priest by Bishop R. O. Hall of the Diocese of Hong Kong and South China as an emergency war measure at Shie Hing in Kwangtung province, China, on 25 January 1944. Owing to the total absence of ordained priests in Macao, Miss Lee had already been granted the authority to celebrate Holy Communion two years earlier, while still a deaconess. In 1946 the Diocesan Synod of Hong Kong and South China endorsed Bishop Hall's action and proposed a draft canon allowing a trial period of twenty years for the ordination of women. The proposal was rejected by the Anglican hierarchy in 1948, by which time Miss Lee, under pressure from the Chinese House of Bishops, had resigned from her priestly ministry. She revitalized a moribund church at Hoppo in mainland China as a deacon, but in 1949, at the time of the Communist takeover, decided she must resume her work as a priest. Between 1958 and 1979 she was forbidden to minister and for most of this time was forced to labor, first on a chicken farm, then in various factories. In 1981 she escaped to Canada, where she died at the age of eighty-five in 1992. By that date there were more than 1,000 women priests in the Anglican Communion.

U.S.: The first women ministers of the Episcopal Church were eleven deacons ordained by four bishops on 13 January 1974 at the Church of the Advocate in Philadelphia. Although the ordinations were invalidated by the Episcopal House of Bishops on 15 August, barely two months later, on 17 October, it voted to accept the principle of ordaining women. First to be ordained with the full authority of the Church was Indianapolis Women's Prison chaplain Jacqueline Means on 1 January 1977. On 8 January Baltimore-born former lawyer and civil-rights activist Dr. Pauli Murray became the first black woman priest when she was ordained at Washington Cathedral. Two days later the Episcopal Church became the first mainstream U.S. denomination to ordain an openly lesbian candidate, Ellen Marie Barrett, who was accepted into the priesthood by Bishop Moore of New York. The first Episcopal woman minister to serve as rector of a church was Beverly Messenger-Harris at Gethsemane Episcopal Church in Sherrill, N.Y., on 1 June 1977.

The first **Woman bishop** in the Anglican/Episcopalian Communion was the Rt. Rev. Barbara Harris, a black woman, consecrated as Suffragan Bishop of Boston before a congregation of 8,000—including two vocal protesters—at the Hynes Convention Center on 12 February 1989. The first full bishop (a suffragan assists a diocesan bishop in a particular part of his or her diocese) was Dr. Penelope Jamieson, consecrated seventh Bishop of Dunedin, New Zealand, on 29 June 1990.

The first **Woman Primate of the Episcopal/ Anglican Church** was the Rt. Rev. Katherine Jefferts Schori, Bishop of Nevada, one of the smallest dioceses in the United States at 6,000 adherents, who was elected Presiding Bishop of the Episcopal Church in the United States at the church's general convention in Columbus, Ohio, on 18 June 2006. Known for views much more liberal than those prevailing in other parts of the 75-million-strong Anglican Communion, her election was widely predicted to create schism within the worldwide church, especially on the issue of practicing gays.

Woman rabbi: The first to be ordained was Regina Jonas of Berlin at Offenbach, Germany, on 27 December 1935 by Rabbi Max Dienemann, head of the Liberal Rabbis' Association. Although she had graduated from Berlin's Higher Institute for Jewish Studies five years earlier with a halachic treatise, *Can Women Serve as Rabbis?*, Jonas was refused ordination both by her Talmud tutor Dr. Hanoch Albeck and by the man she turned to for support, the revered Prof. Leo Baeck, head of the National Representation of Jews in Germany. Despite the shortage of rabbis owing to Nazi persecution, she was unable to secure a position with a congregation and her ministry was largely confined to Jewish hospitals and old-age homes until she was sent to Theresienstadt concentration camp in 1942. There she joined the staff of Austrian psychiatrist Dr. Viktor Frankyl, an inmate who had set up a special unit to help newcomers overcome their shock and despair.

She was assigned the daunting task of meeting new arrivals at the station and offering them spiritual and temporal counsel. Twenty-four of the sermons she preached during her incarceration are preserved in the Theresienstadt archives. In October 1942 Jonas was transferred to the death camp at Auschwitz, where she was shortly to become another victim of the Holocaust. After the war Regina Jonas was virtually erased from the history of Judaism until a resurgence of interest in her pioneering role and heroic life in the 1990s. No other female rabbis were ordained until Sally Priesand in 1972, and none in Germany before 2010.

U.S.: Sally Jane Priesand of Cleveland, Ohio, was ordained by Rabbi Alfred Gottschalk on 3 June 1972 at Reform Hebrew Union College Jewish Institute of Religion in Cincinnati, where she had written her rabbinic thesis, later published as *Judaism and the New Woman*. She subsequently served for seven years as assistant then associate rabbi at Stephen Wise Free Synagogue in New York City and was appointed rabbi of Temple Beth El in Elizabeth, N.J. in 1979. Sally Priesand retired in 2006 after twenty-five years' service at Monmouth Reform Temple in Tinton Falls, N.J. The following year she instituted an archive on the history of female rabbis at the American Jewish Archives in Cincinnati.

Woman Roman Catholic priest: While no woman has been ordained a priest with the approval of the Vatican, it is claimed that Ludmilla Javarova, a schoolteacher of Brno, Czechoslovakia (present Czech Republic), was ordained under "emergency powers" by Bishop Felix Davidek following a secret synod in 1970. Javarova had been prevented from becoming a nun by the communist authorities, but had participated actively in the work of Davidek's diocese, eventually rising to the position of vicar-general. She herself declared that the reason for her ordination was to be able to administer the sacraments to imprisoned women, many of them nuns, denied access to recognized priests.

Women Muslim ministers: The first were fifty *morchidat* who graduated from the Dar al-Hadith al-Hassania seminary in Rabat, Morocco, early in April 2006. All were required to have bachelor of arts degrees and at the end of their course had to be able to recite half the Koran by heart (imams have to be able to recite the whole Koran). On graduation they were assigned to mosques throughout the country at a salary of 5,000 dirhams ($800) a month, with a special remit to minister to women. They were subordinate to the imams particularly in respect of not being able to lead prayers in the mosque.

THE FIRST WOMAN NEWSPAPER EDITOR

was Elizabeth Timothy, Dutch-born publisher and editor of the *South Carolina Gazette* of Charleston for seven years after the death of her husband James in 1738. In the first issue she edited, that of 4 January 1739, she appealed to readers "to continue their Favours and good Offices to this poor afflicted Widow and six small children and another hourly expected." While most of the content of the *Gazette* was lifted from European sources and from other colonial journals, as was customary before the strictures of copyright, she wrote "homilies" herself and selected various literary items—essays, drama, poetry, and prose—for reprinting, as well as original contributions from Southern writers.

Mistress Timothy's first major news story based on eye-witness accounts was the devastating Charleston fire of 18 November 1740, which all but destroyed the major city of the South—two thirds of the town, numbering some three hundred buildings. In the 4 July and 1 August 1741 issues of the *Gazette* she ran what may well have been America's first foray into investigative journalism, an exposé of conditions in and alleged mismanagement of the Bethesda Orphan House in Chatham County, Ga., which had been established three years earlier by Methodist founding father George Whitefield.

The print works were owned by James Franklin, elder brother of the more celebrated Benjamin, who recorded that Elizabeth managed the business with "such success that she not only brought up reputedly a family of children but at the expiration of the term was able to purchase of me the printing house and establish her son in it." This was in May 1746. When the son, Peter, died in 1775 the paper stopped publication, but his widow became the *Gazette*'s second woman editor when she revived it in 1783.

During the colonial period sixteen out of a total of seventy-eight newspapers published in America were edited by women.

Woman editor of a metropolitan daily: The first was twenty-seven-year-old Cornelia W. Walter, who took up the editorship of the *Boston Transcript* on the death of its founding editor, her brother, on 24 July 1842. She was appointed by the senior proprietor Henry W. Dutton, who had been impressed by articles she had contributed, without her brother's knowledge, during his fatal illness. The appointment was made secretly for fear of ridicule and abuse and it was characteristic of the time that the initial approach was made to her father, not to her. The new and anonymous editor's salary was $500 a year, while the services of her two reporters were valued at the higher rate of $572.

Miss Walter was profoundly conservative and deeply religious. She opposed any scientific theory she considered in conflict with the Old Testament; she had no time for upstart literary luminaries of the stamp of Emerson and Lowell, and she vigorously denounced feminism while supporting the idea of "colleges for females." Among those to incur her editorial displeasure was the loose-living Edgar Allan Poe, in Miss Walter's view a Boston boy made bad, who aroused her to further wrath when he called her a "pretty little witch." National and international news found little space in the *Transcript* under her aegis: It was a Boston paper for Bostonians who considered, like Miss Walter, that Boston was the hub of the universe. The hub of Cornelia Walter's universe was the drawing room of her house on Belknap Street, from which she edited the paper, seldom venturing into the office.

After five years in the editor's seat, the talented and comely Miss Walter made a suitable marriage and retired from journalism. Her mentor Henry Dutton said that it had been a great experiment to entrust a lady with the task. "She made the trial with fear and trembling," he wrote, "and her success has been triumphant."

SEE ALSO **woman journalist**.

THE FIRST WOMAN TO WEAR PANTS

as an article of feminine apparel was the French actress Sarah Bernhardt, who was photographed at her Paris studio by Mélandri in 1876 costumed in a jacketed trouser suit of extraordinarily modern style and appearance. It should be noted that the notorious "bloomers" popularized by feminist Amelia Bloomer in 1848 were baggy pantaloons worn beneath a short skirt, and not pants in the generally accepted sense.

Women of fashion, ready enough to follow Sarah Bernhardt's lead in other directions, did not emulate her in this. It was women's entry into the world of organized sports that eventually allowed for a relaxation of the prevailing code on what was acceptable female wear. The first woman known to have adopted trousers for sporting purposes was twenty-five-year-old Miss Eleanora Sears of Boston, great-great-granddaughter of Thomas Jefferson, who in 1909 appeared on the polo ground of the Burlingame Country Club in jacket and trousers and asked to be allowed to participate in a game about to be played against a team from England. It is recorded that the English captain was rendered speechless and that the manager of the American team promptly ordered her from the field. Miss Sears was a superb all-around sportswoman and did much to encourage the active participation of women in sports on a par with men. She also believed passionately that they would never attain equality on the playing field until they discarded the full-length skirts that were still de rigueur for most outdoor activities at this date.

Shortly after Eleanor Sears's daring innovation, fellow Bostonian social luminary Louise Michel became the first woman known to have worn jodhpurs in order to ride astride. She had them specially designed for her in black serge together with a matching jacket that she wore with a cravat and black top hat.

About this time shorts made their first known appearance on female thighs, though in an environment at the opposite end of the social spectrum from that of Miss Sears and Miss Michel. A vaudeville performer with the curious stage name of C' Dora appeared at the New York Hippodrome so attired, looping-the-loop on the "Globe of Death" bestride an Indian motorcycle. She is pictured in costume on the cover of the *Motorcycle News* for April 1909, with a short-sleeved blouse, white shorts cut a couple inches above the knee, and white sneakers worn (even more daringly) with bare legs.

A few colleges and fewer high schools had inaugurated track and field events for girls and young women by the teens of the twentieth century, but for the most part they were obliged to compete in voluminous bloomers that restricted their movement. First to adopt shorts for running was a daring fifteen-year-old English schoolgirl from Leeds called Elaine Burton (later Baroness Burton of Coventry), who risked the taunts of the crowd when she wore them at the 1919 English Northern Counties Ladies' Athletic Championships. The first women known to have worn shorts for a team sport were the members of Canterbury Ladies' Football Association, New Zealand, who were so attired for the first inter-province match against Wellington on 24 September 1921. The baggy black shorts were topped by a red and black sweater and black cap with flowing red tassels. Their opponents wore short skirts over knickers, but the Canterbury girls preserved the proprieties by wearing black silk stockings with their shorts. Generally, however, shorts for women did not invade the sporting arena until the following decade. A Miss G. E. Tomblin appeared on the tennis court in shorts at a tournament held in March 1932 at the Chiswick Hard Court Club in London. They appeared on the championship circuit for the first time the following year worn by Helen Hull Jacobs at Forest Hills.

Golf was a sport quite easy to play in skirts but former conjurer's assistant Gloria Minoprio of Littlestone Golf Club in Kent, England, decided to test the conservative values of the sport's hierarchy by arriving at the English Close Championship of October 1933 in a yellow Rolls-Royce and black slacks. The Ladies' Golf Union responded characteristically with a strongly worded statement that "deplored any departure from the traditional costume of ladies." (The historic pants can be seen at the British Golf Museum at Saint Andrew's in Scotland.)

The earliest known representation of a **women's occupational pants uniform** is a cabinet portrait of c. 1905 taken by H. S. Buss of Fond du Lac, Wis., depicting a woman streetcar conductor. The trousers, of conventional cut, are topped by a brass-buttoned double-breasted reefer jacket with collar and tie and on the lady's head a kepi-style hat. This was exceptional and there are few examples of uniformed women before the First World War. In the summer of 1916 Prussian State Railways ruled that female conductors and guards should be issued with the same costume as men, including "dark gray wide trousers." Similarly in America a group of women engine wipers, known as "the Dirty Dozen," were employed in the depot yard at Livingston, Mont., in 1918 and wore bib overalls with the cuffs of the pants turned over to a depth of about 8 inches (presumably because they were designed for men).

Pants as formal wear: While Eleanor Sears had worn pants for outdoor pursuits, New York socialite Gertrude Vanderbilt Whitney, founder of the Whitney Museum of American Art, was first to wear them in the drawing room. Her 1916 portrait by Robert Henri depicts her in a bohemian but elegant costume of royal blue jacket lined in yellow worn over a pale green oriental blouse and aqua silk pants gathered at the ankle with black ribbons.

Not dissimilar were the pants worn by nineteen-year-old Myrna Loy in her debut role as "the Vamp" in controversial sex movie *What Price Beauty?* of 1925. This was the first time trousers as women's apparel (as opposed to male impersonation by actresses) had been shown on screen. The garment in question had been created by Adrian, destined to become one of Hollywood's most celebrated designers, to demonstrate the dangerous allure of "the Vamp."

Actresses were in the forefront of those who helped to secure the acceptance of pants as fashion wear. The bewitching Louise Brooks, who personified the 1920s look with her bangs and slender, curveless figure, took to wearing silk pants (indoors only) in 1927, about the same time as beach pajamas were becoming fashionable on the French Riviera. The following year the English actress Hermione Baddeley, shortly after marrying and becoming the Honourable Mrs. David Tennant, gave a smart party at which she wore pants expressly designed for evening wear.

Pants for street wear followed the sensational appearance of Marlene Dietrich in slacks in Josef von Sternberg's 1930 film *Morocco*, though the lesbian coda intended by the iconoclastic Austrian director was wholly lost on the housewives of America who dared to emulate her. Short pants for general wear rather than sport became fashionable on the French Riviera in 1934, *l'Illustration* of 15 September commenting that they were to be seen everywhere on city streets and were even worn in the casinos and cocktail bars. In America they were originally seen on American college campuses. *Women's Wear* for 25 May 1937 reported that Vassar College girls had taken to wearing theirs with beer jackets—the same year that *Life* magazine revealed that Vassar drama students were to be seen in blue jeans (qv).

Pants as routine office wear were much longer in coming. Even in the liberated 1960s, when hemlines rose above the knee the solution for secretaries and receptionists worried about too much exposure was modesty boards on their desks rather than the simpler expedient of abandoning miniskirts for pants. In the winter of 1967 a heavy snowstorm in the London area prevented buses from ascending the steep hill to Alexandra Palace, a BBC outstation. BBC employee Amanda Games was on the Sunday duty roster and put on pants to struggle through deep snowdrifts covering the mile-long road up the hill. On arrival at the office she was instructed to return home and come back properly attired.

When the change did come, it happened in a rush in the larger metropolitan centers. In the early fall of 1970 a quiet revolution occurred in New York City as big corporations changed their dress code rules to permit pants at work, prompted by the replacement of the cherished miniskirt by the frumpy midi. At Irving Trust no announcement was made, but word got around. "The first day, I saw two or three girls in pants," a male executive was reported as saying, "the next there were sixty." A week later the female employees of Wall Street brokerage house Dominick & Dominick were debating whether they could adopt the pants look in place of the unpopular midi-skirt and prevailed upon the senior secretary to broach it with CEO Avery Rockefeller. It transpired that he did not like midis either. So if the fashion police would not allow any other skirt length, he opined, it had better be pants. Over at City Hall Mayor John Lindsay pondered the matter for a day and a half before green-lighting pants for municipal women workers.

Pantsuit office uniforms emerged at the same time, adopted for the Gallery Guides at the New York Stock Exchange, for tellers of the National Bank of North America, and as winter wear for Pan Am ground staff. Meanwhile in Washington, D.C., pants were penetrating the seats of power. Senator Jacob Javits declared himself anti-midi and told his female staff he would rather see them in pants, while Democrat Congressman (later mayor) Ed Koch said yes to pants because he wanted his aides to be in fashion. During the last week of September 1970 the first pantsuits in a government department were seen when five secretaries turned up to work in them. In the space of a few weeks women's workwear had changed irrevocably. *Vanity Fair*, the fashion bible that had originally decreed the midi for fashion-conscious middle America, surrendered without a fight to the new legions of betrousered female office workers.

THE FIRST WOMAN TO RECEIVE A PATENT

of invention in America was Sybilla Masters of Philadelphia in respect of a machine for cleaning and cutting Indian corn. The patent, granted by the Patent Office in London on 25 November 1715 in the name of her husband, Thomas, as was customary, was also registered in Pennsylvania. The process involved pounding the corn rather than grinding it and the cornmeal produced by the Masterses using Sybilla's process was sold as "Tuscarora Rice." Promoted as a "cure for consumption," it has been claimed as "the first American patent medicine." If so, then it was also the first quack medicine.

The first woman to receive a U.S. patent was Mary Kies of Killingly, Conn., on 5 May 1809 for an improvement in weaving straw with silk and thread for making bonnets. The first black woman whose invention was patented was Marjorie Stewart Joyner of Chicago, principal of the national chain of Walker Beauty Schools founded by black cosmetician Madame C. J. Walker. She was granted a patent on 27 November 1928 for an improved permanent-wave machine. It was introduced at Madame Walker's beauty salons, which catered to black women, and also in white salons under license.

Significant inventions by women (sometimes in partnership with men) include the jigsaw puzzle (qv), dishwasher (qv), baby incubator (qv), brassiere (qv), luminous watch (Marie Curie, 1904), windshield wiper and turn signal (qv), intravenous drip (ex-Broadway chorine Justine Johnstone, 1931), non-reflecting glass (Katherine Burr Blodgett, 1938), frequency hopping (film star Hedy Lamarr, 1942), typewriter correction fluid (Betty Nesmith Graham, 1956), Kevlar (Stephanie Kwolek, 1963), baby sling (Ann Moore, 1968), and computer screen icons (Susan Kare, 1984). All these inventions originated in the United States except the jigsaw, incubator and luminous watch (all French).

THE FIRST WOMAN PILOT

was Mlle. Élise Deroche, better known by her self-assumed title, Baronne de la Roche, who was taught to fly at Châlons, France, in a Voisin biplane by the Chief Instructor of Voisin Frères; she made her first solo flight—a "straight" of 300 yards—on 22 October 1909. The following year she won her brevet (licence), becoming the world's first qualified woman pilot on 8 March.

U.S.: The first woman to fly solo was Blanche Stuart Scott, the first and last woman to be accepted as a pupil by Glenn Curtiss—who believed, in common with most of his gender, that woman's place was on the ground. She made a number of taxiing runs at the Curtiss Co. airfield at Hammondsport, N.Y., but was unable to leave the ground because Curtiss had thoughtfully blocked the throttle. On 2 September 1910, however, either through the agency of a friendly mechanic or possibly owing to a fortuitous gust of wind, she rose to a height of 40 feet, glided for a short distance, and landed gracefully. There was now no looking back and the chauvinist Curtiss succumbed, allowing her, once she had proved herself fully competent in the air, to join his exhibition flying team. For the next six years, before her sudden retirement from flying in 1916, she thrilled the crowds as the "Tomboy of the Air," earning up to $5,000 a week doing spectacular stunts such as the

Death Dive, a perpendicular plunge from 4,000 feet to as little as 200 feet.

Because Blanche Scott's first solo was unofficial, the title of "First Woman Aviator in America" was accorded to Bessica Raiche of Mineola, N.Y., by the Aeronautical Society. She soloed in a home-built plane on 16 September 1910, two weeks after Blanche.

The first woman to receive a pilot's license in the United States and the second in the world was Harriet Quimby at Moisant Aviation School, Garden City, Long Island, N.Y., on 1 August 1911 flying a Moisant monoplane. She had failed to pass the previous day because of an unsatisfactory landing. Her license was the Fédération Aéronautique International (Aero Club of America) Certificate No. 37. Quimby was drama critic and a feature writer for *Leslie's Weekly*. In April 1912 she became the first woman to fly the English Channel, but only six weeks later, on 1 July, she was killed when her Blériot monoplane went out of control at the Boston Aviation Meet at an altitude of 6,000 feet.

Woman military pilot: There are a number of reports of women serving as pilots on offensive operations during World War I, though in most cases contemporary documentation is lacking. Nothing has been found to substantiate claims that Belgian aviatrix Hélène Dutrieu was accepted into the French air service in 1914 and flew reconnaissance missions from Paris to locate the German advance. (One report states, ambiguously, that she flew "in a non-essential capacity.") The other woman pilot said to have flown for the French was Marie Marvingt, whose Croix de Guerre credited her with bombing missions over German-held territory. According to some sources, in 1915 she bombed Metz, an industrial town in what is now northeastern France but that had been under German control since 1870. There seems little doubt that Marvingt did serve with the French forces and there was indeed a French raid in Metz by six aircraft on 25 March 1915. However, a photograph survives of her in the uniform of the Chasseurs Alpins the same year, so if she was a combat pilot it seems it was only temporarily.

There is rather more consensus that Princess Yevgeniya (aka Eugenie) Shakhovskaya joined the Imperial Russian Air Service in November 1914 with the honorary rank of *Praporshik* (Ensign) and served with the 1st Field Air Detachment on the northwestern front flying reconnaissance missions. Some say that she was a pilot, others that she was an observer. One of the few contemporary references appeared in the French popular weekly *Lectures Pour Tous* for 15 January 1916, in which it was reported: "She executed audacious raids above German lines. In the course of a perilous reconnaissance, her machine was struck by gunshots—the aviatrice was wounded. The tsar decorated her with the Military Order of Saint George." The princess came to a bad end. She was sentenced to death for treason but was reprieved by the tsar. Following the Bolshevik Revolution, she cast her lot with the Reds, serving as chief executioner for the Cheka (secret police) in Kiev. A drug addict, she allegedly shot one of her assistants while under the influence and was herself executed in 1920.

Three other Russian women pilots are said to have served with the military: Nadezhda Degtereva from Kiev, who disguised herself as a man to join up and was wounded in 1915 during a combat mission over the Austrian front in Galicia; Helen P. Samsonova, reconnaissance pilot with the 5th Corps Air Squadron; and Princess Sophie Alexandrovna Dolgorunaya, who flew missions with the 26th Corps Air Squadron for nine months in 1917.

The first woman definitely known to have participated in bombing raids was twenty-two-year-old Sabiha Gokchen, adopted daughter of Turkish president Kemal Atatürk, who was a member of the nine-plane unit of the Turkish Flying Corps that helped quell a revolt of Kurdish tribesmen in the Dersion region during March–June 1937. She was on active service for a month, bombing and strafing the enemy without suffering any personal injury, though her aircraft was peppered by rifle fire. On one occasion she scored a direct hit on the house of one of the rebel leaders, Seyyid Riza. Sabiha is also reputed to have dropped the final bomb that virtually put an end to the insurrection. A trailblazer for Muslim women, she was dubbed the "Amazon of the Air" by the press and she was honored with Turkey's highest aviation award, the Flying Medal set with brilliants. On her return from the conflict, Sabiha became a flying instructor, continuing to fly until 1966.

After World War II, in which Russian women combat pilots participated with conspicuous gallantry, Turkey maintained its lead in women's military aviation. In 1973, when representatives of 28 NATO women's services held a conference in Brussels, the only delegate who was able to declare herself as "combat ready" was a jet pilot serving with the Turkish Air Force.

The first **women pilots to destroy enemy aircraft** were Olga Yamshchikova and Valeria Khomyakova of the 58th Fighter Aviation Regiment of the Soviet Air Force on 24 September 1942, when they shot down, respectively, a Nazi Junkers Ju 88 bomber over Stalingrad and another Ju 88 over western Russia.

U.S.: The first woman pilot in the U.S. armed forces was California-born Lt. Barbara Allen, U.S. Navy, who received her wings at Corpus Christi, Tex., on 22 February 1974. She served with the Pacific Fleet Squadron in California until 1977, when she resigned on becoming pregnant. Recalled to active service in 1981 as a flight instructor, she was killed in a crash at Middleton Field near Evergreen, Ala., on 13 July 1982 while practicing touch-and-go landings.

The first ten women pilots of the U.S. Air Force received their wings at Williams Air Force Base in Mesa, Ariz., on 2 September 1977. On 14 February 1994 the U.S. Air Force announced that the first to qualify as a combat pilot was Lt. Jeannie M. Flynn, who had trained on F15-3s at Luke Air Force Base in Glendale, Ariz. Her intake included Capt. Martha McSally of Warwick, R.I., who in 1995 became the first American woman to fly a combat mission when she participated in the enforcement of the no-fly zone in Iraq piloting an A-16 Thunderbolt. On 19 July 2004 Lt. Col. McSally, despite being an inch below minimum regulation height for pilots, became the first woman to command an air combat unit, 354th Fighter Squadron at Davis-Monthan Air Force Base in Tucson, Ariz.

The first U.S. female combat pilot to go into action against the enemy was Lt. Kendra Williams, U.S. Navy, who took off from the deck of the aircraft carrier USS *Enterprise* in an F-18 Hornet on 16 December 1998 to fire missiles and drop bombs on Iraqi targets during Operation Desert Fox.

Woman airline pilot: The first was the aristocratic Marga von Etzdorf, who was engaged by Lufthansa in April 1928 on a short-term contract to fly a Junkers F13 passenger airliner on the Berlin–Breslau and Berlin–Stuttgart–Basel (Switzerland) routes. The original contract to fly 6,200 miles was extended by a further 3,100 miles. She later wrote:

> Because Lufthansa so far had never employed a woman pilot, I was confronted with incredulous looks of those gentlemen to whom I applied for the job. But even a woman could do no wrong when she was only the co-pilot. That alone was the sentiment which allowed me to get the job.

In 1931 von Etzdorf became the first woman to fly across Siberia to Tokyo. In 1933 she attempted to fly to Australia, but she crash-landed at Aleppo in Syria. Taunted by a French pilot as an incompetent woman, she went into a shed on the airfield and blew her brains out. Adolf Hitler accorded her a state funeral.

U.S.: New York–born Ruth Nichols, in 1931 holder of three women's aviation records simultaneously (speed, altitude, distance), became America's first airline pilot on 29 December 1932, flying the New York–Boston route for New York & New England Airways. The only other American woman to pilot airliners before the jet age, and for reasons that remain obscure usually claimed as first in the world, was the unfortunate Helen "Propeller Annie" Ritchie, who beat seven male applicants for a post with Central Airlines. Her first passenger flight was as Horace Stark's co-pilot in a Fort Tri-Motor from Washington, D.C., to Detroit on 31 December 1934. She earned herself the implacable hostility of her male colleagues (which may be why she has been elevated to premier status) and after representations from the Air Line Pilots' Association, the Air Commerce Bureau "suggested" to Central that women might not be suitable as pilots. Accordingly Helen "resigned" in October 1935.

Outside America the only other woman pilots of propeller-driven airliners were Prem Mathur of Deccan Airways in India in 1951, Maria Atenasova of Balkan Bulgarian Airlines in 1953, Durba Banerjee of Indian Airlines in 1956, Yvonne Pope of Morton Air Services in the United Kingdom in 1963, and the Italian Fiorenza de Bernardí of Aeralpi in 1967.

The first **woman to pilot jet airliners** was Emily Howell, second officer aboard Frontier Airlines

Boeing 737s flying out of Denver, Colo., from 12 January 1973. Three years later, on 6 June 1976, she became the first **woman airline captain**, in command of a Frontier Airlines turbo-prop DMC-6 Twin Otter. In 1984 Betsy Carroll became the first woman to pilot a jumbo jet across the Atlantic when she ferried a People Express Boeing 747 filled with no-frills passengers paying $149 a head from Newark, N.J., to London Gatwick.

THE FIRST **WOMAN PLAYWRIGHT**

to have a play performed was Mrs. Aphra Behn (SEE ALSO **novel: by an American woman; play: play set in America**), whose *Forc'd Marriage: or, the Jealous Bridegroom* ran for six days at the Duke's Theatre, Lincoln's Inn Fields, debuting on 20 September 1670. Described by Montague Summers as "a good tragic-comedy of the bastard Fletcherian Devenant type," the leading roles were taken by Thomas Betterton and his wife Mary Sanderson, one of the first English actresses. A supporting part was played by the dramatist Thomas Otway, then a boy of eighteen just left Winchester College, but he was received so poorly that he abandoned all thoughts of becoming an actor. Mrs. Behn's many plays—she was the most prolific dramatist of her time next to Dryden—are noted for the robustness of their dialogue and the indelicacy of the situations portrayed. Even in her own day this was an occasion for comment. And Alexander Pope composed the apt couplet:

> *The stage how loosely does Astrea tread*
> *Who fairly puts all characters to bed.*

A later age condemned her out of hand, one mid-Victorian female literary critic recoiling from the mention of Mrs. Behn's name with the assertion that "it is amply evident her mind was tainted to the very core." **U.S.:** The first play by an American-born woman was *Angelica: or, Quixote in Petticoats* by New Yorker Charlotte Ramsey Lennox, which was published in London in 1758. The play and the novel (qv) on which it was based, *The Female Quixote: or, The Adventures of Arabella* (1752), were partly set in America. Mrs.

Lennox had left her native country for Britain at the age of fifteen, becoming an actress and the intimate of Johnson, Richardson, Fielding, Goldsmith, and Garrick. Her comedy *The Sister*, an adaptation of her novel *The History of Henrietta* (1758), was given a single performance at Covent Garden on 18 February 1769 but was not well received. It was, however, the first play by an American woman playwright to be performed and also the first by any American to be translated into a foreign language, being published in German in 1776. Sadly she died in penury, despite a long and prolific career devoted to novels, translations, literary criticism, and editing a woman's magazine.

The first play by an American woman written and published in America was *The Adulateur* by Mary Otis Warren of Plymouth, Mass., published anonymously in the *Massachusetts Spy* (Boston) in two parts on 26 March and 23 April 1772. Set in a fictitious Upper Servia, the satire was firmly anchored in the turbulent politics of New England and sought to expose Thomas Hutchinson, governor of Massachusetts ("Rapatio" in the play) as a false patriot. Other thinly veiled portraits in the drama were of such revolutionary luminaries as her brother James Otis, John and Samuel Adams, and John Hancock. The play was never performed and though some authorities believe that her subsequent satire *The Group* (1775) was put on, there is no documentary evidence of this. Since the public performance of plays was illegal in Massachusetts at the time, it seems doubtful.

The first American woman to have a play performed in the United States was Anna Cora Mowatt, whose comic satire *Fashion* debuted at the Park Theatre in her hometown of New York on 26 March 1845. It was an immense success at a time when nearly all drama seen in America came from Britain and it marked a new departure in the comedy of manners. Young, pretty, and vivacious, Mrs. Mowatt also succeeded on the other side of the footlights when she played the role of Pauline in the popular play *The Lady of Lyons* three months later.

THE FIRST
WOMAN CANDIDATE FOR PRESIDENT OF THE UNITED STATES

was the New York stockbroker (SEE **women stockbrokers**) and suffragist Victoria Claflin Woodhull, who announced her intention of running for president in the *New York Herald*, which ran an editorial supporting her, on 2 April 1870. She was nominated for the presidency at a convention of the newly formed Equal Rights Party held at Apollo Hall, New York City, on 10 May 1872. On election day, 2 November 1872, the Equal Rights candidate was languishing in Ludlow Street Jail in New York on charges of obscenity, having published an exposé of the sex life of the noted divine Henry Ward Beecher. How many popular votes she received is not known, because they were included among the two thousand or so "scattering votes" uncounted because of legal impediments of one kind or another.

For the world's first woman president, SEE **woman head of state/government**.

THE FIRST **WOMEN STOCKBROKERS**

were Victoria Claflin Woodhull (SEE ABOVE) and Tennessee Claflin, who opened the brokerage office of Woodhull, Claflin & Co. at the Hoffman House, New York City, on 19 January 1870. The two sisters had been instructed in the art of high finance by Cdre. (Cornelius) Vanderbilt in return for their services as clairvoyant and mistress, respectively. Although neither partner was a member of the New York Stock Exchange, the firm did a brisk business, particularly with lady clients, for whom a special room was reserved when the firm moved to more commodious premises at 44 Broad Street. Here they dispensed champagne and chocolate-covered strawberries to such as Annie Wood and Molly de Ford, two of the wealthiest madams in New York. Mrs. de Ford was a particularly satisfied customer, declaring that the sisters had earned her a profit of $30,000 in one year. "The bewitching brokers," as they were dubbed by the press, sported a business attire of men's jackets and vests though Tennessee discarded the pants she wore 3 inches above the ankle in favor of a broadcloth skirt after a reporter told her the costume would provoke rioting in the streets. Not all their attention was reserved for brokerage, as they also edited a magazine called *Woodhull and Claflin's Weekly*, for the propagation of Free Thought and Free Love, and in April 1870 Victoria offered herself as the first woman candidate for the presidency (SEE ABOVE). They also succeeded in combining stockbroking with an admiration for Marxism, but clients who had been prepared to overlook the sisters' other idiosyncrasies withdrew their support after Victoria had declared herself a free lover from a public platform at Steinway Hall, and business declined sharply. There was a further scandal when Tennessee assumed the honorary colonelcy of two African-American regiments and, after three years in operation, the firm of Woodhull, Claflin & Co. was obliged to close.

Woman member of a stock exchange: The first was Miss Oonagh Keogh of Foxrock, Eire, who was admitted to the Dublin Stock Exchange on 9 July 1925 at age twenty-two and remained an active broker until her resignation in 1939. Miss Keogh was able to make her application under a provision of the Irish Free State Constitution that guaranteed equality of opportunity to every citizen over the age of twenty-one. Since the approval of new members was the responsibility of the minister of finance, the Committee of the Exchange was precluded from barring her on grounds of gender, though a number of brokers declared their intention of ignoring her on the floor. To begin with Miss Keogh confined her activities to recording the deals made by her father, also a member, but when he became ill she took over full responsibility and her aptitude soon won the respect of her male colleagues.

U.S.: In 1965 Phyllis Peterson and Julie Walsh became members of the New York–based American Stock Exchange (AMEX), which traded principally in small to mid-size stocks. Inquiries to all the stock exchanges of the United States have failed to elicit information on earlier women members, though if any is known please contact us. On 28 December 1967 Muriel Siebert became the first woman member of the New York Stock Exchange, having paid $445,000 for her seat.

THE FIRST **WOMEN VOTERS**

....

were enfranchised in the newly independent Republic of Corsica under the Constitution of 18 November 1755. Unmarried women of twenty-five or over were entitled to vote in elections to the Diet. This right was abolished when Corsica was annexed by the French in 1769, restored with the creation of the Anglo-Corsican Kingdom in 1770 and extinguished again with the resumption of French rule in 1796.

U.S.: Under its constitution of 2 July 1776, New Jersey enfranchised all inhabitants aged twenty-one or over with an estate valued at £50 who had been resident for twelve months or more at the date they would exercise their vote. About 95 percent of New Jersey men were able to register as voters under the property qualification, but as women's property was deemed to belong to their husbands, female voters were necessarily spinsters or widows (though in practice some married women did succeed in voting). The first election to the Legislative Council and General Assembly at which women were able to vote was held on Tuesday 13 August 1776. They voted in sufficiently large numbers in the presidential election of 1800 to stir up controversy and the law was amended in 1807 by the use of the prefix *male* in relation to eligible voters. Another significant word was also added: *white*.

No other jurisdiction gave women the right to vote until 1838, when Pitcairn Island, the refuge of the *Bounty* mutineers in the Pacific, became a British colony. In 1867 Y Wladfa, the self-governing Welsh province in Patagonia, gave women the vote, but they were disenfranchised when the community was absorbed into Argentina two years later. In the meantime women ratepayers in the colony of South Australia had been enfranchised for municipal elections on 29 November 1861. Sweden followed suit the following year.

In the United States the first jurisdiction to restore women's right to vote was the Territory of Wyoming on 10 December 1869—according to some authorities as an attraction to women to settle and populate, according to others owing to the machinations of the Democratic party machine, which sought to discredit the Republicans in their attempt to enfranchise blacks. By adding women to the agenda the Democrats hoped to have the whole issue of wider

enfranchisement laughed out of court, but they found themselves hoisted on their own petard. When Wyoming applied for statehood, there was a concerted effort on Capitol Hill to persuade the independently minded territory to enact a disenfranchisement bill. One leading local politician spoke for the majority in Wyoming when he roundly declared "we will remain out of the Union a hundred years rather than come in without the women." Statehood was granted with female suffrage intact on 10 July 1890, making the women voters of Wyoming the first since New Jersey's disenfranchisement who were entitled to vote in national elections.

Country to grant its female citizens the right to vote: The first to do so on a permanent basis was the self-governing colony of New Zealand, the Electoral Reform Act that conferred this privilege receiving the governor's assent on 19 September 1893. There was no qualification other than attainment of the age of majority. Although the enfranchisement of women had been proposed as early as 1843 by Alfred Saunders (who happily lived to see its fulfillment fifty years later), there was no organized campaign until the founding of the Franchise Department of the Women's Christian Temperance Union under Mrs. K. W. Sheppard in 1886. In the comparatively short space of seven years, Mrs. Sheppard and her followers succeeded in winning the support of a majority of the Legislative Council, though not of a minority of dissident members who petitioned the governor against the proposal, on the grounds that votes for women would "seriously affect the rights and property of Her Majesty's subjects not resident in the colony...and may seriously embarrass the finances of the colony." The bill, while drawing support from both the ruling Liberal Party and the opposition Conservative Party, passed its third reading in the upper house by the bare margin of two votes.

The first occasion on which the women of New Zealand went to the polls was the general election of 28 November 1893. William Pember Reeves, the Liberal candidate for Christchurch, wrote:

> The women began to vote early—at about nine o'clock—and by amicable arrangement were allowed in the cities to have certain booths pretty

much to themselves until noon . . . Each woman armed herself conscientiously with her number, and on the whole the novices went through the ordeal with much credit. The proportion of spoiled ballot papers was very little larger than at previous elections. When the polls closed at seven o'clock, 90,000 women had peacefully voted.

New Zealand was at this time still fourteen years away from achieving sovereignty. When Australia became a sovereign nation on the federation of its constituent self-governing colonies in 1901, women of the two states that had already introduced female suffrage, South Australia (1894) and Western Australia (1899), were entitled to vote in federal elections. On 12 June the following year the Commonwealth of Australia enfranchised all women, making it the first fully sovereign nation in the world to do so (Corsica's independent status in 1755 being ambivalent) and also the first to permit women to stand as candidates. The first general election in which women voted was held on 16 December 1903.

Nevertheless, women of Tasmania, Queensland, Victoria were still not entitled to vote in state elections. Queensland not only succumbed (1903), but in 1914 became the first electorate in the world whose women (and their menfolk) were obliged by law to exercise their vote.

U.S.: The Nineteenth Amendment to the Constitution, granting all adult female citizens the right to vote, became law on 26 August 1920. Unlike in New Zealand, where it had taken just seven years to win the vote from the inception of the suffrage movement, it was seventy-two years since women had begun what has been described as "the largest civil rights movement in the history of the world."

Apart from nations without an electoral process, the last to grant votes for women was the United Arab Emirates in 2006. In the western world Liechtenstein had held out until 1984 and in Switzerland the canton of Appenzell Innerrhoden only extended its franchise to women when forced to do so by the federal supreme court in 1990.

THE FIRST WOMEN'S GOLF

precedes any other competitive sporting activity by women. The earliest recorded woman golfer was the first of King Henry VIII's six wives, Catherine of Aragon, daughter of Ferdinand and Isabella of Spain. In the year of her marriage and Henry's accession, 1509, she wrote to her husband's councillor Thomas (later Cardinal) Wolsey that "golfe keeps one busy at court."

According to the *Statistical Account of Scotland*, published in 1792, the game was then being played by the working women of Musselburgh, a fishing port near Edinburgh on the Firth of Forth. It was here that the first women's tournament was organized by Musselburgh Golf Club for the local fishwives and played on 9 January 1811 for a first prize of a creel and "skull" (a small fish basket) and consolation prizes of the best Barcelona handkerchiefs. This was very much a one-off and it was not until 13–15 June 1893 that the first women's all-comers championship was held by the Ladies' Golf Union (SEE BELOW) at Saint Anne's Old Links in Lancashire. It was won by Lady Margaret Scott, whose family estate at Stowell Park, Gloucestershire, had a private golf course.

Golf club to admit women: The first—although it allowed women only as associates—was the Royal and Ancient of Saint Andrew's, Scotland, which built a short course for their use in 1867. This was later reported to be ill-kept and "barely fit for rabbits." North Devon Golf Club at Westward Ho! laid a ladies' course the following year and established a more enduring North Devon Ladies' Golf Club on 8 June 1868. When the Ladies' Golf Union was founded in London on 19 April 1893, there were representatives of sixty-three clubs for ladies or admitting ladies. The LGU was the first **national association governing women's sport** anywhere in the world.

U.S.: The first recorded woman golfer was Mrs. John Reid, sole lady member and one of the founders of the Saint Andrew's Golf Club in Yonkers, N.Y. A Scots linen merchant called Robert Lockhart had brought over some golf clubs and balls from Old Tom Morris's shop at Saint Andrews, Scotland, home of the Royal and Ancient. In a farmer's meadow at Yonkers he and the Reids laid out what must be the shortest golf course of all time, consisting as it did of just three holes, where play commenced on 22 February 1888.

By the time Saint Andrew's Golf Cub organized the first **mixed foursome** in American golfing history, they had already moved to a more capacious 30-acre site at North Broadway and Shonnard Place. On 14 November 1889 Kingman Upham and Mrs. Reid beat John G. Reid and Carrie Low by 1½ holes (each pair scored half a point when a hole was halved).

The first ladies' tournament in the United States was played at Morristown, N.J., on 17–18 October 1894 and won by Hollard A. Ford by 14 strokes in 97 on a double round of 7 holes.

THE FIRST WOMEN'S MAGAZINE

was *The Ladies' Mercury*, a question-and-answer weekly published by the London bookseller John Dunton commencing 27 June 1693. With this periodical Dunton initiated what is now known as a "problem page"—indeed it consisted of only this feature and comprised but a single sheet, printed on both sides. "Ladies are desired to send in their questions to the Latin Coffee House in Ave Mary [*sic*] Lane," wrote Dunton in the first issue. He promised answers "to all the most nice and curious questions concerning love, marriage behaviour, dress and honour of the female sex, whether virgins, wives or widows . . . with the zeal and softness becoming the sex." Both questions and answers were generally couched in frank and forceful language, and the editor evinced no disinclination to admit such subjects as adultery and premarital sex into his columns. This full-blooded approach toward matters affecting the feminine psyche remained characteristic of problem pages in women's magazines until their discontinuance in the latter half of the eighteenth century. The revival of this kind of feature by S. O. Beeton (husband of Mrs. Beeton of culinary fame) in his *Englishwoman's Domestic Magazine* of 1852, under the title "Cupid's Letter Bag," was marked by a far more discreet handling of readers' problems.

The first women's magazine edited by a woman and the first to contain articles on miscellaneous topics was *The Female Tatler*, inaugurated on 8 July 1709 by "Mrs. Crackenthorpe." This pseudonym cloaked the identity of the notorious Mrs. Mary de la Rivière Manley, who was arrested for libel in October of the same year for her scandalous work *Secret Memoirs and Manners of Several Persons of Quality*. Similar intimate revelations in *The Female Tatler* caused the magazine to be indicted as a "nuisance" by a grand jury shortly afterward, and this seems to have effectively altered the character of the paper, which was said to have become "as insipid as anything in print."

U.S.: The first periodical addressed principally to women was the *Gentleman and Lady's Town and Country Magazine* of Boston, which ran for eight monthly issues from May thru December 1784. Despite its title, the content catered more to feminine than masculine proclivities, specializing in light fiction and "advice to the fair sex," mostly about the selection of husbands. The title was revived in February 1789 with a further run to August 1790. The first magazine exclusively for women (i.e., so designated by its title) was the *Lady's Magazine*, published by W. Gibbons of Philadelphia, June 1792 to May 1793.

Two other women's magazine appeared before the close of the eighteenth century and another three dozen or so before 1850. Most of these provided fairly insipid fare for the fair and it was only with the inception of Godey's in 1830, Graham's in 1831, and Peterson's in 1842, all emanating from Philadelphia, that the genre can be said to have become established as a mainstay of the American middle-class lady's regular reading habits. *Ladies* were definitely the target audience. Nearly all the early publications contained the words *Lady's* or *Ladies* in their titles; none contained *Woman's* or *Women's* before the *Pioneer and Woman's Advocate* (Providence, R.I.) in 1852 and the *Woman's Advocate* (Philadelphia) of 1855, both, as their titles suggest, voices of the nascent women's-rights movement. Another targeting women as such was the first **magazine for black women**, *Our Women and Children*, edited by William J. Simmons and issued by the National Publishing Co. of Louisville, Ky., from August 1888. (SEE BELOW for the first black fashion magazine.)

Fashion magazine: The first was *Le Courrier de la mode*, published monthly in Paris from May 1768. The first in English was the *Magazine a-la-Mode or Fashionable Miscellany*, published in London from 29

December 1776 at a price of 6d. The first issue was "Embellished with elegant Engravings, viz. A Lady in full Dress for the Drawing-Room, in the Month of January; a Gentleman in fashionable Undress for the same Month; a representation of Lady's full Dress Cap; the Artois Buckles now in Vogue . . . ; all elegantly engraved by capital Masters."

U.S.: This is difficult to pinpoint, because early American women's magazines tended to focus on literary and domestic content, with fashion as a subordinate element—probably a reflection of Puritan values that still regarded personal adornment as ungodly. The first magazine to contain a fashion plate was *The Port Folio*, Philadelphia, the June 1809 issue illustrating a "woman's day dress, hat, and reticule." The first magazines to contain the word *fashion* in their title were the *Boston Miscellany of Literature and Fashion*, edited by Nathan Hale Jr., and the *Lady's World of Fashion*, Philadelphia, edited by Ann S. Stephens, both of which bowed in January 1842. The latter, published by Charles J. Peterson, became the celebrated *Peterson's*.

The first fashion magazine for black women was *Ringwood's Afro-American Journal of Fashion*, founded by Julia Ringwood Coston at Cleveland, Ohio, in 1891. It is remarkable not only as evidence that the black middle class had advanced sufficiently by the early 1890s to support a fashion magazine, but also for the first appearance in print of the term *Afro-American*.

SEE ALSO **fashion photographs.**

THE FIRST WOMEN'S TRACK AND FIELD

events known were running and jumping contests held for the pupils of Wellington Girls' High School (now Wellington Girls' College) on a piece of open land adjoining the Te Aro Baths (at which swimming races were held on the same occasion) at Wellington, New Zealand, in 1885. The only winner identified by name was Mabel Pownall for the high jump.

U.S.: A 220-yard race for women was held during the Brooklyn Caledonian Club Games on 3 July 1886. There were nine starters and the *New York Times* reported that "prettier girls could not have been found in the whole park." In fact there were two events,

because the race had to be run again after it had been declared a dead heat between Miss Kate McDonald and Miss Bessie Edwards. The two ran against each other in the rerun, Miss Edwards breasting the tape two yards ahead of her rival and winning the trophy, a silver dinner service.

Women's track and field meet: The first was inaugurated at North London Collegiate School for Ladies at Camden Road, Camden Town, in July 1890. Originally these annual sports days involved running, throwing, jumping, and obstacle contests indoors in the gymnasium, but pressure of space soon stimulated a move to an open-air athletics ground in Epping.

U.S.: The first in America and the first anywhere at college level was organized by the Students' Athletic Association at Vassar College, Poughkeepsie, N.Y., on 9 November 1895. Held on the tennis courts in drizzling rain, there were five track and field events: 100-yard dash, won by Elizabeth F. Vassar (granddaughter of Vassar's founder) in 16 seconds; broad jump, won by Emma L. Baker, 11 feet 5 inches; 120-yard hurdle, won by Ida C. Thallon in 25 seconds; high jump, won by Laura C. Bowenell, 3 feet 7 inches; and 220-yard race, won by Helen L. Haight in 36 seconds. It was reported that "the girls were suitably dressed for the sports, bloomers and divided skirts predominating in the costumes." Lest this arouse unseemly interest, no gentlemen were admitted.

Vassar's physical education instructors Harriet Ballintine and Eva G. May, who had organized this first "field day," were sufficiently serious about the sport to attend the Harvard Summer School, which in 1896 hosted the first systematic instruction of women in track and field events. It was on this occasion that Harvard coach James G. Lathrop ordered the first spiked running shoes ever made for a woman, the recipient being Eva G. May. The Vassar Athletic Association subsequently provided spikes for every participant in its field days. When women's track and field records were listed for the first time in *Spalding's Official Athletic Almanac*, in 1904, Vassar held ten out of fifteen and of the other five none was contested at Vassar except the high jump. Five years later they still had eight out of eighteen, but by then Bryn Mawr, Elmira, and Mount Holyoke were taking their share of the honors.

The first open meeting was organized by the Academia Women's Athletics Club at the Stade Brançion in Paris on 1 May 1915. The first **international meet** was held under the auspices of the International Sporting Club of Monaco at Stade du Tir, Monte Carlo, on 25 May 1921, with teams from France, Britain, Switzerland, Italy, and Norway.

America competed internationally for the first time the following year at the Women's World Games in Paris. The meet was held on 20 August at Pershing Stadium, the fifteen-strong U.S. team coming second to Great Britain but achieving two world records, in the 100-yard hurdles and the shot put.

Olympic track and field events for women were first held at the ninth Olympiad at Amsterdam in 1928. The first of the finals, on 31 July, was the 100 meters, which began with Canadian hopeful Myrtle Cook, a "slight attractive lass," being disqualified for twice breaking ahead of the gun, at which she collapsed weeping to the ground. Then at the next attempt Fräulein Schmidt, described in news reports as a "buxom German blonde," was disqualified for the same reason, "but instead of tears . . . shook her fist under the starter's nose and the spectators for the moment thought she might stage a face-scratching and hair-pulling act." Meanwhile the Canadian girl was sobbing so lustily that the starter had her removed to a pile of cushions lest she upset the others. Eventually the race got under way, with sixteen-year-old Riverdale, Ill., high-school junior Elizabeth Robinson, the youngest and the only contestant who had shown no signs of distress by the succession of false starts and dramatics, establishing a world record of 12.5 seconds and becoming the first female Olympian to win a gold in track and field. It was only her fourth track competition. The *New York Times* concluded its report with the information that while the Canadian sprinters tried to comfort their inconsolable team mate, "Fräulein Schmidt departed from the scene, vowing vengeance against the race official the next time they met." Lina Radke of Germany restored her country's honor by winning the 800 meters in 2:16.8—Germany's first-ever gold in track and field by either sex—while the disappointed Canadians also achieved Olympic glory with golds for the 4 x 100-meter relay in 48.4 seconds and the high jump, won by Ethel Catherwood at 1.59 meters. Halina Konopacka of Poland took the discus with a throw of 39.62 meters.

~~~~~~~~~~~~~~~~~~~~~~~~~~~~ X ~~~~~~~~~~~~~~~~~~~~~~~~~~~~~

THE FIRST **X-RAYS**

were discovered on 8 November 1895 by Wilhelm Conrad Röntgen of the Institute of Physics at the University of Würzburg in Germany, using a Crookes cathode-ray tube that had been modified by a younger colleague, Philipp Lenard. The discovery was accidentally made while Röntgen was investigating the conduction of electricity in gases at low pressures. After several weeks of further experimentation, he made the first human X-ray on 22 December, showing the bones in the hand of his Swiss wife, Anna. Six days later Röntgen's friend and former colleague Franz Exner, director of the Physical Institute in Vienna, made the first **clinical X-ray** of a gunshot wound in a forester's hand.

The creation of X-rays did not involve the use of any new technology; rather, Röntgen's achievement was the ability to recognize, and apply, a scientific phenomenon that was to revolutionize medical diagnosis. It would earn him the first Nobel Prize in Physics in 1901, but a jealous Lenard's reaction to the honor was so vindictive that Röntgen abandoned all work on medical imaging. (Only many years later was it revealed that the Nobel committee had recommended both names for a joint award.) Röntgen refused to patent his technique, believing it should be freely available as a benefit for all mankind.

U.S.: On the same day as Exner made the first practical application, 28 December 1895, a "preliminary" report of Röntgen's discovery was published in the *Proceedings* of the Physico-Medical Society of Würzburg. "A mathematics-free paper," commented medical historian Bettyann Holtzmann Kelves in *Naked to the Bone* (1997), "it may have been the last to reveal a major discovery in physics that was accessible to the general public." It did indeed reach the general public via an excited newspaper press, following a report in Vienna's *Neue Freie Presse* on 5 January 1896. A British stringer in Vienna cabled the story to London's *Daily Chronicle*, which ran it the following day, and on 7 January it appeared in the *New York Sun*. Five days later Dr. Henry Louis Smith of Davidson, N.C., shot a bullet into the hand of a corpse and a 15-minute exposure to create America's first X-ray revealed its location.

Seldom has a scientific discovery achieved such instantaneous renown, aided by the fact that it was comparatively easy for even amateurs to replicate, such as the members of the X-ray Boys' Clubs that sprang up in the United States. In Chicago and Lawrence, Kan., there were slot machines that allowed the curious to X-ray their own hands, the dangers of radiation being then unknown. Bloomingdale's of New York hired Columbia University physics senior Herbert Hawks to conduct public demonstrations for the benefit of customers. Not all were equally enchanted by the thrill of seeing inside the body. A New Jersey assemblyman man introduced a bill to ban X-ray opera glasses, should anyone have the temerity to invent them.

During that same month of public announcement two important X-ray innovations were made. In Braunschweig, Germany, the first **dental X-ray** was made by Otto Walkoff. Far away in Chicago, the first use of **radiation treatment** was made by Emile Grubbe on 29 January when he treated Mrs. Rose Lee for a carcinoma of the breast. The next month saw the first diagnostic use of clinical X-rays in the United States. Wealthy New Yorker Prescott Hall Butler had shot himself in the hand with a shotgun and an X-ray made by Michael Pupin with an Edison fluoroscope at his Columbia University laboratory revealed more than a hundred pellets. Butler's surgeon, William Tillinghast Bull, became the first to use an X-ray as an operating guide. Dental X-rays in the United States were pioneered by C. Edmund Kells of New Orleans, who introduced the technique to fellow dental practitioners when he set up a radiography clinic at a convention of the Southern Dental Association in Asheville, N.C., in April 1896.

The first **use of X-rays for battle casualties** followed the Battle of Adowa on 1 March 1896, when invading Italian forces suffered a crushing defeat by the Abyssinians. Two Italian soldiers wounded in the forearm were X-rayed by Lt. Col. Giuseppe Alvaro at the military hospital in Naples. The first field X-ray apparatus was provided for the Greek forces in the Greco-Turkish War of 1897 by the British Red Cross. Another accompanied the British and Indian forces in the Tirah campaign on the North-West Frontier the same year. Manufactured by A. E. Dean of London with tubes by A. C. Cossor, it was in charge of Surgeon-Major W. C. Beevor, who reported at the conclusion of the conflict that all three tubes had survived intact! In July 1898 the first American battle casualties to be X-rayed were those treated at the three U.S. Navy hospital ships equipped with radiography units that were stationed off the Cuban coast during the Spanish-American War. On shore the U.S. Army Hospital Corps also used X-rays.

The first **non-medical use of X-rays** was by French Customs, which used fluoroscopes installed at the Gare du Nord, Paris, in August 1897 to check the contents of baggage or sealed containers. It was not until the 1970s that American Science & Engineering of Cambridge, Mass., succeeded in producing a hand-luggage scanner for airports that could operate without fogging camera film.

Another important non-medical use was the **X-ray analysis of paintings**, pioneered in 1913 by Dr. Alexander Faber of Weimar, Germany, and Professor Maximilian Toepler of Dresden, who separately discovered that it could be used to reveal what lay beneath the surface of old masters. The technique was introduced to the United States by Alan Burroughs in 1923 and over the following years he built up an archive of several thousand X-ray photographs of old masters at Harvard's Fogg Art Museum in Cambridge, Mass. His work came to the attention of the art world when he was able to prove that a portrait of Queen Elizabeth I of England by the sixteenth-century Flemish artist Frans Pourbus, the authenticity of which had been challenged by prominent art critics, was in fact genuine.

Mammograms: High-contrast breast X-rays were first used to detect cancer in 1949 by radiologist Raul Laborgne of Montevideo, Uruguay. He devised an apparatus that would squeeze the patient's breast between a cone and a compression pad while the X-ray was made, the resulting image giving a clearer indication of calcifications. Then as now the technique was far from foolproof, but with a 30 percent success rate in early detection it was adopted in Europe and the United States following publication of Laborgne's results in 1951. The first **mass screening for breast cancer** was of 30,329 women by Health Insurance Plan of New York in 1963, with annual follow-up mammograms and clinical tests. Deaths from cancer detected within five years among this group were 30 percent lower after ten years than the national average.

CAT (Computerized Axial Tomography) scanner: The first X-ray machine capable of cross-sectioning and of seeing deep into the brain, this was developed for British recording and television pioneer EMI by Godfrey N. Hounsfield, a former builder's apprentice and one of the few people to have made a major scientific breakthrough in the twentieth century who had never been to college. (Nor in the previous century had Röntgen, despite becoming a university professor.) The computerized prototype machine was installed at Atkinson Morley's Hospital in the London suburb of Wimbledon and there on 1 October 1971 Hounsfield made the first clinical CAT scan, of a forty-one-year-old woman with symptoms of a brain tumor. Prior to this he had experimented with a pig's head which, in a fit of absentmindedness to which genius is prone, he left on a train seat in the London Underground. The first CAT scanners in the United States were the fifth and sixth in EMI's run of six prototypes, one of which was sold in 1972 to the Mayo Clinic at Rochester, Minn., and the other to Boston's Massachusetts General Hospital, each for $300,000. Godfrey Hounsfield and South African Allan M. Cormack, who had worked out the mathematics for the revolutionary machine, jointly shared the Nobel Prize in Physiology or Medicine 1979. In the meantime the first whole-body scanner, the ACTA (Automated, Computerized, Transverse Axial) scanner, had been completed in Washington, D.C., in 1974 by Georgetown University Medical School professor of biophysics and radiology Robert Ledley and licensed for manufacture to pharmaceuticals giant Pfizer.

The first **MRI (Magnetic Resonance Imaging) scanners,** machines that eliminate bones from the image to reveal areas of soft tissue otherwise concealed, were developed contemporaneously in the 1970s by Armenian-American physician Dr. Raymond Damadian, by Luxembourgian-American chemist Paul Lauterbur, and by English physicist Sir Peter Mansfield, a former printer's assistant who had dropped out of school at fifteen. Lauterbur produced the first MRI image of a living organism, a clam collected by his daughter from a Long Island beach, at the State University of New York at Stony Brook in 1973. The first human MRI scan was made by Sir Peter Mansfield at the University of Nottingham in England and showed the finger of his colleague Dr. Andrew Maudsley, complete with bones, bone marrow, nerves, and arteries. This was submitted to the *British Journal of Radiography* on 1 June 1976. The whole-body MRI scanner built by Dr. Damadian at the SUNY Health Service Center in Brooklyn, N.Y., was first used to make an image of his associate Dr.

Laurence Minkoff's chest cavity on 3 July 1977. The Nobel Prize in Physiology or Medicine was awarded to Lauterbur and Mansfield in 2003 for their individual work on nuclear magnetic resonance imaging, the controversial omission of Dr. Damadian from the honor arousing the ire of his adherents, who placed full-page advertisements of protest in leading newspapers in the United States and Sweden.

Although the theoretical groundwork had been established, by the end of the seventies the clinical application of MRI had yet to be fully realized. This would be achieved on the Pacific Coast at the medical school of the University of California in San Francisco. The head of the Department of Radiology, Alex Margulis, was determined that the lead held by the Mayo Clinic and Massachusetts General in CAT scanning in the United States should be matched by UCSF's lead in MRI. Accordingly he set up a special laboratory in South San Francisco, where in 1981 a team under physicist Leon Kaufman "went clinical" with a machine that could generate whole-body images of high resolution in minutes.

~~~~~~~~~~~~~~~~~~~~~~~~ Y ~~~~~~~~~~~~~~~~~~~~~~~~

THE FIRST YACHTS

recorded were six sailing vessels that took part in a water festival held in Amsterdam in honor of Prince William I of Orange on 17 March 1580. Originally most *jaghts* were small, swift sailing craft employed as escorts to merchant vessels bound for Portugal or the Baltic. The first to be built for purely recreational or sporting purposes followed soon after, when the *Rat o' Wight* was constructed for Queen Elizabeth at Cowes in the Isle of Wight to celebrate the English victory over the Spanish in 1588. By the early seventeenth century yachts were being used in the annual Admiral Sailing in Amsterdam, a kind of water pageant with a competitive element in which maneuvers were carried out by flag signals and mock battles were fought.

The first **yacht race** was held on 21 May 1661 between the English king Charles II in the 49-foot-long *Katherine* and his brother the Duke of York's 52-foot-long *Anne* over a course from Greenwich on the outskirts of London up the Thames to Gravesend on the Kentish coast. Charles, the victor, had twenty-six luxury yachts built for his personal use during his twenty-five-year reign, many of which he named after the royal mistresses. Yachting as a sport was put on an organized basis with the founding of the Cork Harbour Water Club in Ireland by Lord Inchiquin and others in 1720. (This club, the first in the world devoted to a sport, had an excellent rule that is commended to yacht clubs everywhere: Any member who talked about sailing after dinner was fined a bumper.) **U.S.:** The first was the 16-ton *Onrust* ("Restless"), 44 feet 6 inches in length and with beam of 11 feet 6 inches, built by Dutch fur trader Capt. Adrian Block and his crew in the spring of 1614 in pre-settlement Manhattan after their ship *Tiger* had been burned out at its mooring. The site of construction was that now occupied by the historic Fraunces Tavern on Pearl Street and it was named after the island off the Dutch coast that was the last of their homeland they had seen on departure. Block had intended to return to the Netherlands in *Onrust*, but when he encountered fellow fur trader Capt. Hendrick Christiaensen, who was in no hurry to return, he swapped it for the latter's larger and more seaworthy *Fortune*. It was in the *Onrust* that two years later, in August 1616, Capt. Christiaensen discovered the Schuylkill River and explored most of the coast from Nova Scotia to the Capes of Virginia. He then sailed the *Onrust* to Holland, where he was able to present what was then the most accurate chart of the Eastern Seaboard of North America.

An arid Calvinism and Protestant work ethic ordained that recreation did not occupy a prominent place in the life of many seventeenth- and eighteenth-century Americans and it is not until the opening years of the nineteenth century that pleasure craft emerged. The earliest such vessels known by name were the sloop *Diver* and a 56-foot ketch *Trouble*, both built c. 1805 by twenty-year-old John Cox Stevens (SEE **steamboat**) of Hoboken, N.J. He would sail them in New York Bay, challenging local fishermen to impromptu races. Stevens was one of the founders and first commodore of the New York Yacht Club nearly forty years later and leader of the syndicate that built *America*, first winner of the trophy cup named after her (SEE BELOW).

The first luxury yacht built in the United States for pleasure was the oddly named *Cleopatra's Barge*, a sumptuous 100-foot-long floating palace crafted in Salem, Mass., by Retire Becket for the immensely wealthy and flamboyant shipping magnate Capt. George Crowninshield Jr. and launched in December 1816. Her eccentric owner had the starboard topsides painted in bright stripes and those on the port side with a herringbone pattern of vivid hue. Nailed to the deck was a wooden cigar-store Indian. The main saloon and the cabins were furnished with exquisite furniture and appointments in the French Empire style and decorated with Bonapartist emblems, complemented by the steward and four cabin boys who were outfitted in Napoleonic uniforms of imperial gold and green. Crowninshield and a large crew set forth on the *Cleopatra Barge*'s maiden voyage on 30 March 1817 for the Azores, where her sailors succeeded in upsetting the local friars by telling visitors to the strange craft that the cigar-store Indian was an American priest. From there he sailed to Majorca, Barcelona, Toulon, Genoa, Leghorn, Rome, Elba, and Gibraltar before returning to Salem in early October. This was George Crowninshield's first and last voyage in her, for the following month he died suddenly aboard the yacht in Salem harbor. *Cleopatra's Barge*, stripped of her furnishings, which fetched $7,000, was sold by George's starchy and disapproving brother Richard for $15,400 and put into passenger service on the run to Rio. Later she was bought by King Kamehameha II of Hawaii for use as a royal yacht. During his absence in England in 1824 a drunken crew ran her ashore on Kauai, where she broke up. The only surviving fragment of her structure is on display at the Bishop Museum in Honolulu, though there is a full-size replica of the fabled saloon displayed at Salem's Peabody Museum.

The first **yacht club** in America was the short-lived Boston Boat Club, which ran from c. 1832 until 1837. The oldest is the august New York Yacht Club, founded in 1844. (The Detroit Boat Club, founded in 1839, also claims the distinction, but it was founded as a rowing club.)

Steam yacht: The first was the 400-ton *Menai*, built for Thomas Assheton Smith in 1829. Two years earlier the Royal Yacht Club (forerunner of the Royal Yacht Squadron), of which Assheton Smith was a leading member, had attempted to forestall any such blemish upon the seas by instituting a rule that "any member applying steam to his yacht shall be disqualified hereby and shall cease to be a member." Incensed at what he considered an unwarranted interference with personal choice, Assheton Smith built the *Menai* apparently as a gesture of defiance and resigned from the club.

International yacht race: The first was held on 8 May 1849, when Bermuda's *Pearl of Bermuda* beat the American yacht *Brenda* in a contest held off the victor's coast. The first for what would come to be known as the **America's Cup**, originally the Hundred Guinea Cup (its cost), was won by John Cox Stevens' *America*, which beat fourteen competitors from the Royal Yacht Squadron in a race around the Isle of Wight (where the first known pleasure craft was built) on 22 August 1851. U.S. competitors would win every subsequent America's Cup contest until *Australia II* conquered in 1983.

~~~~~~~~~~~~~~~~~~~~~~ Z ~~~~~~~~~~~~~~~~~~~~~~

THE FIRST ZIPPER

was patented by Whitcomb L. Judson of Chicago on 29 August 1893 and consisted of two metal chains that could be joined together in a single movement by a slide fastener. Designed for use on boots and shoes, it was exhibited at the 1893 World's Columbian Exposition in Chicago and attracted the attention of Col. Lewis Walker, who later that year formed the Universal Fastener Co. to undertake manufacture. Judson's device had a number of design defects, the most basic being that it easily came apart. The only order received, twenty fasteners for mailbags in 1896, was not repeated. An improved version produced by Walker's company in 1902 under the brand name C-curity was designed as a "placket fastener" for skirts and dresses and retailed at 25¢. Sadly the device had a distressing tendency to pop open when a lady bent over.

Success was finally achieved after a young Swedish engineer called Gideon Sundback joined the firm and toward the end of 1913 perfected his "Hookless No. 2," a meshed-teeth arrangement that was essentially the zipper in its modern form. Regular production started twelve months later. The Hookless Fastener was sold direct to the garment industry, the first firm to place regular orders, starting in January 1916, being New York sportswear manufacturers Freidenrich & Co., who put them on pants for football, baseball, and other team games. Resistance to the product, which was costlier than conventional fastening devices, remained high and sales remained low until America entered the world war in 1917.

Almost overnight a small manufacturing concern became an industry. The U.S. Navy ordered zippers for flying clothes, the Army used them on the pockets of uniforms, and the Army Air Corps adapted them for airplane fabric. After the war ex-servicemen spread the zipper habit, and zippers were incorporated into leather goods, footwear, sleeping bags, and money belts. In 1920 the Jiffy Lock Co. of New York started to put them on tennis racket covers and bathing suit bags, the latter being the zipper's first application to luggage. Also in that year two competing firms in Gloversville, N.Y., the Wagman Manufacturing Co. and the Van Dreische Co., were applying them to ladies' purses. The biggest customer was another Gloversville firm, the F.S. Mills Co., which introduced the zipped Locktite tobacco pouch. But it was the application to footwear that gave the product what was to become its generic name, when in 1923 the rubber manufacturers B.F. Goodrich Co. changed the name of their Mystik Boot overshoe to the Zipper.

Plastic zippers were produced simultaneously in 1930 by Walker's renamed Hookless Fastener Co., with acrylics supplied by DuPont, and by Kynoch's Lightning Fastener Co. in Britain with plastics from its parent company ICI. These colorful zippers, which could be produced in any hue or color, were the first to be used on couture clothes, Madame Schiaparelli of the eponymous Paris fashion house being attracted to them not simply as a fastener but as an ornamental enhancement to the costume. When she initially used them on the pockets of a beach jacket in 1930, it was also the earliest application of visible zippers to clothing.

Zippers for pants flies: Early slide fasteners were too likely to come undone, while the later, reliable models were too big and cumbersome for the snug fit of a trouser crotch. Only in 1935 was the zipper deemed adequate for protection of male modesty, the pioneers in zip-fly pants being two big Chicago clothiers, Hart, Schaffner & Marx and B. Kuppenheimer. By 1940, according to *Apparel Manufacturer*, nearly 80 percent of all trousers produced in the United States were zipped.

Zippers on jeans (qv) were introduced by Levi Strauss in 1955. This was also a breakout year for jeans as a fashion (or anti-fashion) statement, with a leather-jacketed, bejeaned Marlon Brando rebellious aboard a motorbike in *The Wild One* and James Dean sulking and kicking stones in Levis in *Rebel Without a Cause*. Zippers helped to imbue jeans, formerly regarded as workwear, with an ambience of cool.

THE FIRST **ZOO**

....

as opposed to a royal menagerie (i.e., corporately owned and freely open to the public) was the Jardin des Plantes in Paris, established as a repository for animals—it was already a botanic garden—as a result of the revolutionary fervor of 1792–93. The animals came from several sources. The civic authorities of Paris had decided in 1793 to abolish traveling sideshows in which creatures were pitted against each other in combat, having a higher regard for the lives of the sub-species than they did for those condemned to the guillotine. These were dumped at the Jardin, despite the protests of its staff and of the angry owners of the animals.

Others came from the Royal Menagerie at Versailles. In August 1792 a gang of Jacobins had overrun it and demanded that all the inmates be liberated in accordance with the principles of *liberté* and *égalité* espoused by the revolution. When it was pointed out that the beneficiaries of this animal liberation movement might be so ungracious as to devour their liberators, there were second thoughts and most of the liberated were carted off to the knacker's yard. Those unlikely to make for good eating eventually found their way, in April 1794, to the zoo at the Jardin des Plantes. They included a quagga, a lion, and the lion's best friend, a small dog.

A third source was spoils of war, a valuable collection of beasts brought from the castle at Het Loo in the Netherlands after the French had invaded that country. Citoyen Mordant-Delaunay, a member of the staff of the library of the Musée Nationale d'Histoire Naturelle, of which the Jardin des Plantes was part, put himself in charge of the ramshackle zoo and gave it some order, adding a selection of animals native to France. In spite of its haphazard beginnings, by the early years of the nineteenth century the Jardin des Plantes was on its way toward becoming the world-renowned scientific institution of today.

U.S.: The Philadelphia Zoological Garden, founded by the Philadelphia Zoological Society, opened on a 32-acre site in Fairmont Park on 1 July 1874, admission 25¢ for adults and 10¢ for children. The 282 mammals, 674 birds, and 8 reptiles on display, assembled by superintendent Frank J. Thompson, included lions, zebras, antelope, an elephant, a tiger, a rhinoceros, kangaroos, and 50 monkeys. These were augmented during the early years by a number of donations from the famous: two curassows from President Ulysses S. Grant, two black bears from Mormon prophet Brigham Young, and a noted civil war veteran, a gift from Mrs. William Tecumseh Sherman, the cow "Atlanta" who had accompanied her husband the General on his march across Georgia.

The fortunes of the Philadelphia Zoo waxed and waned; it was practically derelict by the end of the 1920s and during the Depression annual attendance fell to an all-time low of 152,000. Today it flourishes once again as one of the leading zoos of the world. The few buildings surviving as reminders of its beginnings are the two original cottage-style gatehouses on either side of the North Gate, designed by Frank Furness; the 1874 Antelope House by George Hewitt; and the elegant Georgian mansion Solitude, built a hundred years before the zoo by John Penn, grandson of the founder of Pennsylvania, and used until the 1970s as its administration building.

Although Philadelphia's is generally recognized as America's first zoo, several others can claim earlier dates of foundation. Central Park Zoo in New York City began in a very modest way at the start of the Civil War with gifts of unwanted pets to park staff; Lincoln Park Zoo in Chicago had its origins in 1868 with the donation of two pairs of mute swans from Central Park; Roger Williams Park Zoo in Providence, R.I., started in 1872 with a small collection of mainly native mammals. Each, however, was described as a "menagerie" and not as a zoo when it opened and none of the three aspired to that status as a scientific and cultural institution until many years after Philadelphia had blazed the trail.

INDEX

A NOTE ON THE AUTHOR

PATRICK ROBERTSON began compiling his collection of firsts nearly sixty years ago at the age of fourteen. He continued his extensive research in the United States, Canada, New Zealand, Australia, South Africa, and Europe before settling down to a career in government. The first incarnation of the book, *The Shell Book of Firsts*, appeared in 1974 and became an immediate bestseller. Robertson has been a visiting scholar at the University of North Carolina and is a former chairman of the Ephemera Society. He owns the largest private collection of vintage magazines in Britain. He has also written *The Guinness Book of Australian Firsts* and a series of books on movies. His Web site is www.robertsonsfirsts.com.